Rangers

The Complete Record

Rangers
The Complete Record

**BOB FERRIER &
ROBERT McELROY**

The Breedon Books
Publishing Company
Derby

First published in Great Britain by
The Breedon Books Publishing Company Limited
Breedon House, 44 Friar Gate, Derby, DE1 1DA.
1996

© BOB FERRIER &
ROBERT McELROY 1996

ISBN 1 85983 015 3

Printed and bound by Butler & Tanner Ltd., Selwood Printing
Works, Caxton Road, Frome, Somerset.

Colour separations by Colour Services, Wigston, Leicester.

Jackets printed by Lawrence-Allen, Weston-super-Mare, Avon.

Contents

Introduction   6

The Rangers Story

    The First Two Decades   8

    The First of the Great Teams 23

    Days of Disaster 39

    Rangers in World War One 40

    Between the Wars 43

    Rangers in World War Two 58

    The Iron Curtain 61

    From Symon to Souness 75

    Another Great Season 100

    The Way Ahead 106

Riots, Disturbances and Such-Like-Happenings 108

Rangers in Europe 110

Ibrox — a Great Stadium 129

Rangers' Managers 131

Famous Rangers 137

Rangers Season-by-Season 158

Rangers in the Scottish League 285

Top Appearances and Goalscorers 288

Introduction

"There's not a team like the Glasgow Rangers – no not one, no not one …
Follow, follow, we will follow Rangers, everywhere, anywhere, we will follow on …"

THE tribal chants that thunder down the towering sierras of stands at Ibrox Stadium, from thousands of voices in unison, make manifest the uniqueness of Rangers and the intensity of passion with which its supporters identify with the club and what it represents. There is no football club anywhere in the world like Rangers. It has a singular place in the Scottish ethos. It mirrors the life of Scotland in a way that is incomparable, surely not duplicated anywhere else in the world, even by richer clubs in bigger countries.

Its sustained success and achievement over more than 120 years has seen it become institutionalised as the flag carrier of what a majority of Scots would consider to be national virtues – Protestant, Monarchist tradition and Unionist in the literal sense of the Union of Great Britain and Northern Ireland. Red, white and blue are the Rangers colours.

The club was formed by a group of young men, students in Glasgow, who first conceived the idea in 1872 and like very many others, the club was in a sense a product of the Industrial Revolution. The 18th-century 'empires' of cotton, tobacco, spices and commodities in general had made Glasgow a great trading city and entrepôt and brought development to the entire West of Scotland. This was surpassed by the Industrial Revolution of the 19th century in which coal, iron, steel, shipbuilding and engineering were supreme. Glasgow, Clydeside, Lanarkshire and Ayrshire prospered and the consequences spread through every aspect of life.

In sport, it saw clubs being formed and with them, the need for control, for central organisation. National associations, governing bodies, followed. In Glasgow in 1870 there were said to be 35 clubs registered with the Scottish Football Association. Football, Rugby Union, swimming, cricket, rowing, all embraced national organisation. In 1875 there were less than 100 golf clubs in the UK, by 1900 there were 1,000. The population of Glasgow in 1801 had been 77,385. In 1851 it was four times larger at 329,096.

In 1871, Rangers era, it was 477,732. In 1881 it had reached 511,415 (Glasgow topped the 1 million mark in 1921, fell below it only in 1966).

Expansive times – Glasgow then was no mean city in terms of civic pride and achievement, even if in other respects it was no Shangri La. In August 1870, a 'Street Tramways Act' paved the way for one of the wonders of the world, the Glasgow tramway system which brought mobility to the citizens, and incidentally served every major football club in the city, and finally had 36 routes crossing and reaching far beyond the city boundaries. In the same year, the foundations for the Albert Bridge across the River Clyde were laid. In March 1873 'Schools Boards' became a fact. In 1874, the Stephen Mitchell Bequest allowed work to start on the internationally-famous Mitchell Library. All of these were major events in the life of a great and growing city.

As Victoria's empire marched towards its zenith, there were Afghan Wars, Ashanti Wars, Zulu Wars, Boer Wars and needless to say, troubles with the Irish. These were distant happenings, news of which took time to reach 'home'. Communications were far from instant and the world was a good deal more intimate. When sports clubs were being formed back in the 19th century, they were local affairs in the sense that they drew their members from the immediately surrounding population, in a world still short of total mobility. When the new Celtic club was formed, it was perfectly natural that it should be sited in the East End of the city. It was to be the historic process which saw Celtic become the Rangers' alter ego. Founded in 1888 to raise funds to succour the Catholic poor of the East End of the city, it did just that for a season or two before being caught up in the game and its coming professionalism.

The influx of poor Irish to Glasgow probably stretched back to the early 1840s and the 'Potato Famine'. They gravitated to the East End, where the cheapest living accommodation lay, and they took whatever work they could find. The Republic of Ireland did not exist then, and the Irish nationalist and republic movement found support among these immigrants. There was resistance to their presence from the native work people, who saw their jobs in peril from incomers who were prepared to work for lower wages.

By the end of the last century, it was clear that Rangers and Celtic, sustained by clearly defined communities, and with Queen's Park persisting in remaining amateur, would become the two great metropolitan clubs to dominate the Scottish game. The initial relations between the clubs were excellent. Rangers provided the opposition for Celtic's first-ever match in May 1888, and both teams sat down for supper afterwards. 'The Old Firm', a term that dates from the turn of the century, was coined by a sardonic observer who noted that the intensive rivalry between the clubs, everything else apart, was very good for the cash flow in a game that was becoming increasingly commercial.

On the other hand, civil unrest in Ireland, the Easter uprising, the creation of the Republic of Ireland in the early 1920s, hardened attitudes. Following the creation of the Republic, there was an influx of Protestant ship-yard workers from Ulster, settling on Clydeside, gravitating unerringly to the Govan club. Now the divisions were set in stone. Celtic, founded by a Marist Brother to provide healthy recreation 'for Catholic youth', and to succour the Catholic poor of Glasgow's East End, was the Roman club, the Irish Republican club flying at its Parkhead ground the tricolour of Ireland. The Union Flag, the 'Union Jack' was inevitably the flag of establishment Rangers, the club of the Protestant faith, of the monarchy and the union, not to mention of the Masonic order and the Orange movement. These differing identities have led to conflict, riots of one sort or the other over the years, happily abandoned since 1980. In extremes, the Rangers anthem has been 'The Sash my Father Wore'. The Celtic anthem has been 'The Soldier's Song'.

Thus in the story of Rangers, Celtic cannot be ignored. The establishment club always did need a counterweight.

Football has been called the Glory Game – young men play for the glory, older men watch them for the emotion, the passion, the noise, the contest, the victory, the participation, the identification with the team and the colours. Nowhere is there such an intense and intimate identification with the club, the players, the 'jersey', the whole concept, than with Rangers. For Rangers fans, THEY are the club, the team is theirs, the stadium is theirs, the history is theirs. Players and managers come and go, but THEY go on for ever. the very 'idea' of Rangers goes on for ever. The Rangers record epitomises this. The championship win of 1995-96, their 47th, represented victory in 50 per cent of all Scottish League championships ever played. Rangers have won 25 per cent of all Scottish Cup competitions, 39 per cent of all Scottish League Cup competitions. The stronger and more successful Rangers become, the more Scotland's young footballers join them. The more Scotland's young footballers join them, the stronger and more successful do Rangers become. It is a circle of triumph. Rangers can be seen to overwhelm the Scottish game.

Rangers are a football club and an organisation who are at the very heart of the Scottish establishment, their place in the very culture of the nation being as distinctive as that of the Church of Scotland, the Scottish legal system, the Royal and Ancient Golf Club of St Andrew's, their position in society emerging from the historic process that embraced the Masonic Order, the end of the Stuart dynasty of kings all the way back, if you please, to the Reformation. The Rangers club and ethos is supported from every corner of the kingdom and from organised groups in the United States,

Canada, Australia, South Africa and elsewhere. The more pensive friends of the club acknowledge the bigotry of this situation and the tensions between Rangers and Celtic. 'Bigotry' has been defined as '...the condition of being obstinately and blindly attached to some creed, opinion or ritual, and intolerant of others'. But Rangers intellectuals (and Celtic intellectuals for that matter) rationalise the condition by claiming that without it, Rangers v Celtic would be no more than a football match, that it would lose its unique tribal flavour and be as bland as, in their view, Hearts v Hibs.

The 'Blue Nose', the Rangers supporter of club and concept, permeates Scottish life – the judiciary, the police, even the 'state' church, the Church of Scotland. When Graeme Souness signed Maurice Johnston in 1989, a declared Catholic who had made his religion public more than once, it was as much as anything else a declaration of Souness' distaste for the bigotry intrinsic to the Rangers-Celtic relationship, and his determination to put an end to it. It quickly became clear that Souness was not truly aware of the depths of passion involved.

As a Rangers manager, he succeeded in winning trophies. He failed to change the nature of things. He was bucking the Scottish establishment, and the Scottish establishment is blue.

A complete and totally objective record of the history of this great club and institution, of all its personalities and all its happenings, would require volumes by the dozen, indeed an entire library in itself. We trust that the remarkable collection of statistics collated here, of all known games and results, will be recognised as a solid skeleton on which the work hangs, and that the commentary has remained as objective as human frailty permits.

The story of Rangers Football Club is one of sport's great romantic stories: from the humble beginnings in 1872 – four young students who had no pitch, no ball, no strips (playing their very first game in ordinary clothes) – to the multi-million pound organisation of today is a story surely unparalleled in the history of sport.

When yet another League championship had been won in the spring of 1995, Richard Gough, the Rangers captain, said, "When you enter the doors at Ibrox, this club embraces you, looks after you. It is a very special place."

Bob Ferrier
Robert McElroy
Glasgow
July 1996

Acknowledgements

Both authors gratefully acknowledge the assistance of the following in the compilation of this work: Alan & Gary Brown, Jim Gregor, Bill McKenzie, Les Melrose, Neil Stobie, John Taylor, David Wilkes, Gordon Young and the late Sam Johnston.
Photographs supplied by Caledonian Newspapers Ltd., and Empics Ltd.

The Rangers Story

The First Two Decades

IN FEBRUARY 1872, a group of young men were walking in West End Park, a Glasgow open space long since gone, in the present area of Kelvinbridge. They had become intrigued by the growing sport of football, were well aware of its development in England and of the lead taken by Queen's Park in Scotland, and decided to form their own football club. The young men were students in Glasgow, all of them from villages along the Gare Loch, from Rhu to Garelochhead, some 30 miles from the city. They were the brothers Peter and Moses McNeil, Peter Campbell and William McBeath. They decided to call themselves the 'Rangers', from the name of an English rugby club which Moses had noted and liked. They procured an old, well-worn football, and, more or less, were in business. The 'Rangers' were virtually a boys' club – Moses was 16 years old, the others all under 20. The whole thing was to be taken seriously. They set aside three nights each week for training, but in the event so enthusiastic were they that they were out on Glasgow Green, every night save the Sabbath.

After several weeks of concentrated training, it was time to put themselves to the test. Their first serious opposition was to be Callender FC, and Rangers strengthened their side with four 'imports' in Harry McNeil, (brother of Moses, Peter and William) and Willie McKinnon, both of Queen's Park and John Hunter and Willie Miller of the Eastern club. Only these four stripped for action. The others played in street clothes. The match was a ferocious bruising battle, ending 0-0. Willie McBeath was surely man of the match – he collected so many battle scars that he spent a week in bed. Thus towards the end of May 1872, Rangers had played their very first game. It took place on Flesher's Haugh, that section of Glasgow Green, the city's Hyde Park, devoted to football. In those early days, to be sure of having first call on a pitch, Peter McNeil would get down there early on Saturday mornings and plant goal posts on the desired spots, staking his claim as it were. Needless to say there were disputes.

After that a meeting was convened and office bearers elected. In the summer another game was arranged, this time with Clyde (not of course the present Clyde) and it resulted in a massive 11-0 win. The real significance of this game is that Rangers wore for the first time their famous 'light blue' jerseys. Even today their shirts are so described, although the present blue is closer to 'royal' blue than to the Cambridge or Manchester City light blue.

'Use and want' as the lawyers say, saw one particular pitch at Flesher's Haugh accepted as the Rangers' pitch as the new club became better known. It was still a question of changing into the blue shirts and white knickerbockers behind a clump of trees and paying a small boy to keep an eye on the clothes. Tom Vallance, the greatest of the early full-backs, joined in the spring of 1873 and was to have a long career as player and administrator with the club. The first general meeting of the club was held that year and office bearers elected in a proper and satisfactory manner.

With the increase in public interest in the game, arrangements were needed for practice and training nights, and for regular fixtures, and all this was put in hand. Football as an organised game was very much in its infancy; the players were amateurs, the games were 'friendlies', the clubs were not yet organised in leagues. All that was to await William McGregor in Birmingham and his formation of England's Football League in 1888, followed by the Scottish Football League two years later.

Rangers' first full season, 1873-74, was totally successful for the young club, victorious over everyone save Havelock and Star of Leven, both of whom, now long gone, won 1-0. Rangers' main rivals then were the Rovers. Three memorable matches were played against them that season. Crowds flocked to the Queen's Park and the Glasgow Green to see the matches, often flocking over the touchlines in their enthusiasm. The young Rangers enjoyed the presence of the crowds, but not on the playing pitch.

There was a certain amount of criticism of Rangers. With three McNeils, three Campbells and two Vallances in the team, the claim was that the club was too exclusive. Yet these ties of friendship and family meant fame for Rangers as they began to outstrip their opposition. Jealousy is a well-established Scottish trait, persisting with regard to Rangers to the present day. Moses McNeil, one of the founding fathers, was enticed away in fact by Queen's Park for a spell. He was a strong, powerful player with an abundance of stamina, but he soon rejoined Rangers, bringing improved performances to the team.

Rangers had been late in applying for membership of the Scottish Football Association and as a result had to miss the Scottish Cup competition of season 1873-74. They entered the competition the following season and their first competitive game was on 12 October 1874, when they beat Oxford 2-0 on the Queen's Park Recreation Ground in a Scottish Cup first-round tie. Goals came from David Gibb and Moses McNeil. Peter McNeil captained the following team: John Yuil, Tom Vallance, Peter McNeil, William McNeil, William McBeath, Moses McNeil, Peter Campbell, George Phillips, James Watson, David Gibb and J.Campbell. On a later trip to Alexandria, Rangers had a 3-0 win over Vale of Leven in which it was said goalkeeper John Yuil 'never touched the ball'.

On 28 November, Dumbarton were received at Glasgow Green in the second round of the Cup. Rangers were without Willie McBeath, who was ill and were relieved to hold out in a 0-0 draw. In the replay a fortnight later, they went out to a disputed goal. Most people thought that Dumbarton's winning goal had gone over, not under, the bar (no goal nets in those days!) But over or under, Rangers were out of the Cup, not for the last time, in debatable circumstance.

The season went ahead with matches against names long lost in football history – Vale of Leven Rovers, Helensburgh, Barrhead, Havelock, the 23rd Renfrewshire Rifle

Volunteers. The season had been one of encouraging achievement (15 matches had been played, with 12 won and only one lost, that Scottish Cup-tie at Dumbarton. These results had suggested to the young Rangers that the time had come to flex their muscles against better opposition. Queen's Park, the premier Scottish club, the aristocrats of the day – Rangers were after them. The premier club declined to accept. After all these young men had no ground of their own. They were prepared to send their second team, the Strollers, to play the fledgling Rangers, but the Garelochhead lads wanted none of that. They wanted to tackle the best, or no one at all. Their time was coming.

Yet the Queen's Park people had been right – if the young club was to develop, it would need a ground it could call its own. By the summer of 1875, it had been found, at Burnbank, on the south side of Great Western Road near Kelvin Bridge. It was particularly practical, since most of the players lived locally in the Sandyford District. The ground was formally opened on 11 September with a visit from the great Vale of Leven, then second only to Queen's Park in playing ability. Against such opposition, and even if Vale played only ten players, a 1-1 draw was positively heroic. The team that opened the first Rangers ground was: John Yuil; Tom Vallance, Peter McNeil, Willie McBeath, William McNeil, Moses McNeil, Peter Campbell, James Watson, George Phillips, David Gibb, John Campbell.

Burnbank housed its first Scottish Cup-tie on 16 October 1875, when Rangers crushed the 1st Lanarkshire Rifle Volunteers by 7-0. The second round saw Rangers at Cathkin Park to face another of the day's luminaries in Third Lanark, more accurately the 3rd Lanark Rifle Volunteers. Rangers were sure they had triumphed with Peter Campbell's solitary goal, but Thirds launched an appeal which was upheld by the SFA. The result was invalid – Rangers had kicked-off to start both halves. The replay was even more contentious.

Rangers lost 2-1 and immediately protested on three counts: first, they claimed that since the Third Lanark goalkeeper played in plain clothes, he could not be distinguished from the spectators crowding behind the goal; second, the Thirds' first goal was illegal as John Hunter had pushed a Rangers player, and the ball, through the goal with his hands; and lastly, spectators had spilled on to the field causing play to be terminated seven minutes early. Their appeals were rejected. Third Lanark, the 'Warriors' marched on in the Cup, all the way to the Final before yielding to the mighty Queen's Park after a replay.

On 20 November 1875, Rangers achieved one of their earliest ambitions, the game against Queen's Park. It was played at Hampden. Rangers lost 2-0, but their play, and their performances in the Cup-tie with Third Lanark, brought much positive Press comment, and increased their popularity. One feature of the match was a sterling display by Tom Vallance, who kept the idol of the day, Jamie Weir, the 'Prince of Dribblers', in check, The 'gate', affected by the bad weather, was £28 which was donated to the Bridgeton Fire Fund.

On Christmas Day, Caledonian were soundly beaten at Burnbank. Making their debut that day were David Hill at full-back, and Sam Rickets of Stonelaw in midfield. Both contributed a great deal to the making of Rangers. Hill became an international forward of note, while Rickets lived and breathed Rangers, giving his all to the club for many years.

The early part of 1876 was devoted to trial matches for the forthcoming internationals against England and Wales,

and for the highly prestigious Glasgow v Sheffield match. Prominent in all these matches were Tom Vallance, Moses McNeil and Peter Campbell. Rangers lost by the only goal against the Lennox club of Dunbartonshire on 19 February, but it was a historic day for the club – Moses McNeil and Peter Campbell became the first Rangers players to receive representative honours when they played at Bramall Lane and helped Glasgow defeat Sheffield by 2-0. The last match of the season was fateful too. A goalless draw was played with Clydesdale on their Kinning Park ground. They were moving to Titwood (they remain there as a cricket club) and Rangers arranged to 'inherit' Kinning Park for the following season. And a week later, Moses McNeil became Rangers first international player when he played for Scotland against Wales on 25 March.

The annual general meeting was held in April, properly and proudly conducted, and the office bearers were selected for the coming season, all of them drawn from the playing staff. They were: president, George Phillips; vice-president, John Campbell; captain, Tom Vallance; vice-captain, Peter Campbell; 2nd XI captain, Archibald Harkness; 2nd XI vice-captain, Alex Vallance; treasurer, Moses McNeil; secretary, Peter McNeil of 169 Hunter Terrace, Berkeley Street, Glasgow; committee, Messrs William B.McNeil, William D.McBeath, James Watt, James Watson, William Grant.

In August 1876, Rangers moved south of the river Clyde to take up residence in the Kinning Park ground vacated by Clydesdale. At the same time, their playing strength was augmented by the demise of the Sandyford club, many of whose members joined the 'Light Blues'. For the second successive season Vale of Leven found themselves opening a new Rangers ground, on 2 September, before a crowd of 1,500. There were changes in the Rangers line-up. John Watt had supplanted John Yuil in goal. David Hill at full-back was keeping Peter McNeil out of the team. At half-back a fair-haired, fresh-faced youth, George Gillespie in place of Willie McBeath was one of three debutants that day. George who had signed from Rosslyn, had a wonderful career, winning all the honours save an SFA Cup winners' badge, although he appeared in two Finals. Willie Dunlop and Alex Marshall took the places of George Phillips and David Gibb as forwards. The new men were immediately at home with each other and their 2-1 win caused much comment in football circles. It was their finest win to date.

In the Scottish Cup, Queen's Park Juniors, then Towerhill were swept aside. There was a bye in the third round, and in away matches Maunchline and Lennox were eliminated, each by 3-0, and with another bye, in the semi-final, Rangers, in only their third full year of existence, were in the Scottish Cup Final for the first time. Their opponents at Hamilton Crescent were to be the hot favourites, Vale of Leven. Rangers gave as good as they got on 17 March, and came out with a 1-1 draw. Their line up was: James Watt, George Gillespie, Tom Vallance; Willie McNeil, Sam Ricketts, Willie Dunlop, David Hill, James Watson, Alex Marshall, Peter Campbell, Moses McNeil. The crowd was a record 12,000. For the replay, on 7 April, both sides were unchanged and such was the interest that again a record crowd, 14,000 was on hand. Once more it was a tense, close encounter. Rangers led for much of the match by a Willie Dunlop goal, but McDougall of the Vale hit a last-gasp equaliser. Both teams agreed to play an extra 30 minutes, thought to be the first time extra-time was used in the history of the game.

They never did play the 30 minutes. Near the end, Rangers claimed that a shot from Dunlop had crossed the line, struck a spectator and rebounded into the hand of goalkeeper Wood. This, of course, was before goal nets were in use, and in Cup Finals and important matches, the crowd would often gather close behind the goal-line. The umpires could not agree, referee James Kerr of Hamilton decided in favour of Vale of Leven, but since the crowd had encroached on the playing field and refused to be cleared, he terminated the proceedings. The third match in this eventful Final took place on a Friday, again setting a record as being the first midweek evening replay. The venue was switched to First Hampden and yet again there was a record crowd, 15,000 this time. The match was bad-tempered, players freely exchanging punches on the field. Rangers filed a protest, which was not upheld. They led by 2-1 in the second half, but ran out of steam, and the more experienced Vale side won late in the game, 3-2.

Rangers had played the same men in all three games and emerged as highly popular with the football public. Their next appearance was also at Hampden, in another Cup Final, this time the Glasgow Merchant's Charity Cup against Queen's Park. The defeat of Queen's Park by Vale of Leven in the Scottish Cup had led to bad feeling between these clubs, and in order to repair things the Glasgow Merchants put up a trophy in which both teams would play, with the proceeds going to local charities. Vale of Leven refused to enter, Rangers went to the Final against Queen's at Hampden but after their struggles in the Scottish Cup, this was an anticlimax. They were beaten 4-0. It had been a fair season, their first at Kinning Park. In 24 matches, 16 had been won, three drawn and only five lost. The young Rangers were coming along nicely.

Season 1877-78 brought a series of 'firsts' for the young Rangers club. They played in England for the first time, and an English club played Rangers in Scotland for the first time. They made their first appearance in Edinburgh. They set their record of 13 goals scored in a match (twice), they scored in Alexandria for the first time, and avoided defeat by Vale of Leven there (1-1) for the first time. Just as important as all this was the introduction of Hugh McIntyre to a midfield position. He was to make a very marked impression on Rangers and Scottish football.

Rangers ran through September with four high-scoring wins, not least of them a surprising 5-0 over old foes, Vale of Leven. Defeat by Third Lanark at Hampden on 20 October was their first in eight outings. On 6 October, Possilpark came to Kinning Park on Scottish Cup business and were treated mercilessly, Rangers scoring 13 without reply. Seven different players were scorers, with Peter Campbell hitting a hat-trick. In the second round, Alexandra Athletic surrendered eight and in the third Uddingston were the victims. Marshall and Watson had four each, Moses McNeil had two and Davie Hill, John and Peter Campbell one each in Rangers' record 13 goals for a second time. In the fourth round Rangers were again drawn at home, against Vale of Leven, in a meeting of the previous year's Finalists. The match, a goalless draw, was as closely contested as the score suggests, but in the replay, Rangers collapsed and Vale coasted to a 5-0 win.

On New Year's Day 1878, Rangers paid a first visit to Edinburgh, beating Brunswick at Mayfield with a side composed mainly of reserves. February was something of a historic month – Rangers played in England for the first time with matches against Nottingham Forest and The Wednesday. On the 16th, 2,000 saw them beat Forest 4-2 with

Moses McNeil (2), Hugh McIntyre and Marshall scoring. Two days later they beat The Wednesday in Sheffield by 2-1, with goals from Marshall again, and Hill.

After eight straight wins in the New Year, Dumbarton put an end to the streak, winning 2-1 at Boghead over a ten-man Rangers team. For the Glasgow Charity Cup-tie against Third Lanark at Hampden, the Warriors requested that the game should be played as a friendly, since many of their players had been injured in the previous week's Scottish Cup-tie, and were unavailable. The request was not granted, happily for Thirds. They won, 2-1. On 20 April, Nottingham Forest became the first English side to visit a Rangers ground. They went home suitably chastened, losing 2-0. At the Rangers annual general meeting, Archibald Harkness was returned as president with John Watson his vice-president. The club was considered to be on an even keel after five years' existence.

One win from the first five games of the 1878-79 season scarcely confirmed that judgement. This was unacceptable, considering the talent that was available to the club. But it was not to be typical of a season in which Rangers would win its first trophy; play under 'floodlights' for the first time; suffer a 12-week break in a winter of high winds, ice, snow, frost and rainstorms which brought football to a standstill throughout Britain, and reach the Scottish Cup Final for the second time. Cup football seemed to be to the liking of the Kinning Park club. Without being particularly impressive, they disposed of Shaftesbury 3-0 at home, then crushed the Govan side Whitefield by 6-1 at Whitefield Park. On 25 October, Rangers were in London, beating Clapham Rovers 5-1 with goals from Davie Hill, Willie Struthers, Moses McNeil (2) and Archie Steel. This was a notable victory – Rovers were considered a power in London football. Next day, in Nottingham, Rangers beat old friends Forest 2-0, this time goals coming from Willie Dunlop and Willie Struthers.

On the first Saturday of November, Rangers played Parkgrove, another Govan side, in a Scottish Cup rehearsal and were surprisingly beaten 5-1. Peter Campbell's goal was no consolation. Two days later Rangers went to Hampden to play Third Lanark in a game under floodlights, or as the Victorians called it 'Electric Light'. A substantial crowd of 6,000 saw the Soldiers win by 3-2. The innovation was by no means a failure, but was considered rather a novelty. Saturday afternoon was still the time for football.

The Rangers selection for that match showed their top men of the period: George Gillespie, Tom Vallance, Alex Vallance, James Drinnan, Hugh McIntyre, Willie Dunlop, Archie Steel, Willie Struthers, Charles McQuarrie, Moses McNeil, Peter Campbell.

Davie Hill for McQuarrie was the only change for the third round Scottish Cup-tie against Parkgrove at Kinning Park. The 3,000 crowd was delighted – Hill scored a hat-trick, Willie Struthers did the same and other goals came from Dunlop and Campbell in the 8-2 win which raised some eyebrows with regard to the earlier match in which Rangers could score only once and surrendered five goals. The same combination produced much better form in the shape of a 3-0 win over Vale of Leven, 6-1 over Govan and a 3-0 win over Alexandra Athletic in the fourth round of the competition. In that match, Douglas, a former Rangers forward, and James Gossland, a Ranger-to-be, played. After the long winter break, another home draw saw them defeat Partick 4-0, but for the sixth round, the luck of the draw turned against them. They were to face the Spiders of Queen's Park at Hampden, the team which had won all four of their previous Scottish Cup meetings. Indeed, Rangers had failed to score against them in these games. The match was played in a downpour and went goalless until the very last minute, when Willie Dunlop found himself unmarked, unchallenged, in front of the Queen's goal, the ball at his feet. Dunlop had bet a sovereign on Queen's winning the Cup, and as he hammered home the winning goal, he said, "There goes my sov." (A sovereign was a coin of the realm worth 21 shillings, or £1.05.)

On 7 April, newspaper reports announced that the Lancashire club Darwen was planning a tour of Canada and had listed in their pool of players the names Hugh McIntyre and Willie Struthers. The tour never took place, but this was an indication of how desirable these Rangers players could be to English clubs practising even now a veiled professionalism.

As in their first Final appearance a couple of years earlier, Rangers were to meet Vale of Leven. In a warm-up of the Cup Final, they received old friends Nottingham Forest at Kinning Park and won 3-0.

They stepped out before a crowd of 9,000 at Hampden for the Final, on 19 April. Once more there was little between the teams. Willie Struthers gave Rangers the lead after 12 minutes and soon after headed a Dunlop cross past the giant Vale goalkeeper, Parlane. The referee and umpires disallowed the goal for offside. Rangers were incensed. They were even more incensed when three minutes from the end, Ferguson snapped a low cross beyond goalkeeper Gillespie, who seemed to judge that the ball was going wide. Rangers lodged a protest on the grounds that their second goal should stand. The SFA considered this, but decided that the result should stand and ordered a replay for Hampden on 26 April. Rangers promptly announced that they would not turn up for such a match, and meant it. Vale of Leven did turn up, there was no trace of Rangers (their players were all enjoying a day out at Ayr Races!) and Vale of Leven took the Cup for the third year in succession.

The following month saw Rangers beat Third Lanark 4-1 in a Charity Cup-tie which put them into the Final and brought yet another clash with the fearsome Vale of Leven. On 20 May, more than 10,000 turned up at Hampden no doubt expecting fireworks. They were not disappointed. In a bad-tempered match in which two or three players were seen throwing punches, Rangers prevailed this time by 2-1, the winning goal coming from a dreadful scrimmage. Yet again there was controversy, this time Vale of Leven, almost by reflex, claiming for a disallowed goal. The SFA rejected the claim, and Rangers, in half a dozen years of existence had won their first major trophy. Among these trophy winners, in the words of H.H.Bone, eminent Victorian writer and sports historian were: George Gillespie "...was never intended to be anything in the game but a goalkeeper and a brilliant one too. How he kept goal in this great match, and dozens of others, is still fresh in the memory of both old players and spectators".

Tom Vallance "...Who could captain a team like he? When he led Rangers to victory in this Final, he was barely out of his teens. Vallance was a back and for several seasons none in Scotland showed better form. His returns near goal were neat and clean and without being in any way rough with opponents, his length of limb and good judgement often save his club from losing goals."

Alex Vallance "...With quite as much pluck, but wanting in finish and style, the younger of the brothers was nevertheless a fine back, lighter made and more easily tackled

than Tom ...he was in fine form for this tie and some of his returns were splendidly made."

Hugh McIntyre "...Of all the players sent out by Rangers, McIntyre was in many respects the most powerful. He was however, to be outspoken, the coarsest. Woe betide the light and gentle forward who tried to pass Mr Hugh. He pounced on his own man at once and ...meant to have the ball at any cost."

Moses McNeil "...the youngest of a famous football family ...he was quite a boy when this Cup-tie came off, and played with a dash and finish on the left wing that completely astonished all who were present at Old Hampden Park that May evening."

Peter Campbell "...was the life and soul of the forward division and it is not too much to say that it has lasted better than will our contemporary writing."

At the club's annual general meeting on 6 June, it was declared that it had never been in such a flourishing condition since its creation in 1872. Willie Dunlop was elected president, Archie Harkness as vice-president, Tom Vallance club captain, Hugh McIntyre vice-captain.

A charity match in the public park at Rothesay, Isle of Bute, was the unlikely start to season 1879-80. The date was 23 August, the opposition Queen's Park, the result a 1-0 defeat for Rangers. A month later the same teams appeared before a 7,000 crowd at Kinning Park and fought out a 0-0 Scottish Cup draw. The replay a week later on 27 September saw Rangers trounced 5-1 in a match in which they were handicapped by the absence of Tom Vallance, injured. Another more significant fact of the match was the last appearance of Peter Campbell. A founder member of the club, he was a player of outstanding ability and great influence in club affairs. He was the first Rangers player to be lured away to English football. He had a short stay with Blackburn Rovers before going to sea. Sadly he had a tragic end – in 1883 the steamer in which he was chief engineer was sunk in an enormous storm in the Bay of Biscay, with all hands lost.

Rangers were having a hard time getting much change out of Queen's Park – the Spiders went on to win the Scottish Cup for a record fourth time, beating Thornliebank 3-0 in the Final. After their early Cup exit, Rangers were less than convincing in their next match, at home to Parkgrove with whom they drew 1-1. It marked the debut of Willie Corbett in place of Peter Campbell. On 18 October Rangers went to Arbroath and enjoyed the sea air to the extent of a 10-0 win over the home team. A more successful November was rounded out with a 1-0 win over Dumbarton at Kinning Park, the goal coming from John Christie. There were no matches in December. When Rangers did return to action on New Year's Day against a Scotch-Canadian XI, two notable players appeared. James McIntyre, better known as 'Tuck' and younger brother of Hugh, came in at half-back and Willie Pringle, a forward, was the other newcomer. They were both to give Rangers many years of fine service.

The Scotch-Canadians were a scratch international group got together by a Mr Dick of the SFA for a tour of Canada. A series of matches was being played to raise funds. The tour never happened because of the death of Mr Dick. Some 2,500 saw the 'Canadians' win at Kinning Park. The team had some encouraging wins in 1880 – an engrossing 1-1 draw with Vale of Leven at the end of January before 4,000 at Kinning Park; a 3-3 draw with Dumbarton at Boghead; a first match against Hibernian in Edinburgh a 4-1 win, and a 11-0 triumph away to Drumpellier. On 3

April, Vale of Leven were back at Kinning Park but a full-strength Rangers won 2-1, goals coming from their prolific forwards Dunlop and Pringle.

A week later, Rangers fielded three half-backs for the first time, in a 2-3-5 formation, in a Charity Cup-tie against Dumbarton at Hampden. It worked well enough to give them a 3-1 win. Three half-backs were used again in the Charity Cup Final against Queen's Park at Hampden. Willie Pringle scored in a tight match that ended 1-1. In the replay, Rangers lost yet another Cup Final in controversial circumstances. In the 2-1 defeat, they claimed that the ball had crossed the Rangers goal-line by a good yard before it was crossed and ultimately converted.

Just as great a disappointment came when Hugh McIntyre left the club and went south to Blackburn Rovers. An upholsterer by trade, he left Glasgow when trade was slack and by 1884 he was mine host at the Castle Inn, Blackburn. He was to return often to lure the cream of Scottish football talent to the industrial belt of Lancashire, whose teams were all too ready to welcome good players and offer inducements to make them stay.

The new season of 1880-81 was unique in that it opened with a Scottish Cup-tie. At Kinning Park, the guests, Govan, were no match for Rangers, losing 4-1. Other guests were the officers and men of the Russian yacht *Livadia*, docked on the Clyde at the time. Hugh McIntyre's place was taken by his brother Jim, in what was probably Rangers' best team of the time. By the end of the season it was to be much depleted: Watt; A.Vallance, T.Vallance, J.McIntyre, Drinnan, Steel, Hill, Marshall, Struthers, M.McNeil, Pringle.

Queen's Park put a damper on a good start to the season with a 5-0 win at Hampden, Rangers' heaviest defeat in three years. Early in the match captain Tom Vallance went off injured and, despite an outstanding and defiant display by George Gillespie, the ten men wilted late in the match and surrendered four goals. A week later, that defeat was shrugged off. They went to Hydepark, Springburn, for a Scottish Cup second-round tie, and beat the tough northern side with a solitary Willie Struthers goal five minutes from the end, side-footed, following a corner-kick.

When Queen's Park came to Kinning Park, they found Rangers in much better form. A fluctuating game finished 2-2, Rangers' goals coming from Struthers and Angus. One of them was surely one of the best ever scored by Rangers. Picking up the ball close to his own goal, he beat two men and set off into the opposing half, rounding the giant Charlie Campbell, veering left, getting past Watson, and as other defenders closed in on him, blasting the ball high past goalkeeper McCallum from fully 20 yards. In this same match, making his debut, was one John Inglis, a scheming forward signed from Partick and embarking in a career that would bring international honours and an FA Cup winners' medal with Blackburn Rovers.

In the Scottish Cup, Partick Thistle went down to a George Angus hat-trick, at Kinning Park in the third round. At the end of October, Rangers lost to an English team for the first time, going down 2-1 to Forest in Nottingham, and two days later replaying a 0-0 draw with Blackburn Rovers, the English team aided by one Hugh McIntyre. Rangers made the most of their home draw in the fourth round of the Cup. Clyde were overrun 11-0.

On 11 December, despite strong winds and driving rain, 2,000 turned up at Kinning Park to see Nottingham Forest in the return match. An exceptional game between well-matched teams finished 2-2. A trip to Ayrshire for the Cup fifth round saw Hurlford beaten 3-0 on a snow-covered

pitch, but a visit from Dumbarton on Christmas Day in the sixth round was different – nearly 5,000 turned up to see Hugh McIntyre, back on a visit from Blackburn, playing as one of the forwards in place of John Christie, but on a hard, frosty pitch, Rangers were well beaten by a talented Dumbarton side, 3-1. Pringle had headed the home team into the lead early in the second half, but within five minutes, the Sons were level. And five minutes later, they had a two goal lead – too much for Rangers.

Dumbarton went through the Final that year, scheduled for the first time on Rangers' ground, Kinning Park, to meet the holders, Queen's Park. A crowd of 15,000 produced receipts of £450 and saw Queen's Park win 2-1. There was the inevitable protest from Dumbarton, on the grounds that there had been crowd encroachment at the time of the winning goal. In a very controversial decision, the SFA upheld the appeal and ordered a replay on the same ground. Queen's won again, this time by 3-1 before a crowd of 10,000. There was no 'pitch invasion' this time. The SFA had hired 51 members of the Renfrewshire Constabulary who, under the command of one Captain Hunter, had erected boarding to restrain the crowd and raised platforms on three sides of the ground as improved vantage points. Thus for the first, but not the last, time Rangers had hosted the Scottish Cup Final.

They did not play again until 5 February, when they beat Caledonian 8-0 at Burnbank, Struthers scoring four. Next, Dumbarton confirmed that they still had the edge over Rangers with a 1-0 win at Levengrove Park, ground of their town rivals, Lennox. Kennedy and Macadam of Partick Thistle had guested for the club in place of Gillespie and Tom Vallance, who were busy with Glasgow v Sheffield. In Blackburn on 5 March, Rangers lost yet again across the border, 5-4 in a thrilling match in which Rangers had George Kerr and Dr John Smith, Queen's Park's goalscorers in their team, while the Rovers had three Scots in Hugh McIntyre (ex-Rangers), Fergus Suter (ex-Rangers and Partick) and Willie Douglas (ex-Renfrew). When the English team came to Kinning Park two weeks later, it was Rangers' turn, by 2-1.

Hearts came to Kinning Park for the first time and were crushed 7-0, and on 16 April, Rangers turned in a totally unexpected and quite remarkable performance in beating Dumbarton, the Scottish Cup Finalists, by no less than 8-0, in a Charity Cup match at Hampden. Hill, McKinley and Steel each scored twice, Struthers (inevitably) and Pringle getting the others. Next, Hibs were slammed 9-3 at Easter Road, Struthers, in devastating form, this time scoring five.

The Final of the Charity Cup, Rangers v Queen's Park, was played at Hampden on 30 April 1881. Appeals, protests, objections were the order of the day. Rangers objected to the venue, saying that all Finals had been played on neutral grounds and the choice of Hampden would give Queen's an unfair advantage. It seemed a reasonable thought. For a time, it seemed they would refuse to play, but did, since it was a charitable affair. The uncertainty, and bad weather, kept many people away from a 1-1 draw. The replay, at Kinning Park on 7 May, attracted 10,000, was a very much better match, and was won by Queen's, 3-1. But Rangers lost much more than a cup that day, Struthers, Steel and Devlin were lured south by Bolton Wanderers. Struthers, as expected, became a huge success and later managed the club. Another sharp finisher, George Angus, moved to Queen's Park. How then were Rangers to face the 1880s with the loss of these valuable forwards, with their teeth drawn, as it were?

On 27 August 1881, a Rangers team on rather unfamiliar lines opened the new season at Tynecastle, where they were held to a draw by Hearts. A player with the pseudonym 'Petrie' scored the goal. There were three debutants in the team, none of whom ever appeared again. All this was to epitomise Rangers' season.

The next match was on 10 September at Kinning Park in the opening round of the Scottish Cup with Third Lanark in opposition. Gillespie, Tom Vallance and Pringle were all back to strengthen the team, while Robert Young, from Glasgow University, who had played for the club in the past, was there to make his stay more permanent. In a fast, exciting match Rangers won 2-1, with Pringle and Weir scoring. Their opponents in the next round, Harmonic from Dennistoun, scratched.

When William Ness of Glasgow University made his debut in goal against St Bernard's in a home match on 1 October, he was the third goalkeeper used in as many matches. Willie McFarlane was also introduced in one of the forward roles in a match that Rangers won 6-1. The third round home tie against Alexandra Athletic was won 3-1. On 29 October, Rangers were at Trent Bridge to meet Nottingham Forest again, with John Christie and Sam Ricketts playing for the first time that season. The game was played under two sets of rules, the first half under 'Scots' rules, the second under English. One difference concerned the throw-in – the English rules required the ball to be thrown in 'square', *ie* at right angles to the touchline, whereas the 'Scots' allowed for it to be thrown in at any angle. Rangers had the best of a goalless draw. Two days later there was a 2-2 draw with Blackburn Rovers.

Rangers had gone seven successive games without losing when Queen's Park came to Kinning Park on 5 November. Rangers had their strongest team, produced the best performance of the season, and led at half-time by a Corbett goal. But failure to cope with a couple of Queen's corners in the second half meant a 2-1 defeat. A week later, in the Cup, there was a desperate struggle against Thornliebank away. A very late own-goal, and an even later David Hill goal took them through, 2-0. Next, they fared badly against Dunbartonshire teams. Jamestown beat them 3-1, and Vale of Leven 2-1.

On 2 December, they were at Copland Road to beat South Western in the fifth round of the Scottish Cup, by 2-1. The home club immediately protested, this time on the grounds that the throw-in prior to the Rangers' winning goal was not thrown in straight. The SFA agreed. The tie was replayed at Kinning Park, this time Rangers thrashing their near-neighbours 4-0. It was something of a farewell performance from John Christie, one of the goalscorers – he was off to Bolton to join Struthers, Steel and Devlin.

Rangers and Dumbarton met at Boghead on 28 January in the sixth round. A crowd of 5,000 enjoyed a cracking game which the Sons won 2-1. Rangers immediately protested, claiming that the game had ended five minutes too soon. Thus they went at it again, the following Saturday, again at Boghead. Rangers held for much of the match, with Gillespie in the Rangers goal defying Dumbarton, but he turned villain by misjudging a shot which put Dumbarton 2-1 in front. Rangers rather disintegrated, going down 5-1. Dumbarton went on to the Final where after a 2-2 draw, they lost 4-1 to the holders, Queen's Park.

Out of the Cup, apathy seemed to take hold of the club. Only eight players turned up for their next match, against St Mirren, and a 5-2 defeat was no surprise. This match was to be Tom Vallance's farewell to the club. On the following Wednesday, 22 February 1882, he left Glasgow for a position in Calcutta. He was presented with a purse of 50 sovereigns from the club, at Bridge Street Station Hotel, and when he left for London from the Central Station, there was a large turnout of well wishers.

Rangers, dispirited, played only one match in March, on the 25th, against Aston Villa at Perry Barr. Moses McNeil played, for the first time in more than a year, taking the place of David Hill who was playing for Scotland against Wales. Rangers had a good first half and were two up at half-time. In the second half, they faced a strong wind. This and some debatable refereeing decisions saw them go down, 3-2.

Rangers now experienced the worst stage in their ten-year history, losing five games in succession. There were temporary recoveries – the great Queen's Parker, Harry McNeil, helped in a 2-2 draw with Dumbarton in the Glasgow Charity Cup. Two days later Aston Villa came to Kinning Park. Rangers were able to field a strong side, overwhelming Villa 7-1 with Willie Pringle notching a hat-trick. Next up were Blackburn Rovers with John Holm and George Angus (ex-Rangers) coming from Queen's Park and making a powerful contribution to a sparkling 2-2 draw as the goalscorers. For the Charity Cup replay at Hampden, 5,000 turned up to see a Rangers team without the brothers McNeil, Moses and Harry. Drinnan failed to arrive for the kick off. Aitken took his place, played well, but Dumbarton were superior, to the extent of 4-0. This had been a dreadful season. Most of the original band of players had either stopped playing, moved to Queen's Park or crossed the border to one of several Lancashire teams happy to offer them inducements. None of the founder members of the club, that happy band from West End Park, were included in the eleven which lost the ultimate match against Dumbarton. For the first time, Rangers had lost more matches than they had won. Things were bad – they were to get worse.

Rangers started the new season of 1882-83 on 26 August with a home match against Lugar Boswell. There were four new signings in the side – William Ness from Glasgow University in goal, James Duncan (Alexandra Athletic) who had been capped in March against Wales, was at full-back, Charlie Heggie was a reliable midfield player from South Western, and Alick McKenzie from Pilgrims was an attacker. In spite of these new men, all Rangers could manage was a 1-1 draw, thanks to a McKenzie goal. In the rematch at Rosebank a week later, Rangers went down 2-0. These results, against a less fashionable side, proved a sinister overture to the season. It was to prove one of indifferent form on the field, unrest off it.

They mustered up sufficient force to overcome Jordanhill in a first round Scottish Cup-tie on a rutted pitch at Anniesland. Against Dumbarton at Kinning Park on 16 September, another new face was introduced. James Gossland from Alexandra Athletic was a left side forward with exceptional dribbling skills, but no reputation as a goalscorer. Thanks to a Willie Corbett goal, Rangers secured a 1-1 draw. More seriously, the club was informed that Bob Young, on completing his medical studies, would be joining his brother, also a doctor, in practice in Manchester. Young was one of Rangers' best and most popular players.

The following week, Rangers met Queen's Park at Hampden. The Scottish Cup holders were in scintillating form and scored six goals against two from Rangers, by Ramsay and Hill. Goalkeeper Ness had a dreadful game and was faulted for several of the goals. He immediately offered to resign from the club, but was persuaded otherwise. Rangers needed a goalkeeper at the time – George Gillespie, who vied with McAuley of Dumbarton as 'The Prince of Goalkeepers', was not in accord with the committee, John Wallace Mackay in particular annoying him. Gillespie was not to be the only member who crossed swords with the honorary secretary. However, Gillespie donned the jersey for the first time that season a week later in the second round Scottish Cup-tie, against Queen's Park at Hampden. In five games since the start of the season, Rangers had won one, yet on a wet and windy day, they drew most of the 5,000 crowd. During the game when Rangers scored, the crowd was vociferous. When Queen's scored, there was almost total silence. Queen's were the greatest team of the era, but the romantic rise of the young Rangers in the seventies made them popular with the working classes of the city. Goals from Pringle and 'Tuck' McIntyre raised their hopes, but Queen's won 3-2. Rangers disputed one of their goals, but their protest was dismissed by the SFA.

At that time, Rangers decided to change their jersey colours from the 'present shabby blue' to blue and white hoops, the white of half an inch, the blue of one inch. They were worn for the first time in a match against Queen's Park, quite the wrong fixture to introduce them, as they clashed with Queen's black and white hoops. The October holiday weekend saw Rangers again in Lancashire, going down 1-0 to Bolton Wanderers (the goal scored by former Ranger Archie Steel) then holding Blackburn Rovers to 1-1 at Ewood Park.

The match against St Bernard's in Edinburgh scheduled for 11 November was cancelled at the last moment on the death of Rangers' president Archie Harkness. A founder member of the club, he had never reached the first team, although he played many times for the Swifts. The honorary secretary, John Wallace Mackay, was now allowed to dominate the club and wreak havoc. His reign coincided with one of the blackest periods in the entire history of Rangers and the club was forever involved in internal squabbling and disputes, one of the most consistent involving George Gillespie. In addition, Mackay often lambasted the Press, in particular the *Scottish Athletic Journal*, for its reporting of his dealings.

For one match at Cathkin, Gillespie failed to appear. Charlie Heggie played in goal, and saw Third Lanark deposit three past him. For the match against Dumbarton to Boghead, Phillips and Gillespie, again, were missing. George had been so disgusted with recent events that he stayed at Kinning Park to watch a Scottish Cup match between Arthurlie and Hibernian. Over the New Year period, Rangers were in Lancashire. They went down 3-2 to Accrington, then fought an exciting 4-4 draw with Darwen. On 2 January, they met Blackburn Rovers yet again at Ewood Park in dreadful weather conditions. Seven minutes into the second half, with the score 1-1, Rovers' players refused to go on, and the match was abandoned.

Back in Glasgow, the committee discarded George Gillespie for lack of commitment. John Phillips decided that enough was enough and went back to South Western, his first love. Then Gillespie patched up his differences with the club, and came back. There was a splendid run of results in February with four successive wins, the sequence broken only by a narrow 3-2 loss to Blackburn Rovers on 10 March, before a splendid 8,500 Kinning Park crowd. Business pressures broke another link with the foundation for the club when Peter McNeil, one of the West End Park originals, had to resign as match secretary. The honorary

secretary, J.W.Mackay, immediately grabbed the portfolio. Tom Vallance, another name from the earliest days, was back from Calcutta and Assam, but had been suffering from poor health. His best days had gone.

A stuffy performance by Rangers in the Charity Cup-tie against the powerful Vale of Leven at Hampden took Rangers through 3-2. The grand finale to the season was the Charity Cup Final, against Queen's Park at Hampden. Queen's won in a canter, 4-1 – even Rangers' goal was scored by the Hampden men, the great Walter Arnott being the culprit. Thus ended Rangers' worst season in their ten years of existence. In 29 outings, only eight matches had been won, a humiliating 16 lost. Financially, they were £100 in debt, despite £30 having been ploughed in by president George Goudie. Yet the optimists insisted that the good run in February could be repeated, given a settled team. And they decided to revert to the original blue jerseys.

The new season started early, and rancorously. On 31 July 1883, a match at Kinning Park against Dumbarton was played to raise money for the dependents of the 'Daphne Disaster'. A fortnight earlier, on Glasgow Fair Friday, the ship *Daphne* had overturned on her launching into the River Clyde with the loss of 146 of the 200 men working inside her hull. Rangers fielded a strong team and won 4-2, the match realising the sum of £63 8s 6d (approximately £63.45). Not all of it went to charity. Mr Mackay, Rangers' 'chief executive', decided that the club should take their share of match expenses. This decision was treated sensationally by the newspapers, and won no friends for the club. Rangers' response was a statement to the effect that it was all very well for big clubs like to Dumbarton to play for nothing!

On 19 August a massive 9-1 win was recorded at Johnstone in a match arranged to open the home team's new ground. Willie Chalmers made his debut in goal, in place of the discontented (yet again) George Gillespie. St Bernard's were beaten 4-2 in Edinburgh, Jimmy Gossland getting a hat-trick in a game that had grievous consequences for young left-back Fred Gordon. He broke his leg in a tackle, bringing the game to a close in the second half. It was feared that Gordon might lose his leg and it was several years before he reappeared, with the Swifts. Willie Hart came from Clyde to take his place in time to line up against Northern at Hydepark. A Gossland goal in a tough match took Rangers through that first round Cup-tie.

Five straight wins by Rangers pulled out a 6,000 crowd at Kinning Park to see them beat Vale of Leven. Third Lanark were swamped 5-0, then Tom Vallance made a rare appearance in the second round of the Cup. At home, Rangers overran Whitehill by 14-2, a record score which stands to this day. The Whitehill goals came only after goalkeeper Chalmers was injured. Gillespie, whose name was being linked to Queen's Park, was back in the position against Partick at home, Rangers winning 7-1. Chalmers had recovered for the next round of the Cup which saw Falkirk beaten 5-2.

At this time Rangers made another signing which attracted little notice, but was to become one of the most significant in the story of the club. William Wilton, who became a legend as Rangers' first manager achieved no great heights as a player. He played only in minor teams but his contributions, off the field, were to be massive.

The team's good form and impressive scoring continued. At Holm Park on 13 October against Kilmarnock Athletic, they were 4-0 ahead at half-time, only to lose 5-4 in a gale. It was their first defeat of the season. Gillespie was back in goal when Dumbarton won 2-0 at Boghead before a 5,000 crowd in a match which brought the unrest at Kinning Park to a head. Club president Tom Vallance resigned. He had been selected as an umpire for this match, but a deputation of players, said to be led by George Gillespie, opposed this on the grounds that Tom was too honest and would be too soft! Rangers had surely sunk to an all-time low.

At the six-monthly general meeting on 7 November 1883, there was better news. George Goudie the vice-president, took the chair. Mr Crichton, the secretary, reported that the club had been heavily in debt before Mr White had been appointed treasurer. Now, most of the debts had been paid off and only 'trifling sums' remained, which would be paid off over the next two games. George Gillespie had apologised to Tom Vallance, who was invited to resume the president's chair. He accepted, but Gillespie didn't change. The next Saturday, with Rangers winning 6-1 on Cup duty in Dunblane, he was missing. He preferred to referee Pollokshaws Athletic v Our Boys at Haggs Castle.

When Rangers beat St Bernard's 3-0 at Powderhall in the fifth round Scottish Cup, many believed that this could be the season for their first success. There was a set-back at Cathkin when Third Lanark beat them 2-1 in a game that was abandoned six minutes from the end. This followed a fracas in Third's goalmouth when Rangers, en masse, tried to force a loose ball through to level the match. In the scramble, a goal post was broken, the crowd invaded, and that was that!

Bob Young was back from Manchester to play a full-back role in the sixth-round tie at Cambuslang. Rangers were in spanking form, won 5-1 and were in the semi-finals for the first time in five years. Blackburn Rovers were their first foot on 5 January, winning 2-1. Three days later, George Gillespie left, at last, for Queen's Park, where he gave good service for many years. In these days there were no neutral venues for semi-finals, and Rangers were commanded to Alexandria to meet the powerful Vale of Leven. Expectations were high, the following of Rangers supporters huge, but the disappointment intense. They played poorly and were well beaten, 3-0. Attention now centred on the Charity Cup.

John Inglis lost his club membership when he decided to assist Blackburn Rovers in an FA Cup-tie, against the committee's instructions. At Easter, Rangers were yet again in Lancashire, 5,000 seeing their draw 1-1 with Bolton Wanderers, 4,000 a 4-1 defeat by Blackburn Rovers. On their return to Glasgow, the club found an eviction notice at Kinning Park, from their landlords. Possible extinction stared them in the face!

On 29 March, 'Tuck' McIntyre won his one and only cap for Scotland, against Wales. Sam Thomson played in the same match, but was presently 'snatched' by Preston North End for their team which was soon to be famous as 'The Invincibles'. Inglis was reinstated and played in a 5-0 win over Thistle at Kinning Park on 5 April. But he was simply passing through. He was back to help Blackburn win the FA Cup at the end of the season. A massive crowd of 10,000 at Cathkin saw the Charity Cup semi-final, Rangers v Queen's Park. In a rousing tie, Queen's only just edged it, 2-1. There had been a great improvement on the playing side of 36 starts, 22 wins, three draws. And there was financial improvement. Income was £804, expenditure £604, £100 of which was paid to Mr Mackay for advertising! At the annual general meeting president Tom Vallance promised new blood. All seemed well and improving – but the threat of eviction from Kinning Park remained.

The president fulfilled his promise. The summer of 1884 saw a major recruiting drive and many changes among the playing staff. Marshall and McIntyre of Third Lanark were wooed unsuccessfully, but Matt Lawrie, a notable dribbler, was secured from Cessnockbank. Peter Morton, a forward from Dean Park and Alick McKenzie, an outstanding header of the ball from Pilgrims, joined. On the other hand Aitken and Maitland moved on, both to Partick Thistle and David Hill, an international player, decided to retire. So too did full-back Jimmy Duncan, who was to serve on the committee.

The season opened with a 5-2 win over Young Boys in Dundee on 23 August. On their home debut a week later, all the new boys scored, Morton with three, McKenzie and Jimmy Gossland with two each and Lawrie and Willie Pringle counting in a total of nine against Kilmarnock Athletic's one. In the two weeks before their first Scottish Cup-tie, Rangers suffered a distinct loss when their outstanding young forward Alex Hamilton threw in his lot with Queen's Park. Happily their Cup opponents were out of their class and lost 11-0. Home matches against St Mirren (2-1) and the impressive Dumbarton (3-2) made for good preparation for the second round, away to Third Lanark at Cathkin. The biggest crowd of the season so far, 6,000, saw an engrossing match which ended 2-2. Rangers had fielded their former player Sam Thomson, now from Preston, and although his contribution was slight, Thirds quickly lodged a protest on the grounds that he was a professional. This was perfectly true and there is no doubt that Rangers, in the Mackay regime, were breaking the rules. Thirds were quite right – the rule of the time was that only bona fide members of a club could play in a Scottish Cup-tie, and that lists of registered members had to be lodged before a Cup-tie to allow members to play in it. Rangers were dangerously at risk since they could easily have been dismissed from membership of the SFA. Mackay's retort that the entire Thirds team were professional seemed an attempt to make one white equal 11 blacks. Rangers survived. The result stood.

The replay came on the following Saturday at Kinning Park before a crowd of 5,000 and was rough, ending goalless. It featured Lawrie and Kennedy of Thirds in a running feud which ended in a brawl. Much of the bad feeling clearly emanated from the protest. Rangers had played without Thomson but had lined up Archie Steel of Bolton Wanderers, unquestionably a professional.

The rules of the competition permitted both teams to pass into the next round if no decision had been reached and Thirds obviously decided that more protesting was not worth the candle. Nevertheless Rangers, and John Wallace Mackay, were living dangerously.

Before the third round, Vale of Leven came to Kinning Park to win 3-1. Rangers had another new signing that day, 18 October – Alec Peacock of Linthouse, a forward. Next, at the Glasgow October holiday, Rangers disposed of the moderate Fifth Kirkcudbrightshire Rifle Volunteers at Dumfries, by 4-1. The third round Cup draw produced, improbably, Third Lanark v Rangers at Cathkin. Heavy rain held the crowd down to 4,000, who saw a more relaxed Rangers take control and win comfortably, 3-0. Goals came from Lawrie, Morton and new boy Tommy Cook. But that was not the end of it. On checking Rangers' list of eligible players, Thirds were suspicious of Cook; sure enough, they found that name, but it appeared to them that the initial 'J' had been altered to 'T'. It was protest time again. Rangers' 'chief executive', MacKay, was a member of the SFA Committee at the time, yet the suggestion was that it was his hand that had made the alteration! The case provoked much debate and it was widely covered in the Press. The committee found for Rangers, but the whole series of squabbles left the club, so popular in their first decade, with a very tarnished image. They may have suffered from all of this in the very next round.

After a three-week break, it was Scottish Cup time again, this time away to Arbroath at Gayfield. Rangers had William Walker in place of the injured 'Tuck' McIntyre. Goals from Gossland Morton and McKenzie had them three up at half-time but a leg injury to Bob Young, which left him a passenger throughout the second half, brought a dramatic change to the game. Arbroath hit back, Rangers completely lost the initiative and disintegrated, losing 4-3. However, Rangers were past masters at finding loopholes in the rules – as soon as the game was over, they were out measuring the pitch and declaring it to be less than a foot short of the minimum width required. The now-famous telegram went off to Glasgow, 'beaten on a back green'. In went another protest. The SFA agreed, but proceeded with the draw for the next round, with Arbroath's name in the hat. Rangers were furious, made much noise, but no one was interested.

Queen's Park came to Kinning Park, won 3-2, with Rangers goals by Gossland. Jimmy Duncan was coaxed out of retirement in place of Bob Young. And on a bitterly cold day, only 500 spectators saw Rangers beat Third Lanark 6-0 at Cathkin. McKenzie had four goals, Alex Peacock two. Then Jimmy Gossland's goal beat the Pilgrims at Copland Park, Copland. Off the field, Rangers' persistence succeeded. The SFA reversed their decision and decreed that there should be a Cup re-run at Arbroath. On 20 December, Alex Vallance and 'Tuck' were back in the side and 2,000 fans wondered why this 8-1 replay should ever have been thought necessary.

The next round was much more serious – Renton v Rangers at Tontine Park. Rangers scored three goals away from home, McKenzie, Gossland and Peacock counting, but goalkeeper Willie Chalmers, who had been a tower of strength all season, had a disastrous match, conceding five goals. The Scottish Cup dream was over for yet another year. Renton went on to win the Cup that season, beating neighbours Vale of Leven at Hampden after a goalless draw. The crowds were 3,000, then 5,500. Vale at least had turned up for the Final which they had not done the previous season. They had refused to accept the SFA's Final date because of injuries and a family bereavement, and failed to appear. The Cup went by default to Queen's Park and medals were awarded to players who had played in their 5-1 semi-final win over Hibernian.

Rangers' New Year tour in Lancashire brought reasonable results. Preston won 3-1 at Deepdale, Darwen were defeated 5-1 and, the third game in three days, a goalless draw with Blackburn Rovers was creditable. Back at Kinning Park, there were new faces, George Somerville from Hamilton Accies and Jim Mackie from Govanhill in a 3-2 win over Third Lanark. Through February and into March, Rangers were unbeaten against Hibs, St Bernard's, Pollokshields Athletic, Cambuslang, Ayr and Battlefield. In that last match, John Muir and John Allan were introduced. Allan, known as the 'Montcastle Flyer' because of his speed (at one time he held a Scottish national sprint record), was a former Queen's Park player and Scottish international.

The new 'three half-back' system was used for the first time on 4 April 1885, when Rangers beat Cambuslang 4-1 at Westburn Green. The following week they faced Dumbarton at Hampden in the Charity Cup. Cherrie,

Lafferty and Somerville were all ineligible, having played for other clubs in the competition. The match was drawn, 2-2, the 3,500 crowd was increased to 5,000 for the replay. Again the tie was fiercely contested, finishing 1-1 with McKenzie scoring. On 22 April, visitors Blackburn Rovers ended the run of 11 games without defeat, although their 4-3 win was a touch fortunate. Rangers' goals were by Pringle, Mackie and Heggie before a crowd of 6,000.

When Gossland scored twice against Partick Thistle at Muirpark three days later, the home team responded with five, and Rangers' bubble had burst for the season. On 2 May, Dumbarton won the Charity Cup second replay at Hampden by 2-0 before 7,000, and Rangers rounded out their season with a 1-0 win over Queen's at Hampden. With 24 wins in 40 matches and six drawn, it had been a reasonable achievement, although most of the matches were at Kinning Park. At the annual general meeting, Tom Vallance was returned as president and was so enthused with things that he declared that he would speak to the members at the next annual meeting with three trophies on the table – the Scottish Cup, the Charity Cup and the FA Cup, which they had decided to enter.

The first jolt to Rangers' cup winning ambitions came in July 1885. Bob Young had graduated MBChB at Glasgow University and planned to practice in Manchester. Rangers had lost one of their star players. Willie Chambers missed the start of the season, 19 August 1885. Alick McKenzie took his place in goal against Northern at Hydepark. Top-class forwards Marshall and Crawford of Third Lanark made first appearances and Peter Miller of Dumbarton lined up against Hibs in Edinburgh. George Somerville came back to lead the attack and scored twice in a 3-2 defeat. The first home match against Kilmarnock was only won by 4-3, and defeats came at Boghead 4-1 and at, of all places, Cambuslang by 5-2, at Whitefield Park. When Jim Mackie was lost through injury and Marshall and Crawford elected to remain with Thirds, and with the Scottish Cup looming, alarm bells were ringing.

A surprising success came in the Eadie Fraser Benefit match against Queen's Park at Hampden. On a miserably wet night, Somerville struck twice in a 2-1 win. But when Rangers were drawn to meet Clyde at Barrowfield Park, he failed to turn up. John Muir, a half-back, took his place at centre-forward. Rangers played poorly, were deservedly beaten by one goal which of course they disputed vigorously, insisting that the ball never crossed the line and when nothing came of that John Cherrie promptly decided that his future lay with Rangers' conquerors, his old team Clyde, whom he served nobly for years as a player and in committee. Queen's Park were to win the Cup that season, beating Renton in the Final.

On 26 September a crowd of 4,000 was at Hampden for Rangers' match against Queen's Park. Most of them were Rangers fans, in ugly mood throughout a hard physical game. The club was now beset by a foul, loudmouthed support and Kinning Park was fast becoming one of the most disreputable grounds in Scotland. And the residents of Mount Florida were loathe to welcome such hordes to their quiet, douce, respectable suburb. The match itself was won by Queen's Park, 3-2. Rangers' scorers were McKenzie and Somerville. Indeed, Somerville's general play and scoring may have been the one redeeming feature for Rangers in the entire season ...Rangers were not being held in high esteem – at club smokers, players and officials were often said to have been seen in states of intoxication and very few were considered to be 'gentlemen'.

It became a convoluted season. Small attendances were a feature. A series of matches against weak opposition followed – Fifth Kirkcudbrightshire Volunteer Rifles, Falkirk, Battlefield. On 24 October at Cappielow, there was trouble finding a referee. Mr McKay took the field, deputising, but the small crowd of 500 was so hostile that he quickly changed his mind and went off. Morton won 2-1. A few days later, George Somerville, who had missed the game signed for Queen's Park, a move that had been on the cards. By the end of the season, he would be leading Scotland's attack against England, scoring in the 1-1 draw.

One of Tom Vallance's promised trophies had gone. Rangers had entered the FA Cup for the first time and were drawn against Rawtenstall in the first round. It was the tie that never was – Rangers protested to the FA that the English club had professionals on their list of registered players, and refused to play. The FA hit them with a heavy fine.

Jim Buchanan was drafted into the forward line to fill Somerville's place in the Halloween match against Renton at Kinning Park. Charlie Heggie hit a hat-trick in a solid 4-2 win. Heggie and Rangers had a spell of impressive scoring. The forward registered five in a 6-0 win over St Mirren and five in a Boxing Day match at Kinning Park against London Scottish. Beaten 12-2, the guests must have wished they hadn't made the long journey.

In spite of the poor attendances, members were told at the half-yearly meeting in December that the club was flourishing, would show a profit and, under the eye of Willie Wilton, there were many promising junior players coming along. The continued threat of eviction from Kinning Park was the main problem, and hastened the desire for a new ground for the next season.

Four games had seen 26 goals scored and the team continued the trend with an 8-2 win over Cliftonville in Belfast on 2 June, to inaugurate the Irish club's ground. This was the first Rangers overseas trip of any kind, the forerunner of many to almost every quarter of the world. At the end of January, Charlie Heggie's irrepressible scoring form continued. For the third time he scored five goals, in a 6-0 win over Third Lanark. But 6 February was to become a black day in the history of the club. There was a heavy snowfall in Glasgow that day and all matches were off save Rangers v Airdrie at Kinning Park. Rangers were unbeaten in eight games in which they had scored 50 goals and the committee, with an eye on the admission money, decided the game should go on, snow or no snow. Rangers' short-passing game floundered, Airdrie played a hard-driving, volleying game without frills on a snow-covered field, and won 10-2. That remains Rangers' record defeat and may remain so, until the end of time.

In April, at Westmarch Paisley, the Rangers Swifts tackled Abercorn in the Scottish Second Eleven Cup Final. Many thought that the Swifts of this season, under the guidance of Wilton, were a better team than the first team. Alas, another trophy went begging when Abercorn won 2-0. On 16 April, Rangers met Vale of Leven in the Glasgow Charity Cup and went down 1-0. All three of Tom Vallance's cups had gone. The *Scottish Athletic Journal* had a field day. Referring to the close season statement of president Vallance, they said they would present three (tea) cups to place on the table before him at the annual general meeting.

Of very much greater importance however came the resignation of John Wallace Mackay. Pressure had been brought on this controversial character who had once been expelled from the Christian Institute for swearing, and who

shortly lost his position at the SFA. Soon afterwards, he was followed by one of his cronies, W.W.Tait, as Rangers reorganised themselves. These changes brought an immediate upturn in their fortunes. Blackburn Rovers lost an exciting game 4-3, with John Gow (2), Jim Buchanan and Alex Peacock scoring. On the Monday, the game against Nottingham Forest attracted 6,000, the season's biggest attendance, to Kinning Park to see a 2-1 win with goals from Pringle and Heggie. At the same time, Rangers were considering taking a ground near the Third Lanark Rifle Volunteers Drill Hall in Strathbungo, at a rent of £80 per annum. The *Scottish Athletic Journal* commented cryptically that rents in Pollokshields and Strathbungo would tumble if the Kinning Park roughs decided to follow Rangers.

Kinning Park was closed for play on 21 May with the pitch almost devoid of grass and badly in need of a rest. At the annual general meeting members were told that there was in fact a loss on the season of £90, because of the early exit from the Scottish Cup, but the club had funds of £128 2s 3d (£128.11). On 2 June, the Kinning Park ground was re-opened for a game in aid of the local unemployed. Some £18 was raised as Rangers drew 1-1 with a Glasgow Select 'Crusaders'.

The season's conclusion arrived at Hampden on 5 June, in a tournament to raise funds for a new drill hall for Third Lanark Rifle Volunteers. Queen's Park, Third Lanark, Cowlairs and Rangers were to play matches of 20 minutes each half, with ten minutes extra-time and corners to count if necessary. The Finalists were to receive badges. Rangers beat Cowlairs 1-0 and in the Final against Queen's Park there were no goals, two corners each after normal time. A glorious strike from Jim Buchanan in extra-time gave Rangers modest consolation for a modest season.

During the close season of 1886, there were no major departures from the club, but new recruits were Gray, a forward from Partick Thistle, and John McCartney, a burly young full-back from Cartvale as a partner in defence for the 18-year-old Donald Gow, brother of left-winger John. Other good news was that Charlie Heggie, a talented striker who was to have an up and down relationship with the club, announced that after all, although he had married in July, he had 'no intention of giving up playing'.

Rangers started the season at Alexandria on 21 August with the following team: Willie Chalmers, Donald Gow, John McCartney, 'Tuck' McIntyre, John Cameron, Peacock, Gray, Heggie, Jim Buchanan, Willie Pringle and John Gow. In those days, few clubs had much success at the major Dunbartonshire grounds of Vale of Leven, Renton and Dumbarton, so Rangers' 2-1 win over Vale of Leven was an outstanding start. Heggie and Buchanan were the goalscorers. Another strong side, Dumbarton, opened the Kinning Park season and again Rangers prevailed, by 2-1, thanks to Heggie and Peacock goals.

Although Rangers were already planning a move, money was spent on the Kinning Park ground. New grass had been sown in the close season, and a terracing was being raised alongside the pitch to take a further 2,000 spectators. In September the trip to Kirkintilloch was made (considered an expedition into 'the country') and the local team, Central, was dumped 5-0, good practice for the Scottish Cup-tie, due a week later. Against near-neighbours Govan Athletic, Rangers won this in a canter, 9-1.

Their first defeat of the season came on 25 September by Renton, 3-2, on their own Tontine Park. In the second round of the Scottish Cup Rangers made heavy weather of beating Westbourne 5-2; only some 500 fans felt inclined to watch such opposition. On 7 October, as part of an International Exhibition being held in Edinburgh, they played St Bernard's there. The match was significant for the appearance of their latest acquisition from Queen's Park, Bob Fraser. He replaced John Gow, whose injury was to keep him out of football for six months. A tricky winger, Fraser scored in a 4-1 win.

With eight wins and one close defeat behind them, Rangers were set for the first big test of the season. Almost 7,000 were on hand for their home game against Queen's Park, but Rangers went down heavily, by 4-1. Charlie Heggie was an absentee – once more he had fallen out with the club, and indeed went off and played for St Bernard's that same day. He was back in the team to face Cambuslang at Kinning Park in the third round of the Scottish Cup to the exclusion of Bob Fraser but to no great effect. An impressive display by Cambuslang gave them a 2-0 win. The Scottish Cup 'went east' for the first time. Hibs beat Dumbarton at the second Hampden Park on 12 February, before a crowd of 10,000.

With the Scottish Cup beyond them yet again, Rangers turned their attention to the FA Cup. Scheduled to meet Everton, they stayed overnight in a Goodison hotel. Well, not quite overnight – shortly after midnight they were out in the street. The proprietor took exception to their revelry and dumped them out bag and baggage. They had to find refuge in another hotel, but the exploit did nothing to their form. A Charlie Heggie goal took them through to the astonishment of a 6,000 Merseyside crowd. That same week Willie Pringle shocked his teammates by saying he intended to retire from playing. He had made his debut for Rangers on 1 January, 1880 and in recognition, the club presented him with a gold badge.

Dumbarton were bent on revenge for an early season defeat when the teams met on 6 November at Boghead, and in an astonishing match, Rangers were five down at one point but recovered to earn a remarkable 5-5 draw. Matt Lawrie was the hero with a hat-trick. Next, the English side Church came north for the second round of the FA Cup and a match which Rangers won more comfortably than the 2-1 scoreline would suggest. A week later a jaunt to their friends of Cliftonville in Belfast was notable because the temperamental Charlie Heggie did not make the trip. His running feud with the club had reached the point of no return, and the talented goalscorer took himself off permanently to play with St Bernard's of Edinburgh. Young McNab of the Swifts was an instant success as replacement, scoring three goals in the 4-1 success in Ireland. Matt Lawrie had the other goal.

The FA Cup third round saw two Scottish clubs in opposition, Rangers winning a very close match 3-2 against Cowlairs. Donald Gow and Alick McKenzie were back in the team. Following the game, Rangers were notified that Kinning Park would definitely close, and the search for a new ground was intensified. There was cheering news at the half-yearly meeting when it was announced that the club's income had profited by £26. Robert Kerr resigned from the committee, with Bob Fraser taking his place. And when the committee learned that Joe Lindsay, Dumbarton's famous international centre-forward was working in Govan, they decided he was the man to take Charlie Heggie's place. He was transferred and made his debut at Kinning Park on Christmas Day, in a 1-1 draw with Renton.

The holiday season was spent with another visit to Lancashire, better-behaved this time, but not so successful.

On New Year's Day of 1887, Rangers lost to Bolton Wanderers 3-2, then two days later they were trounced by Preston North End 8-1. No doubt they had done some Ne'er Day celebrating. On their return to Glasgow it was learned that there were prospects of settling on some ground at Ibrox, further west, as a successor to Kinning Park. The word 'Ibrox' was to become as much part of the club's history as its name, but Press conjecture at the time was whether or not this venue would be too far from the city! Little could they know that in the 1920s, it would be served directly by bus, tramway, Underground and rail lines.

With a bye in the fourth round, Rangers met Lincoln City in the fifth round of the FA Cup, at home, and won easily by 3-0. Donald Gow so impressed the visitors that they offered him £2 10s (£2.50), a huge sum at the time, to join them. Gow flatly refused. Rangers fourth successive home draw in the competition brought Old Westminsters to Kinning Park on 19 February. The date is significant in the Rangers story. It saw the last official match Rangers played on the ground, after 11 years, fittingly bringing victory over the English team by 5-1 in a splendid performance which gave them a place in the semi-final.

Rangers had been strengthened by the inclusion of John Forbes, a Vale of Leven international and one of the best full-backs of the Victorian era, and Pat Lafferty. The latter, although a club member, normally played only in 'important' Cup-ties. To make room for them, Jim Buchanan was one of the players who had to drop out. Buchanan promptly 'took the huff'. He had been in the team for a year and was a proven goalscorer, but he never again played for Rangers. Thus within a few months, the club had lost the second of two outstanding goalscorers, a state of affairs they would come to regret over the next few seasons.

On 5 March, Rangers met Aston Villa in the FA Cup semi-final, on neutral ground, at Nantwich. The teams had met four times previously, each winning twice, each winning the home matches. If Rangers were unlucky in having to play on a neutral ground which was a lot closer to Birmingham than to Glasgow, they were even more unlucky in meeting their own former player Hugh McIntyre, now of Blackburn Rovers, who turned up to encourage his Glasgow chums. He encouraged some of them too much. On the morning of the match, he entertained some of them to a meal. Willie Chalmers, the goalkeeper, was a man who enjoyed his food and on this occasion he put away a good deal too much. Willie's 'mobility' was lost, Rangers lost 3-1 and the Scots bitterly condemned their goalkeeper for each of the three goals lost.

The Third Lanark club kindly allowed Rangers the use of their Cathkin Park for their home games for the remainder of the season. They lost 2-1 there to Vale of Leven, on 19 March, a date memorable for the return of John Gow after a very long absence. They following week, 5,000 saw Queen's Park give a majestic performance in beating Rangers 4-1. In May, 12,000 crowded Hampden to see the Renton-Rangers Glasgow Merchants' Charity Cup replay, which produced a thrilling match that went to extra-time and yet another 1-1 draw. In the second replay, Rangers went down 2-1.

The last match of the season was against Hibs at Inchview, Partick Thistle's ground at the time. 'Tuck' McIntyre's goal won the match for Rangers and left their fans looking forward to a new season at a new ground.

The 11 men who wore the light blue on 20 August 1887 in the historic opening day of the new Ibrox were: Willie

Chalmers; Donald Gow, John McCartney; John Cameron, 'Tuck' McIntyre, John Muir; Hammy Brown, Andy Peacock, Alick McKenzie, Willie Pringle, Bob Brand. Since the Preston 'Invincibles' clobbered Rangers 8-1, the players had to take a serious slating as their reward. Understandably it was too much for some of them. Hammy Brown went back to his old club Clyde. John McCartney had had enough. He joined Cowlairs. Seven days after the opening match, Morton came to Ibrox and Rangers only just managed a 2-2 draw. After another couple of games, Willie Chalmers turned his back on the abuse and he, too, signed for Clyde. Crowds were disappointing for the owners of this splendid new ground – only 1,000 turned up to see Dumbarton, then close to the peak of their powers.

Rangers had had an easy first round Scottish Cup-tie, their first of the new Ibrox, beating Battlefield 4-1 on 3 September, but chopping and changing the team as they had done, they had some fears of the second round draw, away to Partick Thistle at Inchview. They were right. They had not beaten Thistle since December 1885, and went down again, 2-1, Bob Brand scoring. Another player was lost when Matt Lawrie went off to England and a job in farming.

This was the inaugural season of the Glasgow Cup, a competition not generally welcomed as it was expected to clutter the fixture list. But it caught the public attention and has lasted more than 100 years. Rangers and Third Lanark played a first round 2-2 draw with Bob Fraser and White scoring. Donald Gow was back for the replay, the crowd was a healthy 5,000 and the 2-0 win was well-deserved. Pollokshields Athletic at Pollok Park and Westbourne at Ibrox were disposed of, and when, against St Bernard's, Willie Pringle was back to score once, and John Gow three times in a 5-1 win, Rangers were at last striking some form. There was another 5-1 against Battlefield at Mossfield, then five without replay against Third Lanark at Ibrox. The experiment of playing Bob Fraser at centre-forward and Bob Brand on the left wing had been a success. Fraser had one goal, Brand four.

On 19 November, it was Cowlairs v Rangers at Gourlay Park in the semi-final of the Glasgow Cup and a goalless draw. Port Glasgow were hit for six at Ibrox with Willie Pringle seemingly rejuvenated to the extent of scoring three. The Cowlairs replay at Ibrox was also goalless before 5,000, the second replay at Cathkin before 6,000 produced goals but no result. Fraser and Brand scored in the 2-2 draw. The third replay, on 17 December, went to Barrowfield Park with two Peacock goals giving Rangers a close 2-1 win. But Cowlairs had not finished. They claimed that the match had finished 15 minutes early. They also claimed that Rangers were professionals. They later dropped this generalisation, but then said that Bob Brand, Rangers' pre-season capture from Queen of the South Wanderers, was a professional. They were given time to collate evidence and produced the story that he had been given £1 from the Dumfries club to buy a suit, in 1885! The SFA dismissed this, but suspended the player for two months for receiving £1 from Hearts. He had played for them in an August match, before joining Rangers who were cleared of all blame. But a replay was ordered for 21 January.

In the interval, Rangers at last beat Partick Thistle, 3-1 at Ibrox on Hogmanay, then played a 1-1 draw against Queen's at Hampden. Alick McKenzie, a lad o'pairts, played in goal and 5,000 saw John Gow's goal for Rangers. A 3-2 win against Morton in Greenock set them up for the match with Cowlairs. Feelings ran high among both sets of supporters and 6,000 saw a hard, physical battle decided 3-1 for Rangers with goals from McKenzie, Fraser and Peacock. If after five games the teams were heartily sick of each other, total receipts of £400 was acceptable medicine.

The first Glasgow Cup Final took place at Hampden on 28 January 1888, with Rangers and Cambuslang involved before what was a huge crowd for the time, 11,000. Rangers had gone 16 games without defeat. Cambuslang were in the Scottish Cup Final, due the following week. To the disappointment of the majority of that crowd, Cambuslang dominated and ran Rangers ragged by 3-1. Ironically, Cambuslang were swept away by Renton, 6-1 in what remains the most emphatic Scottish Cup Final defeat.

Rangers, too, lost their edge after that Glasgow Cup Final. They drew with Dumbarton Athletic 1-1 at Ibrox. They went to Birmingham and lost 5-1 to Aston Villa, despite having guest players Bob Smillie (Queen's Park), Neilly McCallum and Campbell of Renton and Buchanan Junior and Gourlay of Cambuslang. They lost 2-0 to Albion Rovers at Whifflets, and Renton came to Ibrox and clobbered them 7-3.

Ibrox staged its first floodlight match on 8 March 1888 against 'Scottish Corinthians', in effect the Scottish national team. They had a good night, winning 4-1. This 'sunlight' match was a success and raised a good deal of money for Govan charities. The lights were installed by Braby & Co and one report said, "When Ibrox was approached, it looked like a large foundry. Inside, the hissing sound suggested the last boat to Rothesay. Play could be followed all over the field. It was much better than previous efforts". Two days later, John Cameron came out of retirement – his last game had been in October – for what he thought would be his final match. Against Dumbarton at Boghead, it was an exciting 4-4 draw before 3,000. The Sons' townies, Dumbarton Athletic, won 2-1 at Ibrox on 24 March. Bob Brand, his suspension over, scored but played poorly and moved on to Hearts. On the first Saturday of April, Rangers were missionaries in the Highlands, beating an Inverness XI 4-0 before 5,000 enthralled spectators. On the Sunday morning, Andy Peacock contributed a different type of entertainment. He went swimming in the River Ness, whose currents carried him far downstream before he scrambled ashore. Undaunted, he marched stark naked back up the road to where his clothes lay, past the douce and startled citizens on their way to the kirk.

Rangers last chance of winning a trophy was in the Charity Cup. In their opening tie, they looked dead and buried, 3-0 down to Vale of Leven. Peacock and Aird pulled goals back before the equaliser was scrambled home by an unidentified player. The replay, also at Hampden, was a thriller, won 5-3 with Nicol (2), Aird (2) and McKenzie scoring. This game had an extraordinary ending. It finished ten minutes early to allow Vale of Leven to catch a train back to Alexandria!

Aston Villa were in Glasgow on Saturday, 5 May to find a Rangers team very different from the one that had lost 5-1 in Birmingham. Two goals from John Gow helped in a fine 3-1 win. Gow scored again in midweek against Renton in the Charity Cup semi-final. The 'Champions of the World' were a class above the Villa and Rangers went down 5-1. Renton, Scottish Cup winners, defeated their English counterparts West Bromwich Albion by 4-1 in a match which had been arbitrarily billed as for the 'Championship of the World'. The end of the season thus came with a rush for Rangers, with four games in ten days. In hindsight, the last of these was one of the most important single football matches played anywhere in the world.

Early in June came the Rangers annual general meeting. Financially, all those Cup-ties meant they were able to pay £1,008 3s 1d (£1,008.15) towards the cost of Ibrox. But many members were unhappy with clashes among the committee of which there had been many. Six committee members failed to be re-elected. Perhaps the changes there, and the appointment of Johnny Taylor from Clyde as a full-time trainer, would have an effect next season.

The First Old Firm Game

What was to become considered by the more chauvinistic, not to say insular, of Scottish football supporters as the 'greatest game in the world', was first played on 28 May 1888 when Rangers went to Celtic Park to meet this new club, Celtic, in its first game, on its own ground.

Within six months of their initial committee meeting, the new Irish club (preceded in the East by Hibernian, on Tayside by Harp of Dundee) had collected a team and a ground at Parkhead (rent of £50 per annum and a ground built by a hoard of the club's volunteer supporters). For this opening match, they recruited a team where they could find it, and in this respect, their greatest capture was the most famous player in the country, James Kelly of Renton. Kelly was an attacking centre-half and an international player. John Glass, the Celtic president, well aware that this superstar's presence in Celtic colours would attract the crowd and just as important in the initial stages of this great adventure, make recruiting other players much simpler, pursued Kelly and after a long courtship, persuaded him to pledge his troth with Celtic.

The Celtic team on that late spring evening was: Dolan; Pearson, McLaughlin; W.Maley, Kelly, Murray; McCallum, T.Maley, Madden, Dunbar, Gorevin. They had been culled from some of the leading clubs in the country. Rangers, too, had some guests, some regulars but more members of their reserve team, known as the Swifts. Rangers were not having the best of times, but then the Celtic team was an unknown quantity. Nevertheless, some 2,000 saw them beat Rangers 5-2, with Neilly McCallum having the distinction of scoring the first Celtic goal, the first goal in an 'Old Firm' game, the first goal at Celtic Park. He also became the first man to play for both clubs – a few months earlier he had played for Rangers against Aston Villa in Birmingham. The Rangers team was: Jimmy Nicol; 'Tuck' McIntyre, John Muir; McPherson, W.McFarlane, Meikle; Robb, McLaren, Alick McKenzie, J.Suter, Wilson. Fittingly, two of the most loyal and talented servants, McIntyre and McKenzie, took part. They had stayed with Rangers through the best of times, the worst of times.

After the game, teams and officials and members gathered in the nearby St Mary's Hall, where they had supper and a concert, joining in several toasts. Early relations between the clubs were thus excellent. John H.McLaughlin, a Celtic committee member and later the club's first chairman, was a talented pianist who accompanied the Rangers Glee Club for several years. Little did these celebrants imagine that all this in the years to come would generate into the most bitter enmity in sport.

Season 1888-89 was disastrous for Rangers, quite the worst in their 17 years of existence. They were beaten in early rounds of both the Scottish Cup and the Glasgow Cup. They were not considered good enough to play in the Glasgow Charity Cup. They lost 6-1 at home in the Glasgow Cup to Celtic, a record away win between the clubs to this day. Third Lanark beat them 5-1. Only nine players turned up for a match against Morton at Greenock, when veterans had to step in. They lost 7-2. In a floodlit exhibition match at Gilmorehill, they lost 8-0 to Vale of Leven. In another match, only ten men turned up. On 4 August they opened the season way to Shettleston, playing under the name of 'Ibroxonians' and lost 3-0, a shocking result against junior opposition. It was an indication of traumas ahead. The Ibrox pitch was criticised as a 'potato patch' and the half-yearly meeting in November was so heated that it was adjourned for a week. The committee had been accused of treating football as a pastime and not a business, perhaps a strange remark for an amateur club. After a nine-hour debate, the committee was increased by two to total seven.

If the top team had been less than convincing, by contrast the reserves, the Swifts under the management of William Wilton, were highly successful and in the opinion of many contemporaries, better than the first XI. They made the point on 11 August at Celtic Park, when they whipped Celtic 9-1. On 25 August Rangers beat Hibernian 3-2 at Ibrox fielding a new right wing of Eaglesham and Sloan. Alex Vallance made a surprise return, after a very long absence. The win glossed over many of Rangers' shortcomings. The Hibernian playing staff had been severely depleted by raids from Celtic, and English clubs. A midweek goalless draw with Clyde at Barrowfield preceded a two-games-in-a-day venture at Ibrox. On 1 September, first Patrick Thistle were beaten 4-2 in the first round of the Scottish Cup. A new right winger Tom Wylie from Maybole, was a flying winger indeed with a hat-trick. That other flying winger, John Gow, had the other goal.

The terraces were then cleared, the gates reopened for a match against Preston North End, seen by 1,500, about half of the Thistle attendance. Guests included George Gillespie, now at Queen's Park, and Johnny Forbes, from Vale of Leven. Preston won easily, 4-0.

A home draw against United Abstainers in the first round of the Glasgow Cup brought no threat and a 10-0 win. A 2-2 draw away to Clyde in the second round of the Scottish Cup left Rangers feeling confident about the replay at Ibrox. Their confidence was misplaced. Clyde strolled through the match, 3-0. Willie Pringle made yet another comeback after a nine-month absence in a 7-1 win over Pollokshields Athletic in the Glasgow Cup second round. Alick McKenzie scored four. At Whiteinch, Patrick Thistle overcame a side that included Maxwell of St Mirren and Stark from Airdrie. Once again the committee was being criticised for chopping and changing the team, and with good reason. The following week there were wholesale changes with no improvement. Third Lanark won 5-1. Five changes were made for the next match, the Glasgow Cup third-round tie against Celtic at Ibrox. Jimmy Wilson scored first to the delight of most of the 4,000 crowd, but Celtic produced a brand of play reflected in the 6-1 result.

Things turned in Rangers' favour on 3 November against Cowlairs at Ibrox. A new left winger, Johnston of Rutherglen, made a pleasing debut with two goals in a 5-2 win. Tom Wylie had a hat-trick, but the meagre crowd was more concerned with booing their former player, John

McCartney, each time he played the ball. The player responded in the Press, complaining that 'the following of Rangers is the worst in Scotland'. Rangers lost at Cambuslang, beat Partick Thistle 4-0 but still the sporting Press was scathing: "The pitch should be used for planting potatoes. The 'Light Blues' may be more successful as potato cultivators than football purveyors".

In December, the match committee was reconstructed and its first selection, with no new faces, was seen on 15 December against Battlefield at Ibrox. There was no improvement. Rangers lost 2-1. Against Queen's at Hampden they lost 3-0. The last Saturday of 1888, and New Year's Day of 1889, saw Rangers at their lowest point. For the match in Greenock, only nine players arrived. Willie Pringle and Jimmy Gossland had to step in. Morton won easily, 7-2. On New Year's Day, Rangers were in Blackburn, losing 6-2 to the Rovers before 7,000, while at the same time Aston Villa arrived in Glasgow, expecting to play Rangers. This was quite scandalous incompetence from the Ibrox club.

The next day Rangers played Bolton Wanderers, but after half an hour, thick fog obscured everything with the score at 1-1. After a 20-minute wait, the referee declared the match a draw, then decided to stage an 'exhibition' for spectators with good eyesight. This, too, was quickly abandoned.

On 12 January, Abercorn thrashed Rangers 6-1 at Blackstoun Park. On a return trip to Nottingham, Forest won 2-1. This time Alick McKenzie was in goal.

After a 2-2 draw with Uddingston, Rangers were criticised for conditions at Ibrox: "Such apathy and the name and fame of grand old Rangers will soon be but a memory". Fortunes for the rest of the season were up and down, in and out – a home loss 4-2 to Partick Thistle before a paltry 500; a 2-1 win at Ayr; a home draw with Port Glasgow 2-2; a 4-1 win at Cambuslang, and a home defeat 2-0 from Morton. The win at Ayr ended a run of nine games without success. Nottingham Forest visited on 20 April, enticed by a guarantee for £25. Rangers won 2-0 with goals from Muir and Dickie, but lost at the gate where only £26 was taken.

A Cowal XI was beaten 9-1 at Dunoon, Blackburn Rovers were held 1-1 at Ibrox, but Queen of the South Wanderers humiliated Rangers in Dumfries, 6-2. Third Lanark won 3-1 at Ibrox and Partick Thistle won 6-2 at Inchview. For this match, Rangers started with ten players, three of whom had not expected to play – they had not brought their boots. It had been that kind of season for the Ibrox club, even if they did surprise Renton there by 3-2. Prominent in this win were the brothers McPherson of Cowlairs, the elder of whom, John, was to feature prominently in Rangers' history.

The annual general meeting was held on 27 May, lasted five hours, the business conducted briskly. The liability of £450 from the construction of the new ground was not considered pressing. A match committee was formed to control all three teams, consisting of Willie Wilton, Alick McKenzie and John M.Grant. The first match under their rein was a 6-0 win over a Falkirk District XI, but that could not disguise a dreadful season in which the club, more than once, had come close to extinction. The men at the helm faced a heavy task in returning the club to its standards of the 1870s.

If season 1889-90 was to start with a mini-tournament, it was to finish with Scottish football convulsed, with the Scottish Football League formed, making professionalism inevitable, and moving the member clubs along to becoming limited companies, not to mention a century on, public

quoted companies. In the case of Rangers, the season was the beginning of a more calculated attitude to team building, no doubt influenced by Willie Wilton, which was to see a first championship won, or at least shared, and a steady development for the club through the decade of the 1890s.

The team was early at work, beating Clyde 9-1 at Irvine in the Sir William Cunningham Cup. The Final was played at Ibrox two weeks later, but Cowlairs knocked out the home team, 4-0. In the Rangers and Clydesdale Harriers Sports Club Cup, first round, Rangers beat Third Lanark 4-0 before a crowd of 8,000. There were new recruits. Robert Marshall, signed from Patrick Thistle, played at wing-half and Jimmy Henderson, a left winger from Fifth Kirkcudbrightshire Rifle Volunteers, scored. Low of Kilbirnie and Wilkie of Uddingston were two other new forwards. These mini-tournaments culminated in a Final against a star-studded Celtic, seen by rather more than 3,000. The Parkhead men were only slightly better, but won by 2-0. A Notts County 'agent' was on hand, keen to sign the Rangers defender, John Hendry, and somehow the crowd became aware of his presence. Identifying the man, they set upon him severely – being a talent scout in these times was a dangerous line of work.

When Maryhill drew 1-1 at Ibrox and Falkirk won 1-0 at Brockville, it was clear that the new Rangers players would need time to settle. David Reid of Maryhill made his debut in goal against St Mirren at Ibrox on 24 August, Alick McKenzie moving out to centre-forward. It was not a winning start for the new man. Rangers lost 2-0. Local team Linthouse had been agitating for a match with Rangers for some time, no doubt seeking to prove that they were the number-one team in Govan and on 28 August, came the day. McKenzie was back in goal, and in came Ralston, McBain and Elspie from the Swifts. John Allan, the' Monkcastle Flyer' and Jimmy Henderson were given a further run on the left wing. This Ibrox match was physical, as local derbies can be, but Rangers came out on top by 2-1. Next came a nightmare match at Barrowfield, Clyde running amok to win 8-2.

September brought the Scottish Cup and Rangers drew a 'rabbit' in United Abstainers at Ibrox. That was 6-2. On 14 September 1889, one of the greatest of Rangers players, Dave Mitchell from Kilmarnock made his debut against Morton at Cappielow. Although Rangers lost 3-2, the new man made a big impression. Next Pollokshaws were disposed of in the Glasgow Cup by 5-1, then in the second round of the Scottish Cup, it was Kelvinside Athletic, at Kelburn Park, shattered 13-0. This equalled the record scores of 1877-78. The line up for this tie was: David Reid; Hay, John Hendry; Robert Marshall, 'Tuck' McIntyre, Davie Mitchell; Tom Wylie, Donald Gow, Johnny Robin, John Allan and Jimmy Henderson. This was to be the nucleus of a settled side for most of the season.

A Donald Gow goal gave Rangers a 1-1 draw at Parkhead and the fans were now coming back. Around 5,000 saw a high-scoring Glasgow Cup victory, 6-3 over Northern at Hydepark. Gow (3) and Robin, Wylie and Allan were the goalscorers. And 9,000 were at Ibrox to see Vale of Leven in the third round Scottish Cup-tie. The match was tremendous, but a goalless draw, and 4,000 fans saw Rangers only just lose the replay 3-2, with Wylie and Gow again doing the scoring. The men from Alexandria went all the way to the Final, held for the first time at Ibrox (Rangers, of course, had staged the 1881 Final at Kinning Park). The Final, scheduled for 8 February, was postponed because of fog and frost. One frustrated supporter scrawled the words, 'Dead Heads,' in the frost on the Press table. A week later the Final was played in drab, dreich conditions, on a heavily-seeded (14 cart loads) surface before 10,000. Queen's Park got a 1-1 draw, thanks to a goal in the 89th minute from Sellar, and won the replay 2-1 before 14,000.

Out of the big Cup, Rangers focussed on the Glasgow Cup and attracted 7,000 to Cathkin for the 1-1 draw with Third Lanark,. The replay saw them weakened by the withdrawals of Hendry and Robin. Meikle and McFarlane came in to replace them. Before 7,000 at Ibrox, Rangers played very well, winning 2-0. Goals from Henderson and Miller gave Thirds, Scottish Cup holders, their first defeat of the season. Rangers' upsurge in form brought 10,000 to Ibrox for a semi-final against Queen's Park. John Hendry resumed at full-back, but Davy Mitchell was unable to play. Meikle moved forward to take his place. The leadership and inspiration of Mitchell was missed. Rangers played well but eventually went down, 2-0.

Much improved as they were over the immediately previous seasons, they soon were to learn that they had a long way to go to compete on a level with the English professionals. On New Year's Day, at Ewood Park, they fought hard before losing 1-0 to Blackburn Rovers. The crowd was 13,000. Next day, before 8,000, they were given both a lesson and a thrashing by Bolton Wanderers, by 4-0. After a day's rest, a commendable 1-1 draw was played with Sunderland, with 10,000 watching. On 15 February, a Rangers team featuring four guest players was totally overwhelmed by Everton – result 8-1. This awful set-back was tempered somewhat by news from home. The Swifts had beaten Dumbarton Rangers 1-0 at Whitefield Park, Copland Road, to win the Scottish 2nd XI Cup. It was Rangers' first success since the Charity Cup win back in 1879, and indeed the first national honour of any kind that the club had won.

With the half-yearly meeting having announced a cut in the deficit, Rangers announced in February that they would erect a new grandstand and bring the ground capacity to 15,000. Included in the plans was a more commodious club house, with the existing one becoming a gymnasium.

Again omitted from the Charity Cup, Rangers went to Inverness to beat a local Select XI by 5-1, but Everton yet again demonstrated how far Rangers would have to go to be the best of the best, and indeed how the game in Scotland had much catching up to do with the English, including the embracing of professionalism. On 19 April, they ran over Rangers, 6-2 at Ibrox. John McPherson of Cowlairs guested and scored, Andrew McCreadie getting the other. The

Scottish League Formed

IN response to a letter from Peter Fairly, secretary of the Renton club, representatives of 12 Scottish clubs met at 7.30 on the evening of 20 March 1890, in Holton's Commercial Hotel, 28 Glassford Street, Glasgow. Fourteen clubs had been invited. The two absentees were Clyde and Queen's Park. The business? – 'to consider the question of organising League matches in Scotland'.

League football in Scotland had become inevitable. The game had expanded, what with Cup-ties and friendly matches, to the extent that some rationalisation of fixtures was essential. The Football League in England, in existence since 1888-89, was an established success. Professionalism was a fact there, and had been since 1885, and English football and its rewards were increasingly attractive to many Scottish players. A League in Scotland meant that professionalism would be inevitable (it came in 1893).

The 12 clubs attending that fateful meeting were: Abercorn, Cambuslang, Celtic, Cowlairs, Dumbarton, Heart of Midlothian, Rangers, Renton, St Bernard's, St Mirren, Third Lanark and Vale of Leven. Clyde joined them subsequently. Queen's Park, the most powerful club in the land, stayed aloof – they were devoted to the principle of amateurism, as they are to this day, but apart from that, they were persuaded that a League system would mean that the weaker clubs would go to the wall. In that they were right. Over the next decade, five of these founder members – Abercorn, Cambuslang, Cowlairs, Renton and Vale of Leven – had gone and in 1900, Queen's Park gave up the struggle for fixtures and joined the Scottish League.

Rangers were represented at that first meeting by their president, John Mellish, and match secretary William Wilton. The 12 founding fathers reached agreement, but started with the odd number of 11, since St Bernard's were not elected. J.H.McLaughlin of Celtic was appointed secretary of the competition, and League matches were to take precedence over all other matches save Scottish Cup-ties.

An opening League programme was played on 16 August 1890 with the following results: Celtic 1 Renton 4; Cambuslang 8 Vale of Leven 2; Dumbarton 1 Cowlairs 1; Rangers 5 Hearts 2. Renton would subsequently be expelled for irregularities.

The Scottish League might just as well have been called the Clydeside League – only Hearts were outside the Glasgow catchment area. For various reasons, the game in Scotland was not particularly healthy. Queen's Park, for so long the bell-weather of the game in Scotland, were deeply concerned at the 'menace' of professionalism and the effect it would have on their recruitment policies. The Rangers club was reasonably healthy, but its current team was not greatly distinguished. The powerful clubs of the day – Vale of Leven, Renton and Dumbarton – would never have the population base to sustain a challenge to the Glasgow clubs, and Hibs and Hearts were fighting it out in Edinburgh, almost in splendid isolation. The new boys of Celtic, however, were very much alive to the facts of life. They decided that professional football could not be resisted, and was bound to come. They reasoned that if they were to become the best club they would have to attract the best players. They simply went out and did just that. They were to find, however, that their first steps along the new League road were to be rocky indeed.

Their second and third League games were solid wins, 5-0 away to Hearts and 5-2 at home to Cambuslang, but the results were wiped out. It seemed they had played an unregistered player, Bell of Hurlford in goal in both games. Two points per game were deducted. Nevertheless, all of this was the start of a decade which consolidated the game in Scotland, saw Celtic emerge as a major presence in the game, and towards its end, brought to Rangers the first of their many 'great' teams, and in 1900, the presence, at last, of Queen's Park in the Scottish League.

Everton match had a postscript which illustrated the state of things in the early 1890s. John Hendry announced that he intended to stop work to make his living by playing football. Everton liked the look of him, and offered him a cash sum of £75 and 30 shillings (£1.50) per week, or alternatively a signing-on fee of £20 and wages of £3 per week. The agreement was that he would meet the English club's representatives at Carlisle on 2 May, and sign. Hendry simply neglected to travel. Instead, he accepted a Celtic offer and, indeed, when Rangers were losing 6-3 to Partick Thistle at Ibrox, he was in the Celtic team against Queen's Park. He then made a complete turn and said that he intended to

play only for Rangers in the coming season. In fact he had played his last game for them. In July, he signed for Notts County, and had a good career with them, playing in their winning FA Cup Final team of 1894.

Rangers lost another player, Wilkie, who signed for Everton in the summer, but their own team-building was under way and so the annual general meeting was more satisfactory than most. Great strides had been made with the ground, good players were joining the club, there was a profit of £31.55. And there was a piece of silverware, however modest, on the table to justify the members' confidence.

The First of the Great Teams

THE Ibrox attendance for Rangers' first match of 1890-91 was a reasonable 4,000 – Edinburgh teams were not considered a big draw in Glasgow. Their scorers were Adams (own-goal), H.McCreadie, Kerr (2), McPherson. John McPherson had finally joined the club from Cowlairs, and was to have 12 years at Ibrox in a career which brought him four championships, three Scottish Cup wins and many international selections.

In the Scottish Cup, Rangers went down at the first hurdle, against Celtic on 6 September. A single Groves goal did it, before 15,000 at Parkhead. The next League game brought a first Rangers' League defeat, a 5-1 shock from Dumbarton at Boghead. These teams in fact were to dominate this first League championship. Rangers beat St Mirren 8-2 and drew 1-1 with Cowlairs before the championship closed down until January. At that point, Rangers had seven points from five games, Dumbarton 13 from seven games. They had won six in succession after an opening draw.

The Glasgow Cup brought a titanic struggle with Third Lanark. A 12-2 win over Carrington preceded a four-game battle with the Cathkin men. Rangers seemed to have the tie won when 3-0 ahead, but the Warriors levelled with two goals in the final eight minutes. The Ibrox replay finished 1-1, the third game back at Cathkin saw Rangers this time come back from 3-0 down in bleak, gale-force winds, with goals from McPherson, Kerr, and Wylie, the last of them three minutes from the end. In the fourth match, Rangers' hopes of a first Glasgow Cup success vanished 3-1. Thirds in turn went down to Celtic in the Hampden Final.

When Dumbarton crushed Cambuslang 5-0 with Rangers merely drawing 1-1 at Abercorn, it seemed that the title would be but a formality for the Sons. They had 17 points from nine games, impressive form and were five ahead of Rangers, who had a game in hand. At last Dumbarton dropped another point, in a 2-2 home draw with Celtic. On the same day, Rangers beat Cambuslang 2-1 at Ibrox. Away wins came for Rangers at St Mirren and Third Lanark, home wins for Dumbarton against Vale of Leven and St Mirren. When Rangers played their game in hand against Abercorn (2-0), the gap was only two points, with six games left to play.

The very first Old Firm League match took place on 21 March 1891 at Celtic Park and was a 2-2 draw. Dowds and Campbell scored for Celtic, Hislop and A.McCreadie for Rangers. Happily, Dumbarton, too, had drawn, 2-2 at Cambuslang. Rangers completed their away programme with a 2-0 win at Cowlairs, while Dumbarton beat Third

Lanark 5-1 in their final home match. Both clubs were a fair distance ahead of the others – it was becoming a thrilling finale to the first Scottish League season. Rangers beat Vale of Leven at Ibrox on 4 April. Their next match was – home to Dumbarton, three weeks ahead! Meanwhile, Dumbarton had to face two fixtures before then. On 11 April, they lost the first of them 1-0, against Celtic at Parkhead. Nine days later, they beat Hearts 4-0 in Edinburgh, and restored a two-point advantage. But Rangers now had a crucial game in hand. The Ibrox clash would surely be the first in a sequence of 'title deciders'.

A 12,000 crowd was on hand to see it. Rangers were without the injured Hugh McCreadie. John McPherson and Neilly Kerr inspired them to a 4-2 win. This incidentally was McPherson's first appearance after his marriage, making the first break in the bachelor ranks of Rangers players. The team that eventful day was: Reid; D.Gow, Hodge, Marshall, A.McCreadie Mitchell, Hislop, Henderson, Kerr, McPherson, Wilson. Two games remained. Rangers met Celtic on 2 May and faltered. John White for Wilson was the only team change. At half-time goals by Henderson and Dowds kept it level at 1-1. A late blunder by D.G.Reid, the Rangers goalkeeper allowed Madden to snatch the winner. Dumbarton won their final game 4-2 in Paisley against St Mirren. Rangers now had to win their final game to tie. This they did in grand style, defeating Third Lanark 4-1 at Ibrox on 9 May. A play-off was ordered to decide the championship. On Thursday, 21 May, 10,000 were at Cathkin to see Rangers lead 2-0 at the interval. But Dumbarton staged a terrific rally, squaring the match at 2-2. The championship was to be shared. Rangers then were joint champions in the very first Scottish League championship. In fairness, on either goal-average or goal-difference, subsequently deciding these matters, Dumbarton would have been champions!

For the second season of League football in Scotland and for the defence of their shared championship, Rangers ranks were decimated. Tom Wylie was off to Everton, Donald Gow to Sunderland, David Hislop to Aston Villa. The affluence of the English professional game was tempting the best of the Scottish players, a trend that was to persist forever more.

David Haddow from Albion Rovers, Robert Scott from Third Lanark and Cullen of Airdrieonians were recruited and a team featuring five half-backs won 4-1 at Tontine Park, Renton, on 15 August 1891. The Renton club had been readmitted to a League which now consisted of 12 clubs. Although the 'landless' Cowlairs club had been suspended for breaches of the rules affecting professionalism, Clyde and Leith Athletic had agreed to join. Clyde had refused to attend the inaugural meeting in March 1890, but probably had noted that the League's first season had produced a profit!

It was soon clear that Rangers new team was struggling. A 23 August defeat by 3-0 at Celtic Park was followed by successive home failures against Third Lanark (3-2) and Dumbarton (3-1). For the Sons, joint champions, John Taylor, soon to join Everton, scored a hat-trick in a period of five minutes. A 6-1 win over Vale of Leven followed, then Rangers opened their Glasgow Cup campaign with an impressive home win over Third Lanark. New signings on hand were Robert Blyth from Glenbuck Athletic, who scored both goals and William McBain, an outside-right who was to die tragically in an accident before the end of the season.

Rangers had been one of the first clubs to provide a press box at their ground, but the *Scottish Referee* of 21 September 1891 complained of the 'invasion' of their area by vociferous Rangers committee members!

A 6-0 win over Abercorn left Rangers with six points from six games. Hearts had 13 from eight games and the title race was on. Everton triumphed at Ibrox by 4-1 on 1 October, before a crowd of 10,000. James Gossland had emigrated to South Africa, Alick Gossland had signed for Glasgow Wanderers when Rangers on 24 October lost 5-1 at home to Clyde. David Mitchell, John McPherson and Hugh McCreadie had all been injured and were replaced by Glass, Steel and Scott, but it was clear that Rangers, with only nine points from ten games, were far adrift in the championship.

A second-round tie in the Glasgow Cup meant Queen's Park at Ibrox, bringing £340 in gate receipts and the appearance of Colonel W.F.Cody, 'Buffalo Bill', who was playing at the East End Exhibition Building. Presented to the crowd at half-time, he was received with cries of "Get your hair cut!" Rangers had new signing Tom Dunbar of Celtic in their ranks, but missed chances cost them dearly and they lost 3-0, Queen's goals coming from W.Berry, J.Hamilton T.S.Waddell.

When St Bernard's of Edinburgh visited Ibrox on Scottish Cup business a week later, things were different. The 1891-92 competition had seen exemptions introduced for the first time, with all the League clubs, plus Kilmarnock, Northern and Queen's Park exempt until the first round proper. Rangers had a convincing win over the Edinburgh team, then concluded their 1891 fixtures with a 4-3 win over St Mirren at the Westmarch grounds, Paisley. Dumbarton led the table at the end of the year, having run up nine successive wins, including 8-0 over local rivals Vale of Leven. The Sons had 28 points from 16 games. It was to be their championship outright, this time.

Kilmarnock were Rangers' second-round opponents and a Scottish Cup marathon tie resulted. After 0-0 at Ibrox, 1-1 in Ayrshire on Boxing Day, Rangers prevailed in the third match 3-2 at Westmarch. Frank Watt, a new signing from Kilbirnie scored in the win against Annbank and Rangers were in their first semi-final since 1884. They lined up against Celtic at Parkhead on 6 February, a day of wild wind and rain which kept the crowd down to 12,000. Winning the toss gave Celtic a first-half advantage. They made the most of it, goals from McMahon, Brady, McCallum and Cunningham giving the home team a 4-0 interval lead. Critical in this first half was the fact that Willie Maley had kept John McPherson completely in

check. When Brady added a fifth early in the second half, a rout seemed in progress, but with Rangers now harnessing the storm, John Law, a Paisley Road boy, got one back. James Henderson scored, and late in the game Neil Kerr made it three, but the Celtic defence held firm for a thrilling 5-3 win. The teams were: Celtic: Cullen; Reynolds, Doyle, Dowds, Kelly, Maley, McCallum, Cunningham, Brady, Campbell, McMahon. Rangers: Haddow; Hodge, Dunbar, Marshall, A.McCreadie, Mitchell, Watt, Henderson, Law, McPherson, Kerr.

The Scottish Cup Final was scheduled for Ibrox Park on 12 March. Rangers had renovated the ground with bankings and two steel-structured stands – 'Glengarnock beams and girders' designed to take 2,000 a a cost of £1,300, all approved by the Govan Dean of Guild Court. A telegraph office and telephone line was installed for the benefit of journalists. The new capacity was estimated at a 'massive' 36,000, in the event hopelessly inadequate. Gates were opened for a 4pm kick off and the crowds poured in. An estimated 12,000 alighted at Ibrox Railway Station, alas no more, from scheduled services and 13 special trains. The Clyde was crossed by ferry and 'Clutha' to Govan and Kinning Park, and hundreds came on foot, by cab and by car.

The attraction was Queen's Park v Celtic – Queen's, the old order, the establishment, persisting as amateurs with the ideal of the game for the game's sake, and Celtic, the thrusting newcomers, founded as Catholic and Irish, in a sense the team of the underdogs, but ultra-professional in all but name and at that time the greatest threat to Queen's Park's dominance of the game. An estimated 40,000 swarmed into Ibrox that day, with 5,000 leaping the barricades after the gates were closed, and 20,000 left outside.

The *Scottish Referee* reported: 'The field was packed to overflowing and the terraces being unable to accommodate more ...it was due most of all to the overcrowding at the pavilion that the spectators, forced from behind by the numbers entering pell-mell into the field, burst aside the feeble resistance of the police, and scampered over the field of play like lunatics let loose ...The orderly spectators, who, hours, before, had taken up their stand around the field, annoyed at the invaders, pelted them with loose snow, but the interest in the match was such that, although pelted right and left, the crowd held their ground and defied all effort to dislodge them. The appearance of the mounted police had an appreciable effect on the disorderly, and before the prancing steeds they fell back as far as the limits of the ground and the crowd behind would permit.'

An attempt to steal the takings from the pavilion was thwarted by Rangers trainer John Taylor, with the aid of a water hose! The pitch was cleared by 150 policemen, plus four on horseback. Queen's had refused to allow the use of goal nets, believing they caused claustrophobia! They became compulsory for semis and Finals the following season.

The crowds encroached the pitch several times and after 20 minutes both captains complained and declared they would protest. The referee accepted and allowed the match to continue as a friendly. Since the Cup presentations at the time were made inside the pavilion, the crowds left imagining that Celtic had won with a Campbell goal after 60 minutes. The protest was upheld, a replay ordered for 9 April, and the SFA decided to double the admission prices, in an effort to control the size of the crowd. That decision was rescinded. The replay crowd was a mere 23,000 and Celtic swept to a 5-1 win. Queen's would never again dominate the Scottish game. Earlier, Ibrox had played host to Scotland v England, its first such fixture. The attendance was 21,000.

Meanwhile, Rangers defeated Everton in Liverpool which marked the debut of Jock Drummond. On 7 May a Rangers-Celtic 1-1 draw, goals by Hugh McCreadie and Campbell, effectively ended the Parkhead club's championship challenge. A week later, Rangers were back in the Glasgow Charity Cup for the first time in four years, playing a 3-3 draw with Queen's Park. The League campaign was wound-up with a 3-1 win at Clyde, to establish a fifth-place finish, 24 points from 22 games and a poor season indeed. It would be more than 30 years before they finished again in such a low position. It was 3-3 again in the Charity Cup replay, but in the third game Rangers inflicted on Queen's their heaviest defeat, 7-1. R.Turnbull had a hat-trick.

This meant the very first Rangers-Celtic Cup Final. On 1 June, at Celtic Park, a huge crowd saw Rangers initially in the ascendant, with McPherson and Turnbull prominent, but Celtic, pushed along by McMahon and Campbell, gradually took control. The deadlock was broken with an hour gone when Campbell headed home a Sandy McMahon cross from the right. McMahon added a second from a Madden cross a few minutes from the end. Celtic thus took the Scottish Cup, the Glasgow Cup, the Glasgow Charity Cup and missed the championship – and a Victorian grand slam – by just two points. For Rangers it was a barren season, but important signings Haddow, Drummond and Barber had been made and financially the club was as sound as could be. Dugald McKenzie was elected president. He served for five years.

Rangers stormed into the 1892-93 championship with four successive wins, Abercorn away, 4-0, Leith Athletic and Dumbarton home, each by 3-2, and Third Lanark at Cathkin, 4-2. Donald Gow was back from Sunderland and in the opening round of the Glasgow Cup, Northern were beaten 6-2 at home. A week later Celtic were at Ibrox for a 2-2 match which left Rangers trailing Hearts, the leaders, by two points, but with a game in hand. Rangers did go top by winning 2-1 against Leith Athletic at Bank Park, while Hearts went down 4-1 at Renton.

Linthouse proved serious opposition in the second round of the Glasgow Cup, then a thrilling win over Queen's Park at Hampden in the quarter-finals gave the Ibrox men hope that a first win of this much sought after trophy was within sight. When the League programme reached halfway in November, Rangers led with 15 points from nine games, two points ahead of Celtic who had a game in hand. For the first time in the Scottish League's short history, the title race had developed into a two-horse race between the Glasgow clubs.

Rangers reached the Glasgow Cup Final, on 12 November, with a 3-2 win over Glasgow Thistle, clearing the way for a Rangers-Celtic Final. A second round Scottish Cup draw took them to 'Fatal Boghead' of all places, where they presented a new right-back in William Hay from London Caledonian, and quickly found themselves under tremendous pressure, with Bell and Taylor quite outstanding for the home team. However, Haddow in goal had a quite magnificent match, stoutly supported by full-backs Hay and Drummond, and with an hour gone, Hugh McCreadie snatched the only goal. The Sons claimed that referee Mr Allison from Port Glasgow, should have allowed at least a full three minutes of injury time. Despite this, the hosts were most generous in congratulating Rangers on their first win at Boghead.

New Logie Green Park, Edinburgh was the venue for Rangers quarter-final match with St Bernard's of the Scottish Alliance. Rangers had Duncan Clark at centre-forward for only his second first-team appearance, and seemed to believe that taking the field would be enough to win. They were soon shocked. The 'Edinburgh Saints' ran all over them, were two up at half-time and three up early in the second half. When Rangers did wake up, it was too late – they were out of the Cup. St Bernard's were not novices – the following season they were in the Scottish League, finishing third, and in 1895 won the Scottish Cup.

By mid-February Rangers were in pole position in the championship when the Glasgow Cup Final took place on the 18th, against Celtic at Cathkin. Celtic had the ex-Rangers Tom Dunbar in their team. Rangers were in superb form that day and a John Barker goal sent them in 1-0 ahead at the interval. Neilly Kerr got a second from a corner. Rangers half-back trio of Bob Marshall, Andrew McCreadie and captain David Mitchell was the linchpin of a famous victory. A Celtic fightback was inevitable of course – goalkeeper Haddow had to head clear one attack and full-back Jock Drummond stopped a Johnny Campbell shot with his knee. McPherson scored a third, Sandy McMahon had a late consolation goal for Celtic near the end. Many of the 10,000 crowd broke in, carrying off Rangers players shoulder high. The road back to the city from Cathkin was a river of blue as the 'Ibroxonians' commandeered every car, cab and brake and celebrated a famous victory.

Rangers players triumphant in this historical, inaugural Glasgow Cup win were: David Haddow; Billy Hay, Jock Drummond; Bob Marshall, Andrew McCreadie, David Mitchell; J.H.Davie, Hugh McCreadie, Neilly Kerr, John McPherson and John Barker. Celtic lined up: Cullen; Reynolds, Doyle, W.Maley, T.Kelly, T.Dunbar, Towie, Blessington, Madden, Campbell, McMahon.

That night both teams were serenaded by the Banjo Band of the Minerva Club in the Alexandra Hotel. Rangers president Baillie John Ure Primrose, in being presented with the Glasgow Cup, in his victory speech thanked Celtic for being such sporting opponents. Celtic president John Glass in response said, "There is no club which the Celts would rather see win the Cup than Rangers." So at the 11th attempt, Rangers had at last beaten Celtic in a competitive fixture. The Parkhead men had won seven of the previous ten matches!

The Glasgow Cup was very important in Victorian times. Only when it had been decided was the venue and date of the Scottish Cup Final settled. It was to be a week later, Celtic v Queen's Park at Ibrox.

It was a day of high wind and rain and Queen's defying the elements led by 2-0 at the interval, with goals from the veteran Sellars. Celtic disputed the second, saying that the ball had not crossed the line. One fan proclaimed: "One can't expect good refereeing and Home Rule for Ireland on the same day." The reference was to Prime Minister Gladstone's Bill, passing through the Commons, later thrown out by the Lords. Paranoia and conspiracy theories abounded, even then.

The championship race was rejoined in March with the Light Blues annexing nine points from a possible ten to lead Celtic by seven, having played three games more. Alas, 'Fatal Boghead' lived up to its name on 22 April when Dumbarton took full revenge for their Scottish Cup defeat with a sweeping 3-0 victory. And when, one week later, Rangers played their first game on the site of the present

Celtic Park, an identical result cast Rangers adrift, a final 2-1 home win over Hearts leaving the Ibroxians one solitary point behind Celtic.

All told, though, Rangers could consider it a successful season. The Glasgow Cup had been won at last. There was a first-ever victory at 'Fatal Boghead', Celtic had been beaten for the first time, and Rangers had finished second in the League championship. Even more momentous with much greater consequences was the decision of the SFA, at its annual meeting in the summer, to legalise professionalism. they were simply acknowledging a practice which had become widespread.

One writer, in *Scottish Sport* (14 October 1892) insisted that he had evidence and wrote: 'A mutual understanding has existed among the League clubs ...in a systematic evasion of the amateur law. The *modus operandi* is simple. Large sums are deducted from gross gate drawings, and set apart especially as a fund for the payment of players. In ordinary League matches last season, in which the Clyde, Celtic, Rangers, Hearts, Dumbarton, Vale of Leven, Leith Athletic, Renton and Third Lanark were concerned, considerable sums were set aside for secret service. £110 was deducted from one game, £100 in three other cases, £70 for another and ranging in intermediate sums as low as £15. In an Edinburgh match where a Glasgow team figured, the gate receipts actually amounted to £115, and were returned at £35...!

'In one club alone last season the money paid to players as professional wages, and other expenses, amounted to £1,150 ...The secretary of a Glasgow League club approached a prominent Rangers player with a view to securing his services. "What are your terms?" enquired the Light Blue. "Well, we can give you 30 shillings (£1.50) per week," was the rejoinder. "Oh, I can get 35 shillings for lying off at Ibrox," came the reply!'

So much for amateurism. Professionalism clearly strengthened the hand of the city clubs. Cambuslang and Vale of Leven a year earlier had withdrawn from the League. The latter had not won a single game in season 1892-93. There were in reality village teams. Dunbartonshire in many ways had been a cradle of the Scottish game. Dumbarton, Renton and Vale of Leven had been giants and founder members of the League, but professionalism and the decline of the textile industry destroyed them. With Queen's Park insisting on remaining amateur, the power base of the game moved to the heart of the industrial population and to Rangers and Celtic, to become the two great metropolitan clubs.

As season 1893-94 dawned, Rangers in their 21 years of existence had come a long way from the 'boy's club' of the Glasgow Green days. Yet apart from sharing that very first Scottish League championship with Dumbarton, there were no national honours to boast about. Not once since the Scottish Cup competition was inaugurated had Rangers won this 'Blue Riband' of Scottish football. Indeed, 15 years had passed since the last of their two losing Final appearances. They lost in the 1878-79 Final against Vale of Leven, who were 'awarded' the Cup when Rangers failed to appear for a replay, after a 1-1 protested game at Hampden. It was clearly time for an improving Rangers team to break some Cup ice.

Bolstering their squad for the new season were John Gray from Albion Rovers and David Boyd from Abercorn. Boyd, a junior internationalist, was the subject of a dispute between Rangers and Bury, the Lancashire club claiming that the Troon lad was their player. True, he had signed pro-fessional forms for Bury and had received wages, but Boyd had simply decided that he wanted to play for Rangers. The notion of professional contracts was less than sophisticated and the matter was settled when H.C.Hammer, the Bury secretary, wrote an apology to Rangers for remarks made by an official of the English club. Robert Blyth returned to Ibrox after spells with Cowlairs and Middlesbrough, but before long went south again, this time to Preston North End. And Donald Gow was to leave the club in October, for Sunderland. The Ibrox club, incidentally, had been censured by the Scottish Amateur Athletics Association who decided that they should forfeit membership because of 'liberal expenses paid to athletes at Rangers Sports'. Rangers later appealed, successfully.

Their championship opened at West Cragie Park, home of Dundee FC. The new Tayside club was facing its first League season as an amalgamation of 'Our Boys' and 'East End'. Before a lively crowd of 6,000, John Gray scored the first League goal on the ground, inspiring Rangers to a 3-1 interval lead, although Dundee fought back to equalise.

Rangers were quickly into a scoring mode. A week later at Ibrox, they beat Renton 5-3, but after a goalless draw in Edinburgh against St Bernard's came the first high point of an eventful season. On 2 September 1893, Celtic, reigning champions who had never lost a League fixture to Rangers, came to Ibrox. A crowd of 18,000 underlined the extraordinary interest in the game among Glasgow's sportsmen. It was hotly contested from the start, but goals from the legendary John McPherson, then Barker and Gray put Rangers three ahead at half-time. Celtic came out for the second half in determined mood and established a good deal of possession, but the famous Rangers full-back partnership of Nichol Smith and Jock Drummond contained them, and the game, played at a fierce pace, turned to Rangers. Goals from Barker again in 60, then 65 minutes underlined the Ibrox team's attacking strength, saw him into the history books as the first Rangers player to notch a hat-trick in an Old Firm game, and produced a famous victory. In defence of the champions, they had clearly missed their seasoned players, Sandy McMahon and Willie Maley. The gate receipts, £360, were an Ibrox record!

This win saw them close in on Celtic in the championship, one point behind them having taken six points from four games. Rangers were in second place and no fewer than seven 'brakes' went with them to Renton for yet another win, 2-1 this time. The defence of the Glasgow Cup had been due to start on 16 September, but when the opponents of Rangers and Third Lanark, respectively Whitefield and Carrington, scratched, a friendly was arranged for Cathkin Park. Rangers led 1-0 at half-time, with 5,000 fans enjoying a fast, open game. Many of them also enjoyed, as the teams went off, John McPherson arguing furiously with the referee, a Mr Allison from Port Glasgow. It was a foretaste of things to come. Thirds scored two quick goals in the second half, and seemed to have taken command of the game. Then when McPherson and Rae of Third Lanark clashed and fell as they chased a loose ball, the Rangers player was promptly ordered off. He went only after a long argument with referee Allison, whereupon a disgusted Hugh McCreadie promptly threw the ball at the referee. He too was invited to leave and did so after what might be called a protracted and heated debate.

It was later said that McPherson had been ordered off for 'kicking' an opponent, although Rae, the Third Lanark man, said the whole thing had been accidental. And McCreadie, showing a neat turn of sardonic remorse, said that he had no personal malice towards Mr Allison – he had thrown the ball at him simply to demonstrate that he had a poor opinion of his talents as a referee. So over the decades, nothing changes.

At the end of September, Rangers and Celtic were equal in the League, both clubs with 11 points from seven games. October saw two friendlies, a 1-0 defeat of Everton, then a superb display against Queen's Park – at the time still not members of the Scottish League – when Rangers inflicted upon them their first defeat of the season. Following a second-round bye, Rangers' defence of the Glasgow Cup started when they trounced Pollokshaws 11-1 at Ibrox, setting up a semi-final against Celtic, a repeat of the previous year's Final. A second successive win over Celtic (1-0 at Ibrox) saw Rangers tighten their hold on the trophy. Their Final opponents were to be Cowlairs, who surprisingly beat Queen's Park in the other semi-final.

First, Cowlairs came to Ibrox in the opening round of the Scottish Cup and were overwhelmed by an 8-0 scoreline which included a David Boyd hat-trick. The Glasgow Cup Final was played at First Cathkin Park, and with Cowlairs this time adopting an out-and-out defensive philosophy, Rangers were limited to a 1-0 victory, the goal coming from John McPherson against his former club. But the Glasgow Cup win turned Rangers' attention to that other Cup, the Scottish, the one they had failed to win in all these years of trying. Leith Athletic were formidable visitors to Ibrox in round two, Rangers winning an exciting game 2-0. In the next round against Clyde away from home, Rangers produced an outstanding display in a 5-0 win, with four goals coming from James Steel and yet another from McPherson. Between these rounds, Rangers won the first ever 'Ne'er Day' clash with Celtic by 3-2, before a 15,000 crowd at Celtic Park, in a friendly match. Other matches on the very next day included scorelines of Rangers 2 Sunderland 2 and Celtic 0 Everton 4.

The Scottish Cup was now becoming an obsession with the Ibrox club, and their League form suffered. Going into their Cup semi-final against Queen's Park, they were third, nine points behind the leading Celtic. Some 15,000 crowded Ibrox for a match in which the Cup holders were without their regulars, Sellars and Lamb. Nevertheless they took the lead through Waddell after 15 minutes. David Boyd headed an equaliser immediately after the interval, Queen's goalkeeper Baird being impeded when he caught his hand in the rigging! A later goal by Barker was disallowed, and the replay was set for Hampden a week later.

Rangers suffered a serious blow before the second match. David Boyd, a ship's carpenter by trade, fell from a staging into the hold of a vessel 20 feet below. His injuries kept him out of the replay, and indeed of the Final. In the meantime, Queen's Park were making the most imaginative attempts to improve their chances by recruiting none other than the legendary, C.B.Fry of the Corinthians. Fry was something of a man for all sporting seasons. He was capped by England at both soccer and cricket, played soccer for the Corinthians and Southampton, played rugby for Blackheath and the Barbarians, and for a long spell held the world long jump record. As a diplomat at the League of Nations in later years, he was offered the throne of Albania. Fry declined.

The replay, without either Boyd or Fry, was a fine match played in windy conditions before a crowd of 16,000. Nicol Smith, with a long punt after 25 minutes gave Rangers the lead, but Gulliland equalised direct from a corner kick, the ball being helped over the line by David Haddow. Queen's

Park dominated early in the second half, but Rangers suddenly broke from defence and John McPherson scored from 20 yards. When Steel, some seven minutes later, scored a third, it was all over. Rangers had reached their first Scottish Cup Final in 15 years. Their opponents were to be Celtic, who had beaten Third Lanark in the other semi-final by 5-3. Celtic were the more experienced side and therefore favourites, but Rangers had won the three previous meetings between the teams, and were brimming with confidence, convinced that this was to be their year.

And Celtic had problems off the field – in the week before the Final, the Celtic Park grandstand was damaged by storms, with debris scattered over the adjoining Janefield cemetery. There was talk of the club being sued for damage done to it! Rain fell continuously before the Final and a crowd of 17,000 turned up on a thoroughly miserable day for this first Old Firm Scottish Cup Final. The first half was close and evenly contested, with no score at the interval. The famed Rangers defence of Smith and Drummond had countered Celtic's attacking ploys and quite outstanding was the Rangers captain, Davy Mitchell – cool, sharp, nimble, inspirational, he targeted the ball into areas which would trouble Celtic most. Mitchell led, quite brilliantly, by example. Conditions deteriorated in the second half and slowly Rangers' superior fitness took effect. Ten minutes into the half, Mitchell placed a free-kick to perfection and Hugh McCreadie volleyed the ball well out of Cullen's reach. Then with 65 minutes gone, John Barker scored one of the great Cup Final goals. Taking possession just inside the Celtic half, he flashed down the left wing, passing man after man, then cutting inside, flattening Reynolds with a shoulder charge and finally driving the ball home fiercely from close range. Three minutes later, John McPherson produced another of his telling strikes from 20 yards and although Celtic, true to their traditions, never gave up and got a consolation goal from Willie Maley, 15 minutes from the end, it was Rangers' trophy, Rangers' day at last, after 21 years of trying.

The trophy was presented to president Dugald McKenzie at the after-match dinner in the Alexandra Hotel; Celtic warmly congratulated the winners; among the telegrams was one from Donald Gow in Sunderland and Baillie John Ure Primrose, committee man and later to be Rangers' president and Lord Provost of Glasgow, apologised to the Christian Institute for his hoarse voice when he spoke to them later that night on 'Rambles with a Camera'!

The teams met a week later at Celtic Park in a League match, yet again in dreadful conditions. Celtic won 3-2, a result which gave the Parkhead men the championship. Since their 5-0 defeat by Rangers back on 2 September, they had won 11 successive League games.

Among the end of season games, Rangers went south to beat Leicester Fosse 2-1, and they had a prestigious 3-1 home win against FA Cup winners Notts County. It was a game of immense future significance for the Ibrox club. It marked the debut of one Alec Smith. A Darvel boy, young Smith had rejected offers from Kilmarnock and Sunderland before signing for Rangers. Working in a Darvel lace mill, he had been invited to play in the Notts County match by the more famous Nicol Smith, and Alec Smith was to become a wonderful player and loyal club servant for Rangers in a career that spanned 21 years. He was to win every club honour and represent his country 34 times, including 20 full international matches, when these were few and far between. He was arguably the finest outside-left the Scottish game had seen before the coming of Alan Morton. His talents and skills seemed inexhaustible.

The Rangers team of 1896-97. Standing: (left to right): McCade (assistant trainer), Oswald, N.Smith, Hyslop, Dickie, Turnbull, Muir (linesman). Seated: McPherson, Miller, McCreadie, Drummond, Mitchell, Gibson, Neil. On ground: Low, A.Smith. This season Rangers won the Scottish Cup, the Glasgow Cup and the Glasgow Merchants' Charity Cup.

On top of all this, in one of Rangers' most successful seasons, club treasurer John Marr was pleased to report that in five years, the club's income had quadrupled from £1,240 to £5,227!

Following the heady triumphs of the two previous seasons, 1894-95 was to prove barren, at least of major trophies. But it was to be significant in Rangers' march towards the turn of the century and the emergence of the first of their truly great teams. Jock Drummond was well established, Nicol Smith was going into his second season, and one of Scottish football's brightest shining lights, Neilly Gibson, made his debut for the club at 'Fatal Boghead'. And the reserve team, the Swifts, won the Kirkwood Shield and the Glasgow Reserve Cup for president MacKenzie's sideboard.

Rangers ran off with their first four matches, but a visit to Celtic Park took some of the steam out of them as they went down 5-3. From then on, a League challenge frittered away as five home games were lost, and the club finished third, nine points behind the champions Hearts, who had developed an impressive team. Rangers were drawn against the same Hearts in their defence of the Scottish Cup, and went down 2-1 at Ibrox to goals from Hogg and Chambers for the Edinburgh side, against a Cowan goal. St Bernard's won the Cup that year, for the first and only time, beating Renton 2-1 in an Ibrox Final before 13,500 spectators.

Defending the Glasgow Cup, Rangers disposed of Queen's Park and Third Lanark before travelling to Inchview to tackle Partick Thistle, something of a bogey team for them at the time. So it seemed as Thistle, inspired by

goalkeeper Smith, took everything Rangers could throw at them to win 1-0. But Rangers discovered that the same Smith had played for Duntocher Harp while a registered Thistle player, a serious offence. Their appeal was upheld. Back at Inchview they won 5-3 this time to go into the Final. Against old rivals and friends, Celtic, Rangers ran into another marvellous goalkeeping display, this time from Dan McArthur. Two goals by Divers, the first hotly disputed, gave Celtic the win. The Charity Cup, too, was lost to Celtic.

In the following season, no better than its predecessor, the loss of goalkeeper David Haddow to Motherwell was a severe blow to Rangers from which it took them virtually the entire season to recover. Several replacements were tried without much success, including one John Bell from Slamannan. He held the position until Rangers faced Hibernian in the third round of the Scottish Cup. In the first Cup match between the sides, the Edinburgh team won 3-2 at Ibrox and John Bell held himself so responsible for the defeat that he walked back to the dressing room, dressed without uttering one single word to anyone, walked out of the ground and was never seen at Ibrox again! Considering that Rangers failed with two penalty kicks, he seems to have been ultra-harsh with himself. Hibernian went on to the Final to face city rivals Hearts in the only Scottish Cup Final played outside Glasgow. Hearts won 3-1 at Logie Green, Edinburgh, before 16,034 spectators.

Rangers' League campaign was spattered with heavy victories, heavy defeats and the goals against told the story of their season. It did have an upbeat ending. The signing of

Matthew Dickie from Renton solved the goalkeeping problem. Alec Miller from Dumbarton, Bob Crawford from Clyde, James Miller from Sunderland, ex-Guardsman Tom Hyslop from Stoke City and Peter Turnbull from Blackburn Rovers arrived to stiffen the side for season 1896-97. When these were supplemented by the arrival of Tommy Low, also from Blackburn Rovers, Rangers were close to having the finest team in their 25 years history. Low was a fast, lightly-built outside-right who was to form a deadly partnership with John McPherson in the championship campaign. Important points were lost early in the season as the team took time to settle, but with Dickie, Neilly Gibson and Nicol Smith finding their feet in defence, goals against were less of a problem and 64 goals in 18 matches was testimony to the striking power. The club finished third, three points behind champions Hearts, but scored 17 goals more than they did.

Cup competition was Rangers' game this season. Clear wins over Third Lanark and Linthouse saw them into a Glasgow Cup Final with Celtic for the third time. Rangers lined up at Cathkin with: Dickie; Nicol Smith, Drummond, Gibson, McCreadie, Mitchell, Low, McPherson, Turnbull, Hyslop and Alec Smith, a team as talented as any Rangers had fielded to that date. Goals from Tommy Hyslop, and McMahon for Celtic, left it at 1-1, and for the replay, Rangers had Hyslop at right-back and James Miller up front.

With goals from Turnbull and Alec Smith, against a Celtic goal by Blessington, Rangers had won the Glasgow Cup for the third time, and beaten Celtic for the first time since February 1894.

League prospects were slipping away, and the Scottish Cup claimed Rangers' attention. There were convincing wins over Partick Thistle and Hibernian before a hazardous trip was scheduled for Dundee. The travelling support that day was reckoned the largest ever to accompany a Scottish club. In gale-force conditions on the waterside Carolina Port ground, Rangers scored an explosive four goals in seven minutes in the second half, against the elements. Next, five special trains followed the team to Greenock, where Rangers had the ball in the Morton net 10 times (three were disallowed). That 7-2 win put them, for the fourth time, into the Scottish Cup Final. Against Dumbarton, they romped through the match at Second Hampden, 5-1, before a crowd of 15,000. Goals came from Miller (2), Hyslop, McPherson and Alec Smith, three of them within five, second-half minutes. As in 1894, Rangers had captured two Cups – could they make it three out of three?

The answer came in two devastating Glasgow Charity Cup displays. Rangers had acquired Bobby Neil, centre-half from Liverpool, and first Celtic went down 4-1, then Third Lanark 6-1. Having beaten Queen's Park in the semi-final, Thirds were considered a real danger, but Rangers were not to be denied, and became known as the 'Three Cup Team'. They had won only four trophies in 25 years existence, but 13 goals in three Cup Finals suggested that more were on the way. Nine Ibrox men represented Scotland that season – Nicol Smith, Gibson, Low, Miller, Hyslop, Dickie, Drummond, McPherson and Oswald – Oswald actually played against Wales on the day of the Scottish Cup Final!

In the new season, after the recent glamour of Cups won, Rangers aim would clearly be the championship. Their opening fixture was encouraging. They went to Meadowside Park, new home of Partick Thistle and won convincingly, 5-1, a match which saw the debut of R.C.Hamilton

from Queen's Park. He became one of Rangers' finest centre-forwards, who won all the honours including 11 international caps. He helped the team to sustain a challenge punctured only when a record attendance of 30,000 saw Celtic win 4-0 at Ibrox. Rangers did not drop another point until the New Year's Day return match. They desperately needed to win that one, but with the score at 1-1, and Rangers piling on the pressure, the crowd invaded the pitch and the match was abandoned. Before the fixture could be replayed Rangers lost 2-1 at Dundee, effectively ceding the championship to Celtic by four points, finishing in second place.

The Glasgow Cup had been retained earlier in the season. An easy 4-0 win over Queen's Park at Cathkin was followed by an immense series with Celtic. After 2-2 at Parkhead, 1-1 at Ibrox, Rangers won 3-1 after extra-time with goals from Hamilton (2) and Hyslop. This fourth Glasgow Cup win equalled Celtic's record. The winning team was: Dickie; Crawford, Drummond, Gibson, Neil, Mitchell, Low, McPherson, Hamilton, Miller, A.Smith.

Nicol Smith and Tom Hyslop were injured for the early rounds of the Scottish Cup, but these were not too taxing. A dazzling display at Hampden overcame Queen's Park by 3-1 and put Rangers into another desperate semi-final struggle, this time with Third Lanark. The Warriors had each of the first two games in their grasp, but a missed penalty when 1-0 ahead at Ibrox allowed Alex Smith to equalise. A late Rangers rally in the second match, after Neil had failed with two penalty kicks, forced a 2-2 draw, then in the third match at Cathkin, Rangers were clear winners 2-0, goals coming from McPherson and Gibson.

On 26 March 1898, Rangers faced Kilmarnock before 14,000 at Second Hampden. Of the 22 players on the field, 16 were from Ayrshire – nine to Kilmarnock seven to Rangers. Goals in the second half from Alex Smith and Hamilton gave Rangers a 2-0 win to retain the Scottish Cup. R.C.Hamilton, incidentally, had sat a three-hours examination at Glasgow University that morning! The Cup-winning team was: Dickie; Nicol Smith, Drummond, Gibson, Neil, Mitchell, Miller, McPherson, Hamilton, Hyslop, A.Smith.

A late goal by Third Lanark's Hannah in the Charity Cup Final dashed Rangers' hopes of being a 'Three Cups Team' for a second year. But it was clear that they had shaken down into a powerful combination for which continuity of selection had been all-important. The defence in particular was clearly a quality unit in the team. Nine Rangers players represented Scotland that season. Seven players in the Scottish League team that faced the Football League team at Villa Park were from Rangers, a club record. They were: Dickie, Nicol Smith, Gibson, Miller, Hamilton, McPherson and Alex Smith. Drummond and Neil were the two others selected during the season. After 25 years, life was healthy for Rangers – income for the season was £13,273, surplus was £4,534.

Possibly the greatest single achievement in the long Rangers story came in season 1898-99. Every one of the 18 League matches was won, a 100% record in championship matches unequalled anywhere in the world, before or since. The team averaged more than four goals per match scored, and the tone was set with the first League match, a thumping 6-2 win at home to Partick Thistle. R.C.Hamilton scored a hat-trick. The season was illuminated by memorable performances. In the sixth match, Celtic were beaten 4-0 at Celtic Park. With ten matches won, the eleventh, against Hibs at Easter Road, was widely taunted as the championship decider. Rangers found themselves two down after 22 minutes, but goals from Miller and Alec Smith brought the score level early in the second half. Hibs regained the lead, but a late goal from Hamilton, then of all things a last minute penalty for Rangers, scored by Neil brought Rangers a thrilling, dramatic and no doubt controversial victory. In his memoirs, Alec Smith wrote 'I can recall, however, our gruelling game against Hibs in Edinburgh during most of which it looked certain that we would be beaten ...it was a desperate encounter'.

The championship was decided by a 7-0 win over Dundee at Ibrox, but the record had still to be preserved. Hibs visit to Ibrox, for game No.15, was sure to be critical. Incredibly, Rangers were five up after 20 minutes. They eventually won 10-0! To this day that score represents a record club defeat for Hibernian. Home wins over St Mirren 3-2 and Celtic 4-1, left the critical final game to be that against Clyde at Shawfield. On 7 January 1899, in dreadful conditions, goals from Alec Smith, Miller and Neil produced a 3-0 victory a hulking ten points ahead of Hearts, the second club.

In spite of the pressures this must have brought, Rangers were finalists in the two big Cup competitions. In the Scottish Cup, they were intent on making it a third successive win, previously achieved only by Queen's Park and Vale of Leven. The first-round draw brought Hearts to Ibrox, about as difficult a tie as could be imagined. It proved combative. Hearts finished with nine men. Hogg and Begbie were ordered off as Rangers ran away with a 4-1 win, goals coming from Gibson (2), Neil and Hamilton. Success against Ayr Parkhouse, Clyde and St Mirren saw Rangers in the final against old rivals Celtic. At Second Hampden Park on 22 April 1899, 25,000 saw Celtic, despite Rangers' two League wins, 4-0 and 4-1 over them, take the Cup with second-half goals from McMahon and Hodge. Celtic's first goal came one minute after a Rangers goal had been ruled out for offside. The decision was not approved by all in the crowd. The Glasgow Cup Final was lost to Queen's Park, the Charity Cup to Celtic, but this season was to be just as significant for Rangers off the field as on. At a special general meeting on 27 March 1899, members voted to adopt the principle of limited liability. On 10 May, 1899, Rangers Football Club became Rangers Football Club Ltd. The first board of directors was appointed. William Wilton, honorary match secretary was appointed manager and secretary and James Henderson became chairman, a post he held until his death on 10 May 1912.

No one could realistically have expected the team to have repeated the achievements of the previous season in the championship, but Rangers none the less were determined to retain their title. An exceptional group of players was strengthened by the signing of Jacky Robertson from Southampton. A Dumbarton man, a half-back, Robertson is generally considered to be one of the finest players in the history of the Scottish game. He represented his country 22 times, including captaining Scotland three times against England. He played for Morton, Everton, Southampton, Chelsea and Glossop. He captained Scotland's great 1900 team against England (4-1) and later became Chelsea manager, and at one time coached abroad. His signing fee was £300!

Rangers' season started with four victories, making a record sequence of 22 wins. It was broken by a 1-1 draw at Tynecastle and the next question was how long they could remain unbeaten in League matches. Their 13th League match was a nostalgic occasion. Kilmarnock were swamped

6-1 in the last match to be played on the first Ibrox Park. The ground had been christened, so to speak, on 20 August 1887, when Preston North End were guests, but in only a dozen years, Rangers had outgrown the ground. On 30 December 1899, the second Ibrox Park (virtually next door to its predecessor) was opened with an Inter-City League fixture against Hearts, won 3-1. John Wilkie scored all three on the new ground. The unbeaten League run went to the 15th game, a New Year fixture at Celtic Park. Celtic won 3-2 with goals from Divers (2) and Bell against those from Alec Smith and Wilkie. Rangers had played seven games in ten days. Thus ended a splendid run of 35 games without defeat – from 12 February 1898 until 1 January 1901. Nevertheless, Rangers were excellent champions, finishing seven points ahead of Celtic. That done, could they win the Scottish Cup and become the first team in Scotland to 'do the double?'

Morton, Maybole and Partick Thistle were disposed of en route to yet another encounter with Celtic in a semi-final, at Ibrox. A last minute score from John McPherson saved Rangers in a 2-2 draw, but in the Celtic Park replay, Rangers for some reason produced their worst performance for many years, and went down 4-0. Celtic beat Queen's Park in the Final at the 'new' Ibrox. In the old one, over 12 years, Rangers had won two championships, three Scottish Cups, the Glasgow Cup five times, the Glasgow League twice and the Charity Cup once.

In 1900, the Glasgow Cup and the Glasgow Charity Cup were won with victories over Celtic in each case by 1-0 and 5-1. Thus in four consecutive seasons, Rangers had reached 11 of the 12 major Cup competitions of the day, winning seven of them.

For season 1900-01, Jamie Stark from the Glasgow Perthshire club was added to the ranks. He became one of their most reliable defenders and his tussles with Jimmy Quin, the powerful Celtic centre-forward, became almost legendary. In the broader sense, this season was distinguished by the acceptance, at last, of League football by Queen's Park. The oldest Scottish club, critical to the very birth and development of the game was amateur, then as now, and had resisted League football for a decade since the Scottish Football League was formed in 1890. Queen's yielded when it was clear that Cup competitions and friendly matches could not sustain a full season of play. Rangers, defending the championship yet again, ripped off four straight wins before going through to Edinburgh to face Hibs, who presented a young, talented and fast-maturing team. Rangers were on the defensive from the very beginning, held Hibs through the first half, but were overrun in the second. The 4-1 defeat represented one of Rangers' biggest-ever League setbacks. Soon afterwards they lost 2-1 at Celtic Park, and briefly, championship hopes seemed to be in the balance. But a particularly sweet revenge of 6-0 was taken over Hibs.

The New Year's Day fixture against Celtic was yet again dubbed a 'championship decider'. Second-half goals from Speedie and McPherson brought a 2-1 win and finally Rangers ran out champions again with 35 points from 20 games, six ahead of Celtic. In the Final of the Glasgow Cup against Partick Thistle, Finlay Speedie from Clydebank Juniors appeared. For seven years, before he moved on to Newcastle United, he formed with Alec Smith one of the finest left-wing partnerships in the club's history.

This decade around the turn of the century is considered one of the outstanding periods in the club's history, comparable with the 1920s, the late 1940s, the early 1960s and the decade of the late 1980s and early 1990s. And Rangers' basic team selection for that Final personified the best of the decade. It was: Dickie; N.Smith, Drummond, Gibson, Stark, Robertson, Campbell, McPherson, Hamilton, Speedie, A.Smith.

They won that Final, 3-1, and in that season, nine players played for an unbeaten Scotland. In the international against Ireland, Robert Hamilton scored four in an 11-0 win, an Ibrox record which stands to this day.

The 1901-02 season was to be one of triumph and tragedy for Rangers. There was triumph in their record fourth successive League championship win, triumph in winning the Glasgow Cup for a record third consecutive time, triumph in winning the unique Glasgow Exhibition Cup. But tragedy came to overshadow all that. During the Scotland-England international match on 5 April 1902, part of the west terracing at Ibrox collapsed, and 25 people were killed (see *Days of Disaster*).

Rangers had started the 1901-02 season in cracking form, winning the Glasgow Exhibition Cup in August. The pick of Scottish clubs were invited, all the ties were played at Gilmorehill in Glasgow, and, it seemed inevitably, the Final came out as Rangers v Celtic. The Rangers team was: Dickie; N.Smith, Drummond, Stark, Neil, Gibson, McDougall, Wilkie, Hamilton, Speedie, A.Smith. Campbell opened the scoring for Celtic who were well on top for a spell, but sterling defending by Drummond and Neil in particular held it at 1-0 down at half-time. Rangers dominated the second half and goals from Neil and Hamilton (two) gave Rangers a 3-1 win and the Glasgow Exhibition Cup, to be held in perpetuity. This at least was the intention.

Presently, the Glasgow Cup was retained in what might be called controversial circumstances. On the vote of the Glasgow FA, the controlling body, the Final against Celtic was ordered for Ibrox Park. When the match ended 2-2, the same committee decided that the replay should also be played at Ibrox. Celtic refused to agree, insisting it should go to Celtic Park. Rangers were prepared to compromise and go to a neutral ground. Celtic were not. The trophy was awarded to Rangers. It can be said that neutral venues for Glasgow Cup Finals were normal, but it was not uncommon for matches to be played on competing team's grounds. Indeed the Scottish Cup Final that very same season, between Celtic and Hibernian, was played at Celtic Park.

Rangers' League campaign had been less than impressive and came the time when Celtic needed but five points from five games to hold them off. Astonishingly, they proceeded to lose to Hearts 2-1 at home, Queen's Park 3-2 away, and draw at home with Hibs. Their five point lead had gone. Victory over Kilmarnock in their last but one game meant that they needed one more win to take the championship – and their next game was to be the Ne'er Day game at home to Rangers! The latter's away form had been much better than their work at home. They had no fears in going to Parkhead. In one of their most famous victories, they won 4-2. It was all, to say the least, controversial. Celtic disputed, hotly, three of Rangers' goals and Celtic's McMahon was ordered off for 'assaulting the referee'. Now Rangers would need five points from their remaining three games to retain their title. They did it. They beat Queen's Park 1-0 at Hampden, St Mirren 3-2 and Dundee 3-1, both at Ibrox.

In the Scottish Cup, Rangers had an easy run to the semi-final but were beaten 2-0 at Ibrox by an excellent Hibernian team. Once again a home team was aggrieved at a referee, in this case Mr Nisbet of Cowdenbeath, the same official who had incurred the wrath of Celtic. Hibs went on to defeat Celtic in the Final at Celtic Park, switched there because of the Ibrox disaster, seen by 16,000 spectators. The scope of the Charity Cup was widened to include non-Glasgow teams, and Hibs won that, and the Rosebery and McCrae Cups in one of their best-ever seasons.

Following the Ibrox disaster, when contributions reached Rangers from clubs and sporting institutions from throughout Britain and beyond, it was decided to have a charity competition with the champions and runners-up from both Scotland and England. Rangers donated their much-prized Glasgow Exhibition Trophy, which became the British League Cup. Rangers, Celtic, Everton and Sunderland competed, producing a Rangers-Celtic Final on 17 June 1902. The game went to extra-time before Jimmy Quinn rounded out the first of his two Cup Final hat-tricks in Old Firm matches, unequalled until the coming of Alistair McCoist. So Rangers prized Glasgow Exhibition Cup went to Parkhead, where it resides to this day. Sadly, this was John 'Kitey' McPherson's last season as a Ranger. Born in Kilmarnock in 1868, he was with the local team at 17. A prolific goalscorer from inside-forward, he was also the most versatile of footballers, having played every position for Rangers, including goal. He won 13 caps, four League and three Scottish Cup medals in 12 years with the club. He then served 20 years as a director.

The shadow of the disaster still hung over Ibrox as yet another season began. To rebuild the ground, a substantial expenditure would be needed and as a result, 22 players were made available for transfer!

The great team of four successive championships was breaking up. Mitchell, McCreadie and McPherson were gone. Within two more years, Matt Dickie, Jock Drummond and Robert Neil would follow as, sadly, would Nicol Smith. As the season progressed, it was clear that new faces would be needed. Alex Fraser from Clydebank Juniors, George Henderson from Dundee, John Walker and Angus McDonald all joined and played important roles as the season developed. This transitional period was reflected in relatively poor League form. Five games were lost, only one fewer than in all of the four previous seasons, and hope of a fifth title withered away. Rangers finished third, eight points behind the champions, Hibernian, whose young side had come to maturity. It lost only one match all season, 1-0 at Cathkin, and had 5-2 and 4-0 wins at Ibrox and Parkhead respectively. Rangers third defence of the Glasgow Cup was short-lived. They went down 1-0 to Third Lanark at Cathkin and by a similar score against St Mirren in the Charity Cup.

The Scottish Cup was a different story. Emphatic wins over Auchterarder Thistle and Kilmarnock brought a quarter-final tie at Celtic Park, the seventh meeting of the clubs in the Scottish Cup. Celtic had won five of the previous six, the only Rangers win coming in the 1894 Final. In the first 20 minutes, goals from Alex Smith, Walker and Hamilton gave Rangers a 3-0 lead which they held comfortably to the end. The semi-final sent them to Larbert to face Stenhousemuir. With an 8,000 crowd packed into the little ground, Rangers won 4-1 in treacherous, icy conditions, Bob Hamilton and Jacky Robertson scoring two each.

Hearts were to be the Final opposition at Celtic Park, on 11 April 1903. On a day of snow and gales, 30,000 saw Rangers take the lead early in the second half with a Stark goal, but with weather conditions becoming intolerable, play was suspended 18 minutes from time. They improved enough to permit a re-start, when a magnificent goal from the peerless Bobby Walker earned Hearts a replay. On the same venue a week later, only 35,000 turned up to see a turgid goalless draw.

Rangers had been unchanged for the replay, fielding: Dickie; Fraser, Drummond, Gibson, Stark, Robertson, McDonald, Speedie, Hamilton, J.Walker, Smith. For the third match, George Henderson and Mackie replaced Neil Gibson and John Walker respectively. The admission price was halved to sixpence (2½p). As a result, 35,000 turned up to see Mackie score in 15 minutes. Drummond went off injured, and with Finlay Speedie moving to full-back, Rangers' backs were against the wall. But against furious Hearts attacks, they held out and a late breakaway goal by R.C.Hamilton settled it.

As they celebrated their fourth Scottish Cup triumph, no one could have imagined that 25 more years would pass before a fifth was won! Jamie Stark, the driving force of the team through the early years of the century had won his solitary Cup medal and Jock Drummond's club record of four medals would stand for more than 30 years.

In 1903-04, a thrilling 4-3 win over Third Lanark at Ibrox and a run of six more undefeated matches represented a determined bid by Rangers to regain the League championship. Then, on the return with Thirds, the Hi Hi's won by a solitary goal, giving them a lead in the race. Although dropping points in drawn games, Rangers lost only one match, in Dundee, in the next 14. An astonishing match at Paisley saw Rangers lead 2-1 at half-time. A second half of four penalties, three for St Mirren scored by Lindsay and the Rangers shot scored by Hamilton, ended in a 5-4 win for the home team. A 2-1 reverse at Tynecastle shortly afterwards really put an end to Rangers' title hopes, and they finished third, five points behind Third Lanark who were champions for the only title won in their history. Thirds, sadly no longer with us, also won the Glasgow Cup repeating their first-round Ibrox win of the previous season, this time by 2-0.

The defence of the Scottish Cup could not have been more testing. A first round repeat of the previous season's Final, Rangers v Hearts, was a thriller, ending 3-2 for the Ibrox men. John Walker (2) and Hamilton scored. Difficult away matches at Easter Road and Paisley brought single goal victories and a place in the semi-final against Greenock Morton at Ibrox. Again two goals from Walker, one from Hamilton meant yet another confrontation with Celtic. The Final, at the new Hampden Park on 16 April 1904, produced a record 64,472 attendance. Celtic played Jimmy Quinn, normally an outside-left, at centre-forward in place of Alec Bennett, said to have influenza. Rangers were badly hit by the absence of Fraser and Hamilton, yet the Cup holders got off to a whirlwind start, with two Finlay Speedie goals in the opening 12 minutes. But the younger, stronger and possibly on the day the more ambitious Celtic team fought back to equality by the interval with two Quinn goals. Jimmy Quinn, carving out a new career in a new position, notched the second-half winner, ensuring himself a place in the history of the game by becoming the first player to score a Scottish Cup Final hat-trick. Swamping Celtic 5-2 in the Charity Cup Final was no great consolation for Rangers. Their goals were from Robertson (2), Mackie, Donnachie and Speedie.

Age had finally overtaken the team that had won four successive League titles. Of the last championship side, Dickie, Drummond, Crawford, Gibson, Neil and McPherson were no longer at Ibrox and for two more, Robertson

and Nicol Smith, this would be a last season. New players to fill gaps included Andrew Easton from Millwall Athletic, John May from Derby County (his brother Hugh had been a Rangers player), Adam Gourlay from Renfrew Victoria, Archie Kyle from Parkhead Juniors and during the season, goalkeeper Tom Sinclair, from Morton and the illustrious former Queen's Parker from Newcastle United, R.S.McColl, then launching out in the confectionery business in Glasgow.

Known inevitably for that reason as 'Toffee' McColl, he was also dubbed with some justification as 'Prince of Centre-Forwards'. Born in Glasgow in 1876, he was with Queen's Park at 18 and had the first of 13 caps at 19. He had speed, swerve, cunning, courage, finishing power – not a bad litany for the position. He had three hat-tricks in internationals, one in the famous 4-1 defeat of England at Celtic Park in 1900, when he scored in the first minute. In spite of its weight, he was an expert at 'bending' the heavy, leather ball of the time. Following his term with Rangers he was reinstated as an amateur with Queen's Park and scored six goals for them in one match. And 'Toffee's' business flourished – even in the 1990s , 173 branches were trading under the name 'Martin McColl'.

Apart from extensive changes in personnel, 1904-05 was a season of severe injuries for Rangers, yet they challenged strenuously for every competition. They went down, ominously, in their first League match, 2-1 at Cathkin, but before September was out, they had beaten Hibs home and away, trounced Partick Thistle 8-1 at Ibrox and had away wins over Dundee and Queen's Park offset only by a 1-1 draw with Hearts. Rangers led the League. But St Mirren of all teams came to Ibrox and won 3-2, their first League win there in 13 years. They completed the double at Paisley, winning 3-0 in the following month, and considering that St Mirren finished tenth of the 14 in the League that season, these four points lost were to cost Rangers the championship.

Three defeats in their first 13 matches cost Rangers pole position, yet they lost only one more match in the remaining 15. That came at Ibrox on 22 February, when Celtic won 4-1. That left the Ibrox men to win three of their final three games to have any chance. They did it, twice against Morton, and with a 5-1 at home against Port Glasgow. Rangers were tied with Celtic on 41 points. They still had neither a better goal-average, nor a better goal-difference than Celtic, but the rules decreed that a play-off should be held, at Hampden on 6 May. Celtic struck twice early in the second half with goals from McMenemy and Hamilton, and although Robertson got one back, the championship was Celtic's, the first of six successive titles. The Rangers team that day, many of them little known, was: Sinclair; Fraser, Craig, Gourlay, Stark, May, Robertson, Speedie, McColl, Donaghy, Smith.

Celtic in fact were to come close to dominating the game in the decade which led up to World War One. They were champions nine times over the next 12 years, and Scottish Cup winners five times in the same period, and they did it with one of the greatest of all Celtic teams. Ever since, Celtic fans have been able to recite full-backs McNair and Dodds, the half-back line of Young, Loney and Hay and above all the brilliant attack of Bennett, McMenemy, Quinn, Somers and Hamilton.

Rangers' Glasgow Cup ambitions had been dumped 2-1 by Celtic at Hampden in October. The 54,613 crowd saw two Alec Bennett goals to Bob Hamilton's one. In the Scottish Cup, Rangers had disposed of Ayr Parkhouse,

Action from the 1905 Scottish Cup Final replay between Rangers and Third Lanark at Hampden Park. Thirds won 3-1.

R.S.McColl, dubbed the 'Prince of Centre-Forwards'. He had speed, swerve, cunning, courage, finishing power.

Morton and Beith without much incident and faced a semi-final at Celtic Park. They did it without Hamilton, McColl and Walker, all injured. Jacky Robertson was played at centre-half and Alec Craig, a youngster only just signed from Rutherglen Glencairn, was drafted in, so Celtic were firm favourites. But then as now, form meant very little in Rangers-Celtic matches. Speedie and Robertson goals had Rangers leading 2-0 with ten minutes remaining. Jimmy Quinn was ordered off. The Celtic fans invaded the pitch. Celtic conceded the tie. Rangers were in their third consecutive Final. They faced Third Lanark, the previous season's champions, at Hampden on 8 April 1905, with 54,000 in attendance. After a goalless draw, 54,000 saw Third Lanark win the replay deservedly, 3-1, taking the Cup for a second and final time. Rangers went all the way to the first round of the Charity Cup, beaten 5-0 by Partick Thistle.

Before the end of the season, Jacky Robertson left to become Chelsea manager, but no doubt the entire second half of the season was a bitter time for Rangers. The much-loved Nicol Smith, as good a player as Rangers ever had, died in January.

Opening season 1905-06 with, basically, the same squad, Rangers won their first two League fixtures, at home to Kilmarnock, then Aberdeen, who were making their First

Division debut. A drastic slump followed. A 5-1 loss at the hands, or rather feet of Airdrie threatened yet another barren season. In the event, the Glasgow Charity Cup was won, but Rangers' heaviest-ever home defeat came on 25 September, a 5-0 drubbing from Hearts. Two such heavy defeats in the opening six matches meant that the championship would be a dreary struggle. Rangers eventually lost eight of their 30 League matches in finishing fourth, no fewer than 12 points behind Celtic.

The ranks had to be stiffened. James Spiers came in August, James Galt and R.G.Campbell in January 1906 and in May 1906, goalkeeper Alex Newbigging from Reading and ex-Ranger James Jackson arrived. Campbell had been transferred from Celtic to ease an injury crisis, a favour Rangers would return the following season. Four matches were played in the Glasgow Cup, two against Clyde, two against Third Lanark. Thirds won the replay 3-1, and a

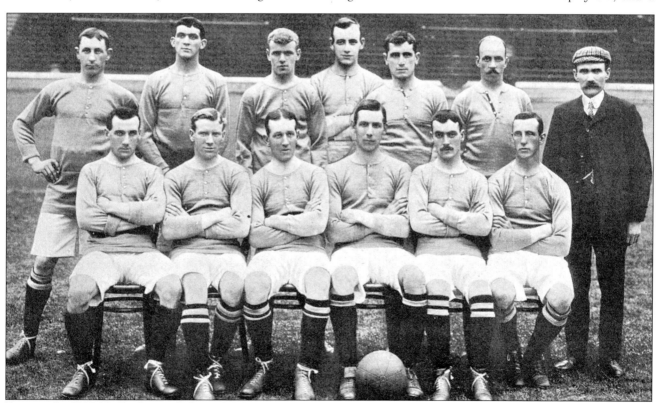

Rangers in 1905-06. Back row (left to right): Fraser, Sinclair, Craig, Speedie, Stark, May, J.Wilson (trainer). Front row: Dalrymple, Gray, McColl, Hamilton, Kyle, Smith.

League double meant that the Hi Hi's were a jinx team for the Ibrox men. Thoughts of a fourth successive Scottish Cup Final appearance were sunk in the 'mud, glue and water' of Clune Park, Port Glasgow. Rangers did everything but score, but ran into goalkeeper Ward having an inspired day in the only Scottish Cup-tie between the clubs. A dramatic 5-3 win in the semi-final of the Charity Cup against Celtic restored some morale and Rangers went on to beat Queen's Park 3-2 in the Final. Three Rangers players represented Scotland that season – Alex Smith, John Hay and Archie Kyle. Half a dozen years earlier, there would have been double that number.

Early in season 1906-07, Finlay Speedie was off to Newcastle United, R.S.McColl, reinstated, back to Queen's Park. New signings were Geordie Livingstone from Manchester City and young players James E.Gordon from Renfrew Victoria and George Law from Arbroath. Both of them would win many honours with the club. Gordon, versatile at either wing or centre-half won every honour in the game save, inevitably, that elusive Scottish Cup medal and was capped 18 times.

The season opened with Finlay Speedie's benefit match at Ibrox, against Celtic. Their goalkeeper David Adams was injured during the match, and Rangers promptly offered the Parkhead men the services of their reserve, Tom Sinclair. In his first eight games for Celtic, he did not concede one single goal. He won a Glasgow Cup medal with them, returned to Ibrox to win a Second XI championship medal and was shortly transferred to Newcastle United, where he won an English League championship, all in that same season!

After a good 2-2 draw at Hampden, Rangers were hammered 3-0 at Ibrox by Queen's Park in the first round of the Glasgow Cup. The League form was less than distinguished. Eight defeats yet again left Rangers in third place with 45 point from 34 matches, ten behind Celtic, champions once more. Their first defeat in 20 League games was Rangers' 2-1 win at New Year, but they took a full revenge in the Scottish Cup, winning 3-0 at Ibrox before a huge 60,000 crowd. Rangers had won impressively at Falkirk in the first round, the improved Brockville team finishing fifth in the League. Celtic were the first club to win the double. Indeed their fine team was thwarted from a clean sweep only by an excellent Rangers display in winning 1-0 in the Charity Cup Final, R.G.Campbell scoring. The Celtic reserves won all their competitions. Rangers' Scotland players were Jamie Stark, George Livingstone, Alex Smith and John May.

Jamie Stark was off to Chelsea, but as it turned out, for only a year. Alec Barrie came from Sunderland and R.C. Hamilton returned for one last season as a 'Light Blue'. Season 1907-08 opened promisingly. A good run in the Glasgow Cup saw Clyde and Third Lanark beaten convincingly with R.G.Campbell, converted the previous season from fullback to centre-forward scoring five of the seven goals. His debut at centre-forward was one of the most exceptional in football. In a benefit match at Ibrox against Morton, he scored seven goals! Over the next three seasons, he was to score 64 goals – a real Rangers find. The Glasgow Cup Final, Rangers v Celtic, was one of the most memorable the competition had known. In the first game, Rangers had the bulk of the pressure, but were held off by sterling defensive work from McNair and Hay. The game ended 2-2, was followed by a goalless replay, then in the third game, Celtic were two up at half-time. Archie Kyle got one back, but Celtic withstood immense Rangers pressure to retain their trophy.

Finlay Speedie from Clydebank Juniors. He formed with Alec Smith one of the finest left-wing partnerships in Rangers' history.

The Rangers team in that third match was: Newbigging; Jackson, Greig, Gordon, May, Galt, Hamilton, Livingstone, Campbell, Kyle, Smith. Alex Smith at outside-left seemed the only connection with the excellent Rangers team of the turn of the century. Serious illnesses to Smith and Jimmy Gordon were more than the team could cope with and twin League defeats by Celtic and Airdrie put an end to title hopes. Its points total improved to 50 from 34 games, but that was good for only a third place, Celtic winning the championship yet again.

The Scottish Cup was something of a re-run of the previous season's experience, Rangers scoring a fine 4-1 replay win over Falkirk before going under to Celtic and a freakish goal from Kivlichen, an ex-Ranger now a doctor in general practice in Glasgow's East End. Celtic won the Cup and with it yet again the double, beating St Mirren in the Final by 5-1 before 60,000 at Hampden. The Charity Cup was lost in disappointing fashion, 3-1 to Queen's Park, a team that Rangers simply could not defeat all season. It ended with a rash of recruitment. James Sharp came from Woolwich Arsenal, Tom Murray from Aberdeen, Tom Gilchrist (Third Lanark), William McPherson (Liverpool), Harry Rennie (Hibs) and by no means least, Alec Bennett from Celtic. R.C.Hamilton, after long service, was given a free transfer. Archie Kyle went to Blackburn Rovers and Spiers and Dickie moved to Clyde. Although far from successful on the field, Rangers remained financially sound – gross receipts from matches alone totalled £14,076. The three-match Glasgow Cup Final had attracted the massive total of 192,000 spectators, grossing receipts of almost £5,000.

For a season that was to end in one of the most notorious of all Scottish Cup Finals (see *Riots, Disturbances and Such-Like Happenings*), season 1908-09 started well enough for Rangers with five straight wins despite the arrival of so many new players. The first point dropped was surprising – a 1-1 home draw with St Mirren. After another home win, 2-0 over Dundee, the first Rangers defeat of the season came not surprisingly from Celtic on 3 October in a Glasgow Cup-tie. After a splendid 2-2 draw at Celtic Park, when Alec Bennett, now wearing blue, had both goals against his former team, 45,000 saw Celtic win convincingly 2-0 in the replay, with goals from Quinn and Somers. A week later, the unbeaten League record went 4-3 at Airdrie but recovering splendidly, Rangers took ten of the next 12 championship points in a six-game unbeaten run. Their challenge was still very much alive when Celtic paid the traditional New Year's visit, with 60,000 on hand at Ibrox. Goals from Hamilton, McMenemy and Munro were more than Rangers could handle. They went down 3-1. Their goal was scored by Tom Murray.

The very next day, Partick Thistle were overwhelmed 6-0 at Ibrox, but a week later, Rangers' title hopes were closely scrutinised when they lost 4-0 at Dundee, who were then close challengers (they were Scottish Cup winners a year later). The rest of Rangers' League results were typified by inconsistency, a fact that their use of 29 players in the season underlined. It was one in which Cup success, however qualified, would redeem things. They did have one outstanding win, 3-2 at Celtic Park, and the events of the Scottish Cup Final should not obscure Rangers' success in getting there. After an easy opener, a second-round tie at Dundee was a little scary and they were happy to come out with a 0-0 draw. At Ibrox, 54,500 saw Rangers win with a solitary goal, from William McPherson. He repeated the feat a week later, on 20 February when Queen's Park went down by the same score before a 45,000 crowd, and incredibly made it three-in-a-row in the semi-final against Falkirk at Brockville.

Following the Scottish Cup Final, a 4-2 win for Rangers at Celtic Park in the Charity Cup Final gave them some silverware and avoided a second barren season. The goals were by Gordon (2), Bennett and May against Celtic's from McLean and Young. Alec Bennett and Jamie Stark both played for Scotland, James Sharp moved to Fulham for a £1,000 fee (!) and George Livingstone moved to Manchester United.

There were impressive new arrivals at Ibrox for the 1909-10 season. Herbert Lock from Southampton, Billy Hogg from Sunderland and William Hunter from Airdrieonians were added to the personnel. Goalkeeper Lock and inside-forward Hogg were established England international players. Lock has the distinction of being the first Englishman signed directly from an English club by Rangers. All three would become important players for the club, but it was to be some time before a settled team was established.

The League programme started with a home win, 3-0 against Kilmarnock, but the away form was appalling – by the turn of the year only six points had been gathered from ten matches, while only two had been lost in nine home games. A Jimmy Quinn goal had won the Glasgow Cup in the Old Firm Final at Hampden, perhaps a touch inconsiderate of the Celtic centre-forward considering that Rangers had supplied the opposition for his benefit match on 18 August, a romp which ended 8-4 to Celtic.

By the turn of the year, the Ibrox players had found some unity and started a surge up the League table with a long succession of wins – only two defeats in the second half of the season, 3-2 against Queen's at Hampden on 12 March and a 1-0 defeat by the sound Falkirk team, at Ibrox in the final game of the season. Ironically, it was Rangers' first home defeat of the season. Such good form had Rangers focussing on a Scottish Cup victory. Inverness Thistle went down in the first round, but the second round brought as tough a draw as they could have wanted – away to Clyde. The Shawfield team had won their home match 1-0. The Cup-tie was a test of stamina in heavy mud, and the home team proved stronger, Chalmers scoring two second-half goals. Clyde went all the way to the Final, going down to Dundee only in a second replay. And Clyde rubbed salt into Rangers' wounds by winning 1-0 in the Glasgow Charity Cup on 7 May.

Early in April 1910, Rangers made a tour of the north, beating Aberdeen 3-1, and Elgin/Forres Select by 6-1 and Inverness Thistle 3-1 in friendly matches. It had been a season of disappointment, but of much promise. Scottish football still marched to the sound of Celtic's drum, but the new Rangers team was coming together, and coming to an end was Celtic's historic sequence of six successive League championships.

A new era of success and prosperity was heralded for Rangers by season 1910-11, not only because they won the championship, but because Celtic's domination of the game had been brought to a halt. Newcomers to Ibrox were George Chapman from Blackburn Rovers, come to captain the team and at 22 reputed to be the finest centre-half in England; Robert Brown, a right-half from Kilwinning Rangers and Robert Parker from Ashfield. Leaving the club were James Stark and John May to join Morton; Harry Rennie and Tom Gilchrist to Kilmarnock and David Taylor, when went to Bradford City.

The season opened with two League victories, 1-0 at home to St Mirren and 2-0 away to Raith Rovers, newcomers replacing Port Glasgow Athletic in the First Division. The first setback was on 3 September when Dundee prevailed at Ibrox, by 2-1. This started a strange run for the Ibrox club, losing three out of four home League matches, yet dropping only one point in five away games. On 26 September, Hibernian were trounced 4-0 in a game marking the debut of outside-left James Paterson. In time he was to make the position his own as successor to the legendary Alex Smith and qualify as a doctor and practice in London.

On 22 October, in a game that lives on in Greenock folklore, a Morton team containing three ex-Rangers (Jackson, Stark and May) came to Ibrox with the promise, by a Greenock butcher, of a lamb for every goal scored. Morton won, 5-1. The butcher's post-match comments have not survived. A 1-0 win at Celtic Park on 29 October, with Hogg scoring meant a second Old Firm win in three weeks, the earlier one being the Glasgow Cup Final at Hampden, when goals from Smith, Reid and Bennett overcame one from Celtic's Johnstone. This 3-1 win gave Rangers the Cup for the first time in nine years. It was something of a momentous triumph for them. They were down to ten men after 37 minutes when right-half Galt went off injured. Veteran Alex Smith, in his 17th season with the club, gave a brilliant display and was the finest player on view.

After their Parkhead League success, Rangers ran up four free-scoring wins and seemed at last to have found consistency. On 3 December, they went north to Pittodrie level on points with Aberdeen at the top. A tense game went to a 1-0 win for the Dons, who thus achieved their first League double over Rangers.

No doubt disturbed by this, Rangers allowed Falkirk to escape from Ibrox with a 1-1 draw, then went down 2-1 against St Mirren at Paisley, and in controversial circumstances. But that St Mirren defeat was to prove the last of the season as Rangers put their head down and took 28 points from the possible 32 in the remaining 16 games. The run started on Christmas Eve with a 2-0 win over Hearts at Ibrox, a game which saw the debut of one James Bowie from Queen's Park, an inside-right who was to have an outstanding career with the club as a player, director and chairman.

Christmas 1910 was busy. On Boxing Day, Rangers fought out a 3-3 draw with old friends Bohemians in Dublin (then of course part of the United Kingdom) in their first visit in four years. They later visited Belfast to defeat a Select XI by 3-0. The New Year fixture against Celtic packed Ibrox, 60,000 witnessing a -1 draw, with Reid and McAteer the respective marksmen. It was a result which effectively ended Celtic's hope of adding to their six successive championships.

The Scottish Cup campaign opened on 28 January, when Rangers beat Kilmarnock 2-1 at Ibrox before 40,000, followed by a home win over Morton, 3-0, which left thousands wondering how the same side could have scored five against Rangers earlier in the season. An unbeaten 13-match run behind them, Rangers went confidently to Dundee for a third-round tie. But a decision by captain Chapman proved fatal – winning the toss, he choose to play against a gale-force wind. Although they snatched a lead after 15 minutes through Hogg, goals by ex-Ranger R.C.Hamilton, and Lee, gave Dundee a 2-1 interval lead. Despite intense Rangers pressure in the second half, it was enough.

Rangers' League form was such that they set a record 52 points from 34 games in winning the championship, four ahead of Aberdeen. And the trophy haul was not complete. After disposing of Clyde and Queen's Park en route, Rangers faced Celtic in the Glasgow Charity Cup Final, yet again. Two goals by Willie Reid, scorer of a startling 48 that season, against one from Nicholl, were enough to take the Cup to Ibrox.

Rejoicing no doubt in their championship success, Rangers set off in May and June for a memorable first visit to Scandinavia, where after a three-day journey, they were warmly welcomed to Christiana. They overwhelmed a provincial select team 12-0, then a Christiana select team 6-0. Next stop was Gothenburg where Orgryte were beaten 7-2, then the full Swedish national side, earlier conquerors of English FA Cup winners Bradford City, by 3-0. In Copenhagen came the sternest test of the tour, 1-1 against the full Danish national side. Before 14,000 Rangers won 3-1 in the final game of a rewarding tour. Much credit for the development of football in Denmark, incidentally, should go to ex-Ranger Alex Hamilton, of Kinning Park days, who did much coaching in the Danish capital.

The calendar year 1911 had been quite magnificent for Rangers. Of 51 matches played, only two were lost. The New Year failed to have a comparable start. In the traditional holiday game against Celtic, they were without James Galt and when his replacement, George Waddell, was lost through injury early in the game, there was no stopping Jimmy Quinn, who notched a hat-trick.

Rangers had started the season in defence of their championship with an unchanged staff, and by winning their first ten competitive matches, including seven in the League. And in defending their Glasgow Cup tenancy, beginning on 9 September, Queen's Park were beaten 6-1 at Hampden, then Clyde, two weeks later, by 1-0 at Ibrox. The Final was to be against Partick Thistle at Celtic Park, on 9 October. Thistle had been putting together good results this early in the season, but Rangers were strong favourites. Nevertheless it took a superb flash of individual skill from Willie Hogg, with a run in which he seemed to beat the entire Thistle team to score. The first trophy of the new season was won, the first League point of the season dropped a week later in a 2-2 draw at Airdrie.

But the team was in devastating form. Celtic were beaten 3-1 at Ibrox with Bowie scoring two, Gordon the other to McAteer's for Celtic. Not until 2 December did the first defeat come, 2-1 at Greenock Morton. In November, 14 goals scored for the loss of one came in just four matches. By the end of the year, Rangers had an eight point lead over Celtic. A surprising 5-0 loss to Hibernian at Easter Road, followed by a home defeat, 2-1, by Clyde had Rangers concerned when the second-round Scottish Cup draw sent them to Shawfield, On 10 February, Clyde swept into a three-goal lead after only half an hour with goals from Morrison (2, one after three minutes) and Carmichael. Joe Hendry got one back early in the second half.

However, in the 73rd minute a foul by McAndrew on Alex Bennett proved to be a flashpoint which led to an estimated 2,000 spectators pouring on to the field of play, obliterating the lines. Whilst no attempt was made to assault any player – indeed, some were carried off shoulder-high – Rangers quickly conceded the tie. Clyde went through to the Final, where they lost 2-0 to Celtic at Ibrox, before 45,000.

Rangers recovered sufficiently to take seven points from their next four League games, and the championship was won, for the seventh time, on 23 March with a 1-0 win over Raith Rovers in Kirkcaldy. With 51 points from the 34 games, they were six ahead of Celtic. Rangers played at Kirkcaldy, during a national coal strike. It was the same day as the Scotland-England international match. They were able to travel only because they supplied their own coal to feed the locomotive of the North British Railway train.

Three friendlies were played in April – on a tour of Ireland, Bohemians were beaten 2-0 in Dublin, but in Belfast, Linfield won 1-0. Woolwich Arsenal came to Ibrox to play a 0-0 draw, no doubt without exciting the players too much. Clyde won 2-1 in a Glasgow Cup-tie, Rangers playing most of the game without a recognised goalkeeper. If it was considered a successful season, it ended on a sad note with the death of Baillie James Henderson. He had been president and chairman of the club for 14 years. He was succeeded as chairman by Sir John Ure Primrose.

With two championships behind them, Rangers had ideas about a hat-trick, but at the same time there were notions of putting an end to a decade without that elusive Scottish Cup. Their start to 1912-13 was excellent, with a home win, 4-2 over Airdrie on 17 August. Two days later Celtic were at Ibrox for the R.G.Campbell benefit, which Rangers won 2-1. Their first setback came from Hearts in late September whose splendid display of attacking football gave them a 4-2 win. Yet Rangers were flying high at the top of the League when the Glasgow Cup came around, and brought with it a massive fixture pile-up and injury crisis to the Govan club, in the form of a three-match semi-final with Partick Thistle.

By this time, Rangers had signed James L.Logan, a former Queen's Park player from Aston Villa. And when Herbert Lock was injured in the second Partick Thistle match – it kept him out for the rest of the season – another signing, that of goalkeeper John Hempsey, was required. They finally got past Thistle to face Celtic in the Glasgow Cup Final at Hampden on 12 October in a game which was to become something of a Rangers legend. One down early in the second half to a Jimmy Quinn goal, they were cut to ten men when John Robertson was injured with a knee injury which was to end his career. Despite this, the ten men surged to a memorable victory with goals from Hogg, Smith and Bennett, winning them the trophy for a record tenth time.

A heavy fixture list which now included the 'Inter City League', played for by the leading clubs of Edinburgh, Glasgow and Aberdeen, compounded Rangers' growing injury list. As the season progressed, Willie Reid, Alex Bennett, Alec Smith and James Galt, as well as Lock and Robertson, were out at various times. On 23 November all three goalkeepers, Lock, Hempsey and Farrington were out, and Rangers were obliged to play R.G.Campbell in goal – Rangers beat Clyde 3-1! By New Year's Day, Rangers had lost four more League games, including a double defeat by Celtic. Jimmy Quinn's solitary goal settled the Ne'er Day match, which left Rangers trailing the leaders Celtic by four points, with 14 League games remaining. And a 5-1 defeat at Ibrox by an international select team in Alec Smith's benefit match, did little to encourage them.

Yet once again the second half of the League season belonged to Rangers. They won 26 of a possible 28 points from these 14 games, claiming their third successive title on 19 April with a goalless draw at Dens Park. From 1 January to 10 May Rangers lost only once in competitive play, that to Falkirk in the Scottish Cup. It was game which Rangers dominated. Falkirk's first corner kick came with 65 minutes gone, but by that time they were three up, thanks to a dreadful exhibition of goalkeeping by Hempsey. Falkirk were inspired by ex-Rangers James Croal, who had been transferred for the grand sum of £10. Falkirk won the Cup, beating Raith Rovers 2-1 at Celtic Park in the Final before a crowd of 45,000.

Rangers did beat Falkirk in the final game, 2-1 at Ibrox to amass a club record of 53 points, four ahead of Celtic. Two days later on 28 April, the Old Firm travelled to Inverness to play each other in a 0-0 friendly. In the Charity Cup Final, two Willie Reid goals were not enough – Celtic goals by Connelly (2) and Gallacher gave them the Cup. In June of 1913, Rangers were in Copenhagen for the second time in three years, recording scores of 2-1 and 1-1 against select teams. James Gordon, James Logan, Willie Reid and Alec Smith represented Scotland, with Alec Smith getting the last of his international honours, a club record that stood for many years.

In the summer of 1913, the First Division was increased to 20 clubs. Rangers set off in pursuit of a fourth successive championship without William Hogg, who had been transferred to Dundee. He was not adequately replaced until September and the coming from Newcastle United of the right-wing partnership of Scott Duncan and James Stewart, the latter a full England international. He remained at Ibrox for only one season, but for all that, made a valuable contribution. Duncan's presence had the extra advantage of allowing James 'Doc' Paterson to switch wings to his natural outside-left position.

The season started well with four League victories. In August, Rangers had the honour of supplying the opposition at Celtic Park and Hampden for the benefit matches of Alec McNair and William Sellar respectively. Both were won, 2-0 and 3-2. The first League defeat came from Hearts at Tynecastle, 2-1 on 13 September, for the second successive season. Two days later there was a 3-0 win at Easter Road before Dundee became the first visitors to Ibrox to take both points, by 1-0 on 20 September. The next six games saw Rangers undefeated, a run which included a 3-0 win over Third Lanark at Hampden in the Glasgow Cup Final. In a match seen as vital to the destiny of the championship, Celtic came to Ibrox on 25 October, with both sides level on points at the top of the table.

A massive crowd of 63,500 saw Celtic win 2-0 with goals by McAteer and Whitehead, although at the height of Rangers' late rally, Celtic goalkeeper Charlie Shaw had to save a penalty from Alec Bennett. Rangers' morale was such that they set out on the kind of run that had brought them previous championships – eight wins from nine matches, the only defeat a 1-0 from Motherwell at Fir Park. The last match of 1913, a visit from Hamilton Accies on 27 December marked the debut of one Tommy Cairns destined to be one of the finest Rangers players of the era. He was renowned for his work rate, his powerful play and scoring talents. He played eight times for Scotland.

That title surge before the end of the year was more than matched by a Celtic team which had dropped only one point in the same period, a goalless draw with Motherwell at Celtic Park. Rangers thus went into the New Year's Day match at Parkhead three points behind, and in the knowledge that failure by them would settle the championship. So it proved. Celtic, shaking down into a team that would dominate the next half-dozen years, won convincingly, 4-0, with goals from Browning (2), Young and McMenemy. They completed a League double over Rangers for the second successive season. It was to be 58 more years before they did it again. The League was effectively won and lost. Rangers were second, with 59 points from 38 games, six behind Celtic's new record of 65.

The Scottish Cup dream yet again was brief. After a 5-0 home win over Alloa, it ended at Easter Road when Hibs won 2-1. Celtic completed the double by winning 4-1 against Hibs at Ibrox, after a goalless first match seen by 55,000. The replay attracted 36,000. At the end of the season, the Charity Cup went down to Third Lanark on the corner kick ruling in a match which saw the return of Alec Craig to the club. At least the Glasgow Cup had been retained for a record-equalling fourth season, and Jimmy Gordon, William Reid and Jimmy Bowie played for Scotland during the season.

Two benefit matches were played at Ibrox. On 2 January, a team of ex-Rangers fought out a lively 4-4 draw in Alec Bennett's benefit. They were: W.Allen (Hibernian); J.Mackenzie (Cowdenbeath), Finlay Speedie (Dumbarton), W.Walker (Clyde), J.Stark (Morton), George Waddell (Kilmarnock), W.Hogg (Dundee), T.Gilchrist (Motherwell), R.C.Hamilton (Elgin City), J.Croal (Falkirk) and W.Hunter (Cowdenbeath). On 28 April, Everton were soundly beaten 6-2 in trainer Jimmy Wilson's benefit match. Wilson, trainer at Ibrox for 17 years, died on 3 May. His replacement, from Clyde, was a man who came with the highest credentials and who was to have a profound impact on the Rangers Football Club, and on Scottish football in general, for many years.

His name was William Struth.

Days of Disaster

LOOKING back to the turn of the 20th century, it is difficult for us to imagine a world without television, radio and the cinema in terms of public entertainment. It was a world without motor cars, without foreign travel, save for the very rich and privileged. Football thus was a major medium for public entertainment and recreation and the new century ushered in an era of vast crowds reaching into six figures with football grounds growing to accommodate them. In 1900, for example, Rangers had spent £20,000, a very considerable sum, on a ground improvement scheme which included two covered stands and behind each goal, huge, inclined, wooden 'scaffolding' terraces.

For the 1902 Scotland-England international, Celtic, Rangers and Queen's Park, all with large capacity grounds, vied to stage the match. It would be worth £1,000 or more to the club concerned. Ibrox Park was chosen because of its capacity of 75,000 following the improvements made. The terracing behind the west goal was 50 feet high and made of open wooden planking on an iron framework. Even by the lax standards of the day, it was regarded by some as suspect, dangerous. One newspaper published a letter from a fan who reported 'vibrations' felt when standing on that West Terrace, and a journalist recorded that many regulars were avoiding that part of the ground.

On 5 April 1902, it was raining heavily in Glasgow as the international kicked-off before a capacity crowd. Although the ground was clearly full, more and more people surged in and those inside began to look for an escape route. Hundreds spilled on to the track, hundreds more left the East Terracing to make for the western end of the ground. They encroached on the playing area. Long narrow stairways serviced the wooden West Terrace. They, too, were packed with men desperate to see this great match. The crowd began to sway at the top of the terracing. At the bottom, people spilled out on to the grass. Suddenly seven rows of planking disappeared. A gap 50 feet long by 12 feet across appeared – according to one witness, it 'collapsed like a trap door'. Without warning, hundreds of people fell 50 feet. In an instant, 26 people were dead, 587 were injured.

The game was stopped, then incredibly, 18 minutes later, restarted, and was played to a finish, the reason being that the officials feared an even greater disaster had it been abandoned. Certainly many spectators in other parts of the huge ground were unaware of what had happened. For the rest of the game, rescue workers coped unseen in the rain with death and injury to the roars of the massive crowd. And, despite the risks, many scrambled back on to the broken terracing. The corridors of the Ibrox stands were used as first-aid stations. The players finished the match in fitful fashion. It ended 1-1, was declared void and a month later an official match at Villa Park replaced it in the records, ending 2-2, from which the £1,000 gate receipts went to the Ibrox Disaster Relief Fund.

It was clear that the construction of football grounds needed completely new thinking, and that solid earth bankings represented the only safe way for clubs to extend their grounds. One Archibald Leitch, a construction engineer who had worked with Celtic and Queen's Park, was retained by Rangers. Ibrox was revamped with an immediate capacity reduced to 25,000. After five years of further work, Leitch's planning had increased the capacity to 63,000 and Ibrox was reinstated as an international venue. Scotland beat Ireland there in March 1909.

If the Ibrox Disaster of 1902 changed the thinking of the Rangers club regarding its stadium, 70 years on the Ibrox Disaster of 1971 had similar but even more far-reaching effects. The awful event of 2 January 1971, following the traditional 'Ne'er Day' Rangers-Celtic match, was a disaster waiting to happen. The simple facts of the matter are that part of the huge crowd of 85,000, leaving at the end of the match from the top of the high Copland Road terracing down Stairway 13, stumbled and fell and, as one report had it, 'the crowd just caved in, like a pack of cards, as if all of them were falling into a huge hole'. As more and more people pushed their way down from the top of the stairway, not knowing what was happening, the pressure became intolerable. People were crushed to death, many of them within seconds, many standing upright. The death toll was 66, with 145 injured. The official cause of the deaths was 'traumatic asphyxiation', or inability to breathe. Sadly, the vast majority of the crowd went home, not realising there had been such a tragedy.

The overture to all this had happened on the field of play, but was rooted in the past. This particular 'Ne'er Day' match had been a tense and rather undistinguished game on a firm surface, play enlivened only by the skills of Jimmy Johnstone and Dave Smith. It trailed towards its end, goalless. Then in the 89th minute, a Bobby Lennox shot from 20 yards rebounded from the crossbar. Jimmy Johnstone got to it first, to head what seemed a dramatic winning goal.

A sensational win for Celtic? So it seemed. In the last few seconds, Jim Craig for Celtic conceded a foul on the left. Dave Smith swept over the free-kick. Derek Johnstone miskicked, but Colin Stein hammered the ball home. Rangers had survived. Celtic were deprived of a first New Year victory at Ibrox, since 1921.

Much was made of this dramatic, even melodramatic, climax to the match, with claims that part of the crowd already leaving down Stairway 13 had turned back on hearing the acclaim for Stein's goal and so caused the turmoil. The fact was that when a crowd was flowing down one of these stairways, 30 feet wide with steel railings and rigid wooden walls held secure by embedded railway sleepers, it would be impossible for anyone to turn against the flow of bodies. Indeed, with a major crowd at Ibrox, leaving by one of these wide stairways meant a complete surrender to the flood, being swept along and down without any control of individual movement, simply swept along by an enormous wave.

The central steel barriers which ran up the length of the stairway were buckled and twisted. The wooden side barriers were so high and rigid that there was no escape that way. Many of the victims were literally squeezed out of their shoes and socks. Bodies were laid out on the grass and on the indoor running track underneath the Ibrox grandstand.

The subsequent inquiry established that the disaster had happened when someone stumbled at the top of the stairway, creating a domino effect that was unstoppable.

It cannot be emphasised too strongly that Colin Stein's equaliser in no way caused the disaster. The Fatal Accident Inquiry clearly established the time of the tragedy as more than five minutes after the final whistle.

The chief constable of Glasgow had immediately put Detective Superintendent Joe Beattie – a spectator at the match – in charge of police operation. Beattie, an experienced policeman, found the Rangers board in disarray, the directors unable to grasp the enormity of the situation.

A sad and unique football photograph. The wreck of the stand at Ibrox which 'collapsed like a trapdoor' during the 1902 Scotland-England international, killing 26 people and injuring 587.

Yet Rangers had had prior warning. There had been three incidents and accidents in the previous ten years on that same Stairway 13. Two people died and 44 were injured in 1961; 11 were injured in 1967; 30 in 1969. On the face of this, it was clear that the club had not heeded expert advice on ground safety, although £150,000 had been spent on improvements during the same period. A Lord Provost's Fund was set up to help the families of the bereaved and injured. Both clubs made substantial donations. Players of both clubs stood together at church funeral services. A memorial service was held in Glasgow Cathedral, a requiem mass at St Andrews Roman Catholic Church, these again attended by players and officials of both clubs, and civic dignitaries.

The official inquiry led by Sheriff Irvine Smith sat for 14 days and was severely critical of Rangers' directors, whose evidence was confused, contradictory, increasingly unimpressive. There was but the vaguest recollection of previous accidents and no one, for example, could remember who had accompanied Chief Superintendent Nicholson in inspecting the stairway some months previously. Sheriff Smith concluded with a savage indictment: "Rarely can an organisation of the size and significance of Rangers Football Club have succeeded in conducting their business with records so sparse, so carelessly kept, so inaccurately written up and so indifferently stored." No action was taken against the club or of any individual in the matter of this specific accident.

Yet from all of this emerged a man of action and an historic turning point in the story of the club and of its stadium. Following the disaster, Willie Waddell, the club manager, worked tirelessly to ensure that the club was represented at every funeral service, that all of the sick were visited, officially, that all of the players were pressed into these duties and that in this and in other ways the club was seen to care.

And Waddell also saw that the perils of these huge terracings, with fans leaning on steel crush barriers and descending en masse, these high, steep exit stair-ways, was no longer acceptable. In 1971, football club grounds were not licensed, as were cinemas and theatres. Police or local authorities had no power to impose regulations on the clubs or force them to make improvements. Lord Wheatly's Commission on ground safety led to the Safety of Sports Ground Act of 1975, but before then, before Bradford and Hillsborough and before the subsequent Taylor Report which demanded from all the leading clubs all-seated stadiums, Waddell saw that the way ahead, for Rangers certainly was just that. The days of 100,000 people standing cramped in the rain were long gone. So he travelled around Europe, visiting the most modern stadiums in Germany and Italy and elsewhere, and throughout the 1970s and 1980s was the driving force in creating the magnificent Ibrox of today, with more than 50,000 seats, all under cover and not one single standing place left. Out of the evil of the 1971 disaster has come an impressive progress.

Rangers in World War One

WHEN Britain declared war on Germany in August 1914, the public hailed the declaration with jingoistic enthusiasm and a massive ignorance. They were ignorant of what modern warfare really meant, ignorant, needless to say, of the appalling slaughter that was to follow in immense battles over the next four years in France and Flanders. On 5 August, the day after war was declared, the Hearts players had a meeting at Tynecastle, and marched as one, with several club supporters, to the nearest recruiting office and enlisted. They were accepted to a man in the Sportmen's Battalion. Many of them did not return and there remains a monument to their memory at the Haymarket Cross in Edinburgh. Yet 'Home by Christmas' was the mood as what was known as the 'Great War' unfolded.

In the context of these events, the world of football was small indeed. Season 1914-15 was ten days old when the war began, and there was some discussion as to what should be done. The government allowed the game to continue. They saw football grounds and football crowds as prime recruitment opportunities – there was no conscription until the last year of the war. Regular Army recruiting sergeants attended grounds on match days, inviting the 'Boys' to take the King's shilling. Progressively, as the seriousness of events became clear, players were not allowed to be full-time footballers. They must either enlist, or work in war-related industry. Football wages came down to a minimum of £1 per week, £2 maximum, and no wages at all in the close season. International matches were abandoned, and for some reason not apparent then or since, the SFA decided to withdraw the Scottish Cup competition for the duration of the war.

The Scottish League continued as normal for season 1914-15, but in 1915-16, the Second Division, mainly clubs from small towns, could not carry on. It was to be six years before it was re-formed. In one match against Falkirk, Rangers had only nine men to field. In April 1916, Hearts scratched from a League fixture because they could not raise a team. Temporary transfers helped clubs field teams of sorts. Players were allowed to change clubs if they could show patriotic or work-related reasons for so doing. By April 1917, Aberdeen, Dundee and Raith Rovers were invited to leave the League – travelling to their grounds for most of the other clubs had become too difficult. So the game soldiered on, so to speak, in a rather haphazard way.

Celtic dominated Scottish football throughout the war, as Rangers were to do during World War Two, retaining the famous defensive unit that was the basis of its pre-war success, and such forwards as Patsy Gallacher and Jimmy McMenemy. Both Celtic and Rangers were criticised during the war, and not without some substance, for not contributing many service personnel and with placing their players in war-related jobs convenient to the grounds which kept them at home and available for football. Yet it could be said that perhaps these clubs, like others contributed to the war effort in other ways. The Celtic club had an association with the City's Stobhill Hospital while Willie Wilton and Bill Struth contributed many voluntary services to Ballahouston Hospital for wounded soldiers. Yet these wartime seasons, in general when they were in the main trekking after Celtic, were to see Rangers assemble a team which with its successors would dominate the entire period between the two world wars.

The first wartime season opened for Rangers on 15 August with a home win over Hamilton Accies, while Hearts were beating Celtic 2-0 at Tynecastle. These were the two clubs most likely to threaten Rangers' title hopes. Three days later Celtic were at Ibrox for Herbert Lock's benefit match, winning 6-4 in a thoroughly relaxed, entertaining match. The next day Rangers were in Greenock for ex-Rangers James Stark's benefit, beating Morton 1-0. After both clubs had made encouraging starts to the season, Hearts came to Ibrox on 1 September and for the third consecutive season, inflicted on Rangers their first League defeat, by 2-1, putting the Edinburgh side clear at the top of the division. A week later, another home defeat came, this time from Partick Thistle in the Glasgow Cup, by 2-0.

October brought four defeats in five League games, and left Hearts, with one of the finest teams in their history, ten points ahead. Although the Light Blues recovered to drop only two points in eight games, this was matched by both Hearts and Celtic. There was a 2-1 win over Celtic at the turn of the year, with goals by Bowie and Reid, but Rangers remained six points behind Celtic, ten behind Hearts. That was the second 'Old Firm' win in two weeks, Rangers having won by the same score in the semi-final of the War Shield at Firhill, earlier.

Three defeats in a week, 2-1 and 5-0 in home games against Clyde and Airdrie and 3-1 away to Partick Thistle put the championship well beyond Rangers reach. But they were to influence its destination. A 1-1 draw at Celtic Park left Hearts with a four-point lead over Celtic with 11 games left. But the combination of the loss of their players to the services, now being felt, and a very consistent Celtic, not to mention Rangers' best performance and result of the season – a 4-3 win at Tynecastle put paid to Hearts.

Of great significance to Rangers were two signings. Bert Manderson from Ulster, who was to prove a superb full-back for club and country, made his debut on 27 March 1915 in a 1-1 draw against Aberdeen at Ibrox. Two weeks later, Andy Cunningham from Kilmarnock appeared at Ibrox on the losing side, 1-0 to Partick Thistle. Already an international player, he became a major Rangers player and one of Scotland's outstanding inside-forwards throughout the 1920s.

And as they arrived, the last of the Victorian Rangers went. Alex Smith, the only remaining player who had graced 'first Ibrox', retired after 21 years with the club.

In 1915, ex-Baillie Joseph Buchanan joined the board. He had been a member of the club since 1894, and had also been involved with the ill-fated Abercorn club, which did not survive the war. They had been founder members of the Scottish Football League.

Rangers opened with eight straight wins, five of them League matches. Celtic did the same. The Glasgow Cup

> In 1914-18, restrictions were not so severe as in 1939-45, but clubs faced difficulties, none greater than Rangers at Falkirk in 1915 – they arrived at Brockville three players short. Messrs Hempsey, Hendry and the great Andy Cunningham were all missing. Nine players took to the field, with inside-forward Alec Bennett in goal. Scott Duncan was injured in the first half and missed all of the second – Rangers played with eight men! Not surprisingly, Falkirk won 2-0.

brought a flood of goals from the Light Blues – 4-1 over Queen's Park at Hampden on 11 September, then 7-2 against Partick Thistle two weeks later. The September holiday weekend brought a 6-1 win over Glasgow Highlanders in a match for War Relief. The Glasgow Cup Final on 9 October, Rangers v Celtic, was their first meeting of the season. The Parkhead men retained their superb championship form from the previous season, and in a closely-fought game, prevailed 2-1. Goals came from Gallacher and Browning, and from Paterson for Rangers. A week later, Hearts were at Ibrox, after an inconsistent start to their season. Yet again they brought Rangers their first League defeat, for a fourth consecutive season. This time by 4-0.

A week later, Celtic were beaten at home for the first time, surprisingly by St Mirren, 2-0. At the end of October, Rangers trounced Celtic 3-0 at Ibrox with goals from Paterson, Reid and Duncan. In November, they overran Queen's Park at Hampden 6-0, then Hamilton Accies 2-0 at Ibrox, and suddenly it seemed they were four points clear of Celtic, and on top. They could not hope to maintain this form, and went to Celtic Park for the Ne'er Day match level on points. The match underlined the equality of the teams, with Rangers goals coming from Cunningham and Duncan, Celtic goals from McAtee and McCollin in the 2-2 draw. On 4 January, Rangers played a Rest-of-Glasgow Select XI at Ibrox, winning 3-2 in a War Relief match.

Their home form was constant. Not another Ibrox League game was lost, but away from home, they were just not good enough to sustain a championship challenge to a Celtic team which, following their defeat by Hearts on 13 November dropped only three points from drawn games from then until the end of the League season! They were runaway champions, with a record 67 points, no fewer than 11 ahead of Rangers.

April 1916 saw James Paterson, a qualified doctor, depart for the front. Happily, he was to return to the club after the war.

Season 1916-17 saw many of the darkest days of World War One, and football in many ways seemed less and less important. On active service were Rangers players James Paterson, Andy Cunningham, Jimmy Gordon and William Reid, and the club had to find youngsters to fill out the team.

On 12 August, they were at Somerset Park for a Red Cross match in which they defeated Ayr United 3-1. In their first League match, the same score beat Dundee at Ibrox. The next match was at Tynecastle. Rangers buried their 'first defeat of the season' hoodoo with a 3-1 win. In the Glasgow Cup, Partick Thistle went down 2-0 at Firhill to set up a Celtic Park semi-final. Both clubs went into the match with a 100% record, but the champions were masters, by 3-0, their goals coming from Browning, O'Kane and Johnstone. In October, both teams dropped their first points, Celtic when they drew 1-1 at Brockville, Rangers a week later in a 1-1 draw at Cathkin with Third Lanark. On 28 October, the teams met at Celtic Park in the League. A goalless draw left Rangers in pole position by one point. It was short-lived. Morton came to Ibrox and won 1-0. It was Rangers' first League defeat and it gave Celtic the leadership, a position they were not to surrender all season.

December brought the now-irritating failings in away matches, defeats in Lanarkshire coming from Airdrie and Motherwell by 2-0 and 2-1 respectively. Rangers went into the New Year trailing Celtic by five points and the 0-0 draw did nothing to resolve that. This was the only season in which both League matches ended scoreless.

January saw Rangers play six League games without leaving Glasgow, without conceding a goal. The run brought them to within two points of Celtic who, unbeaten, nevertheless had dropped three points in drawn games. A 3-1 defeat at Aberdeen dented Light Blue ambitions and 10 March put an end to them. Morton won 1-0 at Cappielow to mark the first and only occasion in League history when they completed a double over Rangers. The Greenock side of the time was probably the best in their history, their second place League finish being the highest they ever achieved.

Celtic finished champions yet again, by ten clear points with a total of 64, but their long unbeaten run came to an end on 21 April (2-0 at Kilmarnock), their penultimate fixture. From 13 November 1915 to 21 April 1917 Celtic played 62 League games without defeat. A stunning record which stands to this day. That same day in April was unique in Rangers history. The team played two League fixtures on the same day – losing 3-1 to Hamilton Accies at Douglas Park in the afternoon and beating Queen's Park 1-0 at Ibrox in the evening. Their season came to a doleful end on 12 May, when they went down 2-0 in the Charity Cup Final at Ibrox.

Rangers welcomed Baillie Duncan Graham to the board of directors before the start of the season 1917-18, but it was new players who were to have a direct impact on the club's fortunes. May 1917 was a significant month in its history. Both Sandy Archibald and Tommy Muirhead were signed. They would win innumerable honours for both club and country. Archibald was a powerful outside right who would score crucial goals for Rangers, while Muirhead, a wing-half or centre-half, was to be the engine room of the team through most of the 1920s. In July Englishman Arthur Dixon arrived, a centre-half who brought solidity to the defence and in time became Rangers' trainer. Another newcomer was George McQueen.

It was to be the most dramatic of seasons, undecided until the very last day. Rangers won it by one point from Celtic, champions for the first time in five years with 56 points from 34 games. And there were tremors galore before the Ibrox club got there.

There was a good start at Kilmarnock, always a difficult place, by 1-0, then a 4-2 win at home against Third Lanark. The first defeat came earlier than usual, however, 2-0 by Partick Thistle and this 'new' Rangers team was having teething troubles, this emphasised at Shawfield in the Glasgow Cup, where it took the corners rule to get past Clyde. The semi-final on 22 September was at Celtic Park. Recent Cup meetings between the clubs had heavily favoured Celtic, but this time goals from Cairns, Archibald and Brown swept them aside. And against Partick Thistle in the Final, Rangers repeated this form, winning comfortably 4-1.

A 1-1 draw at Greenock was an improvement on the previous season, and set up Rangers for the visit of Celtic on 20 October. Celtic had just surrendered their perfect League record when Kilmarnock surprised them 3-2 at Parkhead, but they certainly recovered at Ibrox. A 2-1 win with goals from McAtee and McColl against one from Bowie put them three points ahead. Rangers proceeded to rip off eight wins, at home to Airdrie, Dumbarton, Falkirk and St Mirren, and away to Hearts, Queen's Park, Hamilton Accies and Partick Thistle. But they picked up but one point on Celtic and a 0-0 draw at Celtic Park on 1 January left the hosts favourite. Rangers took seven out of the eight points in the remaining January fixtures and had caught Celtic, who had drawn three consecutive games.

Right: **W.J.Aitken signed for Rangers from Queen's Park but played for only one season before moving to Newcastle United.**

Far right: **James Walls was a new signing towards the end of the war and went on to serve Rangers well in peacetime football.**

The single point Rangers had dropped was 1-1 at Clydebank on 5 January. The Bankies, not of course the present club, had been invited in to balance the League when Aberdeen, Dundee and Raith Rovers went out, temporarily, war victims. Rangers went to Airdrie on 23 March, two points behind and with the suspicion that the championship was slipping away from them. Their stuffy 2-1 win was enhanced when the news came that Celtic had lost at home, 3-1, to lowly Third Lanark. So it was all to play for, with three games left.

All three Rangers games were at home. Clydebank were only just beaten, 1-0, while Celtic had an outstanding away win at third-placed Kilmarnock by 3-1. A week later, Motherwell, in fifth place, were narrowly beaten while Celtic came through 2-0 at Easter Road. Now the championship hung on two final matches, Rangers at home to Clyde, Celtic at home to Motherwell. Rangers won 2-1. What was happening at Celtic Park? No transistor radios then! Despite furious Celtic pressure Motherwell held fast for their 1-1 draw. Rangers were champions! It had been the most marvellous competition between these two great clubs, dominating, as they had done since the turn of the century, the Scottish game.

On 18 September 1917, Rangers Football Club was honoured by the presence of His Majesty King George V at Ibrox Stadium for an investiture in which many medals were presented to war heroes. Both chairman Sir John Ure Primrose and secretary-manager William Wilton, were presented to the King by Lord Provost Thomas Dunlop.

Many with Ibrox connections had served with distinction during the years of conflict. In addition to Messrs Paterson, Cunningham, Gordon and Reid already mentioned, 2nd-Lieut Fred Gray won the Military Cross, James Speirs the Military Medal, 2nd-Lieut James Galt was wounded in action, and, sadly, one Ranger who paid the ultimate price was Walter Daniel Tull, the former Spurs and Northampton man. Whilst stationed at Gailes, Tull became the first coloured player to sign for Rangers. He was posted to Italy with the Middlesex Regiment and distinguished himself in action on New Year's Day 1918, on the River Piana, before returning to France. He was killed in action in the Second Battle of the Somme on 25 March 1918. Tull was awarded the British War and Victory Medals and recommended for the Military Cross. His name is inscribed on the War Cemetery Memorial at Arras, France.

With World War One drawing to an end, Rangers, no doubt like all the other clubs, were concerned about strengthening their squad for peacetime, and what the post-war structure of Scottish football might be. Outside-right W.J.Aitken came from Queen's Park, wing-half James Walls from Baillieston and David McLean, centre-forward, was another new arrival. Walls was to prove himself a fine Ranger, but the two others were to be one-season men. In June 1920, Aitken was transferred to Newcastle United, where made 104 League appearances before going to Preston North End four years later.

Rangers new League campaign began with a close 1-0

home win over Falkirk at Ibrox, then a true champions' performance in a 4-1 win at Tynecastle. Thus began an eight match winning run leaving them with a one-point lead over, yet again, Celtic. A 3-0 home win over Queen's Park put Rangers into the Final of the Glasgow Cup against, yet again, Celtic, in the first Old Firm meeting of the season. Rangers retained the Cup by 2-0 with goals from Jimmy Gordon and 'Daddler' Aitken, and when they went to Celtic Park two weeks later and trounced Celtic 3-0 in a League match (scorers Cairns, Bowie and McDermid), that meant nine successive League wins, a four-point lead and surely another championship secured.

November was a month of anticlimax. Rangers lost their scoring touch, and with it careless points. But they swept through December like real champions, scoring 19 goals with the loss of only one, and winning four matches. They went into the traditional January holiday match with a three-point cushion. A tight match on a difficult surface ended 1-1, goals coming from Bowie and McMenemy. By 11 February, Rangers had lost their lead for the first time in the season, going down 1-0 at Kilmarnock. This was a clear case of over-confidence. The team responded, however, by taking 15 points from the next eight matches. Now they were level on points with Celtic, and four games to play.

In the interim, World War One had ended, with soldiers slowly returning and the 'Victory Cup' was put up to fill out the second half of the season. The Scottish Cup had not yet been re-instated.

The first round saw Rangers beat Hamilton at Douglas Park, 5-1, but this trophy was to prove no more Rangers-friendly than the Scottish Cup. They went down 1-0 at Airdrie in the second round. The League title fight went right down to the last day, Celtic taking the prize with a fine 2-0 win at Ayr on 10 May. Rangers tally of 57 points was one more than the 56 which had won them the previous season's championship, but one meagre point less than Celtic's this time.

For the first time in eight years, the Charity Cup was won. Easy wins over Third Lanark and Clyde brought Rangers into the Final against Queen's Park at Hampden, and a hard-fought 2-1 win. Home and away Victory Internationals were played against England, Ireland and the Football League, and Gordon, Bowie, Cairns, Archibald and Blair wore the national colours.

Between the Wars

AS THE country got back to some kind of peacetime normality, Scottish football did the same. The League was increased by four clubs to 22, with Aberdeen, Dundee and Raith Rovers welcomed back, and the modest Albion Rovers invited to make up the numbers. There was not yet a Second Division – that had to wait two more years before being born again. To Rangers' delight, the Scottish Cup was re-born this season. For too long – 17 years – it had been missing from the Ibrox sideboard.

One important addition to the playing staff was a young man from Govan who would not immediately claim a first-team place but who would be one of the greatest names in the club's history – David Meiklejohn. Willie Reid and Dr Paterson both returned for one final season. Reid played in only nine League games but lost none of his scoring talent – he had nine goals.

Attendances were booming. At Celtic Park on 6 September for a Rangers visit in the Glasgow Cup semi-final, 64,000 packed in to see the home team win with an Adam McLean goal. And when Celtic came to Ibrox on 18 October, 76,000 were on hand to see Rangers win 3-0 with goals by Cunningham (2) and Dr Paterson. Andy Cunningham was leading scorer that season with an impressive tally of 25.

From that day on, Rangers hit majestic form, dropping only two points over the next nine games. Six goals were scored against Third Lanark, seven against Hibs and there was a three-point lead established over Celtic. The Ne'er Day match at Celtic Park, a 1-1 draw, was seen by 80,000! Tommy Muirhead and Willie Cringan were the scorers. By the end of January, Rangers had taken nine points from five games. Celtic dropped two away games, 2-0 at Clydebank and 2-1 at Dundee and Rangers had a lead of seven points.

With the League apparently won, Rangers thoughts had turned to the Scottish Cup. Over the next eight years, these thoughts were to become obsessive. A midweek, afternoon replay against Dumbarton brought 28,000 to Ibrox and questions were asked about absenteeism in the Clyde shipyards. This 1-0 Cup win was the start of a ten-match run in which Rangers did not concede a goal. They had consolidated their championship position, and got past Arbroath and Broxburn to reach the last eight of the Scottish Cup. The quarter-final draw brought Celtic and a Scottish Cup record crowd of 85,000 to Ibrox in what was inevitably dubbed the 'Final before the Final'. A Tommy Muirhead goal after 50 minutes won the match and seemed to unlock the door to the long-awaited Scottish Cup success. The Rangers team that day was Lock; Manderson, Gordon; Bowie, Dixon, Walls; Archibald, Muirhead, Cunningham, Cairns, Paterson. With Celtic out of the way, the remaining opposition was considered to be modest – of the other semi-finalists, Kilmarnock and Morton were at best middle of the road clubs, and the newcomers Albion Rovers were wooden spooners for the entire season.

For the semi-final on 27 March at Celtic Park against the 'Wee Rovers', Rangers were hit by illness and injury. Full-back Gordon had to take Cunningham's place at centre-forward. They were still clear favourites, but a late penalty score by Ribchester tied the game at 1-1. The replay four days later was just as surprising – 0-0. The second replay brought a crowd of 65,000 to Celtic Park, giving an aggregate of 137,000 for the three games. Rangers had

Cunningham back in the team, but were without Dixon and Archibald, and gave a quite jaded performance, losing 2-0 to goals from Hillhouse and Watson. The Final, incidentally was won 3-2 by Kilmarnock before the huge crowd of 95,000 in Hampden.

Rangers' depression was not thrown off by a goalless visit to Tynecastle, plus the fact that Celtic had won seven successive League games. Two home wins over Ayr (2-1) and Queen's Park (3-1), plus the fact that Celtic dropped a point at Motherwell revived them and they eventually led by four points with three games left. The championship was on, for the tenth time, with a 0-0 draw at Boghead. Rangers 71 points from 42 games was a record, for the first time ever Rangers scored a century of League goals, and their championship was won by three points from Celtic.

Alas the death of Willie Wilton took some of the edge of their triumph. The first match of their new manager Bill Struth was won 1-0, against, an International XI for Jimmy Gordon's benefit, but the Charity Cup was not to belong to Rangers. Celtic put them out, 2-1 at Ibrox. The end of the season marked the end of the Ibrox careers of Doc Paterson and Jimmy Gordon. Paterson moved on to Arsenal, and such was his talent that Rangers would surely find it difficult to replace him. In June 1920, they did. They signed one of the greatest of Rangers players – his name was Alan Morton.

Under the new management of Bill Struth, Rangers opened the season with a new goalkeeper in Willie Robb as well as the dapper Alan Morton, but otherwise with the same squad of powerful and successful players. Quickly establishing himself in the team was Geordie Henderson from Forfar, a centre-forward regarded by some old-time Rangers fans as the finest centre-forward the club has ever had.

The team had a comfortable, even privileged, start from the fixture makers – three home games against Airdrie (4-1), Motherwell (2-1) and Aberdeen (2-1). Three away matches followed, producing two League and one Glasgow Cup win, which meant a semi-final against Celtic on 18 September. With nine successive victories behind them, Rangers went to Parkhead cock-a-hoop, but goals from Tommy McInally and Adam McLean were too much for them. Alan Morton did score but the 2-1 meant their second successive Glasgow Cup defeat by Celtic.

When Rangers went back to Celtic Park on League business, on 23 October, despite their cracking form they had a lead of only one point. Alan Morton scored once again against Celtic, adding to an earlier Tommy Cairns goal. Cassidy scored Celtic's only goal, and when they lost three days later at home to Albion Rovers of all people, Rangers had a healthier lead. They set off on a staggering run of 12 consecutive League wins. The only point dropped before 1 January was a 1-1 draw at Ayr on 18 December. In 23 League games, more than half the League programme, Rangers had taken 44 points from a possible 46, and were six ahead of Celtic. Indeed between 27 September 1919 and 31 December, 1920, they had lost only one League match of the 56 played, to Clydebank at Ibrox on 5 April 1920.

A new signing in November 1920, Billy McCandless from Belfast was a full-back who would make an almost immediate impact on the first team. For the New Year game, Rangers were without among others left-half James

Walls, who had broken a leg at Shawfield on Christmas Day. Celtic's Cassidy was the star of 1 January, with two goals on an icy surface in a 2-0 win, Rangers' first defeat of the season. For their next New Year's Day victory at Ibrox, Celtic and their friends would have to wait 62 years!

Rangers proceeded to rip off five League wins in January without losing a goal. They went into the Scottish Cup first round with a six-point League lead and determined that this year the Cup would go to Ibrox. After a first-round bye, Morton were despatched at Ibrox, then came one of the historic Cup scares. Alloa Athletic of the Central League came to Ibrox on 19 February, made a 0-0 draw and scared the life out of Rangers. Alloa agreed to replay at Ibrox, the crowd was 55,000 and Rangers won 4-1. In the last eight, they won at 'Fatal Boghead', and with Celtic losing to Hearts at Parkhead, the Cup seemed even more certainly bound for Ibrox.

They went into the Cup semi-final eight points in the lead. Their opponents were Albion Rovers, their conquerors of the previous season, but this time Rangers made no mistake, winning 4-1. In the other semi-final, Partick Thistle and not the favoured Hearts went through. The Final was set for Celtic Park on 16 April, an inexplicable venue decision by the SFA, who, anxious to keep the attendance lower than the year before (!) also doubled the admission price from one to two shillings (5p to 10p). A national newspaper waged a vigorous campaign against all this, provoking something of a boycott, and only 28,294 turned up.

Rangers were massive favourites, and lined up their most powerful team: Robb; Manderson, McCandless, Meiklejohn, Dixon, Bowie, Archibald, Cunningham, Henderson, Cairns, Morton. They pressed fiercely from the start, but Thistle were superbly marshalled by the veteran Jimmy McMenemy and withstood all the Rangers attacks. And with half an hour gone, and when Bowie was off replacing a torn pair of shorts, they broke away to score a Blair goal! Despite incessant Rangers pressure, Thistle prevailed. The Cup hoodoo had struck Rangers again. It was their first defeat in 20 matches. Jimmy McMenemy said that his medal, his seventh, would be hung on his wall with a horseshoe on either side.

Three days later, the championship title was clinched with a home win over Clyde by 3-1. In winning their 11th title, Rangers amassed 76 points, a record unequalled, ten ahead of Celtic and no fewer than 26 ahead of third-placed Hearts.

Cups were not meant for Rangers this season. Two goals from McInally saw Celtic sweep them away in the Charity Cup Final.

With essentially the same squad of players, Rangers started season 1921-22 in optimistic mood, with such a massive championship win behind them. Their four opening wins put them a point ahead of Celtic that early, then they breezed through September with six victories, including a Glasgow Cup semi-final against Third Lanark. This brought another in the seemingly endless sequence of Rangers-Celtic Finals, on 1 October. A tense tight match in gusty conditions was won by a Davie Meiklejohn goal, giving Rangers a record 14th win. A week later, Hearts brought them back to earth with a 2-0 win at Ibrox. Two weeks later, the Old Firm met in the League at Ibrox, the 1-1 draw leaving Rangers three points clear at the top.

An historic signing took place that October. Carl Hansen from Denmark became the first Scandanavian player to play for Rangers. A centre-forward, he quickly became a firm favourite with the Ibrox fans.

A goalless draw at Celtic Park sent Rangers into the New Year with a lead of three points, and with two trophies already won, their fans had ideas of sweeping the boards for the first time ever, including that elusive Scottish Cup. But January was the worst of times for Rangers. They dropped four points in four games, including a 1-0 home defeat from Raith Rovers. A 5-0 win over Clachnacuddin of Inverness opened the 'big Cup' series, followed by a 1-1 draw at Coatbridge, then a healthy 4-0 win over Albion Rovers in the replay. In the third round, Rangers produced one of their best performances of the season, winning 4-0 over Hearts at Tynecastle. On the same day, Celtic went down 3-1 at home to Hamilton Accies and once again the way seemed to open for a Rangers triumph in the competition. But in the quarter-final against St Mirren at Ibrox, Rangers were down and out until a late equaliser from Geordie Henderson, from an impossible angle, saved them. They made no mistake in the replay, by 2-0.

Club director William R.Danskin, who had served on the board for almost 23 years, died on 20 March.

On 5 March, 60,000 were at Ibrox for the Scottish Cup semi-final with Partick Thistle who for financial reasons had the tie switched from a neutral venue. Rangers won 2-0, then took nine points out of ten in the three weeks before the Final, the one dropped being in a goalless draw at Pittodrie.

Alas, Celtic went one better, winning all five to take a one-point lead with five games remaining. But the Cup was the thing, on 5 April, with Morton the opposition and 75,000 at Hampden. In the first few seconds of the match, Alan Morton shot against a post, and from then on, there was incessant Rangers pressure, relived for the first time after nine minutes when Morton broke upfield, won a free-kick and scored, through Jimmy Gourlay! Eight minutes later, Rangers lost their captain Andy Cunningham, who went off with a broken jaw, but from then on, the ten men laid siege to the Morton goal, only to be defied by a defence that included two full-backs who were former Rangers – John McIntyre and Robert Brown. And goalkeeper Edwards produced saves which a contemporary report described as 'defying the laws of gravity'. In the dying moments, Alan Morton dribbled through the entire defence, and rounded the goalkeeper, only to see his shot scooped off the line by a desperate lunge from Morton's goalscorer, Jimmy Gourlay! Thus the Greenock club achieved the only Scottish Cup victory over Rangers in its entire history, and Rangers would have to wait at least one more long year.

Bill Struth missed most of the action, accompanying Cunningham to hospital, whilst his opposite number, Bob Cochrane, followed much of the progress from the dressing-room, being unable to stand the tension.

Rangers chairman, Sir John Ure Primrose, speaking on behalf of the club afterwards, was said to 'resemble a man reading his own funeral oration'.

They did challenge to the end for the League title, but Celtic refused to falter. Their 1-1 draw at Greenock on the last day, with a late equaliser, took the championship by one point. Rangers total was 66. The Charity Cup was won for the tenth time, with a 3-1 Final win over Queen's Park. Rangers had annexed three trophies – but not the one they wanted desperately.

Rangers' championship win of 1922-23 was the overture to a unique period in Scottish football. Never before, certainly not since the advent of professionalism 30 years ear- lier, had one club so dominated the game over such a long period. In the 17 seasons from 1922-23 to 1938-39, Rangers won the championship 13 times. And after a painful inter- val of 25 years, having won the Scottish Cup in 1928, they repeated that win five times in the next eight years. In the championship, season after season, they achieved impres- sive points totals. In Cup competition, they beat powerful contemporary opposition in Celtic, Kilmarnock, St Mirren, Hamilton Academical and Third Lanark.

Many of these seasons followed a particular pattern, which was of thrilling surging starts, success in the early- season Glasgow Cup competitions, powerful performances up to the end of the year, occasional freewheeling and per- haps the odd lapse in concentration, then, after 1927-28, impressive charges in the Scottish Cup springtimes.

In the first season of this long sequence, they won the championship by five points from Airdrie, a club probably enjoying the best team in its history, one which included Bob McPhail and Hughie Gallacher. The first match was against newly-promoted Alloa Athletic, having their first- ever match in the top division. They were not intimidat- ed and played perfectly well if losing 2-0. The Glasgow Cup proved a lengthy affair. After Partick Thistle went down 3-1 in the first round, Third Lanark in the semi-final, Clyde in the Final, each needed two matches. This Cup marathon had meant Rangers facing five games in 12 days, but their second match in the Final, the 1-0 win, brought them the Cup for a record 15th time.

At Celtic Park on 28 October, Rangers were two points behind Celtic in their first meeting of the season. The pre- lude to the match was a 1-1 draw at home to Albion Rovers, hardly an exciting preparation. Rangers rose from the abject to the sublime with a quite sparkling performance. Superbly orchestrated by Andy Cunningham (two goals) and Alan Morton, who gave a quite brilliant exhibition of wing play, Rangers won 3-1 with their third goal by Geordie Henderson. The legendary Patsy Gallacher scored the Celtic goal.

Rangers were suitably inspired by the win and they fol- lowed with three straight wins over Thistle (4-1), Hamilton (3-0) and Raith Rovers (1-0). On the other hand Celtic slumped, losing 4-1 at home to mid-table Ayr United, then 1-0 at Airdrie. A week later, on 2 December, third-placed Airdrie came to Ibrox in an obviously crucial fixture. Once again Rangers struck top form, in a 4-1 win to be clear lead- ers, two in front of Celtic, six ahead of Airdrie. December was a good month – eight points from five games, includ- ing Aberdeen and Dundee.

Celtic's visit to Ibrox at New Year turned out to be his- toric. Carl Hansen, the 'Great Dane', became the first for- eigner to score in an Old Firm game when he hit the open- ing goal. Sandy Archibald got a second in a 2-0 win which left Rangers five ahead of both their challengers. The Ibrox men promptly won four out of four, with home wins over Motherwell and Hamilton, then away matches at Partick and Kilmarnock. Celtic helped by dropping ten out of 12 possible points and virtually vanished from the champi- onship scene in a manner quite untypical of them, and left Rangers to dream of the Scottish Cup.

The first round was at Shawfield, too often a Rangers graveyard, but the team maintained optimum form and Clyde were swept aside, 4-0. The entire team's thrilling attacking play in mid-winter had brought ten games with- out defeat. The run ended on 27 January in the Cup. Rangers lost 2-0 to Ayr United, at Somerset Park. A team

that was good enough to lead the table by ten points had yielded yet again in the Cup to a middle-of-the-table club. Rangers stumbled. They lost again, at Coatbridge to Albion Rovers of all people. Eventually they were down to a four- point lead with two games left. They steadied and won the championship for a record 12th time with a 1-0 win over Kilmarnock at Ibrox on 21 April.

The Charity Cup was retained comfortably for a record 11th time, with wins over Celtic and Queen's Park. Three of the four major competitions had been won, for the fourth time in the club's history. During the summer, the Ibrox men toured France and Switzerland, winning all six games with 32 goals scored, only two lost. The policies of the mar- tinet manager Bill Struth, of organisation and discipline, were bearing fruit.

In the summer of 1923, Sir John Ure Primrose retired as chairman to make way for a younger man. His association with the club reached back to 1887 when he first became a member. He had been honorary president before succeed- ing to the chair. William Craig JP took his place.

Two important additions to the playing staff were Tully Craig, formerly of Celtic and Alloa, and goalkeeper Tom Hamilton. He would succeed Willie Robb and be remem- bered as one of the finest goalkeepers in the history of the club. Tully Craig had been played at centre-forward by Celtic, but from his debut for Rangers on 24 September, against Clyde at Ibrox, he would be used mainly as an inside-forward or wing-half.

With a 3-0 win at Fir Park on 18 August, Rangers demonstrated that they were serious about retaining their championship. Falkirk, who had finished fourth in the pre- vious season, arrived at Ibrox and well deserved a 2-2 draw. The Glasgow Cup began in September with a 3-0 win over Queen's Park at Hampden, and a 1-0 win over Celtic at Ibrox. Geordie Henderson, something of a scourge to Celtic, was the scorer. The Cup was retained by Rangers, on 29 September with a 3-0 win against Third Lanark at Ibrox. The scorers were Henderson, Archibald and Muirhead and the Rangers team was one of the most powerful the club ever had:- Robb; Manderson, McCandless, Meiklejohn, Dixon, Muirhead, Archibald, Cunningham, Henderson, Cairns, Morton.

It swept through the next seven games like a tornado, taking 13 points from a possible 14 and with them a six- point lead after 14 games. Sadness came to the club with the death of chairman Craig on 20 November. Elected to the general committee in 1897, he had been a director for 20 years. His successor was former Baillie Joseph Buchanan JP.

Before the turn of the year, Rangers took nine of a pos- sible ten points – there was a 1-1 draw with Airdrie at Ibrox – and had an eight-point lead with which to first-foot Celtic at Parkhead. Goals from Cairns and Archibald on the one hand, Thomson and McStay on the other, meant a 2-2 draw. The first defeat of the season, 2-1 came at Ayr on 5 January but did little to impede the flow of goals and points especially since Airdrie contrived to lose to near-neigh- bours Hamilton (5-1) and Motherwell (2-1) and trailed by nine points.

It was Scottish Cup time again. On 26 January, the romantic visit of Lochelly United to Ibrox ended 4-1 for the hosts. At Paisley in the next round, 40,291 packed Love St to see St Mirren go down 1-0. On 16 February, Hibs at Ibrox should have held no fears for Rangers, especially after a Meiklejohn goal had them one up at half-time. But second-half goals from Walker and Murray dumped

Rangers 2-1. Thus a whole generation of Rangers fans had come of age unaware of what it meant to have their team win the national trophy. Hibs reached the Final that year, going down to the excellent Airdrieonians team by 2-0 at Ibrox before 59,218. It was the last Final to be played away from Hampden Park for 69 years.

A severe injury blow hit Rangers, not to say Carl Hansen, when the Dane broke his leg, ending his playing career in Scotland. The team coasted through to the title, clinching it with some irony against Hibs at Ibrox on 5 April with a 2-1 win. They led Airdrie by nine points. The Old Firm brought the curtain down on 10 May in the Charity Cup Final. An Alan Morton goal was topped by scores from Cassidy and Gallacher.

On 29 June 1924, just a year after he left the chair, Sir John Ure Primrose died.

Rangers opened the defence of their title with four straight wins, at home to Raith Rovers and St Johnstone (3-0 and 3-1 respectively) and away to Aberdeen and Queen's Park (1-0 and 3-1 respectively), a pace that might have intimidated the most determined of challengers. Into that category came Airdrie, runners up in the previous season, who dropped only one point, a 1-1 draw at Celtic Park, in the same period. The Ibrox men dropped their first point on 30 August when Kilmarnock escaped with a 1-1 draw, before turning to the Glasgow Cup. Clyde and Partick Thistle – after a replay – were disposed of, setting up a Final against Celtic. The quality of Airdrie was clear in the September fixture at Broomfield. Rangers were handicapped by the loss of Billy McCandless with a severe injury but Bob McPhail and Hughie Gallacher were outstanding in a 1-0 win which left Airdrie and Rangers level on points.

The Glasgow Cup Final teams for 4 October, were stiff with famous names:

Celtic: Shaw; W.McStay, Hilley, Wilson, J.McStay, McFarlane, Cassidy, Gallacher, McGrory, Thomson, McLean.

Rangers: Robb; Manderson, Jamieson, Meiklejohn, Dixon, Craig, Archibald, Cunningham, Henderson, Cairns, Morton.

Celtic led through Adam McLean, but thereafter the match belonged to Rangers. Goals came from Henderson (2), Morton and Cairns, leaving captain Cairns suggesting that they might ease up. Rangers thus equalled their own record of four Glasgow Cup wins in succession. And when Rangers went to Parkhead on 25 October on League business, and won by an Alan Morton goal, Rangers fans were, to coin a phrase, over the moon. Twice in a month.

A scrambled 2-2 draw at Cowdenbeath saw Rangers fall one point behind Airdrie. The Central Park team were making an impressive debut in the First Division. They beat Airdrie in November and finished fifth at the end of the season.

November was a good month for Rangers who took nine points from a possible ten with home wins over Thistle 4-0, Hibs 3-0 and St Mirren 3-1, plus away trips to Cathkin Park 1-1 and Perth 3-1. And, traditionally, December was equally good with seven out of eight points giving them a three-point lead for the January New Year match at Ibrox. Celtic were over-run yet again, 4-1 with Geordie Henderson yet again scoring two. He was to score a record 40 during the season, including 27 in the League.

The Scottish Cup began on 24 January with an easy win over East Fife by 3-1, at Methil, but a week later, Rangers lost for the first time in 21 games, 1-0 to Hamilton at Douglas Park. Cup wins followed over lower-division opponents Montrose and Arbroath before a difficult quarter-final

match at Kilmarnock was only just won, 2-1. Obsession with this elusive Scottish Cup no doubt pre-occupied Rangers. Their League form slumped, with a 1-1 draw at Falkirk and a 4-1 loss at Easter Road. Fortunately, Airdrie were also stumbling, and when 40,000 saw the vital meeting of the teams on 25 February, the 1-1 draw left Rangers two points ahead.

Hampden Park was the venue for the Scottish Cup semifinal on 21 March and a vast crowd, 101,714 – Scottish football's first six-figure attendance – crammed in to see Rangers, clear favourites on their season's results against Celtic, advance to the Final. In the first 30 minutes, they were clearly in control but were perhaps a shade too cocky, and indulgent with their ball work. Celtic broke away to snatch a Jimmy McGrory goal and an interval lead, and inexplicably, the Rangers defence collapsed in the second half. Celtic helped themselves to goals – Adam McLean (2), McGrory and Alec Thomson – in what became a comprehensive win.

In the League Airdrie were matching Rangers stride by stride. It got down to the two final games. Rangers in fact led by three points, but Airdrie had a game in hand. On 18 April, the entire championship centred on Lanarkshire. Airdrie beat Hibs 2-0 and Rangers dropped a point in a 1-1 draw at Motherwell. However, in their game in hand, Airdrie dropped a point, with a 1-1 draw at home to Dundee. A precious free-kick goal from Billy McCandless gave Rangers a win and two points at home to Ayr United, Airdrie went 1-0 down to St Johnstone at Perth, and the title was won for the 14th time. Rangers had 60 points from 38 games, a margin of three. The Charity Cup was won once more 1-0 over Clyde at Ibrox.

Meiklejohn, Cairns and Morton played in the first All-Tartan Scotland team in 30 years, beating England at Hampden by 2-0. Rangers reserves won both their League and Cup and in June two very significant signings were made. Dougie Gray from Aberdeen Muggiemoss and James Marshall from Shettleston came to Ibrox and were to become very fine servants of the club.

Season 1925-26 became one of the poorest in Rangers' history but it began promisingly enough with a 3-0 win in Perth, then home wins over Motherwell and Morton. A visit to Airdrie's Broomfield was scheduled for 5 September, and the home team's 2-1 win was a straw in the wind for Rangers. They were well beaten at Pittodrie and Tynecastle and by the end of September were four points behind the leaders, Celtic.

Drawn against them in the first round of the Glasgow Cup, Rangers produced a stirring performance to draw 2-2, with goals scored by Old Firm legends Jimmy McGrory and Andy Cunningham. Before the replay, Celtic were surprisingly beaten, 5-1 at Airdrie, a result which put the home team into second place, only one point behind Celtic. The Cup replay saw Rangers all but crippled. Severe injuries meant that Meiklejohn, McCandless, Cairns and Morton were missing. In all, seven international players would be out for long spells with injuries – these four plus Muirhead, Archibald and Cunningham – which had a major effect on the season's outcome.

Nevertheless, the team fought hard to make another draw, goals this time from Cunningham and Adam McLean making it 1-1. In the second replay, Rangers were forced to play Dougie Gray, the young full-back signed in the summer, at outside-left, but all the gaps could not be plugged and Celtic were convincing winners by 2-0, goals from McGrory and Gallacher. Celtic were due back at Ibrox a

The Rangers first-team squad at the start of the 1925-26 season, when the club showed off the Scottish League championship trophy and the Glasgow Cup and Glasgow Merchants' Charity Cup which they had won the previous season. Back row (left to right): Hamilton, Archibald, Gray, Osborne, Ireland, Purdon, McGregor, Hodge, Muirhead. Middle row: W.Struth (manager), Henderson, Meiklejohn, A.Kirkwood, D.Kirkwood, Cunningham, Dick, Henderson, Marshall, Robb. Front row: Craig, McCandless, McKay, Cairns, Dixon, Morton, Jamieson, G.Livingstone (trainer).

couple of weeks later, during which time Rangers lost to Thistle at Firhill on 10 October, their fourth game in eight days. But they rose to the Old Firm occasion with a Chalmers goal in a 1-0 win. Rangers were now only two points behind, but they were a beleaguered lot.

December probably saw the championship lost, after three years. It brought only three points to Rangers from a possible eight. The gap was a frightening nine points at the turn of the year, and a 2-2 draw at Celtic Park was commendable if not too productive. The main thrust of Rangers thinking was turned towards the Scottish Cup. Home ties came out against Lochgelly and Stenhousemuir. A third round at Falkirk looked challenging, but Rangers rose to it with a fine 2-0 win. The next round sent them to Greenock. On the day, they were ready, and took out Morton by 4-0.

A desperately close semi-final at Celtic Park saw St Mirren only just prevail, 1-0, to extinguish Rangers dreams yet again. St Mirren went on to beat Celtic 2-0 in a Final seen by a record 98,620 spectators. There were now distinct fears at Ibrox that the club might even finish below midway in the table, the unthinkable, but April shined on them. Seven points from a possible eight dragged them up the ladder to sixth place, their lowest-ever League position. They lost 13 games, a humbling experience for Rangers and took 44 points from 38 games. They were 14 points behind Celtic and that would certainly be considered humiliating by friends of Rangers.

Injuries alone could not account for this. The fact was that many of the stalwarts of previous campaigns were at the veteran stage. It was time for Tom Hamilton, Dougie Gray, James Marshall and Jimmy Fleming, and their like, to take the stage. The Charity Cup came and went, to Clyde by 4-3 to Ibrox. More significantly for the future, the reserves, for the third consecutive year, won their Cup.

On Saturday, 31 July 1926, Rangers director John McPherson collapsed and died whilst watching the Clyde Sports at Shawfield. As a player, director and legislator his career had spanned more than 40 years, but it was as Rangers captain and leading goalscorer that he had left an indelible mark on the game. He won all the honours, and many international caps and was described by one contemporary as 'the finest player in the first 50 years of the club's history'.

It was the improving Motherwell team that made the flying start to this season 1926-27, and having shared the points at Airdrie and lost to St Johnstone at Perth, Rangers found themselves three points behind after only five games. Motherwell went to Ibrox on 11 September in what was an early crunch match. A massive crowd packed the ground and saw Rangers rise to the occasion with an excellent 2-0 win. Motherwell had an emerging team of high quality but in the meantime lacked the consistency needed for a sustained challenge to Rangers and Celtic.

By Glasgow Cup time, the Light Blues had a two point

lead and got past Third Lanark fairly comfortably in the first round. Queen's Park, in the second, was quite different. After a 1-1 draw, Rangers beat them 3-1 to make it yet another Rangers v Celtic Final. It turned out to be a thrilling match which one goal would clearly be enough to settle. It fell to Celtic and Jimmy McGrory, late in the game.

In spite of this 'failure', Rangers ended November level with Motherwell, but December was a dark month for them, with only two points collected from four games, among them a severe defeat, 4-1 by Hamilton Accies, at Ibrox. Going into the New Year match, they were two points behind Motherwell, and the 2-1 win over Celtic indicated a return to some kind of form. The goals were by Sandy Archibald and 'Doc' Marshall against one from Alec Thomson. In January, firepower was demonstrated in four goals scored in each of four consecutive games – 4-1 at Firhill, 4-2 against St Johnstone at Ibrox, 4-1 at Motherwell and 4-1 at Leith Athletic. The win at Motherwell was Rangers finest display of the season. The month gave them a three-point lead, and they were never really caught in the League.

In the Scottish Cup, this phenomenal scoring rate continued. It was 4-1 away to Leith Athletic, 6-0 at home to St Mirren and 4-0 at home against Hamilton. At Falkirk in the quarter-final match, on 5 March, only a Billy McCandless penalty in the dying minutes saved Rangers from defeat, however. More than 80,000 were at Ibrox for the replay, where, only six minutes from the end of extra-time, the legendary Patsy Gallacher split the Rangers defence and let centre-forward Mason score.

Celtic, the Cup winners were to become critical in deciding the championship. Rangers last away game was at Parkhead on Easter Monday 18 April. Celtic paraded their latest trophy before the kick-off with the result that Rangers dumped them with a Jimmy Fleming goal. Two days later at Celtic Park, Motherwell went down 3-2, leaving Rangers three points clear with two games remaining.

That very same Easter Monday, incidentally, saw Rangers make one of the most significant signings in their history. Bob McPhail, the powerful goalscoring inside-left, was bought from Airdrieonians. He would win a vast array of honours at Ibrox, although he arrived there as already a Scottish Cup winner (with Airdrie in 1924). He became Rangers all-time leading goalscorer and formed an outstanding left wing with Alan Morton. His debut came in a Glasgow Charity Cup-tie with Queen's Park on 3 May. He scored after eight minutes as Rangers swamped the amateurs 8-1. And in the semi-final he hit two more in Rangers 4-1 win over Celtic.

The League championship had been won for the 15th time on 28 April when Motherwell dropped a point at Falkirk in a 1-1 draw. Rangers finished five points ahead with 56 from 38 games.

In the Charity Cup Final, Rangers faced Partick Thistle weakened by the absence of Hamilton, Muirhead, Craig, Archibald and Cunningham who had sailed off to Canada on tour with the SFA. A game dominated nevertheless by Rangers ended 3-3 after 90 minutes, but Thistle centre-forward Hair added three goals in extra-time – making his total five – giving Thistle a 6-3 win.

The career of Arthur Dixon, later to become Rangers trainer, came to an end, and Tom Cairns and Bert Manderson both left for Bradford City. At the same time, Rangers signed a young man who would be a mainstay in their teams of the 1930s – centre-half Jimmy Simpson.

Rangers exploded into the defence of their League

championship title with six straight victories in which they scored no fewer than 24 goals, giving them a two-point lead over both Celtic and Motherwell. The first real crunch of the season was a visit to Fir Park on 24 September. The 1-1 draw was considered fair to both teams. Two days later, on holiday Monday, Clyde, at Ibrox on Glasgow Cup business, were swept away, 7-0. Six of the goals were scored by Jimmy Fleming who set a new club scoring record for one game. Fleming, incidentally, was to score 45 goals that season, 33 of them in the League.

That victory over Clyde meant a place in the Final at Hampden on 8 October against – Celtic. Rangers went into the match as League leaders and favourites, but a single Andy Cunningham goal failed to match Celtic scores from Jimmy McGrory and Paddy Connolly. If the Glasgow Cup was lost, there was some consolation a week later. In the League match at Ibrox, a Jimmy Fleming goal dumped the Celts. November and December produced a run of championship quality which produced 16 points from nine games with 28 goals scored and only six lost. On 22 December, incidentally, Rangers signed Jock Buchanan from Morton. He was to become an international player with Rangers. At the turn of the year, the defending champions were three points ahead of Motherwell, no fewer than seven ahead of Celtic, but in the traditional derby match, a Jimmy McGrory goal decided things at Parkhead. On 14 January, Rangers beat Airdrie at Broomfield 7-2, their first win there in six years. There must have been something in the air that day – Celtic beat Dunfermline Athletic 9-0 at Parkhead, with McGrory scoring eight times to establish a new Division One record.

Four points ahead of Celtic, five clear of Motherwell, Rangers' thoughts in the New Year were turning again to that elusive Scottish Cup. Yet another joust at it began in Falkirk, with a 6-0 win against Second Division East Stirlingshire. The next Cup-tie was at home to Cowdenbeath, also Second Division opposition and a 4-2 scoreline. In the first half of February, Rangers wobbled in the League, losing 2-0 to Motherwell at Ibrox, then drawing 3-3 in Paisley. So the championship was wide open again.

The Cup draw continued to favour Rangers, however, the next two rounds producing Second Division opposition yet again – at home to King's Park, then away to Albion Rovers, where Rangers had a fright and won by a solitary goal which took them into the semi-finals. In March, Rangers were fated on three successive Saturdays to travel to Edinburgh – a League match with Hearts (0-0), another with Hibs (1-2), then back to Tynecastle for a semi-final match against the same Hibs! The strain on Rangers' players facing the third of these matches must have been very great, but on the day, they produced the critical result, 3-0. In the other semi-final, Celtic beat Queen's Park at Ibrox, 2-1. It was to be an Old Firm Final, the first in 19 years.

The Easter weekend proved critical in the League, with matches on Saturday and Monday. Rangers won both, against Hamilton Accies and Dunfermline Athletic, while Celtic lost both, going down 3-1 at Motherwell and again at Airdrie.

On the 18 April 1928, a Scottish record attendance of 118,115 packed the soaring slopes of Hampden Park for the Scottish Cup Final. Could Rangers end the hoodoo which had haunted them for 25 years, which had seen them fail in four Finals since they had beaten Hearts in 1903, at the third attempt? The team sent out to do just that was: T.Hamilton; Gray, R.Hamilton, Buchanan, Meiklejohn, Craig, Archibald, Cunningham, Fleming, McPhail, Morton.

Celtic had a strong wind behind them in the first half and had the bulk of the pressure, but the Rangers' defence played with confidence and stood firm, Meiklejohn keeping a tight grip on the dangerous McGrory. Celtic had their chances, never more than when Paddy Connolly struck a ferocious shot and saw Tom Hamilton produce a wonder save that would be remembered forever in Ibrox folklore. So astonished at the save was the Celtic international outside-left Adam McLean that he could only hit the loose ball into the side netting.

With no score in the first half, the general opinion was that the team which scored first would win the match. After half-time, Rangers stretched their stride, began to take some control, and in ten minutes the match was won. An Alan Morton cross was volleyed by Jimmy Fleming. John Thomson in the Celtic goal was hopelessly beaten, but the ball was punched out by Willie McStay, the Celtic defender. Penalty!

Davie Meiklejohn decided that this critical penalty should be the captain's responsibility. Meiklejohn was a powerful personality, one of the greatest captains Rangers ever had, a natural leader of men. As a player he was resolute, skilful, uncompromising, vigorous, and above all, a man for the hour. Yet amidst the tumult of Hampden, as the single focus of that vast throng, what could he have been thinking? Of the job in hand, certainly, but perhaps also of the many great Rangers players who had failed to win a Scottish Cup medal over a quarter century, indeed, won all the honours save this one. He stepped up to the ball, and scored. Rangers were ahead. The entire team went on to play like men possessed. McPhail scored 13 minutes later. Sandy Archibald, two minutes after that blasted in a long-range shot, and repeated the act five minutes from the end! One of the greatest days in the club's history ended with the Scottish Cup bound for Ibrox. At the celebration banquet afterwards, captain Meiklejohn declared, "We have won it at last – we can do it again." They did – five times in the following eight years.

Meiklejohn's example had been that of a true leader. He was not the regular penalty-kicker – Andy Cunningham and Bob McPhail shared that resonsibility – nor was he at that time club captain. Tommy Muirhead, absent through injury, had that honour. Referee Willis Bell later conceded that Jimmy Fleming's shot had indeed crossed the line 'by perhaps a good two feet', but a moment's hesitation led him to award a penalty rather than a goal.

The remaining League matches were run off comfortably. When Kilmarnock went down 5-1 at Ibrox on 21 April, the championship was won. Rangers had done the double for the first time in the club's history. The Charity Cup was retained. The reserves won their 'double' of Alliance championship and 2nd XI Cup. Six Rangers played for Scotland that season – Alan Morton, Davie Meiklejohn, Tommy Muirhead, Tully Craig, Dougie Gray and Andy Cunningham. Morton played in the famous Wembley Wizards team and set a remarkable record of 35 international matches, one more than Alec Smith's 34, for Scotland.

At the end of one of the greatest seasons in Rangers' history, they sailed the broad Atlantic to a North American tour in which they played ten games, won seven, drew three, scoring 46 goals for the loss of seven. No doubt between the football and the journeying, there was time for much revelry.

The world in which Rangers achieved their great successes, in the late 1920s, is difficult for us to comprehend almost 70 years on. It was a world in which a loaf of bread might cost tuppence, rather less than the modern penny. A pint of milk might cost half of that. Paying one shilling (5p) for a packet of cigarettes was considered extravagant, and a new car could be bought for £100. Owning one was a display of personal affluence – the mass automobile culture was a long way ahead, there were no commercial airlines of any consequence, and travel meant the vast network of railways which covered the country. It was a pre-television age and even radio's peak years were yet to come.

And 1929 was also the year of the Wall Street Crash, which led on to the depression years of the early 1930s, when unemployment was rife. On Clydeside, the cruellest monument to that was the great hulk of the Cunarder, the '534' (it became the Queen Mary) overshadowing Clydebank, and left idle for many years.

For Rangers however, it was a time of immense confidence in the team, the club, the future, and it was exemplified by the opening of their huge new grandstand of 10,000 seats (now the 'Main Stand'), the biggest of its kind in the entire country, on New Year's Day, 1929. The Lord Provost of Glasgow, Sir David Mason, did the honours. Paradoxically, a few months earlier, two of the club's pioneers who had been advocates of the move from the Kinning Park ground to the Ibrox area, had passed away in the summer of 1928. Walter Crichton, a former club secretary, had played a leading role in the negotiations to purchase the present site and George Small, still a member of the board at the time of his death, had been a member of committee and director for no fewer than 45 years.

The question for the new season was, where do we go from here? On 1 September, they went down in the Glasgow Cup, first round. Doc Marshall opened the scoring but Thomson, then McGrory late in the game, provided Celtic with yet another Cup win for the Parkhead club. The first League point lost was in a goalless draw at Motherwell on 29 September but Rangers led by two points after seven fixtures, from Celtic. They then produced a stunning run of ten successive wins, scoring 38 goals for the loss of ten. Seven of the games were away from home and included a 2-1 win at Celtic Park.

At the end of the year, Rangers were six points ahead of Hearts (the Edinburgh team had played three games more) and nine ahead of Celtic. And on 1 January, they celebrated the inauguration of their new grandstand by over-running Celtic in the second half for a 3-0 win. Jimmy Fleming, scorer of 41 goals in 45 games that season, scored after 49 and 60 minutes, and Sandy Archibald got a late third. By the middle of January, Rangers were 13 points ahead of Celtic and retaining the Scottish Cup became the more pressing objective. They went at it with ominous power. Edinburgh City went down 11-1, Partick Thistle 5-1, both at Ibrox. Clyde went down 2-0 at Shawfield, then it was Dundee United at Ibrox by 3-1.

A run of home wins against Third Lanark 5-1, Hibs 3-0 and Hearts 2-0 and a 1-1 draw with Falkirk on 16 March clinched the League title. At that stage Rangers had amassed 57 points from 30 League fixtures and were no fewer than 17 points ahead of second club, Celtic. All three points had been dropped at Ibrox, which meant that Rangers had set a record of 15 consecutive away wins. Their remaining targets were clearly the retention of the Scottish and Glasgow Charity Cups and completion of the League programme unbeaten, a feat not achieved this century. A thrilling 3-2 win over St Mirren at Hampden put them into the Scottish Cup Final, while Kilmarnock were defeating Celtic in the other semi, at Ibrox. Four days later, on 27 March, the undefeated League record went, 3-1 at Hamilton. This game marked the debut of young Jimmy Smith at centre-forward. He was to become a prolific scorer and a firm favourite of the Ibrox fans throughout the 1930s. On the day, Rangers were defied by a brilliant goalkeeping display by David Lamont Smith in the Accies goal. He defied all Rangers pressure to allow the Accies forwards to steal upfield three times, and score each time. The irony was that 'Lamie' came from a Rangers diehard family. It was Rangers first League defeat in over a year, since 17 March 1928 in fact, a run of 38 games.

With the championship won, they relaxed and drew four of their last seven games but finished with 67 points from 38 matches, 16 points ahead of second-placed Celtic and champions for a record 17th time.

For the Scottish Cup Final of 6 April 1929, Rangers showed only one change from the 1928 Final team. Tommy Muirhead replaced Andy Cunningham, for most of the 1920s the Rangers captain, who had been transferred to Newcastle United on 30 January. He played his last game a few days earlier, scoring in a 2-0 win over Airdrie. He was Rangers longest-serving player, having spent 14 years at Ibrox during which his 444 games produced 203 goals and 12 caps for Scotland. The first of these came when he was 29 and he was probably the oldest 'debutante' known in the English Football League. He played his first Newcastle game two days after his 38th birthday. He later managed Newcastle United, then Dundee.

Rangers were overwhelming favourites to retain the Cup, and 114,708 went to Hampden to see them do it. They were to see historic happenings. Kilmarnock resisted intense Rangers pressure in the first half, and after 17 minutes, Tully Craig earned the unique distinction of being the first player to fail with a penalty-kick in the Scottish Cup Final. Clemie saved his shot quite brilliantly. Bob McPhail struck the post, but it was goalless at the interval, and when Aitken scored for Kilmarnock three minutes into the second half, they began to believe they could win the Cup. And when Williamson scored after 70 minutes, they had done it. Finally Rangers Jock Buchanan became the first player ever sent off in a Scottish Cup Final, two minutes from the end, for dissent.

The team did rather better in the Charity Cup. Partick Thistle and Third Lanark were disposed of before an Old Firm Final in which on 11 May, Marshall and Muirhead, and McGrory, each scored twice in Rangers 4-2 win. The reserves won their League and Cup, and Gray, Fleming and Craig were in the SFA party making their first-ever Continental tour. Rangers in fact, on their summer tour of 1928 in Canada, had discovered Bob 'Whitey' McDonald, Belfast-born and a capable wing-half or full-back.

At the start of season 1929-30, Rangers announced proudly that 'ordinary spectators' could now have tea at half-time in the enclosure of the new grandstand. There was also the football, and the top dogs of the Scottish game, about to have the most successful season in the club's history, could not have had a more difficult opening fixture – away to Motherwell on 10 August. But Rangers 2-0 victory served notice on all that they were intent on retaining their title, and of equalling the club record of four successive championships.

Over the next half-dozen matches, only one point was dropped, 1-1 at Aberdeen. On 12 October, Glasgow Cup Final day, Rangers were leading the race, by two points from Motherwell. Celtic made it a dour, hard-fought, goalless affair, in which captain Meiklejohn failed from the penalty-spot. The replay was very different. The Rangers

forwards ran riot, with Jimmy Fleming hitting a hat-trick and Sandy Archibald scoring in a 4-0 win. It was a first Glasgow Cup win in five years, but a record 18th win. Celtic were due at Ibrox on 26 October. Rangers had Meiklejohn, Buchanan and Bob Hamilton injured, Gray, Craig, Muirhead and Morton on international duty with Scotland in Cardiff. Rangers could have asked for a postponement but decided to soldier on. Surprisingly, they won 1-0 with a stunning goal from Willie Nicholson.

November brought a deluge of goals, 5-2 and 9-0 respectively against Hamilton and Ayr, then 3-3 and 2-2 against Clyde and Morton. The Ayr match saw the first appearance of one George Brown, a left-half of silky skills from the junior Ashfield, who would win 19 caps for Scotland. He was a Glasgow man, a graduate of Glasgow University, a schoolteacher and therefore, like Alan Morton, always a part-time player. After he retired, he became a director of the club. Joining at the same time was one Jerry Dawson from Camelon Juniors, destined to be one of the greatest of Rangers goalkeepers and an international player for a decade.

Rangers went into December with a four point lead over Motherwell, then set off on a champion's run. Four consecutive wins, including one over Motherwell, 4-2 at Ibrox, led into their first Celtic Park win in the New Year's Day match since 1902. A late George Brown goal made it 2-1, others coming from Morton and Celtic's Charlie Napier.

A 6-1 home win over St Johnstone put Rangers into the Scottish Cup with an eight point League lead. In the event, the draw could not have been more exacting for them. The top division provided all the opposition save for Montrose in the fourth round. A goal from McPhail dumped Queen's Park at Hampden. Cowdenbeath forced a draw at Ibrox with Rangers lucky to survive; in the replay Rangers had control and won easily 3-0. The third round came out 'Motherwell at Fir Park', immediately dubbed by the cognoscenti as 'the Final before the Final'. Rangers produced their finest display of the season, as 5-2 would indicate. The scorers were Fleming (2), McPhail (2) and Archibald.

Montrose in the quarter-final went down 3-0. Continued compelling form in the League saw Rangers step into the semi-final with Hearts 11 points clear of Motherwell with seven games to play – virtually champions. They were irresistible in the semi-final, winning 4-1 with a McPhail goal and a Fleming hat-trick. Within the following week, the championship was won. At Ayr, then at home to Clyde, 3-0 wins secured the 18th success.

Alan Morton on 5 April, playing for Scotland against England at Wembley, collected an injury which kept him out of the Final against Partick Thistle on 12 April. In an exciting game seen by 107,475 at Hampden, Thistle had the better chances in which defences dominated. The game ended goalless and for the replay, Morton was fit, and he and Whitey McDonald replaced Jock Buchanan and Willie Nicholson. A record midweek crowd of 103,688 turned out to see the little outside-left last only 15 minutes before the injury recurred. Doc Marshall opened the scoring for the ten men, Torbet equalised, then only four minutes from the end, Tully Craig's optimistic lob bewitched the Thistle goalkeeper, 'Jakey' Jackson, dazzled by the sun, and Rangers had won the Cup. And Tully had some consolation for his penalty miss a year earlier.

Three major trophies had been won. What was left was the Glasgow Charity Cup and the possibility of a clean sweep for the first time in the club's history. The League was won by five points from Motherwell, with 60 points from 38 games. Home wins over Thistle and Third Lanark brought yet another Celtic-Rangers Cup Final. Marshall and Fleming had Rangers 2-1 ahead until the dying minutes, when Peter Scarff's goal tied the match. Extra time brought no more goals, corners were level, and Rangers won on the toss of a coin – not really satisfactory, but according to the rules of the competition, correct. So the Charity Cup was won, the Grand Slam completed.

A Super Slam was achieved. The reserves won their championship, the Alliance League, by nine points from Aberdeen (a young Jimmy Smith scored 51 goals), and the second XI Cup. Kilmarnock in the Final went down 2-1. Eight players were honoured – Gray, Buchanan, Meiklejohn, Fleming, Morton, Muirhead for Scotland, McCandless and McDonald for Ireland.

Tommy Muirhead and Billy McCandless left the club. Muirhead had played 351 games, McCandless 267. Both would become managers, Muirhead with St Johnstone, McCandless with Dundee.

Rangers embarked on a long, 14-game North American tour, in which all 14 games were won with 68 goals scored for the loss of 20. Significantly, Jimmy Smith had 18 of them, Jimmy Fleming 13.

In a new decade Rangers it seemed were monarchs of all they surveyed, winners of all the prizes, the most powerful club in the land. So much was this so that questions began to be asked about the lack of challenge from their ancient enemy, and of the quality of its management. The Parkhead club, many felt had not yet recovered from that stupefying defeat in the Scottish Cup Final of 1928, reflected in a noticeable inconsistency in their League form ever since, and some felt that the elegant Motherwell team might take their place as principal challengers to the ascendancy of Rangers. But history was on Celtic's side, even if half a dozen years were to pass before their 'rehabilitation'.

More and more the personality and philosophy of Bill Struth, now ten years in the managers chair, became evident. On and off the field, there was a certain hauteur about Rangers men, the attitude that they were the best, and the huge modern grandstand and the sweeping bowl of Ibrox did nothing but sustain that attitude.

They went into season 1930-31 with one addition to the staff, full-back Bob McAulay, opened with a 3-1 win at Cowdenbeath and settled into their competent state. Motherwell on 30 August, with a 1-1 draw at Ibrox, reminded Rangers of their existence. Of the seven games played in September, only one was lost, 2-0 at Celtic Park, underlining the unpredictability of this great fixture. The two Thomsons, Alec and Bertie, had the Celtic goals. October was something of a disaster, with points dropped at Airdrie, defeat at Aberdeen and the loss of the Glasgow Cup on 11 October. An early goal from Charlie 'Happy Feet' Napier, before 71,806 fans, and another from Jimmy McGrory kept Celtic in control. Rangers goal came late, from Jimmy Smith.

There were rumblings among the faithful that the 14-match summer tour had taken the sharpness out of the team but Rangers ran off eight straight wins in November and December. They gained only one point on Celtic, who had a three-point lead going into the New Year match. That was the day of the 'wee blue devil'. Alan Morton's goal, and a brilliant display from the winger, took the points.

A 1-0 Rangers defeat at Fir Park brought Motherwell back into the race in January. At Armadale the locals were crushed 7-1 in the first round of the Scottish Cup. The second round brought the season's greatest anguish to Rangers. At home to Dundee, they lost 2-1 in the match

'that should never have been played'. Incessant rain in Glasgow had made a lake of Ibrox. Huge pools covered the ground. The ball stuck time and again, often requiring three kicks to extract it. The writers all agreed that the game should not have been played. Only the referee disagreed. Eight years had passed since Rangers had gone out of the Cup at such an early stage.

This result stood. One of the two major prizes had been lost. But the championship was very much alive. On 3 March, the Rangers win at Aberdeen, 3-1, was seen as vital, as Celtic went down 1-0 at Firhill. Motherwell were one ahead of Rangers who had a game in hand, two clear of Celtic who had two games in hand. Rangers had the scent of victory. A run of nine successive victories, 11 matches without defeat since 7 February, was almost decisive. Motherwell had faltered, and with all three contenders having two games left, Rangers were one point ahead of Celtic, four ahead of Motherwell. The championship went down to the very last day. Rangers needed an outright victory at East Fife on 25 April. They got it, with a flourish. First-half goals from Smith (2), Marshall and Archibald made it 4-0 and untouchable. They won by two from Celtic, four from Motherwell, and set a club record of five successive League titles, and the 19th overall.

It was Celtic v Rangers in the Charity Cup, first round and a 2-2 draw after extra-time, with Rangers going through 3-1 on corners. Against Queen's Park in the Final, again extra-time was needed, resolved by a Doc Marshall goal at 2-1 for Rangers; thus two of the big four prizes had been won.

Rangers presented one new major signing, centre-forward Sam English signed in July 1931 from Coleraine. He was to break all goalscoring records in his very first season with a total of 56, including 44 League goals, a record to this day. Yet even this was not quite enough to claim a sixth consecutive championship to equal Celtic's 22-year-old record. Rangers first away match was ominously prophetic in this respect. At Fir Park, before a crowd of 25,000, Motherwell won a superb match by 4-2.

At the end of August, Celtic were on top, with 11 points from six games. The first Old Firm game of the season, on 5 September, petered out in a pointless goalless draw following the fatal injury to Celtic goalkeeper John Thomson.

Seven points from the next four matches gave Rangers a point lead over Motherwell, two over Celtic. A 4-1 win over Third Lanark at Ibrox in the Glasgow Cup brought a semi-final against Celtic, a 1-1 draw at Celtic Park a 2-2 draw at Ibrox, then a single Jimmy Smith goal in a third match to settle it. The Final against Queen's Park at Hampden, before 50,376 was a stroll. Despite the Depression and the general state of the nation, big crowds for big games was still the order of the day. Goals by Smith, McPhail and Harvey (own-goal) made it 3-0 and a record 19th win.

A week later, Rangers went down 1-0 at Ibrox to the same Queen's Park. It cost them a championship lead which they were never to retain. Both Morton and Marshall failed with penalty kicks. The leaders, Motherwell, had the finest side in their history, inspired by the left wing partnership of George Stevenson and Bobby Ferrier, with a spearhead in centre-forward Willie McFadyen who scored a record 52 goals that season. They dropped their only home point of the season, to Celtic 2-2, on 31 October and five successive wins saw them three ahead of Rangers, six ahead of Celtic as the holiday season approached. At Ibrox on Boxing Day, a Sam English goal settled the game. Rangers beat Celtic 2-1 at Celtic Park, then Thistle 4-0 at Ibrox to turn the screw on Motherwell, and were to run up a

On 5 September 1931, an undefeated Celtic came to Ibrox to challenge the defending champions before 80,000 people. Five minutes into the second half, Rangers broke away. Jimmy Fleming sent Sam English clear, and as the centre-forward settled himself and shot from around ten yards, John Thomson, the brilliant Celtic goalkeeper, dived at his feet. English, injured, limped out of the collision. The ball went wide. Thom- son lay still. English, realising that Thomson was badly hurt, signalled frantically to the sidelines. Behind the goal, the Rangers fans, not knowing the seriousness of this clash, started to chant. David Meiklejohn, their captain and a forbidding figure, ran behind the goal and silenced them. Thomson, his head swathed in bandages, was stretchered off suffering from a depressed fracture of the skull. He was taken to the Victoria Infirmary where, after unavailing surgery, he died at 9.25pm.

Scottish football was stupefied. John Thomson, 23 years old, was young, slim, handsome, audacious, admired throughout the country, regardless of club allegiances, as a goalkeeper peerless. He had already won eight representative honours. He was agile and graceful, and courageous beyond belief. In February 1930, he had suffered a fractured jaw at

sequence of ten wins, with 39 goals scored. Yet Motherwell equalled that with ten successive wins since the turn of the year. This was a rare vintage in Scotland.

Brechin City and Raith Rovers went down to Rangers in the Scottish Cup before they faced their first serious test, away to Hearts. A tremendous battle, with 53,496 inside Tynecastle, thousands more locked outside, was settled by a Doc Marshall goal. The next round was the plum – at home to Motherwell, who had beaten Celtic 2-0 in the previous round. This time 88,000 were at Ibrox to see the inside-forward James Murray, in his only Scottish Cup-tie of the season, and inevitably Bob McPhail score early goals in each half for an outstanding Rangers win. Hamilton went down 5-2 in the semi-final to goals from Marshall (2), English (2) and Archibald.

Although Motherwell dropped their first point of 1932 in a goalless draw at Firhill on 2 April, the feeling was that it was to be their championship – they needed three points from their two final games to be absolutely sure. Both of these were at home.

The Scottish Cup Final, before 111,982 saw Kilmarnock hustle and bustle Rangers out of their rhythm. 'Bud' Maxwell had them ahead after 41 minutes, but 10 minutes later, one of Bob McPhail's specials from 30 yards tied the score. In the replay, Rangers found a better rhythm. Jimmy Fleming replaced the injured Alan Morton, and his pace brought him a goal after only ten minutes. McPhail and English added goals and Rangers had won their seventh Scottish Cup. Motherwell's championship win, enjoyed by the entire country because of the sustained quality of their play, was confirmed when Rangers drew 1-1 at Shawfield on 23 April. Rangers had finished with 61 points from 38 games, in second place, five behind Motherwell, who had dropped only one point in their final 14 fixtures.

Doc Marshall hit a hat-trick, including two penalties in a 3-1 Charity Cup-tie win over Queen's Park and a week later, Bob McPhail hit three in the Final against Third Lanark. In the 6-1 win were goals from English (2) and Fleming. Nine Rangers players represented Scotland during the season, and Bob Hamilton and Whitey McDonald

Airdrie in making just such a save.

Twenty thousand people packed Queen Street and Queen Street Station in Glasgow as his coffin was on its way to Cardenden, his native village in Fife. Every Celtic player made the journey. Every club in the League, and many others, was represented. Thousands lined the road from his home to the graveyard.

The death of John Thomson touched everyone in the nation in a manner pre-viously unknown and which has perhaps only been equalled by more contemporary tragedies – in a Scottish context – of Jock Stein and Davie Cooper.

In 1931 the tragedy had a profound long-term effect on the career of Rangers player Sam English. In truth, the cumulative effect of the events of 5 September 1931, and of the uneccesary and wholly irresponsible comment of Celtic manager Willie Maley at the subsequent hear-ing – "I hope it was an accident" – haunted English for the rest of his life, even though he was fully exonerated of any blame, both by the inquiry and by those flickering black and white film images of the incident which clearly illustrate that it was the unfortunate Thomson's own forward momentum which caused his head to strike the knee of the Rangers forward.

played for Ireland. And for Alan Morton, it was his final international season, after 35 appearances for Scotland, and 15 for the Scottish League.

In 1932-33, the campaign to recover a League championship which Rangers had come to regard as their own did not get off to a healthy start. They lost the first match against St Mirren at Paisley on 13 August before 25,000. It was the only defeat in the first two months of the season, which brought Glasgow Cup time round again and with it a flood of Rangers goals, 6-2 v Queen's Park at Hampden, 4-0 against Third Lanark at Ibrox. In the Final against Partick Thistle, a Doc Marshall goal won the handsome trophy for Ibrox for a record 20th time.

Motherwell were at Ibrox on 1 October, leading by a point. A monumental match ended 2-2 before 50,000 with goals by Bob McPhail (2) and for Motherwell, the wingers Johnny Murdoch and Bobby Ferrier.

The season was eventful off the field. On 9 November, the club was saddened by the death of ex-Baillie Joseph Buchanan JP. A member of the club since 1894, he had joined the board in 1915, becoming chairman in 1923. And in January 1933, a home win over Airdrieonians, 5-1, saw the retirement of Alan Morton, who fittingly scored in the match, then immediately joined the board of directors.

Saturday, 21 January was a historic occasion when 56,000 at Ibrox saw the first visit by a foreign club side. A thrilling game with the famous Rapid Vienna ended 3-3. Goals were by Smith (2) and McPhail for Rangers, and for Rapid Vienna, Weselik, Osterman and Bican. The teams were:

Rangers: Dawson; Gray, R.Hamilton, Meiklejohn, McDonald, Brown, Archibald, Marshall, Smith, McPhail, English.

Rapid: Raftl; Yastrab, Sejko, Wagner, Smistik, Passer, Osterman, Weselik, Bican, Kabarek, Lyef.

Two days later, the Scottish Cup was under way. Arbroath went down 3-1 at Ibrox, but in the second round three games were needed to dispose of Queen's Park. After 1-1 and 1-1 again, goals by Marshall, Fleming and Smith dumped the amateurs, 3-1. Before the next round, against

A Rangers team for a League game in 1931-32, the season they finished runners-up. Back row (left to right): Meiklejohn, Dawson, McAulay, Marshall, McPhail, Simpson. Front row: Morton, Gray, Brown, Smith, English.

Scottish Cup heroes of 1932. Rangers stars McPhail, English, Meiklejohn and Fleming pictured the day after the club beat Kilmarnock 3-0 in the replayed Final at Hampden. Fleming, McPhail and English scored the goals.

Kilmarnock at Rugby Park, Rangers were at Fir Park, on 11 February. An exceptional performance by the Light Blues brought a 3-1 result that put them ahead in the chase. But the dream of retaining the Scottish Cup for the first time this century perished a week later when 32,745 saw a Liddell goal for Kilmarnock put them out.

Rangers reached a four-point lead with eight games remaining. Motherwell had won six successive games, and it all got down to a Rangers lead of two with two games left. In 22 April, they beat Queen's Park with a Bob McPhail goal. Three days later, Motherwell could do no more than draw 1-1 with Third Lanark. The championship was won. It was Rangers' record 20th win, by three points from Motherwell, with 62 points from 38 games.

The Charity Cup was won for the sixth successive season with wins over Thirds, Thistle and finally Queen's Park. It was a record 18th win. Rangers set off on their most ambitious overseas tour, six games in Germany and Austria, five against German national selects and all in countries making large football strides. The results for Rangers in sequence were 5-1, 3-1, 5-0, 3-2 and 1-2 respectively, watched by an aggregate 125,000. That final defeat in Munich was Rangers' first defeat on foreign soil. The preceding matches had been played in the order of Berlin, Hamburg, Bochum, Dresden. The final game, in Vienna, was a return match with Rapid. Rangers lost an exciting game 4-3, before a crowd of 40,000.

In May 1933, Rangers signed Torrance ('Torry') Gillick from the junior Petershill. Torry was a chunky, versatile inside-forward who would develop into one of the most popular and effective Rangers of his era.

And ...1933 was the year that Adolf Hitler came to power in Germany.

Apart from capturing yet again the League championship, the 1933-34 season for Rangers featured an exceptional demonstration of their finishing skills. With such proven goalscorers as Bob McPhail, Jimmy Fleming and Jimmy Smith on the staff, it may not have been surprising, but the two opening matches set the tone. In the first, a 5-1 win over Airdrie, Smith scored four, Willie Nicholson the other and in the second match, 9-1 over Ayr United, Smith went two better. His six were accompanied by a hat-trick from the Dublin-born Alec Stevenson who had joined the club in August 1932. Stevenson scored again at Fir Park on 2 September, but two goals from Willie McFadyen, in front of 30,000 fans, kept Motherwell's 100 per cent record intact.

On 20 September, Rangers welcomed the legendary Herbert Chapman and his Arsenal team, English champions, for the first leg of the 'British championship'. Rangers in Victorian times had often jousted with Woolwich Arsenal. Goals from Smith and McPhail produced a 2-0 win in front of 40,000, and a week later, 46,000 at Highbury, among them many thousands of exiled Scots, saw a majestic performance and a 3-1 win by Rangers. Two goals came from Fleming, one from Marshall this time.

The Glasgow Cup in October saw Rangers set against Celtic, after a first-round bye. It was 1-1 at Celtic Park, then goals from Marshall and Stevenson took Rangers through at Ibrox. The Celtic goal was by Frank O'Donnell, the result 2-1. The Final against Clyde was an easy win and a 21st Glasgow Cup success. The Final team showed new faces. It was:- Dawson; Gray, McDonald, Meiklejohn, Simpson, Brown, Archibald, Marshall, Gillick, McPhail, Main.

In the championship, Rangers trailed Motherwell by three points, but seven of the next eight games were won,

Jimmy Smith hit successive hat-tricks against Clyde and Queen of the South, but Motherwell matched this, yielding drawn games only at home to Celtic and away to Thirds. Only on 23 December did they suffer their first defeat of the season, 2-1 at home to Clyde. Rangers won 7-2 at Airdrie, beat Hibs 6-0 at Ibrox. In the first of these both McPhail and Fleming hit hat-tricks, in the second Smith did the same. The goals were flooding in.

After the New Year matches against Celtic and Patrick Thistle, Rangers were still three points behind Motherwell. One of the scorers in the 2-2 draw at Celtic Park was Alex Venters, signed from Cowdenbeath in November. A powerful goal-scoring inside-forward, he was already a Scottish international player and would be a distinct asset to Rangers over a dozen years.

At the end of January, Motherwell came to Ibrox. It was clearly the championship decider. Rangers' 4-2 win gave them a lead they would not relinquish.

In the first round of the Scottish Cup, the minor Perthshire team, Blairgowrie, were overwhelmed, 14-2. Fleming scored a club record nine goals. Venters and Marshall scored doubles, Nicholson a single. Rangers scored four in the final four minutes to equal the scoreline of 1883 against Whitehill. This was the greatest number of goals scored by Rangers in a single match. Victories by greater winning margins were 13-0 against Possilpark and Uddingston in 1877 and against Kelvinside in 1889. And a week later, Jimmy Fleming scored five in a 6-0 win over Dundee at Dens Park.

Cup rounds were dramatic and popular – 27,038 were at Cathkin (3-0 over Third Lanark), then 67,543 for a drawn game with Hearts, 47,453 for the replay at Tynecastle, with thousands locked out, then a hulking 53,000 at Ibrox for a narrow win over Aberdeen. The semi-final against St Johnstone at Hampden drew 60,119 to see a poor match decided by a Doc Marshall goal, but no fewer than 113,403 saw the Final against St Mirren, surprising semi-final winners over Motherwell. They were blasted aside 5-0.

Rangers had gone into the field needing two points from three games remaining. Four days later it was done, 3-1 at Brockville. They had 66 points from 38 games, four ahead of Motherwell, having scored 118 goals. That was one goal short of Motherwell's record set in 1931, their championship season. Since 1926-27, the talented Lanarkshire team had finished second, third, third, second, third, first, second, second, a remarkable sequence for a 'provincial' club. But all through their golden years, with one exception, they had to give best to Rangers.

A Robert Main goal against Celtic in the Charity Cup secured the last of the trophies and made 1934, like 1930, a wholly triumphant year.

In July 1934, Rangers lost one of their most valuable players in Dr James Marshall, with his transfer to Arsenal. 'Doc' Marshall, signed in 1925 from Shettleston, had been working in Glasgow Royal Infirmary since his graduation. He took up a medical appointment in London. His 259 appearances for Rangers produced 150 goals and brought him three international appearances for Scotland, six League championship medals and three Scottish Cup wins.

Rangers' defence of the championship could not have had a more sensational start. They beat Dunfermline Athletic 7-1 at East End Park with Jimmy Smith, as he had done in the early match against Ayr United a year previously, scoring six times, equalising his own individual League record. Rapid Vienna were at Ibrox on 14 August, losing 3-1, important home wins were taken over con-

Dr James Marshall of Rangers heads the ball out of the reach of Hearts goalkeeper John Harkness at Ibrox in the 1930s. Other players pictured include Smith and Massie of Hearts and McPhail of Rangers.

tenders Motherwell and Hearts. When Rangers went down by 3-2 to Dundee at Dens, the League battle was joined again. Rangers took part in Jimmy McGrory's benefit match, winning 4-0 at Celtic Park, when one of the goalscorers was Davie Kinnear, signed from Raith Rovers. A lightly-built, swift and skilful outside-left, he was with Rangers for 12 years then came back from 1956 to 1970 as trainer and physiotherapist. A new generation of Rangers was exemplified by the other goalscorers, Gillick, Fiddes and Main.

Rangers were at Highbury on 12 September for another friendly with Arsenal. The 53,000 crowd saw a 1-1 draw with goals from famous names – Bob McPhail and Cliff Bastin. Doc Marshall was in inspired form for the London team. Manchester City went down 1-0 at Ibrox in a home and away series between Scottish and English Cup holders. The scorer, incidentally was Archie McAulay, an inside-forward from Camelon Juniors and not Bob McAuley, who was then with Chelsea. The return at Maine Road saw Rangers go down 4-2. Two days later they were to face Partick Thistle in a bid to equal their own record of four successive Glasgow Cup victories. It was Thistle's day however, and a single goal before a crowd of 28,000 gave them their first Glasgow Cup win.

When, a week later, Rangers went down 2-1 to Clyde at Shawfield, the critics spoke of 'crisis' at Ibrox accusing the team of complacency and lethargy. Rangers' reply was a six-game unbeaten run which produced a five points lead over Hearts, seven over Celtic.

Jimmy Fleming, nine years a Ranger, was transferred to Ayr United. He scored 268 goals in 295 games, winning three international caps, five League championships, three Scottish Cup medals, and set the Ibrox individual scoring record. Also leaving the club was Sandy Archibald, going to Raith Rovers as secretary/manager. After 17 years in the blue shirt, he must be considered one of Rangers' finest players, scoring 170 goals in a total of 665 games, winning a British record of 12 League championships, three Scottish Cup medals and playing in eight representative matches. Davie Meiklejohn, with 15 years of service, became the longest-serving Ranger. One exotic arrival at Ibrox was Mohammed Latif from Cairo, who scored seven goals in 16 reserve matches that season.

On 8 December Hearts blasted the championship wide open with a 4-1 win at Tynecastle and a week later, Rangers lost at home in the League for the first time in three years (Kilmarnock, 3-2). Characteristically, they came back, unbeaten until they entered 1935, including 8-1 against Dunfermline (Jimmy Smith four goals) and 2-1 against Celtic at Ibrox. A massive 83,000 saw Rangers win with goals from Venters and Gillick while Celtic had Napier injured and McGonigle ordered off. A day later, 32,000 at Firhill saw Thistle, not always Rangers' friend, win 1-0. But the reaction was eight consecutive wins, and a lead of eight points with four games left.

In the Scottish Cup, the form was irresistible. Cowdenbeath, Third Lanark, St Mirren, Motherwell (an impressive 4-1 at Fir Park) Hearts after a replay, then Hamilton Accies in the Final. A crowd of 87,740 saw Rangers win the Cup for the ninth time. A week earlier, they had won the championship with a 3-1 at Aberdeen and were three ahead of Celtic, with 55 points from 38 games. The Aberdeen game was the last for 'Tully' Craig. For 12 years a Ranger, he had totalled 306 games, 41 goals, five championships and two Scottish Cups. He won eight representative honours. He was 41 when he left Ibrox to become manager of Falkirk – his nickname came from his original club, Tullibody FC.

After eight years, the Charity Cup was lost. It was Partick Thistle again, winning 1-0 at Firhill.

For the opening of season 1935-36, Rangers had an innovation to offer one particular section of their patrons – the provision of two 'ladies retiring rooms' as they were described, in the enclosure.

It was a season perhaps more important for other happenings. Two Cups were won. The Scottish Cup was won for the third successive season, the first time it had been done in the 20th century. The championship was eventually lost after eight wins in the previous nine years. Torry Gillick was transferred to Everton for a record £8,000. Dougie Gray and Bob McPhail set club records of six Scottish Cup winning appearances and McPhail joined the famous Jimmy McMenemy on seven, one short of the record held by Charles Campbell of Queen's Park. Davie Meiklejohn retired after the Charity Cup Final. And Rangers talked extensively with the SFA about extending Ibrox with a double-decker stand where the Govan Stand now rises, this integrated with the Ibrox railway line that used to run behind it, with a station giving direct access to the stadium. The East and West terraces were to be extended and the talk was of a 200,000 capacity.

Defending their League title, Rangers were a point ahead of Celtic at the end of August. In the challenge between Scottish and English Cup winners, Sheffield Wednesday, they played a 1-1 draw at Hillsborough on 4 September, won 2-0 at Ibrox two weeks later. The first Old Firm match, in Govan in late September with the teams level on points, went to Celtic for their first League win at Ibrox since 1921. Murphy and Crum goals against one by Smith made it 2-1 – goalkeeper Joe Kennaway saved a Meiklejohn penalty in the dying minutes.

Arsenal came to Ibrox for a 2-2 draw, then there was some compensation for Rangers in the Glasgow Cup Final. Goals from Jimmy Fiddes and Torry Gillick gave Rangers a comfortable win over Celtic, and their 22nd Glasgow Cup win. The Rangers defence of the day had an almost timeless look about it, but the forward line demonstrated the new generation at Ibrox. The team was: Dawson; Gray, McDonald, Meiklejohn, Simpson, Brown, Main, Fiddes, Smith, Venters, Gillick.

A seven-game unbeaten stretch saw Rangers nevertheless lose ground. In the same period, Celtic had dropped but one point, 1-1 at Kilmarnock. When Rangers lost 1-0 at Aberdeen on 23 November, the resulting gap of five points looked like the end of the road for Rangers, but it was the last defeat of the year. The Ne'er Day match was of prime importance. It was a Celtic Park classic, with Rangers winning 4-3. In February, Celtic went down at Tynecastle, Rangers had a goalless draw with Motherwell and the teams were level.

The opening rounds of the Cup were straight forward. East Fife and Albion Rovers were knocked over. More testing games came at St Mirren (2-1 and a crowd of 43,308) and Aberdeen (1-0 and 41,663). In the League, both Celtic and Rangers kept winning, point by point. In the semi-final against Clyde at Hampden, 56,243 saw two goals from

Main and one from McPhail give Rangers an easy passage. The Final against Third Lanark, who had beaten Falkirk in a Tynecastle semi-final which drew a remarkable crowd of 47,796, was not distinguished. Thirds went down to a Bob McPhail goal in only 90 seconds.

Rangers had gone into that Final with the championship all but lost. On the same day, Celtic had crushed Ayr United 6-0, and the title was finally surrendered four days later when Rangers were held to a 1-1 draw at Tynecastle. They finished five points behind Celtic who had 66 points in winning their first championship in ten years. They added the Charity Cup, dishing Rangers 4-2 in the Final. Celtic were emerging, gradually welding together a fine team that would come to be remembered as the 'Empire Exhibition' team.

Rangers recaptured the championship in 1936-37. The basis of the achievement was twofold – two long runs of unbeaten games. From the start of the season, they went 17 games without loss. Then from 4 January, the total was 13 undefeated, so Rangers were convincing champions by seven points from Aberdeen. The challenge from the north came perhaps for the first time as Aberdeen became a mainstream 'national' club. Their excellent team were also Scottish Cup Finalists, going down narrowly to Celtic after one of the best Finals on record. Their attractiveness was shown when they brought out 60,000 to Ibrox on 7 November 1936. Rangers won 2-1 with two goals from Bob McPhail. Only Celtic attracted a higher attendance that season. At the heart of the Rangers' success were the goalscorers Jimmy Smith and Bob McPhail, with 31 and 25 respectively. Goalkeeper Jerry Dawson was an ever-present.

The bogey team was Hearts. They inflicted on Rangers their first defeat of the campaign, on 5 December, Rangers' 18th fixture, when they won 5-2 at Tynecastle. This of course was the Hearts of Tommy Walker and Andy Black. One month later, they won 1-0 at Ibrox. These were the only Rangers' defeats in the season until the very last match, when the championship was already won. The Glasgow Cup was won, in a replayed Final against Partick Thistle, by 6-1.

After three successive Scottish Cup wins, from 1934 to 1936, Rangers were aiming for an historic fourth. It had never been done in Scottish Cup history, but this time Rangers' dream was shattered almost before they got started. They lost 1-0 at Dumfries of all places in the first round. It would be 30 years before it happened again, at a place branded into the soul of all Rangers supporters – Berwick. Of course, it was an historic win for the Doonhamers, Queen of the South, seen by 13,000. It was also, to make matters worse, the first time a Rangers game had been recorded on film.

Before the season started, Austria Vienna attracted a 50,000 crowd to Ibrox, on 12 August, Rangers winning 4-1, with a Bob McPhail hat-trick. A new Ibrox record was established on 1 January 1937 when 95,000 saw an Alex Venters goal defeat Celtic 1-0. The next day, at Firhill, one of the great Rangers names was in the team against Partick Thistle. Willie Thornton, aged 16, took part in a 1-0 win. And Archie McAuley was transferred to West Ham United, for £6,000.

The 1937-38 season may well have been the poorest of the 1930s. Third in the championship, a distant 12 points behind Celtic, this was in spite of an unbeaten opening over 16 League fixtures, including a 3-1 home win over Celtic, before 80,000 on 11 September. The first defeat came on 27 November to old bogeys Hearts, by 3-0 at Ibrox. This defeat seemed to unbalance the side. The New Year opened disastrously. Rangers lost 3-0 to Celtic at Parkhead before 83,500, a ground attendance record which stands to this day, then on 3 January, lost 3-1 at home to Partick Thistle. This was bad enough, but for anyone with Rangers in their heart, 5 February was a day of calamity. Dundee beat Rangers 6-1, a Dundee team that was to be relegated at the end of the season. After this, there was never again any serious championship challenge. Hearts again registered a double against the blue shirts, on 23 April in the second last game.

They did at least manage to take the Glasgow Cup with a 2-1 win over Third Lanark in the Final. And for those with a penchant for omens, Rangers were bound to win the Scottish Cup – they had won it every even year since 1926. And when in the semi-final they found themselves in the company of two Second Division clubs (East Fife and St Bernard) and lowly Kilmarnock (they finished 18th of 20 in the First Division), Rangers were massive favourites to win. Contemporary reports record a game which Rangers should have won comfortably but managed to lose 4-3. Kilmarnock proved devastating on the break and also snatched a last minute winner. They in turn became favourites to win the Cup, but after a replay, East Fife made some history by becoming the only Second Division club to win the Scottish Cup.

On 19 October 1937 Rangers played a goalless draw at Stoke City to raise funds for the Holditch Colliery Disaster Fund, and after the match, the Stoke chairman, presented Rangers with 'The Loving Cup', with the injunction that at the first Ibrox game of every year, the guests be invited to toast the health of the Monarch from the Cup. The Cup had been created to commemorate the Silver Jubilee of King George V and all English First Division clubs of the day had been gifted one.

Arrivals at Ibrox were Jock Shaw, signed for £2,000 from Airdrie who went on to have 16 seasons at Ibrox, and Jimmy Duncanson, who also had a long and successful career.

An Empire Exhibition Cup was played at the end of the season, to celebrate a vast Empire Exhibition that was held in Bellahouston Park, quite close to Rangers' ground. All matches were played at Ibrox, where indeed King George VI with Queen Elizabeth had formally opened the exhibition. It was the second royal visit to Ibrox – King George V

had held a 1917 Investiture there. Four of the top teams in Scotland and four from England took part in a Cup competition. Rangers were beaten 1-0 by Everton in the first round, and the Liverpool team went on to the Final, where they were defeated 1-0 by Celtic, with a Johnny Crum goal in extra-time.

It was a tournament of great names – Tommy Lawton and Joe Mercer and Willie Cook of Everton, not to mention Torry Gillick, Raich Carter and Alec Hastings from Sunderland; Dave McCulloch of Brentford and 'Jaikey' Jackson and Joe Payne of Chelsea.

In many ways, the 1938-39 season was one of transition for Rangers. Bob McPhail's career was coming to an end, despite the fact that he scored 13 goals in 23 League games. Great names of the 1930s – Meiklejohn, Simpson, Brown, Gray, McPhail – were going or gone, and with the introduction of young players like Shaw, Willie Woodburn, Willie Waddell and Scot Symon, who came from Portsmouth in August 1938, manager Bill Struth was assembling a new squad which would reign supreme through the war and beyond, as their predecessors had done.

Waddell made an extraordinary debut for the club. At the age of 17, he scored the only goal in a friendly against Arsenal on 29 August 1938, at Highbury, with 41,000 watching. He was to play 37 League games. Leading scorer was Alex Venters with 38 goals. Venters was a Fifer, stocky and powerful, a forceful runner and finisher. If he has not been regarded as a Rangers 'legend', his scoring career is impressive. Until the coming of one Alistair McCoist 50 years on, Venters scored more League goals against Celtic than any other player in the club's history.

The League title was recaptured a hulking 11 points ahead of Celtic, despite losing 6-2 at Celtic Park on 10 September – 1938 must be one of the few, perhaps only, years in which Rangers have conceded six goals in League games, twice! From 10 December, they went 17 games undefeated, the very core of their success. As well as Venters' goals, Willie Thornton had 23. The season was memorable above all for a record attendance at Ibrox on 2 January 1939. For the Celtic match, 118,730 watched, or tried to watch. Contemporary reports had as many as 30,000 locked out. One may well ask, where have they all gone?

Rangers in World War Two

WHEN World War Two broke out on 3 September 1939, five full Scottish League fixtures had been played, leaving a First Division showing Rangers topping the division with eight points, one ahead of Falkirk, and three ahead of Aberdeen, Celtic, Hearts and Partick Thistle.

The wartime period of six years was to be one of the most successful in the club's history, emergency conditions notwithstanding. Rangers won 25 out of 34 first-team competitions played, primarily because they had a talented team which of course was subject to the same restrictions as all the others. For example, Willie Thornton, abroad on active service, went two years without playing a single game for Rangers. The club won seven out of seven League championships, four out of six Southern League Cups, five of seven Glasgow Cups, six of seven Charity Cups, plus one-off tournaments such as the Summer Cup, the Scottish Emergency

War Cup, 1940, the Scottish Victory Cup 1946. On 6 September, the Scottish Football Association suspended all football. The 1939-40 season was abandoned. Players' contracts were declared void. A few days later the Home Secretary gave permission for friendly matches to be played in certain 'safe' areas. With the not uncommon conviction that the German Luftwaffe was about to flatten every urban area in the country gradually fading into the 'Phoney War', authority was given for competitive football to resume.

The clubs agreed on a two-division League structure with an East-North and West-South split. It lasted, unsatisfactorily, for one season. The Edinburgh clubs, Hearts and Hibs insisted that for financial reasons they absolutely had to have fixtures with Rangers and Celtic, otherwise they would have to shut up shop. Other clubs did. Some never returned after the war. For season 1940-41, the divisions became

Jimmy Smith turns away after scoring Rangers' first goal in their 4-1 win over Queen's Park at Hampden Park in a wartime Southern League game in November 1944.

Dinamo Moscow goalkeeper Khomich punches clear from a Rangers attack at Ibrox in November 1945, when a massive crowd of 95,000 saw Rangers fight back against considerable odds to draw 2-2.

North and South, and the Edinburgh clubs were in with the Glasgow clubs in the Southern League. Despite the problems of players, travel and wartime life in general, Rangers maintained a reserve team, playing in the North-Eastern League for a time. This fact and the Rangers' attitude to the game throughout the war, was of the greatest importance to the future of the club. Manager Bill Struth, his energy in organisation and administration, was largely responsible.

The Govan club had dominated the Scottish game throughout the 1920s and most of the 1930s. It was the most powerful single force in the Scottish game. Struth had an immediate awareness of the importance of football as public entertainment in wartime and made no secret of his personal war effort, which was to field teams which were as attractive and efficient as could be, and to maintain Rangers' now-traditional standards of dress, behaviour and as far as possible, a stadium that would remain spick and span if nothing else.

He set about finding employment for his players whose earning capacities at a stroke had been cut to £2 per week maximum, by SFA edict. Struth found 'reserved occupations' as close to Ibrox as possible for them, and they found themselves slaving in shipyards, engineering shops, munitions factories and the like along Clydeside and in the West of Scotland. The myth that all Rangers players were placed in reserved occupations did little to emphasise the importance of such work, and myth it certainly was. Rangers players who were on active service included David Kinnear, Tom McKillop, James Galloway, Willie Thornton, Ian

McPherson, Chris McNee, Eddie Rutherford, Billy Williamson, Alastair McKillop, David Marshall, Willie Paton, Jimmy Parlane. Willie Thornton won a Military Medal in Sicily, Ian McPherson, DFC, was on the first RAF bombing raid on Germany.

And Struth was delighted to welcome guest players as such, from time to time. Stanley Matthews played twice, and won a Glasgow Charity Cup medal for his pains, when Rangers beat Partick Thistle 3-0 in 1940-41. Les McDowell played five times for Rangers, Torry Gillick and Jimmy Caskie were back in Scotland, from Everton, and played. Willie McIntosh from St Johnstone played 66 games and scored 60 goals.

Rangers also entered a reserve team in the North-Eastern League, playing against such opposition as Aberdeen, Dundee, Dunfermline Athletic and Raith Rovers. Their strength in depth was indicated when they won the North-East League championship in 1941-42, the Mitchell Cup and the Supplementary Cup in 1943-44, against the first teams of the other clubs. Their reserve attendance sometimes beat their Southern League attendances; for example on 6 December 1941, St Mirren v Rangers in the Southern League at Paisley was seen by 5,000; A few miles away, the North-Eastern League team, against Aberdeen at Ibrox, attracted 10,000.

Ground capacities were limited early in the war. The Rangers, Celtic and Hampden grounds had a maximum of 15,000 placed on them, all others 8,000. This was quickly relaxed. Later that season, 40,000 was permitted for the

New Year's Day game, and later still, the limit went to 60,000, then 75,000 for the bigger grounds. In general, crowds for routine matches were small – in the Southern League Cup Final of 1942-43, Rangers and Falkirk played to 18,900. And performances and results were far from even and consistent. On 27 September 1941, Hibs 8 Rangers 1 was a scoreline. On 1 January 1943, Rangers 8 Celtic 1 was another. Hibs were emerging as Rangers' greatest challengers during the war, and were to carry that challenge into peacetime.

Nevertheless, Rangers' domination of the wartime scene was evident in the statistics that show of 210 League fixtures played, 155 were won, only 26 lost. An additional 'honour' was reported on 1 November 1942, when it was 'announced' that 'Rangers' had won the championship of a prisoner-of-war camp in Germany. Fourteen teams had competed, all with names of English and Scottish First Division clubs. Preston North End were second, and a cup competition was held, won by Everton. Team selections were not available.

Six years threw up strange doings. On 29 November 1941, when Rangers went to Aberdeen for a North-Eastern League Cup semi-final, they were a man short. They unearthed a spectator, name of Cameron, who had in fact played a trial for Rangers, then became a St Johnstone player who had not played any football in two years! And he played well. Evidence of Rangers' wartime strength was clear on 7 May 1942, when they beat Celtic 2-0 in the Second XI Cup, Celtic playing their first team, their only team, against Rangers' North-Eastern League team. On 6 April 1942. Scot Symon played the full 90 minutes in goal against Clyde at Shawfield. Rangers had no other goalkeeper. They won 8-2.

The club was often called upon to help the war effort with charity matches – on 20 April 1941 Rangers beat the RAF 3-2 at Ibrox, in aid of the Clydeside Air Raid Distress Fund. A trophy was put up – the Sir Archibald Sinclair Cup – which Rangers still hold. On 27 August 1941 Rangers drew 2-2 with a British Army team at Ayr, for the Ayr County Council War Fund. On 1 September 1941, it was Rangers 3 Preston North End 1 in aid of the Lord Provost's Central Relief Fund Benefit and on 25 September 1945, Rangers beat Newcastle United 3-2 in aid of the King George VI Navy Fund.

In 1943, it was revealed that Carl Hansen, Rangers' pre-war Danish player had been arrested and imprisoned in Copenhagen for walking out after curfew. He and a friend had bumped into some German soldiers, a fight broke out, and Hansen collected four months in gaol. And in 1943, Bill Struth the Rangers manager built a personal greenhouse at Ibrox, behind the west terracing, the traditional 'Celtic End'. How times change – for all the years that greenhouse stood behind the Broomloan Road terracing, well into the 1950s, there was not one single report of any damage to it.

One wartime innovation was the Summer Cup. Rangers played three times, were Finalists three times and winners once. And Rangers won the Victory Cup, 3-1 against Hibernian at Hampden before a crowd of 90,000, in 1946. The trophy, which rests in the Trophy Room at Ibrox, had a chequered history. It existed with three different wartime disguises. It was originally the Scottish Emergency War Cup in 1939-40, which Rangers won 1-0 against Dundee United at Hampden. In 1940-41, the Southern League Cup was introduced, and used the same trophy. It was won in four of the six competitions, with Hibernian and Aberdeen each winning once (Aberdeen's was a 3-2 win on 11 May 1946 with 135,000 watching at Hampden!) This was Aberdeen's first national trophy success. It was short-lived. The SFA asked for the return of the trophy to be used for the Scottish Victory Cup, the Final played on 15 June. Aberdeen had held their first trophy for just five weeks!

In November 1945, Soviet giants Dinamo Moscow visited Britain on what turned out to be an unbeaten tour that encompassed fixtures against Rangers, Chelsea, Arsenal and Cardiff City. Their visit to Ibrox at the conclusion of the tour attracted a massive 95,000 crowd for a game that would become part of Rangers' folklore.

The Muscovites led 2-0 early on, Willie Waddell missed a penalty, Torry Gillick at one point counted 12 opponents on the field of play, yet Rangers produced a stirring fightback with goals by Jimmy Smith and a George Young penalty for a memorable draw.

This would by no means be the last time that the Russians featured significantly in Rangers' history.

One downside of 1945-46 for Rangers was that legends Jerry Dawson, Doug Gray and Jimmy Smith had come to the end of their time at Ibrox. But on the other hand, waiting in the wings so to speak, were such names as Bobby Brown, Ian McColl and Sammy Cox.

The Iron Curtain

THE immediate post-war seasons were boom times for football in Scotland. Crowds flocked to the grounds, and nowhere was this greater than at Ibrox. Rangers enjoyed massive attendances. During the 1946-47 season, a Scottish Cup-tie against Hibs drew 95,000. There were 48,816 at the Easter Road replay. A League Cup semi-final, Rangers v Hibs at Hampden, was seen by 125,154. The League Cup Final, Rangers v Aberdeen sold 134,000 tickets, but as an indication of how bad the weather was, 5 April or not 5 April, only (sic) 82,684 attended.

Clearly, Hibs were to be the main challengers to Rangers, this season and beyond. They had the finest team in their history. The immediate post-war forward line of Smith, Combe, Linwood, Turnbull and Ormond quickly transmuted into Smith, Johnstone, Reilly, Turnbull and Ormond. Having challenged Rangers through most of the war, they now came into their own. They made their challenge only too obvious in the second game, when they won 2-1 at Ibrox despite losing a first minute penalty goal by George Young. The Hibernian goalkeeper Jock Kerr was given a standing ovation by the Ibrox crowd.

Nevertheless, Rangers took the League title from them by two points. An 11 game unbeaten run from 30 September to 4 January was the foundation. The 7 September fixture, against Celtic at Parkhead, became a phenomenon. Celtic, very controversially, had decided to increase admission charges for the match. Both Celtic and Rangers Supporters Associations decided to boycott the match, and such was their influence that only 28,000 were on hand to see Rangers win 3-2. Bobby Brown was ever-present – Willie Thornton had 27 goals.

The season saw the inaugural League Cup, offspring of

Rangers in 1946-47. Back row (left to right): Cox, Watkins, Brown, Young, Symon, Jock Shaw. Front row: Waddell. Gillick, Thornton, Duncanson, Caskie.

Boardroom Revolt

In the summer of 1947, the Rangers chairman, Jimmy Bowie, was deposed by a 'Troika' of new directors, John F.Wilson, a Glasgow city councillor who became the new chairman, W.Rogers Simpson, the club's secretary, and Bill Struth, the club's long-serving manager.

Bowie, born in Partick and an engineer by profession, had joined Rangers from Queen's Park in December 1910. For 12 years he was a first-team regular, as wing-half or inside-forward on either side of the team. He won five championships with the club and played five times for Scotland – but for World War One he would have played more often. He retired in 1922, became a Rangers director in 1925, and chairman in 1934.

The fateful sequence of events seemed to have started in April 1947 when Bowie suggested to manager Struth, who was 71, that he should give some thought to retiring (Bowie, 59, was due to retire in rotation at the club's annual meeting in June and would offer himself for re-election in the routine manner). He indicated that Struth was showing signs of strain, and that he should have an assistant who would succeed him and that Struth could then become a director. This would require a change in the Articles of Association of the club, which said that no paid servant could be a director.

At a meeting on 15 May changes meant that there could be five directors and that paid officials could become directors, on a board limited to five. The other 'Bowie' directors were Alan Morton and George Brown, both like Bowie former players. This was said to be harmoniously agreed. Simpson and Struth would come aboard, confirmed at the summer annual meeting. But when John F.Wilson informed Bowie that he intended to stand for election, clearly something would have to give. That something was Bowie.

The board issued a statement condemning this ploy, calling a shareholders meeting for 11 June when an appeal was made for all shareholders to attend the next night at the annual meeting and so withdraw their proxies. The individuals present showed a majority in favour of Bowie, but a card vote, demanded by W.Rogers Simpson, showed that the rebels had a majority shareholding. The annual meeting the following night lasted 15 minutes, the board was enlarged to five members, Wilson became chairman, Bowie was out.

He had been outsmarted. His mistakes were in timing. By suggesting retirement to manager Struth two months before he himself was due for re-election he gave Struth the initiative and time to recruit other major shareholders, and Bowie clearly was innocent regarding the power and intent of major individual shareholders. Bill Struth emerged as the largest single shareholder. He had accumulated his holding of 1,097 shares and explained not unreasonably that they had been bought from his savings from his Ibrox salary, with 'Rangers money' in other words.

So the power went to the big battalions. No longer would the board be made of former players with a particular love for the club they had served. Rangers was no longer a football club – it became a commercial entity. The revolution of 1947 was the first step that took Rangers along a road that led to ownership by the John Lawrence Construction Group in 1985 and eventually, in 1988, to David Murray.

The teams line up before the start of Rangers' friendly match against Benfica in Lisbon in February 1948. Rangers won 3-0, all the goals coming in the last seven minutes of the game.

the Southern League Cup, the very successful wartime competition. Rangers beat Aberdeen in the Final, 4-0 in the dreadful conditions we have noted. In the Scottish Cup, the blue shirts went down 2-1 at Easter Road to Hibernian after a 0-0 draw at Ibrox. Hibs were then clear favourites to win the Cup, for the first time since 1902, but lost 2-1 in the Final to Aberdeen, a first success for the Northern club. In the very last match of the season, Rangers won the Charity Cup with a 1-0 victory over Celtic.

With the League championship and the League Cup won, Rangers fans had no reason to suppose that all was not well at Ibrox, but the summer brought the impossible – a boardroom coup.

The 1947-48 season started with a record attendance for opening day – 80,000 for Rangers v Celtic in a League Cup-tie. Rangers won 2-0, both goals by Billy Williamson. Thus Rangers had made a good start. From 25 October to 31 January 35 points were won from a possible 38, including a 24 games sequence when only one point was dropped. But 31 January was to prove a critical date. Rangers went to Easter Road leading by three points with two games in hand. In losing 1-0 the balance of power changed. From then on, Rangers collected only ten points from ten League games, losing at home to such as Queen of the South, Queen's Park and Hearts, and eventually losing the championship by two points to Hibs.

There was a settled team for much of the season. Bobby Brown, Sammy Cox and Willie Thornton were all ever-present. The League Cup was lost to Falkirk, in the semi-final, for whom former Rangers player Archie Aikman produced a last-minute goal. It was the first time in Southern League Cup or Scottish League Cup competition that Rangers had failed to reach the Final.

The Scottish Cup did come back to Ibrox, however, for the first time in 12 years. In this campaign, Rangers played before more spectators than any other club has done in winning the Scottish Cup – an aggregate of 590,295 in total. This included a British record attendance, save for Cup Finals, of 143,570 for the semi-final with Hibernian at Hampden. This was a titanic struggle between the Hibernian attack (the 'Famous Five') and the Rangers defence ('The Iron Curtain'), and was won by a classic goal of the time. An explosive run down the right by Waddell, a flashing cross and a thundering header from Thornton. Brown in the Rangers goal was quite outstanding, making in particular one world-class save from the great Gordon Smith in the second half. Cox too was outstanding. They had to be, since Hibs had two-thirds of the play.

The Final, over two games with Morton (1-1, then 1-0) saw a total of 265,725 people. The replay 133,750 was a midweek record. The Final was won by a singular goal late in the game with dusk falling and visibility lapsing. Five minutes from the end of extra-time, Billy Williamson flung himself at a cross from the right, and his diving header was in before Jimmy Cowan, the Morton goalkeeper, could move. Williamson was playing his very first Cup-tie for Rangers, replacing Willie Findlay from the first game.

Rangers beat Benfica 3-0 in a friendly. It was a happy trip for Waddell – he met his future wife, a hostess on the flight.

The 1948-49 season was the season of the 'Triple Crown', or the treble as we now call it. Rangers became the first club to win the League championship, the Scottish Cup and the League Cup in the same season. Early in the season, it seemed like a distant dream. Rangers were drawn in a League Cup section of immense proportions – Rangers, Celtic, Hibernian and Clyde, who must have felt like lambs to the slaughter. Yet Rangers seemed to have lost their way when they drew at home to Clyde, drew away to Hibernian, then lost 3-1 at Celtic Park. With three sectional games remaining, Rangers trailed Celtic by three points. They proceeded to lose 4-2 at Easter Road while Rangers won 3-1 at Shawfield. Celtic thereupon lost 6-3 at home to Clyde, a result which astonished Scottish football and which beggars belief even at this span of time. At the same time, Rangers were involved in yet another huge struggle with Hibs. Again it was 1-1, before 76,466, again it was a Willie Thornton goal. This set up an almost unbearable decider, attracting a

Willie Woodburn heads clear from a Clyde attack in the 1949 Scottish Cup Final which Rangers won 4-1.

massive 105,000, the largest crowd that season in the UK outside Cup Finals. Rangers won 2-1 and went on to take the Cup in the spring with a comfortable 2-0 win against Raith Rovers.

The League saw Rangers running neck and neck, this time not with Hibs but with Dundee. It was touch and go throughout the season – One 12 game run without defeat was the foundation. It all came down to Rangers at Coatbridge, Dundee at Falkirk. Dundee had underlined their challenge by comprehensively beating Rangers at Dens Park, 3-1 on 3 January before a 39,000 crowd – huge by Dundee standards. At the finish, Dundee needed a point at Falkirk. They lost their nerve, were beaten 4-1 and Jerry Dawson saved a penalty at a critical point in the match. Rangers won 4-1 at Coatbridge Thornton had a hat-trick, and Rangers the championship.

Having won the Scottish Cup the previous week (4-1 against Clyde), the treble had been achieved at an unlikely setting. The Scottish Cup campaign had been moderate, memorable perhaps only for the Willie Thornton hat-trick against East Fife in the Hampden semi-final, East Fife now being managed by Scot Symon. Rangers had beaten Motherwell at Fir Park, an impressive performance. In the Final itself, George Young scored twice with penalties and Billy Williamson, yet again, in his only Scottish Cup appearance of the season, scored. He went into the history books – two Finals, two goals, two winners medals, only two Cup-ties played in two seasons.

Rangers once more started with a League Cup defeat in 1949-50, this one from Celtic, 3-2 at Parkhead, but the Govan club did qualify from its section. In a quarter-final match, Rangers lost 3-2 at home to Cowdenbeath in the first leg, Cowdenbeath thus becoming the first Second Division club to win at Ibrox. And in the second leg, at Cowdenbeath's Central Park, Rangers were within 30 seconds of elimination when Eddie Rutherford equalised. A Sammy Cox goal in extra-time made it 3-1, and Rangers only just through by a 5-4 aggregate. The crowd of 25,586 set the Central Park record – with 5,000 in that ground today, you would be concerned with your personal safety.

Rangers lost to East Fife, now managed by Scot Symon, in the semi-final. East Fife won 2-1 and went on to an all-Fife Final against Dunfermline Athletic.

In the League, Rangers played touch and go with Hibs all season. The defence remained solid and consistent. Brown, Young, Cox and McColl played in all matches. Shaw and Woodburn missed only one each. The other side of the coin was the use of 13 forwards. A 19 games unbeaten run from 1 December made Rangers persistent challengers, and the visit of Hibs to Ibrox for the second last match was going to be vital. A post war British attendance record for a League match was set by the 101,000 crowd who saw the Iron Curtain defence defy the Famous Five attack and Rangers were left to get one point from their final match, against Third Lanark at Cathkin. They got it with a 2-2 draw after leading 2-0 and seeing Thirds fail with a penalty. The crowd there was 32,800.

The Scottish Cup was won for the third successive season, the third time in Rangers' history. The campaign was prolonged. Three ties were needed to dispose of Raith Rovers in the quarter-finals, two to beat Queen of the South in the semi-final. Cowdenbeath had visited Ibrox yet again,

How good was the much-vaunted 'Iron Curtain' defence, which was the foundation of all Rangers successes from 1946-53? The defence as a unit was essentially Brown; Young and Shaw; McColl, Woodburn and Cox, after Scot Symon retired. If we take six defenders as a collective unit, playing in a 30 game League division, that gives a total of 180 prospective appearances per season. In 1948-49, the unit achieved 175. In 1949-50, with another championship won, they recorded 178. In 1948-49, goals against were 32. In 1949-59, goals against were 26. It is a remarkable record of consistency, and of course of luck in their freedom from compromising injury. In 1950-51, when they finished second in the championship and Willie Rae was becoming an increasingly vital part of the defence they achieved only 150.

But of course as Willie Thornton, tiring of all the talk of the Iron Curtain once said plaintively: "Of course we did manage to score one or two."

but for their League Cup impudence earlier in the season, were put in their place, it was Rangers, 8-0 this time. In the Final, East Fife were demolished, 3-0. Scot Symon, their manager and former Rangers player, said it was the finest Rangers exhibition he had ever seen. Thornton scored two, had another disallowed and so was denied the distinction of being the first Rangers player to score a hat-trick in the Scottish Cup Final.

The 1950-51 season was a disappointing one for Rangers in which they lost the League by ten clear points to Hibs, failed to qualify in their League Cup section for the first time ever, and saw their hopes of a fourth successive Scottish Cup win perish at Ibrox in the second round. Hibs beat them 3-2 before 102,342. One very important signing was that of Billy Simpson from Linfield, for £11,500. He scored 16 goals in that, his first season, and was to go on to be a hard goalscoring attack leader. Brown and Young were ever-present in a season that never really got off the ground for Rangers, after losing to Aberdeen in the League Cup. Beating Third Lanark 2-1 in the Charity Cup Final was poor recompense.

Season 1951-52 was another 'barren' one of the post-war period. There were to be few. It started early, on Glasgow's 'Fair Saturday', 14 July with the St Mungo Cup, marking the Festival of Britain. This was a one-off tournament for all Scottish clubs. Rangers went out at the first round, in Aberdeen, 2-1. It was to prove an omen. Aberdeen lost in the Final 3-2 to Celtic.

The League Cup did see Rangers reach the Final after an outstanding display against Celtic in a Hampden semi-final (83,235), which they won 3-0, but a cultured display by Dundee and a last minute goal from Alfie Boyd won the Final 3-2 for the Dens Park club. This was their first major success since their Scottish Cup win of 1910, achieved by a talented squad that included Boyd, Bobby Flavell and Billy Steel.

Hibernian, defending the championship they had won by ten points, were Rangers' main opponents. They were run much closer this time. Rangers could have won the title if they had won their last four games, all of which were away from home. But a defeat at Motherwell on 22 March, by 2-1, put an end to things. Hibs retained the title, this time by four points.

The Scottish Cup also ended at Fir Park in a quarter-final match which Motherwell won 2-1 yet again. In a first match at Ibrox, before 82,000, a late goal gave Motherwell a 1-1 draw. In the replay, a late goal yet again dumped Rangers, 2-1. This was a very fine Motherwell team of Johnston, Kilmarnock and Shaw, Cox, Paton and Redpath, Sloan, Humphries, Kelly Watson and Aitkenhead. It beat a Dundee team with a quite brilliant display in the Final, before a surprising crowd of 136,274, surely a record in a Final not involving Rangers or Celtic.

On 17 October 1951, Rangers had gone to Highbury to inaugurate the Arsenal floodlights. The home win of 3-2 was witnessed by 62,000. George Niven, goalkeeper and Eric Caldow, full-back, arrived this season and although John Little was replacing Jock Shaw, the team was still very much based on the 'Iron Curtain' defence, which was still in place. The 'unit' played in 172 of a possible 180 League games. Waddell and Thornton were still spearheads, but the rest of the forward line was never really settled.

Seldom can Rangers have made a more disastrous start to a season than they did in 1952-53. They lost 5-0 to Hearts at Tynecastle on opening day, 9 August. Bobby Brown, goalkeeper of distinction and of long-standing, had a nightmare match and was not to play another game that entire season, being replaced immediately by young George Niven. Despite that result, Rangers did contrive to qualify out of their section, but fell to Kilmarnock at the semi-final stage. Yet again it was a solitary late goal, two minutes from the end, which beat Rangers 1-0 at Ibrox, but Kilmarnock, it should be said, gave no indication that they were a Division B team, played perfectly well and deserved their surprising victory.

The championship was a race with Hibernian all season, but Rangers made a bad start here too, losing three of the five opening games, including a home fixture with Hibs, a late goal by Eddie Turnbull, swinging it 2-1 to the Edinburgh team. When they lost successive games, to Hibs and East Fife, still managed by Scot Symon and challenging for the leadership, things were far from promising, but as so often in the past, Rangers set off on a long, unbeaten run. At 31 October, they were nine points behind the leaders, East Fife, with only six points from six games, but with three games in hand. Fifteen unbeaten games through to 7 March took Rangers into the lead. They then dropped four points, to Clyde and Raith Rovers, but steadied and collected 14 points out of a possible 16 to clinch the title – on goal-average from Hibernian. It was done on the very last day, when a Willie Waddell goal 15 minutes from the end gave them the 1-1 draw they needed at Palmerston Park against Queen of the South.

The season was also memorable for the official authorisation of floodlights in Scottish football. Rangers' first domestic game under the lights was in the unlikely setting of Ochilview Park, Stenhousemuir, and a Rangers 2-0 win. The Ibrox club had been experimenting with lights, playing several trial games at Ibrox, but it would be a full year before they had a permanent system in place.

In the Scottish Cup, vast crowds were still the order of the day. Rangers beat Celtic at Ibrox before 95,000. In the next round, the semi-final, it was 116,262 at Hampden for a 2-1 over Hearts. In the first Cup Final match against Aberdeen, it was 129,762 (1-1) and in the replay, it was 113,700. In both matches, Rangers were pinned into their own half by a fluent and adventurous Aberdeen team, and never did Rangers so cherish their magnificent defence.

Remembered to this day is the injury to George Niven, the young Rangers goalkeeper, when he dived at the feet of Aberdeen centre-forward Paddy Buckley. He was carried off, but after 18 minutes, re-appeared wearing a leather protective helmet. Captain George Young held the fort in goal during his absence.

The season ended with the Coronation Cup, held for obvious reasons, and featuring the leading clubs in Scotland and England. Celtic had finished eighth in the League championship – presumably their pulling power at the gate justified their inclusion. They promptly won it. Rangers went down 2-1 in the first round, Celtic beat Hibernian 2-0 in the Final.

Johnny Hubbard from South Africa arrived at Ibrox during the season and quickly forced himself into the team. He was to make a distinctive contribution to the Rangers story.

After a League and Cup double, the 1953-54 season was a disappointment. Rangers were fourth in the championship, nine points behind champions Celtic and for the only time in their history, Rangers were lower than Partick Thistle, who were third. In fact, only a draw in the final game, 2-2 at Easter Road, saved Rangers from finishing in their lowest-ever League position, Five clubs had 34 points – Rangers were in fourth place only on goal-average. Three defeats in the six initial games left Rangers struggling.

There were semi-final defeats in both Cup competitions. In the League Cup, an outstanding display by Ledgerwood the Partick Thistle goalkeeper saw Rangers off, 2-0 and in the Scottish Cup, which required seven games, Rangers were trounced 6-0 in the semi-final by Aberdeen. They were outclassed, but in mitigation could claim that goalkeeper Bobby Brown was injured in the second minute, and John Little, injured early in the first half, hobbled throughout the match. Three Aberdeen goals were scored in the final seven minutes.

John Lawrence, Glasgow builder, joined the board. This was to have a profound effect, good and bad, on Rangers' history. On 8 December, floodlights were inaugurated. Arsenal won 2-1, Jock Shaw and Willie Thornton ended their careers, Thornton becoming manager of Dundee.

Rangers undertook a nine-game tour of North America at the end of the season, winning seven, losing one (to Chelsea) and drawing one (to Chelsea). On 15 June, Bill Struth retired after 34 years as Rangers manager, and Scot Symon, manager of Preston North End, was appointed. Symon had had six very successful years with East Fife, then in his only season, had taken the Deepdale club to a Wembley Final.

Season 1954-55 was one of major change for Rangers, with players going, a new manager coming in. They were further compromised by the *sine die* suspension of Willie Woodburn, their magnificent centre-half, on 14 September. It took Rangers a very long time to come to terms with Woodburn going, and to find a replacement – four years, in fact, in which they failed to find a reliable replacement until the arrival of Willie Telfer from St Mirren. By Rangers' standards, it was not an acceptable season. The League Cup was gone at the quarter-final stage. Motherwell winning on a 3-2 aggregate, and the Scottish Cup, for the second successive season, was lost to Aberdeen, 2-1 at Pittodrie.

The title challenge was vigorous and reasonably prolonged. On Christmas Day Rangers were two points behind the leaders Aberdeen, with a game in hand, but the defeat that day by Hibernian at Easter Road, 2-1, was the first of

six losses in seven games, which really killed off the Rangers' chance. They eventually finished in third position, eight points behind Aberdeen, who were claiming the first League championship in their history.

On 12 January 1955, Jimmy Millar was signed from Dunfermline Athletic for £5,000. He was to be at Ibrox for 12 years, one of the most influential Rangers players for that period, and debatably, Scot Symon's finest signing in terms of value for money. On 9 March 1955, Alex Scott, a young man from Camelon Juniors made his debut against Falkirk at Ibrox – and scored three in the 4-1 win. A flying winger of the old school, Alex had a very successful career at Ibrox, somewhat cut short by the arrival of Willie Henderson and Willie Johnston, considered more talented wingers.

Rangers were due to open the 1955-56 season on 13 August, at Celtic Park in a League Cup-tie, scheduled to coincide with an Orange parade due to pass along Duke Street in the city's east end. The authorities decided it would be unwise to have two such events in close proximity and the fixture was re-scheduled. Rangers opened at Brockville, against Falkirk. This League Cup was memorable if for no other reason than on 27 August, Celtic went to Ibrox and won 4-1. Four days later, in the re-scheduled match, Rangers went to Celtic Park and won 4-0. They qualified handily from their section, but again, went down to Aberdeen in the semi-final. They did eventually beat Aberdeen in a Cup-tie, 2-1 in the fifth round at Ibrox before 66,000. But Hearts in a quarter-final match at Tynecastle were too good for them by 4-0, before 47,258. The Scottish Cup had gone.

In the championship campaign, Rangers won only one of the first six games, one of the last five, but in between such miserable starts and finishes, produced a 23-match unbeaten run which secured yet another title, their 29th, by six clear points from Aberdeen. The 18 April 1-0 win over Aberdeen was probably decisive.

On 28 January 1956, Rangers 4-0 win at Airdrie was notable for the fact that Johnny Hubbard failed with a penalty shot. It was his first miss after 23 successful consecutive conversions.

Arriving at Ibrox this season was the controversial centre-forward Don Kitchenbrand from South Africa, nicknamed the 'Rhino'. He finished leading scorer with 24 goals. Hubbard scored 33 goals in all games – the South African connection was very strong at Ibrox. Kitchenbrand scored five in the 8-0 win over Queen of the South in March – this was the first Scottish League game played under floodlights.

Season 1956-57 marked Rangers' entry into European competition. It also saw them retain the League championship for the first time in seven years. It was a season unsuccessful in the Cup competitions. In the League Cup, a powerful section of Celtic, Rangers, East Fife and Aberdeen – probably the four best teams in the country – saw Celtic overcome a slight League Cup bogey. They had often failed to qualify from their section. This time they did, and the critical game was probably their 0-0 draw at Ibrox, before 84,000.

Celtic also eliminated Rangers from the Scottish Cup, after Rangers had gained some revenge over Hearts from the previous season – a 4-0 win at Tynecastle. Incidentally, after beating Rangers then, Hearts went on to win the Scottish Cup for the first time in 50 years, with a 3-1 win over Celtic.

The sixth round produced a rip-snorting match at Celtic Park. Within 15 minutes, the score was 2-2 as both

Rangers team pictured in May 1957. Back row (left to right): Shearer, Caldow, Niven, McColl, Davis. Front row: Scott, Morrison, Murray, Young, Baird, Hubbard.

attacks went on the rampage. The Final 15 minutes produced yet again four goals. Bobby Collins and Willie Fernie made it 4-2 with seven minutes to play – surely Celtic must win. But Hubbard was flattened, scored inevitably from the penalty spot, and with five minutes left, Rangers' Max Murray side-footed home a Hubbard corner kick. In the Ibrox replay, Celtic were the better team, two up at half-time and never really looked like losing. Celtic won the League Cup for the first time, beating Partick Thistle in the Final.

In the championship, Rangers trailed Hearts for much of the season, diverted by their European adventures and pressure of fixtures – the Glasgow Cup still took precedence over League matches. But a 16 match unbeaten run from 12 January to seasons end, including nine successive away wins saw Hearts overtaken. Rangers were champions by two points.

In the third last League game, on 22 April, Easter Monday at Hampden, Queen's Park led Rangers 4-1 just before half-time, in a match which eventually finished 6-4 to Rangers. In the penultimate match, Rangers' 3-0 win at Dumfries virtually secured the title. One game was left, at Dunfermline. Only a high-scoring win by Dunfermline would have given Hearts the title. Athletic needed a point to escape relegation. A 3-3 result would have given Rangers the title and saved Athletic. But in the last minute goalkeeper Martin dropped a ball at Billy Simpson's feet. He was virtually obliged to score and make it 4-3. He was no

doubt embarrassed. George Young announced his retirement, bringing to an end a distinguished career as captain of Rangers and Scotland.

The absence of George Young during 1957-58 was serious for Rangers. His commanding figure had taken the place of Willie Woodburn at the heart of the defence, but his going led to one of the most traumatic seasons in Rangers' history. They lost three of their first four home games, and 12 goals in the process – not the work of likely contenders. They finished second, but a massive 13 points behind Hearts, who may just have had the best team in their history, or at least since the first decade of the century – Dave Mackay, Alec Young, Willie Bauld, Jimmy Wardhaugh. They lost only one game, taking 62 points from a possible 68, scoring 132 goals in the process. They had scored 100 League goals after only 24 games.

In the League Cup, Rangers struggled to qualify in a section that included Raith Rovers, St Mirren and Partick Thistle. After a 3-0 home defeat by Thistle, they were in danger of elimination at Kirkcaldy. Raith needed to win by two goals to eliminate Rangers and top the section. They came close to doing it, winning 4-3. Rangers were through on goal-average. They had an equally scary time in the quarter-final. After a 2-1 defeat at Rugby Park, they needed two goals in the final 15 minutes to make it 3-1 at Ibrox. Brechin were brushed aside in the semi-final, which meant the very first Old Firm League Cup Final, and a match which was to prove unforgettable, remembered still by the

Harold Davis puts a long, low shot past Clyde goalkeeper McCulloch to level the score at Shawfield in November 1958. It set Rangers up for a 4-1 win as they went on to lift yet another championship.

supporters of each team, if for very different reasons. For Rangers it was a catastrophic 7-1 defeat in which they were outclassed by the high quality of the Celtic football. John Valentine, the centre-half was the scapegoat – Billy McPhail, the skilful Celtic centre-forward had a hat-trick – and the defeat led directly to the purchase of Willie Telfer of St Mirren for £10,000. Telfer at 32 was close to the twilight of his career but nevertheless, his coming stabilised the defence, stabilised the team and he gave good service to Rangers for three years. His signing was followed by a 20-match unbeaten run which took Rangers into second place.

The Scottish Cup was lost to Hibernian after a Hampden replay, with scores of 2-2 and 2-1. The concluding minutes of the second half were clouded with controversy. Referee Bobby Davidson awarded a goal to Max Murray, but after protests by the Hibs players, he consulted a linesman and awarded a free-kick to Hibs. It seemed that the goal was disallowed for handling by Ralph Brand. There was of course no television evidence then to corroborate or otherwise the decision.

Rangers made a good start in 1958-59 with a 3-0 home win over Hearts on League Cup business, before 65,000, but failed to qualify from a group that included Raith Rovers and Third Lanark. They lost at Stark's Park and at Tynecastle and Hearts won the group, going on to win the League Cup, beating Partick Thistle in the Final.

A moderate start was made to the League season. There was one extraordinary match at Airdrie on 20 September, when two Rangers goals in the final four minutes brought some dignity to their score in a 5-4 defeat. The signing of Ian McMillan, the Airdrie inside-forward on 2 October for

£10,000 – it had long been in the pipeline – was to prove decisive in this and other seasons. McMillan, an inside-forward and playmaker of the highest class was to become a mainstay of the team for six years. Already experienced when he arrived at Ibrox, he scored on his debut, a 4-4 draw with Raith Rovers and Rangers, in the next 24 League games suffered only one defeat, that at Firhill by 2-0 on 3 January. From October to April – it took Rangers to the brink of the League championship. With two games remaining, they were four points ahead of Hearts, the defending champions. Only one point would do. The penultimate game was against Hearts at Tynecastle, and was lost, 2-0. One point needed, one game to play. That was Aberdeen at Ibrox. Aberdeen had a very pointed interest in the match. A defeat might see them relegated. They saved themselves, winning 2-1. The Rangers team was booed off the park, their distraught fans sure that the championship had been lost. But Hearts lost by the same score – to Celtic. Quite what Celtic fans thought is not recorded. It was not to be the last time that Hearts would throw away a League title on the last day of the season.

For the second time in three years, Rangers went out of the Scottish Cup at Celtic Park, losing 2-1 in round three after beating Hearts 3-2 at Ibrox in the previous round in a quite excellent game. A two game tour of Denmark brought one specific result. Jimmy Millar right-half, was moved to centre-forward in the second match in emergency, and score all four goals. Thereafter, he was Rangers' centre-forward. Johnny Hubbard, after excellent service, went to Bury on 16 April for £6,000.

Season 1959-60 was one of contrasting fortunes, of

Jimmy Millar, inside the six-yard box, scores the first of his two goals against Kilmarnock in the 1960 Scottish Cup Final. Those goals gave Rangers a 2-0 win.

extreme contrasts in fact. The Scottish Cup was won, the semi-final of the European Cup reached. These were positive achievements, but the League championship was most disappointing. Rangers made a poor defence of their title, perhaps distracted by European excitements, and finished a distant 12 points behind Hearts and Kilmarnock. They had made a very emphatic start with a 6-1 win at Easter Road, with four goals by Ralph Brand, in this League Cup opener on 8 August, but failed to qualify mainly because of defeats home and away from a very fine Motherwell team. On 22 August, when Rangers were beating Hibernian 5-1 at Ibrox, David Meiklejohn, manager of Partick Thistle, Rangers legend, captain of the great teams of the 1920s and 1930s, died.

Although Rangers won their opening three League games, it is fair to say that the League campaign never really looked like being successful. At the heart of the failure was an appalling and quite inexplicable home record. Of 17 games at Ibrox, Rangers won only five, six were drawn, and six lost. From the turn of the year until the end of the season, Rangers did not win one League game at home – of eight played, six were drawn, two lost. In the meantime, two Scottish Cup and two European Cup matches at Ibrox were won.

The Scottish Cup saw Berwick, Arbroath and Stenhousemuir shrugged off before a commendable 3-2 win over Hibernian. The semi-final produced two enthralling matches with Celtic, 1-1, then 4-1, in the latter of which the Celtic defence made embarrassing mistakes. The Final against Kilmarnock was interesting in that Kilmarnock were clear favourites. They were second in the League, and in a 15 match unbeaten run under manager Willie Waddell. A defeat at Dunfermline, now bossed by Jock Stein, lost them their chance. On the day, Rangers took command and won well with two headed goals by Jimmy Millar. Eric Caldow missed with a penalty, and Ian McColl won his fifth Scottish Cup medal. Shortly thereafter, he was Scotland national team manager.

Famous old trophies, old competitions – the Glasgow Cup and the Glasgow Charity Merchants Cup were won, in both cases with wins over Partick Thistle. It was Rangers' last win in the Charity Cup. The first had been back in the fledgling days of the 1870s and Kinning Park. After one more season, the Cup and the competition was abandoned because of lack of interest.

It had been a modest season in terms of League and League Cup. Jimmy Millar led the scorers with 39 in all games. The team at best was hard-working, moderate. It needed a catalyst, that indefinable something extra, to give it an edge. It arrived in the summer of 1960, with the signing of James Curran Baxter from Raith Rovers, for £17,500.

Jim Baxter transformed the Rangers team. It now had midfield creators in Baxter and McMillan, fast goalscoring wingers in Alex Scott and Davie Wilson and two proven strikers in Jimmy Millar and Ralph Brand. But above all the team gelled, the chemistry was right. Baxter was a player of high quality, with an inspired left foot. But of course the magic did not happen immediately – in 1960-61 Rangers got off to a rather stammering start in the League Cup, losing three times in a week, once in the Glasgow Cup. Nevertheless, they qualified despite having trailed Celtic by three points with two games to play. There were two outstanding games in the quarter-final round with Dundee between teams bent on attacking play, the second game, 4-3 to Rangers, remembered on Tayside to this day. The semifinal win of 7-0 over Queen of the South speaks for itself. The Final was a repeat of the Scottish Cup Final earlier that year, 2-0 to Rangers over Kilmarnock.

The first League match of the season was a thumping 6-3 over Partick Thistle at Ibrox. And the second game produced an exceptional scoreline when Rangers won 5-1 at Celtic Park. The Celtic goal, again in the last minute from Chalmers, deprived Rangers of their most emphatic win over Celtic in the 20th century. Rangers won their first five games and were always in pole position, albeit challenged by Kilmarnock. The quality of the team was emerging on 26 October when, at Tynecastle, goalkeeper Billy Ritchie went off after eight minutes with a chipped ankle bone. Shearer took over in goal, and the ten men won 3-1 – no substitutes then. Kilmarnock were entirely worthy challengers, however, particularly on 26 November when they came back from two down at Ibrox to win 3-2.

Other shock results included a 1-0 defeat by Ayr United

on Christmas Eve at Somerset Park – Ayr were bottom of the table then, and were relegated.

Jimmy Millar was out for several months with a slipped disc problem, and National Service deprived Rangers of many Baxter appearances. From 18 March, six points were dropped in four games, including a 2-0 defeat at Kilmarnock where a win would have made Rangers champions, and a 6-1 drubbing at Aberdeen. Yet again, Rangers steadied themselves, beat Hibs at Ibrox with ten men when young Willie Henderson went off with an ankle injury, and won the championship by one point from Kilmarnock, with a 7-3 win over Ayr United at Ibrox.

In the Scottish Cup second round, Rangers were in stunning form at Dundee, winning 5-1 after leading 4-0 at halftime. Alex Scott was a first half scorer – one of his three goals in that final League match with Ayr had been Rangers 5,000th League goal. In the next round, two Max Murray goals gave Rangers a 2-2 draw at Fir Park, but in the replay at Ibrox, Motherwell were quite magnificent, winning 5-2 before 80,000 people. The Army refused to release Baxter for this match.

Rangers played their last-ever Charity Cup match, losing 4-3 at home to Clyde, but a singular achievement, over and above League and League Cup, was in reaching the Final of the European Cup-winners' Cup, going down to Fiorentina.

The success of the 'Baxter Era' in the Rangers story, that of the early 1960s, continued. True the championship was surrendered to Dundee in 1961-62, who led from the start, but both League Cup and Scottish Cup were won and the

Former Airdrie forward Ian McMillan fires in a shot against Third Lanark at Ibrox in January 1961. It was an exciting game which Rangers won by the odd goal in seven.

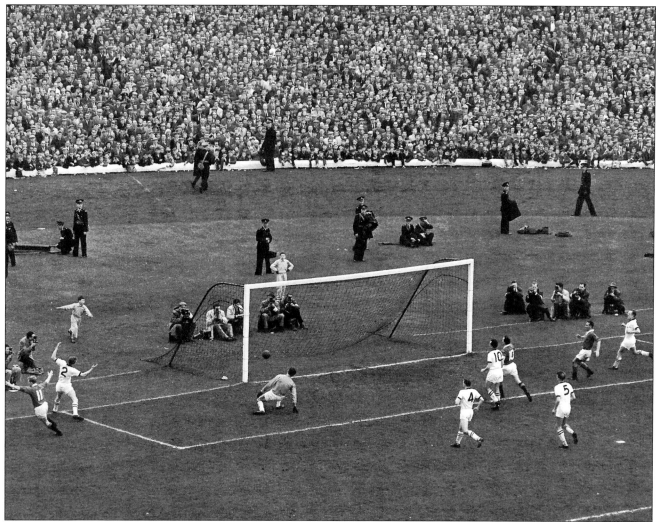

Davie Wilson (11, extreme left) turns away in celebration after his goal effectively ends the hopes of St Mirren in the 1962 Scottish Cup Final.

quarter-finals of the European Cup reached. The team was changing, gradually. Younger players were coming in. John Greig and Ronnie McKinnon replaced Harold Davis and Bill Paterson and Willie Henderson replaced Alex Scott. All of these newcomers were regulars by the end of the season.

The main challengers, Dundee, may well have had the best team in their history with men like Smith, Alan Gilzean, Ian Ure, Alan Cousins, Alec Hamilton. Gordon Smith was having a blazing sunset to his unique career in which he won League championships with three different clubs, not one of them Rangers or Celtic.

Thus he played in the European Cup for three different teams! That Dundee had a very special team was underlined on 11 November when they clobbered Rangers at Ibrox 5-1, one of Rangers most severe defeats for years. It was a day of thick fog, perhaps in the end welcomed by Rangers fans. Gilzean scored four goals at Ibrox that day, only the second player in modern times to do just that. Willie Martin had done the same in a Scottish Cup-tie in 1939, when Clyde won 4-1. Just before Christmas, Rangers lost successive games at Dunfermline and at home to Aberdeen. At the turn of the year Dundee led by six points from Celtic, seven from Rangers, although the Light Blues had a game in hand. A run of League wins by them put pressure on Dundee, including a 7-1 win at Falkirk in March, where Davie Wilson, operating at centre-forward, had six goals.

Rangers then led Dundee by three points. On 14 March,

after a 0-0 draw at Dens Park, Rangers surely were in control, with six games left. But Dundee United did their across-the-street neighbours a large favour by winning 1-0 at Ibrox. The postponed Celtic-Rangers Ne'er Day match was played on 9 April and finished 1-1. That meant advantage to Rangers. They needed to win the two final games. With the Scottish Cup won on 21 April, there seemed no reason why Rangers should not be champions, and win the treble. But Aberdeen, not for the last time, proved no friends of Rangers in these matters. They won 1-0 at Pittodrie. So Dundee needed one point from their final game at Perth. This time, there was no faltering. They won 3-0, took their first and so far only championship, and at the same time, sadly, relegated St Johnstone.

In the League Cup, the closest call had come from the Perth men. In a Celtic Park semi-final, they led 2-0 before Rangers took things into extra-time and won with a Davie Wilson goal in 103 minutes. The first of two Final games against Hearts was pedestrian, 1-1 after extra-time. The second was an exhilarating performance by a Rangers team inspired by Baxter and McMillan which ended 3-1.

In the Scottish Cup, Rangers weathered a trip to Pittodrie, 2-2, then hammered Aberdeen 5-1 at Ibrox in the third round. A vintage display took them past Kilmarnock, 4-2 away, then semi-final and Final matches against Motherwell and St Mirren respectively were routine, and far from classics.

A memorable tour of the USSR ended the season. Ran-

Ralph Brand (10) sets Rangers off to a League and Cup double with an early goal in the 1963 Scottish Cup Final replay against Celtic.

gers beat Lokomotiv Moscow 3-1, Dinamo Tbilisi 1-0 and drew with Dinamo Kiev, this without Baxter. The team had a hysterical reception at Glasgow Airport on return from some 10,000 fans. One wonders what if they were to win the European Cup. John Greig was the success of the tour, and never looked back.

Season 1962-63 was split by the most severe winter weather conditions in living memory, Rangers, after defeating Celtic 4-0 at Ibrox in the New Year match, 1 January, did not play a single game anywhere until they won 2-1 at Dunfermline on 9 March. Almost the whole of Britain, certainly in football terms, came to a standstill in that two-months period. There were several Saturdays when not a single game was played anywhere in mainland Britain.

One of the best of Rangers' teams was falling into place – Ritchie; Shearer, Caldow; Greig, McKinnon, Baxter, Henderson, McMillan, Millar, Brand, Wilson played most of the season, certainly through the first half, with scarcely a break. Rangers dominated Scottish football entirely this season. Clear winners in the championship by nine points from Kilmarnock, they lost only two games, the first at Tannadice on 10 November 2-1 to Dundee United, the second six months later on 13 May, 1-0 at Kilmarnock.

Rangers were beaten in the League Cup semi-final by Kilmarnock, who came from behind with a late goal to win 3-2. Skill and hard work earned the victory, but it was abetted by one Ralph Brand. With Rangers 2-1 up, he actually punched a goal-bound shot across the line. Television evidence showed that the ball would certainly have gone in. The goal was disallowed, Kilmarnock three minutes later broke away and scored and it was 2-2 instead of 3-1. The vagaries of the game, as they say, turned against Kilmarnock when they had a headed goal disallowed in perplexing circumstances, in a 1-0 defeat by Hearts in the Final. The referee Mr Wharton, who was closer to the halfway line than the incident, never spoke of it but seemed to indicate it was disallowed for hands when again television evidence rejected that.

Paradoxically, Rangers' best performance of the season may have been against Kilmarnock when they won 6-1 on 8 December at Ibrox. It was a day of heavy conditions which saw a hat-trick by Ralph Brand. Almost as admirable

was the 4-0 win on 1 January at home to Celtic. During the long winter closure, George McLean was signed from St Mirren for £26,500. Never one of the great Rangers players in later years he was one of the scapegoats for the defeat at Berwick.

Probably the most positive challenge of the season came from Dundee in the fourth round of the Scottish Cup. After a 1-1 draw in Dundee came a monumental match at Ibrox, with 81,190 inside the old stadium, thousands milling around outside. Dundee led 2-1, Rangers equalised with a Ralph Brand penalty – controversial of course with Dundee claiming that Davie Wilson had 'dived', not appreciating that Davie would never do such a thing! – then won with another Brand goal two minutes from time!

Dundee United were beaten handsomely in the semi-final, and it was to be Rangers v Celtic in the Scottish Cup Final, improbably the first since the famous 1928 Final, 35 years earlier. Before the Final, Hearts were beaten 5-1 at Ibrox, thus conceding five goals to Rangers in each League game.

The Scottish Cup Final was not memorable. The wind, the famous 'Hampden Swirl', spoiled things. Frank Haffey, the sometimes-eccentric Celtic goalkeeper, chose to play the game of his life, a preposterous performance in which he stopped everything which Rangers threw at him. In the very last minute, he stopped a Davie Wilson point blank shot. Rangers were equally superior in the replay, winning 3-0. Baxter gave a virtuoso performance and with McMillan back in the team, Rangers outclassed Celtic. The attendances incidentally were 129,643 and 120,273.

The match also featured a mass exodus of Celtic fans when Ralph Brand beat Haffey from 25 yards for the third goal, with 20 minutes left. The King's Park end, the traditional Celtic end at Hampden, was virtually empty when the match ended. Many Rangers fans have felt that this was Rangers' perfect opportunity to go on and wipe out once and for all the memory of the 7-1 defeat by Celtic in the 1957 League Cup Final. Celtic were on their knees – Rangers could have done anything with them, at their leisure. Baxter, of course chose to toy with the opposition, to insult them by a self-indulgent freezing of the ball and posing, instead of driving the team on for goals.

Brand douses his team-mates, Shearer holds the trophy, as Rangers celebrate another hat-trick of Scottish Cup Final triumphs with a 3-1 victory over Dundee in 1964.

With the lifting of the maximum wage in England, Rangers came under increasing pressure from English clubs casting eyes on their players, most particularly of course Jim Baxter. Rangers had been perfectly able to compete with a maximum of £30 per week plus bonuses. Now wages in England increased steadily. Rangers, attracting huge crowds, could have paid more and matched English offers for star players, but they persisted with the Scottish policy of paying all players in the team the same. Baxter in England, of course, would have had superstar compensation. Several Rangers players had gone south – Alex Scott, Billy Stevenson to Everton and Liverpool respectively – and word got back along the players grapevine about payments in England.

Rangers players, Baxter in particular, grew restless about money. He fought a long campaign for either a substantial increase in wages, or a transfer. He simply wanted what he thought he was worth, and was not concerned at what the others were being paid. Rangers had turned down several big money offers from such as Arsenal, Spurs, Manchester United, who obviously thought he was worth superstar compensation. Thankfully for the friends of Rangers, it would be two more seasons before he was allowed to leave.

Young forwards were given chances by Rangers during 1963-64, in the main because goalscorer Jimmy Millar was out for a long spell from the start. Jim Forrest, signed from Glasgow Schools in 1960, grabbed his chance. He would become a prolific goalscorer for Rangers – 145 goals in 164 games is a phenomenal strike rate (in 1964-65 he scored a club record 57 goals in all games, including 40 before Christmas).

He scored twice in the opening game, a 3-0 win at Celtic Park as Rangers qualified unbeaten in a League Cup section that also included Kilmarnock and Queen of the South. East Fife and Berwick Rangers were disposed of in reaching a Final where Rangers faced another Second Division club, but one with a difference. Morton had eliminated First Division Motherwell and Hibernian in reaching the Final and were largely responsible for drawing an astonishing crowd of 104,907 to Hampden. Not even the Old Firm Final of 1957 had matched this. Rangers overwhelmed them, 5-0, with four goals from Forrest and one from his cousin Alec Willoughby. Forrest's goals were a record Cup Final achievement by a Rangers player.

The League championship was carefully protected, Rangers being unbeaten in their opening 13 fixtures. They wobbled slightly towards the end o the year with successive home defeats by Hearts 3-0 and St Johnstone 3-2, for whom one Alec Ferguson scored a hat-trick. Kilmarnock actually led the chase then by one point, a gauntlet thrown down which Rangers quickly picked up, running off with five straight wins. Mid-March was to prove critical. Rangers had suffered severely from injuries. Back in 1963, Eric Caldow had suffered a double fracture of the leg in the England-Scotland match at Wembley. Early in 1963-64, they lost Davie Wilson with a broken ankle in the League Cup semi-final against Berwick Rangers.

All this came to a head at Pittodrie in March, where Henderson and Forrest were stretchered off. Henderson would be out for three weeks, Forrest for the rest of the season. Rangers, with nine men, leading by a point, saw their whole season at risk. But they held out for a 1-1 draw. Kilmarnock lost at Dundee. The next match against Kilmarnock at Ibrox, was won 2-0. Rangers were points clear and the League title had fallen into place.

It was Rangers third championship in four years, their fourth in six years, their sixth in nine years. It was scarcely imaginable that it would be 11 long years before they would again be League champions.

With the Scottish Cup, the first treble in 15 years was on. Five goals at Stenhousemuir, nine at home to Duns, then 3-0 against Partick Thistle and 2-0 against Celtic, both at home, was evidence of Rangers' ambition. Incidentally, they beat Celtic five times during this season – twice in the League, twice in the League Cup, then this tie in the Scottish Cup. The Celtic Cup match, seen by 84,724, is remembered for a classic and dazzling goal from Willie Henderson when, taking possession on the halfway line, he went through the entire Celtic team before scoring from 15 yards.

Jock Stein's Dunfermline Athletic were beaten in the semi-final, leading Rangers into a classic Final with Dundee. Both teams played to prime form with Bert Slater in the Dundee goal time and again defying Rangers until the very last minute when first Millar, then Brand scored to make it 3-1, the treble won, the first since 1949, the first of Scot Symon's management. It gave Ralph Brand a footnote in history. He was the first player to score in three successive Scottish Cup Finals – four if a replay is counted! It was Rangers' third successive Scottish Cup win for the third time in the 20th century. Rangers played Everton in the 'British Championship', with home and away matches. This was the first such fixture in the post-war era, although a similar number of fixtures had been played, particularly with Arsenal in pre-war days. The respective managers, Bill Struth and Herbert Chapman, were close friends.

The great Rangers team of the early 1960s was passing, not just in terms of age, but because of injury, wear and tear, or just the end of a natural cycle. Shearer, Millar, possibly Wilson and certainly Brand, were at their peaks. In terms of injury, Eric Caldow never fully recovered from his 1963 Wembley injury; throughout the 1964-65 season Willie Henderson had several bunion operations and was out for long spells; Baxter's injury, the leg break in Vienna, kept him out and compromised Rangers throughout the season.

After a triple crown victory, motivation may have been difficult for manager Scot Symon, but the League Cup started well with a 4-0 against Aberdeen at Ibrox, then at Muirton Park Perth, St Johnstone were hit by 9-1. Forrest had four of the goals and Rangers qualified, unbeaten, in their section. By contrast, the championship did not have such a glowing start – only one of the first seven League games was won. Rangers lost to Celtic, 3-1 at Parkhead, for the first time in several years. After eight games, they had

won only twice, and trailed Kilmarnock by eight points. Substantial title challenges were coming from various quarters – Hearts and Hibs both had strong teams, and Jock Stein had left Dunfermline Athletic in such fine shape that they mounted their most serious challenge this season. Hibs, now under Jock Stein, were a rejuvenated team.

Rangers however managed to retain their League Cup. In dire straits against Dundee United in the semi-final, they equalised very late, won 2-1 in extra-time thanks to two Jim Forrest goals. The same man brought victory in the Final against Celtic, with two more goals in the 2-1 win. This season he outpaced both Jimmy Millar and Ralph Brand as Rangers top scorer – 30 in the League, 18 in the League Cup, three in the Scottish Cup and six in European Cup matches.

After the League Cup win, 12 unbeaten matches took them close to the top but on 30 January, they went down 1-0 to Hibs at Easter Road, and were left as outsiders.

A Scottish Cup win at least would mean a record four-in-a-row. A fine second round win at Tannadice, 2-0, (two to Forrest again), sent them to Easter Road, and the end of the road. Hibs had already beaten them home and away, and they did it again. A bizarre team selection by manager Scot Symon saw Jim Baxter thrown into this immensely important match, his first in three months since his Vienna injury. Rangers were within two minutes of a replay when the Hibs forward Willie Hamilton headed the winner at 2-1. Hamilton, incidentally, was described by Jock Stein as the finest Scottish player of his (Stein's) time. Hibs under Jock Stein had beaten Rangers for the third time this season, an omen if there ever was one. The Cup match was Stein's last at Easter Road. On the following Monday he arrived at Celtic Park and an astonishing chapter in the long Celtic-Rangers relationship was about to commence.

Rangers, out of the Scottish Cup, faced the possibility of not qualifying for European competition for the first time since season 1957-58. And their League hopes went with a 2-0 defeat at Pittodrie on 13 March. This was Aberdeen's first match under new manager Eddie Turnbull. Rangers finished fifth, a 3-1 defeat at Dunfermline on 14 April making it so. Dunfermline really should have been champions, but a point lost carelessly at St Johnstone, when they were clearly the best team in the country, meant that the entire championship came down to Hearts v Kilmarnock on the last day. Kilmarnock needed to win 2-0 to snatch the title. They did just that! Willie Waddell was their delighted manager. As they had done in 1959, and were to do in 1986, Hearts had 'blown it' on the very last day.

On 25 May, Jim Baxter was transferred to Sunderland for a reported £72,500. This was a massive loss to Rangers, never made good until the coming of Graeme Souness. And Bobby Shearer ended his long Ibrox career with a free transfer.

The post-war period of 1946-65 was probably as successful as most Rangers have had, if it was not absolutely comparable to that between the wars, or that of the brief Souness-Smith era of 1986-96. Of 19 League championships played then, Rangers won ten; of 19 Scottish Cups, eight; of 19 League Cups, six. An analysis of where the other honours went makes interesting reading. Before the war, and in the period from 1965, the vast majority of these honours would have gone to Celtic – this is certainly not the case in the period 1946-65. In just one of those seasons did Celtic win the championship while Hibernian won three, Hearts two, and Aberdeen, Dundee and Kilmarnock won one each. In the Scottish Cup, Celtic, famous Cup fighters, won only three, Clyde won twice and Aberdeen, Dundee, Motherwell, Hearts, Falkirk, St Mirren and Dunfermline Athletic were winners.

It was perhaps the only time this century that the honours had been so widespread. In the past few years, in the Souness-Smith era, the main challengers have not been Celtic – one thinks of Aberdeen and Motherwell in the League. But the spread of challenge could not be compared to the two post-war decades. Celtic's record in this period is surprising. Only twice did they finished above Rangers in the championship, one in winning, 1953-54, then in the following season, when the 1-2-3 was Aberdeen-Celtic-Rangers. Celtic finished in the top three only five times out of 19 tries and seven times in the top four. Indeed in 1947-48 they came very close to relegation. Had they not won their last League game (3-2 at Dundee), and had other results fallen, they would have gone down.

How to account for this, from a great club which had historically always challenged Rangers? The origins may date back to New Year's Day, 1940, when the legendary manager, Willie Maley, left the club. It was not a happy parting. Maley was the great panjandrum of Parkhead. He had served the club for 52 years, having played in its very first match back in 1888. But he was now 71 years old, in failing health. There were differences with the directors and in the end he left, an embittered man. Perhaps he simply could not accept the march of time.

Jimmy McStay, a former captain, succeeded him, but the shadow of Maley the autocrat fell heavily over him during restrictive war years. He was replaced by Jimmy McGrory in 1945. McGrory, one of the greatest of Celtic players, was more than anything a gentleman, and was perhaps so immersed in Celtic that he could not see, or was not allowed to see, the post-war way ahead. Rangers management by contrast remained formidable. When Struth the disciplinarian was succeeded by Scot Symon, conservative and correct, things continued in the Rangers way. Celtic's Empire Exhibition team which won League and Cup in the late 1930s, was highly talented and had younger players like Malcolm McDonald feeding into it. It was allowed to disintegrate during the war years. And Celtic had gained a reputation for selling talented players. Before the war one remembered Charlie Napier and the O'Donnell brothers, Frank and Hugh, after the war Jimmy Delaney, Lou Macari, David Hay, even Kenny Dalglish who gave Liverpool a decade of magnificent service after leaving Parkhead. Rangers by contrast seldom sold a major player with his best days ahead of him. Baxter was probably the exception – he had made it clear that he wanted to go. Pat Crerand at Parkhead was almost forced to go to Manchester United – at gunpoint, so they said, by Robert Kelly, the Celtic chairman. Jock Stein later called Crerand "the finest Celtic play-

er I ever saw". Celtic might claim financial necessity but for much of the early part of this period they played before very large crowds.

Celtic uncovered fine players like Willie Fernie, Bertie Peacock, Bobby Evans, Billy McPhail, who produced fine performances for a Celtic club that was strangely unable to sustain a challenge. So much so that often it seemed that they had become poor relations and had accepted the fact. Before the coming of Jock Stein and the blessed year of 1965, Celtic were being seen as simply an Irish-Catholic football club, inspite of their non-restrictive policies. But society was moving on, and moving away from these associations. On the law of averages, Aberdeen and Dundee, Scotland's third and fourth cities, would surely produce fine teams from time to time. But Motherwell, Kilmarnock and Dunfermline were producing challenges from time to time when Celtic simply were not.

The post-war boom which brought large crowds also meant increased liquidity for these clubs and with part-time football the norm for most of them, they were more able to persuade local boys to play 'at home', and to resist the temptations of the Old Firm.

The end of the period under review came with the arrival of Jock Stein at Celtic Park in 1965. Back in the 1950s, when his playing career ended, he had spent some three years at Parkhead coaching young players who regarded him highly. His was a youth policy which was to stand Celtic in good stead when he returned.

In the early 1960s, Celtic were considered a short-sighted and financially uninspired club. When the chairman Robert Kelly anounced that they would put their faith in youth, the cynics took this as a coded message that he was not going to spend money. It was reported that Leeds United offered Celtic one of their young players, a Scot who was homesick and a Celtic fan. There would be a token fee of £30,000. Kelly said they could not afford it. The player was Billy Bremner.

However, there was some kind of youth system in place which would in time feed through such players as Bobby Lennox, Jimmy Johnston, Steve Chalmers, Bobby Murdoch – many of the team that was to win the European Cup. And at the time, at Ibrox, there was nothing remotely similar.

When Stein arrived at Parkhead, things were so bad that Celtic finished eighth in the championship. He released 25 players at the end of the season. Without Jock Stein, Celtic would at the very least have remained the moderate club they had become. With Stein as catalyst, they embarked on the greatest decade in their history. Rangers dominance over two decades was quickly at risk. Stein was to overtake Rangers, perhaps move ahead of them, but at the same time provoke a Rangers response which established that if they were to play second to Celtic for much of the coming decade, they would be a very, very good second.

From Symon to Souness

JIM Baxter, the flawed genius, had gone to Sunderland in the summer of 1965. New arrivals were two Danish players signed from Greenock Morton, full-back Kai Johansen and inside-forward Jorn Sorenson. Rangers had a fully fit playing staff for the 1965-66 season, and this plus the development of young players Jim Forrest, Alec Willoughby and Bobby Watson gave some hope that the championship

could be recovered from Kilmarnock. Hearts, Hibs and Dunfermline had recorded successful campaigns in 1964-65, but it was correctly anticipated that the main challenge would come from Celtic, now under the guidance of Jock Stein and having won their first trophy for eight years in April, the Scottish Cup.

In a season without European football, Rangers made an

John Greig celebrates after Celtic's Young put through his own goal in the 1965 League Cup Final at Hampden. It was Celtic, though, won lifted the trophy with a 2-1 win.

impressive start, not losing a League match until Christmas Day, at home 3-2 to a fine Dunfermline team. This included an opening sequence of 15 without defeat. Rangers played some impressive attacking football with strikers Forrest and George McLean in sparkling form. Two John Hughes penalties won the League Cup for Celtic and saw Rangers lose a major Cup Final for the first time since 1957.

Rangers were stopped in their tracks on 3 January at Celtic Park, when after leading by a Wilson goal in the first minute, by 1-0 at half-time, they were overwhelmed 5-1. On a frost-bound surface, Rangers played in regular boots, but Jock Stein sent his team out wearing training shoes, showing a little more cuteness than the Rangers management could muster. They then trailed Celtic by four points, but the Parkhead team lost three away games and handed the initiative back. But Rangers suffered an abysmal March, seeing only two points coming from four games and Celtic eventually prevailed by two points, winning their first championship since 1954.

Their 5-1 win at New Year made Celtic overwhelming favourites for the Scottish Cup, but in both Final and Final replay, Rangers as so often produced defiant performances, matching Celtic man for man and tactically. The Cup was won in the 70th minute-of the replay when a 25-yard drive from Johansen beat Ronnie Simpson. Johansen thus became the first foreign player to score the winning goal in a Scottish Cup Final and the first Scandinavian, but not the last, to win a Scottish Cup winners' medal.

Johansen was only partly successful at Ibrox. He was surely inhibited by the restrictions put on his play by manager Scot Symon, who believed that defenders were there to

defend, attackers to attack, and had a horror of seeing defenders cross the halfway line. Johansen had had a gruelling time against Celtic's John Hughes in the League Cup Final, but in the Scottish Cup Final, liberated at last, he had outstanding games and in turn demolished Hughes. This 1966 Final can be seen as the last gesture from the great Rangers team of the early 1960s as the baton was now passing to Celtic, who would go on to have the greatest period in their history. Rangers faced a barren spell – four years to their next trophy in which there were many changes in playing and managerial staffs.

Season 1966-67 was one of the most convulsive in Scottish football that saw Rangers runners-up in League and League Cup to Celtic, beaten and humiliated by Berwick Rangers in the first round of the Scottish Cup, then runners-up yet again, this time in the Final of the European Cup-winners' Cup. And a few miles across the city of Glasgow, Celtic were having the greatest year in their entire history as winners of League Cup, League championship, Scottish Cup and near-miraculously, the European Cup.

The new season presented to Rangers fans two new half-backs, Alec Smith from Dunfermline Athletic for £55,000 and Dave Smith from Aberdeen for £45,000. Both were quality players. Rangers lost to Celtic twice in the opening weeks, first in a Glasgow Cup-tie at Ibrox by 4-0, then 2-0 at Celtic Park in the League. A third loss was the League Cup Final on 29 October, a match which they certainly did not deserve to lose. They controlled much of the play, had most of the pressure, but lost to an opportunist goal from Bobby Lennox after 19 minutes. An equaliser by Bobby Watson was mysteriously disallowed by referee Tiny Wharton. Some scarcely credible Rangers misses were made. One in the closing minutes by Alec Smith when he stumbled with the ball at his feet, in front of an empty net, a few yards out, was bewildering. Thus Celtic had the first trophy of their clean sweep.

Manager Scot Symon was under some pressure in 1966-67. His conservative style of the collar-and-tie, three-piece suit contrasted sharply with the more contemporary track-suited attitude to management of the younger and now much more successful Jock Stein. The Celtic manager worked with his players at every training session, spelling out clearly what he wanted from each of them, what the team had to do on the field, the strengths and mannerisms of the opposition from match to match.

Rangers players line up for the camera before the Scottish Cup Final against Celtic in April 1966. From left to right: Provan, Greig, McKinnon, McLean, Watson, Ritchie, Johansen, Millar, Johnston, Forrest, Sorensen, Willoughby, Wilson, Henderson.

Rangers goalkeeper Billy Ritchie gets across to a shot from Celtic's Jimmy Johnstone (far left) in the 1966 Scottish Cup Final replay at Hampden. Johansen's goal gave Rangers a 1-0 victory.

Approaches were made to Eddie Turnbull, in his time a first-rate inside-forward in the great Hibs post-war team, now a successful manager at Aberdeen. The suggestion was that he would become assistant to, and eventually successor to, Symon in the Rangers managerial chair. Turnbull turned down the offer, and later admitted that it was an error he regretted. Rangers appointed Bobby Seith of Dundee on 16 November 1966.

There was a long unbeaten run of 12 straight League wins in a stretch of 16 unbeaten games in a strong challenge to Celtic. In fact Rangers lost only three League games, two to Dunfermline Athletic and that early-season defeat by Celtic. Although they never really produced much flowing football, they ran Celtic all the way. Comparisons were made with Celtic, a team of flair and pace. The strikers in the first half of the season, Forrest and McLean, scored goals but somehow could not match the magic of such as the Celtic men, Lennox, Chalmers, Wallace and McBride.

However, Rangers were enjoying the League race and an extended run in European competition when calamity – the word is not too strong – struck on 27 January 1967. Rangers lost 1-0 at Berwick in the Scottish Cup, first round – the first time they had lost in the first round in 30 years and the first time this century they had lost to a club from a lower division. And almost 30 years later, people still recall the impact this result had on Scottish, indeed British football. It was the sensation of the 20th century. Comparisons were made with Arthurlie's defeat of Celtic in 1897 and Battlefield's defeat of Queen's Park in the 1880s. In one-off Cup-ties, of course, it can happen. If it is uncommon in the Scottish League (Stenhousemuir beat Aberdeen in 1994-95!), it seems more frequent in the Football League.

Rangers were in a long unbeaten run in a reasonable season, but the result produced alarm, if not panic, within Ibrox. Chairman John Lawrence made statements that certain players who had played at Berwick would never play for Rangers again. That was true of Forrest and McLean, but in the case of Forrest certainly, it was a harsh judgment. It was a decree that might well have cost Rangers the European Cup-winners' Cup, perhaps even the championship itself.

The team proceeded to win the next nine League fixtures, playing with some style. The young Sandy Jardine made his debut one week after Berwick, against Hearts, and he and Alec Willoughby brought some swagger to the team. Willoughby scored goals – two successive hat-tricks immediately after Berwick. For a spell, Willoughby and Alec Smith, contrasted in styles, was a successful partnership, but Rangers were now without an established strike force. They were pipped by Celtic for the title, a 1-0 home defeat by Dunfermline perhaps the decisive result. The date was 1 April. The battle did go to the last day, with Celtic at Ibrox on 6 May. Nothing less than a win would keep Rangers hopes alive. Celtic wanted only a draw. A draw they got, 2-2 and with it they got another championship before 78,000 spectators. It was the first time since 1951-52 that Rangers failed to win a major trophy. The European Cup-winners' Cup Final was played at the end of May, when Rangers went down 1-0 to Bayern Munich in Nuremberg.

The calamitous Berwick Rangers match had even wider ramifications for Rangers. The Berwick goalkeeper's noble efforts in that match had made him a national figure for the first time. It was not to be the last. His name was Jock Wallace.

Jimmy Millar and Davie Wilson, fine long-serving players, both went to Dundee United before the start of 1967-68, Millar on a free transfer, Wilson in part exchange for the Swedish international Orjan Persson. Alex Ferguson came from Dunfermline Athletic for £65,000, Eric Sorensen came from Morton, and Andy Penman from Dundee.

Rangers could not have had a more difficult League Cup qualifying section, one containing Celtic, Aberdeen and Dundee United. On 16 August, the first Rangers-Celtic of the season attracted 94,168 to Ibrox. For the return at Celtic Park ten days later, 75,000 was the count. Ibrox had seen a 1-1 draw. In the decisive return, Rangers led for much of the match with an opportunistic Willie Henderson goal after only eight minutes. They withstood intense Celtic pressure, then 14 minutes from the end were awarded a penalty kick. A conversion would surely have sealed the tie, eliminated Celtic and perhaps compromised their dominance of the Scottish game. Johansen's shot thundered against the crossbar. Two minutes later Willie Wallace had equalised, and in the final seven minutes, Bobby Murdoch and Bobby Lennox made it 3-1. Rangers were out.

On 16 September, they became the first team to defeat Celtic as European Cup holders when a stunning Orjan Persson goal was seen by 90,000 at Ibrox. In a run of some 30 yards, he beat Gemmell, Murdoch, Clark and Gemmell again and from 18 yards and a very tight angle, hit an unstoppable shot past Ronnie Simpson. This result, in but the second League fixture of the season, put Rangers ahead. They stayed there until the very last day of the season, remained unbeaten until the last day. Yet on 1 November, with the team unbeaten and leading the championship, James Scotland Symon parted company with the club.

If David White, his successor, lacked the presence and the stature of what one perceived as a Rangers manager, he nevertheless took Rangers to within touching distance of the championship. With three to play, they had a one point advantage, lost when drawing 3-3 at Greenock. (They were 3-1 down with 20 minutes to play.) Rangers' final game at home to Aberdeen on 27 April, was a few days before Celtic's final game at Dunfermline. They were level on points, Celtic with a better goal-average. Rangers lost 3-2 to Aberdeen, to a last minute goal. A barren season then for David White – not one trophy to show for it. Yet Rangers' points total 61 from 34 games would have won the title in any other season but one, that of 1957-58, in the history of the Scottish League 34 game seasons.

There were no major summer signings in 1968 and again Rangers were drawn in a League Cup section with Celtic for the 1968-69 season, Partick Thistle and Morton were the others.

Davie White tried to introduce a new system of play – the withdrawn centre-forward with Andy Penman and his skill, or even Sandy Jardine in the role. It was not unsuccessful, but such are the pressures that weigh on a Rangers manager that White probably was not allowed enough time to make it bond. Again there was an early League success against Celtic, an excellent 4-2 win at Celtic Park before a capacity 75,000. It was a match that showed to its best advantage a certain flair and style and attacking mood which White had tried to foster. With Henderson and Persson on the wings and the dribbling skills of Johnston, this Rangers team could play some attractive football.

League competition this season was much more competitive, with Aberdeen, Hibernian and Dunfermline Athletic representing stiff opposition. Aberdeen won at Ibrox, for example, on 31 October. Rangers set a Scottish record transfer fee by paying £100,000 for Colin Stein of Hibernian, the first six-figure player in Scotland. Within

Willie Henderson scores Rangers' second goal against Aberdeen in the 1969 Scottish Cup semi-final at Parkhead. Rangers won 6-1 but then lost 4-0 to Celtic in the Final.

weeks Alex McDonald came from St Johnstone for a more modest £50,000 and proved to be of incalculable importance to Rangers for a decade, much more so than Stein. The latter made an immediate impact, scoring hat-tricks in successive games, eight in his first three games, 11 in his first seven. He partnered Willie Johnston, and in particular Alex Ferguson, and at times the combinations were devastating. With goals flowing, friends of Rangers began to suspect that Celtic's power might be broken, but Stein's on-field discipline left much to be desired. Sent off three times in that initial season, his absences at the climax of the championship race, and of the Scottish Cup would prove crippling to Rangers. Away defeats by Airdrie, Dundee United and Dundee in late March, early April left them second, by five points.

The Scottish Cup saw an enthralling 6-1 semi-final win over Aberdeen. featuring a Willie Johnston hat-trick. Rangers crashed to defeat and disaster in the Final, 4-0, their first Scottish Cup Final defeat in 40 years. Celtic scored in the opening minute, two more on the stroke of half-time amid dreadful defensive blunders. It was Alex Ferguson's last match. He was blamed for the first goal, headed in by Billy McNeil. Manager White said Ferguson had been detailed to cover McNeil – and was missing when the fatal corner came over

Jim Baxter came back in the summer of 1969, on a free transfer from Nottingham Forest and was hailed by the Ibrox faithful as prodigal son and messiah combined. This may have been seen as Davie White's major ploy in com-

bating Celtic's superiority, now becoming something of substantial Rangers concern. Baxter initially made something of an impact.

Drawn for the third successive season in the same League Cup qualifying section, Rangers this time did manage to defeat Celtic at Ibrox in the opening fixture by 2-1, inspired as of yore by Jim Baxter. For the return at Celtic Park, Baxter was absent, injured. A late blunder by Gerry Neef, the German goalkeeper, left Celtic's Tommy Gemmell with an open goal. Neef had been signed by White and was in the West German squad for the World Championships in Mexico, where he did not play. He is not remembered as one of the great Rangers goalkeepers.

This match was as controversial as any and had long-term repercussions for referee Jim Callaghan. Celtic's John Hughes had already been booked. Then, involved in an incident with Willie Johnston, Hughes clearly struck the Rangers player. The referee did not see it, but a linesman drew his attention to the incident. Hughes should have been sent off, but Callaghan merely lectured him and allowed him to continue. The referee was subsequently suspended for eight weeks by the SFA. Celtic won the game, the section and the League Cup for the fifth successive year.

A poor start was made in the championship and there were rumblings about the lack of discipline at Ibrox which came to a head when they were at Largs, preparing for a European match with Görnik. Baxter and Henderson both missed training one day, claiming they had overslept. In spite of this, they were selected to play when many people felt they should have been severely disciplined by the club. Defeat by Görnik, who outplayed Rangers, meant the end of manager White's career at Ibrox. Perhaps White's real misfortune was that he found himself head to head, inevitably, with the manager of the hour, Jock Stein at Celtic, who happened to be a giant at his trade, in every respect. Willie Waddell was to be the new manager – he was certainly worthy of Stein's steel. Experienced and able, he had taken Kilmarnock to a League championship. The appointment was acclaimed.

Rangers celebrated with an 11-game unbeaten run which had them challenging for the title in season 1969-70. Sadly, the end of the run came in the quarter-final of the Scottish Cup, at Celtic Park. A very tense competitive game was settled late by a long-range Davie Hay shot which goalkeeper Neef surely should have stopped. He seemed to lose the ball in flight. Rangers were reduced to ten men after an hour with the ordering off of Alex McDonald. It seemed that the Rangers man had been less than discreet in conversation with referee Tiny Wharton.

Celtic seemed on the verge of another clean sweep. They won the championship by 12 points, with Rangers second. But the Parkhead club in the end lost the two big Cup Finals, the Scottish to Aberdeen, the European to Feyenoord. Following their Cup defeat, Rangers season petered out. For the first time since 1926 they lost three successive League matches at Kirkcaldy, Dunfermline and Dundee, each time by 2-1. As new manager Waddell sought to revamp both the playing and coaching staffs, Rangers were in transition. There was a substantial clearance of staff by the end of the season, including the going of Jim Baxter, a classic illustration of the footballer who spurned the footballer's greatest asset, the fitness and conditioning of his body. Jim Baxter's career was over.

Willie Waddell made many changes at Ibrox in the summer of 1970. Davie Kinnear, who had been at Ibrox for 26 years, Harold Davis and Laurie Smith of the backroom staff went, and in came physiotherapist Tom Craig, assistant coach Stan Anderson and most important of all, Jock Wallace from Hearts as coach, the same Wallace who had been the Berwick Rangers player-manager in the infamous Cup-tie at Berwick in 1967.

Under the Waddell-Wallace direction young players were introduced such as Alfie Conn, Derek Johnstone, Graham Fyfe, Ian MacDonald. Others, already with the club but still young – Sandy Jardine, Alex McDonald – were given their heads. Improvement was expected, but the truth was Rangers never really challenged for the League title in the 1970-71 season. Perhaps they lacked the maturity to carry a threat through the entire season. Under Wallace, they were very fit. They trained hard, almost commando-style on the Gullane sand dunes, creating a major media stir.

The playing style was fast, hard-running attacking and Rangers fans enjoyed the fact that at the very least, this team was giving 100 per cent each time it played. The trophy famine ended rather unexpectedly when they won the League Cup. In the Final Celtic were clear favourites – after all, they had won five successive League Cups, five successive League championships, and were at the time ahead of Rangers in the title race. Rangers captain John Greig had flu and the team reshuffle saw the introduction of Derek Johnstone, aged 16. He had made his debut a few weeks earlier, scoring twice against Cowdenbeath in a League match. If his selection was a gamble, it paid off perfectly when he headed the only goal of the game, five minutes before half-time. It was Rangers' first trophy in four years, the first of the Waddell-Wallace era.

Rangers eventually finished fourth in the championship, 15 points behind Celtic who won their sixth successive championship in a row with Aberdeen and St Johnstone if you please between them and Rangers

Wins over Aberdeen and Hibernian graced the road to the Scottish Cup Final and the inevitable and familiar opposition, Celtic. Rangers were compromised by the absence of Sandy Jardine, Dave Smith, Alfie Conn and in the replay Alex Miller, all through injury. Indeed the replay saw reserve player Jim Denny make his first-team debut, the first time a Rangers player had made his debut for the club in a Cup Final since 1909, when Willie Reid did it. Denny's career at Ibrox was not quite as successful as that of Reid, who was a prolific goalscorer.

In the first match, drawn 1-1. Rangers were rescued by another Derek Johnstone goal, this one three minutes from the end. But chances galore had been squandered, none worse than that by Willie Johnston. Presented with an open goal, the goalkeeper stranded, he needed only to tap the ball over the line from a few yards range. Instead, he let the ball squirm under his left foot in what may very well have been the most dreadful miss in the entire recorded history of the game. Celtic commanded the replay, and won more convincingly than the 2-1 result would suggest.

Tommy McLean, bought from Kilmarnock for £65,000, proved to be one of the greatest of all Rangers signings They made an abysmal start to the 1971-72 season, losing three times to Celtic at Ibrox. Indeed they lost four of the five opening League games and were then second from bottom of the League. The first Celtic game at Ibrox was really a home game for the Parkhead men – Celtic Park was under reconstruction. Rangers were beaten 2-0 by two late goals, one of which, the second, was a penalty scored by a young man by name Kenny Dalglish. Celtic were the better team in both League Cup matches, but in the third game, in the League, Rangers came close to winning. After leading 2-1, they lost to a late Jimmy Johnstone goal. At 2-2, Rangers had a Colin Stein goal chalked off. Referee John Paterson of Bothwell later admitted he had been in error. Stein had reached a through ball before goalkeeper Williams and flicked to score over his head. From a good distance back, the referee disallowed the goal for – dangerous play, for Stein lifting his foot. When Paterson saw the television tape, he admitted that Stein was a good five yards short of Williams.

Rangers recovered from one of their worst-ever starts by winning five games and recovering some confidence. As in the previous season, they were never quite consistent enough to pose a challenge for the title. By the end of October, they trailed Aberdeen by seven points, Celtic by six. In the New Year game at Celtic Park, they were cruelly beaten 2-1 by a last minute goal and thus had lost four out of five to Celtic that season.

On 22 January, Rangers produced their finest domestic performance of the season with a 6-0 win over Hearts at Ibrox. All of the goals came in the second half. Derek Johnstone had a hat-trick and five of the goals were laid on by Tommy McLean. More and more as the season progressed, and as each round was passed, Rangers became obsessed with success in the European Cup-winners' Cup and the championship became secondary for them. There was much experimenting with selections and tactics. Thus Rangers finished fourth, a distant 16 points behind Celtic which at the time was a record margin.

In the Scottish Cup, Falkirk and St Mirren were early victims, after forcing an Ibrox replay. Next against

A delighted Jock Wallace greets Alex McDonald after Rangers' 3-2 triumph over Celtic in the 1973 Scottish Cup Final. A crowd of 122,714 saw the game.

Motherwell, Rangers were seven minutes from extinction when Stein forced another Ibrox replay. At the semi-final stage, another replay was needed before Rangers were dumped by a very worthy Hibernian team. They in turn were demolished 6-1 in the Final by a Celtic team giving its finest exhibition since their European Cup win in Lisbon.

Dave Smith was named as Player of the Year in Scotland. Playing as a sweeper, his conversion from mid-field was Waddell's doing just as the manager, equally successfully, had moved Sandy Jardine to full-back from being a front man. Willie Waddell was obviously a man who could see qualities in players that others missed. Similarly he moved Derek Johnstone with outstanding success to centre-half, if only for a couple of seasons. His form in an otherwise barren season helped Rangers to triumph in Barcelona with their European Cup-winners' Cup win.

In the summer of 1972, Willie Waddell moved 'upstairs' to become general manager of Rangers and Jock Wallace became team manager. In true Rangers fashion, these changes were never explained. Waddell had coped with the anguish of the Ibrox Disaster of January 1971 and its aftermath. He had worked hard to resolve the suspension of Rangers – initially for two years – from European competition after the crowd invasions in the European Cup-winners' Final at Barcelona, and he had the suspension reduced to one year. He was now in his 50s, and probably saw that conducting training sessions with the players on a day-to-day basis required a younger man. More than anything else, he may have concluded that his life work would

not be the reconstruction of the once vast, rambling Ibrox Stadium.

He had dented, if not broken, the dominance of Celtic, if not in the championship then certainly in the League Cup, and with European success. He had brought order and discipline to the club. He had forged strong links with supporters' clubs. All told he was probably the most powerful figure at Ibrox through to the mid-1980s.

The Wallace era did not have a sparkling start. Rangers had only five points from the six opening League matches in season 1972-73. The League Cup campaign was notable more for two home defeats by Second Division clubs St Mirren and Stenhousemuir in successive rounds than for any Rangers triumphs. They did get through to the semi-final where their makeshift team lost narrowly to Hibernian, who went on to win the Cup.

Jock Wallace re-shaped the side very much in his own image. Two of the stalwarts of Barcelona were sold to the English Midlands, Colin Stein to Coventry City, Willie Johnston to West Bromwich Albion. Quinton Young arrived from Coventry in part exchange for Stein, Joe Mason came from Morton and Tom Forsyth from Motherwell. Forsyth became a defensive mainstay for the next ten years. Wallace made profits from all his deals and defended the sale of Stein and Johnston by saying they were prima donnas. He wanted a team, not a collection of stars.

Over the balance of the season, Rangers lost only two of 38 games, one being the League Cup semi-final with Hibs, the other a home League match with Hearts on 2 December. From that defeat until the end of the season, they played 26 domestic fixtures without defeat. In 20 League game, 18 were won, two drawn – 38 points from 40, which left them as close as could be, one point, behind Celtic, champions for the eighth consecutive season. Success did come, in the Scottish Cup. Dundee United and Hibernian were overcome, 64,000 watching the first Hibs match at Ibrox, and even more remarkably, almost 50,000 packing into Hibs' Easter Road ground. Twenty years on, it would accommodate scarcely 20 per cent of that figure.

The Final against Celtic was memorable, attended by royalty for the first time in the person of Princess Alexandra and 122,714 others. A splendidly entertaining game was won 3-2 by a goal, his first for the club, from one Tom Forsyth, with the sole of his boot. At that time, Forsyth had not played in a losing Rangers team. His goal followed a McLean free-kick which left him in possession inches from the goal line. It was Rangers' first Scottish Cup win since 1966 and the last played before a six-figure crowd.

John Lawrence retired as chairman before the start of the 1973-74 season, and was appointed honorary president. He was succeeded by his vice-chairman Matt Taylor, and his grandson Lawrence Marlborough was appointed to the board. In time, Marlborough would play a significant role in the renaissance of the club.

At the start of the season, Rangers played Arsenal in a centenary celebration match. Rangers made an exceptional gesture, generating a full house by lowering the admission prices extremely. These ranged from 5p to 20p and attracted 71,000 spectators. Arsenal rather spoiled things by winning 2-1 with two very late goals. The championship start was quite dreadful, seven points dropped in the first four home fixtures without a single-goal scored. They ended this shambles by crushing Hibernian 4-0, but it left Rangers always chasing the game – they eventually finished third in the League, five points behind Celtic.

In the League Cup for the fifth time in seven years, Rangers were paired with Celtic at the sectional stage and for the first time in these five occasions, Rangers finished ahead of Celtic in the group, thanks to a 3-1 win at Celtic Park. Rather ironically, for this season the rules had been changed to permit first and second in each group to go through. Celtic went through, the clubs met in the semi-final and Celtic won 3-1 at Hampden thanks to a Harry Hood hat-trick.

The year of 1974 is remembered as the year of a miners' strike, a 3-day week and two general elections and because of the national crisis all this invoked, floodlighting was banned for a time. Clubs had to play in midweek and crowds plummeted. This led to Sundays being used for domestic fixtures and Rangers' first such Sunday game was on 17 February 1974 when a huge crowd, 64,672, saw a Scottish Cup-tie against a very fine Dundee team featuring Jocky Scott, John Duncan, Ian Phillip, which won handily, 3-0. The following Sunday, in the League, it was Dundee United, and a crowd of 15,500. In one week, Rangers seemed to have misplaced 50,000 people, carelessness indeed.

The rest of Rangers season was concentrated on qualifying for European competition, involving a close fight with Hibernian, which the Edinburgh club won. There would be no European matches at Ibrox in season 1974-75.

This was the last season of the old-style, 18 clubs 34 matches Scottish First Division. For season 1975-76 and henceforth, a new 'Premier' Division of the top ten clubs playing each other four times was established. One of the main reasons for the change came paradoxically from the success of Celtic, who had won the championship in the previous nine seasons, and the thought that this had led to a drop in general interest in the game. Certainly attendances were down. It was also claimed that a division of ten clubs, playing each other four times would create such competition that never again would any club repeat Celtic's achievement.

In July, Alfie Conn had been sold to Tottenham Hotspur for £140,000. Jock Wallace, going into his third season as manager had been gradually putting together a young fit team, without expensive purchases. In the transfer market, he remained in profit. Wallace had built, while others had sought to buy, a team that was about to come good. Many Wallace players had long careers, and many went on to have successful management and coaching success. Long servers included Sandy Jardine, Tommy McLean, Alex MacDonald, John Greig (his career was extended) and Colin Jackson.

At the start of the season Rangers were invited by Barcelona to take part in the 'Juan Camper' tournament. They beat Athletic Bilbao 1-0 with a Sandy Jardine goal, then went down 4-1 in the Final to a Barcelona team of Cruyff, Neeskens and company, a quite brilliant team which had won the Spanish championship the previous season. On their return to Barcelona, Rangers were fine ambassadors and repaired some of the damage that had been done in their European Final of 1972

A 2-1 victory at Celtic Park in the third game of the season was highly significant. Rangers came from behind, after trailing at half-time to a Kenny Dalglish goal. Ian MacDougall and Colin Jackson scored to persuade Wallace's team that they could enter this lion's den and emerge unscathed and victorious. And this match may just have dented Celtic's superiority complex built up over a decade. Rangers then had a long successful run, during which they played some enthralling football. Six goal victories were recorded at Kilmarnock and Dunfermline, the latter match producing five goals for Derek Parlane, the first time a Rangers player had scored five since Jim Forrest in 1966.

The first championship defeat came in the 13th match, when Hibernian won 1-0 at Ibrox. They were a Rangers bogey that season. They had already eliminated them from the League Cup section winning home and away. At the turn of the year, Rangers were two points behind Celtic. The traditional match would be important, and it was – Rangers swept to a 3-0 win to top the table on goal-difference. With both League games against Celtic won, Rangers truly believe that they could put an end to Celtic, particularly as, while in the next fixture Rangers were winning 5-1 at Dumbarton with a Tommy McLean hat-trick, Celtic were losing at home to Motherwell. Advantage Rangers, and the Ibrox club did not lose another match until the title was truly won.

In March, Colin Stein was back from Coventry City, for no other reason that the Midlands club could not keep up payments on his transfer. He bolstered Rangers' firepower for another season, although he had a dramatic start to his second Ibrox career, in only his second match. He was ordered off at Dens Park for 'foul and abusive language' to the referee. The decisive championship match came on 29 March. With Celtic faltering, close to collapse, Rangers needed one point at Easter Road to claim the title for the first time in 11 years. The attendance of 38,585 illustrated the hunger of Rangers fans for the title. It was reckoned that more than 30,000 were Rangers fans. The highway between the cities was stalled with cars and coaches. Train passengers queued for more than an hour at Glasgow's Queen Street station before packing every Edinburgh train. Colin Stein scored in the 1-1 draw which brought the first League championship since 1964, Rangers 35th overall, and at last they had ended Celtic's nine years of supremacy. The title was won by seven points from Hibernian, eleven from Celtic. Only three League games were lost all season, oddly including those of Airdrie, home and away.

Perhaps one player who contributed more than any other to the championship win was goalkeeper Stewart Kennedy, an unsung hero who had been signed from Stenhousemuir for the grand sum of £10,000. His displays this season were of such quality that older Rangers fans compared him with the great Jerry Dawson. He was capped against Wales, Northern Ireland and sadly, England at Wembley. He was blamed unfairly for a 5-1 defeat and was never quite the same afterwards.

At the end of the season Rangers set off on an unlikely tour of Norway, Canada and for the first time Australia and New Zealand. Nine matches were played, two of them lost.

Rangers went into the history books as the first Premier Division champions. They also gave manager Jock Wallace his first treble with a team that was maturing nicely and seemed well equipped in every sector. In goal Peter McCloy and Stewart Kennedy shared the 1975-76 season. At the heart of the defence was the powerful partnership of Colin Jackson and Tom Forsyth. At full-back were Sandy Jardine, young, quick, elegant, accurate, a precise tackler; Alex Miller, steadfast, reliable, a man for all positions, and John Greig, now ripe in football years but as resolute as ever. Iain MacDougall and Alex Macdonald were a powerful midfield. Bobby McKean, Tommy McLean and Quinton Young shared skills and pace on the wing and the strike force of the two Dereks, Parlane and Johnstone, was formidable indeed. Johnstone had 31 goals in all competitive matches.

Rangers won their first Premier Division fixture, against Celtic at Ibrox, coming from behind. The attendance of 69,594 remains a Premier Division record. Steady progress was made through the season. There was some uncertainty in October and November. Successive games were lost at Ayr and Motherwell, Hearts won at Ibrox, then away games were lost at Hibernian and Aberdeen. But from 6 December to the end of the season, Rangers did not lose another League game – 21 successive League matches. Throw in the Scottish Cup and it meant 26 unbeaten.

The League Cup Final, another Old Firm affair, was won by a flying Alex Macdonald header midway through the second half. This win followed a rather disappointing European Cup loss to St Etienne. It was nip and tuck with Celtic, who had a three point lead at New Year, but in the big game a Derek Johnstone goal saw Celtic off at Ibrox, 1-0, narrowing the gap. The title was won at Tannadice on the third last game, a goal from Johnstone yet again – this time in just 22 seconds, beating Dundee United, what time Celtic struggled at home to Ayr United. Rangers were champions by six points. A week later, the third treble was clinched with a 3-1 win over Hearts in the Scottish Cup Final.

The opening goal by Derek Johnstone arrived in 45 seconds – in successive weeks he had scored decisive goals in the first minute, each time in a trophy-deciding match. John Greig was named as Player of the Year, and had had an inspirational season. And Alex MacDonald had yet again been a dynamic in the team. His ability to run on the blind

side of defences, particularly to Tommy McLean crosses created many chances and produced many goals for Rangers.

Rangers presented a well-attended pre-season tournament at Ibrox 1976 in which Southampton, FA Cup holders at the time, rather spurned their hospitality by beating the host team 2-1 in the Final. There was an early and impressive win at Celtic Park in a delayed Glasgow Cup Final, but at the same venue in the opening League match, a Rangers half-time lead of 2-0 was squandered as Celtic fought back to 2-2. Thereafter, strangely, Rangers never quite seemed to be the same confident team. Indeed it was to be a team which went to the extreme, from the triumphs of 1975-76 to winning precisely nothing. The League programme opened with four drawn games in the first five, eight points from the first eight fixtures. From then on, it was always a struggle to a finish of nine points behind Celtic. All this was quite mystifying to Rangers fans. Certainly there were injury problems, but this season became a break between two lavish courses, two treble-winning successes. It was difficult to know how a team could fall away so badly between summits. Perhaps it can only be dismissed with "football's a funny game". In the same way, an outstanding second half of 1972-73, a long unbeaten run that led almost to League and Scottish Cup success, was followed by a disappointing 1973-74.

In the League Cup, qualifying was straightforward, then at the quarter-final stage, facing First Division Clydebank, a club founded only 11 years earlier, Rangers were given a torrid time which extended over four games before they won. Clydebank were inspired by a young winger, Davie Cooper, who scored in three of the four ties needed. In the next round, the semi-final, Rangers were comprehensively routed 5-1 at Hampden by Aberdeen, then managed by Ally McLeod. They beat Celtic 2-1 in the Final.

There was still the Scottish Cup to be defended and with it the chance to salvage something from the season. FC Zürich had ended the European quest. A routine progression to the Final brought the Old Firm face to face again, in probably the poorest Final between the clubs, ever. Heavy rain, live television (the first for 22 years), reduced the attendance to 54,252, a drop of 68,463 from the similar Final four years earlier. The match was decided by a disputed penalty decision awarded for handball against Derek Johnstone by referee Bob Valentine of Dundee, converted by Andy Lynch.

In the summer of 1977, Rangers signed Davie Cooper from Clydebank for £100,000 and Gordon Smith from Kilmarnock for £65,000, at the start of the 1977-78 season. Cooper's arrival was anticipated. He had rejected approaches from major English clubs. Smith was a surprise. He played the same position as Cooper and Rangers had other wingers in Tommy McLean, Bobby McKean, and even young Bill Mackay coming through, but again it demonstrated the ability of Willie Waddell, or Jock Wallace, to spot potential. Smith was never played as a winger. He was a secondary striker, playing off the target man, and successfully – he scored 20 League goals, six League Cup and one European goal for a tally of 27.

These proven, expensive players strengthened the squad. A bonus was the arrival of Robert Russell from Shettleston Juniors in the close season. Played immediately in the team's midfield, he brought craft and skill that had been missing in the previous season. His style was reminiscent of that of the late John White, of Tottenham Hotspur and Scotland, ghosting into free positions, playing the simple

Celebrations are in full swing after Rangers' 3-1 win over Hearts in the 1976 Scottish Cup Final. By now the Hampden crowd had been reduced and 'only' 85,354 saw this latest Rangers success.

ball out of defence, unerring in his passing. There three were skilful players, as were the men in situ – Tommy McLean, and Derek Johnstone and with a steely defence in Greig, Jackson and Forsyth, the balance was close to perfect. It took them some time to bond. In early games, Rangers lost 3-1 at Aberdeen and 2-0 at home to Hibernian. Towards the end of the Hibs game, there were chants from the crowd for the head of Jock Wallace! One week later, Rangers beat Partick Thistle 4-0 at Firhill.

In the opening Old Firm game, at Ibrox on 10 September, Rangers trailed 2-0 down at half-time to two goals by Johannes Edvaldssen, Celtic's Iceland international. Wallace switched the team around at half-time, bringing Greig into defence, moving Johnstone up front and the team was transformed. Celtic were totally outplayed by 45 minutes of quite brilliant attacking football, and a 3-2 scoreline. Rangers lost only one of the next 23 games. By the end of February, they were six points ahead of rivals Aberdeen. Celtic's start had been even worse in the League, they once lost five successive games and were only just above the relegation zone. They eventually finished fifth, 19 points behind Rangers in Jock Stein's last season at Celtic Park.

In March, Aberdeen came to Ibrox and won 3-0 with a very convincing display. Rangers dropped seven points in seven games, and with just three remaining, they led Aberdeen by just one point. But they won difficult fixtures, Dundee United home and away and clinched things with a home win over Motherwell.

The League Cup had been won in yet another Final with Celtic, 2-1 after extra-time, goals by Gordon Smith and Davie Cooper. When Aberdeen were beaten 2-1 in the Scottish Cup Final, Rangers had won their second treble in three years, their fourth overall. In this match, the Rangers performance was impressive, but their outstanding performance of the season had been in the League Cup against Aberdeen, back in October, a 6-1 win at Ibrox. The new team had really found its rhythm. Gordon Smith had three goals in a display orchestrated by Robert Russell. Aberdeen manager Billy McNeil said that in all his time in football, it was the finest display he had seen from any Rangers team.

Jock Wallace, with two trebles in three years, was at the peak of his powers and success in football management. Quite sensationally, on 23 May, he resigned. His decision rocked the club. He moved to Leicester City, then in the English Second Division, He never did reveal his reasons for leaving. Perhaps it was simply a clash of personalities between himself and general manager Willie Waddell – two very strong-willed men. At the time it was suspected that Waddell had vetoed a number of transfers, Andy Gray from Dundee United and Alan Hansen from Partick Thistle among them. David Narey and goalkeeper Jim Stewart were others. Waddell of course was always Rangers spokesman, their public figure doing all the public business. Wallace never did. The board decided on a successor immediately, as they had done when Scot Symon left the club. He was to be John Greig their captain with a lifetime at Ibrox behind him, but without the slightest managerial experience. He was the first Rangers player in more than half a century to be awarded a 'benefit' match. The last one was the famous Davie Meiklejohn, back in the 1920s. The match was Rangers v a Scotland XI. Rangers won 5-0, exposing some shortcomings in the national side all too evident two months later in the World Championships in Argentina.

A continuation of success was the requirement from Greig. Going straight from dressing room to manager's office has seldom worked in football. Rangers might have done better going for the young Alex Ferguson who had success with East Stirlingshire and St Mirren. Five years later he was approached – too late.

Season 1978-79, John Greig's first as manager, almost brought a repeat of the treble. Both the Cups were won, the League was lost very narrowly and the quarter-final round of the European Cup was reached. His first drama was a transfer request from Derek Johnstone – leading goalscorer of the previous season with 38 goals in all. Greig persuaded him to withdraw it. Greig did little to strengthen what was of course a formidable playing staff, but the League programme got off to an abysmal start. After their opening six games, Rangers were without a single win. This did little to suggest they could retain their title although in the end they certainly should have. It all boiled down to a game at Celtic Park on 21 May. Rangers led 1-0 at half-time and Celtic's Johnny Doyle was ordered off early in the second half, but John Greig's ultra-defensive tactics, in vogue for much of the season, allowed Celtic's ten men, spurred on by their captain Roy Aitken, to take control of the game. They won 4-2. Greig had brought to Rangers play a tactical awareness, a sharper perception of the opposition which perhaps had been lacking in Wallace's time, despite his success. Wallace had believed in letting the opposition worry about Rangers. Greig on the other hand perhaps worried too much about the opposition and the dangers it would pose.

The League Cup was won 2-1 against Aberdeen with late goals from Alex McDonald and Colin Jackson after a hugely dramatic semi-final against Celtic. Tommy Burns of Celtic and Alex Miller of Rangers were sent off. An own goal by Celtic substitute Jim Casey deep into extra-time gave it to Rangers, 3-2. Celtic thus missed a place in the League Cup Final for the first time since 1963-64, an astonishing run over 14 years.

The Scottish Cup required nine games for its retention. The Final itself against Hibernian took three games, the first two as tedious as could be imagined, goalless draws without any redeeming points. The third match was much more entertaining, five goals, cut and thrust, extra-time. Alex Miller, Rangers' penalty-kicker, missed one, the fifth Rangers player to miss a Scottish Cup Final penalty. An own-goal deep into extra-time by Arthur Duncan, the Hibs winger, gave Rangers the win 3-2. Thus Greig in consecutive years had captained, then managed Scottish Cup winning teams. His tactical nous took Rangers to the quarter-final round of the European Cup, where they had disposed of Juventus and PSV Eindhoven before going down to 1FC Cologne.

The second season of John Greig's stewardship, 1979-80, was once described as a 'calamitous abomination' of a season. Oddly, it started quite successfully, in the Dryburgh Cup, and Rangers' only win in this sponsored tournament, held for several years in the 1970s, at the start of each season. It was notable not only for the defeat of Celtic in the

Final, 3-1, although that is worthy of note, not to say rejoicing, among all Rangers fans, but the goals scored that day at Hampden were of the highest quality, some of the finest ever seen at the old stadium. For the second, Sandy Jardine ran from penalty area to penalty area, beating several Celtic players en route before shooting home. But the third goal was a classic in which the late Davie Cooper beat four Celtic players in sequence by flicking the ball over their heads, never allowing the ball to touch the ground, before stroking it past the goalkeeper. In its quality, imagination, originality, the goal was breathtaking.

But Rangers fans should have been forewarned by the first Old Firm match of the season, in August. Rangers led a ten-man Celtic team 2-0, late in the game. Roy Aitken had been sent off. Rangers allowed their concentration to lapse and Celtic, inspired by Danny McGrain, saved the match in the last six minutes with goals from Sneddon and Macadam. Rangers never looked like winning anything after that match which incidentally marked the opening of the new Copland Road Stand.

League form was so appalling that the final points total of 37 from 36 games was the worst in the club's history. The away form was shameful by Rangers' standards and expectations. Of 18 matches, 12 were lost, only four won. The fifth place finish, 11 points behind champions Aberdeen, was the lowest in 15 years. The League Cup had been changed to a home and away tie system in a knock-out competition. Aberdeen beat Rangers comfortably in both games, beat Celtic in the next round, then lost to Dundee United in the Final, a first title for the Tannadice club. Rangers had their day in the semi-final of the Scottish Cup, beating Aberdeen 1-0 at Celtic Park. In another Old Firm Final, both sides produced a splendid match of brisk attacking play and solid defence.

The match was won after 107 minutes when a deflected goal by George McCluskey took the Cup to Parkhead and deprived Rangers of their last chance for European competition the following season. Disturbing crowd scenes at the end of the game eventually brought legislation which had profound effects on the Scottish game.

Colin MacAdam was recruited from Partick Thistle for £165,000; Jim Bett from Lokeren for £180,000 and Willie Johnston was back from Vancouver Whitecaps for a fee of £40,000. Macadam was the last Rangers player in living memory to come from Partick Thistle, interesting in itself and he was the first player to move under freedom of contract, his transfer fee decided by an independent tribunal. Thistle wanted £500,000, Rangers thought him worth £80,000, the tribunal compromised. Bett proved to be a quality midfield player for Rangers, and many times for Scotland.

For once under Greig, Rangers got off to a fine start in 1980-81, 15 matches unbeaten, wins home and away over Celtic. The win at Parkhead on 23 August was their first there in the Premier Division. Their home win, 3-0 in November, probably flattered somewhat, but they were playing some lively football, nowhere more than at Kilmarnock in September when they set a Premier Division away record of 8-1, including a John MacDonald hat-trick.

As in the previous season, Rangers were dumped from the League Cup by Aberdeen, this time because of two quite ludicrous penalty awards. They had won 1-0 in the first game at Ibrox, thanks to a Colin MacAdam goal in the very first minute. In the away match, Aberdeen were awarded a penalty when Sandy Jardine, defending himself, fended off with his arm a ball that was blasted straight at his face, and

John McDonald signals his delight as one of his two goals for Rangers in the 1981 Scottish Cup Final leaves the Dundee United defence in tatters.

in the very last minute another following a Colin Jackson foul which was later shown to be clearly outside the penalty area. Gordon Strachan dispatched both penalty kicks.

If all that was unfortunate, defeat in the Anglo-Scottish Cup was ignominious, to say the least. Rangers took part because they had no European football to offer their customers. They were clear favourites to win this Cup. Four teams from each country took part, but not one English First Division club entered. Rangers found themselves playing against Chesterfield – and losing. After a drab 1-1 draw at Ibrox, Rangers were outplayed at Chesterfield's Recreation Ground.

Rangers seemed slightly derailed. A 1-0 defeat at home by Morton ended their unbeaten run. In late November-early December, they took only three points from five matches and the League challenge thereafter was never serious. The Scottish Cup seemed all that was left. International goalkeeper Jim Stewart was signed in mid-March from Middlesbrough for £115,000. Rangers were over-run by Dundee United 4-1 at Ibrox, showing a positive gulf between the teams. Gregor Stevens, just back from suspension – he had been ordered off six weeks earlier against the same opponents – was again ordered off.

In the Scottish Cup, Rangers opened with a very commendable 5-0 win at Airdrie, never an easy venue for them and with the Lanarkshire club enjoying one of their more successful teams. At Perth in the next round, Rangers were cruising 2-0 in front of St Johnstone, deemed the match won, and indulging themselves, suddenly found the home

team 3-2 ahead. Only a goal in injury time from Ian Redford saved them from elimination. The replay at Ibrox was won more handily, 3-1 with the visiting goal scored by one Alistair McCoist.

There was a tempestuous semi-final. Two Morton men, Holmes and Thomson, were ordered off for scything tackles. Rangers won 2-1. For the Final against Dundee United, who started favourites, manager Greig opted for defensive, holding tactics. There were no places for Derek Johnstone's skills, Davie Cooper and John MacDonald were on the bench. United dominated for 80 minutes. Then in an instant the match was transformed. Cooper and MacDonald came on for Johnston and MacAdam. In the final minute, Ian Redford's penalty shot was stopped by the legs of Hamish McAlpine and they went into extra-time, and a 0-0 draw. That penalty miss was therapeutic. Greig went on the attack in the replay. Cooper MacDonald and Johnstone were starters and Rangers out-played United by 4-1, Cooper in particular giving a vintage display.

His goal after ten minutes established the mood of the team, and had many spectators deciding that Davie Cooper, on this form, was the best player in the whole of Britain. Yet never in John Greig's reign did Cooper have a regular place in the team. They were very different personalities – Greig all blood and guts and teeth gritting, Cooper, serene inside his vast talent, laid back and dilettante.

Once again under John Greig in 1981-82, Rangers fell short of mounting a true League championship challenge. Somehow there did not seem to be the depth of squad or quality of player needed to make a serious bid for the title. New signings John McClelland from Mansfield Town (£90,000) and Robert Prytz from Malmö (£100,000) were first-class players, but Craig Paterson and Gregor Stevens for example, other Greig signings, proved disappointing. In August 1981, they almost signed Alistair McCoist. He came two years later at half the fee they had proposed in 1981. For the second successive season, Rangers finished third, again 12 points behind Celtic.

As so often, they found the League Cup more to their liking. Against Dundee United yet again in the Final, they trailed to a Ralph Milne goal. A stunning free-kick score from Davie Cooper, 15 minutes from the end, then a chip from the edge of the penalty area by Ian Redford, with two minutes left, ended United's hopes of making it three Cup wins in a row.

The season marked the completion of Ibrox redevelopment with the opening of the Govan Stand in September 1981. It was celebrated in December with a match against Liverpool, won 2-0 by the visitors. Undersoil heating was installed that summer, and when the winter of 1981-82 was particularly severe, paid for itself quickly – Ibrox did not miss a match. The Liverpool match had attracted 40,000 despite the weather. A reasonable, if temporary, title challenge emerged around the turn of the year, partly because Rangers were able to play without weather interruption. The New Year game against Celtic was won, 1-0 at Ibrox. They did get within touching distance of Celtic without quite being able to strike out for the top. The end of the road came on 13 March with Aberdeen's 3-1 win at Ibrox. Had Rangers won and Celtic lost at Paisley on that same day, Rangers' challenge would have been alive, but that defeat ended it.

One sad note was the enforced retirement of Tom Forsyth because of an injury picked up the previous November. Forsyth had captained the team, played many times for Scotland and was a very popular Rangers servant, playing 324 games for the club.

The defence of the Scottish Cup was not the most enthralling of campaigns. Benevolent draws took Rangers to the Final fairly easily – home matches against Albion Rovers, Dumbarton and Dundee brought an abysmal display against Forfar Athletic which somehow ended in a goalless draw. The replay was won easily, but the attendances of 15,878, then 11,864 illustrated how enchanted the Hampden public was with this affair.

The Final brought the most powerful opposition, Celtic included, that Rangers could have – an Aberdeen team which was coming to full maturity under manager Alex Ferguson. After a League championship win two years earlier, they had finished this time in second place, two points behind Celtic. For the Final, through injury or suspension, Rangers were without Derek Johnstone, Ian Redford, Tom Forsyth, Gregor Stevens. During the match, they lost Sandy Jardine and Alex Miller, severe handicaps indeed. They led through John MacDonald in 15 minutes, a goal equalised spectacularly by Alex McLeish. For the 90 minutes of regulation play, Rangers probably had marginally the better of things. But in extra-time, the strain was too much for what suddenly seemed an ageing Rangers, and Aberdeen ran out deserved 4-1 winners. Rangers played out time with ten men.

Colin Jackson and Sandy Jardine were given testimonials. The two Tommys, McLean and Forsyth, were given free transfers (Jardine had five more years with Hearts, including-another Scottish Cup Final appearance). The final

break-up of the treble winning teams of the mid-1970s was at hand.

Despite reaching both Cup Finals in 1982-83, this was a season of total failure for Rangers. They lost both Finals, to Celtic in the League Cup, to Aberdeen in the Scottish Cup. And in the championship, they only just contrived better than a point a match with 38 from 36 games and a wholly unsatisfactory fourth position. They were an all-time record 18 points behind the champions, Dundee United and their total of 52 goals scored was 38 fewer than United's tally.

Yet at the start of the season, there were no indications that things would become quite so bad. There were expensive new arrivals in Craig Paterson, signed from Hibernian for a club record £225,000, Don McKinnon from Partick Thistle and Robert Prytz from Malmö. Younger players like Dave McPherson and Andy Kennedy were brought into the team.

The early season form was quite successful, if not entirely impressive. An unbeaten run of 20 successive matches in League, League Cup and UEFA Cup, including a splendid 2-0 win over Borussia Dortmund, came to an end in late October. Within a few days – October 30 to November 3 – Rangers were beaten, 3-2 at Parkhead by Celtic in the League, then swept aside 5-0 in Cologne. The League Cup qualifying section, including Hibernian, Clyde and Airdrie was won without losing a match, Kilmarnock and Hearts being clipped before another Final against Celtic. In rather depressing rain, Celtic dominated the first half and scored through Charlie Nicholas and Murdo MacLeod. A goal in the first minute of the second half by Jim Bett kept Rangers in the match with some kind of chance, but their battle to the end was unavailing. This result in early December, following the defeats at Ibrox and Cologne, seemed to knock the stuffing out of the team. With 15 matches played, they were already ten points behind the leaders, Celtic, who had 27.

Manager John Greig sought support for his team. An approach was made to Partick Thistle for their goalkeeper Alan Rough,who went to Hibs for a fee of £60,000. Gordon Smith was brought back from Brighton 'on loan' for the League Cup Final. Sandy Clark, a far-travelled striker was brought in from West Ham, but there was no dramatic improvement in League form. The Scottish Cup, for no apparent reason, was different.

Rangers seemed to potter through the rounds against Falkirk, Forfar Athletic, Queen's Park, then made heavy weather of St Mirren in a twice-played semi-final. Indeed in the replay referee Brian McGinley awarded a winning goal only 90 seconds from the end of extra-time. St Mirren were not best pleased. The Final also went to extra-time, when an Eric Black goal after 116 minutes gave Aberdeen the Cup. Rangers probably played well enough to win, but again their absence of fire power was evident. Aberdeen, ten days earlier, had won the Cup-winners' Cup in Gothenburg against Real Madrid.

An end-of-season signing, however, may have pointed the way to improvement in the Ibrox strike rate. The new boy was Alistair McCoist, from Sunderland, price £185,000.

Season 1983-84 was another eventful, not to say traumatic one in the old club's history. Rangers did win the League Cup, but made no impression on either the championship or the Scottish Cup, and the events on the field were to cause a major upheaval off it. For Rangers, the championship has always been the Holy Grail, but it was now seven years since it rested at Ibrox.

In the opening matches, Rangers failed to beat St Mirren

The joy of winning! Rangers players show their delight after lifting the League Cup in March 1984 by beating arch-rivals Celtic 3-2 after extra-time. Ally McCoist scored a hat-trick, one of his goal coming from the penalty-spot.

at Ibrox, then lost away matches at Celtic Park, Tynecastle and to Dundee. Home defeats by Aberdeen, then Motherwell on 22 October, brought sustained demonstrations against the club management. Six days later, manager John Greig resigned, saying "I am finished with football". For John, time was the great healer – half a dozen years later he was back at Ibrox as Press Attache. But his failure to win, above all, the League championship during his five years term was clearly his undoing. Alex Ferguson, a Goven man, former player and now a successful Aberdeen manager, was approached. He turned down Rangers and promptly signed a new five-year contract with Aberdeen. Jim McLean of Dundee United was approached. He also rejected Rangers.

His brother Tommy had been appointed assistant manager. Three more games were lost before the directors persuaded Jock Wallace, on 10 November, to leave Motherwell for a second spell at Ibrox. Wallace transformed the club. Morale was bolstered, fitness sharpened. There were staff changes. Tommy McLean, Joe Mason, Davie Proven left. Alec Totten was appointed first-team coach. During the season, striker Bobby Williamson came from Clydebank for £100,000. Goalkeeper Nicky Walker came from Motherwell with Kenny Black and Kenny Lyall going to Fir Park and Stuart Munro came from Alloa.

Wallace's first match in charge was a 3-0 defeat at Pittodrie, but Rangers then swept into an unbeaten streak of 22 matches in all competitions through to March and a replay defeat by Dundee at Ibrox in the Scottish Cup. Still, at the end of February Rangers were fourth in the race, 16 points behind Aberdeen. The League Cup was won in a thrilling Final. The faltering Rangers had been in command for the best part of an hour, leading by two goals, but Celtic

rallied and a last minute penalty goal by Mark Reid took then into extra-time. After 104 minutes, McCoist was flattened by Roy Aitken, and took the penalty kick himself. His first shot was blocked by Pat Bonner, but he followed up to complete a hat-trick and win the Cup. McCoist had started his Rangers career in a pre-season tour of Sweden, where his goal count was nine from four games. He was the season's leading scorer with 35 goals in a season in which Rangers could not improve on fourth position, 15 points behind champions Aberdeen. But in a decade and more with Rangers, McCoist was to know the best of times and the worst of times.

The 1984-85 season was all but a carbon copy of its predecessor as the Rangers 'slump' which had depressed the club since the treble season of 1977-78 continued. For the third successive season they finished fourth in the League table, a massive and record 21 points behind the champions Aberdeen. This failure was not from the lack of investment. At a total cost of £465,000, Iain Ferguson and Cammy Fraser came from Dundee and Ted McMinn from Queen of the South. And for a more modest £30,000 Derek Johnstone was back from Chelsea to play out his career.

Ferguson was to have an important part to play in the League Cup Final. Rangers had a routine journey there, disposing of Falkirk, Raith Rovers, Cowdenbeath and Meadowbank Thistle. The Final, against Dundee United, was played in quite atrocious conditions on a skidding surface. Ferguson's goal, which won the match, came importantly one minute before half-time and his crisp shot from 12 yards climaxed an unlikely movement started by Davie Cooper and carried along by Bobby Russell and Ian Redford. Ferguson was a player of exceptional ability and a

Rangers' full squad line up for the photographer before the start of the 1984-85 season. Back row (left to right): Prytz, D.Ferguson, McFarlane, Kennedy, McPherson, McClelland, Paterson, McAdam, Mitchell, E.Ferguson, Munro, Fleck. Middle row: Stan Anderson (youth team coach), Lindsay, Davies, Durrant, S.Fraser, Walker, McCloy, Bruce, Burns, McKinnon, Leeman, Connor and Bob Findlay (physiotherapist). Front row: Redford, Dawson, I.Ferguson, Williamson, Cooper, Alex Totten (first-team coach), Jock Wallace (manager), John Hagart (reserve-team coach), Clark, C.Fraser, McCoist, Russell, McDonald.

That winning feeling again. These rain-soaked Rangers players are all smiles – they have just won not one cup but two. Their victory over Dundee United at Hampden in October 1984 saw them with the Scottish League Cup, which meant that they also lifted the Skol Cup, the new trophy for the competition presented by the sponsors.

thrilling goalscorer who nevertheless seemed short of the commitment needed for the game at the highest level. He managed only 46 games for the club.

A reasonable start was made to the League campaign and with eight matches played, at the end of September Rangers were unbeaten. But on 21 September John McClelland lost the captaincy of the team. This was but a preamble to perhaps the worst piece of Rangers business all season. McClelland was a Northern Ireland international –

more than 50 times – and a solid, reliable, experienced defender for Rangers with 153 games for the club. But he and manager Jock Wallace seemed to be at odds over his value to Rangers and on 8 November, he was transferred to Watford for £265,000.

It was not a move that pleased Rangers fans, and may have anticipated events. At the turn of the year, Rangers were in third position, six points behind Aberdeen, two behind Celtic and therefore still with all to play for. But from 1 January, they won only four of the remaining 16 League fixtures. It was becoming tiresome, and the next season, when Rangers won not one single trophy, it was to become intolerable.

In the Scottish Cup, Morton had taken Rangers to a replay at Ibrox, before Dundee came to the Stadium in the fourth round to defeat Rangers with a ninth minute goal scored by John Brown. His was a name that was to become more widely known to Ibrox fans.

For the friends of Rangers, the 1985-86 season was to become the most dreadful in living memory. For the first time in the club's history, Rangers won less than one point per game – 35 points from 36 League matches. Defeat came in the semi-final of the League Cup when Hibernian prevented Rangers from making a fifth consecutive appearance in the Final. And in the Scottish Cup, Rangers went out in their first match, beaten 3-2 by Hearts at Tynecastle. Certainly this was a much-improved Hearts team, which lost the championship at Dundee in the very last League fixture, and the Scottish Cup in the Final against Aberdeen 3-0. But Rangers' fifth place finish in the championship equalled their worst position in post-war football.

Some kind of promise seemed at hand when the first four League games saw the loss of only one point, but the month of September was a disaster for the club. Both Dundee and Aberdeen won at Ibrox, Hibernian ended any League Cup hopes, and Atlético Osasuna, by no means a stellar name in Spanish football, dumped Rangers at the first time of asking from the UEFA Cup. There was a run of ten League matches that produced only two wins and at the end of the year, Rangers were in fifth position, and there to stay.

Off the field, events were to have a profound effect on the future of the club. On 7 January, the John Lawrence Organisation, a construction company, announced that it held 176,948 shares or 51.2 per cent of the equity of the club. Their man David Holmes became a director. In the following season he succeeded John Paton as chairman. Holmes is on record as saying that "Things could not be allowed to go on".

After a dreadful display in a friendly against Tottenham Hotspur, which Rangers lost 2-0, Jock Wallace resigned on 7 April. Graeme Souness was appointed player-manager, the first in Rangers' history. Walter Smith from Dundee United became assistant manager, Don Mackay the reserve-team coach. Within two weeks an approach of £500,000 for Richard Gough was rejected by Dundee United. A few weeks later this was increased to £625,000 with the same result. Souness had been under contract to Sampdoria, the Genoa club and Rangers paid £300,000 for his transfer. He was part of the Scotland party in the World Cup in Mexico in June 1986, but before leaving he bought Colin West, a striker from Watford for £175,000.

In spite of the fact that McCoist was leading scorer for the season, it became no secret that Souness did not have a high regard for his talents. The first Souness trophy was a Glasgow Cup Final win over Celtic, in which Mr McCoist for the second time hit a hat-trick against the old enemy.

When, in 1963-64 Rangers won the treble and their 34th League championship, including their third in four years, it would have been difficult to envisage the decade to come and the fact that they would not win another League title for 11 years, and indeed would win only three in the next 22 years.

The reasons are varied, and not easily defined, but one of the major, most powerful reasons was the sheer existence

of Jock Stein, as manager of Celtic in the greatest decade of their history.

The 34th League title saw Rangers with an ageing team, one which in any case was on the verge of breaking up. That in itself, given good forward planning, should not have excused the lack of subsequent success. From 1966 to 1970, Rangers did not win one single trophy, far less a championship. One would have to go back before the mid-1960s to find some reasons for this decline. Scot Symon, as we have seen, was an old-school manager, who had failed to move with the times. One of Jock Stein's favourite sayings was that a "moderate team with a good manager will always beat a good team with a bad manager" (that may have summed up where many of Rangers problems lay).

The entire structure of the club required overhaul. Training was unimaginative, consisting of lapping round the track in the main, for 35-year-old veterans and 17-year-old newcomers alike. There was no specialist consideration given to the individual's needs, no sense of using veterans players sparingly, for specific matches and tasks. It did seem that many senior players ceased to be effective, suddenly.

The scouting system was antiquated. Very few talented juniors, or schoolboy players were coming to Ibrox to freshen the top team in a season or two. Paradoxically Bob Macaulay, former Rangers player of the 1920s and 1930s, was successful in the east of Scotland, produced John Greig, Willie Johnston, Sandy Jardine, among others from there, while the West of Scotland and the Glasgow area, the Rangers heartland, seemed to produce little in comparison to these players who would go on and become successful international footballers.

Such talents as Kenny Dalglish, from a Rangers household, and possibly Danny McGrain, both in turn becoming outstanding international players, were allowed to go to Celtic. There was a certain *laissez-faire* attitude about the entire business, the feeling that such youngsters would knock on the door at Ibrox, and did not need to be persuaded to come to the club. Instead, Jock Stein signed both.

Further, the arrival of Stein at Parkhead had transformed Celtic into an exciting, attack-minded club attractive to young players. Stein had paid close attention to the scouting system at Parkhead. Celtic had a fair system in place when he went there, evidenced by a number of young players who came through. Not all that many of the 'Lisbon Lions', Celtic's European Cup-winning team had been signed by Stein, but he was the catalyst that made them an outstanding team and brought the best out of the players.

This was lacking at Rangers – the treble team had senior, experienced players such as Bobby Shearer, Eric Caldow, Jimmy Millar, Ralph Brand, Davie Wilson and Ian McMillan, all of them ending Ibrox careers almost within months of each other.

At the start of Jock Stein's reign at Celtic Park, Rangers were not the club they should have been, or needed to be, to meet his challenge. The way was clear for Celtic to win all the honours. And nine successive championships cannot be denied. No matter how well organised, well equipped Rangers had been, it would have been difficult for them to compromise the Celtic success over the greatest decade in their history.

Nevertheless, if Rangers were not as 'ready' as their motto claims, they consistently finished second in the championship, reached a Final, quarter-final and semi-final of European competitions in successive seasons, so that their 'failure' was neither abject nor absolute. But there was no doubt that the lack of trophy success was seriously undermining Rangers position as the Scottish bellweather club. In 1967, the departure of manager Symon indicated that the club was feeling the pressure from Celtic. Chairman John Lawrence was increasingly criticised, and severely. The board then made an error of judgement in appointing David White as manager. It quickly became clear that he did not have the public persona of Stein who, apart from anything else, was a quite brilliant manipulator of the media. The team played some fine football under White's control, but lack of trophies, in particular that elusive championship, was his undoing.

The appointment of Willie Waddell to succeed White in 1969 was hailed as a second coming, that here was a true blue manager who would match Stein in every respect. He had a sound record, having taken Kilmarnock to a championship four years earlier. Waddell did transform the club, if without instant success. He took a longer view, putting his faith in a youth policy which was beginning to show promise, and in restructuring the staff, cutting out waste and bad administrative practices. He brought in Jock Wallace as coach, and a completely new backroom staff. It took a couple of years to work through. First Rangers won the 1970-71 League Cup, then the 1971-72 European Cup-winners' Cup and finally the 1972-73 Scottish Cup, this last one with Wallace as manager, Waddell as general manager.

Wallace put together a team in his own image, a team of young players most of whom would have long careers, a team that was to win three League championships in four years, including two trebles. If any criticism could be made of Wallace it would be that he too, like Scot Symon 14 years earlier, failed to anticipate the ageing process. In 1978, his second treble team had players – John Greig, Alex Macdonald – who had little time left. They would have to be replaced in a couple of years and the youth policy seemed to be faltering (Jim McLean, the Dundee United manager always said that a youth policy would have an effect on the first team only after ten years).

Wallace probably concentrated overmuch on the first-team squad. The reserve team in his time won almost everything open to them, basically because it was a very experienced group. But there were few youngsters on the horizon. His departure meant that his successor would inherit these problems. Yet again, in hindsight, the board made another error of judgment in appointing John Greig, from the dressing room. Waddell was considered to be behind it, taking his cue from Liverpool, who had appointed from within the club when Bill Shankly resigned in 1974 and Bob Paisley succeeded.

Greig's assets in a strange way were to become his liabilities. Whereas Wallace as a manager let the opposition worry about his players, in the tactical sense Greig took the other view, tending to think too much about the game and the opposition. It produced an over-cautious approach to too many domestic fixtures. It was ludicrous going to Paisley and facing St Mirren with a sweeper behind a defensive line of four, playing it seemed for a goalless draw. This was unheard of from either of the Old Firm teams. Lack of management experience did for Greig and he paid the penalty of Wallace's neglect of a flow of talent through the various elevens to the League team.

In the first few years of his managership, players like Sandy Jardine, Colin Jackson, Tommy McLean and Alex Macdonald all effectively finished their Ibrox careers. Jardine could have continued to play for Rangers for a few more seasons. In the event, he did just that with Hearts, with success.

Greig probably lost the respect of his senior players on tactics. There was one occasion in which Jardine simply revolted, and refused to play Greig's plan, which he thought unworkable.

In addition, Ibrox was being rebuilt between 1978 and 1981 with three new stands being built, a substantial drain on finances. Greig did have money to spend, but it was not always done wisely. Gregor Stevens, Craig Paterson, Sandy Clark and others, were not successes. It was ironic that two outstanding successes for Greig were players that few people had heard of – Jim Bett came from Lokeren, the Belgian club and John McClelland from Mansfield Town. Alistair McCoist, in Greig's time a notable failure, later blossomed into one of Rangers' great success stories, although due credit must be given to Greig for signing the player in the first instance.

Cups were fine, but John Greig's ultimate failure was as ever, in the championship. In October 1983 he made way for the return of Jock Wallace. Before that appointment, Rangers had approached Alex Ferguson at Aberdeen and Jim McLean at Dundee United. Their refusals spoke volumes for the state of affairs at Ibrox, although McLean came very close to accepting.

Wallace's return to Ibrox invigorated the club in the short term. The team went off on a long unbroken run, won the League Cup in successive years, as he introduced many of the characteristics of his former teams. But starting from a low base and with the onset of a long illness which only later became known, his second time round was not successful. By 1985-86, Rangers were in dire straits. The club for the first time in its history failed to secure one point per game in the championship. The team was definitely inferior not only to that of Celtic, but of Aberdeen, Dundee United, even Hearts, who, under the joint management of old Ibrox men Alex Macdonald and Sandy Jardine, came desperately close to winning the double.

Since 1965 Rangers had won but three championships in 22 years, all under manager Jock Wallace. Friends of Rangers began to wonder if the Wallace regimes were interludes in a terminal decline of the club, as gates slumped drastically and as Rangers, despite its fine new stadium, seemed to fall so far behind its rivals. Could the stadium be a white elephant? Some cynics said that when the Copland Road and Broomloan Road stands were completed, there would be no need to build the Govan Stand, opposite the Main stand – the existing capacity of 35,000 would be quite enough for Rangers future needs. They should just built a wall along that far touchline.

From 1981-86, excluding Old Firm games, the stadium would be full only on a handful of occasions. In 1985-86, one of the worst seasons in Rangers history, average attendance was in the region of 25,000.

When Alex Ferguson turned down Rangers offer, it was said that he did so because he believed there were two factions on the Rangers board. No director of Rangers had ever had overall control of the club. They had always held a small number of shareholdings in percentage terms, drawn as they were from Glasgow business men and former players all with Rangers leanings, Rangers' interest at heart. This was to change, in December 1985. Then Lawrence Marlborough, grandson and inheritor of the shares of John Lawrence, chairman for so many years, came to an agreement with Jack Gillespie, a garage owner, to buy his shareholding. This gave Marlborough a controlling shareholding in the club.

He had said he would either buy out Gillespie, or sell out

Ally McCoist is crowned with the trophy after yet another Rangers League Cup Final triumph, in October 1986 when they beat Celtic 2-1. Derek Ferguson and Ian Durant do the honours.

– the drain of Rangers' losses on the John Lawrence group's financial position was such that they had to do something. With a controlling interest, Marlborough was now able to run Rangers as he saw fit. This was not likely to transform Rangers as Marlborough was now resident in Nevada, running down the John Lawrence UK interests and developing business life in Reno.

His first move was to appoint David Holmes to the board, obviously to keep him informed as to what was going on and to decide what action should be taken. Holmes' background was unknown to Rangers' fans. A Falkirk man, he was chief executive of the John Lawrence UK operation, but again, the appointment did not exactly stir true blue blood. Holmes promptly said he would make no moves or take no action possibly for six months until he had studied how things at Ibrox worked, or did not work. Thus the thought was that nothing much would happen, nothing much change.

On the contrary, almost to the day, Holmes was true to his word, and almost everything changed. Holmes approached the club's bankers with a business plan which gave him substantial overdraft-facilities so that he could attract the best management, the best players. At that time, Celtic, Aberdeen and Dundee United players were earning, including bonuses, more than Rangers players! Holmes had looked, listened and learned. In April 1986 he acted. Things changed utterly. Wallace went and the coming of Graeme Souness as player-manager was announced. The entire football world was, to say the least, surprised. Souness had no links with Rangers. He had no managerial experience.

He had spent his entire career outside Scotland, most recently with Sampdoria in Italy. Rangers fans with memories of David White and John Greig wondered just what Souness could bring to the club in management terms.

On the other hand, Rangers fortunes were so dire at the time that Souness as a player of high quality would surely improve the club performance on the field. Nobody was able to anticipate the Souness achievement – his actions as manager were to transform the club.

David Holmes made revolutionary changes to the wage structure. John McClelland, the club captain who was a first-class player for Rangers, had left a club which failed dismally to meet his financial requirement. They refused him a re-signing fee, which may have been morally correct, but which ignored completely current practice in the game. The fact that McLelland moved to a club like Watford showed how naive Rangers had been in these matters, how far they were from the facts of life. Holmes changed all that. Holmes should get much credit. He brought Souness to the club. He put the club on a better financial basis. He changed the wage pattern. He agreed with Souness in the recruitment of the best players.

And he saw clearly the commercial potentiality of the club. He was the first to introduce a corporate hospitality suite, the Thornton Suite, the first of many.

The coming of David Holmes and the appointment of Graeme Souness represented a turning point in the long Rangers story. The great old club had gone into a decline, above all perhaps because of a lack of vision in the board room. But now it had a superb stadium and a dynamic

Aberdeen's Peter Nicholas misses from the spot against Rangers in the 1987 League Cup Final at Hampden. The result was a 3-3 draw but Rangers won the trophy 5-3 on penalties.

management. A long and dark passage in its history was over. For Rangers, the sun was rising again.

The wisdom of David Holmes, Rangers' chairman and chief executive, in selecting Graeme Souness to cure an ailing giant was entirely justified in 1986-87, a season in which Souness transformed Scottish football. After Colin West came a stream of international players of quality such as Chris Woods, Terry Butcher, Jimmy Nichol, not to mention various others which had Rangers fans in a state of permanent animation. Rangers' attendances reached back up to capacity levels as Ibrox became a place of excitement. And Rangers played to similar capacity audiences throughout the country.

The start to the season was not uneventful. Souness was ordered off in his very first game, for a violent foul in the match against Hibernian in Edinburgh. It was clear that Souness would have to learn the ways of Scottish football and Scottish referees. And with one win and two defeats in the initial three League games, it was clear that this 'New Rangers' would need time to bond. But not over-long – before August was out, Celtic had been beaten at Ibrox by an Ian Durrant goal.

At the end of November, Rangers were in fourth position, nine points behind Celtic but with a game in hand. The coming of Graham Roberts transformed the team and its championship challenge. In the interim, the League Cup had been won in 2-1 a thrilling Final against Celtic which featured a late Davie Cooper penalty goal and the ordering off of one Maurice Johnston.

The arrival of Roberts from Spurs was probably the last piece in the design which gave Souness his championship edifice. His first match was on 27 December, a 2-0 win over Dundee United at Ibrox and it set Rangers off on an unbeaten run of 19 League games which swept them into the thick of the fight. The title was won with a thrilling Terry Butcher goal in a 1-1 draw at Pittodrie in the last but one match of the season.

It was Rangers' first League success since 1978, a treble-

winning season, and their 38th title in all. In it, Butcher had been an outstanding player and captain, a man of energy, enthusiasm and inspiration. Souness himself, although a mid-season injury kept his appearances down to 24 and meant him missing the League Cup Final, was a vital part of the pulse of the team.

Any thoughts the rejuvenated Rangers supporters may have had about another treble vanished in the gloom of a January Scottish Cup-tie when central defender David McPherson failed to take care of a through ball, and allowed Adrian Sprott to run on and score the single Hamilton Accies goal that put Rangers out of the Cup and made Sprott the sensation of the hour. In Rangers' long unbeaten run was a record 12 games in which goalkeeper Chris Woods did not concede one solitary goal. It was Sprott's Cup goal that put an end to that record. Yet again Alistair McCoist at the other end of the team was leading scorer, repeating his tally of 41.

Dramatic big-money signings featured in season 1987-88, no doubt in keeping with the Graeme Souness belief that "big clubs need big players". Impressive names came from impressive clubs – Trevor Francis from Sampdoria, Ray Wilkins from Paris St Germain, Richard Gough (at last!) from Tottenham Hotspur as Scotland's first £1 million player. Mark Walters came from Aston Villa, Mark Falco from Watford and John Brown came from Dundee to become a faithful servant of the club in many defensive positions.

The defence of the League title alas foundered in a start of only three points from the first possible ten and it was to be a season in which an unprecedented injury list, plus disciplinary problems and the consequent suspensions were to haunt the club. Rangers never did catch up. They finished third, 12 points behind Celtic who were champions in their centenary season.

The League Cup produced a truly memorable Final, one of thrilling incident, high skills, stunning goals. Aberdeen went down only after extra-time, a 3-3 draw, and a Rangers

Ally McCoist beats Willie Miller to score Rangers' winning goal in the last minute of the League Cup Final of October 1988.

win with penalty shots. If Rangers as Finalists in the League Cup was becoming a commonplace, success in the Scottish Cup continued to elude them. For the second successive year, they went down to a team that was relegated, Dunfermline Athletic, by 2-0.

The season was enlivened however by European competition and exciting successes against Dinamo Kiev, and Górnik Zabrze before losing to the great Steaua Bucharest team, at a time when Terry Butcher and Avi Cohen were injured. Brown, Walters, Bartram and Ferguson were unavailable. McCoist had undergone a cartilage operation only ten days earlier, and the sale of Mark Falco and Robert Fleck between the Górnik and Steaua ties were considered by many Rangers fans as very serious errors of judgment by manager Souness, leaving the club all but bereft of a strike force.

In 1988-89 the recovery of the League championship and victory in the League Cup for a third successive season – the first time Rangers had done this – again justified the Souness policy of importing quality players from England. Gary Stevens came from Everton and played in every League match and Kevin Drinkell arrived from Norwich City as a strong striking force at McCoist's elbow.

After a ten-day pre-season training spell in Italy, Rangers came out like lions, winning five pre-season friendlies then in the space of eight days at the end of August hammering home 15 goals at Ibrox. Clydebank went down 6-0 in a League Cup match, Celtic were mauled 5-1 in the first of the Old Firm League games, then Dundee were beaten 4-1 in the League Cup. Terry Butcher, back after a leg break, added power to the team, demonstrated in yet another first-class League Cup Final against Aberdeen. A last minute McCoist goal gave it to Rangers, 3-2. A few days earlier, Rangers had suffered the loss of Ian Durrant, their skilful midfield player to a tackle by Aberdeen's Neil Simpson, at Pittodrie. Durrant had a dreadful knee injury which

required the most sophisticated surgery and compromised his career for a good three years.

That early season trouncing of Celtic was inspirational to Rangers and gave them an initiative in the League which they never quite surrendered. There was a faltering briefly in December when there were defeats by Dundee United at Ibrox and by Hearts at Tynecastle but the team rallied and won 14 of the final 17 fixtures. Ray Wilkins in midfield disguised the absence of Durrant, and with McCoist injured through most of the winter, Drinkell became top scorer with 12 of the 62 scored.

The Scottish Cup had been long absent from the Ibrox sideboard. Indeed six years had passed since they were Finalists. The campaign was arduous in the extreme. Raith Rovers forced an Ibrox replay. Stranraer were beaten handsomely 8-0 at home. But Dundee United in the quarter-final required a replay as did St Johnstone of all people in the semi-final round. At last Rangers were Finalists. They had to face Celtic without Ray Wilkins and Derek Ferguson, both injured, and were beaten by a Joe Millar goal when he fastened on to a muffed back pass by the largely experienced but stumbling Gary Stevens.

The events of the summer of 1989 were to bring Rangers, a club well acquainted with 'sensations', one of the greatest sensations Scottish football had known.

On 10 July 1989, Rangers signed Maurice Johnston, snatching him from the embrace of Celtic, one of his former clubs, who had arranged his signing from Nantes in France. It was a signing which stunned the Scottish football world since Johnstone was the first acknowledged Roman Catholic to play for Rangers in modern times. As an addition to the playing staff it was a startling manifestation of the Graeme Souness history of purchasing 'famous' players and it split the Rangers following in two. The media reaction was close to hysterical.

But Johnston buckled down, kept his head down off the

Mark Walters and Richard Gough get highest in a crowded goalmouth during the goalless draw between Rangers and St Johnstone in the 1989 Scottish Cup semi-final tie at Celtic Park. Three days later the sides tried again and this time Rangers triumphed easily, 4-0.

pitch and worked unselfishly on it. Over the first few months of the season, judgment was withheld, but when, on 4 November, he scored the goal which beat Celtic at Ibrox, 1-0, and with only two minutes left for play, all was forgiven. Johnston in fact proved a positive asset to the club in his first season.

Almost overlooked in the hullabaloo over Johnston's signing was the arrival of Trevor Steven, for a record £1,525,000 from Everton. A winner of all the prizes with the Liverpool club – FA Cup, Football League championship, European Cup-winners' Cup and many appearances for England – Steven was a player of high skill and

Mel Sterland is happy enough after scoring his second goal in the 4-0 win over Hearts at Ibrox in April 1989.

Trevor Steven and Davie Dodds celebrate Rangers' second goal against Dunfermline at Ibrox in April 1990.

vision, operating on the right side of midfield. He played almost every match, linked perfectly with Ray Wilkins and in a sense succeeded him in the team pattern when Wilkins left in December to return to London.

Rangers contrived to lose their two opening League fixtures, 1-0 at home to St Mirren, 2-0 away to Hibernian, but were quickly into a stride that brought them a third title in four seasons, finishing seven points ahead of Aberdeen, and retaining the championship for the first time since 1976. Five days in January were quite vital. Celtic were beaten 1-0 at Parkhead, Rangers' first win there in the New Year match for more than 20 years. The scorer was Nigel Spackman, arrived at Ibrox from Queen's Park Rangers one month earlier. A 2-0 win at home to Aberdeen five days later confirmed Rangers' championship intentions.

In February at Parkhead, Celtic had some revenge, hustling Rangers, 1-0 out of the Scottish Cup in the fourth round. And Aberdeen had broken Rangers' hold on the League Cup with a 2-1 win after extra-time in the Final.

The 1990-91 season was yet another of sensations which saw Rangers win a third successive championship for the first time since 1945, making a record of 41 wins; the departure of Terry Butcher, their captain, in some acrimony; the abrupt departure of Graeme Souness, the manager; a record 17th win in the League Cup, and a championship won in the most dramatic circumstances imaginable on the very last day.

New signings were in place. Mark Hateley came from Monaco, Pieter Huistra from Twente Enschede, and Oleg Kuznetsov from Dinamo Kiev was promised. Hateley was not welcomed with acclamation by the Ibrox public. He

seemed slow and his ball control was uncertain. Perhaps he had underestimated the pace and vigour of the Scottish game but he settled down under the Ibrox training and coaching systems and became one of Rangers' most successful and important players over the following five years.

Of the 19 League games played to the end of the year twelve were won, only two lost. Rangers' defence of their championship seemed solid. It was compromised by the going of Terry Butcher, one of the best-liked Rangers captains, after a squabble with manager Souness in September and by a fearful succession of injuries. Durrant, Kuznetsov, McCoist, Steven, Brown, Gough, Walters and Ian Ferguson all had absences of various lengths, some too long to contemplate. Kuznetsov, injured at McDirmid Park, Perth, in Rangers' first-ever visit there and in only his second game for the club, was out for the entire season.

In the League Cup, Rangers disposed of Stirling Albion, 5-0 at Ibrox; Kilmarnock 1-0 at Ibrox, and Aberdeen in a 1-0 semi-final, by way of a precious Trevor Steven goal. The Final against Celtic was won 2-1, in extra-time, by a stunning goal at close range from an advanced foraging Richard Gough.

For the second successive season, Celtic triumphed at Parkhead by 2-0 in a Scottish Cup-tie of hatred and indiscipline. Three Rangers players were ordered off for retaliation (Hurlock, Walters, Hateley) and Rangers' disciplinary record, then the best in Scotland, crumbled. In the following four League fixtures, three more players were ordered off and points were frittered away until the championship itself was at risk.

Before its extraordinary climax, Graeme Souness left the

The fans celebrate as Mark Hateley scores the first of his two goals against Aberdeen at Ibrox in May 1991. Rangers won 2-0 and were champions yet again.

club, saying that he had "gone as far as I am allowed to go". Walter Smith, his assistant, was immediately appointed manager, and had to ask the team for one last supreme effort in the final League match against Aberdeen at Ibrox. A draw for the Dons would have given them the title, but in a stadium that throbbed with emotion, Rangers pulled out a stunning performance and a 2-0 win, both goals from Mark Hateley. Aberdeen were devastated.

As Walter Smith, the 'new' manager impressed his character and personality on affairs at Ibrox, 1991-92 was a season of much change in playing personnel. Trevor Steven went to Marseille, Chris Woods to Sheffield Wednesday, Mark Walters to Liverpool and Maurice Johnston to Everton. They were all talented and senior players, and the going of Steven in particular, in spite of the £5.5 million fee, caused much unrest among Rangers' supporters. Incomers were Alexei Mikhailichenko from Sampdoria, Stuart McCall from Everton, David Robertson from Aberdeen, Andy Goram from Hibernian, Dale Gordon from Norwich City and Paul Rideout from Notts County. Smith's juggling act was obviously influenced by the UEFA regulation that teams in European competition could play no more than three 'foreigners'. In addition, he was facing a season of 44 games in a 12 club division – strength in depth would be essential.

A fourth successive championship was secured for the first time in more than 60 years and this one clearly emphasised the superiority which the Ibrox club was building over

all opposition. The Rangers total of 72 points left them nine ahead of second-placed Hearts. They scored 101 goals for the first time since the Premier Division was formed and they won 19 of 22 away fixtures, a remarkable achievement. The absence of Trevor Steven in midfield was often noticeable and September brought the disappointment of a loss in the semi-final of the League Cup to Hibernian, and in the European Cup to Sparta Prague on the 'away' goals rule.

As the season wore on, the team played with increasing confidence, and success, losing only one of their last 24 League games. January was a particularly important month – Celtic were beaten 3-1 at Parkhead, Hibernian and Motherwell at home, and Aberdeen at Pittodrie, in the Scottish Cup. Eleven years had passed since Rangers had won the senior trophy, and the next round brought Motherwell, the holders to Ibrox. A desperately tense match saw Rangers only just prevail by 2-1. An away win over St Johnstone brought a semi-final against Celtic, and one of the greatest achievements in Rangers history. David Robertson was ordered off after only six minutes play. A goal by Alistair McCoist on the stroke of half-time set up Rangers for a second half of defiant defence against all that the full strength of Celtic could throw at them.

After all that, the Final tie against Airdrie had to be something of a let-down. It was one of the poorer Finals, but the Rangers' 2-1 win ended an 11-years jinx. McCoist scored Rangers' second to conclude a golden personal season. He was top scorer with 41 goals, won both Sports

Hateley shows his feelings after scoring against Airdrieonians in the 1992 Scottish Cup Final. Alexei Mikhailichenko shares the Englishman's joy.

Writers' and Managers', Player of the Year awards, and Europe's 'Golden Boot' award. In the last League match, at Aberdeen, he scored his 200th Scottish League goal, and Rangers' 100th of the season. With Graeme Souness gone from the club, Alistair McCoist seemed liberated.

Season 1992-93 was the season of Rangers' fifth successive championship, of their fifth 'treble' and of the confirmation of the status of Walter Smith as a manager, in the best Ibrox tradition.

The first League match was against St Johnstone at Ibrox. A McCoist goal ten minutes from the end gave notice that Rangers were in earnest and that McCoist was to have another glorious season. The bald facts are compelling. In the first 23 games up to the turn of the year, 18 were won, only one lost. Of the 21 games in the second half, 14 were won, only four lost, three of these in May after the championship had been won – by no fewer than nine points from Aberdeen. Indeed since Rangers had lost to Dundee, 4-3 in August in the most freakish result of the season, they had put together a record of 29 unbeaten Premier Division matches, dropping only five points.

In this remarkable season, unprecedented in the history of the club, Rangers had a run of 44 unbeaten matches in all competitions, following the August defeat at Dundee. This embraced 29 League, four League Cup, three Scottish Cup and eight matches in European competition.

At the end of February, they were 11 points ahead. If any one match could have illustrated the quality and the calibre of Rangers' football throughout this season, it was the match at Pittodrie on 2 February. A win for Aberdeen would have cut Rangers' five-point lead to manageable proportions for the Dons. They played marvelously well, dominated much of the game, but were defied by inspired and occasionally fortunate goalkeeping from Andy Goram. And they were beaten, 13 minutes into the second half by a quite magnificent Rangers goal. A probing, incisive cross from

deep on the right by Gary Stevens saw Mark Hateley, with a prodigious leap, rise above the Aberdeen defence to head an inspired goal wide of Theo Snelders' left hand.

Rangers were no friends of Aberdeen in 1992-93. In the League Cup they went past Dumbarton and Stranraer, won 3-2 at Tannadice only with an extra-time goal from Pieter Huistra, then beat St Johnstone to reach their ninth Final in 11 years. Aberdeen got there by way of Arbroath, Dunfermline Athletic, Falkirk and Celtic, a stonier road. The Final was the fourth between the clubs in half a dozen years. They produced a fine match. Stuart McCall took advantage of an untypical error by goalkeeper Snelders to put Rangers in front, Duncan Shearer equalised with an inspired spin and shot. Not surprisingly, the game went into overtime. Seven minutes from the end, Gary Smith, the talented Aberdeen defender, deflected David Robertson's cross past Snelders. It was a cruel finish for the Dons, but over the entire match, Rangers probably deserved the win, particularly since in the preceeding midweek, they had survived an intense match with Leeds United in the European Cup.

The Scottish Cup Final, played at Celtic Park because of Hampden reconstruction, produced the same result. It was Rangers' 42nd Final, Aberdeen's 14th. With the scent of the domestic treble in the wind, Rangers proved irresistible. Goals came from Neil Murray with a wickedly deflected shot for the opener, then a superb Hateley strike making it two. Near the end, Lee Richardson's 25 yarder made for a stirring finish, but Rangers had retained the Cup, rounded out their treble and made it clear yet again that they were the dominant force in Scottish football.

In 1993-94 Rangers were champions yet again – six in a row – but this time with the less than devastating margin of three points over perennial rivals Aberdeen. What was becoming quite striking was the absence of challenge coming from historic rivals Celtic. The Parkhead club was going

You can't keep a good man down. Ally McCoist, the centre of attention all season until breaking a leg, hobbles on to the Celtic Park pitch to join in the celebrations with Ian Ferguson, Davie McPherson, John Brown and Mark Hateley after Rangers' Scottish Cup Final victory of 1993.

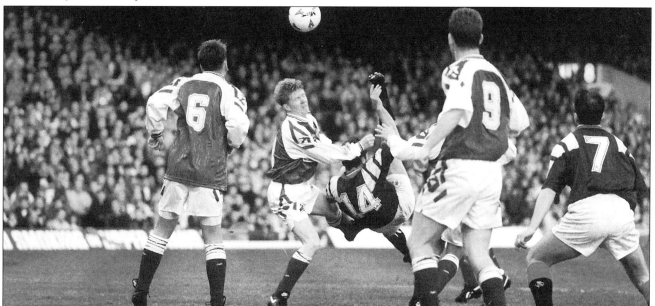

Back to having a ball. Ally McCoist hits his spectacular winning goal against Hibs in the 1993 League Cup Final.

through the most vexed period in its history. The board of directors was swept away, and famous Celtic names – Kelly, White – were no longer listed. The aged creaking stadium had to be rebuilt, managers came and went – Liam Brady, Lou Macari. The shareholding of the club was hugely enlarged. The new directorate had convulsed the club, and serious, sustained challenges for the major honours seemed a long way ahead.

Aberdeen lacked consistency, finding it difficult to string together more than three consecutive wins. Apart from the champions, Motherwell were the team to watch. From toiling in relegation zones for too long, they swept up to third place in a challenge that was to be maintained. But of all Rangers many championships, this may have been one of their greatest in adversity. No fewer than 11 Ibrox squad players underwent surgery during the season. Alistair

McCoist for instance played only 16 League games, Andy Goram 23. But the 'Player of the Year', Mark Hateley with 22 goals from 42 appearances had an outstanding season in spite of constant changes in his striking partners.

In the League Cup, Rangers again disposed of Aberdeen, this time in the quarter-final round at Ibrox. Again it went to extra-time, before an Ian Ferguson goal won it. A tremendous semi-final with Celtic, played at Ibrox because of the Hampden reconstruction, saw Pieter Huistra sent off, and the ten men pull off a notable victory. Ian Durrant on the right dispossessed Celtic defender Mike Galloway, and his cross was swept in for the single goal win, by Mark Hateley.

Rangers were in their seventh Final in eight years, against a Hibernian team there for the first time. It was played at Celtic Park before 47,632 fans. An own goal by

David McPherson equalised an earlier Ian Durrant score. Alistair McCoist was a substitute for the match – he had just recovered from his leg break in Lisbon, playing for Scotland the previous April. He was to settle this Final with one of the most spectacular goals Celtic Park had ever seen. With his back to goal, and only nine minutes left, his overhead, 'bicycletta' shot gave Hibs' goalkeeper Jim Leighton no chance. McCoist called it "the best single moment of the season for me".

Thus Rangers, with the Scottish Cup to come, were on track to repeat their treble. It was to be one of the classic upsets in football when they played the Final. Dundee United had had a very moderate season, winning only 11 of 44 League games. Six times they had been in the Scottish Cup Final, six times they had lost. But after 47 minutes at Hampden, they had won. David McPherson left a pass back to Alistair Maxwell short. The goalkeeper under pressure sought to volley it away, but the ball struck the on-rushing Christian Dailly, who turned it behind Maxwell along the goal line from a narrow angle. The ball struck the far post, rebounded, and Craig Brewster arrived to run the ball home. It was a bewildering end to what was nevertheless a hugely successful domestic season for Rangers.

Glamorous close season signings in Brian Laudrup from Fiorentina and Basile Boli from Marseille had Rangers very optimistic about their prospects in 1994-95 for participation in the Champions League, now becoming something of an obsession with the Ibrox club. A change of regulations for the competition, decided by UEFA, meant that Rangers were forced to play a qualifying round, before the domestic season started. That proved disastrous for the club. Beaten in Athens by AEK, then again in the home leg at Ibrox, Rangers lost three home games in a row for the first time since 1971-72.

On 24 August, they lost the home leg to Athens. On 27 August they lost 2-0 to Celtic at Ibrox. On 31 August they lost 2-1 to Falkirk in the Coca Cola League Cup, also at Ibrox. Three successive home defeats meant 'crisis', Ibrox was rocked. Manager Walter Smith was under pressure from the fans for the first time. But chairman David Murray, pressed for action, said there would be no panic, no "knee-jerk reaction – it will be simply heads down, hard work". If the defeat in European competition so early had provoked a knock-on effect, Rangers steadied themselves with a 3-0 win at home to Hearts, then a week later a win at Falkirk put them in pole position in the championship, a placing they were never to concede.

Craig Moore and Charlie Miller were young players brought into the team, and an important new signing Alan McLaren from Hearts brought some defensive stability. The presence of Laudrup and the re-introduction of Pieter

Huistra brought Rangers some balance and style. They ran off 15 matches unbeaten. Outstanding among these were 3-1 over Celtic at Hampden (Celtic Park was still being rebuilt); a 3-0 win at Tannadice over Dundee United and a 2-0 Boxing Day win over Hibernian at Ibrox.

The skills and vision of Dane Brian Laudrup, the Dutchman Huistra, the graft of Scot Stuart McCall in the middle of the team and the power and pace of Mark Hateley in attack, produced, albeit sporadically, football that brought to mind the halcyon days of the early 1960s.

However, when the Scottish Cup was lost 4-2 in a night of tension and passion to Hearts at Tynecastle, in the fourth round, Rangers' defensive frailties were all too evident. Winning a successive seventh League championship was an achievement in itself. Rangers simply gobbled it up. Early in March, they were 15 points ahead of second placed Motherwell. By the end of April, they were 20 points in front of the Lanarkshire team. This merely reflected the high standards demanded by the club, and expected by its supporters, although it should be said that there was clearly no sustained challenge. Celtic found themselves in an unseemly squabble with the Kilmarnock club after Tommy Burns left Ayrshire to become manager at Parkhead. Aberdeen had a dreadful season which saw the going of manager Willie Miller, and the club only just avoided, on the last day of the season, relegation which it had never previously experienced. Hearts too, only just survived on the last day of the season.

A transfer policy which can attract world-class players such as Brian Laudrup and Paul Gascoigne has also seen errors of judgment. One was the signing of Basile Boli, whose total failure to adapt to Rangers and the requirements of the Scottish game certainly had a bearing on the lack of success in Cup games. An extraordinary amount of money was spent on Duncan Ferguson, in both directions. It seemed that chairman Murray was simply determined to sign him from Dundee United, come what may, and Ferguson's problems on and off the field might suggest that a player's worth, and his value to a club, cannot be measured simply in the size of a transfer fee. Not every signing needs to be in the millions. Many friends of Rangers felt that David McPherson, who was transferred to Hearts, was a better defender for the Scottish game than Boli.

Brian Laudrup's signing on the other hand was a monumental success. His displays lit up the Scottish winter, but for a second successive season, Rangers were handicapped by the absence of a natural right-back and of a replacement striker for Alistair McCoist, whose broken leg injury in Lisbon, 1993 with the Scotland team, cost him the greater part of two years action. The signing of Stephen Wright from Aberdeen may have resolved the first problem. It remains to be seen if the second can be resolved.

1995-96—Another Great Season

AFTER the golden season of 1992-93 when they won the treble and almost reached a place in the European Cup Final, Rangers, in terms of any sustained quality to their play, seemed to suffer a reaction. True, they won both subsequent League championships, but their play was not always impressive by the standards they had reached under Graeme Souness and Walter Smith. There was one golden spell in 1994-95, on either side of the New Year, from November to the end of January. The football was of high quality from a balanced team which had Brian Laudrup on

one wing, Peter Huistra on the other. Team selection was consistent, but the transfer of Huistra to Hiroshima San Frecce in January upset the balance. Huistra was approaching the end of his contract and manager Smith accepted the Japanese approach, but this transfer was not generally approved by Rangers fans. After his departure, the team was never quite the same again, although it went on to win the championship comfortably. In 1994-95, with only Motherwell challenging, the championship was won without too much stress.

Ally McCoist heads the winning goal against Celtic in the Scottish League Cup quarter-final at Parkhead in September 1995.

For many people, 1995-96 brought a better quality of play, principally due to the presence of Paul Gascoigne, and the team played with impressive and successful style and flair. Of Rangers new signings, Gascoigne took longest to settle into form, largely because he had been out of major action for a considerable time. He was not match fit when he came to Ibrox, yet even in his early games, in spite of a rather slow start, he made positive contributions, never more so than in the Coca Cola League Cup quarter-final match at Celtic Park on 20 September. This was a very tight match which could have gone either way, but late in the game it was Gascoigne who produced a stunning cross from the right wing to the far post, giving McCoist the chance to head a solitary winning goal. This of course put Rangers into their first semi-final of the season, but against Aberdeen, with Gascoigne present but Richard Gough absent because of injury, the performance was poor, and Rangers went down 2-1. In late October, this was the first match that Gough had missed. His influence all season, as captain and player, was to be immense.

Rangers' 4-1 win at Easter Road against Hibs at the end of November saw a fulminating performance from Gascoigne, this one match perhaps finally establishing him as the innovative core of the team, and perhaps putting an end to Hibs' ambitions as a force of challenge. Their early form had suggested that they might be. Their 1-0 win at Ibrox in late September was quite inexplicable from a Rangers point of view – a few days earlier the Ibrox side had beaten Celtic in the League Cup at Celtic Park, and a few days later had gone back to Celtic Park and won again, this time in a League match. On 30 December, the Rangers 7-0 win over Hibs at Ibrox left the Edinburgh club shattered for the rest of the season. The Rangers League win at Celtic Park by 2-0, following their League Cup 1-0 success was memorable for a vintage Gascoigne goal, a magnificent effort which started in midfield when he gained possession, sprinted all the way to the Celtic penalty area to take his return pass from McCoist, then clipped a volley past the stranded goalkeeper Gordon Marshall. This was Celtic's only League defeat of the season.

Walter Smith, in re-moulding the team, had changed the basic Rangers defensive structure from a straight line of four to one of three central defenders, with a wide, marauding player on each flank. Gough, Alan McLaren and Goran Petric, all tall, vigorous men, formed the centre of the redoubt, and with Andy Goram behind them playing as well as at any time in his career, Rangers defensive record in the first half of the season was excellent, and in terms of results was as good as anything in the preceding decade. The 1-0 loss to Hibs was the only defeat in that time. In December and January they played seven consecutive games without losing a goal. Indeed at the three-quarter point, they had totalled as many points as in the whole of 1994-95. On a points-per-game basis, they were more consistent than in any of the other seven championship seasons. The second defeat, against Hearts at Ibrox on 20 January was inexplicable. Rangers had an abundance of possession, pressed and compressed Hearts throughout the match, yet lost 3-0 to three counter attacks. Gordon Durie had been having his most profitable spell for Rangers, He had four of the seven goals inflicted on Hibs, only for injury to sideline him after 14 goals in 20 League games.

One very significant fixture, and result, was the 1-0 win at Aberdeen in February. It seemed to epitomise Rangers experience over the entire season and the two previous ones – long lists of injured players and long-term injuries which meant shuffling the club's resources. Rangers went to Pittodrie with something of a makeshift team, without captain Gough, still without Steven Wright and Trevor Steven. Their workhorse player, Ian Ferguson, was asked to play the only forward role and Walter Smith flooded the midfield successfully and brought home a notable win, penalty goal or not. The high incidence of injuries among Rangers players caused much concern among friends of the club, and Walter Smith was closely questioned about this at the 1995 AGM. He said that Rangers had taken the best possible advice about treatment of injuries, about match preparation and the like and had been assured that they were doing things properly. He also expressed the view that a link might be drawn between the number and types of injuries sustained by Rangers players and the intensity with which they are obliged to play their games, that opposition teams play harder against Rangers than against any others.

In the home game against Juventus on 1 November, Steven Wright suffered a knee injury similar to that of Ian Durrant in 1988. It kept him out for the entire season. Trevor Steven played one League game, the opening match against Kilmarnock at Ibrox and the season became a nightmare for him – not until April was he fit for Premier Division play. It is not unfair to say that his absence compromised Walter Smith's planning of the right side of the team all season. Long-term injuries at Ibrox were never better illustrated than in the case of young Derek MacInnes, the talented midfield player who joined from Greenock Morton in late 1995. He was no sooner at Ibrox than he was hospitalised for not one but two operations, the result keeping him out for the balance of the season. Alistair McCoist, at the beginning of the season, seemed to be enjoying an Indian summer to his career, scoring some critical goals for the club and a particularly vital goal for Scotland against Greece in the European Championship, but small, niggling injuries blighted his season, keeping him out for two or three games at a time.

Similarly, there has been much disquiet and concern expressed as to the manner in which certain Rangers players behave beyond the football ground. Too many of them seem too fond of what is euphemistically known as a 'good night out'. A particularly humiliating illustration came early in 1996. During the weekend of the Wales-Scotland Rugby international, when Rangers were without a fixture, several Rangers players including Gascoigne, McCoist, Durrant, Goram and members of the coaching staff in Archie Knox and David Dodds were reported to have spent the weekend on a binge in Cardiff and London. This was later dismissed as a 'youthful prank' by the Rangers vice-chairman Donald Findlay QC, but to the extent that it was widely reported in tabloids and broadsheets alike, it was more serious than that.

This 'machismo' that equates drinking alcohol to excess with manliness is a part of Scottish culture that the nation could well do without. It is an abject philosophy. When the *Daily Mail*, interviewing Ravanelli, the Juventus player, asked him if he drank, he said, "Of course – mineral water". And when he said he would be happy to give them an interview after training, the *Daily Mail* representatives had to wait until 7pm – when training ended! Another instance of lack of discipline at the club came two days before Rangers were due to play Juventus in Turin, illuminating the difference in attitude between these two major clubs. Then, Andy Goram was arrested and charged with drunk driving. Leaving aside the morality, it was highly unprofessional that a player should be in that condition two days before a critical match AND be selected to play. One can hardly imagine a Juventus player, or any senior Italian player, being allowed to play 48 hours after being involved in such an incident. Another Rangers player arrested – and locked in a police cell for four hours – was the full-back David Robertson. After an evening in a city centre pub with McCoist, Goram, Durrant and John Brown, Robertson was seen 'trashing' a car owned by a member of the pub's management. Robertson paid the car owner £2,000 and was given a six-month deferred sentence.

Many Rangers fans were disquieted over all these incidents and in particular, following the Goram affair, felt that a true disciplinarian in the manager's chair would have put Goram on the transfer list immediately, making it clear to him that he had burned his boats and that there was to be no way back for him. He is a first-class goalkeeper and with Richard Gough had been Rangers most consistent player. The club scarcely had a ready-made replacement, but nevertheless it was surely time for the club to make a once and for all example, with immediate and beneficial effect on club discipline. It is difficult to imagine that Bill Struth would have tolerated such behaviour and indiscipline from anyone at Ibrox.

When Mark Hateley left Ibrox abruptly in August 1995 – for domestic reasons it was said – and joined Ray Wilkins at Queen's Park Rangers in London, his absence left a gap in the ranks which left manager Smith with a problem which persisted all season and left him scrambling for alternative attacking formations and tactics. In his five years with Rangers, Hateley had been an outstanding success, in spite of being welcomed with a good deal of suspicion by a coterie of Rangers fans who in fact abused him heartily on his debut, in a friendly against Dynamo Kiev. He was to respond in the best possible manner by scoring vital goals for the club, memorably in a League championship decider against Aberdeen, that stunning opening goal at Elland Road in a European Cup match against Leeds United, and more than one against Celtic. No doubt these early critics saw him as a threat to Alistair McCoist, their darling boy, but in fact they worked up a very successful partnership.

Many people later claimed that Hateley, considered as a 'target striker' or whatever the jargon was for an advanced centre-forward, was the finest such player to have played for the club. Rangers have had many great scoring centre-forwards – Willie Reid, R.C.Hamilton, Jimmy Fleming, Jimmy Smith, Willie Thornton, Jimmy Millar, Derek Johnstone – and Hateley would certainly stand comparison with these. Mark left the club without playing a single League game that season and manager Smith, shuffling all the cards in his pack, was never able to find a comparable replacement.

Smith in fact had been persistently re-shaping the team. There were few if any survivors of the last Souness team, few from the team that Smith had inherited five years earlier. In the summer of 1995, as we have seen, he signed Paul Gascoigne, Steven Wright and Oleg Salenko. Later he tried to sign Ule Kirsten from Bayern Leverkusen and early in 1996, did sign Eric Bo Andersen from Aalborg in Denmark, an international striker. In January of 1996, Salenko went to Istanbulspor of Turkey in exchange for Peter Van Vossen. These newcomers were not perhaps of the very highest quality but manager Smith no doubt had decided that he must have replacements for his strikers Durie and McCoist who were injured.

The Salenko saga brought the age of the agent into sharp focus. With the 'Jean-Marc Bosman' ruling which abolished restrictive contracts and gave players complete freedom at the end of contracts, players' agents became increasingly important in the international 'machinery' of the game. They have a useful function to perform. Club managers can scarcely be expected to know the availability of players throughout Europe, indeed increasingly throughout the world, since footballers are feeding into the British game not only from Europe but from Africa and South America. The result is that managers may be signing players on name and reputation and agents' recommendations without investigating fully how they might adapt to British, to Scottish culture, and the Scottish way of life, much less how the game is played in Scotland.

Some of Rangers signings have been of doubtful quality

in these respects. One thinks of Basile Boli, Salenko, Kuznetsov, even Mikhailichenko. In each case Rangers were signing players of proven international quality. Boli had played many times for France and had been a European Cup winner with Marseille. Salenko had scored five goals in one World Cup match for Russia. Mikhailichenko had captained the Soviet Union in the European Championship finals, and to Olympic gold. Kuznetsov, who suffered a bad injury in but his second match for Rangers, had also won Olympic gold with the USSR.

The questions were – how often had Rangers scouting staff, or the manager for that matter seen these players play, and what consideration was given as to how they might adapt to life in Scotland? There is a risk of course in any signing, particularly those of foreign players. In an interview in *The Scotsman*, Walter Smith said that he had spent much time and effort in trying to sign Floran Raducioiu, a proven international player of tremendous pace and power, who played with Espanol Barcelona. Within 24 hours of 'losing' him, he had contacted a continental agent and asked what strikers were available. He was given the name of Oleg Salenko. Smith said that he had some recollection of seeing Salenko play in the 1994 World Cup finals, knew that he had scored five in the game against Cameroon and on that basis decided to sign him for something around £2.5 million.

Salenko was a fine player – intelligent, thoughtful, someone who could shield the ball, go past a defender, a goalscorer. He did not have pace such as Rudicioiu had. Nor was he as good in the air as Hateley. Few forwards are. Such shortcomings were scarcely Salenko's responsibility and one has to question a policy that permits a jump in 24 hours from signing a player with pace and strength to one with very different qualities – one always imagines that managers buy specific qualities to fit a team pattern.

When early in 1996 Salenko was despatched to Turkey, he was exchanged for Peter Van Vossen. Thus with Hateley gone, with McCoist and Durie injured, Rangers were left without a recognised striker. Van Vossen had played 18 times for Holland and had played for Ajax and Anderlecht. He could scarcely be described as a poor player. Yet when deals are being done for millions of pounds, it behoves the buying club to do its homework thoroughly.

These were some of the matters exercising the many friends, season ticket holders, shareholders, bondholders of the club throughout the season. The wide players complementing the three central defenders in the team structure were Alec Cleland and David Robertson. The pace, and from time to time the menacing shooting power of Robertson on the left were highly acceptable. Cleland worked hard and loyally, but was never quite able to dominate possession of the slot. The skill, class, vision and intelligence of Trevor Steven on that side of the team was missed. Nevertheless success in the shape of results came relentlessly. The traditional short fuse of the Rangers supporter spluttered in late March, when the team seemed to falter. In a home match against the luckless Falkirk, it produced a vintage first-half performance, leading 2-0 and overwhelming the opposition to the point of embarrassment, then in the second half completely losing its pulse and rhythm, eventually winning unimpressively by 3-2. A week later, against Raith Rovers at Kirkcaldy, Rangers were 2-1 down with seven minutes left when McCoist equalised. Then one minute from the end, in a storming finish which belied the first hour of the match, the same man completed

a hat-trick, put Rangers in front, and Durie in extra-time, made it 4-2.

These results and performances in hindsight may be put down to the approaching Scottish Cup semi-final match with Celtic, in which the team again showed great resolution in a major win.

Yet all of these misgivings, for want of a better word, arose from a success which was in many ways unprecedented, and from a growing awareness that in Walter Smith, Rangers may have a manager to be compared with the great ones, Bill Struth and Scot Symon.

The championship was won in a blazing crescendo and a goalscoring tour-de-force by Paul Gascoigne in the last home match. The game at Motherwell on 20 April, the 34th of the season, with Aberdeen at Ibrox and Kilmarnock at Rugby Park to come, was seen by Rangers fans as one of major importance. Motherwell invariably played well against the Govan club and there were disquieting memories of a desperately close 3-2 win over the Motherwell team in an excellent Ibrox match back in February. This time, a goal from Stuart McCall in the opening minutes settled the team and it went on to a solid 3-1 win, demonstrating yet again the powerful desire which seemed to run through the club for the winning of this championship.

Once more in a season's climax it was to be Aberdeen in opposition. The statistics of the affair were that in beating Partick Thistle 4-2 at Firhill, on Saturday, 27 April, Celtic had amassed a remarkable 80 points from 35 matches. Rangers had 81 from 34 matches. Victory over Aberdeen would make them champions. On Sunday, 28 April, with Ibrox bulging with 47,247 spectators, with the match televised live, Rangers won their 46th League championship title in a manner as breathtaking as any in their long history.

Aberdeen brought out in this Rangers team the one quality they had shown throughout the season – resolution. When Aberdeen scored after 19 minutes with Brian Irvine's close-range shot following a right-wing corner-kick, a wave of apprehension swept over Ibrox's towering stands. But within minutes, Gascoigne had produced the first of three gem-like goals to equalise. Brian Laudrup, taking a left-wing corner, cut the ball back low to Gascoigne on the edge of the penalty area. Thrusting through the 'inside-left channel', the Englishman flashed passed two defenders with brilliant ball control and lightning feet. Almost on the dead-ball line, he somehow switched his balance and clipped his shot, right-footed, over the left shoulder of the goalkeeper, Michael Watt, and into the far roof of the net. It was a goal of imagination, control and stunning execution.

Nevertheless, Aberdeen held Rangers off and made an immensely thrilling match of it. Indeed, later in the half, they might well have gone ahead again when Scott Booth broke through the Rangers defensive line and was clear, in the classic one-on-one confrontation with the goalkeeper. But this had become an Andy Goram speciality. His speed of reaction and decision – he came out quickly to reduce Booth's angles – let him parry, and hold, the shot.

With some ten minutes remaining, yet another stunning Paul Gascoigne goal turned the match and won the championship. He found possession ten yards inside his own half and ran at the Aberdeen defence, holding off converging opponents and showing yet again his marvellous close control. Laudrup, ahead of him, made a decoying run to the left. Gascoigne ran on. About 12 yards out, about to be smothered by defenders, he let go a left-foot shot that flashed past Watt's right shoulder. The huge crowd was in uproar, overjoyed by this brilliant and dramatic strike, and with an eighth successive championship won. And when, a few minutes from the end, Gordon Durie was tumbled, and a penalty awarded, it had to be none other than Paul Gascoigne, despatching the kick clinically to make it three, this time right-footed, low, to the goalkeeper's left.

After this bravura performance, Gascoigne celebrated, grandstanding and blowing kisses to the crowd, like a man who had conquered himself. Later, at his press conference, he spoke of how 14 surgical operations – his injuries had included a broken leg and a broken jaw – in three and a half years, this season, this success made it all worthwhile. And he thanked manager Walter Smith for 'giving me back my life'.

If the 1995-96 League championship was settled by Gascoigne's bravura performance against Aberdeen, the Scottish Cup, and the club's 14th 'double' of League and Scottish Cup, was won by a performance, comparable in drama, by Brian Laudrup in the 5-1 Final victory over Hearts. Thus the club's two great international footballers had stood centre stage in Rangers' 47th championship win, their 27th Scottish Cup win.

The Cup campaign had featured three straight rounds away from home, but less than onerous jousts against, twice, Highland League opposition, and against Second Division Clyde. Keith were consumed 10-1 in a match played at Pittodrie, Clyde went down 4-1, and Inverness Caledonian lost 3-0 in a match played at Tannadice in which the Caley players seemed most concerned with claiming Paul Gascoigne's shirt at the finish. The semi-final which followed was somewhat different, a confrontation yet again with the old enemy Celtic. Despite Celtic's very impressive League form, it was a match always controlled by Rangers, with goals coming from McCoist and Laudrup. McCoist's was a close-in crumb to a flashing David Robertson cross shot which goalkeeper Gordon Marshall parried but could not hold. The Laudrup goal was something of a gem. A pass volleyed accurately first time by Gordon Durie, of all people, sent the Dane flashing through the Celtic defensive line. His lob beat the advancing Marshall and bounced dramatically into the net. The Celtic goal a few minutes from the end to make it 2-1 was of no consequence – too little, too late for the Parkhead club,

Paul Gascoigne caps a gloriously happy season for Rangers by lifting the Scottish Cup, won with a resounding 5-1 thrashing of Hearts at Hampden in May 1996.

One of the most striking aspects of Scottish football's 1995-96 season was the 'resurrection' of Celtic. The word is not too dramatic – two seasons earlier, the Celtic Football Club was on the verge of extinction. It was deeply in debt, somewhere in the area of £4 million overdrawn at the bank, with a rundown stadium and a dispirited team. But having won the Scottish Cup in May of 1995, in the following season Celtic were providing the most serious challenge which Rangers had known since Aberdeen had run them so close in 1990-91, and the best from Celtic since they had last won the championship, in 1987-88.

The Celtic club was fortunate in one sense. There were friends of Celtic with funds to invest if the existing board of directors, dominated for so long by the Kelly and White families, and which had brought the club down, could be removed. After a long and bitter and too often public battle, Fergus McCann, a Scot who had made a fortune in the travel business and others in Canada, eventually won control and set about rescuing the club from the very brink of the abyss. He was reported to have provided an immediate £1 million of his own money, to keep the bank at bay.

He made his first priority the rebuilding of the aged Celtic Park and organised a share flotation which raised reportedly the astonishing sum of £14 million, greater than any other British club had achieved. After a year's lodging at Hampden Park, the team returned to a dramatic if spartan stadium which rose in remarkable fashion to dominate the skyline of Glasgow's East End. The rebuilding of the Celtic team has been equally remarkable. Ever since the club was formed it has had a reputation for being rather cheese-paring in its financial treatment of staff, in not competing on players' wages for example and for selling off very many talented players. In more recent times, they have lost, at the very last moment, players who have been tempted to Ibrox for instance, by better wages and conditions. Outstanding cases have been Maurice Johnston back in 1989, and Gordan Petric in 1995.

The latter example may have been due to Fergus McCann's commendably frugal housekeeping but also, on his part, a lack of awareness of how the game in Scotland operates and how it is governed. He was indiscreet in tempting Tommy Burns, manager of Kilmarnock, to leave that job and come to Celtic with the result an inquiry by the governing bodies, and a costly rebuke. When Brian O'Neill, a talented young centre-half was out of contract, one had the impression that McCann felt that the same salary, with perhaps a small cost of living increase would hold a player who had become a first-team regular and was on the brink of international recognition. There were clearly differences of approach. Following Celtic's Cup Final win in 1995, Burns came close to leaving the club. When Petric was 'lost' to Rangers and Burns had asked what had gone wrong, he said "You'll have to ask the president", clearly referring to McCann. Mr McCann, chairman and managing director, quickly reminded him who owned the club and who was paying his wages. Burns had to climb down.

Much of the credit for the resurgence of Celtic on the field was due to Burns, who dealt shrewdly in the transfer market, and to a surprising absence of injuries in 1995-96. He may have had better value from some signings than had Walter Smith. Two major signings from abroad were Pierre van Hoojidonk and Andreas Thom, both of whom adapted well to the Scottish game. Another major achievement was the signing of Jackie Macnamara from Dunfermline Athletic, an exciting and skilled right-back of pace who ideally wanted to go to Ibrox. The call never came.

Celtic certainly had better luck than Rangers in terms of injuries, and there was the impression that their playing resources were limited in such a way that had they suffered a serious level of injuries, the Celtic challenge would not have been as stubborn and sustained as it was.

Just as Rangers fans, with eight consecutive championships won, had become obsessed with winning a ninth to equal the Celtic record of the 1960s and 1970s, so Celtic would be just as determined to protect and preserve that record. All in all, it made the prospect of the 1996-97 season one of the most stirring in Scottish League history.

who suffered their second Cup defeat from Rangers in the season.

The Final turned, to some extent, on two incidents which were quite unpredictable but which at the end saw Rangers triumphant, and Hearts demoralised. With less than five minutes played, Hearts' young captain, Gary Locke, badly twisted his knee and had to be replaced. And with less than five minutes of the second half played, Gilles Rousset, Hearts' French goalkeeper, suffered one of those haunting goalkeeping mistakes which come along only once in a hundred games.

Rangers had opened the match conservatively, playing carefully in defence with Gascoigne obviously withdrawn, keeping Hearts at arm's length, denying them any early success. Nevertheless, over the first 20 minutes, they were still more penetrative than Hearts. After 25 minutes, the Edinburgh team began to throw off its inhibitions over its regrouped pattern, and showed more unity, and imagination. It was a brief interlude. With 35 minutes gone, Durie pitched a ball beyond the defensive line, for Laudrup. The Dane volleyed his shot in full stride, finding the narrowest of gaps between Rousset's diving, reaching right hand, and his right-hand post. It was a stunning strike which put a proper reflection on things at half-time.

Five minutes into the second half, Laudrup struck again. From the right wing, turning his defender again and again, he found room to turn inside and strike, left-footed, a ground shot to Rousset's near post. It was rather a routine shot demanding a routine save, But the big goalkeeper, at 6ft 4in a pillar in every sense of Hearts' revival during the season, in going down to field it, let it slip between his legs and over the line. Rangers were inspired and produced 20 minutes of flowing football that matched their best of the season. Their defensive line of McLaren, Gough and Brown, unmatched in the air, was a perfect platform for an outstanding display of counter-attacking football, and Laudrup and Durie were a perfect strike force.

The Dane set up all three of Durie's goals. The first, from a break down the left, saw Laudrup's low, driven cross volleyed in turn by the Scot, wide of Rousset's left hand. The next, again from Laudrup on the left, was from a little dinked cross which Durie ran in, and the third, the hat-trick goal, came from the right and a cross that found its target so precisely that Durie was able to head the goal without breaking stride.

The explosive nature of the running, the accuracy of delivery and, of course, the relentless finishing, made these goals of wonder.

Brian Laudrup may well have played the best 45 minutes of his career in this second half. His close skills in turning a defender, his acceleration away from the man when once beaten, his body strength in holding off or riding physical challenges, all are features of his repertoire, brilliantly demonstrated here. It was a vintage performance. And set in a team performance that was so encompassing that once again the Ibrox club was confirmed as, by a wide margin, the dominant force in the Scottish game.

The date 16 April 1996, marked the fifth anniversary of Graeme Souness' resignation as Rangers manager, and Walter Smith's succession. Since then, including a title win in the season Souness left (1990-91), Walter Smith has guided the club to six successive championships, three Scottish Cup wins (a trophy which Souness never did win), two League Cup wins and a treble season in 1992-93. Seven of these trophy honours were successive, and in the treble season there was a sequence of ten games undefeated in the

European Cup, four of them drawn, including two drawn games with the winners, Marseille.

Walter Smith, in season 1995-96, proved himself quite outstanding in coping with a sustained and serious injury list, in using tactical acumen in team selection when, for example, he had no fit and recognised striker available, in tolerating a three-months bedding-in period for Paul Gascoigne, for tolerating with calm and in good spirit, the endless torrent of criticism and media demands which come with the job, and above all motivating his playing staff from week to week throughout a long and very demanding season. And that is why, all bickering apart, with eight successive League championship wins behind them, friends of Rangers were more and more obsessed with winning two more – the succession of ten, one more than the historic nine of Celtic, which Rangers themselves, of course, achieved from 1939-47 inclusive, and parity with the world record ten of Dinamo Berlin from 1979-88 inclusive.

The Way Ahead

WHEN four youths, walking in Glasgow's West End Park in 1872 hit upon the idea of forming a football club to take part in the new, growing sport in the city, they could not have begun to imagine that what started as virtually a boys' club would grow into the multi-million pounds business which is Rangers Football club today.

The growth and development of the club is a complex story told we hope accurately and honestly in this book. In the 1880s for instance, Rangers came perilously close to going under, hard to imagine today. So many clubs of the time, scratching for cash subscriptions, amateurs, scratching for pitches to play on, dependent on amateur helpers, not to mention wives and mothers to wash the kit, are no longer with us. Our early statistics show names – Vale of Leven, Renton – once famous, now forgotten. Perhaps only luck allowed Rangers to survive.

It is a romantic story without parallel in Scotland. The historic rivals, Queen's Park, remained outside the initial Scottish League and have persistently spurned professionalism. Celtic, certainly founded for charitable reasons in 1887 when football was close to professionalism, was quickly taken over by business men who from the earliest days organised the club as a business. And Queen's Park, of course, is generally considered to have been run by the professional classes, the middle classes

'The First TwoDecades' will show many differences, discrepancies, with *The Story of Rangers*, published by John Allan, a sports journalist later sports editor of *The Daily Record*. We believe our account to be more reliable, both fair and accurate, based on a study of many of the early documents and contemporary accounts of Scottish football. The prime difference is the date of origin of the club, surely a remarkably easy fact to substantiate. Allan's book said 1873 and from the publication of Allan's book, all the club's literature, letterheads, publications say '1873', to the extent of celebrating a centenary in 1973, with games against Ajax and Arsenal. All publications pre-1923 refer to the formation date as 1872. We suspect that 1873 was chosen simply to defer to the publication date of Allan's book.

The growth of the club is reflected in a sense in the various stadia it has used. When Rangers in their first decade

moved to Kinning Park on the south side of the city, where they have remained, for the first time they began to have a strong identity with the local community. After moving a mile or so to Ibrox, their stadium there grew until it had a 60,000 capacity. With terracing built of scaffolding, the Ibrox disaster of 1902 clearly made that unacceptable, and the stadium was rebuilt with earth terracing. The building of the 10,500 main grandstand in 1929 was an exceptional act of vision on the part of the directors and saw a huge bowl of 80,000 capacity. All of this was based on the continuing success of the team, of course, and its popularity.

In this respect, the late Celtic chairman Bob Kelly related in his autobiography that when Celtic built their stand a little earlier, they had only 3,800 seats and it took them several years for them to even fill it. This perhaps underlines the differences in volume of support between the clubs.

Rangers growth over the years has been tied to the industrial growth of Glasgow. It also contains having over the years a group of players of quality converging at the right time, the vision of the directors in presenting a stadium which meets the demands of its supporters, and the need for a Protestant, Unionist club in Scotland balancing the perceived Catholic, Nationalist Celtic.

Earlier this century, Rangers, Celtic and Queen's Park vied with each other to build Scotland's biggest stadium. The prize was the staging of international matches and Cup Finals. Queen's Park, with the development of Hampden to 150,000 in the 1930s, won. The Ibrox disaster of 1971 sent Rangers off on a different direction, long before the sadness of Bradford and Hillsborough and the Heysel. It was clear that the massed crowds of the post-war era were gone. The need was for a modern comfortable, manageable and SAFE stadium. Rangers created that and now the Ibrox club has the finest stadium in Scotland, one as good as any other in the UK.

In November 1988, David Murray, friend of Graeme Souness and a successful young Scottish entrepreneur in steel stockholding and property, bought the shareholding of Lawrence Marlborough and became virtual owner of Rangers. As chairman of a newly-constructed board, he brought good, sound practical business experience to the club, and broadened the club's horizon far beyond that achieved by David Holmes. He spent many millions of pounds on international footballers under the guidance of first Souness, then Walter Smith; he spent millions on the ground by adding a deck to the main stand, making it all-seated by seating the enclosure in front of it, and extended dramatically the marketing effort of an astonishing range of club products – clothing, tops, shoes, scarves, phone cards, videos, books, pictures, posters, even razors and ashtrays. There seemed almost nothing that could not be sold wearing a Rangers logo.

With the team constantly shown on television, particularly in live matches, sponsors were lining up to do business with Rangers, and with the corporate facilities greatly extended, Rangers are now a multi-million pound enterprise.

In 1996, the 'corners' at Ibrox were 'filled in' – the Copland Road stand was connected to the Govan stand, the Govan stand to the Broomloan Road stand, to give a capacity of 51,000. And in signing Paul Gascoigne the previous summer, Murray said that if the demand was there, he would push the stadium capacity out to around 64,000. How it was to be done remained to be seen, but it was clear that Murray's thinking did not embrace a Rangers team relying on matches against Morton and Falkirk, with respect to these clubs. David Murray clearly envisaged Rangers playing in more embracing competitions than the domestic Scottish League and Cups. Whether these would be British, or European, remained likewise to be seen.

Certainly, trends in European football suggested that UEFA, the continental body wished to create more and more fixtures for the cream of European football. For example, they initiated the Champions League in 1991, and extended from eight to 16 the number of clubs, eight of them given automatic entry, principally because these would come from the major football nations.

More and more it seems that clubs will be in the Champions League not strictly on merit but on the strength of television audiences they can attract. Thus England, Germany, France, Spain and Italy are favoured. UEFA may be more noble than this, but one doubts it – large amounts of money are at stake.

For Rangers to be able to compete on a level field with clubs from these five nations will not be easy. Each of them has a much higher population base than Scotland affords, which is particularly relevant in terms of the supply of native talent.

Short of winning the European Cup, it is difficult to imagine Rangers at any time gaining automatic entry to a Champions League. They will have to qualify their way in.

The wealth in European football is considerable, but only in respect of the privileged clubs. UEFA figures show that European Cup Finalists in 1995, Ajax and AC Milan, each received, exclusive of gate receipts, something in the region of £8 million for their participation in the competition. For a successful club, the money to be earned is considerable indeed. On the other hand AEK Athens and Dinamo Kiev, not so successful, received only £1 million, which might not pay Paul Gascoigne's salary

The fact that Rangers can now attract top-class players from all over Europe speaks volumes for how the club has changed over the past 10 years. Then, Rangers were not able to attract Ian Wallace, a homesick Scot playing for an unfashionable English Midlands club. He was not able to accept the cut in salary involved in coming to Ibrox. Now Rangers can probably compete with any club in Europe, except those in Italy. The signing of Paul Gascoigne underlined this in many ways. His arrival and the media hype which it attracted suggested that Rangers were in line for a substantial increase in commercial turnover, already close to equalling season ticket and admissions income. This may very well have been a factor in his signing. In fact Rangers were said to be anticipating the additional sale, in England, of 50,000 'tops' bearing Gascoigne's name – 'Gazza'.

For the future, Rangers' first priority must be the winning of the Scottish League championship. That opens European doors. Besides, there is an unspoken feeling inside the club, widely discussed in the stands, that Rangers would dearly like to go one better than Celtic's nine championships in a row by retaining their title at least until 1998, not to mention the world record of ten consecutive national championships won by Dinamo Berlin, then of East Germany, between 1979 and 1988.

Questions remain. Can Rangers assemble a playing staff which would compete in, and succeed in, the present domestic competition, provide players for the national team, and at the same time succeed in major European competition?

As things stand, Rangers would have to play 13 games to win the European Cup. If they were playing in some form of midweek European League, with a 20-game schedule played over the whole season, then they would require two different teams.

And how much public interest could be sustained in European League matches if a team languished in mid-table, or in the lower half. In Scotland of course, there must also be the calculation of how much admission money any club can extract from its customers in any one season. There must be a saturation point in a country like Scotland, which is 'Too big to be small, too small to be big'. That may well be the dilemma for this great club in the future.

Riots, Disturbances and

THE first disturbance in the long Rangers story was a good deal short of being a riot, but it certainly was a happening. When Preston North End opened the original Ibrox ground in August 1887, a huge crowd, perhaps 18,000 in a ground measured for 15,000 spilled through the railings, spilled across the field and stopped the game, permanently, 20 minutes early. The fact that Rangers were trailing 8-1 was of course entirely incidental.

After the first Celtic v Rangers match in May 1888, at Celtic Park, both teams and officials sat down to supper and a concert, friendly as could be. Ten years later, things were different.

At the January match in 1898, 50,000 packed into Celtic Park. The match was closely contested, the crowd frequently encroached and with only 40 policemen on hand, the game was abandoned after 70 minutes. Celtic were criticised in the newspapers for lack of crowd control. Celtic in turn blamed the crowd, one editorial describing them as 'the very scum of the city...' Rangers were more concerned about where the gate money went, claiming that before the referee had stopped play, they had agreed with Celtic directors to split the take. Celtic failed to remember this, keeping 80 per cent of the receipts as the regulations permitted, and Rangers felt they were 'cheated out of it'.

In the Glasgow Cup Final of 1901, a drawn game at Ibrox meant a replay also at Ibrox, following the custom of the times. Celtic said it should be at Celtic Park, took a huff and withdrew from the competition.

From a huff to a tiff, and how Rangers won and lost the much-prized Exhibition Cup... In 1901 with the Great Glasgow exhibition taking place at Gilmorehill, the exhibition authorities presented a trophy to the Scottish Football League. The top eight Scottish clubs were to compete and it was agreed that the winners would receive the trophy. A brilliant display by Rangers in the Final against Celtic saw them take the Cup, 3-1. Next, following the Ibrox Disaster of 1902 at the Scotland v England international match, Rangers put up the Cup for a competition to raise funds for the dependents, with Rangers, Celtic, Sun-

derland and Everton competing for what was named the 'British League Cup'.

The two Glasgow teams reached their third Final of the season. It was a tremendous match, won 3-2 for Celtic only after extra-time, and featured a hat-trick by the young Jimmy Quinn, the first of four he would score against Rangers (the others were in a Disaster Fund benefit match at Hampden 1902 (Celtic 7-2), the Scottish Cup Final of 1904 at Hampden (Celtic 3-2) and a 1911-12 League match at Celtic Park (Celtic 3-0). Rangers felt that the Exhibition Cup aka the British League Cup was their property and claimed that there was an agreement that it should be put up for annual competition. Celtic did not agree. Rangers were miffed. The trophy remains to this day on the Parkhead sideboard.

In a Scottish Cup semi-final in 1905 at Celtic Park, Rangers were short of several regular players because of injury or illness, but in a tumultuous match, held out, 0-0 at the interval. Just before half-time, the Celtic fullback McLeod pulled a muscle and left the field. Against the ten-man team, Rangers scored twice, but Celtic, in the formidable form of Jimmy Quinn, their centre-forward, hustled and harassed the Rangers defence. When he was tackle by Craig, who held his legs in a tangle as the ball broke loose, Quinn lashed out, and was ordered off. Unhappy with play, and no doubt uncomfortable in the rain, several Celtic fans invaded the pitch and refused to leave. The game was abandoned. The Celtic directors conceded the tie. Quinn was suspended for four weeks. But something rather worse was to come.

The first decade of the 20th century saw Rangers and Celtic established as the pre-eminent Scottish clubs, and the passing from power and influence of the early leaders Queen's Park, Dumbarton and Vale of Leven. The first of the great Rangers teams held sway from 1898-99 to 1902-03. As it passed, Hibernian and Third Lanark had brief moments of success as the first of the great Celtic teams came to maturity. It was in command until 1910, then again throughout World War One. Rangers challenged them persistently throughout this entire

period, winning three successive championship from 1910-11 to 1912-13. The clubs met in the Scottish Cup Final of 1909. The regulations of the day permitted extra-time to be played only after a second replay. Willie Maley, the Celtic manager, had suggested to a newspaper that it would be sensible if extra-time be played after the first replay. The newspaper proposed the idea.

In the first match, a 2-2 draw was the result of a thriller before 70,000 at Hampden. It had a controversial finish with Celtic 2-1 down and only ten minutes left. Their outside-right Weir swung over a cross which goalkeeper Rennie gathered, with an eye on the onrushing Quinn. To avoid him, he took a step back and half-turned left to clear the ball. The referee awarded a goal, saying that Rennie had carried the ball over the line! The replay a week later ended 1-1. Several of the Celtic players and one or two of the Rangers lingered on the field, not sure if extra-time was to be played, after the speculation in the newspapers. In the same mind, almost all of the 60,000 crowd waited too. When the extra-time did not come, and convinced that a third match was to be played only for financial reasons, they invaded the pitch en masse. When the police, outnumbered of course, tried to restrain them, they were swept aside savagely. The mob broke up barricades and turnstiles, set fires on the running track and fuelled with whisky, attacked the fire brigade by cutting hoses and for four hours, were on the rampage.

Directors of both clubs agreed to petition the Scottish Football Association to abandon the Final. The SFA agreed, withheld Cup and medals, compensated Queen's Park for the damage to the ground and each club was fined £150. There had been no question of a Rangers v Celtic battle – the fury of the crowd, inflamed no doubt by drink, had been aimed at the 'authorities'.

In the second round of the Scottish Cup in 1912, Rangers were drawn against Clyde at Shawfield. A record attendance of 52,000 led to spectator encroachment after 73 minutes and the game was abandoned. Rangers, trailing 3-1, conceded.

RIOTS, DISTURBANCES AND SUCH-LIKE HAPPENINGS

Such-Like Happenings

There was large-scale rioting at a wartime Southern League match between Rangers and Celtic at Ibrox in September 1941. The Lord Provost of Glasgow, Sir Patrick ('Paddy') Dolan, announced:- 'The Chief Constable has powers to prohibit games between Celtic and Rangers until the end of the war, and I have informed him that if he cares to exercise that power, he will have the support of all citizens ...' The 'support of all citizens' was perhaps a very moot point. The trouble in the first place had been caused by Celtic fans, and the SFA War Emergency Committee closed Celtic Park for a month, causing them to play home games at Shawfield, the home of Clyde FC. The committee was also concerned with the level of dissent shown by Rangers players.

On 1 June 1946, Rangers played a 0-0 draw with Celtic at Hampden in the 'Victory Cup' semi-final. The attendance was 90,000. In the midweek replay, before 45,000, Rangers led 1-0 at half-time, but the second half degenerated into a farce. Celtic's Sirrell injured an ankle, and became a passenger. When Rangers were awarded a penalty, George Paterson, the Celtic captain appealed the decision while holding the ball, and was ordered off for not surrendering it quickly enough to the referee. Mallen, obstructing the penalty-spot, was ordered off. Four young men, Celtic supporters needless to say, came 'over the fence' but were mopped up by the police. Celtic's Gallacher had to retire injured and they finished with seven fit players. George Young scored from the penalty-kick, Rangers won 2-0 and Celtic went home persuaded that referee Dale, among other things, had not been entirely sober.

In the League Cup Final of 23 October 1965, Celtic won 2-1 both goals coming from penalties. A massive, indeed record Hampden crowd of 107,609 saw Rangers' Ronnie McKinnon handle a harmless free-kick, after 18 minutes. John Hughes scored from the spot. Ten minutes later, Davie Provan, playing at left-back against the elusive Jimmy Johnstone, fouled the winger – penalty number two, converted once more by Hughes. The Rangers fans were not at all amused by referee Phillips. Rangers

battled fiercely and got a goal back six minutes from the end, too little, too late to save the match.

After the presentation, the Celtic players took to the field again to flaunt the Cup before their supporters and hundreds of infuriated Rangers fans invaded. The police quickly got the players off the field, and eventually restored some order, but the result of it all was 'laps of honour' were banned, a ban which remained effective for many years.

When Rangers went to Dens Park on 15 March 1975 for a League match with Dundee, they led the championship by six points from Celtic, with seven games to play. They had not won the title for 11 years, during which time Jock Stein's fine Celtic teams had won nine in succession. A former Ibrox favourite, centre-forward Colin Stein, had been brought back from Coventry City at a cost of £80,000 ten days earlier.

Rangers were staggered in the very first minute, when they failed to clear a corner from the right and Hutchinson scored. They buckled down to save the game, but found it hard going. Then, after 37 minutes, Colin Stein was ordered off (for the seventh time in his career). His challenge on Tommy Gemmell was penalised. Stein disputed the verdict so vigorously with referee George Smith that he was sent packing. Trouble flared on the terraces as the game re-started, and fans spilled on to the pitch to escape the fighting and flying missiles. Police with dogs brought it all to a halt, making 18 arrests. The ten-strong Rangers team made all the running in the second half. Tommy McLean scored a brilliant individual equaliser after 52 minutes, and with only seven minutes left, Derek Parlane shot home the winner.

If Rangers seemed to be in the lead in the pitch-invasion championship, the events of the Scottish Cup Final of 1980 perhaps put an end to all that nonsense and certainly forced a profound change on the patterns of crowd behaviour in the Scottish game. Before this, in the late 1970s at a Motherwell/Rangers match there had been a crowd invasion and others even earlier. They were not all restricted to the exuberance of a few youths.

The Rangers-Celtic 1980 Final was

an exciting match, one side then the other having spells in control. It went into extra-time, when a Danny McGrain shot, which Rangers goalkeeper Peter McCloy seemed to have covered, was deflected in by George McCluskey. At the end of the match, the Celtic players went to Hampden's King's Park End, the traditional Celtic end, to celebrate with their supporters. With no fences to confine them, their fans came over the wall to join in the dancing and cavorting and proceeded uninhibited to march across the pitch to the Mount Florida End where the Rangers fans, infuriated at the late result and incensed by the Celtic celebrations, flooded on to the field in their hundreds and joined in a pitched battle. The television cameras kept turning. Shameful scenes were broadcast to a nation humiliated by the sight of mounted police charging across the Hampden turf to separate these armies. Only that ended the mayhem.

After the event, it was agreed that the police strategy had been wrong. The Glasgow police, expert at handling large crowds, had long established that in highly-charged matches between these teams, there are two potential war zones – first inside the stadium at the final whistle, and second in the streets around the stadium where fans could clash. On this occasion, perhaps because the match had thrown up no hint of trouble, nothing in the way of misbehaviour, they had withdrawn many of their stadium troops and deployed them in the streets.

Each club was fined £20,000, a trivial sum, but much more important was the subsequent passing of the Criminal Justice (Scotland) Act 1980. This made it an offence to be drunk within a Scottish ground, or when attempting to enter one; to possess alcohol in a ground; to transport alcohol in buses or special trains; to carry any kind of drink container into a ground and many other relevant restrictions.

The Act made a major contribution to the near-elimination of crowd violence that continued through the 1980s and 1990s in England and elsewhere in the world.

Rangers in Europe

IN April 1955, representatives of 18 of Europe's leading clubs met in Paris at the invitation of Gabriel Hanot, doyen of European football writers. He had been proposing in the great French sporting daily, *L'Equipe* and its sister weekly *France Football* that the time was ripe for some form of inter-club competition across the Continent. It was agreed that a 'European Cup' should go ahead on a knock-out basis, although each round would be on a home and away two-match basis, except for the Final, which would be one match at a neutral venue. The champions of each country in the previous season would take part thus, oddly, making qualification for a Cup competition success in a League competition.

On the grounds that they had to start somewhere, some invitations were needed to get the ball rolling truly. Scotland that first year was represented by Hibernian, whose cavalier style was preferred to that of Aberdeen, the champions. The first competition was an outstanding success. So too were Hibs who reached the semi-final round. Oddly, England was not represented in the first year – Chelsea, the champions, were 'forbidden' to compete by Alan Hardaker, the aggressively insular secretary of the Football League in spite of the fact that Joe Mears the Chelsea chairman, was a member of the Football League Executive Committee. He no doubt decided supinely to avoid a conflict with his hired hand! The following year, Rangers started a romance with European football which was to last 40 years, almost unbroken, to the present day.

The European Cup spawned two other competitions, the Cup-winners' Cup in 1960-61 and what is now known as the UEFA Cup, variously called Inter Cities Cup and Fairs Cup, over the years. After all this, the original competition had to become the 'Champions Cup', but in general usage it remains the European Cup. Rangers took part as champions in 1956-57 and only four times since have they failed to appear in one competition or the other. Over such a long period, inevitably, there have been triumphs and tribulations, disasters, hopes raised and dashed. Success has proved elusive. Three appearances in the European Cup-winners' Cup Final, one of them victorious has been the sum total of success and to a club as ambitious as Rangers, this has never seemed quite enough. More objective observers might say that their ambition has outstripped their reason too often in European play. The European Cup has been their Holy Grail, particularly since their rivals, Celtic, succeeded in 1967. There have been hard lessons, some of them learned in facing quality opposition.

For example, too often lack of concentration has meant early goals, or late goals, being lost (Arnold Palmer, the golf champion always said that he concentrated particularly hard over the first few holes and the last few holes of a round). At various times Rangers have been naive in their preparation and dispositions and investigations of opponents. In our view, two principle factors mitigate against sustained success for Rangers in Europe. First is that the quality of domestic opposition that Rangers have to face is not comparable to that experienced in the major countries, England, Italy, Spain, Germany, for example, and it does little to prepare them for the various styles and sophistication they have to cope with in these matches. This is scarcely the fault of the Glasgow club, rather it is a reflection of the size,

the wealth, the affluence of these other countries and the 'three foreigners' rule, which restricted teams in European football to field no more than three of this category, was an added burden to British clubs, since English, Irish and Welsh players were considered foreign. In 1956-57, having drawn a bye in the first round, Rangers first opposition in the second round, was to be OGC Nice. It became an eventful introduction.

The first leg was played at Ibrox on 24 October 1956, before 65,000 on a dark night of heavy rain, some hailstones and an electrifying atmosphere. Rangers were not inexperienced against foreign opposition. They had played splendid matches with Racing Club de Paris, apart from many Scandinavian and German clubs on tour, if seldom against 'Latin' opposition. But friendlies were one thing, Cup-ties another. Nice played in a neat rhythmic patterned style while Rangers were more powerful physically, producing as expected their direct, forceful approach to things. They should have taken more from the match than a 2-1 lead, but Colonna, the Nice goalkeeper was on top form, his defence worked resolutely and indeed the French team scored after only 23 minutes through their outside-left Faivre. A Max Murray header five minutes before half-time levelled things when Rangers really should have been three up. They bombarded Colonna's goal throughout the second half, but against an exceptional defensive performance, only Billy Simpson's goal with an hour gone compensated Rangers. The match was memorable for two refereeing decisions by Arthur Ellis of Halifax, one of England's top officials. After 55 minutes he called all the players together for a resounding lecture. He later revealed that he had become very frustrated by the French body-checking and obstruction. Then with five minutes of time left, he blew for the end of the match! He had to recall the teams. Rangers' Eric Caldow had to be retrieved from his bath.

The Nice leg was set for 1 November, but torrential rain cancelled it. Rangers were back on 14 November, again in heavy rain, tackling the Frenchmen on a quagmire. Only crude tackling and spoiling held off the more powerful Rangers players until the 40th minute, when centre-half Gonzales hacked down Max Murray. The penalty award brought a blatant intimidation of the referee, but Johnny Hubbard, Rangers penalty king, converted. At half-time Murray stabbed home a corner, but the referee, perhaps not surprisingly, ruled that time had elapsed. With an hour gone, a mishit shot by Bravo dribbled over the line and two minutes later, Foix connected with a cross from left winger Faivre. Suddenly the score was level on aggregate. In the closing minutes, the match degenerated into anarchy. Willie Logie was fouled by Muro. Logie, shall we say, defended himself. Bravo dived in to thump Logie and the Italian referee ordered both Bravo and Logie from the field. Bravo took several minutes to go. Near the end, George Niven's goal was bombarded with fireworks and the police were called to escort the referee to safety.

A third match was required. Parc des Princes in Paris was decreed as the venue two weeks later. With 15,000 in attendance, Rangers yet again dominated the first half and should have been goals in front. Again, Colonna made exceptional saves. Close to half-time, Nice broke clear and Foix scored from a dozen yards. Five minutes into the second half a Sammy Baird cross was turned into his own goal by Bonvin, but within a few minutes, Muro had restored the French lead. With 15 minutes left, Bobby Shearer, by no means a polished full-back followed through with a huge lunge that knocked Muro over the touch-line. In the mayhem that followed, Bruno threw a punch at Shearer. He responded and a scrimmage followed. Muro was removed on a trolley, apparently unconscious. The referee, M. Van Nuffel of Belgium booked Ian McColl, the Rangers captain for some reason not very clear and said later that he had ordered both Bruno and Shearer from the field. Neither left it, and Shearer later claimed no knowledge of this. Thus Rangers in their first competitive venture in Europe had been well beaten in a tie which embraced three cities, three visits to France, ten goals and either two or four players ordered off. This was highly educational – there were more lessons to come.

Rangers were back for more French, this time without tears, the following season. Against St Etienne at Ibrox with 85,000 looking on Rangers again, on possession, should have overwhelmed the opposition. They would have to learn to capitalise on such possession, particularly in home matches. They actually lost a goal after 14 minutes, retreating before a brilliant run by Mekloufi, the inside-left. Don Kitchenbrand equalised before half-time, Scott scored a second and critically, eight minutes from the end, Simpson's goal gave Rangers some security for the away leg. There before a crowd of 35,000, young Davie Wilson, taking the place of a sick Hubbard stooped to an Alex Scott centre to head an equaliser. Ferrier scored a second for St Etienne two minutes from the end, but Rangers were through on aggregate, 4-3.

In the next round, Rangers had a different experience. Drawn against AC Milan they were facing a team of the highest class with outstanding defenders in Buffon, Maldini and Bergomaschi and two virtuosi from South America in inside-forwards Schiaffino and Grillo, Uruguay and Argentina, respectively.

Ibrox's statutory 85,000 for European matches saw Milan stroll almost derisorily through the first half, virtually ignoring Murray's goal after 31 minutes. Fifteen minutes from the end, Murray made the mistake of fouling Buffon, the goalkeeper. Almost on cue, in fact within seconds, Grillo, accelerating, floated through the entire Rangers defence in a brilliant dribbling run to score. Milan, in full flight scored three more before the end, from Grillo again, Baruffi and Bean. In the return in Milan two weeks later, a deluge delayed the start for ten minutes, kept the crowd to a mere 2,000 and made the match farcical. Rangers played with spirit in the lost cause, going down 2-0 and 6-1 on aggregate.

The quality of this Milan team was underlined when they beat Manchester United, depleted by the Munich tragedy, in the semi-final and lost the Final to Real Madrid 3-2 only after extra-time. Thus in their first two seasons of the European experience, there were lessons for Rangers. Whether the club, not much given to tactical meditation, learned them or not, is a very moot point. First against the French clubs Nice and St Etienne, they had controlled the play for long periods without turning their superiority into goals. In this type of competition it would be mandatory to create chances and to convert them, ruthlessly. In the games against Milan, it was clear that Rangers, big fish in a small pond, could not hope to compete against any team of outstanding players gathered expensively from major football countries unless they adopted such a policy themselves.

Thirty years were to pass before Graeme Souness showed them the way.

In 1958-59, Rangers did not compete after surrendering their championship, third by 12 points to a Hearts team which lost only one match all season and with their memorable forwards Young, Bauld and Wardhaugh. No European nights at Ibrox this season. In 1959-60, however, they were back, drawn against Anderlecht, the Belgian champions, and found themselves in a war. The visitors were two down in three minutes and lost all control. With half an hour gone they had conceded 12 free kicks to Rangers' two, and when referee Leo Horn disallowed a goal for offside, the entire team surrounded him, manhandling and abusing him. Outside-left Andy Matthew made it three two minutes into the second half – he headed past Meert after the goalkeeper had blocked his penalty shot. Goals from Stockman and de Waele made it 3-2 dangerously close, but Sammy Baird came with two late goals to make it 5-2.

In spite of two penalty awards, the referee had been unacceptably tolerant of dreadful behaviours by Anderlecht players. The second leg, alas was a resumption of the warfare. Just before the interval, Alex Scott was sent crashing over the touch-line and track and into the boundary wall. He was stretchered off, bleeding from a head wound. He reappeared with his head bandaged as play became more and more furious, but a goal by Andy Matthew headed from Scott's cross after 65 minutes and another by Ian McMillan ten minutes later, put an end to it.

In the next round, Red Star Bratislava astonished Rangers with their attacking flair in the first match at Ibrox, raining shots down on George Niven and getting three past him. Just on half-time the half-back Matlak was ordered off and not until Davie Wilson equalised in the 74th minute did Rangers feel relaxed. Ian McMillan had scored in the very first minutes, Eric Caldow missed with a penalty, and Jimmy Millar, much praised, scored in the last minute to make it 4-3. Perversely in the away leg, Rangers defended magnificently and secured the tie with a vintage breakaway goal. Wilson's run and cross saw Scott score with a deliberate header. Miller was ordered off eight minutes from time for punching the obstructionist, Tichy, who tied the match 1-1, but not the tie, with a goal in the last minute.

Sparta Rotterdam received Rangers in the quarter-final, which saw the away team win in each leg, Rangers 3-2 in Rotterdam, Sparta 1-0 in Glasgow. Away goals were not then considered and a third match was scheduled for Arsenal's Highbury. Rangers won 3-2 before 34,176 to reach their first European Cup semi-final. It was a humiliating experience for them. They ran into Eintracht Frankfurt, a team that was clearly a class above Rangers in athleticism, technique, individual skills and tactical awareness. In Frankfurt, 80,000 saw Rangers defeated and outclassed 6-1. In spite of this scoreline 70,000 turned out at Ibrox for the return. They were aptly rewarded. After only eight minutes, the German midfield player Stinka ran 50 yards before beating Niven from outside the penalty area! It finished 6-3 to Eintracht. But this was the team that went on to dispute an historic Final with Real Madrid at Hampden, before 134,000.

In three tries, Rangers had reached the semi-final stage in European competition – perhaps a reasonable progression, considering the quality of much of the opposition. And they had further to go. Season 1960-61 saw the inauguration of the European Cup-winners' Cup and Rangers qualified by a 2-0 win over Kilmarnock.

In 1960-61, Rangers disposed of Ferencváros of Hungary

Rangers goalkeeper George Niven is well-beaten by Scherer for Red Star's first goal in the European Champions' Cup second-round first-leg game at Ibrox in November 1959.

and Borussia Mönchengladbach in jig time, then the unstoppable force ran into the immovable object – they drew Wolverhampton Wanderers. Rangers won 2-0 at Ibrox, then held Wolves 1-1 at Molineux in an April snowstorm, both hard, close matches as one would expect. Rangers then were in their first Final, with a talented team – one that now contained both Jim Baxter and Ian McMillan in midfield, Alex Scott and Dave Wilson on the wings.

The Final was a home and away affair, and Rangers ran into a Fiorentina team that displayed all the cynical irritations of Italian football. Despite their marvellous technical skills, the men from Florence represented the usual programme of body-checking, obstruction, shirt-pulling and the rest, which British footballers find so infuriating. There was a capacity 80,000 at Ibrox for the first match and when Harold Davis half-hit a back pass to goalkeeper Ritchie they were aghast when the outside-left Petris got to the ball first and set up the early goal for inside-left Milan. Six minutes later Rangers were awarded a rather soft penalty when McMillan went down after a tackle by Orzon, the Fiorentina captain. After the usual impassioned Italian protests, Eric Caldow shot wide. Fiorentina were content to contain Rangers and were helped by the naive Rangers tactic of persistently hitting high balls into the penalty area, where big Italian defenders gobbled them up. The visiting wingers, Hamrin of Sweden and Petris were outstanding players of flashing pace. A second goal from Milan in the last minute virtually guaranteed the Italians the Cup – the match in Florence followed the same pattern of Rangers huffing and puffing, the Italians containing and countering. Their 2-1 win meant a 4-1 aggregate, and a proper reflection of the talents of the teams.

In the European Cup next year, AS Monaco went down to a quite brilliant display by Rangers in the away game, considered by many to have been Jim Baxter's finest game for the club. The return at Ibrox, a more ragged match, was won by an Alex Scott goal nine minutes from the end. Both matches finished 3-2, giving Rangers a 6-4 aggregate. The next round took Rangers to East Berlin and a 2-1 win over ASK Vorwaerts. The second leg match was played in Malmö, Sweden – the Cold War at the time was such that East European countries were not given visas to visit NATO countries. It was abandoned because of fog after 45 minutes, with Rangers leading 1-0 from a Willie Henderson goal, before 4,000 people! It was replayed the following day, 23 November, this time before a crowd of 1,781, many of them Rangers supporters, who saw a 4-1 win.

The quarter-final round sent Rangers to Belgium to tackle Standard Liege. Eric Caldow withdrew before the start with an injured toe, and a youngster, Bobby King, took his place at left-back. The right wing of Willie Henderson and John Greig meant that Rangers had at least three teenagers in their team. Standard scored in six minutes when Ritchie parried a powerful shot from inside-right Sztani to the feet of Claesson. The Belgians were off and running. Wilson equalised with 19 minutes gone, but Liege were 2-1 up at half-time, and in the second half the Rangers defence, in particular centre-half Bill Paterson, wilted. It finished 4-1. At Ibrox in slippery conditions Rangers stormed Standard, but got few telling shots at goal as the Belgians held possession and sought to draw the fire out of Rangers. The home team's impatience helped them. Their left-back Heilen played Alex Scott out of the game – if Willie Henderson had played things might have been different. Henderson arrived at Ibrox too late to play, pleading he had

Fiorentina's assistant coach comes on to the field to argue with referee Steiner after he had awarded Rangers a dubious penalty in the first leg of the European Cup-winners' Cup Final at Ibrox in May 1961. He needn't have worried, though, because Eric Caldow put the spot-kick wide.

been caught in match traffic (the crowd was 76,000). In fact, he had probably dallied overlong in the Mitchell Street snooker hall!

Runners-up in the League to Dundee, Rangers' Scottish Cup win over St Mirren put them into the Cup-winners' Cup in 1962-63. Drawn against Seville at Ibrox in the first round, a Jimmy Millar hat-trick including a goal after only 12 minutes, and another by Ralph Brand gave Rangers a 4-0 lead and one or two indications from the Seville players that a warm welcome awaited them in Spain. There, the Spaniards were two up after only nine minutes. Rangers steadied and were only 2-0 down at half-time.

The second half was a tempestuous affair in very hostile atmosphere, with incidents and fights breaking out all over the field. Once, as the media reported, 'all 22 players were involved'. What both goalkeepers were doing then boggles the imagination. The Portuguese referee brought all differences of opinion to an end by wisely finishing the game a few minutes short of time. The Spanish centre-forward attacked Grieg. Many other Rangers players were attacked and inevitably defended themselves, as they were perfectly capable of doing. Happily there was no trouble off the field – apparently the crowd was not too enamoured of their own team's performance. But Davie Wilson was butted, Ronnie McKinnon was bitten, Jim Baxter was kicked, according to contemporary reports. There were no recriminations from either club or governing body. Three days later, in a League match against Dundee at Ibrox, Rangers had an unchanged team!

The next round draw must have been something of a comfort by comparison, not to say relief – Tottenham Hot-

spur. Spurs had won the double in 1961, the first team in England to do it in the 20th century, and had retained the FA Cup in 1962. Blanchflower's team was hugely talented, with David Mackay, John White, Jimmy Greaves, Bill Brown, Cliff Jones household names even in non-football households. A couple of years earlier Rangers had defeated Wolves in the semi-final of the Cup-winners' Cup, and the general feeling amongst their supporters in Glasgow was that they would handle Spurs just as successfully. It was a massive under-estimation of the depth of talent in the London team, and the quality of play they were capable of producing. Against the quicksilver switching of positions by White and Greaves and the pace of Terry Medwin and Cliff Jones on the wings, Rangers were tactically naive. In the first match at White Hart Lane, bulging at the seams with 58,859 present, goals were lost to corner kicks, Rangers being terribly weak defensively in the air. John White of all people had headed home a Greaves corner kick in just five minutes (Greaves was to score only eight minutes into the Ibrox return). In that match, Maurice Norman scored from a corner, underlining a Rangers flaw. In London it was 5-2 for Spurs, in Glasgow 3-2. Spurs went all the way in that competition, beating Atlético Madrid 5-1 in the Final to become the first British team to win a European competition.

In later years Eric Caldow recalled that manager Scot Symon gave his first tactical talk before the London game. Caldow was making his way to the hotel lounge when he bumped into a friend Joe Walsh, who was making for the bar. Walsh asked Eric where he was going. Caldow said the manager was having a tactical talk. Walsh looked at him in disbelief. The talk lasted eight minutes and Caldow was back in the bar before Walsh had ordered his drink! It comprised Symon going through the entire Spurs team and saying what wonderful players they were. It left the Rangers players with the impression that there was not much point in playing this match. In the Ibrox game, play was fast, and fascinating, and friendly drawn between two fine teams. Spurs always kept control of the aggregate situation, and the match was won in the last minute by a vintage, shimmering goal from Greaves in which he glided through the entire Rangers defence.

The draw for the European Cup produced Rangers v Real Madrid, the Real which had dominated the competition since it began in 1955 and which still presented proudly such names as Di Stefano, Puskas, Gento, Santamaria. Rangers played very well in the first leg, Willie Henderson stretching Real even if Baxter contributed little to the match. The Spanish team seemed perfectly content to take the 0-0 draw they were working for when three minutes from the end, Puskas hammered a Gento cross into the roof of the net. Rangers plunged into the cauldron of the Bernabeu Stadium (90,000) with a suicidal team selection. They were without Jimmy Millar, Ralph Brand and Davie Wilson who was injured. They had virtually a teenage forward line. Three minutes into the match, Puskas pulled down a Gento cross with his chest and volleyed an awesome shot past Shearer. Real were four up in 24 minutes, Puskas scored three and the result was 6-0. Jim Forrest had missed a very good chance in the first minute of the match. A Scottish reporter recorded that after the match, manager Scot Symon said that if Forrest had taken the chance, things might have been different. "Yes" said Gair Henderson the journalist, "it would have been 6-1 to Real." The presence of Ian McMillan might have helped, but this was a rout, perhaps a foregone rout.

In 1964-65, Red Star Belgrade in the European Cup were certain to be difficult, gifted opponents. Indeed only last minute goals both home and away provided Rangers with the chance of a deciding third match. At Ibrox, Ralph Brand's second goal in the final minute made it 3-1 to Rangers and a more reassuring margin to take away from home, although the Yugoslavs, controlling much of the second half, were rather unfortunate. In Belgrade, perhaps for the first time, Rangers seemed to apply some tactical sense in a European match. This time they set about defending that lead sensibly, whereas in the past, as most Scottish teams of the time would have done, they would have gone out to attack as they would when playing at Dundee or Tynecastle in a League game. After 1-1 at half-time, a three-goal burst within ten minutes from Red Star seemed to have finished it. The Yugoslavs in their own stadium, which they dubbed the 'Maracana', were always formidable. But in the last minute Forrest headed Wilson's corner against the bar, and McKinnon headed home the rebound.

The deciding match was at Highbury before 34,428 of London Scots and imports from Glasgow and elsewhere, and Rangers rewarded them with a competent performance. Millar and Brand were in the team, Baxter was on top form, and after Jim Forrest's 12th-minute goal Rangers had the initiative, and kept it for a fine 3-1 win.

In the next round, Rapid Vienna at Ibrox threw up an instant defensive wall and never suggested they would dismantle it. It took a subtle Baxter pass which set Wilson through to score in 55 minutes to give Rangers any reward. In Vienna's Prater (now Ernst Happel) stadium, before a Viennese crowd considered one of the most invective in Europe, Rangers produced an outstanding performance in which Jim Baxter was at his most brilliant, all of which provoked a prolonged ovation from the 70,000. Goals from Forrest and Wilson, early in each half, underlined Rangers dominance. They paid a high price for it. In the final minute, with the game lost, Baxter was hit from behind in a tackle from Skocik, suffered a broken leg, and in the opinion of friends of Rangers, after he had been out of action for months, was never as good a player again. His absence was surely a factor in Rangers failure to retain the League championship that season.

In the quarter-finals, Rangers went to Milan. At that time, the clubs arranged the dates of matches and the Italians would normally have sought to play later, to avoid a Scottish winter – the first leg was scheduled for Italy. But shrewd as ever, they opted to play while Baxter was still absent. On 17 February 1965, the Internazionale of Suarez, Mazzola, Facchetti and Sarti – a team of wonderful players well drilled in Helenio Herrera's Cattenachio system of defence and counter-attack play – tackled Rangers in their San Siro Giuseppe Meazza Stadium before 49,520, in defence of their title. In effect, conditions were just as wintry as they might have been in Glasgow. Rangers defended well in the first half, their man-to-man marking, staunch and disciplined, holding Inter at bay, 0-0 at the interval. A bewildering burst of scoring form Suarez and Peiro twice, within three minutes early in the second half, put paid to Rangers. Jim Forrest's late goal gave them some hope for the Ibrox leg.

There, on a bitterly cold night, Forrest's early goal opened things out. But Inter closed ranks, set a phalanx around Picchi in front of Sarti, and gave an impeccable exhibition of defensive play at its best, or worst. They beat Liverpool in controversial semi-finals, on both grounds, then beat Benfica to retain the Cup in a Final in Milan.

In 1965-66 Rangers did not qualify – they finished fifth in the championship, their lowest since 1926 – but in 1966-67 their 1-0 win over Celtic in the Scottish Cup Final qualified them for the Cup-winners' Cup.

The first Irish opposition for Rangers in any European tie was to be Glentoran. The Glentoran manager of the time, one John Colraine, the former Celtic player was quoted before the game as having reminded his players that the fact that they were all Rangers supporters should be forgotten at least for 90 minutes. Rangers were not very impressive in fact. They led by one goal for much of the match, then to the delight of the 40,000 packing into Belfast's Oval ground, lost a late goal to make it 1-1. They won the Ibrox leg easily, 4-0.

Next came the holders, Borussia Dortmund, who had beaten Liverpool in a Hampden Final the previous spring. They had Sigi Held and Lothar Emmerich, who had distinguished careers with West Germany. Rangers played very well at Ibrox, and won 2-1. The game was memorable for a freakish German goal equalising Johansen's earlier score. A German attack frittered out and Sigi Held overran and stayed outside the field of play. Dortmund attacked again, a shot was deflected wide. Held re-entered the field, played the ball before it went out of play, to Trimholdt, who scored. The goal was allowed!

This caused an immense controversy. Rangers protested furiously. The referee rejected all appeals. Jack Mowat, then a highly-respected Scottish referee who saw the match on television, said that he would certainly have disallowed the goal and booked Held for a) going off without permission, b) staying off the field and c) re-entering the field without permission! Now away goals were counting double when

Bayern Munich's Roth scores the winning goal against Rangers in the 1967 European Cup-winners' Cup Final in Nuremburg.

necessary. Thankfully a late goal from Alex Smith let Rangers go to Germany with a 2-1 lead, not too reassuring. But they produced a first-class defensive performance for their 0-0 draw, playing for 50 minutes with ten men; Watson was carried off having been kicked by Emmerich in an off-ball incident.

Quarter-final opposition in Real Zaragoza was just as challenging. Real had been rather a scourge to Scottish teams in Europe, having defeated Dunfermline, Dundee and others. Rangers' great advantage in their first, home, leg was the Scottish weather – rain fell unremittingly throughout the game.

Rangers played magnificently in that first match, goals from Dave Smith after ten minutes, Willoughby after 27 sending them to Spain in front, but not for the first time on foreign soil, they found themselves up against it. They were handicapped by the absence of Ronnie Mckinnon, who had suffered a broken nose in a League match at Ayr in the interim, and when Lapetra scored after 24 minutes, Rangers lived a torrid lifetime in defence. Four minutes from the end, Santos scored with a penalty given for a rather dubious handling offence then Davie Smith saw his extra-time penalty saved by Yarza. Not yet was the 'penalty shoot-out' in vogue. The rules demanded the toss of a coin, or the drawing of straws. So, in the loneliest moment of his career, in the centre-circle, John Greig called, correctly! Rangers were in the semi-final.

Rangers won 1-0 in both matches, playing well, against opponents Slavia Sofia who were slow and cumbersome. Not often could that be said about European teams at such an advanced stage of competition.

The Final was to be against Bayern Munich, a team on the verge of greatness, with youngsters Maier, Roth, Beck-

enbauer, Olk, Müller and Brenninger in place. The venue, Nuremberg, comparatively but a few miles down the autobahn from Munich, made it virtually a home match for Bayern. The vast majority of the 65,000 crowd was for them. The Rangers preparation psychologically was far from ideal. Team selection was bewildering. Alex Willoughby had come into the team following the Scottish Cup defeat at Berwick in January and had been a prolific scorer that season with 17 goals from 1 February to the end of April. He was not selected for the Ibrox match with Slavia, nor for the Final. On Saturday, 29 April Rangers were at Dundee, their reserves at home to Dundee reserves. The centre-forward for the Ibrox game called off. The only player on hand was Roger Hynd, a capable defender, heavily built, solid, short of pace. He was put on, scored four goals in a 5-2 win. On the strength of that and that alone, he found himself selected for a European semi-final (against Slavia at Ibrox).

It was a staggering team selection. Alec Willoughby to this day finds difficulty in comprehending it. In Hynd's defence, he never ceased to work and hustle and hassle the opposition, but his lack of pace was obvious at this level. The Final came six days after Celtic had won the European Cup in Lisbon, which added to the pressure on the Rangers players. On the day before the Nuremberg game, the chairman John Lawrence was quoted as saying that several new forwards would be needed for the new season. Few would disagree, but this was certainly not the time to say so.

Little was known about Bayern – in the first year of the Bundesliga they were not in the top division. Winning promotion, they won the German Cup in 1966, and in fact went all the way to the Final in 1967. The game was none too exciting, with defences dominating. Rangers had been very sound in defence all season, with John Greig and Ronnie McKinnon at the heart of it. They might as easily have won the match. Hynd had a goal disallowed, then missed dreadfully from six yards when Dave Smith gave him an open chance. He took so long to control, turn and shoot that Sepp Maier got a hand to it. The match went into extra-time, and after 11 additional minutes, Roth scored the goal that took the trophy to Munich.

In the 1967-68 Fairs Cities Cup it was back to East Germany for Rangers and a trip to Dresden and a splendid 1-1 draw. Goalkeeper Eric Sorenson was heroic against solid opposition, making several important saves. Alex Ferguson the future Manchester United manager, signed from Dunfermline, scored early in the second half but Reidel equalised. The 1-1 scored reflected the close balance between the teams. At Ibrox Rangers controlled almost the entire match, having Dinamo under persistent pressure with only an early Penman goal to show. Then in the 90th minute, Kreische scored. Sensation! With extra-time looking inevitable, Rangers summoned up one last heave and John Greig knocked in an improbable winner.

West Germany was Rangers' next round destination, specifically Cologne, with the club in turmoil. After 13 years, Scot Symon had been sacked. The new manager was to be David White, his inexperienced assistant. Nevertheless the team played splendidly, winning 3-0, the last of them a spectacular header from Alex Ferguson. For the Cologne match, his first 'European' trip abroad as manager White impressed on the players the importance of not losing an early goal. Result? One down to Wolfgang Overath in 30 seconds. Later, White said he had not had enough time to take his seat on the touch-line. Rangers did very well to survive the resulting onslaught, but lost two goals in eight late minutes by Weber and Ruhl. In extra-time, after 118 minutes, Willie Henderson scored.

It was to be yet another 'Battle of Britain' in the quarter-finals, Rangers v Leeds United. Under Don Revie, Leeds had become very successful if not very popular. Victory was all with the United team, the manner of it secondary. They were not popular. Yet for all that, they were a very fine football team which could produce football both effective and attractive from time to time. The first match at Ibrox was seen by 85,000 with 21,000 back at Elland Road watching on large television screens. Rangers' shortcomings in finishing against a competent Leeds defence centred on Jack Charlton cost them their home advantage. They took to Leeds a 0-0 scoreline and a massive support. There, 50,498 looked on while back at Ibrox 43,177 watched on closed circuit television. Rangers never looked like winning the tie and first-half goals from a John Giles' penalty and Peter Lorimer, put Leeds through.

Back behind the Iron Curtain again went Rangers in the first round of the Fairs Cities Cup in 1968-69, this time to meet Vojvodina from Novi Sad in Yugoslavia. They took a 2-0 lead there after the Ibrox leg, but found Vojvodina at home very difficult opponents in a hostile, forbidding country, before a small (7,000) vociferous audience. Rangers were under pressure for most of the match and were happy to lose 1-0, winning 2-1 on aggregate, Greig and Trivic were ordered off. Greig reported later that Trivic had kicked him, spat at him, pulled his hair, fouled and abused him throughout the entire match. Finally with ten minutes left, Trivic kicked him once too often, Greig retaliated, and they were both sent on their way. As they marched towards the tunnel, Greig, in front, was bombarded with coins, bottles, anything that could be thrown. Several of them hit him, drawing blood. Trivic, seeing this, rushed up and shielded Greig from the missiles, until they were safely in the tunnel!

The next match was fraught in a different way. With the IRA taking to the gun in Ulster, Rangers v Dundalk was guaranteed to be rife with incident. Happily, none of it was serious. For the first match at Ibrox, the Dundalk club wanted the Irish tricolour flag to be flown, and the Republic of Ireland national anthem, 'The Soldier's Song', played. Rangers declined both requests. It was not the custom to play national anthems before European matches.

Rangers won 6-1 at Ibrox. Dundalk, close to the Ulster border and an IRA stronghold and provider of 'safe houses' for them, did not after all prove a tinder box, the match passing off without incident, with Rangers winning 3-0. Another away draw was to Amsterdam, and DWS, one of the lesser-known Dutch clubs. They had eliminated Chelsea, but a 2-0 win for Rangers in the Olympic Stadium there, then 2-1 at Ibrox disposed of DWS. Next came Athletic Bilbao. The first leg at Ibrox was a strange affair, without much of a pattern. Rangers opened strongly, Ferguson scoring after seven minutes and at half-time it was 2-1. The crowd was 63,000, but the second half was so quiet and uneventful that Ronnie Allen, Bilbao's English international manager, said he thought all 63,000 had gone home. A final flurry in the last five minutes brought goals by Persson and Stein and a 4-1 lead that surely would be enough. But Rangers had to work desperately to keep the score in Bilbao at 2-0 for the Basques. Willie Johnston and full-back Betzeun were sent off near the end for fighting.

Newcastle United were in Europe for the first time. For many years a sleeping giant in England, they qualified only because four clubs were permitted from the 'strong' football nations, ie England, Italy, Germany, Spain; a rule said that no more than one club per city could participate. In the first match, at Ibrox, Rangers put unrelenting pressure on Newcastle, who were totally defensive. Rangers missed numerous chances and United never threatened, but they survived at 0-0. In the Newcastle match, with 60,000 packed into the ground, Rangers had a massive support yet again. After 52 minutes, Jim Scott, brother of former Ranger Alex, scored with a glorious shot. Another Scot, Jackie Sinclair, hit a thundering second goal 13 minutes from the end. There was a crowd invasion which took 17 minutes to clear, with the players leaving the field until order was restored. Certainly, Rangers' fans were incensed at the prospect of defeat, but probably the first 'invasion' came from youngsters at the front of the crowd climbing on to the track to avoid a shower of bottles which came pouring down from the crowd at the back. Whatever the origin it brought little credit to the club.

Jim Baxter was back in the ranks of the Rangers, after his sojourn in England, but in the meantime had lost some of his flair and was not really the same player. He did however play well in European games. The first round of the 1969-70 Cup-winners' Cup brought Steau Bucharest to Ibrox, where they dominated the first half, always in control with neat possession football. Rangers scarcely created a chance, yet were two up at half-time from opportunist goals from Johnston, scored from out of nowhere. Rangers played much better in the second half. There were 90,000 in the National Stadium in Bucharest for the return, on a national holiday, and Rangers match was the second game of a double-header, Dinamo Bucharest v Vittoria Setubal being the other. Dinamo produced a home win and the crowd was looking for a double to celebrate. Rangers again played a fine tactical game, Greig mopping up behind Johansen

John Greig misses from the penalty spot against Athletic Bilbao in the Inter-Cities Fairs Cup quarter-final first-leg match at Ibrox in March 1969, but Rangers still won 4-1.

and Provan, the full-backs and Baxter holding things together in midfield. Again a 0-0 draw against a very good team produced a 2-0 aggregate – satisfactory.

Back again in Eastern Europe went Rangers in the next round, this time to Górnik Zabrze in Poland. They had run Manchester United close in the year that United won the European Cup and Matt Busby said they were United's most difficult opponents and if they had not played Górnik in the middle of their winter shutdown, things might have been different. Rangers played them in November in the Slavski Stadium in Chortsow, and manager White decided to attack the Poles. The result was that Rangers lost two goals in the first ten minutes. Górnik were an excellent attacking team, fast, pacy football with a world-class performer in Lubanski and a fearsome defender in Olek, understandably known as 'Gorgon'. Rangers were heartened when Persson scored after 55 minutes, since 2-1 down would not be a bad score to take home with them. They played a disciplined second half until 88 minutes had passed. Górnik won a free-kick just outside the penalty area. Rangers' defensive wall was in place. One man asked the other how much time was left. They both turned to look at the stadium clock, leaving a meagre gap in the line. Lubanski drove the ball unerringly through it for a third goal. Or so said the newspapers, next day.

If 3-1 was much more daunting than 2-1, Rangers remained confident, even if they had never pulled back any deficit in Europe before. The Ibrox game was damned by the controversy that seemed to dog David White's entire

managerial career. Rangers went to Largs for preparation. Jim Baxter and Willie Henderson missed training on Tuesday morning, missed breakfast, missed the team bus. Both later claimed that they had overslept, having taken sleeping pills to make sure they slept. They had not heard the alarm calls. Controversially, they were selected to play. Many friends of Rangers felt that they should certainly have been disciplined. Both did play, and played quite well in the event. Baxter opened the scoring with a well-placed shot after 18 minutes. For more than an hour, Rangers controlled the match. Willie Johnston missed a glorious opportunity on the hour mark. Górnik broke away in 64 minutes, and Olek scored from a narrow angle, when Rangers German goalkeeper Gerhardt 'Gerry' Neef failed to cover his near post. The tie was not yet beyond Rangers. Two goals would have taken it into extra-time. But 15 minutes from the end, Vladimir Lubanski, superstar, scored one of the finest goals ever seen at Ibrox. It was reminiscent of the famous Puskas goal for Hungary against England at Wembley in 1963, when England were beaten 6-3. Lubanski collected on the centre line and drove for goal. He beat McKinnon and Neef, coming out, worked him wide towards the byline. Lubanski went, turned, came back infield by which time two or three defenders were piling in to block his way to goal. He swivelled, unbalancing them. He swivelled again unbalancing them again, then thrashed the ball into the roof of the net. The game was over. The tie was lost. Skowronek, with nine minutes left, broke through the middle and beat Neef with a swerving, unstoppable shot

Barcelona, A Tainted Triumph

In the 1971-72 European Cup-winners' Cup, Rangers, against Rennes, the French club from Brittany, progressed in what was a less than satisfactory manner. The French manager was very critical of their defensive display after their 1-1 draw in France but they had gained an away goal from Johnston. In the home match, Rangers attacked persistently, their only goal coming from Alex McDonald late in the first half. Both of these goalscorers, Johnston and McDonald, were to play significant parts in what was to be Rangers most successful season in Europe.

The second round brought more formidable opposition in Sporting Lisbon. In the first leg on 20 October, Rangers got off to a flying start, three up after half an hour, two from Colin Stein and one from Henderson. At that time the score might have been anything – the Portuguese were down and out, well-beaten, there, it seemed, for the taking. Inexplicably, Rangers in the second half allowed them back into the match. Perhaps Rangers had failed to pace themselves properly, perhaps complacency set in, but Sporting were allowed to snatch late goals from Chico and Gomez. The 3-2 lead did not look like security in such a daunting destination as the Jose Alavalade Stadium in the Portuguese capital. Rangers were not helped by difficulties in getting there... An air traffic control strike in London saw them arrive in Lisbon little more than 24 hours before the match. Nevertheless, they produced one of their finest attacking displays ever in Europe that night. Two goals from Colin Stein wiped out any advantage Sporting had from Ibrox. Rangers twice came from behind, controlled the play in the second half and the tie seemed won on the night, at 5-4 when four minutes from the end, Gomez headed an equaliser. Another late goal lost – extra-time. Yet again Willie Henderson scored a vital late goal in Europe (viz Cologne '67) and again Rangers seemed to have the advantage. But again Sporting scored, this time by Perez, the aggregate was 6-6, and Rangers through on away goals. But the drama was not over. In spite of regulations which now stated clearly that away goals would count double to settle drawn ties, the Dutch referee, Leo Horn, decreed that penalty kicks should be taken! This was won by Sporting. But the official UEFA observer intervened, pointed out the regulations, and the referee apologised – the victory went to Rangers.

In the quarter-final round, it was to be Rangers against Torino, Italian Cup holders and at the time, League leaders. The first leg was in the Stadio Communale, where the previous evening Wolverhampton Wanderers had survived against Juventus. Rangers produced a very fine disciplined performance in which Derek Johnstone was a key figure. He played beside Colin Jackson in central defence, with Dave Smith sweeping behind them. Rangers had lost Ronnie McKinnon in Lisbon, where he suffered a double leg fracture. McKinnon did not play again that season, and never really returned to be a first team player. Derek Johnstone, moved back from centre-forward, would compensate.

In Turin, Johnston scored a breakaway goal in only 12 minutes, and in a second half of almost permanent possession by Torino, Toschi scored with an hour gone. A second goal by Pulici was disallowed for offside. Rangers survived. At Ibrox, Rangers prevailed again by a solitary goal, as they had done against Rennes. This time Alex McDonald repeated his score in the first minute of the second half, following a cross from the right. It seemed to go in off his knee – Alex rejoiced in the old saw that they all count.

Rangers joined Bayern Munich, Dinamo Moscow and Dinamo Berlin. They probably preferred old adversaries Bayern rather than face further trips behind the Iron Curtain, even if Bayern were the most dangerous opponents possible. With the exception of Ajax Amsterdam, who were in the middle of their great run of 'Total Football' and three European Cup wins in succession, Bayern Munich were surely the best team in Europe. As in 1967 and 1970 they had no fewer than seven players who would within the month play for West Germany at Wembley, beat England 3-1 in the European championship, and go on to beat the Soviet Union in the Final in Brussels, 3-0. And two years later, they would help West Germany win the World Cup against Holland.

Rangers' performance in the Grunwald Stadion in Munich was exemplary. For the first 45 minutes, they were under extreme pressure. Bayern attacked ceaselessly, a blitzkreig by any stretch of the imagination. Paul Brietner scored after 23 minutes, but with Derek Johnstone marking Hoeness out of the game, 1-0 at half-time was a job well done. Then early in the second half the game changed dramatically when a Colin Stein cross from the right, driven in hard, was turned into his own goal by Zobel, retreating. Oh, the delights of the away goal. Although Bayern retained the balance of play, Maier had to make two particularly good saves from Mathieson.

Two weeks later at Ibrox, the fixture produced another 80,000 crowd. Rangers were handicapped by the loss of captain Greig, injured in a Scottish Cup semi-final with Hibs. Youngster Derek Parlane was brought in to replace him. Rangers seemed to demoralise the Germans with a goal in the opening 60 seconds. A Sandy Jardine cross-cum-shot from the right came drifting in wide of Sepp Maier, who seemed to think the ball was going past the post. A second goal by Derek Parlane, playing marvellously well, scored after 23 minutes, volleying home a Willie Johnstone corner kick. Johnston and Jackson blotted out the twin threat of Müller and Hoeness, Bayern never really got started, Rangers were in command – and stayed there. So after 15 years of effort, they were in their third European Final.

When Rangers met Dinamo Moscow in the Final of the European Cup-winners' Cup in May 1972, in Barcelona, it was a match that stretched significantly beyond the play and the players. The Rangers experience in European competition had been chequered to say the least. Yielding to no other club anywhere in ambition, they had reached the semi-final of the European Cup at their third try, and never improved on that. In the Cup-winners' Cup, they had reached two previous Finals, home and away against Fiorentina, when a talented Rangers team experienced the worst of Italian football – obstruction, body-checking, shirt-pulling, pushing, spitting and worse and lost – then again in 1967 against a Bayern Munich team a few years short of greatness, but in a match of little distinction which they lost 1-0 in extra-time.

The greatest significance of the Bayern match, in Nuremberg, in Rangers eyes, was that it came only a matter of days after Celtic had won the European Cup in such cavalier fashion in Lisbon against a forbidding Internazionale of Milan. It was considered a humiliation by friends of Rangers, unsupportable, unacceptable, particularly since Celtic were at the height of their domestic League hegemony. Even if the Cup-winners' Cup was not quite the European Cup, nevertheless Barcelona offered them some possibility of a riposte, at least. In the event, the match against Dinamo Moscow turned out to be an explosion waiting to happen. The city and the venue were critical to the events which followed.

Barcelona is a great metropolis, cosmopolitan as all major seaports are, and the centre and heart of a distinctive culture, that of Catalonia. With sunny May weather, with beer and brandy, the San Miguel and Fundador, cheap and plentiful by Scottish standards, it was an altogether agreeable place to spend some time, and support the team. With the USSR remaining an essentially closed country it was

Colin Stein celebrates his goal in Rangers' 3-2 win over Dinamo Moscow in the 1972 European Cup-winners' Cup in Barcelona.

kely that the mass of the attendance would comprise the Rangers legions. So it proved – of the 35,000 total, it was reckoned that close to 30,000 were Scots. It was a home game in effect for Rangers.

The Nou Camp stadium, home of Barcelona FC, is one of the wonders of the football world, its soaring tiers rising to like 90,000 to 100,000 fans (it was later extended to 120,000 for the World Cup of 1982). But in 1972, its security was abysmal, non-existent. There was no moat, no ditch, no fence in place between spectators and arena. From the front row of the seats, a man could take one step and be on the grass, virtually on the playing surface. Thus, astonishingly, one hour before the kick off, hundreds of Rangers fans, not all of them it could be said total abstainers, strolled and cavorted across the field. They embraced the Spanish police, who good-naturedly posed for photographs with them before shepherding them off.

Rangers played perfectly well, and enjoyed an easy control throughout the first half. Their team of the time was one of skilled craftsmen, solid professionals who rejoiced in their unity, their entity, perfect-ly balanced if without having a dazzling figure as such, a Jim Baxter. But the list of their victims en route to the Final – Sporting Lisbon, Torino, Bayern Munich – was evidence of their quality. They were two up at half-time, Dave Smith's inter-ventions from deep defence brought both, first a long ball after 24 minutes liberating Colin Stein for a fierce drive from the

penalty line, then a deep cross for Willie Johnston's head for the second, after 40 minutes. Four minutes into the second half, Johnston went through to make it 3-0.

The Russians had been bewildered by Rangers, the team and the supporters, and must have thought they had been caught up in a whirlwind. But since they had little to lose at 3-0 down, their pride forced them back into the game, Rangers in the meantime, persuaded that a lead of three in a European Final was surely untouch-able, slackened. Their substitute forward Eschtrekov scored in 59 minutes. For the last half-hour Rangers were on the defen-sive as the crowd grew more and more tense. Three minutes from the end Mekovikov scored a second to make it 3-2 and at the final whistle, Rangers fans poured on to the field in their elation. It was the kind of invasion not uncommon in other places, in other sports. Celtic fans had done exactly the same, in their ecstasy in the National Stadium in Lisbon in 1967. The crowd swept across the field to where the presentation had been planned to take place on the field. Unlike the Portuguese police, not to mention the Glasgow police, the Spanish police were uncomfortable. They had lined up, backs to the stand, along the touch-line.

Whereas the Glasgow police, for exam-ple, would have jollied them back to make enough space for the presentation, the Spanish police, without giving the crowd any instruction (there was no English lan-guage broadcast from the stadium sound

system to help) suddenly drew batons and started to smash wildly at the front ranks of the Rangers fans. They were driven back, retreated to the far side of the stadi-um, and since Scottish crowds for better or for worse were never much for spurning a challenge, lost cause or not, tore up seats and anything that might be used as weapons, and took the field again. This battle ebbed and flowed across the pitch until exhaustion set in. The public present-ation for the trophy and medals was aban-doned and the Cup was presented to Rangers captain John Greig in a small room inside the stadium. He and his team-mates had been denied the one thing they wanted to do, the one thing the fans had wanted done – show that the trophy had been well won. It was a tawdry conclusion. The Glasgow police would have controlled the situation, moved the crowd steadily back far enough for the presentation to take place, without one broken head. It was indeed the Spanish police who pro-voked the whole affair, but in the final analysis it was drunken supporters who brought dishonour to the club.

Rangers were suspended from European football for two years, later reduced to one on appeal by Willie Waddell, their manag-er. A few weeks later, he handed over the team reins to Jock Wallace and became general manager. Eighteen months earlier, he had been a critical figure after the 'Stairway 13' Ibrox disaster. On both occa-sions, at Ibrox and at Barcelona, Rangers were lucky to have him.

from 20 yards. The much-maligned Rangers supporters gave Górnik a standing ovation.

If the Rangers fans were appreciative of the Poles, and their skills, they were less than appreciative of David White, their manager. Crowds at the end of the game chanted "White must go". Next morning, he went. Summoned to a board meeting, chairman John Lawrence in White's own words later, "took ten seconds to tell me I was dismissed".

David White may have lacked the man management skills which a Rangers manager needs. He may have lacked the aura, the public persona, of his opposite number at Celtic Park, Jock Stein. But many people to this day will say that he went because of the lack of discipline he showed in the Baxter-Henderson incident of before the Ibrox Górnik match. And, much more importantly, the bad luck – for him – of events in Lisbon that same night. There, Celtic played Benfica in a European tie. They had gone there 3-0 up, but were comprehensively beaten. Billy McNeill, their captain, said later that Benfica's three goals to tie the aggregate might easily have been six. The match hung on the toss of a coin. McNeill called correctly. If the coin had favoured Benfica and not Celtic, Celtic could have been out, and White may have stayed in, at Ibrox. Such are the vagaries of football management, but White's going led to Willie Waddell's coming.

Rangers toured Germany in the 1970 close season, playing in Hamburg and against Kaiserslautern, giving them some taste of West German football. If there is any country with which they were familiar in terms of European football, it was certainly Germany and a first-round Fairs Cup draw against Bayern Munich continued the trend. In the first leg in the Grunwald Stadion in Munich, Rangers played very well, created and missed many chances. Greig hit the bar with a powerful header and goalkeeper Sepp Maier made the kind of stops which would make him increasingly famous. The match turned on a typical Beckenbauer goal. Striding majestically as he did from midfield, he played a wall pass with Paul Breitner, then clipped a ground shot out of Peter McCloy's reach.

The Ibrox game attracted 83,000 who saw the match and the tie turn on what was an 'illegal' goal, scored by Gerd Müller ten minutes from the end. Bayern were awarded a free-kick on the edge of the area. Television and photographic evidence proved beyond doubt that the Swiss referee had raised his arm indicating an indirect free-kick. When Müller shot the ball directly into the net, he awarded a goal. Colin Stein equalised within seconds, but with that incredible away goal, Bayern were through.

In 1972-73 Rangers were banned from European competition, although they contested the 'Super Cup' against Ajax Amsterdam, European Cup winners, in two legs, home and away. In the first match at Ibrox, flags of all the competing countries were carried round the ground and Andy Cunningham, one of Rangers legendary figures from the past, started the game which doubled as a celebration, albeit a year late, of their centenary. It was a superb display of attacking football from both teams. Ajax were the better team but Rangers were not disgraced. Ajax had such outstanding players as Ruud Krol, Gerry Muhren, Arnold Muhren, Johnny Rep, Franz Keizer and above all Johann Cruyff, surely one of the greatest footballers in the entire history of the game. His second goal was a delight. Spinning past Tom Forsyth on the edge of the penalty area, he hit a wicked volley past Peter McCloy. Ajax were comfortable winners, with 60,000 delighting in their skills. In the Olympic Stadium, Amsterdam, 43,000, a healthy crowd for Ajax and Holland, saw Alex McDonald score with a spectacular shot from 20 yards in the third minute. Haan equalised, Quinton Young put Rangers ahead again. A penalty to Ajax meant 2-2 at half-time, but again it was Cruyff who broke away to hit a subtle swerving shot round Peter McCloy. After 3-1 at Ibrox, the aggregate was 6-3 for Ajax, but for a young Rangers team of such as Tom Forsyth, Derek Parlane and Quinton Young, it had been a marvellous experience.

In 1973-74, Rangers qualified for the Cup-winners' Cup by beating Celtic in the 1973 Final for their first win since 1966. And it sent them on their first visit to Turkey against Ankaragücü. This was a new experience, but the Turks have never been a major football power, and Rangers had straightforward wins in Turkey (2-0) and at home (4-0). Their second goal in Ankara's '19th of May' stadium was magnificent. Tom McLean's mazy run took him past three defenders, then he curled his shot home from the penalty area line. And at Ibrox, two Turkish players were sent off.

The next round brought Rangers back to the real world, and a pairing with Borussia Mönchengladbach, away leg first. The German team had excellent players of international quality – Bertie Vogts later captain then team manager of West Germany, Rainer Bonhof, Ruppland Heynckes. This match was infamous for one of the silliest goals lost in Europe. With 20 minutes gone, Rangers had curtailed Borussia and seemed to have settled into a relaxed, if certainly defensive night. Borussia seemed to fret over their lack of scoring chances. After one attack had broken up, Peter McCloy had the ball in his possession and had rolled it forward before clearing it upfield. But he had forgotten that there was a Borussia forward loitering behind him. This dreadful fellow, Rupp, sneaked up on McCloy, flicked the ball away from him passed to Heynckes, who with some glee knocked it into the vacant goal. Rangers protested that McCloy had been obstructed, but it was a classic case of lack of concentration by the goalkeeper. Bobby Davidson, the Scottish referee who was handling Bayern Munich v Dinamo Dresden in the European Cup that same night in Munich, saw the game later on television and could find nothing wrong with the goal.

Losing such a stupid goal was a slap in the face, but with an hour gone, Rangers were still alive. And McCloy went some way to redeeming himself by saving a penalty from Herr Heynckes, but within a few minutes, and when 65 had passed, the same fellow did score to make it 2-0. And sadly, when Rangers were piling forward four minutes from the end to get the insurance of one away goal, Rupp broke away and made it three.

Rangers were out, but at least in the Ibrox match they played very well in an open entertaining game in which both sides attacked without inhibition, and which Rangers won 3-2.

If Rangers lacked the delights of European football in season 1974-75, they more than compensated at home. Their championship win was their first since season 1963-64, and even more important, it brought the historic run of nine successive championships, by arch-rivals Celtic, to an end. Rangers then were in the European Cup after a long interval. They were found to be ring rusty, but at home it was the perfect season as they took all the honours with yet another treble of championship and the two Cups. This was the season of the first 'Premier' Division, as the Scottish League was rearranged.

The first round draw brought to life the Rangers supporters chant, "Follow, follow we will follow Rangers... if they go to Dublin we will follow on." It was to be Rangers v

Bohemians, in the football context no contest. Rangers won 4-1 at Ibrox.

A 1-1 draw in Dublin set Rangers against the French champions, St Etienne, 'Les Verts', so called because of their green shirts. They turned out to be a highly-accomplished team. Rangers, as so often in Europe, got off to a bad start when Peter McCloy was injured during the warm-up for the match – he damaged his wrist, and Stewart Kennedy had to take his place. Wave upon wave of green-shirted attackers broke on the Rangers defence, and a goal was lost to Patrick Revelli in 25 minutes. Rangers often looked like equalising, and at least as the match wore on, they had silenced the fanatical French supporters. But yet again, when it looked like they would take a good result back to Ibrox , lack of concentration condemned them. In the final minute, a sloppy pass from Alex McDonald across the face of the defence towards Sandy Jardine, never had any hope of reaching him. McDonald could have played it into touch, volleyed it upfield, knocked it back to his goalkeeper, or cracked it out of the ground. Inevitably Bathenay seized the chance and gave Kennedy no chance.

At Ibrox, Rangers were outclassed to the extent that the Rangers fans were chanting "What a load of rubbish" long before the end. McDonald did redeem himself with a last minute goal, but by that time, Rangers were two down, and only some 10,000 of the 45,000 crowd were still in the ground. St Etienne went on to the Final that season, losing rather unluckily 1-0 in a Hampden Final to Bayern Munich. Rangers consolation, if any, was that they had lost to a first-class team.

Rangers, against FC Zürich in the European Cup the following season, once more made the worst possible start, losing a goal in less than 60 seconds. Defensive carelessness let Cucinotta steal it. Rangers piled in with the usual British-style energy, power, hard-running game – all good enough to knock over the domestic opposition, but not cute enough, lacking in flair and subtlety against opponents who had such qualities. Derek Parlane scored an equaliser after half an hour. In Zürich it was the same sad tale. A goal was lost – this time Rangers held out for eight minutes before Marinelli scored. Rangers fought the good fight, but discovered that fighting is not enough. They went out 2-1 on aggregate – in fact 1976-77 was a dreadful season for them – they won nothing!

Rangers found their place in the Cup-winners' Cup in 1977-78 by having finished runners up in the Scottish Cup to Celtic, who were in the European Cup. Again Switzerland beckoned, this time Young Boys of Berne. A Greig goal at home gave them a 1-0 lead; in Switzerland they fashioned the required draw 2-2 to take them through. Derek Johnstone was ordered off for the second season in Switzerland, for retaliation. The referee later said he was sorry for Johnstone, who had been kicked "up and down the field all night". One wonders what he thought of the kickers.

Twente Enschede of Holland had some fine players and in the goalless leg at Ibrox, first, Rangers sorely missed Johnstone. In Holland, in truth, they were brushed aside. Dutch football, inspired by Ajax, was very strong at that time.

Back in the European Cup in 1978-79, and with a new manager John Greig in place, Rangers' hopes of success in the competition seemed like so much pie-in-the-sky when they drew Juventus, away, in the first round. The Turin club had players of the calibre of Zoff, Cabrini, Causio, Tardelli, Benetti, Bettega and no fewer than nine of the national

squad that had finished as semi-finalists in the World Cup in Argentina. Before 70,000 in the Stadio Communale, Rangers yet again lost an early goal, to Virdis after eight minutes. With this match, new manager John Greig proved himself as a tactician. He brought in Alex Miller and Kenny Watson to play wide and deep, and used Sandy Jardine as a sweeper. Rangers man-marked the Italians effectively, were well-disciplined and alert and altogether it was a magnificent performance for the 1-0 result.

In more than 20 years in Europe, Rangers had never pulled back a first-round deficit (they had also never lost a first-leg lead), yet with an outstanding performance at Ibrox, perhaps their very best in Europe over all those years, Rangers beat Juventus, one of the finest teams in the world, 2-0. Again, Greig's team selection and tactics were precise and successful. Tommy McLean and Derek Johnstone were back in the team. Alex McDonald in the first half, Gordon Smith in the second, headed goals against the great Dino Zoff. Three months earlier, these players had been playing in the World Cup finals. It was a memorable victory.

In the next round, Rangers faced another group of exceptional players, men who had played in the Final of the same World Cup, for Holland against Argentina. Van der Kerkhof and Brandts were typical members of a fine PSV Eindhoven team. At Ibrox Van Engelen defied Rangers who found themselves taking a 0-0 draw to the Phillips stadium in Eindhoven, where the Dutch team had never lost on their own ground in European play. It didn't seem that this Rangers team would put that record in peril, particularly, since once again, they lost a goal in the first minute, in precisely 34 seconds in fact. As one Rangers fan called to his friend, "That lot started before we were ready!" Rangers held on to 1-0 down at half-time, then produced 45 minutes of dazzling football. Twice they came from behind. Then at 2-2, with but three minutes to play Rangers produced a goal that was a gem supreme. Derek Johnstone headed a Dutch cross out to Gordon Smith, on the edge of the penalty area. Spinning, he drove a long ball out to Tommy McLean on the right, on the halfway line. McLean, one of the greatest of goal makers, held the ball seeing Robert Russell sprinting at the PSV defence, then at the precise moment, hit a pass of killing accuracy round the Dutch defence, freeing Russell. As the goalkeeper came to him, he curled his shot, bent his shot round him, into the net.

It was a stupendous goal, rated by the BBC as the 'Goal of the Year'.

So Rangers were in the quarter-finals of the European Cup for the first time in 14 years. PSV's home record had gone. Juventus had been beaten. Rangers at last had hopes of achieving the impossible dream of winning the European Cup, as Celtic had done. Having eliminated two of the best teams in the competition, they had no reason to fear anyone. Alas, the Scottish winter beat them. So severe was the winter that they played only three League games between 23 December and 4 March, and the fixture pile-up took the edge off their play. Derek Johnstone missed both matches against Cologne, and in fact Rangers were obliged to play players who were not fully fit. A 1-0 loss in Germany did not seem critical, but in the second match at Ibrox, Rangers played poorly, and never stretched the German team. Dieter Müller's goal early in the second half put the tie beyond reach, and Tommy McLean's late goal was no more than a gesture.

Rangers, winners of the Scottish Cup after three games, two lots of extra-time and five and a half hours of play against Hibernian, hauled themselves into the Cup-winners' Cup for 1979-80. It brought a first trip to Norway for competitive play with a preliminary round tie against Lillestroem. The winning aggregate was 3-0. Next came Fortuna Düsseldorf and the familiar Rhine triangle which contained Eindhoven and Mönchengladbach all within an hour's drive of each other. The Allofs brothers were the Fortuna stars. If the season was a poor one for Rangers they produced one of their best displays in the first match at Ibrox, won 2-1. Again they conceded a late goal. McDonald and McLean with second-half goals put them in front, but with nine minutes left, Klaus Allofs made a devastating forward run to set up Wenzel for the goal.

In Düsseldorf, Rangers quite simply survived a siege, with Peter McCloy's goalkeeping being outstanding, all the more so since after being injured in the first half, he had sight only in one eye. It finished goalless.

Rangers now faced a Valencia team which featured Rainer Bonhof and Mario Kempes, the Argentine striker who had been one of the sensations of the 1978 World Cup, but in Spain, they came up with another mature display for a 1-1 draw. John Grieg here had the team playing to rational patterns, but rather surprisingly, Rangers, flat and ill at ease, gave an indifferent performance in the home match against Spaniards who were masters. Rangers were disappointing and went down 3-1, Kempes scoring twice quite brilliantly.

In 1980-81, Rangers did not qualify for Europe but in 1981-82 the Cup-winners' Cup took Rangers to Czechoslovakia for the first time since 1959. In the first-round first match, this time against Dukla Prague, a miserable night of torrential rain saw Rangers produce a performance to match. In four minutes, a goalkeeping error by McCloy cost a goal, two more came in the second half and Rangers never looked like scoring an away goal. Tommy McLean of all people was ordered off near the end. At Ibrox, Rangers won 2-1 but went down to a 4-2 aggregate. It was not the best of seasons. They did win the League Cup, but were beaten Finalists in the Scottish Cup (by Aberdeen) and finished third in the championship. Indeed the first half of the 1980s were not the best of times for Rangers – Dundee United and Aberdeen were emerging to claim their share of the great prizes. The modernisation of Ibrox Stadium had been completed, but Rangers fans demand success. In the two final League matches of the season, with nothing to play for, less than 10,000 attended.

In 1982-83 Rangers for the first time were in the UEFA Cup, successor to the Fairs Cities Cup, and yet again they were ordained to tackle a leading German side, this time Borussia Dortmund. Impressive work under John Greig's direction saw a smooth display at Ibrox when the team inspired by their Swedish international Robert Prytz regaled a capacity crowd. In the Westfalen Stadion, the central defenders John McClelland and Craig Paterson, newly signed from Hibs, were outstanding and Rangers fully deserved the 0-0 result. At Ibrox Davie Cooper had scored an opportunist first goal then laid on the second with a cross for Derek Johnstone to head home. Prytz was the outstanding player over the two matches – he had played in a European Final earlier, for Malmö.

The second round brought Cologne to Ibrox after which, a leading Scottish journalist of the day, John Fairgrieve described Rangers 2-1 win as the best performance he had seen since the days of Jim Baxter. But Rangers only just did it – only five minutes were left when McClelland headed home a Cooper free-kick. Johnstone's goal in nine minutes

was equalised by Klaus Allofs goal after 60- minutes. It was illegal. Television evidence showed that the player taking the free-kick which produced that goal had played the ball twice.

Rangers went to Cologne in the knowledge that they had never surrendered a lead in these competitions, but if they had to surrender a lead, this was how to do it. They were four down after 21 minutes. Ironically, Derek Johnstone almost scored before the first goal went in, hitting a shot which only just cleared the bar. But Rangers were overwhelmed by a Cologne team that was sharp and decisive, converting almost every chance it made, whereas Rangers created quite a few and spurned all of them. The worst Rangers memory was not of the defeat, but of the quite disgraceful foul by Harold Schumacher on Jim Bett. About to head into an empty net, Bett was floored by a karate kick to the chest, reminiscent of his dreadful foul on Patrick Battiston in the 1982 World Cup semi-final match against France. He should certainly have been ordered off in Cologne. The referee did nothing.

The first round, first leg of the European Cup-winners' Cup in 1983-84 meant a pleasant holiday trip for Rangers to Valletta, Malta. In that first match, they were not in holiday mood, running up eight goals quite ruthlessly. A teenage David McPherson, central defender scored four goals if you please. Then ten goals at Ibrox meant a record score in one match, an aggregate record and a Scottish club record in Europe.

The second round brought FC Porto to Ibrox. They were a fine and maturing team which a few years on would win the European Cup itself. Sandy Clark scored after 35 minutes, but in the second half Rangers were overwhelmed by Porto's possession football in every area of the field. Seven minutes from the end Ze Beto, the Portuguese goalkeeper, in running out to volley a pass back, totally missed his kick, allowing the Australian international from Glasgow, David Mitchell to run the ball into the empty goal.

A 2-0 lead would have been more than welcome to take to Oporto, but an even more maddening mistake by Peter McCloy came three minutes from the end when he completely mis-punched a cross and gave Jacques the all-important away goal. Between the two games John Greig resigned as manager and Rangers were under the control of Tommy McLean, his assistant. He had the team well drilled tactically, but Rangers hopes of defending their lead were swept away by a rainstorm over the Antas stadium. They lived on a knife edge as Oporto drove at them relentlessly. A goal from Gomez after 53 minutes gave Oporto the win on that away goal.

When Rangers were drawn to play Bohemians in the first round of the 1984-85 UEFA Cup, crowd trouble seemed inevitable. Terrorist activity in Northern Ireland was at its height, and Rangers' tradition of being a Unionist club was not lost on the republicans in Dublin. The match was played against a background of crowd trouble. Rangers manager Jock Wallace twice made public appeals to the crowd to stop the terracing violence. Rangers goalkeeper Nicky Walker was under attack throughout the entire match from missiles thrown by home supporters. The referee and the Garda did nothing to stop it. Rangers seemed in control at 2-1 ahead, but lost concentration in the midst of the unrest, and lost two more goals. They were on the verge of the club's most humiliating defeat at Ibrox, after losing 3-2 in Dublin. Not until the closing six minutes did goals come, when Cooper fashioned crosses to allow Craig Paterson, then Ian Redford to head goals for a 2-0 win on the night and a 4-3 aggregate victory.

From Dublin and 10,000 to Milan and 65,591 in the San Siro Giuseppe Meazza Stadium, and Internazionale the opposition. They now had Baresi, Altobelli, Liam Brady and Rummenigge on their list. Rangers lost 3-0, were often outplayed but as with Mönchengladbach ten years earlier, lost a late goal to Rummenigge's head only because they were pouring down on Zenga's goal, searching for that critical away goal. Unforgettable in this match was an appalling miss by the young Rangers striker Alistair McCoist. He was later to become an outstanding goalscorer for the Ibrox club, but when Cammy Fraser's shot from 25 yards hit the bar, rebounded, with Zenga hopelessly beaten, it fell down towards McCoist. He froze. Instead of heading the ball he allowed it to hit his head and the chance was gone.

He was dropped for the return leg. Davie Cooper was injured. Rangers gave a fighting display and played well enough to have won the match and the tie, but Altobelli's goal after 15 minutes rally put it beyond their reach. Inter had to defend desperately but a 3-1 Rangers scoreline gave them a 4-3 aggregate win.

If Rangers had gone out in glory in 1984-85 against Inter-Milan, the same could not be said of their failure against the middle-of-the-road Spanish team Atlético Osasuna, from Pamplona the following season. Conditions in the first match were dreadful. A rain-sodden Ibrox was simply not playable. Had it been a domestic game and not a UEFA match, it would not have been started. Paterson headed home a Cooper cross and Rangers took a 1-0 lead to Spain, but there, Osasuna, on a quick, dry pitch in pleasant temperatures had a goal in 12 minutes, were completely at ease and knocked in another before half-time. Rangers could never get to grips with them.

All told, this had been a bad time for the Govan club. But at the end of the season, Graeme Souness was the manager, a different squad of players was put in place for the following season, and the Souness Era, from which one way or the other Rangers would never look back, had begun.

Souness had set about recruiting for Rangers an impressive array of quality players and in the first round of the UEFA Cup, 1986-87, when Rangers were drawn to play in Finland for the first time, among them were Chris Woods, Jimmy Nicholl and Terry Butcher. The first match at Ibrox was won easily, against Ilves Tampere, by 4-0. The away leg Rangers lost 2-0, playing on what amounted to a public park before a crowd of 2,109. For all that, it was a poor Rangers display. Fleck's hat-trick in the Ibrox game came from crosses laid on by Davie Cooper of the unerring left foot. Against Boavista of Oporto in Portugal, Rangers again monotonously lost another early goal, and a 2-1 win did not seem much to take to Portugal. But Boavista were not FC Oporto. A stunning Chris Woods save in the middle of the first half of the away game turned the match, when he twisted in mid-air to turn away a swerving 25-yard shot. A late Derek Ferguson shot made it 1-0.

The third round brought Borussia Mönchengladbach to a packed Ibrox. It was a hugely competitive match, play surging from end to end. Ian Durrant got an early goal, Borussia equalised towards the end of the first half, and so it ended. The German away goal was to prove decisive. In Germany, Rangers played well but could do no better than 0-0. Davie Cooper and Stuart Munro, the least physical of all the Rangers players, were sent off for 'retaliation', goaded into action by the cynical fouling of the Germans and by totally incompetent refereeing by a Belgian. The game ended with senior players like Butcher in tears at the manner of Rangers defeat.

In season 1987-88, having won the championship in Graeme Souness' first year, Rangers were in the European Cup again, for the first time in nine years. They had to face Dinamo Kiev in the Ukraine in the first match. Dinamo had Oleg Kuznetsov and Alexei Mikhailichenko, later to come to Ibrox, in their ranks. The 'Republic Stadium' held a remarkable 100,000 for the match and they saw a disciplined defensive performance from Rangers. The home goal came from a penalty conceded by Graham Roberts, scored by Mikhailichenko, so Rangers came home well pleased with themselves. They could not begin to imagine the gift they would receive from Dinamo at Ibrox.

An attack broke down, their goalkeeper Chanov had the ball. In throwing it to a defender, he mishandled the ball, it bounced off Kuznetsov's behind, falling to McCoist. He fed it across to Mark Falco who tapped it into a vacant net. Midway through the second half Falco repaid the compliment by heading a Trevor Francis cross to McCoist, who headed into the corner of the net. Kiev inevitably stepped up the pace, but without success. Rangers were through. This was the match of the controversial moving of the touch-lines. Souness had become wary of the pace of the Russians' wide players, so he had the Ibrox touch-lines moved in a yard or two, narrowing the field, but staying within the required measurements. No doubt it smacked of gamesmanship. The Russians were not best pleased.

A second round with Görnik Zabrze saw Rangers get through quite easily. They led 3-0 at Ibrox at half-time, lost goal in the second half, but were 3-1 ahead going to Poland. A penalty for the home team there equalised an earlier McCoist score but Rangers were never in danger of being caught.

Souness may well have thought, not unreasonably, having disposed of the quality of Dinamo Kiev and Görnik, that Rangers might go all the way in the competition. Between the second Görnik match and the first against Steau Bucharest, he sold Robert Fleck and Marc Falco, leaving Rangers with only one striker, McCoist. He promptly got injured. He was brought back for the first game, in Bucharest, only one week after a cartilage operation, but was soon seen to be unfit. Butcher had broken his leg. Players were signed – Mark Walters, John Brown, Jan Bartram among them, but none of them eligible to play in the competition. The loss of Avi Cohen through injury just before the game was a serious blow. The Israeli international player had a wide experience of European play. Allowing Piturca to score in just two minutes was another setback. Steau were a first-class team which was unbeaten in a couple of seasons of domestic play. Cause and effect – they were the favourite team of dictator Nicholae Caucescu. They had won the European Cup in 1986 and had outstanding players in Hagi and Lacatus. Rangers were well beaten. Steau scored a second, rather unfortunately when there was a lucky deflection to Iovan's free-kick in the second half.

At Ibrox, there was a full house to see Rangers yet again (this was getting beyond belief) lose a goal in the very first minute. Lacatus from 25 yards, with the defence square seeing Woods out of his goal, lobbed him. Ibrox was silenced. Rangers got to 2-1 at half-time, from a Gough header and a McCoist penalty, but needed two more and no one could imagine how they would get them against such a quality team.

Having failed to win the championship for the only time in the Souness Era, Rangers were in the UEFA Cup of 1988-89, against GKS Katowice, and were rather lucky to win 1-0. The Polish team startled Rangers by attacking them mercilessly, creating good chances and might have had goals. A Mark Walters goal was little enough to take to Poland, particularly when they were hit by a superbly taken free-kick early in the match. Two headed goals from Butcher helped them to a 4-2 win. Next was a fourth visit to Cologne and the Mungersdorf Stadion (visits in 1967-68, 1978-79 and 1982-83 had produced only one Rangers goal). For 75 minutes Rangers controlled the match. Then their legs seemed to go. Souness said later that Scottish clubs were not getting a fair crack of the whip in terms of fixtures. Three days earlier Rangers had played a League Cup Final against Aberdeen. McCoist was sent off for a frustrated challenge on a defender, thus handicapping Rangers further for the return.

Rangers never looked like retrieving the tie despite constant pressure. When Kevin Drinkell scored 15 minutes from time, the Germans promptly equalised in injury time, and the Scots had pressed the self-destruct button yet again.

In 1989-90, Rangers were in the European Cup again, and bound for Germany again. Bayern Munich overwhelmed Rangers with their all round skills and with three goals at Ibrox. The third of them was the best of them, a bewildering long range shot from their captain, Klaus Augenthaler. In Munich's Olympic stadium, Rangers played much more rationally, but without McCoist were clearly lacking in firepower. The Germans simply eased their way through the match, which finished 0-0. Bonny Ginsberg had taken the place of Woods in goal.

In 1990-91 European Cup again, Malta again. It was 4-0 at Valletta, 6-0 at Ibrox. Next was Red Star Belgrade with a team of high quality – Savicevic, Prosinecki and Panchev were the stars. They tore Rangers apart, 3-0, in the first leg in Belgrade, 80,000 in their nicknamed 'Maracana' stadium. An own goal by John Brown after five minutes started the rot. Red Star were an exciting team, a team of flair and pace who gave the impression they could do as they pleased. Prosinecki, with an hour gone, drove in a free-kick from 25 yards, off a post. Five minutes later Panchev scored. Oddly, Richard Gough who was covering him quite suddenly checked and stopped running, as though he had been stricken by some weird and unknown ailment. McCoist did score a late, headed goal, but even at Ibrox, where it finished 1-1, there was no way Rangers could pull back three goals against a team of Red Star's quality. They went on to win the European Cup that season, beating Olympique Marseille in a penalty shoot-out. Two of the most attractive teams in Europe had played, alas, a quite dreadful Final.

Season 1991-92 was Walter Smith's first in command of a European campaign which took Rangers first to Prague, where Sparta won deservedly, 1-0. At Ibrox Rangers took things to extra-time when Stuart McCall scored, then went ahead when he scored again. Rangers looked home and dry, but self-destructed yet again when, in an isolated Czech attack, Goram and Scott Nisbet go in a fearful tangle with across from the right. The ball broke off Nisbet to one of the Czech forwards, who flicked it towards goal. Goram let the gentle shot slip over his hands. Sparta had the vital away goal they needed. They were a fine team – conquerors of Marseille and possibly one of the four best teams in Europe at that time.

The season of the 'Champions League' of 1992-93 was Rangers' finest in Europe for 20 years since the winning of the European Cup-winners' Cup in 1972. The last eight of the competition were to be drawn into two groups of four clubs each, and the home and away matches of each of

these fixtures would produce a leader of each group contesting the Final. In the opening match, Rangers met Lyngby of Copenhagen. At Ibrox, a diving header from Hateley late in the first half, a flick round the goalkeeper from Peter Huistra in the second, let Rangers take a 2-0 scoreline to the Parken Stadium in Copenhagen. There, Ian Durrant's late run from midfield, and round the goalkeeper, made it 1-0.

The next round brought Leeds United, and a 'Battle of Britain' to Ibrox. To anticipate and avoid trouble, the clubs made a decision to 'ban' away supporters at each venue. The supporters promptly got round this by the one set helping the other set to find tickets (both matches were all-ticket affairs). Capacity crowds welcomed the matches and in the first one at Ibrox, Gary McAllister silenced the Rangers fans with a stunning volley, returning a partial clearance from a left-wing corner high beyond Goram's right hand, in the very first minute! It was a night of constant thundering noise from the grandstands as the Rangers faithful ran the gamut of all the emotions in spurring on the team to much derring-do. Leeds goalkeeper, Lukic, was well aware of it – under massive pressure from Rangers corner kicks, he at last mis-punched one into his own goal. Alistair McCoist got his second from a corner, when Lukic parried but could not hold a McPherson effort, and McCoist sneaked in to steal the goal as he often did.

Leeds United went back to Elland Road confident that their away goal from McAllister was the foundation for a victory. Once more it as a night of unbelievable passion. Mark Hateley stunned the Yorkshiremen with a goal that was almost preposterous when he did the unimaginable. From a good 25 yards, with his back to Lukic's goal, he suddenly spun and hooked an innocent and entirely optimistic shot high in the air. The ball soared over Lukic and bounced into the net, cancelling out the Leeds away goal, Leeds pummelled Rangers, but Goram was outstanding, and quite defiant – from time to time, it could be said, lucky. He maintained this into most of the second half, but midway through, Rangers scored a quite magnificent goal.

From midfield, Durrant hit a brilliant pass which released Hateley wide on the left. In full stride he hit an equally brilliant cross to beyond the far post. McCoist, coming in at full speed, headed first time a goal which gave Lukic no chance. In its speed and accuracy and audacity, it was a gem of a goal that left the Leeds crowd and team stunned. For the rest of the match, United, as they had to, attacked, often frantically, but Goram and his defence, in particular Richard Gough, stood fast. Leeds finally scored in the last few minutes, but it was a shattering defeat which took the Leeds team two years to throw off. The Elland Road crowd gave Rangers a standing ovation, which made rather a nonsense of the visitor 'ban'. There was no need for hostility when each set of supporters had helped the other out with tickets.

This famous victory put Rangers into the League system in which they were drawn with Olympique Marseille, CSKA Moscow and Club Brugges. Marseille were first at Ibrox, on a dreadful night of heavy rain and high wind, and a pitch barely playable. For 80 minutes, Marseille were not of Rangers world, comprehensively outclassing them. Alan Boscik and Rudi Voller scored, Goram brought off two breathless saves. McCoist, injured, was missing as was Ian Ferguson, suspended, which made the 'three foreigners' rule more severe. Neil Murray, Steven Pressley and Gary McSwegan, all youngsters, played in their first European game. McSwegan, a substitute, scored with his first touch of the ball, a spectacular header, then late in the game, Hateley headed a second. Rangers were back from the dead. A point salvaged was the most that could be said.

Because of the severity of the Russian winter, the game against CSK Moscow was played at Bochum in the Ruhr, where Rangers had played in 1933. In the first 30 seconds of the match, Rangers had an escape which was beyond belief. Three Russian forwards found themselves with a yard or so of the ball, perhaps four yards from goal, lining up to score. It was a case of 'After you, Sacha'. But somehow David Robertson materialised, from nowhere and flying across, swept the ball away. An Ian Ferguson shot deflected in was the only goal of the game. Rangers deserved their win in a game short of distinction. The Russians did not show much in attack although they had eliminated Barcelona in the previous round. Barcelona, the holders, after a 1-1 draw in Moscow, were 2-0 up in their own Nou Camp – and were beaten 3-2!

Three months later in Brugges, Daniel Amokachi's goal had the home team ahead 1-0 at half-time. Rangers found some rhythm in the second half, took command of the game, and Huistra equalised 12 minutes from the end. It was a good solid result, well-earned and important because that same night Marseille could only draw with Moscow in Berlin. Andy Goram suffered a knee injury in an innocent clash with his own player, David McPherson, had to have surgery, and two years later had still not properly recovered. Goram had attracted much criticism in his early months with Rangers, but lately had been a pillar of defensive virtue for them, with his speed of action, particularly along the ground. He was a vital part of the team that season – it won the treble.

At home to Brugges, heavy rain drenched the scene again. Rangers played very well in the first half and led through an Ian Durrant goal. Mark Hateley was ordered off, rather harshly, after wrestling with a big Brugges central defender, who went down mortally stricken, it appeared. It was a two of a kind situation, but Hateley, a senior and widely experienced player, should have known better. The defender didn't, after all, die. Brugges got an early second half equaliser, then from deep and wide on the right, Scott Nisbet hit blindly a swerver that astonished everyone, the Brugges goalkeeper and Nisbet included. 2-1 to Rangers. The next game, in the Velodrome Marseille, would be critical. The teams were level on points. A win for either side would put them in the Final. A draw might help Rangers – Marseille had still to go to Brugges, while Rangers had a home match with CSKA to come. Marseille certainly commanded the first half. Boscik scored after a mistake by David Robertson. Rangers came back at them in the second half, equalised through Durrant, then fell back on the defensive. It finished 1-1 and left all to play for. It was going to be Marseille or Rangers in the Final..

But something very odd had happened before Marseille's final game in Brugges. There was ill-feeling between the clubs. In the match at Marseille, Brugges fans had been seated in a vulnerable section of the stadium, with home fans above them. The Marseille crowd threw all sorts of missiles and things, some of them unmentionable things, down on them, causing a great deal of trouble. Raymond Goethals, Marseille's Belgian coach, made several disparaging remarks about Brugges. By contrast, Rangers and Brugges got on well. The Brugges players told Rangers, "Get a result in Marseille, because we'll do them when they come to us." Brugges had not lost a home European tie in years, a record they were very proud of.

Suddenly, over the weekend before Marseille were due in Brugges, all that seemed to change. The Brugges manager, coach, chairman, all began to make strange noises, such as that since they were obviously not going to win the European Cup, it was more important for them to qualify for next season by winning their domestic championship – the next League match was more important than the coming European match! The captain suddenly announced he was injured and was not able to play, and in fact they played without three important players, all supposedly injured.

Now, two years later, given what we know about M.Bernard Tapie, the Olympique Marseille president, one wonders what might have made the Brugges people change their attitude to the match. In Brugges, Marseille scored in the first minute. Rangers could do no more than draw with CSKA Moscow, spurning a round dozen of chances. Olympique got to the Final where, against all the odds, they beat AC Milan.

In the following season, 1993-94, against the most modest of opposition, Rangers went out at the first pop. It was a saga of goals surrendered wilfully and scandalously. The draw brought Levski Sofia to Ibrox first. Goals from McPherson and Hateley put Rangers in an easy command, then a goal was lost from indecisive defending before Hateley made it 3-1. So far so good no doubt was the attitude. But in the dying minutes, Duncan Ferguson, playing wide on the left and defending in depth, slipped, allowed a cross to come in. It was headed home. Rangers had played without Goram, and 3-2 away from home, in spite of the fact that Levski were not of their calibre, was precarious for Rangers.

In Sofia, Rangers controlled the first half. It was then 1-1. In the second half, they decided to go on to defence, allowing Levski to come to them. In injury time, Todorov hit a fierce, speculative but devastating shot from 30 yards. It hammered in off the under-side of the bar. Levski were in. Rangers were out. They were without Goram, but in spite of that questions remained. Why was Duncan Ferguson played wide on the left, manifestly not his position? Why did Rangers fall back into defence when they had the measure of Levski? Would Rangers never learn to be other than naive in these European matches?

For the 1994-95 season, UEFA had changed the format of the Champions' Cup to the extent that only 24 teams were permitted entry. This was partly as a consequence of the restructuring of European nations – following the collapse of the Soviet Empire, there were now somewhere in the region of 48 independent states in being. It also reflected UEFA's desire to ensure that the major clubs competed in this premier competition. Too often in the past, even with the advent of the Champions' League, the leading clubs of the leading nations had been eliminated early or indeed had not qualfied for some reason, and there was little commercial advantage to be had from Dinamo Kiev against Spartak Moscow as compared with AC Milan v Barcelona. Thus UEFA decreed that the major nations of Europe in terms of population, economic muscle and football achievement should always be able to compete. So the rules were changed and as of right, the champion clubs of England, France, Italy, Spain and Germany would always be able to compete in the Champions League.

Other clubs from other countries such as Rangers from Scotland would have to pre-qualify for entry into the League. Thus in August 1994, before the Scottish domestic season had started, Rangers found themselves facing very difficult opposition in the Greek champions, AEK Athens, with the first of the two matches in Greece. The new summer signings, Brian Laudrup and Basile Boli would obviously be unfamiliar with the habits of new clubmates. Boli indeed carried over a one-match suspension from the previous season's competition. Rangers would clearly have to be ready, physically, tactically, psychologically for that first early leg in Athens and in preparation, a good programme of pre-season matches was arranged. Two games were played in Denmark, one in Germany, and a tournament was staged at Ibrox involving Sampdoria, Newcastle United and Manchester United.

In spite of all this, for the Athens match a defensive formation was presented which the players had never experienced before, either in pre-season games or at any other time. A three-man central defence was to be Richard Gough, Stephen Pressley and Gary Stevens, with full-backs Neil Murray and David Robertson pushed into wide positions in midfield, giving a 3-5-2 formation. The unfamiliarity was obvious as Rangers were torn apart in the intimidating atmosphere in the Greek capital.

Individual performances were unacceptable – Rangers were fortunate to escape with a 2-0 defeat which on the balance of play could have been five or six. It was a major disappointment to the club, and in particular chairman David Murray. Rangers had invested heavily in new players – Laudrup and Boli had cost in excess of £5 million. A place in the Champions League with three home games guaranteed against top-quality opposition could have recovered most of that expenditure. It was a forlorn hope.

Rangers went into the home match scratching to find some hope and confidence. It was perceived that the Greek champions would not be good travellers. Historically this was surely the case – the Greek team which had played in the World Championships a couple of months earlier had not done particularly well (the fact that they had qualified for the finals, and Scotland had not, was handily ignored). Again the performance was found wanting, and serious questions had to be asked about team selection and tactics. The partnering of Mark Hateley and Duncan Ferguson in forward positions, and the plan of lumping high balls up to them, was naive in the extreme, and on the night there seemed to be no alternative tactic to fall back on. The persistent use of the long ball was a failure and when AEK scored in a breakaway just before half-time, the game was over.

It was the first time since 1963 that Rangers had failed to score in either leg of a European tie and the first time since 1975 that they had lost both legs.

If their European experience in 1994-95 had been a comprehensive disaster, hope springs eternal with the passing seasons. The helter-skelter nature of the domestic game, with a programme of two games each week from August to December, had not changed in the slightest for the 1995-96 season, and emerging from this into the more sophisticated steppes of Europe was still going to pose distinctive challenges to any Scottish, or come to that any English team. But the summer of 1995 saw Rangers yet again, as they had been for nine seasons since the coming of Graeme Souness, very active in the transfer market with an eye on European competition. The most prominent signing, without question, was that of Paul Gascoigne from Lazio in Rome for a reported fee of £4.3 million. The highly-rated England international was, on his best day, one of the finest midfield players in the world. The signing was not without opposition from many quarters among friends of Rangers, not with

regard to his football talents but in terms of his being injury-prone. He had suffered two serious injuries in preceeding years, and his off-the-field antics had been, to say the least, controversial. Nevertheless both David Murray and Walter Smith were persuaded that they were signing a world-class player around whom Rangers could build a team for the coming season.

Also arriving at Ibrox were Stephen Wright from Aberdeen to fill the right-back position. It had been glaringly ill-served since Gary Stevens had suffered a broken leg while on international duty with England in 1992. Oleg Salenko, the Russian forward with the not inconsiderable record of having scored five goals in one World Cup finals match against Cameroon in the USA in 1994, arrived at Ibrox as did Gordan Petric from Dundee United, a Yugoslav international central defender, snatched from under the noses of Celtic as they prepared to sign him. Walter Smith clearly believed that Petric would be crucial to his plan to change the Rangers' defensive system from a final line of four defenders to one of three, centrally, with two full-backs or wide backs given licence to go forward into withdrawn winger positions. Petric was to complete the line of three central defenders with Richard Gough and Alan McLaren.

With such a substantial investment in quality players, the possibility that Rangers, for a third successive season, would fail in Europe was unthinkable. The draw for the qualifying round paired the Ibrox club with Anorthosis Famagusta. It was welcomed. Rangers rightly or wrongly believed that the Cyprus club was among the weakest opposition they could face. Still their hopes of entry into the Champions League and a profitable run there, rested in the first place in defeating the island team. In the event, Rangers did qualify but only after a narrow 1-0 win at Ibrox and a 0-0 draw in Larnaca. The home performance was laboured. A Gordon Durie goal midway through the second half gave them a meagre margin with which to travel and Rangers, not overly impressive, struggled for long periods against a team which was very much better than anyone imagined it could be. Indeed had goalkeeper Goram not been in exceptional form, Rangers might very well have lost the match. A much more disciplined and professional performance was produced in the away leg, and Rangers went through with the scoreless draw on aggregate.

The Champions League draw put Rangers into a group of four which turned out to be the 'Group from Hell'. It included Juventus of Italy (the competition favourites), Borussia Dortmund of Germany, and Steau Bucharest of Romania. If the most pessimistic of Rangers fans had seen the struggles against Anorthosis as an omen, they were quickly proved right. Rangers' opening fixture was in Bucharest against Steau, who had been beaten in a pre-season match in Glasgow, but that was most certainly a friendly and if Rangers had any thought of progressing in this forbidding group and reaching the quarter-final stage, they absolutely had to come home with at least one point from this opening match.

An indication of how perhaps Rangers are regarded on the continent was evident at the press conference before the match, with the Steau coach, Dimitriu Dimitru, who said it was to Steau's advantage that they were playing their opening fixture at home against "the weakest team in the group". Few Rangers people agreed, but there it was.

Rangers were unlucky to lose in Bucharest. They were within five or six minutes of success in a holding operation. Their resolute defence was intent on taking one point from the match, and they seemed to have succeeded with little more than five minutes left. Then Daniel Prodan volleyed, left foot, a blinding shot which rocketed past Goram. It was a strike, hitting first time a left-wing corner, from nowhere. It was a severe blow. Even more severe was the ordering off of Alan McLaren midway through the second half. It followed an infringement in the penalty area at a corner kick when both he and Damian Militaru were sent packing. In the entire stadium, only a linesman had seen an offence, but the consequence was that Mclaren would miss the next three Champions League fixtures.

Rangers were criticised by television viewers at home for the 'negativity' of their performance, their persistent reluctance to attack the Romanian team. Accordingly the next tie, at home to Borussia Dortmund took on an even greater significance. In four previous meetings with the German side, Rangers had never lost, eliminating Borussia on both of the 'two-legged' occasions, so they were not without confidence going into the game. Over the 90 minutes, Rangers did enough to win yet had to settle for a 2-2 draw, with goals from Richard Gough and Ian Ferguson. They were handicapped by the absence of the suspended McLaren, David Robertson was out through injury and they lost Brian Laudrup at half-time with an injury that kept him out of the team for the next dozen matches. Thus with Gascoigne still working up to full match fitness and tempo, Walter Smith's strategy of having the combination and individual skills of Brian Laudrup and Paul Gascoigne as overwhelming factors against European opposition was substantially compromised, almost in tatters in fact. The team now needed nothing less than victory in one of its two games with the Italian champions, Juventus, but any hope of taking anything from the game in Turin vanished within 15 minutes as Rangers were blitzed by a quite superb performance from the Italians.

Rangers were clearly and totally outclassed. The defeat was such an embarrassment that Juventus, 3-0 ahead at halftime, looked quite capable of going on to inflict on Rangers as great a humiliation as had Real Madrid in 1963 (6-0) and Eintracht Frankfurt in 1960 (6-1, 6-3). That they scored one more goal in the second half was a matter of Juventus relaxing more than anything else. Juventus of course had players of the highest quality – del Pierro, Vialli, Ravanelli – throughout the team.

Their performance seemed in character with the quality of life in the Piedmont capital. Turin's department stores, elegant boutiques, cafés and restaurants along the Via Roma and the other main streets led many Rangers supporters to see themselves as poor relations despite the fact that they were following the champion club of Scotland, one which could spend millions of pounds on players. On the field, their team had been outclassed. Off the field they felt they were in a different world – one Rangers stalwart observed that the whole thing was, as far as Rangers were concerned, 'closer to Armenia than Armani'. A late consolation goal by Richard Gough was cheered even by Italian fans who were perhaps more appreciative of the loyalty of the Rangers fans than they were of the quality of Rangers football.

The return match, Rangers v Juventus, was the fourth in the group. Once again, victory was mandatory if Rangers were to have any hope of advancing in the competition. This time the result was 4-0 to Juventus, an even greater margin than in Turin, but it is not unfair to say that the result was a travesty. Rangers certainly did not deserve to lose by such a margin. Juventus again scored early, through

del Pierro, but from then on Rangers pressed, and compressed them. But midway through the second half, Juventus broke upfield. Ravanelli went off on a solo run from a blatantly offside position – later confirmed by the television tape – to score a second goal and effectively leave Rangers without the hope of even taking one point from the game. Had it ended 2-0, Rangers might have felt cross, but what they certainly did not deserve was to lose two more goals in injury time with the game dead. The 4-0 result did no justice to Rangers' performance.

Despite having sustained two drubbings from Juventus, Rangers nevertheless and ironically still had a chance of qualifying from their group, into the quarter-final round. Victories from their two remaining games, Steau at home and Borussia away, and the not unreasonable belief that the vastly talented Juventus team would win its two remaining matches against the Bucharest and Dortmund teams would mean that Rangers would qualify. Sadly for their hopes, Juventus, having already qualified, chose their home game with Borussia to rest several of their leading players with a view to battles still to come. This, and an outstanding display from the German goalkeeper, gave Borussia a 2-1 win in Turin. The television broadcast showed Juventus having most of the play. This result effectively eliminated Rangers from the competition. They could do no more than draw 1-1 with Steau in a match distinguished by a wonder goal from Gascoigne, when he ran 50 yards through the Romanian defence before scoring. Some pride was restored in a meaningless fixture in Dortmund, with a 2-2 draw and goals from Laudrup and Durie.

Rangers could have had the game won in the opening 15 minutes, when they played their finest football of the season to date. On a very difficult surface – this was 6 December – they opened up the German defence at will and missed chances were expensive. The game was marred by the ordering off of Paul Gascoigne, somewhat unfortunately, for two yellow-card offences. In a Rangers attack, Gascoigne had appealed for a penalty. The Spanish referee waved play on, the action broke quickly to the other end, where Dortmund came close to scoring. The referee moved over to Gascoigne, to explain things. The player no doubt said something indiscreet, was shown a second yellow card and had to go off. Thus had the referee not gone to Gascoigne nothing would have come of it. He later said that he had not realised that this was a second yellow-card offence.

Also ordered off in the Champions League was Alec Cleland in the match against Juventus in Turin, for a wild and reckless challenge on the Italian winger Alessandro del Piero, after del Piero had taunted and teased Cleland with his skills throughout the match. The Rangers player finally lost patience and made a wild swiping challenge which fortunately did not make contact. There was considerable sympathy for Cleland from the Italian players, particularly shown by Ravanelli as Cleland left the field.

Thus Rangers had had three players ordered off in eight matches in European competition, all away from home, all by 'foreign' referees. If these Rangers players were behaving as they do in Scottish League matches, that would suggest that Scottish referees are lenient! But this kind of thing is totally unacceptable and does not reflect well on the club. A number of points may be made: Nowadays, the manner in which the laws of the game are applied leads to a much greater number of bookings; it may be true to say that there is more dissent from players concerning refereeing decisions than ever before; it may be true that the conduct of professional footballers has deteriorated in the contemporary world. This may be a reflection of a general decline in morality in Western societies, or the result of the huge salaries the leading players are now paid and their abilities or otherwise to cope with the subsequent responsibilities. And in the mid-1990s, there has been a body of critical opinion claiming that the quality of refereeing has also deteriorated. It is a facile point, much loved of tabloid newspapers. Certainly many decisions are bewildering to the spectator, but the spectator has but a vague grasp of the laws of the game. Not one in ten could list the four ordering off offences, for example.

Alan McLaren's ordering off in Bucharest was seen by no one except a linesman, but he is the referee's assistant and therefore part of the adjudicating team. Cleland's dismissal in Turin was for 'serious foul play'. Gascoigne's dismissal in Dortmund was for a second yellow-card offence, the first for a reckless challenge, to which the Englishman is prone, the second for dissent, to which he is also prone.

In a First Division match at McDirmid Park, Perth, a St Johnstone player was ordered off for time wasting, in the judgement of the referee taking too long over a corner kick and gaining a second yellow card. Since his team was trailing at the time, it seemed less than logical. But as ever, it is well for everyone in football to recall the fifth Law of the Game, which states: 'A referee shall be appointed to officiate in each game. His authority and the exercise of the powers granted to him by the Laws of the Game commence as soon as he enters the field of play... his decision on points of fact connected with the play shall be final... He shall enforce the Laws'.

Thus lack of discipline, injuries and the 'maximum of three non-nationals in the team' at any time, cost Rangers dearly in their European venture. Mclaren, ordered off, was suspended for three European matches, Cleland similarly for two, and Gascoigne must miss the two opening matches of European competition in 1996-97. Wright, Steven, McInnes were out for substantially, the entire season. Robertson, Laudrup and others missed important matches. And with a healthy complement of 'foreign' players – Moore, Petric, Mikhailichenko, Salenko, Gascoigne were mature, senior players – manager Walter Smith often had no sorrows to seek come team selection time, tactical planning time, in accomodating the UEFA edict.

The ruling of the European Court, early in 1996, in favour of the Belgian player Bosman, giving a footballer total freedom from the claims of his club when a specific contract with the club had expired, led also to a relaxing of the 'three foreigners' rule. It was a liberation which sent Walter Smith trawling through Europe in February and March of 1996 when he needed instant replacements for his injured strikers McCoist and Durie.

Elimination from the Champions League was obviously a great disappointment for David Murray, the Rangers chairman at more than one level. Financially it was a severe blow. Many fans view the Champions League as some kind of crock of gold and that participation in itself will coin millions for the club. The fact is that a high proportion of the competition's income, from sponsorship and television rights is paid on results – Swiss francs per point, as it were! Thus the rich get richer. The Champions League Finalists in 1995, Ajax Amsterdam and AC Milan, swept up a total of £15 million each, £8 million from UEFA, the competition's ruling body, plus their retained receipts from five home matches and other peripheral sources.

This, in the contemporary world, is no doubt as it should be. At the other end of the scale, clubs like AEK Athens who took only one point from the Champions League were very much the poor relations and badly rewarded by comparison. For all that, a place in the Champions League remains an ambition for every club.

Given the quality of the opposition which Rangers faced in their group in 1995, it was less than rational for friends of Rangers to suppose they could succeed. It is probably fair to say that had Rangers been drawn in any other section, they could have qualified for a quarter-final place. They would certainly have made a better fist of things than did the English champions, Blackburn Rovers, a team of talented footballers whose failure in this competition was absolute and quite bewildering in a group of much poorer quality. Rangers' lack of success in Europe in recent seasons requires some consideration. They have run into very high-quality opposition. The last time they were a force in the competition was in 1992-93 when they almost reached the European Cup Final – they were 'pipped' as we have seen by the eventual winners, Olympique Marseille. Before then, in 1987-88, they went out in the quarter-final round to Steau Bucharest. Considered over 40 years the club has had its successes and near-successes but these have not been sustained from season to season. Rangers' best European achievements have been followed by failures. It may be that we expect too much from any Scottish club, even one with the resources of Rangers, and a more realistic expectation might be of a Rangers club making a positive challenge every fifth year.

Ibrox—A Great Stadium

THE history of the Rangers' home ground, from the public pitches on Glasgow Green through a brief stay at Burnbank, then the Kinning Park years which led to the first Ibrox Park and the magnificent stadium of today, has been one of a progress and development which has marched side by side with the growing appeal of the game, and the continuing success of a great football club.

Rangers' first home of their own was a field at Burnbank, on the south side of Great Western Road, near Kelvinbridge and not far from West End Park, where the club was first conceived. To this day, Burnbank Street and West End Park Street are names which feature in the area on Glasgow street maps. This ground served for a year after being opened on 11 September 1875 by Vale of Leven with a 1-1 draw.

Early in October, Rangers went south of the river to play Clydesdale, one of the powers of the time at their Kinning Park ground, and held them 1-1. The attractions of that ground stayed in Rangers' memories and a year later, when Clydesdale moved to Titwood, where they remain as a cricket club, Rangers stepped in. On 2 September 1876, Vale of Leven again opened a Rangers ground, this time winning 2-1. Rangers were to stay at Kinning Park for a decade.

That first match was seen by a crowd of 1,500. The ground capacity of 2,000 was steadily increased by Rangers to around 7,000. They made regular improvements, adding sloping terraces and improving the playing surface, although as early as 1884, their landlords were indicating that they would take the ground back, for development. The last official match at Kinning Park was on 26 February 1887, against Old Westminsters in a sixth-round FA Cup-tie.

Rangers played the rest of their matches that season at Cathkin Park, courtesy of the Third Lanark club, then laid claim to a new ground at Ibrox, a few miles west of Kinning Park. It was very advanced for its time.

The playing field was 115 yards long and 71 yards broad, surrounded by a track exactly a quarter of a mile in circumference, perfect for the summer athletics meetings which were to feature in the history of the club. A grandstand 300 feet long with six tiers of seats and accommodation for 1,200 was built. The playing pitch was bordered by a wooden rail about three and a half feet high and painted white and behind it the ground had been raised in ash terraces giving clear views of the field.

A splendid pavilion was built in the north-east corner, by Copland Road, with dressing rooms, bathrooms and a committee room – an altogether splendid place with brick foundations, walls and roofs of corrugated iron sheeting and gas and water supplies in place. The entire property had a perimeter fence of corrugated iron paling eight feet high on wooden frames, and as far as the contractors, Fred Braby and Co of Petershill Road, were concerned, this was an altogether unique creation.

The capacity was estimated at 15,000 and the opening match, a friendly against Preston North End, excited enormous interest. It was a financial success with gate receipts of £350, but in all other respects it was a near-disaster. The size of the crowd, more than 18,000, took everyone by surprise and when a railing broke and the crowd spilled on to the field, the match was halted 20 minutes early. At that point the 'Invincibles' from Preston led by 8-1! There were widespread suggestions that the Kinning Park hooligan element had seen enough. At all events it was a black day for the new arrivals in Govan.

By the end of the century, the game and Rangers' success had outgrown this first ground at Ibrox on the site of the present Edmiston House and the club developed a much grander stadium on a site which was practically adjoining. It was completely different. There was a spacious two-storey pavilion at the south-east corner of the ground and a grandstand, completed in 1900, which seated 4,500, the roof of which came from the First Ibrox Park. Along the opposite touchline was a covered enclosure, dubbed the 'Bovril Stand' from the huge Bovril advertisement displayed at the front of the roof. Covering a total of 14.5 acres, the new site was described, with customary Scottish modesty, as 'the finest football ground in the world'. The estimated capacity of 80,000 was somewhat fanciful. But within two years, it was up to 75,000.

The grandstand and enclosure ran the full length of the ground, accommodating 15,000 spectators – the Rangers management hoped that this facility might attract a better class of spectator! There were two miles of seating and 28 miles of pitch pine needed for standing places, each wide enough for one person only. This provided clear viewing. At the west end of the ground, 100 tiers rose high on scaffolding and an iron framework. This was to have fearful consequences in a couple of years time. Severe weather conditions had delayed things, but in December, Rangers president James Henderson declared the ground formally open. R.C.Hamilton kicked-off in a match against Hearts, which Rangers won 3-1.

By 1902, the ground was named to host both the Scotland-England match and the Scottish Cup Final, but after the former on 5 April 1902 (see *Days of Disaster*) the wooden terracing was removed, and by 1905 Ibrox had been rebuilt on safer lines to hold 25,000. Five years later it had been extended to take 63,000 and into a vast saucer shape which persisted until 1978. Following World War One, the ground capacity was stretched to 80,000 and indeed in the Rangers-Celtic New Year's Day match of January 1939, no fewer than 118,730 packed the stadium for a record in a British club match which will surely never be broken.

The success of Rangers' teams in the 1920s – they won their first League and Cup double in 1928 – saw vaulting ambition soar again, and the club set about building the finest grandstand in Britain. Archibald Leitch, the designer who had worked at Celtic Park and Hampden, produced a

Ibrox, photographed a few years ago before it became an all-seater stadium

design similar to those he had done for Portsmouth's Fratton Park and Everton's Goodison, but for an Ibrox stand which would seat 10,500, with thousands standing in its enclosures. It had – still has – an imposing red brick façade with arched windows on its upper floors, pedimented windows at each end, and on each gable end, the club crest with its Lion Rampant shield and 'Aye Ready' motto was picked out in blue and gold mosaic. No doubt it was Leitch's finest work. His accolade came in 1980, when the façade became a listed building.

The optimism and confidence of the club manifested in this structure was further demonstrated by a lavishly castellated Press Box, long since gone, placed on the roof, and the massive blue ironwork gates at each end of the stand. One other striking feature was the criss-cross balcony wall which survives and which can be seen also at Fratton, Goodison and Sunderland's Roker Park.

On the north side of the ground, the 'Bovril Stand' disappeared, and a barrel roof covered the upper half of the terracing. Inside the new stand, Rangers, in expansive mood, elected for quality. The entrance hall and main staircase were in marble, corridors and boardroom were panelled in expensive wood, carpeting was of the finest. As the years passed, art deco lamps, the Trophy Room and the Alan Morton painting, were added. It was opened by Glasgow's Lord Provost on 1 January 1929. Rangers beat Celtic 3-0. But the events of January 1971 (see *Days of Disaster*) were to put an end to the great sweeping bowl of Ibrox Park and to begin the creation of Ibrox as a modern, compact, sophisticated stadium, just possibly the finest in Britain.

Among short-term measures, 10,000 bench-type seats had been laid on the north terracing in 1973, at a cost of £70,000 and dubbed the Centenary Stand. It was not a success, proving less than popular with the fans. In August 1978, the removal of the entire east terracing began, and a year later the Copland Road Stand rose in its place, opened with a 2-2 League match with Celtic. Next, the vast

sweep of the west terracing went the same way, and in August 1980, Arsenal were the official guests in a 2-0 Rangers win.

Ibrox was becoming a rectangle. The Centenary Stand was demolished, and a new stand, an enlarged version of its two predecessors, rose in its place. The method of construction was a simple 'goalpost' frame in support of the roof. The Copland Road and Broomloan Road stands were 78 metres wide. The Centenary or North Stand, now named the Govan Stand, had a girder 110 metres long supporting the roof, and no fewer than 10,300 seats. It was opened officially by a Liverpool visit in 1981. All of this over a ten years period had cost £10 million, a huge sum made possible only by contributions from Rangers Pools. And when a top deck was added to Leith's South Stand, the Main Stand in 1991, and its enclosure converted to seating, Ibrox, at an overall cost of some £30 million provided an all-seater stadium of 46,836 capacity. The final project, as the club headed towards a new century, was to fill in the corners, *ie* join Copland to Govan and Govan to Broomloan to make a completely enclosed stadium with a capacity of 51,000, one of the largest in Britain. The cost will be £6.5 million.

The present stadium provides executive boxes in the Govan Stand, with the impressive Argyle Restaurant. Executive and sponsors' lounges are in the Main Stand (Waddell, Thornton and McPhail Suites) with function suites in the Govan Stand (Meiklejohn, Morton, Symon and Woodburn Suites). The stadium employs a full-time staff of 150. On match days, 500 personnel are required to provide the catering requirement and the total number of service personnel, including police, will be at least 1,000. Each turnstile is centrally monitored. The stadium is covered by close-circuit television. Match ticketing is computerised. The club has 36,000 season ticket holders and more than 6,500 individual shareholders. Total turnover in 1993-94 was in the region of £15 million.

Rangers' Managers

William Wilton
1899-1920

WILLIAM WILTON was Rangers' first manager, and although his name has drifted away with the mists of time and history, he could be reckoned as effective as any manager the club has ever had.

He joined Rangers as a player in 1883, but never progressed beyond the minor elevens. He did have an eye for talent, though, and when he was appointed match secretary for the Swifts and Shields teams, the fortunes of these reserve sides improved to the extent that many of the players preferred to stay with them, and had the idea that they were often better than the first team.

Wilton's abilities in administration and his foresight saw him on a special committee set up to oversee the move from Kinning Park to the new ground at Ibrox, in 1887. In May 1889, he was elected match secretary, and ten years later, when Rangers became a limited company, he was named as manager

Representing the club, he was elected as the Scottish League's first treasurer in 1890. He was an imaginative and innovative man – the *Rangers Handbook* was his creation and he insisted that the new ground at Ibrox should have a running track. At Rangers Sports through the years, many world records were set. The first Ibrox grandstand was also his conception.

His signings for Rangers were a hall of fame: Davy Mitchell, Andrew McCreadie, John McPherson, Jock Drummond, Nicol Smith, Alec Smith, Neil Gibson, Jacky Robertson, Bobby Neil, R.C.Hamilton, Archie Kyle, John May, Jimmy Gordon, Herbert Lock, Alex Bennett, Willie Reid, Andy Cunningham, Tommy Cairns, Sandy Archibald and many others.

His last trophy success with the club was the Glasgow Charity Cup of 1919, when Rangers beat Queen's Park 2-1 in a memorable match before 70,000 at Hampden. A year later on 2 May 1920, Willie Wilton lost his life tragically when he was lost overboard in heavy seas whilst relaxing on a friend's yacht at Gourock.

William Struth
1920-1954

WILLIAM STRUTH, manager of Rangers for 34 years, will surely be seen by history as one of the greatest of British football managers, surpassing perhaps even the achievements of Jock Stein with Dunfermline and Celtic, Herbert Chapman with Huddersfield Town and Arsenal, and Matt Busby at Manchester United, all of them in differing eras.

The Struth record cannot be denied. In his 34 years in command, Rangers won 18 League championships, ten Scottish Cup Finals, two League Cup Finals; the Glasgow Cup 18 times, the Glasgow Charity Cup 20 times. In season 1929-30, Rangers won every competition the club entered – Scottish Cup, League championship, Reserve Cup, Reserve championship and the Glasgow and Glasgow Charity Cups. All of those included six seasons of World War Two, when football was a secondary affair in the fab-

ric of life. Perhaps the most remarkable statistic in the Struth portfolio is that from season 1920-21, his first in full command, until season 1938-39, Rangers won the championship 14 times. In the other four years, they were second three times, third once.

Bill Struth went a long way to complete the Rangers mystique, the creation of which was started by his predecessor, William Wilton. The Rangers ethos, backed by the club's history, is simply that 'we are the best there is, and we shall always be seen as the best there is'. The result is that

the great mass of Scotland's young footballers hope desperately that one day they will be invited to play for Rangers.

An Edinburgh man, Struth was a stonemason by trade, which no doubt gave him his chunky, deep-chested physique. And as a young man, he was a professional pedestrian, a 'ped', a runner who did the rounds of the athletic tracks up and down the country which offered money prizes for competition. No doubt this sparked his interest in physical fitness and training. At the age of 33, in 1908, he became trainer of Clyde FC, and of Rangers in 1914. On the death of Wilton, the club's secretary-manager, in 1920, Bill Struth took over the job.

He was a strict disciplinarian. He was not much of a football tactician, or analyst. He left much of that to his senior players, but he was a shrewd operator in the recruitment of talent – always concerned for example about a young player's family life – and in the transfer market. He built up a network of informers, a Struth 'mafia', which kept him informed of promising players, of the football gossip and rumours and scandals of the day, and much more important of any Rangers players who were misbehaving away from Ibrox. When that happened, he was quite ruthless in dealing with the offender, laying down the law that Rangers must be first-class in everything. He made sure that Rangers travelled first-class everywhere and had first-class service in all things. That meant that players had to behave accordingly, in their dress, their behaviour and their public lives away from the club.

Struth was something of a dandy. He kept half a dozen suits in his panelled Ibrox office, and would change often more than once a day. All the suits were double-breasted. And he was apt to appear in full dress Highland rig at social functions, weddings and the like. Struth became a director of the club in 1947, retired as manager in the summer of 1954 and died on 21 September 1956, aged 81.

Scot Symon
1954-1967

SCOT SYMON, through his term of 13 years in the 1950s and 1960s, was clearly a success as a Rangers manager. His teams won six championships, five Scottish Cups and four League Cups. Twice the double was won, and in 1964, the 'treble'. Rangers were European Cup-winners' Cup Finalists in 1961 and 1967, and Symon's finest Rangers team included such players as Baxter and McMillan, Greig and McKinnon.

James Scotland Symon from Tayside had a distinguished playing career with Dundee, Portsmouth and Rangers. He lost, of course, six prime years to World War Two. When he retired at Ibrox in season 1946-47, he became manager of East Fife. In his first season there, the modest Fife team won the Scottish League Cup as well as promotion to the

top echelon, Division 'A' as it was then called. In 1949-50, the unpretentious Fifers won the League Cup. And in 1949-50, they reached the Final of the Scottish Cup, only to be hit by a dazzling performance by Rangers, who scored in a matter of seconds and eventually won 3-0. Symon joined Preston North End in March 1953, and saw them to an FA Cup Final, where they lost to a West Bromwich penalty. He was invited back to Ibrox when Bill Struth retired in June 1954.

He has been described as the last of the lounge-suited managers, the waistcoat managers, the Homburg managers. Symon was not a track-suit man who involved himself on the training grounds. Rather he believed in recruiting excellent footballers and allowing them to blend their talents to his thinking about the game, and to each other. He was in one sense a shy, almost introverted man, certainly in his handling of the media, but never less than polite. His departure from the club, on 1 November 1967, was scandalous in the fullest sense of the word. The Rangers board may have been right in deciding that he should go, or possibly move up in the club structure, leaving room for a track-suited tactition to work on the training ground with the players. And the defeat by Berwick Rangers, back in January of that year, was not allowed to be forgotten by influential supporters who had the ears of the directors. But the manner of Symon's going brought no dignity to the club.

Instead of discussing the matter directly with him, as common courtesy would suggest, the club chairman, John Lawrence sent an emissary, a business associate who had no connection with, and no doubt little particular interest in, football, to do it for him. Symon, a proud man, not surprisingly, could not accept that, and resigned. He was a director of Dumbarton for a short time, then manager of Partick Thistle.

David White
1967-1969

DAVID WHITE'S managerial career at Ibrox was the shortest-lived of any. His entire playing career was spent with Clyde FC, where he became player-coach, then manager. In 1967, Rangers and Celtic were both in Finals of European competitions, and White, as an observer, travelled with each party. Perhaps Scot Symon was impressed by the young man's performance at Nuremburg. On their return, White was appointed assistant manager at Ibrox. Perhaps Symon saw in him the track-suited manager which he was not. And when Symon left in November, David White, with less than six months at the club, became manager.

His time at Ibrox was plagued by near-misses. In that first season, 1967-68 , Rangers faced Aberdeen at Ibrox in their final League game. They lost, their only League defeat of the season. It meant that, finishing with 61 points, they were second to Celtic in the championship by two meagre points. In the 1969 Scottish Cup Final, basic mistakes by experienced players allowed Celtic to help themselves to a 4-0 win and inflict on Rangers their heaviest Cup Final defeat. An error by goalkeeper Gerry Neef the next year cost them their place in the League Cup.

In European competition, White's teams reached the quarter-finals and semi-finals of the Inter-Cities Fairs Cup, as it then was, losing to Leeds United, then Newcastle United, respectively. In November 1969, for the European Cup-winners' Cup match in Poland, White seemed to have

unlikely League championship in 1964-65, the Scottish Cup Final of 1960 (0-2 v Rangers), and League Cup Finals in 1960-61 (0-2 v Rangers) and 1962-63 (0-1 v Hearts). He became manager of Rangers in December 1969 following the departure of David White and was to remain at Ibrox for the rest of his life. Little more than a year later, in January 1971, he was to face the greatest challenge of his public life (see *Days of Disasters*).

totally underestimated the opposition, Górnik Zabrze. He announced before the match that Rangers would attack from the first whistle. They did. The result was 3-1 to the Polish team, and when the same result emerged in the Ibrox return – Rangers were two down after 12 minutes, this was too much for the Rangers directors. White was dismissed the next day.

David White was perhaps not tough enough for the job. The management of the Rangers club demands very particular talents and it may be that David White simply lacked the background and the experience of the game at the highest level, which all successful Rangers managers need. And the ever-present Celtic, always part of the Rangers equation, were at their peak under Jock Stein.

As he moved into his 50s (Waddell was born in 1921) he judged that the team needed a coach, a younger, hands-on, everyday track-suit man who would direct the players' preparation. Waddell became general manager, and in Jock Wallace, decided that he had found his man. Wallace became coach in June 1970 and team manager in 1972. Waddell concentrated his energies subsequently on the modernisation of Ibrox (see *Ibrox Stadium*) and lived to see Ibrox become probably the finest club ground in the British Isles. He died in 1992.

Willie Waddell
1969-1972

NO MAN made a greater contribution to the achievements of the Rangers Football Club than did Willie Waddell. As a player, manager, general manager, managing director, director and vice-chairman, and finally as a consultant to the club, Willie Waddell stamped his authority and personality indelibly on Ibrox over a period of 50 scarcely-interrupted years. His name is perpetuated in the 'Waddell Suite' in the contemporary Ibrox Stadium which he did so much to shape.

As a player, he brought pace and power to the right wing in the great Rangers teams of the late 1940s and early 1950s. Before he finished playing, in the summer of 1956, he had become a talented Glasgow journalist. In 1957, he became manager of Kilmarnock and brought exceptional success to the provincial club. Their honours included an

Jock Wallace
1972-1978 & 1983-1986

TWO men, Willie Waddell and Jock Wallace, had much in common. Both were hard men, winners, achievers. In an Army career with the King's Own Scottish Borderers, Wallace had served in Northern Ireland, and fought communist insurgents in Malaysia. He had a remarkable career in football. A goalkeeper from Wallyford in Midlothian (his father kept goal for Raith Rovers, Blackpool and Derby County), Wallace played first for Airdrie, then by way of West Bromwich Albion, Bedford and Hereford he reached Berwick Rangers as player-manager.

On one of Scottish football's historic days, and a black day in Rangers' history, Wallace was in the home goal when Berwick beat Rangers 1-0 in the first round of the Scottish

Cup on 28 January 1967. Within a couple of years at the modest club, Wallace had it challenging for promotion, but was lured away by Hearts as assistant to manager John Harvey. Waddell no doubt saw him as a man after his own heart and brought him to Ibrox in 1970.

Jock Wallace was a motivator supreme. He believed in a high level of physical fitness and in one pre-season programme, controversially, he had Rangers players running up and down the huge sand dunes at Gullane. He brought Rangers success. His League Cup win over Celtic brought the club some hope of catching up with the apparently invincible Celtic of Jock Stein. There was the European Cup-winners' Cup success in 1972, a Centenary Scottish Cup win in 1973, and the winning of the championship of 1974-75, the first in 11 years. He went on to win a 'double treble' of League, Scottish Cup and League Cup in each of two seasons, 1975-76 and 1977-78.

Yet a few days after the second of his trebles, Wallace resigned. Rangers have always maintained some secrecy about their affairs, and Wallace's going was never explained, but it was thought to be the result of a clash with Willie Waddell over the purchase of players which Wallace, in spite of his success, may have seen to be necessary. Waddell, of course, was concerned with the financing of the rebuilding of Ibrox.

Jock Wallace still had miles to go. He took Leicester City to the championship of the English Second Division and the semi-final of the FA Cup. He was back in Scotland in 1982, at Motherwell, and following the resignation of John Greig in October 1983, Jock Wallace was back at Ibrox, the only man who has been a Rangers manager twice. The team by this time was in decline. Wallace won the League Cup in March 1984, beating Celtic in the Final by 3-2, then Dundee United in the 1984-85 Final by 1-0. But with

Aberdeen and Dundee United emerging as powers in the land during the 1980s, the championship proved elusive. Indeed season 1985-86 was in Rangers' terms a disaster. The team finished fifth in the championship in the only season in its history in which it failed to average at least one point per match. Only once before, in 1925-26, had Rangers been worse (they finished sixth that season) and only once before, in 1964-65, had they also finished fifth.

When the John Lawrence organisation bought a majority shareholding in the club, and put their man, David Holmes, in place as chief executive, Wallace's time was up. After a dismal defeat by Tottenham Hotspur in April 1986, he was fired by Holmes, who no doubt already had Graeme Souness in mind as a successor. Unabashed, Wallace went off to Spain to manage Seville, came back to be first manager, then a director of Colchester United. If Jock Wallace's first act in the Rangers story was 'infamous' (the defeat at Berwick when he denied the Rangers attack), his achievements were quite outstanding.

When he died in July 1996 it was a sad day for all Rangers followers.

John Greig
1978-1983

JOHN GREIG was appointed manager of Rangers on 24 May 1978, the day after Jock Wallace's first reign came to an end.

Greig had just finished a season in which he had played 41 games in his total of 753 for the club, becoming the only Scottish player to have won a 'treble of trebles'. Rangers in season 1977-78 had won League, Scottish Cup and League Cup. Thus Greig on the face of it was inheriting an experi-

enced, successful team, which is as much as any incoming manager might hope for.

In his first season, the team won the League Cup, and after three games with Hibs, the Scottish Cup, and in the European Champions' Cup, had good wins over impressive names, Juventus and PSV Eindhoven, before losing to Cologne in the quarter-finals. The championship was lost to Celtic. In what became the decisive game, Colin Jackson, five minutes from the end, headed into his own goal and in the very last minute Murdo McLeod was up to hammer in a fourth. It was to prove ominous for Greig and his men.

The next season, 1979-80 was considered a disaster by Rangers standards. They finished fifth and failed to beat Celtic in any match throughout the season, always a yardstick for the Rangers club and its fans. In addition, they went out of the League Cup in round three, beaten home and away by Aberdeen. Greig splashed out in the hope of refreshing the team. Ian Redford came from Dundee for £210,000, Gregory Stevens from Leicester City for £150,000. Rangers got to the Scottish Cup Final, but it seemed that John Greig did not have what some would say is the greatest of all managerial qualities – luck. Against Celtic in that Final, 17 minutes into extra-time, George McCluskey deflected a Danny McGrain shot which goalkeeper Peter McCloy had covered and Celtic won 1-0.

Colin MacAdam was bought for £165,000 from Partick Thistle, Jim Bett from the Lokeren club of Belgium for £180,000 but in 1980-81, Aberdeen again dumped Greig's team out of the League Cup. They did manage to beat Dundee United (4-1) in a replayed Scottish Cup Final, but yet again the championship, the Holy Grail for Rangers, was beyond them. They finished third. In 1981-82, the League Cup was secured with a late, dramatic goal by Ian Bedford against Dundee United, but both League title and Scottish Cup were lost and at the season's end, experienced

players Sandy Jardine and Colin Jackson left the club. Tommy McLean ended his playing career and stayed at Ibrox as coach and assistant manager to John Greig.

In season 1982-83, John Greig's team reached the Scottish Cup Final for the seventh straight year, but lost yet again to Aberdeen after extra-time, and could do no better than third in the championship. That season, Greig paid a club record £225,000 for Craig Paterson in July. Injuries at Ibrox compromised the promise Paterson had shown at Hibs. Rangers repeated lack of challenge in the championship did little to please their customers and this was being reflected in the attendances. John Greig resigned on 28 October 1983, saying, "I've finished with the game". It was the type of remark any manager, frustrated and under stress is likely to make. Perhaps John's outstanding success as a player made it difficult for him to make the instant transition from dressing-room to manager's office. He was not finished with the only club he had known – he was back early in 1990 as Rangers' public relations manager.

Graeme Souness 1986-1991

RANGERS first player-manager, Graeme James Souness, came to the club in April 1986 with the highest credentials. He had played 54 times for his country and had been Scotland's captain. He had known outstanding success as a player, being a key figures in the successes of Liverpool teams in the 1970s and 1980s, with triumphs in the English League championship and the European Champions' Cup. He had played in World Cup finals campaigns and for two seasons had played for Sampdoria of Genoa in the Italian Serie 'A', perhaps the most sophisticated competition in world football.

David Holmes, chairman of Rangers in the John Lawrence regime, brought Souness back from Italy in the spring of 1986. Thanks to the drive and vision of a predecessor, Willie Waddell, Souness came to a magnificent, modern stadium, and clearly intended his team to be worthy of the new Ibrox. He had known quality in his life. His creed seemed to be, 'If you want to be a big club, you must have big players'. He demonstrated this in a way which convulsed the Scottish game. He spent huge sums for the time, and high salaries to his purchases, his star, international players, in one sense reversing the century-old trend of Scottish players being tempted to England. Souness reversed this, his aim victory in European competition.

He signed Chris Woods, the England international goalkeeper in June 1986 from Norwich City at a price of £600,000. He signed Terry Butcher, captain of England, from Ipswich Town for £750,000 in August 1986. They were the first of a stream of international players brought to Ibrox by Souness – Trevor Steven, Gary Stevens, Trevor Francis, Ray Wilkins, Richard Gough, for whom he paid Tottenham Hotspur £1.1 million.

In his first season, Rangers won the championship for the first time in nine years and won a major trophy each year during his five years at the club. Four championships, four League Cup wins was the count. Rangers were a power in the land yet again. One of his greatest contributions to the well-being of the club may have come in 1988, when he persuaded a friend, David Murray, to join him in buying control of the club from the John Lawrence organisation. David Murray was a millionaire with interests in steel stockholding and property, and one of a new breed of young Scottish entrepreneurs.

But Souness, however, had a brusque, arrogant streak in his character. He was seemingly intolerant of the media, often appearing to be patronising.

He gradually ran down his appearances in the team, but on the field he was over-fierce more than once. Indeed, in his very first game for Rangers he was ordered off the field at Easter Road for kicking George McCluskey of Hibernian.

He was sometimes censured by authority, yet could appear indifferent to the national association and the Scottish League.

It is said that he argued with players, officials, referees and his own staff. And differences of opinion with his own players, such as Terry Butcher, Davie Cooper, David McPherson and Graham Roberts, saw them depart from the club.

Walter Smith
1991-

THREE days after Souness left Rangers, chairman David Murray announced his successor – the assistant manager, Walter Smith. Smith, born in Carmyle, a Glasgow suburb not much more than a mile from Celtic's Parkhead ground, was a 'blue-nose', a dyed-in-the-wool Rangers fan, and had been since boyhood. He had wanted above all else to play for Rangers, but the call never came. Instead, at 18, in November 1966, he left the Glasgow junior club Ashfield and signed for Dundee United. He had a good solid career there as a half-back. From September 1975, he had 18 months with Dumbarton, then went back to Tannadice where manager Jim McLean encouraged his interest in coaching. In March 1982, he was appointed assistant manager, and in April 1986, two months after becoming a Dundee United director, he could not resist the call from Graeme Souness to go to Ibrox, at last!

Smith said once, after becoming Rangers manager, that the greatest pleasure he had in the job was simply 'walking through these big front doors at nine o'clock each morning' – and the worst of it? The expectations of the Rangers fans – "They expect the team to win every match, every competition – not very rational".

On 16 April 1991, Souness himself was off – back to Anfield – only six weeks after saying, "I'll never leave Ibrox. I know in my own mind that I could never contemplate leaving Ibrox." At his final press conference, he remained in character. Entering the room, he said that he was leaving Rangers, going to Liverpool, and would brook no questions. He then walked out. David Murray, his chairman and friend who was present, said "He's making the biggest mistake of his life".

He may have proved a wise prophet. At Liverpool, Souness was succeeding his former teammate Kenny Dalglish, who had resigned 'because of stress' two months earlier.

Souness lasted a couple of years at Anfield, where he won the FA Cup, survived a major heart operation, spent money without producing a team to win the championship and take Liverpool into the European Champions' Cup. He left Anfield late in 1993 and after working in Turkey with Galatasary he took charge at Southampton, back in the FA Premiership.

Outwardly calm and composed most of the time, Walter Smith has a long management experience. He had worked with Jim McLean and Dundee United's championship team, with Scottish national team managers Jock Stein, Alex Ferguson and Andy Roxburgh, and of course at Ibrox through the Souness years. It has shown. Rangers won the 1991 championship, Smith's first, with a dramatic last match win over Aberdeen, and have won the championship in every one of his seasons so far!

Famous Rangers

Sandy Archibald

Sandy Archibald, from Aberdour in Fife, had one of the longest (17 years) and most distinguished careers in the history of the club. A vigorous, free-running goalscoring outside-right, the former miner, born in 1897, arrived at Ibrox from Raith Rovers before he was 20 and was to win 12 League champi-

onships between 1918 and 1934. He was a Scottish Cup winner in 1928 and Finalist in 1921, 1922 and 1929. Archibald played eight times for Scotland. Retiring at the end of November 1934, he became manager of Raith Rovers, then of Dunfermline Athletic from 1937 until his early death in 1946. His 514 League appearances for Rangers are an all-time record excluding the wartime appearances of Dougie Gray.

Jim Baxter

"The most skilful left-half ever produced by Rangers..."
"The best left-sided player Rangers had

seen since Alan Morton..."
"Most extravagantly gifted..."

Such compliments were not overdone. James Curran Baxter was a quite exceptional footballer of world class, and he proved it. His ball skills, particularly with his left foot, were astonishing. He dominated and largely controlled one of Rangers' most successful teams, that of the first half of the 1960s. In his five years at Ibrox, from 1960 to 1965, he won ten of the 15 domestic honours available to the club – three League championship medals, three Scottish Cups, four League Cups. With Ian McMillan, he formed the core of the team and controlled the middle of the field in match after match.

Baxter's arrogance on the field, and on the ball, never was more manifest than in games against Celtic, and in the

blue of Scotland. He played 18 times in Rangers v Celtic matches in the period 1960-65, in ten League matches, five in the League Cup and three in the Scottish Cup, and was on the losing side but twice. In Wembley internationals, he scored both goals in a ten-men Scottish victory over England, by 2-1 in 1963 and by 3-2 in 1967. Another peak appearance, in the highest company, was in the Rest of Europe team v England in the FA Centenary Match at Wembley, in 1963.

Rangers paid a record Scottish fee of £17,500 when signing Baxter from Raith Rovers in June 1960. A Fife boy, he had been a part-time player with Raith, working as a carpenter, then a collier. He was one of the last of the young men to do National Service, which he did in the Black Watch. At Ibrox, he was immediately and continuously successful. Indifferent to serious defensive play, he relied on the pace of Eric Caldow, the left-back, to cover him. Alas, a prodigious career was squandered wilfully by self-indulgence, waywardness, indiscipline and an indifference to his physical conditioning. He had little interest in training, became a heavy drinker and seemed to have a self-destruct button which eventually worked only too well for him. He moved on to Sunderland in May 1965 for £72,500, then to Nottingham Forest in December 1967 for £100,000. He came back to Rangers for an unsuccessful season, then became a publican, near Ibrox.

Jimmy Bowie

Jimmy Bowie, born in Partick, followed one of the classic routes to Ibrox, had a distinguished career on the field, became a director, then chairman, of the club in an association of 37 years and finally suffered the ignominy of being deposed from the chair by a boardroom coup, in 1947. It was said that from then until his death in 1969, aged 81, he never again set foot in Ibrox. From Glasgow Schools, Maryhill Juniors and Queen's Park, Bowie, an engineer by profession, reached Ibrox as a professional in 1910, playing in the championship-winning teams of 1912, 1913, 1918, 1920 and 1921, and in the Scottish Cup Final of 1921. Of medium

build he was an adaptable wing-half or inside-forward who believed in skill and control rather than power. He played twice for Scotland and was president of the Scottish Football League from 1939 to 1946.

Ralph Brand

Ralph Laidlaw Brand arrived in the public domain as it were when he played in the televised England v

Scotland Schoolboys international at Wembley in 1952. That summer, he was provisionally signed by Rangers and became fully-fledged in April 1954, six months before his 18th birthday. And five months later, he made a precocious debut against Kilmarnock. Rangers won 6-0, Brand, an outside-right for the day, scored two. He was on his way, even then, to becoming one for the great Rangers goalscorers. He played 317 games, scored 206 goals in spite of spending most of 1955 and 1956 on National Service.

By the end of the 1950s, the Brand-Millar strike-force was established. In an opening fixture in 1959-60, Rangers beat Hibs at Easter Road, 6-0. The scorers were Brand (4), Millar and Andy Matthew. Brand, like Millar, was simply destined to be a footballer. It was all he ever wanted to do with his life. He was 5ft 7in tall, never weighed more than 150 pounds, but he was fast, sharp and fearless, and quick as a Jimmy Greaves in the penalty area. Above all else, he wanted to be a great player, and was totally immersed in the tactics of the game. In seven Rangers Finals, he scored six goals and was never on the losing side. In eight international matches, he scored eight goals, and in that scene he suffered from being a contemporary of Denis Law.

With a great Rangers team breaking up in the middle 1960s, he moved to Manchester City for two years, then to Sunderland, before ending his career at Raith Rovers in 1970.

Terry Butcher

One of the most dramatic, and significant, signings ever made by Rangers was that of Terry Butcher, of Ipswich Town and England, in August 1986 for £725,000. Coming just two months after the purchase of Chris Woods for £600,000, it was an indication of an entirely new, big-spending policy at Ibrox, and of the audacity of player-manager Graeme Souness in carrying it out.

Butcher was a seasoned international player, deputy captain to Bryan Robson in the England team, and had a reputation respected throughout world football. He was a domineering figure in every respect, a giant of 6ft 4in who played with an enthusiasm and passion which made him an inspirational figure in Rangers teams. Almost unchallengeable in the air, his forays forward for free-kicks and corners made him a huge

attacking factor for the team. He captained England to third place in the 1990 World Cup in Italy, when they lost on penalty kicks against Germany in the semi-final.

He was the perfect leader of the Souness policy of bigger and better – an international star, articulate and intelligent, as gifted on and off the field as any Rangers captain before or since. His first competitive match was the 2-1 defeat at Easter Road on 9 August – when Graeme Souness was ordered off – and a disquieting introduction to Scottish football it must have been. Butcher led the team to the championship, and a League Cup win that season, and to two more championships and another League Cup.

The lowest point of his time in Scotland was surely being ordered off with Chris Woods and Celtic's Frank McAvennie in the infamous match at Ibrox on 17 October 1987. Butcher was all but a bystander when Woods and McAvennie played a barging game, the kind of thing that passes almost every week. Referee Jim Duncan booked Butcher for protesting at the sending off of Woods, then for a second time (which meant automatic dismissal) for a subsequent and fairly routine foul. Astonishingly, the case, such as it was, went to Glasgow Sheriff Court where to charges brought by the Fiscal's office of 'behaviour likely to cause a breach of the peace'. Both Woods and Butcher were fined £250, and McAvennie was found not guilty. The case had been brought by Assistant Procurator Fiscal Sandy Jessop of the Glasgow office. He was a rugby referee!

Both players took their cases to the Court of Appeal, but lost on a split decision, and both thought that they did not need this kind of justice and thought very seriously of saying goodbye to Scottish football.

Terry Butcher's last League game for Rangers was at Tannadice Park, Dundee, on 22 September 1990, when he back-headed a United clearance from 22 yards over Chris Woods for an own-goal. Later in the match he missed a tackle which allowed United to score a second and winning goal. He moved to Coventry City on 15 November for a fee of £500,000, and later spent time with Sunderland before coming back to Scotland to become a hotelier at Bridge of Allan, and a sports reporter. It would be correct to say that the relationship between Butcher and Souness was not of the healthiest when he left. Rangers fans, for whom Butcher was something of a folk hero, had another example of the ruthlessness of their manager. And five years on, these same fans would insist that Rangers have not found a comparable replacement in their defence.

Tommy Cairns

Tommy Cairns, inside-left, was hard, strong, direct without subtleties or grace-notes to his play, and, above all, durable. When he finally retired from a career spent wholly in first-class football, he was within months of his 42nd birthday. Comparison could be made with Jock Shaw, a generation later. Fourteen of Tommy's years were spent

at Ibrox, taking hit through World War One into the 1920s, always in successful Rangers teams and bringing him a lauded left-wing partnership with the famous Alan Morton. From Burnbank Athletic, by way of Bristol City and St Johnstone, he arrived at Ibrox in November 1913. As a Rangers player he won championships in 1918, 1920, 1921 and 1923-24-25, and played in Scottish Cup Finals in 1921 and 1922. He moved to Bradford City in 1927, retired in 1932 and later in the 1930s was Arsenal's chief scout in Scotland. He died in 1967, aged 77.

Eric Caldow

Eric Caldow from Cumnock in Ayrshire had one of the most distinguished of Rangers careers in that he played in not one but two of the greatest of Rangers teams. His first game, a League Cup-tie against Ayr United at Ibrox in September 1953, saw him in the company of giants – McColl, Woodburn, Waddell, Cox. His last game, a League match at Falkirk in March 1966, saw him in the company of latter-day giants – Greig, McKinnon, Johnston, Henderson.

He captained both Rangers and Scotland, for whom he played 40 times. That would have been many more, perhaps a Scottish record, save for a violent tackle he suffered from Bobby Smith, the Tottenham centre-forward, in the England-Scotland match at Wembley in 1963, only a few minutes into the match. Caldow's leg was broken in three places. His international career was over, and he played only reserve football for most of the following season. From April 1957 to April 1963, he had missed only two internationals, and captained his country for three years.

His haul of club honours was spread over nine years, from 1956 to 1965, and brought him five championships, two Scottish and three League Cup medals. At 5ft 8in and around 150 pounds, Caldow was scarcely a physical player. His strength as a full-back was, above all, exceptional pace. Eric was very quick. Wingers might get past him – they could never escape him. He had balance, crisp tackling, adaptability. Twenty-nine of his caps were at left-back, 11 at right-back, testimony to his maturity as a tactician. And he had the most phlegmatic temperament, never being ordered off in his career.

Eric Caldow was totally committed to Rangers, and had been since he was a boy of 14 when he was in schools football. He was farmed out to Muirkirk Juniors for a couple of season before going to Ibrox. But he was there when he was 18, in the team when he was 19, and spent 13 thrilling seasons with the club.

Davie Cooper

Transferred from Clydebank in June 1977 for £100,000, Hamilton-born Davie Cooper was an outrageously gifted outside-left, with a left foot that brought memories of that of Jim Baxter. He was equally perverse. Often his brilliant dribbling runs would scatter entire defences and produce startling goals, but equally often, it seemed, they took him into a cul-de-sac. He was an impeccable crosser of the ball with his left foot, and a menacing finisher from free kicks, examples being a thundering goal against Aberdeen in the 1987 League Cup Final; a decisive strike for Scotland against Australia in a World Championship qualifying match in 1985 and his critical penalty goal against Wales in Cardiff in the same competition.

He played 22 times for Scotland and with Rangers won three League championships, three Scottish Cups and no fewer than seven League Cups. In 1989, he was transferred to Motherwell for £50,000 and with them he won yet another Scottish Cup medal against Dundee United in 1991, and was recalled to the Scotland team. He had planned to end a long playing career back at his first love, Clydebank, at the end of season 1994-95, then concentrate on coaching. On Wednesday, 22 March, at Clyde's Broadwood Stadium in Cumbernauld, he and Charlie Nicholas, of Celtic and Scotland, were taking part in the making of a Scottish Television video on coaching for young people. Tragically, he suffered a massive brain haemorrhage, and died in a Glasgow hospital the next morning, aged a few days after his 39th birthday. His death brought a massive outpouring of sympathy and respect from Rangers fans, and others, among them many Celtic supporters, who made a shrine of the famous blue gates at Ibrox which were smothered in scarves and flags and flowers.

Andy Cunningham

A powerful lad from Galston in Ayrshire, Andy Cunningham was a celebrated name in the famous Rangers forward lines of the 1920s – Archibald, Cunningham, Henderson, Cairns and Morton, which later became Archibald,

Cunningham, Fleming, McPhail and Morton. After five years with Kilmarnock, he was a seasoned player when he arrived at Ibrox in April 1915. Through 1916 and 1917 he was on war service; He quickly established himself in the team in season 1918-19, and went on to win seven championship medals in the decade. He was a Scottish Cup winner in 1928 (at last) and played

in the losing Finals of 1921 and 1922. Cunningham was an inside-forward of skill and purpose, and longevity – when he moved to Newcastle United in January 1929, he became the Football League's oldest debutant, two days after his 38th birthday. He managed Newcastle United from 1930 to 1935, then Dundee 1937-40. After World War Two, he became a successful sports journalist. He had played 12 times for Scotland, and died in 1973, aged 82. That year he had kicked-off the Rangers-Ajax centenary game.

Jerry Dawson

Dawson was one of the truly great goalkeepers in the Scottish game. He played 14 times for Scotland in the period 1934-39, and in several wartime internationals, up to 1943. Born in Falkirk in 1909, he came to Rangers in 1929, and by the early 1930s had succeeded another fine Rangers goalkeeper, Tom Hamilton. During 16 years at Ibrox, Jerry Dawson won five League championships, two Scottish Cup medals, two

Scottish War Cups, two Summer War Cups, one Southern League Cup. And he defended the Rangers goal throughout all their various regional League successes during the war. It clearly denied Jerry – his name was James, his nickname taken from an earlier namesake, the England and Burnley goalkeeper – and many of his contemporaries, several seasons at the peak of

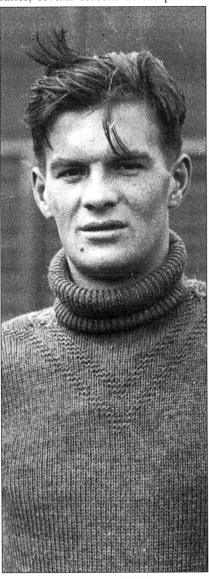

their careers. His first 'Old Firm' match, sadly, was the day the famous Celtic goalkeeper John Thompson was injured at Ibrox and subsequently died, that evening. His last game for Rangers was in the exceptional match against Dinamo Moscow in 1945, when Jerry and Rangers were two down in a matter of 20 minutes. His goalkeeping was unspectacular but above all thoroughly dependable. Perhaps his greatest goalkeeping quality was the speed of his reflexes, and he was a goalkeeper most definitely in command of his area. Perhaps most important of all was the fact that Jerry was a fun person, a happy, outgoing man who rejoiced in being a footballer, who spread his virtues to everyone he met.

He suffered a badly broken leg during the South League Cup Final against Hibs at Hampden in 1944. His injury was serious enough to cast doubts on his career, but he was back in action the following year. Shortly after the Dinamo Moscow match he signed for Falkirk, and played there for manager Tully Craig, the former Rangers and Scotland international, until his retirement in 1949. He was manager of East Fife for five years in the 1950s. One of the legendary Rangers players, Jerry Dawson died on 19 January 1977.

Jock Drummond

Jock Drummond, from Alva in Clackmannanshire, formed with Nicol Smith one of the great full-back partnerships in Rangers' history, and an almost impregnable line in front of goalkeeper Matt Dickie throughout the 1890s. They won honours galore. Drummond was a Scottish Cup winner in 1894, 1897, 1898 and 1903, and championship winner in 1900, 1901, 1902. He had 14 caps and captained his country, but above all was noted for wearing a cloth cap in action. Jock Drummond was a lusty defender, volleying immense clearances and with little concern for knocking opponents over. He came from Falkirk FC to Rangers in March 1892, when the Scottish game was embracing professionalism, and had a dozen years with the club. He went back to Falkirk, as a coach, in 1904 and in retirement became a Falkirk director. He died in 1935, aged 65, on the same day as his former teammate Jacky Robertson.

Paul Gascoigne

When Rangers signed Paul Gascoigne, the England midfield player formerly with Newcastle United, Tottenham Hotspur and Lazio of Rome, they signed a player of the highest quality. Indeed many writers south of the border considered him England's only world-class player in the mid-1990s. Rangers had also signed one of the most controversial characters in the game, a man of boorish conduct and often manic tendencies both on and off the field.

On his arrival at Ibrox Stadium, he was mobbed by welcoming fans reach-

ing out to touch him as though he was some messiah. He arrived with his hair bleached blonde, a statement of sorts, but apart from indicating 'I am Jack the Lad', it was difficult to imagine what it might be. Paul clearly lacked, perhaps understandably, any knowledge of what Glasgow football means when he declared that he was 'looking forward to playing for Glasgow' – it was pointed out to him that the name of his club was 'Rangers' and not 'Glasgow'.

Many Rangers connections had misgivings about his coming and the wisdom of his ever having been considered by the Govan club. His talents on the field were not in question. But his history of injuries, of indiscretions and lack of discipline on and off the field, were disquieting. It is probably fair to say that at the age of 28 when he joined Rangers he had not fulfilled his exceptional talents. Two particularly serious injuries, self-inflicted in a sense, had been major hindrances. In the FA Cup Final of 1991 at Wembley, Gascoigne, playing for Tottenham Hotspur, launched himself against the Nottingham Forest player Gary Charles with what one observer described as a 'kamikaze' tackle. Gascoigne should have been ordered from the field. Instead he was carried off. The tackle put not Charles but Gascoigne out of football with a smashed knee and postponed his departure to Lazio, already agreed, by one year. When he did get to Rome, oddly and somewhat mysteriously, he broke a leg in training with Lazio. This again kept him off the field for several months.

In the 1990 World Cup in Italy, where he first burst into world recognition, he launched into a fierce challenge

on a German player in the semi-final match, bringing the German substitutes storming to their feet in anger. He was booked for this and wept unashamedly at the thought that if England were to qualify for the Final (they lost on penalty kicks), he would be banned. It was in Italy that Bobby Robson, the England team manager described him as 'daft as a brush'.

This 'daftness' lapsed into boorishness on many occasions during his time in Italy, and since joining Rangers, with social gaffes galore in and out of pubs, restaurants and hotels. He seemed addicted to night life and heavy refuelling as one commentator described it.

When Rangers drew 1-1 with Celtic, on 17 March 1996 at Ibrox in a match which had been widely touted in the media as the championship decider, but which merely delayed the decision, Gascoigne was booked for the fifth successive League game, making his 13th booking in domestic play and his 16th in 32 matches for the club. This is not the record of a rational footballer.

What then of this paragon on the field? Without the edge that his physical condition of six years earlier gave him in getting past the opposition, he gave the impression that he should not be tackled, that he was untouchable, that he should be allowed to play his game without any bodily contact. Defending himself from defenders then, he sometimes bullied his way past them, employing a Rugby 'hand-off' technique with arms and particularly elbows widespread, the elbows often finding their way into opposing faces. His other massive shortcoming was dissent. He simply could not resist snarling at referees, and this was good for 50 per cent of his bookings. Paul Gascoigne is no saint. In his defence, it might be suggested that he becomes so involved, so obsessed, with the game, that reason vanishes from his mind. Manager Walter Smith, criticised for signing the player for these reasons, has responded by saying that with someone like Gascoigne, one has to take the full package and there is no point in hoping that you will get only the good – the bad and the ugly come with it.

The good is immense. Gascoigne's footballing talents are abundant and exceptional. One of the greatest is 'heightened peripheral vision' as the pedants would say, meaning that he can see more out of the corners of his eyes than can your average player. This gives Gascoigne a unique awareness of the patterns of play as they constantly unfold and change around him, and of precisely where his teammates are at any moment. His passing, long and short, is killingly accurate, precisely paced. The pass through a defensive line, turning it and liberating a colleague beyond it, indeed the pass forcing his teammate into position, is a distinctive feature of his repertoire. Gascoigne is a footballer of imagination and vision. His ball control on quick, nimble, dainty 'dancing' feet give him an outstanding ability to run at defenders, ghosting past them with shattering changes of direction and balance in the closest of situations.

An indication of Paul Gascoigne's importance to Rangers was shown in results when he was absent – for example, 0-0 at Motherwell in December, then 0-3 at home to Hearts in January. Much of Rangers play has been channelled through Gascoigne. It is true to say that he likes to have the game 'in front of him', doesn't much like defending or tackling back – he doesn't quite know how to do it and is not programmed for it. Rangers have approved his playing from a deep position, just in front of his defence where he picks up possession and deploys a 40 yards pass, a 40 yards run. Given possession, he seldom loses it, or squanders it. Add to all this quite startling finishing power, free-kicks or open shots curved from outside the penalty area, or the deftest of flicks at close range at the end of incisive, tightly-controlled runs.

Yet often, demons seem to drive him. Often he seems to be battling with dark forces within him. Always, he needs to be loved, by turns man-child, little boy lost, enfant terrible. Never can he stop moaning at referees. In his bewildering championship-winning performance

against Aberdeen, when he was one further caution away from suspension, referee Les Mottram more than once had to say, "Behave yourself, son – do you want to miss the Cup Final?" And at the end of that astonishing match he went grandstanding around Ibrox, blowing kisses to the crowd, wearing every ridiculous hat offered to him. And later that day, at a dinner awarding him the Professional Players' 'Player of the Year' award, with everyone else in dinner jackets, Paul appeared draped in a three-piece suit – in tartan

Paul Gascoigne stands as a player of the very highest class – but at the same time a paradox wrapped in an enigma.

Neilly Gibson

"The greatest half-back of Victorian times" (Ivan Sharpe, the finest football critic of his day).

"The greatest of my, and any generation following, in Scottish football". (Willie McCartney, former Hibernian manager).

"The greatest footballer I ever saw" (Steve Bloomer of Derby County and England).

"The greatest half-back I ever saw or played against – most wing-halfs tried to pattern their play on his but none of them remotely hoped to emulate him".

(Jimmy Dickson, wing-half in Hearts' fine Scottish Cup winning team of 1906).

"Pavlova in football boots" (Harry Wood of Sheffield United).

This paragon was Neilly Gibson from Larkhall, who signed for Rangers on 25 November 1894, was in the first team within a few months and held his place in it for ten years until he left for Partick Thistle in 1904. In that time he won four consecutive League championship medals, two Scottish Cup, five Glasgow Cup, two Glasgow Charity Cup, two Glasgow League and one Glasgow Exhibition medals. There were 16 Scottish caps, 11 Scottish League selections, and two caps for Glasgow against Sheffield.

Gibson was born on 23 February 1873 and his first club was Larkhall Thistle, in 1890. He was quickly claimed by Royal Albert, then members of the Scottish Federation League. Although he was slight in build, Gibson always could tackle strongly, but early in his career, he was often played at outside-left.

In December 1893, he was left-half for Lanarkshire against Ayrshire, played at Motherwell. The host team lost but the outstanding player was Neilly Gibson, his ball control and artistry captivating the crowd – as well as several observers from other clubs. His Royal Albert team won the Lanarkshire Cup and the Scottish Alliance League championship that season. There were offers galore, but manager Willie Wilton was beckoning from Ibrox and Gibson said yes.

Within a week, he was making his debut at Boghead in a League match. Dumbarton won 1-0, but a contemporary scribe wrote: 'In young Neilly Gibson, the Rangers have unearthed a star of the first magnitude if we are to take this game as a criterion.' Three months later, he was selected for Scotland against Ireland. A few weeks after that, he played against England and although Scotland were outclassed and lost 3-0, the crowd of 55,000 packed into Everton's Goodison Park were amazed by the array of skills shown by the young half-back.

Gibson could pass the ball with stunning accuracy. But what really endeared him to the fans was his ball control, which he had perfected to a degree which made many of his performances border on arrogance. The obvious comparison would be Jim Baxter, many generations on, in the 1960s. In spite of the heavy leather ball and boots of the time, Gibson could juggle the ball for 20 minutes or more with a succession of flicks, back-heels and headers, and it was said he could do the same thing with other objects such as blocks of wood, tin cans and the like.

He also created a Gibson dynasty. His three sons all played professionally, all were half-backs. Willie won an FA Cup medal with Newcastle United in 1924; Neil junior played for 11 seasons (1923-34) with Clyde; and Jimmy became the most expensive player of his time when Aston Villa paid Partick Thistle £7,500 for his transfer in 1927. He played eight times for Scotland and was one of the Wembley Wizards of the 1928 match. His father had played in a comparable, equally historic, Scottish team, against England (4-1) at Celtic Park in 1900.

Andy Goram

A key figure in Rangers' splendid record in the 1990s has been goalkeeper Andy Goram. Born in Bury, Lancashire, he joined nearby Oldham Athletic as a teenager, where he spent seven seasons and won the first of many caps for Scotland before joining Hibernian in 1987-88. He had four seasons at Easter

Road before signing for Rangers on 27 June 1991.

Although at 5ft 11in, not exceptionally tall for a goalkeeper, Goram perhaps compensates with his single finest quality – quickness: quickness of thought, quickness of feet, quickness in body movement. His anticipation is excellent, and when left stranded and exposed in the classic situation against a single striker, he is quite masterly at exploding from his line, dominating the forward, controlling and making the blocking save.

He is, of course, a double international, for besides his soccer caps he is a fine enough cricketer to have represented Scotland at the summer game.

Jimmy Gordon

Jimmy Gordon was an outstanding figure in the successful Rangers teams just before and just after World War One. He was a Saltcoats man who had played for Renfrew Victoria at the age of 15 and was six times a junior international player. His preferred position was right-half, but such were his talents – he was compared by some to Neilly Gibson – that he played inside-forward, centre-forward, even left-back for the club. Gordon won all the honours with Rangers save that elusive Scottish Cup medal. Between 1911 and 1920 he won five championships. He played in ten full internationals for Scotland, plus various Victory internationals at the end of the war. A commercial traveller by occupation, he was involved in business ventures with club colleague James Galt. Gordon died in 1954, aged 66.

Richard Gough

Richard Gough was born in Stockholm of a Swedish mother and Scottish father. The latter, a Govan man and Rangers fan who had played for Charlton Athletic in the 1960s, was in business in South Africa and Gough spent his early years there. In 1980, he came to Scotland and played a trial for Rangers, who decided he was not good enough. The young man, aged 18, also played a trial for Dundee United. They decided he was good enough, and signed him.

At one point, Gough quit and went back to South Africa – no doubt because of homesickness – but he returned to Tannadice and settled into an international career. Indeed, he

could have played for any one of three countries, the others being Sweden or South Africa. In 1986, Rangers offered £500,000, a huge sum, to buy him but instead he went to Tottenham Hotspur in August that year after Jim McLean, the Dundee United manager, insisted

he would not sell Gough to a Scottish club. In defence of the Rangers decision on Gough back in 1980, it was probably a correct one – he did not play well in the trial. At Spurs, he became captain and led them to a Wembley Cup Final.

In December 1987, Graeme Souness paid £1.1 million for him, and Gough quickly formed an outstanding central defence with Terry Butcher. Gough is a solid tackler with sharp timing and good distribution. He is courageous and strong in spite of a slender physique, and is particularly aggressive in his heading work. Richard Gough has been a positive Rangers captain, but after a Scotland team had disintegrated in a World Cup qualifying match in Portugal, losing by five goals, a difference of opinion with Andy Roxburgh, the national team manager, ended his international career after more than 50 appearances.

Rangers' 1996 Scottish Cup win was reckoned to be Richard's 17th major football honour, a remarkable achievement. His form had been such there was sustained calls for his selection for the national team once more. But Craig Brown, Roxburgh's successor, seemed just as determined to ignore him.

He has been one of the most successful captains in Rangers' history.

Dougie Gray

Dougie Gray, from Alford in Aberdeenshire, was possibly the most durable player in Rangers' history. An active player for 20 years (1925-1945),

when he officially retired in April 1947 he had played 667 League and Cup games for Rangers – a club record – and the massive total of 940 in all matches. He won 16 League championships, including wartime, and six Scottish Cup winners' medals with the club and was additionally a Scottish Cup Finalist in 1929. Gray was a right- back of medium physique who based his defence on interception, with short crisp clearances. In his long career, he played ten times for Scotland.

John Greig

In 18 years as a player at Ibrox, John Greig played in 857 games. He won five League championship medals, six Scot-

tish Cup medals and four League Cup medals. In captaining the team to the 'treble' in 1978, he became the only player to have a hat-trick of trebles, including those of 1964 and 1976. He captained Rangers to victory in the European Cup-winners' Cup of 1972 and played 44 times for Scotland, captaining his country for the best part of three years.

The bald statistics of his career are: 496 League games, 73 in the Scottish Cup, 12 in the League Cup, 16 in the European Champions' Cup, 29 in the European Cup-winners' Cup, 17 in the UEFA Cup, 19 in the Dryburgh Cup, one Texaco Cup match and 79 friendlies, plus his own testimonial match which drew an astonishing 65,000 to Ibrox in 1978. He was twice Scotland's Player of the Year, and was awarded the MBE.

It was a staggering career which has placed him among the very greatest of Rangers players. It began on 2 September 1961, in a League Cup match against Airdrie at Ibrox, when the young Greig, ten minutes into the match, scored the first goal in a 4-1 win.

John was born in Edinburgh, within sound of Hearts' Tynecastle Park, and was initially a Hearts fan. Rangers signed him from Edina Hearts. He was originally an inside-forward, but Rangers moved him back and his great days were as a defensive wing-half, supporting Ronnie McKinnon, a splendid centre-half for much of Greig's career. Indeed the Greig-McKinnon-Jim Baxter half-back line of the mid-1960s could be compared with any other in the club's history.

John Greig was not the most polished of footballers. His ball technique would not survive any serious analysis, and he was not the most incisive passer of the ball. But above all, he was a player of honesty, resolution, integrity. With Greig what you saw was what there was. With Greig, no cause was lost until the game was over. With Greig, the club was the thing and he seemed to epitomise the best of the Rangers ethos, as a captain ranking with such as Davie Meiklejohn.

On his retirement in 1978, he became manager of the club, and served for five years, bringing such players as Derek

Ferguson, Ian Durrant, Robert Fleck and Alistair McCoist to Ibrox. He proved himself an astute tactician in European matches, with successes against Juventus and others, and there were Scottish Cup and League Cup successes. But the championship, the yardstick by which all managers are judged, eluded him and he resigned in November 1983. He took up a career in broadcasting and in the travel industry, but returned to Rangers, his only club in January of 1990 as director of public relations.

R.C.Hamilton

Robert Cumming Hamilton, the famous 'R.C.', was a Rangers celebrity in the years before World War One, which effectively brought his career to a close. An Elgin man, he moved from the local

City club to Queen's Park in 1896, then became a professional with Rangers a year later. A graduate of Glasgow University, he was a schoolmaster who also managed to maintain the family net manufacturing business until his death in 1948, aged 71. 'R.C.' was a goalscorer, hitting lethal long-range shots with his right foot.He had two spells with the club, and appeared variously with Fulham, Hearts, Morton and Dundee. He had 11 caps for Scotland and with Rangers won championships in 1899-92 inclusive and two Scottish Cup Finals, in 1898 and 1903. Above all, his greatest claim to immortality in the story of Rangers is that he captained the most successful of all Rangers teams, the undefeated champions of

1898-99 – played 18, won 18. To this day Hamilton is the leading scorer in Rangers-Celtic games.

Mark Hateley

Mark Wayne Hateley was born, in Liverpool on 7 November 1961, into a football environment. His father Tony had a long career as a centre-forward with several clubs, in particular Aston Villa. The young Hateley started with Coventry City in August 1978, moved to Portsmouth in June 1983, then a year later to AC Milan for £915,000. A £1 million move took him to Monaco four years later, and a similar fee took him to Ibrox, maintaining a high-priced and no doubt profitable, to him, career for another £1 million fee, in the summer of 1990.

He played 32 times for England, scoring nine goals, perhaps the most spectacular of these being the one

headed at the far post from a John Barnes cross, against Brazil in the Maracana Stadium in Rio. For Rangers, he had 136 goals in 241 appearances. His most memorable goals for the club may have been the two scored in the final match of the 1990-1991 season which snatched the championship title from an Aberdeen team which needed only a draw from the match to become champions, and a tremendous volley from beyond the penalty area against Leeds United at Elland Road in the European Champions League of 1991.

Mark Hateley won a French championship medal with Monaco, and five Scottish titles with Rangers. He moved

to Queen's Park Rangers in the summer of 1995, and it became clear that his time at Ibrox, after a tentative start, had seen the full maturity of an incisive and menacing strike forward.

Willie Henderson

Willie Henderson was a prodigy. He was a schoolboy international with Airdrie Schools, in the Rangers team when he was 17, in the Scotland team at the age of 18 years and 269 days. Only Dennis Law in modern times has been a younger international player by about one month. Known fancifully to

some Rangers fans as 'Scotland's Garrincha', Henderson nevertheless was a brilliant dribbler, a winger of crackling pace who could flash through packed defences with swerve and dummy at high speed. Although small (5ft 4in), he was a powerful runner and an accurate crosser of the ball to his high-scoring strikers Brand and Millar, and even to Davie Wilson on the opposite wing.

His emergence at Ibrox hastened the departure of Alex Scott, his talented predecessor, to Everton. Willie had won 21 of his 27 caps before he was 23, but he had more than his share of injuries. Eyesight problems meant he had to wear contact lenses, and once surgery for a bunion problem kept him out for months. He was transferred to Sheffield Wednesday in 1972 and in 1974 was off to Hong Kong, where he was to captain the colony's representative team. He ended a long playing career back at Airdrie.

Sandy Jardine

Sandy Jardine from Edinburgh vies with John Greig, another Edinburgh man, his teammate, captain and manager, and Dougie Gray of the 1920s and 1930s, in the longevity of an Ibrox career. An elegant, composed defender, Sandy played 671 official games with Rangers, then with an Indian summer to his career at Hearts, topped the 1,000 total.

Born close to Hearts' Tynecastle ground, he was snapped up by Rangers and made his debut at the age of 18, one week after Rangers 'Berwick

Disaster', their defeat there in the Scottish Cup in January 1967. Sandy's first match was at Ibrox against – Hearts! Rangers won 5-1.

He played in all the defensive positions at one time or another (under Davie White's management he was a centre-forward for a spell), but he was best used as a full-back, on either flank, or as a sweeper. He and Danny McGrain of Celtic formed a notable full-back partnership for Scotland, playing together 19 times. Jardine made a total of 39 Scotland appearances. He was a cultured player, strong, very fast, scrupulously clean and correct. He was much praised by his opposite number, Franz Beckenbauer of Bayern Munich, after the losing European Cup-winners' Cup Final of 1967, but was in the winning team of 1972. He was in the Scotland squad for the World Championship finals of 1974 and 1978 in Germany and Argentina respectively, and was one of the few players to be twice voted Player of the Year by the sportswriters.

Sandy was released by John Greig after the 1982 Scottish Cup Final, and at the age of 33 went to Hearts, becoming sweeper in their 1985-86 team which almost did the double finishing second in both League and Scottish Cup. He became assistant manager to Alex McDonald, then joint manager before leaving in 1988 for a career in commerce.

Maurice Johnston

The arrival of Maurice Johnston at Ibrox caused a major sensation in Scottish football. The former Partick Thistle, Watford and Celtic player was signed by Graeme Souness from the French club Nantes for £1.5 million on 10 July 1989, and the transfer was sensational on two counts: Johnston was the first known Roman Catholic to play for Rangers in modern times certainly since World War One; and Souness had snatched him from under the very nose of Celtic who had announced that he would be joining them. It was a scenario hard to believe.

It was nevertheless an act of cold courage by manager Souness and his chairman David Murray. The transfer was received with horror by many Rangers fans, and there was talk of a boycott. Souness sought to disarm them by pointing out that he, Souness, had married a Catholic girl and that the club's only concern was to have the services of a quality player. At the same

time, the more perceptive of Rangers' fans saw it as another manifestation of the Souness obsession with bigotry in Glasgow football, and his ambition to put an end to it.

Maurice Johnston was certainly a quality player, a proven goalscorer with all his clubs, a striker of pace and courage prepared to go in close against the most densely-packed defences. Although only 5ft 9in tall, he was surprisingly good in the air. He was an enthusiastic hunter and hustler of defences, and quite unselfish.

He played 110 games for Rangers, scoring an impressive 51 goals, three in particular against Celtic on separate winning occasions. After two and a half years at Ibrox he moved to Everton for yet another large, £1.75 million, fee. After a couple of years, he came back to play for Hearts and in early 1995, in true mercenary style, moved on to Falkirk. And although little was made of it at the time, it took a great deal of moral courage on the part of Maurice Johnston to wear the blue jersey in view of his own background and history.

Derek Johnstone

Something of a boy wonder, Derek Johnstone played for Scotland at schoolboy, youth, amateur, Under-23 and senior international level. He played for senior Scotland in all three sectors of the team – defence, midfield and attack – and did the same for Rangers as one of the most versatile players the club has ever had.

As a local boy, his first love was for Dundee United, and he did some training with them, but he signed schoolboy forms with Rangers in December 1968 and became a full professional in July 1970. And he was still ten days short of his 17th birthday in the following season when he leapt into a place in the history books as surely the youngest player ever to score the winning goal in a national Cup Final. Derek got between Celtic's Billy McNeill and Jim Craig to head the only goal in the League Cup Final of 1970-71.

Even at that age, Derek was a big boy, 6ft tall and powerfully built. Yet he was quick over the ground and a goalscorer of strength and determination. He scored goals in Scottish Cup Finals from centre-half and centre-forward. He won Scottish Cup Finals in three different positions, even if centre-half was his favourite. In his first match for Rangers, a month before that League Cup win, he had two of the goals in a 5-0 win over Cowdenbeath. In 547 games, he had 209 goals, one of a very select band of Rangers players since 1945 who have notched 200 or more goals.

Johnstone was transferred to Chelsea for £30,000 in 1983, came back in January 1985 to play for Jock Wallace but his second stint at Ibrox was not a success and he was released in 1986 by Graeme Souness. After a spell as manager of Partick Thistle, he took up a career in broadcasting.

Willie Johnston

A footballer unique in the annals of the Scottish game, Willie Johnston will be remembered not for a range of exceptional talents, but for one of the worst disciplinary records the game has known. In a long career, he was ordered off at least 20 times. The lowest point was when he failed a drug test at the World Championships in 1978 in Argentina, and was suspended by FIFA. He was sent home by the SFA and banned from further international play.

Glasgow-born, 'Bud' Johnston was signed from the Fife junior club Lochore Welfare at the age of 17, as precocious as Willie Henderson. Such a player was Johnston that he graduated from Scottish Youth international to full international within six months. Early in his career, he played inside-left and made an irresistible wing with Davie Wilson. But it was as an outside-left that Johnston took his world by storm. He was lightning fast, a bewildering dribbler, a more than average goalscorer for a winger – he scored two of the three goals in Rangers' famous European Cup-winners' Cup Final in Barcelona, 1972. He delighted the Ibrox crowds, but a tempestuous temperament became intolerable to the club. The last of several suspensions – nine weeks, following an ordering off against Partick Thistle on 9 September 1972 – led to his transfer in December to West Bromwich Albion for £135,000.

He played well at The Hawthorns, went to Vancouver Whitecaps in March 1979, then to Birmingham City on loan. He came back to Rangers for the period 1980-82 for manager John Greig and was ordered off within a month! When he ended his playing career with Hearts, he was in his 39th year.

Brian Laudrup

Few players have had a more immediate impact on Rangers fans than the Danish forward Brian Laudrup. From his dazzling, diagonal dribbling run against Motherwell in his first Premier Division home match, setting up a last-minute winning goal for Duncan Ferguson in August 1994, Laudrup quickly became an Ibrox darling who sustained his form throughout the 1994-95 season to such effect that he was voted Player of the Year by Scottish football writers and his fellow professional players alike.

As a player of high quality, he had reached Rangers in a costly transfer in July of 1994 at the age of 25, and as a man of many clubs. From Brondby in Denmark, he moved to Germany first in a £650,000 transfer to Bayer Uerlingen, then on to Bayern Munich for £2 million. Next came a move to Italy and Fiorentina AC for £2 million and finally to Rangers for a reported £3.5 million.

Brian is from a football family – his father Finn played 21 times for Denmark, twice against Scotland. His older brother Michael played for Juventus and Barcelona and both were capped many times for Denmark, with the high point for Brian the European Championship victory of 1992.

Fiorentina were relegated in his time there, and Brian moved on loan to AC Milan, where he found himself competing with seven other 'foreign' players on the Milan list for selection and a regular team place, and was inhibited by a restricted tactical role imposed on him by the management. With Rangers,

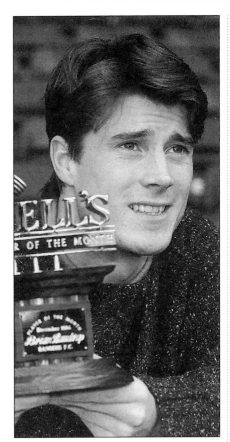

of his goals – flashing drives or subtle swerves – had the Rangers crowd on its feet. Laudrup's game is distinguished by high technical skills which give him close dribbling control and long, penetrating runs in possession. His body strength (he is 6ft tall and weighs 13 stones), particularly his lower body strength, make it immensely difficult for defenders to knock him off the ball. His speed and acceleration, and the precision of his crossing, all told have revolutionised Rangers' attacking options.

His finest hour may well have been the 1996 Scottish Cup Final, when his two goals, and the three he created for striker Gordon Durie, overwhelmed Hearts 5-1.

Peter McCloy

Peter McCloy, at 6ft 4in probably the tallest British goalkeeper of his time, was dubbed the 'Girvan Lighthouse', this in reference to his home town of Girvan on the Ayrshire coast. He was the son of a St Mirren goalkeeper, and started his career with Motherwell. He moved to Rangers in the spring of 1970, as they were putting together their powerful team of the 1970s. In his first match they lost, 2-1 at Dunfermline, but for the next several seasons, Peter was

manager Walter Smith allowed him to 'play as and where he pleased' and in that first season, he turned in 13 goals in 35 matches.

Although he considers himself more of a playmaker than a finisher, several

the goalkeeper in residence. A series of challenges, from Stewart Kennedy, Jim Stewart and others, came and went, and Peter was to play a record number of games for a Rangers goalkeeper, his total of 644 passing the mark of 545 which the famous Jerry Dawson had set. Peter played in the European Cupwinners' Cup team of 1972.

Alistair McCoist

Alistair McCoist from East Kilbride, one of the greatest Rangers personalities of the 1980s and early '90s, has had

a career of extremes, and many distinctions, with the Ibrox club. One of these distinctions, perhaps unique, is that he twice rejected invitations to join Rangers, and signed only at the third time of asking. As a schoolboy he turned down a John Greig approach in favour of going to St Johnstone, signing for them on 1 December 1978, aged 16. On August 1981, he was actually at Ibrox considering yet another offer when Sunderland interrupted the proceedings and tempted him to Roker Park for a fee of £400,000, a huge amount at the time for such a young player.

His time at Sunderland was not successful and in June 1983, he at last signed for John Greig for a fee of £185,000. In turn, his early seasons at Ibrox were not over-successful. The new manager Jock Wallace indeed suggested that he might want to leave and that a transfer back to Sunderland could be arranged. McCoist, determined to prove himself, forced himself into the team in 1984-85. The next season he was a regular and in April of 1986 won his first cap for Scotland.

With the coming of Graeme Souness, the McCoist's career was again in the shadows for a time, with spells out of the team or on the bench, but again McCoist persisted, survived and prospered. His goalscoring was hard to deny. From 1983-84, he was leading scorer with respectively 35, 25, 41, 41, 49 and 25 goals. Maurice Johnston was top man in 1989-90 with 21 and 1990-91 with 19, but 1991-92 was something of an *annus mirabilis* for McCoist. His 41 goals included a personal career total of 200 Scottish League goals, Rangers' 100th goal of the season in their total of 101, and brought McCoist the European award of the 'Golden Boot'. He was voted 'Player of the Year' by the Scottish Football Writers Association and by the Scottish players themselves. And McCoist thereupon did the impossible, winning the award for the next season, with 34 goals in 34 League games, the only player to win the European Golden Boot Award in consecutive years. At the end of 1995-96 he had amassed 319 competitive goals for the Ibrox club.

Alistair McCoist is lively, extrovert, a bubbling personality. Technically, he may not have been the most skilled of Rangers strikers, but his qualities included quickness and the snapping-up of slender chances, half chances. Indeed it was often said that the easier the chance, the more likely he was to

miss it. A severe injury when playing for Scotland in Portugal in 1993 – his leg was badly broken – compromised his career in the mid-1990s

But in 1995-96 he was back with 20 goals, many of them critical for both Rangers and Scotland. Early in the season he passed Bob McPhail's club record, and finished it with a new Rangers record (discounting Jimmy Smith's wartime goals) of 236 League goals. Injuries affected his season, though, and he missed the Scottish Cup Final for the second time.

Ian McColl

Ian McColl was an early-day John Greig, winning honours galore, playing hundreds of games, captaining the club and making his mark in management. He was born in Alexandria, the heartland of the game in its beginnings, in June 1927. He was playing for Queen's Park when only 16, a tall, athletic wing-half who would develop into ball winner extraordinary. He was signed by Rangers before he was 18 and after only

half a season, had succeeded Scot Symon at wing-half in the famous post-war defence. There were similarities between them; both were fierce tack-

lers, and as conservative destroyers, their contributions to attack took the form of long, accurate passes from deep. He was, like Alan Morton another ex-Queen's Parker, always a part-time player, training in the evening, and taking an engineering degree at Glasgow University. Never a goalscorer – only 14 in 526 games – he was nevertheless a rock in Rangers teams from 1946 to 1961.

After six League championship wins, five Scottish Cups, two League Cups with the club and 14 appearances for Scotland, he spent four and a half years as national team manager in the early 1960s. McColl was one of the most successful. His teams won 16 of the 27 games played, helped greatly by a generation of players that included Mackay and White and Brown of Tottenham, Law and Crerand from Manchester United, and such Rangers as Baxter, Caldow, Henderson and Wilson.

Ian rounded out his managerial career with Sunderland in the First Division – he kept them there for three years – then continued a business career outside the game.

Alex McDonald

If never one of the most glamorous of Rangers players, Alex McDonald was

one of their most valuable over a lengthy career. He was bought by Davie White for £50,000 from St Johnstone in November 1968 and went on to play 500 games for the club. A Glasgow man and lifelong 'blue nose', McDonald was small, fiery, combative, a fierce competition and ball-winner, operating on the left of midfield.

After a certain reluctance in accepting him, 'Doddie' became tremendously popular with the Ibrox crowd, for his 'stolen' goals as much as anything else. He was adept at stealing on to the blind side of defences and his tally of 92 goals was impressively high for a midfield ball-winner. One of the most important of these was the one he headed against Celtic in Rangers League Cup win of 1975-76, in a 1-0 match.

Alex was in the Rangers team that won the European Cup-winners' Cup in 1972 and won 12 major honours with Rangers. He played once in 1976 for Scotland. He moved to Hearts, became player-manager in 1981, then manager so successfully that he was named Manager of the Year in 1986. Since then, he has moved on to Airdrie with continuing success.

Ron McKinnon

Ronnie McKinnon was generally accepted as the best centre-half Rangers

had had since Willie Woodburn. He developed with Benburb, the junior club whose ground is a stone's throw from Ibrox. A Glasgow boy, he came to the club as a wing-half but quickly displaced Bill Paterson at centre-half, and became a Scotland player when Celtic's Billy McNeil had to withdraw from an Italy match. From then on they contested the position in the national team, McKinnon eventually winning 28 caps, McNeill 29.

He worked hard at the game, was composed and stylish and never seemed under more pressure than he could handle. The half-back line of Greig-McKinnon-Baxter is famous in club history. McKinnon suffered a leg break in an away European match against Sporting Lisbon, and so missed a place in the Rangers European Cup-winners' Cup victory in May 1972. In the summer of 1973, Ronnie went to South Africa and played for a year, before moving on to Australia.

Tommy McLean

When Willie Waddell signed outside-right Tommy McLean from Kilmarnock for £65,000 in Copenhagen in 1971, he

bought a mature international player who was to be compared very favourably with a line of his peers, Willie Henderson, Alex Scott, Waddell himself. Indeed many Rangers fans were prepared to rate him the best of the four. Waddell, when manager of Kilmarnock, had signed him then as a young player and knew his play intimately.

Tommy McLean was never a player who relied on physical power to advance his game. At 5ft 4in, he was not equipped for that. He was never an intimidating presence. Unlike Henderson, he was not a dribbler. Unlike Scott and Waddell, he was not a power runner. Rather McLean was a meticulous footballer, almost prim in his ball skills, a magnificent passer of the ball, a player of outstanding accuracy with either foot, a precise crosser of the ball possessing a sophisticated tactical sense. The quality of his distribution, in particular in finding the goalscorers Johnstone, Parlane, often Alex McDonald, was critical to the sustained success of Rangers team throughout the 1970s.

Tommy retired after the Scottish Cup Final of 1982, when Rangers lost 4-1 to Aberdeen after extra-time. He had played 449 times for the club. He became assistant manager to John Greig. When he left in October 1983, McLean held the team together very well until Jock Wallace arrived. He became part-time manager of Morton, then in the summer of 1984, manager and subsequently a director of Motherwell. After a decade at Fir Park, with much success, he became manager of Hearts in 1994.

Ian McMillan

When Ian McMillan joined Rangers from Airdrie on 2 October, 1958, he was 27 years old and an international player. From the time of his first match, against Raith Rovers at Ibrox – a 4-4 draw in which he scored the first and the fourth goal – Rangers went 23 matches with only one defeat. Before his arrival they had been having a lean spell. With McMillan, they won the championship by two points from Hearts. Indeed his six years at Ibrox was a period of almost total success for the club.

Ian was the classic Scottish inside-forward, technically skilled with sophisticated but rational ball control, with clever dribbling skills, and highly gifted in the strategy and stratagems of the game. Many Rangers fans thought him their best inside-forward since Torry Gillick, a decade or more earlier, and he may well have been manager Scot Symon's most perceptive signing. When Jim Baxter arrived in the summer of 1960, Rangers had the most devastating inside-forward partnership in the game. They were scarcely midfield players in the modern context. Neither was much concerned with defence. McMillan in this respect was protected by his right-half, Harold Davis, a powerful player.

McMillan, dubbed 'The Wee Prime Minister' because of his control and direction of the team, and of the pre-miership of Harold McMillan at the same time, worked brilliantly in feeding fine outside-rights in Alex Scott then Willie Henderson and in releasing the speed and force of the strikers Jimmy Millar and Ralph Brand. A qualified chartered surveyor, he was always a part-time player with Rangers and later returned to Airdrie as manager, then director.

Moses McNeil

Moses McLay McNeil, born at Rhu on the Gare Loch on 29 October 1855, was a founder member of the Rangers club, as were four of the seven McNeil brothers. Moses is generally credited with suggesting the name 'Rangers' for the new club they were forming, when it was first discussed in 1872. His elder brothers, James, John and Alec, were

never involved in the game, but Moses, Peter, Harry and William all gained some prominence in football. Moses, in fact, was Rangers' first international player. He was capped for Scotland in 1876. A tough, hard-dribbling winger, not afraid to give as good as he got when it came to tackling, Moses played in the Rangers Scottish Cup Finals of 1877 and 1879. A commercial traveller after his student days, he died in 1938 at the age of 83.

Bob McPhail

Bob McPhail was born to football. He was a Scottish schoolboy international. He won a Scottish Cup medal (with Airdrie, 1924), when he was 18 and it

was to be the first of seven. He suc-ceeded Tommy Cairns at inside-left in the Rangers forward line and for the best part of a decade formed an out-standing left-wing partnership with Alan Morton. He was on six Rangers Cup-winning teams, won no fewer than nine League championships, and between 1927 and 1938, when interna-tional honours were hard to come by, played 17 times for Scotland. McPhail was a powerful, hard-hitting goalscorer – 230 in League matches for the club

and a further 70 with Airdrie. He retired in 1941, played a few wartime games for St Mirren and was a Rangers reserve-team trainer for a few seasons.

John McPherson

John 'Kitey' McPherson, born in Kilmarnock on 19 June 1868, was one of the most versatile players ever to grace the club. An inside-forward of strength if not of a great physique, a master dribbler and stealer of goals, in a career of a dozen years he played in

every position including goal for Rangers. He had nine Scottish caps, the first of them with Kilmarnock, from which club he joined Rangers in 1890. He won four League championships and three Scottish Cup medals with the club and after retiring in 1902 – he was a fitter by trade – he was a club director from 1907 until his death in 1926. At the club's jubilee dinner in 1922-23 he was described as the finest player in the 50 years' history of Rangers.

Davie Meiklejohn

David Meiklejohn, born in Govan in 1900, was one of the greatest players and captains that Rangers ever had. He made a total of 635 appearances for the club, a total few have surpassed. He played in 73 Scottish Cup matches and was on five Cup winning teams. He played in no fewer than 12 championship teams. He was with the club from 1919 – he signed from Maryhill Juniors – to 1936, and later managed Partick Thistle.

He was fairly obviously dubbed 'Meek', although it was certainly not a word that could be applied to him. He was as commanding as any Rangers captain must be. As a right-half, and when necessary at centre-half, Davie Meiklejohn was a player of resolution, versatility, composure and great inspiration. The greatest illustration of his control was surely in converting the penalty kick in the 1928 Scottish Cup Final against John Thomson in the Celtic goal. The goal inspired his team to a 4-0 win and Rangers' first Scottish Cup success after 25 barren years.

Meiklejohn had an international career spanning 1922 to 1933 and played 15 times for Scotland. He captained his country twice against England.

Jimmy Millar

Jimmy Millar, an Edinburgh lad, was an outstanding half-back at Dunfermline when Rangers signed him for £5,000 on 17 January 1955. In May 1959, in a tour match in Denmark, he moved up to centre-forward when Max Murray was injured. At half-time the score was 0-0. At full-time it was 4-0 to Rangers, scorer Millar (4)! It would scarcely be true to say that he never looked back, since he won a Scottish Cup medal in 1966,

against Celtic at Hampden, as a half-back, after a dozen years at Ibrox, but that night a centre-forward was born, one who scored 160 goals in his 317 games.

He was a dashing centre-forward, brave and honest. But he was a long way from being a knock 'em down warhorse. At 5ft 6in, he was quite remarkably potent in the air, with a talent for heading balls down to his striking partner, Ralph Brand. They formed a powerful strike partnership, rather as did Mark Hateley and Alistair McCoist briefly in the 1990s. Jimmy Millar was always in control, cool, a positive character who was inspirational to his team mates.

Alan Morton

Alan Lauder Morton, the 'wee blue devil', has a clear claim to be the greatest of Rangers' players. Given that hundreds and hundreds of players have worn the blue shirt over a century and a quarter of the club's existence, it is an extravagant claim. But the supporting evidence is equally extravagant.

Morton was 5ft 4in tall and weighed not much more than 9st, yet over a

dozen years, he earned 31 caps for Scotland at a time when three each season was generally the maximum. It was a record that stood until broken by George Young after World War Two.

From 1921 to 1932, he played 11 times against England, the match of 1926, which Scotland lost 1-0 at Old Trafford was long spoken of by the Scots as 'the year Morton didn't play'. He was to win nine League championship medals with Rangers over 13 years.

When Alan Morton arrived at Ibrox from Queen's Park in 1920, he was already an international player, having played against Wales and Northern Ireland in the previous season. He was born in Glasgow in 1893 and in his teens, joined Queen's Park to keep his brother Bob, a centre-forward, company. During the years of World War One, he became an outstanding player and in 1920, when the highly-thought-of Rangers outside-left, Dr Jim Paterson, left to practise medicine in London, Rangers went for Morton, persuaded him to turn professional, and a brilliant career of a dozen years in the famous blue shirt began.

Alan and Bob were two of the five sons of a coalmaster, and Alan became a mining engineer, a profession he practised throughout his career and beyond.

Alan Morton was a brilliant footballer, brilliant in the fullest sense of the world. He dominated the British football scene of his time as Stanley Matthews, then George Best, were to do for later generations. His dribbling skills were staggering, based on an instant, killing ball control. His balance was superb, allowing him to change direction with a speed that defenders could not hope to anticipate. In spite of his stature, or lack of it, he was surprisingly strong, and took all the knocks from big defenders often enough, but without complaint. He was never guilty of an unsporting action.

His right foot was naturally stronger and he would favour it in carrying the ball. It gave him an edge in moving inside a full-back. He did at the same time have a quite powerful shot in either foot. One particularly baffling facet of his talent was the famous Morton 'floating lob'. This was a high cross which seemed to stop and hang on the face of the crossbar, inflicting a desperate indecision in the minds of goalkeepers.

In the famous 'Wembley Wizards' match of 1928, when an English fan was overheard to call him a 'wee blue devil' (the remark was reported and stayed with Morton forever more), Alec Jackson, the swashbuckling outside-right, scored three goals, each of them from Morton's crosses.

Morton was seldom injured, and despite being a part-timer player, maintained a high level of fitness. His talents were never allowed to become self-indulgent and his accuracy in the pass and the shot were almost prim. He was that kind of person. His age, the 1920s, remained a time of the waistcoat and spats and bowler hat for the professional man. Alan wore a bowler – and was dubbed unerringly by the Glaswegians the 'wee society man', their equivalent of the 'Man from the Pru', the insurance agent who called at the door every week to collect coppers for the policy.

Alan Morton played seven matches at the start of the 1932-33 season then announced his retirement. He was immediately appointed a director of the club and remained one until his death in 1971. He had played a total of 742 competitive games, 247 for Queen's Park, 498 for Rangers, scoring 166 goals. His portrait in oils, in Rangers

football rig, hangs in solitary splendour in the entrance hall to Ibrox Stadium.

Tommy Muirhead

Tommy Muirhead was a wing-half or inside-forward who was happy to play in any creative position provided it also

allowed him to tackle incisively! From Cowdenbeath, he joined Rangers by way of Fife junior football and Hibs, in May 1917. When there was a short-lived attempt to promote the professional game in the cities of the eastern seaboard of the United States, Tommy was one of many who had a brief whirl as a player-manager in Boston, in the mid-1920s. But basically he was a Ranger until he retired in 1930, becoming captain, and playing eight times for Scotland. He collected championships in 1920, 1923, 1924 and 1927-29 inclusive. He was a defeated Scottish Cup Finalist in 1922 and 1929 and although he did not play in the famous 1928 victory, he was awarded a winners' medal. He subsequently managed St Johnstone and Preston North End in the 1930s, before entering sports journalism. He died in 1979 at the age of 82.

Willie Reid

Willie Reid, from Baillieston, was one of the great goalscorers in the club's history. He was at Ibrox from 1909 to

1920 and in season 1910-11, for example, he scored 38 League goals and 52 in all senior matches. Willie Reid was a plain and simple scoring centre-forward, taking balls first time in full stride, with tremendous power of shot. He served in World War One and was lost to football for three seasons, and in 1920 he moved on to Albion Rovers where he eventually became manager. He played nine times for Scotland. Willie Reid died in 1966 at the age of 80.

Jacky Robinson

John Tait Robertson, 'Jacky', was a Dumbarton boy who became one of Rangers' and Scotland's most brilliant players. Making his debut in the second match of the 1899-1900 season, Jacky was never missing from Rangers teams, injuries and international calls apart, until he moved to Chelsea as player-manager six years later. In that concentrated period he won 14 of his 16 Scottish caps, championships in 1900 and 1901, and the Scottish Cup in 1903. In 1904 and 1905 he was in losing Rangers Finals. Robertson played in several positions but he was by far the outstanding left-half of his time, a player of power, of attacking instincts and deadly finish with an exceptional heading ability – a paragon indeed. One of his finest hours was his performance in captaining an outstanding Scottish team to a 4-1 victory over England in

1900. He had taken a devious route to Ibrox – Morton, Everton, Southampton – and after Rangers and Chelsea, to Glossop as player-manager. He then had much success coaching on the Continent.

Jock Shaw

'Tiger' Shaw, alias John Shaw, alias Jock Shaw, got his nickname from the

tigerish nature of his tackling. At 5ft 7in tall and not much more than 11st in weight, he was perhaps under-equipped for an extreme defender, but as a left-back he compensated with speed and exceptional physical fitness and a remarkable durability. When he won a League and Cup double with the club in 1950, he was 38 years old, and when he retired he was 42 years old. His career began with Airdrie in 1933 and his move to Ibrox in July 1938, brought him the first of his four championship titles the following season, 1938-39. The others came after World War Two in the 1940s along with three Scottish Cup and two League Cup successes as captain in the famed 'Iron Curtain' defence. There were four selections for Scotland, each time as captain. After retirement in 1954, Shaw remained associated with the club for a long period as trainer, then groundsman.

Alec Smith

Alec Smith was working in a lace mill in his home town of Darvel when Nicol Smith, no relation, invited him to play for Rangers in a friendly match against Notts County, the FA Cup holders, on 30 April 1894. Rangers won 3-1 in a

match which saw the start of an exceptional career for the 18-year-old outside-left.

He was to play 20 times for his country between 1898 and 1911, and wore Rangers colours for 21 years, a record that stood until Dougie Gray appeared in the 1920s. Smith appeared in 12 consecutive international matches for Scotland and in 1903, he and clubmate Finlay Speedie formed the left wing against England.

Smith graced the great Rangers team of the turn of the century, with four successive championships won. Friends of Rangers players who spanned the careers of Alec Smith and Alan Morton often claimed that the former was the greater, and the 'greatest of all' Rangers outside-lefts was Smith.

Distance always lends enchantment, of course, but what is clear is that Alec Smith was a quite exceptionally talented footballer who held the Rangers outside-left position from 1894 until 1915. He was totally unselfish, and a marvellous provider of chances. It can certainly be said that he was first among equals with regard to the others who starred in the outside-left position for Rangers – Morton, of course, in the 1920s, Davie Wilson in the 1960s, Davie Cooper in the 1970s and 1980s.

Jimmy Smith

Generally remembered by older Rangers fans as the 'biggest' centre-forward Rangers have had, Jimmy Smith, at 6ft 1in and 14 st, although never the silkiest of footballers, was rather more than a battering ram. He is the club's record goalscorer, ahead of such as Alistair McCoist and Bob McPhail , and

he had a very lengthy career. He joined the club in 1928, made his debut in March 1929 at Hamilton, and retired only in 1946. His goals tally was 300 League and a total of 381 in League and Cup, although some were wartime goals. Smith became an outstanding successor to Jimmy Fleming. Their careers overlapped for a few seasons. Jimmy Smith was an Airdrie man and, indeed, when he joined Rangers he was still attending Airdrie Academy. He was to gain nine League championships, including wartime, three Scottish Cup successes, in his golden years, the decade of the 1930s. He played twice for Scotland. On the ground and in the air, the bulk of Smith was a fearful prospect for defences. He had several wartime honours and after he retired in May 1946 he continued with the club as trainer, then chief scout, until 1967.

Nicol Smith

Nicol Smith was born on Christmas Day 1873, in Darvel, Ayrshire, at a time when the McNeil brothers and friends were helping their infant club to its feet. Inevitably, he was to be dubbed the 'Darvel Marvel', forming with Jock Drummond an outstanding full-back partnership which was the foundation of a decade of Rangers success around the turn of the century.

Developing his game with the local Darvel Juniors, he was selected to play a trial match for the Scottish Junior international team, and subsequently, his appointment as captain of that team for a Junior international match against Ireland in 1893 brought him wider publicity. Rangers acted smartly. He was signed and within a few weeks was in the team in place of the regular full-back, Donald Gow, who was injured.

His debut was against Hearts at Tynecastle in March 1893. He was prominent in a 2-1 win, a contemporary account claiming that he was 'a fine tackler with great possibilities'. He was one of the first players to go straight from the junior ranks into a first team of a Scottish League club, and at 5ft 10ins and around 13st, broad in the shoulder, was well equipped to handle a game of hard challenges and hard knocks.

At the start of the 1893-94 season, he had matured to the extent of claiming a regular place in the team, so much so that Donald Gow, an international player, was allowed to move to Sunderland.

In Smith's very first season, Rangers won the Scottish Cup for the very first time, beating Celtic 3-1. Smith's display was one of the features of the game. During his career, Smith's vigorous, powerful if accurate play brought him injuries and he missed many games. But it brought him four League championships, three Scottish Cup victories, five Glasgow Cup, four Charity Cup, two Glasgow League and an Exhibition Cup medal among his trophies.

Rangers was his only club. He played 12 times for Scotland, nine times for the Scottish League, twice for Glasgow against Sheffield and in his time was considered the finest full-back in Britain. Rangers have had outstanding full-back partnerships, Gray and Macdonald, Gray and Shaw, Young and Shaw, Shearer and Caldow, but Nicol Smith and Jock Drummond was the first and possibly the finest.

Yet the black hand of a cruel fate had touched the Smith family of Darvel. Nicol's mother died when he was a young man. Other members of the family died early in life. In November 1904, he wore a Rangers jersey for the last time in a 3-1 win over Third Lanark at Ibrox. A few weeks later, he was stricken with enteric fever. It was scarcely considered to be a life-threatening illness, but his young wife, in nursing him, was infected and died tragically in the pre-Christmas week in Kilmarnock hospital. Smith was devastated. On 4 January, while Rangers were playing Queen's Park in a benefit game for Smith and his dependents, he had a relapse, never recovered and died early on 6 January 1904. He was 32.

William Wilton, Rangers' manager, handed over £384 3s 9d (£384.18) to the trustees on behalf of the couple's five orphaned children. The sum was from the benefit match, and from subscriptions from all over the country. A donation of £6.5s (£6.25p) came from 'employees of the Natal Government Railways'. For the funeral, the entire village of Darvel shut down, and thousands attended.

James Stark

James Stark was a graduate of the Glasgow Perthshire junior club, and joined Rangers in May 1900. He served for seven successful years, went to Chelsea for a year, then from 1910 played out his career, until the coming of World War One, with Morton. He was a centre-half who played simple

economical football, making the game look easy. His anticipation was exceptional and the great Jimmy Quinn, the fearsome Celtic centre-forward, confessed that he could never get the better of Stark. He played twice for Scotland, and Rangers brought him championships in 1901 and 1902, a Scottish Cup win in 1903 and Finalist spots in 1904, 1905 and 1909. One of his unique distinctions was in captaining the Rangers team which won the Glasgow Exhibition Cup in 1901.

Willie Thornton

In March of 1936, two schoolboys played for Rangers for the first time, in a reserve match against Partick Thistle at Firhill. They were Willie Thornton, then 16, and Willie Waddell, then 15. Willie

Thornton was born in Winchburg, West Lothian on 3 March 1920 (almost a year to the day before Willie Waddell's birth in Forth, Lanarkshire). He signed amateur forms on 7 March 1936, and made his first-team debut on 2 January 1937, again at Firhill, at outside-right in a 1-0 Rangers win. He signed professional forms in the spring of that year when he turned 17.

Thus began the career of one of the most honourable footballers the Glasgow club has ever had. He won four championship medals (including pre-war, when our prodigy was but 19), three Scottish Cup and three League Cup medals. He 'won' the inaugural League Cup in 1946-47 and in 1948-49 the first 'treble' won by any club in Scotland.

He was the first post war Rangers player to score 100 goals and in a total of 432 games he scored 255. In his last playing season, he scored eight goals in eight games played! He appeared for Scotland seven times in full international matches, a meagre return, many thought, for his talents.

Willie Thornton was a thoroughbred centre-forward, magnificently skilled in the air, with a deft first touch on the ball, a perceptive passer, stylish and sophisticated. His combination with Waddell made a powerful attacking force in the great Rangers team of the late 1940s. Waddell's power and pace brought him space from which he could deliver precise crosses to the flashing head of Thornton. The centre-forward was also finely tuned to the through passes of Gillick from the deep.

He remained in football all his life. On retirement as a player in 1954, he became manager of Dundee FC (1954-59), introducing to the game such young talent as Andy Penman, Alan Gilzean, Jim Gabriel, Ian Ure, and laying the foundation of the Dundee club's great championship success in 1961-62. The death in office of Davie Meiklejohn, when Partick Thistle manager, led to Willie succeeding him, in September 1959. After nine years there, he returned to Ibrox as an assistant to manager David White, then to Willie Waddell.

Yet Thornton's greatness rested not alone in his playing skills or management talents. He is a legend at Ibrox because of his character. Willie Thornton was a gentleman in the fullest sense of the word. He was never once in his career ordered off, never once 'booked'.

His wartime service merely decorates the point. He served six years with the Duke of Atholl's Scottish Horse, in campaigns through Tripoli, Sicily and Italy, in unforgettable battle sites at Anzio and Monte Cassino. In action in Sicily on 18 November 1943, he won the Military Medal.

Until his final brief illness and death in a Glasgow hospital on 26 August 1991, at the age of 71, Willie Thornton was part of Ibrox, part of Rangers. He

was custodian of the Trophy Room, and on match days, host in the Thornton Suite. He was a man of vintage rare.

Tom Vallance

Tom Vallance, from Renton in the Vale of Leven, was a founder-member of Rangers and captain for the club's first nine seasons. He went to Assam on business in 1882 but returned for health reasons in a year, and thereafter played only in charity matches. He played in Rangers early Scottish Cup Final teams in 1877 and 1879, and seven times for Scotland. At nearly 6ft 2in, Vallance was unusually tall for the times but despite a slim physique, he was a powerful full-back. He was also something of a 'lad of pairts', a Scottish renaissance man. He set a long jump record, was a talented oarsman and had paintings exhibited at the Royal Scottish Academy.

Ray Wilkins

Ray Wilkins was a Rangers player for a mere two years, but when he played his final game at Ibrox, in November 1989, he was given a sustained standing ovation such as few Rangers players have had in the long history of the club.

In that short spell he came to be considered by many serious Rangers observers as the best midfield talent the club had had since Jim Baxter. That need not have surprised them – Wilkins came as the holder of 84 England caps. He had been in the Chelsea first team at the age of 17, and after half a dozen years at Stamford Bridge, he spent a similar period with Manchester United, playing in their FA Cup wins of 1982 and 1983. After that, it was AC Milan and Paris St Germain, the highest of cosmopolitan credentials.

Ray Wilkins was a totally creative player, operating in midfield as a focal point for defensive clearances which he would turn into perceptive attacking passes. He was a complete professional, technically skilled, ice-cold in temperament, not a great ball-winner, but a quite superb ball-user. Graeme Souness had signed him from the French club for £250,000. It proved to be one of his finest investments - Rangers won two League championships (1988-89, 1989-90) and one League Cup (1988-89) during Wilkins' time at the club.

A London boy, he moved to Queen's Park Rangers in December 1989, and

became manager there. Still playing the occasional match in 1995-96, his career had spanned over 20 years. He bought Mark Hateley from Rangers for QPR.

Davie Wilson

Davie Wilson was the outside-left in Scot Symon's great team of the 1960s.

He was considered by many friends of Rangers to be their best outside-left since Alan Morton, although Wilson's football personality was rather different. He was fast, direct, opportunistic in the penalty area, fastening on to crosses from the right wingers, Alec Scott and Willie Henderson. In March 1962, he scored six goals in Rangers 7-1 win at Falkirk.

He scored 155 goals in 373 matches, played 22 times for Scotland, one of his most memorable achievements being in the 1963 match, when he moved to left back after Eric Caldow's injury, and played with great distinction. In 1967, aged 28, he was transferred to Dundee United (prematurely in the opinions of many Rangers fans) and had five successful seasons with them. He was later a successful manager at Dumbarton.

Willie Woodburn

Willie Woodburn was perhaps the most gifted centre-half Rangers ever had, the pivot of their marvellous 'Iron Curtain' defence of Brown; Young and Shaw; McColl, Woodburn and Cox. He was a commander in the air and on the ground, perfectly balanced on either side in interception and tackling. In clear possession, he would go forward confident in his ball control, spreading passes with accuracy and imagination.

Woodburn was a player of high qual-

ity, but alas, is now remembered for his behaviour rather than his talents. After a series of confrontations with authority – he was ordered off five times – he was suspended *sine die* on 14 September 1954. There is no doubt that Woodburn had a ferocious temper which brought this upon himself. He applied it indiscriminately against referees, opponents, even his own players at times, if they were not in accord with his thinking and requirements. These were simply that Rangers should win, everything.

He went to Ibrox directly from his home town Edinburgh Athletic, a juvenile team, signed professional in October 1937 at 18. He left Ibrox effectively in the summer of 1955. The suspension was lifted on 22 April, 1957, but at the age of 38, Woodburn was out of the game. He played 325 games for the club, winning four championships, four Scottish Cups, two League Cups and played for Scotland 24 times.

George Young

George Lewis Young was a Rangers giant. At 6ft 2in and weighing 15st, he was no doubt the biggest captain the club ever had. A Grangemouth boy, born in 1922, he was cornered by Rangers as an amateur at the age of 15, signed as a professional in 1941, and by the end of World War Two, was a mature player ready to take his place in one of the great Rangers team, and eventually captain it.

Dubbed 'Corky' because of a good luck champagne cork he habitually carried, Young, with an angular, top-heavy-in-appearance physique, was not quite poetry in motion, but he was a talented footballer. Powerful in the air as could be imagined, his length of leg allowed him to nail forwards who had passed him, and salvage many a lost cause with a crunching tackle. Right-footed, he could sweep the ball downfield with a casual swing distances of up to 60 yards.

Endless practice brought accuracy with this ball, and time and again it became an attacking gambit as his clearances found quality forwards such as Waddell and Thornton.

He was a natural centre-half who moved to right-back to accommodate Willie Woodburn in the famous 'Iron Curtain' defence. With it, George Young won six League championships, four Scottish Cups and two League Cups and a record 53 Scotland caps. He captained his country 48 times, ending his international career in May 1957. He retired completely that summer and later managed Third Lanark for three years.

Rangers
Season-by-Season

1872-73

May 1872	Callendar	D 0-0 10 known players: Hunter, P.McNeil, W.McBeath, W.McNeil, M.McNeil, P.Campbell, H.McNeil, W.McKinnon, W.Miller, J.Campbell.
	Clyde	W 11-0 No players specified.

Both of the above fixtures played at The Flesher's Haugh, on Glasgow Green.

1873-74

No dates or chronological order of matches is known. Rangers did, however, lose to both Havelock and Star of Leven 'by the odd goal' and also lost 0-4 to Star of Leven. Contemporary reports state that Rangers defeated all other opposition, and that a number of matches were played with the Rovers – but no dates, results or line-ups are recorded.

1874-75

#	Date	Opponent	Result	Scorers	Yuil	Vallance T	McNeil P	McBeath W	McNeil W	McNeil M	Campbell P	Phillips	Gibb	Watson	Campbell J	Rankine	Mackie
1	Sep 19 (h)	Star (Vale of L)	D 0-0		1	2	3	4	5	6	7	8	9	10	11		
2*	Oct 3 (a)	Helensburgh	W 1-0	Gibb	1	2	3	4	5	6	7	8	9	10			
3	24 (a)	Vale of Leven R	W 3-0	M.McNeil, P.Campbell, Gibb	1	2	3	4	5	6	8		9	7	10	11	
4	31 (a)	Star of Leven	W 3-0	J.Campbell 2, Watson	1	2	3	4	5	6	7	9	10	11	8		
5	Nov 7 (h)	Barrhead	W 4-1	Untraced	1	2	3	4	5	6	7	9	10	11	8		
6	Jan 23 (h)	Vale of Leven R	W 2-0	P.Campbell, Watson	1	2	3	4		6	5	8	9	10	7	11	
7	Feb 6 (a)	Sandyford	W 3-0	Untraced	1	2	3	4	5	6	7	10	9	11	8		
8	20 (a)	Barrhead	W 2-0	Untraced	1	2	3	4	5	6	7	10	9		8	11	
9	Mar 6 (a)	Havelock	W 2-0	Untraced	1	2	3		5	6	7	10	9		8	11	4
10	13 (h)	23rd Renfrew RV	W 1-0	Gibb	1	2	3		5	6	7	10	9	4	8	11	
11	20(h†)	Rovers	W 4-0	P.Campbell 2, Phillips, Watson	1	2	3	4	5	6	7	10	9	11	8		
12	27 (h)	Sandyford	W 3-0	M.McNeil 2, P.Campbell	1	2	3	4	5	6	7		9	10	8	11	
				Appearances	12	12	12	10	11	12	12	10	12	10	11	6	1
				Goals						3	5	1	3	3	2		

*Only ten men played
† Played at Queen's Park Recreation Ground

11 goals untraced

Scottish FA Cup

#	Date	Opponent	Result	Scorers	Yuil	Vallance T	McNeil P	McBeath W	McNeil W	McNeil M	Campbell P	Phillips	Gibb	Watson	Campbell J	Rankine	Mackie
1	Oct 10(h*)	Oxford	W 2-0	M.McNeil, Gibb	1	2	3	4	5	6	7	8	9	10	11		
2	Nov 28 (h)	Dumbarton	D 0-0		1	2	3		4	6	8	10	9	7	5	11	
R	Dec 12 (a)	Dumbarton	L 0-1		1	2	3	5	4	6	8	10	9	7		11	
				Appearances	3	3	3	2	3	3	3	3	3	3	2	2	
				Goals						1			1				

*Played at Queen's Park Recreation Ground

1875-76

Honorary Match Secretary: John Campbell

#	Date	Opponent	Result	Scorers	Yul J	Vallance T	McNeil P	McBeath W	McNeil W	McNeil M	Campbell P	Watson J	Phillips G	Gibb D	Campbell John	Campbell James	Watson W	Wight J	Grant J	Hill D	Ricketts S	Watt J	Roche C	Douglas W
1	Sep 11 (h*)	Vale of Leven	D 1-1	Untraced	1	2	3	4	5	6	7	8	9	10	11									
2	18 (h)	Helensburgh	D 1-1	Untraced	1	2	3	4	5	6	7	8	9	10	11									
3	25 (a)	Vale of Leven	L 0-4		1	2	3	4	5	6	7	8	9	10	11									
4	Oct 2 (a)	Clydesdale	D 1-1	James, Campbell	1	2	3	4	5	6	11	8	7			10	9							
5	Nov 6 (a)	Havelock	W 4-0	John Campbell 3, M.McNeil		2	3	4	5	6	11	8	7			10	9	1						
6	20 (a)	Queen's Park	L 0-2		1	2		4	5	6	7					3								
7	Dec 25 (a)	Caledonian	W 4-0	Untraced		2			5	6	7	10	8	9		11				1	3	4		
8	Feb 19 (h†)	Lennox	L 0-1			2			5			10	8	9		11					3			
9	Mar 11 (a)	Lennox	L 1-3	Untraced		2	5		4	6	7	8		9		10				3			1	11
10	18 (a)	Clydesdale	D 0-0			2	5		4	6	7	8		9		10				3			1	11
	Appearances				5	10	7	6	10	9	9	10	8	8	5	7	1	1	1	4	1	2	2	
	Goals										1					3	1							

*Rangers' opening fixture at Burnbank
†Rangers' closing fixture at Burnbank

In Match 8 four players are unknown. 7 goals untraced.

Scottish FA Cup

#	Date	Opponent	Result	Scorers	Att	Yul J	Vallance T	McNeil P	McBeath W	McNeil W	McNeil M	Campbell P	Watson J	Phillips G	Gibb D	Campbell John	Campbell James	Watson W	Watt J
1	Oct 16 (h)	1st Lanark RV	W 7-0	John Campbell 3, Watson 2, Phillips, P.Campbell		1	2	3	4	5	6	11	8	7			10	9	
2	30 (a)	Third Lanark RV	W1-0*	P.Campbell		1	2	3	4	5	6	11	8	7			10	9	
R	Nov 13 (h)	Third Lanark RV	L 1-2	M.McNeil	2,000	1	2	3	4	5	6	7	8	10			9		11
	Appearances					3	3	3	3	3	3	3	3	3			2	3	1
	Goals											1	2	2	1		3		

*3rd Lanarkshire Rifle Volunteers protested, Rangers having kicked off in both halves.

1876-77

Honorary Match Secretary: P.McNeill

#	Date	Opponent	Result	Scorers	Att	Watt J	Vallance T	Hill D	Gillespie G	McNeil W	Campbell James	Dunlop W	Watson J	Marshall A	Campbell P	McNeil M	Tait W	Martin J	Ricketts S	Roche C	Douglas W	Steel A	Kerr R	Primrose W	McNeil P
1	Sep 2 (h*)	Vale of Leven	W 2-1	Marshall, Dunlop	1,500	1	2	3	4	5	6	7	8	9	10	11									
2	16 (h)	Eastern	L 0-2			1	2	3		5	6	7	8	9	10	11	4								
3	23 (a)	Vale of Leven	L 0-4		1,000		2	3	4	5	6	7	8	9	10	11		1							
4	Oct 7 (h)	Northern	W 3-0	Untraced		1	2	3	6	5		7	8	9	10	11			4						
5	14 (h)	Lennox	D 0-0			1	2					7	8	9	10	11			4						
6	28 (h)	Rovers	W 4-0	Untraced		1	2	9	3	5		8		7		6			4	10	11				
7	Nov 4 (h)	Eastern	W 7-0	Untraced		1	2		3	5									4		6				
8	18 (h)	Alexandra A	W 5-0	M.McNeil, Dunlop, Untraced 3		1	2	11	3	5		8	10	9	6	7			4						
9	25 (h)	Queen's Park	L 0-1			1	2	7	3	5		6	9	8	10	11			4						
10	Dec 16 (h)	Partick	W 8-1	Dunlop 3, Marshall, M.McNeil, P.Campbell		1		7	3			6		8	10	11			4			2	9		
11	Jan 6 (a)	Caledonian	W 5-1	M.McNeil, W.McNeil, P.Campbell, Marshall, Dunlop		1		8	3	5	7	6		9	10	11			4			2			
12	13 (a)	Northern	W 4-3	Untraced		1	2	8	3	5		6	7	9	10	11			4						
13	Feb 24 (h)	Caledonian	W 4-0	Marshall 2, P.Campbell, Dunlop		1		7	3	5		6	9	8	10	11			4			2			
14	Mar 10 (h)	Havelock	W 8-0	Untraced		1	2	7	3	5		6	9	8	10	11			4						
15	31 (a)	Clydesdale	W 3-0	P.Campbell 3		1	2	7	3	5		6	9	8	10	11			4						
16	May 12 (a)	Ayr Thistle	W 2-0	Untraced		1	2		3	5					10	11			4						
	Appearances					15	13	13	14	14	4	14	11	14	14	15	1	1	13	1	1	3	1		
	Goals							1			7			5	6	5									

*Rangers' opening fixture at Kinning Park.

In four matches some players are unknown: in Match 5, three players; in Match 7, five players; in Match 10, one player; in Match 16, four players. 31 goals untraced.

Scottish FA Cup

#	Date	Opponent	Result	Scorers	Att	Watt J	Vallance T	Hill D	Gillespie G	McNeil W	Campbell James	Dunlop W	Watson J	Marshall A	Campbell P	McNeil M	Tait W	Martin J	Ricketts S	Roche C	Steel A
1	Sep 30 (h)	Queen's Park J	W 4-1	James Campbell, Untraced 3			2	3	4	5	6	7	8	9	10	11		1			
2	Oct 21 (a)	Towerhill	W 8-0	P.Campbell 2, Dunlop 2, Marshall 2, Watson 2		1	2	8	3			6	7	9	10	11			4		5
4	Dec 9 (a)	Mauchline	W 3-0	Marshall, P.Campbell, Watson		1	2	7	3		5	6	9	8	10	11			4		
QF	30 (a)	Lennox	W 3-0	P.Campbell, Marshall, Dunlop		1	2	8	3	5		6	7	9	10	11			4		
F	Mar 17 (n)	Vale of Leven	D 1-1	McDougall (og)	12,000	1	2	7	3	5		6	9	8	10	11			4		
R	Apr 7 (n)	Vale of Leven	D 1-1*	Dunlop	15,000	1	2	7	3	5		6	9	8	10	11			4		
2R	13 (n)	Vale of Leven	L 2-3	P.Campbell, M.McNeil	15,000	1	2	7	3	5		6	9	8	10	11			4		
	Appearances					6	7	7	7	5	2	7	7	7	7	7		1	6		1
	Goals									1	4	3	4	5	1						

The Scottish Cup Final and first replay were played at West of Scotland Cricket Ground, Hamilton Crescent. The second replay was played at First Hampden Park. *After extra-time Rangers received a bye in the third round and the semi-final.

3 goals untraced. 1 own-goal

Glasgow Merchants' Charity Cup

#	Date	Opponent	Result	Att	Watt J	Vallance T	Hill D	Gillespie G	McNeil W	Dunlop W	Watson J	Marshall A	Campbell P	Ricketts S	Roche C
F	Apr 28 (a)	Queen's Park	L 0-4	10,000	1	2	9	3	5	8	10	6	11	4	7
	Appearances				1	1	1	1	1	1	1	1	1	1	1
	Goals														

Rangers participated as Scottish FA Cup finalists – Vale of Leven having declined invitation.

1877-78

Honorary Match Secretary: P.McNeill

No.	Date	Opponent	Result	Scorers	Att	Hill D	Vallance T	Gillespie G	Ricketts S	McIntyre H	Dunlop W	Campbell James	McDonnet	Marshall A	McNeil M	Campbell P	Watt J	Kerr R	Watson J	Grant J	Vallance A	Struthers W	Bain A	Ricketts G	Harris J	Douglas W	Steel A	Rankine J	McMillan J	McClellan	Martin J	Cairns	McNeil W	Campbell JJ	McDonald J	Holms
1	Aug 25	(a) Beith	W 2-0	McNeil, P.Campbell		1	2	3	4	5	6	7	8	9	10	11																				
2	Sep 1	(h) Ayr Thistle	W 4-2	Dunlop, McNeil 2, P.Campbell		9	2	3		4	6	7		8	10	11	1	5																		
3	15	(h) Parkgrove	W 5-0	James Campbell, McNeil, Marshall 2, P.Campbell		6	2		5	3	4	7		8	10	11	1		9																	
4	22	(h) South Western	W 3-0	P.Campbell, Dunlop 2		6	2		5	3	4	7		8	10	11	1		9																	
5	29	(h) Vale of Leven	W 5-0	McNeil, Hill, Opp own-goal, Watson, Marshall		6	2		5	4	3	7		8	10	11	1		9																	
6	Oct 13	(a) Kilmarnock P	W 8-3	James Campbell, Untraced 7	1,500	6	2		5	3		7			10	11			9																	
7	20	(a) Third Lanark RV	L 0-2			6	2	3	5	4		7		8	10	11			9	1																
8	Nov 3	(h) Northern	W 4-1	Marshall 2, P.Campbell, Watson		6	2		5	4		7		8	10	11	1		9																	
9	17	(a) Vale of Leven	D 1-1	Untraced	4,000	6	2			3	5	7		8	10	11	1				4	9														
10	24	(h) Dumbarton	W 1-0	Marshall		6	2	3	5	4		7		8	10	11	1		9																	
11	Jan 1	(a) Brunswick	W 2-1	McMillan, Untraced	200				2	1				11									3	4	5	6	7	8	9	10						
12	12	(h) Helensburgh	W 4-0	Untraced			2			3						11																				
13	19	(a) Caledonian	W 5-0	Dunlop 2, Watson 2, P.Campbell			2	3		4	6			8	10	11	5		9			7									1					
14	Feb 9	(h) Kilmarnock P	W 4-1	Untraced		6			4	3	7	10		9			1					8				11						2	5			
15	16	(a) Nottingham F	W 4-2	McNeil 2, Marshall, McIntyre	2,000	6	2	3	4	5				8	10	11	1		9															7		
16	18	(a) Sheffield W	W 2-1	Marshall, Hill		6	2	3	4	5	7			8	10	11	1		9																	
17	Mar 9	(a) Alexandra A	W 6-1	Watson, McNeil 3, Hill, P.Campbell		6		3	4	2					10	11	1		9																	
18	16	(h) Havelock	W 8-1	Dunlop 4, Marshall 2, McNeil 2			2	3		5	6	7		9	10	11	1	4	8																	
19	23	(a) Dumbarton	L 1-2	Untraced			2																													
20	30	(a) Govan	W 3-0	Dunlop, P.Campbell, McNeil			2				6				10	11																				
21	Apr 2	(h) Rosslyn	D 0-0			7	2	3	4	5	6	11			10						9	8													1	
22	10	(h) Shaftesbury	D 0-0				2	3		5	6	7			10	11			9		4	8										1				
23	13	(h) Third Lanark RV	W 4-2	Marshall 2, P.Campbell, Untraced		6	2	3		5				7		10			8		4	9														1
24	20	(h) Nottingham F	W 2-0	Hill, James Campbell		6	2	3		5	10	7				11			8		4	9									1					
25	May 11	(a) C & FC Kilmark	W 2-1	Untraced	2,000		2																													
26	20	(h) Vale of Leven	D 0-0		1,500																															
					Appearances	17	22	13	14	22	14	15	1	16	18	20	13	2	15	1	5	7	1	1	1	2	1	1	1	1	2	2	1	1	1	1
					Goals	4				1	10	3		12	13	9			5										1							

In eight matches some players are unknown: in Match 6, three players; in Match 8, one player; in Match 12, eight players; in Match 17, three players; in Match 19, nine players and only 10 played; in Match 20, seven players; in Match 25, 10 players; in Match 26, whole team. Match 23 was ten-a-side. 21 goals untraced. 1 own-goal.

Scottish FA Cup

Rd	Date	Opponent	Result	Scorers	Att	Hill D	Vallance T	Gillespie G	Ricketts S	McIntyre H	Dunlop W	Campbell James	McDonnet	Marshall A	McNeil M	Campbell P	Watt J	Kerr R	Watson J	Grant J	Vallance A	Struthers W	Bain A	Ricketts G	Harris J	Douglas W	Steel A	Rankine J	McMillan J	McClellan	Martin J	Cairns	McNeil W	Campbell JJ	McDonald J	Holms
1	Oct 6	(h) Possilpark	W13-0	Marshall 2, Watson 2, Ricketts, P.Campbell 3, James Campbell 2, Hill 2, McNeil		6	2		5	4	3	7		8	10	11	1		9																	
2	27	(h) Alexandra A	W 8-0	Dunlop, P.Campbell 3, McNeil 3, James Campbell	1,500		2	1	5	4	6	7		8	10	11			9		3															
3	Nov 10	(h) Uddingston	W13-0	Marshall 4, Watson 4, McNeil 2, James Campbell, P.Campbell, Hill		6	2		5	4		7		8	10	11	1		9																	
4	Dec 1	(h) Vale of Leven	D 0-0		4,000	6	2	3	5	4		7		8	10	11	1		9																	
R	15	(a) Vale of Leven	L 0-5		4,000	6	2	3	5	4		7		8	10	11	1		9																	
					Appearances	4	5	3	5	5	2	5		5	5	5	4		5		1															
					Goals	3			1		1	4		6	6	7			6																	

FA Cup Round 3, one player unknown.

Glasgow Merchants' Charity Cup

Rd	Date	Opponent	Result	Scorers	Att	Hill D	Vallance T	Gillespie G	Ricketts S	McIntyre H	Dunlop W	Campbell James	McDonnet	Marshall A	McNeil M	Campbell P	Watt J	Kerr R	Watson J	Grant J	Vallance A	Struthers W	Bain A	Ricketts G	Harris J	Douglas W	Steel A	Rankine J	McMillan J	McClellan	Martin J	Cairns	McNeil W	Campbell JJ	McDonald J	Holms
1	Apr 6	(n*) Third Lanark RV	L 1-2	Struthers			2	3		5	6	7			10	11	1		9		4	8														
					Appearances		1	1		1	1	1			1	1	1		1		1	1														
					Goals																	1														

* Played at First Hampden Park.

1878-79

Honorary Match Secretary: P.McNeill

No.	Date	Opponent	Result	Scorers	Att	Vallance A	Vallance T	Gillespie G	Drinnan J	McNeil W	Dunlop W	Struthers W	Watson J	Marshall A	McNeil M	Campbell P	McIntyre H	Watt J	Steel A	Hozier	Hill D	McDonald J	McQuarrie C	Campbell James	Kerr R	Stewart	McLeish H	Angus G	Cairns J	Hill J	Lummler W	Warner J	McLeish J
1	Sep 14	(a) Govan	L 4-5	Marshall, Untraced 3		1	2	3	4	5	6	7	8	9	10	11																	
2	21	(h) Third Lanark RV	D 2-2	M.McNeil, W.McNeil		1	2	3		5	6	7	8	9	10	11	4																
3	Oct 5	(a) Vale of Leven	L 0-2		2,000	5	2	1	3			8			10	11	4	6	7	9													
4	12	(h) Queen's Park	L 0-1			5	2	1	3			8		9	10	11	4		7		6												
5	25	(a) Clapham R	W 5-1	Hill, Struthers, McNeil 2, Steel		5	2	1	3		11	9		8	10		4		7		6												
6	26	(a) Nottingham F	W 2-0	Dunlop, Struthers		5	2	1	3		11	9		8	10		4		7		6												
7	Nov 2	(a) Parkgrove	L 1-5	Campbell		5		2	3		9	8			10	11	4		7		6	1											
8	4	(n*) Third Lanark RV	L 2-3	Untraced	6,000	3	2	1	4		6	8			10	11	5		7				9										
9	16	(h) Vale of Leven	W 3-0	Dunlop, Struthers 2		3	2	1	4		6	8			10	11	5		9		7												
10	23	(h) Govan	W 6-1	Dunlop, Untraced 5		1	2	3	4		6	8			10		5		11		7		9										
11	Dec 7	(a) First Lanark RV	D 1-1	Dunlop		4	2	3	5		7	9			1	11	8		10					6									
12	Mar 1	(a) Third Lanark RV	L 1-2	Hill		3	2	1	5		10	9			11	6	4		8		7												
13	29	(a) Kilmarnock P	D 1-1	Drinnan		3	2	1	5			9			10	11			8		7				4	6							
14	Apr 5	(h) Third Lanark RV	W 2-0	Struthers, Dunlop	1,000	3		1	5		6	9			11				8		7				4		2	10					
15	9	(a) Caledonian	L 0-2								6	9			10	1			7						4		2		3	5	8		
16	12	(h) Nottingham F	W 3-0	Hill 2, Struthers	5,000	3	2	1	5		6	9			10	11			8		7						4						
					Appearances	15	13	15	14	2	13	16	2	5	16	12	11	1	14	1	10	1	2	1	3	1	3	1	1	1	1		
					Goals				1	1	5	6		1	3	1			1		4												

* Played under electric light at First Hampden Park.

Only 10 men played in Match 15. 10 goals untraced.

Scottish FA Cup

Rd	Date	Opponent	Result	Scorers	Att	Vallance A	Vallance T	Gillespie G	Drinnan J	McNeil W	Dunlop W	Struthers W	Watson J	Marshall A	McNeil M	Campbell P	McIntyre H	Watt J	Steel A	Hozier	Hill D	McDonald J	McQuarrie C	Campbell James	Kerr R	Stewart	McLeish H	Angus G	Cairns J	Hill J	Lummler W	Warner J	McLeish J
1	Sep 28	(h) Shaftesbury	W 3-0	Struthers, Untraced 2								8																					
2	Oct 19	(a) Whitefield	W 6-1	Untraced		5	2	1	3			8		9	10	11	4		7		6												
3	Nov 9	(h) Parkgrove	W 8-2	Struthers 3, Hill 3, Dunlop, Campbell	3,000	3	2	1	4		6	8			10	11	5		9		7												
4	30	(h) Alexandra A	W 3-0	Dunlop, McQuarrie, Untraced		3	2	1	4		6	8			10		5		11		7		9										
5	Mar 8	(h) Partick	W 4-0	Angus 2, Hill, Steel		4	2	3	5		6	9			11				8		7							10				1	
QF	22	(a) Queen's Park	W 1-0	Dunlop		3	2	1	5		6	9			10	11	4		8		7												
F	Apr 19	(n*) Vale of Leven	D 1-1	Struthers	9,000	3	2	1	5		6	9			10	11	4		8		7												
					Appearances	6	6	6	6		5	7		1	6	4	5		6		6		1					1				1	
					Goals						3	5				1			1		4		1					2					

Following an unsuccessful protest, Rangers declined to participate in a replay.

* Played at First Hampden Park. Rangers received a bye in the semi-final.

The team for the FA Cup Round 1 is unknown. 9 goals untraced.

Glasgow Merchants' Charity Cup

Rd	Date	Opponent	Result	Scorers	Att	Vallance A	Vallance T	Gillespie G	Drinnan J	McNeil W	Dunlop W	Struthers W	Watson J	Marshall A	McNeil M	Campbell P	McIntyre H	Watt J	Steel A	Hozier	Hill D	McDonald J	McQuarrie C	Campbell James	Kerr R	Stewart	McLeish H	Angus G	Cairns J	Hill J	Lummler W	Warner J	McLeish J
SF	May 3	(n) Third Lanark RV	W 4-1	Campbell, Untraced 3		3	2		4			9			10	11			6		7							8				1	5
F	20	(n) Vale of Leven	W 2-1	Struthers, Untraced	11,000	3	2	1	4*			9			10	11	5		6		7		8										
					Appearances	2	2	1	2			2			2	2	1		2		2		1					1				1	1
					Goals							1				1																	

Semi-final and Final played at First Hampden Park.

*Drinnan played under the name of 'R Jackson'. 4 goals untraced.

1879-80

Honorary Match Secretary: P.McNeill

No	Date	Opponent	Result	Scorers	Att	Gillespie G	Vallance T	Vallance A	McIntyre H	Drinnan J	Dunlop W	Hill D	Struthers W	Steel A	Angus G	McNeil M	Stewart A	Corbell W	Kerr R	McQuarrie C	Christie J	McKenzie	Marshall A	McIntyre J	Pringle W	Young R	McDonald T	Smith P	Harris J	Martin J	Gow A	Fraser E	Campbell P	Ricketts S	Kennedy A
1	Aug 23	(n*) Queen's Park	L 0-1		1,000	1	2	3	4	5	6	7	8	9	10	11																			
2	Sep 13	(h) Alexandra A	W 1-0	Steel		1	2	3	4	5	6	7	8	9	10	11																			
3	Oct 11	(h) Parkgrove	D 1-1	Opp own-goal		1		2	4	5		7	8	9	6	10	3	11																	
4	18	(a) Arbroath	W10-0	Gillespie, McIntyre, McQuarrie 2, Christie 2, Steel 2, McKenzie, Stewart	3,000	8		2	4	5				9			3		1	6	10	11													
5	25	(a) Blackburn R	W 4-1	Dunlop 2, Untraced 2	2,000	11		2	4	5	6	7		8		10	3		1				9												
6	Nov 1	(a) Third Lanark RV	D 1-1	McNeil					4	5	6	7		8		10	3						9												
7	8	(h) South Western	W 2-1	Christie, Untraced		2			4	5		7				10	3		1		8														
8	15	(h) Kilmarnock P	W 3-1	Dunlop, McNeil, Christie				2	4	5	6	7				10	3			9	8														
9	22	(h) Jamestown	W 3-0	McIntyre, Dunlop, McQuarrie			3	2	4	5	6	7				10				8	9														
10	29	(h) Dumbarton	W 1-0	Christie		1	3	2	4	5	6		8	7		10				11	9														
11	Jan 1	(h) Scotch C XI	L 2-3	Pringle, Untraced	3,000	1	3		2	5		7	8			10				6	9			4	11										
12	31	(h) Vale of Leven	D 1-1	Dunlop	4,000	1	3	2		5	6	7	8			10				9					11	4									
13	Feb 14	(a) Caledonian	W 4-1	Pringle, McQuarrie, Smith, McIntyre				2	4	5		7		8			3			6	9				11		1	10							
14	21	(a) Dumbarton	D 3-3	Untraced		1		3	4		6	7	9	8		10				11				2					5						
15	28	(a) Hibernians	W 4-1	Pringle, McNeil, Untraced 2			3	2				7		8		10				9				4	11					1	5	6			
16	Mar 27	(a) Drumpellier	W11-0	Untraced																															
17	Apr 3	(h) Vale of Leven	W 2-1	Pringle, Dunlop	2,000	1	3	2	4		6	7	9	8		10								5	11										
18	24	(a†) Heart of Mid	D 0-0			1	3	2	4		6	7	9	8		10								5	11										
19	May 22	(a) Vale of Leven	L 1-3	Untraced	1,500																														
					Appearances	12	9	14	15	13	11	15	9	12	3	15	7	1	3	9	7	1	2	5	6	1	1	1	1	1	1	1			
					Goals	1			3		6			3		3	1			4	5	1			4			1							

* Played at Rothesay. † Played at Easter Road

In seven matches some players are unknown: in Match 4, one player; in Match 6, three players; in Match 7, three players; in Match 8, two players; in Match 9, two players; in Match 16, whole team; in Match 19, whole team. 21 goals untraced. 1 own-goal.

Scottish FA Cup

Rd	Date	Opponent	Result	Scorers	Att	Gillespie G	Vallance T	Vallance A	McIntyre H	Drinnan J	Dunlop W	Hill D	Struthers W	Steel A	Angus G	McNeil M	Stewart A	Corbell W	Kerr R	McQuarrie C	Christie J	McKenzie	Marshall A	McIntyre J	Pringle W	Young R	McDonald T	Smith P	Harris J	Martin J	Gow A	Fraser E	Campbell P	Ricketts S	Kennedy A
1	Sep 20	(h) Queen's Park	D 0-0		7,000	1	2		4	5	6	7	8	9		10	3																11		
R	27	(a) Queen's Park	L 1-5	Steel	5,000	1			3	5	2	7	8	9	6	10																	11	4	
					Appearances	2	1		2	2	2	2	2	2	1	2	1																2	1	
					Goals									1																					

Glasgow Merchants' Charity Cup

Rd	Date	Opponent	Result	Scorers	Att	Gillespie G	Vallance T	Vallance A	McIntyre H	Drinnan J	Dunlop W	Hill D	Struthers W	Steel A	Angus G	McNeil M	Stewart A	Corbell W	Kerr R	McQuarrie C	Christie J	McKenzie	Marshall A	McIntyre J	Pringle W	Young R	McDonald T	Smith P	Harris J	Martin J	Gow A	Fraser E	Campbell P	Ricketts S	Kennedy A
SF	Apr 10	(n*) Dumbarton	W 3-1	Struthers 2, Steel		1	3	2	4	6		8	9	10		11								5	7										
F	May 8	(a) Queen's Park	D 1-1	Pringle		1	3	2	5	6		8	9	7		10									11										4
R	12	(h) Queen's Park	L 1-2	Hill		1	3	2	5	6		8		7		10								9	11										4
					Appearances	3	3	3	3	3		3	2	3		3								2	3										2
					Goals							1	2	1											1										

* Played at Hampden

1880-81

Honorary Match Secretary: P.McNeill

No	Date	Opponent	Result	Scorers	Att	McDonald T	Vallance A	Vallance T	McIntyre J	Aitken A	Steel A	Hill D	Marshall A	Struthers W	McNeil M	Pringle W	Gillespie G	Drinnan J	Maitland A	Warner J	Stewart A	McHardy H	Angus G	Inglis J	Weir L	Kerr R	McKenzie	Christie J	Devlin J	Kennedy J	McAdam	McKinlay S	Watt J	Ker G	Smith Dr J	Smith P	McIntyre M
1	Sep 18	(h) Partick Thistle	W 4-1	Struthers 2, Pringle, McNeil		1	2	3	4	5	6	7	8	9	10	11																					
2	25	(a) Queen's Park	L 0-5		3,000		2	3	4		6		8	9	10	11	1	5	7																		
3	Oct 9	(h) Thornliebank	D 1-1	Angus					4		6			9	10	11	3	5		1	2	7	8														
4	16	(h) Queen's Park	D 2-2	Struthers, Angus			3		4		6			9	10	11	1	5			2		8	7													
5	30	(a) Nottingham F	L 1-2	McIntyre			3		4		6	7		9	10	11	1	5			2		8														
6	Nov 1	(a) Blackburn R	D 0-0				5	3	4		6	7		9	10	11	1				2		8														
7	6	(h) Hibernians	W 5-1	Pringle 2, McIntyre, Struthers 2			2	3	4		6			9	10	11	1	5		8					7												
8	27	(a) Hibernians	D 2-2	Pringle, McKenzie				3	4			7		9	10	11					2		5	8		1	6										
9	Dec 4	(h) Third Lanark RV	D 1-1	Pringle				3	4			7		9	10	11	2	5						8		1											
10	11	(h) Nottingham F	D 2-2	McNeil, Hill	2,000		2	3	4		6	7		9	10	11	1	5						8													
11	Feb 5	(a) Caledonian	W 8-0	Struthers 4, Gillespie, Christie, Pringle, McHardy			2	3	4					9		11	6	1				10		7			5	8									
12	12	(a*) Dumbarton	L 0-1				2			4				9		11				1		8						10	3	5	6	7					
13	19	(a) Partick Thistle	W 8-2	Untraced				3	4			7		9	10	11	2	5										8				6	1				
14	Mar 5	(a) Blackburn R	L 4-5	Struthers 2, Smith 2	2,000		5	3	4					10		11				1	2							7				6		8	9		
15	19	(h) Blackburn R	W 2-1	Hill, Pringle	4,000		2	3	4			7		9		11	1	5						8				10				6					
16	Apr 2	(h) Heart of Mid	W 7-0	Hill 2, Pringle, Drinnan, Inglis, McKinlay, Struthers			2		4			7		9		11		5						8				10				6					
17	9	(a) Vale of Leven	L 2-3	Struthers, Steel			2		4		10	7		9		11								8				5	3			6	1				
18	23	(a) Hibernians	W 9-3	Struthers 5, Smith, Devlin, Hill, Gillespie			2	3	5			7		9		11	1				4			8					6							10	
19	May 4	(h) South Western	D 1-1	Christie				3	1		10					11		5	6		2			8				9	4							7	
					Appearances	1	14	13	18	2	10	11	2	18	11	19	12	12	2	4	8	3	5	10	1	2	2	8	4	1	1	6	2	1	1	2	
					Goals				2		1	5		18	2	8	2	1				1	2	1			1	2	1			1			2	1	

* Played at Levengrove Park.

In two matches some players are unknown: in Match 9, one player; in Match 16, two players. 8 goals untraced.

Scottish FA Cup

Rd	Date	Opponent	Result	Scorers	Att	McDonald T	Vallance A	Vallance T	McIntyre J	Aitken A	Steel A	Hill D	Marshall A	Struthers W	McNeil M	Pringle W	Gillespie G	Drinnan J	Maitland A	Warner J	Stewart A	McHardy H	Angus G	Inglis J	Weir L	Kerr R	McKenzie	Christie J	Devlin J	Kennedy J	McAdam	McKinlay S	Watt J	Ker G	Smith Dr J	Smith P	McIntyre M
1	Sep 11	(h) Govan	W 4-1	Untraced			2	3	4		6	7	8	9	10	11		5															1				
2	Oct 2	(a) Northern	W 1-0	Struthers	3,000		2	3	4		6		8	9	10	11	1	5																			
3	23	(h) Partick Thistle	W 3-0	Angus 3	1,000		3		4		6	7		9	10	11	1	5			2		8														
4	Nov 13	(h) Clyde	W11-0	Struthers, Steel, Pringle, Angus, Untraced 7			2	3	4		6			9	10	11	7	5					8			1											
5	Dec 18	(a) Hurlford	W 3-0	Christie, Angus, McNeil			2	3	4			7		9	10	11		5					6					8					1				
QF	25	(h) Dumbarton	L 1-3	Pringle	4,000/5,000		2	3	4		6	7		9	10	11	1	5																			8
					Appearances		6	5	6		5	4	2	6	6	6	4	6			1		3			1		1					2				1
					Goals						1			2	1	2							11					1									

FA Cup Round 2, one player unknown. 4 goals untraced.

Glasgow Merchants' Charity Cup

Rd	Date	Opponent	Result	Scorers	Att	McDonald T	Vallance A	Vallance T	McIntyre J	Aitken A	Steel A	Hill D	Marshall A	Struthers W	McNeil M	Pringle W	Gillespie G	Drinnan J	Maitland A	Warner J	Stewart A	McHardy H	Angus G	Inglis J	Weir L	Kerr R	McKenzie	Christie J	Devlin J	Kennedy J	McAdam	McKinlay S	Watt J	Ker G	Smith Dr J	Smith P	McIntyre M
1	Apr 16	(n*) Dumbarton	W 8-0	Hill 2, Struthers, McKinlay 2, Steel 2, Pringle			2	3	4		10	7		9		11	1	5						8								6					
F	30	(a*) Queen's Park	D 1-1	McKinlay			2	3	4		10	7		9		11	1	5						8								6					
R	May 7	(h) Queen's Park	L 1-3	Untraced	10,000		2	3	4		10	7		9		11	1	5						8								6					
					Appearances		3	3	3		3	3		3		3	3	3						3								3					
					Goals						2	2		1		1																3					

* Played at Hampden

1 goal untraced.

1881-82

Honorary Match Secretary: P.McNeill

#	Date	Opponent	Res	Scorers	Att	McDonald T	Vallance A	Markelyne	McIntyre J	Gilchrist	Hill D	Inglis J	Corbett W	Smith P	Maitland A	Petrie	Ness WF	Young R	Drinnan J	Gillespie G	McFarlane W	Weir CS	Pringle W	Christie J	Ricketts S	Vallance T	Suter	Young A	Ramsay R	McNeil M	McNeil H	Holm JW	Angus G	Thomson T	Aitken A
1	Aug 27 (a)	Heart of Mid	D 1-1	Petrie		1	2	3	4	5	6	7	8	9	10	11																			
2	Oct 1 (h)	St Bernards	W 6-1	Weir 4, Pringle, Untraced			2		4			7	8				1	3	5	6	9	10	11												
3	8 (h)	Vale of Leven	W 1-0	Inglis			2		4		6	7	8					3	5	1	9	10	11	9											
4	29 (a)	Nottingham F	D 0-0		2,000	1	2		4		6	7	8					3			10		11	9	5										
5	31 (a)	Blackburn R	D 2-2	Inglis, Pringle	5,000	1	2		4		6	7	8					3			10		11	9	5										
6	Nov 5 (h)	Queen's Park	L 1-2	Corbett	5,000		2		4		6	7	8					3	5	1	10		11	9											
7	19 (a)	Jamestown	L 1-3	Maitland					4		6	7		8				3		1						2									
8	26 (a)	Vale of Leven	L 1-2	Corbett			2		4		6	7	8				10	5		1			11	9		3									
9	Dec 10 (a)	Kilmarnock P	L 2-4	Corbett 2		1			4		6	7	8					3			11	10		9	5	2									
10	Jan 14 (h)	Thistle	L 1-2	Corbett									8								9					3									
11	Feb 18 (a)	St Mirren	L 2-5	Untraced																						3									
12	Mar 25 (a)	Aston Villa	L 2-3	Ramsay*, Untraced	4,000			2				7						3	4				11		5		1	6	8	10					
13	Apr 5 (h)	South Western	D 0-0				2			5	6	7						3	4	1			11						8	10	9				
14	10 (h)	Aston Villa	W 7-1	Hill, Corbett, Pringle 3, Young, Inglis	1,000		2			5	6	7	10					3	4	1			11						8		9				
15	22 (h)	Blackburn R	D 2-2	Angus, Holm	2,000					5	6	7	10						4	1			11						8			9	3		
		Appearances				4	9	1	13	1	11	13	11	1	2	1	2	11	7	9	7	2	10	6	4	4	1	1	4	2	2	1	1		
		Goals									1	3	6		1	1		1				4	5						1			1	1		

* Ramsay played under the pseudonym, 'Danvers'

In four matches some players are unknown: in Match 7, four players; in Match 10, nine players; in Match 11, seven players and only eight played; in Match 12, one player. 4 goals unknown.

Scottish FA Cup

#	Date	Opponent	Res	Scorers	Att	McDonald T	Vallance A	Markelyne	McIntyre J	Gilchrist	Hill D	Inglis J	Corbett W	Smith P	Maitland A	Petrie	Ness WF	Young R	Drinnan J	Gillespie G	McFarlane W	Weir CS	Pringle W	Christie J	Ricketts S	Vallance T	Suter	Young A	Ramsay R	McNeil M	McNeil H	Holm JW	Angus G	Thomson T	Aitken A
1	Sep 10 (h)	Third Lanark RV	W 2-1	Pringle, Weir	3,000		2		4		6	7	8					5		1		10	11	3											
2		Rangers walkover, Harmonic scratched																																
3	Oct 22 (h)	Alexandra A	W 3-1	Pringle 2, Hill	3,000		2		4		6	7	8					10	5	1	9		11	3											
4	Nov 12 (h)	Thornliebank	W 2-0	Hill, Opp own-goal			6		4			7	8					3	5	1	10		11	9										2	
5	Dec 3 (a)	South Western*	W 2-1	Inglis, McFarlane	3,000		2		4			7	8					5	6	1	10		11	9	3										
R	24 (h)	South Western	W 4-0	Christie, Inglis, McFarlane, Hill	1,000		2		4		6	7		9				5		1	10		11	8	3										
QF	Jan 28 (a)	Dumbarton†	L 1-2	Pringle	5,000		2		8		6	7			10			5	4	1	9		11	3											
R	Feb 4 (a)	Dumbarton	L 1-5	Hill	5,000		2		8		6	7	9					5	4	1			11	3	10										
		Appearances					7		7		7	7	3	2				7	5	7	5	1	7	3	6	1							1	
		Goals									4	2									2	1	4	1										

* South Western protested - upheld. † Rangers protested - upheld.

FA Cup Round 1, one player unknown.

Glasgow Merchants' Charity Cup

#	Date	Opponent	Res	Scorers	McDonald T	Vallance A	Markelyne	McIntyre J	Gilchrist	Hill D	Inglis J	Corbett W	Smith P	Maitland A	Petrie	Ness WF	Young R	Drinnan J	Gillespie G	McFarlane W	Weir CS	Pringle W	Christie J	Ricketts S	Vallance T	Suter	Young A	Ramsay R	McNeil M	McNeil H	Holm JW	Angus G	Thomson T	Aitken A
1	Apr 8 (n*)	Dumbarton	D 2-2	Hill, Ramsay		2			5	6	7						3	4	1			11						8	10	9				
R	29 (n*)	Dumbarton	L 0-4			2		4		6	7	10					3		1			11						8					9	5
		Appearances				2		1	1	2	2	1					2	1	2			2						2	1	1			1	1
		Goals								1																		1						

* Played at Hampden

1882-83

Honorary Match Secretary: P.McNeill

#	Date		Venue / Opponent	Result	Scorers	Att.
1	Aug	26 (h)	Lugar Boswell	D 1-1	McKenzie	
2	Sep	2 (a)	Lugar Boswell	L 0-2		
3		16 (h)	Dumbarton	D 1-1	Corbett	3,000
4		23 (a)	Queen's Park	L 2-6	Ramsay, Hill	3,000
5	Oct	7 (h)	Thistle	L 1-3	Corbett	
6		14 (h)	Queen's Park	W 3-2	Gossland 2, Hill	4,000
7		28 (a)	Bolton W	L 0-1		4,000
8		31 (a)	Blackburn R	D 1-1	Heggie	2,000
9	Nov	18 (a)	Vale of Leven	L 1-3	Untraced	1,500
10		25 (a)	Third Lanark RV	L 0-3		
11	Dec	23 (a)	Dumbarton	L 1-3	Gossland	
12		30 (a)	Accrington	L 2-3	Pringle, Gossland	
13	Jan	1 (a)	Darwen	D 4-4	Duncan, Corbett, Inglis, Gossland	4,000
14		2 (a)	Blackburn R *	D 1-1	Hamilton	2,000
15		6 (h)	Pollokshields A	L 1-2	Gossland	
16	Feb	3 (h)	Partick Thistle	W 3-0	Untraced	
17		10 (a)	Thistle	W 5-1	McGregor, McHardy, Pringle, Gossland, Untraced	
18		17 (a)	Kilmarnock P	W 1-0	McHardy	
19		24 (h)	Thornliebank	W 3-0	Pringle, McHardy, McGregor	
20	Mar	10 (h)	Blackburn R	L 2-3	Hamilton, Untraced	8,500
21		24 (a)	Aston Villa	W 4-1	McHardy, Hamilton, Gossland, Pringle	5,000
22		31 (a)	Aston Villa	L 1-2	Untraced	6,000
23	Apr	7 (a)	Abercorn	L 0-4		
24		14 (a)	Partick Thistle	L 1-2	Untraced	
25		25 (h)	Third Lanark RV	L 1-3	Hamilton	

* Abandoned after 52 minutes due to weather conditions.

Appearances and Goals

Player	App	Goals
Ness WF	8	
Young R	7	
Duncan J	19	1
Heggie C	23	1
McIntyre J	22	
McKenzie AB	4	1
Inglis J	20	1
Watson J	3	
Aitken A	6	
Maitland A	2	
Pringle W	22	4
Corbett W	17	3
Ramsay R	3	1
Gossland J	22	8
McIntyre D	1	
Hill D	6	2
Arnott	1	
Hamilton A	17	4
Young A	1	
Gillespie G	11	
Vallance A	2	
Phillips J	3	
McIntyre R	1	
Kennedy	1	
McHardy R	13	4
Nichol G	4	
Gordon F	11	
MacHolden	1	
Cameron J	2	
Hunli	1	
Nicholls	1	
McGregor W	9	2

D.Smith played number-7 in Match 18; Campbell played number-6 in Match 23; J.W.Holm played number-2 in Match 24; T.Vallance played number-2 in Match 25; In Match 2, five players are unknown. In Matches 10 and 23 only 10 men played. 8 goals untraced.

Scottish FA Cup

#	Date		Venue / Opponent	Result	Scorers	Att.
1	Sep	9 (a)	Jordanhill	W 4-0	Watson 2, Corbett 2	
2		30 (a)	Queen's Park	L 2-3	Pringle, McIntyre	5,000

M.McNeil played number-11 in Round 1 and number-10 in Round 2.

Glasgow Merchants' Charity Cup

#	Date		Venue / Opponent	Result	Scorers	Att.
1	May	5 (n*)	Vale of Leven	W 3-2	Pringle, Gossland, Hamilton	4,500
F		19 (a)	Queen's Park	L 1-4	Arnott (og)	7,500

* Played at First Hampden Park.

J.W.Holm played number-2 in Round 1 and the Final; J.Christie played number-9 in Round 1 and the Final. 1 own-goal.

1883-84

Honorary Match Secretary: J.W.MacKay

#	Date		Opponent	Result	Scorers	Att	Gillespie G	Vallance T	Duncan J	McIntyre J	Heggie C	Hamilton A	Inglis J	Christie J	McHardy H	Pringle W	Gossland J	Chalmers W	MacKay J	McAusland	Gordon F	Maitland A	McGregor W	Hart W	Cameron J	Hendry	Young R	Aitken A	Weir CS	Watson J	Thomson S	Corbett W	Smith DW	Bryden	Hill D	Marshall A	Raeside H
1	Jul 31	(h)	Dumbarton*	W 4-2	McHardy, Christie, Heggie 2	2,500	1	2	3	4	5	6	7	8	9	10	11																				
2	Aug 18	(a)	Johnstone	W 9-1	Untraced					4	5		7			10	11	1		8																	
3		25 (a)	St Bernards	W 4-3	Gossland 3, Maitland					4	5		7		9	10	11	1	2		3	6	8													
4	Sep 1	(h)	Mauchline	W 5-2	Untraced				2	4	5		7		9	10	11	1					8														
5		15 (h)	Vale of Leven	W 2-1	Cameron, Inglis	6,000			2	4	5	6	7		9		11	1					8	3	10												
6		22 (h)	Third Lanark RV	W 5-0	McGregor 3, Inglis, Hamilton	4,000			2	4		6	7		9	10	11	1					8	3	5												
7	Oct 6	(h)	Partick	W 7-1	Untraced	200	1		2	4	5		7		9	10	11						8	3													
8		13 (a)	Kilmarnock A	L 4-5	Untraced		1		2	4	5		7		9	10	11						8	3		6											
9		27 (a)	Dumbarton	L 0-2		5,000	1		2	4	5	6	7		9	10	11						8	3													
10	Nov 3	(h)	Pollokshields A	W 8-2	McHardy, Heggie, Hamilton, McGrgor 2, Gossland, Inglis, Pringle		1		2	4	5	6	7		9	10	11						8	3													
11		17 (h)	Dumbarton	L 2-4	McHardy, McGregor	5,000	1		2	4	5	6	7		9	10	11						8	3													
12		24 (h)	Queen's Park	L 2-5	Hamilton 2	5,000	1		2	4	5	6	7		9	10	11						8	3													
13	Dec 8	(a)	Third Lanark RV	L 1-2	Untraced	3,000			2	4			7	6	9	10	11	1					8	3	5												
14		15 (h)	Pilgrims	W 5-0	Untraced				2	4			7	6	9	10	11	1					8	3	5												
15		29 (h)	Third Lanark RV	D 0-0		5,000			2	4	8	6	7		9	10	11	1							5		3										
16	Jan 5	(h)	Blackburn R	L 1-2	Hamilton				2	4	8	6	7		9	10	11	1							5		3										
17		12 (a)	Battlefield	W 5-3	Inglis 2, McHardy, Untraced 2				2		5	6	7		9	10		1					8				3	4	11								
18	Feb 2	(a)	Thistle	W 4-1	Thomson 2, Watson, Pringle				2	4		6				10	11	1												8	9						
19		9 (h)	Northern	W 2-1	Opp own-goal, Heggie	1,000			2	4	8	6				11		1							5		3			10	9	7					
20		23 (a)	Abercorn	W 10-0	Heggie 6, Untraced 4				3		8	6				10	11	1							5		2				9		7				
21	Mar 8	(h)	Abercorn	W 9-2	Untraced			2		4	8	6				10	11	1							5		3				9		7				
22		15 (a)	Bolton W	D 1-1	Thomson	5,000			3	4	8	6			2	10	11	1							5		7				9						
23		17 (a)	Blackburn R	L 1-4	Pringle	4,000			3	4	8	6			2	10	11	1							5		7				9						
24		22 (a)	Pollokshields A	W 6-1	Heggie 2, Duncan, Gossland, Thomson 2				3	4	8	6				10	11	1							5		2				9						
25		29 (a)	St Mirren	D 0-0					3		8	6			9	10	11	1							5		2				7				4		
26	Apr 5	(h)	Thistle	W 5-0	Untraced				3	4	8	6	7			10	11	1							5		2										
27		19 (a)	Hibernians	L 1-4	Watson	2,000			3	4	8	6					11	1							5		2			10		7		9			
28	May 10	(h)	Queen's Park	L 1-4	Untraced	3,000			3	4		6				10	11	1							5		2				7					8	9
			Appearances				7	2	24	26	24	22	17	3	19	27	25	19	1	1	1	1	13	10	16	1	14	1	1	3	7	3	3	1	1	1	1
			Goals						1		12	5	5	1	4	3	5						6		1					2	5						1

* 'Daphne' Disaster Match

In seven matches some players are unknown: in Match 2, four players; in Match 4, two players; in Match 7, one player; in Match 18, three players; in Match 20, one player; in Match 24, one player; in Match 26, one player. 52 goals untraced. 1 own-goal.

Scottish FA Cup

#	Date		Opponent	Result	Scorers	Att	Gillespie G	Vallance T	Duncan J	McIntyre J	Heggie C	Hamilton A	Inglis J	Christie J	McHardy H	Pringle W	Gossland J	Chalmers W	MacKay J	McAusland	Gordon F	Maitland A	McGregor W	Hart W	Cameron J	Hendry	Young R	Aitken A	Weir CS	Watson J	Thomson S	Corbett W	Smith DW	Bryden	Hill D	Marshall A	Raeside H
1	Sep 8	(a)	Northern	W 1-0	Gossland				2	4	5	6	7		9	10	11	1					8	3													
2		29 (h)	Whitehill	W 14-2	McHardy, Untraced 13			2		4	5	6	7		9	10	11	1					8	3													
3	Oct 20	(a)	Falkirk	W 5-2	McGregor, Hamilton, Gossland, McHardy, Untraced	2,000			2	4	5	6	7		9	10	11	1					8	3													
4	Nov 10	(a)	Dunblane	W 6-1	Untraced				2	4	5	6	7		9	10	11	1					8	3													
5	Dec 1	(a)	St Bernards	W 3-0	McHardy, Gossland, Pringle	2,000			2	4		6	7		9	10	11	1					8	3	5												
QF		22 (a)	Cambuslang	W 5-1	Gossland 2, Pringle, Heggie, Inglis				2	4	8	6	7		9	10	11	1							5		3										
SF	Jan 19	(a)	Vale of Leven	L 0-3		7,000			2	4	5	6	7	8	9	10	11	1									3										
			Appearances				1	6	7	6	7	7	1		7	7	7	7					5	5	2		2										
			Goals								1	1	1		3	2	5						1														

20 goals untraced

Glasgow Merchants' Charity Cup

	Date		Opponent	Result	Scorers	Att	Gillespie G	Vallance T	Duncan J	McIntyre J	Heggie C	Hamilton A	Inglis J	Christie J	McHardy H	Pringle W	Gossland J	Chalmers W	MacKay J	McAusland	Gordon F	Maitland A	McGregor W	Hart W	Cameron J	Hendry	Young R	Aitken A	Weir CS	Watson J	Thomson S	Corbett W	Smith DW	Bryden	Hill D	Marshall A	Raeside H
S	Apr 12	(n*)	Queen's Park	L 1-2	Corbett	10,000			3	4	8	6				10	11	1							5		2					7			9		
			Appearances						1	1	1	1				1	1	1							1		1					1			1		
			Goals																													1					

*Played at Cathkin

1884-85

Honorary Match Secretary: J.W.MacKay

#	Date	V	Opponent	Result	Scorers	Att	Chalmers W	Young R	Vallance A	McIntyre J	McHardy H	Cameron J	Morton P	Pringle W	McKenzie AB	Lawrie M	Gossland J	Corbett W	Duncan J	Peacock A	Young A	Walker	Cook T	Barker	Robertson	Cherry R	Sommerville G	Mackie J	Gray	Ritchie	Ricketts S	Lafferty P	Campbell	Aitken A	Heggie C	Muir J	Allan J	Reid
1	Aug 23	(a)	Our Boys Dun	W 5-2	Untraced																																	
2	30	(h)	Kilmarnock A	W 9-1	Morton 3, Lawrie, McKenzie 2, Pringle, Gossland 2		1	2	3	4	5	6	7	8	9	10	11																					
3	Sep 20	(h)	St Mirren	W 2-1	McKenzie, Lawrie	1,000	1	2		4	3	5	6	8	9	10	11	7																				
4	27	(h)	Dumbarton	W 3-2	Gossland, Morton, Young	3,000	1	2		4	3	5	6	8	9	10	11	7																				
5	Oct 18	(a)	Vale of Leven	L 1-3	Untraced	2,000	1			4	3	5	6	8	9	10				2	7	11																
6	23	(a)	5th Kirk RV	W 4-1	Untraced																																	
7	Nov 22	(h)	Queen's Park	L 2-3	Gossland 2	4,000	1				3	5	6	8	9	10	11			2			4			7												
8	29	(a)	Third Lanark RV	W 6-0	McKenzie 4, Peacock 2	500					3	5		8	6		10	11		7			4	9	1	2												
9	Dec 6	(a)	Pilgrims	W 1-0	Gossland		1				3	5		8	6		10	11		7			4	9		2												
10	13	(h)	Battlefield	L 2-3	Cook, Pringle		1				3	5		8	6		10	11		7			4	9		2												
11	Jan 1	(a)	Preston NE	L 1-3	Gossland	7,000	1			4	3	5		8	6		10	11		7				9		2												
12	2	(a)	Darwen	L 5-1	Peacock, Cook, Untraced 3		1			4	3	5		8	6		10	11		7				9		2												
13	3	(a)	Blackburn R	D 0-0		2,000	1			4	3	5		8	6		10	11		7				9		2												
14	10	(h)	Third Lanark RV	W 3-2	Sommerville, Gossland, McKenzie	1,000	1			4	3	5	6	8			11			7						2	9	10										
15	17	(h)	Thistle	W 4-2	McKenzie, Sommerville 3		1				5				10		6			11			7			2	9	8	1	3	4							
16	24	(a)	St Mirren	L 1-3	Gossland	3,500	1			5	3	4			10		11		6				7			2	9	8										
17	31	(h)	Battlefield	W 4-1	Lafferty, Mackie 2, McKenzie	1,500	1			5	3	4			10	9	11			7						2		8				6						
18	Feb 7	(h)	Hibernians	W 4-3	Mackie 2, Sommerville, Pringle		1			5	3	4			10		6			7						2	9	8					11					
19	14	(a)	St Bernards	W 5-1	McKenzie 2, Lafferty 2, Cook						3	4	11	10	9					8			7	1		2					6	5						
20	21	(a)	Pollokshields A	W 1-0	Pringle		1			5	3	4			9	8	10			6			7			2												
21	28	(h)	Cambuslang	W 3-1	Untraced	2,000	1			5	3	4			10	8	11			7						2	9					6						
22	Mar 7	(a)	Ayr*	W 3-2	Sommerville 2, Untraced						3	4			10	8	11			7		11				2	9					5						
23	21	(a)	Pollokshields A	W 3-2	Heggie 2, Cook	3,000	1			5	3	4			10		11			6			7			2		8							9			
24	26	(h)	Battlefield	W 2-0	Untraced			2			3	4							11	7				1			8	10							9	5	6	
25	Apr 4	(a)	Cambuslang	W 4-1	Untraced					5	3	4			8		6						7															
26	22	(h)	Blackburn R	L 3-4	Pringle, Mackie, Heggie	6,000	1	2		5	3	4			10		6			7							9	11							8			
27	25	(a)	Partick Thistle	L 2-5	Gossland 2			1		5		4			10	11			2	9			7			3	8					6						
28	May 13	(a)	Queen's Park	W 1-0	McKenzie	1,500		2		5		4			10	11				7						9						6			8			1
29	Jun 4	(a)	Falkirk District XI	W 4-0	Untraced						3	4											7															
30	6	(a)	Lugar Boswell	D 1-1	Untraced																																	
				Appearances			18	7	1	18	24	27	7	22	23	12	19	2	3	20	1	4	15	3	1	17	10	9	1	1	1	5	1	2	4	1	1	1
				Goals				1					4	5	13	2	11						3				7	5				3			3			

* Ayr Charity Cup

J.B.Niven played number-3 in Match 28. No team line-ups have been traced for Matches 1, 6 & 30. In three matches some players are unknown: in Match 22, one player; in Match 25, five players; in Match 29, eight players. Only ten men played in Match 20. 28 goals untraced.

Scottish FA Cup

#	Date	V	Opponent	Result	Scorers	Att	Chalmers W	Young R	Vallance A	McIntyre J	McHardy H	Cameron J	Morton P	Pringle W	McKenzie AB	Lawrie M	Gossland J	Corbett W	Duncan J	Peacock A	Young A	Walker	Cook T
1	Sep 13	(h)	Whitehall	W 11-0	Untraced		1	2		4	3	5		7	10	11	8			9			
2	Oct 4	(a)	Third Lanark RV	D 2-2	Gossland, Morton	6,000	1		2	4	3	5	6	7	9	10	11						
R	11	(h)	Third Lanark RV	D 0-0		7,000	1		2	4	3	5	6	7	9	10	11						
3	25	(a)	Third Lanark RV	W 3-0	Lawrie, Cook, Morton	4,000	1	2		4	3	5	6	8	9	10	11						7
4	Nov 15	(a)	Arbroath	L 3-4*	Morton, Gossland, McKenzie	4,000	1	2			3	5	6	8	9	10	11					4	7
R	Dec 20	(a)	Arbroath	W 8-1	Untraced	2,000	1		2	5	3				6		10	11		7		4	9
5			Rangers received a Bye.																				
QF	27	(a)	Renton	L 3-5	Gossland, McKenzie, Peacock	4,000	1		2	4	3	5		8	6		10	11		7			9
				Appearances			7	3	4	6	7	6	4	7	6	7	7	1		2		2	4
				Goals									3		2	1	3			1			1

* Rangers made successful protest over size of the Arbroath pitch.

Lockhart played number-6 in Round 1. S.Thomson played number-8 in Round 2. A.Steel played number-8 in Round 2R. 19 goals untraced.

Glasgow Merchants' Charity Cup

#	Date	V	Opponent	Result	Scorers	Att	Chalmers W	Young R	McIntyre J	McHardy H	Cameron J	McKenzie AB	Gossland J	Corbett W	Peacock A	Sommerville G	Lafferty P	Heggie C	Reid
1	Apr 11	(n)	Dumbarton	D 2-2	Heggie 2	3,500	1	2	5	3	4	10	6		7	8	11	9	
R	18	(n)	Dumbarton	D 1-1	McKenzie	5,000	1	2	5	3	4	10	6	11	7	8		9	
2R	May 2	(n)	Dumbarton	L 0-2		7,000		2	5	3	4	10	6	11	7	8		9	1
				Appearances			2	3	3	3	3	3	3	2	3	3	1	3	1
				Goals								1						2	

All ties played at Second Hampden Park.

1885-86

Honorary Match Secretary: J.Gossland

Player columns (left to right): McKenzie AB, Cherry R, McHardy H, Cameron J, McIntyre J, Marshall A, Peacock A, Crawford, Heggie C, Pringle W, Lawrie M, Barker, Miller P, Sommerville G, Gossland J, Mackie J, Allan J, Chalmers W, Maxwell, Smith, Downs, Muir J, Vallance A, McPhee D, Niven JB, Corney, Campbell, Buchanan J, Cook T, Hume, Gow J, Gow D

#	Date	V	Opponent	Result	Scorers	Att
1	Aug 19	(a)	Northern	L 1-2	Untraced	
2	22	(a)	Hibernians	L 2-3	Sommerville 2	2,500
3	26	(h)	Kilmarnock	W 4-3	Untraced	
4	29	(a)	Dumbarton	L 1-4	Untraced	
5	Sep 5	(a)	Cambuslang	L 2-5	Opp own-goal, Untraced 1	
6	9	(a)	Queen's Park *	W 2-1	Sommerville 2	
7	19	(h)	Arthurlie	W 4-1	Sommerville 2, Muir, McKenzie	
8	26	(a)	Queen's Park	L 2-3	McKenzie, Sommerville	4,000
9	Oct 3	(h)	Battlefield	D 0-0		1,500
10	8	(a)	5th Kirkcud RV	W 2-1	Untraced	
11	10	(a)	Falkirk	W 7-3	Sommerville, Untraced 6	
12	17	(h)	Battlefield	D 1-1	Untraced	2,000
13	24	(a)	Morton	L 1-2	McPhee	500
14	31	(h)	Renton	W 4-2	Heggie 3, Untraced	
15	Nov 7	(h)	Queen's Park	L 0-4		
16	14	(a)	Pollokshields	W 2-1	Untraced	
17	21	(h)	Dumbarton	L 2-5	McKenzie, Heggie	615
18	28	(a)	St Mirren	W 6-0	Heggie 6, Untraced	
19	Dec 12	(a)	Partick Thistle	W 5-0	Pringle, Heggie, Buchanan, Peacock 2	
20	19	(h)	Vale of Leven	D 3-3	Heggie, Peacock, McKenzie	
21	26	(h)	London Scott	W 12-2	Heggie 5, McKenzie 2, Buchanan 2, Pringle 2, Peacock	
22	Jan 2	(a)	Cliftonville	W 8-2	Untraced	
23	16	(a)	Port Glasgow	W 3-2	Heggie, McKenzie, Untraced	
24	23	(h)	Pollokshields A	W 7-1	Buchanan 3, McKenzie, Cochrane 2, Gow	
25	30	(h)	Third Lanark RV	W 6-0	Heggie 5, Buchanan	
26	Feb 6	(h)	Airdrieonians	L 2-10	Buchanan, Untraced	
27	13	(a)	Kilmarnock	L 1-4	McIntyre	
28	27	(a)	Nottingham F	D 2-2	Buchanan, Pringle	2,000
29	Mar 6	(a)	Grennock N	W 7-3	Heggie, Pringle, Buchanan, Untraced 4	
30	11	(h)	Moffat	W 3-2	Untraced	
31	13	(a)	Third Lanark RV	W 3-2	McKenzie, Heggie 2	1,000
32	20	(a)	Renton	D 1-1	McKenzie	
33	27	(a)	St Mirren	L 3-6	Untraced	
34	Apr 3	(a)	Morton	D 1-1	Untraced	
35	9	(h)	Bolton W	L 2-3	Heggie 2	2,000
36	21	(h)	Blackburn R	W 4-3	Gow J 2, Buchanan, Peacock	
37	24	(h)	Nottingham F	W 2-1	Heggie, Pringle	6,000
38	29	(h)	Battlefield	D 1-1	Untraced	
39	May 1	(a)	Partick Thistle	L 1-4	McIntyre	
40	5	(h)	Cowlairs	W 2-0	Heggie, Gow J	
41	8	(h)	Dundee W	L 2-4	Stewart, Untraced	
42	Jun 2	(a)	Crusaders †	D 1-1	Untraced	

* Eadie Fraser Benefit Match.
† Kinning Park Unemployed Benefit Match. § after extra-time

Appearances: 30, 4, 32, 37, 39, 2, 35, 2, 26, 38, 3, 2, 3, 8, 20, 2, 1, 36, 1, 1, 5, 3, 2, 3, 4, 1, 6, 26, 1, 16, 15, 8
Goals: 10, 2, 5, 29, 6, 8, 12, 4

G.Cochrane played number-8 in Match 24 and scored 2 goals. T.Nicol played number-5 in Match 32 and number-2 in Match 41. Graham played number-6 in Match 32. P.Lafferty played number-6 in Match 36. Dougal played number-3 in Match 37 and number-5 in Match 38. Campbell (2) played number-7 in Match 38. W.Hotson played number-7 in Match 39. Calder played number-3 in Match 40. Muray played number-7 in Match 41. J.Stewart played number-11 in Match 41 and scored 1 goal. In 13 matches some players are unknown: in Match 3, whole team; in Match 5, six players; in Match 9, two players; in Match 10, one player; in Match 11, one player; in Match 16, two players – ten a side; in Match 23, one player; in Match 27, one player; in Match 30, one player; in Match 33, four players; in Match 34, five players; in Match 40, three players; in Match 42, one player. 45 goals untraced. 1 own-goal.

Scottish FA Cup

#	Date	V	Opponent	Result	Att
1	Sep 12	(a)	Clyde	L 0-1	1,500

Players: McKenzie 6, Cherry 2, Cameron 4, McIntyre 5, Peacock 7, Pringle 10, Sommerville 11, Barker 1, Muir 8, Vallance 9, McPhee 3.
Appearances: 1 each. Goals: –

Glasgow Charity Cup

#	Date	V	Opponent	Result	Att
1	Apr 16	(n*)	Vale of Leven	L 0-1	

* Played at Cathkin Park.
Players: McHardy 3, Cameron 4, McIntyre 5, Crawford 8, Pringle 10, Barker 1, Corney 6, Campbell 9, Buchanan 7, Gow J 11.
Appearances: 1 each.
D.Gow played number-2.

Third Lanark Rifle Volunteers Drill Hall Fund Benefit Tournament

#	Date	V	Opponent	Result	Att
1	5 (nt)		Cowlairs	W 1-0	Untraced	4,000
2	5 (nt)		Queen's Park	W 1-0*	Buchanan	4,000

† Played at Hampden Park. * after extra-time.
Appearances: 2 each (McKenzie 6, Cameron 4, McIntyre 5, Crawford 8, Pringle 10, Barker 1, Muir 3, Buchanan 9, Gow J 11, Gow D 2).
One player in each Match is unknown. 1 goal untraced.

1886-87

Honorary Match Secretary: J.Gossland

Player columns (left to right): Chalmers W, Gow D, McCartney J, Cameron J, McIntyre J, Gray, Peacock A, Buchanan J, Heggie C, Pringle W, Gow J, Nicol T, Duncan, Park, McKenzie AB, Lawrie M, Fraser R, Muir J, Gossland J, Dougall, McNab A, Hotson W, Lindsay J, Ferguson, Warburton, Mackie, Nicol AJ, Neil Q, Oswald, Wighton, McFarlane A, McIntosh

#	Date		Opponent	Result	Scorers	Att
1	Aug	21 (a)	Vale of Leven	W 2-1	Heggie, Buchanan	
2		28 (h)	Dumbarton	W 2-1	Peacock, Heggie	
3	Sep	4 (a)	Central (K'loch)	W 5-0	Untraced	
4		18 (h)	Northern	W 1-0	Peacock	
5		25 (a)	Renton	L 2-3	Lawrie, Buchanan	
6	Oct	7 (a)	St Bernard's	W 4-1	Lawrie, Fraser, Pringle, McKenzie	
7		9 (a)	Third Lanark RV	W 1-0	McKenzie	6,000
8		16 (h)	Queen's Park	L 1-4	Buchanan	7,000
9	Nov	6 (a)	Dumbarton	D 5-5	Lawrie 3, Buchanan, Untraced	2,000
10		13 (a)	Abercorn	W 4-2	McIntyre, Fraser, Untraced 2	3,000
11		27 (a)	Cliftonville	W 4-1	McNab 3, Lawrie	
12	Dec	11 (h)	Partick Thistle	D 0-0		
13		25 (h)	Renton	D 1-1	Lawrie	
14	Jan	1 (a)	Bolton W	L 2-3	Buchanan 2	5,000
15		3 (a)	Preston NE	L 1-8	Peacock	5,000
16		22 (a)	Linthouse	W 3-0	Peacock, Untraced 2	
17	Feb	5 (h)	Cambuslang	L 0-1		3,000
18		12 (a)	St Bernard's	W 2-0	McKenzie, Untraced	
19	Mar	12 (a)	Grangemouth	W 4-1	Untraced	
20		19 (h*)	Vale of Leven	L 1-2	Peacock	
21	Apr	2 (a)	Queen's Park	L 0-4		5,000
22		9 (h*)	Nottingham F	W 1-0	Untraced	4,000
23		16 (a)	Clyde	W 2-1	Lindsay, Pringle	3,000
24		20 (a)	Whitefield	W 3-1	Lawrie, Cameron, McKenzie	
25		23 (a)	Partick Thistle	D 1-1	Untraced	
26		26 (a)	Shettleston	W 4-2	Untraced	
27		30 (h†)	Partick Thistle	L 1-5	Lawrie	3,000
28	May	7 (a)	Hibernian	D 2-2	Fraser 2	
29		11 (a)	Uddingston	W 4-1	McKenzie 2, Lawrie, Campbell	
30		25 (§)	I Zingari	D 1-1	Untraced	
31	Jun	1 (h‡)	Hibernian	W 1-0	McIntyre	2,000
32		3	A match was scheduled against Northern at Hydepark but there are no reports that it ever took place.				

*Played at Cathkin. †Played at Hampden. ‡Played at Inchview. § Venue unknown.

Appearances: 26 26 21 28 28 5 28 18 5 13 10 3 2 1 14 21 21 18 1 1 1 3 8 1 1 1 4 1 1 1 1 1
Goals: 1 2 5 6 2 2 6 10 4 3 1

Only 10 men played in Match 16. Johnson played number-9 in Match 28; Campbell played number-10 in Match 29 and scored 1 goal; McGregor played number-7 in Match 31. In five matches some players are unknown: in Match 10, one player; in Match 24, four players; in Match 26, three players; in Match 31, four players. The team that played in Match 19 is untraced. 22 goals untraced.

Scottish FA Cup

#	Date		Opponent	Result	Scorers	Att
1	Sep	11 (h)	Govan A	W 9-1	Gray, J.Gow, Peacock, Opp own-goal, Untraced 5	500
2	Oct	2 (h)	Westbourne	W 5-2	Buchanan, McKenzie, Duncan, Lawrie, Untraced 1	600
3		23 (h)	Cambuslang	L 0-2		4,000

Appearances: 3 3 3 3 2 2 3 1 3 1 2 2 2
Goals: 1 1 1 1 1 1

6 goals untraced. 1 own-goal.

FA Cup

#	Date		Opponent	Result	Scorers	Att
1	Oct	30 (a)	Everton	W 1-0	Heggie	6,000
2	Nov	20 (h)	Church	W 2-1	Lawrie 2	
3	Dec	4 (h)	Cowlairs	W 3-2	Fraser, Lawrie, Peacock	
5	Jan	29 (h)	Lincoln C	W 3-0	Fraser, Lindsay, Peacock	
QF	Feb	19 (h*)	Old Westminsters	W 5-1	Lafferty, Lawrie, Lindsay, Fraser, Untraced 1	6,000
SF	Mar	5 (n†)	Aston Villa	L 1-3	Lafferty	

*This was the last match at Kinning Park. †Played at Nantwich Road, Crewe.
Rangers received a bye in round 4.

Appearances: 6 5 4 6 6 6 3 2 1 1 6 6 6 3 1
Goals: 2 1 4 3 2

J.Forbes played number-3 in round 5 and the semi-final; P.Lafferty played number-11 in round 5 and the semi-final and scored 2 goals. 1 goal untraced.

Glasgow Merchants' Charity Cup

#	Date		Opponent	Result	Scorers	Att
1	Apr	6	Cambuslang	W 4-2	McKenzie, J.Gow, Untraced 2	3,000
SF	May	4	H'den Renton	D 1-1	Pringle	4,000
R		14	H'den Renton	D 1-1	McKenzie	12,000
2R		18	H'den Renton	L 1-2	Untraced	5,000

Appearances: 4 4 4 4 4 4 2 4 2 4 2
Goals: 1 1 2 1

3 goals untraced.

1887-88

Honorary Match Secretary: J.Gossland

Player columns (left to right): Nicol J, Gow D, Meikle, Cameron, McIntyre, Muir, Brown, Peacock, Pringle, McCluggage, Brand, Chalmers, McCartney, McKenzie, McFarlane A, Weir, Hotson R, Fraser, Cochrane, Forbes, Sellar, White, Gow J, Eaglesham, Bremner, Nisbet, McDonald, Hotson W, McLellan, Moffat, Sommerville, Robin

No	Date		Venue	Opponent	Result	Scorers	Attendance
1	Aug	13	(a)	Whitefield	D 2-2	Brown, McCluggage	1,500
2		20	(h)	Preston NE*	L 1-8	Peacock	18,000
3		27	(h)	Morton	D 2-2	Peacock 2	2,000
4	Sep	10	(h)	Queen's Park	L 2-4	Fraser, White	3,000
5		17	(h)	Dumbarton	L 2-3	White, Lawrie	1,000
6	Oct	22	(h)	St Bernards†	D 1-1	Brand	
7	Nov	5	(a)	Battlefield	W 5-1	J.Gow 3, Pringle, Untraced	
8		12	(h)	Third Lanark RV	W 5-0	Brand 4, Fraser	
9		26	(h)	Port Glasgow†	W 6-0	Pringle 3, Fraser 2, D.Gow	
10	Dec	31	(h)	Partick Thistle	W 3-1	J.Gow, Untraced 2	1,000
11	Jan	7	(a)	Queen's Park	D 1-1	J.Gow	5,000
12		14	(a)	Morton	W 3-2	Untraced	
13	Feb	11	(h)	Dumbarton A	D 1-1	McLellan	
14		18	(a)	Aston Villa	L 1-5	Untraced	
15		25	(a)	Albion R	L 0-2		
16	Mar	3	(h)	Renton	L 3-7	Aird 2, Untraced	5,000
17		8	(h)	Scottish C§	W 4-1	Untraced	
18		10	(a)	Dumbarton	D 4-4	Untraced	3,000
19		24	(a)	Dumbarton A	L 1-2	Brand	
20		31	(h)	Battlefield	W 5-0	Robin 2, Fraser 2, McKenzie	
21	Apr	7	(a)	Inverness S	W 4-0	Untraced	5,000
22		21	(a)	Thistle	W 4-1	McClellan 2, J.Gow 2	
23		28	(n)	Scottish C‡	W 6-0	Untraced	
24	May	5	(a)	Aston Villa	W 3-1	J.Gow 2, Untraced	
25		12	(a)	Monckcastle K	W 4-2	Sloan, Untraced 3	
26		16	(a)	Uddingston	L 1-2	McIntyre	
27		19	(a)	Camelon	W 3-1	Untraced	
28		21	(a)	Northern	L 1-2	Untraced	
29		24	(n#)	Third Lanark RV	L 0-1		
30		28	(a)	Celtic ¥	L 2-5	Souter 2	2,000

Appearances: 14 14 2 3 18 17 2 16 9 1 13 3 1 11 9 1 9 8 1 3 1 3 9 1 1 2 4 3 1 1 3

Goals: 1 1 1 3 4 1 6 1 6 2 9 3 2

* Official opening of first Ibrox Park. Match abandoned 70 minutes due to spectator encroachment. † 10-a-side fixtures. § 'Sunlight match' under artificial lights provided by Messrs Braby & Co. ‡ Dunfermline Charity Cup-tie, played at Ladysmill, Fife. # Played at the Exhibition Grounds, Gilmorehill. ¥ Cetic's inaugural fixture, played at first Celtic Park.

Lawrie played number-9 in Match 5 scoring 1 goal. Thomson played number-4 in Match 18. Aird played number-11 in Match 16 & 24, number-10 in Matches 18 & 19 and number-7 in Match 20. Hendry played number-2 in Matches 20, 22 & 24. T.J.Nicol played number-5 in Match 20 & number-6 in Match 22. Allan played number-7 in Matches 22 & 24. Calder played number-3 in Match 24. McPhearson played number-4 in Match 30. W.McFarlane played number-5 in Match 30. Robb played number-7 in Match 30. McLaren played number-8 in Match 30. Souter played number-10 in Match 30 and scored 2 goals. Wilson played number-11 in Match 30. R.Smellie, N.McCallum, Campbell, Buchanan and Gourlay played in Match 14. N.Munro played in Match 29. In Match 7, two players are unknown. 34 goals untraced.

Scottish FA Cup

No	Date		Venue	Opponent	Result	Scorers	Attendance
1	Sep	3	(h)	Battlefield	W 4-1	White 2, Brand, Lawrie	3,500
2		24	(a)	Partick Thistle	L 1-2	Brand	5,000

Appearances: 2 1 1 2 1 2 2 2 2 2 2

Goals: 2 2

Lawrie played number-9 in Round 1 & 2 and scored 1 goal. A.Nicol played number-3 in Round 2.

Glasgow Cup

No	Date		Venue	Opponent	Result	Scorers	Attendance
1	Oct	1	(a)	Third Lanark RV	D 2-2	Fraser, White	5,500
R		8	(h)	Third Lanark RV	W 2-0	Brand, Muir	5,000
2		15	(a)	Pollokshields	W 3-2	J.Gow, Turner (og), Untraced	
QF		29	(h)	Westbourne	W 5-1	J.Gow 3, Pringle, Untraced	
SF	Nov	19	(a)	Cowlairs	D 0-0		
R	Dec	3	(n)	Cowlairs	D 0-0		5,000
2R		10	(n)	Cowlairs	D 2-2	Fraser, Brand	6,000
3R		17	(n)	Cowlairs	W 2-1	Peacock 2	
P	Jan	21	(n)	Cowlairs	W 3-1	McKenzie, Fraser, Peacock	6,000
F		28	(n)	Cambuslang	L 1-3	D.Gow	11,000

Appearances: 10 9 1 3 10 9 10 7 7 2 8 10 9 1 3 8

Goals: 1 1 3 1 2 1 3 1 4

Semi-final 2nd replay and protest match both played at first Cathkin Park.
Semi-Final 3rd Replay played at Battlefield Park, Cowlairs successfully protested.
Result on Grounds of a breach of the amateur regulations in respect of Bob Brand of Rangers.
Final played at second Hampden Park.

Bryce played number-9 in Round 1. Wilson played number-10 in Round 1 Replay & number-11 in Round 2. 2 goals unknown. 1 own-goal.

Glasgow Merchants' Charity Cup

No	Date		Venue	Opponent	Result	Scorers	Attendance
1	Apr	14	(n)	Vale of Leven	D 3-3	Peacock, Aird, Untraced	5,000
R		23	(n)	Vale of Leven*	W 5-3	T.J.Nicol 2, Aird 2, McKenzie	3,000
SF	May	8	(n)	Renton	L 1-5	J.Gow	6,000

Appearances: 3 3 3 3 3 3 2 3

Goals: 1 1

*Match concluded ten minutes early to enable Vale of Leven to catch Alexandria train!
All ties played at Second Hampden Park.

Hendry played number-3 in Round 1 Replay and number-2 in the Semi-Final. Allan played number-7 in Round 1 & Replay and number-11 in Semi-Final. Aird played number-10 in Round 1 Replay and number-8 in Semi-Final. T.J.Nicol played number-6 in Round 1 Replay scoring 2 goals.

1888-89

Honorary Match Secretary: J.Gossland

#	Date		Opponent	Result	Scorers	Att.
1	Aug	4 (a)	Shettleston*	L 0-3		
2		11 (a)	Celtic	W 9-1	Untraced	
3		25 (h)	Hibernian	W 3-2	Untraced	
4		28 (a)	Clyde**	D 0-0		3,000
5	Sep	1 (h)	Preston NE†	L 0-4		1,500
6		8 (h)	Canada	D 1-1	Hotson	
7	Oct	13 (a)	Partick Thistle	L 0-2		2,000
8		20 (h)	Third Lanark RV	L 1-5	Untraced	2,000
9	Nov	3 (h)	Cowlairs	W 5-2	Wylie 3, Johnston 2	1,000
10		5 (n)	Vale of Leven ‡	L 0-8		
11		10 (a)	Cambuslang	L 1-3	Wilson	
12		17 (h)	Thistle	W 4-0	Untraced	
13	Dec	1 (h)	Vale of Leven	W 3-2	Johnston, Wylie, Untraced	
14		15 (h)	Battlefield	L 1-2	Johnston	
15		22 (a)	Queen's Park	L 0-3		1,500
16		29 (a)	Morton	L 2-7	Wilson 2	
17	Jan	1 (a)	Blackburn R	L 2-6	Untraced	7,000
18		2 (a)	Bolton W	D1-1§	Untraced	
19		12 (a)	Abercorn	L 1-6	McBain	
20		19 (a)	Nottingham F	L 1-2	Untraced	
21		26 (h)	Uddingston	D 2-2	Wylie, Morgan	
22	Feb	9 (h)	Partick Thistle	L 2-4	J.R.Gow, D.Gow	500
23		16 (a)	Ayr A	W 2-1	Untraced	
24		23 (h)	Port Glasgow	L 2-5	Sutherland, Peacock	
25	Mar	2 (h)	Cambuslang	W 4-1	Wylie, W.Peacock, White, Untraced	
26		9 (a)	Motherwell#	D 3-3	Vallance, Untraced 2	
27		16 (h)	Morton	L 0-2		
28		23 (a)	Sunderland	L 0-3		
29		30 (h)	Ayr U	W 4-2	Wylie, Untraced 3	
30	Apr	6 (a)	Queen's Park	L 2-4	Mackie, Izatt	
31		13 (h)	Dumbarton A	D 3-3	McKenzie 2, Untraced	
32		20 (h)	Nottingham F	W 2-0	Muir, Dickie	
33		22 (a)	Cowal S¥	W 9-1	Untraced	
34		26 (h)	Blackburn R	D 1-1	Oswald	
35		27 (a)	Queen of the S	L 2-6	Untraced	
36	May	1 (h)	Third Lanark RV	L 1-3	Wylie	3,000
37		4 (a)	Partick Thistle	L 2-6	Mackie, Untraced	
38		16 (h)	Renton	W 3-2	Hector, McPherson	
39	Jun	11 (a)	Falkirk DS*	W 6-0	Untraced	

Player appearances (shirt numbers):

#	Nicol J	Gow D	McFarlane A	McIntyre	Hotson R	Muir	Eaglesham	Sloan	McKenzie	Vallance A	Gow JR	McFarlane W	Gillespie	Forbes	Stewart	Alexander	Hamilton	Berry	Fraser	Maclachlan	McAllister	Wylie	Allison	Bremner	Deans	White	Wilson J	Wilson W	Pringle	Thomson	Johnston	Ritchie
3	1	2	3	4	5	6	7	8	9	10	11																					
4	1	3	2	4	5	6	10	7	9		11	8																				
5		2					10				4		1	3	5	6	7	8	9	11												
6		3	2	5	4	6	11	8	9	10											1	7										
8	1	2		5																7		3	4	6	8	9	10	11				
9	1	3		5	6				10	2												7			8	9				4	11	
13		2		9	5																	7		6	8				10	4	11	1
14																															11	
15		2		5	4	6																7			8	9					11	1
16				4	2																	7			8	9		5			11	1
19							1	4	6							5						7			8						11	
20									5													7			8						11	
21	1	3		5	6																	7			8	9					11	
22	1	9			4						3	7										10			11							
24		2		6						4												10			11							
25			5																			7			11							
26			5							4																						
27		3	5		6					4																9						
30		3	5					8																		9				4		1
31								9																								
32		2	5		6																					9		10				1
34		2	5		6																	7										1
36		2	5		6																11	7										1

No further details availabe matches 1-3, 7, 8, 10-13, 17, 18, 20, 21, 23, 25-29, 31, 33, 35, 37-39   Appearances

*Rangers played under title of 'Ibroxonians'. **Sergeant McNeill (8th Lanark Rifle Volunteers)   Goals

Benefit Match. †Evening kick-off. ‡Floodlit exhibition match, courtesy of 'Wells patent light' played at The Exhibition Grounds, Gilmorehill. §Match abandoned 30 minutes due to fog. #Opening fixture at Fir Park, Motherwell. ¥Played Dunoon.

Maxwell played number-3 in Matches 7, 13 & 15. Morgan played number-10 in Matches 15, 16, 19 & 21. Kane played number-3 in Matches 15, 16 & 19, number-4 in Match 21 and number-3 in Match 24. Gossland played number-6 in Match 16. Boyd played number-2 in Matches 19, 21 & 22. McBain played number-9 in Match 19. A.Peacock played number-5 in Match 22, number-9 in Match 23, number-10 in Matches 24, 25 & 27 and number-7 in Match 30. Barclay played number-6 in Match 22 and number-5 in Match 24. Sutherland played number-8 in Match 22 and number-7 in Match 24. McCulloch played number-1 in Matches 23, 24 & 27. W.Peacock played number-8 in Match 24 and number-11 in Matches 25 & 27. Hendry played number-2 in matches 25 & 30 and number-3 in Matches 32, 34 & 36. Izatt played number-8 in Matches 25, 27 & 32 and number-10 in Match 30. Dickie played number-6 in Match 30 and number-4 in Match 32. Mackie played number-11 in Matches 30 & 32 and number-10 in Matches 34, 36 & 37. Robin played number-7 in Match 32. Hall played number-4 in Match 34. Wilkie played number-8 in Matches 34 & 36. Oswald played number-9 in Match 34. Morrison played number-11 in Match 34. Marshall played number-4 in Match 36. Robertson played number-9 in Match 36. Stark played in Match 7. 51 goals untraced.

Scottish FA Cup

#	Date		Opponent	Result	Scorers	Att.
1	Sep	1 (h)	Partick Thistle*	W 4-2	Sloan 2, Wylie, J.R.Gow	3,000
2		22 (a)	Clyde	D 2-2	Aird, Wylie	
R		29 (h)	Clyde	L 0-3		4,000

*Afternoon kick-off

	Nicol J	Gow D	McFarlane A	McIntyre	Hotson R	Muir	Eaglesham	Sloan	McKenzie	Vallance A	Berry	McAllister	Wylie
1		3	2	5	4	6	10	8	9	11		1	7
2	1	3	2	4	5	6	10	8	9				7
R	1	3	2	5	4	6	11		9	10	8		7
Appearances	2	3	3	3	3	3	3	2	3	2	1	1	3
Goals								2	1				2

Aird played number-11 in Round 2 and scored 1 goal.

Glasgow Cup

#	Date		Opponent	Result	Scorers	Att.
1	Sep	15 (h)	United A	W10-0	Wylie 3, J.Gow 2, McKenzie 2, Eaglesham, Untraced 2	
2	Oct	6 (a)	Pollokshields A	W 7-1	McKenzie 4, J.Gow, Wylie 2	
QF		27 (h)	Celtic	L 1-6	Wilson	4,000

	Nicol J	Gow D	McFarlane A	McIntyre	Hotson R	Muir	McKenzie	Vallance A	Gow JR	McFarlane W	Maclachlan	Wylie	Allison	White	Wilson J	Wilson W	Ritchie
1	1	2	3	5	4	6	9	11				7					
2	1	2	3	5	6		9		7		10	11	4			8	
QF				5	4	6	11	2				8			7	9	10
Appearances	3	3	3	3	3	3	1	1	3	1	2	1	3	1	1	1	2
Goals						1	6	3				5			1		

2 goals untraced.

1889-90

Honorary Match Secretary: W.Wilton

League and Friendly Matches

#	Date	Venue	Opponent	Result	Scorers	Att
1	Aug 10	(h)	Maryhill	D 1-1	Untraced	
2	17	(a)	Falkirk	L 0-1		
3	24	(h)	St Mirren	L 0-2		
4	28	(h)	Linthouse	W 2-1	Elspie, Untraced	
5	31	(a)	Clyde	L 2-8	McBain, Allan	5,000
6	Sep 14	(a)	Morton	L 2-3	Untraced	
7	Oct 5	(h)	Celtic	D 1-1	D.Gow	
8	Nov 9	(h)	Morton	D 3-3	Henderson 2, Miller	
9	30	(h)	Partick Thistle	W 5-2	McFarlane 2, Allan 2, Wylie	2,000
10	Dec 7	(h)	Renton	L 2-3	Marshall, Wylie	
11	14	(a)	Cowlairs	L 2-3	Untraced	
12	21	(h)	Clydesdale H	W 2-1	Wylie, McFarlane	
13	28	(h)	Cambuslang	W 3-2	Morton, Robin, Wylie	
14	Jan 1	(a)	Blackburn R	L 0-1		13,000
15	2	(a)	Bolton W	L 0-4		8,000
16	4	(a)	Sunderland	D 1-1	McIntyre	10,000
17	11	(a)	Third Lanark RV	D 3-3	D.Gow 3	
18	18	(a)	St Mirren	W 3-1	D.Gow 2, Marshall	
19	25	(h)	Partick Thistle	W 2-0	D.Gow 2	
20	Feb 1	(h)	Third Lanark RV	L 3-4	H.McCreadie, Henderson, D.Gow	
21	15	(a*)	Everton	L 1-8	Untraced	
22	Mar 1	(h)	Thistle	W 3-1	McFarlane 2, Untraced	
23	8	(h)	Cambuslang	W 5-0	Allan, McFarlane, Untraced 3	
24	15	(a)	Kilmarnock	L 0-2		
25	22	(h)	Battlefield	W 3-0	Henderson, Untraced 2	
26	29	(h)	Queen's Park	D 1-1	Henderson	
27	Apr 5	(a)	Inverness S	W 5-1	Untraced	
28	12	(h)	Third Lanark RV	W 2-0	Allan, Marshall	
29	19	(h)	Everton	L 2-6	John McPherson, A.McCreadie	
30	May 1	(h)	Partick Thistle	L 3-6	Untraced	
31		(h)	Dumbarton	D 1-1	James McPherson	
32			Linthouse	W 4-2	Untraced	
33		(h)	Dumbarton †	L 2-3	Bowie, Hislop	
34	31	(a)	Hearts	L 0-5		
35		(h)	Maryhill	W 4-3	Untraced	

*Played at Anfield. † United Abstainers Tournament.
N.B. No further details available matches 1, 4, 6, 8, 11, 14-16, 19, 21, 27, 30-35.

Player appearances (League/Friendly)

#	McKenzie	Ferguson	Hendry	Marshall	McIntyre	Muir	Wylie	Miller	Berry	Henderson	Wilkie	Reid	Hay	Allan	McBain	Easton	Ralston	Gow D	Mitchell	Robin	McCreadie H	McFarlane A	Gillespie	Meikie	Morton	Low	Nicol	McCorkindale	Hunter	McPherson James	McCreadie A	McIntosh
2	1	2	3	4	5	6	7	8	9	10	11																					
3	9		3	4	5	6	7			10	8	1	2	11																		
4	1									10					9																	
5	1		3	4		6				10			7	11	9	2	5	8														
6		2		4	5		7			10		1	3	11					8	6	9											
7			3	4	5		7			10		1	2	11					8	6	9											
8								8		10																						
9			3	4	5		7			10		1	2	11				6			8	9										
10			3	4	5		7			10			2	11				6			8	9	1									
11	9		3	4	5		7			11		1	2	10				6			8											
12			3	8	5		7			11		1	2					6	10		9		4									
13			3	4	5		7					1	2					6	10	8	9				11							
17			3		5					10		1	2	11				7	6	4		9				8						
18			3	4	5					10			2	11				9	6		8			1								
19																		9														
20			3	4	5		7			10			2	11				9	6		8						1					
21			3	4	5		7			10									11			9				1	2	6				
22	9		3	4	5		7					1	2	11				6		8	10											
23	1		3	7	5					10			2	11				6	4	8		9										
24	1		3	7	5					10			2	11				6	4	8		9										
25			3	4	5		7			10		1	2	11				6			8	9										
26	1		3	4	5					11			2	10				6			8	9									6	7
27	10		3		5			9		8		1	2					7	6	11											4	
28			3	9	5		7	8				1	2	11				6	10												4	
29			3	7	5			8				1	2	11	9			6			8										4	
31																														6		
Appearances	10	1	22	20	22	3	15	2	1	21	4	13	19	18	3	1	1	9	15	9	15	10	1	1	1	2	2	1	1	2	4	1
Goals				3	1		4	1		5				5	1			9		1	1	6			1					1	1	

John McPherson played number-10 in Match 29. Elspie played and scored in Match 4. Bowie and Hislop both played and scored in Match 33. 29 goals untraced.

Scottish FA Cup

#	Date	Venue	Opponent	Result	Scorers	Att
1	Sep 7	(h)	United A	W 6-2	Untraced	
2	28	(a)	Kelvinside A	W 13-0	Allan 2, Wylie 2, Henderson 2, McIntyre, Robin, Mitchell, Untraced 4	2,000
3	Oct 19	(h)	Vale of Leven	D 0-0		8,500
R	26	(a)	Vale of Leven	L 2-3	Wylie, D.Gow	4,500

No further details available Round One.

#	Hendry	Marshall	McIntyre	Muir	Wylie	Miller	Henderson	Wilkie	Reid	Hay	Allan	McBain	Gow D	Mitchell	Robin
1		4		6		10	7	11	1	3	8	5	2		9
2	3	4	5		7			11	1	2	10		8	6	9
3	3	4	5		11	7			1	2	10		8	6	9
R	3	4	5		11	7			1	2	10		8	6	9
Appearances	3	4	3	3	3	1		2	1	4	4	4	1	4	3 / 4
Goals		1			3			2						2	1 1 1

10 goals untraced.

Glasgow Cup

#	Date	Venue	Opponent	Result	Scorers	Att
1	Sep 21	(a)	Pollokshaws	W 5-1	D.Gow, Robin, Wylie, Untraced 2	
2	Oct 12	(a)	Northern	W 6-3	D.Gow 3, Robin, Wylie, Allan	6,000
QF	Nov 2	(a)	Third Lanark RV	D 1-1	Allan	7,000
R	16	(h)	Third Lanark RV	W 2-0	Henderson, Miller	7,000
SF	23	(h)	Queen's Park	L 0-2		10,000

#	Hendry	Marshall	McIntyre	Wylie	Miller	Henderson	Wilkie	Reid	Hay	Allan	Gow D	Mitchell	Robin	McCreadie H	McFarlane A
1	3	4	5	7		10			2	11	8	6	9		1
2	3	4	5	7		10		1	2	11	8	6	9		
QF	3	4	5	7		11		1	2	10	8	6	9		
R		4	5	7	8	11		1	2	10	6			9 3	
SF	3	4	5			11	8	1	2	10			9 6		
Appearances	4	5	5	5	1	5	1	4	5	5	3	4	3	2 2	1
Goals				2	1	1					4		2		

2 goals untraced.

Sir William Cunningham Cup

#	Venue	Opponent	Result
SF	(n)	Clyde	W 9-1
F	(h)	Cowlairs	L 0-4

Semi-final played at Irvine
No further details available

Rangers and Clydesdale Harriers Sports Cup

#	Date	Venue	Opponent	Result	Scorers	Att
SF		(h)	Third Lanark RV	W 4-0	Henderson, Untraced 3	8,000
F	Aug 6	(h)	Celtic	L 0-2		4,000

No further details available

#	McKenzie	Marshall	McIntyre	Muir	Wylie	Miller	Henderson	Wilkie	Allan	Gow D	Low
SF	1		4				10	11			8
F	1	3	4	5	6	7	10	11	2		8
Appearances	2	1	2	1	1	1	2	2	1		2
Goals							1				

J.Hamilton played number-9 in Final.

1890-91

Honorary Match Secretary: W.Wilton

Scottish League

#	Date	V	Opponent	Result	Scorers	Att
1	Aug 16	(h)	Hearts	W 5-2	Kerr 2, H.McCreadie, J.McPherson, Adams (og)	4,000
2	23	(a)	Cambuslang	W 6-2	J.McPherson 4, D.Gow, Marshall	
3	Sep 13	(a)	Dumbarton	L 1-5	Hislop	4,000
4	Oct 4	(h)	St Mirren	W 8-2	J.McPherson 5, Kerr 3	
5	18	(h)	Cowlairs	D 1-1	Hislop	
6	Jan 17	(a)	Vale of Leven	W 3-1	J.McPherson, Hislop, Henderson	
7	24	(a)	Hearts	W 1-0	Kerr	5,000
8	Feb 7	(a)	Abercorn	D 1-1	Marshall	
9	21	(h)	Cambuslang	W 2-1	H.McCreadie, J.McPherson	2,000
10	28	(a)	St Mirren	W 7-3	H.McCreadie 2, Henderson 2, Kerr, J.McPherson, Sloan (og)	
11	Mar 7	(a)	Third Lanark RV	W 4-0	J.McPherson, Untraced 3	
12	14	(a)	Abercorn	W 2-0	H.McCreadie, Henderson	5,000
13	21	(a)	Celtic	D 2-2	A.McCreadie, Hislop	12,000
14	28	(a)	Cowlairs	W 2-0	Henderson, Hislop	
15	Apr 4	(h)	Vale of Leven	W 4-0	Hislop 2, Untraced 2	2,000
16	25	(h)	Dumbarton	W 4-2	A.McCreadie, Hislop, Kerr, J.McPherson	12,000
17	May 2	(h)	Celtic	L 1-2	Henderson	10,000
18	9	(h)	Third Lanark RV	W 4-1	McKenzie 3, Hislop	6,000

FINAL LEAGUE POSITION: 1st (Jointly with Dumbarton)

Player line-ups (shirt numbers by column):

#	Reid	Gow D	Muir	McCreadie A	Marshall	Mitchell	Wylie	Kerr	McCreadie H	McPherson John	Hislop	McIntyre	McKenzie	Henderson	Hodge	White	Wilson
1	1	2	3	4	5	6	7	8	9	10	11						
2	1	2	3	4	5	6	7	8	9	10	11						
3	1	2	3	4	8	6		7	9	10	11	5					
4	1	2	3		4	6	7	9	8	10	11	5					
5		2	3		4	6	7	9	8	10	11	5	1				
6	1	3		2	4	6		9	8	10	7	5		11			
7	1	3		4	2	6		9	11	10	7	5		8			
8		3		4	2	6		9	11	10	7	5	1	8			
9	1		2	5	4	6		9	8	10	11			7	3		
10	1		2	4		6		9	11	10	7	5		8	3		
11	1	2		5	4	6		9	11	10	7			8	3		
12	1	2		5	4	6		9	11	10	7			8	3		
13	1	2		5	4	6		9	11	10	7			8	3		
14	1	2		5	4	6		9	11	10	7			8	3		
15	1	2		4		6		9		10	7	5		8	3	11	
16	1	2		5	4	6		9		10	7			8	3	11	
17	1	2		5	4	6		9		10	7			11	3		8
18	1	2	3		4	6		9		10	11	5	7	8			
Appearances	16	16	8	15	16	18	4	18	14	18	18	9	3	13	9	2	1
Goals		1		2	2			8	5	15	9		3	6			

5 goals untraced. 2 own-goals.

Championship Play-off

Date	V	Opponent	Result	Scorers	Att
May 21	(n*)	Dumbarton	D 2-2	Hislop, H.McCreadie	10,000

*Played at First Cathkin Park, Glagow. Both clubs declared joint champions.

	Reid	Gow D	McCreadie A	Marshall	Mitchell	Kerr	McCreadie H	McPherson John	Hislop	Henderson	Hodge
Line-up	1	2	5	4	6	9	8	10	11	7	3
Appearances	1	1	1	1	1	1	1	1	1	1	1
Goals							1		1		

Scottish FA Cup

Date	V	Opponent	Result	Att
Sep 6	(a)	Celtic	L 0-1	16,000

	Reid	Gow D	Muir	McCreadie A	Marshall	Mitchell	Wylie	Kerr	McCreadie H	McPherson John	Hislop
Line-up	1	2	3	4	5	6	7	8	9	10	11
Appearances	1	1	1	1	1	1	1	1	1	1	1

Glasgow Cup

#	Date	V	Opponent	Result	Scorers	Att
1	Sep 20	(h)	Carrington	W 12-2	J.McPherson 3, Hislop 2, Kerr 2, Allan 2, D.Gow, Marshall, Untraced	
QF	Nov 1	(a)	Third Lanark RVD	3-3	Wylie 2, J.McPherson	15,000
R	15	(h)	Third Lanark RVD	1-1	J.McPherson	15,000
2R	22	(a)	Third Lanark RVD	3-3	Kerr, McPherson, Wylie	6,000
3R	Dec 6	(h)	Third Lanark RVL	1-2	Untraced	10,000

Rangers received Bye in Round Two.

#	Reid	Gow D	Muir	Marshall	Mitchell	Wylie	Kerr	McCreadie H	McPherson John	Hislop	McIntyre	Henderson	Allan	Hay	Sillars
1	1	2	3	4	6		9	8	10	11	5		7		
QF	1	2		4	6	7	9	8	10	11	5				3
R	1	2		4	6	7	9	8	10	11	5				3
2R	1	2		4	6	7	9	8	10	11	5				3
3R	1	2		4	6		9	8	10	7	5	11		3	
Appearances	5	5	1	5	5	3	5	5	5	5	5	1	1	1	3
Goals		1		1		3	3		6	2			2		

2 goals untraced.

Rangers Sports Trophy

	Date	V	Opponent	Result	Scorers
SF	Aug 2	(h)	Linthouse	W 3-2	H.McCreadie, Untraced 2
F	9	(h)	Dumbarton	W 3-1	J.McPherson 2, Hislop

	Reid	Gow D	McCreadie A	Marshall	Mitchell	Wylie	Kerr	McCreadie H	McPherson John	Hislop	Sillars
SF	1	2	4	5	6	7	8	9	10	11	3
F	1	2	4	5	6	7	8	9	10	11	3
Appearances	2	2	2	2	2	2	2	2	2	2	2
Goals								1	2	1	

2 goals untraced.

Other matches

#	Date	V	Opponent	Result	Scorers	Att
1	Aug 30	(h)	Renton*	W 4-1	Kerr, Hislop, J.McPherson, D.Gow	7,000
2	Sep 8	(a)	Uddingston	D 1-1	Untraced	
3	27	(h)	Thistle	D 2-2	Untraced	
4	Oct 2	(n)	Sunderland A†	W 5-1	Kerr 3, J.McPherson 2	6,000
5	11	(h)	Methlan P	W 4-2	Wylie, H.McCreadie, Untraced 2	1,000
6	25	(h)	Partick Thistle	L 2-3	Kerr, Hislop	2,000
7	Nov 8	(a)	Kilmarnock	W 3-1	H.McCreadie, J.McPherson, Wylie	
8	29	(h)	Third Lanark§	L 1-3	Untraced	6,000
9	Dec 13	(a)	Partick Thistle	D 1-1	D.Gow	
10	20	(a)	Clyde	D 2-2	H.McCreadie, Untraced	
11	Jan 1	(a)	Newcastle U	W 3-0	D.Gow, Untraced 2	4,000
12	2	(a)	Sunderand	L 1-3	Untraced	10,000
13	3	(a)	Middlesbrough	W 1-0	Hislop	4,000
14	10	(h)	Nottingham F	L 1-2	D.McPherson	
15	Feb 14	(a)	Cowlairs	W 4-2	Untraced	
16	Apr 11	(a)	Nottingham F	L 0-3		2,000
17	13	(a)	Sheffield W	D 3-3	Hislop 2, J.McPherson	1,000
18	May 16	(n)	Dumbarton#	L 0-1		
19	25	(h)	Govan & Ibrox	W 4-2	Untraced	
20	26	(a)	Thistle			
21	28	(a)	Glasgow Warehousemen			
22	30	(a)	5th King's RV	W 4-2	Untraced	

Appearances (by column: Reid, Gow D, Muir, McCreadie A, Marshall, Mitchell, Wylie, Kerr, McCreadie H, McPherson John, Hislop, McIntyre, McKenzie, Henderson, Hodge, …):
12, 17, 10, 9, 14, 16, 7, 18, 14, 19, 18, 15, 6, 11, 5, … 1, 1, … 1, … 1, 1, 1, 1, 3, 1, 1, 1, 1, 1, 1

Goals: Gow D 3, Wylie 2, Kerr 5, McCreadie H 3, McPherson John 5, Hislop 5, McPherson D 1

N.B. No further details available matches 2, 3, 8, 12, 15, 19, 21. *League fixture declared invalid due to expulsion of Renton. †Edinburgh International Exhibition Fixture.

\# League Charity Cup Match played at first Celtic Park, Glasgow.

§Glasgow Cup-tie declared a friendly due to frost.

Morrison played number-11 in Match 22. 22 goals untraced.

1891-92

Honorary Match Secretary: W.Wilton

Scottish League

Player columns (left to right): Haddow, Hay, Hodge, Marshall, McIntyre, Mitchell, McCreadie H, Henderson, Kerr, Muir, McPherson J, Scott, Cullen, McCreadie A, McKenzie, Tait, Fraser, Fleming, Blyth, Steel, Glass, Dunbar, McGowan, McBain, Law J, Barker, Watt, Drummond, Allan, McPherson D, Turnbull, Deans

#	Date	V	Opponent	Result	Scorers	Att	Had	Hay	Hod	Mar	McI	Mit	McCH	Hen	Ker	Mui	McPJ	Sco	Cul	McCA	McK	Tai	Fra	Fle	Bly	Ste	Gla	Dun	McG	McB	LawJ	Bar	Wat	Dru	All	McPD	Tur	Dea
1	Aug 15 (a)		Renton	W 4-1	Muir 2, Kerr, J.McPherson		1	2	3	4	5	6	7	8	9	10	11																					
2	22 (a)		Celtic	L 0-3		12,000	1		2	4	5	6		8	9		11	3	7	10																	
3	29 (h)		Third Lanark RV	L 2-3	McKenzie 2	5,106	1		2	4		6	11		8		10	3	7	5	9																
4	Sep 5 (h)		Dumbarton	L 1-3	Kerr	5,000	1		2	4		6	11	8	9		10	3	7	5																	
5	12 (a)		Vale of Leven	W 6-1	Untraced		1		2	4		6		8	9		10			5		3	7	11													
6	26 (h)		Abercorn	W 6-2	Fraser 3, J.McPherson 2, Kerr	3,000	1		2	4			11		9	6	10			5		3	8		7													
7	Oct 3 (a)		Leith A	L 1-3	Kerr		1		2			6	11		9	4	10	5				3	7		8													
8	10 (a)		Third Lanark RVD	2-2	H.McCreadie, Fraser	5,000	1		2	4		6	11		10				7	5		3	8		9													
9	17 (h)		Cambuslang	W 2-1	Marshall, Blyth	3,000	1		3	4					8		10	6	11	5		2			7	9												
10	24 (h)		Clyde	L 1-5	Kerr	5,000	1		2	4				8	9				6	5		3			7	10	11											
11	Nov 21 (h)		Hearts	L 0-1		3,000	1		2	4		6	11	10	8		9	5					7				3											
12	Dec 5 (a)		St Mirren	W 4-3	J.McPherson 2, Kerr, McGowan		1		2	4		6	11	8	7		10			5							3		9									
13	Feb 13 (a)		Vale of Lven	W 7-0	Law 3, McBain, Barker, Kerr, A.McCreadie	2,000	1			4		6	10		8				2	5							3			7	9	11						
14	27 (a)		Cambuslang	W 6-0	Barker, J.McPherson, Untraced 4		1		2	4		6			8		10			5							3			9	11	7						
15	Mar 19 (h)		Renton	W 5-2	Barker 3, A.McCreadie, J.McPherson	6,000	1		2			6	8		7		10	4		5							3			9	11							
16	26 (h)		Abercorn	W 1-0	Law		1		2	4		6	8		10					5							3			9	11	7					
17	Apr 16 (a)		Leith A	W 3-2	McBain, J.McPherson, A.McCreadie		1			4		6	8		7		10			5							3	9		11		2					
18	23 (a)		Hearts	L 2-3	Scott, J.McPherson	5,000	1			4		6	8		7		10	9		5							3			11		2					
19	May 4 (a)		Dumbarton	L 0-6		1,000	1			4					7		10			5							3		8	9	11		2	6				
20	7 (h)		Celtic	D 1-1	H.McCreadie		1			4		6	11		9	3	10	2		5							3								7	8		
21	10 (h)		St Mirren	L 2-3	A.McCreadie, Allan		1			4			11			6	10	2		5	9						3								7	8		
22	21 (a)		Clyde	W 3-1	J.McPherson, A.McCreadie (pen), Bowie (og)		1			4		6	8		7		10			5							3				11					9		

FINAL LEAGUE POSITION: 5th
No further details available Match 5.

| | | | | | | Appearances | 22 | 1 | 15 | 20 | 2 | 17 | 16 | 7 | 21 | 5 | 18 | 12 | 5 | 19 | 2 | 6 | 4 | 1 | 5 | 3 | 1 | 11 | 1 | 3 | 5 | 8 | 2 | 4 | 3 | 2 | 1 | |
| | | | | | | Goals | | | 1 | | | 2 | | 7 | 2 | 10 | 1 | | 5 | 2 | | 4 | 1 | | | | | | 1 | 2 | 4 | 5 | | | | 1 | | |

10 goals untraced. 1 own-goal

Scottish FA Cup

#	Date	V	Opponent	Result	Scorers	Att	Had	Hay	Hod	Mar	McI	Mit	McCH	Hen	Ker	Mui	McPJ	Sco	Cul	McCA	McK	Tai	Fra	Fle	Bly	Ste	Gla	Dun	McG	McB	LawJ	Bar	Wat	Dru	All	McPD	Tur	Dea
1	Nov 28 (h)		St Bernard's	W 5-1	Kerr, Blyth, J.McPherson, McBain, Untraced	3,000	1		2	4		6			11		10			5			7		3	9	8											
2	Dec 19 (h)		Kilmarnock	D 0-0		2,000	1		2	4		6	11	8			10			5					3	9	7											
R	26 (a)		Kilmarnock	D 1-1	Kerr	3,000	1		2	4		6	11	8	7		10	5							3	9												
2R	Jan 23 (n*)		Kilmarnock	W 3-2	Henderson 2, J.McPherson	5,000	1		2	4		6	11	8	7		10			5					3		9											
QF	30 (h)		Annbank	W 2-0	Watt, H.McCreadie	5,000	1		2	4		6	11	8	9		10			5					3								7					
SF	Feb 6 (a)		Celtic	L 3-5	Law, Henderson, Kerr	12,000	1		2	4		6		8	11		10			5					3		9					7						

*Played at Westmarch Park, Paisley

| | | | | | | Appearances | 6 | | 6 | 6 | | 6 | 4 | 5 | 5 | | 6 | 1 | | 5 | | | 1 | | 6 | 2 | 3 | 2 | | | | 2 | | | | | | |
| | | | | | | Goals | | | | | | | 1 | 3 | 3 | | 2 | | | 1 | | | | | | 1 | 1 | 1 | | | | | | | | | | |

1 goal untraced

Glasgow Cup

#	Date	V	Opponent	Result	Scorers	Att	Had	Hay	Hod	Mar	McI	Mit	McCH	Hen	Ker	Mui	McPJ	Sco	Cul	McCA	McK	Tai	Fra	Fle	Bly	Ste	Gla	Dun	McG	McB	LawJ	Bar	Wat	Dru	All	McPD	Tur	Dea
1	Sep 19 (h)		Third Lanark RV	W 2-0	Fraser, Marshall	10,000	1		2	4		6	11		9		10			5			3	7	8													
QF	Nov 7 (h)		Queen's Park	L 0-3		10,000	1		2	4				10	11	9		8	6	5			7		3													

Rangers received a Bye in Round Two

| | | | | | | Appearances | 2 | | 2 | 2 | | 1 | 2 | 1 | 2 | 1 | 1 | 2 | 1 | 2 | | | 2 | 1 | 2 | | | | | | | | | | | | | |
| | | | | | | Goals | | | | 1 | | | | | | | | | | | | | 1 | | | | | | | | | | | | | | | |

Glasgow Merchants' Charity Cup

#	Date	V	Opponent	Result	Scorers	Att	Had	Hay	Hod	Mar	McI	Mit	McCH	Hen	Ker	Mui	McPJ	Sco	Cul	McCA	McK	Tai	Fra	Fle	Bly	Ste	Gla	Dun	McG	McB	LawJ	Bar	Wat	Dru	All	McPD	Tur	Dea
SF	May 14 (a)		Queen's Park	D 3-3	H.McCreadie, A.McCreadie, Deans	8,000	1			4		6	8		9		11	2		5					3							7						10
R	23 (h)		Queen's Park	D 3-3	Kerr, D.Gow, J.McPherson	5,000	1			4		6			9		10			5					3							11	7					
2R	28 (n*)		Queen's Park	W 7-1	Turnbull 2, McInnes 2, Watts, J.McPherson, Mitchell	5,000				4		6			9		11			5	1				3								7				10	
F	Jun 1 (a)		Celtic	L 0-2		8,000	1			4					7	6	11			5					3												10	

*Played at First Celtic Park.

| | | | | | | Appearances | 3 | | | 4 | | 3 | 1 | | 4 | 1 | 4 | 1 | | 4 | 1 | | | | 4 | | | | | | | 1 | 3 | | | | 2 | 1 |
| | | | | | | Goals | | | | 1 | | 1 | 1 | | | | 2 | | | 1 | | | | | | | | | | | | | 1 | | | | 2 | 1 |

D.Gow played number-2 in Matches 2, 3, 4 and scored 1 goal; McInnes played number-8 in Matches 2, 3, 4 and scored 2 goals; Gibb played number-9 in Match 4.

Other matches

#	Date	V	Opponent	Result	Scorers	Att	Had	Hay	Hod	Mar	McI	Mit	McCH	Hen	Ker	Mui	McPJ	Sco	Cul	McCA	McK	Tai	Fra	Fle	Bly	Ste	Gla	Dun	McG	McB	LawJ	Bar	Wat	Dru	All	McPD	Tur	Dea
1	Aug 8 (a)		Caledonian	W 9-0																																		
2	Oct 1 (h)		Everton	L 1-4	McBain	10,000			2	4		6	11		9		10			5		3	7							8								
3	Nov 14 (h)		Battlefield	D 2-2	Henderson, Untraced		1				5			10	9	4	8	6					7		3													
4	Dec 7 (h)		Renton*	D 2-2	Kerr, J.McPherson					4		6	11		9		10	2		5	1		7		3	8												
5	Jan 2 (h)		Partick Thistle	W 3-1	Law, Untraced 2	2,000	1		2	4				8	11	6	10						7		3					9								
6	4 (a)		Celtic	L 0-2																																	
7	Apr 2 (a)		Everton	W 2-0	Burke, Untraced					4			8			6	10			5	1				3					9		7	2					
8	9 (a)		Dumbarton†	L 1-4	J.McPherson		1			4			8				10	6		5					3					9	11	7	2					
9	30 (a)		Woolwich A	W 3-2	Kerr, Barker, McBain	6,000				4		6		8	9		10			5	1				3					7	11		2					

No further details available matches 1 & 6. *League fixture abandoned 75 minutes due to heavy snow. †League fixture declared invalid due to non-appearance of Referee.

| | | | | | | Appearances | 3 | | 2 | 6 | 1 | 3 | 4 | 3 | 5 | 3 | 7 | 3 | | 5 | 3 | 1 | 4 | | 6 | | | | | 3 | 3 | 2 | 2 | 3 | | | | |
| | | | | | | Goals | | | | 1 | | | 2 | | 2 | | | | | | | | 1 | | | | | | | 2 | 1 | 1 | | | | | | |

D.Reid played number-1 in Match 2; Neil played number-2 in Match 3; Ross played number-11 in Match 3; Roberts played number-5 in Match 5; Burke played number-11 in Match 7 and scored 1 goal. 5 goals untraced.

1892-93

Honorary Match Secretary: W.Wilton

Scottish League

No	Date	Venue/Opponent	Result	Scorers	Att	Haddow	Scott	Drummond	Marshall	McCreadie A	Mitchell	McPherson D	McInnes	Bruce	McPherson J	Barker	Turnbull	Gow	McCreadie H	Kerr N	Martin	Clark	Freebairn	Davie	Muir	Dick	Steel	Smith N	Reid R	Hay	McKenzie	Hyslop	McPherson D	Wild	Gray
1	Aug 20 (a)	Abercorn	W 4-0	Bruce 2, J.McPherson, Barker		1	2	3	4	5	6	7	8	9	10	11																			
2	22 (h)	Leith A	W 3-2	McInnes 2, D.McPherson	5,000	1	2	3	4	5	6	7	8	9	11		10																		
3	Sep 3 (h)	Dumbarton	W 3-2	Bruce 2, Barker	6,000	1	2	3	4	5	6	7	8	9	10	11																			
4	10 (a)	Third Lanark RV	W 4-2	A.McCreadie (pen), Bruce, H.McCreadie, Untraced	8,000	1		3	4	5	6		8	7	9	11		2	10																
5	24 (h)	Celtic	D 2-2	Turnbull, H.McCreadie	14,000	1		3	4	5	6		8		11		7	2	10	9															
6	Oct 1 (a)	Leith A	W 2-1	H.McCreadie 2	5,000	1		3	4	5	6		8		10			2	11	7	9														
7	15 (h)	St Mirren	D 0-0		4,000	1		3	4	5	6		8		10			2	11	7	9														
8	22 (h)	Clyde	W 4-1	J.McPherson 2, Kerr, Mitchell		1	5	3	4		6		8		10	11		2	7	9															
9	Nov 5 (a)	Renton	D 2-2	Clark, H.McCreadie		1		3	4	5	6				10	11		2	7	8		9													
10	Feb 4 (h)	Abercorn	W 4-3	H.McCreadie 2, J.McPherson, Kerr (pen)		1	5	3	4		6				10	11			8	9			2	7											
11	Mar 11 (a)	Clyde	W 3-0	H.McCreadie, Kerr, J.McPherson		1		3	4	5	6				10	11			7	9				8	2										
12	18 (h)	Hearts	W 2-1	Kerr, Steel		1		3	2	11		4			8				6	7							5	9	10						
13	25 (a)	St Mirren	D 2-2	J.McPherson, Dick		1	6	3	4	5					10	11			8	9				7		2									
14	Apr 1 (h)	Third Lanark RV	W 2-1	H.McCreadie, Barker	3,000	1	6	3	4	5					10	11			8				2	7					9						
15	15 (h)	Renton	W 2-0	Drummond, Scott		1	5	3	4		6				10			2	8	9				7							11				
16	22 (a)	Dumbarton	L 0-3			1		3	4	5	6				10	11		2	8	9				7											
17	29 (a)	Celtic	L 0-3			1		3	4	5	6				10	11		2	8	9				7											
18	May 6 (h)	Hearts	W 2-1	J.McPherson, H.McCreadie		1		3	4	5	6				10	11		2	8	7									9						
				Appearances		18	10	17	18	14	16	8	4	4	18	11	2	10	15	13	2	1	2	6	1	2	2	2	2						
				Goals			1	1		1	1	1	2	5	7	3	1		10	4		1				1	1								

FINAL LEAGUE POSITION: 2nd

1 goal untraced

Scottish FA Cup

No	Date	Venue/Opponent	Result	Scorers	Att	Haddow	Drummond	Marshall	McCreadie A	Mitchell	McPherson D	Bruce	McPherson J	Barker	Gow	McCreadie H	Kerr N	Clark
1	Nov 26 (h)	Annbank	W 7-0	N.Kerr 4, H.McCreadie 2, Clark		1	3	4	5	6			10	11	2	7	8	9
2	Jan 21 (a)	Dumbarton	W 1-0	H.McCreadie		1	3	4	5	6	9		10	11	2	8	7	
QF	28 (a)	St Bernard	L 2-3	Barker, Untraced	8,000	1	3	4	5	6			10	11	2	8	7	9
				Appearances		3	3	3	3	3	1		3	3	3	3	3	2
				Goals										1		3	4	1

1 goal untraced

Glasgow Cup

No	Date	Venue/Opponent	Result	Scorers	Att	Haddow	Scott	Drummond	Marshall	McCreadie A	Mitchell	McPherson D	McInnes	McPherson J	Barker	Gow	McCreadie H	Kerr N	Clark	Reid R
1	Sep 7 (h)	Northern	W 6-2	H.McCreadie 3, J.McPherson, D.McPherson, A.McCreadie	1,000	1	2		4	5	6	7	8	10		3	11	9		
2	Oct 8 (h)	Linthouse	W 3-2	D.McPherson, J.McPherson, Untraced		1		3	4	5	6		8	10	9	2	11	7		
QF	29 (a)	Queen's Park	W 4-2	H.McCreadie 2, J.McPherson 2	12,000	1		3	4	5	6		8	10	11	2	7	8	9	
SF	Dec 19 (a)	Glasgow T	W 3-2	H.McCreadie 3		1		3	4	5	6			10	11	2	8	7	9	
F	Feb 18 (n)	Celtic	W 3-1	Barker, Kerr, J.McPherson	10,000	1		3	4	5	6			10	11		8	9	7	2
				Appearances		5	1	4	5	5	5	2	1	5	4	4	5	5	2	1
				Goals						1		2		5	1		8	1		

Final played at First Cathkin Park.

1 goal untraced

Glasgow Merchants' Charity Cup

No	Date	Venue/Opponent	Result	Scorers	Att	Haddow	Scott	Drummond	McCreadie A	Mitchell	McInnes	McPherson J	Barker	Gow	McCreadie H	Kerr N	Davie
SF	May 20 (h)	Third Lanark RV	W 3-2	J.McPheson, Davie, Kerr	4,000	1	4	3	5	6	8	10	11	2		9	7
F	27 (a)	Celtic	L 0-5			1	4	3	5	6	8	10		2	11	9	7
				Appearances		2	2	2	2	2	2	2	1	2	1	2	2
				Goals								1				1	1

1 goal untraced

Other matches

No	Date	Venue/Opponent	Result	Scorers	Att	Haddow	Scott	Drummond	Marshall	McCreadie A	Mitchell	McPherson D	McInnes	Bruce	McPherson J	Barker	Gow	McCreadie H	Kerr N	Clark	Davie	Muir	Dick	Hay	McKenzie	Wild	Gray
1	Aug 13 (h)	Linthouse	W 5-2	J.McPherson, Barker, Marshall, Cameron (og), Untraced	1,000	1	2	3	4	5	6	7	8	9	10	11											
2	Sep 17 (a)	Queen's Park	L 1-3	Untraced	13,500		5	3	4		6	7	8	9	11		2	10						1			
3	Nov 12 (h)	Abercorn*	W 3-0	Cuthertson (og), Untraced 2		1	6	3	4				8		10	11	2			9					7		
4	19 (h)	Glasgow T	W 2-1	Clark, Barker		1		3	4	5	6		8		10	11	2			9	7						
5	Dec 3 (a)	Glasgow T	L 2-3	H.McCreadie, Clark		1		3	4	5					10	11	2	7	8	9		6					
6	Jan 2 (a)	Middlesbrough	D 6-6	J.McPherson 3, Barker, Kerr, Untraced	1,000																						
7	3 (a)	Newcastle U	L 0-4		3,000																						
8	Mar 4 (a)	Morton	W 4-2	Barker, Untraced 3																							
9	Apr 3 (h)	Celtic	W 3-1	Barker 2, J.McPherson	7,000	1	5	3	4				8		10	11					7			2		6	9
10	26 (h)	Sunderland	L 2-6	Kerr, A.McCreadie	5,000	1		3	4	5	6		8		10	11	2		9		7						
11	May 13 (a)	Linthouse	D 3-3	Kerr, Davie, Untraced		1			4	5					10	11	6	8			7	3	2				9
				Appearances		7	4	7	8	6	4	6	2	2	8	7	5	3	4	3	3	2	1	1	1	1	1
				Goals				1							5	6		1	3	2	1						

No further details available matches 2, 6-8.

*League fixture abandoned due to bad light.

9 goals untraced. 2 own-goals

1893-94

Honorary Match Secretary: W.Wilton

Scottish League

No	Date	Opponent	Result	Scorers	Att
1	Aug 12 (a)	Dundee	D 3-3	Gray 3	6,000
2	19 (h)	Renton	W 5-3	Gray 2, Kerr, Barker, Steel	5,000
3	26 (a)	St Bernard's	D 0-0		5,000
4	Sep 2 (h)	Celtic	W 5-0	Barker 3, McPherson, Gray	18,000
5	9 (a)	Renton	W 2-1	Steel, Barker	
6	23 (h)	Dumbarton	W 4-0	H.McCreadie 2, Marshall, Untraced	
7	30 (a)	Leith A	D 2-2	Steel 2	4,000
8	Oct 14 (a)	Hearts	L 2-4	Blyth, Gray	8,000
9	Nov 4 (h)	Leith A	W 1-0	McPherson	3,000
10	11 (a)	Third Lanark RV	W 2-1	McPherson, Boyd	
11	Dec 23 (h)	Third Lanark RV	L 0-3		5,000
12	Jan 20 (a)	Dumbarton	L 0-2		
13	27 (a)	St Mirren	D 2-2	Boyd, Crawford (og)	
14	Feb 24 (a)	Celtic	L 2-3	Gray, Barker	10,000
15	Mar 10 (h)	Dundee	W 7-2	Boyd 2, Steel 2, Barker, A.McCreadie, Mitchell	3,000
16	Apr 14 (h)	Hearts	L 1-2	Boyd	4,000
17	21 (h)	St Mirren	W 5-0	Steel, Untraced 4	4,000
18	May 2 (h)	St Bernard's	L 1-2	Gray	1,000

FINAL LEAGUE POSITION: 4th

Appearances: Haddow 15, Smith N 17, Drummond J 17, Marshall 18, McCreadie A 18, Mitchell 15, Steel 14, McCreadie H 9, Gray 18, McPherson J 15, Barker 13, Kerr N 6, McKenzie A 1, Blyth 5, Boyd 10, Muir 4, Drummond R 1, Johnstone 1, Montgomery 1

Goals: Marshall 1, McCreadie A 1, Mitchell 1, Steel 7, McCreadie H 2, Gray 9, McPherson J 3, Barker 7, Kerr N 1, Blyth 1, Boyd 5

5 goals untraced. 1 own-goal

Scottish FA Cup

No	Date	Opponent	Result	Scorers	Att
1	Nov 25 (h)	Cowlairs	W 8-0	Boyd 3, McPherson 2, H.McCreadie 2, Kerr	5,000
2	Dec 16 (h)	Leith A	W 2-0	McPherson, Blyth	2,500
QF	Jan 13 (a)	Clyde	W 5-0	Steel 4, McPherson	10,000
SF	Feb 3 (h)	Queen's Park	D 1-1	Boyd	15,000
R	10 (a)	Queen's Park	W 3-1	Smith, McPherson, Steel	16,000
F	17 (n)	Celtic	W 3-1	H.McCreadie, Barker, McPherson	17,000

Final played at second Hampden Park.

Appearances: Haddow 6, Smith N 6, Drummond J 6, Marshall 6, McCreadie A 6, Mitchell 5, Steel 5, McCreadie H 5, Gray 5, McPherson J 6, Barker 3, Kerr N 1, Blyth 1, Boyd 4, Montgomery 1

Goals: Smith N 1, Steel 5, McCreadie H 3, McPherson J 6, Barker 1, Kerr N 1, Blyth 1, Boyd 4

Glasgow Cup

No	Date	Opponent	Result	Scorers	Att
QF	Oct 28 (h)	Pollokshaws	W 11-1	Untraced	1,000
SF	Nov 18 (h)	Celtic	W 1-0	McPherson	14,000
F	Dec 9 (n*)	Cowlairs	W 1-0	McPherson	

Round One - Rangers Walkover, Whitefield scratched.
Round Two - Rangers received Bye. * Played at first Cathkin Park.

Appearances: Haddow 3, Smith N 3, Drummond J 3, Marshall 3, McCreadie A 3, Mitchell 3, Steel 2, McCreadie H 2, Gray 3, McPherson J 3, Barker 2, Boyd 3

Goals: McPherson J 2

11 goals untraced

Glasgow Merchants' Charity Cup

No	Date	Opponent	Result	Scorers	Att
SF	Apr 28 (n)	Queen's Park	L 0-2		15,000

Played at first Cathkin Park.

Appearances: Haddow 1, Smith N 1, Drummond J 1, Marshall 1, Steel 1, Gray 1, McPherson J 1, Barker 1, Boyd 1, Muir 1

Goals: —

Other matches

No	Date	Opponent	Result	Scorers	Att
1	Aug 5 (a)	Abercorn	L 1-2	Mitchell	
2	9 (h)	Linthouse	W 4-0	McPherson 3, Mathieson (og)	
3	15 (a)	King's Park	W 6-1	Blyth, McPherson, Untraced 4	
4	Sep 16 (a)	Third Lanark RV	L 2-3	Untraced	5,000
5	28 (h)	Everton	W 2-1	Barker, A.McCreadie	7,000
6	Oct 7 (h)	Queen's Park	W 3-0	Gray 2, Barker	12,000
7	21 (a)	Linthouse	W 4-2	Marshall, Blyth, Mitchell, Gray	2,000
8	Dec 2 (a)	St Mirren*	L 0-3		
9	25 (a)	Everton	W 2-1	Boyd, Steel	14,000
10	30 (h)	Renton	W 3-0	Kerr, Blyth, Steel	1,000
11	Jan 1 (a)	Celtic	W 3-2	Gray 2, McPherson	15,000
12	2 (h)	Sunderland	D 2-2	McPherson 2	10,000
13	Mar 17 (a)	Queen's Park	W 4-1	Boyd 2, Gray, Smellie (og)	10,000
14	24 (h)	Hibernian	W 2-0	McPherson, Gray	
15	26 (h)	Third Lanark RV	W 4-1	Barker 2, McPherson, Untraced	
16	27 (a)	Aston Villa	L 1-3	Untraced	5,000
17	28 (n)	Leicester F	W 2-1	Untraced	
18	Apr 7 (a)	Aberdeen	W 2-1	Untraced	
19	30 (h)	Notts C	W 3-1	H.McCreadie, McPherson, Boyd	3,000
20	May 5 (a)	Darvel	W 5-3	Untraced	
21	7 (h)	Clyde	D 1-1	Gray	
22	12 (a)	Motherwell	W 3-1	Marshall, Barker, Gray	
23	17 (a)	Falkirk	W 6-1	McPherson 2, A.McCreadie, Steel, Barker, Boyd	
24	19 (a)	Kilmarnock	L 1-3	Untraced	
25	24 (a)	Celtic	D 1-1	Untraced	
26	26 (a)	Dundee	L 2-3	McPherson, Untraced	

*League fixture declared a friendly due to frost.
No further details available for Matches 4, 16-18, 20, 24 and 25.

Appearances: Haddow 13, Smith N 16, Drummond J 19, Marshall 19, McCreadie A 17, Mitchell 15, Steel 12, McCreadie H 14, Gray 17, McPherson J 18, Barker 12, Kerr N 4, McKenzie A 4, Blyth 7, Boyd 12, Muir 5, Johnstone 3, Davie 2, Cameron 2, Scott 1, Freebairn 1, Neil 1, Smith A 3, Cowan 2, Gibson W 1

Goals: Marshall 2, McCreadie A 2, Mitchell 2, Steel 3, McCreadie H 1, Gray 9, McPherson J 13, Barker 6, Kerr N 1, Blyth 3, Boyd 5

20 goals untraced. 2 own-goals

1894-95

Honorary Match Secretary: W.Wilton

Scottish League

Player columns: Haddow, Crawford, Drummond, Marshall, Gibson W, Mitchell, Cowan, McCreadie H, Boyd, McPherson, Barker, Smith N, Gray, Pray, Montgomery, Hamilton, Smith A, Gibson N, Gardiner, King, McNeish, Spiers, McIntyre, McKay, Miller J, Jackson, Stevenson, Mann

#	Date	Venue/Opponent	Res	Scorers	Att	Had	Cra	Dru	Mar	GbW	Mit	Cow	McC	Boy	McP	Bar	SmN	Gra	Pra	Mon	Ham	SmA	GbN	Gar
1	Aug 18 (h) Dumbarton	W 3-0	Barker 2, Untraced		1	2	3	4	5	6	7	8	9	10	11								
2	25 (a) St Benard's	W 4-1	McPherson 2, Barker 2		1		3	4	5	6	7	8	9	10	11	2							
3	Sep 1 (h) Dundee	W 1-0	Gibson	4,000	1		3	4	5	6	7		8	10	11	2	9						
4	8 (a) Leith A	W 4-3	Barker 2, Mitchell, Cowan		1		3	4	5	6	7	8		10	11	2	9						
5	22 (a) Celtic	L 3-5	Gray, Barker, McPherson	20,000	1		3	4	5	6		7	8	11	10	2	9						
6	29 (h) St Mirren	W 4-3	McPherson 2, Cowan, Goldie (og)	5,000	1		3	4		6	7		8	10	11	2	9	5					
7	Oct 13 (a) Third Lanark RV	W 2-0	Hamilton, Untraced	10,000			3	4		6	7		8	10	11	2		5	1	9			
8	20 (h) Hearts	L 0-1		10,000			3	4	5	6	7	11	8	10		2			1	9			
9	Nov 3 (h) Leith A	W 5-1	A.Smith 2, Gray, McPherson, H.McCreadie				3	4		6	7	8		10		2	9	5	1		11		
10	Dec 1 (a) Dumbarton	L 0-1					3			6	7		10	11		2	9		1		8	4	5
11	8 (a) Clyde	W 5-1	Barker 2, Gray 2, Cowan				3		5	6	7			10	11	2	9		1		8	4	
12	22 (a) Clyde	W 4-1	McPherson, Untraced 3			2	3	4	5		7	8	10	9	11				1		6		
13	Jan 19 (a) Hearts	D 0-0		10,000		2	3	4		6	7		9	10	11				1		8	5	
14	26 (a) Dundee	L 1-2	H.McCreadie	6,000	1	2	3	4		6	7	8	9	10	11						5		
15	Feb 16 (h) Third Lanark RV	L 0-1		4,000	1	11	3	4	5	6			8	9		2					7	10	
16	Mar 9 (a) St Mirren	L 2-4	McPherson, Boyd		1		3	4			7	8	9	10	11	2					6	5	
17	23 (h) Celtic	D 1-1	McPherson		1	2	3	4		6	7	8	9	10	11						5		
18	Apr 27 (h) St Bernard's	W 2-1	Boyd, A.Smith	5,000	1		3		5	6	7	8	9	10	4	2					11		
	FINAL LEAGUE POSITION: 3rd			**Appearances**	11	6	16	15	17	11	16	13	13	17	15	13	7	3	7	2	6	8	2
				Goals					1	1	3	2	2	9	9		4			1	3		

5 goals untraced. 1 own-goal

Scottish FA Cup

#	Date	Venue/Opponent	Res	Scorers	Att	Had	Dru	Mar	Mit	Cow	McC	McP	Bar	SmN	Gra	Pra	Mon
1	Nov 24 (h) Hearts	L 1-2	Cowan	12,000	1	3	4	6	7	8	10	11	2	9	5	
				Appearances	1	1	1	1	1	1	1	1	1	1	1	
				Goals					1							

Glasgow Cup

#	Date	Venue/Opponent	Res	Scorers	Att	Had	Dru	Mar	GbW	Mit	Cow	McC	Boy	McP	Bar	SmN	Gra	Pra	Mon	Ham	SmA
1	Sep 15 (h) Queen's Park	W 2-0	McPherson 2	17,000	1	3	4	5	6	8	7	9	10	11	2					
QF	Oct 6 (h) Third Lanark RV	W 3-2	McPherson, Hamilton, Untraced	8,000		3	4		6	7	8		10	11	2		5	1	9	
SF	27 (a) Partick Thistle	L 0-1				3	4		6	7	8		10		2	9	5	1		11
R*	Nov 10 (a) Partick Thistle	W 5-3	Gray 3, Cowan, H.McCreadie		1	3	4		6	7	8		10		2	9	5			11
F	17 (n†) Celtic	L 0-2		20,000	1	3	4		6	7	8		10		2	9	5			11
				Appearances	3	5	5	5	1	5	5	1	5	2	5	3	4	2	1	3
				Goals						1	1		3			3			1	

*Semi-final replayed after protest. † Final played at first Cathkin Park.

1 goal untraced

Glasgow Merchants' Charity Cup

#	Date	Venue/Opponent	Res	Scorers	Att	Had	Cra	Dru	GbW	Mit	Cow	McC	Boy	McP	Bar	SmN	SmA	GbN	Gar
SF	May 18 (n) Third Lanark RV	W 4-0	Cowan 2, Barker, Drummond	15,000	1		3	5	6	7	8	9	10	11	2		4	
F	25 (n) Celtic	L 0-4			1	2		5	6	7	8	9			3		4	10
				Appearances	2	2		2	2	2	2	2	1	2			2	1
				Goals			1			2				1				

Semi-final played at second Hampden Park.
Final played at first Cathkin Park.

Other matches

#	Date	Venue/Opponent	Res	Scorers	Att	Had	Cra	Dru	Mar	GbW	Mit	Cow	McC	Boy	McP	Bar	SmN	Gra	Pra	Mon	SmA	GbN	Gar	Kin	McN	Spi	McI	McK	MiJ	Jac	Ste	Man
1	Aug 11 (h) Renton	W 8-4	Gray, Untraced 7	5,000	1		3	4	5	6	7	8		10		2	9			11											
2	14 (h) Hibernian	L 1-2	A.Smith	3,000	1		3	4	5	6	7	8		10		2	9			11											
3	Sep 3 (a) Sunderland	D 1-1	Untraced																												
4	27 (h) Everton	L 1-4	H.McCreadie	6,000	1	2	3		5	6	7	8	9	10	11				4												
5	Dec 15 (a) Queen's Park	W 4-2	Boyd 2, Cowan, Barker			2	3		5	6	7		9	10	11				1	8	4										
6	29 (h) Third Lanark RV	W 2-0	Boyd 2			2	3		5	6	7	8	9	10	11				1		4										
7	Jan 1 (h) Celtic	L 2-3	McPherson (pen), Boyd	16,000		2	3	4	5		7		9	10	11				1	8	6										
8	Feb 2 (h) Third Lanark RV	W 3-0	Boyd 3	4,000	1		3	4	5	6	7	8	9	10		2				11											
9	23 (a) St Mirren	W 4-3	Cowan 2, H.McCreadie, Barker		1		3	4	5	6	7	8	9	10	11	2															
10	Mar 2 (h) Hearts	W 2-1	Boyd, Untraced		1		3			6						2	9		4		5		7	8	11						
11	16 (h) Queen's Park	D 2-2	Marshall, Boyd		1		3	4	5		7		9	10	11	2			6				8								
12	Apr 6 (h) Renton	W 2-1	Untraced		1	3		4	5	6	7	8		11	2							9					10				
13	12 (a) Everton	W 4-0	Untraced		1	3				6	7	8	10		4	2				11						9		5			
14	13 (a) Aston Villa	W 3-2	Untraced																												
15	15 (a) Notts C	L 0-1																												
16	16 (a) Leicester F	W 2-1	Untraced																												
17	20 (a) Clyde	D 1-1	A.Smith		1	3			5		7	11		4	2					10	6			9	8						
18	30 (a) Newcastle U	W 5-2	Untraced																												
19	May 1 (h) St Mirren	D 0-0		1,000	1	2	3	4	5			8	10		11				6			7		9						
20	4 (h) Leith A	W 3-0	Untraced		1		2	4	6		7		9	3					11			10				8	5			
21	8 (a) Linthouse	W 5-1	McPherson 3, Miller 2	2,000	1	2	3		5				10	4					11	6				7		8	9			
	No further details available matches 3, 4, 10, 13-16, 18, 20.			**Appearances**	13	9	13	9	14	10	12	10	11	10	12	10	3	2	3	9	7	1	2	2	1	2	4	3	2	1	1
				Goals				1			3	2	10	4	2		1			2											

28 goals untraced

1895-96

Honorary Match Secretary: W.Wilton

Scottish League

No	Date		Opponent	Result	Scorers	Att	Murdoch	Smith N	Drummond	Marshall	Mathie	Gibson N	McIntyre	Miller T	Barker	Boyd	Smith A	Wilson	Oswald	McPherson	Russell	Stewart	McLeod	Crawford D	Mitchell	Burns	McCreadie H	Bell	Muir	Yuille	McAllan
1	Aug 17	(a)	Dumbarton	W 5-3	Miller 2, Barker 2, A.Smith		1	2	3	4	5	6	7	8	9	10	11														
2	24	(h)	Third Lanark RV	L 0-4				2	3	4		6	7	8	5		11	1	9	10											
3	31	(a)	Hearts	W 2-1	Oswald, Untraced			2	3		5			8	4		11	1	9	10	6	7									
4	Sep 7	(h)	Celtic	L 2-4	Stewart, A.Smith	16,000		2	3		5			8	4		11	1	9	10	6	7									
5	14	(a)	St Bernards	W 4-3	McPherson, Miller, A.Smith, Untraced				3		5			8	4		11		9	10		7	1	2	6						
6	Oct 5	(a)	St Mirren	W 7-1	A.Smith 4, McPherson, Oswald, H.McCreadie			2	3			6					11		9	10		7	1		4	5	8				
7	12	(h)	St Bernards	W 2-0	A.Smith, McPherson	4,000		2	3	4		6				7	11		9	10			1			5	8				
8	26	(a)	Hibernian	D 1-1	Barker	8,000		2	3	4		5	8	7			11		9	10					6			1			
9	Nov 9	(h)	Clyde	D 4-4	Oswald 2, McPherson, Mitchell	4,000		2	3	4		5		7					9	10					6		8	1	11		
10	23	(h)	Hibernian	W 4-0	Oswald 2, Barker, McPherson	6,000		2	3	4		5	8	7			11		9	10					6			1			
11	30	(a)	Dundee	W 3-1	Marshall, Barker, Oswald	3,000		2	3	4		5		7			11		9	10					6		8	1			
12	Dec 7	(h)	Hearts	W 7-2	Oswald 3, Gibson, Barker, McPherson, Untraced			2	3	4		5		7			11		9	10					6		8	1			
13	14	(a)	Celtic	L 2-6	A.Smith, H.McCreadie	25,000		2	3	4		5		7			11		9	10			1		6		8				
14	21	(a)	Third Lanark RV	W 3-2	A.Smith, H.McCreadie, Boyd	5,000		2		4		6				8	11		9	10			3			5	7	1			
15	Jan 4	(h)	Dumbarton	W 3-1	Oswald, H.McCreadie, Miller (og)	2,000		2		4						10	11		9	3		7			6	5	8	1			
16	Feb 8	(a)	Clyde	D 2-2	Stewart, A.Smith			2	3	4		5					11		9	10		7			6		8		1		
17	22	(h)	St Mirren	D 3-3	A.Smith 2, Miller	3,000		2	3			4		8			10	11		9			7			6	5				1	
18	29	(h)	Dundee	W 3-1	H.McCreadie 2, McPherson	3,000		2	3			4	7				11		9	10			1			6	5	8			
			Appearances				1	17	16	12	1	17	3	8	12	4	17	3	17	16	2	7	5	2	12	6	10	7	1	1	1
			Goals							1		1		4	6	1	13		11	7		2			1		6				

FINAL LEAGUE POSITION: 2nd

3 goals untraced. 1 own-goal

Scottish FA Cup

No	Date		Opponent	Result	Scorers	Att	Smith N	Marshall	Barker	Smith A	Oswald	McPherson	Stewart	Crawford D	Mitchell	McCreadie H	Bell
1	Jan 18	(a)	Dumbarton	D 1-1	Stewart		2	4	5	11	9	10	7	3	6	8	1
R	25	(a)	Dumbarton	W 3-1	A.Smith 2, Oswald	6,000	2	4	5	11	9	10	7	3	6	8	1
2	Feb 1	(h)	St Mirren	W 5-0	Oswald 3, McPherson, H.McCreadie	4,500	2	3 4	5	11	9	10	7		6	8	1
QF	15	(h)	Hibernian	L 2-3	A.Smith, H.McCreadie	18,000	2	3 4	5	11	9	10	7		6	8	1
			Appearances				4	2 4	4	4	4	4	4	2	4	4	4
			Goals							3	4	1	1			2	

Glasgow Cup

No	Date		Opponent	Result	Scorers	Att	Smith N	Marshall	Barker	Miller T	Gibson N	Smith A	Oswald	McPherson	Stewart	Crawford D	Mitchell	Burns	McCreadie H
1	Sep 21	(a)	Queen's Park	D 2-2	A.Smith 2	12,000	2 3	5	8 4			11	9	10	7	1	6		
R	28	(h)	Queen's Park	L 2-3	H.McCreadie 2	20,000	2 3	4				11	9	10	7	1	6	5	8
			Appearances				2 2	2	1 1			2	2	2	2	2	2	1	1
			Goals									2							2

Glasgow League

No	Date		Opponent	Result	Scorers	Att	Drummond	Marshall	McIntyre	Barker	Smith A	Oswald	McPherson	Stewart	Crawford D	Mitchell	McCreadie H	Muir	McAllan	Pray
1	Mar 14	(h)	Third Lanark RV	W 6-2	Untraced		2 3	4 7	11			9	10			6	8	1	5	
2	21	(a)	Celtic	L 2-3	H.McCreadie, Oswald	12,001	2 3	4 7	11			9	10			6	8	1	5	
3	28	(a)	Queen's Park	W 7-2	A.Smith 3, Untraced 4	5,000	2 3	7	4	11		9	10	1		6	8		5	
4	Apr 6	(a)	Third Lanark RV	W 3-1	McPherson, A.Smith, Draper (og)	5,000	2 3	6 7	4	11		9	10				8	1	5	
5	11	(h)	Celtic	D 2-2	H.McCreadie, McPherson		2	7		10 11		9			3 6		8	1	5	4
6	18	(a)	Queen's Park	W 2-1	McIntyre 2	8,000	2 3	4 7	9	11		10				6	8	1	5	
			Appearances				6 5	4 6	5	1 4		4	6	1	1 5	6	1 4 6 1			
			Goals					2			4	1 2			2					

FINAL LEAGUE POSITION: 1st

10 goals untraced. 1 own-goal

Glasgow Merchants' Charity Cup

No	Date		Opponent	Result	Scorers	Att	Smith N	Marshall	Barker	Smith A	McPherson	Crawford D	Mitchell	McAllan	Pray
SF	May 9	(n*)	Celtic	L 1-6	McPherson	20,000	2 3	4	9	11	8	6	7	1	5
			Appearances				1 1	1	1	1	1	1	1	1	1
			Goals								1				

*Played at Second Hampden Park.

Hyslop played number-10 in Semi-Final.

Other matches

No	Date		Opponent	Result	Scorers	Att
1	Aug 7	(h)	Hibernian	L 2-5	H.McCreadie, Boyd	4,000
2	10	(h)	Renton	W 4-1	McIntyre 2, Miller, A.Smith	3,000
3	14	(h)	Linthouse	W 4-3	Untraced	
4	19	(h)	Partick Thistle	W 5-1	Untraced	
5	Sep 16	(a)	Hibernian	L 1-3	Untraced	3,000
6	26	(a)	Everton	W 3-1	Gibson (pen), Boyd, McGowan	3,000
7	Oct 19	(a)	Dundee	L 2-3	Miller, A.Smith	
8	Nov 2	(h)	Third Lanark RV	W 6-1	Untraced	
9	16	(a)	Orion	W 7-2	Untraced	
10	Dec 25	(a)	Everton	L 1-5	A.Smith	5,000
11	Jan 1	(a)	Celtic	D 3-3	A.Smith, Oswald, Barker	10,000
12	2	(a)	Third Lanark RV	L 3-4	Oswald 2, A.Smith	5,000
13	Apr 21	(a)	Linthouse	D 2-2	McNeish, Gibson	
14	25	(a)	Hibernian	W 4-1	McNeish 2, Gibson, Oswald	2,000
15	29	(h)	Sunderland	L 1-3	McPherson	1,000
16	May 2	(a)	Hearts*	D 2-2	A.Smith, Untraced	4,000
17	4	(h)	Renton	L 2-5	Oswald 2	
18	11	(a)	Partick Thistle	D 2-2	Turnbull, Miller	
19	20	(a)	Clyde	D 3-3	Untraced	
20	23	(a)	Morton	W 7-1	Untraced	
21	25	(a)	Falkirk	W 5-0	Untraced	
22	28	(a)	Royal Albert	W 4-1	Untraced	

*Glasgow - Edinburgh League Champions Challenge Match

No further details available for matches 2-4, 8, 9, 13-15, 18-21.

Thomson played number-6 in Match 5; McGowan played number-9 in Match 6; Fulton played number-9 in Match 10; McKenzie played number-1 in Match 12; Gillespie played number-8 in Match 12; Cram played number-2 in Match 17; R.Crawford played number-7 in Matches 17 & 18; Turnbull played number-10 in Match 17 and number-9 in Match 18; Hyslop played number-10 in Match 18; Jackson played number-5 in Match 18. 43 goals untraced.

1896-97

Honorary Match Secretary: W.Wilton

Player columns (left to right): Dickie, Miller A, Drummond, Gibson, McCreadie A, Mitchell, Crawford R, Crawford J, Miller J, Turnbull, Hyslop, Smith A, Crawford D, Smith N, Oswald, McPherson, Jackson, Low, Hay, Glen, Neil, McNicol, McAllan, Hogg, McDonald, Gibb, Tinto, Phillip

Scottish League

No	Date	Opponent	Result	Scorers	Att
1	Aug 15 (h)	St Mirren	W 5-1	Turnbull 2, Hyslop, R.Crawford, J.Miller	8,000
2	22 (a)	Third Lanark RV	D 1-1	Gibson	15,000
3	29 (h)	Dundee	W 3-1	Hyslop, D.Crawford, Burgess (og)	13,000
4	Sep 5 (a)	Hibernian	L 3-4	J.Miller 2, Turnbull	
5	12 (h)	Hearts	W 5-0	R.Crawford, A.Smith, Oswald, Hyslop, J.Miller	14,000
6	21 (a)	Hearts	L 1-2	Gibson	7,000
7	26 (a)	Abercorn	W 9-2	McPherson 5, Turnbull 2, J.Miller, R.Crawford	
8	Oct 3 (h)	Hibernian	W 4-3	Turnbull 3, McCreadie	20,000
9	10 (a)	Celtic	D 1-1	McPherson	24,000
10	17 (h)	Clyde	W 2-1	McPherson 2	4,000
11	24 (h)	Third Lanark RV	W 6-1	Low 3, McPherson 2, Oswald	5,000
12	Nov 7 (a)	St Mirren	D 2-2	A.Smith, Mitchell	
13	28 (a)	Dundee	L 2-3	J.Miller, A.Smith	10,000
14	Dec 5 (a)	Clyde	W 7-2	Hyslop 4, Untraced 3	4,000
15	12 (h)	Abercorn	W 6-1	Turnbull 2, Hyslop, A.Smith, Untraced	2,000
16	19 (h)	Celtic	W 2-0	Low, J.Miller	15,000
17	26 (a)	St Bernards	L 2-3	J.Miller, Hyslop	2,000
18	Feb 20 (h)	St Bernards	W 3-2	A.Smith, McPherson, Russell (og)	

FINAL LEAGUE POSITION: 3rd

Appearances: 18 2 16 17 18 17 7 15 11 17 17 7 9 5 10 1 9 1 1
Goals: 2 1 1 3 8 10 10 5 1 2 11 4

4 goals untraced. 2 own-goals.

Scottish FA Cup

No	Date	Opponent	Result	Scorers	Att
1	Jan 9 (a)	Partick Thistle	W 4-2	Hyslop 2, N.Smith, Gibson	6,000
2	23 (h)	Hibernian	W 3-0	Low 2, McPherson	22,000
QF	Feb 13 (a)	Dundee	W 4-0	Gibson, Hyslop, McCreadie, J.Miller	16,000
SF	Mar 13 (a)	Morton	W 7-2	McPherson 2, Low, Gibson, J.Miller, Hyslop, A.Smith	12,000
F	20 (n)	Dumbarton	W 5-1	J.Miller 2, Hyslop, McPherson, A.Smith	15,000

Final played at Second Hampden Park.

Appearances: 5 5 5 5 5 5 5 5 5 1 4 5
Goals: 3 1 4 5 2 1 4 3

Glasgow Cup

No	Date	Opponent	Result	Scorers	Att
1	Sep 19 (h)	Third Lanark RV	W 5-1	Hyslop 2, R.Crawford 2, Oswald	13,000
SF	Oct 31 (h)	Linthouse	W 3-0	Turnbull 2, A.Smith	6,000
F	Nov 14 (n)	Celtic	D 1-1	Turnbull	13,000
R	21 (n)	Celtic	W 2-1	Turnbull 2	15,000

No further details available round one & semi-final.
Final and final replay both played at First Cathkin Park.

Appearances: 4 4 4 4 4 1 2 3 4 4 3 1 3 3
Goals: 2 5 2 1 1

Glasgow Merchants' Charity Cup

No	Date	Opponent	Result	Scorers	Att
SF	May 11 (n)	Celtic	W 4-1	Low, McPherson, Miller, A.Smith	20,000
F	15 (n)	Third Lanark RV	W 6-1	McPherson 2, Low, A.Smith, Hyslop, Gibson	10,000

Semi-final and Final both played at Second Hampden Park.

Appearances: 2 2 2 2 2 2 2 2 2 2 2
Goals: 1 1 1 2 3 2

Glasgow League

No	Date	Opponent	Result	Scorers	Att
1	Jan 2 (h)	Celtic	W 3-0	Low, J.Miller, McPherson	26,000
2	Feb 27 (a)	Queen's Park	D 1-1	A.Smith	15,000
3	Apr 10 (h)	Queen's Park	L 0-3		16,000
4	28 (h)	Clyde	W 4-0	McNicol, J.Miller, Hyslop. A.Smith	
5	May 1 (a)	Celtic	D 1-1	J.Miller	20,000
6	4 (a)	Third Lanark RV	L 3-4	Hyslop 2, Gibson	
7	8 (a)	Clyde	W 7-0	A.Smith 3, Hyslop 3, McPherson	
8	12 (h)	Third Lanark RV	W 4-1	Oswald 2, Turnbull 2	3,000

FINAL LEAGUE POSITION: 2nd

Appearances: 7 4 6 3 7 1 5 2 6 7 2 7 2 6 2 7 6 1 3 1 1 1 1
Goals: 1 3 2 6 5 2 2 1

Other matches

No	Date	Opponent	Result	Scorers	Att
1	Aug 19 (h)	Renton	W 4-1	Untraced	
2	24 (h)	Hibernian	W 2-1	Untraced	
3	Sep 1 (a)	Everton	D 2-2	Turnbull, A.Smith	
4	28 (h)	Blackburn R	L 3-4	Hyslop 2, McPherson	9,000
5	Jan 1 (a)	Hearts	W 6-4	Turnbull 2, Oswald, A.Smith, Hyslop, Untraced 1	4,000
6	4 (h)	Everton	D 4-4	Hyslop, Oswald, J.Miller, Low	15,000
7	Feb 6 (a)	Dundee*	D 1-1	A.Smith	10,000
8	Mar 27 (a)	Hibernian	L 0-2		
9	Apr 3 (h)	Third Lanark RV	D 1-1	Tinto	
10	16 (a)	Blackburn R	W 5-1	Untraced	
11	17 (a)	Millwall A	L 0-1		
12	19 (a)	Chatham	D 3-3	Worsell, Low, Smith	5,000
13	20 (a)	Leicester F	D 1-1	Gibson	2,000
14	24 (a)	Newcastle U	L 1-3	Untraced	
15	26 (h)	Dumbarton A	W 2-1	Untraced	
16	May 25 (h)	Internationalists†	W 4-0	Untraced	

N.B. No further details available matches 1, 2, 5, 10, 11, 12, 14, 15, 16.
*Scottish Cup-tie declared a friendly due to state of pitch. † John Taylor Benefit Match.

19 goals untraced.

1897-98

Manager: W.Wilton

Scottish League

No	Date		Opponent	Result	Scorers	Att	Dickie	Smith N	Drummond	McCreadie	Neil	Mitchell	Low	Miller J	Hamilton	Hyslop	Smith A	Gibson	McPherson	Glen	Turnbull	Crawford D	Oswald	Jamieson	Murray	Yuille	Turner
1	Sep	4 (a)	St Bernard's	W 4-2	Hamilton 2, Miller, Hyslop	7,000	1	2	3	4	5	6	7	8	9	10	11										
2		11 (h)	Hibernian	W 1-0	Hamilton	15,000	1	2	3		5		6	7	8	9	10	11	4								
3		20 (a)	Hearts	D 2-2	Hamilton, A.Smith	13,000	1	2	3				7	8	9	10	11	4	5	6							
4		25 (a)	Third Lanark RV	W 3-0	Hyslop (pen), A.Smith, Hamilton	15,000	1	2	3		5		7	8	9	10	11	6		4							
5		27 (h)	Celtic	L 0-4		30,000	1	2	3		5		7	8	9	10	11	4		6							
6	Oct	2 (h)	Hearts	W 2-0	Hamilton 2	15,000	1	2	3			6	7	8	9		11	4	5			10					
7		9 (a)	Partick Thistle	W 5-1	Mitchell, Gibson, Neil, Hamilton, Hyslop	8,000	1	2	3		5	6	7		9	10	11	4	8								
8		16 (a)	Clyde	W 8-1	A.Smith 3, Miller 2, Hamilton, Hyslop, McPherson	6,000	1	2	3		5	6		9	7	10	11	4	8								
9		23 (h)	Clyde	W 7-0	Hyslop 3 (1 pen), McPherson, Hamilton, Miller, A.Smith	3,000	1		3				7	9	10	11		4	8	6		2	5				
10	Nov	6 (a)	St Mirren	W 5-1	Turnbull 2, Low, McPherson, Hamilton		1		3		5	6	7		9		11	4	8		10		2				
11	Dec	4 (h)	St Mirren	W 9-0	Hamilton 4, McPherson 3, Neil, Miller	5,000	1	2	3		5	6	7	9	10	11		4	8								
12		11 (a)	Hibernian	W 3-0	Hamilton 3, Hyslop, A.Smith	9,000	1	2	3		5	6	7		9	10	11	4	8								
13		25 (h)	Dundee	W 5-0	Miller 4, A.Smith	6,000	1	2			5		7	9		10	11	4	8			3			9		6
14	Jan	3 (h)	Partick Thistle	W 6-1	A.Smith 2, McPherson 2, Miller, Hyslop	4,000	1	2	3		5		7	9		10	11	6	8	4							
15	Feb	12 (a)	Dundee	L 1-2	A.Smith	11,000	1		3		5	6	7	10	9		11	4	8				2				
16	Mar	19 (a)	St Bernard's	W 8-1	Hyslop 3, McPherson 2, A.Smith, Neil, Turnbull	5,000	1		3		5	6	7			10	11	4	8		9	2			4		
17	Apr	9 (h)	Third Lanark RV	D 0-0		3,000			3		5	6	7						10	2	9		4	1	8	11	
18		11 (a)	Celtic	D 0-0		15,000	1	2			5	6	7		9	10		4	8			3					
					Appearances		17	13	16	4	12	11	12	15	15	13	17	15	12	5	4	6	4	1	3	1	1
					Goals						3	1	1	10	18	12	12	1	10		3						

FINAL LEAGUE POSITION: 2nd

Scottish FA Cup

No	Date		Opponent	Result	Scorers	Att	Dickie	Smith N	Drummond	Neil	Mitchell	Low	Miller J	Hamilton	Hyslop	Smith A	Gibson	McPherson	Glen	Crawford D	Oswald	Murray	Kerr	Scott	Goudie
1	Jan	8 (h)	Polton Vale	W 8-0	Miller 2, McPherson 2, A.Smith, Hamilton, Goudie, Neil	3,000	1	2		5		7	10	9		11		8		4				3	6
2		22 (h)	Cartvale	W 12-0	Hamilton 4, A.Smith 2, Neil (pen), Mitchell, Kerr, Gibson, Miller, Coulrough (og)		1			5	6		10	9		11	4	8		2			7	3	
QF	Feb	5 (a)	Queen's Park	W 3-1	McPherson, Hamilton, Miller	20,000	1		3	5	6	7	10	9		11	4	8		2					
SF		19 (h)	Third Lanark RV	D 1-1	A.Smith	20,000	1	2	3	5	6		7	9		11	4	8	10						
R		26 (a)	Third Lanark RV	D 2-2	Hamilton, A.Smith	16,000	1		3	5	6		7	9	10	11	4	8		2			7		
2R	Mar	12 (a)	Third Lanark RV	W 2-0	McPherson, Gibson (pen)	12,000	1		3	5	6		10	9		11	4	8		2					
F		26 (n*)	Kilmarnock	W 2-0	A.Smith, Hamilton	14,000	1	2	3	5	6		7	9	10	11	4	8							
					Appearances		7	3	5	7	6	2	7	7	2	7	6	7	1	4	1		2	2	1
					Goals					2	1		4	8		6	2	4					1		1

* Played at second Hampden Park

1 own-goal

Glasgow Cup

No	Date		Opponent	Result	Scorers	Att	Dickie	Smith N	Drummond	Neil	Mitchell	Low	Miller J	Hamilton	Hyslop	Smith A	Gibson	McPherson	Glen	Crawford D	Oswald	Murray
1	Sep	18 (a)	Partick Thistle	W 6-0	Miller 4, Hyslop 2 (1 pen)	14,000	1	2	3			7	8	9	10	11	4	5	6			
SF	Oct	30 (a)	Celtic	D 2-2	McPherson, Hamilton	36,000	1	2	3	5	6	7		9	10	11	4	8				
R	Nov	13 (h)	Celtic	D 1-1	Neil (pen)	30,000	1		3	5	6	7		9		11	4	8		10	2	
2R		20 (h)	Celtic	W 3-1	Hamilton 2, Hyslop	25,000	1		3	5	6	7		9	10	11	4	8			2	
F		27 (n*)	Queen's Park	W 4-0	Neil (pen), McPherson, A.Smith, Hamilton	15,000	1		3	5	6	7	10	9		11	4	8			2	
					Appearances		5	2	5	4	4	4	3	5	3	5	5	5	5	1	1	3
					Goals					2			4	4	3	1		2				

* Played at first Cathkin Park

Glasgow Merchants' Charity Cup

No	Date		Opponent	Result	Scorers	Att	Dickie	Smith N	Neil	Mitchell	Low	Miller J	Hamilton	Hyslop	Gibson	McPherson	Glen	Oswald
SF	May	7 (n*)	Celtic	W 2-0	Miller, Hamilton	20,000	1	2	5	6	7	8	9		11	4	10	3
F		14 (a)	Third Lanark RV	L 0-1		6,000	1	2	5	6	7	8	9		11	4	10	3
					Appearances		2	2	2	2	2	2	2		2	2	2	2
					Goals							1	1					

* Played at first Cathkin Park

Glasgow League

No	Date		Opponent	Result	Scorers	Att	Dickie	Smith N	Drummond	Neil	Mitchell	Low	Miller J	Hamilton	Hyslop	Smith A	Gibson	McPherson	Glen	Turnbull	Crawford D	Oswald	Murray	Yuille	Kerr	Goudie	Sharp A	Sharp J
1	Jan	29 (h)	Clyde	W 5-3	McPherson 2, Oswald 2, Goudie		1		3	5		7	10				4	11		2	9			8		6		
2	Apr	4 (a)	Clyde	L 2-3	McPherson, A.Smith	5,000	1	2				7	5		9	11		10	3			6	8		4		7	8
3		13 (a)	Third Lanark RV	W 5-0	Hamilton 2, McPherson 2, Hyslop	1,000	1			5	6			9	11		4	10	3		2						7	8
4		16 (h)	Queen's Park	W 2-0	Hamilton 2	10,000	1	2		5	6	7		10		11	4	8			3	9						
5		20 (a)	Celtic	L 2-3	McPherson, Hamilton	5,000	1	2		5	6	7	8	9		11	4	10			3							
6		23 (h)	Third Lanark RV	W 3-1	Gibson, Hamilton, Miller	3,000	1	2		5		7	8	9	11		4	10			3					6		
7		27 (a)	Queen's Park	W 4-2	Hamilton 3, Miller	7,000	1	2		5	6	7	8	9		11	4	10			3							
8		30 (h)	Celtic	W 4-3	McPherson, A.Smith, Hamilton, Low	15,000	1	2		5	6	7	8	9		11	10	3		2	4							
					Appearances		8	5	1	7	5	7	6	6	3	5	6	8	3	7	3	1	1	1	3	1	1	
					Goals					1		2	10	1	2	1	7	2								1		

FINAL LEAGUE POSITION: 1st

Other matches

No	Date		Opponent	Result	Scorers	Att	Dickie	Smith N	Drummond	McCreadie	Neil	Low	Miller J	Hamilton	Hyslop	Smith A	Gibson	McPherson	Glen	Turnbull	Crawford D	Oswald	Murray	Kerr	Scott	Sharp J
1	Sep	1 (a)	Partick Thistle*	W 5-1	Hamilton 2, Neil, A.Smith, McPherson	7,000	1	2	3	4	5		7		9	10	11	6	8							
2		7 (a)	Celtic†	W 3-1	Hamilton 2, Hyslop	10,000	1		3	5			8	9	10	11	4	7	6		2					
3		14 (a)	Stenhousemuir	W 13-1	Hamilton 7, A.Smith 2, Low 2, Glen, Hyslop	4,000	1	2	3			7	8	9	5	11	4	10	6							
4	Dec	18 (h)	Queen's Park	W 3-2	Turnbull 2, Hyslop	5,000	1	2	3				7		9	10		4	11	5		6				8
5	Jan	1 (a)	Celtic‡	D 1-1	Hamilton	50,000	1	2	3		5		7	9	10	11	4	8	6							
6		4 (h)	Everton	W 5-3	Low 3, A.Smith, Hamilton	6,500		2	3			7	10	9		11	4				5		6	1	8	
					Appearances		5	5	6	2	2	4	4	6	5	5	5	4	4	1	1	2	2	1	1	1
					Goals						1	5	13	3	4	1	1	2								

* Opening of Meadowside Park, Glasgow. † James Madden Benefit Match.
‡ League fixture abandoned after 70 minutes due to spectator encroachment.

1898-99

Manager: W.Wilton

Scottish League

Player columns: Dickie, Crawford, Drummond, Gibson, Neil, Mitchell, Sharp J, Miller J, Hamilton, McPherson, Smith A, Campbell, Wilkie, Smith N, Sharp A, Miller JE

#	Date	Venue/Opponent	Result	Scorers	Att	Dic	Cra	Dru	Gib	Nei	Mit	SJ	MJ	Ham	McP	SA	Cam	Wil	SN	SpA	MJE
1	Aug 20 (h)	Partick Thistle	W 6-2	Hamilton 3, J.Sharp, Neil, J.Miller	7,000	1	2	3	4	5	6	7	8	9	10	11					
2	27 (a)	St Mirren	W 3-1	A.Smith, Hamilton, McPherson		1	2	3	4	5	6			9	8	11	7	10			
3	Sep 3 (a)	Hearts	W 3-2	Hamilton 2, Wilkie	17,000	1	2		4	5	6		8	9	3	11	7	10			
4	10 (h)	Third Lanark RV	W 4-1	J.Miller, McPherson, Campbell, Neil (pen)	18,000	1	2	3	4	5	6		10	9	8	11	7				
5	19 (h)	St Bernard's	W 2-0	A.Smith, Neil (pen)	8,000	1	2	3	4	5	6		8	9	10	11	7				
6	24 (a)	Celtic	W 4-0	Neil (pen), McPherson, Campbell, J.Miller	45,000	1	3		4	5	6		10	9	8	11	7		2		
7	26 (a)	Third Lanark RV	W 3-2	Campbell 2, McPherson	14,000	1	3		4	5	6		10	9	8	11	7		2		
8	Oct 1 (h)	Hearts	W 3-1	Hamilton 2, A.Smith	25,000	1	3		4	5	6		10	9	8	11	7		2		
9	8 (a)	Dundee	W 2-1	Hamilton, Wilkie	7,500	1	3		4	5	6			9	8	11	7	10	2		
10	Nov 5 (a)	Partick Thistle	W 5-0	Hamilton 2, J.Miller 2, A.Sharp	5,000	1		3	4	5	6		7	9	10	11			2	8	
11	19 (a)	Hibernian	W 4-3	J.Miller, A.Smith, Hamilton, Neil (pen)	10,000	1	3		4	5	6		10	9	8	11	7		2		
12	26 (h)	Clyde	W 8-0	J.Miller 3, A.Sharp 2, Gibson 2, Watson (og)	4,000	1	3		4	5	6		10	9		11	7		2	8	
13	Dec 3 (h)	St Bernard's	W 5-2	Campbell 4, Hamilton	3,000	1	3		4	5	6		10	9		11	7		2	8	
14	17 (h)	Dundee	W 7-0	Hamilton 3, A.Smith 2, McPherson 2	3,000	1	3		4	5			10	9	8	11	7		2		6
15	24 (h)	Hibernian	W 10-0	A.Smith 4, Hamilton 2, McPherson, J.Miller, Gibson (pen), Campbell	7,000	1	3		4	5			10	9	8	11	7		2		6
16	31 (h)	St Mirren	W 3-2	Campbell 2, A.Smith	5,000	1	3		4	5			10	9		11	7		2	8	6
17	Jan 2 (h)	Celtic	W 4-1	Hamilton 3, Campbell	30,000	1	3		4	5			10	9	8	11	7		2		6
18	7 (a)	Clyde	W 3-0	A.Smith, J.Miller, Neil (pen)	4,000	1	3		4	5			10	9	8	11	7		2		6
		Appearances				18	17	5	18	18	13	1	16	18	15	18	16	3	13	4	5
		Goals							3	6		1	11	21	7	12	12	2		3	

FINAL LEAGUE POSITION: 1st

Scottish FA Cup

Player columns: Dickie, Crawford, Drummond, Gibson, Neil, Mitchell, Miller J, Hamilton, McPherson, Smith A, Campbell, Wilkie, Smith N, Low, Oswald

#	Date	Venue/Opponent	Result	Scorers	Att	Dic	Cra	Dru	Gib	Nei	Mit	MJ	Ham	McP	SA	Cam	Wil	SN	Low	Osw
1	Jan 14 (h)	Hearts	W 4-1	Gibson 2, Neil (pen), Hamilton	20,000	1	3		4	5	6	10	9	8	11	7		2		
2	Feb 11 (a)	Ayr Parkhouse	W 4-1	Hamilton 2, Campbell, A.Smith	5,000	1	3			5	6	11	9	4	10	7	8	2		
QF	18 (h)	Clyde	W 4-0	Low, McPherson, Gibson (pen), Hamilton	6,000	1	3		4		6	10	9	8	11			2	7	5
SF	Apr 15 (n)	St Mirren	W 2-1	McPherson, J.Miller	10,000	1	2	3	4	5	6		9	8	11	7				
F	22 (n)	Celtic	L 0-2		25,000	1	3		4	5	6	10	9	8	11	7		2		
		Appearances				5	5	1	4	4	5	5	5	5	5	4	5	1	4	1	1
		Goals							3	1		1	4	2	1	1			1	

Final played at second Hampden Park, Glasgow.

Glasgow Cup

Player columns: Dickie, Crawford, Drummond, Gibson, Neil, Mitchell, Miller J, Hamilton, McPherson, Smith A, Campbell, Wilkie, Smith N, Low

#	Date	Venue/Opponent	Result	Scorers	Att	Dic	Cra	Dru	Gib	Nei	Mit	MJ	Ham	McP	SA	Cam	Wil	SN	Low
1	Sep 17 (a)	Cameronians	W 4-0	McPherson 2, A.Smith, J.Miller		1	2	3	4	5	6		9	8	11	7	10		
SF	Oct 15 (h)	Celtic	D 1-1	Campbell	35,000	1	3		4	5	6	10	9		11	7	8	2	
R	22 (a)	Celtic	W 2-1	Hamilton 2	30,000	1	3		4	5	6	8	9	10	11			2	7
F	Nov 12 (n*)	Queen's Park	L 0-1		16,000	1	3		4	5	6	10	9	8	11	7		2	
		Appearances				4	3	2	4	4	4	4	3	2	3	4	3	3	1
		Goals										1	2	2	1	1			

*Played at first Cathkin Park

Glasgow Merchants' Charity Cup

Player columns: Dickie, Crawford, Gibson, Neil, Mitchell, Miller J, Hamilton, McPherson, Smith A, Campbell, Smith N

#	Date	Venue/Opponent	Result	Scorers	Att	Dic	Cra	Gib	Nei	Mit	MJ	Ham	McP	SA	Cam	SN
SF	May 22 (n*)	Third Lanark	W 4-1	Neil, A.Smith, Hamilton, Campbell	5,000	1	3	4	5	6	10	9	8	11	7	2
F	27 (h)	Celtic	L 0-2		28,000	1	3	4	5	6	10	9	8	11	7	2
		Appearances				2	2	2	2	2	2	2	2	2	2	2
		Goals							1			1		1	1	

*Played at second Hampden Park

Glasgow League

Player columns (as printed): Dickie, Crawford, Drummond, Gibson, Neil, Mitchell, Miller J, Hamilton, McPherson, Smith A, Campbell, Wilkie, Smith N, Miller JE, Low, Oswald, Wylie, Hyslop, Taylor

#	Date	Venue/Opponent	Result	Scorers	Att	Dic	Cra	Dru	Gib	Nei	Mit	MJ	Ham	McP	SA	Cam	Wil	SN	MJE	Low	Osw	Wyl	Hys	Tay
1	Jan 3 (a)	Partick Thistle	W 8-2	Hamilton 3, McPherson 3, Campbell 2	4,000	1	3		4	5		10	9	8	11	7		2	6					
2	21 (a)	Third Lanark RV	W 2-1	Hamilton, A.Smith	8,000	1	3		4	5			9	8	11	7	10	2	6					
3	Mar 11 (h)	Third Lanark RV	D 0-0		7,000	1	3		4		6	10	9		11	7	8	2					5	
4	18 (h)	Partick Thistle	W 4-1	McPherson 2, J.Miller, Auchincloss (og)	4,000	1	3			5	6	9		11		10				8	4	7	2	
5	Apr 8 (a)	Clyde	W 3-1	McPherson, Wilkie, J.Miller	4,000	1	3			5		9		11		10			6	8		7	4	2
6	29 (h)	Queen's Park	D 1-1	Gibson	11,000	1	2	3	4	5		10	9	11	7	8			6					
7	May 6 (a)	Celtic	L 1-4	Wilkie	18,000	1	2	3	4	5		9	10	11	7	8			6					
8	9 (h)	Clyde	W 4-1	McPherson 2, J.Miller 2	3,000	1	2	3	4	5	6	10	9	11	7	8								
9	13 (h)	Celtic	D 1-1	J.Miller	12,000	1	3			5	6	10	9	11	7	8		2	4					
10	15 (a)	Queen's Park	W 4-3	Hyslop 2, Wilkie, Campbell	4,000	1	3		4	5	6		9	11	7	8		2					10	
		Appearances				10	5	8	7	9	5	8	3	10	7	8	9	5	2	7	2	3	1	1
		Goals							1			5	4	8	1	3	3						2	

FINAL LEAGUE POSITION: 2nd

Other matches

Player columns (as printed): Dickie, Crawford, Drummond, Gibson, Neil, Mitchell, Miller J, Hamilton, McPherson, Smith A, Campbell, Smith N, Sharp A, Wylie, Hyslop, Taylor, Scott, Murray, Baird

#	Date	Venue/Opponent	Result	Scorers	Att	Dic	Cra	Dru	Gib	Nei	Mit	MJ	Ham	McP	SA	Cam	SN	SpA	Wyl	Hys	Tay	Sco	Mur	Bai
1	Aug 16 (h)	Hearts	D 2-2	Hamilton, J.Miller	5,000	1	2	3	4	5	6	8	9	10	11				7					
2	17 (h)	Linthouse	W 7-1	Wilkie 4, Hamilton 3		1	2	3	4	5		7	9	8	11	10			6					
3	23 (h)	Hibernian	W 2-0	Hamilton 2	4,000	1		3	4	5	6	8	9	11	7	10	2							
4	Sep 5 (h)	Liverpool	L 0-3		6,000	1			4	5		7	9	11	10	8				2	3	6		
5	Oct 29 (h)	Kilmarnock	W 5-0	Hamilton 2, McPherson, Drummond, Busby (og)	6,000	1		3	4	5		9	11	10	2	8		7						6
6	Dec 10 (h)	Queen's Park	L 1-2	Hamilton	3,000		3			5	6	10	9	11	7		2	8			4	1		
7	Feb 25 (h)	Aston Villa	W 3-1	Campbell, Hamilton, McPherson	16,000	1	3		4		6	10	9	11	7	8	2						5	
8	Mar 31 (a)	Liverpool	W 2-0	Untraced	12,000																			
9	Apr 1 (a)	Millwall A	L 1-5	Oswald	7,000																			
10	3 (a)	Southampton	W 1-0	Oswald	10,000																			
		Appearances																							
		Goals																							

NB. No further details available for matches 8, 9, 10.

2 goals untraced

1899-1900

Manager: W.Wilton

Player column headers (left to right): Dickie, Smith N, Drummond, Gibson, Neil, Dunlop, Campbell, Miller J, Hamilton, Hyslop, Smith A, Robertson J, McPherson, Wilkie, Crawford, Graham, Mitchell, Sharp A, McKinlay, Howden, Robertson R, Millar, Wilson, Urquhart, Stark, Cameron, Miller JE, Robertson, Taylor, Duncan, Tutty, Reid

Scottish League

#	Date		Opponent	Result	Scorers	Att
1	Aug	19 (a)	Third Lanark RV	W 5-1	Campbell 2, J.Miller, Hyslop, N.Smith	16,000
2		26 (a)	Clyde	W 6-2	Hyslop 2, McPherson, A.Smith, J.Robertson, Untraced 1	10,000
3	Sep	2 (h)	Hearts	W 4-3	Campbell 2, Hamilton 2	20,000
4		9 (a)	Kilmarnock	W 4-2	Campbell, A.Smith, McPherson, Hamilton	10,000
5		18 (a)	Hearts	D 1-1	Hamilton	15,000
6		25 (h)	Hibernian	W 3-2	Hamilton, A.Smith, Wilkie	12,000
7	Oct	7 (h*)	Celtic	D 3-3	Graham 2, A.Smith	40,000
8		14 (h)	Clyde	W 7-0	McPherson 3, A.Smith 2, Sharp, Hamilton	5,000
9		21 (a)	Hibernian	W 2-0	A.Smith 2	16,000
10	Nov	4 (h)	Dundee	W 6-0	A.Smith 3, Hamilton, Wilkie, Watson (og)	6,000
11		25 (h)	St Bernard's	W 4-3	McPherson 2, Hamilton, J.Robertson	5,000
12	Dec	2 (a)	St Mirren	W 3-1	Hamilton 3	
13		9(h†)	Kilmarnock	W 6-1	Wilkie 2, Hamilton 2, J.Robertson, Graham	5,000
14		16(h‡)	St Mirren	W 4-1	Neil 2 (1 pen), A.Smith, Hamilton	2,000
15	Jan	1 (a)	Celtic	L 2-3	A.Smith, Wilkie	20,000
16		6 (h)	Third Lanark RV	W 2-1	Neil, McPherson	4,000
17		20 (a)	Dundee	W 3-2	Hamilton 3	12,000
18	Feb	3 (a#)	St Bernard's	W 4-1	McPherson, Campbell, Gibson, Wilkie	4,000

FINAL LEAGUE POSITION: 1st * Played at Celtic Park, Glasgow.
† Final fixture at first Ibrox Park. ‡ Played at Meadowside Park, Glasgow. # Played At Ibrox Stadium.

1 goal untraced. 1 own-goal.

Scottish FA Cup

#	Date		Opponent	Result	Scorers	Att
1	Jan	13 (h)	Morton	W 4-2	McPherson 2, Wilkie, A.Smith	7,000
2		27 (h)	Maybole	W12-0	Hamilton 4, Wilkie 3, A.Smith, Robertson, Hyslop, Neil, Gibson	3,000
QF	Feb	17 (a)	Partick Thistle	W 6-1	Hamilton 2, A.Smith, McPherson, Wilkie, Graham	10,000
SF		24 (h)	Celtic	D 2-2	A.Smith, McPherson	33,000
R	Mar	10 (a)	Celtic	L 0-4		32,000

Glasgow Cup

#	Date		Opponent	Result	Scorers	Att
1	Sep	16 (a)	Third Lanark RV	D 0-0		15,000
R		23 (h)	Third Lanark RV	W 5-0	A.Smith 2, Hamilton 2, Graham	15,000
SF	Oct	28 (h)	Queen's Park	W 7-3	Wilkie 2, Hamilton 2, Neil (pen), A.Smith, McPherson	18,000
F	Nov	11 (n*)	Celtic	D 1-1	Wilkie	10,000
R		18 (n*)	Celtic	W 1-0	Neil (pen)	8,000

* Played at first Cathkin Park

Glasgow Merchants' Charity Cup

#	Date		Opponent	Result	Scorers	Att
SF	May	10 (n*)	Third Lanark RV	W 2-0	Hamilton, A.Smith	4,000
F		12 (n*)	Celtic	W 5-1	Campbell, Gibson, Hamilton, J.Miller, Battles (og)	15,000

* Played at second Hampden Park

1 own-goal.

Inter-City League

#	Date		Opponent	Result	Scorers	Att
1	Dec	30 (h)	Hearts*	W 3-1	Wilkie 3	8,000
2	Jan	2 (h)	Hibernian	W 3-0	A.Smith 2, J.Miller	5,000
3	Mar	3 (h)	Queen's Park	L 1-3	Campbell	12,000
4		24 (h)	Third Lanark RV	W 4-1	Wilkie, A.Smith, Gibson, Campbell	5,000
5		31 (h)	Celtic	L 1-2	Hamilton	15,000
6	Apr	7 (a)	Hearts	L 1-4	J.Miller	
7		14 (a)	Hibernian	W 1-0	Wilson	6,000
8		16 (a)	Celtic	L 1-2	Hamilton	11,000
9		25 (a)	Third Lanark RV	D 4-4	A.Smith 2, Hyslop, McPherson	2,000
10	May	5 (a)	Queen's Park	W 2-1	J.Robertson (pen), McPherson	6,000

FINAL LEAGUE POSITION: 3rd * Opening fixture at second Ibrox (the present Ibrox stadium).

Other matches

#	Date		Opponent	Result	Scorers	Att
1	Aug	15 (h)	Hibernian	W 3-2	McPherson, Hyslop, Neil (pen)	5,000
2	Aug	16 (a)	Clydebank J	W 5-1	Untraced	
3		21 (h)	St Mirren	W 4-0	Hamilton 2, McPherson, Wilkie	5,000
4		23 (a)	Partick Thistle	D 2-2	J.Miller, Sharp	2,000
5		28 (a)	Celtic*	D 2-2	Hamilton 2	10,000
6	Sep	4 (h)	Liverpool	D 2-2	A.Smith, J.Miller	4,000
7	Dec	23 (a)	St Bernard's†	W 1-0	Wilkie	4,000
8		25 (a)	Preston NE	L 0-4		8,000
9		26 (a)	Liverpool	L 2-3	Untraced	
10	Jan	3 (a)	Everton	L 2-4	Hyslop 2	7,000
11	Mar	17 (a)	Manchester C	W 3-0	Campbell, Hyslop, Wilkie	
12	Apr	2 (a)	Dunf'line & Dis	W 4-2	Untraced	
13	Apr	21 (h)	Hibernian	L 0-3		4,000
14		23 (a)	Renton	W 5-1	Sharp 2, Wilkie 2, Hyslop	
15		28 (h)	Sheffield U	L 0-1		11,000
16		30 (h)	Aston Villa	D 0-0		5,000
17	May	3 (a)	Johnstone	W 5-2	Untraced	
18	May	7 (a)	Orion	W 4-1	Untraced	
19		8 (a)	Elgin City	W 8-3	Untraced	
20		14 (a)	Arthurlie	W 4-1		
21		15 (a)	Renfrew V‡	D 2-2	Wilkie, Hamilton	
22		26 (h)	Dunbartonshire#	W 5-3	Campbell 2, J.Robertson, Neil, Tutty	

* Sandy McMahon Benefit match. † League fixture abandoned after 83 minutes due to bad light.
‡Councillor Clarke's Poor Children Fund Benefit Match. #Benefit match for the widow and children of James Wilson.
NB. No further details are available for matches 7, 8, 14, 15, 17, 18, 30, 21.

28 goals untraced.

1900-01

Manager: W.Wilton

Scottish League

No	Date		Opponent	Result	Scorers	Att	Dickie	Smith N	Drummond	Gibson	Neil	Robertson	Campbell	Cameron	Hamilton RC	McPherson	Smith A	Stark	Tutty	Crawford	Speedie	Graham	Sharp A	Brown
1	Aug	18 (h)	Third Lanark RV	W 4-0	Gibson, Cameron 2, McPherson	10,000	1	2	3	4	5	6	7	8	9	10	11							
2		25 (a)	Hearts	W 1-0	Neil	10,000	1	2	3	4	5	6	7	9	8	10	11							
3	Sep	1 (h)	Kilmarnock	W 5-1	Campbell 2, R.C.Hamilton, Cameron, A.Smith	9,500	1	2	3	4	5	6	7	9	10	8	11							
4		8 (a)	Partick Thistle	W 2-1	A.Smith, Cameron	9,000	1	2	3	4		6	7	9		10	11	5	8					
5		17 (a)	Hibernian	L 1-4	Campbell		1	2		4		6	7	8	9	10	11	5		3				
6		24 (h)	Hearts	W 1-0	A.Smith	6,000	1	2	3	4		6	7	8	9	10	11	5						
7		29 (a)	Queen's Park	W 3-2	Robertson (pen), McPherson, Russell (og)	16,000	1	2	3	4		6	7	8	9	10	11	5						
8	Oct	6 (a)	Celtic	L 1-2	Cameron	12,000	1	2	3	4		6	7	8	9	10	11	5						
9		13 (a)	Third Lanark RV	D 1-1	McPherson	5,000	1		3	4		6	7	8	9	10	11	5			2			
10		20 (h)	Dundee	W 4-2	R.C.Hamilton 3, A.Smith	9,000	1	2	3	4		6	7		9	8	11	5			10			
11	Nov	3 (h)	Partick Thistle	W 4-1	R.C.Hamilton 3, A.Smith	7,000	1	2	3	4		6	7		9	8	11	5			10			
12		17 (a)	Morton	W 3-1	R.C.Hamilton, Speedie, McPherson	7,000	1	2	3	4		6	7		9	8	11	5			10			
13		24 (h)	St Mirren	W 5-2	R.C.Hamilton 4, Graham	6,000	1	2	3	4		6			9	8	11	5			10	7		
14	Dec	1 (a)	Kilmarnock	W 2-1	Speedie, McPherson	10,000	1	2	3	4	5	6	8		9	7	11				10			
15		15 (a)	Dundee	W 5-1	Campbell 2, R.C.Hamilton, Robertson, A.Smith	10,000	1	2	3	4	5	6	7		9	8	11				10			
16		29 (h)	Queen's Park	W 3-2	Robertson, Graham, Speedie	11,000	1	2	3	4	5	6			9	8	11				10	7		
17	Jan	1 (h)	Celtic	W 2-1	Speedie, McPherson	30,000	1	2	3	4	5	6	11		9	8					10	7		
18		5 (a)	St Mirren	W 4-1	R.C.Hamilton 3, McPherson	6,000	1	2		4		6	11		9			5		3	10	7		
19		26 (h)	Hibernian	W 6-0	R.C.Hamilton 2, Sharp, A.Smith, Handling (og)		1	2	3	4	5	6	7		9		11				10		8	
20	Feb	16 (h)	Morton	W 3-2	R.C.Hamilton 2, Speedie	5,000	1		3		5	6	11		9					4	2	10	7	8
				Appearances			20	18	18	19	9	20	18	9	19	18	17	12	1	4	11	5	2	
				Goals						1	1	3	5	5	20	7	7				5	2	2	

FINAL LEAGUE POSITION: 1st

2 own-goals

Scottish FA Cup

No	Date		Opponent	Result	Att	Dickie	Smith N	Drummond	Gibson	Neil	Robertson	Campbell	Hamilton RC	Smith A	Speedie	Sharp A
1	Jan	12 (a)	Celtic	L 0-1	28,000	1	2	3	4	5	6	7	9	11	10	8
				Appearances		1	1	1	1	1	1	1	1	1	1	1
				Goals												

Glasgow Cup

No	Date		Opponent	Result	Scorers	Att	Dickie	Smith N	Drummond	Gibson	Robertson	Campbell	Cameron	Hamilton RC	McPherson	Smith A	Stark	Crawford	Speedie
1	Sep	15 (a)	Celtic	D 3-3	R.C.Hamilton, Robertson, A.Smith	30,000	1	2		4	6	7	9	10	8	11	5	3	
R		22 (h)	Celtic	W 4-3	R.C.Hamilton 2, Cameron, Campbell	30,000	1	2	3	4	6	7	8	9	10	11	5		
SF	Oct	27 (h)	Third Lanark RV	W 2-1	Cameron, McPherson	12,000	1	2	3	4	6	7	9	10	8	11	5		
F	Nov	10 (n*)	Partick Thistle	W 3-1	McPherson, Robertson, R.C.Hamilton	7,000	1	2	3	4	6	7		9	8	11	5		10
				Appearances			4	4	3	4	4	4	3	4	4	4	4	1	1
				Goals							2	1	2	4	2	1			

*Played at Celtic Park.

Glasgow Merchants' Charity Cup

No	Date		Opponent	Result	Att	Dickie	Smith N	Drummond	Gibson	Neil	Robertson	Campbell	Hamilton RC	McPherson	Smith A	Speedie	Graham	Sharp A
1	May	2 (n*)	Celtic	D 0-0	12,000	1	2	3	4	5	6	7	9	8	11	10		
R		3 (n*)	Celtic	L 0-1	4,000	1	2	3	4	5	6	11	9			10	7	8
				Appearances		2	2	2	2	2	2	2	2	1	1	2	1	1
				Goals														

*Played at the Exhibition Grounds, Gilmorehill.

Inter-City League

No	Date		Opponent	Result	Scorers	Att	Dickie	Smith N	Drummond	Gibson	Neil	Robertson	Campbell	Cameron	Hamilton RC	McPherson	Smith A	Stark	Speedie	Graham	Sharp A	Brown	Hamilton JR	Munsie	McIntyre	McKinlay
1	Jan	2 (h)	Hibernian	W 2-1	J.R.Hamilton, R.C.Hamilton	10,000	1	2			5	11			9	10		4	3		7		6	8		
2		19 (h)	Third Lanark RV	L 0-2		2,500	1		3	4		6	8		9		11	5	2	10	7					
3	Mar	2 (h)	Hearts	D 2-2	Sharp, R.C.Hamilton (pen)	2,000	1		3		5		7		9		11	4	2	10		8	6			
4		9 (h)	Queen's Park	D 2-2	Speedie, R.C.Hamilton	10,000		2	3	4	5	6			9	8	11		10	7					1	
5		23 (a)	Third Lanark RV	W 4-1	R.C.Hamilton 2, A.Smith, Graham	7,000	1	2			5	6			9		11	4	3	10	7	8				
6	Apr	8 (h)	Celtic	W 4-3	R.C.Hamilton 3, Graham	5,000	1		3	4	5	6	11		9	10	8		2	7						
7		13 (a)	Celtic	L 0-1		10,000	1	2			5	6			9	8	11	4	3	10	7					
8		15 (a)	Hibernian	L 0-1		4,000	1	2	3		5	6	7		9	8	11	4	10							
9		20 (a)	Queen's Park	W 3-1	Sharp 2, Campbell	11,000	1	2	3		5	6	7		9	8	11		10			8				
10		27 (a)	Hearts	D 1-1	A.Smith	6,000	1	2	3	4	5	6	7		9	8	11		10							
				Appearances			9	7	7	7	9	6	6	2	9	6	7	7	6	7	6	4	2	1	1	1
				Goals									1		8		2		1	2	3		1			

FINAL LEAGUE POSITION: 3rd

Further match details for this season are continued on page 277

1901-02

Manager: W.Wilton

Scottish League

Player columns: Dickie, Smith N, Drummond, Gibson, Neil, Robertson, Campbell J, McDougall L, Hamilton RC, Speedie, Smith A, Crawford, Stark, Wilkie, Goudie, Morton, McPherson J, Graham, McPherson N, Young, Hamilton JR, Lennie, Walker J, Mackie, Sharp, Miller, Campbell, Buchan, Wood, May, Grant, Richmond

#	Date		Opponent	Result	Scorers	Att.
1	Aug 17	(a)	Kilmarnock	L 2-4	R.C.Hamilton, McDougall	6,000
2	24	(h)	Hearts	W 2-1	Speedie, R.C.Hamilton	17,000
3	31	(a)	Dundee	W 3-0	McDougall 2, Speedie	12,000
4	Sep 7	(h)	Kilmarnock	W 3-2	Campbell, A.Smith, Gibson	16,000
5	16	(a)	Hearts	W 2-0	Neil, R.C.Hamilton	
6	21	(a)	St Mirren	W 5-1	Campbell 2, A.Smith, Wilkie, Jackson (og)	10,000
7	23	(h)	Hibernian	L 0-2		10,000
8	28	(a)	Third Lanark RV	D 2-2	A.Smith, R.C.Hamilton	16,000
9	Oct 5	(h)	Celtic	D 2-2	Neil, Speedie	30,000
10	19	(a)	Hibernian	W 3-2	Wilkie, R.C.Hamilton (pen), Neil	12,000
11	Nov 2	(h)	Queen's Park	W 2-1	J.McPherson, R.C.Hamilton	12,000
12	9	(a)	Morton	W 3-2	J.McPherson 2, Wilkie	7,000
13	16	(h)	Third Lanark RV	L 1-4	Robertson	5,000
14	Dec 7	(a)	Morton	W 2-1	A.Smith, R.C.Hamilton	3,000
15	Jan 1	(a)	Celtic	W 4-2	N.Smith, Campbell, Robertson, R.C.Hamilton	40,000
16	4	(a)	Queen's Park	W 1-0	Robertson	20,000
17	18	(h)	St Mirren	W 3-2	Speedie 2, Cameron (og)	12,000
18	Mar 29	(h)	Dundee	w 3-1	R.C.Hamilton, A.Smith, Speedie	13,000

FINAL LEAGUE POSITION: 1st

Appearances: 15 15 12 13 16 8 12 4 16 16 18 8 16 14 1 2 5 3 2 1 1
Goals: 1 1 3 3 4 3 9 6 5 3 3

2 own-goals

Scottish FA Cup

#	Date		Opponent	Result	Scorers	Att.
1	Jan 11	(h)	Johnstone	W 6-1	Howie (og), Speedie, A.Smith, J.R.Hamilton, Robertson, Graham	2,000
2	25	(h)	Caledonian	W 5-1	Wilkie, A.Smith 2, Campbell, J.R.Hamilton	5,000
QF	Feb 22	(h)	Kilmarnock	W 2-0	Speedie, A.Smith	10,000
SF	Mar 22	(h)	Hibernian	L 0-2		35,000

Appearances: 4 4 3 4 1 4 3 2 4 4 1 3 2 1 1 1 2
Goals: 1 1 2 4 1 1 2

1 own-goal

Glasgow Cup

#	Date		Opponent	Result	Scorers	Att.
1	Sep 14	(h)	Normal A	W 5-0	Untraced	
SF	Oct 12	(h)	Partick Thistle	W 4-1	Gibson, R.C.Hamilton, A.Smith, Wilkie	5,000
F	26	(h)	Celtic*	D 2-2	Speedie, Wilkie	40,000

* Rangers were awarded the trophy, Celtic refusing to replay at Ibrox Stadium.

Appearances: 3 3 3 2 3 1 2 3 2 2 3 3 1 1 1
Goals: 1 1 1 1 2

5 goals untraced

Glasgow Merchants' Charity Cup

#	Date		Opponent	Result	Scorers	Att.
1	May 17	(h*)	Hibernian	L 0-1		10,000

* Played at first Cathkin Park, Glasgow.

Appearances: 1 1 1 1 1 1 1 1 1 1 1
Goals:

Glasgow International Exhibition Cup

#	Date		Opponent	Result	Scorers	Att.
1	Aug 13	(n*)	St Mirren	W 8-1	R.C.Hamilton 4, Gibson 2, Speedie, Cambell	7,000
SF	29	(n*)	Third Lanark RV	W 4-1	R.C.Hamilton 2, A.Smith, Neil	7,000
F	Sep 9	(n*)	Celtic	W 3-1	R.C.Hamilton 2, Neil	16,000

* Played at the Exhibtion Grounds, Gilmorehill.

Appearances: 3 3 2 3 3 1 1 2 3 3 3 1 2 2 1
Goals: 2 2 1 8 1 1

British League Cup

#	Date		Opponent	Result	Scorers	Att.
SF	May 1	(a)	Everton	D 1-1	R.C.Hamilton	8,000
R	3	(h*)	Everton	W 3-2	Speedie, R.C.Hamilton, Walker	12,000
F	June 17	(a)	Celtic	L 2-3	R.C.Hamilton, Speedie	12,000

Ibrox Disaster Fund Benefit Tournament.. * Played at Celtic Park, Glasgow.
† Played at first Cathkin Park, Glasgow. Delayed in order to coincide with coronation of King Edward VII.

Appearances: 3 2 1 3 2 2 1 3 2 2 2 3 2 1 2 1 1
Goals: 3 2 1

Inter-City League

#	Date		Opponent	Result	Scorers	Att.
1	Dec 28	(a)	Hearts	D 2-2	R.C.Hamilton 2	2,500
2	Mar 1	(h)	Celtic	L 0-5		12,000
3	8	(h)	Third Lanark RV	D 2-2	Graham, J.R.Hamilton	5,000
4	31	(a)	Third Lanark RV	L 2-5	Speedie, Graham	7,000
5	Apr 19	(h*)	Hearts	L 0-2		5,000
6	21	(a)	Hibernian	L 0-1		5,000
7	May 7	(h†)	Hibernian	D 1-1	May	2,000
8	9	(a)	Celtic	L 0-2		4,000
9	10	(a)	Queen's Park‡	D 1-1	Walker	8,000

FINAL LEAGUE POSITION: 5th

Appearances: 6 5 2 6 7 5 4 3 4 8 5 8 5 3 2 7 2 3 6 1 1 1 2 1 1
Goals: 2 1 2 1 1 1

* Played at Tynecastle Park, Edinburgh. † Played at first Cathkin Park, Glasgow.
‡ All clubs played Queen's Park once only, each fixture's points counting double.

Knowe played number-6 in Match 8.

Further match details for this season are continued on page 277

1902-03

Manager: W.Wilton

Scottish League

#	Date		Opponent		Result	Scorers	Att
1	Aug	16 (a)	Third Lanark RV	L	2-4	Hamilton 2	13,000
2		23 (h)	Partick Thistle	W	9-0	Hamilton 4, Neil 2, Lennie 2, Mackie	7,000
3		30 (a)	Port Glasgow A	W	3-0	Stark, Neil (pen), Hamilton	7,000
4	Sep	6 (a)	Hearts	L	1-2	Neil (pen)	14,000
5		15 (a)	Hibernian	L	0-1		6,500
6		20 (h)	Morton	W	4-1	Fraser, Hamilton, McDonald, A.Smith	6,000
7		27 (a)	Queen's Park	W	2-0	Mackie, Hamilton	12,000
8		29 (h)	Hibernian	L	2-5	J.Walker, Stark	15,000
9	Oct	4 (h)	Hearts	W	2-1	Speedie 2	11,000
10		11 (a)	Morton	W	4-0	J.Robertson, Hamilton, McDonald 2	7,000
11		18 (a)	Celtic	D	1-1	A.Smith	25,000
12	Nov	1 (h)	Third Lanark RV	W	2-0	Mackie 2	12,000
13		8 (a)	Partick Thistle	W	4-2	J.Walker, Neil (pen), A.Smith 2	7,000
14		15 (h)	Queen's Park	W	3-2	Speedie, J.Robertson, Neil	10,000
15		22 (a)	St Mirren	W	1-0	A.Smith	
16		29 (h)	Kilmarnock	W	5-0	A.Smith, Hamilton, J.Walker 2, McDonald	4,500
17	Dec	6 (a)	Dundee	L	1-3	Neil	12,000
18		13 (h)	Port Glasgow A	W	4-2	Brodie, Hamilton 2, Speedie	3,000
19		20 (a)	Kilmarnock	D	0-0		4,000
20	Jan	1 (h)	Celtic	D	3-3	J.Walker 2, Neil	25,000
21		3 (h)	St Mirren	D	2-2	McDonald, J.Walker	6,000
22		17 (h)	Dundee	D	1-1	Gibson	10,000

FINAL LEAGUE POSITION: 3rd

#	Dickie	Crawford	Drummond	Gibson	Neil	Robertson J	Graham	Walker J	Hamilton RC	Mackie	Smith A	Lennie	Smith N	Stark	Walker W	Speedie	Fraser	McDonald	Wallace	Henderson	Brodie	McMurray
1	1	2	3	4	5	6	7	8	9	10	11											
2	1	2	3	4	5	6		8	9	10	11	7										
3	1		3	4	5	10		8	9		11	7	2	6								
4	1		3	4	5				10	9	11	7	2	6	8							
5	1		3	4	5		7		9	8	11			2		6		10				
6	1		3			6			9		11			2	5	8	10	4	7			
7	1		3	4	5	6			9	10	11			2		8			7			
8	1				5	6		8	9		11	7	2	4	10	3						
9	1		3	4		6			9	10	11			5		8	2	7				
10	1		3	4	5	10			9		11			6		8	2	7				
11	1		3	4		6			9	10	11		2	5		8		7				
12	1		3	4	5	6			9	10	11					8	2	7				
13	1		3		5	6		10	9		11			4		8	2	7				
14			3	4	5	9				10	11			6		8	2	7		1		
15	1		3	4	5	6		10	9		11					8	2	7				
16	1		3	4	5	6		10	9		11					8	2	7				
17	1		3	4	5	6		10	7	9	11					8	2					
18	1	2				6		10	9		11			5		8	3				4	7
19	1		3	4	5	6		10	9		11					8	2	7				
20	1		3	4	5	6		10	9		11	7				8	2					
21	1	2			5	6		10	9		11					8	3	7		4		
22	1		3	4		6		10	9		11			5		8	2	7				
Appearances	21	4	19	17	17	20	2	17	19	8	22	5	7	12	2	18	15	13	1	2	1	
Goals				1	8	2		7	13	4	6	2		2		4	1	5			1	

Scottish FA Cup

#	Date		Opponent		Result	Scorers	Att
1	Jan	10 (h)	Auchterarder T	W	7-0	Speedie 3, McDonald 2, Hamilton, Gibson	2,000
2		24 (h)	Kilmarnock	W	4-0	J.Walker 2, J.Robertson, McDonald	7,500
QF	Feb	28 (a)	Celtic	W	3-0	A.Smith, J.Walker, Hamilton	40,000
SF	Mar	7 (a*)	Stenhousemuir	W	4-1	J.Robertson 2, Hamilton 2	8,000
F	Apr	11 (n*)	Hearts	D	1-1	Stark	30,000
R		18 (n*)	Hearts	D	0-0		35,000
2R		25 (n*)	Hearts	W	2-0	Mackie, Hamilton	35,000

* Played at Celtic Park, Glasgow.

#	Dickie	Crawford	Drummond	Gibson	Neil	Robertson J	Walker J	Hamilton RC	Mackie	Smith A	Stark	Speedie	Fraser	McDonald	Henderson
1	1	2		4		6		9		11	5	8	3	7	10
2	1		3	4		6	10	9		11	5	8	2	7	
QF	1		3	4		6	10	9		11	5	8	2	7	
SF	1		3	4		6	10	9		11	5	8	2	7	
F	1		3	4		6	10	9		11	5	8	2	7	
R	1		3	4		6	10	9		11	5	8	2	7	
2R	1		3			6		9	8	11	5	10	2	7	4
Appearances	7	1	6	6		7	5	7	1	7	7	7	7	7	1
Goals				1		3	3	5	1	1	1	3		3	

Glasgow Cup

#	Date		Opponent		Result	Scorers	Att
1	Sep	13 (a)	Third Lanark RV	L	0-1		12,000

#	Dickie	Drummond	Neil	Robertson J	Walker J	Hamilton RC	Mackie	Smith A	Stark	Speedie	Fraser
1	1	3	5	6	10	9	8	11	7	2	4
Appearances	1	1	1	1	1	1	1	1	1	1	1
Goals											

Glasgow Merchants' Charity Cup

#	Date		Opponent		Result	Scorers	Att
1	May	16 (h)	St Mirren	L	0-1		5,000

#	Dickie	Robertson J	Graham	Walker J	Smith A	Smith N	Stark	Speedie	Fraser	McDonald	Paton
1	1	6	7	8	11	2	5	10	3	4	9
Appearances	1	1	1	1	1	1	1	1	1	1	1
Goals											

The Rangers Benefit Tournament

#	Date		Opponent		Result	Scorers	Att
1	Aug	20 (n*)	Celtic	L	2-7	Hamilton, J.Walker	5,000

* Played at second Hampden Park, Glasgow, Ibrox Disaster Fund Benefit Tournament.

#	Dickie	Crawford	Drummond	Gibson	Neil	Robertson J	Graham	Walker J	Hamilton RC	Smith A	Mackie
1	1	2	3	4	5	6	7	8	9	11	10
Appearances	1	1	1	1	1	1	1	1	1	1	1
Goals								1	1		

Inter-City League

#	Date		Opponent		Result	Scorers	Att
1	Jan	31 (h)	Hearts	D	4-4	Hamilton 2, Speedie 2	6,000
2	Mar	21 (a)	St Mirren	L	0-4		2,000
3		28 (h)	Hibernian	W	5-2	A.Smith 2, Hamilton, Speedie, Mackie	8,000
4	Apr	4 (a)	Partick Thistle	L	0-2		3,000
5		13 (h)	Celtic	D	2-2	McMurray, Speedie	12,000
6	May	2 (h)	Third Lanark RV	D	0-0		6,000
7		9 (h)	Queen's Park	W	4-1	Speedie, A.Smith, Paton, Hamilton	6,000
8		11 (a)	Dundee	W	2-0	A.Smith, Speedie	

FINAL LEAGUE POSITION: 5th

#	Dickie	Crawford	Drummond	Gibson	Neil	Robertson J	Graham	Walker J	Hamilton RC	Mackie	Smith A	Smith N	Stark	Walker W	Speedie	Fraser	McDonald	Henderson	Brodie	McMurray	Paton	Rankin
1	1		3			6			10	9	11	7	2	5	8			4				
2	1				5				10	9	11	2	6			3	7	4	8			
3	1		2	4		6		7	9	8	11		5		10	3		4				
4	1		3	6	5			7		8		11		9	2			4	10			
5	1	3		6					9		11	2	5		8			4	10		7	
6	1				6			8	9		11	2			10	3		4			7	5
7	1	3			6			7	8		11	2	5		10			4			9	
8	1				6			8			11	7	2	5	10	3		4				
Appearances	8	2	3	3	2	5		7	6	2	7	3	6	6	1	6	5	1	7		3	2
Goals					4	1		4			6							1	1			

Further match details for this season are continued on page 277

1903-04

Manager: W.Wilton

Scottish League

Player columns: Dickie M, Smith N, Fraser, Gibson N, Stark J, Robertson JT, Walker J, Mackie, Hamilton RC, Speedie FB, Smith A, Henderson GH, Drummond J, McDonald, Hartley, Campbell D, Dinsmore HR, Watson HR, Neil RG, Gray J, Chalk C, Paton T, Donaghy, Findlay J, Lloyd F, Gibson W, Lorimer J, McGraw, Gilchrist, Speedie W, Johnstone, Clark

#	Date		Opponent	Result	Scorers	Att.
1	Aug	15 (h)	Third Lanark	W 4-3	Hamilton 3 (1 pen), A.Smith	7,000
2		22 (a)	Airdrieonians	W 3-1	Stark, Speedie, Hamilton	10,000
3		29 (a)	St Mirren	D 2-2	Hamilton, Walker	10,000
4	Sep	5 (a)	Motherwell	W 5-2	Hamilton 4, Speedie	6,000
5		19 (h)	Hearts	W 5-1	Hamilton 3, Walker 2	9,000
6		26 (h)	Queen's Park	W 5-0	Hamilton 2, Robertson (pen), Walker, Mackie	14,000
7		28 (a)	Partick Thistle	W 4-1	Speedie, Walker, Robertson (pen), A.Smith	8,000
8	Oct	10 (a*)	Third Lanark	L 0-1		25,000
9		17 (a)	Celtic	D 0-0		25,000
10		24 (a)	Morton	W 3-1	Speedie, Walker, Robertson	4,000
11		31 (h)	Dundee	W 6-1	Mackie, Walker 2, Hamilton 2, Jeffrey (og)	10,300
12	Nov	7 (a)	Queens Park	W 3-2	Speedie, Hamilton, Drummond	16,000
13		14 (h)	Hibernian	1-1	Hamilton	8,000
14		21 (a)	Dundee	L 1-3	A.Smith	14,400
15		28 (h†)	Morton	W 5-0	Hamilton 2, Speedie, Walker 2	3,000
16	Dec	5 (a)	Kilmarnock	D 2-2	N.Smith, Untraced	3,000
17		12 (h)	Motherwell	W 3-0	Hamilton, Mackie 2	3,000
18		19 (a)	Port Glasgow A	D 1-1	Mackie	4,000
19		26 (a)	Hibernian	W 2-1	Hamilton, Robertson	6,000
20	Jan	1 (a)	Celtic	D 2-2	Speedie, Mackie	30,000
21		2 (h)	Partick Thistle	W 2-0	Walker, Hamilton	6,000
22		9 (a)	St Mirren	L 4-5	Mackie 2, Hamilton 2 (1 pen)	
23		16 (h)	Kilmarnock	W 3-0	Mackie, Hamilton, Donaghy	4,000
24		30 (a)	Hearts	L 1-2	Mackie	12,000
25	Feb	13 (h)	Port Glasgow A	W 8-1	Speedie 3, A.Smith, Hamilton 2, Campbell, Gibson	3,500
26	Mar	26 (a)	Airdrieonians	W 5-0	Donaghy, Chalk, Mackie 2, Stark	6,000

FINAL LEAGUE POSITION: 3rd

*Played at Ibrox Stadium. †Played at Cappielow Park, Greenock.

Appearances: 15 22 14 17 22 18 21 23 24 23 16 18 14 1 4 4 1 11 5 1 4 2 5 1

Goals: 1 1 2 4 11 12 28 10 4 1 1 1 2

1 own-goal. 1 goal untraced

Scottish FA Cup

#	Date		Opponent	Result	Scorers	Att.
1	Jan	23 (h)	Hearts	W 3-2	Hamilton, Walker 2	30,000
2	Feb	6 (a)	Hibernian	W 2-1	Mackie, Walker	17,000
QF		20 (a)	St Mirren	W 1-0	Hamilton	17,000
SF	Mar	5 (h)	Morton	W 3-0	Walker 2, Hamilton	10,000
F	Apr	16 (n)	Celtic	L 2-3	Speedie 2	64,472

Final played at third Hampden Park, Glasgow (The present stadium)

Appearances: 5 4 5 5 5 5 4 5 5 5 1 5 1

Goals: 5 1 3 2

Glasgow Cup

#	Date		Opponent	Result		Att.
1	Sep	12 (h)	Third Lanark	L 0-2		20,000

Appearances: 1 1 1 1 1 1 1 1 1 1 1

Goals:

Inter-City League

#	Date		Opponent	Result	Scorers	Att.
1	Mar	12 (a)	Queen's Park	L 0-2		10,000
2		19 (a)	Hearts	L 0-1		6,000
3	Apr	2 (a)	Dundee	L 1-3	Mackie	2,000
4		4 (h)	St Mirren	L 1-2	Speedie	4,500
5		18 (a)	Hibernian	L 0-3		3,000
6		23 (h)	Partick Thistle	D 1-1	Speedie	3,000
7		30 (a)	Celtic	L 0-2		10,000
8	May	10 (h)	Third Lanark	W 4-1	Collins 3, Mackie	1,000

Appearances: 3 5 4 5 6 2 1 7 1 5 8 7 1 1 5 4 3 2 2 1 1 2 4 2 1 1 1

Goals: 2 2 1

Bolton played number-10 in Match 7; Kerr played number-7 in Match 8; Collins played number-10 in Match 8 and scored 3 goals.

Glasgow Merchants' Charity Cup

#	Date		Opponent	Result	Scorers	Att.
SF	May	7 (n)	Third Lanark	W 1-0	Speedie	17,000
F		14 (n)	Celtic	W 5-2	Mackie, Robertson 2, Donaghy, Speedie (pen)	26,000

Both matches played at third Hampden Park, Glasgow.

Appearances: 2 2 2 2 1 2 1 2 2 2 1 2 1

Goals: 2 1 2 1

Further match details for this season are continued on page 278

1904-05

Manager: W.Wilton

Scottish League

Player columns: Allan, Fraser, Gilchrist, Henderson, May, Robertson, Kyle, Mackie, Hamilton, Speedie, Smith A, Smith N, Stark, Easton, McColl, Donaghy, Walker John (t), Turnbull, Watson, Gourlay, Sinclair, McEwan, Campbell, Craig, Low, Chalmers, Steel, Chapman, Gibson, Galbraith, Lawrie, Chalk

#	Date	Opponent	Result	Scorers	Att
1	Aug 20 (a)	Third Lanark	L 1-2	Mackie	20,000
2	27 (h)	Hibernian	W 4-0	Hamilton 2, Mackie, Kyle	12,000
3	Sep 3 (h)	Partick Thistle	W 8-1	Stark, Speedie 3, Kyle 2, Hamilton 2	7,000
4	10 (a)	Dundee	W 3-0	Hamilton 2, Chaplin (og)	14,760
5	17 (a)	Queens Park	W 4-0	Kyle 2, A.Smith, Hamilton	30,231
6	19 (a)	Hibernian	W 2-1	Hamilton, McColl	
7	26 (h)	Hearts	D 1-1	Speedie	20,188
8	Oct 1 (h)	St Mirren	L 2-3	Mackie, Turnbull	10,000
9	15 (a)	Celtic	D 2-2	Hamilton, Mackie	25,000
10	22 (h)	Queens Park	W 5-0	Mackie 2, Walker, McColl, Hamilton	15,000
11	29 (h)	Dundee	W 2-1	McColl, Mackie	13,000
12	Nov 5 (a)	Hearts	W 5-0	A.Smith, Walker 2, Speedie, Hamilton	10,000
13	12 (a)	St Mirren	L 0-3		
14	19 (h)	Third Lanark	W 3-1	Kyle 2, A.Smith	
15	Dec 3 (a)	Kilmarnock	W 4-0	Kyle 2, Hamilton, Robertson	6,500
16	10 (a)	Motherwell	W 2-0	McLean (og), Hamilton	5,000
17	17 (h)	Airdireonians	W 4-1	Speedie, Hamilton, Kyle, Mackie	4,000
18	31 (a)	Airdireonians	D 2-2	May, Speedie (pen)	8,000
19	Jan 3 (a)	Partick Thistle	W 4-1	Kyle, Hamilton 2, Robertson	11,000
20	14 (h)	Motherwell	W 3-2	Speedie 2 (1 pen), McColl	6,000
21	21 (h)	Kilmarnock	W 6-2	May, Walker, Speedie 2, McColl, Mackie	
22	Feb 4 (a)	Port Glasgow A	W 3-0	Walker, McColl 2	7,000
23	18 (a)	Celtic	L 1-4	Kyle	30,000
24	Mar 18 (h)	Port Glasgow A	W 5-1	A.Smith 2, Hamilton, Speedie, Low	5,000
25	Apr 1 (h)	Morton	W 5-0	Hamilton 2, A.Smith 2, Kyle	5,000
26	29 (h)	Morton	W 2-0	Speedie, Kyle	3,000

FINAL LEAGUE POSITION: 2nd

Appearances: 8 13 1 14 21 20 23 20 17 26 26 12 13 9 12 1 12 1 2 3 16 9 2 3 1 1
Goals: 2 2 14 8 19 13 7 1 7 5 1 1

2 own-goals

Championship Play-off

Date	Opponent	Result	Scorers	Att
May 6 (n)	Celtic	L 1-2	Robertson	30,000

League decider played at Hampden Park, Glasgow.
Fixture doubled as Rangers' home game in Glasgow League.

Appearances: 1 1 1 1 1 1 1 1 1 1 1
Goals: 1

Scottish FA Cup

#	Date	Opponent	Result	Scorers	Att
1	Jan 28 (h)	Ayr Parkhouse	W 2-1	Robertson, Chalmers	7,000
2	Feb 11 (a)	Morton	W 6-0	McColl 2, Speedie 2 (1 pen), Kyle, Walker	9,000
QF	25 (h)	Beith	W 5-1	Kyle 2, Speedie 2, Chalmers	4,000
SF	Mar 25 (a)	Celtic	W 2-0	Speedie, Robertson	36,000
F	Apr 8 (n)	Third Lanark	D 0-0		54,000
R	15 (n)	Third Lanark	L 1-3	A.Smith	55,000

Semi-final abandoned 78 minutes due to crowd invasion - Celtic conceded tie.
Final and Final Replay both played at Hampden Park, Glasgow.

Appearances: 3 3 4 6 5 1 1 6 6 6 4 1 2 6 3 3 3 1 2
Goals: 2 3 5 1 2 1 2

Glasgow Cup

#	Date	Opponent	Result	Scorers	Att
SF	Sep 24 (h)	Third Lanark	W 3-0	Hamilton, A.Smith, McColl	27,837
F	Oct 8 (n)	Celtic	L 1-2	Hamilton	54,613

Final played at Hampden Park

Appearances: 2 2 2 2 2 2 2 2 2 2 2
Goals: 2 1 1

Glasgow Merchants' Charity Cup

#	Date	Opponent	Result	Att
1	May 15 (a)	Partick Thistle	L 0-5	

Appearances: 2 4 6 10 11 9 1 3 5 7 8
Goals: 1 1 1 1 1 1 1 1 1

Glasgow League

#	Date	Opponent	Result	Scorers	Att
1	Mar 4 (a)	Partick Thistle	L 0-1		2,000
2	Apr 19 (a)	Third Lanark	W 4-1	Speedie, Kyle, McColl, Walker	
3	22 (h)	Partick Thistle	L 3-4	McColl, Kyle, Robertson	5,000
4	24 (h)	Queen's Park	W 3-2	McColl 2 (1 pen), A.Smith	4,000
5	May 3 (h)	Third Lanark	D 0-0		2,000
6	6 (h)	Celtic	L 1-2	*Robertson	30,000
7	8 (a)	Queen's Park	W 2-0	A.Smith, Speedie	3,000
8	13 (a)	Celtic	W 2-0	Low, McColl	7,000

FINAL LEAGUE POSITION: 2nd

*Played at Hampden Park. Fixture doubled as Scottish League Championship decider.

Appearances: 4 3 5 2 4 2 6 7 7 1 7 2 1 6 7 2 4 5 3 2 3 2
Goals: 2 2 2 2 5 1 1

Croal played number-2 in Match 3; McMillan played number-5 in Match 5; Pekarna played number-1 in Match 7.

Further match details for this season are continued on page 278

1905-06

Manager: W.Wilton

Scottish League

#	Date	Venue / Opponent	Result	Scorers	Att.
1	Aug 19	(h) Kilmarnock	W 3-2	McColl (pen), Hamilton 2	10,000
2	26	(h) Aberdeen	W 1-0	McMillan	8,000
3	Sep 2	(a) Airdrieonians	L 1-5	Hamilton	12,000
4	11	(a) Hibernian	W 2-1	Hamilton, Low	6,000
5	16	(a) St Mirren	W 1-0	Stark	15,000
6	25	(h) Hearts	L 0-5		18,000
7	Oct 7	(a) Port Glasgow A	W 4-1	Kyle, Stark, Hamilton, Speirs	3,000
8	14	(h) Dundee	D 1-1	Shaw	9,500
9	21	(h) Celtic	W 3-2	Kyle, Shaw, May	30,000
10	28	(a) Falkirk	W 6-1	Ruddiman 3, May, Kyle (pen), Shaw	6,000
11	Nov 4	(h) Queen's Park	W 2-1	Hawthorne (og), Speirs	13,000
12	11	(h) Third Lanark	L 2-4	Kyle 2 (1 pen)	10,000
13	18	(a) Motherwell	D 3-3	Kyle 3 (1 pen)	5,000
14	25	(h) Morton	L 1-2	Hamilton	4,000
15	Dec 2	(h) Queen's Park	W 3-1	Kivlichan 2, Smith	7,000
16	9	(a) Morton	W 3-0	Speirs, May, Hamilton	5,000
17	16	(a) Aberdeen	D 1-1	Rankine	10,000
18	23	(h) Motherwell	W 2-1	McColl, Smith	6,000
19	30	(h) Airdrieonians	L 1-3	Speirs	8,000
20	Jan 1	(a) Celtic	L 0-1		40,000
21	2	(h) Partick Thistle	W 1-0	McColl	
22	6	(a) Kilmarnock	W 3-1	Hamilton, Dalrymple, McColl	6,000
23	13	(a) St Mirren	L 2-3	Smith, McColl	
24	20	(h) Port Glasgow A	W 4-0	Dalrymple 3, McColl	8,000
25	Feb 3	(a) Third Lanark	L 0-3		13,000
26	17	(a) Dundee	D 1-1	Kivlichan	10,000
27	Mar 3	(h) Hibernian	D 1-1	Hamilton	7,000
28	17	(h) Partick Thistle	D 1-1	Speirs	8,000
29	24	(a) Falkirk	W 3-1	Stark, Kivlichan, McFie	7,000
30	Apr 7	(h) Hearts	D 2-2	Speirs, Untraced	6,000

FINAL LEAGUE POSITION: 4th

Player appearances / goals (Scottish League):

Player	Apps	Goals
Sinclair, Thomas S.	30	
Fraser	2	
Gourlay	6	
Gray, Josiah	26	
Stark, James	28	3
May, John	21	3
Dalrymple	13	4
Kyle, Archibald	22	8
Hamilton, Robert C.	20	9
McColl, Robert S.	13	6
Smith, Alexander	24	3
Croal, James	3	
Cochrane, Andrew	10	
McMillan, David	9	1
Steel	2	
Craig, A	25	
Low	2	1
Speirs	18	6
Walker, John (2)	14	
McFie	4	1
Shaw H.C.	6	3
Ruddiman T.	4	3
Kivlichan	9	4
Rankine	8	1
Campbell	6	
Miller	1	
Craig J.	1	
Speedie	2	
McGhee	1	

1 goal untraced. 1 own-goal

Scottish FA Cup

#	Date	Venue / Opponent	Result	Scorers	Att.
1	Jan 27	(a) Arthurlie	W 7-1	Speirs 3, McColl, Dalrymple 2, May	6,000
2	Feb 10	(a) Aberdeen	W 3-2	Dalrymple 2, Hamilton	14,000
QF	Mar 10	(a) Port Glasgow A	L 0-1		11,000

Appearances: Sinclair 3, Gray 3, Stark 3, May 3, Dalrymple 3, Kyle 2, Hamilton 2, McColl 3, Smith 2, Craig A 3, Speirs 3, Kivlichan 3.
Goals: May 1, Dalrymple 4, McColl 1, Hamilton 1, Speirs 3.

Glasgow Cup

#	Date	Venue / Opponent	Result	Scorers	Att.
1	Sep 9	(a) Clyde	D 0-0		
R	23	(h) Clyde	W 2-1	Smith, McFie	17,000
SF	30	(a) Third Lanark	L 1-3	Speirs	12,000

Appearances: Sinclair 3, Gray 3, Stark 3, May 3, Dalrymple 3, Kyle 3, Hamilton 2, McColl 1, Smith 3, Croal 3, Craig A 3, McFie 2, Speirs 1.
Goals: Smith 1, McFie 1, Speirs 1.

Glasgow Merchants' Charity Cup

#	Date	Venue / Opponent	Result	Scorers	Att.
SF	May 5	(a) Celtic	W 5-3	Speirs 2, May, Kyle, A.Smith	
F	12	(a) Queen's Park	W 3-2	Speirs 2, Kyle	25,000

Appearances: 2 each — Sinclair, Gray, Stark, McColl, Smith, Craig A, Speirs, McFie, Kivlichan, Rankine, Young.
Goals: May 1, Kyle 2, Smith 1, Speirs 4.

Glasgow League

#	Date	Venue / Opponent	Result	Scorers	Att.
1	Mar 21	(h) Third Lanark	L 0-2		2,000
2	31	(a) Celtic	W 3-0	Speirs 2, McFie	12,000
3	Apr 14	(a) Clyde	D 0-0		4,000
4	16	(h) Partick Thistle	W 1-0	Kivlichan	2,000
5	May 1	(a) Queen's Park	W 3-0	Smith 2, Kivlichan	1,500

FINAL LEAGUE POSITION: 2nd

Appearances: Sinclair 5, Stark 3, May 5, Dalrymple 3, Kyle 2, Hamilton 4, McColl 1, Smith 1, Craig A 5, Speirs 2, McFie 4, Shaw 4, Ruddiman 1, Kivlichan 3, Rankine 3, Campbell 2, Miller 3, Young 1, Blyth 1.
Goals: Speirs 2, McFie 1, Smith 2, Kivlichan 2.

Other matches

#	Date	Venue / Opponent	Result	Scorers	Att.
1	Aug 16	(h) Hibernian	L 0-1		3,000
2	21	(h) Hearts*	L 2-3	Kyle, Hamilton	6,000
3	22	(a) Arthurlie	L 1-3	Untraced	
4	30	(a) Dundee†	W 5-1	Kyle 2, Steel, Untraced 2	4,000
5	Sep 4	(a) Celtic	L 0-1		
6	Dec 25	(a) Blackburn R	L 1-4	Speirs	16,000
7	Jan 3	(h) Hearts‡	W 4-1	McColl 2, Dalrymple, Hamilton	4,000
8	Apr 2	(a) Cowdenbeath	W 3-0	Untraced	
9	13	(h) West Norwood	W 3-0	McColl 3 (1 pen)	
10	21	(a) Dundee	W 1-0	McColl	
11	23	(a) Albion R	W 4-0	Untraced	
12	25	(a) Border Counties	W 6-1	Untraced	
13	30	(a) Clydebank & D	D 2-2	Untraced	
14	May 7	(a) Alloa Athletic	W 6-3	Untraced	
15	14	(a) Caledonian	W 4-1	McColl 3 (1 pen), Hamilton	
16	15	(a§) Morayshire S	W 7-1	Untraced	

*Charles Thomson Benefit Match; †Fred McDiarmid Benefit Match; ‡Robert Cumming Hamilton Benefit Match; §Played at Elgin.

Blair played number-6 in Match 7; Brebner played number-1 in Matches 7 & 9; Galt played number-6 in Matches 9 & 10; Thomson played number-7 in Match 9; Spence played number-11 in Match 9. 20 goals untraced.

1906-07

Manager: W.Wilton

Scottish League

#	Date		Opponent	Result	Scorers	Att.
1	Aug	18 (h)	Falkirk	D 2-2	Smith, Speirs	13,000
2		25 (a)	Port Glasgow A	W 2-0	Mainds, Kyle	8,000
3	Sep	1 (h)	Aberdeen	W 6-2	Stark 2, Kyle, Smith, Rankine, Speirs	10,000
4		22 (a)	Dundee	L 0-2		14,600
5		24 (h)	Hearts	D 1-1	McFie	10,000
6		29 (a)	Partick Thistle	L 1-2	Hamilton	12,000
7	Oct	13 (a)	Kilmarnock	W 5-1	Speirs 2, Smith, Kyle, Rankine	7,000
8		20 (h)	Morton	W 2-0	Kivlichan, Speirs	9,000
9		27 (a)	Celtic	L 1-2	Kyle	30,000
10	Nov	3 (h)	St Mirren	D 1-1	Kyle (pen)	12,000
11		10 (a)	Third Lanark	W 2-0	Kyle (pen), Law	16,000
12		17 (h)	Queen's Park	W 3-2	Dickie, Kyle, Cunningham	14,000
13		24 (a)	Hibernian	W 3-1	Kyle, McFie, Smith	
14	Dec	1 (h)	Airdrieonians	W 2-1	Speirs, Kyle	13,000
15		8 (a)	Clyde	W 5-1	Smith 2, Speirs, Kyle, Dickie	
16		15 (h)	Motherwell	L 0-1		5,000
17		22 (a)	Aberdeen	W 3-0	Kyle 2, Smith	7,000
18		29 (h)	Hamilton A	L 0-1		5,000
19	Jan	1 (h)	Celtic	W 2-1	Dickie, Kivlichan	50,000
20		2 (a)	Partick Thistle	D 2-2	Campbell 2	7,000
21		5 (a)	Morton	L 1-2	Speirs	5,000
22		12 (h)	Hibernian	W 1-0	Speirs	7,000
23		19 (a)	Airdrieonians	W 3-2	Cunningham, Speirs, Campbell (pen)	8,000
24	Feb	2 (h)	Third Lanark	D 0-0		10,000
25		9 (a)	Hamilton A	W 3-0	Speirs 2, Cunningham	6,000
26		23 (a)	St Mirren	D 0-0		7,000
27	Mar	2 (a)	Motherwell	L 0-1		5,000
28		16 (a)	Falkirk	L 1-2	Kivlichan	7,000
29		23 (h)	Clyde	W 4-0	Campbell 3, Stark	7,000
30		30 (h)	Port Glasgow A	W 5-0	Campbell 3, Kyle, Livingstone	5,000
31	Apr	1 (h)	Dundee	D 2-2	Campbell 2 (1 pen)	12,000
32		6 (a)	Queen's Park	W 2-1	Livingstone, Campbell	18,000
33		13 (h)	Hearts	W 1-0	Smith	9,000
34		20 (h)	Kilmarnock	W 3-0	Livingstone 2, Speirs	2,500

FINAL LEAGUE POSITION: 3rd

League appearances/goals by player (Newbigging · Campbell · Jackson · Mainds · Gray · May · Rankine · Speedie · Speirs · Kyle · Smith · Galt · McFie · Stark · Kivlichan · McColl · Taylor · Hendry · Hamilton JR · Ruddiman · Craig · Cunningham · Menzies · Dickie · Law · McDonald · Livingstone · McFarlane · Gordon · Sinclair · Gibson · Nelson):

Appearances: 34, 26, 16, 13, 20, 17, 7, 1, 22, 27, 25, 21, 12, 22, 11, 1, 9, 19, 2, 3, 12, 10, 1, 20, 6, 5, 10, 1, 1

Goals: Campbell 12, Jackson 1, Speedie 2, Speirs 13, Kyle 13, Smith 8, Stark 2, Kivlichan 3, Hendry 3, Cunningham 1, Dickie 3, Law 3, McDonald 1, Livingstone 4

Scottish FA Cup

#	Date		Opponent	Result	Scorers	Att.
1	Jan	26 (a)	Falkirk	W 2-1	Campbell (pen), McFie	16,000
2	Feb	16 (a)	Galston	W 4-0	Livingstone 2, Dickie, Speirs	4,000
QF	Mar	9 (h)	Celtic	L 0-3		60,000

Appearances: Newbigging 3, Campbell 3, Mainds 3, Gray 2, Speirs 3, Kyle 1, Smith 3, Galt 1, McFie 2, Stark 3, Craig 3, Dickie 3, Livingstone 3
Goals: Campbell 1, Speirs 1, McFie 1, Dickie 1, Livingstone 2

Glasgow Cup

#	Date		Opponent	Result	Scorers	Att.
1	Sep	8 (a)	Queen's Park	D 2-2	Speirs, Kyle	28,000
R		15 (h)	Queen's Park	L 0-3		26,000

Appearances: Newbigging 2, Campbell 2, Jackson 2, Mainds 1, Gray 1, May 2, Rankine 2, Speedie 1, Speirs 2, Kyle 2, Smith 2, McFie 2, Stark 1
Goals: Speirs 1, Kyle 1

Glasgow Merchants' Charity Cup

#	Date		Opponent	Result	Scorers	Att.
1	Apr	10 (h)	Partick Thistle	W 3-0	Stark, Livingstone, McDonald	2,000
SF	May	4 (h)	Third Lanark	W 1-0	Campbell	10,000
F		18 (n*)	Celtic	W 1-0	Campbell	38,000

*Played at Cathkin Park.

Appearances: Newbigging 3, Campbell 3, Jackson 2, Mainds 1, Gray 1, Speirs 3, Kyle 2, Smith 3, Galt 2, McFie 1, Hendry 1, Craig 2, Dickie 1, Law 3, McDonald 3, Livingstone 2
Goals: Campbell 2, Law 1, McDonald 1

Other matches

#	Date		Opponent	Result	Scorers	Att.
1	Aug	16 (h)	Celtic*	W 4-2	Speedie 2, Smith, Spiers	6,000
2		20 (h)	Benburb	D 0-0		
3		21 (a)	St Mirren†	W 3-0	McFie 3	
4	Nov	14 (a)	Morton‡	W 7-0	Campbell 7 (2 pens)	
5	Dec	25 (a)	Preston NE	W 3-1	Kyle 2, Smith	5,000
6	Jan	3 (h)	Hearts#	D 3-3	McColl 2 (1 pen), Richardson	3,000
7	Mar	18 (a)	Bohemians	D	W 3-1	Gordon, Untraced 2
8	Apr	22 (a)	Morton§	D 0-0		
9		24 (h)	Newcastle U	W 3-0	Livingstone, McDonald, Kivlichan	15,000
10		27 (a)	Maxwelltown V	W 4-0	Untraced	
11	May	2 (a)	Vale of Leven+	W 2-0	Untraced	
12		6 (a)	Celtic¥	W 2-1	Livingstone, Kyle	
13		11 (a)	Arbroath	W 3-2	Untraced	
14		14 (a)	Clydesbank Dist	W 2-1	Untraced	
15		29 (n)	St Mirren¶	W 2-0	Untraced	

No further details available for Matches 2, 5, 7, 10, 11, 13, 14 & 15.
*Finlay Speedie benefit match. †Donald Greenleas benefit match. ‡Clyde Boilermakers strike distress fund benefit match. #James Stark benefit match. §John Walker benefit match. +Alex Galbraith benefit match. ¥St Mary's (Lanark) Convalescent Home benefit match. ¶Stevenston (Ayrshire) Sick Nursing Association benefit match.

Other matches appearances: Newbigging 9, Campbell 8, Jackson 7, Mainds 3, Gray 4, May 5, Rankine 1, Speirs 3, Kyle 5, Smith 8, Galt 7, McFie 4, Stark 1, Kivlichan 3, McColl 3, Taylor 1, Hendry 4, Craig 5, Cunningham 2, Dickie 2, Law 2, McDonald 3, Livingstone 3, Gordon 5, Sinclair 1, Gibson 1, Nelson 1
Goals: Campbell 7, Speedie 2, Smith 1, Kyle 3, McFie 2, McColl 3, Kivlichan 1, Livingstone 2, McDonald 1, Gordon 1

Currie played number-11 in Match 2; Rollo played number-7 in Match 6; Bell played number-8 in Matches 6 & 8; Richardson played number-9 in Match 6 and scored 1 goal; Murray played number-6 in Match 8; Robertson played number-7 in Match 8. 15 goals untraced.

1907-08

Manager: W.Wilton

Scottish League

Player columns: Newbigging, Jackson, Craig, Gordon, May, Galt, McDonald, Livingstone, Campbell, Kyle, Smith A, Dickie, Law, Hamilton, Hendry, Taylor, Steven, Speirs, McArthur, Bovill, Barrie, Hadden, Cunningham, Noble, Sharp, Rennie, Douglas, Gilchrist, Murray, McPherson, Butler, Houston

#	Date	Opponent	Result	Scorers	Att
1	Aug 15 (h) Morton	W 3-0	Smith 2, Campbell	7,000
2	17 (a) Port Glasgow A	W 6-1	Campbell 2, Livingstone 2, McDonald, Thomson (og)	6,000
3	24 (h) Aberdeen	W 4-0	Campbell 3, Livingstone	20,000
4	31 (a) Falkirk	D 4-4	Campbell, Galt, May, Livingstone	14,000
5	Sep 7 (h) Kilmarnock	W 1-0	Campbell	14,000
6	21 (a) Morton	W 3-2	Galt, Campbell, Kyle	10,000
7	30 (h) Queen's Park	D 1-1	Livingstone	17,000
8	Oct 5 (h) Airdrieonians	L 1-2	McDonald	22,000
9	Nov 2 (a) Queen's Park	L 1-3	Livingstone	20,000
10	9 (h) St Mirren	D 2-2	Kyle, Hamilton	15,000
11	16 (a) Partick Thistle	W 2-1	Steven, Campbell	8,000
12	23 (h) Hibernian	D 1-1	Campbell	11,000
13	30 (a) Third Lanark	W 5-3	Kyle 3, Speirs, Hamilton	9,000
14	Dec 7 (a) Hearts	W 2-1	Kyle, Hamilton	11,000
15	14 (h) Motherwell	W 4-2	Speirs 2, May, Kyle	10,000
16	21 (a) Dundee	W 2-1	Campbell, May	15,000
17	28 (a) Falkirk	D 2-2	Speirs, Campbell	25,000
18	Jan 1 (a) Celtic	L 1-2	Kyle	60,000
19	2 (h) Partick Thistle	W 3-2	Livingstone 2, Kyle	5,000
20	4 (a) Airdrieonians	L 0-3		7,000
21	11 (h) Third Lanark	W 2-0	Speirs, Kyle	8,000
22	18 (a) Aberdeen	D 0-0		10,000
23	Feb 15 (a) Hamilton A	D 2-2	Livingstone, McDonald	6,000
24	29 (h) Hearts	W 2-1	Campbell, Barrie	6,000
25	Mar 7 (a) Kilmarnock	W 2-0	Livingstone, Smith	8,000
26	14 (a) Clyde	W 2-0	Kyle, Gordon	9,000
27	21 (h) Hamilton A	W 1-0	Campbell	6,000
28	28 (a) Hibernian	W 3-0	Campbell 3	9,000
29	Apr 4 (a) Motherwell	W 2-1	Campbell 2	3,000
30	11 (h) Clyde	D 1-1	Campbell	6,000
31	13 (a) St Mirren	W 2-0	Campbell, Kyle	4,000
32	18 (h) Port Glasgow A	W 5-1	Campbell 3, McDonald, May	2,500
33	20 (h) Dundee	W 2-0	Noble, May (pen)	12,000
34	25 (h) Celtic	L 0-1		40,000

FINAL LEAGUE POSITION: 3rd

Appearances: 26 14 23 22 26 27 19 24 32 27 22 9 13 11 12 12 9 13 6 2 11 2 3 8 1

Goals: 1 5 2 4 10 25 12 3 · 3 · 1 5 · 1 · 1

1 own-goal

Scottish FA Cup

#	Date	Opponent	Result	Scorers	Att
1	Jan 25 (a) Falkirk	D 2-2	Livingstone, May	20,000
R	Feb 1 (h) Falkirk	W 4-1	Smith 2, Kyle, Speirs	52,000
2	8 (h) Celtic	L 1-2	Kyle	23,000

Appearances: 3 3 3 3 3 3 3 3 3 3 3

Goals: 1 1 2 2 1

Glasgow Cup

#	Date	Opponent	Result	Scorers	Att
1	Sep 14 (a) Clyde	W 4-0	Campbell 2, Livingstone 2	27,000
SF	28 (h) Third Lanark	W 3-0	Campbell 3	25,000
F	Oct 12 (n) Celtic	D 2-2	Campbell, Smith	81,000
R	19 (n) Celtic	D 0-0		52,000
2R	26 (n) Celtic	L 1-2	Kyle	56,000

Final, Replay and Second Replay all played at Hampden Park, Glasgow.

Appearances: 4 4 5 5 5 5 5 2 5 5 5 5 1 1 2 1

Goals: 2 6 1 1

Glasgow Merchants' Charity Cup

#	Date	Opponent	Result	Scorers	Att
1	May 2 (n) Third Lanark	D 1-1	Galt	22,000
R	6 (n) Third Lanark	W 3-1	Gordon, Murray, Campbell	12,000
SF	9 (h) Queen's Park	L 1-3	Murray	21,000

First round and first round replay both played at Hampden Park.

Appearances: 2 3 2 2 2 2 2 2 3 1 2 3 2 2 2 1

Goals: 1 1 1 2

Other matches

#	Date	Opponent	Result	Scorers	Att
1	Aug 19 (a) Celtic *	L 2-3	Campbell, Hamilton	6,000
2	26 (a) St Mirren **	D 0-0		
3	Dec 25 (a) Fulham	W 1-0	Hamilton	6,000
4	Feb 22 (a) Motherwell †	D 2-2	Cunningham, Speirs	5,000
5	Apr 6 (h) Forres Mech.	W 6-0	Campbell 3, Galt 2, Taylor	1,000
6	28 (h) W Arsenal	D 1-1	Campbell	2,000
7	May 5 (h) Celtic ‡	D 0-0		
8	11 (n) St Mirren §	W 5-1	Untraced	

No further details available matches 3 & 8. *William Loney Benefit Match. **Robertson Benefit Match. †League fixture abandoned 75 mins, due to waterlogged pitch.
‡R.Robertson Benefit Match. § Stevenson (Ayrshire) Sick Nursing Asociation Benefit Match.

Appearances: 4 4 3 2 3 4 1 5 1 2 3 3 3 2 3 1 5 1 5 2 1 1 1 2 2

Goals: 2 5 1 2 1 1 1 2 2

McCabe played number-6 in Match 7; McCallum played number-7 in Match 7; Bell played number-10 in Match 7; Currie played number-11 in Match 7. 5 goals untraced.

1908-09

Manager: W.Wilton

Scottish League

Player columns (left to right): Rennie, Law, Sharp, Gordon, Campbell, Galt, Bennett, McPherson, Murray, McDonald, Smith A, Craig, Livingstone, May, McArthur, Smith J, Noble, Stark, Taylor, Yuille, Gilchrist, Reid, McKenzie, McLean, Jackson, Waddell, Miller, Steel, Currie, Neil, Logan, Houston.

No	Date		Opponent	Result	Scorers	Att
1	Aug 15	(h)	Port Glasgow A	W 7-0	McDonald 3, McPherson 2, Murray, Bennett	15,000
2	22 (a*)		Partick T	W 2-0	McPherson, Murray	12,000
3	29	(h)	Falkirk	W 4-1	A.Smith 2, Bennett, McDonald	30,000
4	Sep 5	(a)	Aberdeen	W 2-0	Campbell, Bennett	9,000
5	12	(a)	Kilmarnock	W 5-0	Murray 2, A.Smith, Bennett, McPherson	9,000
6	19	(a)	St Mirren	D 1-1	Campbell	27,000
7	28	(h)	Dundee	W 2-0	Bennett, Campbell	35,000
8	Oct 10	(a)	Airdrieonians	L 3-4	Gordon, Campbell, McPherson	11,000
9	17	(h)	Motherwell	W 3-1	Livingstone, A.Smith, J.Smith	11,000
10	24	(a)	Airdrieonians	W 2-0	J.Smith 2	18,000
11	31	(h)	Third Lanark	D 2-2	J.Smith, Livingstone	24,000
12	Nov 7	(a)	Morton	W 8-0	Murray 3, Bennett 2, McPherson 2, A.Smith	10,000
13	14	(a)	Queen's Park	D 1-1	Murray	32,000
14	21	(a)	Clyde	W 1-0	Bennett	18,000
15	28	(h)	Hearts	W 4-3	Campbell 2, May, Bennett	9,000
16	Dec 5	(a)	Falkirk	L 0-1		10,000
17	12	(a)	Hamilton A	W 7-0	Campbell 4, A.Smith, Yuille, Gordon	8,000
18	19	(a)	Kilmarnock	D 1-1	May	8,000
19	26	(h)	St Mirren	W 3-1	Bennett, McPherson, Murray	12,000
20	Jan 1	(h)	Celtic	L 1-3	Murray	60,000
21	2	(h)	Partick T	W 6-0	Livingstone 4, A.Smith, J.Smith	5,000
22	9	(a)	Dundee	L 0-4		16,000
23	30	(a)	Motherwell	W 5-2	McPherson 2, A.Smith, Bennett, Campbell	7,000
24	Feb 27	(a)	Port Glasgow A	L 0-2		4,000
25	Mar 6	(a)	Hibernian	D 0-0		4,000
26	13	(a)	Celtic	W 3-2	Yuille, McDonald, Murray	28,000
27	27	(h)	Aberdeen	W 3-1	Bennett, Campbell, Gilchrist	10,000
28	30	(h)	Hamilton A	W 4-0	Gordon 3, Campbell (pen)	8,000
29	Apr 3	(a)	Hearts	D 0-0		11,000
30	12	(h)	Clyde	D 2-2	Gilchrist, McPherson	15,000
31	19	(h)	Hibernian	L 0-1		6,000
32	24	(a)	Third Lanark	L 0-1		11,000
33	26	(h)	Queen's Park	L 2-3	Bennett, McPherson	1,000
34	28	(h)	Morton	W 7-1	Campbell 3, A.Smith, Gordon, Stark, McDonald	2,000

FINAL LEAGUE POSITION: 4th
*Played at Ibrox Stadium.

League totals

	Ren	Law	Sha	Gor	Cam	Gal	Ben	McP	Mur	McD	SmA	Cra	Liv	May	McA	SmJ	Nob	Sta	Tay	Yui	Gil	Rei	McK	McL	Jac	Wad	Mil
Appearances	31	20	18	25	22	24	28	26	14	22	28	28	13	21	3	7	2	17	6	3	8	2	2	1	1	1	1
Goals				6	16		13	12	11	6	9		6	2		5		1		2	2						

Scottish FA Cup

No	Date		Opponent	Result	Scorers	Att
1	Jan 23	(a)	St.Johnstone	W 3-0	Stark, Bennett, Campbell	7,000
2	Feb 6	(a)	Dundee	D 0-0		31,000
R	13	(h)	Dundee	W 1-0	McPherson	54,500
QF	20	(h)	Queen's Park	W 1-0	McPherson	45,000
SF	Mar 20	(a)	Falkirk	W 1-0	McPherson	12,000
F	Apr 10	(n)	Celtic	D 2-2	Gilchrist, Bennett	70,000
R	17	(n)	Celtic	D 1-1	Gordon	60,000

Final and Final Replay both played at Hampden Park, Glasgow.
Competition abandoned and trophy withheld following riot at replay.

	Ren	Law	Gor	Cam	Gal	Ben	McP	Mur	McD	SmA	Cra	Liv	Sta	Tay	Yui
Appearances	7	7	2	5	7	7	7	1	2	7	7	5	7	5	1
Goals			1	1		2	3						1		1

Scottish National Exhibition Tournament

No	Date		Opponent	Result	Scorers	Att
SF	Aug 5	(a)	St Bernard's	W 1-0	Livingstone	9,000
F	12	(n)	Dundee	D 1-1	Livingstone	10,000

Both ties played at Saughton Park, Edinburgh. Rangers won Final on toss of a coin.

	Ren	Sha	Gor	Cam	Gal	Mur	McD	SmA	Cra	Liv	May	Sta	Tay	Yui
Appearances	2	2	2	1	2	2	2	2	2	1	2	2		2
Goals										2				

Glasgow Cup

No	Date		Opponent	Result	Scorers	Att
SF	Sep 26	(a)	Celtic	D 2-2	Bennett 2	44,000
R	Oct 3	(h)	Celtic	L 0-2		45,000

	Ren	Law	Sha	Gor	Cam	Gal	Ben	McP	Mur	McD	SmA	Cra	Liv
Appearances	2	1	1	2	2	2	1	2	2	2	2	1	1
Goals							2						

Glasgow Merchants' Charity Cup

No	Date		Opponent	Result	Scorers	Att
1	May 1	(h)	Partick Thistle	W 3-1	Gordon 3	7,000
SF	8	(a)	Third Lanark	W 3-2	Gordon 2, McPherson	17,000
F	15	(a)	Celtic	W 4-2	Gordon 2, Bennett, May (pen)	25,000

	Ren	Law	Gor	Ben	McP	SmA	Cra	Liv	Sta	Tay	Yui	Gil
Appearances	3	3	3	3	3	2	3	3	3	1	2	1
Goals			7	1	1			1				

Other matches

No	Date		Opponent	Result	Scorers	Att
1	Aug 18	(h)	Queen's Park *	W 4-0	Murray 2, A.Smith, McPherson	8,000
2	26	(a)	Celtic †	L 1-3	Craig	5,000
3	31	(a)	Third Lanark ‡	D 2-2	Livingstone, Murray	2,000
4	Sep 30	(a)	Newcastle U §	L 1-4	Pudan (og)	5,000
5	Oct 7	(h)	Newcastle U §	L 2-4	McPherson, Livingstone	9,000
6	Jan 4	(h)	Falkirk #	L 2-4	May, Robey	5,000

*Alex Smith Benefit Match. †Peter Somers Benefit Match. ‡Tod Sloan Benefit Match.
§Unemployed Relief Fund Benefit Match. #John May Benefit Match.

	Ren	Law	Sha	Gor	Cam	Gal	Ben	McP	Mur	McD	SmA	Cra	Liv	May	McA	SmJ	Nob	Sta	Gil	Rei
Appearances	3	4	3	4	4	1	3	3	3	3	3	4	4	5	2	2	4	3	2	
Goals							2	3		1	1	2	1							

Robey played number-10 in Match 6 and scored 1 goal. 1 own-goal.

1909-10

Manager: W.Wilton

Scottish League

No	Date	Opponent	Result	Scorers	Att	Lock	McKenzie	Craig	May	Stark	Galt	Bennett	Hogg	Reid	Hunter	Smith A	McPherson	Law	Gilchrist	Gordon	Campbell	Miller	Jackson	Waddell	Ramage	McLean	Rennie	Bell	Yuille	Hendry	Taylor	Riley
1	Aug 16 (h)	Kilmarnock	W 3-0	Smith, Reid, Hunter	18,000	1	2	3	4	5	6	7	8	9	10	11																
2	21 (a)	Airdrieonians	L 1-2	Hogg	13,000	1	2	3	4	5	6	7	8	9	10	11																
3	28 (h)	St Mirren	D 1-1	Bennett	16,000	1	2	3	4	5	6	7	8	9		11	10															
4	Sep 4 (a)	Dundee	L 2-4	McPherson, Bennett	22,000	1	2	3	4	5	6	7	8	9		11	10															
5	18 (a)	Aberdeen	W 2-1	Gordon, Gilchrist	16,000	1		3	4	5	6	7			11		10	2	8	9												
6	20 (a)	Hibernian	L 0-1		10,000	1		3			6	7		9	11		10	2	8	4	5											
7	27 (h)	Dundee	W 2-1	McPherson, Reid	30,000	1		3		5	6	7		9	11		10	2	8	4												
8	Oct 2 (a)	Port Glasgow A	D 1-1	Hunter	5,000	1		3		5	6	7		9	11		10	2	8	4												
9	16 (h)	Hamilton A	W 5-1	Hunter 5	9,000	1		3		6	5	11		7	9			2	8	4					10							
10	23 (h)	Kilmarnock	W 2-0	Hunter 2	9,500	1		3		5	6	7		9	11			2	8	4					10							
11	30 (h)	Celtic	D 0-0		45,000	1		3		5	6	8	7	9			10	2		4	11											
12	Nov 6 (h)	Partick Thistle	D 0-0		30,000	1		3		5	6	8	7	11	9			2		4	10											
13	13 (a)	Clyde	L 0-1		18,000	1		3			6	8	7	11	9		4	2		5	10											
14	20 (h)	Queen's Park	W 7-1	Hunter 3, Ramage, May, Gilchrist, McPherson	14,000	1	2	3	6	5		7			9		10		8	4					11							
15	27 (h)	Motherwell	W 4-1	Hunter 3, Gilchrist	7,000	1		3	6	5		7			9		10	2	8	4					11							
16	Dec 4 (a)	Morton	W 4-1	Bennett 2, McPherson, Ramage	6,000	1		3	6	5		7			9		10	2	8	4					11							
17	11 (a)	Third Lanark	L 1-2	Hunter	6,000	1		3		5	6	7			9		10	2	8	4					11							
18	18 (h)	Partick Thistle	W 2-1	Gilchrist, McPherson	16,000	1		3		5	6	7		9		11	10	2	8													
19	25 (a)	Falkirk	L 1-3	McPherson	7,000	1		3		5	6	7		9		11	10	2	8	4												
20	Jan 1 (a)	Celtic	D 1-1	Hogg	47,000	1		3		5	6	7		9		11	10	2	8	4												
21	3 (h)	Port Glasgow A	W 4-0	Reid 2, McLean, McPherson	8,000	1		3		5	6	7		9			10	2		4					11	8						
22	8 (h)	Hearts	W 1-0	McPherson	8,000	1		3		5	6	7		9		11	10	2		4	8											
23	15 (a)	Hamilton A	W 3-2	Hunter 3 (1 pen)	8,000	1		3		6	5	7		9	10	11		2	8	4												
24	29 (a)	Motherwell	W 3-2	Miller, McPherson, Hogg	8,000	1		3	4	5	6	7		9		11	8	2				10										
25	Feb 19 (h)	Morton	W 2-1	Hogg, Bennett	8,000	1		3		5	6	7		9			10	2	8	4					11							
26	26 (a)	St Mirren	W 6-1	Reid 3, Hogg 2, McPherson	8,000	1		3		5	6	7		9		11	10	2	8	4												
27	Mar 5 (a)	Aberdeen	D 1-1	Reid	8,000			3		5		7		9		11	10	2	8	4	6		1									
28	12 (a)	Queen's Park	L 2-3	Reid 2	16,000	1		3		6	5	7		9		11	10	2	8	4												
29	19 (h)	Airdrieonians	W 3-0	Yuille 2, Bennett	5,000					5	6	7	8	9		11		2		4								1	3	10		
30	26 (h)	Hibernian	W 1-0	Smith	15,000	1				6	5	7		9		11		2	8	3	4								10			
31	28 (h)	Third Lanark	W 1-0	McPherson	12,000	1			4	5	6	7		9		11	10	2	8	3												
32	Apr 18 (a)	Hearts	W 3-1	Reid 2, McPherson	7,000	1			6	5		7		9		11	10	2	4	3									8			
33	23 (h)	Clyde	W 1-0	Gordon	10,000	1			4	5		7		9		11		2	8	3									10	6		
34	30 (h)	Falkirk	L 0-1		15,000	1			4	5		7		9		11		2	8	3									10	6		
				Appearances		32	24	9	23	24	25	22	26	20	17	21	25	22	13	19	14	9	1	11	6	1	2	1	5	2		
				Goals			1					6	6	12	19	2	12		4	2		1			2	1			2			

FINAL LEAGUE POSITION: 3rd

Scottish FA Cup

No	Date	Opponent	Result	Scorers	Att	Lock	McKenzie	Craig	May	Stark	Galt	Bennett	Hogg	Reid	Hunter	Smith A	McPherson	Law	Gilchrist	Gordon	Campbell
1	Jan 22 (h)	Inverness T	W 3-1	Gilchrist, May, Reid	10,000	1		3	4	5	6	7		9		11	10		8		2
2	Feb 5 (a)	Clyde	L 0-2		35,000	1		3	4	5	6	7		9	10	11	8	2			
				Appearances		2		2	2	2	2	1		2	1	2	2	1	1		1
				Goals					1					1					1		

Glasgow Cup

No	Date	Opponent	Result	Scorers	Att	Lock	McKenzie	Craig	May	Stark	Galt	Bennett	Hogg	Reid	Hunter	Smith A	McPherson	Law	Gilchrist	Gordon	Campbell	Miller
1	Sep 11 (h)	Partick Thistle	W 2-1	Hogg 2	18,000	1		3	4	5	6	7	8			11	10	2				9
SF	25 (a)	Third Lanark	W 2-1	Reid, Bennett	30,000	1		3		5	6	7		9		11	10	2	8	4		
F	Oct 9 (n*)	Celtic	L 0-1		55,000	1		3		5	6	7		9		11	10	2	8	4		
				Appearances		3		3	1	3	3	2	2	2	2	2	1	3	3	2		3
				Goals								1	2	1								

*Played at Hampden Park, Glasgow.

Glasgow Merchants' Charity Cup

No	Date	Opponent	Result	Scorers	Att	Lock	Galt	Bennett	Reid	McPherson	Law	Gilchrist	Campbell	Yuille	Hendry	Taylor
SF	May 7 (h)	Clyde	L 0-1		14,000	1	6	9	7	11	2	8	5	10	3	4
				Appearances		1	1	1	1	1	1	1	1	1	1	1
				Goals												

Other matches

No	Date	Opponent	Result	Scorers	Att	Lock	McKenzie	Craig	May	Stark	Galt	Bennett	Hogg	Reid	Hunter	Smith A	McPherson	Law	Gilchrist	Gordon	Campbell	Miller	Jackson	Waddell	Ramage	Yuille	Hendry	Taylor
1	Aug 18 (a)	Celtic *	L 4-8	Gordon 2, Hunter, Weir (og)	8,000		2	3	4				8			11	10		7	9	5	6		1				
2	25 (a)	Clyde †	W 2-1	McKenzie, Yuille	5,000	1	2										10		8	9	5	6		11	4	3		7
3	Jan 4 (h)	Falkirk ‡	W 5-1	Reid 3, Miller, Yuille	5,000	1						7		9				2		5	8	6		11	4	3	10	
4	Apr 4 (a)	Aberdeen	W 3-1	Reid, Hogg, May (pen)		1			5	3	6	7		9		11	10	2	8	4								
5	5 (a §)	Elgin/Forres Sel	W 6-1	Reid 4, Gordon, May		1		3	4	5	6	7		9		11	10	2	8									
6	6 (a)	Inverness Sel	W 3-1	Hogg, Bennett, Untraced								8	7															
7	11 (a)	Morton #	W 5-1	Hogg 2, Miller, Reid, Gordon				3		5		7		9			2		8		10	6	1	11	4			
8	14 (a +)	Berwick R	W 6-1	Reid 3, Bennett, Galt, Gordon	2,000						6	7		9					8									
9	27 (a)	Ayr U	W 3-0	Reid 2, Hogg	3,000	1		3	4	5	6	7		9		11	10	2	8									
10	May 4 (a)	Kilmarnock ¥	D 1-1	Galt							6																	
				Appearances		5	5	1	4	4	5	3	6	6	1	3	5	5	2	7	3	2	1	5	2	3	2	2
				Goals			1	1	2		2	2	5	14	1		5		2							2		

*Jimmy Quinn Benefit Match. † William Walker Benefit Match. ‡ Alec Craig Benefit Match. § Played at Elgin. # McIntosh Benefit Match. + Played at Tweedmouth, Berwickshire. ¥ Ardrossan, Saltcoats & Stevenston Sick Nursing Association Benefit Match, played at Stevenston, Ayrshire. No further details are available for Matches 6, 8 & 10. 1 goal untraced. 1 own-goal.

1910-11

Manager: W.Wilton

Scottish League

#	Date	Opponent	Res	Scorers	Att	Lock	Law	Campbell	Brown R	Chapman	Hendry	Hogg	Gordon	Reid	Bennett	Smith	Galt	Richmond	Gibson	Parker	Taylor	Paterson	McAulay	Yuille	Bowie	Goodwin	Craig	Brown A
1	Aug 20 (h)	St Mirren	W 1-0	Gordon	25,000	1	2	3	4	5	6	7	8	9	10	11												
2	27 (a)	Raith Rovers	W 2-0	Gordon, Smith	10,000	1	2	3		5	6	7	8	9	10	11	4											
3	Sep 3 (h)	Dundee	L 1-2	Reid	30,000	1	2	3		5	6	7	8	9	10	11	4											
4	10 (a)	Hamilton A	W 4-2	Gibson 2, Reid, Bennett	10,000	1	2			5	6		8	9	7	11	4	3	10									
5	17 (h)	Aberdeen	L 2-4	Reid 2	19,000	1	2			5	6			9	7	11	4	3	10	8								
6	19 (a)	Hearts	W 4-1	Reid 4	9,000	1	2			5	6	7	8	9	10	11	4	3										
7	26 (h)	Hibernian	W 4-0	Reid 3, Gibson	15,000	1		2	4			7	8	9			6	3	10	5	11							
8	Oct 1 (a)	Motherwell	W 2-1	Reid, Hogg	12,000	1	2		4	5	6	7	8	9	10	11		3										
9	15 (a)	Third Lanark	D 1-1	Gordon	30,000	1	2			5	6	7	4	9	10	11		3		8								
10	22 (h)	Morton	L 1-5	Reid	15,000	1	2		4	5	6	7	8	9	10	11		3										
11	29 (a)	Celtic	W 1-0	Hogg	35,000	1	2			5	6	7	4	9	10			3			11				8			
12	Nov 5 (h)	Airdrieonians	W 7-1	Hogg 2, Reid 2, Bennett (pen), Gordon, Yuille	12,000	1	2			5	6	7	4	9	10	11		3						8				
13	12 (h)	Kilmarnock	W 3-0	Hogg 2, Reid	7,000	1	2			5	6	7	4	9	10	11		3							8			
14	19 (a)	Queen's Park	W 4-0	Reid 2, Hogg, Bennett	18,000	1	2			5	6	7	4	9	10	11		3							8			
15	26 (h)	Motherwell	W 7-1	Reid 4, Chapman 2, Hogg	6,000	1	2	3		5	6	7	4	9	10	11									8			
16	Dec 3 (a)	Aberdeen	L 0-1		14,000	1	2	3		5	6	7	4	9	10	11									8			
17	10 (h)	Falkirk	D 1-1	Reid	10,000	1		2		5	6	7	4	9	10	11		3							8			
18	17 (a)	St Mirren	L 1-2	Hogg	10,000	1		2		5	6	7	4	9	10	11		3							8			
19	24 (h)	Hearts	W 2-0	Reid, Galt	9,000	1	2	3			6	7	4	9			11	5							8	10		
20	31 (a)	Kilmarnock	W 2-0	Reid, Gibson	12,000	1	2	3		5	6	7	4	9			11			10					8			
21	Jan 2 (h)	Celtic	D 1-1	Reid	60,000	1	2	3		5	6	7	4	9			11			10					8			
22	3 (a)	Partick Thistle	D 2-2	Bowie, Reid	35,000	1		2		5	6	7		9			11	4	3						8	10		
23	7 (h)	Clyde	W 6-1	Hogg 2, Goodwin 2, Reid, Chapman	10,000	1		2		5	6	7					11	4	3						8	10		
24	14 (a)	Hamilton A	W 4-0	Gibson, Smith, Hogg, Hendry	8,000	1		2			6	7	4	9			11	5	3	10					8			
25	21 (a)	Airdrieonians	W 4-1	Reid 2, Bennett (pen), Hogg	10,000	1	2	3			6	7	4	9	10	11		5							8			
26	Feb 4 (h)	Raith Rovers	W 4-1	Reid 2, Bowie, Gordon	8,000	1	2			5		7	4	9	10	11	6								8			3
27	18 (h)	Partick Thistle	W 2-0	Reid, Bennett (pen)	8,000	1	2	3		5	6			9	10	11									8	7		
28	Mar 11 (a)	Hibernian	W 3-1	Smith, Reid, Hogg	12,000	1	2	3		5	6	7	4	9			11								8	10		
29	18 (a)	Queen's Park	W 4-0	A.Brown, Goodwin, Parker, Bowie	6,000	1	2	3		5	6	7	4							9					8	10		11
30	25 (a)	Morton	D 2-2	Reid, Bowie	10,000	1	2	3		5	6	7	4	9			11								8	10		
31	Apr 8 (a)	Dundee	W 2-0	Goodwin, A.Brown	12,000	1	2				6	7	4	9				5	3						8	10		11
32	15 (a)	Falkirk	D 2-2	Reid, Campbell	10,000	1	2				6		4	9		7		5	3						8	10		11
33	20 (h)	Third Lanark	W 3-1	Reid, Bennett, Smith	10,000	1		2		5		7	4	9	10	11	6		3						8			
34	22 (a)	Clyde	W 1-0	Reid	10,000	1		2		5	6	7		9	10	11	4		3						8			
	FINAL LEAGUE POSITION: 1st				**Appearances**	34	24	23	4	28	31	30	28	33	23	29	18	20	6	2	1	2	1	6	17	10	1	3
					Goals		1			3	1	14	5	38	6	4	1		5	1				1	4	4		2

Scottish FA Cup

#	Date	Opponent	Res	Scorers	Att	Lock	Law	Campbell	Brown R	Chapman	Hendry	Hogg	Gordon	Reid	Bennett	Smith	Galt	Richmond	Gibson	Bowie
1	Jan 28 (h)	Kilmarnock	W 2-1	Hogg, Reid	40,000	1	2	3			6	7	4	9	10	11		5		8
2	Feb 11 (h)	Morton	W 3-0	Reid 2, Bowie	39,000	1	2			5		7	4	9	10	11	6	3		8
QF	25 (a)	Dundee	L 1-2	Hogg	30,000	1	2	3		5	6	7	4	9	10	11				8
					Appearances	3	3	2		2	2	3	3	3	3	3	2	1		3
					Goals							2		3						1

Glasgow Cup

#	Date	Opponent	Res	Scorers	Att	Lock	Law	Chapman	Hendry	Hogg	Gordon	Reid	Bennett	Smith	Galt	Richmond
SF	Sep 24 (a)	Clyde	D 1-1	Reid	42,000	1	2	5	6	7	8	9	10	11	4	3
R	28 (h)	Clyde	W 3-0	Bennett 2 (1 pen), Gordon	12,000	1	2	5	6	7	8	9	10	11	4	3
F	Oct 8 (n*)	Celtic	W 3-1	Smith, Reid, Bennett	65,000	1	2	5	6	7	8	9	10	11	4	3
					Appearances	3	3	3	3	3	3	3	3	3	3	3
					Goals						1	2	3	1		

*Played at Hampden Park, Glasgow.

Glasgow Merchants' Charity Cup

#	Date	Opponent	Res	Scorers	Att	Lock	Law	Chapman	Hendry	Hogg	Gordon	Reid	Bennett	Smith	Galt	Richmond	Gibson	Bowie	Goodwin
1	May 3 (h)	Clyde	W 3-2	Reid 2, Bennett	8,000	1	2	5		7	4	9	10	11	6	3		8	
SF	6 (a)	Queen's Park	W 1-0	Reid	15,000	1	2	5	6	7	4	9	10	11		3		8	
F	10 (n*)	Celtic	W 2-1	Reid 2	22,000	1	2	5		7	4	9			11	6	3	8	10
					Appearances	3	3	3	1	3	3	3	2	3	2	3		3	1
					Goals							5	1						

*Played at Hampden Park, Glasgow.

Other matches

#	Date	Opponent	Res	Scorers	Att
1	Aug 29 (a)	Partick Thistle*	W 2-1	Parker, Yuille	
2	Nov 2 (h)	Partick Thistle†	W 3-2	Parker 2, Paterson	
3	Dec 26 (a)	Bohemians	D 3-3	Goodwin, Reid, Gibson	
4	Jan 4 (h)	Clyde §	D 1-1	Yuille	6,000
5	Mar 20 (a)	Utd Belfast Sel‡	W 3-0	Chapman, Parker, Hogg	
6	Apr 1 (h)	Third Lanark	W 4-2	Parker 2, Bowie, Goodwin	
7	26 (a#)	Stirlingshire Jn	D 0-0		
8	27 (a)	Beith +	W 4-1	Galt 3, Hogg	
9	29 (a$)	5th Kings Own	W 6-1	Reid 2, Smith, Dunn, Bennett, Hogg	
10	May 15 (a)	Morton ¶	D 1-1	Reid	5,000
11	28 (a¥)	Grenland Sel	W 12-0	Reid 3, Hendry 3, Gordon 2, Hogg, Bennett, Galt, Waddell	6,000
12	30 (a¥)	Christiana Sel	W 6-0	Reid 5, Galt	6,000
13	Jun 2 (a)	Örgryte IS	W 7-2	Reid 2, Bennett 2 (2 pens), Gordon, Hogg, Smith	4,000
14	5 (aø)	Sweden	W 3-0	Reid 2, Smith	
15	8 (a√)	Denmark	D 1-1	Chapman	9,000
16	11 (a√)	Denmark	W 3-1	Chapman 2, Hendry	11,000

Other matches — **Appearances:** 12, 10, 7, 2, 12, 8, 14, 10, 9, 10, 7, 12, 5, 5, 5, …, 3, …, 3, 4, 3, 4, 5, 1, 1, 8, 1, 2, 1, 2
Other matches — **Goals:** 4, 4, 5, 3, 16, 4, 3, 5, …, 1, 6, …, 1, …, 2, 1, 2, …, 1, …, 1

*Archie McKenzie Benefit Match. †Boilermakers' Lock-out Benefit Match.
§James Galt Benefit Match. ‡Municipal Milk Fund Benefit Match, played at Grosvenor Park, Belfast.
#Played at Brockville Park, Falkirk. +Hugh McPherson Benefit Match. $Played at Palmerston Park, Dumfries.
¶Greenock Infirmary Benefit Match. ¥Played at Christiana, Norway. øPlayed at Gothenburg, Sweden.
√Played at Copenhagen, Denmark.

No further details available for Match 8.

1911-12

Manager: W.Wilton

Scottish League

#	Date	Opponent	Result	Scorers	Att	Lock	Law	Campbell	Gordon	Galt	Hendry	Hogg	Bowie	Reid	Bennett A	Smith	Richmond	Goodwin	Ormond	Chapman	Waddell	Brown A	Brown R	Brown J	Allan	Paterson	Parker	Farrington	Robertson	Gibson	Riddell	Cameron	Boden	Thomson	Bennett	Connor	Lawrie
1	Aug 16 (h)	Raith Rovers	W 5-0	Reid 2, Hogg, Bennett, Galt	11,000	1	2	3	4	5	6	7	8	9	10	11																						
2	19 (h)	Morton	W 6-1	Reid 2, Bennett 2, Hogg, Gordon	25,000	1	2	3	4	5	6	7	8	9	10	11																						
3	26 (a)	Clyde	W 2-0	Bennett, Hogg	35,000	1	2	3	4	5	6	7	8	9	10	11																						
4	Sep 2 (h)	Dundee	W 2-1	Bennett 2	30,000	1		2	4	5	6	7		9	10	11	3	8																				
5	16 (a)	Aberdeen	W 2-1	Goodwin, Reid	16,000	1		2	4	5	6	7		9	10	11	3	8																				
6	25 (h)	Hibernian	W 2-0	Bennett (pen), Chapman	40,000	1		2	4			7		9	10	11	3	8		5	6																	
7	30 (h)	Third Lanark	W 4-0	Reid 4	22,000	1		2	4		6	7		9	10	11	3	8			5																	
8	Oct 14 (a)	Airdrieonians	D 2-2	Hogg, Reid	18,000	1		2	4	5	6	7	8	9	10	11	3																					
9	21 (h)	Celtic	W 3-1	Bowie 2, Gordon	47,000	1		2	4	5	6	7	8	9	10	11	3																					
10	28 (a)	Partick Thistle	W 1-0	Reid	30,000	1		2	4		6	7	8	9	10		3				5	11																
11	Nov 4 (h)	St Mirren	W 4-1	Bowie, Goodwin, Reid, Hogg	13,000	1		2	4		6	7	8	9			3	10			5	11																
12	11 (a)	Motherwell	W 2-1	Hogg, Reid	15,000	1		2	4	5	6	7	8	9	10	11	3																					
13	18 (h)	Queen's Park	W 1-0	Goodwin	20,000	1	2	3	4	5	6	7	8	9		11		10																				
14	25 (a)	Hamilton A	W 7-0	Reid 4, Hogg, Bowie, Goodwin	12,000	1	2	3	4	5	6	7	8	9		11		10																				
15	Dec 2 (a)	Morton	L 1-2	Hogg	15,000	1	2	3	4	5	6	7	8	9		11		10																				
16	9 (a)	St Mirren	W 5-1	Reid 3, Hogg, Goodwin	15,000	1	2	3	4		6	7	8	9		11		10			5																	
17	16 (h)	Hearts	W 2-1	Reid, Hogg	22,000	1	2	3	4	5	6	7	8	9	10	11																						
18	23 (a)	Falkirk	W 2-0	Bennett, Smith	10,000	1	2	3	4	5	6	7	8	9	10	11																						
19	30 (h)	Kilmarnock	W 6-1	Hogg 3, Bennett, A.Brown, Reid	15,000	1	2	3		5	6	7		9	10			8				11	4															
20	Jan 1 (a)	Celtic	L 0-3		70,000	1		2	4		6	7	8	9	10	11	3				5																	
21	2 (h)	Partick Thistle	W 4-1	Reid 3, Galt	20,000	1		2	4	5	6	7	8	9	10		3					11																
22	6 (a)	Hibernian	L 0-5		13,000	1		2	4	5	6	7		9	10	11	3	8											3									
23	13 (a)	Clyde	L 1-2	Reid	30,000	1		2		5	6	7		9	10		3	8				11	4															
24	20 (h)	Aberdeen	W 2-0	Parker, Goodwin	20,000	1		2	4	5	6				10	11	3	8									7	9										
25	Feb 3 (a)	Hamilton A	D 1-1	Reid	10,000	1		5	4		6	7	8	9	10		3		2			11																
26	17 (a)	Third Lanark	W 3-1	Reid, Hogg, Bowie	25,000	1		5			6	7	10	9		11	3	8	2								4											
27	24 (h)	Airdrieonians	W 4-1	Hogg 2, Reid, Smith	15,000	1		2	4	5	6	7	8	9	10	11	3																					
28	Mar 2 (a)	Queen's Park	D 0-0		25,000	1		2	4	5	6	7	8	9		10	3					11																
29	9 (h)	Falkirk	W 4-0	Hogg 2, Reid 2	8,000	1		2	4	5	6	7	8	9	10	11	3																					
30	16 (a)	Dundee	L 1-2	Parker	8,000	1		2		5	6	7	8		11	10	3						4				9											
31	23 (a)	Raith Rovers	W 1-0	Goodwin	6,000	1		2		5	6	7	8	9	10		3						4															
32	30 (a)	Kilmarnock	L 2-3	Reid, Goodwin	4,000	1		5	4		6			9	10	11	8	2									7		1	3								
33	Apr 15 (a)	Hearts	L 1-2	Reid	8,000	1			4	5	6			9	10		2					11					7	8	3									
34	27 (h)	Motherwell	W 3-1	Bennett 2, Hendry	6,000	1	2		4	5	6			8	9	10	11	3									7											
	FINAL LEAGUE POSITION: 1st				**Appearances**	33	11	32	29	26	32	30	24	32	25	27	12	17	12	2	5	8	5	1	1	4	3	1	2								
					Goals				2	2	1	18	5	33	11	2		8		1		1					2										

Scottish FA Cup

#	Date	Opponent	Result	Scorers	Att	Lock	Law	Campbell	Gordon	Galt	Hendry	Hogg	Bowie	Reid	Bennett A	Smith	Richmond	Goodwin	Ormond	Chapman	Waddell	Brown A	Brown R	Brown J	Allan	Paterson	Parker	Farrington	Robertson
1	Jan 27 (h)	Stenhousemuir	W 3-1	Paterson 2, Reid	7,500	1		2	4	5	6		8	9	10	11										3	7		
2	Feb 10 (a)	Clyde	L 1-3*	Hendry	52,000	1		2	4	5	6	7	8	9	10	11	3												
	*Match abandoned after 75 minutes due to crowd invasion. Rangers conceded the tie.				**Appearances**	2		2	2	2	2	1	2	2	2	2	1									1	1		
					Goals						1			1												2			

Glasgow Cup

#	Date	Opponent	Result	Scorers	Att	Lock	Law	Campbell	Gordon	Galt	Hendry	Hogg	Bowie	Reid	Bennett A	Smith	Richmond	Goodwin	...	Gibson
1	Sep 9 (a)	Queen's Park	W 6-1	Reid 3, Gibson, Bennett, Hendry	25,000	1		2	4	5	6	7		9	10	11	3			8
SF	23 (h)	Clyde	W 1-0	Bennett (pen)	28,000	1		2	4	5	6	7		9	10	11	3	8		
F	Oct 7 (n*)	Partick Thistle	W 1-0	Hogg	58,000	1		2	4	5	6	7		9	10	11	3	8		
	*Played at Celtic Park, Glasgow.				**Appearances**	3		3	3	3	3	3		3	3	3	3	2		1
					Goals						1	1		3	2					1

Glasgow Merchants' Charity Cup

#	Date	Opponent	Result	Scorers	Att	Campbell	Gordon	Hendry	Bowie	Reid	Bennett A	Smith	Richmond	Goodwin	...	Paterson	Parker	...	Robertson
1	May 4 (n*)	Third Lanark	W 1-0	Reid	14,000	2	4	6	10	9		11		8	3	7	1		5
SF	8 (n†)	Clyde	L 1-2	Reid	7,000	2	4	6	8	9	10	11	3			7	1		5
	*Played at Celtic Park, Glasgow. †Played at Hampden Park, Glasgow.				**Appearances**	2	2	2	2	2	1	2	1	2		2	2		2
					Goals					2									

Other matches

#	Date	Opponent	Result	Scorers	Att
1	Aug 21 (a)	Celtic *	D 0-0		4,000
2	23 (a)	Third Lanark §	W 3-1	Reid 2, Gibson	2,000
3	Jan 3 (h)	Clyde †	D 2-2	Parker 2	5,000
4	Apr 8 (a)	Bohemians D	W 2-0	Reid, Paterson	6,000
5	9 (a)	Linfield	L 0-1		4,000
6	20 (h)	W Arsenal	D 0-0		12,000
7	22 (a)	Ayr U ‡	W 7-2	Reid 6, Goodwin	
8	29 (a)	Partick Thistle+	W 2-1	Reid, A.Bennett	4,000

*Jim Young Benefit Match. §Robert Ferguson Benefit match. †Jimmy Gordon Benefit Match.
‡Troon Navigation Lodge No.86 Building Fund Benefit Match.
+ Benefit Match for the widows of Glasgow Junior players Hislop & Smith.

Risk played number-11 in Match 8. No further details available for Matches 5 & 7.

1912-13

Manager: W.Wilton

Scottish League

No	Date		Opponent	Result	Scorers	Att	Lock	Campbell	Robertson	Gordon	Galt	Bowie	Hogg	Montgomery	Reid	Bennett	Smith	Brown A	Ormond	Hendry	Farrington	Paterson	Logan	Parker	Goodwin	Brown R	Ramsay	Gibson	Hempsey	Waddell	Riddell	Muir H	Ferguson	Boden	Lawrie	Daniels
1	Aug 17	(h)	Airdrieonians	W 4-2	Montgomery, Hogg, Reid, Gordon	25,000	1	2	3	4	5	6	7	8	9	10	11																			
2	24	(a)	Hamilton A	W 2-0	Reid, A.Brown	18,000	1	2	3	4	5	6	7	8	9	10		11																		
3	31	(h)	Dundee	D 3-3	Reid 2, Hogg	40,000	1	2	3	4	5	6	7	8	9	10		11																		
4	Sep 7	(a)	St Mirren	W 3-0	Smith, Montgomery, Hogg	20,000	1	2		4	5	10	7	8	9		11	3	6																	
5	14	(a)	Motherwell	W 2-1	Bennett, Smith	20,000		2			4	5		7	8	9	10	11	3	6	1															
6	21	(h)	Hearts	L 2-4	Reid 2	50,000		2			4	5		7	8	9	10		3	6	1	11														
7	30	(h)	Kilmarnock	W 3-0	Parker, Hogg, Bowie	14,000	1		3	2	4	8	7			10				6			5	9	11											
8	Oct 5	(a)	Aberdeen	W 3-1	Reid 2, A.Brown	20,000	1		3	2	4	8	7		9	10				6			5													
9	19	(a)	Hibernian	W 1-0	Reid	16,000		2				6	7	8	9			11	3	1			4	10												
10	26	(a)	Celtic	L 2-3	Reid 2	45,000		2			4	6			9	10	11		3		1		7	5	8											
11	Nov 2	(h)	Morton	D 1-1	Reid	18,000		2			4	6	10	7	9			11	3		1		5		8											
12	9	(a)	Queen's Park	W 3-2	Reid, Bowie, Smith	10,000		2			4	6	8	7	9			11	3		1		5	10												
13	16	(h)	Third Lanark	W 2-1	Reid, Bowie	20,000		2			4	6	8		9	10	11		3		1		5	7												
14	23	(a)	Clyde	W 3-1	Paterson, Reid, Bowie	18,000	1			2	4	8			9	10	11		3	6		7	5													
15	30	(a)	Falkirk	L 0-2		15,000		2	3		4	8			9	10	11			6		7	5					1								
16	Dec 7	(h)	Raith Rovers	D 2-2	Reid, Smith	12,000		2	3	4		6	8		9	10	11					7	5					1								
17	14	(h)	St Mirren	W 2-1	Reid, Smith	12,000			3	4		10			9		11		2	6		7	5	8				1								
18	21	(a)	Airdrieonians	L 0-3		7,000		2	3	4		6	8		9	10	11					7	5					1								
19	28	(h)	Aberdeen	W 3-1	Goodwin, Bowie, Parker (pen)	15,000		2	3			6	8	7								11	5	9	10	4		1								
20	Jan 1	(h)	Celtic	L 0-1		67,000		2	3			6	8	7								11	5	9	10	4		1								
21	2	(a)	Partick Thistle	W 3-2	Bowie, A.Brown, Goodwin	25,000			3			8						11	2			7	6	9	10	4		1	5							
22	4	(a)	Hibernian	W 5-3	Parker 3, Paterson, A.Brown	20,000			3			6	8					11	2			7		9	10			1	4	5						
23	11	(a)	Motherwell	W 3-1	Parker 3	8,000		2				8	6					11				7		9	10	4		1	5							
24	25	(a)	Morton	W 3-0	Goodwin, Paterson, Reid	15,000				2		6	8		9			11	3			7	5	10	4			1								
25	Feb 1	(a)	Raith Rovers	W 4-0	Reid 2, Goodwin 2	8,000				2		6	10		9			11	3			7	5	8	4			1								
26	Mar 1	(a)	Kilmarnock	W 3-2	Parker, Paterson	6,000		2			5		7			10			3	6		11		9	8	4		1								
27	8	(h)	Hamilton A	W 3-2	Goodwin, Reid, Bennett	12,000		2		4			7		9	10			3	6		11	5	8	4			1								
28	15	(a)	Hearts	D 1-1	Logan	18,000		2		4			7					11	3	6			5	9	10	8		1								
29	22	(h)	Partick Thistle	W 2-0	Bennett, Paterson	12,000		2		4					9	10	11		3	6		7	5	8				1								
30	24	(a)	Third Lanark	W 1-0	Hogg	25,000		2					7		9	10	11		3	6			5	8	4			1								
31	Apr 5	(h)	Queen's Park	W 4-0	Parker 2, Paterson 2	10,000		2				6				10	11		3			7		9	8	4		1	5							
32	15	(a)	Clyde	W 1-0	Reid	10,000		2				6			9	10	11		3			7	5	8	4			1								
33	19	(a)	Dundee	D 0-0		12,000				4		6	8		9	10	11		2			7	5					1			3					
34	26	(h)	Falkirk	W 2-1	Goodwin, Bennett (pen)	16,000				4		6			9	10	11		2			7	5	8				1			3					
	FINAL LEAGUE POSITION: 1st					Appearances	6	22	12	28	27	22	16	7	25	22	6	24	13	7	21	24	9	19	12	3	3	17	4	1	2					
						Goals				1		6	5	2	22	4	5	4				7	1	12	7											

Scottish FA Cup

No	Date		Opponent	Result	Scorers	Att	Gordon	Bowie	Hogg	Reid	Brown A	Ormond	Paterson	Logan	Parker	Goodwin	Gibson
2	Feb 8	(a)	Hamilton A	D 1-1	Reid	16,000	2	6	10	9	11	3	7	5	8	4	1
R	15	(h)	Hamilton A	W 2-0	Goodwin, Parker (pen)	37,000	2	6		9	11	3	7	5	8 10	4	1
3	22	(h)	Falkirk	L 1-3	Parker	48,000	2	6		9	11	3	7	5	8 10	4	1
					Appearances		3	3	1	3	3	3	3	3	2 3	3	3
					Goals					1					2	1	

Glasgow Cup

No	Date		Opponent	Result	Scorers	Att	Lock	Campbell	Robertson	Gordon	Galt	Bowie	Hogg	Montgomery	Reid	Bennett	Smith	Hendry	Logan	Brown R	Gibson
SF	Sep 28	(a)	Partick Thistle	D 0-0		35,000	1	2	3	4	5	8	7		9	10	11	6			
R	Oct 7	(h)	Partick Thistle	D 1-1	Smith	18,000	1	2	3	4	5	8	7		9	10	11	6			
2R	9	(a)	Partick Thistle	W 2-0	Hogg, Bennett	18,000		2	3	4			7	8	9	10	11	6	5		1
F	12 (n*)		Celtic	W 3-1	Hogg, Smith, Bennett	90,000		2	3	6			7	8	9	10	11		5	4	1
					Appearances		2	4	4	4	2	2	4	2	4	4	4	3	2	1	2
					Goals								2			2	2				

*Played at Hampden Park, Glasgow.

Glasgow Merchants' Charity Cup

No	Date		Opponent	Result	Scorers	Att	Gordon	Bowie	Hogg	Reid	Brown A	Ormond	Paterson	Logan	Parker	Goodwin	Gibson	Riddell
SF	May 3	(h)	Partick Thistle	W 3-1	Gordon 2, Reid	10,000	4	6	10	9	11	2	7	5	8		1	3
F	10	(a)	Celtic	L 2-3	Reid 2	30,000	2	6	10	9	11	3	7	5	8	4	1	
					Appearances		2	2	2	2	2	2	2	2	2	1	2	1
					Goals		2			3								

Inter-city League

No	Date		Opponent	Result	Scorers	Att
1	Oct 15	(h)	Aberdeen	W 5-2	Parker, Goodwin, Paterson, Hogg, Campbell (pen)	2,000
2	22	(a)	Hearts	L 0-3		4,000
3	29	(h)	Hibernian	W 2-1	A.Brown, Hogg	2,000
4	Nov 5	(h)	Celtic	W 4-0	Reid 3, Paterson (pen)	7,000

Competition abandoned due to lack of interest

	Appearances	2			1	3	2	1	2	1	2	4		2	4	2	3	1	3		1	1	3	3		1	1	1			
	Goals	1						2		3					1			2		1	1											

Other matches

No	Date		Opponent	Result	Scorers	Att
1	Aug 19	(h)	Celtic *	W 2-1	Parker, A.Brown	5,000
2	Sep 2	(a)	Hibernian †	D 0-0		2,000
3	11	(a)	Lochgelly	W 5-0	Galt, Gordon, Hogg, Bennett, Waddell	
4	Jan 6	(h)	Internationalists‡	L 1-5	Parker	35,000
5	18	(a)	Clyde §	D 0-0		18,000
6	Apr 16	(a)	Kilmarnock +	D 1-1	Paterson	
7	23	(a)	Border Counties	W 2-0	Parker, A.Brown	
8	28 (n#)		Celtic	D 0-0		3,000
9	Jun 5 (a¥)		Denmark	W 2-1	Parker, Reid	12,000
10	8 (a¥)		Denmark	D 1-1	Reid	15,000

	Appearances	2	4	1	7	8	1	4	4	5	2	8	10	5	1	9	2	9	2	3			7	7	1	2	1		1		
	Goals			1	1		1		2	1		2				1		4						1							

*R.G.Campbell Benefit Match. †Paddy Cannon Benefit Match. ‡Alec Smith Benefit Match.
§Scottish League fixture abandoned 70 minutes due to adverse weather conditions.
+Kilmarnock Farmers' Society Benefit Match. #Played at Kingsmill Park, Inverness. ¥Played at Copenhagen, Denmark.

1913-14

Manager: W.Wilton

Scottish League

Player columns (left to right): Hempsey, Campbell, Ormond, Gordon, Logan, Hendry, Paterson, Bowie, Reid, Bennett, Brown A, Muir H, Galt, Duncan, Stewart, Parker, Goodwin, Glenn, Brown R, Ferguson, Fulton, Cairns, Smith, Lock, Scott, Waddell, Cresswell, Pollock, Ramsay, Menzies, Muir J, Noble

#	Date		Opponent	Result	Scorers	Att	Hempsey	Campbell	Ormond	Gordon	Logan	Hendry	Paterson	Bowie	Reid	Bennett	Brown A	Muir H	Galt	Duncan	Stewart	Parker	Goodwin	Glenn	Brown R	Ferguson	Fulton	Cairns	Smith	Lock	Scott
1	Aug 16	(a)	Kilmarnock	W 6-1	Reid 2, Gordon, Paterson, Bowie, Bennett (pen)	9,000	1	2	3	4	5	6	7	8	9	10	11														
2	23	(h)	St Mirren	W 2-1	Reid, Bowie	35,000	1	2	3	4	5	6	7	8	9	10	11														
3	30	(a)	Hamilton A	W 1-0	Reid	20,000	1	2		4	5	6	7	8	9	10	11		3												
4	Sep 6	(h)	Aberdeen	W 5-1	Reid 2, Bennett, Bowie, Paterson	20,000	1	2		4	5	6	7	8	9	10	11		3												
5	13	(a)	Hearts	L 1-2	Logan	12,000	1	2		4	5	6	7	8	9	10	11		3												
6	15	(a)	Hibernian	W 3-0	Reid 2, Logan	12,000	1	2		4	5		7	8	9	10	11		3	6											
7	20	(h)	Dundee	L 0-1		45,000	1	2		3	5	6		11	9	10				4	7	8									
8	22	(a)	Aberdeen	D 0-0		18,000	1	2	3	4	5	6		11							7	8	9	10							
9	29	(h)	Queen's Park	W 3-0	Reid, Hendry, Stewart	25,000		2		4	5	6	7	8	9		11		3		10	1									
10	Oct 4	(a)	Morton	W 1-0	Duncan	18,000	1	2		4	5	6		11	8	9	10		3		7										
11	18	(a)	Third Lanark	W 4-2	Logan, Bowie, Parker, Paterson	30,000	1		2		5	6	11	8					3	4	7	10	9								
12	25	(h)	Celtic	L 0-2		63,500	1	2			5	6	11	8	9	10			3	4	7										
13	Nov 1	(a)	Raith Rovers	W 3-0	Bennett, Reid, Duncan	14,000	1	2			5		11	4	9	10			3	6	7	10	9		4						
14	8	(h)	Dumbarton	W 3-2	Parker, Bowie, Gordon (pen)	12,000	1			2	5		11	8					3	6	7	10	9		4						
15	15	(a)	Airdrieonians	W 2-0	Reid, Gordon (pen)	20,000	1	2		4	5		11	6	9	10					7	8			3						
16	22	(a)	Motherwell	L 0-1		16,000	1	2		4	5		11	6	9	10			3		7	8									
17	29	(a)	Clyde	W 1-0	Reid	26,000	1	2		4		6	11		9	10			3	5	7	8									
18	Dec 6	(h)	Morton	W 1-0	Craig (og)	25,000	1		2	4		6	11	8	9	10				5	7								3		
19	13	(h)	Falkirk	W 3-2	Bowie 2, Paterson	24,000	1		2	5		6	11	8	9	10					7				4				3		
20	20	(a)	Dundee	W 2-0	Duncan, Stewart	18,000	1		2	4	5	6	11		9	10					7	8							3		
21	27	(h)	Hamilton A	W 3-0	Reid, Stewart, Duncan	6,000	1		2	4	5	6	11		9						7	8					3	10			
22	Jan 1	(a)	Celtic	L 0-4		80,000	1		2	4	5	6	11	8	9	10					7						3				
23	3	(a)	St Mirren	W 1-0	Fulton	16,000		2		6	5		11	8	9			6			7	10			1	4	3				
24	5	(h)	Partick Thistle	D 0-0		10,000		2		4	5		7	8	9	10		6							1		3		11		
25	10	(a)	Ayr U	W 2-1	Reid, Gordon	10,000	1	2		6				8	9	10			5	7					4		3		11		
26	17	(h)	Motherwell	D 0-0		25,000		2		4	5		11	8	9				6	7	10						3			1	
27	31	(h)	Raith Rovers	W 4-0	Reid 2, Stewart 2	10,000		2		4	5	6		8	9		11		7	10							3			1	
28	Feb 14	(a)	Airdrieonians	W 3-0	Reid, Cairns, Paterson	15,000		2			4	6	7		9		11		5		8						3	10		1	
29	28	(a)	Queen's Park	W 6-0	Reid 4, Stewart, Smith	30,000		2		4	5	6	7		9				3		8							10	11	1	
30	Mar 7	(h)	Clyde	W 2-1	Paterson, Stewart	12,000		2		4		6	7		9					5	8						3	10	11	1	
31	14	(a)	Dumbarton	W 3-0	Stewart 3	8,000			2	6	7	8			10					5	9				4				11	1	3
32	21	(a)	Kilmarnock	W 1-0	Hendry	18,000			5	6					10					4	7	9					2	8	11	1	3
33	25	(h)	Ayr U	W 5-2	Reid 3, Duncan, Bennett	10,000			2	5	6			8	9	10				4	7						3		11	1	
34	Apr 1	(a)	Falkirk	L 1-4	Smith	5,000	2				6	7	8	9	10					5							4		11	1	3
35	7	(h)	Hibernian	D 1-1	Cairns	4,000		2			5	6	7		9	8	11	3				1	4					10			
36	13	(a)	Partick Thistle	D 1-1	Smith	12,000			2	5	6			8	9	7		3					4					10	11	1	
37	18	(h)	Third Lanark	W 2-0	Bennett, Logan	12,000			2	5	6			8	9	7		3					4					10	11	1	
38	25	(h)	Hearts	W 3-2	Smith 2, Logan	10,000			2	5	6	7		8	9	10		3					4						11	1	

FINAL LEAGUE POSITION: 2nd

Appearances	22	17	17	31	31	29	32	28	33	27	10	17	17	21	19	3	1	4	10	1	14	8	11	12	3
Goals				4	5	2	6	7	24	5				5	10	2					1	2	5		

1 own-goal

Scottish FA Cup

#	Date		Opponent	Result	Scorers	Att	Campbell	Gordon	Logan	Hendry	Bennett	Reid	Brown A	Galt	Stewart	Parker	Cairns	Smith
2	Feb 7	(h)	Alloa A	W 5-0	Stewart 3, A.Brown, Bowie	8,000	2	4	5	6	10	9	11		7	8	3	1
3	21	(a)	Hibernian	L 1-2	Reid	30,000	2	4	6		10	9	11	5	7	8	3	1
					Appearances		1	2	2	1	2	2	2	1	2	2	2	2
					Goals						1	1	1		3			

Glasgow Cup

	Date		Opponent	Result	Scorers	Att	Hempsey	Campbell	Gordon	Logan	Brown A	Bowie	Reid	Bennett	Galt	Stewart	Parker
SF	Sep 27	(a)	Clyde	W 1-0	Reid	36,000	1	2	4	5	11	8	9	10	3	6	7
F	Oct 11 (n*)		Third Lanark	W 3-0	Reid 2, Bennett	60,000	1	2	4	5	11	8	9	10	3	6	7
					Appearances		2	2	2	2	2	2	2	2	2	2	2
					Goals								3	1			

*Played at Hampden Park, Glasgow.

Glasgow Merchants' Charity Cup

#	Date		Opponent	Result	Scorers	Att	Campbell	Paterson	Bowie	Reid	Bennett	Galt	Duncan	Fulton	Smith	Lock
1	May 2 (n*)		Clyde	W 2-1	Reid, Bennett	20,000	2	6	7	8	9 10	3	5	4	11	1
SF	9	(h)	Third Lanark	D 1-1†	Bennett	14,000		5	6	7	9 10	2		4	8 11	1
					Appearances		1	1	2	2	1 2	2	1	2	1 2	2
					Goals					1	2					

*Played at Celtic Park, Glasgow. †Third Lanark won 4-3 on corners.

Craig played number-3 in semi-final.

Other matches

#	Date		Opponent	Result	Scorers	Att
1	Aug 18	(a)	Celtic *	W 2-0	Pollock 2	3,000
2	20	(a)	Queen's Park †	W 3-2	Bowie, Gordon, A.Brown	12,000
3	26	(a)	Partick Thistle§	L 0-1		5,000
4	Sep 9	(a)	Stenhousemuir‡	W 4-1	Gordon 2, Reid, A.Brown	
5	Dec 25	(a)	Hibernian+	W 2-0	Robinson, Paterson	1,500
6	Jan 2	(h)	Ex-Rangers$	D 4-4	J.Muir, Stewart, Bennett, Smith	15,000
7	Mar 28	(a)	Newcastle U	D 1-1	Stewart	12,000
8	Apr 6	(a)	Dunfermline A#	W 4-3	A.Brown, Stewart, Duncan, Thomson	
9	8	(a)	Ayrshire Jnrs±	W 8-1	Duncan 4, Hendry 2, Logan, Paterson	
10	15	(a)	Gala Fairydean	W 7-0	Stewart 4, Hendry 2, Duncan	
11	20	(a)	Abercorn	L 1-2	Stewart	
12	28	(h)	Everton @	W 6-2	Reid 3, Paterson, Bowie, Smith	15,000

Appearances	2	7	4	6	8	4	6	2	5	7	8	4	6	5	2	2	5	5	3	1	4	3	4	4	2	1	2	1	2	4	1
Goals				3	1	4	3	2	4	1	2			6	8								2					2			1

*Alec McNair Benefit Match. †William Sellar Benefit Match. §Frank Branscombe Benefit Match. ‡William Niven Benefit Match. +Willie Smith Benefit Match. $Alex Bennett Benefit Match. #James Thomson Benefit Match. ±John Robertson Benefit Match, played at Patna, Ayrshire. @James Wilson Benefit Match.

Wilson played number-7 in Match 2; Robinson played number-9 in Match 5 and scored one goal; Thomson played number-10 in Match 8 and scored one goal;. Walker played number-10 in Match 12; One player is unknown in Match 8.

1914-15

Manager: W.Wilton

Scottish League

#	Date	Opponent	Result	Scorers	Att	Lock	Kelso	Craig	Brown R	Logan	Gordon	Paterson	Bowie	Reid	Bennett	Smith	Cairns	Hendry	Duncan	Pursell	Hempsey	Muir H	Thomson	Anderson	Baird	Manderson	Cunningham	Muir J	Gilchrist	Hamilton	Lister
1	Aug 15 (h)	Hamilton A	W 1-0	Reid	20,000	1	2	3	4	5	6	7	8	9	10	11															
2	22 (a)	Aberdeen	W 2-0	Reid, Paterson	15,000	1	2	3	4	5	6	7	10	9			11	8													
3	29 (h)	Kilmarnock	W 2-1	Reid, Bennett	15,000	1	2	3	4	5	6	11	10	9	7			8													
4	Sep 5 (h)	Falkirk	W 3-1	Reid, Cairns, Bennett	10,000	1	2	3	4	5	6		10	9	7	11		8													
5	12 (a)	Dundee	D 1-1	Reid	15,000	1	2	3	4	5	6		8	9	7	11	10														
6	19 (h)	Hearts	L 1-2	Bowie	41,000	1	2	3		5	4		8	9	7	11	10	6													
7	28 (h)	Hibernian	W 4-2	Bowie, Reid, Cairns, Paterson	14,000	1	2	3		5	4	11	8	9			10	6	7												
8	Oct 3 (h)	Morton	L 0-2		16,000	1		2		5	4	11	8	9			10	6	7	3											
9	10 (a)	Raith Rovers	W 2-1	Bennett, Gordon	7,000		2	3	4		9	11			8		10	6	7	5	1										
10	17 (a)	Ayr U	L 0-2		13,000		2	3	4				8	9		11	10	6	7	5	1										
11	24 (h)	Raith Rovers	L 1-2	Cairns	14,000	1	2	3	4			7	8	9		11	10	6		5											
12	31 (a)	Celtic	L 1-2	Reid	35,000	1	2	3			4	11	8	9			10	6	7	5											
13	Nov 7 (a)	Queen's Park	W 4-1	Reid 2, Gordon 2	20,000	1	2	3			10	11	4	9	7		6		8	5											
14	14 (a)	Dumbarton	D 1-1	Reid	10,000	1	2	3			8	11	4	9	7		6		10	5											
15	21 (h)	Airdrieonians	W 2-1	Duncan, Reid	8,000	1	2	3	6		4	11	8	9			10		7	5											
16	28 (h)	Third Lanark	W 3-0	Reid 2, Gordon	6,000	1	2	3	6		4	11	8	9	7		10			5											
17	Dec 5 (h)	St Mirren	W 5-0	Logan, Cairns, Reid, Bowie, Paterson	8,000	1	2	3		6	4	11	8	9	7		10			5											
18	12 (a)	Kilmarnock	W 1-0	Cairns	5,000	1		2		6	4	11	8	9			10		7	5		3									
19	19 (h)	Motherwell	W 5-0	Gordon 2, Bowie, Reid, Paterson	6,000		2			6	4	7	8	9			10			5	1	3	11								
20	26 (a)	Third Lanark	D 1-1	Reid	6,000		2				4	7	8	9			10	6		5	1	3	11								
21	Jan 1 (h)	Celtic	W 2-1	Bowie, Reid	50,000		2			6	4	7	8	9			10			5	1	3	11								
22	2 (a)	Partick Thistle	L 1-3	Duncan	18,000		2		4				8	9			10	6	7	5	1	3	11								
23	4 (h)	Airdrieonians	L 0-5		12,000		2			4		11	8	9	7		10	6		5	1	3									
24	9 (h)	Clyde	L 1-2	Cairns	8,000		2			4		11	8	9			10	6	7	5	1	3									
25	16 (a)	Morton	W 1-0	Reid	10,000	1	2	3	4	6		7	8	9			10	11		5											
26	23 (h)	Dumbarton	W 1-0	Cairns	8,000	1	2	3	4	6		7	8	9			10	11		5											
27	30 (a)	Hibernian	W 2-1	Anderson, Gordon (pen)	8,000	1	2	3		6	4		8	9			10		7	5				11							
28	Feb 6 (h)	Falkirk	W 3-0	Cairns 2, Reid	8,000	1	2	3		6	4		8	9			10		7	5				11							
29	13 (a)	Ayr U	L 1-3	Reid	10,000	1	2	3			4	7	8	9			10			5						11	6				
30	20 (h)	Hearts	W 4-3	Reid 3, Cairns	15,000	1	2				4	11	8	9			10	6	7	5		3									
31	27 (a)	Motherwell	W 4-2	Cairns 2	8,000	1	2				4	11	8	9			10	6	7	5		3									
32	Mar 6 (h)	Dundee	W 2-1	Cairns, Paterson	12,000	1	2			6	4	11	8	9			10		7	5		3									
33	13 (a*)	Clyde	W 2-1	Cairns, Paterson	12,000	1	2			6	4	11	8	9			10		7	5		3									
34	27 (h)	Aberdeen	D 1-1	Hendry	10,000	1		3		6	4		8	9			10	11	7	5					2						
35	Apr 3 (h)	Hamilton A	L 3-4	Bowie, Cairns, Paterson	6,000		2			4		11	8	9			10	6		5	1	3									
36	5 (h)	Partick Thistle	L 0-1		12,000		2				4	11	6	9	7		8			5	1	3					10				
37	10 (a)	St Mirren	W 2-0	Reid 2	12,000		2				4	11	6	9	7		8			5	1	3					10				
38	24 (a)	Queen's Park	W 4-0	Cunningham 2, Reid, Gordon	10,000		2				4	11	6	9			10		7	5	1	3					8				
		Appearances				26	22	37	15	20	30	30	36	37	17	7	36	17	19	31	12	15	3	3	1	1	3				
		Goals								1	8	7	6	28	3		15	1	2					1			2				

FINAL LEAGUE POSITION: 3rd
*Played at Ibrox Stadium, Glasgow.

Glasgow Cup

#	Date	Opponent	Result	Att	Lock	Kelso	Craig	Logan	Gordon	Paterson	Bowie	Reid	Bennett	Smith	Hendry
SF	Sep 26 (h)	Partick Thistle	L 0-2	20,000	1	2	3	5	4	7	8	9	10	11	6
		Appearances			1	1	1	1	1	1	1	1	1	1	1
		Goals													

Glasgow Merchants' Charity Cup

#	Date	Opponent	Result	Scorers	Att	Kelso	Gordon	Paterson	Reid	Cairns	Hendry	Duncan	Pursell	Hempsey	Muir H	Cunningham
SF	May 4 (a)	Third Lanark	W 3-0	Cairns 2, Reid	7,000	2	4	11	9	10	6	7	5	1	3	8
F	8 (h)	Celtic	L 2-3	Cairns, Cunningham	30,000	2	4	11	9	10	6	7	5	1	3	8
		Appearances				2	2	2	2	2	2	2	2	2	2	2
		Goals							1	3						1

Belgian Relief War Fund Shield

#	Date	Opponent	Result	Scorers	Att	Lock	Kelso	Craig	Brown R	Gordon	Paterson	Bowie	Reid	Smith	Cairns	Hendry	Duncan	Pursell	Hempsey	Muir H	Cunningham
1	Oct 20 (a)	Third Lanark	W 4-0	Reid 3, Pursell	5,000		2	3	4		7	8	9	11	10	6		5	1		
SF	Dec 15 (n*)	Celtic	W 2-1	Reid, Bowie	9,000	1		2		4	11	8	9		10	6	7	5		3	
F	Apr 28 (n*)	Morton	L 1-2	Bennett	16,000	1		2		4	11	6	9		10		7	5		3	8
		Appearances				2	1	3	1	2	3	3	3	1	3	2	2	3	1	2	1
		Goals								1	4	1					1	2			1

*Played at Firhill Park, Glasgow.

Other matches

#	Date	Opponent	Result	Scorers	Att
1	Aug 18 (h)	Celtic *	L 4-6	Cairns 2, Bowie, Gilchrist	10,000
2	19 (a)	Morton §	W 2-1	Reid 2	
3	25 (h)	Clydebank †	W 3-1	Reid 2, Bennett	1,000
4	26 (a)	Vale of Leven ‡	W 2-1	Thomson, Logan	
5	Apr 13 (a)	Partick Thistle +	D 2-2	Lister 2	3,000
6	17 (a)	Notts C #	D 1-1	Smith (pen)	10,000

*Herbert Lock Benefit Match. §James Stark Benefit Match. †Clydebank Prize Band Benefit Match. ‡Opening of Millburn Park Pavilion. +Grand Orange Lodge of Scotland, Hall Building Fund Benefit Match. #Alec Smith Benefit Match.

No further details available for Matches 2 & 4.

1915-16

Manager: W.Wilton

Scottish League

No	Date	Opp	Result	Scorers	Att	Lock	Manderson	Muir H	Gordon	Pursell	Bowie	Duncan S	Cunningham	Reid	Cairns	Paterson J	Hempsey	Craig	Logan	Hendry	Fleming	Bennett	Parker	Branscombe	Sneddon	Lister	McCrae	Bone	Ballantyne	Brander	Taylor
1	Aug 21 (a) Dumbarton	W 3-1	Reid 2, Cunningham	6,000	1	2	3	4	5	6	7	8	9	10	11															
2	28 (h) Third Lanark	W 4-0	Cunningham 2, Reid 2	16,000	1	2	3	4	5	6	7	8	9	10	11															
3	Sep 4 (a) Kilmarnock	W 3-0	Reid, Cunningham, Cairns	8,000	1	2	3	4	5	6	7	8	9	10	11															
4	18 (h) Ayr U	W 5-2	Reid 2, Duncan, Cairns, Cunningham	16,000	1	2	3	4	5	6	7	8	9	10	11															
5	Oct 2 (a) Airdrieonians	W 1-0	Cunningham	7,000		2		4	5	6	7	8	9	10	11	1	3													
6	16 (h) Hearts	L 0-4		15,000	1	2	3	4		6	7	8	9	10	11			5												
7	23 (a) Raith Rovers	W 3-1	Reid 2, Hendry	3,000		2	3	4	5		7	8	9	10	11	1			6											
8	30 (h) Celtic	W 3-0	Duncan, Reid, Paterson	45,000	1	2	3	4			7	8	9	10	11			5	6											
9	Nov 6 (a) Queen's Park	W 6-0	Cairns 2, Cunningham 2 (1 pen), Fleming, Duncan	14,000		2	3	4			7	8		10	11	1		5	6	9										
10	13 (h) Hamilton A	W 3-0	Cunningham 2 (1 pen), Duncan	15,000		2	3	4			7	8		10	11	1		5	6	9										
*11	20 (a) Falkirk	L 0-2		3,000		2	3	4	5		7		9	10						6		1								
12	27 (h) Hibernian	W 4-2	Cunningham 3, Paterson	7,000		2	3	4	5			8	9	10	11	1			6		7									
13	Dec 4 (a) Morton	L 0-2		10,000	1	2			7	3	4	8	9	10	11			5	6											
14	11 (h) St Mirren	W 4-0	Gordon 2, Cunningham 2	6,000	1	2	4	3	6	7		8		10	11			5		9										
15	18 (a) Clyde	W 2-0	Reid, Cairns	12,000	1	2	3	4			7	8	9	10	11			5	6											
16	25 (h) Falkirk	W 1-0	Paterson	10,000		2	3	4			7	8	9	10	11	1		5	6											
17	Jan 1 (h) Celtic	D 2-2	Cunningham, Duncan	40,000		2	3	4			10	7	8	9	11	1		5	6											
18	3 (h) Partick Thistle	L 0-1		20,000	1			4	3		10	7	8		11		2	5	6				9							
19	8 (h) Motherwell	W 4-1	Reid 3, Cairns	10,000	1	2	3	4			7	8	9	10	11			5	6											
20	15 (a) Dundee	L 0-2		10,000		2	3	4				8	9	10	11	1		5	6		7									
21	22 (h) Kilmarnock	W 3-1	Bennett 2, Gordon	4,000	1		3	4	2	6	7		9	10	11			5			8									
22	29 (a) Motherwell	D 2-2	Cairns, Reid	10,000	1	2	3	4	6		7		9	10	11			5			8									
23	Feb 5 (h) Morton	W 1-0	Cairns	25,000		2	3	4			7		9	10	11	1		5	6		8									
24	12 (h) Hearts	W 2-1	Gordon 2 (1 pen)	15,000		2	3	4			7		9	10	11	1		5	6		8									
25	19 (h) Aberdeen	W 4-0	Cunningham 2 (1 pen), Reid, Cairns	15,000		2	3	4			7	8	9	10	11	1		5	6											
26	26 (a) Ayr U	L 0-1		7,000		2			6	4	7		9	10	11	1	3	5			8									
27	Mar 4 (h) Airdrieonians	W 3-0	Gordon, Duncan, Reid	12,000	1	2	3	4		6	7		9	10	11			5			8									
28	11 (a) Hibernian	W 3-2	Paterson 2, Reid	5,000		2	3	4			7		9	10	11	1		5	6		8									
29	18 (a) Third Lanark	W 1-0	Branscombe	22,000	1	2	3	4			8	7		10	11			5	6				9							
30	Apr 1 (h) Hamilton A	W 1-0	Sneddon	10,000		2	3	4	5		8	7		10		1			6				9	11						
31	8 (h) Raith Rovers	W 3-0	Gordon 2, Paterson	10,000		2	4	3			10	7	9		11	1		5	6		8									
32	10 (h) Dundee	W 3-2	Lister, Cairns, Branscombe	5,000		2			5	4				10		1	3				8		9	11	6	7				
33	15 (a) Partick Thistle	L 2-5	Cairns 2	30,000		2	3	4	5	6	7			10	11	1					8		9							
34	17 (a) St Mirren	D 1-1	Paterson	4,000				4			8			10	11	1	3	5	6				9		2	7				
35	20 (h) Dumbarton	D 2-2	Duncan, Branscombe	3,000	1	2		4		6	7							5			10		11		9	3	8			
36	22 (h) Clyde	D 2-2	Duncan, Branscombe	5,000		2	3	4			7			10		1		5			8		9	11	6					
37	24 (h) Queen's Park	W 6-0	Reid 3, Duncan 2, Branscombe	6,000		2	3	4		6	7		9	10		1		5			8		11							
38	29 (a) Aberdeen	D 0-0		6,000		2	5	4			7					1							10	6	9	11	8		3	
	Appearances					16	32	30	31	20	26	32	20	25	34	31	21	5	26	18	4	17	1	7	5	5	3	2	1	3	1
	Goals								8			10	18	21	12	7				1	1	2		5	1	1					

FINAL LEAGUE POSITION: 2nd

*Rangers played with nine players. Hempsey, Hendry and Cunningham missed their train connection in Glasgow due to fog.

Glasgow Cup

No	Date	Opp	Result	Scorers	Att	Lock	Manderson	Muir H	Gordon	Pursell	Bowie	Duncan S	Cunningham	Reid	Cairns	Paterson J	Hempsey	Hendry	Fleming
1	Sep 11 (a) Queen's Park	W 4-1	Reid 2, Cunningham, Paterson	40,000	1	2	3	4	5	6	7	8	9	10	11			
SF	25 (h) Partick Thistle	W 7-2	Reid 3, Cairns 3, Paterson	20,000	1	2	3	4	5		7	8	9	10	11			6
F	Oct 9 (n*) Celtic	L 1-2	Paterson	70,000	1		3	4	5	6	7	8	9	10	11	2		
	Appearances					3	2	3	3	3	2	3	3	3	3	3	1		1
	Goals												1	5	3	3			

*Played at Hampden Park, Glasgow.

Glasgow Merchants' Charity Cup

No	Date	Opp	Result	Att	Manderson	Muir H	Duncan S	Cairns	Hempsey	Logan	Hendry	Bennett	Brander	Taylor
SF	May 6 (a) Celtic	L 0-3	30,000	2	3	7	10	1	4	6	8	5	9
	Appearances				1	1	1	1	1	1	1	1	1	1
	Goals													

Seymour played number-11.

Other matches

No	Date	Opp	Result	Scorers	Att	Lock	Manderson	Muir H	Gordon	Cunningham	Reid	Cairns	Paterson J	Craig	Logan	Bennett	Branscombe	Lister	McKenna	Sibbald	Leitch
*1	Sep 27 (h) Glasgow Highs	W 6-1	Lister 3, Gordon, Cunningham, Paterson	6,000			3	4	8		10	11	2	5	7	9		1	6	
†2	Jan 4 (h) Rest of Glasgow	W 3-2	Reid 2, Leitch	12,000	1	2		3		9		11		5	8			6	7	10
	Appearances					1	1	1	1	1	1	1	2	1	2	2	1	1	2	1	1
	Goals								1	1	2		1					3			1

*Red Cross funds & 9th HLI Benevolent Funds Benefit Match.

†Lord Provost's Belgian Refugee Relief Fund Benefit Match.

1916-17

Manager: W.Wilton

Scottish League

#		Date	V	Opponent	Result	Scorers	Att	Lock	Manderson	Blair	Pursell	Logan	McKenna	Duncan S	Bell	Duncan C	Cairns	Archibald R	Riddell	Lawson	Phillip	Paterson W	Hempsey	Law	Bennett	Bowie	Martin	Hamilton	Hendry	Gordon	Croot	Livingston	Gray	Rutherford	Anderson	Harris	Dick	Archibald A	Lindsay
1	Aug	19	(h)	Dundee	W 3-0	C.Duncan 2, S.Duncan	12,000	1	2	3	4	5	6	7	8	9	10	11																					
2		26	(a)	Hearts	W 3-1	Cairns, S.Duncan, R.Archibald	8,000	1	2	3	4	5	6	7	8	9	10	11																					
3	Sep	2	(h)	Dumbarton	W 6-0	C.Duncan 3, Logan, Cairns, S.Duncan (pen)	10,000	1	2		3	5	6	7	8	9	10	11	4																				
4		16	(a)	Kilmarnock	W 3-0	S.Duncan 2 (1 pen), C.Duncan	10,000	1	2	3	4	5	6	7	8	9	10				11																		
5		30	(h)	St Mirren	W 1-0	Cairns	12,000	1	2	3	4	5	6	7			10	8				11	9																
6	Oct	7	(a)	Ayr U	W 3-1	Paterson 2, S.Duncan	6,000	1	2	3	4		6	7			10	8	5			11	9																
7		14	(h)	Motherwell	W 2-1	Cairns 2	5,000		2	3	4		6	7			10	8	5			11	9	1															
8		21	(a)	Third Lanark	D 1-1	Paterson	30,000		2	3	4		6	7			10	8	5			11	9	1															
9		28	(a)	Celtic	D 0-0		40,000	1	2	3		5	6	7			10					11	9		4	8													
10	Nov	4	(h)	Morton	L 0-1		30,000	1	2	3		5	6	7			10		4			11	9			8													
11		11	(a)	Hibernian	D 0-0		10,000	9		3	4	5	6	7			10					11	1	2		8													
12		18	(h)	Clyde	W 1-0	S.Duncan	8,000		2	3	4	5	6	7	8	9						11	1			10													
13		25	(a)	Raith Rovers	W 4-1	R.Archibald 2, Riddell, Bennett	5,000		2	3	4					9	10	11	5	7			1		6	8													
14	Dec	2	(h)	Falkirk	W 3-1	S.Duncan 2, Cairns	7,000		2	3	4		6	7		9	10	11	5				1			8													
15		9	(a)	Airdrieonians	L 0-2		8,000		2	3	4	5	6	7		9	10	11					1			8													
16		16	(h)	Hibernian	W 5-1	Martin 2, Manderson, C.Duncan, Dornan (og)	10,000		2	3	4		6	7		9		11	5				1			8	10													
17		23	(a)	Motherwell	L 1-2	Blair (pen)	8,000		2	3	4			7		9		11	5				1			8	10		6											
18		30	(h)	Airdrieonians	W 3-0	C.Duncan 2, Lawson	12,000		2	3	4		6	7		9		11	5				1			8	10													
19	Jan	1	(h)	Celtic	D 0-0		50,000		2	3	4		6	7		9		11	5				1			8	10													
20		2	(a)	Partick Thistle	W 1-0	Martin	12,000		2	3	6	5				9				7			1			8	10			4	11									
21		6	(h)	Hearts	W 1-0	Martin	12,000		2	3	4		6	7		9			5				1			8	10				11									
22		13	(a)	Clyde	W 1-0	Riddell	15,000		2	3	4			7		9		11	5				1			8	10		6											
23		20	(h)	Partick Thistle	W 3-0	C.Duncan 2, Riddell			2	3	4		6	7		9			5				1			8	10				11									
24		27	(h)	Hamilton A	W 2-1	Blair (pen), Pursell	8,000		2	3	7				8	9			5				1			4	10		6		11									
25	Feb	3	(a)	Aberdeen	L 1-3	C.Duncan	6,000		2	3			6		8	9	7		5				1	4			10				11									
26		10	(h)	Ayr U	W 1-0	Manderson	12,000	9	3	2				7	8		10		5				1			4	6				11									
27		17	(a)	Dumbarton	W 3-0	Bell, Cairns, Croot	5,000	1	2	3				7	8	9	10		5							4	6				11									
28		24	(a)	St Mirren	D 1-1	Cairns	12,000		2	3				7	8		10		5				1			4	6			9	11									
29	Mar	3	(h)	Aberdeen	W 1-0	Gordon	8,000	1	2	3				7	8				5							4	6			10	9	11								
30		10	(a)	Morton	L 0-1		7,000		2	3		5		7		9			4			11	1			8	6			10										
31		17	(a)	Falkirk	W 2-0	Cairns 2	5,000		2	3				7		9	8		5			11	1				6			4	10									
32		24	(h)	Raith Rovers	W 4-3	Livingston 3, Cairns	5,000		2	3	4			7	8	9			5			11	1				6				10									
33		31	(a)	Kilmarnock	L 1-4	Cairns	5,000		2	3	9	5		7	8							11	1			4	6				10									
34	Apr	7	(h)	Third Lanark	L 0-2		15,000	1	2	3			6			9	10					11				8	5			4			7							
35		9	(a)	Queen's Park	W 4-1	C.Duncan 2, Gray, Rutherford	10,000	1	2	3			6		8	9						11				4	6						7	10						
36		21	(a)	Hamilton A	L 1-3	C.Duncan	7,000	1	2	3		5			8	9	10					11				4		6							7					
37		21	(h)	Queen's Park	W 1-0	Harris	7,000	1	2	3	5		6		8							11				4						10				7	9			
38		28	(a)	Dundee	L 1-2	Blair (pen)	9,000	1	2	3		5				9						11				4	6			8	10						7			
				Appearances				16	38	35	30	12	24	28	14	25	24	12	23	24	1	5	21	4	7	20	21	1	6	6	9	5	2	1	2	1	1		
				Goals					2	3	1	1		9	1	15	12	3	3	1		3			1		4			1	1	3	1	1		1	1		

FINAL LEAGUE POSITION: 3rd

Matches 36 & 37, both played on 21 April, at 3.30 and 6.45pm respectively.

1 own-goal

Glasgow Cup

#		Date	V	Opponent	Result	Scorers	Att	Lock	Manderson	Blair	Pursell	Logan	McKenna	Duncan S	Bell	Duncan C	Cairns	Archibald R	Riddell	Lawson	Phillip	Paterson W	Hempsey
1	Sep	9	(a)	Partick Thistle	W 2-0	Cairns 2	30,000	1	2		3	5	6	7	8	9	10	11	4				
SF		23	(a)	Celtic	L 0-3		60,000	1	2	3		5	6	7			10	8	4			11	9
				Appearances				2	2	1	1	2	2	2	1	1	2	2	2			1	1
				Goals													2						

Glasgow Merchants' Charity Cup

#		Date	V	Opponent	Result	Att	Manderson	Blair	Pursell	Cairns	Paterson W	Hempsey	Bowie	Martin	Gordon	Archibald A	Lindsay
SF	May	12	(h)	Celtic	L 0-2	30,000	2	3	5	10	11	1	4	6	9	7	8
				Appearances			1	1	1	1	1	1	1	1	1	1	1
				Goals													

Other matches

#		Date	V	Opponent	Result	Scorers	Att	Lock	Manderson	Blair	Pursell	Logan	Duncan S	Bell	Duncan C	Riddell	Paterson W	Bowie	Martin	Gordon	Rutherford	Dick
1	Aug	12	(a)	Ayr U *	W 3-1	Untraced 3	1,500	1	2	3	6	5	7	8	9							
2	Apr	14	(h)	British Army §	W 3-1	Bell 2, C.Duncan	15,000	1	2	3	6			8	9	5	11	4		10	7	
3	May	5	(a)	Morton †	L 0-1				2	3	6		7				11	4	5	10		8
				Appearances				2	3	3	3	1	2	2	2	1	2	2	1	2	1	1
				Goals										2	1							

*Red Cross funds Benefit Match. §Red Cross & Soldiers Comfort Fund Benefit Match.
†Greenock Infirmary Benefit Match.

McConnell played number-4 in Match 1; Clark played number-10 in Match 1; McNaughton played number-11 in Match 1; Bruce played number-1 in Match 3; Steel played number-9 in Match 3. 3 goals untraced.

1917-18

Manager: W.Wilton

Scottish League

#	Date		Opponent	Result	Scorers	Att	Hempsey	Manderson	Blair	Pursell	Dixon	Martin	Archibald A	Bowie	McDermid	Cairns	Lawson	Cunningham	McQueen	Gordon	Muirhead	McKenna	Brown	Bell	Reid	Dick	Riddell	Singleton	Young	Lock	McCulloch	Hart	Pollock	Higgenbotham	Miller	Duward
1	Aug 18	(a)	Kilmarnock	W 1-0	McDermid	10,000	1	2	3	4	5	6	7	8	9	10	11																			
2	25	(h)	Third Lanark	W 4-2	Cunningham 3 (1 pen), Cairns	18,000	1	2	3	4	5	6	7	8	11	10		9																		
3	Sep 1	(a)	Partick Thistle	L 0-2		20,000	1	2	3	4	5	6	7	8	9	10	11																			
4	15	(h)	Hibernian	W 3-0	Bowie, Cairns, Gordon (og)	10,000	1		3		5	6	7	8	11	9		2	4	10																
5	24	(h)	Queen's Park	W 3-0	Muirhead 2, Lawson	12,000	1	2	3	4	5	6	7	8	9		11				10															
6	29	(a)	Dumbarton	W 4-2	Cairns 2, Muirhead 2	8,000	1		3	4	5		7	8	11	9		2		10	6															
7	Oct 13	(a)	Morton	D 1-1	Brown	10,000	1	2	3	4	5	6	7	8	11	10							9													
8	20	(h)	Celtic	L 1-2	Bowie	45,000	1	2	3	6	5		7	8	11	10				4			9													
9	27	(h)	St Mirren	D 0-0		10,000	1	2	3	6	5	10	7		11	9				4		8														
10	Nov 3	(h)	Ayr U	D 0-0		8,000	1	2			5		7	4	9	10	11		3	8		6														
11	10	(a)	Hearts	W 3-0	Gordon 2, Archibald	12,000	1		3	4	5		7	8	10	11			2	9		6														
12	17	(h)	Airdrieonians	W 4-0	Brown 3, Cairns	12,000	1	2		4	5		7	8	11	10			3			6	9													
13	24	(a)	Queen's Park	W 3-2	Gordon (pen), Archibald, Brown	12,000	1	2	3	6	5		7	8	11	10				4			9													
14	Dec 1	(h)	Dumbarton	W 2-1	Cairns 2	7,000	1	9	3		5		7	8	11	10		2		4		6														
15	8	(a)	Hamilton A	W 2-1	Reid 2	9,000	1	2	3	4	5		7	8	11	10						6			9											
16	15	(h)	Falkirk	W 4-1	Brown 2, Archibald, Bowie	8,000	1	2	3	6	5		7	8	11	10				4			9													
17	22	(a)	Third Lanark	W 1-0	Muirhead	12,000	1	2	3	6	5		7	8	11	10					9	4														
18	29	(h)	St Mirren	W 2-0	Bowie, Cairns	12,000	1	2			5		7	8	11	10			3	9	6	4														
19	Jan 1	(a)	Celtic	D 0-0		55,000	1	2	3	4	5		7	8	11	10						6	9													
20	2	(h)	Partick Thistle	W 1-0	Blair (pen)	18,000	1	2	3		5		7	8	11	10						6	9						4							
21	5	(a)	Clydebank	D 1-1	Archibald	14,700	1	2	3	4	5		7	8	11	10						6	9													
22	12	(h)	Hearts	W 2-0	Gordon 2	8,000	1	2	3	4	5		7	8	11	10				9		6														
23	26	(a)	Ayr U	W 2-0	Cairns, McDermid	5,000		2	3		5	7	6	11	10	8				4	9						1									
24	Feb 2	(h)	Morton	W 4-2	Gordon 4	25,000		2		6	5	7	4	11	10	8			3	9							1									
25	9	(a)	Hibernian	W 1-0	McDermid	8,000	1	2			5	6	7	8	11	10			3	9									4							
26	16	(a)	Clyde	W 3-0	Brown 2, Cairns	8,000	1	2			5	6	7	4		10			3	8			9					11								
27	23	(a)	Motherwell	D 0-0		12,000	1	2			5	6	7	4		10			3	8			9					11								
28	Mar 2	(h)	Kilmarnock	W 3-0	Archibald 2, McCulloch	20,000		2	3		5	6	7	4		10				8								11		1	9					
29	9	(a)	Falkirk	L 0-2		8,000		2	3	4	5	6	7	8		10												11		1	9					
30	16	(h)	Hamilton A	W 4-2	McDermid, Hart, Archibald, Martin	10,000		2	3	4	5	6	7	8	11	10														1		9				
31	23	(a)	Airdrieonians	W 2-1	Hart, Cairns	10,000			3	4	5	6	7	8	11	10		2												1		9				
32	30	(h)	Clydebank	W 1-0	Cunningham	10,000		2	3		5	6	7	4	11	10		9		8										1						
33	Apr 6	(h)	Motherwell	W 2-1	Gordon 2	25,000		2	3		5	6	7	4	11	10		9		8										1						
34	13	(h)	Clyde	W 2-1	Archibald, Bowie	10,000		2	3	4	5	6	7	8	11	10														1		9				
	FINAL LEAGUE POSITION: 1st				Appearances		25	29	27	24	32	18	34	33	28	34	5	4	12	16	7	12	11	1	1	1	2	2	4	7	2	3				
					Goals				1			1	8	5	4	11	1	4		11	5		9		2						1	2				

1 own-goal

Glasgow Cup

#	Date		Opponent	Result	Scorers	Att	Hempsey	Manderson	Blair	Pursell	Dixon	Martin	Archibald A	Bowie	McDermid	Cairns	Lawson	Gordon	Brown
1	Sep 8	(a)	Clyde	D 0-0*		20,000	1	2	3	4	5	6	7	8	9	10	11		
SF	22	(a)	Celtic	W 3-0	Cairns, Archibald, Brown	40,000	1	2	3	6	5		7	8	11	10		4	9
F	Oct 6	(h)	Partick Thistle	W 4-1	Brown 2, Gordon, McDermid	45,000	1	2	3	6	5		7	8	11	10		4	9
				Appearances			3	3	3	3	3	1	3	3	3	3	1	2	2
				Goals									1		1	1		1	3

*Rangers won 14-2 on corners.

Glasgow Merchants' Charity Cup

#	Date		Opponent	Result	Scorers	Att	Manderson	Blair	Dixon	Martin	Archibald A	Bowie	McDermid	Cairns	Cunningham	McCulloch	Hart
1	May 11	(n*)	Partick Thistle	L 0-2		16,000	2	3	5	6	7	4	11	10	8	1	9
				Appearances			1	1	1	1	1	1	1	1	1	1	1
				Goals													

*Played at Celtic Park, Glasgow.

Army & Navy War Relief Fund Shield

#	Date		Opponent	Result	Scorers	Att	Manderson	Blair	Pursell	Dixon	Archibald A	Bowie	Cairns	Gordon	Singleton	Young	Hart
QF	Apr 20	(h)	Partick Thistle	W 3-0	Hart 2, Cairns	16,000	2	3	4	5	7	8	10	6	11	1	9
SF	27	(h)	Morton	L 1-3	Young	23,000	2	3	4	5	7	8	10	6	11	1	9
				Appearances			2	2	2	2	2	2	2	2	2	2	2
				Goals									1			1	2

Other matches

#	Date		Opponent	Result	Scorers	Att	Manderson	Blair	Martin	Archibald A	Bowie	McDermid	Singleton	Pollock	Higgenbotham	Miller	Duward
1	May 18	(a)	Renfrewshire Sel	L 1-4	Untraced		2	3	6	8	5	10	1	4	7	9	11
				Appearances			1	1	1	1	1	1	1	1	1	1	1
				Goals													

Red Cross War Fund Benefit Match played at St Mirren Park, Paisley.

1 goal untraced

1918-19

Manager: W.Wilton

Scottish League

#		Date		Opponent	Result	Scorers	Att.	Hempsey	Manderson	Blair	Pursell	Dixon	Wallis	Aitken	Bowie	McLean	Cairns	McDermid	Cunningham	Gordon	Archibald	McQueen	Hart	Lawson	Riddell	Brown	Lock	Duncan S	Donnachie	Miller
1	Aug	17	(h)	Falkirk	W 1-0	McLean (pen)	30,000	1	2	3	4	5	6	7	8	9	10	11												
2		24	(a)	Hearts	W 4-1	McLean 3, Cairns	15,000	1	2	3	4	5	6	7	8	9	10	11												
3		31	(h)	St Mirren	W 2-0	Aitken, McLean	12,000	1	2	3		5	6	7	4	9	10					8	11							
4	Sep	7	(a)	Hamilton A	W 3-0	McLean 2, Manderson	12,000	1	2		4	5	6		8	9	10					11	3	7						
5		14	(h)	Partick Thistle	W 2-0	McLean 2	25,000	1	2	3	4	5	6	7	8	9	10	11												
6		28	(h)	Ayr U	W 6-2	Bowie 3, Hart 2, Cairns	10,000	1	2		4	5	6	7	8		10	11				3	9							
7		30	(a)	Queen's Park	W 2-0	Hart, Cairns	25,000	1	2		4	5	6	7	8		10					3	9	11						
8	Oct	12	(h)	Dumbarton	W 3-0	McLean 2, Aitken	12,000	1	2	3	4	5	6	7	8	9	10						11							
9		19	(a)	Celtic	W 3-0	Cairns, Bowie, McDermid	36,000	1	2	3		5	6	7	8		10	11						9		4				
10		26	(h)	Motherwell	D 0-0		22,000	1		3		5	6	7	8	9	10	11							2	4				
11	Nov	2	(a)	Third Lanark	W 2-1	Bowie, McLean	25,000	1		3	4	5	6	7	8	9	10					11			2					
12		9	(h)	Clyde	W 3-0	Cairns 2, McLean	20,000	1		3	4	5	6	7	8	9	10	11												
13		16	(a)	Airdrieonians	D 0-0		7,000	1	2	3	4	5	6	7	8	9	10							11						
14		23	(a)	Morton	L 0-1		10,000	1	2	3	4	5	6	7	8	10	11									9				
15	Dec	7	(h)	Hibernian	W 5-1	Bowie 3, McLean, Cairns	12,000	1	2	3	4	5	6	7	8	9	10							11						
16		14	(a)	Clydebank	W 5-0	McLean 3, Cairns, Lawson	20,000	1	2	3		5	6	7	8	9	10							11		4				
17		21	(h)	Kilmarnock	W 8-0	McLean 4, Bowie 2, Cairns, Lawson	15,000	1	2			5	6	7	8	9	10					3		11		4				
18		28	(h)	Motherwell	W 1-0	Bowie	20,000	1	2	3		5	6	7	8		10				4			11		9				
19	Jan	1	(h)	Celtic	D 1-1	Bowie	65,000	1	2	3		5	6		8	9	10				4			7		11				
20		2	(a)	Partick Thistle	L 0-1		30,000	1	2	3		5	6		8	9	10				4			7		11				
21		4	(a)	Airdrieonians	W 2-1	Blair 2 (2 pens)	18,000	1		3	4	5	6				10		8		7	2		11		9				
22		11	(a)	Kilmarnock	L 0-1		10,000	1	2	3	4	5	6	7	8	9	10							11						
23		18	(h)	Queen's Park	W 4-0	Cunningham 3, Gordon	20,000	1	2	3	4	5	6	11		9			10	8	7									
24		25	(a)	Hibernian	W 2-1	Archibald, Gordon	12,000	1	2	3	4	5	6	11		9			10	8	7									
25	Feb	1	(a)	Dumbarton	W 2-0	Cairns, McLean	10,000	1	2	3	4	5	6		8	9	11		10		7									
26		8	(h)	Morton	W 1-0	McLean	40,000	1	2	3	4	5	6			9	11		10	8	7									
27		15	(a)	St Mirren	D 2-2	Cairns, Manderson	15,000	1	2	3	4	5	6				10		8	9	7			11						
28		22	(h)	Clydebank	W 3-0	Brown 3	14,000		2	3	4	5	6	8			11		10							9	1	7		
29	Mar	1	(h)	Hearts	W 3-2	Brown, Archibald, Cunningham	35,000	1	2	3	4	5	6				11		10	8	7					9				
30		8	(h)	Hamilton A	W 3-0	Archibald, Brown, Dixon	15,000	1	2		4	5	6						10	3	7					9			11	
31		22	(a)	Ayr U	D 1-1	Blair (pen)	12,000		2	3	4	5	6						10	8	7					9	1		11	
32	Apr	12	(a)	Falkirk	W 4-0	Gordon 2, McLean, Bowie	12,000		2	3		5	6		8	9			10	4	7						1		11	
33		21	(h)	Third Lanark	W 4-0	McLean 2, Dixon, Gordon	15,000			3		5	6		8	9			10	4	7	2							11	1
34	May	10	(a*)	Clyde	W 4-0	McLean 3, Bowie	35,000		2	3		5	6		8	9			10	4	7								11	1
				FINAL LEAGUE POSITION: 2nd		Appearances		29	30	29	23	34	34	21	26	24	28	7	15	16	15	7	3	9	4	9	4	1	5	1
				*Played at Celtic Park, Glasgow.		Goals			2	3		2			2	14	29	11	1	4	5	3		3	2		5				

Glasgow Cup

#		Date		Opponent	Result	Scorers	Att.	Hempsey	Manderson	Blair	Pursell	Dixon	Wallis	Aitken	Bowie	McLean	Cairns	McDermid	Cunningham	Gordon	Archibald	McQueen	Hart
SF	Sep	21	(h)	Queen's Park	W 3-0	Bowie 2, McDermid	32,000	1	2	3	4	5	6	7	8		10	11					9
F	Oct	5	(n*)	Celtic	W 2-0	Gordon, Aitken	65,000	1	2	3	4	5	6	7	8	9	10					11	
				*Played at Hampden Park, Glasgow.		Appearances		2	2	2	2	2	2	2	2	1	2	1				1	1
						Goals								1	2			1					1

Glasgow Merchants' Charity Cup

#		Date		Opponent	Result	Scorers	Att.	Manderson	Blair	Dixon	Wallis	Aitken	Cunningham	Archibald	Gordon	McQueen	Brown	Lock	Duncan S
1	May	17	(n*)	Third Lanark	W 3-0	Brown 2, Bowie	25,000		3	4	5	6	8	10	2	7	11	9	1
SF		24	(h)	Clyde	W 2-0	Lawson, Archibald	20,000	2	3	5	6	8	10	4	7		11	9	1
F		31	(a)	Queen's Park	W 2-1	Bowie, Brown	65,000	2	3	5	6	8	10	4	7		11	9	1
				*Played at Hampden Park, Glasgow.		Appearances		2	3	1	3	3	3	3	3	3	3	3	3
						Goals						2		1	1		3		

Victory Cup

#		Date		Opponent	Result	Scorers	Att.	Hempsey	Manderson	Blair	Dixon	Wallis	Aitken	Cunningham	Archibald	Gordon	McQueen	Brown	Lock	Donnachie
2	Mar	15	(a)	Hamilton A	W 5-1	Archibald 2, Gordon, Cunningham, Brown	15,000	1	2	3	5	6	8	10	4	7		9		11
QF		29	(a)	Airdrieonians	L 0-1		20,000		2		5	6	8	10	4	7	3	9	1	11
						Appearances		1	2	1	2	2	2	2	2	2	1	2	1	2
						Goals								1	1	2		1		

Other matches

#		Date		Opponent	Result	Scorers	Att.	Manderson	Blair	Pursell	Dixon	Wallis	Aitken	Bowie	McLean	Cairns	Cunningham	Gordon	Archibald	McQueen	Hart	Lawson	Brown	Lock	Donnachie	Miller	Dick	Martin	Dominy	Roberts	Ritchie	Reid	McKenna
1	Apr	1	(h)	3rd Canadian CDW	6-2	Roberts 3, Dominy 2, Cunningham	4,000			4	5		7				10		2		11		1				3	6	8	9			
2		14	(a)	Dundee	L 1-2	Aitken	11,000				5	4	8		6			3	7	2		10	1	11						9			
3		29	(h)	Everton	W 4-0	Archibald 2, Pursell 2	20,000		3	4	5	6		8			10		7				1	11							2	9	
4	May	3	(a)	Everton*	L 3-4	McLean 3	20,000	2			4	6			9	8	10		7				1	11							3		5
				*St Dunstan Hospital for Blinded Servicemen Benefit Match.		Appearances		1	1	3	3	3	2	1	2		3	1	3	2	1	1	4	3		1	1	1	2	2	1	1	
						Goals				2			1		3		1		2										2	3			

1919-20

Manager: W.Wilton

Scottish League

Player columns (left to right): Lock, Manderson, Ritchie, Gordon, Dixon, Walls, Archibald, Bowie, Reid W, Cunningham, Muirhead, Cairns, Smith James, Paterson, Meiklejohn, Low, Henderson, Robb, McDonald, Johnston, Houghton, Stewart, Hutchinson, Reid T, Laird

#	Mth	Date	Opponent	Res	Scorers	Att	Lock	Manderson	Ritchie	Gordon	Dixon	Walls	Archibald	Bowie	Reid W	Cunningham	Muirhead	Cairns	Smith J	Paterson	Meiklejohn	Low	Henderson	Robb	McDonald	Johnston
1	Aug	16 (a) Airdrieonians	W 1-0	Bowie	12,000	1	2	3	4	5	6	7	8	9	10	11									
2		23 (h) Aberdeen	W 3-2	Cunningham 2, Reid	22,000	1	2	3	4	5	6	7	8	9	10	11									
3		26 (h) Albion Rovers	W 3-0	Reid 2, Bowie	10,000	1	2	3	4	5	6	7	8	9	10	11									
4		30 (a) St Mirren	W 4-0	Bowie 2, Muirhead, Cairns	20,000	1	2	3	4	5	6	7	8		10	11	9								
5	Sep	9 (h) Raith Rovers	W 3-2	Archibald, Cunningham, Paterson	12,000	1	2		4	5	6	7	8		10			9	3	11					
6		13(a*) Clyde	D 0-0		12,000	1	2	3	4	5	6	7	8		10			9		11					
7		15 (a) Kilmarnock	W 7-1	Gordon 2 (1 pen), Cunningham 2, Paterson, Bowie, Cairns	15,000	1	2	3	4	5	6		8		10	11		9	7						
8		20 (h) Dumbarton	W 4-0	Gordon 3, Muirhead	10,000	1	2	3	9	5	6	7	4		10	8			11						
9		27 (a) Motherwell	L 0-1		20,000	1	2	3	9	5	6	7	4		10	8			11						
10		29 (h) Hearts	W 3-0	Reid 2, Archibald (pen)	40,000	1	2	3		5	6	7	4	9	10	8			11						
11	Oct	4 (h) Kilmarnock	W 5-0	Reid 2, Paterson, Archibald, Bowie	15,000	1	2	3			6	7	4	9	10	8	5		11						
12		11 (a) Raith Rovers	W 2-1	Gordon (pen), Archibald	15,000	1	2	3	4		6	7	8	9	5	11	10								
13		18 (h) Celtic	W 3-0	Cunningham 2, Paterson	76,000	1	2	3		5	6	7	4		9	8	10		11						
14		25 (a) Dundee	W 2-0	Cunningham 2	30,000	1	2	3		5	6	7	4		9	8	10		11						
15	Nov	1 (h) Third Lanark	W 6-1	Cunningham 3, Cairns, Paterson, McCormack (og)	20,000	1	2	3		5	6	7	4		9	8	10		11						
16		8 (a) Partick Thistle	W 2-1	Cunningham, Cairns	45,000	1	2	3		5	6	7	4		9	8	10		11						
17		22 (a) Queen's Park	D 0-0		45,000	1		3	2	5	6	7	4		9	8	10		11						
18		29 (a) Albion Rovers	W 4-0	Cunningham 2, Cairns, Bowie	16,000	1	2	3	4	5	6	7	8		9		10		11						
19	Dec	6 (h) Hibernian	W 7-0	Cunningham 4, Muirhead, Archibald, Cairns	14,000	1	2	3		5	6	7	4		9	8	10		11						
20		13 (a) Clydebank	D 0-0		20,000	1	2	3		5	6	7	4		9	8	10		11						
21		20 (h) Hamilton A	W 4-1	Cunningham 2, Archibald, Muirhead	14,000	1	2	3		5	6	7	4		9	8	10		11						
22		27 (a) Ayr U	W 3-0	Bowie, Muirhead, Cairns	10,000	1	2	3		5	6	7	4		9	8	10		11						
23	Jan	1 (a) Celtic	D 1-1	Muirhead	80,000	1	2	3		5	6	7	4		9	8	10		11						
24		3 (h) Falkirk	W 3-1	Cairns 2, Gordon (pen)	25,000	1	2	3		5	6	7	4		9	8	10		11						
25		5 (h) Partick Thistle	D 2-2	Muirhead, Paterson	15,000	1	2	3		5	6	7	4		9	8	10		11						
26		10 (a) Hamilton A	W 2-1	Bowie, Cairns	10,000	1	2	3		5	6	7	4		9	8	10		11						
27		17 (h) St Mirren	W 3-1	Archibald 2, Paterson	10,000	1	2	3		5	6	7	4		9	8	10		11						
28		31 (a) Falkirk	W 3-0	Paterson, Archibald, Gordon	12,000	1	2	3	4	5	6	7	8		9		10		11						
29	Feb	14 (a) Morton	W 2-0	Reid, Muirhead	20,000	1		3	2		6	7	4	9	5	8	10		11						
30		28 (h) Clyde	W 1-0	Walls	20,000	1	2	3			6	7	4	9	5	8	10		11						
31	Mar	16 (h) Motherwell	D 0-0		20,000	1	2		3	5	6	7	4		9	8	10		11						
32		20 (a) Aberdeen	W 2-0	Paterson, Walls	24,000	1	2	3		5	6		8		10				11	4	7	9			
33	Apr	3 (h) Airdrieonians	W 3-2	Cairns 2, Henderson	25,000	1	2	3		5		7	6		8	10			11	4		9			
34		5 (h) Clydebank	L 1-2	Muirhead	25,000	1	2	3		5		7	6		8	10			11	4		9			
35		10 (a) Hearts	D 0-0		24,000	1	2	3			6	7		9	5	8	10		11	4					
36		13 (h) Ayr U	W 2-1	Cunningham, McDonald	15,000		2		3		6		4		10	8			7	5		9	1	11	
37		17 (h) Queen's Park	W 3-1	Cunningham (pen), Henderson, Muirhead	15,000		2		3		6		4		5	8	10		7			9	1	11	
38		21 (a) Hibernian	D 1-1	Meiklejohn	12,000		2		4		6	7			9	8	10	3		5			1	11	
39		24 (h) Dundee	W 6-1	Gordon 2, Bowie 2, Cairns, Paterson	25,000		2		9		6	7	8		5		10	3	11	4			1		
40		27 (a) Third Lanark	W 2-0	Meiklejohn, Bowie	35,000		2		9		6	7	8		5		10	3	11	4			1		
41		28 (a) Dumbarton	D 0-0		6,000		2		9		6	7	8		5		10	3	11	4			1		
42	May	1 (h) Morton	W 3-1	Archibald 2, Paterson	30,000		2					7	8		5		10	3	11	4		9	1		6
		Appearances				35	40	21	33	30	39	38	39	9	39	34	35	6	36	10	1	6	7	3	1
		Goals							10		2	11	12	8	23	10	13		11	2		2		1	

FINAL LEAGUE POSITION: 1st
*Played at Celtic Park, Glasgow.

1 own-goal

Scottish FA Cup

#		Date	Opponent	Res	Scorers	Att	Lock	Man	Rit	Gor	Dix	Wal	Arch	Bow	RW	Cun	Mui	Ca	SJ	Pat	Me
1	Jan	24 (h) Dumbarton	D 0-0		28,000	1	2	3	4	5	6	7	8		9		10		11	
R		27 (h) Dumbarton	W 1-0	Cairns	28,000	1	2	3	4	5	6	7	8		9		10		11	
2	Feb	7 (h) Arbroath	W 5-0	Muirhead 2, Archibald, Bowie, Cunningham	25,000	1	2	3	5		6	7	4		9	8	10		11	
3		21 (h) Broxburn U	W 3-0	Muirhead, Cunningham, Dixon	16,000	1	2		3	5	6	7	4		9	8	10		11	
QF	Mar	6 (h) Celtic	W 1-0	Muirhead	85,000	1	2		3	5	6	7	4		8	10			11	
SF		27(n*) Albion Rovers	D 1-1	Paterson	32,000	1	2	3	9	5	6	7	4		8	10			11	
R		31(n*) Albion Rovers	D 0-0		40,000	1	2	3		5	6	7	4		8	10			11	9
2R	Apr	7(n*) Albion Rovers	L 0-2		65,000	1	2		3		6		4		9	8	10		11	5	7
		Appearances				8	8	5	7	6	8	7	8		6	6	8		8	1	2
		Goals								1		1	1		2	4	1		1	

*Played at Celtic Park, Glasgow.

Glasgow Cup

#		Date	Opponent	Res		Att	Lock	Man	Rit	Gor	Dix	Wal	Arch	Bow	Cun	Mui	Ca
1	Sep	6 (a) Celtic	L 0-1		64,000	1	2	3	4	5	6	7	8	10	11	9
		Appearances				1	1	1	1	1	1	1	1	1	1	1
		Goals														

Glasgow Merchants' Charity Cup

#		Date	Opponent	Res	Scorers	Att	Man	Rit	Gor	Dix	Wal	Arch	Bow	Cun	Mui	Ca	SJ	Pat	Me	Hen
1	May	5 (h) Partick Thistle	W 4-0	Bowie, Muirhead, Cairns, Paterson	15,421	2				6	7	8	5	9	10	3	11	4	1
SF		8 (h) Celtic	L 1-2	Muirhead	45,000	2		3	5	6	7		9	8	10		11	4	1
		Appearances				2		1	1	2	2	1	2	2	2	1	2	2	2
		Goals									1		2	1	1			

Other matches

#		Date	Opponent	Res	Scorers	Att	Lock	Man	Rit	Gor	Dix	Wal	Arch	Bow	Cun	Mui	Ca	Pat	Me	Hen	McD	Jo	Ho	St	Hu	RT	La
1	Aug	21 (h) Partick Thistle*	W 3-1	Cairns 3	12,000	1	2		4	5	6	7	8	10	11	9					3					
2		27 (a) Morton §	D 0-0		6,000		3		5	4	7	8		10		9	11					6	2	1		
3	Sep	22 (a) Cowdenbeath	W 7-1	Muirhead 3, Hutchinson 3, McDonald	1		5			4	7			8	10	2					11	6	3		9	
4	Jan	7 (h) Internationalists‡	D 1-1	Cunningham	15,000	1	2			3	5	6	7	4		9	8	10	11						
5	May	3 (h) Internationalists‡	W 1-0	Muirhead	15,954			3			6	7		5	9	10		11	4	1				2	8
6		15 (h) Arran Select #	W 4-0	Untraced 4															1						
7		22 (h) Kilmarnock +	W 5-0	Cunningham 2, Archibald, Muirhead, Cairns	14,000		2				5	6	7	9	8	10	3	11	4	1					
		Appearances				3	3	2	3	4	6	6	3	5	5	6	3	3	2	3	1	2	3	1	1	1
		Goals										1		3	5	4				1			3			

*Willie Reid Benefit Match. §Jackie Wright Benefit Match. †James Bowie Benefit Match.
‡Jimmy Gordon Benefit Match. #Arran War Memorial Fund Benefit Match.
+Scottish War Memorial Fund Benefit Match.

No further details for Match 6. 4 goals untraced.

1920-21

Manager: W.Struth

Scottish League

Player columns (left to right): Robb, Manderson, Smith James, Bowie, Dixon, Walls, Archibald, Muirhead, Cunningham, Cairns, Morton AL, Meiklejohn, McKenna, Low, McQueen, Reid T, McCandless, Henderson, McDonald T, Morton J, Johnston, Lawson, McDermid, Lock, McMillan, Laird, McGibbon, Gordon, Dickson, Morrison, Gibson, Wilson

No	Date	Venue/Opponent	Result	Scorers	Att.	Robb	Mand	Smith	Bowie	Dixon	Walls	Arch	Muir	Cunn	Cairns	MortAL	Meik	McKn	Low	McQ	Reid	McCa	Hend	McDT	MortJ	Johns	Laws	McDm
1	Aug 17 (h)	Airdrieonians	W 4-1	Cunningham 2, Archibald, Cairns	12,000	1	2	3	4	5	6	7	8	9	10	11												
2	21 (h)	Motherwell	W 2-1	Walls, Cunningham	45,000	1	2	3	8	5	6	7		9	10	11	4											
3	24 (h)	Aberdeen	W 2-1	Cunningham, Cairns	20,000	1	2	3	8	5	6	7		9	10	11	4											
4	28 (a)	Kilmarnock	W 2-1	Archibald, Cunningham	15,000	1	2	3		5	6	7	8	9	10	11												
5	Sep 1 (a)	Motherwell	W 2-0	Muirhead, Cunningham	25,000	1	2	3		5	6	7	8	9	10	11				4								
6	7 (h)	Albion Rovers	W 2-1	Archibald, Cunningham	12,000	1	2	3		5	6	7	8	9	10	11	4											
7	11 (h)	Morton	W 2-0	Cunningham 2	41,000	1	2	3	8	5	6	7		9	10	11	4											
8	20 (a)	Hearts	W 4-0	Cunningham 2, Cairns, Bowie	30,000	1	2	3	8	5	6			9	10	11	4		7									
9	25 (a)	Aberdeen	D 1-1	Cunningham	21,800	1	2		4	5	6	7	8	9	10	11	3											
10	27 (h)	Hibernian	W 1-0	Cairns	20,000	1	2		4	5	6	7	8	9	10	11	3											
11	Oct 2 (h)	St Mirren	W 2-0	Archibald (pen), Cunningham	20,000	1	2		8	5	6	7		9	10	11	4		3									
12	9 (a)	Dumbarton	W 5-2	Cunningham 2, Meiklejohn, Cairns, A.L.Morton	10,000	1	2		8	5	6	7		9	10	11	4		3									
13	16 (a)	Partick Thistle	W 3-0	Archibald 2, Cunningham	30,000	1	2		4	5	6	7	9	8	10	11			3									
14	23 (a)	Celtic	W 2-1	Cairns, A.L.Morton	65,269	1	2		4	5	6	7	9	8	10	11			3									
15	30 (h)	Third Lanark	W 2-1	Cunningham, A.L.Morton	25,000	1	3		10	5	6	7	9	8		11	4				2							
16	Nov 6 (h)	Dundee	W 5-0	Henderson 4, Archibald	43,000	1	2			5	6	7			8	10	11	4				3	9					
17	13 (a)	Clydebank	W 4-2	Henderson 4	22,000	1	2			5	6	7			8	10	11	4				3	9					
18	20 (h)	Hamilton A	W 4-0	Henderson 2, Cunningham, Bowie	25,000	1	2		10	5	6	7			8		11	4				3	9					
19	27 (a)	Albion Rovers	W 2-1	Cairns, Muirhead	22,000	1	2			5	6	7	8	9	10	11	4					3						
20	Dec 4 (h)	Queen's Park	W 3-1	Muirhead 2, Meiklejohn	30,000	1	2		4	5	6	7	9	10		11	8					3						
21	11 (h)	Falkirk	W 2-0	Henderson, Cunningham	25,000	1	2		4	5	6			8	10	11					7	3	9					
22	18 (a)	Ayr U	D 1-1	Cunningham	13,000	1	2		4	5	6	7		8	10	11						3	9					
23	25 (a)	Clyde	W 3-1	Walls, Cunningham (pen), Henderson	36,000	1	2		4	5	6	7		8	10							3	9	11				
24	Jan 1 (h)	Celtic	L 0-2		69,260	1	2			5		7	6	8	10	11	4					3	9					
25	3 (a)	Partick Thistle	W 2-0	Archibald, Cairns	42,000	1	2			5		7	6	8	10	11	4					3	9					
26	8 (h)	Kilmarnock	W 2-0	Henderson 2	15,000	1	2			5		7	6	8	10	11	4					3	9					
27	15 (a)	Hamilton A	W 1-0	A.L.Morton	20,000	1	2			5		7	6	8	10	11	4					3	9					
28	22 (h)	Dumbarton	W 2-0	Cunningham, Cairns	15,000	1	2			5		7	6	8	10	11	4					3	9					
29	29 (a)	Airdrieonians	W 3-0	Archibald, Henderson, A.L.Morton	17,000	1	2			5		7	6	8	10	11	4					3	9					
30	Feb 9 (h)	Raith Rovers	W 1-0	Archibald	15,000	1	2		6	5		7		8	10	11	4					3	9					
31	12 (a)	Dundee	W 2-1	Henderson, Cairns	23,000	1	2		6					10	7	4		8				3	9	11	5			
32	Mar 2 (a)	Falkirk	W 2-0	Cairns, Cunningham (pen)	9,000	1				5		7		8	10	11	4	6				2	3	9				
33	9 (h)	Ayr U	W 7-2	Henderson 4, Archibald, Cunningham (pen), Cairns	8,000	1	2			5		7		8	10	11	4					3	9	6				
34	19 (h)	Clydebank	W 1-0	Archibald	15,000	1	2		6	5		7		8	10		4					3	9		11			
35	28 (h)	Queen's Park	D 1-1	Dixon	18,000	1	2			5		7		8	10	11	4					3	9	6				
36	Apr 2 (a)	Morton	D 0-0		15,000	1	2		6	5		7		8	10	11	4					3	9					
37	9 (a)	Hibernian	D 1-1	Archibald (pen)	18,000	1	3		4	5		7			10		8				2		9		6	11		
38	19 (h)	Clyde	W 3-1	Meiklejohn, Archibald, Henderson	10,000	1	2			5		7		8	10	11	4	6				3	9					
39	21 (a*)	St Mirren	W 1-0	Meiklejohn	10,000	1	2			5		7		8	10	11	4	6				3	9					
40	23 (a)	Third Lanark	W 1-0	A.L.Morton	30,000	1	2			5		7		8	10	11	4					3	9	6				
41	27 (h)	Hearts	D 0-0		10,000	1	2	11		5				6	8	10	7	4				3					9	
42	30 (a)	Raith Rovers	W 1-0	Dixon	15,000	1	2		6	5				7	10	8		11	4			3					9	
		FINAL LEAGUE POSITION: 1st			Appearances	42	41	9	23	41	23	38	19	40	38	39	35	4	3	4	3	26	23	2	2	3	2	2
		*Played at Hampden Park, Glasgow.			Goals				2	2	2	14	4	24	12	6	4						21					

Scottish FA Cup

No	Date	Venue/Opponent	Result	Scorers	Att.	Robb	Mand	Dixon	Walls	Arch	Cairns	MortAL	Meik	McCa	Hend
2	Feb 5 (h)	Morton	W 2-0	A.L.Morton, Henderson	67,000	1	2	6	5	7	8	10 11 4		3	9
3	19 (h)	Alloa A	D 0-0		60,000	1	2	6	5	7	8	10 11 4		3	9
R	26 (h)	Alloa A	W 4-1	Cairns 2, Cunningham, Archibald	55,000	1	2	6	5	7	8	10 11 4		3	9
QF	Mar 5 (a)	Dumbarton	W 3-0	Bowie, Cunningham, Henderson	6,000	1	2	6	5	7	8	10 11 4		3	9
SF	Mar 26 (n*)	Albion Rovers	W 4-1	Cairns 2, Cunningham, Archibald	65,000	1	2	6	5	7	8	10 11 4		3	9
F	Apr 16 (n*)	Partick Thistle	L 0-1		28,294	1	2	6	5	7	8	10 11 4		3	9
		*Played at Celtic Park, Glasgow.		Appearances		6	6	6	6	6	6	6 6 6		6	6
				Goals					1		2	3 4 1			2

Glasgow Cup

No	Date	Venue/Opponent	Result	Scorers	Att.
1	Sep 4 (a)	Queen's Park	W 2-1	Archibald, Henderson	40,000
SF	18 (a)	Celtic	L 1-2	A.L.Morton	65,082

Line-ups (match 1): Robb1, Manderson2, Smith3, Archibald5, Muirhead6, Cunningham7, Cairns8, MortonAL10, Meiklejohn4, Henderson9.
Line-ups (SF): Robb1, Manderson2, Smith3, Bowie8, Dixon5, Walls6, Cunningham9, Cairns10, MortonAL11, Meiklejohn4, Low7.

Appearances: Robb 2, Manderson 2, Smith 2, Bowie 1, Dixon 2, Walls 2, Archibald 1, Muirhead 1, Cunningham 2, Cairns 1, Morton AL 2, Meiklejohn 2, Low 1, Henderson 1.
Goals: Cunningham 1, Archibald 1, Henderson 1.

Glasgow Merchants' Charity Cup

No	Date	Venue/Opponent	Result	Scorers	Att.
1	May 3 (h)	Queen's Park	W 5-0	Henderson 3, Cunningham, A.L.Morton	14,000
SF	7 (n*)	Clyde	W 2-0	Cunningham 2	28,000
F	14 (n*)	Celtic	L 0-2		55,000

*Played at Hampden Park, Glasgow.

Line-ups: Robb1, Manderson2, Dixon5, Archibald7, Muirhead6, Cunningham8, Cairns10, MortonAL11, Meiklejohn4, McCandless3, Henderson9.

Appearances: Robb 3, Manderson 3, Dixon 3, Archibald 3, Muirhead 3, Cunningham 3, Cairns 3, Morton AL 3, Meiklejohn 3, McCandless 3, Henderson 3.
Goals: Cunningham 3, Cairns 1, Henderson 3.

Other matches

No	Date	Venue/Opponent	Result	Scorers	Att.
1	Aug 25 (a)	Airdrieonians *	D 1-1	McGibbon	5,000
2	30 (h)	Celtic §	W 2-1	Laird 2	20,000
3	Sep 13 (a)	Third Lanark †	D 1-1	McDonald	3,000
4	Mar 30 (a)	Linfield	W 2-0	Meiklejohn, J.Morton	15,000
5	Apr 26 (h)	Newcastle U ‡	D 0-0		30,000
6	Jun 1 (a)	AB (Akademisk)	W 2-0	Henderson, Moltke (og)	16,000
7	3 (a)	B1903 (Hellerup)	W 2-1	Cunningham, Poul Christiansen (og)	20,000
8	5 (a)	Copenhagen Sel	W 2-1	Cunningham 2	20,000

*James Reid Benefit Match. §Bert Manderson Benefit Match.
†Bobby Orr Benefit Match. ‡Tommy Cairns Benefit Match.

Appearances: Robb 5, Manderson 4, Smith 1, Bowie 3, Dixon 4, Walls 4, Archibald 3, Muirhead 3, Cunningham 3, Cairns 4, Morton AL 5, Meiklejohn 4, McKenna 3, Low 3, McQueen 2, Reid 5, McCandless 7, Henderson 1, McDonald T 1, Morton J 3, Johnston 2, Lawson 2, McDermid 3, Lock 4, McMillan 3, Laird 1, McGibbon 1, Gordon 1, Dickson 1, Morrison 1, Gibson 1, Wilson 1.
Goals: Cunningham 3, Meiklejohn 1, J.Morton 1, McGibbon 1, Laird 2, McDonald 1.

2 own-goals

1921-22

Manager: W.Struth

Scottish League

#	Date		Opponent	Result	Scorers	Att	Robb	Manderson	McCandless	Meiklejohn	Dixon	Muirhead	Archibald	Cunningham	Henderson	Cairns	Morton AL	Bowie	McDermid	Nicholson	Lawson	Hansen	Jamieson	Smith James	Laird	Smith JR
1	Aug	16 (a)	Third Lanark	W 3-1	Archibald, Cunningham, A.L.Morton	29,000	1	2	3	4	5	6	7	8	9	10	11									
2		20 (a)	Clydebank	W 7-1	Henderson 3, Cairns 2, Archibald, A.L.Morton	22,000	1	2	3		5	6	7	8	9	10	11		4							
3		23 (h)	Albion Rovers	W 3-1	Cunningham, Cairns, Henderson	31,000	1	2	3		5	6	7	8	9	10	11		4							
4		27 (h)	Motherwell	W 2-1	McDermid, Cunningham	40,000	1	2	3	4	5	6	7	8		10	11		9							
5	Sep	3 (a)	St Mirren	W 2-1	Cunningham, Cairns	35,290	1	2	3	4	5	6	7	8	9	10	11									
6		10 (h)	Kilmarnock	W 1-0	Cunningham	20,000	1	2	3	4	5	9	7	8		10	11			6						
7		19 (a)	Hearts	W 2-1	McDermid 2	22,000	1	2	3	4	5	6	7	8		10			9	11						
8		24 (a)	Aberdeen	W 1-0	Henderson	26,000	1	2	3	4	5	6	7	8	9	10				11						
9		26 (h)	Clyde	W 3-0	Henderson 3	38,000	1	2	3	4	5	6	7	8	9	10				11						
10	Oct	8 (h)	Hearts	L 0-2		40,000	1	2	3	4	5	6	7	8	9	10				11						
11		15 (a)	Airdrieonians	W 2-1	Henderson, Cunningham	15,000	1	2	3	4	5	6	7	8	9	10	11									
12		22 (h)	Celtic	D 1-1	Henderson	50,000	1	2	3	4	5	6	7	8	9	10	11									
13		29 (h)	Queen's Park	W 4-2	Henderson 2, A.L.Morton, Cunningham	32,000	1	2	3	4	5	6	7	8	9	10	11									
14	Nov	5 (a)	Dundee	D 0-0		39,000	1	2	3		5	6	7	8	9	10		11		4						
15		12 (h)	Dumbarton	D 1-1	Cairns	16,000	1	2	3		5	6	7	8	9	10		11		4						
16		19 (a)	Morton	W 2-1	Cunningham, Henderson	20,000	1	2	3	4	5	6	7	8	9	10		11								
17		26 (h)	Hamilton A	W 5-0	Archibald 2 (1 pen), Cunningham 2, Henderson	20,000	1	2	3	4	5	6	7	8	9	10		11								
18	Dec	3 (a)	Falkirk	L 0-1		18,000	1	2	3	4	5	6	7	8	9	10	11									
19		10 (h)	Third Lanark	W 2-1	Cairns, Bowie	20,000	1	2	3		5	6	7	8	9	10	11	4								
20		17 (a)	Albion Rovers	W 5-0	Cairns 3, Henderson, Cunningham	10,000	1	2	3		5	6	7	8	9	10	11		4							
21		24 (a)	Hibernian	D 0-0		25,000	1	2	3		5	6	7	8	9	10	11		4							
22		26 (h)	Dundee	W 2-1	Hansen, Cairns	10,000	1	2	3		5	6	7	8		10	11		4			9				
23		31 (h)	St Mirren	W 4-1	Henderson 2, Cunningham, Cairns	30,000	1	2	3	4	5	6	7	8	9	10	11									
24	Jan	2 (a)	Celtic	D 0-0		60,000	1		3	4	5	6	7	8	9	10	11							2		
25		3 (h)	Partick Thistle	D 2-2	Cairns, Meiklejohn	35,000	1		3	4	5	6	7	8	9	10	11							2		
26		7 (a)	Ayr U	W 1-0	Archibald	12,000	1		3	4	5	6	7	8		10	11					9		2		
27		14 (a)	Raith Rovers	L 0-1		20,000	1	2	8	4	5	6	7			10	11					9	3			
28		21 (a)	Hamilton A	D 0-0		20,000	1	2	3	4	5	8	7			10	11			6		9				
29	Feb	4 (a)	Motherwell	L 0-2		10,000	1	2	3		5	6			9	10			8	4	11	7				
30		18 (a)	Partick Thistle	W 1-0	A.L.Morton	53,000	1	2	3	4	5	6	7	8	9	10	11									
31		21 (h)	Clydebank	W 6-1	McDermid 2, Cunningham 2, Manderson, Meiklejohn	5,000	1	2	3	4	5	6	7	8		10	11		9							
32		28 (h)	Falkirk	D 0-0		18,000	1		3	4	5		7	8		10	11		9	6				2		
33	Mar	4 (h)	Morton	W 3-0	Archibald 2 (1 pen), James Smith	18,000	1	2		4	5		7		9	10	8		6					3		11
34		28 (h)	Hibernian	W 2-0	Henderson, Nicholson	13,000	1	2	3	4	5		7	8	9	10	11			6						
35		Apr 1 (h)	Ayr U	W 2-0	Archibald, Hansen	20,000	1	2	3	4	5		7			10	11		6			9				
36		3 (a)	Raith Rovers	W 3-0	Henderson 2, Archibald	20,000	1	2	3	4	5		7	8	9	10	11		6							
37		5 (a)	Aberdeen	D 0-0		20,000	1	2	3	4	5		7	10			11		6			9			8	
38		8 (a)	Dumbarton	W 4-0	Meiklejohn, McCandless (pen), Henderson, McDermid	7,000	1	2	3	4	5		7		9			8	10	6				11		
39		17 (h)	Queen's Park	W 2-1	Hansen 2	15,000	1	2	3		5	6	7			10	11		8	4		9				
40		22 (h)	Airdrieonians	W 3-0	Hansen 3	18,000	1	2	3	4	5	6	7			10	11					9			8	
41		24 (a)	Kilmarnock	W 2-1	Hansen, McDermid	12,000	1	2	3	4	5	6	7			10	11		8			9				
42		29 (a)	Clyde	D 0-0		30,000	1	2	3	4	5	8	7			10	11		6			9				
			Appearances				42	38	41	32	42	36	40	32	28	40	31	5	15	17	2	11	6	2	2	
			Goals					1	1	3			9	14	21	12	4	1	7	1		8		1		

FINAL LEAGUE POSITION: 2nd

Scottish FA Cup

#	Date		Opponent	Result	Scorers	Att	Robb	Manderson	McCandless	Meiklejohn	Dixon	Muirhead	Archibald	Cunningham	Henderson	Cairns	Morton AL	Bowie	McDermid	Nicholson	Lawson	Hansen	Jamieson	Smith James
1	Jan	28 (a)	Clachnacuddin	W 5-0	Henderson 3, McDermid, A.L.Morton	4,000	1	2	3	4	5	6	7		9	10	11		8					
2	Feb	11 (a)	Albion Rovers	D 1-1	Archibald	20,000	1	2	3	4	5	6	7		9	10	11		8					
R		15 (h)	Albion Rovers	W 4-0	A.L.Morton 2, Meiklejohn, Archibald	35,000	1	2	3	4	5	6	7	8	9	10	11							
3		25 (a)	Hearts	W 4-0	Cunningham 2, Dixon, McDermid	40,000	1		3	4	5	6	7	8		10	11		9					2
QF	Mar	11 (h)	St Mirren	D 1-1	Henderson	67,700	1	2	3	4	5	6	7	8	9	10	11							
R		14 (a)	St Mirren	W 2-0	Henderson, Cunningham	38,027	1	2	3	4	5	6	7	8	9	10	11							
SF		25 (h)	Partick Thistle	W 2-0	Henderson, Archibald (pen)	60,000	1	2	3	4	5	6	7	8	9	10	11							
F	Apr	15 (n*)	Morton	L 0-1		70,000	1	2	3	4	5	6	7	8	9	10	11							
			Appearances				8	7	8	8	8	8	8	6	7	8	8		3					1
			Goals							1	1		3	3	6		3		2					

*Played at Hampden Park, Glasgow.

Glasgow Cup

#	Date		Opponent	Result	Scorers	Att	Robb	Manderson	McCandless	Meiklejohn	Dixon	Muirhead	Archibald	Cunningham	Henderson	Cairns	Morton AL	Bowie	McDermid
SF	Sep	17 (a)	Third Lanark	W 2-0	A.L.Morton, McDermid	40,000	1	2	3	4	5	6	7	8		10	11		9
F	Oct	1 (n*)	Celtic	W 1-0	Meiklejohn	76,828	1	2	3	4	5	6	7	8	9	10		11	
			Appearances				2	2	2	2	2	2	2	2	1	2	1	1	1
			Goals							1							1		1

*Played at Hampden Park, Glasgow.

Glasgow Merchants' Charity Cup

#	Date		Opponent	Result	Scorers	Att	Robb	Manderson	McCandless	Meiklejohn	Dixon	Muirhead	Archibald	Cairns	Morton AL	Hansen	Jamieson	Smith James
SF	May	6 (n*)	Celtic	D 0-0†		33,000	1	2	3	4	5	8	7	10	11	9	6	
F		13 (a)	Queen's Park	W 3-1	Archibald 3	43,000	1	2	3	4	5	8	7	10	11	6		9
			Appearances				2	2	2	2	2	2	2	2	2	2	1	1
			Goals										3					

*Played at Hampden Park, Glasgow. †Rangers won 10-6 on corners.

Lord Provost's Rent Relief Fund Cup

#	Date		Opponent	Result	Scorers	Att	Robb	Manderson	McCandless	Meiklejohn	Dixon	Muirhead	Archibald	Cunningham	Henderson	Cairns	Morton AL	Bowie	McDermid	Nicholson	Hansen
1	Nov	22 (a)	Queen's Park	W 3-2	Hansen 3 (1 pen)	7,000	1	2	3	4		8	7			10		6	11	5	9
SF	Dec	6 (h)	Partick Thistle	W 2-0	Archibald, Hansen	10,000	1	2	3		5		7		8	10	11	4	6		9
F		13 (n*)	Celtic	W 2-0	Hansen (pen), Cairns	25,000	1	2	3		5		7	8		10	11		6	4	9
			Appearances				3	3	3	1	2	1	3	1	1	3	2	2	3	2	3
			Goals										1			1					5

* Played at Hampden Park, Glasgow.

Further match details for this season are continued on page 278

1922-23

Manager: W.Struth

Scottish League

Player columns (left → right): Robb, Manderson, McCandless, Meiklejohn, Dixon, Muirhead, Archibald, Cunningham, Smith JR, Cairns, Morton AL, Hansen, Henderson, Nicholson, Johnston, Lawson, Reid, Jamieson, Walls, Kilpatrick, Laird, Rollo, Gould, Kirkwood, Booth, Walker, Blair, Kinloch, Paterson, Hamilton, Ireland, McDonald M

No	Date	Opponent	Result	Scorers	Att	Robb	Mand	McCa	Meik	Dixo	Muir	Arch	Cunn	Smit	Cair	Mort	Hans	Hend	Nich	John	Laws	Reid	Jami	Wall	Kilp
1	Aug 15 (h) Alloa A		W 2-0	Cunningham, Smith	30,000	1	2	3	4	5	6	7	8	9	10	11									
2	19 (h) Third Lanark		W 5-1	Hansen 2, Cunningham, Cairns, Morton	30,000	1	2	3	4	5	6	7	8		10	11	9								
3	26 (a) Motherwell		W 4-0	Cunningham 2, Smith, Cairns	16,000	1	2	3	4	5	6	7	8	9	10	11									
4	Sep ( ) (a) Falkirk		L 0-2		18,000	1	2	3	4	5	6	7	8	9	10	11									
5	18 (h) Hearts		D 0-0		20,000	1	2	3	4	5	6	7	8		10	11	9								
6	23 (h) Morton		D 0-0		30,000	1	2	3	4	5	6	7	8		10	11	9								
7	25 (a) Clyde		W 2-1	Muirhead, Cairns	31,000	1	2	3	4	5		7	8		10	11		9	6						
8	Oct 7 (h) Hibernian		W 2-0	Cunningham, Henderson	22,000	1	2	3		5		6	7	8	10			9				4	11		
9	14 (a) Aberdeen		D 0-0		26,294	1	2	3		5		6	7	8	10			9				4	11		
10	21 (h) Albion Rovers		D 2-2	Dixon, Henderson	18,000	1	2	3	4	5	6	7	8		10	11		9							
11	28 (a) Celtic		W 3-1	Cunningham 2, Henderson	55,000	1	2	3	4	5	6	7	8		10	11		9							
12	Nov 4 (h) Partick Thistle		W 4-1	Henderson 2, Muirhead, Cunningham	30,000	1		3	4	5	8	7	10			11		9	6			2			
13	11 (a) Hamilton A		W 3-0	Henderson 2, Cairns	10,000	1	2	3	4	5	6	7	8		10	11		9							
14	18 (h) Raith Rovers		W 1-0	Johnston	18,000	1	2	3	4	5		7	8		10	11		9		6					
15	25 (a) St Mirren		L 0-1		30,000	1	2	3	4	5	6	7	8		10	11		9							
16	Dec 2 (h) Airdrieonians		W 4-1	Henderson 3, Archibald	30,000	1		3	4	5	6	7	8		10	11		9				2			
17	9 (h) Dundee		W 4-1	Henderson 2, Muirhead, Archibald	35,000	1		3	4	5	6	7	8		10	11		9				2			
18	16 (a) Ayr U		D 1-1	Henderson	10,000	1		3	4	5	6	7	8		10	11		9				2			
19	23 (a) Alloa A		W 2-0	Henderson, Morton	8,000	1		3		5	6	7	8		10	11		9	4			2			
20	30 (h) Aberdeen		D 1-1	Cunningham (pen)	22,000	1	2			5	6	7	8		10	11		9	4				3		
21	Jan 1 (h) Celtic		W 2-0	Hansen, Archibald	50,000	1		3		5	6	7	8		10	11	9		4			2			
22	2 (a) Partick Thistle		W 1-0	Archibald	36,000	1		3	4	5	8	7	10			11	9		6			2			
23	6 (h) Motherwell		W 2-1	Meiklejohn, Cairns	35,000	1		3	4	5	8	7			10	11	9		6			2			
24	20 (a) Kilmarnock		W 2-1	Henderson, Cairns	16,000	1			5	6	7	8			10	11		9	4			2	3		
25	Feb 3 (h) Hamilton A		W 3-0	Hansen 2, Cunningham	13,000	1	2		4	5	6		8		10	11	9	7					3		
26	6 (a) Third Lanark		D 2-2	Muirhead, Hansen	10,000	1		4	5	8					10	11	9	7				2	3	6	
27	10 (a) Airdrieonians		L 0-1		12,000	1	2	4	5	6		8			10	11	9	7					3		
28	24 (a) Morton		D 1-1	Dixon	16,000	1	3	4	5		7	8			10	11		9	6			2			
29	Mar 3 (h) Clyde		W 2-1	Henderson 2	15,000	1	3	4	5		8				10			9	6	11	2		7		
30	10 (a) Raith Rovers		L 0-2		10,000	1	2	4	5		7	8			10	11	9		6			3			
31	14 (h) Ayr U		W 2-1	Henderson 2	8,000	1	2	4	5		7	8			10	11		9	6			3			
32	24 (a) Dundee		W 2-1	Henderson, Cairns	20,000	1	2	4	5		7	8			10	11		9		6		3			
33	27 (h) Falkirk		W 2-0	Cunningham (pen), Henderson	15,000	1	2	4	5	6	7	8			10	11		9				3			
34	31 (a) Albion Rovers		L 1-2	Cairns	10,000	1	2	4			8	7	5		10	11		9	6			3			
35	Apr 2 (h) St Mirren		D 1-1	Morton	10,000	1	2	5			6	7	8		10	11	9		4			3			
36	7 (a) Hibernian		L 0-2		16,000	1	2	4	5		6	7	8		10	11	9					3			
37	21 (h) Kilmarnock		W 1-0	Henderson	16,000	1	2	4	5	6	7	8			10	11		9				3			
38	28 (h) Hearts		W 3-0	Cairns 2, Henderson	8,000	1	2	4	5		7	8			10	11		9		6	3				

FINAL LEAGUE POSITION: 1st

| | | | | Appearances | | 38 | 28 | 22 | 34 | 34 | 31 | 34 | 35 | 3 | 36 | 35 | 10 | 28 | 10 | 9 | 3 | 13 | 13 | 1 | 1 |
| | | | | Goals | | | | | 1 | 2 | 4 | 4 | 11 | 2 | 10 | 3 | 6 | 23 | | 1 | | | | | |

Scottish FA Cup

No	Date	Opponent	Result	Scorers	Att	Robb	Mand	McCa	Meik	Dixo	Muir	Arch	Cunn	Smit	Cair	Mort	Hans	Hend	Nich	John	Laws	Reid
1	Jan 13 (a) Clyde		W 4-0	Cunningham 2, Henderson, Morton	40,000	1		3	4	5	6	7	8		10	11		9				2
2	27 (a) Ayr U		L 0-2		16,000	1	2	3	4	5	6	7	8		10	11		9				
				Appearances		2	1	2	2	2	2	2	2		2	2		2				1
				Goals									2			1		1				

Glasgow Cup

No	Date	Opponent	Result	Scorers	Att	Robb	Mand	McCa	Meik	Dixo	Muir	Arch	Cunn	Smit	Cair	Mort	Hans	Hend	Nich	John
1	Sep 2 (h) Partick Thistle		W 3-1	Cairns 2, Cunningham	36,000	1	2	3		5	6	7	8	9	10	11				4
SF	16 (a) Third Lanark		D 2-2	Muirhead, Cunningham	47,000	1	2	3	4	5	6	7	8		10	11		9		
R	27 (h) Third Lanark		W 2-1	Henderson 2	27,000	1	2	3	4	5		7	8		10	11		9	6	
F	30 (n*) Clyde		D 0-0		37,000	1	2	3		5		7	8		10	11		9	6	4
R	Oct 4 (n*) Clyde		W 1-0	McCandless (pen)	30,000	1	2	3		5	6	7	8		10	11		9		4

*Played at Celtic Park, Glasgow.

| | | | | Appearances | | 5 | 5 | 5 | 2 | 5 | 3 | 5 | 5 | 1 | 5 | 5 | | 4 | 4 | 1 |
| | | | | Goals | | | | 1 | | | 1 | | 2 | | 2 | | | 2 | | |

Glasgow Merchants' Charity Cup

No	Date	Opponent	Result	Scorers	Att	Robb	Mand	McCa	Meik	Dixo	Muir	Arch	Cunn	Smit	Cair	Mort	Hend	Nich
SF	May 5 (a) Celtic		W 1-0	Henderson	26,000	1	2		4	5		7	8		10	11	9	6
F	12 (h) Queen's Park		W 4-0	Henderson 2, Cunningham, Morton	35,000	1	2		4	5		7	8		10	11	9	6
				Appearances		2	2		2	2		2	2		2	2	2	2
				Goals									1			1	3	

Other matches

No	Date	Opponent	Result	Scorers	Att
1	Aug 16 (a) Celtic *	L 1-3	Hansen	5,000
2	22 (a) Clyde †	D 1-1	Rollo	500
3	Sep 5 (a) Burnley ‡	L 0-3		
4	7 (a) Preston NE	D 1-1	Johnston	30,000
5	12 (h) Burnley §	W 2-0	Smith 2	8,000
6	20 (a) Newcastle U	L 1-4	Smith	10,000
7	26 (h) Preston NE +	L 0-1		5,000
8	Feb 17 (h) Ayr U	W 1-0	Hansen	
9	Apr 4 (a) Linfield #	W 1-0	McDonald	10,000
10	25 (a¶) Wigtownshire XI	W 3-0	Hansen 2, Henderson	3,000
11	May 24 (a°) CAP Olympique G	W 6-1	Henderson 2, Hansen 2, Cunningham, Archibald	
12	26 (a) FC St Gallen	W 7-0	Henderson 5, Cunningham, Craig	
13	27 (a) FC Basel	W 3-0	Henderson, Cunningham, Archibald	
14	30 (a°) Les Coqs	W 6-1	Henderson 2, Cunningham 2, Archibald, Hansen	
15	Jun 3 (a) FC Berne	W 7-0	Untraced 7	10,000
16	4 (a±) La Chaux de Fondes	W 3-0	Untraced 3	

*Willie McStay Benefit Match. †Harry Rae Benefit Match. ‡Burnley Hospital Benefit Match.
§Sandy Archibald Benefit Match. +Tommy Muirhead Benefit Match. #John Campbell Benefit Match.
¶Played at Holm Park, Creetown. °Played at Paris, France. ±Played at Geneva, Switzerland.

No further details available for Matches 2 and 10-16. 10 goals untraced.

1923-24

Manager: W.Struth

Scottish League

#	Date	Venue/Opponent	Result	Scorers	Att.	Robb	Manderson	McCandless	Meiklejohn	Dixon	Muirhead	Archibald	Cunningham	Henderson	Cairns	Morton AL	Johnston	Reid	Craig	Wallis	Lawson	Nicholson	Hansen	Kirkwood A	McDonald	Jamieson	McGregor	Kilpatrick
1	Aug 18	(a) Motherwell	W 3-0	Cunningham 2, Morton	22,000	1	2	3	4	5	6	7	8	9	10	11												
2	21	(h) Falkirk	D 2-2	Cunningham (pen), Morton	18,000	1	2	3	4	5	6	7	8	9	10	11												
3	25	(h) St Mirren	W 5-0	Cairns 2, Muirhead, Cunningham, Henderson	20,000	1	2	3	4	5	6	7	8	9	10	11												
4	Sep 8	(a) Morton	W 1-0	Cunningham	15,000	1	2	3	4	5	6	7	8	9	10	11												
5	17	(a) Hearts	D 0-0		24,000	1	2	3	4	5		7	8	9	10	11	6											
6	22	(h) Aberdeen	W 2-0	Cunningham (pen), Henderson	20,000	1	3		4	5	6	7	8	9	10	11		2										
7	24	(h) Clyde	W 2-1	Cairns, Craig	12,000	1	3		4	5	6	7		9	10	11		2	8									
8	Oct 6	(a) Dundee	W 4-1	Henderson 3, Archibald	22,000	1	2	3	4	5	6	7	8	9	10	11												
9	13	(a) Ayr U	W 5-0	Meiklejohn 2, Henderson 2, Craig	15,000	1	2	3	4	5	6	7		9	10	11			8									
10	20	(a) Hibernian	W 3-1	Meiklejohn, Henderson, Morton	22,000	1	2	3	4	5	6	7	10	9			11		8									
11	27	(h) Celtic	D 0-0		38,000	1	2	3	4	5	10		8	9			11	6	7									
12	Nov 3	(a) Partick Thistle	W 6-0	Morton 3, Cunningham, Henderson, Cairns	35,000	1	2	3	4	5	6	7	8	9	10	11												
13	10	(h) Third Lanark	W 2-0	Meiklejohn, Muirhead	15,000	1	2	3	4	5	6	7	8	9	10	11												
14	17	(a) Falkirk	W 1-0	Cunningham (pen)	16,000	1	2	3	4	5	6	7	8	9	10	11												
15	24	(h) Airdrieonians	D 0-0		20,000	1	2	3	4	5	6	7	8	9	10	11												
16	Dec 1	(a) Clydebank	W 2-1	Cunningham, Cairns	10,000	1	2	3	4	5	6	7	8	9	10	11												
17	8	(h) Queen's Park	D 1-1	Meiklejohn	15,000	1	2	3	4	5	6	7	8	9	10	11												
18	15	(h) Raith Rovers	W 1-0	Henderson	20,000	1	2	3	4	5		7	8	9			11					10	6					
19	22	(h) Hamilton A	W 4-0	Henderson 3, Archibald	10,000	1	2	3		5	6	7	8	9			4					10		11				
20	29	(a) St Mirren	D 0-0		12,000	1	2	3	4	5	6	7	8	9								10		11				
21	Jan 1	(a) Celtic	D 2-2	Cairns, Archibald	60,000	1	2	3	4	5		7	8	9	10	11	6											
22	2	(h) Partick Thistle	W 1-0	Cunningham	30,000	1	2	3	4	5		7	8	9	10	11				6								
23	5	(a) Ayr U	L 1-2	Cairns	14,000	1	2	3	4	5		7	8		10	11	6				9							
24	12	(h) Dundee	D 1-1	Craig	10,000	1	2	3	4	5	6	7		9	10	11			8									
25	19	(a) Hamilton A	W 3-2	Craig 2, Cairns	12,000	1	2	3	4	5	6	7		9	10	11			8									
26	Feb 2	(h) Motherwell	W 3-0	Craig 2, Cunningham	20,000	1	2	3	4	5	6	7	8		10	11												
27	12	(a) Queen's Park	W 2-0	Henderson 2	10,000	1		3	4		6	7		9	10	11		2	8							5		
28	19	(h) Kilmarnock	W 2-0	Henderson 2	10,000	1	2	3	4	5	6	7		9	10	11									8			
29	26	(h) Clydebank	W 3-0	Craig 3	6,000	1		3	4	5		7	8		10	11	6	2	9									
30	Mar 5	(a) Kilmarnock	D 1-1	Archibald	10,000	1	3			5		7	8		10	11	6	2		4				9				
31	11	(h) Hearts	W 1-0	Henderson	6,000	1	2		4	5	10	7	8	9			6										3	11
32	19	(a) Aberdeen	L 0-1		16,000	1	2	3	4	5	7			9	10	11	6		8									
33	22	(a) Third Lanark	W 3-1	Cunningham, Henderson, Cairns	10,000	1	2	3	4	5			8	9	10	11	6											
34	29	(h) Raith Rovers	L 0-1		10,000	1		3	4	5		7	8	9	10	11	6	2										
35	Apr 5	(h) Hibernian	W 2-1	Meiklejohn (pen), Cunningham	12,000	1		3	4	5	6	7	10	9			2	8										
36	12	(h) Morton	W 2-1	Craig, Cairns	8,000	1		3	4	5	8				10		2	9						6			11	7
37	18	(a) Clyde	L 1-3	Craig	10,000	1	3		4	5		7	8		10	11	6	2	9									
38	26	(a) Airdrieonians	D 0-0		8,000	1		3		5		7	8		10	11		2	9		4	6						
		FINAL LEAGUE POSITION: 1st			Appearances	38	32	33	35	37	34	30	31	31	34	12	10	17	1	2	3	2	3	1	1	2	2	
					Goals				6		2	4	13	19	10	6			12									

Scottish FA Cup

#	Date	Venue/Opponent	Result	Scorers	Att.	Robb	Manderson	McCandless	Meiklejohn	Dixon	Muirhead	Archibald	Cunningham	Henderson	Cairns	Morton AL	Johnston	Reid	Craig
1	Jan 26	(h) Lochgelly U	W 4-1	Henderson 3, Craig	6,000	1		3	4	5	6	7		9	10	11		2	8
2	Feb 9	(a) St Mirren	W 1-0	Henderson	40,291	1	2	3	4	5	6	7		9	10	11			8
3	23	(h) Hibernian	L 1-2	Meiklejohn	54,000	1	2	3	4	5	6	7	8		10	11			9
					Appearances	3	2	3	3	3	3	3	1	2	3	3		1	3
					Goals				1					4					1

Glasgow Cup

#	Date	Venue/Opponent	Result	Scorers	Att.	Robb	Manderson	McCandless	Meiklejohn	Dixon	Muirhead	Archibald	Cunningham	Henderson	Cairns	Morton AL
1	Sep 1	(a) Queen's Park	W 3-0	Archibald, Cunningham, Morton	38,000	1	2	3	4	5	6	7	8	9	10	11
SF	15	(h) Celtic	W 1-0	Henderson	40,000	1	2	3	4	5	6	7	8	9	10	11
F	29	(h) Third Lanark	W 3-1	Muirhead, Archibald, Henderson	25,000	1	2	3	4	5	6	7	8	9	10	11
					Appearances	3	3	3	3	3	3	3	3	3	3	3
					Goals						1	2	1	2		1

Glasgow Merchants' Charity Cup

#	Date	Venue/Opponent	Result	Scorers	Att.	Robb	Manderson	McCandless	Meiklejohn	Dixon	Muirhead	Archibald	Cunningham	Henderson	Cairns	Morton AL	Johnston	Reid	Craig	Nicholson	Kirkwood A
1	May 3 (n*)	Clyde	W 3-0	Meiklejohn, Archibald, Morton	9,000	1		3	4	5	6	7		9	10	11		2	8		
SF	7	(h) Partick Thistle	W 1-0	Craig	10,000	1	2	3	4	5		7			10	11			8	6	9
F	10 (n†)	Celtic	L 1-2	Morton	30,000	1	2	3	4		6	7		9	10	11			8	5	
					Appearances	3	2	3	3	2	2	3		2	3	3		1	3	2	1
					Goals				1			1				2			1		

*Played at Celtic Park, Glasgow. †Played at Hampden Park, Glasgow.

Other matches

#	Date	Venue/Opponent	Result	Scorers	Att.	Robb	Manderson	McCandless	Meiklejohn	Dixon	Muirhead	Archibald	Cunningham	Henderson	Cairns	Morton AL	Johnston	Reid	Craig	Wallis	Lawson	Nicholson	Hansen	Kirkwood A	McDonald	Jamieson	McGregor	Kilpatrick	Chalmers	Hamilton T	Ireland	Rollo	Gibson	Curran	Wilkinson	McPherson
1	Aug 16	(a) Celtic *	L 1-2	Hansen	1,000													3		6	11	5	9		8	2		7		1	4	10				
2	Sep 6	(n) Queen's Park †	W 4-0	McDonald, Craig, Henderson, Morton	3,000	1						7		9	10	11	6		8					2	4	3						5					
3	10	(h) Liverpool ‡	D 1-1	Hansen	10,000		2	3	4	5	6	7	8		10	11						9					1										
4	Mar 25	(h) Clyde §	D 2-2	Wilkinson, McGregor									9						2	10	6		5			11		1	4			3	7	8		
5	Apr 17	(a) Forfar A	W 3-2	Cairns, Craig, Meiklejohn	3,000	1	2		4	5		7			10	11			9	6				8										3		
6	21	(a) Liverpool +	W 2-0	Cunningham, Henderson	38,000	1		3	4	5		7	8	9	10	11	2				6															
7	23	(a) Manchester U	D 1-1	Archibald	10,000	1		3	4	5	6	7			10		2	9			8					11										
8	28	(a) Ayr U #	W 1-0	Craig	4,000	1		3								11	2	8	6		5	9	10			7		4								
					Appearances	5	2	4	4	4	2	5	2	3	5	5	1	5	5	4	1	2	2	5	4	2	2	2		3	3	1	1	2	1	1	
					Goals				1			1	1	2	1	1			3			2			1		1									1	

*Adam McLean Benefit Match. †Gartshore Pit Disaster Fund Benefit Match played at Haugh Park, Kilsyth. ‡Arthur Dixon Benefit Match. §Harry Cowan Benefit Match. +British Championship.

Phil McCloy Benefit Match.

1924-25

Manager: W.Struth

Player columns (in order): Rb=Robb, Mn=Manderson, McC=McCandless, Mk=Meiklejohn, Dx=Dixon, Cg=Craig, Ar=Archibald, Cn=Cunningham, Hn=Henderson, Cr=Cairns, MoA=Morton A.L., Rd=Reid, KwA=Kirkwood A, Jm=Jamieson, Ch=Chalmers, McG=McGregor, Ir=Ireland, MoAr=Morton Archie, Mu=Muirhead, Dk=Dick, HmT=Hamilton T, Hg=Hodge, KwD=Kirkwood D, St=Stevenson, Pn=Purdon

Scottish League

#	Date		Opponent	Result	Scorers	Att	Rb	Mn	McC	Mk	Dx	Cg	Ar	Cn	Hn	Cr	MoA	Rd	KwA	Jm	Ch	McG	Ir	MoAr	Mu	Dk
1	Aug 16	(a)	Raith Rovers	W 3-0	Henderson 3	15,000	1	2	3	4	5	6	7	8	9	10	11									
2	20	(h)	St Johnstone	W 3-1	A.L.Morton 2, Henderson	30,000	1	2	3	4	5	6	7	8	9	10	11									
3	23	(a)	Aberdeen	W 1-0	Meiklejohn	23,000	1	2	3	4	5	6	7	8	9	10	11									
4	26	(a)	Queen's Park	W 3-1	Cunningham 2, Archibald	30,000	1		3	4	5	6	7	8	9	10	11	2								
5	30	(h)	Kilmarnock	D 1-1	Henderson	18,000	1		3	4	5	6	7	8	9	10	11	2								
6	Sep 13	(a)	Ayr U	W 4-0	McCandless (pen), Archibald, Cairns, A.L.Morton	20,000	1	2	3	4	5		7	8	9	10	11		6							
7	15	(a)	Hearts	W 2-1	Henderson, A.L.Morton	22,000	1	2	3	4	5		7	8	9	10	11		6							
8	27	(a)	Airdrieonians	L 0-1		27,000	1	2	3	4	5		7	8	9	10	11		6							
9	29	(h)	Hearts	W 4-1	Cairns 2, Meiklejohn, Archibald	12,000	1			4	5		7	8	9	10	11	2	6	3						
10	Oct 11	(a)	Cowdenbeath	D 2-2	Cunningham 2	20,000	1	2		4	5	6	7	8	9	10	11			3						
11	18	(h)	Falkirk	W 3-1	Henderson 2 (1 pen), Archibald	10,000	1	2		4	5	6	7	8	9		11			3	10					
12	25	(a)	Celtic	W 1-0	A.L.Morton	40,000	1	2		4	5	6	7	8	9		11			3	10					
13	Nov 1	(h)	Partick Thistle	W 4-0	Craig, Cunningham, Henderson, Chalmers	25,000	1	2		4	5	6	7	8	9		11			3	10					
14	8	(a)	Third Lanark	D 1-1	Craig	23,000	1	2		4	5	6	7	8	9		11			3	10					
15	15	(h)	Hibernian	W 3-0	Meiklejohn, Cunningham (pen), Henderson	30,000	1	2	3	4	5	6	7	8	9	10	11									
16	22	(a)	St Johnstone	W 3-1	Henderson 2, A.L.Morton	10,000	1	2	3	4	5	6	7	8	9	10	11									
17	29	(h)	St Mirren	W 3-1	Cairns 2, Archibald	26,000	1	2	3	4	5	6	7	8	9	10	11									
18	Dec 6	(a)	Dundee	D 0-0		20,000	1	2	3	4	5	6	7	8	9	10							11			
19	13	(h)	Hamilton A	W 2-0	Henderson 2	10,000	1	2	3		5	6	7	10	9						8			4	11	
20	20	(a)	St Mirren	W 4-1	Henderson 3, Archibald	20,000	1	2	3	4	5	6	7	8	9		11					10				
21	27	(h)	Motherwell	W 1-0	Henderson	15,000	1	2	3		5	6	7	8	9		11								4	
22	Jan 1	(h)	Celtic	W 4-1	Henderson 2, Cunningham, McCandless (pen)	34,000	1	2	3	4	5		7	8	9		11								6	
23	3	(h)	Morton	W 2-0	Cairns, A.L.Morton	17,000	1	2	3	4	5		7		9	10	11				8				6	
24	5	(a)	Partick Thistle	W 1-0	Henderson	25,000	1		3	4	5		7	8	9	10	11		2						6	
25	10	(a)	Morton	D 1-1	A.L.Morton	10,000	1	2	3		5		7	8	9	10	11		6					4		
26	17	(h)	Queen's Park	D 1-1	Cairns	20,000	1	2	3	4	5	6	7	8	9	10	11									
27	31	(a)	Hamilton A	L 0-1		15,000	1	2	3	4	5		7		9	10	11				8				6	
28	Feb 10	(h)	Dundee	W 2-0	McCandless (pen), Chalmers	5,000	1	2	3	4	5	6	7		9	10	11				8					
29	18	(a)	Falkirk	D 1-1	Henderson	12,000	1	2	3	4	5	6	7		9	10	11				8					
30	25	(h)	Airdrieonians	D 1-1	Archibald	40,000	1	2	3	4	5		7	8	9	10	11								6	
31	Mar 11	(a)	Hibernian	L 1-4	Dick	23,000	1	2	3	4	5		7	8		10	11								6	9
32	25	(a)	Raith Rovers	W 4-0	Henderson 3, Archibald		1	2	3	4	5		7	8	9	10	11								6	
33	28	(a)	Kilmarnock	D 0-0		12,000	1	2	3	4	5		7	8	9	10	11								6	
34	Apr 1	(h)	Cowdenbeath	W 1-0	McCandless (pen)	5,000	1	2	3	4			7		9	10	11				8		5		6	
35	7	(h)	Aberdeen	W 2-0	Cairns 2	8,000	1	2	3	6	5		7	8	9	10	11							4		
36	11	(h)	Third Lanark	W 5-2	Henderson 2, Cairns 2, Archibald	12,000	1	2	3	6	5		7	8	9	10	11							4		
37	18	(a)	Motherwell	D 1-1	Archibald	7,000	1	2	3	5		4	7	8	9	10	11								6	
38	25	(h)	Ayr U	W 1-0	McCandless	10,000	1	2	3	4	5		7	8	9	10	11								6	
	FINAL LEAGUE POSITION: 1st				Appearances		38	34	32	35	36	21	38	33	37	31	36	3	5	7	12	1	5	1	12	1
					Goals				5	3		2	10	7	27	11	8				2					1

Scottish FA Cup

#	Date		Opponent	Result	Scorers	Att	Rb	Mn	McC	Mk	Dx	Cg	Ar	Cn	Hn	Cr	MoA	KwA	Ch	McG	MoAr
1	Jan 24	(a)	East Fife	W 3-1	Archibald 2, Henderson	10,000	1	2	3	4	5		7		9	10	11		8		6
2	Feb 7	(a)	Montrose	W 2-0	Chalmers 2	4,000	1	2	3	6	5		7		9	10	11		8	4	
3	21	(h)	Arbroath	W 5-3	Henderson 3, Cairns, Cunningham	15,000	1	2	3	4	5		7	8	9	10	11				6
QF	Mar 7	(a)	Kilmarnock	W 2-1	Henderson, Cunningham	31,502	1	2	3	4	5		7	8	9	10	11				6
SF	21	(n*)	Celtic	L 0-5		101,714	1	2	3	4	5	6	7	8	9	10	11				
	*Played at Hampden Park, Glasgow.				Appearances		5	5	5	5	5	1	5	3	5	5	5	2	1	3	
					Goals								2	2	5	1			2		

Glasgow Cup

#	Date		Opponent	Result	Scorers	Att	Rb	Mn	McC	Mk	Dx	Cg	Ar	Cn	Hn	Cr	MoA	Rd	KwA	Jm
1	Sep 6	(a)	Clyde	W 1-0	Archibald	20,000	1		3	4	5	6	7	8	9	10	11	2		
SF	20	(h)	Partick Thistle	D 0-0		30,000	1	2	3	4	5		7	8	9	10	11		6	
R	23	(a)	Partick Thistle	W 2-0	Henderson 2	20,000	1	2	3	4	5		7	8	9	10	11		6	
F	Oct 4	(a)	Celtic	W 4-1	Henderson 2, A.L.Morton, Cairns	73,941	1	2		4	5	6	7	8	9	10	11			3
					Appearances		4	3	3	4	4	2	4	4	4	4	4	1	2	1
					Goals								1		4	1	1			

Glasgow Merchants' Charity Cup

#	Date		Opponent	Result	Scorers	Att	Mn	McC	Mk	Dx	Ar	Cn	Hn	MoA	McG	MoAr	HmT
1	May 2	(h)	Third Lanark	W 4-1	Henderson 2, Meiklejohn, Cunningham	10,000	2	3	6	5	7	8	9	11	10	4	1
SF	9	(n*)	Partick Thistle	W 2-1	Cunningham, Henderson	16,000	2	3	6	5	7	8	9	10 11		4	1
F	16	(h)	Clyde	W 1-0	Henderson	15,756	2	3	6	5	7	8	9	10 11		4	1
	*Played at Hampden Park, Glasgow.				Appearances		3	3	3	3	3	3	3	2 3	1	3	3
					Goals				1			2	4				

Other matches

#	Date		Opponent	Result	Scorers	Att
1	Aug 27	(a)	Airdrieonians *	L 3-4	Chalmers 2, Dick	4,000
2	Sep 2	(n†)	Partick Thistle	W 6-1	Henderson 4, Archibald 2	8,000
3	Dec 25	(a)	Hibernian ‡	W 4-2	Dick 3, D.Kirkwood	6,000
4	Apr 27	(h)	Newcastle U §	W 1-0	Henderson	4,000

Appearances: 2 2 2 2 1 1 2 2 2 2 2 1 3 2 3 1 2 2 2 2 2 2 1 1
Goals: 2 5 2 4 1

*George Carroll Benefit Match. †Opening of Helenvale Park, Glasgow, HRH The Duke of York officiating. ‡Willie Dornan Benefit Match. §James 'Fister' Walls Benefit Match.

1925-26

Manager: W.Struth

Scottish League

Player columns: Robb, Jamieson, McCandless, Meiklejohn, Dixon, Craig, Archibald, Cunningham, Henderson, Cairns, Morton AL, Ireland, Manderson, Muirhead, McKay, McGregor, Hamilton J, Gray, Chalmers, Kirkwood A, Hodge, Fleming, Hamilton T, Malone, Osborne, Marshall, Weir, Kirkwood D, Smith Jamie, Dick

No	Date	Venue	Opponent	Result	Scorers	Att
1	Aug 15	(a)	St Johnstone	W 3-0	Cunningham 2, Henderson	15,848
2	22	(h)	Motherwell	W 1-0	Cunningham	
3	29	(h)	Morton	W 4-1	Henderson 2, Archibald, Cunningham	
4	Sep 5	(a)	Airdrieonians	L 1-2	Henderson	27,000
5	12	(a)	Aberdeen	L 1-3	McCandless (pen)	26,000
6	19	(h)	St Mirren	W 4-1	Archibald, McKay, Henderson, Cairns	40,000
7	21	(a)	Hibernian	W 2-0	Cunningham, McKay	20,000
8	26	(a)	Hearts	L 0-3		30,000
9	Oct 3	(h)	Kilmarnock	W 3-0	Chalmers 2, McKay	20,000
10	10	(a)	Partick Thistle	L 0-2		35,000
11	17	(h)	Celtic	W 1-0	Chalmers	35,000
12	24	(h)	Dundee	L 1-2	Fleming	12,000
13	31	(a)	Raith Rovers	L 0-1		10,000
14	Nov 7	(a)	Queen's Park	W 6-3	Fleming 4, Cunningham, Morton	35,000
15	14	(h)	Cowdenbeath	W 3-0	McKay 2, Fleming	14,000
16	25	(a)	Motherwell	W 3-1	Morton, Malone, McKay	8,000
17	28	(h)	Falkirk	L 2-3	Cunningham 2 (1 pen)	16,000
18	Dec 5	(a)	Kilmarnock	D 2-2	Cunningham 2 (1 pen)	10,000
19	12	(h)	Hibernian	W 3-1	Fleming 2, Morton	22,000
20	19	(a)	Dundee U	L 1-2	Cunningham (pen)	12,000
21	26	(h)	St Johnstone	L 0-1		7,000
22	Jan 1	(a)	Celtic	D 2-2	Cunningham, Muirhead	60,000
23	2	(h)	Partick Thistle	W 2-1	Cunningham, Cairns	20,000
24	4	(h)	Clydebank	W 3-1	Henderson 2, Cunningham	15,000
25	9	(a)	Hamilton A	D 3-3	Fleming, Cairns, Morton	12,000
26	16	(h)	Hearts	D 2-2	Craig, Morton	25,000
27	30	(a)	Cowdenbeath	W 3-2	Muirhead, Cunningham, Cairns	8,000
28	Feb 10	(a)	Airdrieonians	L 1-2	Cunningham (pen)	14,000
29	13	(h)	Raith Rovers	W 4-2	Fleming 2, J.Hamilton (pen), Cunningham	15,000
30	24	(a)	Falkirk	D 1-1	Malone	5,000
31	27	(a)	Dundee	W 5-1	Fleming 5	14,000
32	Mar 10	(h)	Queen's Park	L 1-2	J.Hamilton (pen)	6,000
33	23	(a)	St Mirren	L 2-3	Osborne, Cunningham	6,000
34	27	(h)	Aberdeen	L 0-1		12,000
35	Apr 3	(a)	Morton	W 3-1	Marshall 2, Fleming	7,000
36	5	(h)	Dundee U	W 2-1	Craig, Marshall	12,000
37	10	(a)	Clydebank	D 2-2	Marshall 2	6,000
38	17	(h)	Hamilton A	W 2-0	Marshall 2	

FINAL LEAGUE POSITION: 6th

Appearances: Robb 22, Jamieson 5, McCandless 7, Meiklejohn 12, Dixon 37, Craig 31, Archibald 18, Cunningham 31, Henderson 13, Cairns 17, Morton AL 29, Ireland 2, Manderson 15, Muirhead 27, McKay 22, McGregor 6, Hamilton J 29, Gray 21, Chalmers 6, Kirkwood A 1, Hodge 2, Fleming 21, Hamilton T 16, Malone 15, Osborne 9, Marshall 4

Goals: Jamieson 1, Archibald 2, Cunningham 2, Henderson 18, Cairns 7, Morton AL 4, McKay 5, Muirhead 2, Hamilton J 6, Chalmers 2, Fleming 3, Fleming(col) 17, Malone 2, Osborne 1, Marshall 7

Scottish FA Cup

No	Date	Venue	Opponent	Result	Scorers	Att
1	Jan 23	(h)	Lochgelly U	W 3-0	Fleming 2, Archibald	5,700
2	Feb 6	(h)	Stenhousemuir	W 1-0	Henderson	14,000
3	20	(a)	Falkirk	W 2-0	McKay, Cunningham	22,000
QF	Mar 6	(a)	Morton	W 4-0	Morton 2, Fleming, Cunningham (pen)	15,000
SF	20(n*)		St Mirren	L 0-1		61,000

*Played at Celtic Park, Glasgow.

Appearances: Dixon 5, Craig 5, Archibald 2, Cunningham 4, Henderson 1, Cairns 2, Morton AL 5, Manderson 1, Muirhead 4, McKay 4, Hamilton J 5, Gray 4, Fleming 4, Hamilton T 5, Malone 3, Osborne 1

Goals: Archibald 1, Cunningham 2, Henderson 1, Morton AL 2, Fleming 3

Glasgow Cup

No	Date	Venue	Opponent	Result	Scorers	Att
SF	Sep 28	(a)	Celtic	D 2-2	Cunningham 2	65,000
R	Oct 6	(h)	Celtic	D 1-1	Cunningham	55,000
2R	8	(h)	Celtic	L 0-2		40,000

Appearances: Robb 3, Jamieson 3, Dixon 3, Craig 3, Archibald 3, Cunningham 3, Henderson 1, Cairns 1, Manderson 1, Muirhead 3, McKay 2, McGregor 3, Hamilton J 2, Hodge 1, Fleming 1

Goals: Cunningham 3

Glasgow Merchants' Charity Cup

No	Date	Venue	Opponent	Result	Scorers	Att
1	May 1	(h)	Clyde	L 3-4	D.Kirkwood, Marshall (pen), McKay	12,000

Appearances: Archibald 1, Manderson 1, Muirhead 1, McKay 1, Hamilton J 1, Hamilton T 1, Malone 1, Osborne 1, Marshall 1, Weir 1, Kirkwood D 1

Goals: McKay 1, Marshall 1, Kirkwood D 1

Other matches

No	Date	Venue	Opponent	Result	Scorers	Att
1	Aug 18	(a)	Clyde *	W 3-1	Hodge, Henderson, Morton	7,000
2	26	(a)	Morton §	W 3-2	Craig, Archibald, Cunningham	5,000
3	Sep 2	(a)	Newcastle U	W 2-0	Archibald, Muirhead	10,000
4	22	(h)	Huddersfield T‡	L 1-5	D.Kirkwood	2,000
5	Nov 21	(a)	Motherwell	D 0-0 †		12,000

*Mattha Gemmell Benefit Match. §George French Benefit Match. ‡Davie Meiklejohn
Benefit Match. †League fixture abandoned after 54 minutes due to bad light. Rangers arrived 45 minutes late.

Appearances: Jamieson 4, McCandless 3, Meiklejohn 1, Dixon 2, Craig 4, Archibald 4, Cunningham 3, Henderson 3, Cairns 1, Morton AL 3, Ireland 3, Manderson 1, Muirhead 3, McKay 4, Hamilton J 2, Gray 3, Chalmers 1, Kirkwood A 2, Hodge 1, Fleming 1, Hamilton T 1, Malone 1, Osborne 2, Kirkwood D 1, Dick 1

Goals: Archibald 1, Cunningham 2, Henderson 1, Morton AL 1, Muirhead 1, Kirkwood D 1

1926-27

Manager: W.Struth

Scottish League

Player columns (left to right): Hamilton T, Gray, Manderson, Craig, Dixon, Shaw, Archibald, Cunningham, Marshall, Cairns, Morton, Meiklejohn, Smith Jamie, Fleming, Muirhead, Kirkwood D, Weir, McKay, Purdon, McCandless, Henderson, Ireland, McMillan, Hair, Moyies, Hamilton J, Hamilton R, McPhail, Chalmers, Osborne

#	Date	Match	Result	Scorers	Att	HamT	Gray	Mand	Craig	Dixon	Shaw	Arch	Cun	Mar	Cairns	Morton	Meik	SmJ	Flem	Muir	Kirk	Weir	McKay	Purdon	McCand	Hend	Irel	McMil	Hair	Moyies	HamJ	HamR	McPhail	Chalm	Osb
1	Aug 14 (h)	Dundee U	W 2-0	Marshall 2	20,000	1	2	3	4	5	6	7	8	9	10	11																			
2	17 (h)	Dunfermline A	W 2-0	Shaw, Archibald	16,000	1	2	3	4		6	7	8	9		11		5	10																
3	21 (a)	Airdrieonians	D 3-3	Marshall, Cairns, Fleming	20,000	1	2	3	4		6	7	8	9	10		5		11																
4	28 (h)	Partick Thistle	W 2-1	Marshall 2	22,000	1	2	3	6			7		9	10				5	11	4	8													
5	Sep 4 (a)	St Johnstone	L 1-2	Morton	5,000	1	2	3		5	6		8	9	10	11			7	4															
6	11 (h)	Motherwell	W 2-0	Archibald, Cunningham	18,000	1	2			5	6	7	8	9	10		4			11			3												
7	18 (a)	Hearts	W 2-0	Fleming, Cairns	30,000	1	2	3	4		6		9	10	11		5	8	7																
8	25 (h)	Aberdeen	W 3-2	Shaw, McKay, Cunningham	23,000	1	2		4		6		10	9			11	5	7				3	8											
9	Oct 2 (a)	St Mirren	W 7-3	Henderson 3, Fleming 2, Craig, Archibald	34,000	1			4		5	7	10						11	6					8	2	3	9							
10	16 (h)	Queen's Park	L 0-1		19,000	1			4		5		8	7		10			11	6					2	3		9							
11	23 (a)	Morton	W 8-2	Marshall 5, Morton, Fleming, Cairns	5,000	1	2		6		5	7	8	9		10	4		11						3			5							
12	Nov 6 (h)	Cowdenbeath	W 4-1	Morton 2, Craig, Fleming	15,000	1	2		6		5	7	8	9		10	4		11						3										
13	13 (a)	Hibernian	D 2-2	Cunningham, Marshall	18,000	1	2		6		5	7	8	9		10	4		11						3										
14	20 (h)	Falkirk	W 2-1	Marshall, Muirhead	25,000	1	2		6		5	7	8	9			4		11	10					3										
15	27 (h)	Clyde	W 6-0	Marshall 3, McCandless (pen), Muirhead, Cunningham	10,000	1	2		6		5	7	8	9			4		11	10					3										
16	Dec 4 (h)	Hamilton A	L 1-4	Muirhead	10,000	1	2		6		5	7		9	10		4		11	8					3										
17	11 (a)	Dundee	D 1-1	Marshall	20,000	1	2		6		5	7	8	9	10		4		11						3										
18	18 (a)	Kilmarnock	D 0-0		12,000	1	2		6		5	7	8	9	10		4		11						3										
19	25 (a)	Dundee U	L 0-2		15,000	1	2		6		5	7	8				4		11	10					3			9							
20	Jan 1 (h)	Celtic	W 2-1	Archibald, Marshall	63,000	1	2		6		5	7		9		10	4		11						3			8							
21	3 (a)	Partick Thistle	W 4-1	McMillan 2, Marshall, Cunningham	40,000	1	2		6		5	7		9		10	4		11						3			8							
22	8 (h)	St Johnstone	W 4-2	Morton 3, Jamieson (og)	8,000	1	2		6		5	7				10	11			4					3	9		8							
23	15 (a)	Motherwell	W 4-1	Mieklejohn, Archibald, Fleming, Cunningham	32,000	1	2		6		5	7	10				11		4		9				3			8							
24	29 (h)	Hearts	W 1-0	McMillan	15,000	1	2				5	7	10	9			11		4			6			3			8							
25	Feb 12 (h)	St Mirren	W 4-0	Fleming 2, Morton 2	20,000	1	2		6		5	7	10				11			9	4				3			8							
26	16 (a)	Aberdeen	D 2-2	Hair 2	16,000	1	2	3	6		5	7					11		4		9	10							8						
27	23 (a)	Dunfermline A	W 3-1	Fleming 3	4,000		2				6	7		8	10	11	4		9						3	5				1					
28	Mar 1 (h)	Queen's Park	W 2-1	Archibald, McMillan	18,000	1		2			5	7				10	11		4		9	6			3			8							
29	12 (h)	Airdrieonians	D 1-1	Fleming	27,000	1		2	6		5	7	10				11		4		9							8			3				
30	16 (h)	Morton	W 2-1	Cunningham, Morton	8,000	1	2		10		5	7	8				11		4		9	6			3							3			
31	23 (a)	Cowdenbeath	L 0-1		3,000	1	2		10		5	7	8	9			11		4			6										3			
32	29 (h)	Hibernian	W 2-0	McMillan, Marshall	5,000	1			6		5			10	9		2		11	4						8	7				3				
33	Apr 2 (a)	Falkirk	D 3-3	McMillan, Marshall, Meiklejohn	5,000	1	2		6		5	7		9			10		11	4						8					3				
34	9 (a)	Clyde	D 0-0		20,000	1	2				5	7	10	9			11		4			6				8					3				
35	16 (a)	Hamilton A	D 1-1	Fleming	10,000	1	2		6		5	7				11	10		9	4					8					3					
36	18 (a)	Celtic	W 1-0	Fleming	40,000	1	2		6		5	7	10				11	8	9	4					3										
37	23 (h)	Dundee	D 0-0		10,000	1	2		6		5	7	10				11	8	9	4					3										
38	30 (h)	Kilmarnock	W 1-0	Fleming	10,000	1	2		6			7	10				11	4	9						3		5	8							
	FINAL LEAGUE POSITION: 1st				**Appearances**	37	30	12	30	3	36	28	29	25	15	31	30	2	26	24	1	2	3	2	22	4	3	13	2	1	6	1			
					Goals				2		2	6	7	20	3	10	2		16	3			1		1	3		6	2						

1 own-goal

Scottish FA Cup

#	Date	Match	Result	Scorers	Att	HamT	Gray	Mand	Craig	Shaw	Arch	Morton	Meik	Flem	McCand	McMil								
1	Jan 22 (a)	Leith A	W 4-1	Morton 2, Fleming, Craig	14,130	1	2		6	5	7	10	4	11	3	8								
2	Feb 5 (h)	St Mirren	W 6-0	Fleming 2, Morton 2, Archibald, Cunningham	56,000	1	2		6	5	7	10	4	11	3	8								
3	19 (h)	Hamilton A	W 4-0	Fleming 2, Cunningham, Archibald	53,000	1		2	6	5	7	10	4	11	3	8								
QF	Mar 5 (a)	Falkirk	D 2-2	Archibald, McCandless (pen)	20,233	1		2	6	5	7	10	4	11	3	8								
R	9 (h)	Falkirk	L 0-1		80,000	1		2	6	5	7	10	4	11	3	8								
				Appearances		5	3	2	5	5	5	5	5	5	5	5								
				Goals					1		3	2		4		5								

Glasgow Cup

#	Date	Match	Result	Scorers	Att	HamT	Gray	Mand	Craig	Dixon	Shaw	Arch	Cun	Mar	Cairns	Morton	Meik	Flem	Muir	Weir	McKay	Purdon	McCand	Hend	Irel
1	Sep 7 (h)	Third Lanark	W 4-2	Shaw, Archibald, Cunningham, Marshall	7,000	1	2	3			6	7	8	9	10	11	5	4							
SF	27 (h)	Queen's Park	D 1-1	Cunningham (pen)	22,240	1			4		6		10			11	5		7		3	8	2	9	
R	29 (a)	Queen's Park	W 3-1	McKay 2, Marshall	16,500	1			4	5	6	7		9			11	10		3	8	2			
F	Oct 9 (n*)	Celtic	L 0-1		55,000	1			4		5	7	10			11	6			8	2	3	9		
				Appearances		4	1	1	3	1	4	3	3	2	1	2	2	3	3	2	3	2	2	2	
				Goals					1		1	2	2								2				

*Played at Hampden Park, Glasgow.

Glasgow Merchants' Charity Cup

#	Date	Match	Result	Scorers	Att	HamT	Gray	Craig	Shaw	Arch	Cun	Flem	Muir	McKay	Purdon	McCand	McMil	Hair	Moyies	HamJ	McPhail
1	May 3 (h)	Queen's Park	W 8-1	Fleming 4, Cunningham 2, McPhail, Archibald	5,500	1	2		5	7	8	11	4	9	6	3					10
SF	7 (a)	Celtic	W 4-1	McPhail 2, Fleming, Archibald	36,000	1	2	6	5	7	8	11	4	9		3					10
F	14 (n*)	Partick Thistle	L 3-6	Morton 2, McPhail	18,520		2		6			11	4	9		3	5	8	7	1	10
				Appearances		2	3	1	3	2	2	3	3	3	1	3	1	1	1	1	3
				Goals					2	2	2	5									4

* Played at Hampden Park, Glasgow.

Other matches

#	Date	Match	Result	Scorers	Att	HamT	Gray	Craig	Shaw	Arch	Mar	Flem	Weir	McKay	Purdon	McCand	Hend	Irel	McMil	Hair	HamJ	HamR	McPhail	Chalm	Osb
1	Sep 21 (a)	Huddersfield T*	W 2-1	Henderson, Morton	15,000	1	2	4	6	7		11		8	3	9	5						10		
2	Apr 27 (a)	Ayr U †	W 4-1	Chalmers 2, Ireland (pen), Hair	1,000				9		11		2	10		5		7	1	6	3		8	4	
				Appearances		1	1	1	1	2	1	1	1	1	1	1	1	2	1	1	1	1	2	1	
				Goals								1					1	1		1				2	

*Hospital Challenge Cup. †Tom Kilpatrick Benefit Match.

1927-28

Manager: W.Struth

No.	Date	Opponent	Result	Scorers (Scottish League)	Att	Hamilton T	Gray	McCandless	Muirhead	Meiklejohn	Craig	Archibald	Cunningham	Fleming	McPhail	Morton	McMillan	Osborne	Simpson	Chalmers	Moyies	Hamilton R	Buchanan	Haddow	Marshall	Yuill	Ireland	Hamilton J	Docherty	Lockie	Hair	Stewart	Hutchinson
1	Aug 13	(a) Aberdeen	W 3-2	Fleming 2, Morton	25,000	1	2	3	4	5	6	7	8	9	10	11																	
2	20	(h) Hearts	W 4-1	Fleming 2, Archibald, Morton	25,000	1	2	3	4	5	6	7	8	9	10	11																	
3	27	(a) Cowdenbeath	W 4-1	Fleming 3, Morton	12,000	1	2	3	4	5	6	7	8	9	10	11																	
4	Sep 3	(h) St Johnstone	W 5-1	Fleming 2, McPhail 2, Morton	25,000	1	2	3	4	5	6	7	8	9	10	11																	
5	10	(a) Partick Thistle	W 6-0	Craig, Archibald, Cunningham, Fleming, McPhail, Morton	45,000	1	2	3	4	5	6	7	8	9	10	11																	
6	17	(h) Airdrieonians	W 2-1	Meiklejohn, McPhail	37,000	1	2	3	4	5	6	7	8	9	10	11																	
7	24	(a) Motherwell	D 1-1	McPhail (pen)	30,000	1	2	3	4	5	6	7	8	9	10	11																	
8	Oct 1	(h) St Mirren	W 4-2	McPhail 2, Cunningham, Fleming	30,000	1	2	3	4	5	6	7	8	9	10	11																	
9	15	(h) Celtic	W 1-0	Fleming	60,000	1	2	3	4	5	6	7	8	9	10	11																	
10	22	(h) Raith Rovers	W 7-0	Fleming 3, McMillan 2, Archibald, Morton	10,000	1	2	3	4	5	6	7		9	10	11	8																
11	29	(a) Queen's Park	L 1-3	McPhail	25,000	1	2	3			6	7	8	9	10			4	5	11													
12	Nov 5	(a) Dunfermline A	W 5-0	Archibald 2, Cunningham, Fleming, Morton		1	2	3	4	5	6	7	8	9	10	11																	
13	12	(h) Hibernian	W 4-1	McMillan 2, Fleming, Cunningham	15,000	1	2	3	4	5	6	7	10	9		11	8																
14	19	(a) Falkirk	W 2-1	Fleming, Morton	15,000	1	2	3	4	5	6	7		9	10	11	8																
15	26	(a) Clyde	W 4-1	McPhail 2 (1 pen), Craig, Fleming	18,000		2	3	4	5	6	7	8	9	10	11					1												
16	Dec 3	(a) Hamilton A	D 1-1	Archibald	15,000	1	2	3		5	6	7	10	9	4	11	8																
17	10	(h) Dundee	W 5-1	Simpson, Archibald, Fleming, McPhail, Morton	10,000	1	2	3		4	6	7	8	9	10	11			5														
18	17	(a) Kilmarnock	D 1-1	Archibald	14,440	1	2		4	5	6	7	8	9	10	11						3											
19	24	(h) Aberdeen	W 5-0	Fleming 3, Archibald, Morton	15,000	1	2		6	5		7	8	9	10	11						3	4										
20	31	(a) St Johnstone	W 1-0	Morton	10,000	1	2		4	5	6	7	8	9	10	11						3											
21	Jan 2	(a) Celtic	L 0-1		70,000	1	2		4	5	6	7	8	9	10	11						3											
22	3	(h) Partick Thistle	W 2-1	Archibald, Fleming	20,000	1	2		4	5	6	7	8	9	10							3		11									
23	7	(h) Cowdenbeath	D 2-2	Cunningham, Marshall	10,000	1	2			5	6	7	8	11	10							3	4		9								
24	14	(a) Airdrieonians	W 7-2	McPhail 2, Cunningham, Craig, Fleming, Muirhead, Archibald	8,000		2		4	5	6	7	8	9	10	11					1	3											
25	28	(h) Boness U	W 3-1	Archibald, Marshall, McPhail (pen)	12,000		2		4		6	7			10	11	8		5			3			9	1							
26	Feb 11	(h) Motherwell	L 0-2		45,000		2		4	5	6	7	8	9	10	11						3				1							
27	15	(a) St Mirren	D 3-3	Archibald, Cunningham, Marshall	15,000		2		4	5	6	7	8		10	11						3			9	1							
28	28	(h) Queen's Park	W 4-0	Marshall 2, Cunningham, Morton	10,000	1	2			5	6	7	8		10	11						3	4		9								
29	Mar 7	(a) Hearts	D 0-0		20,000	1	2			5	6	7		9	10	11	8					3	4										
30	17	(a) Hibernian	L 1-2	Archibald	18,000	1	2			5	6	7			10	11	8					3	4		9								
31	28	(h) Falkirk	W 4-0	Fleming 3, Buchanan	10,000	1	2			5	6	7	8	9	10	11						3	4										
32	31	(h) Clyde	W 3-1	Fleming 2, Marshall	18,000	1	2		6	5		7	8	9	10							3	4		11								
33	Apr 2	(a) Raith Rovers	D 0-0		10,000	1	2				6	7		9	10	11	8		5			3	4										
34	7	(h) Hamilton A	W 3-1	Archibald 2, McPhail	15,000	1	2			5	6	7		9	10	11			8			3	4										
35	9	(h) Dunfermilne A	W 4-0	Cunningham 3, McPhail	10,000	1	2		8			7	10	9	6	11			5			3	4										
36	18	(a) Dundee	W 1-0	McPhail	12,000	1	2			6		7	8	9	10	11			5			3	4										
37	21	(h) Kilmarnock	W 5-1	Fleming 3, Cunningham 2	28,000	1	2			5	6	7	8	9	10	11						3	4										
38	28	(a) Boness U	D 1-1	Cunningham	4,000	1	2		10	5	6	7	8	9		11						3	4										
FINAL LEAGUE POSITION: 1st					Appearances	33	38	17	26	34	34	38	31	34	36	34	8	1	7	1	2	21	13	1	6	3							
					Goals				1	1	3	16	14	33	17	12	4		1				1		6								

Scottish FA Cup

Rd	Date	Opponent	Result	Scorers	Att	Hamilton T	Gray	McCandless	Muirhead	Meiklejohn	Craig	Archibald	Cunningham	Fleming	McPhail	Morton	McMillan	Osborne	Simpson	Chalmers	Moyies	Hamilton R	Buchanan	Haddow	Marshall	Yuill	Ireland	Hamilton J	Docherty	Lockie	Hair	Stewart	Hutchinson
1	Jan 21	(a) East Stirling	W 6-0	Fleming 3, McPhail (pen), Cunningham, Archibald	5,500		2		4	5	6	7	8	9	10	11						3				1							
2	Feb 4	(h) Cowdenbeath	W 4-2	McPhail 3, Fleming	30,226		2		4	5	6	7	8	9	10	11						3				1							
3	18	(h) King's Park	W 3-1	Morton 2, Cunningham	20,000	1	2			5	6	7	8	9	10	11						3	4										
QF	Mar 3	(a) Albion Rovers	W 1-0	Cunningham	25,000	1	2			5	6	7	8	9	10	11						3	4										
SF	24	(n*) Hibernian	W 3-0	Archibald, McPhail, Simpson	43,129	1	2			5	6	7		9	10	11			8			3	4										
F	Apr 14	(n†) Celtic	W 4-0	Archibald 2, Meiklejohn (pen), McPhail	118,115	1	2			5	6	7	8	9	10	11						3	4										
*Played at Tynecastle Park, Edinburgh. †Played at Hampden Park, Glasgow.					Appearances	4	6		2	6	6	6	5	6	6	6			1			6	4			2							
					Goals					1		4	3	4	6	2			1														

Glasgow Cup

Rd	Date	Opponent	Result	Scorers	Att	Hamilton T	Gray	McCandless	Muirhead	Meiklejohn	Craig	Archibald	Cunningham	Fleming	McPhail	Morton	McMillan	Osborne	Simpson	Chalmers	Moyies	Hamilton R	Buchanan	Haddow	Marshall	Yuill	Ireland	Hamilton J	Docherty	Lockie	Hair	Stewart	Hutchinson
SF	Sep 26	(h) Clyde	W 7-0	Fleming 6, McPhail	23,000	1	2	3	4	5	6	7	8	9	10	11																	
F	Oct 8	(n*) Celtic	L 1-2	Cunningham	84,536	1	2	3		4	6	7	8	9	10	11			5														
*Played at Hampden Park, Glasgow.					Appearances	2	2	2	1	2	2	2	2	2	2	2			1														
					Goals								1	6	1																		

Glasgow Merchants' Charity Cup

Rd	Date	Opponent	Result	Scorers	Att	Hamilton T	Gray	McCandless	Muirhead	Meiklejohn	Craig	Archibald	Cunningham	Fleming	McPhail	Morton	McMillan	Osborne	Simpson	Chalmers	Moyies	Hamilton R	Buchanan	Haddow	Marshall	Yuill	Ireland	Hamilton J	Docherty	Lockie	Hair	Stewart	Hutchinson
SF	May 5	(a) Celtic	W 2-0	Fleming, McPhail (pen)	27,000	1	2				6	7	8	9	10	11						3	4				5						
F	12	(n*) Queen's Park	W 3-1	Archibald, Fleming, Wiseman (og)	27,000	1	2			5	6	7	8	9	10	11						3	4										
*Played at Celtic Park, Glasgow.					Appearances	2	2			1	2	2	2	2	2	2						2	2				1						
					Goals							1		2	1																		

1 own-goal

Other matches

No.	Date	Opponent	Result	Scorers	Att	Hamilton T	Gray	McCandless	Muirhead	Meiklejohn	Craig	Archibald	Cunningham	Fleming	McPhail	Morton	McMillan	Osborne	Simpson	Chalmers	Moyies	Hamilton R	Buchanan	Haddow	Marshall	Yuill	Ireland	Hamilton J	Docherty	Lockie	Hair	Stewart	Hutchinson
1	Sep 5	(a) Hibernian *	W 3-2	Stewart 2, Chalmers	1,000	1											8		5	9		3			11			2	4	6	7	10	
2	19	(a†) E Scotland Jun	W 7-2	Marshall 4, Hair 2, McMillan													10	7			1	3			9		5	2	4	6	8		11
3	May 30	(a‡) Nat League Sel	W 8-2	McPhail 3, Fleming 2, Buchanan, Morton, Cunningham		1	2			5	6	7	8	9	10	11						3	4										
4	Jun 2	(a) Brooklyn W	W 4-0	Fleming 4	20,000	1	2			5	6	7	8	9	10	11						3	4										
5	3	(a) Fall River	D 0-0		15,000	1	2		10	5	6	7	8	9		11						3	4										
6	9	(a) Pittsburgh	W 9-0	McPhail 3, Marshall 2, Morton 2, Fleming, Craig	8,000	1	2	3	4	5	6	7		9	10	11									8								
7	10	(a) Detroit Select	D 1-1	Hair	15,000	1		2			6		8	9	10	11			5			3	4								7		
8	13	(a§) Ulster U	W 7-0	McPhail 4, Fleming 2, Cunningham	10,000	1	2		4	5	6	7	8	9	10	11						3											
9	16	(a) Montreal	W 5-1	Cunningham 2, Marshall 2, McPhail		1	2	3	11	5	6	7	8		10								4		9								
10	18	(a) Boston	D 2-2	Marshall, Cunningham		1	2	3	11	5	6	7	8		10								4		9								
11	20	(a#) Illinois AllStars	W 4-1	McPhail 2, Cunningham, Marshall		1	2	3	11	5		7	8		10				6				4		9								
12	23	(a+) America Lgue	W 6-0	Cunningham 2, Archibald, Buchanan, Marshall, McPhail	18,000	1	2	3	11	5	6	7	8		10								4		9								
*John Halligan Benefit Match. †Played at Tynecastle Park, Edinburgh. ‡Played at Philadelphia. §Played at Toronto. #Played at Chicago. +Played at Brooklyn, New York.					Appearances	11	9	6	7	9	9	9	9	6	9	6	2	1	3	1	1	7	8		7		1	2	2	2	3	1	1
					Goals						1	1	8	9	14	3	1			1			2		11						3	2	

1928-29

Manager: W.Struth

	Date	Opponent	Result	Scorers	Scottish League	Hamilton T	Gray	Hamilton R	Muirhead	Meiklejohn	Craig	Archibald	Cunningham	Fleming	McPhail	Morton	Marshall	Buchanan	Ireland	McMillan	Simpson	Smith, Jimmy	McDonald	Osborne	Purdon	McCandless	McPherson J	McPherson A	McGowan	Hamilton J	Hair	Lockie	Moyies
1	Aug 11	(h) Kilmarnock	W 4-2	Fleming 2, Archibald, Morton	20,000	1	2	3	4	5	6	7	8	9	10	11																	
2	18	(a) St Mirren	W 5-1	McPhail 3, Marshall 2	22,000	1	2	3	4	5	6	7	8		10	11	9																
3	25	(h) Cowdenbeath	W 3-1	Morton 2, Meiklejohn (pen)	20,000	1	2	3		5	6	7		9	10	11	8	4															
4	Sep 8	(a) Dundee	W 3-2	Meiklejohn 2 (1 pen), Morton	16,000	1	2	3		6		7		9	10	11	8	4	5														
5	15	(a) Hearts	W 1-0	Fleming	45,000	1	2	3		5	6	7		9	10	11		4		8													
6	22	(h) Raith Rovers	W 7-1	Fleming 3, McPhail 2, McMillan, Morton	16,000	1	2	3		5	6	7		9	10	11		4		8													
7	29	(h) Motherwell	D 0-0		40,000	1	2	3		5	6	7		9	10	11		4		8													
8	Oct 6	(a) Third Lanark	W 5-2	Muirhead 2, Meiklejohn, McPhail, Morton	22,000	1	2	3	8	5	6	7		9	10	11		4															
9	13	(h) St Johnstone	W 8-0	Fleming 3, Morton 3, Archibald, Muirhead	25,000	1	2	3	8	5	6	7		9	10	11		4															
10	20	(a) Celtic	W 2-1	McMillan, Archibald	35,000	1	2	3	6	5		7		9	10	11		4		8													
11	Nov 3	(a) Hibernian	W 2-1	Craig, Archibald	22,000	1	2	3	8		6	7		9	10	11		4	5														
12	10	(a) Falkirk	W 4-1	Fleming 3, Buchanan	15,000	1	2	3	8		6	7	10	9		11		4	5														
13	17	(h) Hamilton A	W 4-0	Fleming 3, Cunningham	14,000	1	2	3	8	5	6	7	10	9		11		4															
14	24	(a) Clyde	W 3-2	Craig, Fleming, Cunningham	15,000	1	2	3	8	5	6	7	10	9		11		4															
15	Dec 1	(a) Ayr U	W 3-1	Fleming 3	18,500	1	2	3	8	5	6	7		9	10	11		4															
16	8	(h) Aberdeen	W 2-0	Muirhead, McPhail	15,000	1	2	3	8	5	6	7		9	10	11		4															
17	15	(a) Airdrieonians	W 5-2	Fleming 3, Archibald, Morton	8,000	1	2	3		5	6	7	8	9	10	11		4															
18	22	(h) St Mirren	D 1-1	Archibald	15,000	1	2	3	10		6	7	8	9		11		4	5														
19	29	(a) Kilmarnock	W 3-1	Archibald 2, Fleming	30,000	1	2	3	8	5	6	7		9	10	11		4															
20	Jan 1	(h) Celtic	W 3-0	Fleming 2, Archibald	60,000	1		3	4	5	6	7		9	10	11	8	2															
21	2	(h) Partick Thistle	W 1-0	Meiklejohn (pen)	10,000	1		3	4	5	6	7			10	11	9	2		8													
22	5	(a) Cowdenbeath	W 2-0	Fleming, McPhail	5,000	1	2	3	4	5	6	7		9	10	11	8																
23	12	(a) Queen's Park	W 4-0	McPhail 3, Fleming	60,000	1	2	3	4		6	7		9	10	11	8				5												
24	26	(h) Airdrieonians	W 2-0	Archibald, Cunningham	25,000	1	2	3		5	6	7	8	9	10	11		4															
25	Feb 9	(a) Raith Rovers	W 3-1	Muirhead, Fleming, McPhail	9,000	1	2	3	8	5	6	7		9	10	11		4															
26	26	(h) Third Lanark	W 5-1	Craig 2, McPhail 2, Archibald	6,000	1	2		4	5	6	7		9	10	11		3		8													
27	Mar 6	(a) St Johnstone	W 3-1	Craig, Marshall, McPhail	8,000	1	2		8	5	6			9	10	11	7	4			3												
28	9	(h) Hibernian	W 3-0	Buchanan, Fleming, McPhail	15,000	1	2	3	8	5	6			9	10	11	7	4															
29	12	(h) Hearts	W 2-0	Marshall, Fleming	12,000	1	2	3	8	5	6			9	10	11	7	4															
30	16	(h) Falkirk	D 1-1	Marshall	20,000	1		3	4	5	6	7		9	10	11	8	2															
31	27	(a) Hamilton A	L 1-3	Morton	12,000	1	2	3	8		6	7			10	11		4			5	9											
32	30	(h) Clyde	D 0-0		12,000	1	2	3	8	5				9	10	11	7	4			6												
33	Apr 1	(h) Queen's Park	W 2-1	Fleming 2	22,000	1	2	3		5				9	10	11	8				6		4	7									
34	10	(h) Ayr U	D 0-0		5,000	1	2	3			6	7		11	10		8		5			9	4										
35	17	(a) Motherwell	W 4-2	Morton 2, Craig, McPhail	6,000	1	2			5	6	7		9	10	11	8	3					4										
36	20	(a) Aberdeen	D 2-2	Archibald, Morton	18,000	1	2		4	5	6	7		9	10	11	8	3															
37	24	(a) Partick Thistle	D 1-1	Muirhead	10,000	1	2	3	10		6	7		9		11	8	4	5														
38	27	(h) Dundee	W 3-0	Marshall, Fleming, McPhail	5,000	1	2	3	7		6			9	10	11	8	4	5														
FINAL LEAGUE POSITION: 1st					Appearances	38	35	34	28	30	34	32	8	35	33	37	18	32	7	6	5	2	3	1									
					Goals				6	5	6	12	3	33	18	14	6	2		2													

Scottish FA Cup

	Date	Opponent	Result	Scorers	Att	Hamilton T	Gray	Hamilton R	Muirhead	Meiklejohn	Craig	Archibald	Cunningham	Fleming	McPhail	Morton	Marshall	Buchanan	Ireland	McMillan	Simpson	Smith, Jimmy	McDonald	Osborne	Purdon	McCandless	McPherson J	McPherson A	McGowan	Hamilton J	Hair	Lockie	Moyies
1	Jan 19	(h) Edinburgh C	W11-1	Fleming 3, Craig 2 (1 pen), McPhail 2, Morton 2, Cunningham, Archibald	10,500	1	2	3			6	7	8	9	10	11		4			5												
2	Feb 2	(h) Partick Thistle	W 5-1	Fleming 3, Craig, Morton	67,000	1	2	3	8	5	6	7		9	10	11		4															
3	16	(a) Clyde	W 2-0	Muirhead, Archibald	34,000	1	2	3	8	5	6	7		9	10	11		4															
QF	Mar 2	(h) Dundee U	W 3-1	Marshall, Fleming, McPhail	49,000	1	2		4	5	6	7		9	10	11	8	3															
SF	23	(n*) St Mirren	W 3-2	Muirhead, Archibald, Morton	69,727	1	2	3	8	5	6	7		9	10	11		4															
F	Apr 6	(n*) Kilmarnock	L 0-2		114,780	1	2	3	8	5	6	7		9	10	11		4															
*Played at Hampden Park, Glasgow.					Appearances	6	6	5	5	5	6	6	1	6	6	6	1	6			1												
					Goals				2		3	3	1	7	3	4	1																

Glasgow Cup

	Date	Opponent	Result	Scorers	Att	Hamilton T	Gray	Hamilton R	Muirhead	Meiklejohn	Craig	Archibald	Cunningham	Fleming	McPhail	Morton	Marshall	Buchanan	Ireland	McMillan	Simpson	Smith, Jimmy	McDonald	Osborne	Purdon	McCandless	McPherson J	McPherson A	McGowan	Hamilton J	Hair	Lockie	Moyies
1	Sep 1	(h) Celtic	L 1-2	Marshall	80,000	1	2	3	4	5	6	7	8		10	11	9																
					Appearances	1	1	1	1	1	1	1	1		1	1	1																
					Goals												1																

Glasgow Merchants' Charity Cup

	Date	Opponent	Result	Scorers	Att	Hamilton T	Gray	Hamilton R	Muirhead	Meiklejohn	Craig	Archibald	Cunningham	Fleming	McPhail	Morton	Marshall	Buchanan	Ireland	McMillan	Simpson	Smith, Jimmy	McDonald	Osborne	Purdon	McCandless	McPherson J	McPherson A	McGowan	Hamilton J	Hair	Lockie	Moyies
1	May 4	(h) Partick Thistle	W 2-1	Meiklejohn (pen), Morton	12,000	1	2	3		4	6			9		11	10	8	5								7						
SF	7	(n*) Third Lanark	W 2-1	Buchanan, Marshall	3,175	1	2			5	6			7		11	10	4								3		8	9				
F	11	(h) Celtic	W 4-2	Muirhead 2, Marshall 2	25,288	1	2		10	5	6	7		9		11	8	4								3							
*Played at Firhill Park, Glasgow.					Appearances	3	3	1	1	3	3	1		3		3	3	3	1							2	1	1	1				
					Goals				2	1						1	3	1															

Glasgow Dental Cup

	Date	Opponent	Result	Scorers	Att	Hamilton T	Gray	Hamilton R	Muirhead	Meiklejohn	Craig	Archibald	Cunningham	Fleming	McPhail	Morton	Marshall	Buchanan	Ireland	McMillan	Simpson	Smith, Jimmy	McDonald	Osborne	Purdon	McCandless	McPherson J	McPherson A	McGowan	Hamilton J	Hair	Lockie	Moyies
SF	Dec 5	(h) Clyde	W 6-0	Marshall 2, Morton 2, Archibald, McMillan	3,000	1	2			5		7	8			11	9			10	6		4		3								
F	11	(n*) Partick Thistle	L 0-2		5,000	1	2			5	6	7	8	9	10	11		4							3								
*Played at Hampden Park, Glasgow.					Appearances	2	2			2	1	2	2	1	1	2	1	1		1	1		1		2								
					Goals							1				2	2			1													

Other matches

	Date	Opponent	Result	Scorers	Att	Hamilton T	Gray	Hamilton R	Muirhead	Meiklejohn	Craig	Archibald	Cunningham	Fleming	McPhail	Morton	Marshall	Buchanan	Ireland	McMillan	Simpson	Smith, Jimmy	McDonald	Osborne	Purdon	McCandless	McPherson J	McPherson A	McGowan	Hamilton J	Hair	Lockie	Moyies
1	Sep 11	(n*) Celtic	W 3-2	Lockie 2, McMillan	5,000	1											9		5	8			4		2	6	10			3	7	11	
2	19	(a) Kilmarnock †	L 2-7	Hair, Simpson	2,000				6								9		5		8		4		3	2	10				7	11	1
*Dunnoon Festival. †Mattha Smith Benefit Match.					Appearances	1			1								2		2	1	1		2		2	2	2			1	2	2	1
					Goals															1	1										1	2	

1929-30

Manager: W.Struth

	Date	Opponent	Result	Scorers	Scottish League	Hamilton T	Gray	Buchanan	Muirhead	Meiklejohn	Craig	Archibald	Marshall	Fleming	McPhail	Nicholson	McPherson	Morton	Hamilton R	McMillan	Purdon	McCandless	McDonald	Ireland	Simpson	Brown	Osborne	Lockie	Smith	Main
1	Aug 10 (a)	Motherwell	W 2-0	Archibald, Fleming	25,000	1	2	3	4	5	6	7	8	9	10	11														
2	17 (h)	Hibernian	W 3-0	McPhail, Marshall, Nicholson	18,000	1	2	3	4	5	6	7	8	9	10	11														
3	24 (a)	St Johnstone	W 1-0	Marshall	10,000	1	2	3	4	5	6	7	8	9			10	11												
4	31 (h)	Falkirk	W 4-0	Fleming, Marshall, McPherson, Craig	28,000	1	2	4		5	6	7	8	9			10	11	3											
5	Sep 3 (h)	Queen's Park	W 1-0	Archibald	18,000	1	2	4	6	5		7	8	9			10	11	3											
6	7 (a)	Aberdeen	D 1-1	Morton	36,000	1	2	4	8	5	6	7		9			10	11	3											
7	14 (h)	St Mirren	W 2-1	Marshall, Archibald	25,000	1	2		4	5	6	7	9		10		8	11	3											
8	21 (a)	Kilmarnock	L 0-1		23,000	1	2	4		5	6	7	9	10				11	3	8										
9	28 (h)	Dundee U	W 3-1	Archibald 2, McPhail	20,000	1	2	4		5	6	7	9	8	10			11	3											
10	Oct 5 (a)	Hearts	L 0-2		41,000	1	2	4	8	5	6	7	9		10			11	3											
11	19 (a)	Partick Thistle	W 1-0	Fleming	40,000	1	2	4		5	6	7	8	9	10			11			3									
12	26 (h)	Celtic	W 1-0	Nicholson	50,000	1						7	8	9	10	11					2	3	4	5	6					
13	Nov 9 (h)	Hamilton A	W 5-2	Fleming 3, Archibald, McPherson	12,000	1	2		6	5		7	8	9			10	11	3				4							
14	16 (h)	Ayr U	W 9-0	Fleming 4, Archibald 2, Marshall 2, Brown	12,000	1	2			5	6	7	10	9				11	3				4			8				
15	23 (a)	Clyde	D 3-3	Brown, Morton (pen), Fleming	25,000	1	2			5	6	7	10	9				11	3				4			8				
16	30 (a)	Morton	D 2-2	Fleming 2	18,000	1	2				6	7	10	9				11	3				4		5	8				
17	Dec 7 (h)	Dundee	W 4-1	Brown, Craig, Fleming, Archibald	12,000	1	2	3		5	6	7		9	10			11					4			8				
18	14 (h)	Airdrieonians	W 2-0	McPhail, Brown	11,000	1	2	3	6	5		7		9	10			11					4			8				
19	21 (h)	Motherwell	W 4-2	McPhail 2, Brown, Fleming	22,000	1	2	4		5	6	7		9	10			11	3							8				
20	28 (a)	Hibernian	W 2-0	Fleming, Brown	18,000	1	2	4		5	6	7		9	10			11	3							8				
21	Jan 1 (a)	Celtic	W 2-1	Morton (pen), Brown	40,000	1	2	4		5	6	7		9	10			11	3							8				
22	2 (h)	Partick Thistle	W 2-1	Archibald, McPhail	35,000	1	2		4	5	6	7		9	10	11			3							8				
23	4 (h)	St Johnstone	W 6-1	Fleming 3, Marshall 2, Morton (pen)	15,000	1	2		6	5		7	10	9				11	3				4			8				
24	25 (h)	Aberdeen	W 3-1	Archibald 2, McPhail	45,000	1	2	4		5	6	7	9		10			11	3							8				
25	Feb 8 (h)	Kilmanock	W 4-0	Morton (pen), Fleming, McPhail, Brown	25,000	1	2	4		5	6	7		9	10			11	3							8				
26	11 (a)	St Mirren	W 1-0	Fleming	10,000	1	2		6			7	10	9		11			3	8			4		5					
27	19 (a)	Dundee U	W 1-0	Fleming	8,000	1	2		6	5		7	8	9	10	11			3				4							
28	22 (h)	Hearts	L 1-3	McPhail	10,000	1		4	6			7		9	10	11					2	3			5	8				
29	Mar 4 (a)	Queen's Park	W 3-1	Fleming, McPhail, Marshall	13,000	1	2	4			6	7	8	9	10			11	3						5					
30	8 (h)	Cowdenbeath	W 5-0	McPhail 2, Fleming 2, Marshall	12,000	1	2	4		5	6	7	8	9	10			11	3											
31	15 (a)	Hamilton A	D 1-1	McPhail	18,000	1	2	4		5	6	7		9	10			11	3							8				
32	26 (a)	Ayr U	W 3-0	Marshall (pen), Fleming, Brown	6,000	1	2		7		6		10	9		11			3				4		5	8				
33	29 (h)	Clyde	W 3-0	Marshall 2 (1 pen), Muirhead	10,000	1	2	4	7	5	6		10	9		11			3	8										
34	Apr 19 (a)	Airdrieonians	L 0-1		4,000	1	2		6	5		7	8	9	10				3								4	11		
35	21 (h)	Morton	W 3-0	Brown, Fleming, Marshall	10,000	1			6	5		7	10	9		11			3		2		4			8				
36	23 (a)	Dundee	W 3-1	McPhail 2, Smith	8,000	1	2	4	6	3		7			8	11				10					5				9	
37	26 (a)	Cowdenbeath	L 2-3	McPhail 2	2,500	1	2	4	7	5	6			9	10				3	8								11		
38	30 (a)	Falkirk	L 1-2	Brown	5,000	1		2			6		10	9		11			3				4		5	8				7
FINAL LEAGUE POSITION: 1st					Appearances	38	34	25	20	31	27	34	26	34	23	12	6	24	29	5	4	2	13	1	8	17	1	2	1	1
					Goals				1		2	12	14	27	17	2	2	5								11			1	

Scottish FA Cup

	Date	Opponent	Result	Scorers	Att	Hamilton T	Gray	Buchanan	Muirhead	Meiklejohn	Craig	Archibald	Marshall	Fleming	McPhail	Nicholson	McPherson	Morton	Hamilton R	McMillan	Purdon	McCandless	McDonald	Ireland	Simpson	Brown	Osborne	Lockie	Smith	Main
1	Jan 13 (a)	Queen's Park	W 1-0	McPhail	95,722	1	2	4		5	6	7		9	10			11	3							8				
2	Feb 1 (h)	Cowdenbeath	D 2-2	Morton 2	40,000	1	2	4		5	6	7	9		10			11	3							8				
R	5 (a)	Cowdenbeath	W 3-0	McPhail 2, Fleming	18,754	1	2	4		5	6	7		9	10			11	3							8				
3	15 (a)	Motherwell	W 5-2	Fleming 2, McPhail 2, Archibald	27,500	1	2	4		5	6	7		9	10			11	3							8				
QF	Mar 1 (h)	Montrose	W 3-0	Morton 2, Brown	12,500	1	2	4		5	6	7		9	10			11	3							8				
SF	22 (n*)	Hearts	W 4-1	Fleming 3, McPhail	92,084	1	2	4		5	6	7	8	9	10			11	3											
F	Apr 12 (n*)	Partick Thistle	D 0-0		107,475	1	2	4		5	6	7	8	9	10	11			3											
R	16 (n*)	Partick Thistle	W 2-1	Marshall, Craig	103,688	1	2			5	6	7	8	9	10			11	3				4							
*Played at Hampden Park, Glasgow.					Appearances	8	8	7		8	8	8	4	7	8	1		7	8				1			5				
					Goals						1	1	1	6	6			4								1				

Glasgow Cup

	Date	Opponent	Result	Scorers	Att	Hamilton T	Gray	Buchanan	Muirhead	Meiklejohn	Craig	Archibald	Marshall	Fleming	McPhail	Nicholson	McPherson	Morton	Hamilton R	McMillan	Purdon	McCandless	McDonald	Ireland	Simpson	Brown	Osborne	Lockie	Smith	Main
SF	Sep 30 (a)	Partick T	W 2-0	Marshall, Meiklejohn (pen)	48,000	1	2	4	8	5	6	7	9		10			11	3											
F	Oct 12 (n*)	Celtic	D 0-0		74,399	1	2	4		5	6	7	8	9			10	11	3											
R	16 (n*)	Celtic	W 4-0	Fleming 3, Archibald	41,500	1	2	4		5	6	7	8	9			10	11	3											
1	*May 3 (a)*	*Partick Thistle*	*W 2-1*	*Marshall 2*	*23,617*	1	2			5	6	7	10	9	8	11			3							4				
SF	*7 (h)*	*Third Lanark*	*W 5-1*	*Smith 2, McPhail, Brown, Nicholson*	*5,000*	1			6	2		7	8		10	11			3						5	4			9	
F	*10 (n*)*	*Celtic*	*D 2-2†*	*Marshall, Fleming*	*35,647*	1		2		5	6	7	8	9	10	11			3							4				
					Appearances	6	4	4	2	6	5	6	6	4	4	3	2	3	6						1	3			1	
					Goals					1		1	4	4	1	1										1			2	

*Played at Hampden Park, Glasgow. *Games in italic in Glasgow Merchants' Charity Cup.*
†Rangers won by the toss of a coin after extra-time.

Other matches

	Date	Opponent	Result	Scorers	Att	Hamilton T	Gray	Buchanan	Muirhead	Meiklejohn	Craig	Archibald	Marshall	Fleming	McPhail	Nicholson	McPherson	Morton	Hamilton R	McMillan	Purdon	McCandless	McDonald	Ireland	Simpson	Brown	Osborne	Lockie	Smith	Main
1	Sep 11 (a)	Kilmarnock*	D 1-1	Fleming	4,000	1						7	9	10		11			3	8	2		4	5	6					
2	May 21 (a†)	Ulster U	W 4-3	Fleming 2, Morton 2		1	2		10		6	7		9				11	3				4		5	8				
3	24 (a)	Hamilton T	W 3-0	Fleming 2, Nicholson	10,000	1	2		10	5	6	7		9		11			3				4			8				
4	25 (a)	New York Nat	W 5-4	McPhail 2, Smith 2, Morton	21,000	1	2	4		5	6	7			10			11	3							8			9	
5	30 (a‡)	Fall River	W 3-2	Brown, Meiklejohn, Smith	10,000	1	2	3		5	6	7	10			11							4			8			9	
6	31 (a§)	Car Steel	W 5-2	Smith 3, Brown, McPhail	10,000	1	2	6		5				7	10			11	3						4	8			9	
7	Jun 3 (a#)	Fort Range R	W 4-2	Fleming 2, Archibald, McPhail	10,000	1	2	3	6	5		7	8	9	10	11										4				
8	5 (a+)	Edmonton U	W 5-0	Smith 3, Marshall, Archibald	6,000	1	2	3			6	7	8		10	11									5	4			9	
9	7 (a+)	St Andrew's	W 7-1	Fleming 3, Morton, Muirhead, Archibald, Marshall	10,000	1	2	4	10	5	6	7	8	9				11	3											
10	9 (a)	Victoria West	W 8-1	Smith 3, Marshall 2, McPhail, Morton, Nicholson	5,000	1		2					8		10	11		7	3				4		5	6			9	
11	11 (a)	Calgary U	W 8-1	Marshall 3, Brown 2, Craig, Archibald, Fleming	7,000	1	2			5	6	7	10	9		11			3				4			8				
12	15 (a)	Chicago Sparta	W 4-1	Morton (pen), McPhail, Fleming, Marshall	7,000	1	2			5	6	7	8	9	10			11	3				4							
13	18 (a)	Detroit	W 3-1	McPhail, Nicholson, Brown	8,000	1	2			5		7	8	9	10	11			3						6	4				
14	20 (a¥)	Bruells	W 3-1	Smith 2, Nicholson	7,000	1		2	7		6				10	11			3				4		5	8			9	
15	22 (a¶)	Fall River	W 6-1	Smith 4, Fleming 2	20,000	1	2	3		5	6			7	10			11					4			8			9	
					Appearances	15	12	9	5	10	10	11	9	10	9	9		7	11	1	1		9	1	7	12			7	
					Goals				1	1	1	4	8	14	7	4		6								5			18	

* John McWhinnie Memorial Fund Benefit Match. †Played in Toronto. ‡ Played in New Bedford.
§ Played in Montreal. # Played in Winnipeg. + Played in Vancouver. ¥ Played in Cleveland.
¶ Played in New York.

In Match 15 number-11 was substituted by Nicholson.

1930-31

Manager: W.Struth

Scottish League

#	Date		V	Opponent	Result	Scorers	Att	Hamilton T	Gray	Buchanan	McDonald	Meiklejohn	Brown	Archibald	Marshall	Smith	McPhail	Morton	Craig	Fleming	Hamilton R	Simpson	McAulay R	McMillan	Main	Murray	Nicholson	McGowan	Conlin	Dawson	Purdon	Lockie
1	Aug	9	(a)	Cowdenbeath	W 3-1	Smith 2, Marshall	12,000	1	2	3	4	5	6	7	8	9	10	11														
2		16	(h)	Hearts	W 4-1	Smith 2, Archibald, Morton (pen)	40,000	1	2	3	4	5	6	7	8	9	10	11														
3		23	(a)	Dundee	W 1-0	Smith	22,000	1	2	3		5	4	7	8	9	10	11	6													
4		30	(h)	Motherwell	D 1-1	Marshall	40,000	1	2	3		5	4	7	8		10	11	6	9												
5	Sep	2	(h)	Hamilton A	W 1-0	Brown	30,000	1	2		4			8	7	9	10	11	6		3	5										
6		6	(a)	St Mirren	D 1-1	Smith	20,000	1	2		4				8	9	10	11	6	7	3	5										
7		13	(h)	Leith A	W 4-1	Fleming 2, McPhail 2	15,000	1	2		4	5		7	8		10	11	6	9	3											
8		20	(a)	Celtic	L 0-2		70,000	1	2			5	4	7	10			11	6	9	3	8										
9		27	(h)	Partick Thistle	W 3-1	Smith 2, Morton	25,000	1	2	3		5	4		8	9	10	11	6						7							
10	Oct	4	(a)	Airdrieonians	D 3-3	Smith, McPhail, Gray (pen)	15,000	1	2	3	4	5		7	8	9	10										6	11				
11		18	(a)	Kilmarnock	L 0-1		15,000	1	2	3		5	4	7	8	9	10	11	6													
12	Nov	1	(h)	Aberdeen	W 4-0	Fleming, Morton, McGowan, McPhail	12,000	1	2		4	5			8		10	11	6	7		3						9				
13		8	(a)	Falkirk	W 3-1	McGowan 2, Brown	12,000	1	2		4	5			8		10	11	6	7		3						9				
14		15	(a)	Queen's Park	W 2-0	Marshall 2	25,000	1	2		4	5			8		10	11	6	7		3						9				
15		22	(h)	Morton	W 7-1	McGowan 2, McPhail, Craig, Morton, Marshall, Gray (pen)	10,000	1	2	3	4	5			8		10	11	6	7								9				
16		29	(h)	Clyde	W 5-1	McPhail 2, McGowan, Marshall, Fleming	10,000	1	2		4	5	6		8		10	11		7		3						9				
17	Dec	6	(a)	Hibernian	W 2-1	McPhail 2	20,000	1	2		4	5	6	7	8		10	11				3						9				
18		13	(h)	East Fife	W 4-0	Marshall 2, McGowan 2	10,000	1	2		4	5	6	7	8			11				3						9	10			
19		20	(h)	Cowdenbeath	W 7-0	McGowan 2, Marshall 2, McPhail 2, Archibald	16,000	1	2		4	5	6	7	8		10	11				3						9				
20		27	(a)	Hearts	L 0-3		37,000	1	2		4	5	6	7	8		10	11				3						9				
21	Jan	1	(h)	Celtic	W 1-0	Morton	83,500	1	2		4				8		10	11		7	3	5					6	9				
22		3	(h)	Dundee	W 3-0	Marshall, Fleming, McPhail	20,000	1	2	6	4			7	8		10	11		9	3	5										
23		10	(a)	Motherwell	L 0-1		26,000	1	2	6	4			7	8		10	11			3	5						9				
24		24	(h)	St Mirren	D 1-1	McPhail	15,000		2		4	5			8		10	11		9	3				7	6						1
25	Feb	7	(h)	Airdrieonians	L 0-1		14,000		2		4	5			8			11		7	3						6	9	10			
26		14	(a)	Clyde	W 8-0	Smith 5, Meiklejohn, Marshall, McPhail	15,000	1	2		4		6	7	8	9	10				3	5					11					
27		18	(a)	Ayr U	D 2-2	Smith, Marshall	7,000	1	2	6	4			7	8	9	10				3	5					11					
28		21	(h)	Kilmarnock	W 1-0	Marshall	10,000	1	2	6	4			8	7	10	9				3	5					11					
29		28	(a)	Hamilton A	W 3-0	Marshall 2, Smith	10,000	1	2		4		6	7	8	9	10				3	5					11					
30	Mar	7	(a)	Aberdeen	W 3-1	Smith, Archibald, Marshall	10,000	1	2		4		6	7	8	9	10	11			3	5										
31		14	(a)	Leith A	W 3-1	McPhail, Archibald, Morton	9,000	1	2		4		6	7		9	10	11	8		3	5										
32		18	(h)	Falkirk	W 1-0	Smith	9,000	1	2		4		6	7	8	9	10	11			3	5										
33	Apr	1	(h)	Queen's Park	W 2-0	Smith, McPhail	10,000	1	2		4	5	6	7	8	9	10	11			3											
34		4	(a)	Morton	W 2-1	Archibald, Brown	14,000	1	2		4	5	6	7	8	9	10	11			3											
35		6	(h)	Air U	W 5-1	McPhail 2, Marshall 2, Morton	14,000	1	2		4	5	6	7	8	9	10	11			3											
36		18	(h)	Hibernian	W 1-0	Smith	10,000	1	2		4	5	6	7	8	9	10				3						11					
37		22	(a)	Partick Thistle	D 1-1	McPhail	43,400	1	2		4	5	6	7	8	9	10	11							3							
38		25	(a)	East Fife	W 4-0	McPhail, Smith, Marshall, Archibald	8,000	1	2			5	4	7	8	9	10	11	6						3							
				FINAL LEAGUE POSITION: 1st			Appearances	37	38	26	13	31	29	28	32	21	34	32	14	13	27	12	3	1	2	4	6	12	2	1		
							Goals		2			1	3	6	20	21	20	7	1	5								10				

Scottish FA Cup

#	Date		V	Opponent	Result	Scorers	Att	Hamilton T	Gray	Buchanan	McDonald	Meiklejohn	Brown	Archibald	Marshall	Smith	McPhail	Morton	Craig	Fleming	Hamilton R	Simpson	McAulay R	McMillan	Main	Murray	Nicholson	McGowan	Conlin	Dawson	Purdon	Lockie
1	Jan	17	(a)	Armadale T	W 7-1	Fleming 3, McPhail 2, Morton (pen), Marshall	5,527	1	2	6	4			7	8		10	11		9	3	5										
2		31	(h)	Dundee	L 1-2	Fleming	17,000	1	2	6	4	5			8		10	11		7	3							9				
							Appearances	2	2	2	2	1			1	2		2	2		2	2	1					1				
							Goals								1		2	1		4												

Glasgow Cup

#	Date		V	Opponent	Result	Scorers	Att	Hamilton T	Gray	Buchanan	McDonald	Meiklejohn	Brown	Archibald	Marshall	Smith	McPhail	Morton	Craig	Fleming	Hamilton R	Simpson	McAulay R	McMillan	Main	Murray	Nicholson	McGowan	Conlin	Dawson	Purdon	Lockie
1	Sep	9	(h)	Third Lanark	W 2-1	McPhail, Nicholson	8,000	1	2		4				8	9	10		6	7	3	5					11					
SF		29	(h)	Queen's Park	W 1-0	Smith	30,000	1	2	3	4				8	9	10	11	6			5			7							
F	Oct	11	(n*)	Celtic	L 1-2	Smith	71,806	1	2	3		5	4	7	8	9	10	11	6													
	*Played at Hampden Park, Glasgow.						Appearances	3	3	3	1	1	2	1	2	3	3	2	3	1	1	2			1							
							Goals									2	1										1					

Glasgow Merchants' Charity Cup

#	Date		V	Opponent	Result	Scorers	Att	Hamilton T	Gray	Buchanan	McDonald	Meiklejohn	Brown	Archibald	Marshall	Smith	McPhail	Morton	Craig	Fleming	Hamilton R	Simpson	McAulay R	McMillan	Main	Murray	Nicholson	McGowan	Conlin	Dawson	Purdon	Lockie
1	May	2	(n*)	Celtic	D 2-2	Morton (pen), Smith	40,012	1	2		4	5	6	7	8	9	10	11				3										
SF		6	(h)	Partick Thistle	W 1-0	Smith	16,000	1	2		4	5	6	7		9	10	11	8			3										
F		9	(a)	Queen's Park	W 2-1	Smith, Marshall	26,000	1	2		4	5		7	8	9	10	11	6			3										
	*Played at Hampden Park, Glasgow. Rangers won 3-1 on corners.						Appearances	3	3		3	3	3	3	2	3	2	3	2			3										
							Goals								1	3		1														

Other matches

#	Date		V	Opponent	Result	Scorers	Att	Hamilton T	Gray	Buchanan	McDonald	Meiklejohn	Brown	Archibald	Marshall	Smith	McPhail	Morton	Craig	Fleming	Hamilton R	Simpson	McAulay R	McMillan	Main	Murray	Nicholson	McGowan	Conlin	Dawson	Purdon	Lockie
1	Aug	12	(a)	Dumbarton	W 3-1	McGowan 2, McMillan	3,000													4	3	8	7	6	11	9	10	1	2	5		
2		19	(a)	Partick Thistle*	D 1-1	Nicholson	1,000				4		8							5	3		7	6	11	9	10	1	2			
3	Sep	15	(a)	Linfield	D 0-0		15,000	1	2		4			7	8	9	10		6		3	5					11					
	* David Ness Benefit Match.						Appearances	1	1	1	1		1	1	1	1	1		1	1	3	2	2	1	2	3	2	2	2	2	1	
							Goals																	1		1	2					

1931-32

Manager: W.Struth

Column headers (players): Hamilton T, Gray, McAulay R, McDonald, Meiklejohn, Brown, Archibald, Marshall, English, McPhail, Nicholson, Hamilton R, Craig, Smith, Morton, Dawson, Fleming, Simpson, Murray, Deans, Main

Scottish League

#		Date		Opponent	Result	Scorers	Att	HamiltonT	Gray	McAulayR	McDonald	Meiklejohn	Brown	Archibald	Marshall	English	McPhail	Nicholson	HamiltonR	Craig	Smith	Morton	Dawson	Fleming	Simpson	Murray	Deans	Main
1	Aug	8	(h)	Dundee	W 4-1	English 2, Marshall, Nicholson	30,000	1	2	3	4	5	6	7	8	9	10	11										
2		11	(h)	Airdrieonians	W 2-1	Smith 2	10,000	1		2		5	4	7	8		10		3	6	9	11						
3		15	(a)	Motherwell	L 2-4	Fleming, Smith	25,000		2	3	4	5	8			10	11			6	9		1	7				
4		18	(h)	Morton	W 7-3	English 5, McPhail 2	10,000		2	3	4	5	6			8	9	10	11				1	7				
5		22	(h)	St Mirren	W 4-0	English, Brown, Meiklejohn, Nicholson	25,000		2	3		4	6			8	9	10	11				1	7	5			
6		25	(h)	Leith A	W 4-0	Fleming 2, McPhail, English	6,000		2	3		4	6			8	9	10				11	1	7	5			
7		29	(a)	Ayr U	W 3-1	English 2, McPhail	13,000		2	3		4	6			8	9	10	11				1	7	5			
8	Sep	2	(a)	Falkirk	W 2-1	English, McPhail	13,000		2	3		4	6			8	9	10	11				1	7	5			
9		5	(h)	Celtic	D 0-0		80,000		2	3		4	6			8	9	10				11	1	7	5			
10		12	(a)	Partick Thistle	W 3-1	McPhail, Fleming, Calderwood (og)	30,000		2	3		4	6			8	9	10	11				1	7	5			
11		15	(h)	Aberdeen	W 4-1	Fleming 2, Nicholson, McPhail	10,000		2	3			6			8	9	10	11	4			1	7	5			
12		26	(a)	Hearts	D 0-0		32,000		2	3		4	6			8	9	10	11				1	7	5			
13	Oct	3	(a)	Cowdenbeath	W 6-1	Meiklejohn 2, Marshall 2, English 2	8,000	1	2			4	6	7	8	9	10			3		11			5			
14		17	(h)	Queen's Park	L 0-1		20,000		2	3		4	6			8	7	10			9	11	1		5			
15		24	(a)	Hamilton A	W 2-1	English, Marshall		1	2	3		4	6	7	8	9	10					11			5			
16		31	(h)	Dundee U	W 5-0	English 3, Murray 2		1	2		4				7	8	9		11	3	6				5	10		
17	Nov	14	(h)	Clyde	D 2-2	McPhail, English	6,000		2	3		4	6	7	8	9	10					11	1		5			
18		21	(a)	Morton	W 2-1	Meiklejohn, English	15,000		2	3		4	6	7	8	9	10							11	5			
19		28	(a)	Leith A	W 5-2	English 3, Craig, Fleming	7,000	1	2	3		4			8	9	10			6	7			11	5			
20	Dec	5	(a)	Falkirk	W 4-0	English 3, Smith	5,000	1	2	3		4	6			8	9	10			7	11			5			
21		12	(a)	Aberdeen	D 0-0		24,000	1	2	3		4	6			8	9	10			7	11			5			
22		19	(a)	Dundee	L 2-4	McPhail, English	15,000	1	2	3		4	8				9	10			6	7			11	5		
23		26	(h)	Motherwell	W 1-0	English	50,000	1	2	3		4	6	7	8	9	10							11	5			
24	Jan	1	(a)	Celtic	W 2-1	Archibald, Marshall	55,000	1	2	3		4	6	7	8	9	10							11	5			
25		2	(h)	Partick Thistle	W 4-0	Fleming 2, McPhail, Marshall (pen)	20,000	1	2	3	4		6	7	8	9	10							11	5			
26		9	(a)	St Mirren	W 2-0	Fleming 2	15,000	1	2	3		4	6	7	8	9	10							11	5			
27		23	(h)	Ayr U	W 6-1	English 3, McPhail 2, Fleming	15,000		2		4	6	7	8	9	10		3					1	11	5			
28	Feb	6	(h)	Hearts	W 4-2	McPhail, Marshall, English, Fleming	30,000	1	2	3		4	6	7	8	9	10							11	5			
29		20	(h)	Third Lanark	W 6-1	McPhail 2, English 2, Archibald, Marshall	25,000	1	2	3		4	6	7	8	9	10					11			5			
30		27	(a)	Queen's Park	W 6-1	English 4, McPhail, Marshall	30,000	1	2	3		4	6	7	8	9	10					11			5			
31	Mar	12	(a)	Dundee U	W 5-0	English 2, Fleming 2, Archibald		1	2	3		4	6	7		9	10							11	5	8		
32		19	(h)	Kilmarnock	W 3-0	McPhail, English, Marshall	25,000	1	2	3		4	6			8	9	10				11		7	5			
33		28	(a)	Third Lanark	L 3-4	English 2, Marshall	40,000	1	2	3		4			7	8	9	10			6	11			5			
34	Apr	2	(a)	Cowdenbeath	W 7-1	McPhail 3, Marshall 2, English, Fleming	7,000	1	2	3		4			7	8	9	10						11	5	6		
35		23	(a)	Clyde	D 1-1	Marshall (pen)	15,000	1	2	3		4	6	7	8	9								11	5	10		
36		25	(a)	Airdrieonians	L 0-3		6,000	1	2	3		4			7	8	9		11		10				5	6		
37		27	(h)	Hamilton A	W 1-0	Meiklejohn	6,000	1		2	5	8				9	10		3			11				6	4	7
38		30	(a)	Kilmarnock	W 4-2	McPhail 2, Marshall, Smith	10,000	1	2	3	4		6	7	8		10				9			11	5			
						Appearances		25	35	36	7	34	32	21	34	35	35	11	5	8	14	13	24	33	6	1	1	
						Goals						5	1	3	15	44	22	3		1	5			16		2		

FINAL LEAGUE POSITION: 2nd

1 own-goal

Scottish FA Cup

#		Date		Opponent	Result	Scorers	Att	HamiltonT	Gray	McAulayR	McDonald	Meiklejohn	Brown	Archibald	Marshall	English	McPhail	Nicholson	HamiltonR	Craig	Smith	Morton	Dawson	Fleming	Simpson
1	Jan	16	(h)	Brechin C	W 8-2	English 3, McPhail 2, Fleming 2, Marshall	6,000	1		2		4	6	7	8	9	10		3					11	5
2		30	(a)	Raith Rovers	W 5-0	English 3, Archibald, Fleming	18,052	1	2	3		4	6	7	8	9	10							11	5
3	Feb	13	(a)	Hearts	W 1-0	Marshall	53,496	1	2	3		4	6	7	8	9	10							11	5
QF	Mar	5	(h)	Motherwell	W 2-0	Murray, McPhail	88,000	1	2	3		4	6			9	10				11		7	5	8
SF		26	(n*)	Hamilton A	W 5-2	Marshall 2, English 2, Archibald	53,000	1	2	3		4	6	7	8	9	10				11				5
F	Apr	26	(n†)	Kilmarnock	D 1-1	McPhail	111,982	1	2	3		4	6	7	8	9	10				11				5
R		20	(n†)	Kilmarnock	W 3-0	Fleming, McPhail, English	105,695	1	2	3		4	6	7	8	9	10							11	5
						Appearances		7	6	7		7	7	6	6	7	7		1		3			5	7
						Goals								2	4	9	5							4	

*Played at Celtic Park, Glasgow. †Played at Hampden Park, Glasgow.

(Goals columns: Murray 1)

Glasgow Cup

#		Date		Opponent	Result	Scorers	Att	Gray	McAulayR	McDonald	Meiklejohn	Brown	Archibald	Marshall	English	McPhail	Nicholson	HamiltonR	Smith	Morton	Dawson	Fleming	Simpson	Murray
1	Sep	10	(h)	Third Lanark	W 4-1	Marshall 2, McPhail, English	10,000	2	3		4	6			8	9	10				11	1		5		7
SF		28	(a)	Celtic	D 1-1	Marshall (pen)	50,160	2	3	4	5	6			8	9	10	11				1	7		
R	Oct	6	(a)	Celtic	D 2-2	Marshall, Archibald	40,000	2	3		4	6	7	8	9	10				11	1		5	
2R		7	(h)	Celtic	W 1-0	Smith	32,000	2	3	4		7	8		10			6	9	11	1		5	
F		10	(a)	Queen's Park	W 3-0	Smith, McPhail, T.M.Harvey (og)	50,376	2	3		4	6		8	6	7	10		9	11	1		5	
						Appearances		5	5	2	4	4	2	5	4	5	1	1	2	4	5	1	4	1
						Goals					1	4	1	2					2					

1 own-goal

Glasgow Merchants' Charity Cup

#		Date		Opponent	Result	Scorers	Att	HamiltonT	Gray	Meiklejohn	Archibald	Marshall	English	McPhail	Nicholson	HamiltonR	Fleming	Simpson
SF	May	7	(h)	Queen's Park	W 3-1	Marshall 3 (2 pens)	14,000	1	2	4	8	6	7	10	9	3	11	5
F		14	(n†)	Third Lanark	W 6-1	McPhail 3, English 2, Fleming	26,710	1	2	5	4	6	7	8	9	10	11	3
						Appearances		2	2	2	2	2	2	2	1	1	2	2
						Goals					3	2	3				1	

†Played at Hampden Park, Glasgow.

1932-33

Manager: W.Struth

Scottish League

FINAL LEAGUE POSITION: 1st

#	Date	V	Opponent	Res	Scorers	Att	Dawson	Gray	Hamilton R	Meiklejohn	Simpson	Brown	Archibald	Marshall	English	McPhail	Morton	Kennedy	Smith	McDonald	Main	Fleming	Hamilton T	Mason	Deans	Stevenson	Craig	Campbell	Russell	Nicholson	Calder
1	Aug 13	(a)	St Mirren	L 0-2		25,000	1	2	3	4	5	6	7	8	9	10	11														
2	17	(a)	Morton	W 3-1	Smith 2, McPhail	16,000	1	2	3		5	6	7	8		10	11	4	9												
3	20	(h)	Ayr U	W 4-1	English 2, McPhail, McLeod (og)	17,000	1	2		3	5	6	7		9	10	11	4	8												
4	23	(h)	Clyde	D 2-2	McPhail, McDonald (pen)	8,000	1	2		3		6		8	9	10		4	5	7	11										
5	27	(a)	Airdrieonians	W 2-1	Fleming 2	12,000		2		3	5	6	7		9			4	8			11	1								
6	31	(h)	Third Lanark	W 5-0	Smith 2, Archibald 2, McPhail	10,000		2		4	5	6	7	8		10			9			11	1	3							
7	Sep 3	(h)	East Stirling	W 4-0	Smith 3, McPhail	10,000		2		4	5	6	7	8		10			9			11	1	3							
8	10	(a)	Celtic	D 1-1	McPhail	60,000		2		4	5	6	7	8	9	10				3		11	1								
9	17	(h)	Partick Thistle	W 3-0	Smith 2, Morton	13,000				4	5	6	7	10			11		9	3			1			2	8				
10	24	(a)	Cowdenbeath	W 3-2	McPhail, Morton, Smith	5,000		2			5	6	7	8		10	11	4	9	3			1								
11	Oct 1	(h)	Motherwell	D 2-2	McPhail 2	55,000		2		4	5	6	7	8	9	10			11	3			1								
12	8	(a)	Dundee	W 3-0	Smith 2, McPhail	6,600		2		4	5	6	7	8	9	10			11	3			1								
13	22	(a)	Hearts	L 0-1		25,000		2		4	5	6	7	8	9	10			11	5			1								
14	29	(h)	Kilmarnock	W 2-0	Archibald, Marshall	9,000		2	3	4		6	7	8	9				11	5			1				10				
15	Nov 5	(a)	Clyde	W 5-0	Marshall 3, McPhail, English	20,000		2		4	5	6	7	8	9	10			11	3			1								
16	12	(h)	Morton	W 6-1	Meiklejohn, English, McPhail, Marshall, Fleming, Smith			2		4	5	6	7	9	8	10				3		11	1								
17	19	(h)	St Johnstone	W 3-0	McPhail 2, Smith			2		4	5	6		8	9	10			7	3			1		11						
18	26	(a)	Falkirk	W 4-1	English, Meiklejohn, Smith, Marshall	12,000		2		4	5	6	7	8	9	10			11	3			1								
19	Dec 3	(h)	Aberdeen	W 3-1	English 2, Marshall	20,000		2		4	5	6	7	8	9	10			11	3			1								
20	10	(a)	Queen's Park	D 0-0		16,000		2			5	6	7	8	9	10		4		3		11	1								
21	17	(h)	Hamilton A	D 4-4	Marshall 2, McPhail, Smith	8,000		2		4	5	6	7	8	9	10			11	3			1								
22	24	(h)	St Mirren	W 4-0	Marshall 2, McPhail, English	15,000		2		4	5	6	7	8	9	10			11	3			1								
23	31	(a)	Ayr U	D 3-3	Smith, Archibald, Fleming	10,000	1	2		4	5	6	7	8					9	3		11					10				
24	Jan 2	(h)	Celtic	D 0-0		42,000	1	2			5	6		8	9	10		4	11	3	7										
25	3	(a)	Partick Thistle	D 0-0		40,000	1	2			5	6		8	9	10		4	11	3	7										
26	7	(h)	Airdrieonians	W 5-1	Smith 2 (1 pen), McPhail 2, Morton	7,000	1	2			5	6		8		10	11	4	9	3		7									
27	14	(a)	East Stirling	W 3-2	Smith 2, Campbell	5,000	1	2			5	6	7	8		10		4	9	3								11			
28	28	(h)	Cowdenbeath	W 4-1	Smith 3, Fleming	7,000	1	2	3	4		6	7	8					9	5		11					10				
29	Feb 11	(a)	Motherwell	W 3-1	Fleming 2, Smith (pen)	30,000	1	2			5	6		8	9	10		4		7		11							3		
30	25	(h)	Dundee	W 6-4	Marshall 2, Fleming 2, Smith, Nicholson	8,000	1	2		4	5	6	7	8		10			9										3	11	
31	Mar 4	(a)	Third Lanark	W 3-1	McPhail 2, English	15,000	1	2			5	6	7	4	9	10			8			11							3		
32	11	(h)	Hearts	D 4-4	McPhail 3, Fleming	28,000	1	2		4	5	6		8		10			9			7							3	11	
33	18	(a)	Kilmarnock	W 6-2	Smith 3, McPhail 2, English	7,000	1	2		4	5	6	7		8	10			9	3		11									
34	25	(a)	St Johnstone	W 2-0	Smith 2	12,000	1	2		4	5	6	7			10			9	3		11						8			
35	Apr 8	(a)	Falkirk	W 5-1	Marshall 2, McPhail, Smith, Fleming	12,000	1	2		4	5	6	7	8		10			9	3		11									
36	15	(a)	Aberdeen	D 1-1	Smith	22,000	1	2		4	5	6	7	8		10			9	3		11									
37	22	(h)	Queen's Park	W 1-0	McPhail	22,000	1	2		4	5	6	7	8	9	10				3		11									
38	29	(a)	Hamilton A	W 4-2	McPhail 2, Fleming, Marshall	4,000	1	2			5	6	7	8		10			9	4		11							3		
			Appearances				20	37	4	31	32	38	28	34	25	31	6	10	34	29	3	21	18	2	1	1	4	2	5	2	
			Goals					2					4	16	10	29	3		33	1		12						1		1	

1 own-goal

Scottish FA Cup

#	Date	V	Opponent	Res	Scorers	Att	Dawson	Gray	Hamilton R	Meiklejohn	Simpson	Brown	Archibald	Marshall	English	McPhail	Morton	Kennedy	Smith	McDonald	Main	Fleming	Hamilton T	Mason	Deans	Stevenson	Craig	Campbell	Russell	Nicholson	Calder
1	Jan 23	(h)	Arbroath	W 3-1	Marshall 2, Smith	5,000	1	2	3	4				8	11	10			9	5	7						6				
2	Feb 4	(h)	Queen's Park	D 1-1	English	30,006	1	2		4	5	6	7	8	9				11	3							10				
R	8	(a)	Queen's Park	D 1-1	Marshall	31,805	1	2			5		7	8		10		4	9	3							6		11		
2R	13	(a)	Queen's Park	W 3-1	Marshall, Fleming, Smith	45,217	1			4	5			8	9	10				3	7	11					6			2	
3	18	(a)	Kilmarnock	L 0-1		32,745	1	2		4	5	6		8	9	10				3	7	11									
			Appearances				5	4	1	4	4	2	2	5	5	1		1	5	5	3	2					4		1	1	
			Goals											4	1				2			1									

Glasgow Cup

#	Date	V	Opponent	Res	Scorers	Att	Dawson	Gray	Hamilton R	Meiklejohn	Simpson	Brown	Archibald	Marshall	English	McPhail	Morton	Kennedy	Smith	McDonald	Main	Fleming	Hamilton T	Mason	Deans	Stevenson	Craig	Campbell	Russell	Nicholson	Calder
1	Sep 7	(a)	Queen's Park	W 6-2	English 3, Fleming 2, Marshall	17,200		2			5	6	7	8	9	10		4		3		11	1								
SF	26	(h)	Third Lanark	W 4-0	English 2, Marshall, McPhail	22,000		2		4	5	6	7	8	9	10	11			3			1								
F	Oct 15 (n*)		Partick Thistle	W 1-0	Marshall	35,552		2		4	5	6	7	8	9	10			11	3			1								
			Appearances					3		2	3	3	3	3	3	3	1	1	1	3		1	3								
			Goals											3	5	1						2									

*Played at Hampden Park, Glasgow.

Glasgow Merchants' Charity Cup

#	Date	V	Opponent	Res	Scorers	Att	Dawson	Gray	Hamilton R	Meiklejohn	Simpson	Brown	Archibald	Marshall	English	McPhail	Morton	Kennedy	Smith	McDonald	Main	Fleming	Hamilton T	Mason	Deans	Stevenson	Craig	Campbell	Russell	Nicholson	Calder
1	May 3	(h)	Third Lanark	W 3-1	Smith, McPhail, Marshall	2,000	1	2			5	6	7	8		10			9	4		11							3		
SF	6	(h)	Partick Thistle	W 2-0	Marshall, Nicholson	8,627	1	2			5	6	7	8		10				4	9								3	11	
F	13	(a)	Queen's Park	W 1-0	Marshall	26,194	1	2			5	6		8		10		4		3	7	9								11	
			Appearances				3	3			3	3	2	3		3		1	1	3	1	3							2	2	
			Goals											3		1			1											1	

Other matches

#	Date	V	Opponent	Res	Scorers	Att	Dawson	Gray	Hamilton R	Meiklejohn	Simpson	Brown	Archibald	Marshall	English	McPhail	Morton	Kennedy	Smith	McDonald	Main	Fleming	Hamilton T	Mason	Deans	Stevenson	Craig	Campbell	Russell	Nicholson	Calder
1	Sep 14	(h)	Newcastle U	W 4-1	English 2, Archibald, McPhail	31,000		2		4	5	6	7	8	9	10				3		11	1								
2	21	(a)	Newcastle U	L 0-5		22,000		2		4	5	6	7	8	9	10	11			3			1								
3	Jan 21	(a)	Rapid Vienna	D 3-3	Smith 2 (1 pen), McPhail	56,000	1	2	3	4		6	7	8	11	10			9	5											
4	Apr 10	(a)	Dolphins	W 3-1	English 2, Simpson	30,000		2		4	5	6	7		9	10	11									8	3				
5	May 17 (a*)		DFB Select	W 5-1	Smith 3, McPhail, Fleming	40,000	1	2			5	6	7	8		10		4	9	3		11									
6	21 (a†)		DFB Select	W 3-1	Smith 2, Marshall (pen)	20,000	1	2			5	6	7	8		10		4	9	3		11									
7	25 (a‡)		DFB Select	W 5-0	Smith, McPhail 2, Fleming	5,000	1	2				6		8	9	10		4	5		7	11							3		
8	28 (a§)		DFB Select	W 3-2	Smith 3	30,000	1	2				6	7	8		10		4	9	5		11							3		
9	31 (a#)		DFB Select	L 1-2	McPhail	30,000	1	2			5	6	7	8		10		4	9	3		11									
10	Jun 4	(a)	Rapid Vienna	L 3-4	Brown, Marshall, McDonald	40,000	1	2			5	6	7	8	9	10		4		3		11									
			Appearances				8	10	1	4	7	10	9	9	6	10	2	6	5	9	1	7	2		1		3				
			Goals								1	1	1	2	6	6			10	1		2									

* Played in Berlin. † Played in Hamburg. ‡ Played in Bochum. § Played in Dresden.
# Played in Munich.

1933-34

Manager: W.Struth

Scottish League

Player columns (left→right): Dawson, Gray, Russell, Meiklejohn, McDonald, Brown, Archibald, Stevenson, Smith, McPhail, Nicholson, Kennedy, Mason, Marshall, Fleming, Cheyne, Simpson, Main, McAuley, Gillick, Venters, Craig, Jenkins, Hamilton T

No	Date		Opponents	Result	Scorers	Att	Daw	Gra	Rus	Mei	McD	Bro	Arc	Ste	Smi	McP	Nic	Ken	Mas	Mar	Fle	Che	Sim	Mai	McA	Gil	Ven	Cra	Jen	Ham
1	Aug 12	(h)	Airdrieonians	W 5-1	Smith 4, Nicholson	10,000	1	2	3	4	5	6	7	8	9	10	11													
2	15	(h)	Ayr U	W 9-1	Smith 6, Stevenson 3	8,000	1	2			5	3	6	7	8	9	10	11	4											
3	19	(a)	Hibernian	D 0-0		21,000	1				5	3	6	7	8	9		4		2	10	11								
4	22	(a)	Clyde	W 6-1	Smith 2, McPhail 2, Archibald, Stevenson	20,000	1	2			5	6	7	8	9	10	11	4				3								
5	26	(h)	Cowdenbeath	W 3-1	Archibald, Smith (pen), McPhail	7,000	1	2		4	5	6	7	8	9	10	11					3								
6	Sep 2	(a)	Motherwell	L 1-2	Stevenson	30,000	1	2	3		5	6	7	8	9	10		4						11						
7	9	(h)	Celtic	D 2-2	McPhail, Smith (pen)	49,000	1	2	3	4	5	6	7	8	9	10	11													
8	13	(h)	Queen of South	W 5-1	Nicholson 3, Stevenson, Smith	7,000	1	2		4	3	6		8	9	10	11						5	7						
9	16	(a)	Ayr U	W 2-0	Fleming 2		1	2		4	3	6				10		11			9		5	7	8					
10	23	(h)	Dundee	W 1-0	McPhail	14,000	1	2			3	6	7	8	9	10	11	4					5							
11	30	(a)	Partick Thistle	W 4-3	Main, Fleming, Brown, Stevenson	20,000	1	2		4	3	6		10						8	9		5	7	11					
12	Oct 7	(h)	St Mirren	W 3-0	McPhail 2, Main	14,000	1	2		4	3	6	7			10				8	9		5	11						
13	21	(h)	Hearts	W 3-1	Smith 2 (1 pen), McPhail	30,000	1	2		4	3	6	7		9	10				8			5	11						
14	28	(a)	Kilmarnock	W 3-1	McPhail, Smith, Marshall	16,000	1	2		4	3	6	7		9	10				8			5	11						
15	Nov 4	(h)	Clyde	W 3-1	Smith 3	10,000	1	2		4	3	6	7		9	10				8			5	11						
16	11	(a)	Queen of South	W 4-0	Smith 3, McPhail	11,040	1	2		4	3	6		8	9	10				7			5	11						
17	18	(a)	St Johnstone	L 1-3	Smith	6,000	1	2		4	3	6	7		9	10				8			5	11						
18	25	(h)	Falkirk	W 3-1	McPhail 2, Smith	12,000	1	2		4	3	6			9	10	11						5	7			8			
19	Dec 2	(a)	Aberdeen	W 2-1	Marshall, Smith (pen)	21,000	1	2		4	3	6			9		11			8			5	7			10			
20	9	(h)	Queen's Park	W 4-0	Smith 2, McPhail, Meiklejohn	10,000	1	2		4	3				9	10	11						5	7			8	6		
21	23	(a)	Airdrieonians	W 7-2	McPhail 3, Fleming 3, Nicholson			2		4	3	6				10	11				9		5	7			8		1	
22	30	(h)	Hibernian	W 6-0	Smith 3, McPhail 2, Venters	6,000		2		4	3				9	10	11						5	7			8	6	1	
23	Jan 1	(a)	Celtic	D 2-2	Venters, McPhail	40,000		2		4	3	6			9	10	11						5	7			8		1	
24	2	(h)	Partick Thistle	D 2-2	Marshall, Main	20,000		2		4	3	6			9	10	11			8			5	7					1	
25	6	(a)	Cowdenbeath	W 4-3	Fleming, Simpson, McPhail, Nicholson	2,000		2		4	3	6				10	11				9		5	7			8			1
26	13	(h)	Motherwell	W 4-2	McPhail 2, Fleming 2	67,000	1	2		4	3	6				10	11			8	9		5	7						
27	27	(h)	Dundee	W 6-0	Fleming 5, Smith	20,000	1	2		4	3	6		11	10					8	9		5	7						
28	Feb 24	(a)	St Mirren	W 2-1	Marshall, Smith	14,000	1	2			3	6			9			4		8	11		5	7			10			
29	Mar 10	(a)	Hearts	W 2-1	Smith, Marshall	26,000	1	2			3	6			9		11			8			5	7			10	4		
30	14	(a)	Hamilton A	W 2-1	McAuley, Main	10,000	1	2			3	6			9		11	4		10			5	7	8					
31	17	(h)	Kilmarnock	D 2-2	Nicholson, Fleming	7,000	1	2		4	3					10	11				9		5	7	8					
32	21	(a)	Third Lanark	W 1-0	Venters	4,000	1	2		4	3	6	7		9		11			8			5				10			
33	24	(h)	St Johnstone	W 3-0	Venters, Smith, Fleming	13,000	1	2		4	3	6			9					8	11		5			7	10			
34	Apr 2	(a)	Third Lanark	W 1-0	Marshall	18,000	1	2			5	3	6		9		11			8				7			10	4		
35	7	(h)	Aberdeen	W 2-1	Smith, Falloon (og)	18,000	1	2			5	3	6		9	10	11			8						7		4		
36	25	(a)	Falkirk	W 3-1	Smith 2, Marshall	15,000		2			3	6			9		11			8			5	7			10	4	1	
37	28	(h)	Hamilton A	W 4-2	Nicholson, Venters, Smith, Meiklejohn			2		4	3	6			9		11			8			5	7			10		1	
38	30	(a)	Queen's Park	D 1-1	Smith	8,000		2		4			7		9		11						3 5	8			10	6	1	

FINAL LEAGUE POSITION: 1st

							Daw	Gra	Rus	Mei	McD	Bro	Arc	Ste	Smi	McP	Nic	Ken	Mas	Mar	Fle	Che	Sim	Mai	McA	Gil	Ven	Cra	Jen	Ham
Appearances							30	37	3	29	38	35	15	11	32	25	26	7	1	21	13	3	29	25	5	2	15	8	7	1
Goals								2				1	2	7	41	22	8			7	16		1	4	1		5			

1 own-goal

Scottish FA Cup

No	Date		Opponents	Result	Scorers	Att	Daw	Gra	Rus	Mei	McD	Bro	Arc	Ste	Smi	McP	Nic	Ken	Mas	Mar	Fle	Che	Sim	Mai	McA	Gil	Ven	Cra	Jen	Ham
1	Jan 20	(h)	Blairgowrie	W 14-2	Fleming 9, Venters 2, Marshall 2, Nicholson	5,000	1	2	3	4							11			8	9		5	7			10	6		
2	Feb 3	(a)	Third Lanark	W 3-0	Smith 3	27,038	1	2		4	3	6			11	10				8	9		5	7						
3	17	(h)	Hearts	D 0-0		69,543	1	2		4	3	6			11	10				8	9		5	7						
R	21	(a)	Hearts	W 2-1	McPhail, Fleming	47,453	1	2			3	6			9	10				8	11		5	7			4			
QF	Mar 3	(h)	Aberdeen	W 1-0	Main	53,000	1	2			3	6			9	10				8	11		5	7			4			
SF	31	(n*)	St Johnstone	W 1-0	Marshall	60,119	1	2		4	3	6			9	10	11			8			5		7					
F	Apr 21	(n*)	St Mirren	W 5-0	Nicholson 2, McPhail, Main, Smith	113,403		2		4	3	6			9	10	11			8			5	7					1	

*Played at Hampden Park, Glasgow.

							Daw	Gra	Rus	Mei	McD	Bro	Arc	Ste	Smi	McP	Nic	Ken	Mas	Mar	Fle	Che	Sim	Mai	McA	Gil	Ven	Cra	Jen	Ham
Appearances							6	7	1	5	6	6			6	6	3			7	5		7	6	1		1	3	1	
Goals															5	2	3			3	10			1			2			

Glasgow Cup

No	Date		Opponents	Result	Scorers	Att	Daw	Gra	Rus	Mei	McD	Bro	Arc	Ste	Smi	McP	Nic	Ken	Mas	Mar	Fle	Che	Sim	Mai	McA	Gil	Ven	Cra	Jen	Ham
SF	Sep 25	(a)	Celtic	D 1-1	Smith	39,763	1	2			3	6		8	9	10		4					11				5	7		
R	Oct 11	(h)	Celtic	W 2-1	Marshall, Stevenson	24,000	1	2		4	3	6		8		10	11			9							5	7		
F	14	(n*)	Clyde	W 2-0	Main, McPhail	23,439	1	2		4	3	6	7			10				8			5	11	9					

*Played at Hampden Park, Glasgow.

							Daw	Gra	Rus	Mei	McD	Bro	Arc	Ste	Smi	McP	Nic	Ken	Mas	Mar	Fle	Che	Sim	Mai	McA	Gil	Ven	Cra	Jen	Ham
Appearances							3	3		2	3	3	1	2	1	3	1	1		2	1		3	3	1					
Goals												1		1	1					1				1						

Glasgow Merchants' Charity Cup

No	Date		Opponents	Result	Scorers	Att	Daw	Gra	Rus	Mei	McD	Bro	Arc	Ste	Smi	McP	Nic	Ken	Mas	Mar	Fle	Che	Sim	Mai	McA	Gil	Ven	Cra	Jen	Ham
SF	May 5	(h)	Partick Thistle	D 1-1†	Smith	14,000	1	2		4	3	6			9		11			8			5	7			10			
F	12	(n*)	Celtic	W 1-0	Main	35,000	1	2		4	3	6			9	10	11			8			5	7						

†Rangers won 7-4 on corners. *Played at Hampden Park, Glasgow.

							Daw	Gra	Rus	Mei	McD	Bro	Arc	Ste	Smi	McP	Nic	Ken	Mas	Mar	Fle	Che	Sim	Mai	McA	Gil	Ven	Cra	Jen	Ham
Appearances							2	2		2	2	2			2	1	2			2			2	2			1			
Goals															1									1						

Other matches

No	Date		Opponents	Result	Scorers	Att	Daw	Gra	Rus	Mei	McD	Bro	Arc	Ste	Smi	McP	Nic	Ken	Mas	Mar	Fle	Che	Sim	Mai	McA	Gil	Ven	Cra	Jen	Ham
1	Sep 20	(h)	Arsenal *	W 2-0	Smith, McPhail	40,000	1	2		4	3	6		8	9	10	11						5	7						
2	27	(a)	Arsenal *	W 3-1	Fleming 2, Marshall	46,000	1	2		4	3	6	7		9	10				8	11		5							

* British Championship.

							Daw	Gra	Rus	Mei	McD	Bro	Arc	Ste	Smi	McP	Nic	Ken	Mas	Mar	Fle	Che	Sim	Mai	McA	Gil	Ven	Cra	Jen	Ham
Appearances							2	2		2	2	2	1	1	2	2	1			1	1		2	1						
Goals															1	1				1	2									

1934-35

Manager: W.Struth

Scottish League

#	Date	Opponent	Result	Scorers	Att	Dawson	Gray	McDonald	Meiklejohn	Simpson	Brown	Main	Macauley	Smith	McPhail	Nicholson	Fleming	Craig	Kinnear	Venters	Cheyne	Gillick	Kennedy	Jenkins	Hay	Roberts	Fiddes	Winning	Drysdale
1	Aug 11 (a)	Dunfermline A	W 7-1	Smith 6, Main	14,000	1	2	3	4	5	6	7	8	9	10	11													
2	18 (h)	Motherwell	W 1-0	Meiklejohn	51,000	1	2	3	4	5	6	7	8	9	10	11													
3	22 (h)	Hearts	W 2-1	Main 2	30,000	1	2	3	4	5	6	7	8		10	11	9												
4	25 (a)	Dundee	L 2-3	Craig, Brown	19,000	1	2	3	4	5	6	7	8	9				10	11										
5	Sep 1 (h)	Partick Thistle	W 4-0	Main, McPhail, Macauley, Smith	20,000	1	2	3	4	5	6	7	8	9	10				11										
6	4 (a)	Kilmarnock	W 3-1	Smith, McPhail, Venters	13,000	1	2	3		5	6	7		9	10	11		4		8									
7	8 (a)	Celtic	D 1-1	Smith	40,000	1	2	3		5	6	7		9	10			4	11	8									
8	15 (h)	Ayr U	W 2-0	McPhail, Macauley	10,000	1	2	3	4	5	6	7	8	9	10	11													
9	22 (a)	St Mirren	W 2-0	McPhail, Smith	10,000	1	2	3		5	6	7	8	9	10	11		4											
10	29 (h)	Hibernian	W 4-2	Smith 2, Meiklejohn, Main	10,000	1	2		4	5		7	8	9	10			6			3	11							
11	Oct 6 (a)	Airdrieonians	W 2-1	Fleming, Simpson	10,000	1	2			5	6	7	8		10		9				3	11	4						
12	20 (a)	Clyde	L 1-2	McPhail	30,000		2		4	5	6	7	8		10		9				3	11		1					
13	27 (a)	Queen of South	W 3-2	Gillick 2, Venters	12,100	1	2	3	4	5	6	7			10	11				8		9							
14	Nov 3 (h)	St Johnstone	W 3-1	Venters 2, Gillick	20,000	1	2	3	4	5	6	7			10	11				8		9							
15	10 (a)	Albion R	W 5-1	Smith 3, Venters, McPhail		1	2	3	4	5	6	7		9	10					8		11							
16	17 (h)	Aberdeen	D 2-2	Smith 2	18,000	1	2	3	4	5	6	7		9	10					8		11							
17	24 (a)	Queen's Park	W 4-0	Smith 3, Gillick	16,000	1	2	3	4	5	6	7	8	9						10		11							
18	Dec 1 (h)	Hamilton A	D 1-1	Gillick	14,000	1	2	3	4	5	6	7		9	10					8		11							
19	8 (a)	Hearts	L 1-4	Gillick	35,000	1	2	3	4	5	6	7		9	10					8		11							
20	15 (h)	Kilmarnock	L 2-3	Venters, Gillick	18,000	1	2		4	5	6	7		9	10					8	3	11							
21	22 (a)	Dunfermline	W 8-1	Smith 4, Macauley, Meiklejohn, Gillick, Crawford (og)	7,000	1	2	3	4	5	6		8	9		11				10		7							
22	25 (h)	Falkirk	W 1-0	Smith	10,000	1	2	3		5	6		8	9		11				10		7	4						
23	29 (a)	Motherwell	D 2-2	Gillick 2	25,000	1	2	3	4	5	6	7			10	11				8		9							
24	Jan 1 (h)	Celtic	W 2-1	Venters, Gillick	83,000	1	2	3		5	6			9	10	11				8		7	4						
25	2 (a)	Partick Thistle	L 0-1		32,000	1	2	3		5	6			9	10	11				8		7	4						
26	5 (h)	Dundee	W 3-1	Gillick, Venters, Macauley (pen)	16,000	1	2	3		5	6	7			10	11				8		9	4						
27	12 (a)	Ayr U	W 4-2	Smith 2, Nicholson, Venters	12,000	1	2	3		5	6		8	9		11				10		7	4						
28	19 (h)	St Mirren	W 1-0	Smith		1	2	3		5	6			9	10	11				8		7	4						
29	Feb 2 (a)	Hibernian	W 2-1	Smith 2	23,000	1	2	6		5		7		9						8		10	4		3	11			
30	16 (a)	Airdrieonians	W 3-1	McPhail 2, Roberts	10,000	1	2		4	5	6	7		9	10					8	3					11			
31	Mar 2 (a)	Falkirk	W 3-0	Smith, Venters, McPhail	15,000	1	2	3	4	5	6			9	10					8		7				11			
32	16 (h)	Queen of South	W 5-0	McPhail 3 (1 pen), Smith 2	10,000	1	2	3	4	5	6	7		9	10					8		11							
33	20 (h)	Clyde	W 4-2	Gillick 2, Smith, McPhail	5,000	1	2	3		5	6	7		9	10					8		11	4						
34	23 (a)	St Johnstone	L 0-2		11,700	1	2	3	4	5	6	7	8	9	10							11							
35	Apr 13 (a)	Aberdeen	W 3-1	Smith, McPhail, Gillick	17,000	1	2	3		5				9	10			6		8		11	4			7			
36	24 (h)	Albion Rovers	D 2-2	Gillick 2	8,000	1	2	3		5	6	7		9	10					8		11	4						
37	27 (a)	Hamilton A	L 1-2	Smith	9,000	1	2			5				9	10					8	3	11	4			7	6		
38	30 (h)	Queen's Park	L 0-1		6,000	1	2	3		5	6			9						10		7	4			11	8		
	FINAL LEAGUE POSITION: 1st			Appearances		37	36	35	22	37	34	27	16	32	30	13	4	6	4	28	6	27	13	1	1	5	3	1	
				Goals					3	1	1	5	4	36	14	1	1	1		10		17				1			

1 own-goal

Scottish FA Cup

#	Date	Opponent	Result	Scorers	Att	Dawson	Gray	McDonald	Meiklejohn	Simpson	Brown	Main	Macauley	Smith	McPhail	Nicholson	Fleming	Craig	Kinnear	Venters	Cheyne	Gillick	Kennedy	Jenkins	Hay	Roberts	Fiddes	Winning	Drysdale
1	Jan 26 (h)	Cowdenbeath	W 3-1	Gillick 2, Main	16,000	1	2	3	4	5	6	7			10					8		9				11			
2	Feb 9 (h)	Third Lanark	W 2-0	Smith 2 (1 pen)	25,000	1	2	3		5	6			9	10					8		7	4			11			
3	23 (h)	St Mirren	W 1-0	Gillick	42,000	1	2	3	4	5	6	7			10					8		9				11			
QF	Mar 9 (a)	Motherwell	W 4-1	Smith 4	29,777	1	2	3	4	5	6	7		9	10					8		11							
SF	30 (n*)	Hearts	D 1-1	Gillick	102,661	1	2	3	4	5	6	7		9	10					8		11							
R	Apr 10 (n*)	Hearts	W 2-0	McPhail, Main	90,428	1	2	3	4	5	6	7		9	10					8		11							
F	20 (n*)	Hamilton A	W 2-1	Smith 2	87,740	1	2	3		5	6	7		9	10					8		11	4						
				Appearances		7	7	7	4	7	7	6		5	7					7		7	2		1	3			
				Goals								2		8	1							4							

*Played at Hampden Park, Glasgow.

Glasgow Cup

#	Date	Opponent	Result	Scorers	Att	Dawson	Gray	McDonald	Meiklejohn	Simpson	Brown	Main	Macauley	Smith	McPhail	Nicholson	Fleming	Craig	Kinnear	Venters	Cheyne	Gillick	Kennedy	Jenkins	Hay	Roberts	Fiddes	Winning	Drysdale
SF	Sep 24 (a)	Celtic	W 2-1	Macauley, Gillick	31,332	1	2		4	5	6	7	8	9	10						3	11							
F	Oct 13 (n*)	Partick Thistle	L 0-1		28,000	1	2	3	4	5	6	7	8	9	10							11							
				Appearances		2	2	1	2	2	2	2	2	2	2						1	2							
				Goals									1									1							

*Played at Hampden Park, Glasgow.

Glasgow Merchants' Charity Cup

#	Date	Opponent	Result	Scorers	Att	Dawson	Gray	McDonald	Meiklejohn	Simpson	Brown	Main	Macauley	Smith	McPhail	Nicholson	Fleming	Craig	Kinnear	Venters	Cheyne	Gillick	Kennedy	Jenkins	Hay	Roberts	Fiddes	Winning	Drysdale
1	May 4 (h)	Third Lanark	W 3-1	Smith, Simpson, Gillick	7,500	1	2	3		5	6		8	9	10							7	4			11			
SF	6 (a)	Partick Thistle	L 0-1		11,800	1	2	3		5	6		8	9	10							7	4			11			
				Appearances		2	2	2		2	2		2	2	2							2	2			2			
				Goals						1				1								1							

Other matches

#	Date	Opponent	Result	Scorers	Att	Dawson	Gray	McDonald	Meiklejohn	Simpson	Brown	Main	Macauley	Smith	McPhail	Nicholson	Fleming	Craig	Kinnear	Venters	Cheyne	Gillick	Kennedy	Jenkins	Hay	Roberts	Fiddes	Winning	Drysdale
1	Aug 14 (h)	Rapid Vienna	W 3-1	Smith, Nicholson, Macauley (pen)	50,000	1	2	3	4	5	6	7	8	9	10	11													
2	27 (a)	Celtic*	W 4-0	Gillick, Main, Fiddes, Kinnear	7,500	1				5		7					6	11	10		3	9	4			8	2		
3	Sep 12 (a)	Arsenal	D 1-1	McPhail	53,000	1	2	3		5	6	7	8		10	11	9	4											
4	18 (h)	Manchester C	W 1-0	Macauley	30,000	1	2	3	4	5	6	7	8	9		11				10									
5	Oct 3 (a)	Manchester C	L 2-4	Fleming, McPhail	25,000	1	2			5	6	7			10		9	4		8	3	11							
				Appearances		5	4	2	2	4	4	5	3	3	3	2	2	3	1	3	2	2	1			1	1		
				Goals								1	2	1	2	1	1		1			1					1		

*Jimmy McGrory Benefit Match.

1935-36

Manager: W.Struth

	Date	Opponents	Result	Scorers	Scottish League	Dawson	Gray	Cheyne	McDonald	Simpson	Brown	Gillick	Venters	Smith	McPhail	Kinnear	MacAuley	Main	Meiklejohn	Roberts	Kennedy	Winning	Latif	Fiddes	McKillop	Drysdale	Wallace	Turnbull	Hill	Ross J	Jenkins	Hay	Campbell	McHarg	Galloway	Stewart J	Stewart E
1	Aug 10 (h)	Arbroath	W 6-0	Smith 3, Gillick, McPhail, Brown	11,000	1	2	3	4	5	6	7	8	9	10	11																					
2	14 (a)	Albion R	W 2-1	Smith, Kinnear	10,000	1	2	3	4	5	6	7	10	9		11	8																				
3	17 (a)	Ayr U	D 2-2	McPhail 2	20,000	1	2	3	4	5	6	11	8	9	10			7																			
4	24 (h)	Dundee	W 4-3	Smith 2, Meiklejohn (pen), McPhail	20,000	1	2	3		5	6	8		9	10	11		7	4																		
5	28 (h)	St Johnstone	W 7-0	Smith 3, Venters 2, McPhail, Gillick		1	2		3	5	6	7	8	9	10				4	11																	
6	31 (a)	Partick Thistle	W 3-1	Smith 2, McPhail	30,000	1	2		3	5	6	7	8	9	10				4	11																	
7	Sep 7 (h)	Airdrieonians	W 5-3	Smith 2, McPhail, Main, Gillick	18,000	1	2		3	5	6	11		9	10		8	7			4																
8	14 (a)	Hibernian	D 1-1	Smith	20,000	1	2		3	5		11		9	10			7	4			6	8														
9	21 (h)	Celtic	L 1-2	Smith	72,000	1	2		3	5	8	10		9				7	4	11		6															
10	28 (a)	Motherwell	W 2-0	Smith, Winning	15,000	1	2	3		5	6	11		9				7	4			10		8													
11	Oct 5 (h)	Dunfermline A	W 6-2	McPhail 2, Gillick 2, Venters, Main	12,000	1	2		3			9	8		10	11		7	4			6			5												
12	19 (h)	Hearts	D 1-1	Brown	26,000	1	2		3	5	6	11	10	9				7	4					8													
13	26 (a)	Clyde	W 4-1	Venters 2 (1 pen), Drysdale 2	14,000	1	2		3	5	6		10			11		7	4					8		9											
14	Nov 2 (h)	Quen's Park	D 3-3	Drysdale 2, Venters	16,000	1	2		3	5	6		10					7						8	4	9	11										
15	9 (a)	Queen of South	W 2-0	McPhail 2	10,700	1	2		3	5	6	11	8		10			7	4							9											
16	16 (h)	Hamilton A	W 3-1	Gillick, Fiddes, Venters	20,000	1	2		3	5	6	11	8	9	10				4					7													
17	23 (a)	Aberdeen	L 0-1		34,500	1	2		3	5	6	11	8		10			7	4							9											
18	30 (h)	Kilmarnock	W 2-1	Main, Venters	8,000	1	2		3	5	6	11	10					7	4					8		9											
19	Dec 7 (a)	St Johnstone	W 2-1	Smith, Gillick	10,000	1	2		3	5	6	11	10	9				7	4					8													
20	14 (h)	Albion R	W 5-1	Main 3, Smith, Venters	9,000	1	2	3		5	6		10	9		11		7	4					8													
21	21 (a)	Arbroath	D 0-0		10,000	1	2	3		5	6		10	9				7	4					8				11									
22	28 (h)	Ayr U	W 6-1	Smith 5, Turnbull	7,000	1	2	3		5	6		8	9	10			7	4									11									
23	Jan 1 (a)	Celtic	W 4-3	McPhail 2, Smith 2	65,000	1	2		3	5			8	9	10				4			6		7				11									
24	2 (h)	Partick Thistle	W 3-1	Smith 2, McPhail	25,000	1	2		3	5			8	9	10						4	6		7				11									
25	4 (a)	Dundee	W 3-0	Venters, McPhail, Smith	25,000	1	2		3	5			8	9	10						4	6		7				11									
26	11 (a)	Airdrieonians	W 2-0	Venters 2	12,000	1	2		3	5			8	9	10				4			6		7				11									
27	Feb 1 (h)	Motherwell	D 0-0		35,000	1	2		3	5	6		8	9	10			7	4									11									
28	15 (a)	Dunfermline A	W 6-2	Fiddes 3, Turnbull, Drysdale, McPhail	9,000	1	2	3			6		8		10				5		4			7		9		11									
29	29 (h)	Third Lanark	W 4-2	Fiddes 2, Meiklejohn (pen), McPhail	15,000	1	2	3		5	6		8	9	10				4					7				11									
30	Mar 14 (h)	Clyde	W 4-1	Smith 2, Turnbull, Venters	21,000	1	2	3		5	6		10	9			8		4					7				11									
31	18 (h)	Hibernian	W 3-0	Venters, Smith, McPhail (pen)	7,000	1	2	3		5			8	9	10						4	6		7				11									
32	21 (a)	Queen's Park	W 3-1	McPhail, Venters, Main	26,000	1	2	3			6		8	9	10	11		7	4							5											
33	Apr 8 (h)	Queen of South	W 2-1	McPhail, Turnbull	5,000	1	2	3		5	6		8		10			7			4					9		11									
34	11 (a)	Hamilton A	L 0-1		12,000	1	2	3		5	6		8	7	10	11					4					9											
35	13 (a)	Third Lanark	W 3-1	McPhail 2, Kinnear	15,000	1	2	3		5					10	11	8				4	6						9	7								
36	22 (a)	Hearts	D 1-1	Turnbull	48,000	1	2	3		5	6		10		9	11	8		4									7									
37	25 (a)	Kilmarnock	W 3-0	Kinnear, Venters, Macauley	8,000	1	2	3		5			10	9		11	8				4	6						7									
38	29 (h)	Aberdeen	L 2-3	McPhail, Venters	12,000	1	2	3		5			8	9	10	11					4	6						7									
	FINAL LEAGUE POSITION: 2nd				Appearances	38	38	19	22	35	28	17	32	28	26	12	6	20	25	3	10	12	1	17	2	9	1	16	1								
					Goals						2	7	17	31	23	3	1	7	2			1		6		5		5									

Scottish FA Cup

	Date	Opponents	Result	Scorers	Att	Dawson	Gray	Cheyne	McDonald	Simpson	Brown	Gillick	Venters	Smith	McPhail	Kinnear	MacAuley	Main	Meiklejohn	Roberts	Kennedy	Winning	Latif	Fiddes	McKillop	Drysdale	Wallace	Turnbull	Hill	Ross J	Jenkins	Hay	Campbell	McHarg	Galloway	Stewart J	Stewart E
1	Jan 29 (h)	East Fife	W 3-1	Smith 2, Venters	3,000	1	2		3	5	6		8	9	10				4					7				11									
2	Feb 8 (a)	Albion R	W 3-1	Smith 3	27,381	1	2		3	5	6		8	9	10				4					7				11									
3	22 (a)	St Mirren	W 2-1	McPhail, Smith	43,308	1	2	3		5	6		8	9	10				4					7				11									
QF	Mar 7 (a)	Aberdeen	W 1-0	Turnbull	41,663	1	2	3		5	6		8	9	10				4					7				11									
SF	28(n*)	Clyde	W 3-0	Meiklejohn, McPhail, Main	56,243	1	2	3		5	6		8	9	10			7	4									11									
F	Apr 18(n*)	Third Lanark	W 1-0	McPhail	88,859	1	2	3		5	6		8	9	10				4					7				11									
	*Played at Hampden Park, Glasgow.				Appearances	6	6	4	2	6	6		6	6	6			1	6					5				6									
					Goals								1	6	3			1	1									1									

Glasgow Cup

	Date	Opponents	Result	Scorers	Att	Dawson	Gray	Cheyne	McDonald	Simpson	Brown	Gillick	Venters	Smith	McPhail	Kinnear	MacAuley	Main	Meiklejohn	Roberts	Kennedy	Winning	Latif	Fiddes	McKillop	Drysdale	Wallace	Turnbull	Hill	Ross J	Jenkins	Hay	Campbell	McHarg	Galloway	Stewart J	Stewart E
1	Sep 11 (h)	Queen's Park	W 2-0	McPhail, Smith	13,000	1	2		3	5		11		9	10		8	7	4			6															
SF	30 (h)	Clyde	W 2-0	Meiklejohn, Gillick	15,000	1	2	3		5	6	11	10	9				7	4					8													
F	Oct 12(n*)	Celtic	W 2-0	Fiddes, Gillick	50,000	1	2		3	5	6	11	10	9				7	4					8													
	*Played at Hampden Park, Glasgow.				Appearances	3	3	1	2	3	2	3	2	3	1		1	3	3			1		2													
					Goals							2		1	1				1					1													

Glasgow Merchants' Charity Cup

	Date	Opponents	Result	Scorers	Att	Dawson	Gray	Cheyne	McDonald	Simpson	Brown	Gillick	Venters	Smith	McPhail	Kinnear	MacAuley	Main	Meiklejohn	Roberts	Kennedy	Winning	Latif	Fiddes	McKillop	Drysdale	Wallace	Turnbull	Hill	Ross J	Jenkins	Hay	Campbell	McHarg	Galloway	Stewart J	Stewart E
1	May 2 (h)	Third Lanark	W 1-0	Ross	12,000	1	2	3		5	6		8	9	10	11			4											7							
SF	5(n†)	Clyde	W 1-0	Smith	4,933	1	2	3		5	6		8	9	10						4							11		7							
F	9(n*)	Celtic	L 2-4	Turnbull, McPhail	43,162	1	2	3		5			8	9	10				4			6						11		7							
	†Played at Cathkin Park. *Played at Hampden Park, Glasgow.				Appearances	3	3	3		3	2		3	3	3	1			2		1	1						2		3							
					Goals									1	1													1		1							

Other matches

	Date	Opponents	Result	Scorers	Att	Dawson	Gray	Cheyne	McDonald	Simpson	Brown	Gillick	Venters	Smith	McPhail	Kinnear	MacAuley	Main	Meiklejohn	Roberts	Kennedy	Winning	Latif	Fiddes	McKillop	Drysdale	Wallace	Turnbull	Hill	Ross J	Jenkins	Hay	Campbell	McHarg	Galloway	Stewart J	Stewart E
1	Sep 4 (a)	Sheffield W	D 1-1	Main	23,986	1	2		3	5	6	11		9	10		8	7	4																		
2	18 (h)	Sheffield W	W 2-0	Smith 2	30,000	1			3	5	4	11		9	10		8	7				6				2											
3	25 (h)	Arsenal	D 2-2	Smith, Kinnear	30,000	1	2	3		5	6	9		10		11		7	4					8													
4	Oct 7 (a)	Raith Rovers	W 4-1	Galloway 2, Wallace, Kinnear				3			7					11									6	5	8				1	2	4	9	10		
5	Apr 30 (a)	Falkirk*	L 0-3			1			3													6	7		4	5	11								10	2	9
	* Hugh Hamill Benefit Match				Appearances	4	2	2	3	3	4	3		3	2	2	2	3	2			2	1	1	2	3	2				1	1	1	1	2	1	1
					Goals									3		2		1									1								2		

McKenzie played number-8 in Match 5 and was substituted by Hart.

1936-37

Manager: W.Struth

Scottish League

No.	Date	Opponent	Result	Scorers	Att	Dawson	Gray	Cheyne	Kennedy	Simpson	Brown	Soutar	Venters	Smith	McPhail	Kinnear	McKillop	Main	Drysdale	Fiddes	Macauley	Reid	McDonald	Thornton	Winning	Turnbull
1	Aug 8 (a)	Dundee	D 0-0		22,000	1	2	3	4	5	6	7	8	9	10	11										
2	15 (h)	Third Lanark	W 3-1	McPhail 3	16,000	1	2	3	4		6		8	9	10	11	5	7								
3	19 (h)	Dundee	W 3-0	Smith 2, McPhail	12,000	1	2	3	4		6		8	9	10	11		7	5							
4	22 (a)	Falkirk	W 2-0	Smith, McPhail	22,000	1	2	3	4		6		8	9	10	11		7	5							
5	29 (h)	Hibernian	W 4-0	Smith 2, McPhail, Main	12,000	1	2	3	4		6		8	9	10	11		7	5							
6	Sep 5 (a)	Arbroath	D 0-0		7,000	1	2	3	4		6	7	10	9		11			5	8						
7	9 (a)	Third Lanark	D 0-0		25,000	1	2	3	4	5	6	7	10						9		8	11				
8	12 (h)	Motherwell	W 3-2	Venters 3	45,000	1	2	3	4		6		10	9		11			5	7	8					
9	19 (a)	Celtic	D 1-1	Venters	60,000	1	2	3	4	5	6		10	9		11		8		7						
10	26 (h)	Dunfermline A	W 5-3	McPhail 3 (1 pen), Fiddes, Smith	8,000	1	2	3		5	6		4	9	10	11		8		7						
11	Oct 3 (a)	St Mirren	W 4-1	Smith 2, Kinnear, Venters	25,000	1	2	3	4	5	6	7	10	9		11		8								
12	17 (h)	Queen's Park	D 1-1	Cheyne	18,000	1	2	3	4	5	6	7	8	9	10	11										
13	24 (a)	Queen of South	D 1-1	McPhail	5,000	1	2	3	4	5	6	7	8	9	10	11										
14	Nov 7 (h)	Aberdeen	W 2-1	McPhail 2	60,000	1	2		4	5	6	7	8	9	10	11							3			
15	14 (a)	Kilmarnock	W 2-1	Smith, Main	15,000	1	2			5	4		6	9	10	11		7			8		3			
16	21 (h)	St Johnstone	D 0-0		10,000	1	2		4	5	6		8	9	10	11		7					3			
17	28 (a)	Albion R	W 3-2	Kinnear, Smith, Simpson		1	2		4	5	6			9	10	11		7			8		3			
18	Dec 5 (a)	Hearts	L 2-5	Smith, Kinnear	40,000	1	2			4	5		6	9	10	11		7			8		3			
19	12 (h)	Clyde	W 2-0	Smith, Brown	10,000	1			4	5	6	7	10	9	8	11			2				3			
20	19 (h)	Falkirk	W 3-0	Smith 2, McPhail	10,000	1		3		5	6	7	10	9	8	11	4						2			
21	26 (h)	Hibernian	W 4-1	McPhail (pen), Smith, Main, Venters	25,000	1	2			5	6		10	9	8	11	4	7					3			
22	Jan 1 (h)	Celtic	W 1-0	Venters	95,000	1	2			5	6		10	9	8	11	4	7					3			
23	2 (a)	Partick Thistle	W 1-0	Kinnear	25,000	1	2		4	5	6		10	9	8	11							3	7		
24	4 (h)	Hearts	L 0-1		31,000	1	2	3		5	6	7	10	9	8	11	4									
25	9 (a)	Arbroath	W 4-0	Smith 2, McPhail (pen), Thornton	14,000	1	2	3		5	6		10	9	8	11	4							7		
26	16 (a)	Motherwell	W 4-1	Smith, McKillop, McPhail	22,000	1	2	3		5	6		10	9	8	11	4							7		
27	23 (h)	St Mirren	W 2-0	Venters, Smith	16,000	1	2			5			10	7	8	11	4						3	9	6	
28	Feb 6 (a)	Dunfermline A	W 3-2	Kinnear, Smith, McPhail	8,000	1	2		4		6		10	9	8	11	5	7					3			
29	20 (h)	Queen's Park	D 1-1	Smith	12,000	1	2			5	6		10	9	8	11	4	7					3			
30	27 (h)	Kilmarnock	W 8-0	Smith 3, McPhail 3, Macauley, Main	7,000	1	2			5	6			9	10	11	4	7			8		3			
31	Mar 6 (a)	Queen of South	W 1-0	Smith	11,000	1	2			5	6			9	10	11	4	7			8		3			
32	20 (a)	Aberdeen	D 1-1	Main	30,000	1	2			5	6		8	9	10	11	4	7					3			
33	24 (a)	Hamilton A	W 4-0	Venters, McPhail (pen), Smith, Simpson	6,000	1	2		4	5	6		8	9	10	11		7					3			
34	29 (h)	Partick Thistle	W 3-1	Venters, Kinnear, McPhail	18,000	1	2			5	6		8	9	10	11	4						3	7		
35	Apr 3 (a)	St Johnstone	W 2-1	McPhail, Smith	8,000	1	2			5	6		8	9	10	11	4	7					3			
36	7 (a)	Hamilton A	W 5-1	Smith 2, McPhail, Main, Kinnear	5,000	1	2			5				9	10	11	4	7			8		3		6	
37	10 (h)	Albion R	W 1-0	McPhail (pen)	5,000	1	2		4	5	6			9	10	11		7			8		3			
38	23 (a)	Clyde	L 2-3	Smith, Kinnear	9,000	1	2			5	6		8	9	10	11	4	7					3			
	FINAL LEAGUE POSITION: 1st				Appearances	38	36	17	21	31	35	10	33	37	33	37	17	23	7	4	9	1	22	5	2	
					Goals			1		2	1		10	31	25	8	1	6		1	1			1		

Scottish FA Cup

No.	Date	Opponent	Result	Att	Dawson	Gray	Cheyne	Kennedy	Simpson	Brown	Soutar	Venters	Smith	McPhail	Kinnear	McKillop	Main	Drysdale	Fiddes	Macauley	Reid	McDonald	Thornton	Winning	Turnbull
1	Jan 30 (a)	Queen of South	L 0-1	13,000	1	2			5	6		10	9	8	11	4	7					3			
			Appearances		1	1			1	1		1	1	1	1	1	1					1			
			Goals																						

Glasgow Cup

	Date	Opponent	Result	Scorers	Att	Dawson	Gray	Cheyne	Kennedy	Simpson	Brown	Soutar	Venters	Smith	McPhail	Kinnear	McKillop	Main	Drysdale	Fiddes	Macauley	Reid	McDonald	Thornton	Winning	Turnbull
1	Aug 26 (h)	Queen's Park	W 4-1	McPhail 2 (1 pen), Venters, Smith	18,000	1	2	3	4		6		8	9	10	11		7	5							
SF	Sep 28 (h)	Celtic	W 2-1	Smith, McPhail	65,000	1	2	3		5	6		4	9	10	11		8		7						
F	Oct 10 (h)	Partick Thistle	D 2-2	McPhail, Smith	40,000	1	2	3	4	5	6		8	9	10	11		7								
R	Nov 11 (h)	Partick Thistle	W 6-1	Smith 3, McPhail, Main, Kinnear	15,000	1	2		4	5			6	9	10	11		7			8		3			
			Appearances			4	4	3	3	3	3		4	4	4	4		4	1	1	1		1			
			Goals										1	6	5	1		1								

Glasgow Merchants' Charity Cup

	Date	Opponent	Result	Att	Dawson	Gray	Cheyne	Kennedy	Simpson	Brown	Soutar	Venters	Smith	McPhail	Kinnear	McKillop	Main	Drysdale	Fiddes	Macauley	Reid	McDonald	Thornton	Winning	Turnbull
1	May 1 (h)	Queen's Park	L 0-3	10,000	1	2			5	6		8	9		11	4						3	7	10	
			Appearances		1	1			1	1		1	1		1	1						1	1	1	
			Goals																						

Other matches

	Date	Opponent	Result	Scorers	Att	Dawson	Gray	Cheyne	Kennedy	Simpson	Brown	Soutar	Venters	Smith	McPhail	Kinnear	McKillop	Main	Drysdale	Fiddes	Macauley	Reid	McDonald	Thornton	Winning	Turnbull
1	Aug 12 (h)	Austria Vienna	W 4-1	McPhail 3 (1 pen), Simpson	50,000	1	2	3		5	6		8	9	10	11	4	7								
2	Sep 23 (a)	Arsenal	L 1-2	Kinnear	35,000	1	2	3	4	5			6	9		11			7	8				10		
3	Apr 27 (a)	Irish League*	D 1-1	Smith	10,000	1	2			5			6	9	10	11	4	7			8		3			
* Distillery Football Club Benefit Match played at Windsor Park, Belfast.				Appearances		3	3	2	1	3	1		3	3	2	3	2	2		1	2		1		1	
				Goals						1				1	3	1										

1937-38

Manager: W.Struth

Scottish League

Player columns: Dawson, Gray, McDonald, McKillop, Simpson, Brown, Main, Venters, Smith, McPhail, Kinnear, Reid, Cheyne, Ross R, Thornton, Winning, Jenkins, Fiddes, Harrison, Drysdale, Turnbull, Galloway, Sowerby, Lyness, Little

#	Date	Opponent	Result	Scorers	Att	Dawson	Gray	McDonald	McKillop	Simpson	Brown	Main	Venters	Smith	McPhail	Kinnear	Reid	Cheyne	Ross R	Thornton	Winning	Jenkins	Fiddes	Harrison	Drysdale	Turnbull	Galloway	Sowerby	Lyness	Little
1	Aug 14 (h) Falkirk	D 0-0		20,000	1	2	3	4	5	6	7	8	9	10	11														
2	18 (h) Motherwell	W 2-1	Smith, McPhail	22,000	1	2	3	4	5	6	7	8	9	10		11													
3	21 (a) Hibernian	D 0-0		31,000	1	2			5	6	7	8	9	10		11	3	4											
4	25 (a) Falkirk	W 1-0	Reid	24,000	1	2		4	5	6	7	8		10		11	3		9										
5	28 (h) St Johnstone	D 2-2	Thornton, Main	20,000	1	2		4	5	6	7	8		10		11	3		9										
6	Sep 4 (a) Motherwell	D 1-1	Main	25,000	1	2			5	6	7	10		8	11		4	9	3										
7	11 (h) Celtic	W 3-1	Venters 2, Thornton	80,000	1	2		4	5	6	7	10		8	11			9	3										
8	15 (h) Hibernian	W 2-0	Kinnear, Smith (pen)	12,000	1	2			5	6	8	10	9		11		4	7	3										
9	18 (a) Ayr U	D 1-1	McPhail	16,000	1	2			5	6	7	10		8	11		4	9	3										
10	25 (h) St Mirren	W 4-0	Smith 2, Kinnear, McPhail	12,000	1	2			5	6	7	10	9	8	11		4		3										
11	Oct 2 (a) Third Lanark	W 2-1	Smith, McPhail	19,000		2			5	6	7	10	9	8	11		4		3	1									
12	9 (h) Dundee	W 6-0	Smith 4, Kinnear, Venters	30,000	1	2		4	5	6	7	10	9		11			3			8								
13	23 (h) Hamilton A	D 2-2	Reid, Smith	12,000	1	2		4	5	6	7		9	10		11			3		8								
14	Nov 6 (h) Kilmarnock	W 4-1	Smith 2, Venters 2	12,000	1	2		4	5	6		10	9	8	11			3		7									
15	13 (a) Arbroath	D 1-1	Smith	9,000	1	2		4	5	6	7	10	9		11			3		8									
16	20 (h) Morton	W 3-1	Smith 2, Kinnear	8,000	1	2		4	5	6	8	10	9		11			3	1	7									
17	27 (h) Hearts	L 0-3		51,000	1	2		4	5	6	7	10	8		11			9	3										
18	Dec 4 (a) Clyde	D 1-1	Smith	20,000		2		4	5	6		10	9		11			7	3	1	8								
19	11 (h) Queen's Park	W 2-1	Smith, Venters	10,000		2		4	5	6		10	9		11			7	3	1	8								
20	25 (a) St Johnstone	W 5-1	Venters 3, Kinnear 2	10,000		2		4	5	6		8	9		11			3	1	7	10								
21	Jan 1 (a) Celtic	L 0-3		83,500		2		4	5	6		8	9	10	11			3	1	7									
22	3 (h) Partick Thistle	L 1-3	Harrison	20,000			3	4	5	6		8	9			11		7		1			10	2					
23	8 (h) Ayr U	D 2-2	Thornton, Reid	20,000				4	5	6	7			8		11		9	3	1			10	2					
24	15 (a) St Mirren	D 1-1	Smith	20,000		2		4	5	6			9	10		11		7	3	1			8						
25	29 (h) Third Lanark	W 3-0	Thornton 2, Harrison	12,000		2		4	5	6	7	8	11					9	3	1			10						
26	Feb 5 (a) Dundee	L 1-6	Venters	12,000		2		4	5	6	7	8	11					9	3	1			10						
27	19 (a) Hamilton A	D 2-2	McPhail, Smith			2		4	5		7	8	9	10			3		6	1					11				
28	26 (h) Aberdeen	D 2-2	Smith 2	35,000	1	2			5		7	6	9	10			3	4							11	8			
29	Mar 5 (a) Queen of South	W 2-0	Main, Kinnear		1	2			5		4	7	6	9	10	11	3								8				
30	12 (a) Kilmarnock	L 1-2	Kinnear	25,000	1			2	5	6			9		11		3					4	10				7	8	
31	23 (a) Arbroath	W 3-1	Lyness (pen), Sowerby, Kinnear		1	2		5				6	9		11		3					4	10				7	8	
32	26 (a) Morton	W 3-2	Kinnear, Main, Venters	8,000	1	2		4	5	6	7	8	9	10	11				3										
33	Apr 9 (a) Clyde	W 1-0	McPhail	7,000	1	2		5			8	6	9	10	11				3		4					7			
34	13 (a) Aberdeen	W 3-0	McPhail, Smith, Main	18,000	1	2		8	5		7	6	9	10			3				4								
35	16 (a) Queen's Park	W 3-0	Kinnear, Venters, McPhail	20,000	1	2			5	4	7	6	9	10	11				3		8								
36	18 (a) Partick Thistle	D 1-1	McPhail	20,000	1	2			5	4	7	6	9	10	11				3			8							
37	23 (a) Hearts	L 2-3	Kinnear, Main	25,000	1	2		5		4	7	6	9	10	11				3			8							
38	30 (a) Queen of South	L 2-3	McPhail, Turnbull	12,000	1	2		5		4	7	6	9	10	11				3						8				
	FINAL LEAGUE POSITION: 3rd			Appearances	26	35	3	29	34	32	29	34	32	25	26	8	9	7	14	27	12	14	10	2	3	2	3	2	
				Goals					6		12	22	10	12	3			5			2			1		1	1	

Scottish FA Cup

#	Date	Opponent	Result	Scorers	Att	Dawson	Gray	McDonald	McKillop	Simpson	Brown	Main	Venters	Smith	McPhail	Kinnear	Reid	Cheyne	Ross R	Thornton	Winning	Jenkins	Fiddes	Harrison	Drysdale	Turnbull	Galloway	Sowerby	Lyness	Little
1	Jan 22 (a) Alloa A	W 6-1	Smith 3, Venters, McPhail, Reid	9,400		2		4	5	6		8	9	10		11		7	3	1									
2	Feb 12 (h) Queen of South	W 3-1	McPhail 2, Reid	50,000		2		4	5	6		10	9	8		11		7	3	1									
QF	Mar 19 (a) Falkirk	W 2-1	Venters, Thornton	20,058	1	2		4	5	6		8						9	3		7	10							
SF	Apr 2 (n*) Kilmarnock	L 3-4	Venters 2, Thornton	70,833	1	2		4	5	6	7	8		10	11			9	3										
	Rangers received a bye in round three.			Appearances	2	4		4	4	4	1	4	2	3	2	2		4	4	2	1	1							
	*Played at Hampden Park, Glasgow.			Goals								4	3	3		2		2											

Glasgow Cup

#	Date	Opponent	Result	Scorers	Att	Dawson	Gray	McDonald	McKillop	Simpson	Brown	Main	Venters	Smith	McPhail	Kinnear	Reid	Cheyne	Ross R	Thornton	Winning	Jenkins	Fiddes	Harrison	Drysdale	Turnbull	Galloway	Sowerby	Lyness	Little
1	Aug 31 (a) Clyde	W 3-1	Venters, Thornton, Main	15,000	1	2			5	6	7	10		8	11		4	9	3										
SF	Sep 27 (a) Celtic	W 2-1	Smith, Venters	55,000	1	2			5	6	7	10	9	8	11		4		3										
F	Oct 16 (n*) Third Lanark	W 2-1	Venters, Smith	39,699	1	2		4	5	6		10	9	8					3		7		11						
	*Played at Hampden Park, Glasgow.			Appearances	3	3		1	3	3	2	3	2	3	2		2	1	3		1		1						
				Goals							1	3	2						1										

Glasgow Merchants' Charity Cup

#	Date	Opponent	Result	Scorers	Att	Dawson	Gray	McDonald	McKillop	Simpson	Brown	Main	Venters	Smith	McPhail	Kinnear	Reid	Cheyne	Ross R	Thornton	Winning	Jenkins	Fiddes	Harrison	Drysdale	Turnbull	Galloway	Sowerby	Lyness	Little
1	May 3 (h) Clyde	W 4-1	Smith 2, Kinnear, McKillop (pen)	6,000	1	2		4	5	6		8	9		11		3				7	10							
SF	7 (h) Third Lanark	W 1-0	Smith	12,000	1	2		4	5	6		8	9		11		3				7	10							
F	14 (n*) Celtic	L 0-2		40,052	1	2		4	5			6	9	8	11		3		7			10							
	*Played at Hampden Park, Glasgow.			Appearances	3	3		3	3	2		3	3	1	3		3		1		2	3							
				Goals				1					3		1														

Empire Exhibition Cup

#	Date	Opponent	Result	Att	Dawson	Gray	McDonald	McKillop	Simpson	Brown	Main	Venters	Smith	McPhail	Kinnear	Reid	Cheyne	Ross R	Thornton	Winning	Jenkins	Fiddes	Harrison	Drysdale	Turnbull	Galloway	Sowerby	Lyness	Little
1	May 30 (h) Everton	L 0-2		47,692	1	2		4	5	6	7	10			11				9	3				8					
				Appearances	1	1		1	1	1	1	1			1				1	1				1					
				Goals																									

Other match

#	Date	Opponent	Result	Att	Dawson	Gray	McDonald	McKillop	Simpson	Brown	Main	Venters	Smith	McPhail	Kinnear	Reid	Cheyne	Ross R	Thornton	Winning	Jenkins	Fiddes	Harrison	Drysdale	Turnbull	Galloway	Sowerby	Lyness	Little
1	Oct 19 (a) Stoke C*	D 0-0		30,000	1	2	3	4	5		7	10	9		11							8					6		
	*Holditch Colliery Disaster Relief Fund Benefit Match.			Appearances	1	1	1	1	1		1	1	1		1							1					1		
				Goals																									

1938-39

Manager: W.Struth

Scottish League

#	Date		Opponents	Res	Scorers	Att.	Dawson	Gray	Shaw	McKillop	Simpson	Brown	Main	Galloway	Smith	Venters	Kinnear	Woodburn	Thornton	McPhail	Ross R	Waddell	Fiddes	Symon	Little	Cheyne	Harrison	Jenkins	Lyness	Turnbull	Reid	Gilmour
1	Aug 13	(a)	St Johnstone	D 3-3	Venters 2, Brown	15,000	1	2	3	4	5	6	7	8	9	10	11															
2	20	(h)	Motherwell	D 2-2	Kinnear 2	25,000	1	2	3	4		6	7	8			11	5	9	10												
3	24	(h)	St Johnstone	W 4-2	Venters 2 (1 pen), McPhail, Thornton	18,000	1	2	3			6	7			8	11	5	9	10	4											
4	27	(a)	St Mirren	W 5-1	Thornton 2, Main 2, McPhail	20,000	1	2	3	4		6	7			8	11	5	9	10												
5	Sep 3	(h)	Ayr U	W 4-1	McPhail 2, Thornton, Brown	10,000	1	2	3	4		6					11	5	9	10		7	8									
6	10	(a)	Celtic	L 2-6	Smith, Thornton	74,500	1	2	3	4		6	7		9		11	5	8	10												
7	14	(a)	Motherwell	W 5-0	Thornton 3, Fiddes, Kinnear	16,000	1	2	3	4		6	7				11	5	9	10			8									
8	17	(h)	Third Lanark	W 5-1	Venters 2, Thornton 2, Black (og)	20,000	1	2	3	4		6	7			8	11	5	9	10												
9	24	(a)	Arbroath	D 3-3	Venters, Harrison, Main	10,000	1	2					7			8	11	5	9					4	6	3	10					
10	Oct 1	(h)	Hibernian	W 5-2	Thornton, Symon, Venters, Waddell, Kinnear	15,000	1	2	3		5	6				8	11		9			7		4			10					
11	8	(a)	Falkirk	D 2-2	Venters 2			2		4	5					8	11		9	10		7			6	3		1				
12	15	(h)	Partick Thistle	W 4-1	Venters 2, McPhail, Thornton	30,000	1	2	3		5	6				8	11		9	10		7		4								
13	22	(a)	Kilmarnock	L 1-3	Kinnear	18,000	1	2	3		5					8	11		9	10		7	4	6								
14	29	(h)	Raith Rovers	W 4-0	Venters 3, Thornton	12,000		2	3		5					8	11		9	10		7	4	6				1				
15	Nov 5	(a)	Albion R	W 7-2	Waddell 2, Thornton 2, McPhail, Venters, Kinnear	10,000		2	3		5					8	11		9	10		7	4	6				1				
16	12	(a)	Hearts	W 3-1	Waddell, McPhail, Venters	40,000		2	3		5					8	11		9	10		7	4	6				1				
17	19	(h)	Clyde	W 2-0	Venters, Waddell (pen)	13,000		2	3		5					8	11		9	10		7	4	6				1				
18	26	(a)	Queen's Park	W 3-1	Kinnear, Waddell, Venters	40,000	1	2	3		5					8	11		9	10		7	4	6								
19	Dec 3	(h)	Queen of South	W 4-1	McPhail 3, Kinnear	16,000	1	2	3		5					8	11		9	10		7	4	6								
20	10	(a)	Hamilton A	L 1-2	Venters	17,500	1	2	3		5					8	11		9	10		7	4	6								
21	17	(h)	Aberdeen	W 5-2	Fiddes 4, Venters	30,000	1	2	3	4	5				9	10			8			11	7	6								
22	26	(h)	St Mirren	W 3-0	Thornton, Fiddes, Venters	18,000	1	2	3	4	5					10	11		9			7	8	6								
23	31	(a)	Ayr U	W 4-3	Thornton 2, Venters, Symon	20,000	1	2	3		5	6				10	11		9			7	8	4								
24	Jan 2	(h)	Celtic	W 2-1	Kinnear, Venters	118,730	1	2	3	4	5					10	11		9			7		6	8							
25	3	(a)	Partick Thistle	W 4-2	Venters 2, Turnbull, Lyness	35,000	1	2	3	4	5	6				10			9			7							8	11		
26	11	(a)	Arbroath	W 4-0	Thornton 2, Lyness, Venters	5,000	1	2	3	4	5	6				10			9			7							8	11		
27	14	(a)	Hibernian	D 1-1	Venters	31,000	1	2	3	4	5	6				10			9			7							8	11		
28	28	(h)	Falkirk	W 2-1	Thornton, Smith	30,000	1	2	3		5	6			9	10			8			7		4						11		
29	Feb 11	(a)	Third Lanark	W 2-1	Harrison 2	20,000	1	3	2		5	6							9			7		4			10		8	11		
30	25	(h)	Kilmarnock	D 2-2	McPhail, Smith	10,000	1	3	2		5				9		11		8	10		7	4	6								
31	Mar 4	(a)	Raith Rovers	W 2-0	Thornton, Venters	18,000	1	2	3	4	5	6				10			9	8		11	7									
32	11	(h)	Albion R	W 5-0	Venters 3, McPhail, Thornton	10,000	1	2	3	4	5	6				10			9	8		11	7									
33	18	(h)	Hearts	D 1-1	Smith	40,000	1	2	3	4	5	6			9	10				8		11	7									
34	28	(a)	Clyde	D 1-1	McPhail	10,000	1	2	3	4		6				10		5	9	8		7									11	
35	Apr 1	(h)	Queen's Park	W 1-0	Venters (pen)	20,000	1	2	3	4						10		5	9	8		7		6							11	
36	8	(a)	Queen of South	D 1-1	Symon	9,000	1	2	3	4	5				9	10				8		7		6			11					
37	21	(h)	Hamilton A	W 3-2	Venters 2, Waddell	10,000	1	2	3							10	11	5	9			7		4	6							8
38	29	(a)	Aberdeen	L 0-2		15,002	1	2	3	4						10	11	5	9			7		6								8
			Appearances				33	35	36	25	25	19	8	2	7	33	26	12	36	23	1	27	19	22	4	2	4	5	4	6	2	2
			Goals									2	3		4	35	9		23	13		7	6	3			3		2	1		

FINAL LEAGUE POSITION: 1st

1 own-goal

Scottish FA Cup

#	Date		Opponents	Res	Scorers	Att.	Dawson	Gray	Shaw	McKillop	Simpson	Brown	Main	Venters	Thornton	McPhail	Waddell	Fiddes	Symon	Lyness	Turnbull
1	Jan 21	(a)	Raith Rovers	W 1-0	Venters	21,747	1	2	3	4	5			10	9		7	8	6		11
2	Feb 4	(h)	Hamilton A	W 2-0	Lyness, Venters	75,000	1	3	2		5	6		10	9		7		4	8	11
3	18	(h)	Clyde	L 1-4	Lyness (pen)	63,000	1	3	2		5	6	7		9	10			4	8	11
			Appearances				3	3	3	1	3	2	1	2	3	1	2	1	3	2	3
			Goals											2						2	

Glasgow Cup

#	Date		Opponents	Res	Scorers	Att.	Dawson	Gray	Shaw	McKillop	Simpson	Brown	Main	Venters	Kinnear	Thornton	McPhail	Waddell	Fiddes	Symon
1	Sep 6	(a)	Queen's Park	D 0-0		12,921	1	2	3		5	6	7		11	9	10	8		4
R	21	(h)	Queen's Park	L 2-3	Venters (pen), Fiddes	10,000	1	2	3	4	5			8	11	9	10		7	6
			Appearances				2	2	2	1	2	1	1	1	2	2	2	1	1	2
			Goals											1					1	

Glasgow Merchants' Charity Cup

	Date		Opponents	Res	Scorers	Att.	Gray	Shaw	Smith	Venters	Kinnear	Woodburn	Thornton	McPhail	Waddell	Fiddes	Symon	Little	Jenkins
SF	May 6	(h)	Queen's Park	W 2-1	Waddell, Smith	17,000	3	2	9	10		5		8	11	7	4	6	1
F	13 (n*)		Third Lanark	D 0-0†		29,448	3	2		10	11	5	9	8	7		4	6	1
			Appearances				2	2	1	2	1	2	1	2	2	1	2	2	2
			Goals						1						1				

†Rangers won 7-4 on corners. *Played at Hampden Park, Glasgow.

Other match

#	Date		Opponents	Res	Scorers	Att.	Dawson	Gray	Shaw	McKillop	Simpson	Brown	Smith	Kinnear	McPhail	Waddell	Fiddes
1	Aug 29	(h)	Arsenal	W 1-0	Waddell	41,000	1	2	3	4	5	6	9	11	10	7	8
			Appearances				1	1	1	1	1	1	1	1	1	1	1
			Goals													1	

1939-40

Manager: W.Struth

Player columns (left to right): Dawson, Gray, Shaw, Bolt, Woodburn, Symon, Waddell, Fiddes, Thornton, Venters, Kinnear, McNee, Cowan, McPherson, Gilmour, Simpson, Smith, McKillop, Galloway, Finley, Jenkins, Brown, Little, Duncanson, Ross S, Matthews, Forshaw, McPhail, Nimmo, Marshall, Caskie

Scottish League

No	Date		Venue/Opponent	Result	Scorers	Att.
1	Aug	12	(h) St Mirren	W 5-1	Venters 2 (1 pen), Thornton, Woodburn, Fiddes	35,000
2		19	(a) Ayr U	W 4-0	Thornton 2, Waddell, Venters	20,000
3		22	(a) St Mirren	D 0-0		25,000
4		26	(h) Arbroath	W 3-1	Waddell, Thornton, Venters	15,000
5	Sep	2	(a) Third Lanark	W 2-1	Thornton, Gilmour	30,000

Competition suspended following outbreak of World War Two.

Appearances: 5 5 4 5 4 5 5 3 5 5 1 4 1 1 1 1
Goals: 1 2 1 5 4 1

Scottish Regional League Western Division

No	Date		Venue/Opponent	Result	Scorers	Att.
1	Oct	21	(a) Motherwell	W 1-0	Smith	8,000
2		28	(h) Third Lanark	W 6-0	Smith 3, Thornton 2, McNee	15,000
3	Nov	4	(a) Ayr U	W 2-0	Gilmour, Galloway	8,000
4		11	(h) St Mirren	W 4-0	Thornton, Gilmour, Finlay, McNee	6,000
5		18	(a) Airdrieonians	W 1-0	Venters (pen)	9,000
6		25	(h) Dumbarton	W 2-1	Thornton, Venters	8,000
7	Dec	2	(h) Kilmarnock	W 4-1	Smith 2, Waddell, McNee	5,500
8		9	(a) Clyde	W 1-0	Smith	15,000
9		16	(h) Albion R	W 2-1	Thornton, McNee	13,000
10		23	(a) Hamilton A	L 0-2		12,000
11		30	(a) Morton	L 0-3		8,000
12	Jan	1	(h) Celtic	D 1-1	Waddell	40,000
13		6	(h) Queen's Park	W 4-0	Duncanson 2, Venters, Waddell	
14		13	(a) Queen of South	W 2-1	Venters, Waddell	8,200
15		20	(h) Motherwell	L 1-2	Thornton	3,000
16	Feb	10	(a) St Mirren	W 6-4	Venters 3, Duncanson, McNee, Thornton	11,000
17		17	(h) Airdrieonians	W 3-1	Venters (pen), McKillop, Thornton	10,000
18	Mar	16	(a) Albion R	D 3-3	Thornton, Venters, McNee	10,000
19		25	(h) Partick Thistle	D 2-2	Thornton, Galloway	12,000
20		30	(h) Morton	W 1-0	Venters	20,000
21	Apr	6	(a) Celtic	W 2-1	Venters (pen), Brown	30,000
22		17	(h) Ayr U	W 3-1	McPherson 2, Smith	
23		20	(a) Queen's Park	W 3-2	Smith, Little, Venters	20,000
24		22	(a) Third Lanark	W 1-0	McPhail	
25		24	(a) Dumbarton	W 3-2	McPherson 2, McPhail	
26		27	(a) Queen of South	W 5-1	Smith 3, McPherson, Thornton	
27	May	8	(h) Clyde	W 3-1	McPherson 3	2,000
28		15	(a) Kilmarnock	L 1-3	McPhail	
29		18	(h) Hamilton A	D 2-2	Smith, McPherson	
30		25	(a) Partick Thistle	W 3-1	McPherson 2, Little	6,000
PO*	Jun	1	(h) Falkirk	W 2-1	Venters, Little	15,000

FINAL LEAGUE POSITION: 1st
*Regional League Play-off match

Appearances: 26 26 29 10 30 16 22 1 23 22 3 19 5 11 4 1 16 26 2 3 5 7 10 10 3 1 3 5 1 1
Goals: 4 11 13 6 11 2 13 1 2 1 1 3 3 3

Scottish Emergency War Cup

No	Date		Venue/Opponent	Result	Scorers	Att.
1	Feb	24	(a) Alloa A	W 4-1	Duncanson 2, Thornton 2	7,000
	Mar	2	(h) Alloa A	D 2-2	Venters (pen), Waddell	8,000
2		9	(a) Falkirk	D 0-0		16,000
R		13	(h) Falkirk	W 3-2	Thornton 2, Venters	50,000
QF	Mar	23	(h) St Mirren	W 3-1	Thornton, McNee, Smith	60,000
SF	Apr	13	(n*) Motherwell	W 4-1	Smith 2, Thornton, Venters	57,000
F	May	4	(n*) Dundee U	W 1-0	Smith	90,000

*Played at Hampden Park, Glasgow.

Appearances: 7 7 7 1 7 5 6 7 7 6 3 7 1 1 4 1
Goals: 1 6 3 1 4 2

Glasgow Cup

No	Date		Venue/Opponent	Result	Scorers	Att.
1	Aug	29	(a) Partick Thistle	W 4-0	Thornton 2, McNee, Bolt	22,000
SF	Oct	7	(h) Third Lanark	D 2-2	Gilmour, Thornton	15,000
R		14	(h) Third Lanark	W 2-1	Waddell, Gilmour	15,000
F	Dec	25	(h) Queen's Park	W 3-1	Gilmour, Thornton, McNee	15,000

Appearances: 3 4 4 3 4 1 4 4 4 2 2 4 1 1 2 1
Goals: 1 1 4 2 3

Glasgow Merchants' Charity Cup

No	Date		Venue/Opponent	Result	Scorers	Att.
SF	May	22	(h) Celtic	W 5-1	Caskie 2, Thornton 2, Venters	21,000
F		29	(n*) Clyde	D 1-1†	Venters	12,924

†Rangers won 7-2 on corners. *Played at Hampden Park, Glasgow.

Appearances: 2 2 2 2 2 2 2 2 2 2 1 1 1
Goals: 2 2 2

Other matches

No	Date		Venue/Opponent	Result	Scorers	Att.
1	Sep	23	(h) Falkirk	L 1-4	Venters (pen)	9,000
2		30	(a) Morton	L 2-4	Thornton, Kinnear	5,000

Appearances: 1 2 2 2 2 1 2 1 2 2 2 1 1 1
Goals: 1 1 1

1940-41

Manager: W.Struth

Southern League

No	Date	Venue	Opponent	Result	Scorers	Att
1	Aug 10	(a)	Falkirk	W 3-1	Smith, Johnston, Gillick	12,000
2	17	(h)	Hibernian	W 5-1	Gillick 2, McPherson 2, Marshall	15,000
3	24	(a)	Motherwell	W 3-2	Gillick 2, Johnston	11,000
4	31	(h)	Partick Thistle	W 3-1	Smith 2, Gillick	12,000
5	Sep 7	(a)	Celtic	D 0-0		40,000
6	14	(h)	Airdrieonians	W 2-0	Hamilton, Johnston	
7	21	(h)	St Mirren	W 3-0	Waddell, Venters (pen), Johnston	
8	Oct 5	(h)	Hamilton A	W 2-0	Venters, Johnston	10,000
9	12	(a)	Hearts	D 1-1	Duncanson	
10	19	(h)	Albion R	W 2-0	Venters, Duncanson	
11	26	(a)	Dumbarton	W 4-1	Smith 3, Waddell	10,000
12	Nov 2	(a)	Queen's Park	W 5-0	Smith, Waddell, Johnston, Marshall, Venters	6,000
13	9	(h)	Clyde	W 3-2	Marshall 3	21,000
14	16	(h)	Morton	W 5-4	Smith 3, Bolt (pen), Johnston	
15	23	(h)	Falkirk	W 4-0	Smith 2, Thornton, Venters	10,000
16	30	(a)	Hibernian	L 0-1		15,000
17	Dec 7	(h)	Motherwell	L 2-3	Venters 2	
18	14	(a)	Partick Thistle	W 4-1	Johnston, Gillick, Marshall, Venters	8,000
19	21	(a)	St Mirren	L 0-2		9,000
20	28	(a)	Airdrieonians	W 2-0	Smith 2	9,000
21	Jan 1	(h)	Celtic	L 2-3	Venters, Johnston	33,168
22	4	(a)	Third Lanark	W 1-0	Waddell	6,000
23	18	(h)	Hearts	W 3-0	Beattie, Venters, Smith	
24	25	(a)	Albion R	W 7-2	Smith 5, Beattie 2	7,000
25	Feb 1	(h)	Dumbarton	D 1-1	Smith	7,500
26	8	(h)	Queen's Park	D 1-1	Gillick	8,000
27	15	(a)	Clyde	W 3-0	Smith 2, Gillick	20,000
28	22	(a)	Morton	W 4-2	Johnston 2, Brown, Smith	8,000
29	Apr 12	(a)	Hamilton A	W 4-1	A.McKillop 2, Galloway, Johnston	6,000
30	26	(h)	Third Lanark	L 0-3		5,000

FINAL LEAGUE POSITION: 1st

Player appearances (shirt numbers by match) and totals:

	Dawson	Gray	Shaw	Bolt	Woodburn	Thomson	Waddell	Gillick	Smith	Marshall	Johnston	Jenkins	McPherson	Duncanson	Hamilton	McKillop T	Symon	Venters	Thornton	McIntosh	Brown	Beattie	McKillop A	Galloway	Cowan	Little	Matthews	McDowell
Appearances	25	29	30	27	29	7	13	22	19	17	26	5	2	8	3	4	22	22	2	2	4	5	5	1	1			
Goals				1			4	9	24	6	12		2	2	1			10	1		1	3	2	1				

Southern League Cup Section Three

No	Date	Venue	Opponent	Result	Scorers	Att
1	Mar 1	(h)	Falkirk	W 4-0	Symon, Bolt, Smith, Gillick	12,000
2	8	(a)	Dumbarton	W 8-1	Brown 3, Smith 3, Johnston, Venters	6,000
3	15	(h)	Third Lanark	W 3-0	Venters, Gillick, Brown	8,000
4	22	(a)	Falkirk	L 0-2		9,000
5	29	(h)	Dumbarton	W 6-3	Smith 2, Johnston 2, Gillick, Marshall	4,000
6	Apr 5	(a)	Third Lanark	W 2-1	Venters, Symon	12,000
SF	19	(n*)	St Mirren	W 4-1	Johnston, Thornton, Waddell, Smith	36,823
F	May 10	(n*)	Hearts	D 1-1	Marshall	75,000
R	17	(n*)	Hearts	W 4-2	Venters, Smith, Thornton, Johnston	70,000

*Played at Hampden Park, Glasgow.

	Dawson	Gray	Shaw	Bolt	Woodburn	Waddell	Gillick	Smith	Marshall	Johnston	Symon	Venters	Thornton	Brown
Appearances	9	9	9	9	9	2	8	8	3	9	9	7	4	4
Goals				1		1	3	8	2	5	2	4	2	4

Glasgow Cup

No	Date	Venue	Opponent	Result	Scorers	Att
1	Aug 21	(a)	Third Lanark	W 5-2	McPherson 2, Marshall, Hamilton, Johnston	4,000
SF	Sep 4	(h)	Partick Thistle	W 1-0	Waddell	7,000
F	28	(h)	Celtic	L 0-1		50,000

	Dawson	Gray	Shaw	Bolt	Woodburn	Thomson	Waddell	Gillick	Smith	Marshall	Johnston	Jenkins	McPherson	McKillop T	Symon	Venters	Thornton
Appearances	2	3	3	2	3	2	2	2	1	2	3	1	2	2	1	1	1
Goals							1			1	1		2		1		

Glasgow Merchants' Charity Cup

No	Date	Venue	Opponent	Result	Scorers	Att
SF	May 24	(h)	Third Lanark	W 3-1	Gillick, McIntosh, Johnston	7,331
F	31	(n*)	Partick Thistle	W 3-0	Gillick 2, Venters	25,000

*Played at Hampden Park, Glasgow.

	Dawson	Gray	Shaw	Bolt	Woodburn	Thomson	Waddell	Gillick	Smith	Marshall	Johnston	Symon	Venters	Thornton	Galloway	Cowan
Appearances	2	2	2	1	2	1	2	1	1	2	1	2	1	1	1	1
Goals								3			1		1	1		

Summer Cup

No	Date	Venue	Opponent	Result	Scorers	Att
1	Jun 7	(a)	Falkirk	W 3-2	Venters 2, Johnston	10,000
	14	(h)	Falkirk	W 3-1	Gillick, Duncanson, McIntosh	6,000
QF	21	(a)	Hamilton A	W 3-1	Gillick 2, Duncanson	8,000
	28	(h)	Hamilton A	D 5-5	Smith 3, McIntosh 2	8,000
SF	Jul 5	(n*)	Hearts	W 4-2	McIntosh 2, Venters, Thornton	40,000
F	12	(n*)	Hibernian	L 2-3	Gillick, McIntosh	37,200

*Played at Hampden Park, Glasgow.

	Dawson	Gray	Shaw	Bolt	Woodburn	Gillick	Smith	Marshall	Johnston	Duncanson	Symon	Venters	Thornton	McIntosh	Galloway	Little
Appearances	6	6	6	6	6	6	1	1	5	2	5	6	2	6	1	1
Goals						4	3	1		2		3	1	6		

Other match

No	Date	Venue	Opponent	Result	Scorers	Att
1	Apr 23	(h)	RAF*	W 3-2	Venters, Johnston, Smith	25,500

*Sir Archibald Sinclair Cup in aid of the Clydeside Air Raid Distress Fund.

	Dawson	Gray	Shaw	Bolt	Woodburn	Waddell	Smith	Johnston	Symon	Venters	Thornton
Appearances	1	1	1	1	1	1	1	1	1	1	1
Goals							1	1		1	

1941-42

Manager: W.Struth

Southern League

#	Date	Venue/Opponent	Result	Scorers	Att	Dawson	Gray	Shaw	Bolt	Woodburn	Symon	McIntosh	Gillick	Smith	Venters	Johnston	Duncanson	Thomson	Little	Beattie	Jenkins	Marshall	McDowall	McKillop A	Young	Waddell	Thornton	Williamson	Dempster	Watkins	Grant
1	Aug 9 (h)	Motherwell	W 3-0	Smith 2, Gillick	20,000	1	2	3	4	5	6	7	8	9	10	11															
2	16 (a)	Partick Thistle	W 3-2	Smith 2, Venters	10,000	1	2	3	4	5	6		8	9	10	11		7													
3	23 (h)	St Mirren	W 8-1	Smith 4, Venters 2, Johnston 2	10,000	1	2	3	4	5		7	8	9	10	11			6												
4	30 (a)	Airdrieonians	W 6-1	Gillick 3, Smith 2, McIntosh	6,000	1	2	3		5	6	7	8	9	10					4	11										
5	Sep 6 (h)	Celtic	W 3-0	Beattie, Gillick, Venters	60,000	1	2	3		5	6	7	8	9	10					4	11										
6	13 (a)	Third Lanark	W 2-0	Symon (pen), Gillick	15,000	1	2	3		5	6	7	8	9	10	11				4											
7	20 (h)	Falkirk	W 5-2	Smith 2, McIntosh, Gillick, Venters	10,000	1	2	3		5	6	7	8	9	10	11				4											
8	27 (a)	Hibernian	L 1-8	Venters (pen)	14,800	1	2	3	4	5		7	8	9	10	11			6												
9	Oct 4 (a)	Albion R	W 1-0	Thomson (pen)	7,000		2	3			6	7		9		10	11		5	4		1	8								
10	11 (h)	Dumbarton	W 7-0	Thomson 2 (2 pens), Gillick 2, Shaw, Marshall, McIntosh	8,000		2	3			6	7		9		11			5	4		1	10	8							
11	25 (h)	Queen's Park	W 3-0	Gillick 2, Johnston	8,000	1	2	3			6	7		9		11			5	4			10	8							
12	Nov 1 (a)	Morton	L 1-2	A.McKillop	9,000	1	2	3			6	7		9		11			5	4			10		8						
13	8 (a)	Hamilton A	W 3-2	Bolt, Smith, Johnston	7,000	1	2	3	4					8	9			11	10	6						5	7				
14	15 (h)	Hearts	W 5-2	Gillick 2, Smith, Johnston, McIntosh	20,000		2	3	4			7	8	9		11			5	6		1	10								
15	22 (a)	Motherwell	D 1-1	Smith	12,000	1	2	3	4			7	8	9		11			5	6			10								
16	29 (h)	Partick Thistle	W 6-0	Gillick 3, Marshall 2, Thornton	20,000	1	2	3			6	7		9		11			5	4			10				8				
17	Dec 6 (a)	St Mirren	L 1-3	Gillick	5,000	1	2	3			6	7		9		11	8		5	4			10								
18	13 (h)	Airdrieonians	W 3-0	Waddell, Gillick, Williamson	4,000	1	2	3			6			9		11				4			10			5	7	8			
19	20 (a)	Falkirk	D 2-2	Marshall, Symon (pen)	7,000	1	2	3			6			9		11				4			10			5	7		8		
20	27 (h)	Hibernian	L 0-1		25,000	1	2	3			6		9	8		11				4			10			5	7				
21	Jan 1 (a)	Celtic	W 2-0	Waddell, Marshall	30,000	1	2	3			6		9			11				4			10			5	7	8			
22	3 (h)	Third Lanark	W 6-1	Gillick 2, Smith, Symon (pen), Johnston, Marshall		1	2	3			6		9	8		11				4			10			5	7				
23	17 (a)	Dumbarton	D 3-3	Marshall, Smith, Hickie (og)	6,000	1	2	3			6			8						4	11	1	10			5	7	9			
24	31 (h)	Clyde	D 0-0		10,000	1	2	3			6			9							11		10			5	7		8	4	
25	Feb 14 (h)	Hamilton A	W 6-0	Beattie 2, Waddell, Marshall, Smith, Shaw (pen)	6,000	1	2	3			6			9	8					4	11		10			5	7				
26	21 (a)	Hearts	W 1-0	Thornton	10,000	1	2	3			6			9	10	11				4						5	7	8			
27	Apr 6 (a)	Clyde	W 8-2	Venters 3, McIntosh 2, Shaw (pen), Waddell, Johnston			2	3	4	5	1	9			8	11			6				10				7				
28	14 (h)	Morton	W 3-0	McIntosh 2, Beattie				3		2	6	7		9	8				5	4	11	1	10								
29	21 (a)	Queen's Park	W 2-1	McIntosh, Marshall	5,000		2	3			6	9			8					4	11	1	10			5	7				
30	28 (h)	Albion R	W 2-1	Marshall, Grant				3	4	2			9			10	11		5		1	6		7							8

FINAL LEAGUE POSITION: 1st

| Appearances | | | | | | 22 | 28 | 30 | 9 | 11 | 24 | 19 | 24 | 16 | 15 | 23 | 3 | 11 | 25 | 7 | 7 | 20 | 2 | 2 | 11 | 12 | 4 | 1 | 2 | 1 | 1 |
| Goals | | | | | | | | 3 | 1 | | | 3 | 9 | 20 | 18 | 9 | 7 | | 3 | | 4 | | 10 | 1 | | | 4 | 2 | 1 | | 1 |

1 own-goal

Southern League Cup Section Four

#	Date	Venue/Opponent	Result	Scorers	Att	Dawson	Gray	Shaw	Bolt	Woodburn	Symon	McIntosh	Gillick	Smith	Venters	Johnston	Duncanson	Thomson	Little	Beattie	Jenkins	Marshall	McDowall	McKillop A	Young	Waddell	Thornton	Williamson	Dempster	Watkins	Grant
1	Feb 28 (h)	Third Lanark	W 5-1	Waddell 2, Marshall 2, Venters	8,000	1	2	3			6		9		8	11				4			10			5	7				
2	Mar 14 (a)	Motherwell	W 3-1	Gillick, Marshall, Waddell	10,000	1	2	3			6		9		8	11				4			10			5	7				
3	21 (a)	Third Lanark	W 5-2	Venters 2, Gillick, Waddell, Marshall	15,000	1	2	3	4				9		8	11				6			10			5	7				
4	28 (h)	Hearts	W 2-1	Gillick, Venters	20,000	1	2	3			6		9		10	11				4						5	7	8			
5	Apr 4 (h)	Motherwell	W 3-0	Gillick 2, Johnston	15,000	1	2	3			6		9		8	11				4			10			5	7				
6	11 (a)	Hearts	W 2-0	Gillick 2	16,000	1	2	3			6		9		8	11				4			10			5	7				
SF	May 2 (n*)	Celtic	W 2-0	Johnston, Venters	60,000	1	2	3			6		9		10	11				4						5	7	8			
F	9 (n*)	Morton	W 1-0	Gillick	43,000	1	2	3					9	8	10	11			6	4						5	7				

*Played at Hampden Park, Glasgow.

| Appearances | | | | | | 8 | 8 | 8 | 1 | | 6 | | 8 | 1 | 8 | 8 | | | 1 | 8 | | | 5 | | | 8 | 8 | 2 | | | |
| Goals | | | | | | | | | | | | | 8 | | 5 | 2 | | | | | | | 4 | | | | 4 | | | | |

Glasgow Cup

#	Date	Venue/Opponent	Result	Scorers	Att	Dawson	Gray	Shaw	Bolt	Woodburn	Symon	McIntosh	Gillick	Smith	Venters	Johnston	Duncanson	Thomson	Little	Beattie	Jenkins	Marshall	McDowall	McKillop A	Young	Waddell	Thornton	Williamson	Dempster	Watkins	Grant
SF	Sep 29 (n*)	Celtic	W 3-2	Johnston, McIntosh, Thomson (pen)	15,000	1	2	3			6	7		9		11			5	4			10					8			
F	Oct 18 (n*)	Clyde	W 6-0	McIntosh 2, McDowall, Thomson (pen), Gillick, Johnston	40,000	1	2	3			6	7		9		11			5	4			10	8							

*Played at Hampden Park, Glasgow.

| Appearances | | | | | | 2 | 2 | 2 | | | 2 | 2 | | 2 | | 2 | | | 2 | 2 | | | 2 | 1 | | | | 1 | | | |
| Goals | | | | | | | | | | | | 3 | | 1 | | 2 | | | | | | | | 1 | | | | | | | |

Glasgow Merchants' Charity Cup

#	Date	Venue/Opponent	Result	Scorers	Att	Dawson	Gray	Shaw	Bolt	Woodburn	Symon	McIntosh	Gillick	Smith	Venters	Johnston	Duncanson	Thomson	Little	Beattie	Jenkins	Marshall	McDowall	McKillop A	Young	Waddell	Thornton	Williamson	Dempster	Watkins	Grant
1	Apr 25 (a)	Queen's Park	W 1-0	Smith	8,000	1	2	3			6			9	8	11				4			10			5	7				
SF	May 13 (n*)	Celtic	W 2-1	Duncanson 2	26,000	1	2	3			6	9			10	11	8			4						5	7				
F	16 (n*)	Clyde	W 3-1	Venters, Waddell, Duncanson	25,000	1	2	3			6		9		10	11	8			4			1			5	7				

*Played at Hampden Park, Glasgow.

| Appearances | | | | | | 3 | 3 | 3 | | | 3 | 1 | 1 | 1 | 3 | 3 | 2 | | | 3 | | | 1 | | | 3 | 3 | | | | |
| Goals | | | | | | | | | | | | | | 1 | 1 | | 3 | | | | | | | | | | 1 | | | | |

Summer Cup

#	Date	Venue/Opponent	Result	Scorers	Att	Dawson	Gray	Shaw	Bolt	Woodburn	Symon	McIntosh	Gillick	Smith	Venters	Johnston	Duncanson	Thomson	Little	Beattie	Jenkins	Marshall	McDowall	McKillop A	Young	Waddell	Thornton	Williamson	Dempster	Watkins	Grant
1	May 30 (a)	Hamilton A	W 7-1	McIntosh 3, Waddell 2, Duncanson, Johnston	8,000	1	2	3			6	9			10	11	8			4						5	7				
	Jun 6 (h)	Hamilton A	W 3-2	Johnston 2, Venters	6,000	1	2	3			6	9			10	11	8			4						5	7				
QF	13 (a)	Falkirk	L 0-1		10,000	1	2	3			6		9	10	11	8				4						5	7				
	20 (h)	Falkirk	W 3-0	Gillick 2, Marshall	20,000	1	2	3			6		9		8	11				4			10			5	7				
SF	27 (n*)	Albion R	W 3-2	Gillick 2, Symon	20,000	1	2	3			6		9		8	11				4			10			5	7				
F	Jul 4 (n*)	Hibernian	D 0-0†		60,000	1	2	3			6		9		10	11				4						5	7	8			

*Played at Hampden Park, Glasgow.
†Rangers won Final by the toss of a coin, after 2-2 tie on corner-kicks in extra-time.

| Appearances | | | | | | 6 | 6 | 6 | | | 6 | 2 | 3 | 1 | 6 | 6 | 3 | | | 6 | | | 2 | | | 6 | 6 | 1 | | | |
| Goals | | | | | | | | | | | | 1 | 3 | | 4 | | 1 | | 3 | | 1 | | | | 2 | | | | | |

Other matches

#	Date	Venue/Opponent	Result	Scorers	Att	Dawson	Gray	Shaw	Bolt	Woodburn	Symon	McIntosh	Gillick	Smith	Venters	Johnston	Duncanson	Thomson	Little	Beattie	Jenkins	Marshall	McDowall	McKillop A	Young	Waddell	Thornton	Williamson	Dempster	Watkins	Grant
1	Aug 27 (a*)	British Army	D 2-2	Johnston, Gillick	4,000	1	2	3	5			7	9		10	11		6				4						8			
2	Sep 1 (h)	Preston NE†	W 3-1	Gillick, Smith, McIntosh	35,000	1	2	3	5	6	7	8	9	10						4	11										

*Played Somerset Park, Ayr in aid of the Ayr County Council War Fund.
†Lord Provost's Central Relief Fund Benefit Match.

| Appearances | | | | | | 2 | 2 | 2 | | 2 | 1 | 2 | 2 | 1 | 2 | 1 | 2 | | 1 | 1 | 1 | 1 | | | 1 | | | | 1 | |
| Goals | | | | | | | | | | | | 1 | 2 | 1 | | 1 | | | | 1 | | | | | | | | | | |

1942-43

Manager: W.Struth

Southern League

No	Date		Opponent	Result	Scorers	Att	Dawson	Gray	Shaw	Little	Young	Symon	Waddell	Venters	Gillick	Marshall	Johnston	Williamson	Duncanson	Smith	Kinnear	Bolt	Woodburn	Jenkins	Beattie	McIntosh	Gunn	Thornton	Bell	Watkins
1	Aug 8	(a)	St Mirren	W 1-0	Johnston	10,000	1	2	3	4	5	6	7	8	9	10	11													
2	15	(h)	Airdrieonians	W 4-1	Johnston 2, Williamson, Gillick	7,000	1	2	3	4	5	6	7	10	9		11	8												
3	22	(a)	Falkirk	W 5-0	Young 2 (2 pens), Waddell 2, Johnston	8,000	1	2	3	4	5	6	7	10	9		11		8											
4	29	(h)	Third Lanark	W 4-2	Waddell 3, Duncanson	10,000	1	2	3	4	5	6	7	10	9		11		8											
5	Sep 12	(h)	Hibernian	D 1-1	Venters	25,000	1	2	3	4	5	6	7	10						8	9	11								
6	19	(h)	Albion R	W 3-0	Gillick 2, Johnston	7,000	1	2	3	6	5		7		9	10	11			8		4								
7	26	(a)	Dumbarton	W 2-1	Duncanson, Gillick	10,000	1	2	3	6	5		7	10	9		11		8			4								
8	Oct 3	(a)	Queen's Park	L 0-1		8,000	1	2	3	6			7	10	9		11		8			4	5							
9	17	(h)	Morton	W 7-0	Gillick 4, Johnston 2, Waddell	11,000	1	2	3	4	5	6	7	10	9		11		8											
10	24	(h)	Hamilton A	W 4-2	Gillick 3, Marshall	6,000	1	2	3	4	5	6	7		9	10	11		8											
11	31	(a)	Hearts	W 3-0	Duncanson 2, Williamson	18,000	1	2	3	4	5	6	7		9		11	8	10											
12	Nov 7	(a)	Motherwell	W 2-0	Duncanson, Waddell	10,000	1	2	3	4	5	6	7	10	9		11		8											
13	14	(h)	Partick Thistle	W 4-1	Duncanson 2, Gillick, Venters	9,000	1	2	3	4	5	6	7	10	9		11		8											
14	21	(h)	St Mirren	W 5-1	Johnston 2, Gillick 2, Young (pen)	6,000	1	2	3	4	5	6	7	10	9		11		8											
15	28	(a)	Airdrieonians	W 7-1	Williamson 3, Duncanson, Johnston, Venters, Waddell	6,000	1	2	3	4	5	6	7	10			11	9	8											
16	Dec 5	(h)	Falkirk	D 1-1	Venters	7,000		2	3	4	5	6		10			11		8					1	7	9				
17	12	(a)	Third Lanark	W 3-0	Gunn, Smith, Venters	10,000	1	2	3	4	5	6		10			11			8					9		7			
18	19	(a)	Albion R	W 4-0	Venters 2, Waddell, Duncanson		1	2	3	4	5	6	7	10			11		8	9										
19	26	(a)	Hibernian	D 1-1	Venters	30,000	1	2	3	4	5	6	7	10	9		11		8											
20	Jan 1	(h)	Celtic	W 8-1	Gillick 3, Waddell 2, Young 2 (1 pen), Duncanson	30,000	1	2	3	4	5	6	7	10	9		11		8											
21	2	(h)	Queen's Park	W 5-2	Venters 2, Duncanson, Johnston, Thornton		1	2	3	4	5	6	7	10			11		8									9		
22	9	(h)	Dumbarton	W 1-0	Duncanson	7,000	1	2	3	4	5	6	7	10	9		11		8						4					
23	16	(a)	Clyde	W 3-1	Johnston 2, Venters	25,000	1	2	3	4	5	6	7	10			11	9	8											
24	23	(a)	Morton	D 1-1	Venters	15,000	1	2	3	4	5	6	7	10			11			9								8		
25	30	(a)	Hamilton A	W 3-0	Thornton 2, Young (pen)	8,000	1	2	3	4	5	6	7			10	11		8									9		
26	Feb 6	(h)	Hearts	D 1-1	Duncanson	10,000	1	2	3	4	5	6	7	10	9		11		8											
27	13	(h)	Motherwell	W 2-1	Gillick 2	8,000	1	2	3	4	5	6	7	10	9		11		8											
28	20	(a)	Partick Thistle	W 2-0	Gillick, Venters	12,000	1	2	3	4	5	6	7	10	9		11	8												
29	Apr 10	(a)	Celtic	D 2-2	Venters, Duncanson	34,000	1	2	3	4	5	6	7	10	9		11		8											
30	26	(h)	Clyde	L 0-1		5,000		2	3		5	6	7	10	9		11		8										1	4
	Appearances						28	30	30	28	29	27	28	26	21	4	28	4	26	5	1	4	1	1	2	1	1	3	1	1
	Goals										6		11	14	20	1	13	5	14	1							1	3		

FINAL LEAGUE POSITION: 1st

Southern League Cup Section D

No	Date		Opponent	Result	Scorers	Att	Dawson	Gray	Shaw	Little	Young	Symon	Waddell	Venters	Gillick	Marshall	Johnston	Williamson	Duncanson	Smith
1	Feb 27	(a)	St Mirren	W 3-0	Gillick, Young (pen), Little	12,000	1	2	3	4	5	6	7	10	9		11		8	
2	Mar 6	(h)	Celtic	W 3-0	Gillick 2, Duncanson	40,000	1	2	3	4	5	6	7	10	9		11		8	
3	13	(a)	Hibernian	W 2-0	Gillick, Duncanson	25,000	1	2	3	4	5	6	7	10	9		11		8	
4	20	(a)	St Mirren	W 3-1	Duncanson 2, Young (pen)	8,000	1	2	3	4	5	6	7	10	9		11		8	
5	27	(a)	Celtic	W 2-0	Venters 2	30,000	1	2	3	4	5	6	7	10	9		11		8	
6	Apr 3	(h)	Hibernian	W 1-0	Gillick	20,000	1	2	3	4	5	6	7	10	9		11		8	
SF	24	(n*)	Hamilton A	W 3-0	Gillick 2, Young (pen)	60,000	1	2	3	4	5	6	7	10	9		11		8	
F	May 8	(n*)	Falkirk	D 1-1†	Gillick	18,900	1	2	3	4	5	6	7	10	9		11		8	
	Appearances						8	8	8	8	8	8	8	8	8		8		8	
	Goals									1	3			2	8				4	

*Played at Hampden Park, Glasgow.
†Rangers won 11-3 on corners.

Glasgow Cup

No	Date		Opponent	Result	Scorers	Att	Dawson	Gray	Shaw	Little	Young	Symon	Waddell	Venters	Gillick	Johnston	Duncanson	Smith	Bolt	Woodburn	Jenkins	Thornton
1	Sep 5	(h)	Celtic	W 2-1	Thornton, Duncanson	30,000	1	2	3	4	5	6	7	10		11	8					9
SF	28	(a)	Partick Thistle	W 2-0	Waddell, Gillick	22,000	1	2	3	6			7	10	9	11	8		4	5		
F	Oct 10	(n*)	Third Lanark	W 5-2	Venters 2, Young (pen), Gillick, Johnston	18,000		2	3	4	5	6	7	10	9	11	8				1	
	Appearances						2	3	3	3	2	2	2	3	2	3	3	1	1	1	1	1
	Goals										1			2	2	1						1

*Played at Hampden Park, Glasgow.

Glasgow Merchants' Charity Cup

No	Date		Opponent	Result	Scorers	Att	Dawson	Gray	Shaw	Young	Symon	Waddell	Venters	Gillick	Johnston	Duncanson	Bolt
1	May 1	(h)	Clyde	L 1-2	Venters	15,000	1	2	3	5	6	7	10	9	11	8	4
	Appearances						1	1	1	1	1	1	1	1	1	1	1
	Goals												1				

Summer Cup

No	Date		Opponent	Result	Scorers	Att	Dawson	Gray	Shaw	Little	Young	Symon	Waddell	Venters	Gillick	Johnston	Williamson	Duncanson	McIntosh
1	May 29	(h)	Hearts	W 2-0	Venters 2	10,000	1	2	3	4	5	6		10	9	11		8	7
	Jun 5	(a)	Hearts	W 2-1	Duncanson, Gillick	10,000	1	2	3	4	5	6	7	10	9	11		8	
QF	12	(a)	Celtic	W 4-0	Duncanson 2, Williamson, Young (pen)	25,000	1	2	3	4	5	6	7	10		11	9	8	
	19	(a)	Celtic	W 4-1	McIntosh 3, Johnston	15,000	1	2	3	4	5	6	7	10		11		8	9
SF	26	(n*)	Hibernian	W 3-1	Duncanson, Little, Johnston	40,000	1	2	3	4	5	6	7	10		11	9	8	
F	Jul 10	(n*)	St Mirren	L 0-1		45,000	1	2	3	4	5	6	7	10	9	11		8	
	Appearances						6	6	6	6	6	6	5	6	3	6	2	6	2
	Goals									1	1			2	1	2	1	4	3

*Played at Hampden Park, Glasgow.

1943-44

Manager: W.Struth

Southern League

Player column legend (left→right): Dawson, Gray, Shaw, Little, Young, Symon, Waddell, Williamson, Gillick, Duncanson, Johnston, Venters, Jenkins, Marshall, McIntosh, Kinnear, Nimmo, Watkins, Woodburn, Parlane, Houliston, Smith, McCormack, Bolt, McKinnon, Cargill, Lindsay, McMoran, Neil, Craven

#	Date		Opponent	Result	Scorers	Att	Daw	Gra	Sha	Lit	You	Sym	Wad	Wil	Gil	Dun	Joh	Ven	Jen	Mar	McI	Kin	Nim	Wat	Woo	Par	Hou	Smi	McC	Bol	McK	Car	Lin	McM	Nei	Cra
1	Aug 14	(h)	Hibernian	W 4-0	Duncanson 2, Gillick 2	20,000	1	2	3	4	5	6	7	8	9	10	11																			
2	21	(a)	Motherwell	W 5-0	Venters 3, Duncanson, Gillick	7,000	1	2	3	4	5	6	7		9	8	11	10																		
3	28	(h)	Clyde	W 3-2	Gillick, Little, Young (pen)	10,000	1	2	3	4	5	6	7		9	8	11	10																		
4	Sep 4	(a)	Airdrieonians	W 3-1	Waddell, Duncanson, Marshall	5,000		2	3	4	5	6	7		9	8	11			1	10															
5	11	(h)	Celtic	L 0-1		30,000		2	3	4	5	6	7		9	8	11			1	10															
6	18	(a)	Third Lanark	W 6-0	McIntosh 4, Gillick, Young (pen)	10,000		2	3	4	5	6	7		8	10	11			1	9															
7	25	(h)	Falkirk	W 2-0	McIntosh, Waddell	6,000		2	3	4	5	6	7		8	10			1		9	11														
8	Oct 2	(a)	St Mirren	W 4-1	McIntosh 3, Duncanson	14,000		2	3	4	5	6	7		8	10			1		9		11													
9	16	(h)	Hearts	L 1-3	McIntosh	15,000		2	3			6		10	7		11		1		9				4	5	8									
10	23	(a)	Morton	D 1-1	Waddell		1	2	3	4	5	6	7		8		11				9			10												
11	30	(h)	Hamilton A	W 6-0	Johnston 3, Gillick 2, McIntosh	9,000	1	2	3	4	5	6	7		8	10	11				9															
12	Nov 6	(a)	Albion R	W 5-1	McIntosh 2, Johnston, Gillick, Waddell	4,000	1	2	3	4	5	6	7		8	10	11				9															
13	13	(a)	Queen's Park	W 4-1	McIntosh 4	8,000	1	2	3	4	5	6	7		8	10	11				9															
14	20	(h)	Dumbarton	W 2-0	Duncanson 2	20,000	1	2	3	4	5	6	7		8	10	11				9															
15	27	(a)	Hibernian	W 4-3	McIntosh, Waddell, Johnston, Duncanson	30,000	1	2	3	4	5	6	7		8	10	11				9															
16	Dec 4	(h)	Motherwell	W 2-0	Duncanson, McIntosh	15,000	1	2	3	4	5	6	7		8	10	11				9															
17	11	(a)	Partick Thistle	W 2-1	Williamson, Gillick	12,000	1	2	3	4	5	6	7	8	9	10							11													
18	18	(h)	Airdrieonians	W 3-0	Duncanson 2, Smith	8,000	1	2		4	5	6	7		8	10						3						9	11							
19	25	(h)	Third Lanark	W 3-1	Waddell, Smith, Duncanson	10,000	1	2	3	4	5	6	7		8	10	11											9								
20	Jan 1	(a)	Celtic	W 3-1	Gillick, McCormack, Duncanson	60,000	1	2	3	4	5	6	7	9	8	10													11							
21	3	(a)	Dumbarton	D 1-1	Smith		1	2	3	4	5	6			8	10	11											9								
22	8	(a)	Falkirk	W 2-0	Duncanson, McCormack	10,000			3	4	5	6	7	8		10			1		9								11	2						
23	15	(h)	St Mirren	L 1-2	Duncanson	20,000		2	3	4	5	6	7	8		10			1		9								11							
24	22	(a)	Clyde	W 3-0	McIntosh 2, Young (pen)	12,000		2	3	4	5	6	7		8	10	11		1		9															
25	29	(a)	Hearts	W 3-1	McIntosh 2, Gillick	25,000		2	3	4	5	6	7		8	10	11		1		9															
26	Feb 5	(h)	Morton	W 4-1	Duncanson 3, Young (pen)	8,000		2	3	4	5	6	7		8	10	11		1		9															
27	12	(a)	Hamilton A	W 4-1	McIntosh 2, Duncanson, McKinnon	14,000	1	2	3	4	5	6			8	10	11				9										7					
28	19	(h)	Albion R	W 5-0	McIntosh 3, McKinnon 2	5,000	1	2	3	4	5	6			8	11	10				9										7					
29	26	(h)	Queen's Park	D 1-1	McKinnon	10,000	1	2	3	4	5	6				11	10				9										7	8				
30	Apr 10	(h)	Partick Thistle	D 3-3	Little, Johnston, Neil	15,000	1	2		4	5	6			8		11	10															3	7	9	

FINAL LEAGUE POSITION: 1st

| | | | | | | Appearances | 18 | 29 | 28 | 29 | 29 | 30 | 23 | 4 | 25 | 28 | 23 | 6 | 12 | 3 | 20 | 2 | 2 | 1 | 1 | 1 | 1 | 3 | 4 | 1 | 3 | 1 | 1 | 1 | 1 | 1 |
| | | | | | | Goals | | | | 2 | 4 | | 6 | 1 | 11 | 19 | 6 | 3 | | 1 | 27 | | | | | | | 3 | 2 | | 4 | | | | 1 | |

Southern League Cup Section A

#	Date		Opponent	Result	Scorers	Att	Daw	Gra	Sha	Lit	You	Sym	Wad	Wil	Gil	Dun	Joh	McI	Smi	Bol	McK
1	Mar 4	(a)	Hearts	W 4-2	McIntosh 2, Duncanson, McKinnon	20,000	1	2	3	4	5	6			8	10	11	9			7
2	11	(h)	Motherwell	L 0-1		20,000	1	2	3	4	5	6			8	10	11	9			7
3	18	(h)	Airdrieonians	W 1-0	McKinnon	12,000	1	2	3	4	5	6		8		10	11	9			7
4	25	(h)	Hearts	W 2-0	Duncanson 2	40,000	1	2	3	4	5	6	7		8	10	11	9			
5	Apr 1	(a)	Motherwell	W 3-2	McIntosh, Johnston, Gillick	20,000	1	2	3	4	5	6	7		8	10	11	9			
6	8	(h)	Airdrieonians	W 4-0	Smith 2, Young (pen), Duncanson	8,000	1	2		4	5	6	7		8	10	11		9	3	
SF	29	(n*)	Celtic	W 4-2	Duncanson 2, Smith 2	90,000	1	2	3	4	5	6	7		8	10	11		9		
F	May 20	(n*)	Hibernian	D 0-0†		63,000	1	2	3	4	5	6	7		8	10	11		9		

*Played at Hampden Park, Glasgow. † Hibernian won 6-5 on corners.

| | | | | | | Appearances | 8 | 8 | 7 | 8 | 8 | 8 | 5 | 1 | 7 | 8 | 8 | 5 | 3 | 1 | 3 |
| | | | | | | Goals | | | | | 1 | | | | 1 | 6 | 1 | 3 | 4 | | 2 |

Glasgow Cup

Player legend: Gray, Shaw, Little, Young, Symon, Waddell, Gillick, Duncanson, Johnston, Marshall, McIntosh, Kinnear, Watkins

#	Date		Opponent	Result	Scorers	Att	Gra	Sha	Lit	You	Sym	Wad	Gil	Dun	Joh	Mar	McI	Kin	Wat
SF	Sep 27	(a)	Partick Thistle	W 3-0	McIntosh 2, Gillick	28,000	2	3	4	5	6	7	8			1	9	11	10
F	Oct 9	(n*)	Clyde	W 2-0	McIntosh 2	40,000	2	3	4	5	6	7	8	10	11	1	9		

*Played at Hampden Park, Glasgow.

| | | | | | | Appearances | 2 | 2 | 2 | 2 | 2 | 2 | 2 | 1 | 1 | 2 | 2 | 1 | 1 |
| | | | | | | Goals | | | | | | | 1 | | | | 4 | | |

Glasgow Merchants' Charity Cup

Player legend: Dawson, Gray, Shaw, Little, Young, Symon, Waddell, Gillick, Duncanson, Johnston, Marshall, Smith, McMoran

#	Date		Opponent	Result	Scorers	Att	Daw	Gra	Sha	Lit	You	Sym	Wad	Gil	Dun	Joh	Mar	Smi	McM
SF	May 13	(h)	Partick Thistle	W 3-0	Waddell 2, Little	13,000	1	2	3	4	5	6	7	8	10	11			9
F	27	(n*)	Clyde	W 2-1	Smith 2	38,549		2	3	4	5	6	7	8	10	11	1	9	

*Played at Hampden Park, Glasgow.

| | | | | | | Appearances | 1 | 2 | 2 | 2 | 2 | 2 | 2 | 2 | 2 | 2 | 1 | 1 | 1 |
| | | | | | | Goals | | | | 1 | | | 2 | | | | | 2 | |

1944-45

Manager: W.Struth

Southern League

#		Date		Opponent	Result	Scorers	Att.	Jenkins	Gray, Douglas	Shaw, Jock	Little	Young	Symon	Waddell	Duncanson	Gillick	Venters	Johnston	Watkins	Smith	Woodburn	McKinnon	Craven	Williamson	McCormack	Dawson
1	Aug	12	(a)	Falkirk	W 3-2	Gillick, Venters, Waddell	16,000	1	2	3	4	5	6	7	8	9	10	11								
2		19	(h)	St Mirren	W 6-1	Venters 3, Gillick 2, Johnston	20,000	1	2	3	4	5	6	7	8	9	10	11								
3	Sep	2	(h)	Third Lanark	D 0-0		12,000	1	2	3	4	5	6	7	8	9	10	11								
4		9	(a)	Celtic	W 4-0	Watkins 2, Waddell, Johnston	50,000	1	2	3	4	5	6	7	10	9		11	8							
5		16	(h)	Airdrieonians	W 2-0	Smith, Gillick	15,000	1	2	3	4	5	6	7	10	8		11		9						
6		23	(a)	Hibernian	L 1-4	Smith	30,000	1	2	3	4	5	6	7	10	8		11		9						
7		30	(h)	Motherwell	D 1-1	Symon	25,000	1	2	3		5	6	7	10	8		11	4	9						
8	Oct	14	(a)	Hamilton A	W 4-2	Gillick 2, Venters, McKinnon	10,000	1	2	3		5	6		8	9	10	11	4			7				
9		21	(h)	Albion R	W 3-0	Venters 2, Gillick	7,000	1	2			4	5	6	7	8	9	10	11					3		
10		28	(a)	Hearts	D 1-1	Duncanson	20,000	1	2	3	4	5	6	7	8	9	10	11								
11	Nov	4	(h)	Morton	L 2-4	McKinnon 2	10,000	1	2	3	4	5	6	9	10	8		11				7				
12		11	(h)	Dumbarton	W 5-2	Waddell 2, Duncanson, Symon, Watkins	12,000	1	2	3	4	5	6	7	10			11	8	9						
13		18	(a)	Queen's Park	W 4-1	Waddell 2, Smith, Duncanson	10,000	1	2	3	4	5	6	7	10	8		11		9						
14		25	(h)	Falkirk	W 4-0	Smith 2, Waddell, Young (pen)	18,000	1	2	3	4	5	6	7	10	8		11		9						
15	Dec	2	(a)	St Mirren	W 1-0	Little	10,000	1	2	3	4	5	6	7	10	8		11		9						
16		9	(h)	Partick Thistle	W 2-0	Gillick, Waddell	15,000	1	2	3	4	5	6	7	10	8		11		9						
17		16	(h)	Third Lanark	W 4-1	Duncanson, Waddell, Young (pen), Bowman (og)	10,000	1	2	3	4	5	6	7	10	8		11		9						
18		23	(h)	Hibernian	W 5-0	Johnston, Young (pen), Duncanson, Smith, Waddell	35,000	1	2	3	4	5	6	7	10	8		11		9						
19		30	(a)	Airdrieonians	W 3-1	Waddell, Gillick, Smith	9,000	1	2	3	4	5	6	7	10	8		11		9						
20	Jan	1	(h)	Celtic	L 0-1		70,000	1	2	3	4	5	6	7	10	8		11		9						
21		2	(h)	Queen's Park	L 0-1			1	2	3	4	5	6	11		8	10					7	9			
22		6	(a)	Motherwell	W 4-0	Johnston 2, Waddell, Symon	18,000	1	2	3	4	5	6	7		8		11		9				10		
23		13	(a)	Clyde	W 2-0	Waddell, Smith	30,000	1	2	3		5	6	7		8	10	11	4	9						
24		20	(h)	Hamilton A	W 2-0	Smith, Waddell	12,000	1	2	3		5	6	7	10	8			4	9					11	
25		27	(a)	Albion R	W 4-0	McCormack 2, Duncanson, Smith	6,000	1	2	3			6	7	10	8			4	9	5				11	
26	Feb	3	(h)	Hearts	W 4-0	Duncanson 2, Venters, McCormack	18,000	1	2	3	4	5	6		7	8	10			9					11	
27		10	(a)	Morton	W 4-1	Duncanson 2, Venters, Waddell	15,000	1	2	3	4	5	6	7	9	8	10								11	
28		17	(a)	Dumbarton	W 6-3	Duncanson 3, Gillick 2, Young (pen)	4,000	1	2	3	4	5	6	7	9	8	10								11	
29	Apr	2	(a)	Partick Thistle	W 4-1	Duncanson 2, Smith, Johnston	15,000			3	4	2	6	7	8		10	11		9	5					1
30		7	(h)	Clyde	W 3-0	Venters 2, Waddell	15,000	1		3	4	2	6	7		8	10	11		9	5					
						Appearances		29	28	29	25	29	30	28	26	28	13	24	7	18	4	3	1	2	5	1
						Goals					1	4	3	16	15	11	11	6	3	11		3			3	

FINAL LEAGUE POSITION: 1st

1 own-goal

Southern League Cup Section A

#		Date		Opponent	Result	Scorers	Att.	Jenkins	Gray, Douglas	Shaw, Jock	Little	Young	Symon	Waddell	Duncanson	Gillick	Venters	Johnston	Watkins	Smith	Woodburn	McKinnon	Craven	Williamson	McCormack	Dawson
1	Feb	24	(h)	Albion R	W 2-1	Young (pen), McCormack	10,000	1	2	3	6	5		7	9	8	10		4						11	
2	Mar	3	(a)	Hibernian	D 1-1	Duncanson	20,000	1	2	3	4	5	6	7	10	8				9					11	
3		10	(h)	Third Lanark	W 2-0	Young (pen), Smith	18,000	1	2	3		5	6	7		8	10		4	9					11	
4		17	(a)	Albion R	W 3-1	Venters 2, Gillick	9,000	1	2	3	4	5	6	7		8	10								11	
5		24	(h)	Hibernian	W 2-0	Smith 2	35,000	1		3	4	2	6	7		8	10	11		9	5					
6		31	(a)	Third Lanark	W 4-2	Smith 2, Venters 2	7,000	1		3	4	2	6	7	8		10	11		9	5					
SF	Apr	21	(a)	Queen's Park	W 3-0	Waddell, Smith, Venters	87,000	1		3	4	2	6	7		8	10	11		9	5					
F	May	12	(n*)	Motherwell	W 2-1	Gillick, Venters	69,879	1		3	4	2	6	7		8	10	11		9	5					
						Appearances		8	4	8	7	8	7	8	3	7	7	4	2	7	4				4	
						Goals						2		1	1	2	6			6					1	

*Played at Hampden Park, Glasgow.

Glasgow Cup

#		Date		Opponent	Result	Scorers	Att.	Jenkins	Gray, Douglas	Shaw, Jock	Little	Young	Symon	Waddell	Duncanson	Gillick	Venters	Johnston	Watkins	Smith	Woodburn	McKinnon	Craven
1	Aug	26	(a)	Partick Thistle	W 2-1	Gillick, Duncanson	22,000	1	2	3	4	5	6	7	8	9	10	11					
SF	Sep	25	(a)	Queen's Park	W 3-0	Duncanson, Smith, Young (pen)	20,000	1	2	3		4	6	7	10			11	8	9	5		
F	Oct	7	(n*)	Celtic	W 3-2	Waddell, Symon, Young (pen)	48,000	1	2	3		5	6	9	10	8		11	4			7	
						Appearances		3	3	3	1	3	3	3	3	2	1	3	2	1	1	1	1
						Goals						2	1	1	2	1				1			

*Played at Hampden Park, Glasgow.

Glasgow Merchants' Charity Cup

#		Date		Opponent	Result	Scorers	Att.	Jenkins	Gray, Douglas	Shaw, Jock	Little	Young	Symon	Waddell	Duncanson	Gillick	Venters	Johnston	Watkins	Smith	Woodburn	McKinnon	Craven	Williamson	McCormack
1	Apr	28	(h)	Queen's Park	W 1-0	Venters	12,000	1		3	4	2	6	7		8	10	11		9	5				
SF	May	5	(h)	Clyde	W 4-0	Waddell 2, Gillick, McCormack	10,000	1		3	4	2	6	7	9	8	10				5			11	
F		21	(n*)	Celtic	W 2-1	Duncanson, Venters	50,000	1		3	4	2	6	7	8	9	10	11			5				
						Appearances		3		3	3	3	3	3	2	3	3	2		1	3			1	
						Goals								2	1	1	2							1	

*Played at Hampden Park, Glasgow.

1945-46

Manager: W.Struth

Southern League

Player columns: Jenkins, Young, Shaw Jock, Little, Woodburn, Symon, Waddell, Gillick, Williamson, Venters, Johnston, McColl, Smith, Stead, Dawson, Gray Douglas, Duncanson, McCormack, Watkins, Gray David, Shaw John, McMaster, Lindsay, Rae, Caskie, Thornton, McKillop T, Gudmundsson, Dougal, Parlane, Arnison, Grant

#	Date	Opponent	Result	Scorers	Att.
1	Aug 11 (h) Motherwell	L 0-3			35,000
2	16 (h) Partick Thistle	W 4-2	Waddell 2, Gillick, Smith	
3	18 (a) Hibernian	L 1-2	Williamson	30,000
4	Sep 1 (a) Kilmarnock	W 7-0	Johnston 2, Duncanson 2, Gillick, Williamson, Horton (og)	20,000
5	8 (h) Celtic	W 5-3	Williamson 2, Duncanson, Johnston, Venters	51,000
6	15 (a) Third Lanark	W 5-1	Gillick 2, Venters, McCormack, Williamson	22,000
7	22 (h) Falkirk	W 1-0	Young (pen)	10,000
8	29 (a) St Mirren	D 2-2	Young (pen), Williamson	20,000
9	Oct 13 (h) Aberdeen	W 3-1	Waddell 2 (1 pen), Smith	66,000
10	20 (a) Queen's Park	W 2-0	Waddell (pen), Williamson	40,000
11	27 (a) Morton	D 2-2	Gillick, McCormack	16,000
12	Nov 3 (h) Hamilton A	W 5-1	Gillick 2, Williamson 2, Waddell	12,000
13	10 (a) Queen of South	W 4-2	McCormack 2, Gillick, McMaster	14,500
14	17 (h) Hearts	D 1-1	Waddell	18,000
15	24 (a) Motherwell	W 2-1	Waddell (pen), Johnston	15,000
16	Dec 1 (h) Hibernian	W 3-2	Caskie, Gillick, Duncanson	25,000
17	8 (a) Partick Thistle	W 5-1	Gillick 2, Young (pen), Waddell, Smith	25,000
18	15 (h) Kilmarnock	W 5-1	Gillick 2, Williamson, Caskie, Waddell	
19	22 (h) Third Lanark	W 1-0	Waddell	12,000
20	25 (h) Clyde	W 3-1	Waddell 2 (1 pen), Watkins	
21	29 (a) Falkirk	W 3-0	Gillick, Waddell, Thornton	20,000
22	Jan 1 (a) Celtic	W 1-0	Thornton	70,000
23	2 (h) St Mirren	W 3-1	Williamson, Waddell (pen), Caskie	
24	5 (a) Clyde	W 1-0	Thornton	25,000
25	12 (a) Aberdeen	L 1-4	Waddell (pen)	35,000
26	19 (h) Queen's Park	W 2-1	Gillick, Waddell	12,000
27	26 (h) Morton	D 4-4	Williamson, McColl, Caskie, Waddell	28,000
28	Feb 2 (a) Hamilton A	W 4-1	Duncanson 2, Smith, Williamson	8,000
29	9 (h) Queen of South	W 5-2	Caskie 2, Waddell, Duncanson, Williamson	12,000
30	16 (a) Hearts	L 0-2		40,000

FINAL LEAGUE POSITION: 1st

Appearances: 3 12 27 8 21 22 26 27 25 4 8 11 5 4 9 7 16 6 20 17 18 3 4 1 14 7 2 1 2

Goals: 3 — — — — — 19 15 14 2 4 1 4 — — 7 4 1 — — — — — 1 6 3 — —

1 own-goal

Southern League Cup Section B

#	Date	Opponent	Result	Scorers	Att.
1	Feb 23 (h) Queen of South	W 4-0	Caskie, Gillick, Symon, Williamson	15,000
2	Mar 2 (a) Motherwell	W 3-0	Smith, Williamson, Gillick	20,000
3	9 (h) Morton	W 1-0	Waddell	55,000
4	16 (a) Queen of South	W 2-0	Johnston, Smith	12,500
5	23 (h) Motherwell	W 4-2	Williamson, Young (pen), Waddell, Duncanson	30,000
6	30 (a) Morton	D 1-1	Duncanson	17,000
QF	Apr 6(n*) Dundee	W 3-1	Gillick, Young (pen), Duncanson	50,000
SF	27(n*) Hearts	W 2-1	Thornton, Gillick	75,000
F	May 11(n*) Aberdeen	L 2-3	Duncanson, Thornton	135,000

*Played at Hampden Park, Glasgow.

Appearances: 9 9 — 9 9 5 8 — 5 — 4 — — 6 — 9 9 9 — — 4 2 — — 1 1

Goals: 2 — — 1 2 4 3 — 1 — 2 — — 4 — — — — — — 1 2

Glasgow Cup

#	Date	Opponent	Result	Scorers	Att.
1	Aug 25 (h) Celtic	W 3-1	Williamson 2, Young (pen)	50,000
SF	Sep 24 (a) Clyde	L 3-4	Gillick, Williamson, Venters	30,000

Appearances: 2 2 1 — 1 2 2 2 1 1 2 — — 2 2 2

Goals: 1 — — — — — 1 3 1

Glasgow Merchants' Charity Cup

#	Date	Opponent	Result	Scorers	Att.
1	May 6 (h) Queen's Park	W 4-1	Arnison 3, Thornton	16,000
SF	13 (a) Celtic	W 3-1	Duncanson 2, Thornton	40,374
F	Jun 8(n*) Third Lanark	W 2-0	Thornton 2	51,287

*Played at Hampden Park, Glasgow.

Appearances: 1 2 — 2 — 3 1 2 — — 2 1 2 1 — 1 2 1 3 — 1

Goals: — — — — — — — — 2 — — — — — — — — 4 — 3

Brown played number-1 in all matches; Cox played number-2 in round One and semi-final & number-6 in Final; Laurie played number-4 in round One; McNee played number-11 in semi-final.

Victory Cup

#	Date	Opponent	Result	Scorers	Att.
1	Apr 20 (a) Stenhousemuir	W 4-1	Duncanson 2, Arnison 2	4,903
	22 (a) Stenhousemuir	W 4-1	Arnison 2, Johnston, Williamson	
2	May 4 (a) Airdrieonians	W 4-0	Waddell 2, Smith, Thornton	21,600
QF	18 (a) Falkirk	D 1-1	Gillick	20,000
R	25 (a) Falkirk	W 2-0	Gillick, Symon	61,000
SF	Jun 1(n*) Celtic	D 0-0		90,000
R	5(n*) Celtic	W 2-0	Waddell, Young (pen)	50,000
F	15(n*) Hibernian	W 3-1	Duncanson 2, Gillick	100,000

*Played at Hampden Park, Glasgow.

Appearances: 8 8 — 7 8 5 4 — 2 1 1 — — 5 — 8 1 2 — 1 5 6 — 2 1

Goals: 1 — — 1 3 3 1 — 1 — 1 — — 4 — — — — — — 1 — — 4

Brown played number-1 and Cox number-2 in every round except One; McNee played number-11 in the quarter-final first game.

Other matches

#	Date	Opponent	Result	Scorers	Att.
1	Sep 25 (h) Newcastle U‡	W 3-2	Williamson 2, Duncanson	50,000
2	Oct 17(a*) Comb Services	L 1-6	Waddell	50,000
3	Nov 28 (h) Dinamo Moscow	D 2-2	Smith, Young (pen)	95,000
4	Apr 15 (n) Celtic	W 2-1	Arnison, McCormack	12,000
5	30(n†) Everton	L 2-3	Symon, Arnison	26,500

‡King George VI Navy Fund Benefit. *Played in Hanover, Germany.
†Played Windsor Park, Belfast – Jack Price Benefit Match.

Appearances: 3 4 — 1 4 4 3 5 1 2 1 2 — 4 2 2 1 4 2 1 — 1 1 — 1 2

Goals: — 1 — — — 1 1 1 — 2 — — — 1 — 1 1 — — — — — — 1

McNee played number-11 in Match 1; Robb played number-2 in Match 4; McIntyre played number-7 in Match 4.

1946-47

Manager: W.Struth

Scottish League

#	Date	Opponent	Res	Scorers	Att	Brown	Cox	Shaw, Jock	Watkins	Young	Symon	Waddell	Gillick	Thornton	Duncanson	Caskie	Gray, David	Williamson	Arnison	Stead	Parlane	Woodburn	McColl	Rae	McNee	Rutherford	Lindsay	Shaw, John
1	Aug 10 (a)	Motherwell	W 4-2	Duncanson 2, Thornton, Waddell	30,000	1	2	3	4	5	6	7	8	9	10	11												
2	14 (h)	Hibernian	L 1-2	Young (pen)	50,000	1	6	3	4	5		7	8	9	10	11	2											
3	17 (h)	Kilmarnock	W 3-2	Cox, Gillick, Waddell	25,000	1	6	3	4	5		7	8	9	10	11	2											
4	21 (a)	Falkirk	W 5-0	Thornton 3, Duncanson, Waddell		1	4	3		5	6	7	8	9	10	11												
5	28 (h)	Third Lanark	W 8-1	Thornton 3, Caskie 3, Gillick, Duncanson	22,000	1	4	3		5	6		8	9	7	11	2	10										
6	31 (h)	Queen's Park	W 2-0	Duncanson 2	20,000	1	4	3		5	6	7	8		10	11	2		9									
7	Sep 4 (a)	Aberdeen	L 0-1		35,000	1	4	3	7	5	6		8		10	11	2		9									
8	7 (a)	Celtic	W 3-2	Duncanson 2, Parlane	28,000	1	4	3		5	6		8		10	11	2			7	9							
9	14 (h)	St Mirren	W 4-0	Duncanson 3, Gillick	15,000	1	4	3		5	6		8		10	11	2		9	7								
10	30 (a)	Partick Thistle	L 2-3	Gillick, Duncanson	36,000	1	4	3			6	7	8	9	10	11	2					5						
11	Nov 2 (h)	Morton	W 2-1	Thornton, Cox	40,000	1	8	3		2		7		9				10				5	4	6	11			
12	9 (a)	Hamilton A	W 6-0	Thornton 3, McNee, Gillick, Duncanson	15,000	1	2	3		5		7	8	9	10								4	6	11			
13	16 (a)	Clyde	W 4-2	McNee, McColl, Duncanson, Thornton	27,000	1		3		2		7	8	9	10							5	4	6	11			
14	23 (h)	Queen of South	W 2-1	Thornton, Gillick	10,000	1		3		5	6		8	9	10								4	2	11	7		
15	30 (a)	Hearts	W 3-0	Duncanson, McNee, Thornton	45,000	1				2		7	8	9	10							5	4	6	11		3	
16	Dec 7 (h)	Motherwell	W 2-1	Thornton, Young (pen)	35,000	1		3		2		7	8	9	10							5	4	6	11			
17	14 (a)	Hibernian	D 1-1	Duncanson	41,378	1		3		2		7	8	9	10							5	4	6	11			
18	21 (h)	Falkirk	W 2-1	Duncanson, Gillick	15,000	1		3		2		7	8	9	10	11						5	4	6				
19	28 (a*)	Third Lanark	D 1-1	Gillick	35,000	1		3		2		7	8	9	10					11		5	4	6				
20	Jan 1 (h)	Celtic	D 1-1	Gillick	85,000	1		3		2		7	8	9	10							5	4	6	11			
21	2 (a)	Kilmarnock	W 2-0	Gillick 2	32,325	1		3		2		7	8	9	10							5	4	6	11			
22	4 (a)	St Mirren	L 0-1		18,000	1		3		2		7	8	9	10							5	4	6	11			
23	11 (h)	Partick Thistle	W 4-0	Waddell, Thornton, Young (pen), Gillick	18,000	1		3		2		11	8	9							10	5	4	6		7		
24	18 (h)	Aberdeen	W 1-0	Waddell	60,000	1		3		2		11	8	9							10	5	4	6		7		
25	Feb 1 (a)	Queen's Park	D 0-0		40,000	1		3		2		7	8		10	11			9			5	4	6				
26	8 (a)	Queen of South	W 2-0	Young (pen), Arnison	11,000	1		3		2		7	8		10	11			9			5	4	6				
27	15 (a)	Morton	W 1-0	Thornton	18,000	1		3		2		7	8		10	11			9			5	4	6				
28	Mar 29 (h)	Clyde	W 5-0	Williamson 4, Rutherford	15,000	1		3	4	2			8		10	11		9				5		6		7		
29	Apr 7 (h)	Hearts	L 1-2	Thornton	12,000	1		3		2				10	7	11		8	9			5	4	6				
30	12 (h)	Hamilton A	W 4-1	Williamson 2, Parlane, Duncanson	8,000	1	2		4		6				10	11		9			8	5				7	3	
	FINAL LEAGUE POSITION: 1st			Appearances		30	13	28	6	28	10	22	27	25	27	13	9	5	7	3	4	18	19	19	10	5	2	
				Goals			2			4		5	12	18	18	3		6	1		2		1		3	1		

*Played at Hampden Park, Glasgow.

Scottish FA Cup

#	Date	Opponent	Res	Scorers	Att	Brown	Cox	Shaw, Jock	Watkins	Young	Symon	Waddell	Gillick	Thornton	Duncanson	Caskie	Gray, David	Williamson	Arnison	Stead	Parlane	Woodburn	McColl	Rae
1	Jan 25 (h)	Clyde	W 2-1	Duncanson, Thornton	74,606	1		3		2		11	8	10	7						9	5	4	6
2	Feb 22 (a)	Hibernian	D 0-0		95,000	1		3		2		7	8	10	11				9			5	4	6
R	Mar 8 (a)	Hibernian	L 0-2		48,816	1		3	6	2		7		9	10	11					8	5	4	
				Appearances		3		3	1	3		3	2	3	3	1			1		2	3	3	2
				Goals										1	1									

Scottish League Cup Section B

#	Date	Opponent	Res	Scorers	Att	Brown	Cox	Shaw, Jock	Watkins	Young	Symon	Waddell	Gillick	Thornton	Duncanson	Caskie	Gray, David	Williamson	Arnison	Stead	Parlane	Woodburn	McColl	Rae	McNee	Rutherford	Lindsay	Shaw, John
1	Sep 21 (h)	St Mirren	W 4-0	Arnison 2, Cox, Stead	20,000	1	4	3		5	6		8		10	11	2		9	7								
2	28 (a)	Queen's Park	W 4-2	Duncanson 2, Gillick, Thornton	30,000	1	4	3			6	7	8	9	10	11	2				5							
3	Oct 5 (h)	Morton	W 3-0	Duncanson, Caskie, Thornton	50,000	1	6	3	4	5		7	8	9	10	11	2											
4	12 (h)	St Mirren	W 4-0	Gillick 2, Thornton 2	20,000	1		3	6	2		7	8	9	10	11						5	4					
5	19 (h)	Queen's Park	W 1-0	Arnison	20,000	1	8	3		2						11		10	9			5	4	6		7		
6	26 (a)	Morton	W 2-0	Young (pen), Thornton	18,000		8	3		2		7		9		11		10				5	4	6				1
QF1	Mar 1 (h)	Dundee U	W 2-1	Waddell, Caskie	40,000	1		3		2		7	8	9	10	11						5	4	6				
QF2	5 (a*)	Dundee U	D 1-1	Duncanson	18,000	1		3		2		7	8	9	10	11						5	4	6				
SF	22 (n†)	Hibernian	W 3-1	Gillick, Thornton, Waddell	125,154	1		3		2		7	8	10	11			9				5	4	6				
F	Apr 5 (n†)	Aberdeen	W 4-0	Duncanson 2, Gillick, Williamson	82,684	1		3		2			8	10	11			9				5	4	6		7		
				Appearances		9	5	10	2	9	2	7	8	8	8	8	3	4	2	1		8	7	6		2		1
				Goals			1			1		2	5	6	6	2		1	3	1								

*Played Dens Park, Dundee. † Played at Hampden Park, Glasgow.

Glasgow Cup

#	Date	Opponent	Res	Scorers	Att	Brown	Cox	Shaw, Jock	Watkins	Young	Symon	Waddell	Gillick	Thornton	Duncanson	Caskie	Gray, David	Williamson	Arnison	Stead
SF	Sep 17 (a)	Clyde	D 2-2	Arnison 2	28,000	1	4	3		5	6		8		10	11	2		9	7
R	25 (h)	Clyde	L 2-4	Arnison, Gillick	40,000	1	4	3		5	6		7		10		2	8	9	11
				Appearances		2	2	2		2	2		2		2	1	2	1	2	2
				Goals									1						3	

Glasgow Merchants' Charity Cup

#	Date	Opponent	Res	Scorers	Att	Brown	Cox	Shaw, Jock	Watkins	Young	Symon	Waddell	Gillick	Thornton	Duncanson	Caskie	Gray, David	Williamson	Arnison	Stead	Parlane	Woodburn	McColl	Rae
SF	May 7 (h)	Partick Thistle	W 4-0	Williamson 3 (1 pen), Gillick	25,000	1	2	3					8	10	7	11		9				5	4	6
F	14 (h)	Celtic	W 1-0	Caskie	38,000	1		3		2			8	10	7	11		9				5	4	6
				Appearances		2	1	2		1			2	2	2	2		2				2	2	2
				Goals									1			1		3						

Other matches

#	Date	Opponent	Res	Scorers	Att	Brown	Cox	Shaw, Jock	Watkins	Young	Symon	Waddell	Gillick	Thornton	Duncanson	Caskie	Gray, David	Williamson	Arnison	Stead	Parlane	Woodburn	McColl	Rae
1	Oct 14 (h)	Sparta Prague	W 3-1	Arnison, Caskie, Gillick	50,000	1		3		2		7	8	10		11			9			5	4	6
2	Apr 26 (a)	Manchester C	L 1-2	Thornton	46,570	1		3		2		7*	8	10	11	12		9				5	4	6
				Appearances		2		2		2		2	2	2		1		1	1			2	2	2
				Sub Appearances													1							
				Goals									1	1		1			1					

1947-48

Manager: W.Struth

Scottish League

No	Month	Day	Opponent	Result	Scorers	Att	Brown	Cox	Shaw, Jock	McColl	Woodburn	Rae	Waddell	Gillick	Williamson	Thornton	Duncanson	Young	Findlay	Paton	Rutherford	Marshall	Parlane	Caskie	Lindsay	Little	Watkins	Johnson	McPherson
1	Aug	13	(h) Third Lanark	W 5-2	Thornton 3, Williamson, Waddell		1	2	3	4	5	6	7	8	9	10	11												
2		27	(a) Partick Thistle	W 1-0	Thornton	35,000	1	2	3	4	5	6	7	8	9	10	11												
3	Sep	20	(h) Celtic	W 2-0	Williamson, Findlay	50,000	1	6	3	4	5		7		9	10	11	2	8										
4	Oct	18	(h) Hibernian	W 2-1	Paton, Williamson	55,000	1	6	3	4	5				9	10	11	2		8	7								
5		25	(a) St Mirren	L 1-2	Thornton	24,000	1	2	3	4	5	6			9	10	11			8	7								
6	Nov	1	(h) Airdrieonians	W 3-0	Thornton, Shaw (pen), Marshall	15,000	1	2	3	4	5	6				9	11		8		7	10							
7		8	(a) Queen of South	W 3-0	Findlay 2, Marshall	21,000	1	2	3	4	5	6	7			9	11		8			10							
8		15	(a) Clyde	W 2-1	Thornton, Marshall	30,000	1	2	3	4	5	6				9	11		8		7	10							
9		22	(h) Morton	D 1-1	Duncanson	25,000	1	2	3	4	5	6		7		9	11		8			10							
10		29	(a) Queen's Park	W 4-1	Gillick 2, Parlane, Duncanson	28,000	1	2	3	4	5	6		8		10	11				7		9						
11	Dec	6	(a) Hearts	W 2-1	Duncanson, Rutherford	40,000	1	2	3	4	5	6		8		9	10				7			11					
12		13	(h) Aberdeen	W 4-0	Gillick 2, Rutherford, Thornton	30,000	1	2	3	4	5	6		8		9	10				7			11					
13		20	(a) Third Lanark	W 1-0	Gillick	20,000	1	2	3	4	5	6		8		9	10				7			11					
14		25	(a) Dundee	W 3-1	Duncanson 3	25,000	1	2	3	4		6		8		9	10	5			7			11					
15		27	(h) Partick Thistle	W 2-1	Rutherford, Gillick	20,000	1	2	3	4	5	6		8		9	10				7			11					
16	Jan	2	(a) Celtic	W 4-0	McColl, Thornton, Rutherford, Duncanson	60,000	1	2	3	4		6		8		9	10	5			7			11					
17		3	(h) Dundee	W 2-1	Thornton 2	35,000	1	2	3	4		6		8		9	10	5			7			11					
18		10	(a) Falkirk	W 5-1	Gillick 2, Duncanson 2, Waddell	22,000	1	6	3	4	5		7	8		9	10	2						11					
19		17	(h) Motherwell	W 2-0	Thornton, Young	35,000	1	6	3	4	5		7	8		9	10	2						11					
20		31	(a) Hibernian	L 0-1		52,750	1	6	3	4	5		7	8		9	10	2						11					
21	Feb	14	(h) St Mirren	W 3-2	Thornton 3	20,000	1	6	3	4	5		7	8		9	10	2						11					
22		28	(h) Queen of South	L 2-3	Gillick, Thornton	34,000	1	6	3	4	5	7		8		9	10	2						11					
23	Mar	13	(a) Morton	W 1-0	Thornton	18,000	1	2	3	4		6	7	8		9	10	5			11								
24		20	(h) Queen's Park	L 1-2	Rutherford	37,000	1	2	3	4		6	7	8		9	10	5			11								
25		29	(h) Falkirk	D 1-1	Duncanson		1	4	3		5	6	7	8		9	10	2			11								
26	Apr	3	(a) Aberdeen	D 1-1	Duncanson	43,800	1	6	3	4	5		7	8		9	10	2			11								
27		24	(a) Motherwell	D 1-1	Duncanson	25,000	1	2		5					9	10	11			8	7				3	4	6		
28		26	(h) Clyde	W 2-1	McPherson, Cox		1	11	3	4						10				8	7				2		6	5	9
29	May	1	(a) Airdrieonians	W 2-1	Findlay 2	18,000	1	6	3	4	5				9	10	11	2	8		7								
30		3	(h) Hearts	L 1-2	Findlay	10,000	1	2		4	5			8		10	11		9		7				3		6		
FINAL LEAGUE POSITION: 2nd						Appearances	30	30	28	29	23	19	12	21	7	30	29	15	7	4	20	4	1	12	3	1	3	1	1
						Goals		1	1	1			2	9	3	17	12	1	6	1	5	3	1						1

Scottish FA Cup

Rd	Month	Day	Opponent	Result	Scorers	Att	Brown	Cox	Shaw, Jock	McColl	Woodburn	Rae	Waddell	Gillick	Williamson	Thornton	Duncanson	Young	Findlay	Paton	Rutherford	Marshall	Parlane	Caskie	Lindsay	Little	Watkins	Johnson	McPherson
1	Jan	24	(a) Stranraer	W 1-0	Thornton	6,000	1	6	3	4	5		7	8		9	10	2						11					
2	Feb	7	(h) Leith Athletic	W 4-0	Thornton, Waddell, Cox, Rutherford	17,000	1	6	3	4	5		11	8		9	10	2			7								
3		21	(h) Partick Thistle	W 3-0	Young (pen), Duncanson, McGowan (og)	68,000	1	6	3	4	5			8		9	10	2			7			11					
QF	Mar	6	(h) East Fife	W 1-0	Duncanson	90,000	1	2	3	4		6		8		9	10	5			7			11					
SF	Mar	27	(n*) Hibernian	W 1-0	Thornton	143,570	1	6	3	4	5		7	8		9	10	2			11								
F	Apr	17	(n*) Morton	D 1-1	Gillick	131,975	1	6	3	4	5			8		9	11	2	10		7								
R		21	(n*) Morton	W 1-0	Williamson	133,750	1	6	3	4	5			11	9	8	10	2			7								
*Played at Hampden Park, Glasgow.						Appearances	7	7	7	7	6	1	3	7	1	7	7	7	1		6			3					
						Goals		1					1	1	1	3	2	1			1								

1 own-goal

Scottish League Cup Section C

Rd	Month	Day	Opponent	Result	Scorers	Att	Brown	Cox	Shaw, Jock	McColl	Woodburn	Rae	Waddell	Gillick	Williamson	Thornton	Duncanson	Young	Findlay	Paton	Rutherford	Marshall	Parlane	Caskie	Lindsay	Little	Watkins	Johnson	McPherson
1	Aug	9	(h) Celtic	W 2-0	Williamson 2	80,000	1	2	3	4	5	6	7	8	9	10	11												
2		16	(a) Third Lanark	W 3-1	Williamson 2, Duncanson	25,000	1	2	3	4	5	6	7	8	9	10	11												
3		23	(h) Dundee	W 3-0	Williamson, Gillick, Thornton	25,000	1	2	3	4	5	6	7	8	9	10	11												
4		30	(a) Celtic	L 0-2		60,000	1	2	3		5	6	7	8	9	10	11										4		
5	Sep	6	(h) Third Lanark	W 3-0	Findlay 2, Gillick	20,000	1	6	3	4	5		7	8		9	11	2	10										
6		13	(a) Dundee	D 1-1	Paton	39,000	1	6	3	4	5		7			9	11	2	10	8									
QF		27	(h) Stenhousemuir	W 2-0	Findlay, Thornton	25,000	1	6	3	4	5		7	8		9	11	2	10										
SF	Oct	11	(n*) Falkirk	L 0-1		44,432	1	6	3	4	5			8		9	11	2	10		7								
*Played at Hampden Park, Glasgow.						Appearances	8	8	8	7	8	4	7	7	4	8	8	4	4	1	1						1		
						Goals								2	5	2	1		3	1									

Glasgow Cup

Rd	Month	Day	Opponent	Result	Scorers	Att	Brown	Cox	Shaw, Jock	McColl	Woodburn	Rae	Waddell	Gillick	Williamson	Thornton	Duncanson	Young	Findlay	Paton	Rutherford	Marshall	Parlane	Caskie	Lindsay	Little	Watkins	Johnson	McPherson
1	Aug	20	(h) Partick Thistle	W 1-0	Thornton	50,000	1	2	3	4	5	6	7	8	9	10	11												
SF	Sep	9	(a) Queen's Park	D 2-2	Thornton, Cox	16,000	1	6	3	4	5		7	8		9	11	2	10										
R		17	(h) Queen's Park	W 3-1	Thornton 2, Findlay		1	6	3	4	5		7			9	11	2	10	8									
F		29	(n*) Third Lanark	W 4-1	Duncanson, Rutherford, Findlay, Gillick	47,000	1	6	3	4	5			8		9	11	2	10		7								
*Played at Hampden Park, Glasgow.						Appearances	4	4	4	4	4	1	3	3	1	4	4	3	3	1	1								
						Goals		1						1		4	1		2		1								

Glasgow Merchants' Charity Cup

Rd	Month	Day	Opponent	Result	Scorers	Att	Brown	Cox	Shaw, Jock	McColl	Woodburn	Rae	Waddell	Gillick	Williamson	Thornton	Duncanson	Young	Findlay	Paton	Rutherford	Marshall	Parlane	Caskie	Lindsay	Little	Watkins	Johnson	McPherson
SF	May	5	(h) Partick Thistle	W 3-0	Findlay 3	31,000	1	6	3	4	5				9	10	11	2	8		7								
F		8	(n*) Celtic	W 2-0	Williamson, Duncanson	69,500	1	6		4	5				9	10	11	2	8		7				3				
*Played at Hampden Park, Glasgow.						Appearances	2	2	1	2	2				2	2	2	2	2		2				1				
						Goals									1		1		3										

Other matches

No	Month	Day	Opponent	Result	Scorers	Att	Brown	Cox	Shaw, Jock	McColl	Woodburn	Rae	Waddell	Gillick	Williamson	Thornton	Duncanson	Young	Findlay	Paton	Rutherford	Marshall	Parlane	Caskie	Lindsay	Little	Watkins	Johnson	McPherson
1	Feb	10	(a) Benfica	W 3-0	Duncanson 2, Thornton	60,000	1	6	3	4	5		7	8		9	10	2						11					
						Appearances	1	1	1	1	1		1	1		1	1	1						1					
						Goals										1	2												

1948-49

Manager: W.Struth

Scottish League

Player columns (left→right): Brown, Young, Shaw, McColl, Woodburn, Cox, Waddell, Findlay, Thornton, Duncanson, Caskie, Rutherford, Gillick, Lindsay, Frame, Marshall, Williamson, Rae, Paton, Wainsley, Little

#	Date	V	Opponent	Result	Scorers	Att	Brown	Young	Shaw	McColl	Woodburn	Cox	Waddell	Findlay	Thornton	Duncanson	Caskie	Rutherford	Gillick	Lindsay	Frame	Marshall	Williamson	Rae	Paton	Wainsley	Little
1	Aug 14	(a)	Motherwell	D 1-1	Thornton	35,000	1	2	3	4	5	6	7	8	9	10	11										
2	18	(h)	Falkirk	W 4-3	Gillick 2, Thornton, Findlay	40,000	1	2	3	4	5	6		10	9	11			7	8							
3	21	(a)	Celtic	W 1-0	Findlay	50,000	1	2	3	4	5	6		10	9	11			7	8							
4	28	(h)	Dundee	D 1-1	Findlay	55,000	1	2		4	5	6		10	9	11			8	3	7						
5	Sep 1	(a)	Partick Thistle	D 1-1	Thornton	40,000	1	2		4	5	6		10	9	11			7	8	3						
6	4	(h)	Third Lanark	W 2-1	Williamson, Duncanson	35,000	1	2		4	5		7		10	11			8	3			6	9			
7	Oct 23	(a)	Hearts	L 0-2		42,000	1		3	4	5	2		10	8	11			7				9	6			
8	Nov 6	(h)	Hibernian	L 2-4	Thornton, Gillick	50,000	1		3	4	5	6		8	10			11	7	2			9				
9	13	(a)	St Mirren	W 2-0	Gillick, Waddell	40,000	1	2	3	4	5	6	7		9	10		11	8								
10	27	(a)	East Fife	W 2-1	Thornton, Duncanson	20,737	1	2	3	4	5	6		8	9	11		7							10		
11	Dec 4	(a)	Clyde	W 3-1	Thornton 2, Paton	25,000	1	2	3	4	5	6		8	9	11		7							10		
12	11	(h)	Morton	W 4-1	Thornton 2, Findlay, Rutherford	25,000	1	2	3	4	5	6		8	9	11		7							10		
13	18	(a)	Queen of South	W 2-0	Thornton, Rutherford	20,200	1	2	3	4	5	6	7	8	9			11							10		
14	25	(a)	Falkirk	D 2-2	Paton, Waddell	21,000	1	2	3	4	5	6	7	8	9			11							10		
15	Jan 1	(h)	Celtic	W 4-0	Duncanson 3, Thornton	95,000	1	2	3	4	5	6	7		9	10		11							8		
16	3	(a)	Dundee	L 1-3	Marshall	39,000	1	2	3	4	5	6	7		9			11				10			8		
17	8	(h)	Motherwell	W 2-0	Paton, Thornton	55,000	1	2	3	4	5	6	7		9			11				10			8		
18	15	(a)	Third Lanark	L 1-2	Thornton	35,000	1	2	3	4	5	6	7		9			11	8						10		
19	29	(h)	Partick Thistle	D 2-2	Thornton, Cox	55,000	1	2	3	4	5	6	7		9	10		11							8		
20	Feb 12	(a)	Aberdeen	W 2-0	Thornton, Paton	42,000	1	2	3	4	5	6	7		9	10		11							8		
21	19	(a)	Hibernian	W 1-0	Paton	50,000	1	2	3	4	5	6	7		9	10		11							8		
22	26	(a)	St Mirren	W 2-1	Thornton, Duncanson	40,000	1	2	3	4	5	6	7		9	10		11							8		
23	Mar 19	(a)	Clyde	W 4-1	Paton 2, Thornton, Duncanson	50,000	1	2	3	4	5	6			9	10		7							8		11
24	Apr 2	(h)	Queen of South	W 3-0	Thornton 2, Duncanson	28,000	1	2	3	4	5	6	7		9	10		11							8		
25	5	(h)	Hearts	W 2-1	Cox, Paton	45,000	1	2	3	4	5	6	7		9	10		11							8		
26	13	(h)	East Fife	W 3-1	Young 2 (2 pens), Paton	35,000	1	2	3	4	5	6	7		9	10		11							8		
27	16	(h)	Aberdeen	D 1-1	Duncanson	45,000	1	2	3	4	5	6	7		9	10		11							8		
28	18	(h)	Albion R	W 3-1	Williamson, Waddell, Young (pen)	16,000	1	2	3	4	5	6	7			10		11					9		8		
29	25	(a*)	Morton	W 1-0	Thornton	40,000	1	2	3	4	5	6	7	8	9			11							10		
30	30	(a)	Albion R	W 4-1	Thornton 3, Duncanson	15,000	1	2	3	4	5	6	7		9	8		11							10		
					Appearances		30	28	27	30	30	29	20	12	29	24	1	27	8	4	1	3	6	1	19		1
					Goals			3				2	3	4	23	10		2	4			1	2		9		

FINAL LEAGUE POSITION: 1st
*Played at St Mirren Park, Paisley.

Scottish FA Cup

#	Date	V	Opponent	Result	Scorers	Att	Brown	Young	Shaw	McColl	Woodburn	Cox	Waddell	Thornton	Duncanson	Rutherford	Williamson	Paton
1	Jan 22	(h)	Elgin C	W 6-1	Thornton 2, Duncanson 2, Cox, Rutherford	29,000	1	2	3	4	5	6	7	9	10	11		8
2	Feb 5	(a)	Motherwell	W 3-0	Young (pen), Paton, Thornton	31,000	1	2	3	4	5	6	7	9	10	11		8
QF	Mar 5	(h)	Partick Thistle	W 4-0	Thornton 2, Duncanson, Paton	65,000	1	2	3	4	5	6	7	9	10	11		8
SF	26	(n*)	East Fife	W 3-0	Thornton 3	104,958	1	2	3	4	5	6	7	9	10	11		8
F	Apr 23	(n*)	Clyde	W 4-1	Young 2 (2 pens), Williamson, Duncanson	120,162	1	2	3	4	5	6	7	9	8	11	10	
					Appearances		5	5	5	5	5	5	5	5	5	5	1	4
					Goals			3				1		8	4	1	1	2

Rangers received Bye in Round Three.
*Played at Hampden Park, Glasgow.

Scottish League Cup Section A

#	Date	V	Opponent	Result	Scorers	Att
1	Sep 11	(h)	Clyde	D 1-1	Findlay	50,000
2	18	(a)	Hibernian	D 0-0		47,000
3	25	(a)	Celtic	L 1-3	Findlay	65,000
4	Oct 2	(a)	Clyde	W 3-1	Waddell 3 (2 pens)	27,000
5	9	(h)	Hibernian	W 1-0	Thornton	76,466
6	16	(h)	Celtic	W 2-1	Williamson, Waddell	105,000
QF	30	(h)	St Mirren	W 1-0	Thornton	50,000
SF	Nov 20	(n*)	Dundee	W 4-1	Rutherford, McColl, Duncanson, Thornton	50,996
F	Mar 12	(n*)	Raith Rovers	W 2-0	Gillick, Paton	57,450

Appearances: Brown 9, Young 9, Shaw 9, McColl 6, Woodburn 7, Cox 9, Waddell 8, Findlay 4, Thornton 9, Duncanson 8, Caskie 1, Rutherford 3, Gillick 4, Lindsay 2, Marshall 3, Williamson 4, Rae 3, Paton 1
Goals: McColl 1, Waddell 4, Findlay 2, Thornton 3, Duncanson 1, Rutherford 1, Gillick 1, Williamson 1, Paton 1

*Played at Hampden Park, Glasgow.

Glasgow Cup

#	Date	V	Opponent	Result	Scorers	Att
1	Aug 25	(a)	Clyde	W 2-1	Thornton, Findlay	24,000
SF	Sep 7	(a)	Third Lanark	L 1-4	Thornton	22,000

Appearances: Brown 2, Young 2, Shaw 1, McColl 2, Woodburn 2, Cox 2, Waddell 1, Findlay 1, Thornton 2, Duncanson 2, Caskie 1, Rutherford 1, Lindsay 1, Marshall 1, Williamson 1, 1
Goals: Findlay 1, Thornton 2

Glasgow Merchants' Charity Cup

#	Date	V	Opponent	Result	Att
SF	May 4	(h)	Partick Thistle	L 0-1	30,000

Appearances: Brown 1, Young 1, Shaw 1, McColl 1, Woodburn 1, Cox 1, Waddell 1, Thornton 1, Duncanson 1, Caskie 1, Marshall 1
Goals: —

1949-50

Manager: W.Struth

Scottish League

No	Date	Opponent	Result	Scorers	Att	Brown	Young	Shaw	McColl	Woodburn	Cox	Waddell	Findlay	Williamson	Duncanson	Hubbard	Rae	Rutherford	Paton	Thornton	Gillick	Johnson	McCulloch	Marshall	McIntyre	Lindsay	Little	Forbes
1	Sep 10 (h)	Partick Thistle	W 2-0	Waddell, Findlay	60,000	1	2	3	4	5	6	7	8	9	10	11												
2	24 (h)	Celtic	W 4-0	Rutherford, Findlay, Waddell (pen), Williamson	64,000	1	2	3	4	5	10	7	8	9			6	11										
3	Oct 15 (a)	Falkirk	W 2-0	Williamson, Rutherford	20,000	1	2	3	4	5	6		8	9		11		7	10									
4	22 (a)	Hearts	W 1-0	Findlay	50,000	1	2	3	4	5	6		8	10	11			7		9								
5	29 (a)	Aberdeen	W 3-1	Findlay, Thornton, Rutherford	40,000	1	2	3	4	5	6		8	10				11	7	9								
6	Nov 5 (a)	Hibernian	L 0-1		51,500	1	2	3	4	5	6		8	10			11	7		9								
7	12 (h)	St Mirren	W 1-0	Johnson	45,000	1	2	3	4	5	6		8					11	7	9		10						
8	19 (a)	Raith Rovers	W 3-1	Williamson 2, Thornton	24,800	1	2	3	4	5	6			9				7	11	8		10						
9	26 (h)	Stirling Albion	W 2-1	Thornton, Williamson	45,000	1	2	3	4	5	6			9	11			7		8		10						
10	Dec 3 (h)	Clyde	W 5-4	Thornton 2, Cox 2, Johnson	25,000	1	2	3	8	5	6						4	11		9		10	7					
11	10 (a)	Motherwell	L 0-4		28,000	1	2	3	8	5	6						4	11		9		10	7					
12	17 (h)	Queen of South	W 1-0	Thornton	18,000	1	2	3	4	5	6				8			11		9		10	7					
13	24 (h)	Partick Thistle	W 3-1	Johnson 2, Thornton	35,000	1	2	3	4	5	6		8			11		7		9		10						
14	31 (h)	Dundee	D 2-2	Thornton, Findlay	35,000	1	2	3	4	5	6		8			11				9		10	7					
15	Jan 2 (a)	Celtic	D 1-1	McCulloch	65,000	1	2	3	4	5	6		8							9		10	7		11			
16	3 (h)	Third Lanark	W 3-1	Thornton 2, Johnson	30,000	1	2	3	4	5	6			9						8		10	7		11			
17	7 (a)	East Fife	W 2-0	Williamson, Rutherford	18,674	1	2	3	4	5	6		8	9				11				10	7					
18	14 (a)	Falkirk	W 3-0	Young (pen), Rutherford, Williamson	35,000	1	2	3	4	5	6		8	9				11				10	7					
19	21 (a)	Hearts	W 1-0	Findlay	49,000	1	2	3	4	5	6		8	9	11							10	7					
20	Feb 4 (h)	Aberdeen	D 2-2	Young 2 (2 pens)	50,000	1	2	3	4	5	6		8	9					11			10	7					
21	18 (a)	St Mirren	W 2-1	Rutherford, Waddell	40,000	1	2		4	5	6	7		9				11	8			10		3				
22	25 (h)	Raith Rovers	W 2-0	Williamson, Waddell	35,000	1	2	3	4	5	6	7		9				11	8			10						
23	Mar 4 (a)	Stirling Albion	W 2-0	Williamson, Paton	25,000	1	2	3	4	5	6	7		9	11				8			10						
24	18 (h)	Motherwell	W 2-0	Findlay, Rutherford	38,000	1	2	3	4	5	6		8	9				7				10			11			
25	25 (a)	Queen of South	W 2-1	Thornton, Williamson	18,000	1	2	3	4	5	6		8	10	11			7		9								
26	Apr 8 (h)	East Fife	D 2-2	Cox, Findlay	40,000	1	5	3	4		6	7	8					11		9		10			2			
27	10 (a)	Clyde	W 2-1	Rae, Cox	25,000	1	2	3	4	5	6	7	8		10		11			9								
28	17 (a)	Dundee	W 1-0	Duncanson	32,000	1	2	3	4	5	6		8		10		11	7		9								
29	29 (h)	Hibernian	D 0-0		101,000	1	2	3	4	5	6		8		10		11	7		9								
30	May 1 (a)	Third Lanark	D 2-2	Williamson, Paton	32,800	1	2	3	4	5	6			10				7	8	9		11						
				FINAL LEAGUE POSITION: 1st	Appearances	30	30	29	30	29	30	7	20	19	12	2	7	22	7	19	2	20	10	1	2	2		
					Goals		3				4	4	8	11	1		1	7	2	11		5	1					

Scottish FA Cup

No	Date	Opponent	Result	Scorers	Att	Brown	Young	Shaw	McColl	Woodburn	Cox	Waddell	Findlay	Williamson	Duncanson	Hubbard	Rae	Rutherford	Paton	Thornton	Gillick	Johnson	McCulloch	Marshall				
1	Jan 28 (a)	Motherwell	W 4-2	Williamson, Paton, McCulloch, Findlay	32,000	1	2	3	4	5	6		8	9				11				10	7					
2	Feb 11 (h)	Cowdenbeath	W 8-0	McCulloch 2, Williamson 2, Johnson 2, Paton, Rutherford	24,000	1	2		4	5	6			9				11	8			10	7	3				
QF	Mar 11 (h)	Raith Rovers	D 1-1	Findlay	43,080	1	2	3	4	5	6	7	10	9				11	8									
R	15 (a)	Raith Rovers	D 1-1	Williamson	28,500	1	2	3	4	5	6	7	8	10	11					9								
2R	27 (h)	Raith Rovers	W 2-0	Findlay, Cox	63,000	1	2	3	4	5	6		8	10			11	7		9								
SF	Apr 1 (n*)	Queen of South	D 1-1	Rutherford	52,924	1	2	3	4	5	6	7	8	10				11		9								
R	5 (n*)	Queen of South	W 3-0	Williamson, Young (pen), Findlay	58,975	1	2	3	4	5	6		10	9			11	7	8									
F	22 (n*)	East Fife	W 3-0	Thornton 2, Findlay	120,015	1	2	3	4	5	6		8		10		11	7		9								
		Rangers received a bye in round three.			Appearances	8	8	7	8	8	8	3	7	7	2		3	5	3	6		2	2	1				
		*Played at Hampden Park, Glasgow.			Goals		1				1		5	5				2	2	2		2	3					

Scottish League Cup Section A

No	Date	Opponent	Result	Scorers	Att	Brown	Young	Shaw	McColl	Woodburn	Cox	Waddell	Findlay	Williamson	Duncanson	Hubbard	Rae	Rutherford	Paton	Thornton	Gillick	Johnson	McCulloch	Marshall				
1	Aug 13 (a)	Celtic	L 2-3	Waddell (pen), Thornton	71,000	1	2	3	4	5	6	7	8		10			11		9								
2	17 (h)	St Mirren	W 5-1	Waddell 2 (1 pen), Rutherford, Findlay, Thornton	50,000	1	2	3	4	5	6	7	8		10			11		9								
3	20 (h)	Aberdeen	W 4-2	Findlay 2, Duncanson 2	50,000	1	2	3	4	5	6	7	8		10			11		9								
4	27 (h)	Celtic	W 2-0	Findlay, Waddell	95,000	1	2	3		5	4	7	8		10		6	11		9								
5	30 (a)	St Mirren	D 1-1	Duncanson	45,000	1	2	3	4	5	6	7	8	9				11										
6	Sep 3 (a)	Aberdeen	D 1-1	Findlay	43,000	1	2	3	4	5	6	7	8	9	11						10							
QF1	17 (h)	Cowdenbeath	L 2-3	Williamson, Marshall	46,670	1	2	3	4	5	6	7	8	9				11						10				
QF2	21 (a)	Cowdenbeath	W 3-1	Cox 2, Rutherford	25,586	1	2	3	4	5	10	7	8	9			6	11										
SF	Oct 8 (n*)	East Fife	L 1-2	Marshall	74,507	1	2	3	4	5	6	7	8	9				11						10				
		*Played at Hampden Park, Glasgow.			Appearances	9	9	9	8	9	9	9	9	5	6		2	8		4	1			2				
					Goals						2	4	5	1	3			2		2				2				

Glasgow Cup

No	Date	Opponent	Result	Scorers	Att	Brown	Young	Shaw	McColl	Woodburn	Cox	Waddell	Findlay	Williamson	Duncanson	Hubbard	Rae	Rutherford	Paton	Thornton	Gillick	Johnson						
SF	Sep 13 (a)	Celtic	W 2-1	Williamson, Findlay	55,000	1	2	3	4	5	6	7	8	9	10			11										
F	26 (n*)	Clyde	D 2-2	Rutherford, Waddell (pen)	53,177	1	2		4	5	3	7	10	9			6	11		8								
R	Oct 12 (n*)	Clyde	W 2-1	Gillick 2	40,000	1	2	3	4	5	6	7			10			11	9	8								
		*Played at Hampden Park, Glasgow.			Appearances	3	3	2	3	3	3	3	2	3	1		1	3	1		2							
					Goals							1	1	1				1			2						

Glasgow Merchants' Charity Cup

No	Date	Opponent	Result	Scorers	Att	Brown	Young	Shaw	McColl	Woodburn	Cox	Waddell	Findlay	Williamson	Duncanson	Hubbard	Rae	Rutherford	Paton	Thornton	Gillick	Johnson	McCulloch	Marshall	McIntyre	Lindsay	Little	
SF	May 3 (h)	Partick Thistle	W 4-0	Thornton 3 (1 pen), Duncanson	22,000	1		3		5					10	11		7	8	9		6				2	4	
F	6 (n*)	Celtic	L 2-3	Gillick, Thornton	81,672	1		3		5	6				10	11			8	9	7					2	4	
		*Played at Hampden Park, Glasgow.			Appearances	2		2		2	1				2	2		1	2	2	1	1				2	2	
					Goals										1					4	1							

Other matches

No	Date	Opponent	Result	Scorers	Att	Brown	Young	Shaw	McColl	Woodburn	Cox	Waddell	Findlay	Williamson	Duncanson	Hubbard	Rae	Rutherford	Paton	Thornton	Gillick	Johnson	McCulloch	Marshall	McIntyre	Lindsay	Little	
1	May 9 (a)	Malmö FF	W 1-0	Findlay	18,200	1	2	3	4	5	6		8		10	11		7		9								
2	11 (a)	Staevnet	W 2-0	Findlay, Thornton	20,000	1	2	3	4	5	6		8		10	11		7		9								
3	17 (a)	Akademisk	L 1-2	Findlay	20,000	1	2		4	5	6		8			11				9	10			3		7		
					Appearances	3	3	2	3	3	3		3		2	1	2	3		3				1		1		
					Goals								3							1								

1950-51

Manager: W.Struth

Scottish League

Player columns (left to right): Brown, Young, Shaw, McColl, Woodburn, Cox, Waddell, Findlay, Thornton, Paton, Rutherford, Rae, Duncanson, Lindsay, Johnson, Simpson R, Simpson W, Williamson, Little A, Hubbard, Dunlop, Marshall, Beckett, Prentice, McCulloch, Wright

#	Date		Opponent	Result	Scorers	Att	Br	Yo	Sh	Mc	Wo	Cx	Wa	Fi	Th	Pa	Ru	Rae	Dun·n	Lin	Joh	SiR	SiW	Wil	LiA	Hub	Dun·p	Mar	Bec	Pre	McC	Wr
1	Sep	9 (a)	East Fife	W 3-0	Thornton, Findlay, Waddell	26,000	1	2	3	4	5	6	7	8	9	10	11															
2		16 (h)	Dundee	D 0-0		40,000	1	2	3	4	5			8	9	10	7	6	11													
3		23 (a)	Celtic	L 2-3	Rae, Thornton	53,789	1	2		4	5	6		8	9		7	11		3	10											
4		30 (h)	Airdrieonians	W 4-1	Thornton 2, R.Simpson 2	20,000	1	2		4	5	6	7		9	10	11			3		8										
5	Oct	7 (a)	Partick Thistle	L 1-2	Thornton	33,000	1	2		4	5	6	7		9	10	11			3		8										
6		14 (h)	Third Lanark	W 2-1	Cox, Rutherford	35,000	1	2		4	5	6	7	8	9		11			3	10											
7		28 (h)	Aberdeen	L 1-2	Thornton	50,000	1	2	3	4	5		7	8	10		11	6						9								
8	Nov	4 (h)	Hibernian	D 1-1	Paterson (og)	80,000	1	2	3	4	5		7	8	10		11	6						9								
9		11 (a)	St Mirren	W 2-0	Paton, Thornton	20,000	1	5	3	4			7	8	10		11	6		2			9									
10		18 (h)	Raith Rovers	W 4-1	Thornton, Paton, Williamson, Young (pen)	25,000	1	2	3	4	5		7	8	10		11	6						9								
11		25 (a)	Falkirk	D 1-1	Thornton	20,000	1	2	3	4	5		7	8	10		11	6						9								
12	Dec	2 (a)	Clyde	L 1-2	Williamson	22,000	1	2	3	4	5		7	8	10		11	6						9								
13		9 (h)	Morton	W 2-0	Paton 2	35,000	1	2	3		5		7	8	10			6					9		4	11						
14		23 (h)	East Fife	W 5-0	W.Simpson 3, Rae, Hubbard	25,000	1	2	3	4	5		7	8	10			6					9			11						
15		30 (a)	Dundee	L 0-2		37,400	1	2	3	4	5	6	7	8	10		11						9									
16	Jan	1 (h)	Celtic	W 1-0	Waddell	55,000	1	2	3	4	5	6	7	8	10		11						9									
17		6 (h)	Partick Thistle	L 1-3	Waddell	40,000	1	5	3			6	7	8	10		11			2			9							4		
18		20 (h)	Hearts	W 2-1	Thornton, W.Simpson	54,000	1	2	3	4	5		7	8	10			6					9				11					
19	Feb	3 (a)	Aberdeen	W 4-2	Thornton 2, Paton, W.Simpson	42,000	1	2	3	4	5		7	8	10		11	6					9									
20		17 (h)	St Mirren	D 1-1	W.Simpson	20,000	1	2	3	4	5		7	8	10		11	6					9									
21		24 (a)	Raith Rovers	L 1-3	Waddell	25,000	1	2	3	4	5		7	8			11	6					10	9								
22	Mar	3 (h)	Falkirk	W 5-2	Findlay 3, W.Simpson, Marshall	20,000	1	2	3	4	5		7	8			11	6					9					10				
23		10 (h)	Clyde	W 4-0	Findlay 2, McColl, Waddell	20,000	1	2	3	4	5		7	8				6					9					10	11			
24		17 (a)	Morton	W 2-0	Marshall, Findlay	22,000	1	2	3	4	5		7	8			11	6					9					10				
25		24 (h)	Motherwell	W 3-0	Findlay, Hubbard, W.Simpson	30,000	1	2	3	4	5		7	8				6					9			11		10				
26		31 (a)	Airdrieonians	L 1-2	Waddell	20,000	1	2	3	4	5		7	8				6					9			11		10				
27	Apr	7 (a)	Motherwell	W 3-2	Rutherford, Woodburn, Findlay	18,000	1	2	3	4	5		7	8			10	6					9			11						
28		21 (a)	Hearts	W 1-0	Findlay	35,000	1	2	3	4	5		7	8			10	6					9			11						
29		25 (a)	Third Lanark	W 5-1	W.Simpson 4, Rutherford	25,000	1	2	3	4	5		7	8			10	6					9			11						
30		28 (a)	Hibernian	L 1-4	W.Simpson	40,000	1	2	3	4	5		7	8			10	6					9			11						
				FINAL LEAGUE POSITION: 2nd		Appearances	30	30	18	25	28	19	28	16	21	19	17	25	1	6	2	2	19	6	1	8	2	5	1	1		
						Goals		1		1	1	1	6	10	12	5	3	2				2	13	2		2		2				

1 own-goal

Scottish FA Cup

#	Date		Opponent	Result	Scorers	Att	Br	Yo	Sh	Mc	Wo	Cx	Wa	Fi	Th	Pa	Ru	Rae	SiW
1	Jan	27 (h)	Queen of South	W 2-0	W.Simpson, Waddell	40,000	1	2	3	4	5		7	8	10		11	6	9
2	Feb	10 (h)	Hibernian	L 2-3	W.Simpson 2	102,342	1	2	3	4	5	6	7	8		10	11		9
					Appearances		2	2	2	1	2	2	2	1	2	1	1	2	2
					Goals								1						3

Scottish League Cup Section D

#	Date		Opponent	Result	Scorers	Att	Br	Yo	Sh	Mc	Wo	Cx	Wa	Fi	Th	Pa	Ru	Lin
1	Aug	12 (a)	Morton	W 2-1	Rutherford, Findlay	18,500	1		3	4	5	6	7	8	9	10	11	2
2		16 (h)	Aberdeen	L 1-2	Findlay	40,000	1	2	3	4	5	6	7	8	9	10	11	
3		19 (h)	Clyde	W 4-0	Thornton 3, J.Dunn (og)	45,000	1	2	3	4	5	6	7	8	9	10	11	
4		26 (h)	Morton	W 6-1	Findlay 2, Thornton 2, Paton 2	35,000	1	2	3	4	5	6	7	8	9	10	11	
5		30 (a)	Aberdeen	L 0-2		42,000	1	5	3	4		6	7	8	9	10	11	2
6	Sep	2 (a)	Clyde	W 5-1	Thornton 2, Findlay 2, Paton	31,000	1	2	3	4	5	6	7	8	9	10	11	
					Appearances		6	5	6	6	5	6	6	6	6	6	6	2
					Goals									6	7	3	1	

Rangers failed to qualify for the quarter-final.

1 own-goal

Glasgow Cup

#	Date		Opponent	Result	Scorers	Att	Br	Yo	Sh	Mc	Wo	Cx	Wa	Fi	Th	Ru	Rae	Lin	Joh	SiW	Pre
SF	Sep	12 (h)	Partick Thistle	D 2-2	Paton, Cox	14,000	1	2	3	4	5	6		8	9	11					7
R		20 (a)	Partick Thistle	D 1-1*	Johnson	30,000	1	2		4	5		7	8		11	6	3	10	9	
					Appearances		2	2	1	2	2	1	1	2	1	2	1	1	1	1	1
					Goals							1							1		

*Partick Thistle won on the toss of coin.

Glasgow Merchants' Charity Cup

#	Date		Opponent	Result	Scorers	Att	Br	Yo	Sh	Mc	Wo	Cx	Wa	Fi	Th	Rae	SiR	Wil	Hub	Mar
1	May	2 (n*)	Celtic	W 2-1	Thornton, Findlay	70,000	1	2	3	4	5	6	7	8	9	11	10			
SF		5 (n*)	Third Lanark	D 1-1†	Waddell	36,533	1	2	3	4	5	6	7	8	9			11	10	
F		7 (n*)	Partick Thistle	W 2-0	Findlay 2	35,000	1	2	3	4	5	6	7	8	9				10	11
					Appearances		3	3	3	3	3	3	3	3	3	1	1	1	2	1
					Goals								1	3	1					

†Rangers won on the toss of a coin.
*Played at Hampden Park, Glasgow.

Other match

#	Date		Opponent	Result	Scorers	Att	Br	Yo	Mc	Wo	Cx	Wa	Fi	Th	Pa	Ru	Lin	McC
1	Aug	14 (h)	Akademisk	W 2-1	Findlay, Rutherford	50,000	1	2	4	5	6	7	8	9	10		3	11
					Appearances		1	1	1	1	1	1	1	1	1	1	1	1
					Goals							1		1				

1951-52

Manager: W.Struth

Scottish League

Player columns (left to right): Brown, Young, Little PJ, McColl, Woodburn, Cox, Waddell, Findlay, Simpson W, Thornton, Rutherford, Gardiner, Hubbard, Rae, Johnson, Prentice, Liddell, Paton, Pryde, Shaw, McCulloch, Stanners, Boyd, Neillands, Marshall, Niven, Frame, Scobie

#	Date	Opponent	Result	Scorers	Att	Brn	You	Lit	McC	Woo	Cox	Wad	Fin	Sim	Tho	Rut	Gar	Hub	Rae	Joh	Pre	Lid	Pat	Pry	Sha	Mcu	Sta	Boy	Nei	Mar	Niv	Fra	Sco
1	Sep 8 (h)	Partick Thistle	W 4-1	Findlay 3, Rutherford	60,000	1	2	3	4	5	6	7	8	9	10	11																	
2	22 (h)	Celtic	D 1-1	Findlay	86,000	1	2	3	4	5	6	7	8		10					9	11												
3	29 (a)	Dundee	L 0-1		31,000	1	2	3	4	5	6	11	8		10	9				7													
4	Oct 10 (h)	East Fife	D 1-1	Waddell	20,000	1	2	3	4	5		7	8			11		9		6	10												
5	20 (h)	Hearts	W 2-0	Waddell	40,000	1	2	3	4	5	6	7	8				9			11	10												
6	Nov 3 (h)	Hibernian	D 1-1	Findlay	55,000	1	2	3	4	5	6	7	8	9	10	11																	
7	10 (h)	St Mirren	W 5-1	Thornton 3, Johnson, Findlay	25,000	1	2	3	4	5	6	7	8		10					9	11												
8	17 (a)	Raith Rovers	L 1-3	Liddell	21,000	1	2	3	4	5	6	7	8		10					9		11											
9	24 (h)	Stirling Albion	W 3-0	Johnson 2, Waddell	20,000	1	2	3	4	5	6	7			10					9		11	8										
10	Dec 1 (h)	Third Lanark	D 1-1	Thornton	20,000	1	2	3	4	5	6	7			10					9		11	8										
11	8 (a)	Morton	W 1-0	McColl	14,000	1	2	3	4	5	10	7			9						6	11	8										
12	15 (h)	Motherwell	W 3-0	Thornton, Liddell, Cox	40,000	1	2	3	4	5	10	7			9						6	11	8										
13	22 (a)	Partick Thistle	W 3-1	Cox 2, Paton	35,000	1	2	3		5	10	7			9						6	11	8				4						
14	29 (h)	Queen of South	W 3-2	Thornton, Young (pen)	30,000	1	2	3	4	5	10	7			9						6	11	8										
15	Jan 1 (a)	Celtic	W 4-1	Paton 2, Liddell, Waddell	45,000	1	2		4	5	10	7			9						6	11	8	3									
16	2 (h)	Dundee	L 1-2	Thornton	35,000	1	2	3	4	5	10	7			9						6	11	8										
17	5 (a)	East Fife	L 1-2	Thornton	18,000	1	2	3	4	5	10				9						6	11	8			7							
18	12 (h)	Airdrieonians	W 1-0	Thornton	45,000	1	2	3	4	5	10	7			9						6	11	8										
19	19 (a)	Hearts	D 2-2	Findlay 2	47,600	1	2	3	4	5			8		9						6	11	10			7							
20	26 (a)	St Mirren	W 5-0	Thornton 2, Liddell 2, Paton	32,000	1	2	3	4	5			8		9						6	11	10			7							
21	Feb 2 (h)	Aberdeen	W 3-2	Thornton, Paton, Young (pen)	40,000	1	2	3	4	5			8		9						6	11	10			7							
22	13 (h)	Hibernian	D 2-2	McCulloch, Young (pen)	45,000	1	2	3	4	5			8		9						6	11	10			7							
23	16 (a)	Airdrieonians	W 1-0	Thornton	24,000	1	2	3	4	5			8		9						6	11	10			7							
24	27 (h)	Raith Rovers	W 1-0	Thornton	20,000	1	2		4	3	7		8		9						6	11	10						5				
25	Mar 1 (a)	Stirling Albion	W 5-1	Prentice, Waddell, Rae, Cox (pen), Thornton	14,000	1	2	5		3	6	7			9		10		4		6	11	8										
26	15 (h)	Morton	W 1-0	Thornton	35,000	1	5	2	4	3		7			9		10				6	11	8										
27	22 (a)	Motherwell	L 1-2	W.Simpson	22,200	1	2	3	4	5		7		8	9		10				6	11											
28	29 (a)	Queen of South	D 2-2	Marshall, Thornton	12,000	1	2	3	4	5	6	7			9							11								8	10		
29	Apr 16 (a)	Third Lanark	D 1-1	Prentice	15,000	1	2	3	4	5	6	7			9						10	11						8					
30	19 (a)	Aberdeen	D 1-1	Liddell	20,000		2		4	5	6	7			9						10	11		3								8	1

FINAL LEAGUE POSITION: 2nd

	Brn	You	Lit	McC	Woo	Cox	Wad	Fin	Sim	Tho	Rut	Gar	Hub	Rae	Joh	Pre	Lid	Pat	Pry	Sha	Mcu	Sta	Boy	Nei	Mar	Niv	Fra	Sco
Appearances	29	28	28	29	27	23	24	14	3	28	4	4	1	2	9	19	24	15	3	2	6	1	2	3	1	1		
Goals		3		1		4	5	9	1	18	1			1	3	2	6	5			1				1			

Scottish FA Cup

Rnd	Date	Opponent	Result	Scorers	Att	Brn	You	Lit	McC	Woo	Wad	Fin	Tho	Gar	Pre	Lid	Pat	Mcu
2	Feb 9 (h)	Elgin C	W 6-1	Findlay 2, Paton, Waddell, Liddell, Thornton	36,324	1	2	3	4	5	7	8	9		6	11	10	
3	23 (a)	Arbroath	W 2-0	Thornton 2	13,510	1	2	3	4	5		8	9		6	11	10	7
QF	Mar 8 (h)	Motherwell	D 1-1	Thornton	82,000	1	5	2	4	3	7		9	8	6	11	10	
R	12 (a)	Motherwell	L 1-2	Thornton	36,632	1	5	2	4	3		8	9		6	11	10	7

	Brn	You	Lit	McC	Woo	Wad	Fin	Tho	Gar	Pre	Lid	Pat	Mcu
Appearances	4	4	4	4	4	2	3	4	1	4	4	4	2
Goals						1	2	5			1	1	

Scottish League Cup Section D

#	Date	Opponent	Result	Scorers	Att
1	Aug 11 (a)	East Fife	D 0-0		18,500
2	15 (h)	Aberdeen	W 2-1	Rutherford, Paton	60,000
3	18 (a)	Queen of South	W 3-0	W.Simpson 2, Waddell	19,000
4	25 (h)	East Fife	W 4-1	W.Simpson 2, Waddell (pen), Findlay	28,000
5	29 (a)	Aberdeen	L 1-2	W.Simpson	28,000
6	Sep 1 (h)	Queen of South	W 5-2	Thornton 3, McColl, W.Simpson	40,000
QF1	15 (h)	Dunfermline A	L 0-1		20,000
QF2	19 (h)	Dunfermline A	W 3-1	Findlay 2, Gardiner	45,000
SF	Oct 13 (n*)	Celtic	W 3-0	Thornton, Johnson, Findlay	83,235
F	27 (n*)	Dundee	L 2-3	Findlay, Young	95,325

*Played at Hampden Park, Glasgow.

	Brn	You	Lit	McC	Woo	Cox	Wad	Fin	Sim	Tho	Rut	Gar	Joh	Pre	Lid	Pat
Appearances	10	9	10	10	10	8	10	10	6	6	6	8	2	3	2	5
Goals		1		1			2	5	6	4	1	1	1			1

Glasgow Cup

#	Date	Opponent	Result	Scorers	Att	Brn	You	Lit	McC	Woo	Cox	Wad	Fin	Sim	Rut	Pre
1	Aug 21 (a)	Clyde	L 1-2	Rutherford	17,000	1	2	3	5	4	6	7	8	9	11	10

	Brn	You	Lit	McC	Woo	Cox	Wad	Fin	Sim	Rut	Pre
Appearances	1	1	1	1	1	1	1	1	1	1	1
Goals										1	

Glasgow Merchants' Charity Cup

#	Date	Opponent	Result	Scorers	Att	Brn	You	Lit	McC	Woo	Sim	Gar	Pre	Lid	Mcu	Mar	Fra
1	May 3 (h)	Partick Thistle	W 4-3	Liddell 2, McColl, W.Simpson	28,000	1	2	3	4	5	9	11	6	10	7	8	
SF	7 (h)	Third Lanark	L 0-1		15,000	1	2	3	4	5	9	11	6	10	7	8	7

	Brn	You	Lit	McC	Woo	Sim	Gar	Pre	Lid	Mcu	Mar	Fra
Appearances	2	2	2	2	2	2	2	2	2	1	2	1
Goals				1		1			2			

St Mungo Cup

#	Date	Opponent	Result	Scorers	Att	Brn	You	Lit	McC	Cox	Wad	Fin	Sim	Tho	Pre	Sha
1	Jul 14 (a)	Aberdeen	L 1-2	Findlay	35,000	1	5	2	4	6	7	8	9	10	11	3

	Brn	You	Lit	McC	Cox	Wad	Fin	Sim	Tho	Pre	Sha
Appearances	1	1	1	1	1	1	1	1	1	1	1
Goals							1				

Other matches

#	Date	Opponent	Result	Scorers	Att
1	Aug 22 (a)	Caledonian	W 5-3*	Paton 2, Findlay, Simpson, Rutherford	12,000
2	Oct 17 (a)	Arsenal	L 2-3	Findlay, Johnson	62,000
3	Apr 21 (a)	Deveronvale	W 4-0	Gardiner 2, Prentice 2	6,000
4	23 (a)	Elgin C	D 1-1†	Prentice	8,000
5	25 (a)	Inverness S	W 2-0	Gardiner, Prentice	7,500

Players (other matches): Brown1, Young2, Little3, McColl4, Woodburn5, Cox6, Waddell7, Findlay8, Simpson W9, Thornton, Rutherford11, Gardiner10, Johnson, Prentice, Liddell, Paton, Pryde3, Shaw, McCulloch, Marshall, Niven, Frame, Scobie

*Bobby Bolt Benefit Match. †Johnny Logie and Stuart McLachlan Benefit Match.
Matches 1 and 5 both played at Grant Street Park, Inverness.

	Brn	You	Lit	McC	Woo	Cox	Wad	Fin	Sim	Tho	Rut	Gar	Joh	Pre	Lid	Pat	Sha	Mcu	Mar	Niv	Fra	Sco
Appearances	2	5	2	5	4	5	5	2	1	1	2	2	1	3	3	1	3	3	3	3	2	
Goals								2	1		1	3	1	4		2						

1952-53

Manager: W.Struth

Scottish League

No	Date	Opponent	Result	Scorers	Att	Niven	Young	Little	McColl	Woodburn	Cox	Waddell	Grierson	Thornton	Prentice	Liddell	McCulloch	Hubbard	Simpson W	Shaw	Paton	Rae	Gardiner	Stanners	Pryde	Dunlop	Brown	Marshall	McMillan PH	Woods
1	Sep 6 (a)	St Mirren	W 3-2	Grierson 2, Thornton	45,000	1	2	3	4	5	6	7	8	9	10	11														
2	20 (a)	Celtic	L 1-2	Liddell	48,000	1	2	3	4	5	6		8	9	10	11	7													
3	27 (h)	Third Lanark	W 4-1	Thornton 2, Grierson 2	25,000	1	2	3	4	5	6		8	9	10	11	7													
4	Oct 11 (h)	Hibernian	L 1-2	Grierson	65,000	1	2	3	4	5	6		8		10	11	7		9											
5	18 (a)	East Fife	L 2-3	Thornton, Grierson	20,000	1	2		4	5			8	10	6	11	7		9	3										
6	Nov 1 (h)	Queen of South	W 3-1	Liddell, W.Simpson, Paton	20,000	1	2	3	4	5	6		8		10	11			9		7									
7	8 (a)	Falkirk	W 2-1	Prentice, W.Simpson	18,500	1	2	3	4	5	6		8		10	11	7		9											
8	15 (a)	Clyde	W 6-4	W.Simpson 3, Prentice, Waddell, Grierson	28,000	1	2	3	4	5	6	7	8		10			11	9											
9	22 (h)	Raith Rovers	W 3-2	Grierson 2, Prentice	30,000	1	2	3	4	5	6		8		10		7	11	9											
10	Dec 6 (h)	Aberdeen	W 4-0	McCulloch 2, W.Simpson, Young (pen)	35,000	1	2	3	4	5	6		8		10		7	11	9											
11	13 (a)	Hearts	D 2-2	W.Simpson, Grierson	27,000	1	2	3	4	5	6	7	8		10			11	9											
12	20 (h)	St Mirren	W 4-0	W.Simpson 4	35,000	1	2	3	4	5	6	7	8		10			11	9											
13	27 (a)	Airdrieonians	D 2-2	Grierson, W.Simpson	20,000	1	2	3	4	5	6	7	8		10			11	9											
14	Jan 1 (h)	Celtic	W 1-0	W.Simpson	80,000	1	2	3	4	5	6	7	8		10			11	9											
15	3 (a)	Third Lanark	W 2-0	Prentice 2	20,581	1	2	3	4	5	6	7	8		10			11			9									
16	10 (h)	Partick Thistle	D 2-2	Paton, Grierson	30,000	1	2	3	4	5			9		10		7	11			8	6								
17	17 (a)	Hibernian	D 1-1	Grierson	60,500	1	2	3	4	5	6		8		10		7	11	9											
18	31 (h)	East Fife	W 4-0	McColl 2, W.Simpson, Grierson	52,000	1	2	3	4	5	6	7	8		10			11	9											
19	Feb 14 (a)	Dundee	D 1-1	Cowie (og)	24,000	1	2	3	4	5	6	7	8		10			11	9											
20	28 (h)	Falkirk	W 4-0	W.Simpson 3, Prentice	35,000	1	2	3	4	5	6	7	8		10			11	9											
21	Mar 7 (h)	Clyde	L 1-2	Young (pen)	55,000	1	2	3	4	5	6		8		10		7	11	9											
22	18 (a)	Raith Rovers	L 1-3	W.Simpson	18,000	1	2	3	4	5	6		8		10			11	9		7									
23	21 (h)	Motherwell	W 4-1	Grierson 2, McCulloch, W.Simpson	35,000	1	2	3	4	5	6		8		10		7	11	9											
24	28 (a)	Aberdeen	D 2-2	Grierson, Gardiner	35,000	1	2	3	4	5			8		10		7	11				6	9							
25	Apr 6 (h)	Hearts	W 3-0	W.Simpson, Prentice, McColl	40,000	1	2	3	4	5			8		10			11	9			6								
26	11 (a)	Partick Thistle	W 2-1	Gardiner, Young (pen)	25,500	1	2	3	4		6	7	8		10			11					9	5						
27	15 (h)	Airdrieonians	W 8-2	Grierson 4, Prentice, Paton, Young (pen), Cross (og)	20,000	1	2	3	4		6	7	8		10			11			9			5						
28	20 (a)	Motherwell	W 3-0	Paton 2, Young (pen)	30,720	1	2	3	4			7	8		10			11			9			5	6					
29	May 2 (h)	Dundee	W 3-1	Grierson 2, W.Simpson	45,000	1	2	3	4	5		7	8		10			11	9						6					
30	7 (a)	Queen of South	D 1-1	Waddell	17,000	1	2	3		5		7	8		10			11	9						6	4				
		Appearances				30	29	30	29	27	23	16	30	4	30	6	12	24	21	1	6	3	2	3	3	1				
		Goals					5		3			2	23	4	8	2	3		21		5		2							

FINAL LEAGUE POSITION: 1st

2 own-goals

Scottish FA Cup

No	Date	Opponent	Result	Scorers	Att	Niven	Young	Little	McColl	Woodburn	Cox	Waddell	Grierson	Thornton	Prentice	Liddell	McCulloch	Hubbard	Simpson W	Shaw	Paton	Rae	Gardiner	Stanners	Pryde	Dunlop
1	Jan 24 (h)	Arbroath	W 4-0	Hubbard, Prentice, McCulloch, W.Simpson	44,000	1	2	3	4	5	6		8		10		7	11	9							
2	Feb 7 (a)	Dundee	W 2-0	Hubbard, Grierson	43,024	1	2	3	4	5	6	7	8		10			11	9							
3	21 (a)	Morton	W 4-1	Grierson 2, W.Simpson, Prentice	23,000	1	2	3	4	5	6	7	8		10			11	9							
QF	Mar 14 (h)	Celtic	W 2-0	Prentice, Grierson	95,000	1	2	3	4	5	6		8		10			11	9		7					
SF	Apr 4 (n*)	Hearts	W 2-1	Grierson, Prentice	116,262	1	2	3	4	5	6	7	8		10			11	9							
F	25 (n*)	Aberdeen	D 1-1	Prentice	129,762	1	2	3	4			7	8		10			11			9			5	6	
R	29 (n*)	Aberdeen	W 1-0	W.Simpson	113,700	1	2	3	4	5		7	8					11	9		10				6	
		Appearances				7	7	7	7	6	5	5	7		6		1	7	6		3			1	2	
		Goals											5		5		1	2	3							

*Played at Hampden Park, Glasgow.

Scottish League Cup Section C

No	Date	Opponent	Result	Scorers	Att	Niven	Young	Little	McColl	Woodburn	Cox	Waddell	Grierson	Thornton	Prentice	Liddell	McCulloch	Hubbard	Simpson W	Shaw	Paton	Rae	Gardiner	Stanners	Pryde	Dunlop	Brown	Marshall
1	Aug 9 (a)	Hearts	L 0-5		41,000		2	3	4	5	6	7	8	9		11											1	10
2	13 (h)	Motherwell	W 2-0	Thornton, Liddell	50,000	1	2	3	4	5	6	7	8	9	10	11												
3	16 (h)	Aberdeen	W 3-1	Grierson 2, Thornton	40,000	1	2	3	4	5	6	7	8	9	10	11												
4	23 (h)	Hearts	W 2-0	Thornton, Liddell	75,000	1	2	3	4	5	6	7	8	9	10	11												
5	27 (a)	Motherwell	D 3-3	Prentice, Thornton, Paton	35,000	1	2	3	4	5	6	7		9	10	11					8							
6	30 (a)	Aberdeen	W 2-1	Waddell, Thornton	35,000	1	2	3	4	5	6	7		9	10	11					8							
QF1	Sep 13 (h)	Third Lanark	D 0-0		50,000	1	2	3	4	5	6	7	8	9	10	11												
QF2	17 (a)	Third Lanark	W 2-0	Grierson, Prentice	42,000	1	2	3	4	5	6	7	8	9	10	11												
SF	Oct 4 (n*)	Kilmarnock	L 0-1		45,715	1	2	3	4	5	6	7	10	9				11			8							
		Appearances				8	9	9	9	9	9	9	7	9	7	8		1			3						1	1
		Goals										1	3	5	2	2					1							

*Played at Hampden Park, Glasgow.

Glasgow Cup

No	Date	Opponent	Result	Scorers	Att	Niven	Young	Little	McColl	Woodburn	Cox	Waddell	Grierson	Thornton	Prentice	Liddell	McCulloch	Hubbard
SF	Sep 9 (a)	Queen's Park	W 2-0	Grierson 2	27,000	1	2	3	4	5	6	7	8	9	10	11		
F	29 (n*)	Partick Thistle	L 1-3	Hubbard	46,000	1	2	3	4	5	6		8	9	10		7	11
		Appearances				2	2	2	2	2	2	1	2	2	2	1	1	1
		Goals											2					1

*Played at Hampden Park, Glasgow.

Glasgow Merchants' Charity Cup

No	Date	Opponent	Result	Scorers	Niven	Young	Little	Woodburn	Waddell	Grierson	Prentice	Hubbard	Simpson W	Brown	Marshall
SF	May 4 (h)	Queen's Park	D 1-1	Grierson	1	2	3	5	7	8	10	11	9	6	4
		Appearances			1	1	1	1	1	1	1	1	1	1	1
		Goals								1					

Queen's Park won on the toss of a coin.

Coronation Cup

No	Date	Opponent	Result	Scorers	Att	Niven	Young	Little	Woodburn	Waddell	Prentice	Hubbard	Simpson W	Brown	Marshall	McMillan PH
1	May 13 (n*)	Manchester U	L 1-2	P.H.McMillan	75,546	1	2	3	5	7	10	11	9	6	4	8
		Appearances				1	1	1	1	1	1	1	1	1	1	1
		Goals														1

*Played at Hampden Park, Glasgow.

Other match

No	Date	Opponent	Result	Scorers	Att	Young	McColl	Hubbard	Simpson W	Shaw	Paton	Rae	Gardiner	Stanners	Pryde	Brown	Woods
1	Nov 19 (a)	Stenhousemuir	W 2-0*	Woods 2	7,500	2	4	11	7	3	10	6	9	5		1	8
		Appearances				1	1	1	1	1	1	1	1	1		1	1
		Goals															2

*Floodlit Friendly

1953-54

Manager: W.Struth

Player columns (left to right): Niven, Young, Little, McColl, Woodburn, Cox, Waddell, Grierson, Paton, Prentice, Hubbard, Simpson W, Caldow, Liddell, Stanners, Findlay, McMillan PH, Thornton, Brown, McCulloch, Rae, Gardiner, Rodgers, Neillands, Shaw, McKenzie, Gordon, Pryde

Scottish League

#	Date		Opponent	Res	Scorers	Att
1	Sep	5 (h)	Partick Thistle	W 3-0	Grierson, Paton, Prentice	60,000
2		19 (h)	Celtic	D 1-1	Paton	60,000
3		26 (a)	Stirling Albion	L 0-2		24,000
4	Oct	17 (h)	East Fife	W 2-0	W.Simpson, Grierson	40,000
5		24 (a)	Dundee	L 0-1		34,000
6		31 (h)	Hearts	L 0-1		30,000
7	Nov	7 (a)	Aberdeen	D 1-1	W.Simpson	30,000
8		14 (h)	Hamilton A	W 8-1	Thornton 3, Waddell 2 (1 pen), Paton, Hubbard, W.Simpson	25,000
9		21 (a)	Raith Rovers	W 2-1	Thornton, W.Simpson	18,000
10		28 (h)	Clyde	D 1-1	Thornton	40,000
11	Dec	12 (a)	Queen of South	L 1-2	McColl	18,500
12		19 (a)	Partick Thistle	W 1-0	Thornton	20,000
13		26 (h)	Hibernian	W 3-0	Gardiner 2, Prentice	28,000
14	Jan	1 (a)	Celtic	L 0-1		65,000
15		2 (h)	Stirling Albion	W 3-1	Paton, Prentice, McCulloch	28,000
16		9 (a)	St Mirren	W 1-0	Paton	37,500
17		16 (h)	Airdrieonians	W 3-0	Gardiner 2, Thornton	19,000
18		23 (a)	East Fife	L 1-2	Grierson	18,000
19	Feb	6 (a)	Dundee	W 2-0	Grierson, McCulloch	38,000
20		20 (a)	Hearts	D 3-3	Waddell, Gardiner, Paton	49,000
21	Mar	6 (a)	Hamilton A	D 1-1	Little	16,500
22		17 (h)	Raith Rovers	D 2-2	Caldow (pen), Paton	12,000
23		20 (a)	Clyde	W 5-2	W.Simpson 2, Prentice 2, Grierson	29,919
24		27 (a)	Falkirk	L 3-4	W.Simpson 2, Grierson	20,000
25	Apr	3 (h)	Queen of South	W 2-0	W.Simpson, McColl	10,000
26		14 (a)	St Mirren	D 1-1	W.Simpson	12,000
27		17 (h)	Aberdeen	L 1-3	Paton	45,000
28		21 (h)	Falkirk	W 3-0	Caldow (pen), W.Simpson, Grierson	22,000
29		24 (a)	Airdrieonians	L 0-2		8,000
30		26 (a)	Hibernian	D 2-2	Grierson, Paton	17,300

FINAL LEAGUE POSITION: 4th

Appearances: Niven 9, Young 20, Little 25, McColl 27, Woodburn 21, Cox 28, Waddell 29, Grierson 21, Paton 19, Prentice 18, Hubbard 15, Simpson W 8, Caldow 18, Liddell 5, Stanners 8, Findlay 1, McMillan PH 1, Thornton 8, Brown 21, McCulloch 9, Rae 8, Gardiner 8, Rodgers 1, Neillands 2

Goals: Little 1, McColl 2, Waddell 3, Grierson 8, Paton 9, Prentice 5, Hubbard 1, Simpson W 2, Caldow 2, Thornton 7, McCulloch 2, Gardiner 5

Scottish FA Cup

#	Date		Opponent	Res	Scorers	Att
1	Jan	30 (h)	Queen's Park	W 2-0	Waddell, Gardiner	34,133
2	Feb	13 (h)	Kilmarnock	D 2-2	Grierson, Gardiner	40,000
R		17 (a)	Kilmarnock	W 3-1	Paton 2, McCulloch	33,545
3		27 (a)	Third Lanark	D 0-0		45,591
R	Mar	3 (h)	Third Lanark	D 4-4	Prentice 2, W.Simpson 2	17,000
2R		8 (h)	Third Lanark	W 3-2	Caldow (pen), Paton, Prentice	31,000
QF		13 (h)	Berwick R	W 4-0	W.Simpson, Paton, Liddell, Caldow (pen)	60,245
SF	Apr	10 (n*)	Aberdeen	L 0-6		110,939

*Played at Hampden Park, Glasgow.

Appearances: Niven 4, Young 7, Little 8, McColl 8, Woodburn 6, Cox 7, Waddell 6, Grierson 6, Paton 6, Prentice 5, Simpson W 1, Caldow 3, Liddell 4, Stanners 2, Findlay 1, Brown 4, McCulloch 7, Rae 1, Gardiner 2

Goals: Waddell 1, Grierson 1, Paton 4, Prentice 3, Simpson W 2, Caldow 1, Liddell 1, McCulloch 2, Gardiner 2

Scottish League Cup Section C

#	Date		Opponent	Res	Scorers	Att
1	Aug	8 (a)	Raith Rovers	W 4-0	Young (pen), Prentice, W.Simpson, Grierson	24,807
2		12 (h)	Hearts	W 4-1	W.Simpson, Hubbard, Young (pen), Grierson	60,000
3		15 (h)	Hamilton A	W 5-1	Grierson 3, Paton 2	35,000
4		22 (h)	Raith Rovers	W 3-1	Paton 2, McCulloch	38,000
5		26 (a)	Hearts	D 1-1	Grierson	35,000
6		29 (a)	Hamilton A	W 5-0	Paton 4, Waddell	25,000
QF1	Sep	12 (h)	Ayr U	W 4-2	Prentice 3, Grierson	30,000
QF2		16 (a)	Ayr U	L 2-3	Waddell (pen), Paton	20,000
SF	Oct	10 (n*)	Partick T	L 0-2	48,064

*Played at Hampden Park, Glasgow.

Appearances: Niven 9, Young 7, Little 9, McColl 9, Woodburn 9, Cox 9, Waddell 8, Grierson 9, Paton 7, Prentice 9, Hubbard 9, Simpson W 2, Caldow 2, McCulloch 1

Goals: Young 2, Waddell 2, Grierson 7, Paton 9, Prentice 4, Hubbard 1, Simpson W 2, McCulloch 1

Glasgow Cup

#	Date		Opponent	Res	Scorers	Att
1	Aug	19 (a)	Clyde	W 2-1	Paton 2	30,000
SF	Sep	1 (h)	Celtic	D 1-1	Hubbard	55,500
R		3 (a)	Celtic	W 4-0	Paton 2, Grierson, Prentice	
F		28 (n*)	Third Lanark	W 3-0	Prentice 2, Paton	35,807

*Played at Hampden Park, Glasgow.

Appearances: Niven 4, Young 4, Little 4, McColl 4, Woodburn 4, Cox 4, Waddell 3, Grierson 4, Paton 4, Prentice 4, Hubbard 4, McCulloch 1

Goals: Grierson 1, Paton 5, Prentice 3, Hubbard 1

Glasgow Merchants' Charity Cup

#	Date		Opponent	Res	Scorers	Att
1	May	1 (n*)	Celtic	W 1-0	Prentice	44,674
SF		3 (a*)	Queen's Park	W 2-0	Grierson, W.Simpson	10,000
F		7 (n*)	Third Lanark	L 0-1		18,140

*Played at Hampden Park, Glasgow.

Appearances: Niven 3, Young 3, Waddell 3, Grierson 3, Paton 3, Prentice 3, Simpson W 3, Liddell 3, McCulloch 3, Rae 3, Gardiner 3

Goals: Prentice 1, Simpson W 1, Liddell 1

Further match details for this season are continued on page 279

1954-55

Manager: J.S.Symon

Scottish League

No		Date		Opponent	Result	Scorers	Attendance
1	Sep	11	(h)	Hibernian	D 1-1	Grierson	54,000
2		18	(a)	Celtic	L 0-2		45,000
3	Oct	2	(a)	East Fife	W 7-2	Grierson 2, Paton 2, Gardiner, Young (pen), McCulloch	16,500
4		9	(h)	Stirling Albion	W 6-1	Gardiner 4, Grierson 2	20,000
5		16	(a)	Partick Thistle	W 5-2	W.Simpson 2, Hubbard 2 (1 pen), Grierson	35,741
6		23	(h)	Dundee	W 3-0	Grierson, Hubbard (pen), Rae	30,000
7		30	(a)	St Mirren	L 1-2	Hubbard (pen)	35,054
8	Nov	6	(h)	Kilmarnock	W 6-0	W.Simpson 2, Brand 2, Paton, Hubbard (pen)	40,000
9		13	(a)	Falkirk	W 3-0	W.Simpson 2, Prentice	20,000
10		20	(a)	Clyde	D 1-1	Gardiner	32,000
11		27	(h)	Raith Rovers	W 1-0	Hubbard (pen)	25,000
12	Dec	4	(a)	Queen of South	W 2-1	W.Simpson 2	12,500
13		11	(h)	Aberdeen	W 3-1	W.Simpson 2, Grierson	45,800
14		18	(a)	Hearts	W 4-3	Grierson 2, W.Simpson 2	40,000
15		25	(h)	Hibernian	L 1-2	Grierson	43,000
16	Jan	1	(h)	Celtic	W 4-1	Hubbard 3 (1 pen), W.Simpson	65,000
17		3	(a)	Motherwell	L 0-2		25,000
18		8	(h)	East Fife	W 2-0	Gardiner, W.Simpson	28,000
19		29	(a)	Dundee	L 1-2	W.Simpson	28,000
20	Feb	12	(h)	St Mirren	D 1-1	McCulloch	40,000
21		26	(a)	Kilmarnock	L 0-1		25,000
22	Mar	5	(a)	Stirling Albion	W 2-0	Prentice, Gardiner	9,000
23		9	(h)	Falkirk	W 4-1	Scott 3, Gardiner	8,000
24		12	(h)	Clyde	W 1-0	W.Simpson	60,000
25		19	(a)	Raith R	L 0-1		14,500
26		26	(h)	Queen of South	W 1-0	Hubbard (pen)	15,000
27	Apr	2	(a)	Aberdeen	L 0-4		32,000
28		9	(h)	Hearts	W 2-1	Hubbard, W.Simpson	30,000
29		11	(h)	Partick Thistle	W 3-1	Hubbard 2 (1 pen), W.Simpson	28,000
30		30	(h)	Motherwell	W 2-0	Hubbard, P.H.McMillan	30,000

FINAL LEAGUE POSITION: 3rd

Appearances: Niven 22, Young 28, Little 21, McColl 26, Woodburn 1, Rae 19, McCulloch 12, Grierson 18, Gardiner 11, Prentice 18, Hubbard 23, Stanners 7, Simpson W 25, Paton 19, Waddell 11, Brown 8, McKenzie Gordon 9, McKenzie George 1, Cox 12, Brand 3, Rodger 2, Pryde 5, Caldow 11, Millar 2, Neillands 1, Cunning 3, Scott 7, McMillan PH 4, Woods 1

Goals: Young 1, McCulloch 1, Grierson 2, Gardiner 11, Prentice 9, Hubbard 2, Simpson W 14, Paton 18, Waddell 3, Cox 2, Scott 3, McMillan PH 1

Scottish FA Cup

No		Date		Opponent	Result	Scorers	Attendance
5	Feb	5	(h)	Dundee	D 0-0		58,000
R		9	(a)	Dundee	W 1-0	Gallagher (og)	25,600
6		19	(a)	Aberdeen	L 1-2	Neillands	44,647

Appearances: Niven 3, Young 3, Little 3, McColl 3, Rae 3, McCulloch 2, Gardiner 1, Hubbard 1, Simpson W 3, Paton 2, Waddell 3, Cox 3, Brown 1, Neillands 1, Cunning 1

Goals: Neillands 1

1 own-goal

Scottish League Cup Section C

No		Date		Opponent	Result	Scorers	Attendance
1	Aug	14	(a)	Stirling Albion	W 5-0	W.Simpson 3, Prentice 2	24,000
2		18	(h)	Partick Thistle	D 1-1	Davidson (og)	45,000
3		21	(h)	Clyde	L 1-3	Grierson	50,000
4		28	(h)	Stirling Albion	W 2-0	Paton, Hubbard (pen)	30,000
5	Sep	1	(a)	Partick Thistle	W 2-1	Prentice, W.Simpson	26,883
6		4	(a)	Clyde	W 2-1	W.Simpson, Paton	32,700
QF1		22	(a)	Motherwell	L 1-2	Prentice	24,000
QF2		25	(h)	Motherwell	D 1-1	Paton	55,000

Appearances: Niven 8, Young 7, Little 8, McColl 6, Woodburn 6, Rae 6, McCulloch 7, Grierson 4, Prentice 5, Hubbard 1, Simpson W 8, Paton 3, Waddell 2, Brown 5, McKenzie Gordon 5, Cox 4, Pryde 2, Menzies 3, Walker 1

Goals: Grierson 1, Prentice 4, Hubbard 1, Simpson W 5, Paton 3

1 own-goal

Glasgow Cup

No		Date		Opponent	Result	Scorers	Attendance
1	Aug	25	(a)	Third Lanark	W 2-0	McCulloch, Paton	30,000
SF	Sep	8	(h)	Clyde	D 1-1	McCulloch	20,000
R		9	(a)	Clyde	W 3-2	Gardiner 2, Prentice	9,000
F		27 (n*)		Partick Thistle	L 0-2		45,800

*Played at Hampden Park, Glasgow.

Appearances: Niven 4, Young 3, Little 3, McColl 4, Woodburn 2, McCulloch 4, Grierson 2, Gardiner 1, Prentice 2, Hubbard 2, Simpson W 2, Paton 1, Waddell 3, McKenzie Gordon 1, Cox 2, Scott 1, McMillan PH 1, Woods 2, Menzies 2, Walker 2

Goals: McCulloch 2, Gardiner 2, Prentice 1, Paton 1

Glasgow Merchants' Charity Cup

No		Date		Opponent	Result	Scorers	Attendance
1	May	3	(h)	Third Lanark	W 3-1	W.Simpson 2, Paton	
SF		7	(a)	Celtic	W 1-0	W.Simpson	44,400
F		9	(a)	Queen's Park	W 3-1	Hubbard, P.H.McMillan, Scott	20,000

Appearances: Niven 3, Young 1, Little 2, McColl 3, Rae 3, McCulloch 3, Grierson 3, Gardiner 2, Prentice 3, Simpson W 1, Paton 3, Scott 3, McMillan PH 3

Goals: McCulloch 1, Simpson W 3, Paton 1, Scott 1, McMillan PH 1

Other matches

No		Date		Opponent	Result	Scorers	Attendance
1	Oct	5	(h)	British Army	W 3-0	Grierson (2), Waddell	30,000
2		27	(h)	Manchester C	L 1-4	W.Simpson	40,000
3	Dec	15	(h)	Rapid Vienna	W 1-0	Prentice	50,000
4	Mar	15	(h)	Arsenal	D 3-3	Scott 2, Hubbard	28,123
5	Apr	13	(h)	Racing Club P	W 5-1	W.Simpson 2, P.H.McMillan 2, Hubbard	30,000
6	May	10	(h)	Linfield*	W 2-0	Waddell, Hubbard	30,000
7		19	(a)	Racing Club P	L 1-4	Hubbard (pen)	

*Sandy Row Orange Hall Benefit Match.

Appearances: Niven 4, Young 4, Little 2, McColl 7, Rae 6, McCulloch 1, Grierson 4, Gardiner 2, Prentice 4, Hubbard 6, Simpson W 5, Paton 6, Waddell 3, Brown 3, McKenzie Gordon 3, Cox 2, Rodger 1, Scott 1, McMillan PH 1, Woods 5, Menzies 4, Liddell 2, Walker 1

Substitutes: Simpson W 1, Cox 1

Goals: McCulloch 2, Grierson 1, Prentice 4, Hubbard 3, Simpson W 2, Scott 2, McMillan PH 2

1955-56

Manager: J.S.Symon

Scottish League

No	Date	Opponent	Res	Scorers	Att	Niven	Caldow	Little	McColl	Thomson	Rae	Scott	Simpson	Murray	Baird	Hubbard	Young	Prentice	Stanners	Millar	Kichenbrand	Queen	Paton	Elliott	Brown	Shearer	McMillan PH	Arnison	Pryde	Ritchie	Grierson	Waddell
1	Sep 10 (h)	Stirling Albion	D 0-0		25,000	1	2	3	4	5	6	7	8	9	10	11																
2	24 (h)	Celtic	D 0-0		47,000	1	2	3	4		6	7		9	8	11	5	10														
3	Oct 8 (h)	Airdrieonians	D 4-4	Hubbard 2 (1 pen), Murray, Baird	25,000	1	2		4	3	7			9	10	11	6	8	5													
4	15 (a)	Partick Thistle	W 3-1	Hubbard, Scott, Baird	40,000	1	2	3	4			7	8		10	11	5	6			9											
5	22 (a)	Stirling Albion	D 2-2	Scott, Kichenbrand	15,000	1	2	3		5		7	8		4	11		6			9	10										
6	29 (a)	Queen of South	L 1-2	Simpson	16,500	1	2	3	4		6	7	10		8	11	5				9											
7	Nov 5 (a)	Falkirk	W 2-1	Paton, Scott	20,000	1	2	3	4		6	7	10			11	5				9		8									
8	12 (h)	Hearts	W 4-1	Kichenbrand 2, Baird, Simpson	51,000	1	2	3	4		6	7	10		8	11	5				9											
9	19 (a)	Kilmarnock	W 2-1	Kichenbrand, Baird	25,600	1	2	3	4		6	7	8		10	11	5				9											
10	26 (h)	Motherwell	D 2-2	Hubbard (pen), Kichenbrand	40,000	1	2		4	3		7	8		10	11	5	6			9											
11	Dec 3 (h)	Raith Rovers	W 4-0	Simpson 2, Kichenbrand, Scott	26,000	1	2	3	4		6	7	8		10	11	5				9											
12	10 (a)	Aberdeen	D 0-0		25,000	1	2	3	4		6	7	8		10	11	5				9											
13	17 (h)	Hibernian	W 4-1	Hubbard 2 (1 pen), Kichenbrand, Simpson	50,000	1	2	3	4		6	7	8		10	11	5				9											
14	24 (h)	Dunfermline A	W 6-0	Kichenbrand 2, Baird 2, Scott, Hubbard	30,000	1	2	3	4		6	7	8		10	11	5				9											
15	31 (a)	Clyde	W 4-0	Scott, Simpson, Kichenbrand, Baird	31,000	1	2	3	4		6	7	8		10	11				5	9											
16	Jan 2 (h)	Celtic	W 1-0	Kichenbrand	47,000		2	3	4		6	7	8		10	11					9		5	1								
17	7 (h)	Dundee	W 3-1	Hubbard 2 (1 pen), Scott	46,000		2	3	4		6	7	8		10	11	5				9				1							
18	21 (h)	East Fife	W 3-0	Baird, Hubbard (pen), Kichenbrand	30,000		2	3	4		6	7	8		10	11	5				9				1							
19	28 (a)	Airdrieonians	W 4-0	Baird 3, Hubbard	22,000	1		3	4		6	7	8		10	11	5				9					2						
20	Feb 11 (h)	Partick Thistle	W 1-0	Kichenbrand	45,000	1		3	4		6	7	8		10	11	5				9					2						
21	25 (a)	St Mirren	W 1-0	Kichenbrand	43,000	1		3	4		6	7	8		10	11	5				9					2						
22	Mar 7 (h)	Queen of South	W 8-0	Kichenbrand 5, Simpson 2, Scott	30,000	1		3	4		6	7	8		10	11	5				9					2						
23	10 (h)	Falkirk	W 4-0	McColl, Simpson, Baird, Rae	45,000	1		3	4		6	7	8		10	11	5				9					2						
24	17 (a)	Hearts	D 1-1	Hubbard (pen)	50,000	1		3	4			7	8		10	11	5	6			9					2						
25	21 (h)	St Mirren	W 4-1	Kichenbrand 3, Prentice	30,000	1		3	4		6	7			10	11	5	8			9					2						
26	24 (h)	Kilmarnock	W 3-2	Kichenbrand 2, Hubbard (pen)	30,000	1		3	4		6	7	8		10	11	5				9					2						
27	31 (a)	Motherwell	W 2-1	Murray 2	27,500	1						7	8	9	10	11	5	6								2						
28	Apr 2 (a)	Dundee	W 3-0	Hubbard 2, Simpson	18,500	1		3	4		6	7	8	9	10	11	5									2						
29	7 (a)	Raith Rovers	W 5-0	Murray 2, Hubbard 2 (1 pen), Leigh (og)	20,000	1		3	4			7	8	9	10	11	5	6								2						
30	9 (a)	East Fife	L 1-2	Baird	10,000	1		3	4			7	8		10	11	5	6			9					2						
31	18 (h)	Aberdeen	W 1-0	Scott	45,000	1		3	4			7	8	9	10	11	5									2						
32	21 (h)	Hibernian	D 2-2	Murray, Baird	30,000	1		3	4		6	7	8	9	10	11	5									2						
33	25 (a)	Dunfermline A	L 0-1			1		3	4		6	7	8	9	10	11	5									2						
34	28 (h)	Clyde	L 0-1		25,000	1	2	3	4			7	8		10	11	5									6						
		Appearances				31	26	25	34	1	27	34	32	8	33	34	29	10	1	1	25	1	1	2	3	16					
		Goals							1		1	9	10	6	14	17		1			24					1					

FINAL LEAGUE POSITION: 1st

1 own-goal

Scottish FA Cup

No	Date	Opponent	Res	Scorers	Att	Niven	Caldow	Little	McColl	Thomson	Rae	Scott	Simpson	Murray	Baird	Hubbard	Young	Prentice	Stanners	Millar	Kichenbrand	Queen	Paton	Elliott	Brown	Shearer
5	Feb 5 (h)	Aberdeen	W 2-1	Scott, Kichenbrand	66,000	1		3	4		6	7	8		10	11	5				9					2
6	18 (a)	Dundee	W 1-0	Kichenbrand	42,500	1		3	4		6	7	8		10	11	5				9					2
QF	Mar 3 (a)	Hearts	L 0-4		47,258	1		3	4		6	7	8		10	11	5				9					2
		Appearances				3		3	3		3	3	3		3	3	3				3					3
		Goals										1									2					

Scottish League Cup Section 4

No	Date	Opponent	Res	Scorers	Att	Niven	Caldow	Little	McColl	Rae	Scott	Simpson	Murray	Baird	Hubbard	Young	Prentice	Millar	Kichenbrand	Arnison	McMillan PH
1	Aug 13 (a)	Falkirk	W 5-0	Hubbard 2, Scott, Murray, McMillan	21,000	1	2	3	4		7	10	9		11	5	6				8
2	17 (h)	Falkirk	W 4-3	Hubbard 2 (1 pen), Scott, Murray	35,000	1	2	3	4		7	8	9		11	5	6				10
3	20 (a)	Queen of South	W 2-1	Hubbard, Scott	15,000	1	2	3	4		7	8	9	10	11	5	6				
4	27 (h)	Celtic	L 1-4	Scott	75,000	1	2	3	4		7	8	9	6	11	5					10
5	31 (a)	Celtic	W 4-0	Baird 2, Simpson, Murray	61,000	1	2	3	4	6	7	8	9	10	11	5					
6	Sep 3 (h)	Queen of South	W 6-0	Arnison 2, Scott 2, Hubbard, Simpson	50,000	1	2	3	4	6	7	8		10	11	5				9	
QF1	14 (a)	Hamilton A	W 2-1	Hubbard, Simpson	18,000	1	2	3	4	6	7		9	8	11	5	10				
QF2	17 (h)	Hamilton A	W 8-0	Scott 3, Simpson 2, Hubbard 2, Prentice	40,000	1	2	3	4	6	7		9	8	11	5	10				
SF	Oct 1 (n*)	Aberdeen	L 1-2	Hubbard	79,500	1	2	3	4	6	7			10	11	5		9			8
		Appearances				9	9	9	9	5	9	8	5	7	9	9	5	1		2	3
		Goals									9	5	3	2	10		1			2	1

*Played at Hampden Park, Glasgow.

Glasgow Cup

No	Date	Opponent	Res	Scorers	Att	Niven	Caldow	Little	McColl	Rae	Scott	Simpson	Baird	Hubbard	Young	Millar	Kichenbrand	Arnison	Pryde
SF	Sep 5 (h)	Third Lanark	W 6-0	Scott 2, Arnison 2, Hubbard 2	25,000	1		3	4	6	7	8	10	11	5			9	2
F	26 (n*)	Celtic	D 1-1	McColl	53,000	1	2	3	4	6	7	8	10	11	5	9			
R	Dec 26 (n*)	Celtic	L 3-5	Kichenbrand, Hubbard (pen), Fallon (og)	39,078	1	2	3	4	6	7	8	10	11	5		9		
		Appearances				3	2	3	3	3	3	3	3	3	3	1	1	1	1
		Goals							1		2			3			1	2	

*Played at Hampden Park, Glasgow.

1 own-goal

Glasgow Merchants' Charity Cup

No	Date	Opponent	Res	Scorers	Att	Caldow	Little	McColl	Scott	Simpson	Baird	Hubbard	Kichenbrand	Paton	Elliott	Shearer
1	May 5 (h)	Third Lanark	D 1-1*	Kichenbrand	16,000	2	3	4	7	8	10	11	9	5	6	1
		Appearances				1	1	1	1	1	1	1	1	1	1	1
		Goals											1			

Third Lanark won on the toss of a coin

Other matches

No	Date	Opponent	Res	Scorers	Att	Niven	Caldow	Little	McColl	Thomson	Rae	Scott	Simpson	Murray	Baird	Hubbard	Young	Prentice	Kichenbrand	Queen	Paton	Shearer	McMillan PH	Arnison	Pryde	Grierson	Waddell
1	Oct 12 (a)	Manchester C	W 2-1	Baird, Queen	17,000	1	2	3	4		**6**	7	8		10		5			9	12						11
2	Nov 2 (h)	British Army	W 2-0	Baird, Simpson	18,000	1	2	3	4		6	7	10		8	11	5		9								
3	21 (h)	Arsenal	W 2-0	McColl, Kichenbrand	40,000	1	2	3	4		6	7	8		10	11	5		9								
4	Jan 23 (h)	San Lorenzo	W 4-3	Hubbard 2, Kichenbrand, Baird	36,000	1	2	3	4		6	7	8		10	11	5		9			1		2			
5	Mar 28 (h)	Dinamo Zagreb	D 3-3	Simpson, Grierson, Murray	45,000	1		3	4		6	7	**8**	9	10	11	5	12				2				14	
6	May 20 (h)	Valencia	D 1-1	Simpson	36,000	1		3	4		**6**	7	8	14	10	11	5	12	**9**			2					
7	24 (a)	De Mahon*	W 2-1	Simpson 2	2,000	1		3	4		6	7	8	**9**	10	11	5			12		2					
8	27 (a)	Valencia	D 1-1	Shearer	55,000	1	12	3	4		6	7	8	**9**	10	11	5		14			2					
9	Jun 2 (a)	Barcelona	L 0-3		60,000	1	2	3	4	12	7	**8**		9	10	11	5		14			6					
10	3 (a)	Valencia	L 1-4	Hubbard	60,000	1	2	3	4		6	7	8		10	11	12		9		5						
		Appearances				9	6	9	10		9	10	9	4	10	9	8	1	6	1	1	6		1		1	1
		Sub Appearances					1			1				1			4	3	1							1	
		Goals							1				5	1	3	3			2	1		1				1	

* Union Deportiva De Mahon

1956-57

Manager: J.S.Symon

Scottish League

#	Date		Venue/Opponent	Result	Scorers	Att.	Niven	Caldow	Little	McColl	Young	Shearer	Scott	Simpson	Murray	Paton	Hubbard	Logie	Grierson	Baird	Davis	Walker	Wilson	Morrison
1	Sep	8	(a) Airdrieonians	D 3-3	Murray 2, Hubbard	18,000	1	2	3	4	5	6	7	8	9	10	11							
2		15	(h) Kilmarnock	L 0-1		30,000	1		3	4	5	2	7	8	9		11	6		10				
3		22	(a) Celtic	W 2-0	Murray, Scott	53,000	1		3	4	5	2	7		9		11	6	8	10				
4		29	(h) Ayr United	W 3-1	Scott 2, Hubbard (pen)	27,000	1		3	4	5	2	7		9		11	6	8	10				
5	Oct	6	(a) St Mirren	W 2-1	Baird, Scott	28,700	1	3		4	5	2	7	8	9		11	6		10				
6		13	(h) Partick Thistle	W 4-1	Simpson 2, Baird, Hubbard (pen)	38,000	1	3		4	5	2	7	8	9		11	6		10				
7	Nov	3	(h) Hibernian	W 5-3	Murray 2, Scott, Hubbard (pen), Simpson	45,000	1	3		4	5	2	7	8	9		11	6		10				
8		10	(h) Motherwell	L 2-3	Baird 2	63,000	1	3		4	5	2	7	8	9		11	6		10				
9		17	(a) Falkirk	W 2-0	Murray 2	19,000	1	3		4	5	2	7	8	9		11	6		10				
10		24	(a) Aberdeen	W 3-1	Simpson, Hubbard (pen), Murray	29,100	1	3		4		2	7	8	9		11	6		10	5			
11	Dec	1	(h) East Fife	W 6-1	Scott 2, Baird 2, Hubbard 2	26,000	1	3		4		2	7	8			11	6		10	5	9		
12		8	(a) Raith Rovers	L 1-5	Simpson	20,000	1	3		4	5	2	7	8			11	6		10		9		
13		15	(h) Hearts	W 5-3	Murray 2, Hubbard, Davis, Simpson	45,000	1	3		4	5	2	7	8	9					10	6			
14		22	(a) Kilmarnock	L 2-3	Simpson, Murray	22,436	1	3		4	5	2	7	8	9		11			10	6			
15		29	(h) Queen of South	W 4-0	Simpson 2, Murray 2	30,000	1	3		4	5	2	7	8	9		11	6		10				
16	Jan	1	(h) Celtic	W 2-0	Murray, Simpson	60,000	1	3		4	5	2	7	8	9		11	6		10				
17		2	(a) Dundee	W 3-1	Scott, Simpson, Young (pen)	28,500	1	3		4	5	2	7	8	9					10	6			11
18		12	(a) Ayr United	L 0-1		15,000	1	3		4	5	2	7	8	9		11			10	6			
19		19	(h) St Mirren	W 1-0	Murray	33,000	1	3		4	5	2	7	8	9		11			10	6			
20		26	(a) Partick Thistle	W 3-0	Murray 2, Simpson	35,000	1		3	4	5	2	7	8	9		11			10	6			
21	Feb	9	(h) Dunfermline A	W 2-1	Murray, Simpson	40,000	1	3		4		2	7	8	9		11	6		10	5			
22		23	(h) Queen's Park	D 3-3	Murray, Morrison, Hubbard (pen)	19,000	1	3		4		2		8	9		11	6	5				7	10
23	Mar	2	(h) Hibernian	W 3-2	Murray 2, Morrison	40,000	1	3		4		2		8	9		11	6	5				7	10
24		9	(a) Motherwell	W 5-2	Murray 2, Morrison, Hubbard, Wilson	30,000	1	3		4		2		8	9		11	6	5				7	10
25		16	(h) Falkirk	D 1-1	Murray	35,000	1	3		4	5	2		8	9		11			10	6		7	
26		20	(h) Dundee	W 4-0	Simpson, Murray, Baird, Ferguson (og)	25,000	1	3		4	5	2		8	9		11			10	6		7	
27		23	(a) Aberdeen	W 2-1	Hubbard, Simpson	26,500	1	3		4	5	2	7	8	9		11			10	6			
28		30	(a) East Fife	W 3-0	Morrison 2, Simpson	13,000	1	3		4	5	2	7		9		11			10	6			8
29	Apr	2	(h) Raith Rovers	W 3-1	Morrison, Scott, Simpson	50,000	1	3		4	5	2	7		9		11			10	6			8
30		13	(a) Hearts	W 1-0	Simpson	49,000	1	3		4	5	2	7	8	9		11			10	6			
31		17	(h) Airdrieonians	W 3-2	Baird 2, Simpson	25,000	1	3		4	5	2	7	8	9		11			10	6			
32		22	(a) Queen's Park	W 6-4	Murray 2, Hubbard 2, Simpson, Scott	33,786	1	3		4	5	2	7	8	9		11			10	6			
33		27	(a) Queen of South	W 3-0	Murray 2, Hubbard (pen)	14,500	1	3		4	5	2	7	8	9		11			10	6			
34		29	(a) Dunfermline A	W 4-3	Scott 2, Hubbard, Simpson	10,000	1	3		4	5	2	7	8	9		11			10	6			
					Appearances		34	30	5	34	28	34	29	32	30	1	33	16	3	32	20	2	6	5
					Goals					1			12	21	29		15			9	1		1	6

FINAL LEAGUE POSITION: 1st

1 own-goal

Scottish FA Cup

#	Date		Venue/Opponent	Result	Scorers	Att.	Niven	Caldow	McColl	Young	Shearer	Scott	Simpson	Murray	Hubbard	Logie	Grierson	Baird	Davis	Morrison
5	Feb	2	(a) Hearts	W 4-0	Hubbard (pen), Murray, Scott, Simpson	47,484	1	3	4	5	2	7	8	9	11			10	6	
6		16	(a) Celtic	D 4-4	Morrison, Simpson, Hubbard (pen), Murray	55,000	1	3	4		2	7	8	9	11	6	5			10
R		20	(h) Celtic	L 0-2		88,000	1	3	4		2	7	8	9	11	6	5			10
					Appearances		3	3	3	1	3	3	3	3	3	3	3			2
					Goals							1	2	2	2					1

Scottish League Cup Section Two

#	Date		Venue/Opponent	Result	Scorers	Att.	Niven	Caldow	Little	McColl	Young	Shearer	Scott	Simpson	Murray	Paton	Hubbard	Baird	Rae	Ritchie
1	Aug	11	(h) East Fife	W 3-0	Simpson 2, Hubbard (pen)	51,000	1		3	4	5	2	7	8	9		11	10	6	
2		15	(a) Celtic	L 1-2	Murray	45,000	1		3	4	5	2	7	8	9		11	10	6	
3		18	(a) Aberdeen	W 6-2	Simpson 2, Murray 2, Shearer, Hubbard	35,000	1	2	3	4	5	6	7	8	9		11	10		
4		25	(a) East Fife	W 4-1	Murray, Simpson, Hubbard (pen), Rae	18,000		2	3	4	5	8	7	10	9		11		6	1
5		29	(h) Celtic	D 0-0		84,000	1	2	3	4	5	6	7	10	9	8	11			
6	Sep	1	(h) Aberdeen	W 4-1	Simpson 2, Hubbard (pen), Scott	48,000	1	2	3	4	5	6	7	10	9	8	11			
					Appearances		5	4	6	6	6	6	6	6	6	2	6	3	3	1
					Goals							1	1	7	4		4		1	

Rangers failed to qualify for Quarter-final

European Champions' Cup

#	Date		Venue/Opponent	Result	Scorers	Att.	Niven	Caldow	McColl	Young	Shearer	Scott	Simpson	Murray	Hubbard	Logie	Baird	Davis
2	Oct	24	(h) OGC Nice	W 2-1	Murray, Simpson	65,000	1	3	4	5	2	7	8	9	11	6	10	
	Nov	14	(a) OGC Nice	L 1-2	Hubbard (pen)	12,000	1	3	4	5	2	7	8	9	11	6	10	
R		28	(n*) OGC Nice	L 1-3	Bonvin (og)	15,000	1	3	4		2	7	8	9	11	6	10	5
					Appearances		3	3	3	2	3	3	3	3	3	3	3	1
					Goals								1	1	1			

* Played at Parc des Princes, Paris

1 own-goal

Glasgow Cup

#	Date		Venue/Opponent	Result	Scorers	Att.	Niven	Caldow	Little	McColl	Young	Shearer	Scott	Simpson	Murray	Hubbard	Logie	Grierson	Baird	Wilson
1	Aug	22	(a) Celtic	W 4-3	Simpson, Murray, Scott, Hubbard	41,000		2	3	4	5	6	7	8	9	11			10	1
SF	Sep	17	(h) Partick Thistle	W 5-0	Hubbard 2 (1 pen), Grierson 2, Murray	41,000		3		4	5	2	7		9	11	6	8	10	
F	Oct	10	(h) Clyde	W 2-0	Murray, Hubbard (pen)	28,000	1	3		4	5	2	7	8	9	11	6		10	
					Appearances		2	2	2	3	3	3	3	2	3	3	2	1	3	1
					Goals								1	1	3	4		2		

Glasgow Merchants' Charity Cup

#	Date		Venue/Opponent	Result	Scorers	Att.	Niven	Caldow	Little	McColl	Young	Shearer	Scott	Simpson	Murray	Hubbard	Baird	Davis	Walker	Wilson	Morrison	Valentine	Kichenbrand	Moles
1	May	1	(h) Celtic	W 1-0	Baird	30,000	1	3		4	5	2	7		9	11	10	6		8				
SF		4	(h) Clyde	W 2-0	Morrison, Baird	35,000	1			4	5	2	7		9	11	10	6		8		3		
F		6	(h) Queen's Park	W 2-1	Morrison, Kichenbrand	20,000	1	3				2		10		11		6	7	8		4	5	9
					Appearances		3	1	1	2	2	3	2	2	1	3	2	3	1	3	1	1	1	1
					Goals									2			2						1	

Other matches

#	Date		Venue/Opponent	Result	Scorers	Att.	Little	McColl	Shearer	Baird	Davis	Walker	Wilson	Morrison	Rae	Ritchie	Kichenbrand	Moles	McCulloch	Melrose
1	Dec	18	(h) British Army	L 1-3	Wilson	20,000	3	4	2	6	8	10	9	11		1		5	7	12
2	Jan	23	(h) Scotland U-23	D 3-3	Scott, Walker, Morrison	15,000	3	2	7	14	6	12	9	11	8	1	4	5		10
					Appearances		1	2	1	1	1	2	1	1	2	2	1	2	1	2
					Substitutes						1			1						1
					Goals				1			1	1	1						

1957-58

Manager: J.S.Symon

Scottish League

Player columns (left→right): Ritchie, Little, Caldow, Shearer, McColl, Baird, Scott, Simpson, Kichenbrand, Murray, Hubbard, Valentine, Austin, Niven, Davis, Moles, Millar, Telfer, Brand, Wilson, Queen, Duncan, Smith, Morrison, Robertson, Melrose, Hogg

No	Date	V	Opponent	Result	Scorers	Att
1	Sep 7	(h)	Queen of South	W 4-2	Simpson 2, Shearer, Hubbard (pen)	25,000
2	21	(h)	Celtic	L 2-3	Simpson 2	60,000
3	Oct 12	(a)	St Mirren	W 3-1	Baird, Hubbard, Murray	30,000
4	26	(h)	Hearts	L 2-3	Simpson 2	62,000
5	Nov 2	(a)	Queen's Park	W 4-2	Baird, Kichenbrand, Hubbard (pen), Simpson	30,824
6	9	(h)	Kilmarnock	L 3-4	Hubbard 2 (1 pen), Kichenbrand	45,000
7	16	(h)	Clyde	W 2-0	Baird 2	65,000
8	23	(a)	Falkirk	W 4-0	Hubbard 4 (2 pens)	22,000
9	30	(h)	East Fife	D 3-3	Murray, Baird, Davis	26,000
10	Dec 7	(a)	Motherwell	D 2-2	Baird, Murray	25,000
11	14	(a)	Dundee	W 2-1	Hubbard (pen), Cowie (og)	20,000
12	21	(h)	Third Lanark	W 5-1	Murray 2, Shearer, Wilson, Brand	22,000
13	28	(a)	Aberdeen	W 2-1	Brand, Scott	21,000
14	Jan 1	(a)	Celtic	W 1-0	Scott	50,000
15	2	(h)	Partick Thistle	W 2-0	Murray, Scott	30,000
16	4	(a)	Queen of South	D 1-1	Murray	13,000
17	11	(h)	Hibernian	W 3-1	Baird, Simpson, Muir (og)	47,000
18	18	(a)	Airdrieonians	W 4-3	Brand, Scott, Murray, Simpson	20,000
19	Feb 22	(a)	Queen's Park	W 5-1	Murray 2, Hubbard 2 (1 pen), Brand	30,000
20	Mar 8	(a)	Clyde	W 3-1	Duncan 2, Brand	31,500
21	10	(a)	Kilmarnock	D 3-3	Hubbard 2 (2 pens), Murray	15,335
22	19	(h)	Falkirk	W 3-2	McColl, Brand, Millar	25,000
23	22	(a)	East Fife	W 1-0	Brand	12,000
24	29	(h)	Motherwell	D 2-2	Millar, Duncan	40,000
25	Apr 12	(a)	Third Lanark	W 5-1	Hubbard 2 (2 pens), Simpson 2, Brand	36,000
26	16	(h)	Raith Rovers	W 4-1	Murray 2, Hubbard, Millar	16,000
27	21	(h)	Hibernian	L 1-3	Murray	25,000
28	23	(a)	Raith Rovers	W 3-1	Millar 2, Baird	10,000
29	26	(h)	Aberdeen	W 5-0	Murray 3, Brand 2	15,000
30	28	(h)	St Mirren	W 1-0	Murray	—
31	30	(a)	Hearts	L 1-2	Brand	30,000
32	May 3	(a)	Airdrieonians	L 1-2	Hubbard (pen)	25,000
33	5	(a)	Partick Thistle	W 2-1	Murray, Wilson	6,500
34	10	(h)	Dundee	L 0-1		11,000

FINAL LEAGUE POSITION: 2nd

Appearances: Ritchie 29, Little 12, Caldow 29, Shearer 28, McColl 32, Baird 31, Scott 23, Simpson 16, Kichenbrand 4, Murray 28, Hubbard 24, Valentine 2, Austin 1, Niven 5, Davis 9, Moles 3, Millar 25, Telfer 28, Brand 22, Wilson 12, Queen 1, Duncan 8, Smith 2

Goals: Shearer 2, McColl 1, Baird 8, Scott 4, Simpson 11, Kichenbrand 2, Murray 19, Hubbard 18, Davis 1, Millar 5, Brand 11, Wilson 2, Duncan 3

2 own-goals

Scottish FA Cup

No	Date	V	Opponent	Result	Scorers	Att
1	Feb 1	(a)	Cowdenbeath	W 3-1	Murray 2, Simpson	16,866
2	15	(a)	Forfar A	W 9-1	Murray 3, Brand 2, Simpson 2, Hubbard, McColl	8,066
3	Mar 1	(a)	Dunfermline A	W 2-1	Murray, Brand	24,377
QF	15	(a)	Queen of South	W 4-3	Murray 2, Millar 2	23,000
SF	Apr 5	(n*)	Hibernian	D 2-2	Millar, Murray	76,727
R	9	(n*)	Hibernian	L 1-2	Baird (pen)	75,000

*Played at Hampden Park, Glasgow.

Appearances: Ritchie 6, Caldow 6, Shearer 6, McColl 6, Baird 6, Scott 4, Simpson 3, Murray 6, Hubbard 2, Telfer 3, Millar 6, Brand 6, Duncan 4, Wilson 2

Goals: McColl 1, Simpson 1, Baird 1(?), Murray 9, Hubbard 1, Millar 3, Brand 3

1 own-goal

Scottish League Cup Section Two

No	Date	V	Opponent	Result	Scorers	Att
1	Aug 10	(h)	St Mirren	W 6-0	Murray 3, Simpson 3	55,000
2	14	(a)	Partick Thistle	W 1-0	Baird	35,000
3	17	(h)	Raith Rovers	W 4-3	Scott, Hubbard, Murray, Simpson	47,000
4	24	(a)	St Mirren	W 4-0	Murray 2, Scott, Baird	23,000
5	28	(h)	Partick Thistle	L 0-3		40,000
6	31	(a)	Raith Rovers	L 3-4	Scott 2, Hubbard (pen)	24,000
QF1	Sep 11	(a)	Kilmarnock	L 1-2	Kichenbrand	26,803
QF2	14	(h)	Kilmarnock	W 3-1	Hubbard (pen), Scott, Simpson	78,000
SF	28	(n*)	Brechin City	W 4-0	Melrose 2, Shearer (pen), Paterson (og)	28,453
F	Oct 19	(n*)	Celtic	L 1-7	Simpson	82,293

*Played at Hampden Park, Glasgow.

Appearances: Ritchie 3, Caldow 10, Shearer 10, McColl 10, Baird 8, Scott 9, Simpson 9, Kichenbrand 3, Murray 9, Hubbard 7, Valentine 6, Niven 7, Davis 8, Moles 2, Millar 3, Melrose 3, Morrison 1, Robertson 1, Hogg 1

Goals: Scott 1, Baird 2, Simpson 5, Kichenbrand 6, Murray 1, Hubbard 3, Melrose 2

1 own-goal

European Champions' Cup

No	Date	V	Opponent	Result	Scorers	Att
1	Sep 4	(h)	AS Saint-Etienne	W 3-1	Kichenbrand, Scott, Simpson	85,000
	25	(a)	AS Saint-Etienne	L 1-2	Wilson	35,000
2	Nov 27	(h)	AC Milan	L 1-4	Murray	85,000
	Dec 11	(a)	AC Milan	L 0-2		3,000

Appearances: Ritchie 2, Little 1, Caldow 4, Shearer 3, McColl 4, Baird 4, Scott 4, Simpson 3, Kichenbrand 2, Murray 3, Hubbard 3, Niven 1, Davis 2, Millar 1, Telfer 3, Brand 2, Wilson 2

Goals: Simpson 1, Kichenbrand 1, Scott 1, Murray 1, Wilson 1

Glasgow Cup

No	Date	V	Opponent	Result	Scorers	Att
1	Aug 19	(h)	Celtic	W 2-0	Baird 2	45,000
SF	Oct 23	(h)	Partick Thistle	D 1-1	Kichenbrand	31,000
R	30	(a)	Partick Thistle	W 6-3	Simpson 3, Kichenbrand 2, Scott	30,000
F	Dec 18	(h)	Third Lanark	D 1-1	Lewis, (og)	15,000
R	Mar 31	(h)	Third Lanark	W 4-2	Brand 3, Millar	25,000

Appearances: Ritchie 1, Little 2, Caldow 5, Shearer 3, McColl 5, Baird 5, Scott 4, Simpson 4, Kichenbrand 2, Murray 3, Hubbard 4, Valentine 1, Niven 4, Davis 2, Moles 2, Millar 2, Telfer 4, Brand 2, Wilson 1, Queen 1

Goals: Baird 2, Scott 1, Simpson 3, Kichenbrand 3, Millar 1, Brand 3

1 own-goal

Further match details for this season are continued on page 279

1958-59

Manager: J.S.Symon

Scottish League

#	Date	V	Opponent	Res	Scorers	Att	Niven	Shearer	Caldow	McColl	Telfer	Baird	Scott	Millar	McEwan	Brand	Wilson	Davis	Murray	Hubbard	Paterson	Hogg	Simpson	Matthew	Duncan	Little	McMillan I	Stevenson	Orr	Provan
1	Aug 20	h	Third Lanark	D 2-2	Baird (pen), Millar	35,000	1	2	3	4	5	6	7	8	9	10	11													
2	Sep 6	a	Celtic	D 2-2	Hubbard (pen), Brand	50,000	1	2	3	4	5		7			8	10	6	9	11										
3	13	h	Partick Thistle	W 2-1	Hubbard (pen), Brand	41,000	1	2	3	4			7			8	10	6	9	11	5									
4	20	a	Airdrieonians	L 4-5	Hubbard 3 (1 pen), Hogg	20,000	1	2	3	4	5		7				10	6		11		8	9							
5	27	h	Dundee	L 1-2	Baird	35,000	1	2	3	4	5	10	7			9	6	8		11										
6	Oct 4	a	Dunfermline A	W 7-1	Hubbard 3 (1 pen), Brand, Baird, Duncan, Scott	17,000	1	2	3	4	5	8	9			10		6		11					7					
7	11	h	St Mirren	W 2-1	Duncan, Brand	40,000	1	2	3	4	5	8	9			10		6		11					7					
8	18	a	Raith Rovers	D 4-4	I.McMillan, Scott, Baird, Hubbard	35,000	1	2		4	5	10	9					6		11					7	3	8			
9	25	a	Stirling Albion	D 2-2	Brand, I.McMillan	17,475	1	2	3		5		7			10		4	9					11			8	6		
10	Nov 1	h	Hibernian	W 4-0	Simpson 4	20,000	1	2	3		5		7			10		4	9				11				8	6		
11	8	a	Clyde	W 4-1	Brand 2, Davis, Simpson	25,000	1	2	3		5		7			10		4	9				11				8	6		
12	15	h	Falkirk	W 3-0	Simpson 2, Scott	35,000	1	2	3		5		7			10		4	9				11				8	6		
13	22	a	Kilmarnock	W 3-0	Brand 2, Wilson	25,672	1	2	3		5		7			10	11	4	9								8	6		
14	29	a	Motherwell	D 2-2	Brand, Hubbard	32,977	1	2	3		5		7			10		4	9	11							8	6		
15	Dec 6	a	Queen of South	W 6-3	Brand 3, Scott, Murray, I.McMillan	10,000	1	2	3				7			10	11	4	9		5						8	6		
16	13	h	Hearts	W 5-0	Murray 3, Brand 2	66,000	1	2	3		5		7			10		4	9					11			8	6		
17	20	a	Aberdeen	W 3-1	Murray, Brand, Scott	18,000	1	2	3		5		7			10		4	9					11			8	6		
18	27	a	Third Lanark	W 3-2	Murray 2, Brand	30,000	1	2	3		5		7			10		4	9					11			8	6	4	
19	Jan 1	h	Celtic	W 2-1	Matthew, Caldow (pen)	55,000	1	2	3	4	5		7			10			9					11			8	6		
20	3	a	Partick Thistle	L 0-2		37,000	1	2	3	4	5		7			10			9					11			8	6		
21	21	a	Airdrieonians	W 2-1	Davis, I.McMillan	40,000	1	2	3		5		7			10		4	9					11			8	6		
22	24	h	Dunfermline A	W 1-0	Murray	30,000	1	2	3		5		7			10		4	9					11			8	6		
23	28	a	Dundee	W 3-1	Murray 2, Millar	16,000	1	2	3		5		7	10				4	9					11			8	6		
24	Feb 7	a	St Mirren	W 3-1	Matthew, Scott, Murray	29,000	1	2	3		5		7			10		4	9					11			8	6		
25	18	a	Raith Rovers	D 2-2	Matthew 2	8,000	1	2	3		5		7	10				4	9					11			8	6		
26	21	h	Stirling Albion	W 3-0	Caldow (pen), Wilson, Murray	30,000	1	2	3	4	5		7	8		10	11		9									6		
27	Mar 4	a	Hibernian	D 2-2	Matthew, I.McMillan	32,000	1	2	3				7			10		4	9		5			11			8	6		
28	7	h	Clyde	W 3-1	I.McMillan, Scott, Murray	33,000	1	2	3		5		7			10	11	4	9								8	6		
29	14	a	Falkirk	D 5-5	Murray 2, Caldow (pen), Brand, I.McMillan	15,000	1	2	3		5		7			10	11	4	9								8	6		
30	21	h	Kilmarnock	W 1-0	Murray	30,000	1	2	3		5		7			10	11	4	9								8	6		
31	28	h	Motherwell	W 2-1	Brand, Murray	50,000	1	2	3		5		7			10	11	4	9								8	6		
32	Apr 6	h	Queen of South	W 3-1	Brand, I.McMillan, Caldow (pen)	15,000	1	2	3		5		7			10	11	4	9								8	6		
33	11	a	Hearts	L 0-2		30,000	1	2			5		7	10			11	4	9								8	6		3
34	18	h	Aberdeen	L 1-2	Brand	41,000	1	2	3		5		7			10		4	9					11			8	6		
	Appearances						34	34	32	11	31	6	34	5	1	25	15	29	22	8	3	2	6	18	3	1	26	26	1	1
	Goals								4			4	7	2		21	2	2	17	10		1	7	5	2		8			

FINAL LEAGUE POSITION: 1st

Scottish FA Cup

#	Date	V	Opponent	Res	Scorers	Att	Niven	Shearer	Caldow	Telfer	Scott	Millar	Brand	Davis	Murray	Matthew	McMillan I	Stevenson
1	Jan 31	a	Forfar A	W 3-1	Murray, Millar, Scott	9,813	1	2	3	5	7	10		4	9	11	8	6
2	Feb 14	h	Hearts	W 3-2	Matthew 2, Kirk (og)	55,000	1	2	3	5	7		10	4	9	11	8	6
3	28	a	Celtic	L 1-2	Murray	45,500	1	2	3	5	7		10	4	9	11	8	6
	Appearances						3	3	3	3	3	1	2	3	3	3	3	3
	Goals										1	1			2	2		

1 own-goal

Scottish League Cup Section One

#	Date	V	Opponent	Res	Scorers	Att	Niven	Shearer	Caldow	McColl	Telfer	Baird	Scott	Millar	Brand	Wilson	Davis	Murray	Hubbard	Simpson	Provan
1	Aug 9	h	Hearts	W 3-0	Wilson, Hubbard, Millar	65,000	1	2	3	4	5	6	7	8		10		9	11		
2	13	a	Raith Rovers	L 1-3	Hubbard (pen)	12,000	1	2	3	4	5	6	7	8		10		9	11		
3	16	h	Third Lanark	D 2-2	Brand, Murray	40,000	1	2	3	4	5	6	7		10		8	9	11		
4	23	a	Hearts	L 1-2	Hubbard (pen)	42,000		2	3	4	5	6	7	8		10		9	11		1
5	27	h	Raith Rovers	W 6-0	Simpson 3, Murray, Wilson, Hubbard (pen)	25,000	1	2	3	4	5		7			10	6	9	11	8	
6	30	a	Third Lanark	W 3-0	Murray 3	28,000	1	2	3	4	5		7			10	6	9	11	8	
	Appearances						5	6	6	6	6	4	6	3	1	6	2	6	6	2	1
	Goals													1	1	2		5	4	3	

Rangers failed to qualify for quarter-final.

Glasgow Cup

#	Date	V	Opponent	Res	Scorers	Att	Niven	Shearer	Caldow	McColl	Telfer	Baird	Scott	Brand	Wilson	Davis	Murray	Hubbard	Simpson	Duncan
SF	Sep 1	a	Third Lanark	W 3-1	Murray, Hubbard (pen), Scott		1	2	3	4	5		7		10	6	9	11	8	
F	29 (n*)		Clyde	D 0-0		35,000	1	2	3	4	5	8	9	10		6		11		7
R	Oct 22	h	Clyde	L 0-1		27,162	1	2	3		5	6	9	10		4		11	8	7
	Appearances						3	3	3	2	3	2	3	2	1	3	1	3	1	2
	Goals												1				1	1		

*Played at Hampden Park, Glasgow.

Glasgow Merchants' Charity Cup

#	Date	V	Opponent	Res	Scorers	Att	Niven	Shearer	Caldow	Telfer	Scott	Brand	Davis	Murray	Matthew	McMillan I	Stevenson
SF	May 2	h	Celtic	D 1-1	Brand	38,000	1	2	3	5	7	10	4	9	11	8	6
	Appearances						1	1	1	1	1	1	1	1	1	1	1
	Goals											1					

Celtic won by the toss of a coin.

Other matches

#	Date	V	Opponent	Res	Scorers	Att
1	Sep 16	h	British Army	L 0-1		20,000
2	Nov 11	h	Napoli	W 5-2	Wilson 2, Davis, Murray, Matthew (pen)	30,760
3	25	a	Grasshoppers	W 3-0	Murray, Hubbard (pen), Brand	35,000
4	Apr 21	a	Arsenal	W 3-0	Brand 2, Caldow (pen)	34,500
5	May 12	a	Staevnet	W 4-0	Millar 4	14,000
6	14	a	Vejle BK	D 2-2	Millar, Caldow (pen)	12,000

Appearances: 5 5 5 1 3 1 5 1 6 1 5 5 1 5 1 1 5 5 1 1 1
Substitutes: 1 1
Goals: 2 5 3 2 1 2 1 1

1959-60

Manager: J.S.Symon

					Scottish League	Niven	Shearer	Caldow	Davis	Paterson	Stevenson	Duncan	McLean G (I)	Millar	Baird	Wilson	Little	Telfer	Scott	Matthew	McMillan	McColl	Brand	Murray	Hume	Ritchie	Franks	Anderson	Grant
1	Aug 19	(a) Stirling Albion	W 3-2	Millar 2, Wilson		1	2	3	4	5	6	7	8	9	10	11													
2	Sep 5	(h) Celtic	W 3-1	Wilson, Scott, Millar	65,000	1	2		4		6			9	10	8	3	5	7	11									
3	12	(a) Hibernian	W 1-0	Millar	31,500	1	2		4		6			9	10	8	3	5	7	11									
4	19	(h) Ayr U	L 0-3		32,000	1	2		4		6			9	10		3	5	7	11	8								
5	26	(a) Partick Thistle	W 3-0	Matthew, McMillan, Scott	30,500	1	2		4		6				10	9	3	5	7	11	8								
6	Oct 3	(h) Dunfermline A	W 4-1	McMillan 2, Millar, Scott	25,000	1	2		4		6			9		10	3	5	7	11	8								
7	10	(a) Dundee	W 3-1	Baird (pen), Millar, Matthew	22,000	1	2				6			9	10		3	5	7	11	8	4							
8	17	(h) St Mirren	L 1-3	Millar	45,000	1	2		4		6			9	10		3	5	7	11	8								
9	24	(a) Aberdeen	W 5-0	Scott 2, Brand, Millar, McMillan	25,000	1	2	3	4	5	6			9					7	11	8		10						
10	31	(h) Hearts	L 0-2		70,000	1	2	3	4	5	6			9					7	11	8		10						
11	Nov 7	(h) Clyde	W 6-0	Millar 3, Caldow (pen), Baird, McMillan	40,000	1		2	4		6			9	10	11	3	5	7		8								
12	14	(a) Arbroath	W 4-0	Millar 4	6,025	1		2	4	5	6			9	10	11	3		7		8								
13	21	(h) Raith Rovers	L 2-3	Wilson, Scott	30,000	1	2		4		6			9	10	11	3	5	7		8								
14	28	(a) Motherwell	L 1-2	Baird	22,000	1	2		4		6			9	10	11	3	5	7		8								
15	Dec 5	(h) Kilmarnock	W 5-0	McMillan 2, Wilson, Scott, Murray	20,000	1	2		4	5	6					10	3		7		8			9	11				
16	12	(a) Third Lanark	W 2-0	McMillan, Millar	25,000	1	2		4	5	6			9		10	3		7		8				11				
17	19	(a) Airdrieonians	W 5-0	Scott 2, Stevenson, Hume, Millar	20,000	1	2		4	5	6			9		10	3		7		8				11				
18	26	(h) Stirling Albion	W 3-0	Scott, Wilson, Hume	21,000	1	2		4	5	6			9		10	3		7		8				11				
19	Jan 1	(a) Celtic	W 1-0	Millar	50,000	1	2		4	5	6			9	8	10	3						7		11				
20	2	(h) Hibernian	D 1-1	McMillan	60,000	1	2		4	5	6			9	10		3				8		7		11				
21	9	(a) Ayr U	W 4-2	Millar 2, Hume, McMillan	23,000	1	2		4	5	6			9		10	3		7		8				11				
22	16	(h) Partick Thistle	D 1-1	Caldow (pen)	40,000	1		2	4	5	6			9		10	3		7		8				11				
23	23	(a) Dunfermline A	W 5-0	Scott 2, Millar, McMillan, Wilson	16,000	1		2		5	6			9	4	10	3		7		8				11				
24	Feb 9	(h) Dundee	D 0-0		22,000	1		2	4	5	6			9	8	10	3		7						11				
25	Mar 1	(h) Aberdeen	D 2-2	Caldow (pen), McMillan		1		2	4	5	6			9		10	3		7		8				11				
26	5	(a) Hearts	L 0-2		45,000	1		2	4	5	6			9		11	3		7		8		10						
27	19	(h) Arbroath	D 1-1	McMillan	15,000	1		2	4	5	6					10	3		7		8			9	11				
28	26	(a) Raith Rovers	W 2-1	McMillan, Baird	11,000			2	4	5	6			9	10	11	3		7		8					1			
29	Apr 16	(a) Kilmarnock	D 1-1	Caldow (pen)	26,925	1		2		5	6			9	10	11	3		7		8	4							
30	18	(h) Motherwell	L 0-2		30,000	1	2			5	6			9	10	11	3				8		7				4		
31	25	(a) St Mirren	D 1-1	Wilson	14,000	1		2		5	6			9	10	11	3		7		8	4							
32	27	(a) Clyde	L 1-4	Brand (pen)	10,000	1	2				10		8				3	5		11			7				4	6	9
33	30	(h) Airdrieonians	D 0-0		13,000	1		2		5	6			9		11	3		7		8	4	10						
34	May 7	(h) Third Lanark	L 1-2	Wilson	8,500	1		2		5	6			9		11	3		7			4	10				8		
FINAL LEAGUE POSITION: 3rd					Appearances	33	21	16	26	23	34	1	2	30	19	27	31	11	29	10	27	5	9	2	12	1	3	1	1
					Goals			4			1			21	4	8			12	2	14		2	1	3				

Scottish FA Cup

						Niven	Shearer	Caldow	Davis	Paterson	Stevenson	Duncan	McLean G (I)	Millar	Baird	Wilson	Little	Telfer	Scott	Matthew	McMillan	McColl	Brand	Murray	Hume	Ritchie	Franks	Anderson	Grant
1	Jan 30	(a) Berwick R	W 3-1	Wilson 3	16,000	1		2	4	5	6			9		10	3		7		8				11				
2	Feb 13	(h) Arbroath	W 2-0	Scott, McMillan	30,000	1		2	4	5	6			9		10	3		7		8				11				
3	27	(a) Stenhousemuir	W 3-0	Millar, McMillan, Wilson	12,300	1		2	4	5	6			9		10	3		7		8				11				
QF	Mar 12	(h) Hibernian	W 3-2	Baird, Wilson, Millar	63,000	1		2	4	5	6			9	8	11	3		7				10						
SF	Apr 2	(n*) Celtic	D 1-1	Millar	79,786	1		2	4	5	6			9	10	11	3		7		8								
R	6	(n*) Celtic	W 4-1	Wilson 2, Millar 2	70,977			2	4	5	6			9	10	11	3		7		8					1			
F	23	(n*) Kilmarnock	W 2-0	Millar 2	108,017	1		2		5	6			9	10	11	3		7		8	4							
*Played at Hampden Park, Glasgow.					Appearances	6		7	6	7	7			7	4	7	7		7		6	1	1		3	1			
					Goals									7	1	7			1		2								

Scottish League Cup Section Four

						Niven	Shearer	Caldow	Davis	Paterson	Stevenson	Duncan	McLean G (I)	Millar	Baird	Wilson	Little	Telfer	Scott	Matthew	McMillan	McColl	Brand	Murray	Hume	Ritchie	Franks	Anderson	Grant
1	Aug 8	(a) Hibernian	W 6-1	Brand 4, Matthew, Millar	44,700	1	2	3	4		6			9				5	7	11	8		10						
2	12	(h) Motherwell	L 1-2	Scott	65,000	1	2	3	4		6			9		11		5	7		8		10						
3	15	(h) Dundee	W 2-0	Brand, Wilson	37,000	1	2	3	4		6	7		9		11		5			8		10						
4	22	(h) Hibernian	W 5-1	Wilson 2, Millar 2, Baird	35,000	1	2	3			6			9	10	8		5	7	11		4							
5	26	(a) Motherwell	L 1-2	Millar	37,000	1	2		4					9	6	8	3	5	7	11			10						
6	29	(a) Dundee	W 3-2	Millar, Wilson, Baird	20,000	1	2		4		6			9	10	8	3	5	7	11									
Rangers failed to qualify for Quarter-final					Appearances	6	6	4	5		5	1		6	3	5	2	6	5	4	3	1	4						
					Goals									5	2	4			1	1			5						

European Champions' Cup

						Niven	Shearer	Caldow	Davis	Paterson	Stevenson	Duncan	McLean G (I)	Millar	Baird	Wilson	Little	Telfer	Scott	Matthew	McMillan	McColl	Brand	Murray	Hume	Ritchie	Franks	Anderson	Grant
1	Sep 16	(h) RSC Anderlecht	W 5-2	Baird 2 (1 pen), Millar, Scott, Matthew	80,000	1	2		4		6			9	10		3	5	7	11	8								
	23	(a) RSC Anderlecht	W 2-0	Matthew, McMillan	40,000	1	2		4		6				10	9	3	5	7	11	8								
2	Nov 11	(h) Red S Bratislava	W 4-3	McMillan, Scott, Wilson, Millar	80,000	1		2	4		6			9	10	11	3	5	7		8								
	18	(a) Red S Bratislava	D 1-1	Scott	60,000	1	2		4		6			9	10	11	3	5	7		8								
QF1	Mar 9	(a) Sp Rotterdam	W 3-2	Wilson, Baird, Murray	50,000	1		2	4	5	6				10	11	3		7		8			9					
QF2	16	(h) Sp Rotterdam	L 0-1		82,587			2	4	5	6			9	8	11	3		7				10			1			
R	30	(n*) Sp Rotterdam	W 3-2	Baird 2, Millar	34,176	1		2	4	5	6			9	10	11	3		7		8								
SF1	Apr 13	(a) Eintracht Fr'furt	L 1-6	Caldow (pen)	80,000	1		2		5	6			10	4	11	3		7		8			9					
SF2	May 5	(h) Eintracht Fr'furt	L 3-6	McMillan 2, Wilson	70,000	1		2	4	5	6			9	10	11	3		7		8								
*Played at Arsenal Stadium, Highbury, London.					Appearances	8	3	6	8	5	9			7	9	8	9	4	9	2	8		1	2		1			
					Goals			1						3	5	3			3	2	4			1					

Glasgow Cup

						Niven	Shearer	Caldow	Davis	Paterson	Stevenson	Duncan	McLean G (I)	Millar	Baird	Wilson	Little	Telfer	Scott	Matthew	McMillan	McColl	Brand	Murray	Hume	Ritchie	Franks	Anderson	Grant
1	Aug 17	(a) Celtic	W 2-1	Baird, Millar	38,000	1	2	3	4		6	7		9	10	11		5			8								
SF	24	(a) Queen's Park	W 5-1	Millar 2, Scott, Baird, Matthew	8,000	1	2			5	6			9	10	8	3		7	11		4							
F	Sep 28	(n*) Partick Thistle	W 2-1	Baird, Scott	38,807	1	2	3	4		6				10	9		5	7	11	8								
*Played at Hampden Park, Glasgow.					Appearances	3	3	2	2	1	3	1		2	3	3	1	2	2	2	2	1							
					Goals									3	3				2	1									

Glasgow Merchants' Charity Cup

						Niven	Shearer	Caldow	Davis	Paterson	Stevenson	Duncan	McLean G (I)	Millar	Baird	Wilson	Little	Telfer	Scott	Matthew	McMillan	McColl	Brand	Murray	Hume	Ritchie	Franks	Anderson	Grant
SF	May 9	(h) Celtic	D 1-1	Brand	14,500	1		2		5	6			9		11	3		7		8	4	10						
F	11	(n*) Partick Thistle	W 2-0	Millar, Brand	8,296	1		2		5	6			9		7	3				8	4	10		11				
Rangers won semi-final on the toss of a coin.					Appearances	2		2		2	2			2		2	2		1		2	2	2		1				
*Played at Hampden Park, Glasgow.					Goals									1									2						

1960-61

Manager: J.S.Symon

Scottish League

#	Date	Opponent	Result	Scorers	Att	Ritchie	Shearer	Caldow	Davis	Paterson	Baxter	Scott	McMillan	Millar	Brand	Wilson	Stevenson	McLean	Niven	Murray	Penman	Provan	Baillie	McKinnon	Henderson	Hume
1	Aug 24 (h) Partick Thistle	W 6-3	Wilson 2, Caldow (pen), Davis, Millar, Brown (og)	17,000	1	2	3	4	5	6	7	8	9	10	11										
2	Sep 10 (a) Celtic	W 5-1	Scott, Millar, Brand, Wilson, Davis	43,000	1	2	3	4	5	6	7	8	9	10	11										
3	17 (h) Airdrieonians	W 3-0	Wilson 2, Brand (pen)	25,000	1	2	3	4	5		7	8	9	10	11	6									
4	24 (a) St Johnstone	W 5-2	Scott 2, Brand, Millar, McMillan	19,000	1	2	3	4	5	6	7	8	9	10	11										
5	Oct 1 (a) Third Lanark	W 4-2	Brand 2 (1 pen), Scott, Wilson	32,500	1	2	3	4	5	6	7	8	9	10	11										
6	8 (h) Dundee	L 0-1		45,000	1	2	3	4	5	6	7	8	9	10	11										
7	15 (h) Dunfermline A	W 3-0	Brand 2, Millar	30,000	1	2	3	4	5	6	7		9	10	11			8							
8	26 (a) Hearts	W 3-1	Scott, Brand, Wilson	30,000	1	2	3	4	5	6	7	8	9	10	11										
9	Nov 2 (h) Raith R	W 3-0	McMillan, Wilson, McNaught (og)	10,000		2	3	4	5	6	7	8	9	10	11			1							
10	5 (a) Clyde	W 3-1	Scott, Baxter, Brand	27,000		2	3	4	5	6	7	8	9	10	11			1							
11	12 (h) Dundee U	W 4-0	Millar 2, McMillan, Scott	25,000		2	3	4	5	6	7	8	9	10	11			1							
12	26 (h) Kilmarnock	L 2-3	Wilson, McMillan	55,000		2	3	4	5	6	7	8	9	10	11			1							
13	Dec 3 (a) Aberdeen	W 4-0	McMillan 2, Wilson, Brand	25,132		2	3	4	5	6	7	8	9	10	11			1							
14	10 (a) Hibernian	W 2-1	Wilson, Brand	35,000		2	3	4	5	6	7	8	9	10	11			1							
15	17 (h) St Mirren	W 5-1	Millar 2, Wilson, Brand, Clunie (og)	35,000		2	3	4	5	6	7	8	9	10	11			1							
16	24 (a) Ayr U	L 0-1		15,500		2	3	4	5	6	7	8	9	10	11			1							
17	26 (a) Motherwell	W 2-1	McMillan, Brand	22,000		2	3	4	5	6	7	8	9	10	11			1							
18	31 (a) Partick Thistle	W 3-0	Wilson, Millar, Brand	31,478		2	3	4	5	6	7	8	9	10	11			1							
19	Jan 2 (h) Celtic	W 2-1	Brand, Wilson	79,000		2	3	4	5	6	7	8	9	10	11			1							
20	7 (a) Airdrieonians	D 1-1	Wilson	26,000		2	3	4	5	6	7	8	9	10	11			1							
21	14 (h) St Johnstone	W 1-0	Caldow (pen)	42,000		2	3	4	5	6	7	8	9	10	11			1							
22	21 (h) Third Lanark	W 4-3	Brand 3, Murray	40,000		2	3	4	5		7	8		10	11	6		1	9						
23	28 (a) St Mirren	D 1-1	Murray	34,000		2	3	4	5	6	7			10	11			1	9	8					
24	Feb 8 (a) Dundee	L 2-4	Murray 2	22,000			3	4	5	6	7			10	11			1	9	8	2				
25	18 (a) Dunfermline A	D 0-0		20,000		2	3	4	5	6	7	8		10	11			1	9						
26	Mar 4 (a) Raith R	W 3-2	Brand 2, Wilson	14,000		2	3	4			7	8		10	11	6	9	1			5				
27	8 (h) Hearts	W 3-0	McLean 2, Brand	35,000		2	3				7	8		10	11	6	9	1			5	4			
28	11 (h) Clyde	W 2-1	Wilson, McLean	22,000		2	3					8		10	11	6	9	1			5	4	7		
29	18 (a) Dundee U	D 1-1	Brand	17,300		2	3	4	5			9	8	10	11	6		1					7		
30	25 (h) Motherwell	D 2-2	Scott, Murray	42,000		2	3	4	5	6	7			10	11			1	9	8					
31	Apr 1 (a) Kilmarnock	L 0-2		29,528	1	2	3		5	6	7			10	8	4	9							11	
32	8 (a) Aberdeen	L 1-6	Scott	21,000	1	2	3	4			7	8		10	11	6	9				5				
33	11 (h) Hibernian	W 1-0	McMillan	45,000	1	2		4	5	6	9	8		10										7	
34	29 (h) Ayr U	W 7-3	Scott 3, Wilson 2, Brand 2	45,000	1	2	3	4	5	6	9	8		10	7									11	
		Appearances				12	33	33	31	30	27	33	28	21	34	34	8	6	22	5	3	2	5	2	3	2
		Goals						2	2		1	12	8	9	24	19		3		5						

FINAL LEAGUE POSITION: 1st

3 own-goals

Scottish FA Cup

#	Date	Opponent	Result	Scorers	Att	Shearer	Caldow	Davis	Paterson	Baxter	Scott	McMillan	Brand	Wilson	Stevenson	Niven	Murray
2	Feb 11 (a) Dundee	W 5-1	Murray 2, Brand 2, Scott	32,000	2	3	4	5	6	7	8	10	11		1	9
3	25 (a) Motherwell	D 2-2	Murray 2	31,958	2	3	4	5	6	7	8	10	11		1	9
R	Mar 1 (h) Motherwell	L 2-5	Wilson, McMillan	90,000	2	3	4	5		7	8	10	11	6	1	9
		Appearances			3	3	3	3	2	3	3	3	3	1	3	3
		Goals								1	1	2	1			4

Scottish League Cup Section Two

#	Date	Opponent	Result	Scorers	Att	Ritchie	Shearer	Caldow	Davis	Paterson	Baxter	Scott	McMillan	Millar	Brand	Wilson	Stevenson	McLean	Provan	McKinnon
1	Aug 13 (h) Partick Thistle	W 3-1	Millar 2, Scott	51,000		2		4	5	10	7	8	9		11	6	1	3	
2	17 (a) Third Lanark	L 1-2	Millar		1			2	4	5	8	7	9	10	11	6		3	
3	20 (h) Celtic	L 2-3	Millar, Brand	60,000	1	2	3	4			6	7	9	10	11			5	8
4	27 (a) Partick Thistle	W 4-1	McMillan 2, Millar, Brand	35,000	1	2	3	4	5	6	7	8	9	10	11				
5	31 (h) Third Lanark	W 3-2	Millar 2, Brand		1	2	3	4	5	6	7	8	9	10	11				
6	Sep 3 (a) Celtic	W 2-1	Davis, Brand	50,000	1	2	3	4	5	6	7	8	9	10	11				
QF	14 (h) Dundee	W 1-0	Scott	40,000	1	2	3	4	5	6	7	8	9	10	11				
	21 (a) Dundee	W 4-3	McMillan 2, Wilson, Brand	32,000	1	2	3	4	5	6	7	8	9	10	11				
SF	Oct 19 (n*) Queen of Sth	W 7-0	Brand 3, Millar 2, McMillan, Scott	17,000	1	2	3	4	5	6	7	8	9	10	11				
F	29 (n†) Kilmarnock	W 2-0	Brand, Scott	82,063		2	3	4	5	6	7	8	9	10	11		1		
		Appearances			8	8	10	10	9	10	10	8	10	9	10	2	2	2	1
		Goals						1			4	5	9	9	1				

*Played at Celtic Park, Glasgow. †Played at Hampden Park, Glasgow.

European Cup-winners' Cup

#	Date	Opponent	Result	Scorers	Att	Ritchie	Shearer	Caldow	Davis	Paterson	Baxter	Scott	McMillan	Millar	Brand	Wilson	Niven	Provan	Henderson
1	Sep 28 (h) Ferencváros	W 4-2	Millar 2, Davis, Brand	36,000	1	2	3	4	5	6	7	8	9	10	11			
	Oct 12 (a) Ferencváros	L 1-2	Wilson	25,000	1	2	3	4	5	6	7	8	9	10	11			
QF	Nov 15 (a*) Bor M-Gladbach	W 3-0	Millar, Scott, McMillan	50,000		2	3	4	5	6	7	8	9	10	11	1		
	30 (h) Bor M-Gladbach	W 8-0	Brand 3, Millar 2, Baxter, Scott, Davis	38,174		2	3	4	5	6	7	8	9	10	11	1		
SF	Mar 29 (h) Wolves	W 2-0	Scott, Brand	79,229	1	2	3	4	5	6	7			10	8		9	11
	Apr 19 (a) Wolves	D 1-1	Scott	45,163	1	2	3	4	5	6	9	8		10	7			11
F	May 17 (h) Fiorentina	L 0-2		80,000	1	2	3	4	5	6	9	8		10	7			11
	27 (a) Fiorentina	L 1-2	Scott	50,000	1	2	3	4	5	6	7	8	9	10	11			
		Appearances			6	8	8	8	8	8	8	7	5	8	8	2	1	3
		Goals						2		1	5	1	5	5	1			

*Played at the Rheinstadion, Düsseldorf, West Germany.

Glasgow Cup

#	Date	Opponent	Result	Scorers	Att
1	Aug 15 (a) Celtic	L 2-4	Millar 2	36,000
1	*Apr 25 (h) Clyde*	*L 3-4*	*McLean 2, Scott*	*10,000*

Games in italic in Glasgow Merchants' Charity Cup

Appearances: 1 1 1 2 1 2 1 1 | 2 2 1 2 | 1 1 | 1 | 1 1
Goals: 1 2 | 2

Other matches

#	Date	Opponent	Result	Scorers	Att	Shearer	Caldow	Davis	Paterson	Baxter	Scott	McMillan	Millar	Brand	Wilson	Stevenson	Niven
1	Nov 19 (a) Motherwell	W 1-0	Brand	32,000	2	3	4	5	6	7	8	9	10	11		1
2	Dec 13 (a) Arsenal	W 4-2	Brand 2 (1 pen), Millar, Wilson	42,173	2	3	4	5		7	8	9	10	11	6	1
3	20 (h) British Army	W 2-0	McLean, Brand (pen)	7,000	2						9	10	11	6	8	

Appearances: 3 2 2 2 1 3 2 3 3 3 2 1 2 | 1 1 1 | 1
Goals: 1 4 1 | 1

241

1961-62

Manager: J.S.Symon

Scottish League

	Date		Opponent	Result	Scorers	Att.	Ritchie	Shearer	Caldow	Davis	Paterson	Baxter	Scott	McMillan	Millar	Brand	Wilson	Christie	Provan	Stevenson	McKinnon	Baillie	Henderson	Greig	Murray	Hume	King	Martin
1	Aug 23	(h)	Hibernian	W 3-0	Brand 2 (1 pen), Wilson	40,000	1	2	3	4	5	6	7	8	9	10	11											
2	Sep 9	(a)	Partick Thistle	W 4-1	Wilson, Millar, Scott, Brand	31,500	1	2	3	4	5	6	7	8	9	10	11											
3	16	(h)	Celtic	D 2-2	Christie, Baxter	70,000	1	2	3	4	5	6	7	8		10	11	9										
4	23	(a)	St Mirren	D 1-1	Scott	34,000	1	2	3	4	5	6	7	8	9	10	11											
5	30	(h)	Stirling Albion	W 4-1	Millar 2, McMillan, Brand	30,000	1	2	3	4	5	6	7	8	9	10	11											
6	Oct 14	(h)	Raith Rovers	W 6-0	Brand 4, Wilson, McMillan	34,500	1	2		4	5		7	8	9	10	11		3	6								
7	21	(a)	Motherwell	D 2-2	Wilson, Brand	24,500	1	2	3	4	5	6	7	8	9	10	11											
8	Nov 4	(a)	Third Lanark	W 3-0	Christie 2, Brand	30,000	1	2	3	4	5	6	7	8		10	11	9										
9	11	(h)	Dundee	L 1-5	Brand	38,000	1	2	3	4	5	6	7	8		10	11	9										
10	18	(h)	Falkirk	W 4-0	Millar 3, Wilson	35,000	1	2							9	10	11		3	6	4	5	7	8				
11	25	(a)	Dundee U	W 3-2	Caldow (pen), Greig, Murray	20,000	1	2	3	4		6				10						5	7	8	9	11		
12	Dec 2	(h)	St Johnstone	W 2-0	Wilson, Brand	30,000	1	2		4				8		10	11		3	6		5	7		9			
13	16	(a)	Dunfermline A	L 0-1		16,000	1	2	3	4			7		9	10	11			6		5		8				
14	23	(h)	Aberdeen	L 2-4	Brand, Greig	28,000	1	2	3	4		6	9			10						5	7	8		11		
15	30	(a)	Kilmarnock	W 1-0	Millar	21,992	1	2	3	4		6	7		9	10	11					5		8				
16	Jan 6	(a)	Hibernian	D 0-0		35,000	1	2	3	4		6	7	8	9	10	11					5						
17	10	(h)	Hearts	W 2-1	Scott, Holt (og)	25,000	1	2	3	4		6	7	8	9	10	11					5						
18	13	(h)	St Mirren	W 4-0	Caldow (pen), McMillan, Henderson, Murray	36,000	1	2	3	4		6		8		10	11					5	7		9			
19	20	(a)	Stirling Albion	W 6-0	Millar 3, Brand 2, Caldow (pen)	20,000	1	2	3	4		6		8	9	10	11					5	7					
20	24	(h)	Partick Thistle	W 2-1	Brand, Millar		1	2	3	4		6		8	9	10	11					5	7					
21	31	(a)	Airdrieonians	W 5-2	Greig 2, Millar 2, Brand	12,000	1	2	3	4	5	6			9	10	11						7	8				
22	Feb 3	(h)	Airdrieonians	W 4-0	Brand 2, Millar, Greig	22,000	1	2		4	5	6	7		9	10	11							8			3	
23	10	(a)	Raith Rovers	W 3-1	Brand 2, Scott	13,000	1	2		4		6	7	8		10	11					5			9		3	
24	24	(a)	Hearts	W 1-0	McMillan	30,000	1	2	3	4		6		8	9	10						5	7			11		
25	28	(h)	Motherwell	W 2-1	Millar, Scott	40,000	1	2	3	4			7	8	9	10				6		5			11			
26	Mar 3	(h)	Third Lanark	W 3-1	Brand, Baxter, Scott	35,000	1	2	3	4		6	7		9	10						5	11	8				
27	14	(a)	Dundee	D 0-0		35,000	1	2	3	4		6	7	8	9	10	11					5						
28	17	(a)	Falkirk	W 7-1	Wilson 6, Scott	18,000	1	2	3	5		6	7	8	4	10	9						11					
29	24	(h)	Dundee U	L 0-1		35,000	1	2	3	5		6	7	8	4	10	9						11					
30	Apr 4	(a)	St Johnstone	W 4-0	Greig 2, Wilson, Brand	15,500	1	2	3	4		6				10	11				5		7	8	9			
31	7	(h)	Dunfermline A	W 1-0	Murray	41,000	1	2	3	4		6	7	8			11				5			10	9			
32	9	(a)	Celtic	D 1-1	Wilson	50,000	1	2	3	4		6			9	10	11				5		7	8				
33	25	(a)	Aberdeen	L 0-1		22,000	1	2	3	4		6		8	9	10	11				5		7					
34	28	(h)	Kilmarnock	D 1-1	Wilson	39,848	1	2	3	4		6	7	8		10	11				5				9			
FINAL LEAGUE POSITION: 2nd						Appearances	34	34	29	33	11	29	23	24	23	33	29	3	3	5	6	16	15	11	8	3	2	
						Goals			3			2	7	4	15	23	15	3					1	7	3			

1 own-goal

Scottish FA Cup

	Date		Opponent	Result	Scorers	Att.	Ritchie	Shearer	Caldow	Davis	Paterson	Baxter	Scott	McMillan	Millar	Brand	Wilson	Christie	Provan	Stevenson	McKinnon	Baillie	Henderson	Greig	Murray	Hume	King	Martin
1	Dec 13	(a)	Falkirk	W 2-1	Millar, Wilson	11,500	1	2	3	4			7	8	9	10	11			6		5						
2	Jan 27	(h)	Arbroath	W 6-0	Millar 4, Brand 2	31,908	1	2	3	4	5	6		8	9	10	11						7					
3	Feb 17	(a)	Aberdeen	D 2-2	Caldow (pen), Brand	41,359	1	2	3	4		6			9	10	11					5	7	8				
R	21	(h)	Aberdeen	W 5-1	Millar 2, McMillan, Wilson, Brand	57,600	1	2	3	4		6		8	9	10	11					5	7					
QF	Mar 10	(a)	Kilmarnock	W 4-2	McMillan 2, Caldow (pen), Brand	35,995	1	2	3	4		6	7	8	9	10	11					5						
SF	31	(n*)	Motherwell	W 3-1	Murray 2, Wilson	84,321	1	2	3	4	5			8		10	11				6		7		9			
F	Apr 21	(n*)	St Mirren	W 2-0	Brand, Wilson	127,940	1	2	3	4		6		8	9	10	11				5		7					
*Played at Hampden Park, Glasgow.						Appearances	7	7	7	7	2	5	2	6	6	7	7			1	2	4	5	1	1			
						Goals			2					3	7	6	4								2			

Scottish League Cup Section Three

	Date		Opponent	Result	Scorers	Att.	Ritchie	Shearer	Caldow	Davis	Paterson	Baxter	Scott	McMillan	Millar	Brand	Wilson	Christie	Provan	Stevenson	McKinnon	Baillie	Henderson	Greig	Murray	Hume	King	Martin
1	Aug 12	(a)	Third Lanark	W 2-0	Wilson 2	37,000	1	2	3	4	5	6	7	8	9	10	11											
2	16	(h)	Dundee	W 4-2	Brand 2, Wilson, Millar	40,000	1	2	3	4	5	6	7	8	9	10	11											
3	19	(a)	Airdrieonians	W 2-1	Brand, Davis	20,000	1	2	3	4	5	6	7	8	9	10	11											
4	26	(h)	Third Lanark	W 5-0	Wilson 3, Millar, Brand	40,000	1	2	3	4	5	6	7	8	9	10	11											
5	30	(a)	Dundee	D 1-1	Brand	20,000	1	2	3	4	5	6	7	8		10	11	9										
6	Sep 2	(h)	Airdrieonians	W 4-1	Brand 2, Greig, Christie	35,000	1	2	3		5	6	7			10	11	9		4				8				
QF1	13	(h)	East Fife	W 3-1	Christie 2, Davis	20,000	1	2	3	4	5	6	7			10	11	9						8				
QF2	20	(a)	East Fife	W 3-1	Wilson, Scott, Brand	15,000	1	2	3	4	5	6	7	8		10	11	9										
SF	Oct 11	(n*)	St Johnstone	W 3-2	Wilson 2, Caldow (pen)	41,000	1	2	3		5	6	7	8	9	10	11			4								
F	28	(n†)	Hearts	D 1-1	Millar	88,635	1	2	3	4	5	6	7	8	9	10	11											
R	Dec 18	(n†)	Hearts	W 3-1	Millar, Brand, McMillan	47,522	1	2	3	4		6	7	8	9	10	11					5						
*Played at Celtic Park, Glasgow.						Appearances	11	11	11	9	10	11	11	9	7	11	11	4		2		1		2				
†Played at Hampden Park, Glasgow.						Goals			1	2			1	1	4	9	9	3						1				

European Champions' Cup

	Date		Opponent	Result	Scorers	Att.	Ritchie	Shearer	Caldow	Davis	Paterson	Baxter	Scott	McMillan	Millar	Brand	Wilson	Christie	Provan	Stevenson	McKinnon	Baillie	Henderson	Greig	Murray	Hume	King	Martin
1	Sep 5	(a)	AS Monaco	W 3-2	Scott 2, Baxter	6,024	1	2	3	4	5	6	7	8	9	10	11											
	12	(h)	AS Monaco	W 3-2	Christie 2, Scott	67,501	1	2	3	4	5	6	7	8		10	11	9										
2	Nov 15	(a)	Vorwärts Berlin	W 2-1	Caldow (pen), Brand	14,268	1	2	3	4	5	6	7	8	9	10	11											
	23	(h*)	Vorwärts Berlin	W 4-1	McMillan 2, Henderson, Kalinke (og)	1,781	1	2	3	4	5	6		8	9	10	11						7					
QF1	Feb 7	(a)	Standard Liège	L 1-4	Wilson	35,891	1	2		4	5	6			9	10	11						7	8			3	
QF2	14	(h)	Standard Liège	W 2-0	Brand, Caldow (pen)	76,730	1	2	3	4		6	7	8	9	10	11					5						
*Played at Malmö, Sweden.						Appearances	6	6	5	6	5	6	4	5	5	6	6	1				1	2	1			1	
						Goals			2			1	3	2		2	1	2					1					

1 own-goal

Glasgow Cup

	Date		Opponent	Result	Scorers	Att.	Ritchie	Shearer	Caldow	Davis	Paterson	Baxter	Scott	McMillan	Millar	Brand	Wilson	Christie	Provan	Stevenson	McKinnon	Baillie	Henderson	Greig	Murray	Hume	King	Martin
SF	May 1	(a)	Third Lanark	L 1-4	Shearer	6,000		2		4				10	6						5		7	8	9	11	3	1
						Appearances		1		1				1	1						1		1	1	1	1	1	1
						Goals		1																				

Other matches

	Date		Opponent	Result	Scorers	Att.	Ritchie	Shearer	Caldow	Davis	Paterson	Baxter	Scott	McMillan	Millar	Brand	Wilson	Christie	Provan	Stevenson	McKinnon	Baillie	Henderson	Greig	Murray	Hume	King	Martin
1	Oct 18	(n)	Eintracht F*	L 2-3	Davis 2	104,679	1	2	3	4	5	6	7	8	9	10	11											
2	Nov 22	(h†)	Vorwarts Berlin	W 1-0	Henderson	3,012	1	2	3	4	5	6		8	9	10	11						7					
3	Jun 2	(a)	Lokomotiv M	W 3-1	McMillan, Brand, Wilson	21,000	1	2	3	4			**7**	8	9	10	11				5		12	6				
4	6	(a)	Dinamo Tbilisi	W 1-0	Henderson	30,000	1	2	3	4			7	**8**	9	10	11				5		**12**	6	14			
5	9	(a)	Dinamo Kiev	D 1-1	Brand	60,000	1	2	3	4			**7**	**8**	9	10	11				5		**12**	6	14			
* Inauguration of Hampden Park floodlights.						Appearances	5	5	5	5	2	2	4	5	5	5	5				3		1	3				
†Played in Malmö, Sweden, match abandoned at half-time due to weather conditions.						Sub appearances																	3		2			
						Goals				2				1		2	1						2					

1962-63

Manager: J.S.Symon

	Date	Opponent	Result	Scorers	Scottish League	Ritchie	Shearer	Caldow	Davis	McKinnon	Baxter	Henderson	McMillan	Millar	Brand	Scott	Greig	Wilson	Baillie	Forrest	McLean G (2)	Provan	Watson C	Martin	Hunter	Willoughby	Penman	King	Murray
1	Aug 22 (h)	St Mirren	W 3-0	Brand, Millar, J.Wilson (og)	46,000	1	2	3	4	5	6	7	8	9	10	11													
2	Sep 8 (a)	Celtic	W 1-0	Henderson	72,000	1	2	3	4	5	6	7		9	10		8	11											
3	15 (h)	Partick Thistle	W 2-1	Millar 2	52,000	1	2	3		5	6	7	8	9	10		4	11											
4	22 (a)	Hibernian	W 5-1	Millar 2, Wilson 2 (1 pen), Baxter	28,000	1	2	3		5	6	7	8	9	10		4	11											
5	29 (h)	Dundee	D 1-1	Millar	57,000	1	2	3	4	5	6	7		9	10		8	11											
6	Oct 6 (a)	Queen of South	W 4-0	Millar 2, Brand 2	20,000	1	2	3	4	5	6	7		9	10		8	11											
7	13 (h)	Airdrieonians	W 5-2	Millar 2, Wilson (pen), McMillan, Greig	28,000	1	2	3		5	6	7	8	9	10		4	11											
8	23 (a)	Third Lanark	W 4-1	Henderson 2, Wilson, Brand	20,000	1	2	3	4	5	6	7	8	9	10			11											
9	27 (a)	Aberdeen	W 3-2	Millar, Wilson, Greig	40,000	1	2	3	4	5	6	7		9	10		8	11											
10	Nov 3 (h)	Dunfermline A	D 1-1	Wilson (pen)	38,000	1	2		4	3	6	7		9	10		8	11	5										
11	10 (a)	Dundee U	L 1-2	Greig	24,000	1	2	3	4	6	10	7		9			8	11	5										
12	17 (h)	Falkirk	W 4-0	Millar 2, Wilson, Greig	20,000	1	2	3		4	6	7		10			8	11	5	9									
13	24 (h)	Clyde	W 3-1	Brand 2, Millar	28,000	1	2	3	4		6	7	8	9	10			11	5										
14	Dec 1 (a)	Motherwell	D 1-1	Davis	18,000	1	2	3	4	5			8	9	10	7	6	11											
15	8 (h)	Kilmarnock	W 6-1	Brand 3, Wilson, Millar, Henderson	40,319	1	2	3	4	5	6	7	8	9	10			11											
16	15 (h)	Raith Rovers	W 4-2	Brand 3 (1 pen), Wilson	20,000	1	2		4	3	6	7	8		10			11	5	9									
17	29 (a)	St Mirren	W 2-0	Scott, Millar	28,000	1	2	3	4	5	6		8	9	10	7		11											
18	Jan 1 (h)	Celtic	W 4-0	Davis, Millar, Greig, Wilson	55,000	1	2	3	4	5	6			9	10	7	8	11											
19	Mar 9 (a)	Dunfermline A	W 2-1	Wilson, Millar	22,500	1	2	3		5	6	7		9	10		4	11			8								
20	16 (h)	Dundee U	W 5-0	Millar 4, Brand	35,000	1	2	3		5	6	7		9	10		4	11			8								
21	23 (a)	Falkirk	W 2-0	Henderson, McLean	16,500	1	2	3		5	6	7		9	10		4	11			8								
22	27 (a)	Hearts	W 5-0	Millar 2, Wilson 2, McLean	35,000	1	2	3		5	6	7		9	10		4	11			8								
23	Apr 10 (h)	Hibernian	W 3-1	Wilson 2, Brand	25,000	1	2			5	6	7		9	10		4	11			8	3							
24	17 (a)	Partick Thistle	W 4-1	Wilson 4	32,000	1	2			5	6	7		9	10		4	11			8	3							
25	20 (a)	Raith Rovers	D 2-2	Baxter, Millar	11,000	1	2			5	6	7		9	10		4	11			8	3							
26	27 (h)	Hearts	W 5-1	Baxter 2, Brand, Wilson, Holt (og)	40,000	1	2			5	6	7		9	10		4	11			8	3							
27	29 (h)	Motherwell	D 1-1	Wilson	25,000	1	2			5	6	7			10		4	11		9	8	3							
28	May 6 (a)	Airdrieonians	W 2-0	Baxter, Brand	6,500	1	2			5	6	7		9	10		4	11				3	8						
29	11 (h)	Third Lanark	W 1-0	Brand	34,000	1	2			5	6	7	8	9	10		4					3	11						
30	13 (a)	Kilmarnock	L 0-1		12,801		2		4						10		8	11	5	9		3	7	1	6				
31	18 (h)	Queen of South	W 3-1	Millar 2, Brand	20,000	1	2		4	5	6	7		9	10			11				3				8			
32	22 (a)	Clyde	W 3-1	Willoughby 2, Brand	6,000	1	2			5	6			9	10		4	11				3	7			8			
33	25 (a)	Dundee	D 0-0		18,000	1	2			5	6		8	9	10		4	11				3	7						
34	27 (h)	Aberdeen	D 2-2	Wilson 2	14,000	1	2			5	6			9	10		4	11				3	7			8			
FINAL LEAGUE POSITION: 1st					Appearances	33	34	20	16	32	32	27	12	31	32	4	27	32	6	4	9	12	6	1	1	3			
					Goals				2		5	5	1	27	19	1	5	23			2					2			

2 own-goals

Scottish FA Cup

	Date	Opponent	Result	Scorers	Att	Ritchie	Shearer	Caldow	Davis	McKinnon	Baxter	Henderson	McMillan	Millar	Brand	Scott	Greig	Wilson	Baillie	Forrest	McLean G (2)	Provan	Watson C	Martin	Hunter	Willoughby	Penman	King	Murray
2	Mar 13 (a)	Airdrieonians	W 6-0	Wilson 3, Brand (pen), Henderson, Thompson (og)	17,823	1	2	3		5	6	7	8	9	10		4	11											
3	20 (h)	East Stirling	W 7-2	Brand 4, Wilson, Millar, McLean	35,000	1	2	3		5	6	7		9	10		4	11			8								
QF	30 (a)	Dundee	D 1-1	Brand (pen)	36,839	1	2	3		5	6	7		9	10		4	11			8								
R	Apr 3 (h)	Dundee	W 3-2	Brand 2 (1 pen), Hamilton (og)	81,190	1	2	3		5	6	7		9	10		4	11			8								
SF	13(n*)	Dundee U	W 5-2	Millar 3, Brand, McLean	56,391	1	2			5	6	7		9	10		4	11			8	3							
F	May 4(n*)	Celtic	D 1-1	Brand	129,643	1	2			5	6	7		9	10		4	11			8	3							
R	15(n*)	Celtic	W 3-0	Brand 2, Wilson	120,273	1	2			5	6	7	8	9	10		4	11				3							
*Played at Hampden Park, Glasgow.					Appearances	7	7	4		7	7	7	2	7	7		7	7			5	3							
					Goals							1		4	12			5			2								

2 own-goals

Scottish League Cup

	Date	Opponent	Result	Scorers	Att	Ritchie	Shearer	Caldow	Davis	McKinnon	Baxter	Henderson	McMillan	Millar	Brand	Scott	Greig	Wilson	Baillie	Forrest	McLean G (2)	Provan	Watson C	Martin	Hunter	Willoughby	Penman	King	Murray
1	Aug 11 (a)	Hibernian	W 4-1	Brand 2 (1 pen), Henderson, Wilson	36,500	1	2	3	4	5	6	8		9	10	7		11											
2	15 (h)	Third Lanark	W 5-2	Millar 3, Scott, Wilson	25,000	1	2	3	4	5	6	8		9	10	7		11											
3	18 (a)	St Mirren	L 1-2	Murray	37,000	1	2	3	4	5	6	8			10	7		11											9
4	25 (h)	Hibernian	D 0-0		45,000	1	2	3	4	5	6	7	8	9	10	11													
5	29(a*)	Third Lanark	W 5-2	Millar 3, Scott 2		1	2	3	4	5	6	7		9	10	11	8												
6	Sep 1 (h)	St Mirren	W 4-0	Greig 3, Millar	50,000	1	2	3	4	5	6	7		9	10		8	11											
QF	12 (a)	Dumbarton	W 3-1	Millar, Greig, Wilson (pen)	19,000	1	2	3	4	5	6	7		9	10		8	11											
	19 (h)	Dumbarton	D 1-1	Greig	17,500	1	2	3		5	6		8	9	10	7	4	11											
SF	Oct 10(n*)	Kilmarnock	L 2-3	Brand 2	76,043	1	2	3	4	5	6	7		9	10		8	11											
*Played at Hampden Park, Glasgow.					Appearances	9	9	9	8	9	9	8	2	8	9	6	5	7											1
					Goals							1		8	4	3	5	3											1

European Cup-winners' Cup

	Date	Opponent	Result	Scorers	Att	Ritchie	Shearer	Caldow	Davis	McKinnon	Baxter	Henderson	McMillan	Millar	Brand	Scott	Greig	Wilson	Baillie	Forrest	McLean G (2)	Provan	Watson C	Martin	Hunter	Willoughby	Penman	King	Murray
1	Sep 5 (h)	Sevilla FC	W 4-0	Millar 3, Brand	60,500	1	2	3	4	5	6	7		9	10		8	11											
	26 (a)	Sevilla FC	L 0-2		25,000	1	2	3	4	5	6	7		9	10		8	11											
2	Oct 31 (a)	Tottenham H	L 2-5	Henderson, Millar	58,859	1	2	3	4	5	6	7	8	9	10			11											
	Dec 11 (h)	Tottenham H	L 2-3	Brand, Wilson	80,000	1	2	3	4	5	6	7	8	9	10			11											
					Appearances	4	4	4	4	4	4	4	2	4	4		2	4											
					Goals							1		4	2			1											

Glasgow Cup

	Date	Opponent	Result	Scorers	Att	Ritchie	Shearer	Caldow	Davis	McKinnon	Baxter	Henderson	McMillan	Millar	Brand	Scott	Greig	Wilson	Baillie	Forrest	McLean G (2)	Provan	Watson C	Martin	Hunter	Willoughby	Penman	King	Murray
1	Oct 15 (h)	Celtic	D 2-2	Wilson, Millar	50,000	1	2	3		5	6	7	8	9	10		4	11											
R	Nov 21 (a)	Celtic	L 2-3	Henderson, Brand	24,000	1	2	3		4	6	7		9	10		8	11	5										
					Appearances	2	2	2		2	2	2	1	2	2		2	2	1										
					Goals							1		1	1			1											

Other matches

	Date	Opponent	Result	Scorers	Att	Ritchie	Shearer	Caldow	Davis	McKinnon	Baxter	Henderson	McMillan	Millar	Brand	Scott	Greig	Wilson	Baillie	Forrest	McLean G (2)	Provan	Watson C	Martin	Hunter	Willoughby	Penman	King	Murray
1	Jul 28(a*)	BorMGladbach	D 1-1	Brand	20,000	1	2		4	5		8	12	**9**	10	**7**	6	11									15	3	14
2	Nov 29 (h)	Torpedo Moscow	L 1-2	Millar	47,000	1	2	3	4	5	6	7	8	**9**	10	12		**11**											14
3	May 20 (a)	Arsenal †	D 2-2	Baxter, Brand	30,000	1	2			5	6		**8**	9	10		4	11				3	7				12		
*Opening of Bökelberg Stadion					Appearances	3	3	1	2	3	2	2	2	3	3	1	2	3				1	1					1	
†Jack Kelsey Testimonial Match					Sub appearances								1			1											2		2
					Goals						1			1	2														

1963-64

Manager: J.S.Symon

Player columns (left → right): Ritchie, Shearer, Provan, Greig, McKinnon, Baxter, Henderson, McLean, Forrest, Brand, Wilson, Millar, Willoughby, Hynd, Watson C, Trail, Baillie, McMillan, Wood, Caldow, Davis, Hunter.

Scottish League

#	Date	V	Opponent	Result	Scorers	Att
1	Aug 21	(a)	Dundee	D 1-1	Brand (pen)	34,500
2	Sep 7	(h)	Celtic	W 2-1	McLean, Brand	57,000
3	14	(a)	Partick Thistle	W 3-0	Forrest 3	35,000
4	21	(h)	Hibernian	W 5-0	Brand 2, McLean, Forrest, Henderson	50,000
5	28	(a)	Third Lanark	W 5-0	Forrest 4, Baxter	25,000
6	Oct 5	(h)	Falkirk	W 4-0	McLean 3, Henderson	36,000
7	12	(a)	St Mirren	W 3-0	Brand, Willoughby, Forrest	35,000
8	19	(h)	East Stirling	W 3-1	Forrest 2, Watson	20,000
9	30	(a)	Queen of South	W 2-0	Forrest, Brand	15,000
10	Nov 2	(a)	Airdrieonians	W 4-0	Willoughby, Forrest, Baxter, Watson	20,000
11	9	(h)	Aberdeen	D 0-0		34,000
12	16	(a)	Kilmarnock	D 1-1	Brand (pen)	27,624
13	23	(a)	Dunfermline A	D 4-1	Watson 2, Henderson, Forrest	21,000
14	30	(h)	Hearts	L 0-3		25,000
15	Dec 7	(a)	Dundee U	W 3-2	McLean 2, Brand	20,000
16	14	(a)	Motherwell	D 3-3	Provan (pen), Greig, Brand	16,500
17	21	(h)	St Johnstone	L 2-3	Brand, Provan (pen)	14,000
18	28	(h)	Dundee	W 2-1	Forrest, Provan (pen)	43,000
19	Jan 1	(a)	Celtic	L 1-0	Millar	65,000
20	2	(h)	Partick Thistle	W 4-3	Brand 2, Greig, Millar	30,000
21	4	(a)	Hibernian	W 1-0	Millar	19,000
22	18	(h)	Third Lanark	W 2-1	Brand 2	17,000
23	Feb 1	(a)	Falkirk	W 1-0	Brand	16,000
24	8	(h)	St Mirren	L 2-3	Millar, Wilson	35,000
25	19	(a)	East Stirling	W 5-0	Wilson 2, Forrest 2, Miller (og)	6,000
26	22	(a)	Queen of South	W 4-1	Forrest 2, Wilson, Willoughby	9,500
27	29	(h)	Airdrieonians	W 4-1	Forrest 2, Baxter (pen), Greig	26,500
28	Mar 11	(a)	Aberdeen	D 1-1	Baxter (pen)	22,000
29	14	(h)	Kilmarnock	W 2-0	McLean, Wilson	45,870
30	21	(h)	Dunfermline A	W 2-1	Wilson, McMillan	30,000
31	Apr 1	(a)	Hearts	W 2-1	Brand, Millar	29,000
32	4	(h)	Dundee U	W 2-0	Brand, McLean	28,000
33	18	(h)	Motherwell	W 5-1	Brand 2, Greig, Millar, McLean	39,000
34	29	(a)	St Johnstone	L 0-1	12,000

FINAL LEAGUE POSITION: 1st

Appearances (by player): Ritchie 34, Shearer 31, Provan 33, Greig 34, McKinnon 32, Baxter 26, Henderson 30, McLean 19, Forrest 24, Brand 31, Wilson 16, Millar 22, Willoughby 6, Hynd 1, Watson C 7, Trail 3, Baillie 4, McMillan 10, Wood 4, Caldow 3, Davis 4.

Goals (by player): Provan 3, Greig 4, Baxter 4, Henderson 3, McLean 10, Forrest 21, Brand 19, Wilson 6, Millar 6, Willoughby 3, Watson C 4, McMillan 1. (1 own-goal)

Scottish FA Cup

#	Date	V	Opponent	Result	Scorers	Att
1	Jan 11	(a)	Stenhousemuir	W 5-1	Greig 2, Millar, Provan (pen), Brand	10,384
2	25	(h)	Duns	W 9-0	Millar 4, Brand 3, McLean, Henderson	17,350
3	Feb 15	(h)	Partick Thistle	W 3-0	Wilson 2, Forrest	62,000
QF	Mar 7	(h)	Celtic	W 2-0	Forrest, Henderson	84,724
SF	28	(n*)	Dunfermline A	W 1-0	Wilson	67,823
F	Apr 25	(n*)	Dundee	W 3-1	Millar 2, Brand	120,982

*Played at Hampden Park, Glasgow.

Appearances: 6, 5, 6, 6, 6, 6, 5, 3, 2, 6, 4, 4, 1, 1, 3, 1, 1

Goals (by player): Provan 1, Greig 2, Henderson 2, McLean 1, Forrest 2, Brand 5, Wilson 3, Millar 7.

Scottish League Cup

#	Date	V	Opponent	Result	Scorers	Att
1	Aug 10	(a)	Celtic	W 3-0	Forrest 2, McLean	60,000
2	14	(h)	Queen of South	W 5-2	Wilson 2, McLean, Forrest, Provan	30,800
3	17	(a)	Kilmarnock	W 4-1	Brand 2, Henderson, McLean	34,246
4	24	(h)	Celtic	W 3-0	Wilson, Brand (pen), Forrest	70,000
5	28	(a)	Queen of South	W 5-2	Forrest 4, Wilson	10,000
6	31	(h)	Kilmarnock	D 2-2	Wilson, Forrest	34,570
QF	Sep 11	(a)	East Fife	D 1-1	Forrest	15,000
	18	(h)	East Fife	W 2-0	Brand (pen), Forrest	25,000
SF	Oct 2	(n*)	Berwick R	W 3-1	Wilson, Brand, Forrest	16,000
F	26	(n*)	Morton	W 5-0	Forrest 4, Willoughby	105,907

*Played at Hampden Park, Glasgow.

Appearances (by player): Ritchie 10, Shearer 10, Provan 10, Greig 10, McKinnon 9, Baxter 10, Henderson 10, McLean 7, Forrest 10, Brand 10, Wilson 9, Willoughby 2, Watson C 1, Baillie 1, McMillan 1.

Goals (by player): Provan 1, Henderson 1, McLean 3, Forrest 16, Brand 5, Wilson 6, Willoughby 1.

European Champions' Cup

#	Date	V	Opponent	Result	Att
1	Sep 25	(h)	Real Madrid	L 0-1	81,215
	Oct 9	(a)	Real Madrid	L 0-6	90,000

Appearances: 2, 2, 2, 2, 2, 2, 2, 2, 1, 1, 1, 1

Goals: —

British Championship

#	Date	V	Opponent	Result	Scorers	Att
1	Nov 27	(h)	Everton	L 1-3	Greig	64,006
2	Dec 2	(a)	Everton	D 1-1	Brown (og)	42,000

Appearances: 2, 2, 2, 2, 2, 1, 2, 1, 1, 2, 2, 1, 1, 1

Sub appearances: 1

Goals: 1

(1 own-goal)

Glasgow Cup

#	Date	V	Opponent	Result	Scorers	Att
1	Nov 13	(h)	Queen's Park	W 1-0	McLean	4,900
Sf	Jan 15	(h)	Clyde	L 0-1		10,000

Appearances: 2, 1, 1, 1, 2, 1, 2, 1, 1, 1, 1, 1, 1, 2, 2, 1

Goals: 1

1964-65

Manager: J.S.Symon

Scottish League

No	Date	Venue / Opponent	Result	Scorers	Att	Ritchie	Hynd	Provan	Greig	McKinnon	Baxter	Henderson	McLean	Forrest	Brand	Wilson	Martin	Willoughby	Shearer	Millar	Johnston	Watson C	Caldow	Wood	Beck	Mathieson	Watson R
1	Aug 19 (h)	Dunfermline A	D 0-0		30,000	1	2	3	4	5	6	7	8	9	10	11											
2	Sep 5 (a)	Celtic	L 1-3	Wilson	58,000	1	2	3	4	5	6	7	8	9	10	11											
3	12 (h)	Partick Thistle	D 1-1	McLean	35,000		2	3	4	5	6	7	10	9		11	1			8							
4	19 (a)	Dundee	L 1-4	Forrest	28,700			3	4	5	6	7		9	10	11	1			2	8						
5	26 (h)	Airdrieonians	W 9-2	Forrest 3, Brand 3, Greig, Wilson, Baxter (pen)	30,000	1	2	3	4	5	6	7		9	10	11				8							
6	Oct 7 (a)	St Johnstone	W 1-0	Baxter		1		3	4	5	6	8	7	10						2	9	11					
7	10 (h)	Hibernian	L 2-4	Johnston 2	40,000	1		3	4	5	6			9	10					2	8	11	7				
8	17 (a)	Hearts	D 1-1	Johnston	35,000	1		2	4	5	10	7		9		11				8			3	6			
9	27 (a)	St Mirren	W 7-0	Forrest 4, Baxter, Millar, Brand	15,000	1		2	4	5	10	7		9		11				8			3	6			
10	31 (h)	Clyde	W 6-1	Millar 2, Forrest, Greig, Johnston, Wood	35,000	1		2	4	5	10			9		11				8	7		3	6			
11	Nov 7 (h)	Aberdeen	D 2-2	Baxter, Forrest	40,000	1		2	4	5	10	7		9		11				8			3	6			
12	14 (a)	Kilmarnock	D 1-1	Baxter	32,021	1		2	4	5	10	7		9		11				8			3	6			
13	21 (h)	Motherwell	W 1-0	Forrest	33,000	1	3	2	4	5	10	7		9		11				8				6			
14	28 (a)	Falkirk	W 5-0	Forrest 2, Greig, Baxter, Wilson	14,000	1		2	4	5	10	7		9		11				8			3	6			
15	Dec 12 (a)	Dundee U	W 3-1	Forrest 3	25,000	1		2	4	5				9		11				8	7		3	6	10		
16	19 (h)	Third Lanark	W 5-0	Forrest 2, Wilson 2, Beck	22,000	1		2	4	5				9		11				8	7		3	6	10		
17	Jan 1 (h)	Celtic	W 1-0	Forrest	64,400	1		2	4	5				9		11				8	7		3	6	10		
18	2 (a)	Partick Thistle	D 1-1	Caldow (pen)	28,700	1		2	4	5				9		11				8	7		3	6	10		
19	9 (h)	Dundee	W 4-0	Forrest 3, Millar	30,000	1		2	4	5				9		11				8	7		3	6	10		
20	16 (a)	Airdrieonians	W 4-0	Wilson, Johnston, Caldow (pen), Forrest	18,000	1		2	4	5				9		11				8	7		3	6	10		
21	30 (a)	Hibernian	L 0-1		44,300	1		2	4	5		7		9		11				8			3	6	10		
22	Feb 13 (h)	Hearts	D 1-1	Forrest	50,000	1		2	4	5				9	10	11				8			3	6			
23	27 (h)	St Mirren	W 1-0	Wood	30,000	1	6	2	4	5		7		9		11							3	8	10		
24	Mar 10 (h)	Clyde	W 3-0	McLean 2, Greig	18,000	1	6	2	4	5		7	10	9		11				8			3				
25	13 (a)	Aberdeen	L 0-2		25,000	1	6	2	4	5		7	10	9		11							3	8			
26	20 (h)	Kilmarnock	D 1-1	Brand (pen)	30,574	1		2	4	5		7		9		11				8			3	6	10		
27	24 (h)	St Johnstone	W 2-1	Wilson, Forrest	5,800	1		2	4	5		7	10	9		11				8			3	6			
28	30 (h)	Morton	L 0-1		25,000			2	4	5		7		9	10	11	1	8					3	6			
29	Apr 3 (h)	Falkirk	W 6-1	Forrest 4, Willoughby 2	14,000			2	4	5		7		9	10	11	1	8					3	6			
30	7 (a)	Morton	W 3-1	Wilson 2, Forrest	18,000			2	4	5		7		9	10	11	1	8					3	6			
31	14 (a)	Dunfermline A	L 1-3	Wilson	16,000			2	4	5		7		9	10	11	1	8					3	6			
32	17 (h)	Dundee U	L 0-1		15,000			2	4	5		7		9	10	11	1	8					3	6			
33	21 (a)	Motherwell	W 3-1	McLean, Wood, Henderson	10,000		4	2	6	5		7	10	9		11	1						3	8			
34	23 (a*)	Third Lanark	W 1-0	Brand	5,000		4	2	6	5		7	10	9		11	1						3	8			
	FINAL LEAGUE POSITION: 5th				Appearances	25	10	34	34	34	22	18	8	30	17	25	9	5	3	21	17	1	26	26	9		
	*Rangers' final game at Cathkin Park, Glasgow.				Goals				4		6	1	4	30	6	10		2		4	5		2	3	1		

Scottish FA Cup

No	Date	Venue / Opponent	Result	Scorers	Att	Ritchie	Hynd	Provan	Greig	McKinnon	Baxter	Henderson	McLean	Forrest	Brand	Wilson	Martin	Willoughby	Shearer	Millar	Johnston	Watson C	Caldow	Wood	Beck	Mathieson	Watson R
1	Feb 6 (h)	Hamilton A	W 3-0	Brand, Millar, Forrest	22,184	1		2	4	5		7		9	10	11				8			3	6			
2	20 (a)	Dundee U	W 2-0	Forrest 2	23,000	1	6	2	4	5		7		9		11							3	8	10		
QF	Mar 6 (a)	Hibernian	L 1-2	Hynd	47,363	1	6	2	4	5		7	10	9		11				8			3				
					Appearances	3	2	3	3	3		3	1	3	1	3				2			3	2	1		
					Goals		1							3	1					1							

Scottish League Cup

No	Date	Venue / Opponent	Result	Scorers	Att	Ritchie	Hynd	Provan	Greig	McKinnon	Baxter	Henderson	McLean	Forrest	Brand	Wilson	Martin	Willoughby	Shearer	Millar	Johnston	Watson C	Caldow	Wood	Beck	Mathieson	Watson R
1	Aug 8 (h)	Aberdeen	W 4-0	McLean 2, Forrest, Wilson	45,000	1		3	4	5	6	7	8	9	10	11				2							
2	12 (a)	St Mirren	D 0-0		21,000	1		3	4	5	6	7	8	9	10	11				2							
3	15 (a)	St Johnstone	W 9-1	Forrest 4, McLean 2, Brand 2, Baxter	15,000	1		3	4	5	6	7	8	9	10	11				2							
4	22 (a)	Aberdeen	W 4-3	Forrest 3, Brand	30,000	1	2	3		5	6	7	8	9	10	11								4			
5	26 (h)	St Mirren	W 6-2	Baxter, Forrest, McLean, Brand, Henderson, Wilson	35,000	1	2	3		5	6	7	8	9	10	11								4			
6	29 (h)	St Johnstone	W 3-1	Forrest 3	28,000	1	2	3		5	6	7	8	9	10						11			4			
QF	Sep 14 (a)	Dunfermline A	W 3-0	Brand, Forrest, McLean (og)	20,000			3	4	5	6	7		9	10	11	1			2	8						
	16 (h)	Dunfermline A	D 2-2	Millar, Forrest	30,000			3	4	5	6	7		9	10	11	1			2	8						
SF	30 (n*)	Dundee U	W 2-1	Forrest 2	39,584	1		3	4	5	6			9	10	11			7	2	8						
F	Oct 24 (n*)	Celtic	W 2-1	Forrest 2	91,423	1			4	5	10	7		9		11				8			3	6			
	*Played at Hampden Park, Glasgow.				Appearances	8	3	10	7	10	10	7	6	10	10	9	2		6	4	2		1	1	1		3
					Goals						2	1	5	18	5	2				1							

1 own-goal

European Champions' Cup

No	Date	Venue / Opponent	Result	Scorers	Att	Ritchie	Hynd	Provan	Greig	McKinnon	Baxter	Henderson	McLean	Forrest	Brand	Wilson	Martin	Willoughby	Shearer	Millar	Johnston	Watson C	Caldow	Wood	Beck	Mathieson	Watson R
1	Sep 2 (h)	Red Star B'grade	W 3-1	Brand 2, Forrest	77,669	1	2	3	4	5	6	7	8	9	10	11											
	9 (a)	Red Star B'grade	L 2-4	Greig, McKinnon	42,939	1		3	4	5	6	7		9	10	11				2	8						
R	Nov 4 (n*)	Red Star B'grade	W 3-1	Forrest 2, Brand	34,428	1		2	4	5	10	7		9		11				8			3	6			
2	18 (h)	Rapid Vienna	W 1-0	Wilson	50,788	1		2	4	5	10	7		9		11				8			3	6			
	Dec 8 (a)	Rapid Vienna	W 2-0	Forrest, Wilson	69,272	1		2	4	5	10			9		11				8	7		3	6			
QF	Feb 17 (a)	Internazionale	L 1-3	Wilson	49,520	1	2	6		5		7		9	10	11							3	4			
	Mar 3 (h)	Internazionale	W 1-0	Forrest	78,872	1	6	2	4	5		7	8	9		11				10			3				
	*Played at Arsenal Stadium, Highbury, London.				Appearances	7	2	7	7	7	5	4	2	7	4	5				1	6		4	5	4		
					Goals				1	1				6	3	2											

Glasgow Cup

No	Date	Venue / Opponent	Result	Scorers	Att	Ritchie	Hynd	Provan	Greig	McKinnon	Baxter	Henderson	McLean	Forrest	Brand	Wilson	Martin	Willoughby	Shearer	Millar	Johnston	Watson C	Caldow	Wood	Beck	Mathieson	Watson R
1	Apr 30 (a)	Celtic	L 1-2	Henderson	41,000		4	2	6	5		7	10	9		11	1						3	8			
					Appearances		1	1	1	1		1	1	1		1	1						1	1			
					Goals							1															

1965-66

Manager: J.S.Symon

Scottish League

Player columns (left→right): Ritchie, Johansen, Provan, Watson R, McKinnon, Greig, Henderson, Willoughby, Forrest, Sorensen, Johnston, McLean, Hynd, Wood, Wilson, Caldow, Jackson, Setterington, Beck, Trail, Mathieson, Millar, Martin, Watson C

#	Date		Opponent	Result	Scorers	Att	Rit	Joh	Pro	WaR	McK	Gre	Hen	Wil	For	Sor	Jon	McL	Hyn	Woo	Wls	Cal	Jac	Set	Bec	Tra	Mat	Mil	Mar	WaC
1	Aug 25	(h)	St Johnstone	W 3-2	Forrest 2, Johnston	25,000	1	2	3	4	5	6	7	8	9	10	11													
2	Sep 11	(a)	Partick Thistle	D 1-1	McLean	29,789	1	2	3	4	5	6	7	8		10	11	9												
3		18 (h)	Celtic	W 2-1	Forrest, McLean (pen)	76,000	1	2	3	4	5	6	7		9	8	11	10												
4		25 (a)	Dundee	D 1-1	McLean	22,000	1	2	3	8	5	6	7		9		11	10	4											
5	Oct 2	(h)	Stirling Albion	W 6-0	Wilson 2, Sorensen, Willoughby, Wood, Johnston	20,000	1	2	3	4	5			8	9	10	11			6	7									
6		9 (a)	St Mirren	W 6-1	Forrest 3, McLean 2 (1 pen), Johnston	22,500	1	2	3		5	6	7		9		11	10	4											
7		16 (a)	Hibernian	W 2-1	Willoughby 2	38,000	1	2	3		5	6		8	9		11	10	4	7										
8		27 (h)	Dundee U	W 2-0	Johnston, Forrest	19,000	1	2	3		5	6	7	8	9	10	11		4											
9		30 (a)	Hamilton A	W 7-1	Forrest 5, Henderson, Wilson	12,000	1	2	3		5	6	7	8	9	10			4		11									
10	Nov 6	(h)	Falkirk	W 3-0	McLean, Henderson, Markie (og)	18,000	1	2	3	4	5	6	7	8	9		11	10												
11		13 (a)	Hearts	W 2-0	Henderson, McLean	33,225	1	2	3	4	5	6	7	8	9		11	10												
12		20 (h)	Kilmarnock	W 5-0	McLean 3 (1 pen), Johnston 2	30,000	1	2	3	4	5	6	7	8	9		11	10												
13		27 (a)	Motherwell	W 3-0	Forrest 2 (1 pen), R.Watson	18,000	1	2	3	4	5	6	7	8	9		11	10												
14	Dec 11	(h)	Morton	W 3-1	Greig 2, McLean	25,000	1	2	3	4	5	6	7	8	9		11	10												
15		18 (a)	Clyde	D 2-2	McLean, Forrest	18,000	1		3	4	5	6	7	8	9		11	10				2								
16		25 (h)	Dunfermline A	L 2-3	Forrest, McLean	35,000	1		3	6	5		7	8	9		11	10	4			2								
17	Jan 1	(h)	Partick Thistle	W 4-0	Johnston, Greig, Willoughby, McLean	15,000	1	2	3	4		6	7	8	9		11	10					5							
18		3 (a)	Celtic	L 1-5	Wilson	65,000	1	2	3		5	6			9		11	10	4	7	8									
19		8 (a)	St Johnstone	W 3-0	McLean 3	12,500	1	2	3	4	5	6		8	9		11	10		7										
20		22 (a)	Stirling Albion	W 2-0	Forrest, Willoughby	18,000	1	2	3	4	5	6	7	8	9		11	10												
21		29 (h)	St Mirren	W 4-1	McLean 2, Beck, Greig	20,000	1	2	3	4	5	6			9			10		7					8	11				
22	Feb 12	(h)	Hibernian	W 2-0	McLean, Sorensen	27,000	1	2	3	4	5	6	7	11	10	9									8					
23		26 (h)	Hamilton A	W 4-0	Forrest 2, McLean 2	25,000	1	2	3	4	5	6	7		9	8	11	10												
24	Mar 9	(a)	Falkirk	L 2-3	Forrest, Markie (og)	10,000	1	2		4	5	6	7	8	9	10	11							3						
25		12 (h)	Hearts	D 1-1	Forrest	40,000	1	2	3		5	4	7	8		10	11										9	6		
26		19 (a)	Kilmarnock	D 1-1	Forrest	25,372	1	2	3		5	4	7		9		11	10									8	6		
27		21 (a)	Dundee U	L 0-1		17,000		2	3		5	4	7		9		11	10									8	6	1	
28	Apr 6	(h)	Dundee	W 1-0	Greig	15,000	1	2	3		5	4	7	8		10	11											6		
29		9 (h)	Aberdeen	W 1-0	Greig	18,000	1	2	3		5	4	7	8	9	10					11							6		
30		13 (a)	Aberdeen	W 2-1	Johnston, Willoughby	20,000	1	2	3		5	4	7	8	9	10					11							6		
31		16 (a)	Morton	W 5-0	Johnston, Wilson, Forrest, Greig, Madsen (og)	15,000	1	2	3		5	4	7	8	9		10				11							6		
32		19 (h)	Motherwell	W 2-1	Sorensen, Forrest	15,000	1	2	3		5	4	7	8	9		10				11							6		
33		30 (a)	Dunfermline A	W 2-1	R.Watson, McLean	16,000	1	2	3	8	5	4	7		9			10			11							6		
34	May 4	(h)	Clyde	W 4-0	McLean 2, Millar, Wilson	12,000	1	2	3	8	5	4	7		9			10			11							6		

FINAL LEAGUE POSITION: 2nd

| Appearances | | | | | | | 33 | 32 | 33 | 21 | 33 | 32 | 28 | 23 | 30 | 12 | 31 | 24 | 4 | 5 | 12 | 2 | 1 | 1 | 2 | 1 | 3 | 10 | 1 | |
| Goals | | | | | | | | | 2 | | | 7 | 3 | 6 | 24 | 3 | 9 | 25 | | 1 | 6 | | | | 1 | | | 1 | | |

3 own-goals

Scottish FA Cup

#	Date		Opponent	Result	Scorers	Att	Rit	Joh	Pro	WaR	McK	Gre	Hen	Wil	For	Sor	Jon	McL	Hyn	Woo	Wls	Cal	Jac	Set	Bec	Tra	Mat	Mil	Mar	WaC
1	Feb 5	(h)	Airdrieonians	W 5-1	McLean 3 (1 pen), Wilson, Johnston	16,500	1	2	3	4	5	6				10	11	9		7				8						
2		28 (a)	Ross County	W 2-0	Johnston, McLean	8,500	1	2	3	4	5	6		9	8	11	10			7										
QF	Mar 5	(h)	St Johnstone	W 1-0	Willoughby	32,000	1	2	3	4	5	6	7	8	9	10	11													
SF		26 (n*)	Aberdeen	D 0-0		49,360	1	2	3	5	4		7		10	11	9										6	8		
R	Mar 29	(n*)	Aberdeen	W 2-1	Forrest, McLean	40,852	1	2	3	5	4	7	8	9	11	10											6			
F	Apr 23	(n*)	Celtic	D 0-0		126,599	1	2	3	8	5	4	7		9		10			11							6			
R		27 (n*)	Celtic	W 1-0	Johansen	98,202	1	2	3	8	5	4	7			10	9			11							6			

*Played at Hampden Park, Glasgow.

| Appearances | | | | | | | 7 | 7 | 7 | 5 | 7 | 7 | 5 | 2 | 4 | 4 | 7 | 5 | | 4 | | | | 1 | | | 1 | 4 | | |
| Goals | | | | | | | | 1 | | | | | | 1 | 1 | | 2 | 5 | | 1 | | | | | | | | | | |

Scottish League Cup Section Two

#	Date		Opponent	Result	Scorers	Att	Rit	Joh	Pro	WaR	McK	Gre	Hen	Wil	For	Sor	Jon	McL	Hyn	Woo	Wls	Cal	Jac	Set	Bec	Tra	Mat	Mil	Mar	WaC
1	Aug 14	(a)	Hearts	L 2-4	Forrest 2 (1 pen)	32,859		2			5	4			9		11		6		3			10			8	1	7	
2		18 (h)	Clyde	W 3-0	Willoughby 2, Forrest	25,000		2	3		5	4		8	9		11		6	10								1	7	
3		21 (a)	Aberdeen	L 0-2		25,000		2	3	4	5	6			10	9	11		8	7								1		
4		28 (h)	Hearts	W 1-0	Johnston	40,000	1	2	3	4	5	6	7	8	9		11			10										
5	Sep 1	(a)	Clyde	W 3-1	Johnston, Willoughby, Forrest	15,000	1	2	3	4	5	6		8	9		11	10		7										
6		4 (h)	Aberdeen	W 4-0	McLean 3, Forrest	45,000	1	2	3	4	5	6	7	8	9		11	10												
QF1		15 (a)	Airdrieonians	W 5-1	McLean 2, Greig, Forrest, Willoughby	15,000	1	2	3	4	5	6	7	8	9		11	10												
QF2		22 (h)	Airdrieonians	W 4-0	Forrest 3, McLean	10,000	1	2	3	4	5	6	7	8	9		11	10												
SF	Oct 6	(n*)	Kilmarnock	W 6-4	McLean 3 (1 pen), Willoughby, Forrest, Henderson	54,702	1	2	3		5	6	7	8	9		11	10	4											
F		23 (n*)	Celtic	L 1-2	Young (og)	107,609	1	2	3		5	6	7	8	9		11	10	4	10										

*Played at Hampden Park, Glasgow.

| Appearances | | | | | | | 7 | 10 | 9 | 6 | 10 | 10 | 6 | 9 | 10 | | 10 | 5 | 5 | 5 | 1 | | | 1 | | | 1 | 3 | 2 | |
| Goals | | | | | | | | | | | | 1 | 1 | 5 | 10 | | 2 | 9 | | | | | | | | | | | | |

1 own-goal

Glasgow Cup

#	Date		Opponent	Result	Scorers	Att	Rit	Joh	Pro	WaR	McK	Gre	Hen	Wil	For	Sor	Jon	McL
1	Nov 3	(a)	Clyde	W 4-0	Forrest 2, Henderson, Sorensen	12,000	1	2	3	4	5	6	7	8	9	10	11	

Competition not concluded.

| Appearances | | | | | | | 1 | 1 | 1 | 1 | 1 | 1 | 1 | 1 | 1 | 1 | 1 | |
| Goals | | | | | | | | | | | | | 1 | | 2 | 1 | | |

Other matches

#	Date		Opponent	Result	Scorers	Att	Rit	Joh	Pro	WaR	McK	Gre	Hen	Wil	For	Sor	Jon	McL	Hyn	Woo	Wls	Mat	Mil
1	Sep 28	(h)	Benfica	W 3-1	Forrest 2, McLean	37,535	1	2	3	**4**	5	6	7	14	9	**8**	11	10	12				
2	May 6	(a)	Staevnet	L 1-3	Millar	10,000	1	2	3	**8**	5	4	7			12	10	9		11			6
3		10 (a)	Haederslev	W 5-2	Sorensen 2, McLean, Wilson, Forrest	5,000	1	2	3		5	4	7	15	14	**8**	10	9		11	12		6

Appearances							3	3	3	2	3	3	3	1	2	3	3						2
Sub appearances										2				1	1		1		1				
Goals															3	2		2			1		1

1966-67

Manager: J.S.Symon

Scottish League

Column headers (left→right): Ritchie, Johansen, Provan, Millar, McKinnon, Smith D, Wilson, Smith A, Forrest, McLean, Johnston, Greig, Henderson, Setterington, Martin, Watson R, Willoughby, Jardine, Jackson, Paul, Reid, Hynd, Matheson

#	Date		Opponent	Res	Scorers	Att	Ri	Jo	Pr	Mi	McK	SD	Wi	SA	Fo	McL	Jn	Gr	He	Se	Ma	WR	Wy	Ja	Jk	Pa	Re	Hy	Mt
1	Sep 10	(h)	Partick Thistle	W 6-1	McLean 4, A.Smith, D.Smith	24,000	1	2	3	4	5	6	7	8	9	10	11												
2	17	(a)	Celtic	L 0-2		70,000	1	2		4	5	6	7	8	9	10	11	3											
3	24	(h)	Aberdeen	W 3-0	Henderson, Johnston, McLean	40,000	1	2	3	4	5	6				10		9	11	8	7								
4	Oct 1	(a)	Dundee U	W 3-2	Johansen, A.Smith, Setterington	18,000	1	2	3		5	6		8		9		11	4	7	10								
5	8	(h)	Falkirk	W 5-0	Provan (pen), Millar, Henderson, Johnston, A.Smith	25,000	1	2	3	12	5	6		11	8	9			10	4	7								
6	15	(a)	Hearts	D 1-1	Millar	30,000	1	2	3	9	5	6		11	8				10	4	7								
7	Nov 2	(a)	St Mirren	W 6-1	Henderson 2, Johnston 2, A.Smith, Provan (pen)	10,000		2	3		5	6	12	10	9			11	4	7		1	8						
8	5	(h)	Motherwell	W 5-1	Forrest 2, A.Smith 2, Setterington	30,000		2	3		5	6		8	9			11	4	7	10	1							
9	9	(h)	Kilmarnock	W 3-0	A.Smith, Setterington, Provan (pen)	28,839		2	3		5	6	12	8	9			11	4	7	10	1							
10	12	(a)	St Johnstone	D 1-1	Forrest	12,500		2	3	8	5	6			9			11	4	7	10	1							
11	19	(h)	Ayr U	W 4-0	A.Smith 2, Forrest, Provan (pen)	22,000		2	3		5	6		10	9			11	4	7		1	8						
12	26	(a)	Hibernian	W 2-1	Forrest 2	25,798		2	3		5	6		10	9			11	4	7		1	8						
13	Dec 3	(a)	Dunfermline A	L 2-3	Forrest, A.Smith	18,000		2	3		5	6		10	9			11	4	7		1	8						
14	10	(h)	Stirling Albion	W 4-0	Henderson 2, Greig, Forrest	25,000		2	3		5	6		8	9			11	4	7	10	1							
15	17	(h)	Airdrieonians	W 3-0	A.Smith 2, Keenan (og)	18,000		2	3		5	6		8	9			11	4	7	10	1		12					
16	31	(h)	Dundee	D 2-2	McKinnon, A.Smith	25,000		2	3		5	6		8	9	10	11	4	7		1								
17	Jan 2	(a)	Partick Thistle	D 1-1	A.Smith	27,000		2	3		5	6		8	9			11	4	7		1							
18	14	(h)	Dundee U	W 3-1	Greig, Johnston, McLean	36,000		2	3		5	6		8	10	9	11	4	7		1								
19	18	(a)	Aberdeen	W 2-1	McLean 2	31,000		2	3		5	6		8	10	9	11	4	7		1								
20	21	(a)	Falkirk	W 1-0	A.Smith	17,000		2	3		5	6		8	10	9	11	4	7		1								
21	Feb 4	(h)	Hearts	W 5-1	Willoughby 3, Henderson, Wilson	33,087		2	3		5	10	11	9					6	7	1		8	4	12				
22	8	(a)	Clyde	W 5-1	Willoughby 3, Henderson, Wilson	20,000		2	3		5	10	11	9					7		1		8	4	6	12			
23	11	(a)	Kilmarnock	W 2-1	Wilson, Willoughby	31,551		2	3		5	10	11	9					6	7	1		8	4					
24	25	(h)	St Mirren	W 3-0	Reid 2, A.Smith	23,000		2	3		5	10	11	9					6	7	1		4			8			
25	Mar 4	(a)	Motherwell	W 5-1	Willoughby 4, A.Smith	25,000		2	3		5	10	11	9					6	7	1		8	4					
26	7	(a)	Airdrieonians	W 1-0	D.Smith (pen)	20,000		2	3		5	10	11	9					6	7	1		8	4					
27	18	(a)	Ayr U	W 4-1	Willoughby 2, Jardine, Oliphant (og)	18,000		2	3		5	10	11	9					6	7	1		8	4			12		
28	25	(h)	Hibernian	W 1-0	A.Smith	30,000		2	3			10	11	9					6	7	1		8	4	5				
29	29	(h)	St Johnstone	W 4-3	Wilson 2, A.Smith, Willoughby	20,000		2	3			10	11	9					6	7	1		8	4	5				
30	Apr 1	(h)	Dunfermline A	L 0-1		30,000	2	3				10	11	9					6	7	1		4	5		8	12		
31	8	(a)	Stirling Albion	W 1-0	Willoughby	8,500	2				5	10	11	9					6	7	1		8	4				3	
32	22	(h)	Clyde	D 1-1	Wilson	25,000		2	3		5	10	11	9					6	7	1		8	4					
33	29	(a)	Dundee	D 1-1	Willoughby	20,000		2	3		5	10	11	9					6	7	1		8	4					
34	May 6	(h)	Celtic	D 2-2	Jardine, Hynd	78,000		2	3		5	10		8				11	6	7	1							9	

FINAL LEAGUE POSITION: 2nd

	Ri	Jo	Pr	Mi	McK	SD	Wi	SA	Fo	McL	Jn	Gr	He	Se	Ma	WR	Wy	Ja	Jk	Pa	Re	Hy	Mt
Appearances	6	33	33	5	31	34	17	33	17	9	21	32	32	6	28	4	11	14	4	2	1	1	
Sub appearances							1				2						1	1	1	1	1		
Goals		1	4	2	1	2	6	19	8	8	5	2	8	3			16	2			2	1	

2 own-goals

Scottish FA Cup

#	Date		Opponent	Res	Att	Ri	Jo	Pr	Mi	McK	SD	Wi	SA	Fo	McL	Jn	Gr	He	Se	Ma
1	Jan 28	(a)	Berwick R	L 0-1	13,283		2	3		5	6	12	8	10	9	11	4	7		1

	Ri	Jo	Pr	Mi	McK	SD	Wi	SA	Fo	McL	Jn	Gr	He	Se	Ma
Appearances		1	1		1	1		1	1	1	1	1	1		1
Sub appearances							1								
Goals															

Scottish League Cup Section Two

#	Date		Opponent	Res	Scorers	Att	Ri	Jo	Pr	Mi	McK	SD	Wi	SA	Fo	McL	Jn	Gr	He	Se	Ma	WR	Wy
1	Aug 13	(h)	Hibernian	W 1-0	McLean	40,000	1	2		4	5	6	11	8	9	10			3	7			
2	17	(a)	Stirling Albion	W 8-0	Forrest 5, McLean 2 (1 pen), Wilson	16,000	1	2		4	5	6	11	8	9	10			3	7			
3	20	(h)	Kilmarnock	D 0-0		51,765	1	2	3	4	5	6		8	9			11	10	7			
4	27	(a)	Hibernian	L 2-3	McLean, A.Smith	32,913	1	2	3	4	5	6		8	9	10	11		7				
5	31	(h)	Stirling Albion	D 1-1	A.Smith	20,000	1	2	3	4	5	6		8	9	10	11		7				
6	Sep 3	(a)	Kilmarnock	W 1-0	Forrest	29,743	1	2	3	4	5	6	12	8	9	10	11		7				
QF	14	(a)	Ayr U	D 1-1	Johnston	14,250	1		2	4	5	6	7	8	9	10	11	3					
	21	(a)	Ayr U	W 3-0	McLean 2, Greig	32,000	1	2	3	4	5	6			10	9	11	8	7				
SF	Oct 19	(n*)	Aberdeen	D 2-2	Henderson 2	38,623	1	2	3	9	5	6	12	8			10	11	4	7			
R	24	(n*)	Aberdeen	W 2-0	Johnston, A.Smith	38,086		2	3		5	6	7	10			9	11	4			1	8
F	29	(n*)	Celtic	L 0-1		94,532		2	3		5	6		10			9	11	4	7		1	8

*Played at Hampden Park, Glasgow.

	Ri	Jo	Pr	Mi	McK	SD	Wi	SA	Fo	McL	Jn	Gr	He	Se	Ma	WR	Wy
Appearances	9	10	9	9	11	11	4	11	7	10	9	8	9			2	2
Sub appearances							2										
Goals							1	3	6	6	2	1	2				

Glasgow Cup

#	Date		Opponent	Res	Att	Ri	Jo	Pr	Mi	McK	SD	Wi	SA	Fo	McL	Jn	Gr	He	Se
1	Aug 23	(h)	Celtic	L 0-4	76,456	1	2	3	10	5	6			8	9			11	4	7

	Ri	Jo	Pr	Mi	McK	SD	Wi	SA	Fo	McL	Jn	Gr	He	Se
Appearances	1	1	1	1	1	1			1	1			1	1
Sub appearances														
Goals														

European Cup-winners' Cup

#	Date		Opponent	Res	Scorers	Att	Ri	Jo	Pr	Mi	McK	SD	Wi	SA	Fo	McL	Jn	Gr	He	Se	Ma	WR	Wy	Ja	Jk	Pa	Re	Hy
1	Sep 27	(a)	Glentoran	D 1-1	McLean	40,000	1	2	3	4	5	6			10			9	11	8	7							
	Oct 5	(h)	Glentoran	W 4-0	Johnston, D.Smith, Setterington, McLean	33,473	1	2	3		5	6		8		9	11	4	7	10								
2	Nov 23	(h)	Borussia Dort	W 2-1	Johansen, A.Smith	65,000		2	3		5	6		10	9			11	4	7		1	8					
	Dec 6	(a)	Borussia Dort	D 0-0		45,000		2	3		5	6		10	9			11	4	7		1	8					
QF	Mar 1	(h)	Real Zaragoza	W 2-0	D.Smith, Willoughby	65,000		2	3		5	10	11	9					6	7	1		8	4				
	22	(a)	Real Zaragoza	L 0-2*		40,000		2	3			10	11	9					6	7	1		8	4	5			
SF	Apr 19	(a)	Slavia Sofia	W 1-0	Wilson	48,000		2	3		5	10	11	9					6	7	1		8	4				
	May 3	(h)	Slavia Sofia	W 1-0	Henderson	71,000		2	3		5	10		8				11	6	7	1		4					9
F	31	(nt)	Bayern Munich	L 0-1		69,500		2	3		5	10		8				11	6	7	1		4					9

* Rangers won on the toss of a coin.
† Played at Nuremberg, West Germany.

	Ri	Jo	Pr	Mi	McK	SD	Wi	SA	Fo	McL	Jn	Gr	He	Se	Ma	WR	Wy	Ja	Jk	Pa	Re	Hy
Appearances	2	9	9	1	8	9	3	9	2	2	6	9	9	1	7	2	3	5	1		2	
Sub appearances																						
Goals		1				2	1	1		2	1		1	1			1					

Further match details for this season are continued on page 279

1967-68

Manager: J.S.Symon/D.White

Scottish League

Player columns (left→right): Sorensen, Johansen, Provan, Jardine, McKinnon, Greig, Henderson, Penman, Ferguson, Smith D, Johnston, Persson, Hynd, Watson, Mathieson, Martin, Willoughby, Smith A, Semple, Jackson

#	Date	Opponent	Res	Scorers	Att	Sor	Joh	Pro	Jar	McK	Gre	Hen	Pen	Fer	SmD	Jon	Per	Hyn	Wat	Mat	Mar	Wil	SmA	Sem	Jac
1	Sep 9 (a)	Partick Thistle	W 2-0	Penman 2	31,000	1	2	3	4	5	6	7	8	9	10	11									
2	16 (h)	Celtic	W 1-0	Persson	90,000	1	2	**3**	4	5	6	7	8	9	10	12	11								
3	23 (a)	Falkirk	W 1-0	Penman	25,000	1			10	5	3		8	9	6	11	7	2	4						
4	30 (h)	Hearts	D 1-1	Ferguson	40,000	1	2			4	5	3	7	8	9	6	11	10		12					
5	Oct 7 (a)	Motherwell	W 2-0	Ferguson, Greig	20,500	1	2		12	5	4	7	8	9	6	11	10			3					
6	14 (a)	Clyde	W 3-1	Greig, Persson, Ferguson	26,000		2			5	4		8	9	6	11	7			3	1	10			
7	23 (h)	Dundee	W 2-0	Mathieson, Hynd	30,000		2			5	4		8	9	6	11	**7**	12		3	1	10			
8	28 (a)	Dunfermline A	D 0-0		40,000		2			5	4		12	9	6	7	11		8	3	1	**10**			
9	Nov 4 (a)	St Johnstone	W 3-2	Johnston, Ferguson, Persson	20,000	1	2			5	4	7	8	9	6	10	11			3					
10	11 (h)	Morton	W 1-0	Johnston	38,000	1	2			5		7	8	9	6	10	11			3	4				
11	18 (a)	Stirling Albion	W 4-2	McKinnon, Penman, Henderson, Persson	22,000	1	2		12	5	4	7	8	9	6	10	11			**3**					
12	25 (h)	Hibernian	W 2-0	Greig (pen), Willoughby	55,000	1	2			5	4	7	8	9	6		11			3		10			
13	Dec 2 (a)	Airdrieonians	W 2-1	Johnston, Ferguson	35,000	1	2			5	4	7	8	9	6	10	**11**			3	12				
14	16 (h)	Raith Rovers	W 10-2	Ferguson 3, Johnston 2, Persson 2, Greig 2(1 pen), Willoughby	35,000	1	2			5	4		7	9	6	10	11			3		8			
15	23 (h)	Kilmarnock	W 4-1	Willoughby 2, Johnston, Greig	33,239	1	2			5	4		7		6	10	11			3		8	9		
16	30 (a)	Aberdeen	W 4-1	Penman, Watson, Johnston, Willoughby	23,000	1	2			5	3		7		6	10	11		4			8	9		
17	Jan 1 (h)	Partick Thistle	W 5-2	Hynd 2, Johnston 2, Penman	31,000	1	2			5	4		7		6	10		9		3		8		11	
18	2 (a)	Celtic	D 2-2	Johnston, Johansen	75,000	1	2		4	5	3		7		6	10	11	9	**8**		12				
19	6 (h)	Falkirk	W 2-0	Ferguson, Penman	37,000	1	2			5	4		7	9	6	10	11			3		8			
20	13 (a)	Hearts	W 3-2	Johnston 2, Ferguson	40,000	1	2			5	3		7	9	6	10	11		4			8			
21	20 (h)	Motherwell	W 2-0	Willoughby, Greig (pen)	40,000	1	2			5	3		8	9	6		11		4			10	12	7	
22	Feb 3 (h)	Clyde	W 1-0	Greig	45,000	1	2			5	4		7	9	6	10	11			3		8			
23	10 (a)	Dundee	W 4-2	Johnston 2, Greig (pen), Persson	30,000	1	2		12	5	4		7	9	6	10	11			3		8			
24	Mar 2 (h)	St Johnstone	W 6-2	Ferguson 4 (1 pen), Willoughby, Persson	35,000	1	2		4	5		7		9	6	10	**11**		12	3		8			
25	6 (a)	Dunfermline A	W 2-1	Ferguson, Persson	24,000	1	2			5	4	7		9	6		11		8	3		10			
26	16 (h)	Stirling Albion	W 5-0	Persson 3, Ferguson, Corrigan (og)	18,000	1	2			5	4	7		9	6	10	11			3		8			
27	23 (a)	Hibernian	W 3-1	Persson, Henderson, Johnston	27,195	1	2			5	4	7		9	6	10	11			3			8		
28	30 (a)	Airdrieonians	W 2-1	Johnston, A.Smith	18,000	1	2			5	4	7		**9**	6	10	11			3		12	8		
29	Apr 3 (a)	Dundee U	D 0-0		10,000	1	2			5	4	7		9	6	10	11			3			8		
30	6 (h)	Dundee U	W 4-1	Ferguson 2, Willoughby, Johnston	33,000	1	2			5	4	7		10	6	9	11			3		8			
31	13 (a)	Raith Rovers	W 3-2	D.Smith, Willoughby, Penman	24,000	1	2			5	4	7	12	9	6	10	**11**			3		8			
32	17 (a)	Morton	D 3-3	Greig 2, Johnston	18,500		2			5	4	7	8		6	9	11			3	1	10			
33	20 (a)	Kilmarnock	W 2-1	Persson, Willoughby	17,286	1	2			5	4	7	8	9	6	10	**11**			3		12			
34	27 (h)	Aberdeen	L 2-3	D.Smith, Ferguson	50,000	1	2			5	4	7		9	6	10	11			3					
		Appearances				30	33	2	6	34	32	20	24	29	34	30	32	3	7	26	4	20	6	2	
		Sub appearances						3					2					1		1	2		3	2	
		Goals					1			1	11	2	8	19	2	18	14	3	1	1		10	1		

FINAL LEAGUE POSITION: 2nd

1 own-goal

Scottish FA Cup

#	Date	Opponent	Res	Scorers	Att	Sor	Joh	Pro	Jar	McK	Gre	Hen	Pen	Fer	SmD	Jon	Per	Hyn	Wat	Mat	Mar	Wil	SmA	Sem	Jac
1	Jan 27 (h)	Hamilton A	W 3-1	Greig 2, Johnston	27,500	1	2			5	4		7	9	6	**10**	11	3				8	12		
2	Feb 17 (a)	Dundee	D 1-1	Stewart (og)	33,000	1	2				4	7	8	9	6	10	11	5		3					
R	Mar 4 (h)	Dundee	W 4-1	Watson 2, Persson, Easton (og)	53,875	1	2		4	5		7		9	6	10	11		8	3					
QF	9 (h)	Hearts	D 1-1	Persson	57,521	1	2			5	4	7		9	6		11		8	3		10			
R	13 (a)	Hearts	L 0-1		44,094	1	2			5	4	7		9	6	10	11		8	3					
		Appearances				5	5		1	4	4	4	2	5	5	4	5	2	3	4		2			
		Sub appearances																				1			
		Goals									2					1	2		2						

2 own-goals

Scottish League Cup Section Two

#	Date	Opponent	Res	Scorers	Att	Sor	Joh	Pro	Jar	McK	Gre	Hen	Pen	Fer	SmD	Jon	Per	Hyn	Wat	Mat	Mar	Wil	SmA	Sem	Jac
1	Aug 12 (a)	Aberdeen	D 1-1	Persson	44,000	1	2	3	4	5	6	7	8	9	10		11								
2	16 (h)	Celtic	D 1-1	Penman	94,168	1	2	3	4	5	6	7	8	9	10		11								
3	19 (h)	Dundee U	W 1-0	Johansen (pen)	55,000	1	2	3	4	5	6	7	8	9	10		11								
4	26 (a)	Aberdeen	W 3-0	Penman 2, Jardine	50,000	1	2	3	4	5	6	7	8	9	10		11								
5	30 (a)	Celtic	L 1-3	Henderson	75,000	1	2	3	4	5	6	7	8	9	10	11									
6	Sep 2 (a)	Dundee U	W 3-0	Ferguson 2, Johnston	18,000	1	2	3	4	5	6	7	8	9	10	11									
		Appearances				6	6	6	6	6	6	6	6	6	6	2	4								
		Sub appearances																							
		Goals					1		1			1	3	2		1	1								

Rangers failed to qualify for quarter-finals.

Inter-Cities Fairs Cup

#	Date	Opponent	Res	Scorers	Att	Sor	Joh	Pro	Jar	McK	Gre	Hen	Pen	Fer	SmD	Jon	Per	Hyn	Wat	Mat	Mar	Wil	SmA	Sem	Jac
1	Sep 20 (a)	Dyna Dresden	D 1-1	Ferguson	50,000	1	2		4	5	3	7	8	9	6	11	10								
	Oct 4 (h)	Dyna Dresden	W 2-1	Penman, Greig	60,000	1	2			5	4	7	8	9	6	11	10			3					
2	Nov 8 (h)	1.FC Cologne	W 3-0	Ferguson 2, Henderson	60,000	1	2			5	**4**	7	8	9	6	10	11			3	12				
	28 (a)	1.FC Cologne	L 1-3	Henderson	46,000	1	2			5	4	7	8	9	**6**	10	11	12	3						
QF	Mar 26 (h)	Leeds U	D 0-0		85,000	1	2			5	4	7		9	6	10	11			3		8			
	Apr 9 (a)	Leeds U	L 0-2		50,498	1	2			5	4	7	12	9	6	10	11			3	**8**				
		Appearances				6	6		1	6	6	6	4	6	6	6	6			5	1	1			
		Sub appearances																1			1		1		
		Goals							1		2	1	3												

Rangers received a bye in round three

Other matches

#	Date	Opponent	Res	Scorers	Att	Sor	Joh	Pro	Jar	McK	Gre	Hen	Pen	Fer	SmD	Jon	Per	Hyn	Wat	Mat	Mar	Wil	SmA	Sem	Jac
1	Aug 5 (a)	Arsenal	L 0-3		34,586	1	2	3		5	6	7	8	9	10	11					4				
2	9 (h)	Ein't Frankfurt	W 5-3	Ferguson 3, Penman, Persson	60,000	1	2	3	4	5	6	7	8	9	10	**11**	12								
3	May 13 (a)	Morton	L 0-2		5,000	1		3		5	4	7	8	**9**	6	11					10		12	2	
4	20 (a)	BK Frem	W 4-1	McKinnon, Henderson, Penman, Semple	10,700					8	**5**	4	7	9		6	10			3	12		11		
5	22 (a)	OB Odense	W 2-0	Greig 2	6,000	1	**2**	12	8	5	4	7	9		6	10				3			11		
6	27 (a)	Sydjysk A	W 3-1	Greig 2, Henderson	3,600	**1**		3	2	5	4	7	9	8	6	10					12		11		
7	Jun 4 (a)	Gothenburg A	W 5-1	Penman 2, Persson 2, Johnson	8,000			3	2	5	4	7	9	14	6	**10**	11				1	12	**8**	15	
		Appearances				6	4	5	5	7	7	7	7	4	7	7	1			2	1	1	2	3	1
		Sub appearances					1							1							1	2		2	
		Goals							1	4	2	4	3			1	3							1	

1968-69

Manager: D.White

Scottish League

Players (in column order): Martin, Jackson, Mathieson, Greig, McKinnon, Hynd, Henderson, Willoughby, Jardine, Smith D, Persson, Penman, Johnston, Johansen, Ferguson, Stein, McDonald A, Provan, Watson, Conn, Neef, Miller, McPhee, Smith A, Sorensen

#	Date		Venue	Opponent	Result	Scorers	Attendance
1	Sep	7	(h)	Partick Thistle	W 2-0	Jardine 2	32,000
2		14	(a)	Celtic	W 4-2	Johnston 2, Penman, Persson	75,000
3		21	(h)	Kilmarnock	D 3-3	Johnston, Jardine, Henderson	39,407
4		28	(a)	Hearts	D 1-1	Penman	33,000
5	Oct	5	(h)	Falkirk	W 2-1	Persson, Johnston	40,000
6		12	(a)	St Johnstone	L 0-2		20,000
7		19	(h)	Dunfermline A	W 3-0	Persson, Jardine, Ferguson	35,000
8		26	(a)	Aberdeen	L 2-3	Ferguson, Henderson	40,000
9	Nov	2	(a)	Arbroath	W 5-1	Stein 3, Johnston 2	9,653
10		9	(h)	Hibernian	W 6-1	Stein 3, Johnston, Henderson, Persson	60,000
11		16	(a)	St Mirren	L 0-1		43,500
12		23	(a)	Clyde	D 1-1	Stein	25,000
13		30	(h)	Airdrieonians	D 1-1	Stein	25,000
14	Dec	7	(a)	Raith Rovers	W 3-0	A.McDonald, Stein, Watson	15,000
15		14	(h)	Dundee U	W 2-1	Greig, Johnston	32,000
16		28	(a)	Morton	W 2-0	Penman, Johnston	21,000
17	Jan	1	(a)	Partick Thistle	W 2-0	Johnston, Stein	24,000
18		2	(h)	Celtic	W 1-0	Greig (pen)	85,000
19		4	(a)	Kilmarnock	D 3-3	Penman, Johnston, Persson	32,893
20		11	(h)	Hearts	W 2-0	Penman, Johnston	50,000
21		18	(a)	Falkirk	W 3-0	Penman 2, Johnston	22,000
22	Feb	1	(h)	St Johnstone	W 3-0	Penman, Ferguson, Henderson	33,000
23	Mar	5	(a)	Hibernian	W 2-1	Greig (pen), Johnston	31,000
24		8	(h)	St Mirren	W 6-0	Johansen, D.Smith, Greig (pen), Ferguson, Persson, Penman	40,000
25		11	(h)	Arbroath	W 2-0	Persson, Penman	25,000
26		15	(h)	Clyde	W 6-0	Stein 3, D.Smith, Penman, Ferguson	42,000
27		24	(a)	Airdrieonians	L 2-3	Penman, Caldwell (og)	20,000
28		29	(h)	Raith Rovers	W 2-1	Penman, Johnston	28,000
29	Apr	5	(a)	Dundee U	L 1-2	Greig	21,000
30		9	(a)	Aberdeen	D 0-0		23,000
31		19	(h)	Morton	W 3-0	Ferguson, Persson, Penman	28,000
32		22	(a)	Dundee	L 2-3	Greig, Henderson	7,000
33		28	(h)	Dundee	D 1-1	Johnston	6,800
34		30	(a)	Dunfermline A	W 3-0	Johnston 2, Penman	11,700

FINAL LEAGUE POSITION: 2nd

Summary (Scottish League):

	Martin	Jackson	Mathieson	Greig	McKinnon	Hynd	Henderson	Willoughby	Jardine	Smith D	Persson	Penman	Johnston	Johansen	Ferguson	Stein	McDonald A	Provan	Watson	Conn	Neef
Appearances	31	10	26	33	28	10	32	2	15	22	28	26	29	27	7	18	8	8	10	1	3
Sub appearances									1	3		1			3			5		1	1
Goals				6			5		4	2	8	15	18	1	6	13	1		1		

1 own-goal

Scottish FA Cup

#	Date		Venue	Opponent	Result	Scorers	Attendance
1	Jan	25	(h)	Hibernian	W 1-0	Stein	58,141
2	Feb	24	(h)	Hearts	W 2-0	Johnston, Persson	47,337
QF	Mar	1	(h)	Airdrieonians	W 1-0	Greig (pen)	46,726
SF		22	(n*)	Aberdeen	W 6-1	Johnston 3, Penman 2, Henderson	66,197
F	Apr	26	(n†)	Celtic	L 0-4		132,870

*Played at Celtic Park, Glasgow.
†Played at Hampden Park, Glasgow.

Summary (Scottish FA Cup):

	Martin	Mathieson	Greig	McKinnon	Henderson	Jardine	Smith D	Persson	Penman	Johnston	Johansen	Ferguson	Stein	Provan	Watson
Appearances	5	5	5	4	5	3	5	5	5	5	1	4		3	
Sub appearances							2				1				
Goals		1			1			1	2	4			1		

Scottish League Cup Section Four

#	Date		Venue	Opponent	Result	Scorers	Attendance
1	Aug	10	(h)	Celtic	L 0-2		35,000
2		14	(a)	Partick Thistle	W 5-1	A.Smith 2, Ferguson 2, Persson	28,000
3		17	(h)	Morton	W 2-0	Jackson 2	45,000
4		24	(a)	Celtic	L 0-1		75,000
5		28	(h)	Partick Thistle	W 2-1	Henderson, Jardine	25,000
6		31	(a)	Morton	W 5-0	Jardine 2, Hendersson 2, Penman	15,000

Rangers failed to qualify for quarter-finals

Summary (Scottish League Cup):

	Martin	Jackson	Mathieson	Greig	McKinnon	Hynd	Henderson	Willoughby	Jardine	Persson	Penman	Johnston	Ferguson	Stein	Watson	McPhee	Smith A
Appearances	6	6	6	6	6	3	4	1	1	4	6	5	3	4		2	3
Sub appearances									1				1				
Goals		2					3		3	1	1		2				2

Inter-Cities Fairs Cup

Rd	Date		Venue	Opponent	Result	Scorers	Attendance
1	Sep	18	(h)	Vojvodina NS	W 2-0	Greig (pen), Jardine	70,000
	Oct	2	(a)	Vojvodina NS	L 0-1		12,000
2		30	(h)	Dundalk	W 6-1	Henderson 2, Ferguson 2, Greig, Brennan (og)	30,000
	Nov	13	(a)	Dundalk	W 3-0	Stein 2, Mathieson	10,000
3	Jan	15	(a)	DWS Amsterdam	W 2-0	Johnston, Henderson	18,000
		22	(h)	DWS Amsterdam	W 2-1	D.Smith, Stein	62,000
QF	Mar	19	(h)	Athletic Bilbao	W 4-1	Ferguson, Penman, Persson, Stein	62,842
	Apr	2	(a)	Athletic Bilbao	L 0-2		40,000
SF	May	14	(h)	Newcastle U	D 0-0		75,518
		21	(a)	Newcastle U	L 0-2		61,000

Summary (Inter-Cities Fairs Cup):

	Martin	Jackson	Mathieson	Greig	McKinnon	Hynd	Henderson	Jardine	Smith D	Persson	Penman	Johnston	Johansen	Ferguson	Stein	McDonald A	Provan	Watson	Conn	Neef
Appearances	8	5	8	9	8	3	10	3	7	7	9	9	8	3	7	1	1	2		2
Sub appearances								1	2	1						1	1			
Goals			1	2			3		1	1	1	1		3	4					

1 own-goal

Glasgow Cup

	Date		Venue	Opponent	Result	Scorers	Attendance
1	Oct	14	(h)	Queen's Park	W 7-1	Jardine 4, Johnston 2, Greig	7,000
SF	Apr	11	(a)	Celtic	W 4-3	Johnston 3, Ferguson	40,000
F		15	(h)	Partick Thistle	D 2-2	Johnston, Persson	21,000

Final replay postponed until season 1969-70.

Summary (Glasgow Cup):

	Martin	Jackson	Mathieson	Greig	McKinnon	Hynd	Henderson	Willoughby	Jardine	Smith D	Persson	Penman	Johnston	Johansen	Ferguson	Stein	Miller
Appearances	3	3	3	1	1	1	1	1	3	3	3	2	3	2	2		
Sub appearances																	1
Goals			1						4		1		6		1		

Further match details for this season are continued on page 279

1969-70

Manager: D.White/W.Waddell

Scottish League

Player columns (left to right): Neef, Johansen, Provan, Greig, McKinnon, Baxter, Henderson, McDonald A, Stein, Smith D, Johnston, Penman, Jardine, Mathieson, Watson R, McPhee, Martin, Heron, Persson, Watson K (1), Setterington, Conn, Semple, McDonald I, McCloy, Fyfe, White, Jackson, Miller, Stevenson N, Stevenson D

#	Date		Venue/Opponent	Res	Scorers	Att
1	Aug	30	(a) Dundee U	D 0-0		22,000
2	Sep	3	(h) Aberdeen	W 2-0	Provan (pen), Stein	45,000
3		6	(h) St Mirren	W 2-0	Johnston, Provan (pen)	41,000
4		13	(a) Ayr U	L 1-2	Stein	25,250
5		20	(h) Celtic	L 0-1		84,000
6		27	(a) Partick Thistle	W 2-1	Henderson, Johnston	21,000
7	Oct	4	(h) St Johnstone	W 3-1	Stein 2, Baxter	20,000
8		11	(h) Hibernian	L 1-3	Johnston	54,000
9		25	(h) Dunfermline A	W 2-0	Penman, Johansen	32,998
10		29	(a) Motherwell	D 2-2	Stein 2	25,000
11	Nov	1	(h) Dundee	W 3-1	Penman 2 (1 pen), Johnston	30,000
12		8	(a) Airdrieonians	W 3-1	Penman, Henderson, Johnston	12,200
13		15	(a) Kilmarnock	W 5-3	Stein 3, Penman (pen), Johnston	35,499
14		22	(a) Morton	D 2-2	Johnston	18,000
15		29	(h) Raith Rovers	W 3-0	Johnston, Stein, A.McDonald	25,000
16	Dec	6	(a) Hearts	W 2-1	Stein, Johnston	36,000
17		13	(h) Dundee U	W 2-1	Henderson, Stein	45,000
18		20	(a) Aberdeen	W 3-2	Stein 2, Johnston	22,000
19		27	(h) Clyde	W 3-0	Setterington, Penman (pen), Greig	35,000
20	Jan	1	(h) Partick Thistle	W 3-1	Johnston, Semple, Stein	40,000
21		3	(a) Celtic	D 0-0		75,000
22		17	(h) Ayr U	W 3-0	Stein, Greig, I.McDonald	32,000
23		31	(a) St Mirren	W 4-0	Stein 2, Greig, A.McDonald	48,000
24	Feb	25	(a) St Johnstone	W 3-1	Greig 2, Semple	25,000
25		28	(h) Hibernian	D 2-2	Stein, Greig	31,332
26	Mar	7	(h) Motherwell	W 2-1	Stein 2	31,000
27		11	(a) Raith Rovers	L 1-2	Penman	6,500
28		14	(a) Dunfermline A	L 1-2	Stein	16,000
29		21	(a) Dundee	L 1-2	Stein	17,000
30		25	(h) Hearts	W 3-2	Penman 2, Johnston	14,000
31		28	(h) Airdrieonians	D 1-1	Penman	16,700
32		31	(a) Clyde	L 0-1		14,000
33	Apr	4	(a) Kilmarnock	D 2-2	Greig, Henderson	11,135
34		18	(h) Morton	L 0-2		20,000

FINAL LEAGUE POSITION: 2nd

Appearances: Neef 26, Johansen 33, Provan 9, Greig 30, McKinnon 30, Baxter 14, Henderson 27, McDonald A 15, Stein 33, Smith D 22, Johnston 29, Penman 25, Jardine 10, Mathieson 14, Watson R 5, McPhee 1, Martin 1, Heron 7, Persson 9, Watson K 2, Setterington 4, Conn 8, Semple 4, McDonald I 1, McCloy 7, Fyfe 4, White 1, Jackson 3

Sub appearances: Smith D 3, Jardine 5, Mathieson 4, Heron 3, Setterington 1, Conn 2, Semple 4

Goals: Johansen 1, Provan 2, Greig 7, Baxter 1, Henderson 4, McDonald A 2, Stein 24, Johnston 12, Penman 10, Setterington 1, Semple 2, McDonald I 1

Scottish FA Cup

#	Date		Venue/Opponent	Res	Scorers	Att
1	Jan	24	(h) Hibernian	W 3-1	A.McDonald 2, Penman	73,716
2	Feb	7	(a) Forfar A	W 7-0	Greig 2, A.McDonald, Stein, Penman, Johansen (pen), Jardine	10,800
QF		21	(a) Celtic	L 1-3	Craig (og)	75,000

Appearances: Neef 3, Johansen 3, Greig 3, McKinnon 3, Baxter 1, Henderson 3, McDonald A 3, Stein 3, Johnston 2, Penman 3, Mathieson 3, Setterington 2, Watson K 1

Sub appearances: Smith D 1, Heron 1, Setterington 1

Goals: Johansen 1, Greig 2, Henderson 3, McDonald A 1, Penman 2, Stein 1

1 own-goal

Scottish League Cup Section One

#	Date		Venue/Opponent	Res	Scorers	Att
1	Aug	9	(a) Raith Rovers	W 3-2	Johansen, Stein, A.McDonald	21,000
2		13	(h) Celtic	W 2-1	Persson, Johnston	71,645
3		16	(a) Airdrieonians	W 3-0	Persson, Jardine, Watson	23,000
4		20	(h) Celtic	L 0-1		70,000
5		23	(a) Raith Rovers	D 3-3	Penman, A.McDonald, Polland (og)	40,000
6		27	(h) Airdrieonians	W 3-0	Stein, Johnston, Penman	18,000

Rangers failed to qualify for quarter-finals.

Appearances: Neef 6, Johansen 6, Provan 6, Greig 6, McKinnon 6, Baxter 4, Henderson 2, McDonald A 3, Stein 6, Smith D 4, Johnston 6, Penman 2, Jardine 4, Mathieson 2, Persson 3

Sub appearances: Henderson 1, Stein 1, Johnston 1, Mathieson 1, Persson 1

Goals: Johansen 1, McDonald A 2, Stein 2, Johnston 2, Penman 2, Jardine 1, Persson 1, Watson 2

1 own-goal

European Cup-winners' Cup

#	Date		Venue/Opponent	Res	Scorers	Att
1	Sep	17	(h) Steaua Bucharest	W 2-0	Johnston 2	43,346
	Oct	1	(a) Steaua Bucharest	D 0-0		90,000
2	Nov	12	(a) Górnik Zabrze	L 1-3	Persson	72,000
		26	(h) Górnik Zabrze	L 1-3	Baxter	70,000

Appearances: Neef 4, Johansen 4, Provan 2, Greig 4, McKinnon 4, Baxter 4, Henderson 4, Stein 4, Johnston 4, Penman 2, Jardine 2, Persson 2, Watson K 3

Sub appearances: Stein 1, Johnston 2, Persson 1

Goals: Johnston 2, Baxter 1, Persson 1

Glasgow Cup

#	Date		Venue/Opponent	Res	Scorers	Att
FR	Aug	11	(a) Partick Thistle*	W 3-2	Persson, Jardine, Provan	19,000
1	Oct	7	(h) Queen's Park	W 2-0	Setterington, Watson	10,000
SF	Feb	2	(a) Partick Thistle	W 4-2	Greig 2, A.McDonald, McKinnon	20,000

*1968-9 Final replay.

1969-70 Final postponed until season 1970-71.

Appearances: Neef 3, Johansen 3, Provan 2, Greig 3, McKinnon 3, Henderson 1, McDonald A 2, Stein 2, Johnston 3, Penman 3, Jardine 1, Watson R 1, Martin 2, Setterington 1, Conn 1, Semple 2

Sub appearances: Watson R 1, McDonald I 1

Goals: Provan 1, Greig 2, McKinnon 1, McDonald A 1, Stein 1, Jardine 1, Setterington 1, Watson 1

Other matches

#	Date		Venue/Opponent	Res	Scorers	Att
1	Aug	2	(a) Queen's Park R	D 3-3	Henderson, D.Smith, Hunt (og)	16,725
2		4	(h) Tottenham H	L 0-1		55,500
3	Dec	16	(a) Queen of South	W 5-2	Conn 2, Setterington, A.McDonald, Greig	3,000
4	Jan	19	(a) East Fife	L 0-1		4,000

Appearances: Neef 2, Johansen 2, Greig 3, McKinnon 2, Baxter 1, Henderson 2, McDonald A 1, Stein 2, Johnston 2, Penman 2, Jardine 1, Mathieson 3, Watson R 3, Heron 1, Persson 3, Conn 1, Semple 1, McDonald I 2, McCloy 2, Fyfe 1, White 2, Jackson 2, Miller 1, Stevenson N 1

Sub appearances: Mathieson 1, Martin 1, Heron 1, Fyfe 1, Stevenson N 1

Goals: Greig 1, Henderson 1, Conn 2, Setterington 1, McDonald A 1, D.Smith 1

1 own-goal

1970-71

Manager: W.Waddell

Scottish League

	Date		Opponent	Result	Scorers	Att	McCloy	Jardine	Miller	Greig	McKinnon	Jackson	Fyfe	Conn	Stein	McDonald A	Johnston	Penman	Henderson	Johnstone	Smith	McCallum	Parlane	Semple	Neef	Mathieson	Watson K (1)	McDonald I	Alexander	Denny	Watson RM
1	Aug	29 (a)	St Mirren	D 0-0		27,400	1	2	3	4	5	6	7	8	9	10	11														
2	Sep	5 (h)	Falkirk	W 2-0	Johnston 2 (1 pen)	39,000	1	2	3	4	5	6	7	8	9	10	11	12													
3		12 (a)	Celtic	L 0-2		75,000	1	2	3	4	5	6	7	11	9	8	10	12													
4		19 (a)	Cowdenbeath	W 5-0	Johnstone 2, Greig 2, A.McDonald	31,000	1	2	3	4	5	6	11	8		10				7	9										
5		26 (a)	Dundee U	W 2-0	Conn, Fyfe	23,000	1	2	3	4	5	6	7	8	9	10	11														
6	Oct	3 (h)	Motherwell	W 3-1	A.McDonald, Stein, Johnston	37,000	1	2	3		5	6	8	4	9	10	11			7	12										
7		10 (a)	Hearts	W 1-0	Johnston (pen)	32,500	1	2	3	4	5	6	12	8	9	10	11			7											
8		17 (a)	Aberdeen	L 0-2		39,763	1	2	3	4	5	6	8		9	10	11			7		12									
9		31 (h)	Airdrieonians	W 5-0	Johnston 2 (1 pen), Stein 2, Conn	28,788	1	2	3		5	6		4	10	8	11			7	9										
10	Nov	7 (a)	Dunfermline A	D 1-1	Jackson	20,000	1	2	3	4	5	6		8	10	12	11			7	9										
11		14 (h)	Clyde	W 5-0	Stein 2, Johnston (pen), Johnstone, Mulheron (og)	25,915	1	2	3		5	6	12	4	10	8	11			7	9										
12		21 (a)	Ayr U	L 1-2	Young (og)	20,000	1	2	3		5	6	10	4	9	8	11			7	12										
13		25 (h)	Hibernian	L 2-3	Johnstone, Stein	18,770	1	2	3		5	6		4	10	8	11			7	9										
14		28 (a)	Morton	W 2-1	Conn, Fyfe	15,000	1	2	3		5	6	11	4	10	8				7	9	12									
15	Dec	5 (h)	Dundee	D 0-0		25,420	1	2	3		5	6	12	4	10	8	11			7	9										
16		12 (a)	St Johnstone	L 1-2	Fyfe	10,500	1	2	3	4	5	6	10	8	9	11				7											
17		19 (h)	Kilmarnock	W 4-2	Johnstone 2, Jackson, A.McDonald	19,450	1	2	3	4	5	6		11	9	8				7	12	10									
18		26 (h)	St Mirren	W 1-0	Greig	25,000	1	2	3	4	5	6			8	11				7	9	10									
19	Jan	1 (a)	Falkirk	L 1-3	Conn	18,000	1	2	3			6	7	4		10				9			5	8	11						
20		2 (h)	Celtic	D 1-1	Stein	85,000		2		4	5	6		8	11	12				7	9	10				1	3				
21		16 (a)	Dundee U	D 1-1	Greig	27,776		2		4	5	6		8	11	12				7	9	10				1	3				
22		30 (a)	Motherwell	W 2-1	Matthieson, Stein	17,500		2		4	5	6		8	9	12	11			7		10				1	3				
23	Feb	6 (h)	Hearts	W 1-0	Henderson	29,398	1	2		4	5	6		8	9	12	11			7		10					3				
24		20 (a)	Aberdeen	D 0-0		36,000	1	2		4	5	6		12		8	11			7	9	10					3				
25		27 (h)	Hibernian	D 1-1	Greig	30,644	1	2		4	5	6		8	9	10	11			7	12						3				
26	Mar	10 (a)	Airdrieonians	L 3-4	A.McDonald 2, Stein	15,000	1	2		4		5			9	8				7		10		12			3	6	11		
27		13 (h)	Dunfermline A	W 2-0	Henderson, Greig	21,580	1	2		4	5	6			9	8	11			7		10		12			3				
28		20 (a)	Clyde	D 2-2	Johnston, Stein	10,500	1	2		4	5	6			9	8	10			7							3		11		
29		27 (h)	Ayr U	W 2-0	Greig, Johnston	22,000	1	2		4	5	6			10	9	8	11	12	7							3				
30	Apr	3 (h)	Morton	D 0-0		13,986	1	2	3	4	5	6				12	10	8	7		9								11		
31		10 (a)	Dundee	L 0-1		18,000	1	2		4	5	6			12	9		11	8	7	10						3				
32		14 (a)	Cowdenbeath	W 3-1	Jardine, Greig, Stein	3,396	1	4		10	5	6			9	8	11	12	7								3			2	
33		17 (h)	St Johnstone	L 0-2		17,566	1		4	5	6				9	8	11	12	7			10					3			2	
34		24 (a)	Kilmarnock	W 4-1	Miller, Henderson, A.McDonald, Stein	8,544	1		2	4	5	6			9	10	11	8	7								3				
			FINAL LEAGUE POSITION: 4th			Appearances	31	32	21	26	32	34	11	23	30	27	25	3	29	13	9	1	2	2	3	14	1	3	2		
						Sub appearances							3	2		6		5		4	2		2								
						Goals	1	1	8		2	3	4	12	6	9			3	6						1					

2 own-goals

Scottish FA Cup

	Date		Opponent	Result	Scorers	Att	McCloy	Jardine	Miller	Greig	McKinnon	Jackson	Fyfe	Conn	Stein	McDonald A	Johnston	Penman	Henderson	Johnstone	Smith	McCallum	Parlane	Semple	Neef	Mathieson	Watson K (1)	McDonald I	Alexander	Denny	Watson RM
3	Jan	23 (h)	Falkirk	W 3-0	Johnston 2, Conn	42,000	1	2		4	5	6		8	9		11			7		10					3				
4	Feb	13 (a)	St Mirren	W 3-1	Stein 2, Johnston (pen)	32,373	1	2		4	5	6		8	9		11			7		10					3				
QF	Mar	6 (h)	Aberdeen	W 1-0	Jackson	60,584	1	2		4	5	6		8	9	12	11			7		10					3				
SF		31 (n*)	Hibernian	D 0-0		69,429	1	2		4	5	6		8	9	10	11			7							3				
R	Apr	5 (n*)	Hibernian	W 2-1	Henderson, Conn	54,435	1	2		4	5	6		10	9	8	11			7							3				
F	May	8 (n*)	Celtic	D 1-1	Johnstone	120,092	1		2	4	5	6			9	10	11	8	7	12							3				
R		12 (n*)	Celtic	L 1-2	Craig (og)	103,332	1			4	5	6			9	10	11	8	7	12							3		2		
*Played at Hampden Park, Glasgow.						Appearances	7	5	1	7	7	7		5	7	4	7	2	7	3							7		1		
						Sub appearances										1				2											
						Goals						1		2	2		3		1	1											

1 own-goal

Scottish League Cup Section Two

	Date		Opponent	Result	Scorers	Att	McCloy	Jardine	Miller	Greig	McKinnon	Jackson	Fyfe	Conn	Stein	McDonald A	Johnston	Penman	Henderson	Johnstone	Smith	McCallum	Parlane	Semple	Neef	Mathieson	Watson K (1)	McDonald I	Alexander	Denny	Watson RM
1	Aug	8 (h)	Dunfermline A	W 4-1	Stein 2, Jardine, Johnston (pen)	45,056		2		4	5			8	9	10	11		7		6				3					1	
2		12 (a)	Motherwell	W 2-0	Fyfe, Henderson	25,000	1	2	12	4	5	6	10	8	9		11		7						3						
3		15 (h)	Morton	D 0-0		45,000	1	2	3	4	5	6	10	8	9	12	11		7												
4		19 (h)	Motherwell	W 2-0	Penman, Stein	35,000	1	2	3	4	5	6		12	9		10	8	7							11					
5		22 (a)	Dunfermline A	W 6-0	Johnston 3 (1 pen), Jackson, Fyfe, Stein	17,000	1	2	3	4	5	6	7	8	9	10	11														
6		26 (a)	Morton	W 2-0	Johnston, Conn	18,000	1	2	3		5	6	7	4	9	10	11					8									
QF1	Sep	9 (h)	Hibernian	W 3-1	Fyfe 2, Conn	37,355	1	2	3	4	5	6	8	10	7	11	9														
QF2		23 (h)	Hibernian	W 3-1	A.McDonald, Greig, Fyfe	54,000	1	2	3	4	5	6	7	8	9	10	11	12													
SF	Oct	14 (n*)	Cowdenbeath	W 2-0	Johnston (pen), Stein	35,000	1	2	3	4	5	6		8	9	10	11		7												
F		24 (n*)	Celtic	W 1-0	Johnstone	106,263	1	2	3		5	6		4	10	8	11		7	9											
*Played at Hampden Park, Glasgow.						Appearances	9	10	8	8	10	9	6	9	10	7	10	1	6	1	1		1		2	1		1		1	
						Sub appearances			1					1		1		1													
						Goals		1				1	5	2	5	1	6	1	1	1											

European Fairs Cup

	Date		Opponent	Result	Scorers	Att	McCloy	Jardine	Miller	Greig	McKinnon	Jackson	Fyfe	Conn	Stein	McDonald A	Johnston	Penman	Henderson	Johnstone	Smith	McCallum	Parlane	Semple	Neef	Mathieson	Watson K (1)	McDonald I	Alexander	Denny	Watson RM
1	Sep	16 (a)	Bayern Munich	L 0-1		30,000	1	2	3	4	5	6	7	8	9	10	11		12												
		30 (h)	Bayern Munich	D 1-1	Stein	82,743	1	2	3	4	5	6	7	8	9	10	11		12	14											
						Appearances	2	2	2	2	2	2	2	2	2	2	2														
						Sub appearances													2	1											
						Goals									1																

Glasgow Cup

	Date		Opponent	Result	Scorers	Att	McCloy	Jardine	Miller	Greig	McKinnon	Jackson	Fyfe	Conn	Stein	McDonald A	Johnston	Penman	Henderson	Johnstone	Smith	McCallum	Parlane	Semple	Neef	Mathieson	Watson K (1)	McDonald I	Alexander	Denny	Watson RM
F	Aug	10 (n*)	Celtic	L 1-3	Greig	58,144		2	12	4		5		8	9	10	11		7		6				3					1	
SF	May	1 (a)	Queen's Park	W 2-1	Stein, A.McDonald	7,479	1		2	4	5	6		8	9	10	11	7		12					3						
*1969-70 Final played at Hampden Park.						Appearances	1	1	1	2	1	2		2	2	2	2	1	1		1				2				1		
1970-71 Final postponed until season 1971-72.						Sub appearances			1											1											
						Goals			1						1	1															

Further match details for this season are continued on page 279

1971-72

Manager: W.Waddell

Scottish League

Player columns: McCloy, Jardine, Mathieson, Greig, McKinnon, McDonald A, McLean, Penman, Stein, Denny, Johnston, Conn, Jackson, Henderson, Smith, Fyfe, Johnstone, McDonald I, Miller, Parlane

#	Date	Venue/Opponent	Result	Scorers	Att	McCloy	Jardine	Mathieson	Greig	McKinnon	McDonald A	McLean	Penman	Stein	Denny	Johnston	Conn	Jackson	Henderson	Smith	Fyfe	Johnstone	McDonald I	Miller	Parlane
1	Sep 4	(a) Partick Thistle	L 2-3	A.McDonald, Stein	30,000	1	2	3	4	5	6	7	8	9	10	11	12								
2	11	(h) Celtic	L 2-3	Johnston (pen), Stein	80,000	1	2	3	4		6	7	8	9		11	10		5	12					
3	18	(a) Falkirk	W 3-0	Greig 2, Stein	24,000	1	2	3	4	5	10	7		9		11	8		6						
4	25	(h) Aberdeen	L 0-2		41,236	1	2	3	4		10	7		9		11	8		5	6					
5	Oct 2	(a) Hearts	L 1-2	Johnston	29,000	1	2	3	4	5	10	8	12	9		11			6	7					
6	9	(h) East Fife	W 3-0	Jardine (pen), Fyfe, A.McDonald	25,000	1	4	3	2	5	11			9			8			7	6	10			
7	16	(a) Dundee U	W 5-1	A.McDonald 2, Stein, Greig, Jardine	17,000	1	4	3	2	5	11		8	9						7	6	10			
8	23	(h) Motherwell	W 4-0	Fyfe 2, A.McDonald, Jardine	25,000	1	4	3	2	5	11			9			8			7	6	10			
9	30	(h) Kilmarnock	W 3-1	A.McDonald 2, Stein	25,442	1	4	3	2	5	11		8	9						7	6	10			
10	Nov 6	(a) St Johnstone	W 4-1	Johnston 3 (2 pens), A.McDonald	27,000	1	4	3	2		11			9		12	8	5		7	6	10			
11	13	(h) Dundee	L 2-3	Johnston 2	33,200	1	4	3	2		11			9		10	8	5		7	6				
12	20	(a) Morton	W 2-1	Johnston, Greig	12,500	1	2	3	4		10	7		9		11	12	5			6	8			
13	27	(a) Ayr U	W 2-1	Stein, Henderson	15,100	1	2	3	4		10			9		11	8		7	6		5			
14	Dec 4	(h) Clyde	W 1-0	Stein	25,000	1	4	3			10			9	2	11			7	6	8	5			
15	11	(a) Dunfermline A	W 2-0	Greig, Johnston	13,500	1	2	3	4		10	8		9		11			7	6	12	5			
16	18	(h) Airdrieonians	W 3-0	Stein, Jardine (pen), Fyfe	25,000	1	2	3	4		11	7		9			8	5	12	6	10				
17	25	(a) Hibernian	W 1-0	Stein	30,000	1	2		4		10	7		9	3	11	8	5		6					
18	Jan 1	(h) Partick Thistle	W 2-1	Greig, Johnston	38,200	1	2		4		10	7		9	3	8		5		6			12	11	
19	3	(a) Celtic	L 1-2	Stein	77,811	1	2	3	4		10	7		9		11		5		6	8				
20	8	(h) Falkirk	W 3-1	Greig, Jackson, I.McDonald	23,000	1	2	3	4		10	7		9		8		5		6			11		
21	15	(a) Aberdeen	D 0-0		33,608	1	2	3	4		8	7		9		10		12		6		5	11		
22	22	(h) Hearts	W 6-0	Johnstone 3, Johnston, Greig, Conn	35,000	1	2	3	4		10	7				11	8	5		6		9			
23	29	(a) East Fife	W 1-0	Johnstone	12,018	1	2	3	4		10	7				11	8	5		6		9			
24	Feb 12	(a) Dundee U	W 1-0	Smith	25,000	1	2	3	4		10	7			12		8	5		6		9	11		
25	19	(a) Motherwell	L 0-2		16,192	1	2		4		12	7		9			8	5		6		10	11	3	
26	Mar 4	(a) Kilmarnock	W 2-1	Jardine, Conn	14,707	1	2	3	4		10	7		9		11	8	5		6					
27	11	(h) St Johnstone	W 2-0	Johnstone, McLean	25,000	1		3	4			7			2	10	8	5		6	12	9	11		
28	25	(h) Morton	L 1-2	Jackson	20,000	1		3			10	7	9	2		4	5			6	12	8	11		
29	Apr 8	(a) Clyde	D 1-1	Johnston	7,500	1	2	3	4			7				11	10	5		6	12	9		8	
30	10	(a) Dundee	L 0-2		13,000	1	2	3	4		11	8		9				5	7	6				10	
31	22	(a) Airdrieonians	W 3-0	Penman 2, Fyfe	10,000	1			11			8	2			4	5	7	6	9	10	3			
32	27	(h) Dunfermline A	L 3-4	A.McDonald 2, Stein	5,000	1	2	3			11			9		10	4	5	7	6		8			
33	29	(h) Hibernian	L 1-2	Johnston	11,000	1	2	3			10	7	4	9	12	11		5		6		8			
34	May 1	(h) Ayr U	W 4-2	Conn, Penman, A.McDonald, Fyfe	4,000	1	2	3			10	7	8	9		11	4			6	12	5			

FINAL LEAGUE POSITION: 3rd

						McCloy	Jardine	Mathieson	Greig	McKinnon	McDonald A	McLean	Penman	Stein	Denny	Johnston	Conn	Jackson	Henderson	Smith	Fyfe	Johnstone	McDonald I	Miller	Parlane
Appearances						34	31	30	28	7	31	21	10	28	7	23	21	24	13	30	9	16	7	2	2
Sub appearances												1	1		2	1	2	1	2		5	1			
Goals							5		8		11	1	3	11		11	3	2	1	1	6	7	1		

Scottish FA Cup

#	Date	Venue/Opponent	Result	Scorers	Att	McCloy	Jardine	Mathieson	Greig	McDonald A	McLean	Stein	Johnston	Conn	Jackson	Smith	Johnstone	Parlane
1	Feb 5	(a) Falkirk	D 2-2	Johnstone, Greig	20,000	1	2	3	4	10	7		11	8	5	6	9	
R	9	(h) Falkirk	W 2-0	Stein, McLean	43,000	1	2	3	4	10	7	9	11	8		6	5	
2	26	(h) St Mirren	W 4-1	McLean 2 (1 pen), A.McDonald, Stein	29,376	1	2	3	4	10	7	9	11	8		6	5	
QF	Mar 18	(a) Motherwell	D 2-2	A.McDonald, Stein	28,577	1	2	3	4	10	7	9	11		5	6	8	
R	27	(h) Motherwell	W 4-2	Stein 2, McLean, Fallon (og)	44,800	1	2	3	4	10	7	9	11		5	6	8	
SF	Apr 15(n*)	Hibernian	D 1-1	A.McDonald	75,884	1	2	3	4	10	7	9	11		5	6	8	
R	24(n*)	Hibernian	L 0-2		67,547	1	2	3		10	7	9	12	11	5	6	8	4

*Played at Hampden Park, Glasgow.

						McCloy	Jardine	Mathieson	Greig	McDonald A	McLean	Stein	Johnston	Conn	Jackson	Smith	Johnstone	Parlane
Appearances						7	7	7	6	7	7	6	7	3	5	7	7	1
Sub appearances													1					
Goals									1	3	4	5					1	

1 own-goal

Scottish League Cup Section Four

#	Date	Venue/Opponent	Result	Scorers	Att	McCloy	Jardine	Mathieson	Greig	McKinnon	McDonald A	McLean	Penman	Stein	Denny	Johnston	Conn	Henderson	Johnstone
1	Aug 14(a*)	Celtic	L 0-2		72,500	1	2	3	4	5	11	7		12		10	8	6	9
2	18	(h) Ayr U	W 4-0	Johnstone 2, Stein, McLean (pen)	33,000	1	2	3	4	5	12	7		9		11	8	6	10
3	21	(h) Morton	W 2-0	Johnstone, A.McDonald	41,000	1	2	3	4	5	12	7		9	8	11		6	10
4	25	(a) Ayr U	W 4-0	Stein 2, A.McDonald, Johnstone	20,000	1	2	3	4	5	8	7		9		11	12	6	10
5	28	(h) Celtic	L 0-3		85,000	1	2	3	4	5	8	7		9		11	12	6	10
6	Sep 1	(a) Morton	W 1-0	Stein	7,000	1	2	3	4	5	8	7	12	9		11		6	10

*Played at Ibrox Stadium, Glasgow.
Rangers failed to qualify for quarter-finals

						McCloy	Jardine	Mathieson	Greig	McKinnon	McDonald A	McLean	Penman	Stein	Denny	Johnston	Conn	Henderson	Johnstone
Appearances						6	6	6	6	6	4	6		5	1	6	2	6	6
Sub appearances											2		1	1			2		
Goals											2	1		4					4

European Cup-winners' Cup

#	Date	Venue/Opponent	Result	Scorers	Att	McCloy	Jardine	Mathieson	Greig	McKinnon	McDonald A	McLean	Penman	Stein	Denny	Johnston	Conn	Jackson	Henderson	Smith	Johnstone	Parlane
1.1	Sep 15	(a) Stade Rennes	D 1-1	Johnston	13,993	1	2	3	4	5	8	7	10	9	12	11			6			
1.2	28	(h) Stade Rennes	W 1-0	A.McDonald	42,000	1	2	3	4	5	10			9		11	8		6	7		
2.1	Oct 20	(h) SC de Portugal	W 3-2	Stein 2, Henderson	50,000	1	4	3	2	5	11		8	9			12		7	6	10	
2.2	Nov 3	(a) SC de Portugal	L 3-4	Stein 2, Henderson	60,000	1	4	3	2	5	11	14		9		10	8		6	7	12	
QF1	Mar 8	(a) Torino	D 1-1	Johnston	40,000	1	2	3	4		10	7		9		11		5		6	8	
QF2	22	(h) Torino	W 1-0	A.McDonald	75,000	1	2	3	4		10	7		9		11		5		6	8	
SF1	Apr 5	(a) Bayern Munich	D 1-1	Zobel (og)	44,000	1	2	3	4		10	7		9		11		5		6	8	
SF1	19	(h) Bayern Munich	W 2-0	Jardine, Parlane	80,000	1	2	3			10	7		9		11		5		6	8	4
F	May 24(n*)	Dinamo Moscow	W 3-2	Johnston 2, Stein	45,000	1	2	3	4		10	7		9		11	8			6	5	

*Played at the Nou Camp Stadium, Barcelona.

						McCloy	Jardine	Mathieson	Greig	McKinnon	McDonald A	McLean	Penman	Stein	Denny	Johnston	Conn	Jackson	Henderson	Smith	Johnstone	Parlane
Appearances						9	9	9	8	4	9	6	2	9		8	3	7	3	6	1	5	1
Sub appearances							1								1		1	1		1		1
Goals						1					2			5		4			2			1

1 own-goal

Glasgow Cup

#	Date	Venue/Opponent	Result	Scorers	Att	McCloy	Jardine	Mathieson	Greig	McKinnon	McLean	Stein	Johnston	Conn	Henderson	Smith	Johnstone
F	Aug 16	(h) Clyde *	W 2-0	Stein 2	12,500	1	2	3	4	5	7	9	10	8	6	11	

*1970-71 Final

						McCloy	Jardine	Mathieson	Greig	McKinnon	McLean	Stein	Johnston	Conn	Henderson	Smith	Johnstone
Appearances						1	1	1	1	1	1	1	1	1	1	1	
Sub appearances																	
Goals												2					

Further match details for this season are continued on page 280

1972-73

Manager: J.Wallace

Scottish League

Players: McCloy, Jardine, Mathieson, Greig, Jackson, Johnstone, McLean, Denny, Johnston, Stein, Fyfe, McDonald A, Smith, Conn, Parlane, Donaldson, Young, Forsyth, Mason, Neef, Miller, Penman, McDonald I, Bonnyman

#	Date		Opponent	Res	Scorers	Att.	McCloy	Jardine	Mathieson	Greig	Jackson	Johnstone	McLean	Denny	Johnston	Stein	Fyfe	McDonald A	Smith	Conn	Parlane	Donaldson	Young	Forsyth	Mason	Neef	Miller	Penman	McDonald I	Bonnyman
1	Sep	2 (a)	Ayr U	L 1-2	Johnston	14,500	1	2	3	4	5	6	7	8	9	10	11	12												
2		9 (h)	Partick Thistle	W 2-1	A.McDonald, Johnston	35,000	1	2	3	4	5	9	7	8	11					10	6									
3		16 (a*)	Celtic	L 1-3	Greig	50,416	1	2	3	4	5	9		8	11	7				10	6	12								
4		23 (h)	Falkirk	W 1-0	McLean (pen)	18,000	1	2	3	4	5	9	7		11					10	6	8								
5		30 (a)	Kilmarnock	L 1-2	McLean	10,643	1	2	3	4	5	9	7		12	11				6	10	8								
6	Oct	7 (h)	Morton	D 1-1	Fyfe	30,000	1	8	3	4	5	9	2			7	10			12	6	11								
7		14 (a)	Motherwell	W 2-0	Young, Parlane (pen)	17,621	1	2	3	4		5							6	7	9		11	8	10					
8		21 (a)	Arbroath	W 2-1	Parlane, Mason	8,400		2	3	4		5							6	7	9		11	8	10	1				
9		28 (h)	St Johnstone	W 5-1	Conn 2, Parlane 2, Johnstone	21,000	1	2	3	4		5							6	7	9	12	11	8	10					
10	Nov	4 (a)	Dundee	D 1-1	Conn	19,600	1	2	3	4		5							6	7	9	8	11		10					
11		11 (h)	Airdrieonians	W 1-0	Conn	17,000	1	2	3	4		5					12	11	6	7	9	8			10					
12		18 (a)	Hibernian	W 2-1	Conn, Fyfe	33,356	1	2	3	4		5					8	11	6	7	9				10					
13		25 (h)	Dumbarton	W 3-1	Young, Conn, Parlane	14,500	1	2	3	4		5	12						8	6	9		11	10						
14	Dec	2 (h)	Hearts	L 0-1		30,000	1	2	3	4		5	12						8	6	7		11	10						
15		9 (a)	Dundee U	W 4-1	Parlane 2, Conn, Jardine	12,500	1	2	3			5	7						4	6	8	9	11	10						
16		16 (a)	Aberdeen	D 0-0		26,375	1	2	3			5	7				12	4	6	8	9		11	10						
17		23 (a)	East Fife	W 4-0	Johnstone 2, Young, Parlane	8,608	1	2	3	10		5	7					4			9		11	6	8					
18		30 (h)	Ayr U	W 2-1	Conn, Parlane	17,653	1	2	3	4	5							12	6	7	9		11	8	10					
19	Jan	1 (a)	Partick Thistle	W 1-0	Young	18,500	1	2	3	4		5	7						10	6			11	8						
20		6 (h)	Celtic	W 2-1	Parlane, Conn	72,000	1	2	3	4		5							10	6	7	9	11	8						
21		13 (h)	Falkirk	W 4-2	Young 2, Parlane (pen), Conn	17,000	1	2	3	4			7						10	6	8	9	11	5						
22		20 (h)	Kilmarnock	W 4-0	Parlane 2, Young, Greig	14,515	1	2	3	4		5	7						10	6		9	12	11	8					
23		27 (a)	Morton	W 2-1	A.McDonald, Young	16,000	1	2	3	4		5	7					12	10	6	9									
24	Feb	10 (h)	Motherwell	W 2-1	Young, Jardine	27,000	1	2	3	4			7	8					10	6		9		11	5					
25		19 (a)	Arbroath	W 5-0	Parlane 2, Young, Greig, Miller	15,000	1	2	3	4		5	7						6		9		11	8	12		10			
26	Mar	3 (h)	St Johnstone	W 2-1	Miller, Mason	12,000	1	2	3			5	7						4	6		9	11	8	12		10			
27		10 (h)	Dundee	W 3-1	Parlane 2, A.McDonald	32,500	1	4	3			5	7	2					10	6		9	11	8			12			
28		20 (a)	Airdrieonians	W 6-2	Parlane, Greig, Johnstone, McLean, A.McDonald, Young	20,000	1	2	3	4		5	7						10	6		9	11	8						
29		24 (h)	Hibernian	W 1-0	McLean	51,200	1	2	3	4		5	7						10	6		9	11	8						
30		31 (a)	Dumbarton	W 2-1	Young, Parlane	13,000	1	2	3	4		5	7						10	6		9	11	8	12					
31	Apr	7 (a)	Hearts	W 1-0	Greig	24,000	1	2	3	4		5	7						10	6	12	9	11	8						
32		14 (h)	Dundee U	W 2-1	Greig 2	38,000	1	2	3	4		5	7						6		10	9	11	8						
33		21 (a)	Aberdeen	D 2-2	McLean, Conn	33,000	1	2	3	4		5	7						10	6	11	9		8						
34		28 (h)	East Fife	W 2-0	Young, Conn	27,544	1	2	3	4		5	7						6		10	9		11	8					
			Appearances				33	34	34	30	7	31	22	6	4	2	3	27	29	18	29	3	26	21	12	1	2			
			Sub appearances												2		1	3	2			2	1	2			4	1		
			Goals					2		7		4	5		2		2	4		12	19		13		2		2			

FINAL LEAGUE POSITION: 2nd
*Played Hampden Park, Glasgow

Scottish FA Cup

#	Date		Opponent	Res	Scorers	Att.	McCloy	Jardine	Mathieson	Greig	Johnstone	McLean	McDonald A	Smith	Conn	Parlane	Young	Forsyth	Mason	Miller
3	Feb	3 (h)	Dundee U	W 1-0	Young	35,657	1	2	3	4	5	7	10	6		9	11	8	12	
4		24 (h)	Hibernian	D 1-1	Johnstone	63,889	1	2	3	4	5	7		6	12	9	11	8		10
R		28 (a)	Hibernian	W 2-1	McLean 2 (1 pen)	49,007	1	2	3	4	5	7	10	6		9	11	8		
QF	Mar	17 (h)	Airdrieonians	W 2-0	Parlane (pen), Young	35,500	1	2	3	4	5	7	10	6		9	11	8		
SF	Apr	4 (n*)	Ayr U	W 2-0	Parlane 2	51,815	1	2	3	4	5	7	10	6		9	11	8		
F	May	5 (n*)	Celtic	W 3-2	Parlane, Conn, Forsyth	122,714	1	2	3	4	5	7		6	10	9	11	8		
			Appearances				6	6	6	6	6	6	5	5	1	6	6	6		1
			Sub appearances												1				1	
			Goals								1	2			1	4	2	1		

*Played at Hampden Park, Glasgow.

Scottish League Cup Section Three

Players: McCloy, Jardine, Mathieson, Greig, Jackson, Johnstone, McLean, Denny, Johnston, Stein, Fyfe, McDonald A, Smith, Conn, Parlane, Donaldson, Young, Forsyth, Miller, Penman

#	Date		Opponent	Res	Scorers	Att.	McCloy	Jardine	Mathieson	Greig	Jackson	Johnstone	McLean	Denny	Johnston	Stein	Fyfe	McDonald A	Smith	Conn	Parlane	Donaldson	Young	Forsyth	Miller	Penman
1	Aug	12 (h)	Clydebank	W 2-0	Conn, A.McDonald	26,240	1	2	3	4	5		7		8	9		11	6	10						
2		16 (a)	St Mirren	W 4-0	Johnston, Greig, Stein, Conn	15,000	1	2	3	4	5		7	12	10	9		11	6	8						
3		19 (h)	Ayr U	W 2-1	Johnston, Parlane	25,000	1	2	3	4	5		7		8	9		11	6	10	12					
4		23 (h)	St Mirren	L 1-4	Conn	20,000	1	2	3	4		5			11	9			6	8	10				7	12
5		26 (h)	Clydebank	W 5-0	Greig, McLean (pen), Smith, Johnstone, Stein	9,000	1	2	3	4	5	8	7			9		11	10	6						
6		30 (a†)	Ayr U	W 2-1	Johnston, Johnstone	15,000	1	2	3	4		5	7	8	9			10	11	6						
R2.1	Sep	20 (a)	Stenhousemuir	W 5-0	Johnston 3, Parlane, Greig	3,650	1	2	3	4	5	9	7					11	10	6					7	8
R2.2	Oct	4 (a)	Stenhousemuir	L 1-2	Fyfe	6,000	1	2	3	4	5	6					9	11			10	12			7	8
QF1		11 (h)	St Johnstone	D 1-1	Parlane	15,000	1	8	3	4		5		2			7		10	9	6	11				
QF2	Nov	1 (a)	St Johnstone	W 2-0	Young, Parlane (pen)	12,300	1	2	3	4		5						10	6	7	9	8	11			
SF		22 (n*)	Hibernian	L 0-1		46,513	1	2	3			4	5					8	11	6	7	9	10	12		
			Appearances				11	11	11	10	7	8	6	2	5	5	6	9	9	7	6	3	2		2	1
			Sub appearances										1									1	1	1		1
			Goals						3		5	1			3	2	1	1	1	3	4					

†Played at Rugby Park, Kilmarnock.
*Played at Hampden Park, Glasgow.

European Super Cup

#	Date		Opponent	Res	Scorers	Att.	McCloy	Jardine	Mathieson	Greig	Johnstone	McLean	McDonald A	Smith	Conn	Parlane	Donaldson	Young	Forsyth
1	Jan	16 (h)	Ajax Amsterdam	L 1-3	A.McDonald	60,000	1	2	3	4	5	12	14	10	6	7	9	11	8
2		24 (a)	Ajax Amsterdam	L 2-3	A.McDonald, Young	43,000	1	2	3	4	5	7	10	6		9	11	8	
			Appearances				2	2	2	2	2	1	2	2	1	2	2	2	
			Sub appearances									1			1				
			Goals										2				1		

Drybrough Cup

#	Date		Opponent	Res	Scorers	Att.	McCloy	Jardine	Mathieson	Greig	Jackson	McLean	Denny	Johnston	McDonald A	Smith	Young	Miller
1	Jul	29 (h)	Stirling Albion	W 3-1	Stein 2, A.McDonald	30,000	1	2	3	4	5	7	8	9	11	6	10	12
SF	Aug	2 (a)	Hibernian	L 0-3		27,111	1	2	3	4	5	7	8	9	11	6	10	
			Appearances				2	2	2	2	2	2	2	2	2	1	2	1
			Sub appearances															1
			Goals										2	1				

Other matches

#	Date		Opponent	Res	Scorers	Att.	McCloy	Jardine	Mathieson	Greig	Jackson	McLean	Johnston	Stein	Fyfe	McDonald A	Smith	Conn	Young	McDonald I	Bonnyman
1	Jul	22 (a*)	Stjarn Komb	W 5-2	Stein 3, A.McDonald, Fyfe	5,000	1	2	12	5		7		9	11	10	6	4		3	8
2		26 (a)	Malmö	W 4-2	Greig, Conn, A.McDonald, Johnston	5,000	1	2	3	4	5	7	11	9		10	6	8			12
3	Aug	7 (a)	Wolves	L 0-2		10,600	1	2	3	4	5	7		8	9	14	11	6	10		
			Appearances				3	3	2	2	3	3	2	3	1	3	3	3		1	1
			Sub appearances						1							1					1
			Goals						1	1			1	3	1	2		1			

* Played at Trollhatten, Sweden

1973-74

Manager: J.Wallace

Scottish League

Player columns (left to right): McCloy, Jardine, Mathieson, Greig, Johnstone, McDonald A, McLean, Forsyth, O'Hara, Parlane, Smith, Conn, Denny, Scott, Young, Houston, Kennedy, Fyfe, Jackson, Hamilton, Morris, Hunter, McDougall, Mason, Donaldson

#	Date	Venue/Opponent	Result	Scorers	Att.
1	Sep 1	(h) Ayr U	D 0-0		30,000
2	8	(a) Partick Thistle	W 1-0	Scott	22,000
3	15	(h) Celtic	L 0-1		70,000
4	29	(h) Hearts	L 0-3		35,000
5	Oct 6	(a) Arbroath	W 2-1	O'Hara 2	7,710
6	13	(h) East Fife	L 0-1		25,000
7	20	(a) Dundee U	W 3-1	Conn 2, O'Hara	11,000
8	27	(h) Hibernian	W 4-0	Jardine 2 (2 pens), Conn, Greig	35,000
9	Nov 3	(a) Dunfermline A	D 2-2	Jackson, O'Hara	20,000
10	10	(h) Morton	W 1-0	Greig	20,000
11	17	(h) Falkirk	W 2-1	Greig 2	15,000
12	24	(a) Clyde	W 2-0	Jackson, McDonald	15,000
13	Dec 15	(h) St Johnstone	W 5-1	Conn, Young, McDonald, Parlane, Smith	8,200
14	22	(a) Dumbarton	W 2-0	Parlane, Young	7,500
15	29	(a) Ayr U	W 1-0	Parlane	17,000
16	Jan 1	(h) Partick Thistle	D 1-1	Parlane (pen)	20,000
17	5	(a) Celtic	L 0-1		55,000
18	12	(h) Aberdeen	D 1-1	McLean	16,000
19	19	(a) Hearts	W 4-2	Parlane 4	25,000
20	Feb 2	(h) Arbroath	L 2-3	McLean, Parlane (pen)	22,000
21	9	(a) East Fife	W 3-0	Hamilton, Scott, McLean	8,499
22	24	(a) Dundee U	W 3-1	Parlane 2 (1 pen), Young	15,500
23	Mar 2	(a) Hibernian	L 1-3	McLean	23,149
24	16	(a) Morton	W 3-2	Jackson 2, Parlane (pen)	9,000
25	23	(a) Falkirk	D 0-0		10,000
26	30	(h) Clyde	W 4-0	Johnstone, Greig, McDonald, Scott	15,000
27	Apr 2	(a) Dunfermline A	W 3-0	Parlane (pen), Scott, Fyfe	12,000
28	6	(a) Motherwell	W 4-1	Young 2, Scott, Fyfe	13,346
29	13	(h) Dundee	L 1-2	Jardine (pen)	25,000
30	17	(a) Aberdeen	D 1-1	Greig	18,000
31	20	(a) St Johnstone	W 3-1	Fyfe 2, Young	7,500
32	24	(h) Motherwell	W 2-1	Scott, Parlane	10,000
33	27	(h) Dumbarton	W 3-1	Scott 2, Fyfe	20,000
34	29	(a) Dundee	W 3-2	Fyfe 2, Young	10,578

FINAL LEAGUE POSITION: 3rd

	McCloy	Jardine	Mathieson	Greig	Johnstone	McDonald A	McLean	Forsyth	O'Hara	Parlane	Smith	Conn	Denny	Scott	Young	Houston	Kennedy	Fyfe	Jackson	Hamilton	Morris	Hunter	McDougall	Mason	Donaldson
Appearances	30	34	26	30	31	29	21	18	18	28	7	7		21	19	9	1	7	18	4	5	3			8
Sub appearances		2			1	3		1	1	2	4	1		3	1		6		3	1		1			
Goals		3		6	1	3	4		4	14	1	4		8	7			7	4	1					

Scottish FA Cup

#	Date	Venue/Opponent	Result	Scorers	Att.
3	Jan 26	(h) Queen's Park	W 8-0	Parlane 3, McLean 3, Scott, Morris	19,000
4	Feb 17	(h) Dundee	L 0-3		64,672

	McCloy	Jardine	Mathieson	Greig	Johnstone	McDonald A	McLean	Forsyth	O'Hara	Parlane	Smith	Conn	Denny	Scott	Young	Houston	Kennedy	Fyfe	Jackson	Hamilton	Morris	Hunter
Appearances	1	2	2	1	2		2		2	2	1			2					1	2	1	1
Sub appearances															1							
Goals							3			3				1							1	

Scottish League Cup Section One

#	Date	Venue/Opponent	Result	Scorers	Att.
1	Aug 11	(h) Falkirk	W 3-1	Scott 2, Conn	35,000
2	15	(a) Arbroath	W 2-1	Conn, Parlane	6,677
3	18	(h) Celtic	L 1-2	Scott	63,173
4	22	(h) Arbroath	W 3-0	McDonald, Conn, Smith	14,000
5	25	(a) Celtic	W 3-1	McDonald, Parlane, Conn	65,000
6	29	(a) Falkirk	W 5-1	Conn 2, O'Hara, McLean, Forsyth	12,000
2.1	Sep 12	(h) Dumbarton	W 6-0	Parlane 3 (1 pen), Young 2, Greig (pen)	25,000
2.2	Oct 10	(a) Dumbarton	W 2-1	Scott, Fyfe	6,000
QF1	Oct 31	(h) Hibernian	W 2-0	Greig, Schaedler (og)	35,000
QF2	Nov 21	(a) Hibernian	D 0-0		19,245
SF	Dec 5 (n*)	Celtic	L 1-3	McDonald	54,864

*Played at Hampden Park, Glasgow.

	McCloy	Jardine	Mathieson	Greig	Johnstone	McDonald A	McLean	Forsyth	O'Hara	Parlane	Smith	Conn	Denny	Scott	Young	Houston	Kennedy	Fyfe	Jackson	Hamilton	Morris	Hunter	McDougall	Mason	Donaldson
Appearances	9	11	11	10	8	11	11	11	2	8	1	5		6	3	4	2	1	3		1		2	1	
Sub appearances				1							5	5		2				1							
Goals			2		3	1	1	1	5	1	6		4	2			1								

1 own-goal

European Cup-winners' Cup

#	Date	Venue/Opponent	Result	Scorers	Att.
1	Sep 19	(a) Ankaragücü	W 2-0	Conn, McLean	45,000
	Oct 3	(h) Ankaragücü	W 4-0	Greig 2, O'Hara, Johnstone	30,000
2	24	(a) BorMGladbach	L 0-3		35,000
	Nov 7	(h) BorMGladbach	W 3-2	Conn, Jackson, McDonald	40,000

	McCloy	Jardine	Mathieson	Greig	Johnstone	McDonald A	McLean	Forsyth	O'Hara	Parlane	Smith	Conn	Denny	Scott	Young	Houston	Kennedy	Fyfe	Jackson
Appearances	4	4	4	4	2	3	4	4	2	2	1	4		1	3				2
Sub appearances										1									
Goals			2	1	1	1		1				2							1

Drybrough Cup

#	Date	Venue/Opponent	Result	Scorers	Att.
1	Jul 28	(h) Montrose	W 3-0	Parlane 2, Hamilton	30,000
SF	Aug 1	(a) Hibernian	L 1-2	Parlane	28,089

	McCloy	Jardine	Mathieson	Greig	Johnstone	McDonald A	McLean	Forsyth	O'Hara	Parlane	Smith	Conn	Denny	Scott	Young	Houston	Kennedy	Fyfe
Appearances	2	2	2	2	1	2	2	2		2				2	2			1
Sub appearances												1				1		2
Goals										3								1

Further match details for this season are continued on page 280

1974-75

Manager: J.Wallace

Scottish League

#	Date		Opponent	Res	Score	Scorers	Att	Kennedy	Jardine	Miller	Johnstone	Jackson	Forsyth	McLean	Young	Parlane	Fyfe	Scott	McDougall	McDonald	Greig	McKean	Denny	O'Hara	Hamilton	Stein	Mathieson	Sharp	Morris	Hunter	Steele	Henderson	McCloy	Dawson
1	Aug 31	(a)	Ayr U	D	1-1	Jardine (pen)	20,000	1	2	3	4	5	6	7	8	9	10	11																
2	Sep 7	(h)	Partick Thistle	W	3-2	Fyfe 2, Young	25,000	1	2	3	8	5	6		7	9	11				4	10												
3	14	(a)	Celtic	W	2-1	McDougall, Jackson	65,000	1	2	3	8	5	6	12	7	9	11		4	10														
4	21	(h)	Dumbarton	W	3-2	Johnstone 2, Scott	18,000	1	2		4	5	6	8	10	12	11	9		14	3	7												
5	28	(a)	Kilmarnock	W	6-0	Young 2, Jardine (pen), McKean, Johnstone, McLean	19,609	1	2		4	5	6	8	11		9			10	3	7												
6	Oct 5	(h)	Morton	W	2-0	Forsyth, McLean	25,000	1	2		4	5	6	8	11	9				10	3	7												
7	12	(a)	Dunfermline A	W	6-1	Parlane 5, Johnstone	18,000	1	2		4	5	6	8	11	9			12	10	3	7												
8	19	(h)	Clyde	W	3-1	Jardine (pen), Fyfe, Johnstone	25,000	1	2	3	4	5		8	11	9				10		7		6										
9	26	(a)	Hearts	D	1-1	Jardine (pen)	29,000	1	2		4	5	6	8	11		9			10	3	7		12										
10	Nov 2	(a)	St Johnstone	W	2-1	McLean, Young	13,260	1	2		4	5	6	8	11	9				10	3	7												
11	9	(h)	Dundee	W	1-0	McKean	25,000	1	2		4	5	6	8	11	9				10	3	7												
12	16	(a)	Motherwell	W	5-0	Johnstone, Young, McDonald, Parlane, McKean	19,409	1	2		4	5	6	8	11	9			12	10	3	7												
13	23	(h)	Hibernian	L	0-1		31,500	1	2		4	5	6	8	11	9			12	10	3	7												
14	30	(h)	Dundee U	W	4-2	Jardine 2 (1 pen), Parlane, McLean	26,000	1	2			5	6	8	11	9			4	10	3	7	12											
15	Dec 7	(a)	Aberdeen	W	2-1	Johnstone, McLean	26,000	1	2		4	5	6	8	11	9				10	3	7												
16	14	(h)	Arbroath	W	3-0	Parlane 2, Jackson	20,000	1	2		4	5		8	11	9				10	3	7	6											
17	21	(a)	Airdrieonians	L	3-4	Jardine 2 (1 pen), Johnstone	19,500	1	2		4	5		8	11	9	14			10	3	7	6		12									
18	28	(a)	Ayr U	W	3-0	McLean, Jardine (pen), Parlane	22,000	1	2	10	4	5		7		9			11	8		3		6										
19	Jan 1	(a)	Partick Thistle	W	4-0	Jackson, McLean, McDougall, Greig	22,000	1	2	10	8	5	6	7		9			11	4		3												
20	4	(h)	Celtic	W	3-0	Johnstone, McLean, Parlane	71,000	1	2	12	4	5	6	7	14	9			11	8	10	3												
21	11	(a)	Dumbarton	W	5-1	McLean 3, Parlane, Johnstone	15,800	1	2		8	5		7	12	9			11	4	10	3		6										
22	Feb 1	(a)	Morton	D	1-1	Fyfe	17,000	1	2	3		5	6	7	11	9	12		4	10		8												
23	8	(h)	Dunfermline A	W	2-0	McLean, McDonald	23,500	1	2	3		5	6	7	11	9			4	10		12	8											
24	15	(a)	Kilmarnock	D	3-3	Parlane 3	27,157	1	2	3	8	5	6	7		9			12	4		11			10									
25	22	(a)	Clyde	W	2-1	McKean, O'Hara	20,000	1	2	3		5	6	7		9			12	10		8		4	11									
26	Mar 1	(h)	Hearts	W	2-1	McKean, McLean	40,000	1	2	3		5	6	8	11	9				4	10	7												
27	8	(h)	St Johnstone	W	1-0	Young	42,500	1	2			5	6	7	11	9				10	3	4				8								
28	15	(a)	Dundee	W	2-1	McLean, Parlane	22,700	1	2	12		5	6	7	11	9				10	3	4				8								
29	22	(a)	Motherwell	W	3-0	Johnstone 2, Miller	36,500	1	2	3	11	5	6	7	12	9				10		4				8								
30	29	(h)	Hibernian	D	1-1	Stein	38,585	1	2	3	11	5	6	7						10	12	4				8								
31	Apr 5	(a)	Dundee U	D	2-2	McLean, Johnstone	12,000	1	2	3	11	5	6	7	14	9				10		4			12	8								
32	12	(h)	Aberdeen	W	3-2	Johnstone, Stein, Miller (pen)	41,000	1	2	3	11	5	6	7		9	12			10		4				8								
33	19	(a)	Arbroath	W	2-1	Stein, Parlane	6,393	1	2	3	11	5	6	7	14	9	12			10		4				8								
34	26	(h)	Airdrieonians	L	0-1		65,000	1	2	12	11	5	6	7	14	9				10	3	4				8								
	Appearances							34	34	15	27	33	30	32	22	30	6	7	11	29	21	25	6	2	2	8								
	Sub appearances									3					1	6	1	4	2	3	1	1	1	1	2	1								
	Goals								9	2	14	3	1	14	6	17	4	1	2	2	1	5				1	3							

FINAL LEAGUE POSITION: 1st

Scottish FA Cup

#	Date		Opponent	Res	Score	Scorers	Att	Kennedy	Jardine	Miller	Johnstone	Jackson	Forsyth	McLean	Young	Parlane	Fyfe	Scott	McDougall	McDonald	Greig	McKean	Denny	O'Hara
3	Jan 25	(a)	Aberdeen	D	1-1	Scott	30,000	1	2	3	8	5	6	7		9		11	4	10		12		
R	Feb 10	(h)	Aberdeen	L	1-2	McKean	53,000	1	2	3	4	5	6	8		9	14	11		10		7	12	
	Appearances							2	2	2	2	2	2	2		2		2	1	2		1		
	Sub appearances																1					1	1
	Goals																	1			1		

Scottish League Cup Section Two

#	Date		Opponent	Res	Score	Scorers	Att	Kennedy	Jardine	Miller	Johnstone	Jackson	Forsyth	McLean	Young	Parlane	Fyfe	Scott	McDougall	McDonald	Greig	McKean	Denny	O'Hara	Hamilton	Stein
1	Aug 7	(h)	St Johnstone	W	3-2	Scott, Jardine, Parlane	25,000	1	2	14	6	5		7	12	9	8	11		4		10		3		
2	10	(a)	Hibernian	L	1-3	Scott	23,539	1	2		6		5	7	4	8	11		10		12			3	9	
3	14	(a)	St Johnstone	W	6-3	Young 2, Jardine 2, Scott, Forsyth	5,800	1	8	3	6	5	4	7	9	10	11			2						
4	17	(h)	Dundee	W	2-0	Jardine, Fyfe	18,548	1	8	3	6	5	4	7	9	10	11			2						
5	24	(h)	Dundee	W	4-0	Johnstone 2, Jardine (pen), Scott	35,000	1	8	3	6	5	4	7	9	10	11			2						
6	28	(a)	Hibernian	L	0-1		60,000	1	8	3	6	5	4	7	9	12	10	11		2	14					
	Appearances							6	6	4	6	5	5	6	5	5	6		1	6				4	1	
	Sub appearances									1					1	1					1	1		2	1	
	Goals								5			2	1		2	1	1	4								

Rangers failed to qualify for quarter-finals

Glasgow Cup

#	Date		Opponent	Res	Score	Scorers	Att	Kennedy	Jardine	Miller	Johnstone	Jackson	Forsyth	McLean	Young	Parlane	Fyfe	Scott	McDougall	McDonald	Greig	McKean	Denny	O'Hara	Hamilton	Stein	Mathieson
SF	Oct 15	(a)	Queen's Park	W	3-1	Parlane, Fyfe, Johnstone	5,737	1	2	3	4	5		12		9	8	11		10		7	6				
F	May 10	(n)	Celtic*	D	2-2	Stein, McLean	70,494	1	2		11	5	6	7		9				10	3	4				8	
	Appearances							2	2	1	2	2	1	1		2	1	1		2	1	2	1			1	
	Sub appearances													1												
	Goals										1			1		1	1								1	

*Rangers and Celtic declared joint holders in Final played at Hampden Park

Texaco Cup

#	Date		Opponent	Res	Score	Scorers	Att	Kennedy	Jardine	Miller	Johnstone	Jackson	Forsyth	McLean	Young	Parlane	Fyfe	Scott	McDougall	McDonald	Greig	McKean
1.1	Sep 18	(h)	Southampton	L	1-3	Jackson	40,000	1	2		8	5	6	12	7	9	11		4	10	3	
1.2	Oct 1	(a)	Southampton	L	0-2		23,000	1	2		4	5	6	8	11	12		9		10	3	7
	Appearances							2	2		2	2	2	1	2	1	1	1	1	2	2	1
	Sub appearances													1		1						
	Goals											1										

Drybrough Cup

#	Date		Opponent	Res	Score	Scorers	Att	Kennedy	Jardine	Miller	Johnstone	Jackson	Forsyth	McLean	Young	Parlane	Fyfe	Scott	McDougall	McDonald	Greig	McKean	Denny	O'Hara	Hamilton
1	Jul 27	(a)	Stirling Albion	W	2-0	Fyfe 2	12,000	1	4		5		7		9	11	2			6	10	8		3	
SF	31	(a)	Hibernian	W	3-2	McDonald, Parlane, Fyfe	28,000	1	2		12	5	7		9	11	8		10		6	4		3	
F	Aug 3	(n)	Celtic	D	2-2	Scott, Parlane	57,558	1	2		6	5		7	12	9	11	8		10	4	14		3	
	Appearances							3	3		1	3		3	3	3	2	1	2	1	2	2	1	3	
	Sub appearances										1				1						1				
	Goals										2	3	1			1									

Celtic won 4-2 on penalties in Final played at Hampden Park, Glasgow.

Further match details for this season are continued on page 280

1975-76

Manager: J.Wallace

	Date	Scottish League	Result	Scorers	Att	McCloy	Jardine	Greig	Forsyth	Jackson	McDonald	McLean	McKean	Stein	Johnstone	Young	O'Hara	Miller	Parlane	Denny	Fyfe	Dawson	McDougall	Scott	Kennedy	Boyd	Henderson	Hamilton	Armour
1	Aug 30	(h) Celtic	W 2-1	Johnstone, Young	69,594	1	**2**	3	4	5	6	7	8	9	10	11	12												
2	Sep 6	(a) Hearts	W 2-0	Anderson (og), Murray (og)	28,000	1		3	**4**	5	6	7	**8**	14	10	11		2	9	12									
3	13	(h) St Johnstone	W 2-0	Stein, Johnstone	25,000	1	2	4		5	6		**7**	14	10	11	8	3	**9**	12									
4	20	(h) Hibernian	D 1-1	Blackley (og)	37,000	1		4		5	6	**7**	8	14	10	**11**		3	9	2	12								
5	27	(a) Dundee	D 0-0		15,087	1		4		5	6	7			10	11		2	9			3	8						
6	Oct 4	(h) Aberdeen	W 1-0	McDougall	22,000	1	2	4		5		7			10	11		6	9			3	8						
7	11	(a) Ayr U	L 0-3		20,000	1	2	4		5	6	7	14		10			12	**9**			3	**8**	11					
8	18	(a) Motherwell	L 1-2	Johnstone	18,925	1	2	3	4	5	6	7	8	10	11				9										
9	Nov 1	(a) Celtic	D 1-1	Parlane	60,000		2	3	4	5	6	7		8	10	11			9						1				
10	8	(h) Hearts	L 1-2	Henderson	30,000		2	3	4	5	6	12	8		14				9		**7**				1	**10**	11		
11	12	(h) Dundee U	W 4-1	Parlane, Johnstone, Jackson, McDonald	11,000		4	10	6	5	12	7	**8**		**11**			3	9	2					1		14		
12	15	(a) St Johnstone	W 5-1	Parlane, McKean, McLean, Jardine, McDonald (og)	9,500		4	3	6	5	10	7	8		11				9	2					1				
13	22	(a) Hibernian	L 1-2	Young	26,547		4	3	6	5	10	7	**8**		11	12			**9**	2					1		14		
14	29	(h) Dundee	W 2-1	Henderson 2	16,500		2	3	4	5	6	10	7		11										1		9	8	
15	Dec 6	(a) Aberdeen	L 0-1		19,565		2	3	4	5	6	10	7		11										1		9	8	
16	13	(h) Ayr U	W 3-0	Jardine (pen), Henderson, McKean	15,500		2	3	4	5	6	10	7		11										1		9	8	
17	20	(h) Motherwell	W 3-2	Johnstone 2, Henderson	25,000		**2**	3	4	5	6	10	7		11			12							1		9	8	
18	27	(a) Dundee U	D 0-0		11,500			3	**4**	5	6	10	7		11			2			12				1		9	8	
19	Jan 1	(h) Celtic	W 1-0	Johnstone	57,839	1		3	4	5	6	10	**7**		11		14	2						12			9	**8**	
20	3	(a) Hearts	W 2-1	Henderson 2	24,000	1		3	4	5	6	10	7		11		12	2									9	**8**	
21	10	(h) St Johnstone	W 4-0	Miller (pen), Hamilton, Johnstone, McKean	20,000	1		3	4	5	6	10	7		11			2									9	8	
22	17	(h) Hibernian	W 2-0	Parlane, McLean	40,000	1		3	4	5	6	10	7					2	11								9	8	
23	31	(a) Dundee	D 1-1	Johnstone	14,407	1		3	4	5	6	10	7		11			2	**9**								12	8	
24	Feb 7	(h) Aberdeen	W 2-1	Henderson, McDonald	35,000	1	12	3	4	5	6	10	7		11			2	14								**9**	**8**	
25	21	(a) Ayr U	W 1-0	McKean	18,000	1	12	3	4	5	6	10	7					2	11								9	**8**	
26	28	(a) Motherwell	W 1-0	Johnstone	25,241	1	14	3	4	5	6	10	**7**		11			2	12								9	**8**	
27	Mar 20	(h) Hearts	W 3-1	Johnstone, Jackson, McLean	30,000	1		3	4	5	6	10	7		11			2									9	8	
28	27	(a) St Johnstone	W 3-0	Johnstone 2, Greig	9,079	1	12	3	4	5	6	10	**7**		11			2	14								**9**	8	
29	Apr 3	(a) Hibernian	W 3-0	McDonald, Henderson, Johnstone	18,820	1		3	4	5	6	10	7		11			2	12								**9**	8	
30	10	(h) Dundee	W 3-0	McKean, Greig, Johnstone	25,000	1	14	3	4	5	6	**10**	7		11			2	12								9	**8**	
31	14	(a) Aberdeen	D 0-0		17,968	1	14	3	4	5	6	**10**	**7**		11			2	12								9	8	
32	17	(h) Ayr U	W 2-1	McDonald, Parlane	25,000	1	12	3	4	**5**	6	10	7		11			2	14								**9**	8	
33	21	(h) Motherwell	W 2-1	McLean, Henderson	27,000	1	4	3	**5**		6	10	7		11			2		12							9	8	
34	24	(a) Dundee U	W 1-0	Johnstone	17,000	1	8	4		5	6	10	7		11			3		2							9		
35	26	(a) Celtic	D 0-0		51,000	1	2	4			6	10	7		5			3	11								9	8	
36	May 4	(h) Dundee U	D 0-0		50,000		4	3			6	10	7					2	11	**5**			12		1		9	8	
FINAL LEAGUE POSITION: 1st					Appearances	25	18	36	28	33	34	34	32	3	32	7	1	25	17	6	1	3	3	1	11	1	23	22	
					Sub appearances		7				1	1	1	3	1	1	3	2	7	3	2		1	1			3		
					Goals		2	2		2	4	4	5	1	16	2		1	5				1				10	1	

4 own-goals

Scottish FA Cup

	Date	Opponent	Result	Scorers	Att	McCloy	Jardine	Greig	Forsyth	Jackson	McDonald	McLean	McKean	Stein	Johnstone	Young	O'Hara	Miller	Parlane	Denny	Fyfe	Dawson	McDougall	Scott	Kennedy	Boyd	Henderson	Hamilton	Armour
3	Jan 24	(h) East Fife	W 3-0	McDonald, Henderson, Hamilton	30,000	1		3	4	5	6	7	11					2	10								9	8	
4	Feb 14	(h) Aberdeen	W 4-1	Johnstone, McDonald, Henderson, Parlane	60,000	1	14	3	**4**	5	6	10	7		11			2	12								9	**8**	
QF	Mar 6	(a) Queen of South	W 5-0	McKean 2, Johnstone 2, Henderson	18,700	1		3	4	5	6	10	7		11			2									9	8	
SF	31	(n*) Motherwell	W 3-2	Johnstone 2, Miller (pen)	48,915	1	14	3	4	5	6	**10**	7		11			2	12								**9**	8	
F	May 1	(n*) Hearts	W 3-1	Johnstone 2, McDonald	85,354	1	12	3	4	5	6	10	7		11			2									9	**8**	
*Played at Hampden Park, Glasgow.					Appearances	5		5	5	5	5	5	5		4			5	1								5	5	
					Sub appearances		3												2										
					Goals						3		2		7			1	1								3	1	

Scottish League Cup Section One

	Date	Opponent	Result	Scorers	Att	McCloy	Jardine	Greig	Forsyth	Jackson	McDonald	McLean	McKean	Stein	Johnstone	Young	O'Hara	Miller	Parlane	Denny	Fyfe	Dawson	McDougall	Scott	Kennedy	Boyd	Henderson	Hamilton	Armour
1	Aug 9	(h) Airdrieonians	W 6-1	Jardine 3 (2 pens), Stein, Parlane, Miller (pen)	45,000	1	2	4		5	6	7		8	**10**			3	9	12	11								
2	13	(a) Clyde	W 1-0	Johnstone	28,000	1	2	4		5	6	7	11	8	10			3	9										
3	16	(h) Motherwell	D 1-1	Greig	31,500	1	2	4		5	6	7		8	10	11		3	9										
4	20	(h) Clyde	W 6-0	Parlane 2, Jackson, Miller (pen), Young, Johnstone	16,000	1	2	4		5	6	7	8		10	11		3	9										
5	23	(a) Motherwell	D 2-2	Jardine, Miller (pen)	20,561	1	2	4		5	6	7	8		10	11		3	9										
6	27	(a) Airdrieonians	W 2-1	Johnstone, Young	20,000	1		2	4	5	6		7	9	10	11	8	3											
QF1	Sep 10	(h) Queen of South	W 1-0	Johnstone	12,000	1		4		5	6	**7**	**8**	12	10	11	14	3	9	2									
QF2	24	(a) Queen of South	D 2-2	Johnstone, McDonald	7,500	1		4		5	6	7			10	11		2	9			3	8						
SF	Oct 8	(n*) Montrose	W 5-1	Parlane, Johnstone, Miller (pen), Scott, Jardine	20,319	1	2	4		5		7			10			6	9			3	8	11					
F	25	(n*) Celtic	W 1-0	McDonald	58,806		2	3	4	5	6	7		8	10	11			9						1				
*Played at Hampden Park, Glasgow.					Appearances	9	7	10	2	10	9	9	5	5	10	7	1	9	9	1	1	2	2	1	1				
					Sub appearances									1			1			1									
					Goals		5	1		1	2			1	6	2		4	4					1					

European Champions' Cup

	Date	Opponent	Result	Scorers	Att	McCloy	Jardine	Greig	Forsyth	Jackson	McDonald	McLean	McKean	Stein	Johnstone	Young	O'Hara	Miller	Parlane	Denny	Fyfe	Dawson	McDougall	Scott	Kennedy	Boyd	Henderson	Hamilton	Armour
1	Sep 17	(h) Bohemians D	W 4-1	Fyfe, O'Hara, Johnstone, Burke (og)	25,000	1		4		6				10	5	**11**	**8**	3	9	2	7		12				14		
	Oct 1	(a) Bohemians D	D 1-1	Johnstone	8,000	1		4		5	8	7			10	6		2	9		11	3							
2	22	(a) AS Saint-Etienne	L 0-2		28,394		2	4	6	5	10	**7**		8	11	12		3	**9**						1		14		
	Nov 5	(h) AS Saint-Etienne	L 1-2	McDonald	51,000		2	3	4	5	6	7		8	10	11			9						1				
					Appearances	2	2	4	2	4	3	3		3	4	3	1	3	4	1	2	1			2				
					Sub appearances											1							1				2		
					Goals						1				2		1				1								

1 own-goal

Glasgow Cup

	Date	Opponent	Result	Scorers	Att	McCloy	Jardine	Greig	Forsyth	Jackson	McDonald	McLean	McKean	Stein	Johnstone	Young	O'Hara	Miller	Parlane	Denny	Fyfe	Dawson	McDougall	Scott	Kennedy	Boyd	Henderson	Hamilton	Armour
1	Sep 2	(h) Queen's Park	W 3-0	McDonald, Young, McKay (og)	6,000	1		4	5		6	7		12	10	11	8					**3**					9		2
SF	Mar 23	(a) Partick Thistle	W 1-0	Miller (pen)	15,000	1	5	3	4		6	10	7					2	11								9	8	
1975-76 Final postponed until 1976-77 season.					Appearances	2	1	2	2		2	2	1		1	1	1	1	1			1					2	1	1
					Sub appearances									1															
					Goals						1					1		1											

1 own-goal

Further match details for this season are continued on page 280

1976-77

Manager: J.Wallace

Scottish League

Player columns (left→right): McCloy, Miller, Greig, Forsyth, Denny, McDonald, McLean, Jardine, Parlane, Munro, Johnstone, Henderson, McKean, Hamilton, Jackson, Kennedy, Watson K (2), Dawson, McDougall, Robertson, Steele, Stein, O'Hara, Morris, Armour

No	Date	Opponent	Result	Scorers	Att	McC	Mil	Grg	For	Den	McD	McL	Jar	Par	Mun	Joh	Hen	McK	Ham	Jck	Ken	Wat	Daw	McDo	Rob	Ste	Stn	O'H	Mor	Arm
1	Sep 4 (a)	Celtic	D 2-2	Johnstone, Parlane	62,000	1	2	3	4	5	6	7	8	9	10	11														
2	11 (h)	Kilmarnock	D 0-0		23,430	1	2	3	4	5	6	7	8	14	10	11	9	12												
3	18 (a)	Hibernian	D 1-1	Parlane	19,606	1		3	4	5	6	7	2	9		11				10	8									
4	25 (h)	Hearts	W 4-2	Hamilton, Miller (pen), Parlane, Johnstone	25,000	1		3	4		6	7	2	9		11				8	5									
5	Oct 2 (a)	Ayr U	D 1-1	Parlane	18,000	1		3	4	6	10	7	2	9	12	11				8	5									
6	16 (h)	Aberdeen	W 1-0	McDonald	21,800			3	4	6	10	7	2	9		11	14	12		8	5	1								
7	23 (a)	Motherwell	L 1-3	Hamilton	15,857			3	4		7	2	9		14	11			8	5	1	6	10	12						
8	30 (a)	Partick Thistle	L 1-2	Watson	16,900			3	4		6	11	7	2	9			8		5	1	10		12						
9	Nov 9 (h)	Dundee U	W 3-0	Jackson, McKean, Parlane	16,000	12		3			10	7	2	9		11	8	5	1	6			4							
10	13 (a)	Kilmarnock	W 4-0	Jackson 2, McKean, Parlane	14,717	12		3			10	7	2	9		11	8	5	1	6			4							
11	20 (h)	Hibernian	D 1-1	Parlane	24,621	12		3			10	7	2	9		11	8	5	1	6			4							
12	24 (h)	Celtic	L 0-1		43,500			3			10	7	2	9		11	8	5	1	6			4	12						
13	27 (a)	Hearts	W 1-0	Parlane	19,000			3			10	7	2	9			8	5	1	6			4	11						
14	Dec 26 (h)	Motherwell	W 1-0	O'Hara	28,000	12		3	4			7	2	9	11	10		5	1	6				8						
15	Jan 1 (h)	Partick Thistle	W 1-0	Johnstone	20,000			3		4		7	2		11	9	10	5	1	6			12	8						
16	8 (h)	Kilmarnock	W 3-0	Parlane 2, O'Hara	18,189			3		4		7	2	9	11	12	10	5	1	6				8						
17	11 (a)	Celtic	L 0-1		60,000			3		4		7	2	9	11		10	5	1	6				8						
18	19 (a)	Aberdeen	D 3-3	Miller (pen), McDonald, Johnstone	21,591			3	10	4		12	7	2	9	11	14	5	1	6				8						
19	22 (h)	Hearts	W 3-2	McDonald 2, Johnstone	19,700			3	4		10	7	2	11		12	8	5	1	6			9							
20	Feb 5 (a)	Ayr U	W 2-0	Johnstone, McLean	12,800	12		3	4		10	7	2		11		8	5	1	6			9							
21	12 (h)	Dundee U	L 2-3	Jackson, McDonald	16,000	12		3		4	10	7	2	14	11		8	5	1	6			9							
22	16 (a)	Hibernian	D 0-0		12,452			3	4		10	7	2	9		11	12	8	5	1	6									
23	19 (h)	Aberdeen	W 1-0	Miller (pen)	17,000			3	4		10	7	2	9		11	12	8	5	1	6	14								
24	Mar 5 (a)	Motherwell	W 2-0	McDonald, Watson	15,468	12		3	4		10	7	2	9		14		5	1	6	8	11								
25	8 (a)	Dundee U	D 0-0		10,250			3	4		10	7	2	9		8	5	1	6	12	11									
26	15 (a)	Partick Thistle	L 3-4	Johnstone, Watson, Parlane	17,000			3	4		10	7	2	9		11	8	1	6	12					5					
27	19 (h)	Celtic	D 2-2	Parlane 2	55,500			3	4		10	7	2	9		11	8	5	1	6	12									
28	23 (h)	Ayr U	D 1-1	Johnstone	10,000			3	4		10	7	2	9		11	8	5	1	6										
29	26 (a)	Kilmarnock	L 0-1		8,037			3	4		10	7	2	9		11	8	12	5	1	6									
30	Apr 2 (h)	Hibernian	W 2-1	Parlane, Johnstone	11,500			3	4		10	7	2	9		11	8	5	1	6										
31	9 (a)	Hearts	W 3-1	Johnstone, Parlane, Jardine (pen)	12,500			3	4		10	7	2	9		11	12	8	5	1	6									
32	13 (h)	Partick Thistle	W 2-1	Johnstone, Jardine (pen)	8,000			3	4		10	7	2	9		11	8	5	1	6										
33	16 (h)	Ayr U	W 5-1	McDonald 2, Johnstone, Hamilton, Miller (pen)	10,000		3		4		10	7	2	9		11	8	5	1	6	12									
34	20 (h)	Motherwell	W 4-1	Johnstone, McDonald, Parlane, Robertson (pen)	8,000		3		4		10	7	2	9		5	8	1	6	11										
35	23 (a)	Dundee U	W 1-0	Johnstone	8,000		3		4		10	7	2	9	12	5	8	1	6	11									
36	30 (a)	Aberdeen	L 1-2	Johnstone	13,484			3	4		10	7	2	9		11	8	5	1	6				12						

FINAL LEAGUE POSITION: 2nd

	McC	Mil	Grg	For	Den	McD	McL	Jar	Par	Mun	Joh	Hen	McK	Ham	Jck	Ken	Wat	Daw	McDo	Rob	Ste	Stn	O'H	Mor	Arm
Appearances	5	17	30	25	5	29	36	36	31	3	27	4	14	22	30	31	30	1	1	7	5	1	5	1	
Sub appearances	7					1				2		2		3				8	1	3	4		1		1
Goals		4				9	1	2	16		15		2	3	4		3			1			2		

Scottish FA Cup

Rd	Date	Opponent	Result	Scorers	Att	Grg	For	McD	McL	Jar	Par	Joh	Hen	Jck	Ken	Wat	Daw	McDo
3	Jan 29 (h)	Falkirk	W 3-1	Jardine (pen), Johnstone, McDonald	17,500	3	4	10	7	2		11		8	5	1	6	9
4	Feb 26 (h)	Elgin City	W 3-0	Jackson, McLean (pen), McDonald	18,000	3	4	10	7	2	9	11		5	1	6	8	
QF	Mar 12 (h)	Motherwell	W 2-0	McKean, Watson	35,572	3	4	10	7	2	9	11	8	5	1	6		
SF	30 (n*)	Hearts	W 2-0	Jackson, Jardine (pen)	23,222	3	4	10	7	2	9	11		8	5	1	6	
F	May 7 (n*)	Celtic	L 0-1		54,252	3	4	10	7	2	9	11		8	5	1	6	12

*Played at Hampden Park, Glasgow.

	Grg	For	McD	McL	Jar	Par	Joh	Hen	Jck	Ken	Wat	Daw	McDo
Appearances	5	5	5	5	5	4	5	1	3	5	5	5	1
Sub appearances													1
Goals			2	1	2			1	1	2	1		

Scottish League Cup Section Four

Rd	Date	Opponent	Result	Scorers	Att	McC	Mil	Grg	For	Den	McD	McL	Jar	Par	Mun	Joh	Hen	McK	Ham	Jck	Ken	Wat	Daw	McDo	Rob
1	Aug 14 (h)	St.Johnstone	W 5-0	Jardine 2, Johnstone, Miller (pen), Henderson	31,000	1	2	3	4	5	6	7	8	9	10	11	14	12							
2	18 (a)	Hibernian	D 1-1	Munro	26,000	1	2	3	4	5	6	7	8	9	10	11									
3	21 (h)	Montrose	W 4-0	Johnstone 2, Jardine, McDonald	18,500	1	2	3	4	5	6	7	8	9	10	11	12								
4	25 (h)	Hibernian	W 3-0	Miller (pen), Jardine, McLean	45,000	1	2	3	4	5	6	7	8	9	10	11			12						
5	28 (a)	Montrose	W 3-0	Johnstone, Parlane, Jardine	8,000	1	2	3	4	5	6	7	8	9	10	11									
6	Sep 1 (a)	St Johnstone	W 1-0	Jardine	4,070	1	2	3	4	5	6	7	8	9		11		10							
QF1	22 (h)	Clydebank	D 3-3	Johnstone, McDonald, Hamilton	15,000	1		3	4		6	7	2	9		11		10	8	5					
QF2	Oct 6 (a)	Clydebank	D 1-1	Greig	10,000		3	4	6	12	10		2	9		11	14	7	8	5	1				
R	18 (h)	Clydebank	D 0-0		15,000		3	4		6	10	7	2	9	11		12	8		5	1	14			
2R	19 (n*)	Clydebank	W 2-1	Parlane, McLean	14,000		3	4		6	10	7	2	9		14	8			1	5	11	12		
SF	27 (n†)	Aberdeen	L 1-5	McDonald	20,990		3	4			10	7	2	9		11	8	12	5	1	6			

*Played at Firhill Park, Glasgow.
†Played at Hampden Park, Glasgow.

	McC	Mil	Grg	For	Den	McD	McL	Jar	Par	Mun	Joh	Hen	McK	Ham	Jck	Ken	Wat	Daw
Appearances	7	10	11	8	8	11	10	11	11	6	8	1	6	2	4	4	2	1
Sub appearances						1						4	2	2			1	1
Goals	2	1				3	1	6	2	1	5	1	1	1				

European Champions' Cup

Rd	Date	Opponent	Result	Scorers	Att	McC	Mil	Grg	For	Den	McD	McL	Jar	Par	Joh	Hen	McK	Ham	Jck
1	Sep 15 (h)	FC Zürich	D 1-1	Parlane	35,000	1	2	3	4	5	6	7	8	9	11		10		
	29 (a)	FC Zürich	L 0-1		28,500	1		3	6	4	12	10	7	2	9	11	14	8	5

	McC	Mil	Grg	For	Den	McD	McL	Jar	Par	Joh	McK	Ham	Jck
Appearances	2	2	2	2	1	2	2	2	2	2	1	1	1
Sub appearances						1					1		
Goals									1				

Tennent Caledonian Cup

Rd	Date	Opponent	Result	Scorers	Att	McC	Mil	Grg	For	McD	McL	Jar	Par	Mun	Joh	Hen	McK	Ham	Jck	Ken
SF	Aug 2 (h)	Partick Thistle	W 2-0	Johnstone 2	35,000	1	2	3	4	6	10	12			11	9	7	8	5	
F	3 (h)	Southampton	L 1-2	Parlane	40,000	1	2	3	4	6	10	8	9	12	11	14	7		5	

	McC	Mil	Grg	For	McD	McL	Jar	Par	Joh	Hen	McK	Jck
Appearances	2	2	2	2	2	2	1	1	2	1	2	2
Sub appearances						1		1		1		
Goals						1		2				

Glasgow Cup

Rd	Date	Opponent	Result	Scorers	Att	McC	Mil	Grg	For	McD	McL	Jar	Par	Mun	Joh	Jck
F	Aug 10 (a)	Celtic*	W 3-1	Jardine, Jackson, Miller (pen)	60,000	1	2	3	4	6	7	8	9	10	11	12	5

*1975-76 Final

	McC	Mil	Grg	For	McD	McL	Jar	Par	Mun	Joh	Jck
Appearances	1	1	1	1	1	1	1	1	1	1	1
Sub appearances											1
Goals		1					1				1

Further match details for this season are continued on page 281

1977-78

Manager: J.Wallace

Scottish League

	Date	Opponent	Result	Scorers	Att	McCloy	Jardine	Miller	Forsyth T	Jackson	McDonald A	McKay	Russell	Parlane	Robertson	Cooper	McKean	McLean	Smith	Johnstone	Greig	Watson K (2)	Kennedy	Dawson	Hamilton	Morris	Henderson	Strickland
1	Aug 13	(a) Aberdeen	L 1-3	Russell	21,500	1	2	3	4	5	6	**7**	8	9	10	11	12											
2	20	(h) Hibernian	L 0-2		20,800	1	2	3	4	5	6		8	9	10	**11**		7	12									
3	27	(a) Partick Thistle	W 4-0	Smith 2, Miller (pen), Russell	18,584	1	2	3	4	5	6		8			11		7	10	9								
4	Sep 10	(h) Celtic	W 3-2	Smith 2, Johnstone	48,788	1	2	3	4		**6**		8	**9**		11	7	12	10	5	14							
5	17	(a) St Mirren	D 3-3	Jardine, Cooper, Johnstone	26,000	1	2	12	4	5			8			11	7		10	9	**3**	6						
6	24	(h) Ayr U	W 2-0	Smith 2	20,000		2	3	4	5	6		8			11	7		10	9			1					
7	Oct 1	(h) Clydebank	W 4-1	Cooper 2, Smith 2	13,250		2	3	4	5	6		8			11	**7**	12	10	9			1					
8	8	(a) Dundee U	W 1-0	Russell	18,658		2	3	4	5	6		8			11		7	10	9			1					
9	15	(a) Motherwell	W 4-1	Johnstone 3, Smith	20,050			3	4	5	6		8			11		7	10	9	2		1					
10	22	(h) Aberdeen	W 3-1	Jardine (pen), Smith, McDonald	40,000		2		4	5	6		8			11		7	10	9	3		1					
11	29	(a) Hibernian	W 1-0	Jardine (pen)	22,750		2		4	5	6		8			11		7	10	9	3		1					
12	Nov 5	(h) Partick Thistle	D 3-3	Parlane 2, McDonald	28,200		2		4	**5**	6		8	9	12	11		7	10		3		1					
13	12	(a) Celtic	D 1-1	Johnstone	57,000		2		4	5	6		8			11		7	10	9	3		1					
14	19	(h) St Mirren	W 2-1	Johnstone, Miller (pen)	25,000		2	3		5	6		8	12		11		7	**10**	9	4		1					
15	26	(a) Ayr U	W 5-0	Johnstone 3, Jackson, Parlane	15,300		2	3		5	6		8	14		11	12	**7**	**10**	9	4		1					
16	Dec 10	(h) Dundee U	W 2-0	McLean, Smith	25,000		2	3		**5**	6		8	12		11	14	**7**	10	9	4		1					
17	17	(h) Motherwell	W 3-1	Smith 2, Johnstone	19,750		2		4	5	6		8			11	7		10	9	3		1					
18	24	(a) Aberdeen	L 0-4		21,000		2		4	5	6		8	12		11		7	**10**	9	3		1					
19	31	(h) Hibernian	D 0-0		25,000		2		4	5	6		8	12		11		7	10	**9**	3		1					
20	Jan 2	(a) Partick Thistle	W 2-1	Johnstone, Smith	30,000		2	3	4	5	6		8	12		**11**		7	10	9			1					
21	7	(h) Celtic	W 3-1	Smith, Greig, Parlane	54,000		2	12	4	5	6		8	14		**11**		**7**	10	9	3		1					
22	14	(a) St Mirren	W 2-0	Johnstone, Smith	24,300		2		4	5	6		8			11	7		10	9	3		1					
23	Feb 4	(h) Clydebank	W 1-0	Johnstone	16,492	1	2	4		5	6		8	14		**11**	12	**7**	10	9	3							
24	19	(a) Clydebank	W 3-0	Johnstone 2, Cooper	10,000			2		5	6		8			11		7	10	9	4		1	3				
25	25	(a) Motherwell	W 5-3	Johnstone 2, Smith, Cooper, McVie (og)	20,387			2	4	5	6		8	12		11		**7**	10	9	3		1					
26	Mar 4	(h) Aberdeen	L 0-3		34,500			2	4	5	6		**8**	14		11		7	**10**	9	3		1	12				
27	21	(h) Partick Thistle	W 2-1	McDonald, Jardine	20,000		2	14	4	5	6			12		11		**7**	10	9	3		1		**8**			
28	25	(a) Celtic	L 0-2		51,000		2	12	4	5	6		**8**	14		**11**		7	10	9	3		1					
29	29	(a) Hibernian	D 1-1	Parlane	21,245	1	2	12	4	5	6			11				**7**	10	9	3				8			
30	Apr 1	(h) St Mirren	D 1-1	Johnstone	20,500	1	2	14	4	5	6			11		12		**7**	10	9	3				**8**			
31	8	(a) Ayr U	W 5-2	Johnstone 2, Smith 2, Greig	13,400	1	2	14	4	5	6		**8**	12		11		**7**	10	9	3							
32	12	(h) Ayr U	D 1-1	Johnstone	12,282	1	2	14	4	5	6		**8**	12		11		**7**	10	9	3							
33	15	(a) Clydebank	W 2-0	Johnstone 2	9,800	1	2		4	5	6		**8**	14		11		7	**10**	9	3				12			
34	19	(a) Dundee U	W 1-0	Johnstone	17,293	1	2		4	5			8			11		7	10	9	3	6						
35	22	(h) Dundee U	W 3-0	Jackson, Jardine (pen), Cooper	27,050	1	2		4	5	6		8	12		11		**7**	**10**	9	3	14						
36	29	(h) Motherwell	W 2-0	Jackson, Smith	43,500	1	2		4	5	6		8			11		**7**	10	9	3	12						
FINAL LEAGUE POSITION: 1st					Appearances	14	32	16	31	35	34	1	33	6	2	34	6	29	34	33	28	2	22	1	3			
					Sub appearances			8						16	1	1	4	2	1		1	2		1	1			
					Goals		5	2		3	3		3	5		6		1	20	25	2							

1 own-goal

Scottish FA Cup

	Date	Opponent	Result	Scorers	Att	McCloy	Jardine	Miller	Forsyth T	Jackson	McDonald A	McKay	Russell	Parlane	Robertson	Cooper	McKean	McLean	Smith	Johnstone	Greig	Watson K (2)	Kennedy	Dawson	Hamilton	Morris	Henderson	Strickland
3	Jan 28	(a) Berwick R	W 4-2	Jackson 2, Johnstone 2	10,500		2		4	5	6		8	12		11		7	10	**9**	3		1					
4	Feb 18	(h) Stirling A	W 1-0	Johnstone	15,500		**2**	3		5	6		8	14		**11**		7	10	9	4		1			12		
QF	Mar 11	(h) Kilmarnock	W 4-1	Johnstone, Hamilton, McDonald, Cooper (pen)	28,000		2		4	5	6					11		7	10	9	3		1		8			
SF	Apr 5	(n*) Dundee U	W 2-0	Johnstone, Greig	25,619	1	2	14	4	5	6		8	12		11		7	**10**	**9**	3							
F	May 6	(n*) Aberdeen	W 2-1	McDonald, Johnstone	61,563	1	2		4	5	6		8			**11**		7	10	9	3	12						
*Played at Hampden Park, Glasgow.					Appearances	2	5	1	4	5	5		4			5		5	5	5	5		3		1			
					Sub appearances			1						3								1				1		
					Goals					2	2					1				6	1				1			

Scottish League Cup

	Date	Opponent	Result	Scorers	Att	McCloy	Jardine	Miller	Forsyth T	Jackson	McDonald A	McKay	Russell	Parlane	Robertson	Cooper	McKean	McLean	Smith	Johnstone	Greig	Watson K (2)	Kennedy	Dawson	Hamilton	Morris	Henderson	Strickland
2	Aug 24	(h) St.Johnstone	W 3-1	Johnstone 2, Miller (pen)	10,000	1	2	3	4	5		7	8			11			10	9		6						
	Sep 3	(a) St.Johnstone	W 3-0	Parlane, Miller (pen), Smith	11,200	1	2	3		**5**	6		8	9		11	7		10	**4**		12					14	
3	Oct 5	(h) Aberdeen	W 6-1	Smith 3, Johnstone, Miller (pen), McDonald	25,000		2	3	4	5	6		8			11		7	10	9			1					
	26	(a) Aberdeen	L 1-3	Smith	15,600		2	**3**	4		6		8	12		11	14	7	**10**	9	5		1					
QF1	Nov 9	(h) Dunfermline A	W 3-1	McLean 2, Jackson	12,000		2		4	5	6		8			11		7	10	9	3		1					
QF2	16	(a) Dunfermline A	W 3-1	Greig, Jardine (pen), Johnstone	8,274		2	12	**4**	5	6		8			11		7	10	9	3		1					
SF	Feb 27	(n*) Forfar A	W 5-2	Johnstone 2, Parlane 2, McDonald	12,799			2	4	5	6		8	12		**11**		7	10	9	3		1					
F	Mar 18	(n*) Celtic	W 2-1	Cooper, Smith	60,168		2	12	4	5	6			14		**11**		7	10	9	3		1		**8**			
*Played at Hampden Park, Glasgow.					Appearances	2	7	5	7	7	7	1	7	1		8	1	6	8	8	5	1	6		1			
					Sub appearances			2						3			1					1					1	
					Goals		1	3		1	2			3		1		2	6	6	1							

European Cup-winners' Cup

	Date	Opponent	Result	Scorers	Att	McCloy	Jardine	Miller	Forsyth T	Jackson	McDonald A	McKay	Russell	Parlane	Robertson	Cooper	McKean	McLean	Smith	Johnstone	Greig	Watson K (2)	Kennedy	Dawson	Hamilton	Morris	Henderson	Strickland
PR1	Aug 17	(h) BSC Young Boys	W 1-0	Greig	30,000	1	2		4	5	6	14	8	**9**	10	11		**7**	12		3							
	31	(a) BSC Young Boys	D 2-2	Johnstone, Smith	21,000	1	2	14	4	5	6		**8**			11	12	**7**	10	9	3							
1	Sep 14	(h) FC Twente	D 0-0		40,000	1	2	3	4	5			8			11	7		10			6					9	
	28	(a) FC Twente	L 0-3		20,000		2	3	4	5	6		8	9		11	7		10				1					
					Appearances	3	4	2	4	4	3		4	2	1	4	2	2	3	1	2	1	1				1	
					Sub appearances			1				1					1		1									
					Goals														1	1	1							

Tennent Caledonian Cup

	Date	Opponent	Result	Scorers	Att	McCloy	Jardine	Miller	Forsyth T	Jackson	McDonald A	McKay	Russell	Parlane	Robertson	Cooper	McKean	McLean	Smith	Johnstone	Greig	Watson K (2)	Kennedy	Dawson	Hamilton	Morris	Henderson	Strickland
SF	Aug 6	(h) Southampton	W 3-1	McDonald, Parlane, Cooper	40,000	1	2	3	5		6		8	9		11	10	7			4							
F	7	(h) West Brom A	L 0-2		40,000	1	2	3	5		6		8	9	14	11	**10**	**7**			4				12			
					Appearances	2	2	2	2		2		2	2		2	2	2			2							
					Sub appearances										1										1			
					Goals						1			1		1												

Glasgow Cup

	Date	Opponent	Result	Scorers	Att	McCloy	Jardine	Miller	Forsyth T	Jackson	McDonald A	McKay	Russell	Parlane	Robertson	Cooper	McKean	McLean	Smith	Johnstone	Greig	Watson K (2)	Kennedy	Dawson	Hamilton	Morris	Henderson	Strickland
SF	Oct 18	(h) Partick Thistle	D 2-2*	McLean, Forsyth	9,000			3	4	5	6	7	8			11	12	10		**9**	2		1					
*1976-77 tournament. Rangers won 4-3 on penalties. Competition not concluded.					Appearances			1	1	1	1	1	1			1		1		1	1		1					
					Sub appearances												1											
					Goals				1									1										

Further match details for this season are continued on page 281

1978-79

Manager: J.Greig

Scottish League

Player columns: McCloy, Jardine, Forsyth A, Forsyth T, Jackson, McDonald A, McLean, Russell, Johnstone, Smith, Watson K (2), Urquhart, Parlane, Miller, Cooper, Dawson, Robertson, McDonald J, Armour, McKay, Morris, Strickland, Denny, Kennedy, McLaren, Richardson, Dalziel

#	Date		Opponent	Result	Scorers	Att.
1	Aug	12 (h)	St Mirren	L 0-1		28,000
2		19 (a)	Hibernian	D 0-0		23,000
3		26 (h)	Partick Thistle	D 0-0		24,500
4	Sep	9 (a)	Celtic	L 1-3	Parlane	60,000
5		16 (h)	Aberdeen	D 1-1	A.Forsyth (pen)	27,000
6		23 (a)	Morton	D 2-2	Parlane, Johnstone	16,500
7		30 (h)	Motherwell	W 4-1	Smith 2, McLean, Johnstone	26,000
8	Oct	7 (h)	Dundee U	D 1-1	A.McDonald	27,000
9		14 (a)	Hearts	D 0-0		18,159
10		21 (a)	St Mirren	W 1-0	A.Forsyth (pen)	26,000
11		28 (h)	Hibernian	W 2-1	A.Forsyth (pen), Smith	24,750
12	Nov	4 (a)	Partick Thistle	L 0-1		20,641
13		11 (h*)	Celtic	D 1-1	A.Forsyth (pen)	52,330
14		18 (a)	Aberdeen	D 0-0		26,000
15		25 (h)	Morton	W 3-0	Johnstone, Cooper, Smith	21,500
16	Dec	9 (a)	Dundee U	L 0-3		15,247
17		16 (h)	Hearts	W 5-3	Johnstone 4, K.Watson	16,250
18		23 (h)	St Mirren	W 1-0	Johnstone	22,500
19	Jan	20 (a)	Morton	W 2-0	A.McDonald, K.Watson	16,500
20	Feb	10 (a)	Dundee U	W 1-0	Robertson	23,500
21		24 (a)	Hearts	L 2-3	Smith, Parlane	16,500
22	Mar	14 (h)	Hibernian	W 1-0	Smith	16,000
23		17 (a)	Partick Thistle	W 2-0	Cooper, Urquhart	18,685
24		27 (a)	St Mirren	W 2-1	Urquhart 2	20,000
25	Apr	7 (h)	Morton	D 1-1	Cooper	15,750
26		10 (h)	Motherwell	W 3-0	Cooper, A.McDonald, Smith	12,000
27		14 (a)	Motherwell	L 0-2		14,612
28		21 (a)	Dundee U	W 2-1	Dawson, Smith	20,264
29		25 (a)	Aberdeen	L 1-2	Smith	20,000
30		28 (h)	Hearts	W 4-0	Russell 3, Parlane	20,050
31	May	2 (h*)	Motherwell	W 2-1	Smith, Jackson	13,052
32		5 (h*)	Celtic	W 1-0	A.McDonald	52,841
33		7 (h)	Aberdeen	W 2-0	Smith, Cooper	32,000
34		21 (a)	Celtic	L 2-4	A.McDonald, Russell	52,000
35		23 (h)	Partick Thistle	W 1-0	Johnstone	6,000
36		31 (a)	Hibernian	L 1-2	Urquhart	5,000

FINAL LEAGUE POSITION: 2nd
*Played at Hampden Park, Glasgow.

Appearances: 36 35 16 17 28 33 34 36 31 31 11 6 21 10 26 23 ... 1 1
Sub appearances: 1 ... 2 2 4 3 8 4 ... 2 2 2 1
Goals: 4 ... 1 5 1 4 9 11 2 4 4 ... 5 1 1

Scottish FA Cup

#	Date		Opponent	Result	Scorers	Att.
3	Feb	12 (h)	Motherwell	W 3-1	Johnstone, Jackson, Cooper	19,000
4		21 (h)	Kilmarnock	D 1-1	A.McDonald	17,500
R		26 (a)	Kilmarnock	W 1-0	Urquhart	19,493
QF	Mar	10 (h)	Dundee	W 6-3	Jardine (pen), A.McDonald, Smith, T.Forsyth, Russell, Cooper	28,000
SF	Apr	4 (n*)	Partick Thistle	D 0-0		26,232
R		16 (n*)	Partick Thistle	W 1-0	Johnstone	32,294
F	May	12 (n*)	Hibernian	D 0-0		50,610
R		16 (n*)	Hibernian	D 0-0		33,504
2R		28 (n*)	Hibernian	W 3-2	Johnstone 2, Duncan, (og)	30,602

*Played at Hampden Park, Glasgow.

Appearances: 9 9 ... 4 8 9 8 9 8 6 3 3 4 ... 9 9 ... 1
Sub appearances: 1 ... 2 ... 4
Goals: 1 ... 1 1 2 ... 1 4 1 ... 1 ... 2

1 own-goal

Scottish League Cup

#	Date		Opponent	Result	Scorers	Att.
1	Aug	16 (h)	Albion R	W 3-0	Parlane, Johnstone, Smith	10,000
		23 (a)	Albion R	W 1-0	Parlane	6,500
2		30 (h)	Forfar A	W 3-0	Cooper, McLean, Smith	9,000
	Sep	2 (a)	Forfar A	W 4-1	Smith 2, A.McDonald, Cooper	5,919
3	Oct	4 (h)	St Mirren	W 3-2	Cooper, Miller, Johnstone	20,000
		11 (a)	St Mirren	D 0-0		24,000
QF1	Nov	8 (h)	Arbroath	W 1-0	Wells (og)	10,000
QF2		15 (a)	Arbroath	W 2-1	Smith, Russell	4,000
SF	Dec	13 (n*)	Celtic	W 3-2	Jardine (pen), Jackson, Casey (og)	49,432
F	Mar	31 (n*)	Aberdeen	W 2-1	A.McDonald, Jackson	60,000

*Played at Hampden Park, Glasgow.

Appearances: 10 10 8 6 5 9 8 10 10 8 3 3 7 5 5 2 ... 1
Sub appearances: 1 ... 2 1 2 2 3 3 ... 1 ... 1
Goals: 1 ... 2 2 1 1 2 5 ... 2 1 3

2 own-goals

European Champions' Cup

#	Date		Opponent	Result	Scorers	Att.
1	Sep	13 (a)	Juventus	L 0-1		70,000
		27 (h)	Juventus	W 2-0	A.McDonald, Smith	44,000
2	Oct	18 (h)	PSV Eindhoven	D 0-0		44,000
	Nov	1 (a)	PSV Eindhoven	W 3-2	A.McDonald, Johnstone, Russell	29,000
QF1	Mar	6 (a)	1.FC Cologne	L 0-1		50,000
QF2		22 (h)	1.FC Cologne	D 1-1	McLean	44,000

Appearances: 6 6 4 6 5 6 5 6 3 6 2 1 5 1 1 2 ... 1
Sub appearances: 1 ... 1 1 2 1
Goals: 2 1 1 1 1

Tennent Caledonian Cup

#	Date		Opponent	Result	Scorers	Att.
SF	Aug	5 (h)	Hearts	W 3-1	Smith 2, A.McDonald	30,000
F		6 (h)	Southampton	W 4-1	Russell, Parlane, A.Forsyth, A.McDonald	32,000

Appearances: 2 1 2 2 1 2 2 2 2 2 2 ... 2
Sub appearances: 1 ... 2
Goals: 1 ... 2 1 2 ... 1

Further match details for this season are continued on page 281

1979-80

Manager: J.Greig

Scottish League

Player columns (left to right): McCloy, Miller, Dawson, Jardine, Jackson, Watson K (2), McLean, Russell, Johnstone, McDonald A, Cooper, McDonald J, Smith, Stevens, Parlane, Forsyth A, Urquhart, Dalziel, McKay, Forsyth T, Young, Redford, Robertson, Richardson, Davies, Boyd G, McLaren, Watson G, Matthew, Stirton

#	Date	Venue	Opponent	Result	Scorers	Att.
1	Aug 11	(a)	Hibernian	W 3-1	A.McDonald, Cooper, Russell	17,731
2	18	(h)	Celtic	D 2-2	J.McDonald, Russell	36,000
3	25	(a)	Partick Thistle	L 1-2	Johnstone	20,000
4	Sep 8	(h)	St Mirren	W 3-1	Johnstone, Smith, Miller (pen)	31,000
5	15	(a)	Aberdeen	L 1-3	Johnstone	25,000
6	22	(h)	Dundee	W 2-0	Johnstone, Glennie (og)	25,000
7	29	(a)	Kilmarnock	L 1-2	Johnstone	15,479
8	Oct 6	(a)	Dundee U	D 0-0		19,464
9	13	(h)	Morton	D 2-2	Johnstone 2	25,000
10	20	(h)	Hibernian	W 2-0	Smith, Miller (pen)	25,000
11	27	(a)	Celtic	L 0-1		61,000
12	Nov 3	(h)	Partick Thistle	W 2-1	Urquhart 2	18,400
13	10	(a)	St Mirren	L 1-2	A.Forsyth	17,362
14	17	(h)	Aberdeen	L 0-1		18,500
15	24	(a)	Dundee	L 1-3	Jackson	13,342
16	Dec 1	(h)	Kilmarnock	W 2-1	Johnstone, Russell	16,557
17	8	(a)	Morton	W 1-0	Johnstone	14,750
18	15	(h)	Dundee U	W 2-1	Johnstone, Kopel (og)	19,240
19	22	(a)	Hibernian	L 1-2	McLean	18,740
20	29	(h)	Celtic	D 1-1	Johnstone	34,500
21	Jan 5	(h)	St Mirren	L 1-2	Jardine (pen)	19,000
22	12	(a)	Aberdeen	L 2-3	J.McDonald, Jackson	19,250
23	Feb 23	(h)	Morton	W 3-1	Russell, Smith, J.McDonald	28,000
24	Mar 1	(h)	Hibernian	W 1-0	Johnstone	29,500
25	12	(h)	Dundee	W 1-0	Stevens	17,000
26	15	(h)	Partick Thistle	D 0-0		22,000
27	19	(a)	Dundee U	D 0-0		9,533
28	29	(h)	Aberdeen	D 2-2	Jardine (pen), J.McDonald	25,000
29	Apr 2	(a)	Celtic	L 0-1		60,000
30	5	(a)	Dundee	W 4-1	Johnstone 2, Cooper, Smith	12,948
31	19	(a)	Morton	W 1-0	Russell	15,000
32	23	(a)	Kilmarnock	L 0-1		8,504
33	26	(h)	Dundee U	W 2-1	Jardine (pen), McLean	19,000
34	30	(h)	Kilmarnock	W 1-0	J.McDonald	7,655
35	May 3	(a)	Partick Thistle	L 3-4	Russell 2, Johnstone	15,000
36	7	(a)	St Mirren	L 1-4	Miller	12,000

FINAL LEAGUE POSITION: 5th

	McCloy	Miller	Dawson	Jardine	Jackson	Watson K	McLean	Russell	Johnstone	McDonald A	Cooper	McDonald J	Smith	Stevens	Parlane	Forsyth A	Urquhart	Dalziel	McKay	Forsyth T	Young	Redford
Appearances	34	13	32	35	29	12	22	22	31	23	25	21	20	31	2	8	4	1	16	2	13	
Sub appearances		5				3	6	1	2	3	5	6	10		1				2			
Goals		3		3	2		2	7	15	1	2	5	4	1		1	2					

2 own-goals

Scottish FA Cup

#	Date	Venue	Opponent	Result	Scorers	Att.
3	Jan 26	(a)	Clyde	D 2-2	Jardine (pen), Jackson	12,500
R	30	(h)	Clyde	W 2-0	J.McDonald 2	12,000
4	Feb 16	(h)	Dundee U	W 1-0	Johnstone	29,000
QF	Mar 8	(h)	Hearts	W 6-1	J.McDonald 2, Cooper, Jardine (pen), Russell, Johnstone	36,000
SF	Apr 12 (n*)		Aberdeen	W 1-0	Johnstone	50,000
F	May 10 (n*)		Celtic	L 0-1		70,303

*Played at Hampden Park, Glasgow.

	McCloy	Miller	Dawson	Jardine	Jackson	McLean	Russell	Johnstone	McDonald A	Cooper	McDonald J	Smith	Stevens	McKay
Appearances	6	3	5	6	5	1	1	5	6	1	5	6	4	6
Sub appearances		1					2			2	1		1	
Goals				2	1		1	3		1	4			

Scottish League Cup

#	Date	Venue	Opponent	Result	Scorers	Att.
2	Aug 29	(a)	Clyde	W 2-1	Dawson, Robertson	5,021
	Sep 1	(a)	Clyde	W 4-0	McKay 2, Smith, O'Neill (og)	16,000
3	26	(a)	Aberdeen	L 1-3	Johnstone	22,000
	Oct 10	(h)	Aberdeen	L 0-2		35,000

	McCloy	Miller	Dawson	Jardine	Jackson	Watson K	McLean	Russell	Johnstone	McDonald A	Cooper	McDonald J	Smith	Stevens	Parlane	Forsyth A	Urquhart	McKay	Robertson
Appearances	4	1	4	4	4	4	1	2	2	4	4	1	3	2	1			1	2
Sub appearances		2				1					1				1	1		2	
Goals			1						1			1					2		1

1 own-goal

European Cup-winners' Cup

#	Date	Venue	Opponent	Result	Scorers	Att.
PR1	Aug 21	(h)	Lillestrøm SK	W 1-0	Smith	25,000
	Sep 5	(a)	Lillestrøm SK	W 2-0	A.McDonald, Johnstone	6,175
1	19	(h)	Fortuna Düss'dorf	W 2-1	A.McDonald, McLean	36,000
	Oct 3	(a)	Fortuna Düss'dorf	D 0-0		47,000
2	24	(a)	Valencia CF	D 1-1	McLean	61,000
	Nov 7	(h)	Valencia CF	L 1-3	Johnstone	36,000

	McCloy	Miller	Dawson	Jardine	Jackson	Watson K	McLean	Russell	Johnstone	McDonald A	Cooper	McDonald J	Smith	Stevens	Parlane	Forsyth A	Urquhart
Appearances	6	5	4	6	4	5	6	3	6	6	4		6		1	2	2
Sub appearances		1			1					2	1		2	1		1	
Goals						2	2	2			1						

Drybrough Cup

#	Date	Venue	Opponent	Result	Scorers	Att.
1	Jul 29	(h)	Berwick R	W 1-0	A.McDonald	15,000
SF	Aug 1	(a)	Kilmarnock	W 2-0	J.McDonald 2	10,035
F	4 (n*)		Celtic	W 3-1	J.McDonald, Jardine, Cooper	40,609

*Played at Hampden Park, Glasgow.

	McCloy	Miller	Dawson	Jardine	Jackson	Watson K	McLean	Russell	Johnstone	McDonald A	Cooper	McDonald J	Smith	McKay
Appearances	3	1	3	3	3	2	2	3	2	3	3	1	1	1
Sub appearances										1			2	2
Goals			1							1	1	3		

Further match details for this season are continued on page 281

1980-81

Manager: J.Greig

Scottish League

Player columns: McCloy, Jardine, Forsyth A, Forsyth T, Jackson, Bett, Cooper, Russell, McAdam, Redford, McDonald J, Johnstone, McLean, Miller, Stevens, Dawson, McKay, Clark, Stewart, McDonald A, Dalziel, Robertson, Davies

#	Date	Opponent	Result	Scorers	Att
1	Aug 9 (a)	Airdrieonians	D 1-1	J.McDonald	16,000
2	16 (h)	Partick Thistle	W 4-0	Cooper, McAdam, J.McDonald, Jardine	25,898
3	23 (a)	Celtic	W 2-1	Bett, Miller	58,000
4	Sep 6 (a)	Dundee U	W 4-2	Cooper, McAdam, J.McDonald, Hegarty (og)	16,269
5	13 (h)	Aberdeen	D 1-1	McAdam	34,000
6	20 (a)	Kilmarnock	W 8-1	J.McDonald 3, Redford 2 (1 pen), McAdam, Jardine, Bett	15,021
7	27 (h)	St Mirren	W 2-0	Bett, Cooper	30,000
8	Oct 4 (a)	Morton	D 2-2	Miller (pen), McAdam	15,000
9	11 (h)	Hearts	W 3-1	McAdam 2, Jeffries (og)	23,350
10	18 (h)	Airdrieonians	D 0-0		23,000
11	25 (a)	Partick Thistle	D 1-1	McAdam	14,250
12	Nov 1 (h)	Celtic	W 3-0	McAdam 2, J.McDonald	35,000
13	8 (a)	St Mirren	D 0-0		17,362
14	15 (h)	Kilmarnock	W 2-0	Johnston, Jardine	15,791
15	22 (a)	Hearts	D 0-0		16,315
16	29 (h)	Morton	L 0-1		20,000
17	Dec 13 (a)	Aberdeen	L 0-2		22,500
18	20 (a)	Kilmarnock	D 1-1	Russell	9,172
19	Jan 1 (h)	Partick Thistle	D 1-1	McAdam	18,000
20	3 (a)	Airdrieonians	D 1-1	Dawson	11,800
21	10 (a)	Morton	W 2-0	J.McDonald, Redford	13,000
22	31 (h)	Aberdeen	W 1-0	Johnstone	32,500
23	Feb 7 (a)	Dundee U	L 1-2	J.McDonald	14,328
24	21 (a)	Celtic	L 1-3	Johnstone	52,800
25	28 (h)	Airdrieonians	W 2-0	J.McDonald, Redford	12,200
26	Mar 14 (a)	Hearts	L 1-2	Redford	11,500
27	18 (h)	Dundee U	L 1-4	McAdam	14,000
28	21 (h)	Kilmarnock	W 2-0	Redford, Russell	8,488
29	28 (a)	St Mirren	L 1-2	Dawson	9,988
30	Apr 1 (h)	Morton	W 4-0	Johnstone 2, Redford, J.McDonald	7,000
31	4 (h)	Dundee U	W 2-1	Russell, Redford (pen)	16,000
32	15 (h)	St.Mirren	W 1-0	Russell	10,000
33	18 (h)	Celtic	L 0-1		35,000
34	22 (a)	Aberdeen	D 0-0		11,500
35	25 (a)	Partick Thistle	D 1-1	Russell	7,077
36	May 2 (h)	Hearts	W 4-0	Bett, Russell, Redford, Johnston	8,000

FINAL LEAGUE POSITION: 3rd

Appearances: 26 29 1 15 29 34 17 23 31 35 26 21 23 23 24 7 22 — 10 — — — —
Sub appearances: 3 — — 7 — — 8 5 — — — 4 6 3 5 1 2 — 6 1 — — —
Goals: 3 — — — — 4 3 6 12 9 11 2 4 — 2 — 2 — — — — — —

2 own-goals

Scottish FA Cup

#	Date	Opponent	Result	Scorers	Att
3	Jan 24 (a)	Airdrieonians	W 5-0	Johnstone 2, Stevens, Redford, Bett	16,054
4	Feb 14 (a)	St Johnstone	D 3-3	Redford 2, McAdam	17,595
R	18 (h)	St Johnstone	W 3-1	McAdam 2, Stevens	30,000
QF	Mar 7 (h)	Hibernian	W 3-1	Russell, McAdam, J.McDonald	26,345
SF	Apr 11 (n*)	Morton	W 2-1	Jackson, Russell	27,050
F	May 9 (n†)	Dundee U	D 0-0		53,346
R	12 (n†)	Dundee U	W 4-1	J.McDonald 2, Cooper, Russell	43,099

*Played at Celtic Park, Glasgow.
†Played at Hampden Park, Glasgow.

Appearances: 4 6 — 4 5 7 1 6 4 7 4 6 4 2 3 4 7 — 3 — — — —
Sub Appearances: — — — — — — 4 — 1 — 1 — — 1 — — — — — — — — —
Goals: — — — 1 1 1 3 4 3 3 — 2 — — 2 — — — — — — — —

Scottish League Cup

#	Date	Opponent	Result	Scorers	Att
2	Aug 27 (a)	Forfar A	W 2-0	McAdam 2	4,500
	30 (h)	Forfar A	W 3-1	Miller (pen), Johnstone, McAdam (pen)	15,500
3	Sep 3 (a)	Aberdeen	W 1-0	McAdam	33,000
	24 (a)	Aberdeen	L 1-3	McAdam	23,926

Appearances: 4 4 — 4 4 4 4 — 4 4 2 3 2 1 4 — — — — — — — —
Sub Appearances: — — — — — — — 1 — — — 1 1 1 3 — 1 — — — — — —
Goals: — — — — — — — — 5 — — — 1 — — 1 — — — — — — —

Anglo-Scottish Cup

#	Date	Opponent	Result	Scorers	Att
1	Jul 30 (h)	Partick Thistle	W 3-1	J.McDonald 2, Jardine (pen)	10,000
	Aug 6 (a)	Partick Thistle	L 2-3	McAdam, Russell	11,000
QF1	Oct 13 (h)	Chesterfield	D 1-1	Dalziel	13,000
QF2	28 (a)	Chesterfield	L 0-3		13,914

Appearances: 4 4 2 3 2 2 2 3 4 4 1 1 4 2 1 2 1 1 — 1 — — —
Sub Appearances: — — — — — — — — — — — 3 — 1 — — — 1 — 1 — — —
Goals: — 1 — — — — 1 1 2 — — — — — — 1 — — — — — — —

Glasgow Cup

#	Date	Opponent	Result	Scorers	Att
SF	Jan 12 (a)	Partick Thistle	L 0-1		4,000

Appearances: 1 1 — 1 1 — 1 1 — 1 — — 1 1 1 — — — 1 — — — —
Sub Appearances: — — — — — — — — — — — — 1 — — — — — 1 — — — —
Goals:

Other matches

#	Date	Opponent	Result	Scorers	Att
1	Aug 1 (h)	Arsenal	W 2-0	J.McDonald 2	27,000
2	4 (h)	Tottenham H	W 2-1	Redford, McAdam	35,000
3	Mar 25 (a)	GD Estoril Praia	W 1-0	Jardine	4,000

Appearances: 2 3 — 3 3 3 3 3 3 3 2 — 1 3 — — — 1 — — — — —
Sub Appearances: — — — — — — — — — — — 1 1 — — — — — — — — — —
Goals: — 1 — — — — — 1 1 2 — — — — — — — — — — — — —

1981-82

Manager: J.Greig

Player columns (left to right): McCloy, Jardine, Miller, Stevens, Forsyth T, Bett, Cooper, Russell, McAdam, Johnstone, McLean, Redford, McDonald J, Dawson, Johnston, McClelland, Jackson, Stewart, McKay, Black, Dalziel, Davies, Lyall, Robertson, McIntyre, McPherson, Clark R, Bruce, Forsyth A, Ferguson E, Watson G

Scottish League

No	Date		V	Opponent	Result	Scorers	Att
1	Aug	29	(a)	Partick Thistle	W 1-0	McLean (pen)	15,352
2	Sep	5	(h)	Hibernian	D 2-2	Bett, Cooper	23,500
3		12	(a)	St Mirren	D 1-1	McDonald	15,652
4		19	(h)	Celtic	L 0-2		40,900
5	Oct	3	(a)	Airdrieonians	W 4-1	Bett 2, Johnstone, Jardine	12,500
6		10	(h)	Aberdeen	D 0-0		30,000
7		17	(a)	Dundee	W 3-2	McDonald 2, Russell	11,956
8		24	(h)	Morton	D 1-1	Russell	21,000
9		31	(h)	Partick Thistle	L 0-2		17,000
10	Nov	7	(a)	Hibernian	W 2-1	Bett 2 (1 pen)	14,685
11		11	(a)	Dundee U	L 0-2		16,138
12		14	(h)	St Mirren	W 4-1	Johnstone, Russell, Bett (pen), Cooper	18,000
13		21	(a)	Celtic	D 3-3	Dalziel, Bett, McDonald	48,600
14	Dec	5	(a)	Airdrieonians	D 2-2	McDonald, Russell	13,750
15		19	(h)	Dundee	W 2-1	Bett, McAdam	11,000
16	Jan	9	(h)	Celtic	W 1-0	Bett (pen)	44,000
17		16	(h)	Dundee U	W 2-0	Dalziel, Cooper	23,000
18		30	(h)	Hibernian	D 1-1	Johnstone	20,000
19	Feb	17	(a)	Partick Thistle	L 0-2		6,513
20		20	(a)	Dundee U	D 1-1	Dawson	12,945
21		27	(h)	Morton	W 3-0	McDonald, Dalziel, McKay	10,200
22	Mar	10	(a)	St Mirren	W 3-2	Johnstone 2, Bett (pen)	8,633
23		13	(h)	Aberdeen	L 1-3	Johnstone	25,000
24		17	(a)	Morton	D 0-0		4,579
25		20	(h)	Partick Thistle	W 4-1	Johnstone, Russell, Bett (pen), McDonald	13,000
26		27	(a)	Hibernian	D 0-0		12,390
27		31	(a)	Airdrieonians	W 1-0	McDonald	8,000
28	Apr	10	(a)	Celtic	L 1-2	Johnstone	49,144
29		14	(a)	Dundee	L 1-3	McDonald	7,975
30		17	(a)	Airdrieonians	W 1-0	McDonald	10,000
31		21	(a)	Aberdeen	L 1-3	Johnstone	15,700
32		24	(h)	Dundee U	D 1-1	McDonald	12,000
33	May	1	(a)	Morton	W 3-1	McDonald 2, Russell	6,500
34		5	(h)	St Mirren	W 3-0	McDonald, McAdam, Redford	6,000
35		8	(h)	Dundee	W 4-0	Dalziel 3, Redford	8,500
36		15	(a)	Aberdeen	L 0-4		16,200

FINAL LEAGUE POSITION: 3rd

	McCloy	Jardine	Miller	Stevens	Forsyth T	Bett	Cooper	Russell	McAdam	Johnstone	McLean	Redford	McDonald J	Dawson	Johnston	McClelland	Jackson	Stewart	McKay	Black	Dalziel	Davies	Lyall	Robertson
Appearances	10	36	14	13	12	35	29	32	15	27	2	20	32	25	6	14	21	26	1	7	14	1	3	1
Sub appearances		2							1			7	1	2	12	4		2			6	2	4	5	1	1	1
Goals		1				11	3	6	2	9	1	2	14	1						1	6			

Scottish FA Cup

No	Date		V	Opponent	Result	Scorers	Att
3	Feb	6	(h)	Albion R	W 6-2	Johnstone, McDonald, Russell, McAdam, McPherson (pen), Redford	9,200
4		13	(h)	Dumbarton	W 4-0	Jardine 2, McAdam, Johnstone	15,000
QF	Mar	6	(h)	Dundee	W 2-0	Johnstone, McAdam	16,500
SF	Apr	3	(n*)	Forfar A	D 0-0		15,878
R		6	(n*)	Forfar A	W 3-1	Johnstone, Bett, Cooper	11,864
F	May	22	(n*)	Aberdeen	L 1-4	McDonald	53,788

*Played at Hampden Park, Glasgow.

	Appearances / Sub / Goals per player (see grid)
Appearances	6, 2, 5, 5, 6, 4, 4, 4, 6, 6, 3, 5, 6, 1, 2, 1
Sub appearances	2, 1, 1, 1, 2, 2, 1, 1, 1
Goals	2, 1, 1, 1, 3, 4, 1, 2, 1

Scottish League Cup

No	Date		V	Opponent	Result	Scorers	Att
1	Aug	8	(a)	Morton	D 1-1	McAdam	11,500
2		12	(h)	Dundee	W 4-1	McAdam, Johnstone, Miller, McDonald	13,500
3		15	(h)	Raith R	W 8-1	Redford 4, Russell 2, Jardine, McAdam	18,000
4		19	(a)	Dundee	W 2-1	Stevens, McGeachie (og)	9,124
5		22	(h)	Morton	W 1-0	Johnstone	30,000
6		26	(a)	Raith R	W 3-1	Redford, Johnstone, McDonald	6,000
QF1	Sep	2	(a)	Brechin C	W 4-0	Russell, Jackson, McLean (pen), Redford	7,000
QF2		23	(h)	Brechin C	W 1-0	McDonald	5,000
SF1	Oct	7	(a)	St Mirren	D 2-2	McAdam, McDonald	14,058
SF2		28	(h)	St Mirren	W 2-1	Bett (pen), McDonald	28,000
F	Nov	28	(n*)	Dundee U	W 2-1	Cooper, Redford	53,777

*Played at Hampden Park, Glasgow.

	Appearances / Sub / Goals per player (see grid)
Appearances	2, 8, 6, 8, 7, 9, 11, 9, 7, 7, 6, 8, 6, 4, 4, 3, 4, 9, 2, 1
Sub appearances	1, 1, 3, 4, 1, 4, 1, 1, 1
Goals	1, 1, 1, 1, 1, 3, 4, 3, 1, 7, 5, 1

1 own-goal

European Cup-winners' Cup

No	Date		V	Opponent	Result	Scorers	Att
1	Sep	16	(a)	Dukla Prague	L 0-3		22,500
		30	(h)	Dukla Prague	W 2-1	Bett, McDonald	35,000

	Appearances / Sub / Goals per player (see grid)
Appearances	1, 2, 2, 2, 1, 2, 2, 1, 1, 1, 2, 1, 2, 1, 1
Sub appearances	1, 1, 2
Goals	1, 1

Glasgow Cup

No	Date		V	Opponent	Result	Scorers	Att
SF	Dec	12	(h)	Clyde	W 2-0	Redford 2	4,500
F	May	13	(h)	Celtic	L 1-2	Garner (og)	5,000

	Appearances / Sub / Goals per player (see grid)
Appearances	1, 2, 1, 1, 1, 1, 1, 1, 1, 1, 1, 1, 1, 1, 1, 1, 1, 1, 1, 1
Sub appearances	2, 1, 1
Goals	2

1 own-goal

Further match details for this season are continued on page 282

1982-83

Manager: J.Greig

Player columns (left to right): Stewart, McKinnon, Dawson, McClelland, Paterson, Bett, Cooper, Prytz, McAdam, Redford, McDonald, Johnstone, Russell, McKay, Black, McPherson, Stevens, Robertson, Dalziel, Kennedy, Smith, McCloy, Davies, Lyall, Clark A, Bruce, Miller, Forsyth T, Ferguson D

Scottish League

#	Date		Opponent	Result	Scorers	Att.
1	Sep	4 (a)	Motherwell	D 2-2	Prytz (pen), Redford	19,159
2		11 (h)	Dundee U	D 0-0		22,200
3		18 (h)	Kilmarnock	W 5-0	McDonald 2, Russell, Johnstone, McClelland	17,350
4		25 (a)	Aberdeen	W 2-1	Johnstone, Prytz	20,300
5	Oct	2 (h)	Dundee	D 1-1	Johnstone	18,100
6		9 (a)	Morton	D 0-0		11,500
7		16 (a)	St Mirren	D 2-2	Bett, McKinnon	12,121
8		23 (h)	Hibernian	W 3-2	Johnstone 2, McNamara (og)	16,250
9		30 (a)	Celtic	L 2-3	Prytz, Cooper	60,408
10	Nov	6 (a)	Motherwell	W 4-0	McDonald 2, Dalziel 2	17,000
11		13 (a)	Dundee U	L 2-4	Cooper, Johnstone	16,470
12		20 (a)	Kilmarnock	D 0-0		9,194
13		27 (h)	Aberdeen	L 0-1		27,000
14	Dec	11 (a)	Morton	D 1-1	Prytz (pen)	9,500
15		18 (h)	St Mirren	W 1-0	McDonald	10,500
16		27 (a)	Hibernian	D 0-0		15,900
17	Jan	1 (h)	Celtic	L 1-2	Black	45,000
18		3 (a)	Motherwell	L 0-3		11,383
19		8 (a)	Dundee U	W 2-1	Prytz, Kennedy	15,500
20		15 (h)	Kilmarnock	D 1-1	McDonald	11,223
21		22 (a)	Aberdeen	L 0-2		21,600
22	Feb	5 (h)	Dundee	D 1-1	McPherson	8,500
23		12 (a)	Morton	W 5-0	Bett 2, Kennedy 2, McDonald	6,900
24		26 (a)	St Mirren	L 0-1		11,484
25	Mar	2 (a)	Dundee	L 0-1		6,624
26		5 (h)	Hibernian	D 1-1	Dalziel	10,975
27		19 (a)	Motherwell	W 1-0	McClelland	18,000
28		23 (a)	Celtic	D 0-0		51,062
29		26 (a)	Kilmarnock	W 1-0	McDonald	6,648
30	Apr	2 (a)	Dundee U	L 1-3	Clark	14,142
31		9 (h)	Aberdeen	W 2-1	Redford, Bett	19,800
32		23 (h)	Morton	W 2-0	McDonald, Redford	9,500
33		30 (a)	St Mirren	W 4-0	Bett 2, McDonald, Clark	9,321
34	May	4 (a)	Dundee	L 1-2	Clark	4,788
35		7 (a)	Hibernian	W 2-1	Cooper 2	10,500
36		14 (h)	Celtic	L 2-4	Clark 2	40,500

FINAL LEAGUE POSITION: 4th

Scottish League totals:

	Ste	McK	Daw	McCl	Pat	Bet	Coo	Pry	McA	Red	McD	Joh	Rus	McKay	Bla	McP	Stev	Rob	Dal	Ken	Smi	McCl	Dav	Lya	ClkA	Bru
Appearances	18	30	24	35	20	35	26	24	2	29	27	16	18	2	11	15	10	2	7	12	1	17	2	2	10	1
Sub appearances	1	1					5	7	2	5	3			3	3	4	5	2	8	1	1		2	2		
Goals		1			2	6	4	5		3	10	6	1		1	1			3	3					5	

1 own-goal

Scottish FA Cup

#	Date		Opponent	Result	Scorers	Att.
3	Jan	29 (a)	Falkirk	W 2-0	Kennedy, Oliver (og)	14,700
4	Feb	19 (a)	Forfar A	W 2-1	McDonald 2	14,500
QF	Mar	12 (a)	Queen's Park	W 2-1	Dalziel, Cooper	13,716
SF	Apr	16(n*)	St Mirren	D 1-1	Clark	31,102
R		19(n†)	St Mirren	W 1-0	Clark	25,725
F	May	21(n†)	Aberdeen	L 0-1		62,979

*Played at Celtic Park, Glasgow.
†Played at Hampden Park, Glasgow.

Scottish FA Cup totals:

	Ste	McK	Daw	McCl	Pat	Bet	Coo	Pry	McA	Red	McD	Joh	Rus	McKay	Bla	McP	Stev	Rob	Dal	Ken	Smi	McCl	Dav	Lya	ClkA	Bru
Appearances	4	5	6	4	6	5	3		5	2	1	3		2	5	1			2	3		6			3	
Sub appearances								1	1		1						1	2				1	1			
Goals							1				2								1	1					2	

1 own-goal

Scottish League Cup

#	Date		Opponent	Result	Scorers	Att.
1	Aug	14 (a)	Hibernian	D 1-1	McDonald	15,980
2		18 (h)	Airdrieonians	W 3-1	Bett, Paterson, Black	9,500
3		21 (a)	Clydebank	W 4-1	McDonald 2, Prytz, McClelland	7,090
4		25 (a)	Airdrieonians	W 2-1	Dalziel, Paterson	6,476
5		28 (h)	Hibernian	D 0-0		17,600
6	Sep	1 (h)	Clydebank	W 3-2	McDonald, Prytz (pen), Redford	6,300
QF1		22 (a)	Kilmarnock	W 6-1	Cooper 4, McDonald 2	7,903
QF2	Oct	6 (h)	Kilmarnock	W 6-0	McDonald 2, Johnstone 2, McPherson, Bett (pen)	5,342
SF1		27 (h)	Hearts	W 2-0	Cooper, Bett	25,500
SF2	Nov	10 (a)	Hearts	W 2-1	Bett (pen), Johnstone	18,983
F	Dec	4(n*)	Celtic	L 1-2	Bett	55,372

*Played at Hampden Park, Glasgow.

Scottish League Cup totals:

	Ste	McK	Daw	McCl	Pat	Bet	Coo	Pry	McA	Red	McD	Joh	Rus	McKay	Bla	McP	Stev	Rob	Dal	Ken	Smi	McCl	Dav	Lya	ClkA	Bru
Appearances	11	11	3	11	9	11	9	9	5	10	9	5	5		5	1	2		2	1	1				1	
Sub appearances			3						1	1		2		2	1	1			1	1			3	1		
Goals				1	2	5	5	2		1	8	3			1	1				1						

UEFA Cup

#	Date		Opponent	Result	Scorers	Att.
1	Sep	15 (a)	Borussia Dortmund	D 0-0		54,000
		29 (h)	Borussia Dortmund	W 2-0	Cooper, Johnstone	44,500
2	Oct	20 (h)	1.FC Cologne	W 2-1	Johnstone, McClelland	30,420
	Nov	3 (a)	1.FC Cologne	L 0-5		61,000

UEFA Cup totals:

	Ste	McK	Daw	McCl	Pat	Bet	Coo	Pry	McA	Red	McD	Joh	Rus	McKay	Bla	McP	Stev	Rob	Dal	Ken	Smi	McCl	Dav	Lya	ClkA	Bru
Appearances	4	4	4	4	3	4	4	4		3	1	4	4			1									1	
Sub appearances									1	1	2					1										
Goals			1		1						2															

Tournoi De Nord (Lille, France)

#	Date		Opponent	Result	Scorers	Att.
SF	Jul	27 (a)	AS Saint-Etienne	D 0-0*		10,000
F		29(n†)	SC Lokeren	L 1-2	Paterson	12,000

*Rangers won 6-5 on penalties.
†Played at Lille, France.

Tournoi De Nord totals:

	Ste	McK	Daw	McCl	Pat	Bet	Coo	Pry	McA	Red	McD	Joh	Rus	McKay	Bla	McP	Stev	Rob	Dal	Ken	Smi	McCl	Dav	Lya	ClkA	Bru
Appearances	1	2	2	2	2	2			2	2	2														1	2
Sub appearances												2													1	
Goals					1																					

Further match details for this season are continued on page 282

1983-84

Manager: J.Greig/J.Wallace

Scottish League

Player columns (left to right): McCloy, Dawson, McClelland, McPherson, Paterson, Redford, Prytz, McCoist, Clark, Russell, Cooper, McDonald, Davies, McKinnon, Mitchell, Stewart, Nicholl, Lyall, Stevens, Ferguson D, Kennedy, McAdam, Williamson, Walker, Burns, Fraser S, McKay, Munro, Fleck, Ferguson E, Black, Leeman

#	Date		Opponent	Result	Scorers	Att.
1	Aug	20 (h)	St Mirren	D 1-1	Prytz (pen)	21,500
2	Sep	3 (a)	Celtic	L 1-2	McCoist	50,662
3		10 (a)	Hearts	L 1-3	Mitchell	16,173
4		17 (a)	Aberdeen	L 0-2		27,500
5		24 (h)	St Johnstone	W 6-3	McCoist 2, McClelland, Prytz (pen), Cooper, Clark	12,500
6	Oct	1 (a)	Dundee U	W 2-0	Clark, Hegarty (og)	16,738
7		8 (h)	Hibernian	W 1-0	McClelland	21,800
8		15 (a)	Dundee	L 2-3	Russell, Redford	11,945
9		22 (h)	Motherwell	L 1-2	McCoist (pen)	15,000
10		29 (h)	St Mirren	L 0-3		12,068
11	Nov	5 (h)	Celtic	L 1-2	Clark	42,000
12		12 (a)	Aberdeen	L 0-3		22,771
13		19 (h)	Dundee U	D 0-0		27,800
14		26 (a)	St Johnstone	W 1-0	Redford	9,740
15	Dec	3 (h)	Hearts	W 3-0	Clark 2, McDonald	22,500
16		10 (a)	Motherwell	W 3-0	McAdam, Cooper, Mitchell	13,586
17		17 (h)	Dundee	W 2-1	Russell, Williamson	16,500
18		27 (a)	Hibernian	W 2-0	Williamson, Cooper	20,820
19		31 (h)	St Mirren	D 1-1	Clark	21,200
20	Jan	7 (a)	Aberdeen	D 1-1	Cooper (pen)	37,500
21		21 (h)	St Johnstone	W 2-0	Clark, Russell	18,001
22	Feb	4 (h)	Motherwell	W 2-1	McCoist, Prytz (pen)	17,000
23		11 (a)	Hearts	D 2-2	McCoist, Williamson	18,063
24		25 (a)	Dundee	W 3-1	Russell, Cooper, McPherson	11,750
25	Mar	3 (h)	Hibernian	D 0-0		17,000
26		6 (a)	St Johnstone	W 4-1	Redford, Clark, Davies, McCoist	5,293
27		31 (h)	Motherwell	W 3-0	Paterson, McPherson, Burns	8,574
28	Apr	2 (a)	Celtic	L 0-3		53,229
29		7 (h)	Hearts	D 0-0		22,000
30		21 (h)	Celtic	W 1-0	Williamson	40,260
31		28 (a)	St Mirren	D 1-1	Williamson	8,092
32	May	2 (a)	Dundee U	D 2-2	Clark, Williamson	7,500
33		5 (h)	Dundee	D 2-2	Redford, Cooper	17,000
34		9 (a)	Aberdeen	D 0-0		16,200
35		12 (a)	Hibernian	D 0-0		10,567
36		14 (a)	Dundee U	W 2-1	Prytz (pen), McCoist	6,457

FINAL LEAGUE POSITION: 4th

Appearance summary (by player column):

	McCloy	Dawson	McClelland	McPherson	Paterson	Redford	Prytz	McCoist	Clark	Russell	Cooper	McDonald	Davies	McKinnon	Mitchell	Stewart	Nicholl	Lyall	Stevens	Ferguson D	Kennedy	McAdam	Williamson	Walker	Burns	Fraser S	McKay	Munro	Fleck	Ferguson E	Black	Leeman
Appearances	26	28	36	32	21	28	22	29	27	27	32	2		12	7	2	17	1	1		8	16	8		7	1	2	1	2			
Sub appearances				4		4	4	1	3	4	2	16	3	5	5					2		1	5			1	3	2				
Goals		2	2	1	4	4	8	9	4	6	1	1			2							1	6		1							

1 own-goal

Scottish FA Cup

#	Date		Opponent	Result	Scorers	Att.
3	Jan	21 (h)	Dunfermline A	W 2-1	McAdam, McCoist	17,500
4	Feb	18 (a)	Caledonian	W 6-0	Williamson 2, McCoist 2, Redford, Russell	5,500
QF	Mar	10 (a)	Dundee	D 2-2	Russell, McGeachie (og)	17,097
R		17 (h)	Dundee	L 2-3	McPherson, McClelland	25,000

Appearances: 1 3 4 3 1 4 3 3 1 4 3 1 — 4 — 1 3 3 — 1 1 (by column)
Sub appearances: 1 — 1 1 3 — 1 1 —
Goals: 1 1 1 3 2 — 1 2

1 own-goal

Scottish League Cup

#	Date		Opponent	Result	Scorers	Att.
2	Aug	24 (h)	Queen of South	W 4-0	McDonald 2, Clark, Prytz (pen)	8,000
		27 (a)	Queen of South	W 4-1	Mitchell, McKinnon, Cooper, McCoist	7,350
1		31 (h)	Clydebank	W 4-0	McCoist 2, Russell, Prytz	8,500
2	Sep	7 (a)	Hearts	W 3-0	Clark 2, Gauld (og)	11,287
3	Oct	5 (h)	St Mirren	W 5-0	McCoist 2, Clark, McClelland, Paterson	11,500
4		26 (h)	Hearts	W 2-0	Prytz, Mitchell	12,000
5	Nov	9 (a)	Clydebank	W 3-0	Cooper, McCoist, McPherson	3,612
6		30 (a)	St Mirren	W 1-0	Cooper	5,446
SF1	Feb	15 (a)	Dundee U	D 1-1	Mitchell	14,569
SF2		22 (h)	Dundee U	W 2-0	Clark, Redford	35,950
F	Mar	25 (n*)	Celtic	W 3-2	McCoist 3 (1 pen)	66,369

*Played at Hampden Park, Glasgow.
All but first two games in Section Two

Appearances: 10 10 11 9 8 7 6 10 8 9 9 4 — 4 6 1 5 1 1 1 1 (by column)
Sub appearances: 1 — 1 2 — 2 1 2 1 — 2 — 1 1 — 1 — 2 1 — 1
Goals: 1 1 1 1 3 9 5 1 3 2 — 1 3

1 own-goal

European Cup-winners' Cup

#	Date		Opponent	Result	Scorers	Att.
1	Sep	14 (a)	Valletta FC	W 8-0	McPherson 4, Prytz 2 (1 pen), Paterson, McDonald	18,213
		28 (h)	Valletta FC	W 10-0	McDonald 3 (1 pen), Mitchell 2, Redford 2, Dawson, McKay, Davies	11,500
2	Oct	19 (h)	FC Porto	W 2-1	Clark, Mitchell	27,800
	Nov	2 (a)	FC Porto	L 0-1*		63,000

*Rangers lost on the away-goals rule

Appearances: 3 4 4 4 4 3 4 2 3 2 4 2 1 2 1 1 (by column)
Sub appearances: 1 — 1 1 2 — 2 — 1
Goals: 1 — 4 1 2 2 — 1 — 4 1 3 — 1

World Soccer Series

#	Date		Opponent	Result	Scorers	Att.
1	May	27 (a*)	Australia 'B'	D 0-0		15,000
2		31 (a†)	Australia 'B'	W 2-1	Clark, I.Ferguson	10,000
3	Jun	2 (a‡)	Australia	L 2-3	McCoist 2 (1 pen)	9,000
4		5 (a§)	Australia 'B'	D 1-1	McClelland	5,000

* Played at Melbourne; †Played at Brisbane; ‡Played at Sydney; §Played at Adelaide.

Appearances: 3 2 2 4 4 3 4 2 2 2 2 3 2 1 2 2 1 (by column)
Sub appearances: 1 1 1 1 1 1 1
Goals: 2 1 1

I.Ferguson played number-9 in Match 1, number-8 in Match 2, scoring one goal, number-9 in Match 3 and number-12 in Match 4.

Further match details for this season are continued on page 282

1984-85

Manager: J.Wallace

	Date	Opponent	Result	Scorers	Scottish League	Walker	Burns	Dawson	McKinnon	McClelland	Redford	McDonald	Fraser C	Ferguson I (1)	McCoist	Cooper	Fraser S	Ferguson E	Paterson	Russell	Clark	McPherson	Mitchell	McCloy	Prytz	McMinn	Fleck	Munro	Ferguson D	Johnstone	Williamson	McFarlane	Bruce	Durrant	Davies
1	Aug 11	(h) St Mirren	D 0-0		22,398	1	**2**	3	4	5	6	**7**	8	9	10	11	14	12																	
2	18	(a) Dumbarton	W 2-1	McCoist, Redford	9,607	1	2	3	4	5	6	12	8	**9**	10	11	14	**7**																	
3	25	(h) Celtic	D 0-0		43,500	1	14	3	2	4	6		8	10	12	11			5	**7**	**9**														
4	Sep 1	(a) Dundee	W 2-0	I.Ferguson, Redford	14,156	1		3	2	4	6		8	9	**10**	11			5	**7**		14	12												
5	8	(h) Hibernian	W 2-0	Paterson, McDonald	22,601	1		3	2	4	6	14	8	**10**		11			5	7		12	**9**												
6	15	(a) Aberdeen	D 0-0		23,500	1		3	2	4	6	14	8	**9**	10	11			5	**7**		12													
7	22	(h) Morton	W 2-0	McCoist, C.Fraser	16,995			3	2		6	12	8	9	10	11			5	**7**		4		1											
8	29	(h) Dundee U	W 1-0	Paterson	29,232			3	2	4	6	14	**8**	9	**10**	11			5	12		7		1											
9	Oct 6	(a) Hearts	L 0-1		18,097			3	2	4	6	**10**	14	12	8	11			5	7			**9**	1											
10	13	(a) St Mirren	W 2-0	Redford, I.Ferguson	14,389				2	3	6		8	9	**10**	11			5	12		4		1	**7**	14									
11	20	(h) Dumbarton	D 0-0		16,521			2		3	6		**8**	**9**	10	11			5	12		4		1		7	14								
12	Nov 3	(h) Dundee	D 0-0		14,588			2		3	6		8	9	**10**	11			5	**7**		4	14	1	12										
13	10	(a) Hibernian	D 2-2	C.Fraser, Cooper	14,000				2		6		8	**9**		11			5	12		4	10	1	**7**		14	3							
14	17	(h) Aberdeen	L 1-2	Mitchell	44,000			3	2		6		8	**10**		11			5	12		4	9	1	**7**	14									
15	24	(a) Morton	W 3-1	Redford 2, Dawson	11,000			3	2		6		8	12		11			5			4	9	1		7	**10**								
16	Dec 1	(a) Dundee U	D 1-1	Mitchell	16,477			3	**2**		6	10	8			11			5			4	9	1	12	7									
17	8	(h) Hearts	D 1-1	Mitchell	16,700			3	2		6	12	**8**			11			5			4	**9**	1	10	7			14						
18	15	(h) St Mirren	W 2-0	C.Fraser, McDonald	12,763			3	2		6	14	8	**11**					5			**4**	9	1	12	7			10						
19	22	(a) Celtic	D 1-1	Cooper	43,748		2		5		**6**	7	8			11						4	**9**	1	14	12		3	10						
20	29	(h) Dumbarton	W 4-2	I.Ferguson, McMinn, Mitchell, Cooper	7,800		2		5			**10**		9	14	11						4	12	1	6	7		3	**8**						
21	Jan 1	(h) Celtic	L 1-2	Cooper	45,000		2	14	5		6	12		9		11						4		1	10	**7**		3	**8**						
22	5	(a) Dundee	D 2-2	I.Ferguson 2	11,991		**2**	3	4					10	14	11			5			12	**9**	1	6	7			8						
23	12	(h) Hibernian	L 1-2	I.Ferguson	18,500			3	2			12		10		**11**			5	14		4	9	1	6	**7**			8						
24	19	(a) Aberdeen	L 1-5	Prytz	23,000	1		3	2		14	**10**			7	11			5			4			6	12			**8**	9					
25	Feb 2	(h) Morton	W 2-0	McDonald, Johnstone	14,121	1			2		**6**	10	8		7	11			5			4				12		3		9					
26	9	(h) Dundee U	D 0-0		19,370	1			2		6	**10**	8		7	11			5			4						3		9	12				
27	23	(a) Hearts	L 0-2		14,004		2	3	4		10	12	8	9		11				14				1	**6**	**7**				5					
28	Mar 2	(h) Dumbarton	W 3-1	McCoist 2, E.Ferguson	8,424		2		3				6	10	8	**11**		9				4		1		7	14			**5**		12			
29	16	(a) St Mirren	L 1-2	McCoist	8,608		2						**6**	10	8			9				4			11	7	12			5		3	1		
30	23	(h) Dundee	L 1-3	McCoist	9,954	1	2						6	10	8			**9**		14		4			**11**	7	12	3		5					
31	Apr 6	(h) Aberdeen	L 1-2	Prytz	23,437	1		2			**6**		8	9	**10**	11				12		4			7		14	3		5					
32	20	(a) Morton	W 3-0	McCoist 3	7,000	1		2			12		8	9	10	11						4			7			3		5				**6**	
33	27	(h) Hearts	W 3-1	McCoist, Prytz (pen), Cooper	12,913		14	2	5				8	12	10	11		**9**				4		1	7			**3**						6	
34	May 1	(a) Celtic	D 1-1	McCoist (pen)	40,079		14	2	8					12	10	11		**9**		**7**		4		1				3		5				6	
35	4	(a) Dundee U	L 1-2	McCoist	10,251	1	2		8						10			**9**		7		4			11	14	12	3		**5**				6	
36	11	(a) Hibernian	L 0-1		7,149	1	14	2	8						10	11		**9**	5			4			7	12		**3**						6	
FINAL LEAGUE POSITION: 4th					Appearances	14	11	25	30	11	24	8	27	24	22	32		8	22	9	1	27	11	21	17	13	1	13	7	11		1	1	5	
					Sub appearances		4	1			2	10	1	4	3		2	1		9		4	3		4	7	7		1		1	1			
					Goals			1			5	3	3	6	12	5		1	2				4		3	1				1					

Scottish FA Cup

	Date	Opponent	Result	Scorers	Att	Walker	Burns	Dawson	McKinnon	McClelland	Redford	McDonald	Fraser C	Ferguson I	McCoist	Cooper	Fraser S	Ferguson E	Paterson	Russell	Clark	McPherson	Mitchell	McCloy	Prytz	McMinn	Fleck	Munro	Ferguson D	Johnstone	Williamson	McFarlane	Bruce	Durrant	Davies
3	Jan 26	(a) Morton	D 3-3	Prytz, McDonald, McPherson	12,012	1			2			10	8		7	11						5	**9**		6		12	3				4			
R	30	(h) Morton	W 3-1	Mitchell, C.Fraser, McDonald	18,166	1			2			**10**	8		**7**	11			4	12		5	9		6		14	3							
4	Feb 16	(h) Dundee	L 0-1		26,619				2		6	**10**	8	14	7	11			**5**			4		1	12			3		9					
					Appearances	2			3		1	3	3		3	3			2			3	2	1	2			3		1		1			
					Sub appearances									1						1					1		2								
					Goals							2	1									1	1		1										

Scottish League Cup

	Date	Opponent	Result	Scorers	Att	Walker	Burns	Dawson	McKinnon	McClelland	Redford	McDonald	Fraser C	Ferguson I	McCoist	Cooper	Fraser S	Ferguson E	Paterson	Russell	Clark	McPherson	Mitchell	McCloy	Prytz	McMinn	Fleck	Munro	Ferguson D	Johnstone	Williamson	McFarlane	Bruce	Durrant	Davies
2	Aug 22	(h) Falkirk	W 1-0	McPherson	10,429	1	12		2	3	**6**		8	9	10	11			5	**7**	14	4													
3	29	(h) Raith Rovers	W 4-0	McCoist 2 (1 pen), Paterson, Redford	10,132	1		3	**2**	4	6		8	9	10	**11**			5	7		12	14												
QF	Sep 5	(a) Cowdenbeath	W 3-1	I.Ferguson, Russell, Redford	9,925	1		3	2	4	6		**8**	10	**9**	11			5	7		12	14												
SF1	26	(h) Meadowbank T	W 4-0	McCoist 2, I.Ferguson, C.Fraser	12,600			3	2	4	6	12	8	10	7	11					**9**	5		1											
SF2	Oct 9	(a*) Meadowbank T	D 1-1	McCoist	5,100			3	2		6		8	**9**	10	14			5	12		4		1	**7**			11							
F	28	(n†) Dundee U	W 1-0	I.Ferguson	44,698			2		3	6		8	**9**	10	11			5	**7**		4	14	1	12										
					Appearances	3		5	5	5	6		6	6	6	5			5	4	1	4		3	1			1							
					Sub appearances		1					1				1				1	1	2	3		1										
					Goals						2		1	3	5				1	1		1													

*Played at Tynecastle Park, Edinburgh.
†Played at Hampden Park, Glasgow.

UEFA Cup

	Date	Opponent	Result	Scorers	Att	Walker	Burns	Dawson	McKinnon	McClelland	Redford	McDonald	Fraser C	Ferguson I	McCoist	Cooper	Fraser S	Ferguson E	Paterson	Russell	Clark	McPherson	Mitchell	McCloy	Prytz	McMinn	Fleck	Munro	Ferguson D	Johnstone	Williamson	McFarlane	Bruce	Durrant	Davies
1	Sep 18	(a) Bohemians D	L 2-3	McCoist, McPherson	10,000	1		3	2	4	6	14	8	12	**10**	11			5		**9**	7													
	Oct 3	(h) Bohemians D	W 2-0	Paterson, Redford	31,000			3	2	4	6		14	**9**	**10**	11			5	7		8	12	1											
2	24	(a) Internazionale	L 0-3		65,591			2		3	6		8	12	**9**	11			5	**7**		4		1	10		14								
	Nov 7	(h) Internazionale	W 3-1	I.Ferguson 2, Mitchell	30,594			2	7	3	6		8	**9**	12				5			4	10	1	**11**			14							
					Appearances	1		4	3	4	4		3	2	3	3			4	2	1	4	1	3	2										
					Sub appearances							1	1	2	1								1				1	1							
					Goals						1			2	1				1			1	1												

Glasgow Cup

	Date	Opponent	Result	Scorers	Att	Walker	Burns	Dawson	McKinnon	McClelland	Redford	McDonald	Fraser C	Ferguson I	McCoist	Cooper	Fraser S	Ferguson E	Paterson	Russell	Clark	McPherson	Mitchell	McCloy	Prytz	McMinn	Fleck	Munro	Ferguson D	Johnstone	Williamson	McFarlane	Bruce	Durrant	Davies
SF	May 13	(a) Partick Thistle	W 2-1	McPherson, McCoist	3,264	1	**2**	3	8					12	10	**11**			5	7		4				14				9				6	
Final postponed until 1985-86 season.					Appearances	1	1	1	1						1	1			1	1		1								1				1	
					Sub appearances									1												1									
					Goals										1							1													

Further match details for this season are continued on page 283

1985-86

Manager: J.Wallace/G.Souness

Scottish League

#	Date	V	Opponent	Result	Scorers	Att
1	Aug 10	(h)	Dundee U	W 1-0	McCoist	28,035
2	17	(a)	Hibernian	W 3-1	McCoist, McPherson, Williamson	14,500
3	24	(h)	Hearts	W 3-1	Williamson 2, Burns	35,483
4	31	(a)	Celtic	D 1-1	McCoist	58,365
5	Sep 7	(h)	St Mirren	W 3-0	Fleck, Cooper, Burns	27,707
6	14	(a)	Clydebank	W 1-0	Williamson	9,980
7	21	(h)	Dundee	L 0-1		23,600
8	28	(h)	Aberdeen	L 0-3		37,599
9	Oct 5	(a)	Motherwell	W 3-0	McCoist 2, McPherson	12,711
10	12	(h)	Dundee U	D 1-1	McCoist	15,821
11	19	(h)	Hibernian	L 1-2	Cooper (pen)	23,478
12	26	(a)	St Mirren	L 1-2	McCoist	13,911
13	Nov 2	(h)	Clydebank	D 0-0		16,943
14	9	(h)	Celtic	W 3-0	Durrant, Cooper, McCoist	42,045
15	16	(h)	Hearts	L 0-3		23,083
16	23	(a)	Dundee	L 2-3	McCoist 2	10,798
17	Dec 7	(h)	Motherwell	W 1-0	McCoist	12,872
18	14	(h)	Dundee U	D 1-1	McCoist	17,786
19	21	(a)	Hibernian	D 1-1	Cooper	10,823
20	28	(h)	Hearts	L 0-2		33,410
21	Jan 1	(a)	Celtic	L 0-2		49,812
22	4	(h)	Dundee	W 5-0	McCoist 3, Williamson, Fleck	13,954
23	11	(h)	Clydebank	W 4-2	Paterson, McPherson, Williamson, McCoist	12,731
24	18	(h)	St Mirren	W 2-0	McCoist, McPherson	17,528
25	Feb 1	(h)	Aberdeen	D 1-1	Burns	29,887
26	8	(a)	Motherwell	L 0-1		11,619
27	19	(a)	Aberdeen	L 0-1		19,500
28	22	(a)	Dundee U	D 1-1	McCoist	14,644
29	Mar 1	(h)	Hibernian	W 3-1	McCoist 3 (1 pen)	16,574
30	15	(a)	Dundee	L 1-2	McCoist	10,965
31	22	(h)	Celtic	D 4-4	Fraser 2, McCoist, Fleck	41,006
32	29	(a)	Hearts	L 1-3	McCoist (pen)	24,735
33	Apr 12	(a)	Clydebank	L 1-2	Durrant	7,027
34	19	(a)	St Mirren	L 1-2	Dawson	9,760
35	26	(a)	Aberdeen	D 1-1	McMinn	17,000
36	May 3	(h)	Motherwell	W 2-0	McPherson, McCoist (pen)	21,500

Final League Position: 5th

	Walker	Burns	Munro	McPherson D	Paterson	Durrant	McCoist	Russell	Williamson	Ferguson D	Cooper	McMinn	McKinnon	Bell	Fleck	Dawson	Ferguson I (†)	Fraser C	Beattie	Johnstone	Nisbet	Miller	Ferguson E	McDonald	McCloy	Bruce	McFarlane	Davies
Appearances	34	26	28	34	18	30	33	17	20	12	28	15	18	20	9	23	1	7	5	8	4	2		2	2			
Sub appearances		2	1					10	3	7	4	13	6	3	6	1	3	1		1		1						
Goals		3		5	1	2	25		6		4	1			3	1		2										

Scottish FA Cup

#	Date	V	Opponent	Result	Scorers	Att
3	Jan 25	(a)	Hearts	L 2-3	McCoist, Durrant	27,500

	Walker	Burns	Munro	McPherson D	Paterson	Durrant	McCoist	Russell	Williamson	Ferguson D	Cooper	McMinn	McKinnon	Bell	Fleck	Dawson	Ferguson I	Fraser C	Beattie	Johnstone
Appearances	1	1		1	1	1	1		1	1	1							1		1
Sub Appearances											1									
Goals						1	1													

Scottish League Cup

#	Date	V	Opponent	Result	Scorers	Att
2	Aug 21	(h)	Clyde	W 5-0	Williamson 3 (1 pen), McCoist, Paterson	11,350
3	27	(a*)	Forfar A	D 2-2	Cooper (pen), Williamson	7,283
QF	Sep 4	(a†)	Hamilton A	W 2-1	Williamson 2	12,392
SF1	25	(a)	Hibernian	L 0-2		17,916
SF2	Oct 9	(h)	Hibernian	W 1-0	Cooper	39,282

*Played at Dens Park, Dundee, Rangers won 6-5 on penalties.
†Played at Fir Park, Motherwell.

	Walker	Burns	Munro	McPherson D	Paterson	Durrant	McCoist	Russell	Williamson	Ferguson D	Cooper	McMinn	McKinnon	Bell	Fleck	Dawson	Ferguson I	Fraser C
Appearances	5	4	5	5	4	5	4	4	5		4	1	2	4		1	1	1
Sub Appearances									1		1		1	1		1	1	
Goals					1		1		6		2							

UEFA Cup

#	Date	V	Opponent	Result	Scorers	Att
1	Sep 18	(h)	CA Osasuna	W 1-0	Paterson	29,479
	Oct 2	(a)	CA Osasuna	L 0-2		25,600

	Walker	Burns	Munro	McPherson D	Paterson	Durrant	McCoist	Russell	Williamson	Ferguson D	Cooper	McMinn	McKinnon	Bell	Fleck	Dawson
Appearances	2	2	2	2	2	1	2	2	1		2		2		1	1
Sub appearances									1			2				1
Goals					1											

Glasgow Cup

#	Date	V	Opponent	Result	Scorers	Att
F*	Sep 9	(a)	Queen's Park	W 5-0	Fraser 3, McCoist (pen), I.Ferguson	3,584
SF	Nov 12	(a)	Queen's Park	W 2-1	McCoist 2	1,724
F	May 9	(h)	Celtic	W 3-2	McCoist 3	40,741

*1984-85 Final

	Walker	Burns	Munro	McPherson D	Paterson	Durrant	McCoist	Russell	Williamson	Ferguson D	Cooper	McMinn	McKinnon	Bell	Fleck	Dawson	Ferguson I	Fraser C	Beattie	Johnstone	Nisbet	Miller	Ferguson E	McDonald	McCloy
Appearances	2	1	2	2		1	3	1	1	1	3	2	1	3	1	2		1		1		1		1	1
Sub Appearances									1								1	1							1
Goals							6										1	3							

Other matches

#	Date	V	Opponent	Result	Scorers	Att
1	Jul 27	(a)	Ross C	W 5-1	McCoist 2, Burns, Russell, D.Ferguson	2,700
2	29	(a)	Caledonian	W 6-0	McMinn 2, McCoist, Durrant, Williamson, Russell	3,000
3	Aug 3	(a)	Ayr U	W 2-1	Durrant, D.Ferguson	4,685
4	6	(h)	FC Twente	W 2-1	Paterson, McCoist	10,994
5	Nov 28	(a)	Hamrun Spartans	W 4-1	Nisbet 2, McCoist 2	1,200
6	Dec 1	(a)	Valletta FC	W 7-0	Nisbet 3, McCoist 2, Fleck, McKinnon	1,200
7	Feb 14	(h)	Chelsea	W 3-2	Paterson, Bell, Burns	17,512
8	Mar 11	(a)	Elgin City *	D 1-1	McMinn	2,500
9	Apr 6	(h)	Tottenham H	L 0-2		12,665

*Charles McHardy Testimonial Match.

	Walker	Burns	Munro	McPherson D	Paterson	Durrant	McCoist	Russell	Williamson	Ferguson D	Cooper	McMinn	McKinnon	Bell	Fleck	Dawson	Ferguson I	Fraser C	Beattie	Johnstone	Nisbet	Miller	Ferguson E	McDonald	McCloy	Bruce	McFarlane	Davies
Appearances	8	7	7	9	4	6	8	4	3	7	6	6	1	4	3	2	2	2	3	2	2	1		1	1			
Sub Appearances					1		2	4	2			1			1			1							1		2	
Goals		2		2	2	8	2	1	2			3	1	1	1						5							

1986-87

Manager: G.Souness

Scottish League

Player columns: Woods C, Dawson, Munro, Souness, McPherson D, Butcher, Russell, West, McCoist, Durrant, McMinn, Ferguson D, Fleck, Nicholl, Fraser, Cooper, Burns, Walker, Nisbet, McFarlane, Bell, Paterson, Roberts, Woods N, Phillips, Kirkwood, Williamson, Cohen, McCloy, Miller

#		Date	Opponent	Res	Scorers	Att	WoodsC	Dawson	Munro	Souness	McPhersonD	Butcher	Russell	West	McCoist	Durrant	McMinn	FergusonD	Fleck	Nicholl	Fraser	Cooper	Burns	Walker	Nisbet	McFarlane	Bell	Paterson	Roberts	WoodsN	Phillips	Kirkwood	Williamson	Cohen	McCloy	Miller
1	Aug	9 (a) Hibernian	L 1-2	McCoist (pen)	24,576	1	2	3	4	5	6	7	8	9	10	11	12	14																	
2		13 (h) Falkirk	W 1-0	McCoist (pen)	27,362	1		3		5	6		8	9	10	11	4			2	7														
3		16 (h) Dundee U	L 2-3	McCoist 2	43,995	1		3	4	5	6		8	9	10		12			2	7	11													
4		23 (a) Hamilton A	W 2-1	Fraser, West	10,000	1	3			5	6		8	9	10		4			7	11	2													
5		31 (h) Celtic	W 1-0	Durrant	43,502	1								9	10	8	4			2	7	11													
6	Sep	6 (a) Motherwell	W 2-0	Cooper, D.McPherson	17,013			3	4	5	6			9	10	8			12	2	7	11		1											
7		13 (h) Clydebank	W 4-0	Fleck 3, McMinn	26,433			3	4	5	6			**9**	10	14	12	8		2	7	**11**		1											
8		20 (a) Dundee	L 0-1		17,132	1	6	3		5				9	10		4		8	2	7	11			12										
9		27 (h) Aberdeen	W 2-0	Souness, McCoist	40,155	1	12	3	4	5	6			9	10	**8**			14	2	7	11													
10	Oct	4 (a) Hearts	D 1-1	Cooper	28,637	1		3		5	6			9	10				8	2	7	11					4	12							
11		8 (a) St Mirren	W 1-0	Cooper	16,861	1		3	12	5	6			9	10			7	8	2		11					4								
12		11 (h) Hibernian	W 3-0	D.McPherson, Fleck, Bell	38,196	1		3	**4**	5	6			9	10			7	8	2		**11**					12	14							
13		18 (a) Falkirk	W 5-1	Fleck 3 (1 pen), Cooper (pen), McCoist	16,800	1		3		5	6			9	10			4	8	2		11					7								
14		29 (a) Dundee U	D 0-0		20,179	1	5	3			6			9	10	**8**			14	2	4	11					12	7							
15	Nov	1 (a) Celtic	D 1-1	McCoist	60,000	1		3		5	6			9	10	14	4	8	2	7	**11**						12								
16		8 (h) Motherwell	L 0-1		33,966	1		3		5	6			9	10			4	8	2	7	11					12								
17		15 (a) Clydebank	W 4-1	McCoist 2, D.McPherson, Durrant	9,906	1		3		5	6			9	**10**	12			8	2	4	11					7								
18		19 (h) Dundee	W 2-1	McCoist, D.McPherson	22,992	1		3		5	6			9	**10**	12			8	2	4	11					7								
19		22 (a) Aberdeen	L 0-1		21,733	1		3		5	6			9	10			4	12	2	7	11					8								
20		29 (h) Hearts	W 3-0	McCoist, Cooper, Durrant	38,733	1		3			6		14	9	**10**			7	8	2		11	4				12	5							
21	Dec	3 (h) St Mirren	W 2-0	D.McPherson, Cooper	23,110	1		3		5	6			9		10	7	8				11	2				4								
22		6 (a) Hibernian	D 0-0		18,536	1		3		5	6			9		12	7	8				11	2				10	4							
23		13 (h) Falkirk	W 4-0	Fleck 2, Cooper, Butcher	24,177	1	2	3		5	6			9		10	4	8		7	11															
24		20 (a) Hamilton A	W 2-0	Fleck, McCoist	10,000			3	4	5	6		12	9		10	7	8	2			11														
25		27 (h) Dundee U	W 2-0	McCoist, Fleck	42,165	1		3	4	5	6			9	10			7	8			11						2								
26	Jan	1 (h) Celtic	W 2-0	Fleck, McCoist	43,206	1		3	4	5	6			9	10			7	8			11						2								
27		6 (a) Motherwell	W 1-0	Roberts	19,658	1		3	4	5	6			9	10			7	8			11						2								
28		10 (h) Clydebank	W 5-0	Fleck 3, McCoist 2 (1 pen)	36,397	1		3	4	5	6			9	10	12	7	8				**11**						2								
29		17 (h) Hamilton A	W 2-0	Durrant, McCoist	43,052	1		3		5	6			9	10			7	**8**	4		11						2	12							
30		24 (h) Aberdeen	D 0-0		43,211	1	10	3	4	5	6			**9**				7	8	2		11							12							
31	Feb	7 (a) Hearts	W 5-2	Fleck 2, Roberts, McCoist, Black (og)	29,000	1		3	4	5	6			9	10			8	7			11						2								
32		14 (a) St Mirren	W 3-1	McCoist 3 (1 pen)	21,399	1		3	4	5	6			9	10			**8**	7			11						2	12							
33		28 (h) Hibernian	D 1-1	D.McPherson	38,630	1		3	4	5	6			9	10			8	7			11						2								
34	Mar	7 (a) Falkirk	W 2-1	McCoist 2	18,000	1		3	4	5	6			9	10			8	7			11						2								
35		14 (h) Hamilton A	W 2-0	Cooper, McCoist	33,486	1		3	4	5	6			9	10			8	7			11						2								
36		17 (a) Dundee	W 4-0	McCoist 2, D.McPherson, Fleck	18,723	1		3	4	5	6			9	10			8	7			11						2								
37		21 (a) Dundee U	W 1-0	D.McPherson	21,275	1		3	4	5	6			9	10			8	7			11						2								
38		28 (h) Motherwell	W 1-0	McCoist	37,305	1		3	4	5	6		14	9	10		12	8	**7**			11						2								
39	Apr	4 (a) Celtic	L 1-3	McCoist	60,800	1		3	4	**5**	6			9	10		7	8	12			**11**						2		14						
40		14 (h) Dundee	W 2-0	Cooper, McCoist	42,427	1		3	**4**	5	6			9	10		2	8	7			11							12							
41		18 (a) Clydebank	W 3-0	McCoist 2 (1 pen), West	9,950	1		3		5	6		14	9	10		2	**8**	7			11						4	12							
42		25 (h) Hearts	W 3-0	McCoist 3 (1 pen)	43,205	1		3	4	5	6			9	10		2	8				11						7	12							
43	May	2 (a) Aberdeen	D 1-1	Butcher	22,568	1		3	4	5	6		14	**9**	10			**8**	7			11						2	12							
44		9 (h) St Mirren	W 1-0	Fleck	43,510	1		3		5	6			9	10		2	8	7			11						4	12	14						

Final League Position: 1st

	WoodsC	Dawson	Munro	Souness	McPhersonD	Butcher	Russell	West	McCoist	Durrant	McMinn	FergusonD	Fleck	Nicholl	Fraser	Cooper	Burns	Walker	Nisbet	McFarlane	Bell	Paterson	Roberts	WoodsN	Phillips	Kirkwood	Williamson	Cohen	McCloy	Miller
Appearances	42	6	43	24	42	43	1	4	44	39	9	26	35	33	16	42	4	2			2	7	2	18						
Sub appearances		1		1				5				6	4	5	1				1	2	5				3	6	1			
Goals				1	8	2			34	4	1		19			9					1		2							

1 own-goal

Scottish FA Cup

#	Date	Opponent	Res		Att	WoodsC	Munro	Souness	McPhersonD	Butcher	McCoist	Durrant	McMinn	Nicholl	Fraser	Cooper	Roberts
3	Jan 31 (h) Hamilton A		L 0-1		35,462	1	**3**	4	5	6	12	9	10	8	7	11	2
	Appearances					1	1	1	1	1		1	1	1	1	1	1
	Sub appearances										1						
	Goals																

Scottish League Cup

#	Date	Opponent	Res	Scorers	Att	WoodsC	Dawson	Munro	Souness	McPhersonD	Butcher	West	McCoist	Durrant	McMinn	FergusonD	Fleck	Nicholl	Fraser	Cooper	Nisbet
2	Aug 20 (a‡) Stenhousemuir	W 4-1	Souness, West, Cooper, McCoist	9,052	1		3		4	5	6	8	9	10		12		2	7	11	
3	27 (a) East Fife	D 0-0*		8,835	1	3	12			5	6	**8**	9	10	14	4			7	11	2
QF	Sep 3 (h) Dundee	W 3-1	Fraser, Souness, McMinn	33,750	1		3		4	5	6		9	10	8		12	2	7	11	
SF	24 (n†) Dundee U	W 2-1	McCoist, McMinn	45,249	1		3	4	5	6		9	10	8			12	2	7	11	
F	Oct 26 (n†) Celtic	W 2-1	Durrant, Cooper (pen)	74,219	1	5	3			6		9	10	8	7	14	2	4	11	

*Rangers won 5-4 on penalties. ‡Played at Brockville Park, Falkirk.
†Played at Hampden Park, Glasgow.

	WoodsC	Dawson	Munro	Souness	McPhersonD	Butcher	West	McCoist	Durrant	McMinn	FergusonD	Fleck	Nicholl	Fraser	Cooper	Nisbet
Appearances	5	3	3	3	4	5		2	5	5	3	2		4	5	5	1
Sub appearances			1								1	1	3		1	
Goals				2			1	2	1	2				1	2	

UEFA Cup

#	Date	Opponent	Res	Scorers	Att	WoodsC	Dawson	Munro	Souness	McPhersonD	Butcher	Russell	McCoist	Durrant	McMinn	FergusonD	Fleck	Nicholl	Fraser	Cooper	Nisbet	McFarlane	Miller
1	Sep 17 (h) Ilves Tampere	W 4-0	Fleck 3, McCoist	27,436	1		3		4	5	6		9	10	12		8	2	7	11			
	Oct 1 (a) Ilves Tampere	L 0-2		2,109	1		3			5	6	7	9	**10**			8	2		**11**	14	12	4
2	23 (h) Boavista	W 2-1	D.McPherson, McCoist	38,772	1		3	4	5	6		9	10	12	8	**7**	2		11	14		
	Nov 4 (a) Boavista	W 1-0	D.Ferguson	23,000	1		3		5	6		9	10		4	12	2	7	11		8	
3	26 (h) BorMGladbach	D 1-1	Durrant	44,000	1		3		5	6	12	9	10	8	4		2	7	11			
	Dec 10 (a) BorMGladbach	D 0-0*		36,000	1	2	3	4	5	6	12	9		10	8				11		7	

*Rangers lost on the away-goals rule

	WoodsC	Dawson	Munro	Souness	McPhersonD	Butcher	Russell	McCoist	Durrant	McMinn	FergusonD	Fleck	Nicholl	Fraser	Cooper	Nisbet	McFarlane	Miller
Appearances	6	1	6	3	6	6	1	6	5	2	4	3	5	3	6		2	1
Sub appearances							2			2		1		2	1			
Goals				1				2	1		1	3						

Further match details for this season are continued on page 283

267

1987-88

Manager: G.Souness

No.	Month	Date	Opponent	Result	Scorers	Scottish League	Woods C	Nicholl	Munro	Ferguson D	McGregor	Cohen	Kirkwood	Falco	McCoist	Phillips	Cooper D	Durrant	Fleck	McFarlane	Nisbet	West	Roberts	Butcher	Souness	McCall	Francis	Gough	Wilkins	Walters	Walker	Brown	Bartram	Ferguson I (2)	McSwegan
1	Aug	8	(h) Dundee U	D 1-1	McCoist (pen)	39,120	1	2	3	4	5	6	7	8	9	10	11	12	14																
2		12	(a) Hibernian	L 0-1		22,000	1		3		5	6	7	8	9	11		10	7	2	12	14													
3		15	(a) Aberdeen	L 0-2		22,568	1	2	3		5		7	12	9	11		10	14				4	6	8										
4		22	(h) Falkirk	W 4-0	McCoist 3, Falco	32,340	1	2		7	12			8	9	3	11	10	14				4	6	5										
5		29	(a) Celtic	L 0-1		60,800	1	2	3	7	6			8	9		11	10					4		5	12									
6	Sep	5	(h) Dundee	W 2-1	Fleck, McCoist	38,302	1	2			6				9	3	11	7	8				4		5	10									
7		12	(h) Dunfermline A	W 4-0	McCoist 3, Souness	39,749	1	2		5					9	3	14	11	8				4	6	12	10	7								
8		19	(a) Motherwell	W 1-0	Philliben (og)	19,480	1	2			12				9	3	14	11	8				4	6	5	10	7								
9		26	(h) Morton	W 7-0	McCoist 3, Falco 3, Fleck	35,843	1	2			5	12		8	9	3		11	14				4	6		10	7								
10	Oct	3	(a) Hearts	D 0-0		29,000	1	2	5		4			8	9	3	7	11	14					6		10	12								
11		6	(h) St Mirren	W 3-1	Falco, Butcher, Souness	39,298	1	2			4			8	9	3	11	10						6	5	12	7								
12		10	(a) Dundee U	L 0-1		18,214	1	11	3		7	5		8	9				14				4	6		10	12	2							
13		17	(h) Celtic	D 2-2	McCoist, Gough	44,500	1			5	11	12		8	9	3	14	10					4	6			7	2							
14		28	(a) Dunfermline A	W 4-0	Durrant 2, McCall (pen), McCoist	18,070	1	2		5		14		12	9	3	11	7	8					6		10		4							
15		31	(h) Motherwell	W 1-0	McCoist	36,583	1	2		11		3		14	9		12	10	8				4		5		7	6							
16	Nov	7	(h) Hibernian	W 1-0	Fleck	37,571	1	2		7	3				9		11	10	8				4		5		12	6							
17		14	(a) St Mirren	D 2-2	McCoist 2	20,649	1	2			5				9	3	11	7	8				4			10	12	6							
18		17	(h) Aberdeen	L 0-1		41,371	1		12	5	2			14	9		11	10	8				4	6			7	3							
19		21	(a) Falkirk	W 1-0	Fleck	17,500	1			7	5				9	3	11	10	8		2		4					6							
20		24	(a) Morton	W 3-0	D.Ferguson, Fleck, McCoist	16,500	1			7	5			14	9	3	11	10	8		2		4				12	6							
21		28	(h) Hearts	W 3-2	Fleck, Durrant, Levein (og)	43,557	1			7	14				9	3	11	10	8		2		4				12	6	5						
22	Dec	5	(h) Dundee U	W 1-0	McCoist (pen)	41,159	1			11					9	3	12	10	8		2		4				7	6	5						
23		12	(a) Hibernian	W 2-0	Gough, Fleck	21,000	1			11	3				9		7	10	8		2		4					6	5						
24		15	(h) Dunfermline A	D 2-2	D.Ferguson, McCoist	31,687	1			11	3				9		7	10	8		2		4		12			6	5						
25		19	(a) Motherwell	W 2-0	McCoist (pen), Philliben (og)	15,436	1		3	11					9		7	10			2		4		8			6	5						
26		26	(h) Dundee	W 2-0	McCoist 2 (1 pen)	40,938	1		3	11					9		7	10			2		4		8		12	6	5						
27	Jan	2	(a) Celtic	L 0-2		60,800	1		3		14				9		11	10			2		4		8		12	6	5	7					
28		6	(a) Dundee	W 1-0	McCoist	17,450			3		7				9			10			2		4		8			6	5	11	1				
29		9	(h) Morton	W 5-0	McCoist 3, Durrant 2	38,349		2	3	7	8				9			10			14		4				12	6	5	11	1				
30		16	(a) Hearts	D 1-1	Durrant (pen)	28,967			3		14				9			10			2		4		7		12	6	5	11	1	8			
31		23	(h) Falkirk	W 3-1	Bartram, Brown, Durrant (pen)	41,088				7					9		12	10			2		4					6	5	11	1	8	3		
32	Feb	6	(a) Aberdeen	W 2-1	McCoist, Gough	22,500	1			7	8				9		14	10					4		12			2	5	11		6	3		
33		13	(h) St Mirren	W 4-0	Cooper, Walters, Wilkins, Gough	41,664	1	12		8							7	10			2		4		9	14		6	5	11			3		
34		27	(a) Dundee U	D 1-1	Walters	20,846	1	2		7							12	10			9		4					6	5	11			3	8	
35	Mar	5	(a) Dunfermline A	W 3-0	McCoist (pen), Walters, Gough	19,017	1			7					9		12	10			2		4					6	5	11			3	8	
36		12	(h) Motherwell	W 1-0	Durrant	39,650	1			7					9		14	10			2		4		12			6	5	11			3	8	
37		20	(h) Celtic	L 1-2	Bartram	43,650	1			7					9			10			2		4					6	5	11			3	8	
38		26	(a) Dundee	W 3-2	Roberts, Walters, Durrant (pen)	14,879	1			7					9		12	10			2		4					6	5	11			3	8	
39	Apr	2	(h) Hearts	L 1-2	Bartram	41,125	1			7								10			2		4					6	5	11		9	3	8	
40		9	(a) Morton	L 2-3	I.Ferguson, Durrant	12,000	1			12					9	8		10			2		4			14			5	11		6	3	7	
41		16	(h) Hibernian	D 1-1	D.Ferguson	32,218		2	3	7							12	10			4								5	11	1	6	8	9	14
42		23	(a) St Mirren	W 3-0	Walters, Brown, McCoist	13,809	1	2	3	7					9		11						4					6	5	8		10			
43		30	(h) Aberdeen	L 0-1		36,010	1	2	3	7					9		11				12		4					6	5	8		10			
44	May	7	(a) Falkirk	W 5-0	Walters 2, McCoist 2 (1 pen), D.Ferguson	14,500	1	2	3	7			12		9	10					8							4	5	11		6			
						Appearances	39	21	16	31	20	4	3	9	40	19	21	39	15	1	22		37	11	14	8	8	31	24	18	5	9	11	8	
						Sub appearances		1	1	1	5	3	1	5			12	1	6		3	1			4	4	10								1
						Goals				4				5	31		1	10	7				1	1	2	1		5	1	7		2	3	1	

Final League Position: 3rd

3 own-goals

Scottish FA Cup

Round	Month	Date	Opponent	Result	Scorers	Attendance	Woods C	Nicholl	Munro	Ferguson D	McGregor	Cohen	Kirkwood	Falco	McCoist	Phillips	Cooper D	Durrant	Fleck	McFarlane	Nisbet	West	Roberts	Butcher	Souness	McCall	Francis	Gough	Wilkins	Walters	Walker	Brown	Bartram	Ferguson I (2)	McSwegan
3	Feb	8	(a) Raith Rovers	D 0-0		9,500	1	2		8					9		7	10					4		12				5	11		6	3		
R		10	(h) Raith Rovers	W 4-1	Durrant 2 (1 pen), Walters, McCoist	35,144	1			8					9		14	10			7		4		12			2	5	11		6	3		
4		20	(a) Dunfermline A	L 0-2		19,360	1			8							7	10			12		4		9		14	2	5	11		6	3		
						Appearances	3	1		3					2		2	3			1		3		1			2	3	3		3	3		
						Sub appearances											1				1				2		1								
						Goals									1			2												1					

Scottish League Cup

Round	Month	Date	Opponent	Result	Scorers	Attendance	Woods C	Nicholl	Munro	Ferguson D	McGregor	Cohen	Kirkwood	Falco	McCoist	Phillips	Cooper D	Durrant	Fleck	McFarlane	Nisbet	West	Roberts	Butcher	Souness	McCall	Francis	Gough	Wilkins	Walters	Walker	Brown	Bartram	Ferguson I (2)	McSwegan
2	Aug	19	(a*) Stirling Albion	W 2-1	Falco, McCoist	13,000	1	2	3		12		7	8	9	11		10					4	6	5										
3		26	(a) Dunfermline A	W 4-1	McCoist 3 (1 pen), Falco	18,070	1	2		7	12			8	9	3	11	10	14				4	6	5										
QF	Sep	2	(h) Hearts	W 4-1	Durrant 2, McCoist 2 (1 pen)	39,303	1	2	3	7	6	12			9	5	11	10	8				4												
SF		23	(n†) Motherwell	W 3-1	Fleck, Falco, Kirk (og)	45,938	1	2						12	9	3	11	10	8				4	6	5		7								
F	Oct	25	(n†) Aberdeen	D 3-3‡	Cooper, Durrant, Fleck	71,961		2	3	5	7	14			9		11	10	8				4				12	6			1				
						Appearances	4	5	3	3	2		1	2	5	4	4	5	3				5	3	3		1	1			1				
						Sub appearances					2	2		1					1								1								
						Goals								3	6		1	3	2																

*Played at Brockville Park, Falkirk. †Played at Hampden Park, Glasgow.
‡Rangers won 5-3 on penalties.

1 own-goal

European Champions' Cup

Round	Month	Date	Opponent	Result	Scorers	Attendance	Woods C	Nicholl	Munro	Ferguson D	McGregor	Cohen	Kirkwood	Falco	McCoist	Phillips	Cooper D	Durrant	Fleck	McFarlane	Nisbet	West	Roberts	Butcher	Souness	McCall	Francis	Gough	Wilkins	Walters	Walker	Brown	Bartram	Ferguson I (2)	McSwegan
1	Sep	16	(a) Dinamo Kiev	L 0-1		100,000	1	2		7	11	8	12		9	3		10					4	6	5										
		30	(h) Dinamo Kiev	W 2-0	Falco, McCoist	44,500	1	2			4	11	14	8	9	3		10	12					6	5		7								
2	Oct	21	(h) Górnik Zabrze	W 3-1	McCoist, Durrant, Falco	41,366	1	2		5		12		8	9	3		10	14				4	6	11		7								
	Nov	4	(a) Górnik Zabrze	D 1-1	McCoist (pen)	23,250	1	2		8	7				9	3	11	10	12				4	6	5										
QF1	Mar	2	(a) Steaua Bucharest	L 0-2		33,000	1	7	3	12					9		11	10			6		4		8		14	2	5						
QF2		16	(h) Steaua Bucharest	W 2-1	Gough, McCoist (pen)	44,000	1		3	7					9		11	10			2		4		8		12	6	5						
						Appearances	6	5	2	4	3	2		2	6	4	3	6			2		5	4	6		2	2	2						
						Sub appearances				1		1	2						3								2								
						Goals								2	4			1										1							

Further match details for this season are continued on page 283

1988-89

Manager: G.Souness

Scottish League

#	Date	Venue / Opponent	Result	Scorers	Att.	Woods C	Stevens	Munro	Gough	Wilkins	Butcher	Drinkell	Brown	McCoist	Durrant	Walters	Ferguson D	Cooper D	Souness	Ferguson I	Nisbet	Gray	Cooper N	Walker	McDonald	McCall	McSwegan	Nicholl	Cowan	Sterland	Kirkwood	Robertson A	Phillips	Spencer	McPherson A	McGregor
1	Aug 13	(a) Hamilton A	W 2-0	Stevens, McCoist	10,500	1	2	3	4	5	6	7	8	9	10	11	12		14																	
2	20	(h) Hibernian	D 0-0		41,955	1	2		4	5	6	7	3	9	10	11	8		14	12																
3	27	(h) Celtic	W 5-1	McCoist 2, Wilkins, Drinkell, Walters	42,858	1	2		4	5	6	7	3	9	10	11			14	12	8															
4	Sep 3	(a) Motherwell	W 2-0	Drinkell, Durrant	20,112	1	2		4	5	6	7	3		10	11			9																	
5	17	(a) Hearts	W 2-1	Durrant (pen), Nisbet	25,501	1	2		4	5	6	7	3		10	11			9	12	8	14														
6	24	(h) St Mirren	W 2-1	D.Cooper (pen), Walters	35,523	1	2		4	5	6		3		10	11			9	12	8	7	14													
7	27	(a) Dundee U	W 1-0	I.Ferguson	20,071	1	2	3	4	5	6			9	10	11			12		8	7														
8	Oct 1	(h) Dundee	W 2-0	Drinkell, Walters	40,768	1	2	3	4	5	6	7	10	9		11			12		8		14													
9	8	(a) Aberdeen	L 1-2	N.Cooper	23,370	1	2	12	4		6	7	3	9	10	11			14		8		5													
10	12	(h) Hibernian	W 1-0	McCoist	26,000	1	2		4	5	6	7	3	9		11			12		8		10													
11	29	(a) St Mirren	D 1-1	Gray	20,903	1	2	3	4	5	6	7	11	9		12					8	14	10													
12	Nov 1	(h) Hearts	W 3-0	Gough, Walters (pen), Gray	36,505	1	2		4	5	6	7	3			11					8	9	12	10												
13	5	(h) Motherwell	W 2-0	Brown, Drinkell	36,060	1	2		4	5	6	7	3			11	12				8	9	14	10												
14	12	(a) Celtic	L 1-3	Walters	60,113	1	2		4	5	6	7	3			11	9				8		12	10												
15	16	(h) Hamilton A	W 3-1	Gray, I.Ferguson, Drinkell	33,864		2	3	4	5	6	7				11			14		8	12	9	10	1											
16	19	(a) Dundee	D 0-0		16,514		2	3	4	5	6	7	10						11		8	9	12		1											
17	26	(h) Aberdeen	W 1-0	Gough	42,239		2		4	5	6	7	3			11			9		8		10	1	12											
18	Dec 3	(h) Dundee U	L 0-1		39,123		2		4	5	6	7	3						9		8	12	10	1	11											
19	10	(a) Hearts	L 0-2		26,424		2		4	5	6	7	3			11			9		8	12		1	10											
20	17	(h) Hibernian	W 1-0	McCall	36,672		2	3	4	5	6	7	9						11	12	8		1		10											
21	31	(a) Hamilton A	W 1-0	D.Ferguson	10,500		2	3	4	5	6	7					12				8	9	11	1		10	14									
22	Jan 3	(h) Celtic	W 4-1	Walters 2 (1 pen), Butcher, I.Ferguson	42,515		2	3	4	5	6	7	10			11	9				8		12	1		14											
23	7	(a) Motherwell	L 1-2	Drinkell	19,275		2	3	4	5	6	7	10			11	9				8			1		12											
24	14	(a) Aberdeen	W 2-1	Munro, D.Ferguson	23,000		2	3	4	5	6	7	10			11	9				8		12	1													
25	21	(h) Dundee	W 3-1	I.Ferguson, Butcher, McCoist	43,202		2	3		5	6	7	10	14		11	9				8		12	1					4								
26	Feb 11	(a) Dundee U	D 1-1	Munro	22,019		2	3	4	5	6	7	10			11	9				8			1													
27	25	(h) St Mirren	W 3-1	I.Ferguson, McCoist, Walters	39,021		2	3	4	5	6			9		10	11	14			8		12	7													
28	Mar 11	(a) Hamilton A	W 3-0	I.Ferguson, Sterland, Gough	35,733	1	2		4		6	7		9		10	11				8									3	5						
29	25	(a) Hibernian	W 1-0	Drinkell	23,321	1	2	3	4	12	6	7		9		10	11				8										5						
30	Apr 1	(a) Celtic	W 2-1	Drinkell, I.Ferguson	60,171	1	2	3	4	5	6	7	10	9		11		14			8										12						
31	8	(h) Motherwell	W 1-0	McCoist	33,782	1	2	3	4	5	6	7	10	9		11	12														8						
32	22	(a) St Mirren	W 2-0	I.Ferguson, McCoist	22,096	1	2		4	5	6	7	3	9		10	11	14		8											12						
33	29	(h) Hearts	W 4-0	Sterland 2, Drinkell 2	42,856	1	2	3	4	5	6	7		9		10	11	14												12	8						
34	May 2	(a) Dundee U	W 2-0	Drinkell, McCoist	39,068	1	2	3	4			7	6	9		11		14	12											10	8	5					
35	6	(a) Dundee	W 2-1	Gray 2	14,889	1	2	3	4			6	9			11						7			14					10	8	5	12				
36	13	(h) Aberdeen	L 0-3		42,480	1		3	4		6	7	10	9		11		12		8		14								2		5					

FINAL LEAGUE POSITION: 1st

						Woods C	Stevens	Munro	Gough	Wilkins	Butcher	Drinkell	Brown	McCoist	Durrant	Walters	Ferguson D	Cooper D	Souness	Ferguson I	Nisbet	Gray	Cooper N	Walker	McDonald	McCall	McSwegan	Nicholl	Cowan	Sterland	Kirkwood	Robertson A	Phillips	Spencer	McPherson A	McGregor
Appearances						24	35	21	35	30	34	32	29	18	8	30	12	9		30	5	3	11	12	2	2		1	3	7	2	1				
Sub appearances							1		1							1	1	4	14	6		2	11	3		1	3	1		1	2		1			
Goals							1	2	3	1	2	11	1	9	2	8	2	1		8	1	5	1			1			3						

Scottish FA Cup

#	Date	Venue / Opponent	Result	Scorers	Att.	Woods C	Stevens	Munro	Gough	Wilkins	Butcher	Drinkell	Brown	McCoist	Durrant	Walters	Ferguson D	Cooper D	Souness	Ferguson I	Nisbet	Gray	Cooper N	Walker	McDonald	McCall	McSwegan	Nicholl	Cowan	Sterland	Kirkwood	Robertson A
3	Jan 28	(a) Raith R	D 1-1	I.Ferguson	10,500		2	3		5	6	7	10	12		11	9			8				1			4					
R	Feb 1	(h) Raith R	W 3-0	Walters, Drinkell, Fraser (og)	40,307		2	12	4		6	7	3	9		10	11			8		5	1									
4	18	(h) Stranraer	W 8-0	Drinkell 2, Brown 2, McCoist 2 (1 pen), I.Ferguson, Walters	41,198	1	2	14	4	5	6	7	3	9		10	11			8					12							
QF	Mar 21	(h) Dundee U	D 2-2	Drinkell, McCoist	42,177	1	2	3	4	12	6	7		9		11				8		10						5				
R	27	(a) Dundee U	W 1-0	McCoist	21,872	1	2	3	4	5	6	7	12	9		11				8								10				
SF	Apr 15(n*)	St Johnstone	D 0-0		47,374	1	2	3	4	5	6	7	10	9		11		12										8				
R	18(n*)	St Johnstone	W 4-0	Walters, Stevens, Drinkell, McCoist	44,205	1	2	3	4	5	6	7	10	9		11	8	12				14						5				
F	May 20(n†)	Celtic	L 0-1		72,069	1	2	3	4		6	7	10	9		11		12	14	8								5				

*Played at Celtic Park, Glasgow.
†Played at Hampden Park, Glasgow.

						Woods C	Stevens	Munro	Gough	Wilkins	Butcher	Drinkell	Brown	McCoist	Durrant	Walters	Ferguson D	Cooper D	Souness	Ferguson I	Nisbet	Gray	Cooper N	Walker	McDonald	McCall	McSwegan	Nicholl	Cowan	Sterland	Kirkwood	Robertson A
Appearances						6	8	6	7	5	8	8	6	7		8	4			6		2	2				1	4				
Sub appearances							2		1			1	1					3	1			1		1								
Goals						1					5	2	5	3		2															

1 own-goal

Scottish League Cup

#	Date	Venue / Opponent	Result	Scorers	Att.	Woods C	Stevens	Munro	Gough	Wilkins	Butcher	Drinkell	Brown	McCoist	Durrant	Walters	Ferguson D	Cooper D	Souness	Ferguson I	Nisbet	Gray	Cooper N	Walker	McDonald	McCall	McSwegan	Nicholl
2	Aug 17(a*)	Clyde	W 3-0	Drinkell, Walters, D.Ferguson	14,699	1	2	3	4	5	6	7	8	9	10	11	12	14										
3	24	(h) Clydebank	W 6-0	McCoist, Gough, Walters, Wilkins, Drinkell, Durrant	34,376	1	2	3	4	5	6	7	8	9	10	11		14	12									
QF	31	(h) Dundee	W 4-1	McCoist (pen), Walters, I.Ferguson, Forsyth (og)	39,667	1	2		4	5	6	7	3	9	10	11		12	14	8								
SF	Sep 21(n†)	Hearts	W 3-0	Walters 2, Nisbet	53,623	1	2		4	5	6		3		10	11		9	14	8	7	12						
F	Oct 23(n†)	Aberdeen	W 3-2	McCoist 2 (1 pen), I.Ferguson	72,122	1	2		4	5	6	7	3	9		11				10								

*Played at Firhill Park, Glasgow.
†Played at Hampden Park, Glasgow.

						Woods C	Stevens	Munro	Gough	Wilkins	Butcher	Drinkell	Brown	McCoist	Durrant	Walters	Ferguson D	Cooper D	Souness	Ferguson I	Nisbet	Gray
Appearances						5	5	2	5	5	5	4	5	4	4	5		1		3	1	1
Sub appearances																	1	3	3		1	
Goals							1	1		2		4	1	5	1			2	1			

1 own-goal

UEFA Cup

#	Date	Venue / Opponent	Result	Scorers	Att.	Woods C	Stevens	Munro	Gough	Wilkins	Butcher	Drinkell	Brown	McCoist	Durrant	Walters	Ferguson D	Cooper D	Souness	Ferguson I	Nisbet	Gray	Cooper N	Walker	McDonald	McCall	McSwegan	Nicholl	Cowan	Sterland	Kirkwood	Robertson A	Phillips	Spencer	McPherson A	McGregor
1	Sep 7	(h) GKS Katowice	W 1-0	Walters	41,120	1	2		4	5	6	7	3		10	11	12	9		8																
	Oct 5	(a) GKS Katowice	W 4-2	Butcher 2, Durrant, I.Ferguson	40,000	1	2	3	4	5	6			9	10	11		7		8															12	
2	26	(a) 1.FC Cologne	L 0-2		42,000	1	2	3	4	5	6	7			11	10			8	12																
	Nov 9	(h) 1.FC Cologne	D 1-1	Drinkell	42,204	1	2	3	4		6	9			11	10	7		8	14			12	5											1	

						Woods C	Stevens	Munro	Gough	Wilkins	Butcher	Drinkell	Brown	McCoist	Durrant	Walters	Ferguson D	Cooper D	Souness	Ferguson I	Nisbet	Gray	Cooper N	Walker
Appearances						4	4	3	4	3	4	3	1	2	2	4	2	3	4					1
Sub appearances																		1		2			1	
Goals											2	1			1	1			1					

Further match details for this season are continued on page 284

1989-90

Manager: G.Souness

No.	Date	Opponent	Result	Scorers	Scottish League	Woods	Stevens	Munro	Gough	Wilkins	Butcher	Steven	Ferguson I	McCoist	Johnston	Walters	Drinkell	Ferguson D	Ginzburg	Brown	Nisbet	Cowan	Dodds	Cooper N	McCall	Spackman	Vinnicombe	Robertson A	Souness	McPherson	Rouse	Morrow	Murray N	McGregor	Hamilton	Howard	McSwegan
1	Aug 12	(h) St Mirren	L 0-1		39,951	1	2	3	4	5	6	7	8	9	10	11	14	12																			
2	19	(a) Hibernian	L 0-2		22,500		2	3	4	5	6	7	8	9	10	11	12		1																		
3	26	(a) Celtic	D 1-1	Butcher	54,000		2	3	4	5	6	7	8	12	10		9		1	11																	
4	Sep 9	(h) Aberdeen	W 1-0	Johnston	40,283	1	2	3		5	6	7	8	14	10	11	9			4	12																
5	16	(h) Dundee	D 2-2	McCoist 2	35,836	1	2	3		5	6	7	12	9	10	11		8			4																
6	23	(a) Dunfermline A	D 1-1	McCoist	17,765	1	2	3	4	5	6	7	12	9	10	11		8																			
7	30	(h) Hearts	W 1-0	Johnston	39,554		2	3	4	5	6	7	8	9	10	11			1			12	14														
8	Oct 3	(a) Motherwell	L 0-1		17,667		2	3	4	5	6	7		9	10				1				8	11	12												
9	14	(h) Dundee U	W 2-1	Johnston, McCoist	36,062	1	2	3	4	5	6	7		9	10	11							12	8	14												
10	25	(a) St Mirren	W 2-0	McCoist, Johnston	15,130	1	2	3	4	5	6	7	8	9	10										11												
11	28	(h) Hibernian	W 3-0	McCoist 2, Johnston (pen)	35,260	1	2	3	4	5	6	7	8	9	10							14	12		11												
12	Nov 4	(h) Celtic	W 1-0	Johnston	41,598	1	2	3		5	6	7	8	9	10	11				4																	
13	18	(a) Dundee	W 2-0	Johnston, Walters	14,536	1	2	3		5	6	7	8	9	10	11				4	14		12														
14	22	(a) Aberdeen	L 0-1		22,500	1	2	3		5	6	7	8	9	10	11				4																	
15	25	(h) Dunfermline A	W 3-0	Johnston, Butcher, McCoist	39,131	1	2	3		5	6	7	8	9	10	11				4																	
16	Dec 2	(a) Hearts	W 2-1	Walters, Steven	24,771	1	2	3			6	7	8	9	10	11				4						5											
17	9	(h) Motherwell	W 3-1	Butcher, McCoist, Brown	33,549	1	2	3	4		6	7	8	9	10					11						5	12										
18	16	(a) Dundee U	D 1-1	Johnston	15,947	1	2	3	4		6	7	8	9	10					11						5											
19	23	(h) St Mirren	W 1-0	Dodds	31,797	1	2	3	4		6	7	8	9	10					11			12			5	14										
20	30	(a) Hibernian	D 0-0		24,500	1	2	3	4		6			9	10	7				11		8				5											
21	Jan 2	(a) Celtic	W 1-0	Spackman	54,000	1	2	3	4		6	7		9	10	8				11						5	12										
22	6	(h) Aberdeen	W 2-0	Walters, McCoist	41,351	1	2	3	4		6	7		9	10	8				11						5	12										
23	13	(h) Dundee	W 3-0	McCoist, Dodds, Johnston	36,993	1	2	3	4		6	7		9	10	8				11			12			5											
24	27	(a) Dunfermline A	W 1-0	Stevens	17,380	1	2	3	4			7		9	10	8				11	6					5											
25	Feb 3	(h) Dundee U	W 3-1	Walters, McCoist, Johnston	39,058	1	2	3	4			7		9	10	8				11						5	6	12									
26	10	(a) Motherwell	D 1-1	Johnston	17,647	1	2	3			6	7	4	9	10	8				11			12			5											
27	17	(h) Hearts	D 0-0		41,884	1	2	3			6	7	4	9	10	8				11						5											
28	Mar 3	(a) Dundee	D 2-2	Johnston, Dodds	12,743	1	2	3			6	7	8		10					11	4		9			5	12										
29	17	(a) St Mirren	D 0-0		16,129	1	2	3	4		6	7	8		10					11	9		12			5											
30	24	(h) Hibernian	L 0-1		37,542	1	2	3	4		6	7	12	9	10	8				11						5											
31	Apr 1	(h) Celtic	W 3-0	Walters (pen), Johnston, McCoist (pen)	41,926	1	2	3	4		6	7	8	9	10	11				12						5											
32	8	(a) Aberdeen	D 0-0		23,000	1	2	3	4		6	7	8	9	10	11				14			12			5											
33	14	(h) Motherwell	W 2-1	Steven, Johnston	39,305	1		3	4		6	7		9	10	11		14		2	12		8			5											
34	21	(a) Dundee U	W 1-0	Steven	15,995	1	2	3	4		6	7		9	10	11		8		12						5											
35	28	(h) Dunfermline A	W 2-0	McCoist, Dodds	40,769	1	2	3	4		6	7		9	10	11				8			12			5			14								
36	May 5	(a) Hearts	D 1-1	Munro	20,283	1	2	3	4		6			9	10	11				8			7	14		5	12										
					Appearances	32	35	36	26	15	34	34	21	32	36	27	2	3	4	24	4	1	4	2	2	21	1										
					Sub appearances								3	2			2	2		3	3	2	10	1	2		6	1	1								
					Goals		1	1			3	3		14	15	5				1			4			1											

FINAL LEAGUE POSITION: 1st

Scottish FA Cup

Rd	Date	Opponent	Result	Scorers	Att.	Woods	Stevens	Munro	Gough	Wilkins	Butcher	Steven	Ferguson I	McCoist	Johnston	Walters	Drinkell	Ferguson D	Ginzburg	Brown	Nisbet	Cowan	Dodds	Cooper N	McCall	Spackman	Vinnicombe	Robertson A	Souness	McPherson	Rouse	Morrow	Murray N	McGregor	Hamilton	Howard	McSwegan
3	Jan 20	(h) St Johnstone	W 3-0	Johnston, Brown, Walters	39,003	1	2	3	4		6	7		9	10	8				11						5	12										
4	Feb 25	(a) Celtic	L 0-1		52,565	1	2	3			6	7	4	9	10	8				11			14			5	12										
					Appearances	2	2	2	1		2	2	1	2	2	2				2						2											
					Sub appearances																		1				2										
					Goals										1	1				1																	

Scottish League Cup

Rd	Date	Opponent	Result	Scorers	Att.	Woods	Stevens	Munro	Gough	Wilkins	Butcher	Steven	Ferguson I	McCoist	Johnston	Walters	Drinkell	Ferguson D	Ginzburg	Brown	Nisbet	Cowan	Dodds	Cooper N	McCall	Spackman	Vinnicombe	Robertson A	Souness	McPherson	Rouse	Morrow	Murray N	McGregor	Hamilton	Howard	McSwegan
2	Aug 15	(h) Arbroath	W 4-0	McCoist 3, I.Ferguson	31,762		2	3	4	5	6	7	8	9	10	11	14	12	1																		
3	23	(a) Morton	W 2-1	Walters, Pickering (og)	11,821		2	3		5	6	7	8		10	11	9		1		4																
QF	30	(a) Hamilton A	W 3-0	Walters 2 (1 pen), Steven	9,162		2	3		5	6	7	8	9	10	11			1	4																	
SF	Sep 19	(n*) Dunfermline A	W 5-0	Steven, Johnston, Walters, McCoist, I.Ferguson	41,643	1	2	3	4	5	6	7	12	9	10	11		8																			
F	Oct 22	(n*) Aberdeen	L 1-2	Walters (pen)	61,190	1	2	3	4	5	6	7	8	9	10	11									12												
					Appearances	2	5	5	3	5	5	5	4	4	5	5	1	1	3	1	1																
					Sub appearances								1				1	1							1												
					Goals							2	2	4	1	5																					

*Played at Hampden Park, Glasgow.

1 own-goal

European Champions Cup

Rd	Date	Opponent	Result	Scorers	Att.	Woods	Stevens	Munro	Gough	Wilkins	Butcher	Steven	Ferguson I	McCoist	Johnston	Walters	Drinkell	Ferguson D	Ginzburg	Brown	Nisbet	Cowan	Dodds	Cooper N	McCall	Spackman	Vinnicombe	Robertson A	Souness	McPherson	Rouse	Morrow	Murray N	McGregor	Hamilton	Howard	McSwegan
1	Sep 13	(h) Bayern Munich	L 1-3	Walters (pen)	40,253	1	2	3		5	6	7	8		10	11		9			4																
	27	(a) Bayern Munich	D 0-0		40,000		2	3	4	5	6	7	8		10	11	12		1			9															
					Appearances	1	2	2	1	2	2	2	2		2	2		1	1		1	1															
					Sub appearances												1																				
					Goals											1																					

Other matches

No.	Date	Opponent	Result	Scorers	Att.	Woods	Stevens	Munro	Gough	Wilkins	Butcher	Steven	Ferguson I	McCoist	Johnston	Walters	Drinkell	Ferguson D	Ginzburg	Brown	Nisbet	Cowan	Dodds	Cooper N	McCall	Spackman	Vinnicombe	Robertson A	Souness	McPherson	Rouse	Morrow	Murray N	McGregor	Hamilton	Howard	McSwegan
1	Jul 29	(a) Airdrieonians *	W 3-1	Steven, Brown, Drinkell	11,500	1	2	3	4		6	5		9	10	11	7			8		12															
2	31	(a) Kilmarnock †	W 3-0	Drinkell, Johnston, Steven	11,333	1	2	3	4	5	6	8	16	9	10	11	7	15				12			14												
3	Aug 2	(a) Partick Thistle	W 4-2	Johnston 2, McCoist 2 (1 pen)	11,500	1	2		4	5		11	8	9	10	14	7				6	3			12												
4	5	(a) Clydebank	W 4-2	Nisbet, Madigage, McSwegan, McPherson	2,192													7			5	3			10			6		2	12				1		9
5	6	(h) Tottenham H	W 1-0	Steven	41,214	1	2	3	4	5	6	7	8	9	10	11		14				12															
6	8	(a‡) Clyde	W 5-2	McSwegan 3, McCall 2	3,500					6							8	7			5	3			10					2	15				1	4	9
7	Dec 19	(h) Arsenal §	L 1-2	Johnston	31,118	1	2	3	4		6	7	8		10	9			12	11		14	15			5											
8	Jan 8	(a) Kilmarnock #	W 1-0	Morrow	4,371													6	1		5	3	9	4			10	12	8	2	7	11	14	15			
					Appearances	5	5	4	5	4	4	5	3	4	5	4	4	3	1	2	4	4	1	1	2	1	1	1	1	3	1	1			2	1	2
					Sub appearances								1			1		2	1			4	1		2			1			2		1	1			
					Goals							3		2	4		2			1	1				2					1		1					4

*Brian McKeown and John Martin Testimonial Match. †Alan McCulloch Testimonial Match. ‡Played at Firhill Park, Glasgow. §British Championship (Zenith Data Systems Cup) #Stuart McLean Testimonial Match.

D.Cooper played number-11 in Matches 4 & 6; Madigage played number-8 in Match 4, scoring once and number-12 in Match 6; McFadyen played number-4 in Match 4 and number-14 in Match 6; Playle played number-14 in Match 4; Makalakalane played number-15 in Match 4.

1990-91

Manager: G.Souness/W.Smith

Scottish League

No	Date	Opponent	Result	Scorers	Att	Woods	Stevens	Brown	Gough	Spackman	Butcher	Steven	Ferguson I	Hateley	Johnston	Walters	McCoist	Huistra	Hurlock	Munro	Kuznetsov	Nisbet	Robertson A	McSwegan	Vinnicombe	Dodds	Cowan	Spencer	Reid	Durrant	Ginzburg	Cooper N	Hagen	Trimboli	Murray	Souness	Robertson L
1	Aug 25	(h) Dunfermline A	W 3-1	Hateley, Johnston, Walters	39,951	1	2	3	4	5	6	7	8	9	10	11	12	14																			
2	Sep 1	(a) Hibernian	D 0-0		17,500	1	2	3	4	5	6	7	8	9	10		12		11																		
3	8	(a) Hearts	W 3-1	McCoist 2, Huistra	22,101	1	2		4	5	6	7		9	10	12	8	11	3																		
4	15	(h) Celtic	D 1-1	Hurlock	38,543	1	2	12	4	5	6	7		9	10	14	8	11	3																		
5	22	(a) Dundee U	L 1-2	Johnston	16,270	1	2	12	4	5	6	7		9	10	14	8	11	3																		
6	29	(h) Motherwell	W 1-0	Brown	34,863	1	2	6	4	5		7		12	10	8	9	11		3																	
7	Oct 6	(a) Aberdeen	D 0-0		19,500	1	2	6	4	5		7		12	10	11	9		8	3																	
8	13	(h) St Mirren	W 5-0	McCoist 2 (1 pen), Walters 2, Johnston	38,031	1	2		4	5		7			10	11	9	12	8	3	6																
9	20	(a) St Johnstone	D 0-0		10,504	1	2		4	5		7		14	10	11	9	12	8	3	6																
10	Nov 3	(h) Hibernian	W 4-0	Hateley 2, Walters, Steven	35,925	1	2		4	5		7	12	10		11	9	14	8	3		6															
11	10	(h) Dundee U	L 1-2	McCoist	36,995	1	2	6		5		7		10		11	9		8	3		4	12	14													
12	17	(a) Motherwell	W 4-2	Stevens 2, Walters, Johnston	16,457	1	2	6		5				9	10	11	12					4	8		3	7											
13	20	(a) Dunfermline A	W 1-0	Hateley	14,480	1	2	6		5				8	10		9		7			4			3	11											
14	25	(a) Celtic	W 2-1	Johnston, McCoist	52,565	1	2	6		5				9	10	11	14	12	7	3		4	8														
15	Dec 1	(h) Hearts	W 4-0	Johnston, Hurlock, McCoist, Walters (pen)	37,623	1	2	6		5				9	10	11	12		7	3		4	8														
16	8	(h) St Johnstone	W 4-1	Walters 2, Johnston (pen), Stevens	34,610	1	2	6		5		7		9	10	11	14	12	8	3		4															
17	15	(a) St Mirren	W 3-0	Walters, Johnston (pen), Hateley	15,197	1	2	6	4	5		7		9	10	11	12		8	3																	
18	22	(h) Aberdeen	D 2-2	McCoist 2	37,998	1	2	6	4			7		9	10	11	14	12	8	3			5														
19	29	(a) Dundee U	W 2-1	Johnston, Walters	17,564	1	2	6	4	5				9	10	11	14	12		3			8		7												
20	Jan 2	(h) Celtic	W 2-0	Walters, Hateley	38,399	1	2	6	4	5				9	10	7		11	8	3			12														
21	5	(a) Hearts	W 1-0	Hateley	20,956	1	2	6	4	5				9	10	7		11	8	3			12														
22	12	(h) Dunfermline A	W 2-0	Huistra, Johnston	35,120	1	2	6	4	5				9	10	7		11	8				12		3												
23	19	(a) Hibernian	W 2-0	Johnston, Houchen (og)	15,500	1	2		4	5				9	10	7	14	11	8				6		3		12										
24	Feb 9	(h) St Mirren	W 1-0	McCoist	31,769	1	2	6	4	5		7				8	9	11					12		3			10									
25	16	(h) Motherwell	W 2-0	McCoist, Hateley	32,192	1	2	6	4	5		7		9		11	10	12	8			3															
26	26	(a) St Johnstone	D 1-1	Huistra	10,721	1	2	6	4	5		7		9	8	14	10	12	11			3															
27	Mar 2	(a) Aberdeen	L 0-1		22,500	1	2	6	4	5		7		9	10	11		12	8			3															
28	9	(h) Hearts	W 2-1	Steven, Walters	36,128	1	2		4	5		7	6	9		11	10	12	8			3															
29	24	(a) Celtic	L 0-3		52,000	1	2		4	5			8		10		9					6	12			7	3	11									
30	30	(a) Dunfermline A	W 1-0	Stevens	14,256	1	2		4	5			8	9	10	11		14	7						3			12	6								
31	Apr 6	(h) Hibernian	D 0-0		35,507	1	2		4	5				9	8			11	7						3			12	6	10							
32	13	(h) St Johnstone	W 3-0	Durrant, Spencer, Huistra	35,930	1	2	4		5			8	9				12	7					14	3			11	6	10							
33	20	(a) St Mirren	W 1-0	A.Robertson	18,473	1	2	6		5			8	9				12	7			4	14	11	3					10							
34	24	(h) Dundee U	W 1-0	Ferguson	32,397	1	2	6	4	5			8	9	10	7		12					11				3										
35	May 4	(a) Motherwell	L 0-3		17,672	1	2	6		5			8	9	10	11		12	7			4	14				3										
36	11	(h) Aberdeen	W 2-0	Hateley 2	37,652	1	2	6		5			8	9	10	11	14		7			4					3			12							
					Appearances	36	36	25	26	35	5	19	10	30	29	26	15	10	29	14	2	15	7	1	10	3	4	3	3	3							
					Sub appearances			2					1	3		4	11	17					8	2			1	2		1							
					Goals		4	1				2	1	10	11	12	11	4	2				1					1		1							

FINAL LEAGUE POSITION: 1st

1 own-goall

Scottish FA Cup

Round	Date	Opponent	Result	Scorers	Att	Woods	Stevens	Brown	Gough	Spackman	Butcher	Steven	Ferguson I	Hateley	Johnston	Walters	McCoist	Huistra	Hurlock	Munro	Kuznetsov	Nisbet	Robertson A	McSwegan	Vinnicombe	Dodds	Cowan	Spencer	Reid	Durrant	Ginzburg	Cooper N	Hagen	Trimboli	Murray	Souness	Robertson L
3	Jan 29	(h) Dunfermline A	W 2-0	Huistra, Spackman	29,003	1	2		4	5		7		9	10		14	11				6	8		3	12											
4	Feb 23	(h) Cowdenbeath	W 5-0	Hateley 2, Nisbet, McCoist, Walters (pen)	29,527	1	2	6	4	5		7		9	14	11	10	12	8			3															
QF	Mar 17	(a) Celtic	L 0-2		52,286	1	2		4			7	8	9	10	11		14	6	3		5					12										
					Appearances	3	3	1	3	2		3	1	3	2	2	1	1	2	1		3	1		1												
					Sub appearances										1		1	2								1	1										
					Goals					1				2		1	1	1				1															

Scottish League Cup

Round	Date	Opponent	Result	Scorers	Att	Woods	Stevens	Brown	Gough	Spackman	Butcher	Steven	Ferguson I	Hateley	Johnston	Walters	McCoist	Huistra	Hurlock	Munro	Kuznetsov	Nisbet	Robertson A	McSwegan	Vinnicombe	Dodds	Cowan	Spencer	Reid	Durrant	Ginzburg	Cooper N	Hagen	Trimboli	Murray	Souness	Robertson L
2	Aug 21	(h) East Stirling	W 5-0	Hateley 2, Steven, Walters, Johnston	25,595	1	2	3	4	5	6	7		9	10	8		11																			
3	28	(h) Kilmarnock	W 1-0	Johnston	32,671	1	2	3	4	5	6	7	8	14	10		9	11	12																		
QF	Sep 4	(h) Raith Rovers	W 6-2	McCoist 3, Johnston, Butcher, Steven	31,320	1	2		4	5	6	7		9	10		8	11	3																		
SF	26	(n*) Aberdeen	W 1-0	Steven	40,855	1	2	6	4	5		7			10	11	9		8	3																	
F	Oct 28	(n*) Celtic	W 2-1	Walters, Gough	62,817	1	2	6	4	5		7	14	10		11	9	12	8	3																	
					Appearances	5	5	4	5	5	3	5	1	3	4	3	4	3	3	2																	
					Sub appearances								1	1				1	1																		
					Goals				1		1	3		2	3	2	3																				

*Played at Hampden Park, Glasgow.

European Champions' Cup

Round	Date	Opponent	Result	Scorers	Att	Woods	Stevens	Brown	Gough	Spackman	Butcher	Steven	Ferguson I	Hateley	Johnston	Walters	McCoist	Huistra	Hurlock	Munro	Kuznetsov	Nisbet	Robertson A	McSwegan	Vinnicombe	Dodds	Cowan	Spencer	Reid	Durrant	Ginzburg	Cooper N	Hagen	Trimboli	Murray	Souness	Robertson L
1	Sep 19	(a) Valletta FC	W 4-0	Johnston 2, McCoist (pen), Hateley	8,000	1	2	12	4	5	6	7		9	10	11	8			3																	
	Oct 2	(h) Valletta FC	W 6-0	Johnston 3 (1 pen), Dodds, Spencer, McCoist	20,627	1	2	6				7			10	8	14	11		3			12			5	4	9									
2	24	(a) Red Star Belgrade	L 0-3		82,500	1	2	6	4	5		7	8		10	9	12	11		3																	
	Nov 7	(h) Red Star Belgrade	D 1-1	McCoist	23,831	1	2	6	4	5		7		10		11	9			3		12	14			8											
					Appearances	4	4	3	3	3	1	4	1	2	3	4	2	2		4						2	1	1									
					Sub appearances			1									2					1	2														
					Goals									1	5		3									1		1									

Other matches

No	Date	Opponent	Result	Scorers	Att	Woods	Stevens	Brown	Gough	Spackman	Butcher	Steven	Ferguson I	Hateley	Johnston	Walters	McCoist	Huistra	Hurlock	Munro	Kuznetsov	Nisbet	Robertson A	McSwegan	Vinnicombe	Dodds	Cowan	Spencer	Reid	Durrant	Ginzburg	Cooper N	Hagen	Trimboli	Murray	Souness	Robertson L
1	Jul 31	(a*) Queen's Park	W 1-0	Spencer	300			6	4	5					10			11		3						8	12	9			1	2	7	14			
2	Aug 2	(a) Raith R	L 1-2	Trimboli	1,390			6										11		3					14	9	7	16			1		8	10			15
3	4	(a) Dundee	D 2-2	Souness, Hateley	7,000			6						8	10		9	11		3					7		12				1	4			2	5	14
4	11	(h) Dinamo Kiev	L 1-3	Brown	21,461		2	6	4	5		7		8	10	11	9	15		3					12			14			1						
5	13	(a) Kilmarnock †	W 3-1	McCoist, Murray, Spencer	7,000	1											9	11				5	6	14		8	3	10				4			7		
6	15	(h) Manchester U	L 0-1		31,818	1	2	6	4	5		7		9	10	8	14	12		3					11												
7	17	(a) Morton ‡	W 4-0	Spencer 2, Huistra, McSwegan	6,000	1		3	4	5	6		8			7		11						9	14			10							12		
8	Sep 10	(a) East Stirling	W 6-0	Spencer 4, Walters, I.Ferguson (pen)				6					8			7				3		4				9	11	10				5					
9	Apr 29	(a) Brechin C §	L 4-6	Durrant 2, Morrow, Spencer	2,000											11			4			6		9		5		8		10							
					Appearances	3	2	7	4	4	1	2	2	3	4	5	3	5	1	6		3	1	2	2	5	3	5		1	4	4	2	1	2	1	
					Sub appearances												1	2						1	3		2	2						1	1		2
					Goals			1					1	1		1	1	1						1				9		2				1	1	1	

*Played at Lesser Hampden. †Walter McCrae Testimonial Match. ‡John McNeil Testimonial Match. §Dougie Scott Testimonial Match.

McPherson played number-2 in Matches 2, 5, 7 & 8; Howard played number-12 in Matches 2 & 5; Rouse played number-4 in Match 2; McGregor played number-5 in Match 2; Scott played number-1 in Matches 8 & 9; Morrow played number-12 in Match 8 & number-7 in Match 9, scoring once; Pressley played number-2 in Match 9; Watson played number-3 in Match 9.

1991-92

Manager: W.Smith

Scottish League

No	Date	V	Opponent	Result	Scorers	Att
1	Aug 10	(h)	St Johnstone	W 6-0	Hateley 3, Johnston 2 (2 pens), Ferguson	35,109
2	13	(h)	Motherwell	W 2-0	Steven, Maaskant (og)	35,322
3	17	(a)	Hearts	L 0-1		22,534
4	24	(h)	Dunfermline A	W 4-0	Huistra, Johnston, Spencer, McCoist	35,559
5	31	(a)	Celtic	W 2-0	Hateley 2	51,382
6	Sep 7	(a)	Falkirk	W 2-0	Nisbet, Huistra	13,088
7	14	(h)	Dundee U	D 1-1	McCoist	36,347
8	21	(a)	St Mirren	W 2-1	Huistra, Nisbet	14,503
9	28	(h)	Aberdeen	L 0-2		36,330
10	Oct 5	(a)	Airdrieonians	W 4-0	McCoist 2, Nisbet, Johnston	11,101
11	8	(h)	Hibernian	W 4-2	McCoist 2, Huistra, Tortolano (og)	35,368
12	12	(a)	St Johnstone	W 3-2	McCoist 2, Nisbet	10,323
13	19	(h)	Hearts	W 2-0	McCoist, Mikhailichenko	36,481
14	26	(h)	Falkirk	D 1-1	Johnston	36,441
15	29	(a)	Dundee U	L 2-3	McCoist 2	15,041
16	Nov 2	(h)	Celtic	D 1-1	McCoist	37,387
17	9	(a)	Dunfermline A	W 5-0	Gordon 2, Gough, Hateley, McCoist	13,351
18	16	(h)	Airdrieonians	W 4-0	Hateley 2, D.Robertson, McCoist	36,934
19	19	(a)	Hibernian	W 3-0	McCoist 2, Hateley	16,833
20	23	(h)	St Mirren	L 0-1		36,272
21	30	(a)	Motherwell	W 2-0	Gordon, Gough	15,350
22	Dec 4	(a)	Aberdeen	W 3-2	Hateley 2, McCoist	20,081
23	7	(h)	St Johnstone	W 3-1	Mikhailichenko, Brown, Hateley	35,784
24	14	(a)	Falkirk	W 3-1	McCoist, Hateley, McCall	11,801
25	21	(h)	Dundee U	W 2-0	McCoist 2	41,448
26	28	(a)	Dunfermline A	W 3-1	Stevens, Gordon	41,328
27	Jan 1	(a)	Celtic	W 3-1	McCoist, Hateley (pen), Brown	51,789
28	4	(a)	Airdrieonians	D 0-0		12,276
29	11	(h)	Hibernian	W 2-0	Gordon, McCoist	40,616
30	18	(h)	Motherwell	W 2-0	McCoist, Mikhailichenko	38,217
31	Feb 1	(h)	Hearts	W 1-0	McCoist	24,356
32	8	(a)	St Mirren	W 2-1	McCoist, Mikhailichenko	16,638
33	25	(h)	Aberdeen	D 0-0		38,513
34	29	(a)	Airdrieonians	W 5-0	Hateley 3 (2 pens), Brown, Rideout	40,568
35	Mar 10	(a)	Hibernian	W 3-1	Hateley 2 (1 pen), McCoist	13,387
36	14	(a)	Dunfermline A	W 3-1	Mikhailichenko 2, Nisbet	12,274
37	21	(h)	Celtic	L 0-2		42,160
38	28	(a)	St Johnstone	W 2-1	Hateley 2	9,697
39	Apr 7	(h)	Falkirk	W 4-1	McCoist 3, Mikhailichenko	36,832
40	11	(a)	Dundee U	W 2-1	Mikhailichenko, Brown	11,713
41	18	(h)	St Mirren	W 4-0	McCoist 2, Stevens, Huistra	40,362
42	23	(a)	Motherwell	W 2-1	Mikhailichenko 2	12,515
43	28	(h)	Hearts	D 1-1	McCoist	36,129
44	May 2	(a)	Aberdeen	W 2-0	McCoist 2	16,580

FINAL LEAGUE POSITION: 1st

Player appearance summary (Scottish League):

	Goram	Stevens	Robertson D	Gough	Spackman	Nisbet	Steven	Ferguson	Hateley	Johnston	Huistra	Robertson A	Spencer	McCall	Durrant	McCoist	Michailichenko	Kuznetsov	Brown	Vinnicombe	McSwegan	McGregor	Morrow	Gordon	Rideout	Pressley	Robertson L
Appearances	44	43	42	33	42	20	2	12	29	10	25	3	4	35	9	37	24	16	18	1		1	3	23	7		1
Sub appearances								4	1	1	7	3	4	1	4	1	3	2	7	1	4			4	1		
Goals		2	1	2		5	1	1	21	5	5		1	1		34	10		4					5	1		

2 own-goals

Scottish FA Cup

Rd	Date	V	Opponent	Result	Scorers	Att
3	Jan 22	(a)	Aberdeen	W 1-0	McCoist	23,000
4	Feb 15	(h)	Motherwell	W 2-1	Mikhailichenko 2	38,444
QF	Mar 3	(a)	St Johnstone	W 3-0	McCoist, Gough, Hateley	10,107
SF	31	(n*)	Celtic	W 1-0	McCoist	45,191
F	May 9	(n*)	Airdrieonians	W 2-1	Hateley, McCoist	44,045

*Played at Hampden Park, Glasgow.

	Appearances	Sub appearances	Goals
(summary)	5 5 5 5 5 / 3 2 / 2 / 3 2 5 3 / 5 / 4 1	1 / 4 2 / 1 / 1 1	1 / 2 / 4 2

Scottish League Cup

Rd	Date	V	Opponent	Result	Scorers	Att
2	Aug 20	(h)	Queen's Park	W 6-0	Johnston 4, Durrant, Spackman	32,230
3	28	(a)	Partick Thistle	W 2-0	Johnston, D.Robertson	12,587
QF	Sep 4	(a)	Hearts	W 1-0	McCoist	22,878
SF	25	(n*)	Hibernian	L 0-1		40,901

*Played at Hampden Park, Glasgow.

	Appearances	Sub appearances	Goals
(summary)	4 4 4 3 4 4 / 1 2 4 3 / 2 4 3 1 / 1	1 / 1 1 / 3	1 1 / 5 / 1 1

European Champions' Cup

Rd	Date	V	Opponent	Result	Scorers	Att
1	Sep 18	(a)	Sparta Prague	L 0-1		11,053
	Oct 2	(h)	Sparta Prague	W 2-1	McCall 2	34,260

	Appearances	Sub appearances	Goals
(summary)	2 2 2 1 2 2 / 1 1 1 1 / 2 / 2 1 1 1	1 2 / 1	2

Further match details for this season are continued on page 284

1992-93

Manager: W.Smith

Scottish League

Player columns (left to right): Goram, Nisbet, Robertson D, Gough, McPherson, Brown, Durrant, McCall, McCoist, Hateley, Huistra, Rideout, Kuznetsov, Gordon, Michaillichenko, Steven, Maxwell, Ferguson I, Spackman, Hagen, Robertson A, Stevens, McSwegan, Pressley, Murray, Watson, Reid, Robertson L

#	Date		Opponent	Result	Scorers	Att.
1	Aug	1 (h)	St Johnstone	W 1-0	McCoist	38,036
2		4 (h)	Airdrieonians	W 2-0	Gordon, Hateley	34,613
3		8 (a)	Hibernian	D 0-0		17,044
4		15 (a)	Dundee	L 3-4	McCoist 2, Ferguson	12,807
5		22 (h)	Celtic	D 1-1	Durrant	43,239
6		29 (h)	Aberdeen	W 3-1	Durrant, McCoist, Mikhailichenko	41,636
7	Sep	2 (a)	Motherwell	W 4-1	McCoist 3, Brown	10,074
8		12 (a)	Partick Thistle	W 4-1	McPherson, McCall, Gough, Hateley	18,460
9		19 (h)	Hearts	W 2-0	McCall, McCoist	41,888
10		26 (a)	Dundee U	W 4-0	Huistra 2, Steven, McCoist	13,515
11	Oct	3 (h)	Falkirk	W 4-0	McCoist 4	40,691
12		7 (a)	St Johnstone	W 5-1	McCoist 2, Hateley 2, Ferguson	9,532
13		17 (h)	Hibernian	W 1-0	McCoist	40,978
14		31 (h)	Motherwell	W 4-2	McCoist 3 (1 pen), Brown	38,719
15	Nov	7 (a)	Celtic	W 1-0	Durrant	51,958
16		11 (h)	Dundee	W 3-1	McCoist 2, Hateley	33,497
17		21 (a)	Hearts	D 1-1	McCoist	20,831
18		28 (h)	Partick Thistle	W 3-0	Steven, McSwegan, McPherson	40,939
19	Dec	1 (a)	Airdrieonians	D 1-1	Brown	8,000
20		12 (a)	Falkirk	W 2-1	Hateley, McCoist	12,000
21		19 (h)	St Johnstone	W 2-0	Gough, D.Robertson	35,369
22		26 (a)	Dundee	W 3-1	Hateley 2, McCoist	13,983
23	Jan	2 (h)	Celtic	W 1-0	Steven	46,039
24		5 (h)	Dundee U	W 3-2	Hateley, McCall, McCoist	40,239
25		30 (a)	Hibernian	W 4-3	Hateley 2, Steven, McCoist	17,444
26	Feb	2 (a)	Aberdeen	W 1-0	Hateley	15,500
27		9 (h)	Falkirk	W 5-0	Hateley 2, D.Robertson, Steven, Huistra	34,780
28		13 (h)	Airdrieonians	D 2-2	McCoist 2	39,816
29		20 (a)	Dundee U	D 0-0		13,234
30		23 (a)	Motherwell	W 4-0	Hateley 2, McCoist, Mikhailichenko	14,006
31		27 (h)	Hearts	W 2-1	McCoist, D.Robertson	42,128
32	Mar	10 (a)	St Johnstone	D 1-1	McCoist	9,210
33		13 (h)	Hibernian	W 3-0	Hagen, Hateley, McCoist	41,076
34		20 (a)	Celtic	L 1-2	Hateley	53,241
35		27 (h)	Dundee	W 3-0	McCall, McCoist, Ferguson	40,294
36		30 (a)	Aberdeen	W 2-0	Ferguson, McCoist	44,570
37	Apr	10 (h)	Motherwell	W 1-0	Brown	41,353
38		14 (a)	Hearts	W 3-2	Hateley 2, McCall	14,622
39		17 (h)	Partick Thistle	W 3-1	McSwegan 2, Hagen	42,636
40	May	1 (a)	Airdrieonians	W 1-0	McSwegan	11,830
41		4 (a)	Partick Thistle	L 0-3		9,834
42		8 (h)	Dundee U	W 1-0	Huistra	42,917
43		12 (a)	Aberdeen	L 0-1		13,500
44		15 (a)	Falkirk	W 2-1	Mikhailichenko, Hateley	8,517

FINAL LEAGUE POSITION: 1st

Appearances: 34 10 39 25 34 39 19 35 32 36 27 · 8 18 16 24 10 29 2 5 · 9 8 8 11 3 2 1
Sub appearances: · 11 1 2 1 3 · 1 4 13 · · 1 · 3 2 · 1 5
Goals: · · 3 2 2 4 3 5 34 21 4 · 1 3 5 · 4 · 2 · 4

Scottish FA Cup

#	Date		Opponent	Result	Scorers	Att.
3	Jan	9 (a)	Motherwell	W 2-0	McCoist 2	14,314
4	Feb	6 (a)	Ayr U	W 2-0	McCoist, Gordon	13,176
QF	Mar	6 (a)	Arbroath	W 3-0	Hateley, Murray, McCoist (pen)	6,488
SF	Apr	3 (n*)	Hearts	W 2-1	McPherson, McCoist	41,738
F	May	29 (n*)	Aberdeen	W 2-1	Murray, Hateley	50,715

*Played at Celtic Park, Glasgow.

Appearances: 4 3 5 2 4 5 1 5 4 5 2 · 2 3 3 1 2 · 1 · 1 · · 2
Sub appearances: · · · · · 2 · · · 1 · · · · · · · · · · 1 1
Goals: · · 1 · · · · 5 2 · · 1 · · · · · · 2

Scottish League Cup

#	Date		Opponent	Result	Scorers	Att.
2	Aug	11 (a*)	Dumbarton	W 5-0	Durrant, Gordon, Hateley, McCoist, Mikhailichenko	11,091
3		19 (a)	Stranraer	W 5-0	McCoist 3, Hateley 2	4,500
QF		26 (a)	Dundee U	W 3-2	McCoist, Gough, Huistra	15,716
SF	Sep	22 (n*)	St Johnstone	W 3-1	McCoist 3	30,062
F	Oct	25 (n*)	Aberdeen	W 2-1	McCall, Smith (og)	45,298

*Played at Hampden Park, Glasgow.

Appearances: 4 1 5 5 5 3 5 4 5 4 3 · 1 1 1 1 4 1 · 1 1
Sub appearances: · 1 · · · 2 · · · · 1 · 1 1 1
Goals: · · · 1 · · 1 1 8 3 1 · 1 1

1 own-goal

European Champions' Cup

#	Date		Opponent	Result	Scorers	Att.
1	Sep	16 (h)	Lyngby BK	W 2-0	Hateley, Huistra	40,036
		30 (a)	Lyngby BK	W 1-0	Durrant	4,273
2	Oct	21 (h)	Leeds U	W 2-1	McCoist, Lukic (og)	43,251
	Nov	4 (a)	Leeds U	W 2-1	Hateley, McCoist	25,118

CHAMPIONS LEAGUE GROUP A

#	Date		Opponent	Result	Scorers	Att.
1	Nov	25 (a*)	Marseille	D 2-2	McSwegan, Hateley	41,624
2	Dec	9 (a*)	CSKA Moscow	W 1-0	Ferguson	9,000
3	Mar	3 (a)	Club Brugge KV	D 1-1	Huistra	19,000
4		17 (h)	Club Brugge KV	W 2-1	Durrant, Nisbet	42,731
5	Apr	7 (a)	Marseille	D 1-1	Durrant	46,000
6		21 (h)	CSKA Moscow	D 0-0		43,142

*Played at Bochum, Germany.

Appearances: 10 2 9 7 10 10 9 9 9 8 5 · 1 4 7 7 · · · · 3
Sub appearances: · · · · · · · · · · 1 · · 1 · · 1 · 3 2 1
Goals: · 1 · · · 3 · 2 3 2 · · · · · 1

1 own-goal

Further match details for this season are continued on page 284

1993-94

Manager: W.Smith

Scottish League

Player columns (left to right): Maxwell, McCall, Wishart, Gough, Pressley, Brown, Murray, Ferguson I, Hagen, Hateley, Mikhailichenko, Durrant, Huistra, Steven, Vinnicombe, McPherson, Ferguson D, Stevens, Robertson D, Kuznetsov, Morrow, Miller, McCoist, Scott, Durie, Goram, Moore

No	Date		Opponent	Result	Scorers	Att.
1	Aug	7 (h)	Hearts	W 2-1	Hagen, Hateley	43,261
2		14 (a)	St Johnstone	W 2-1	Gough, I.Ferguson	10,152
3		21 (a)	Celtic	D 0-0		47,942
4		28 (h)	Kilmarnock	L 1-2	Pressley	44,243
5	Sep	4 (a)	Dundee	D 1-1	Hateley	14,211
6		11 (h)	Partick Thistle	D 1-1	Hateley	40,988
7		18 (a)	Aberdeen	L 0-2		19,138
8		25 (h)	Hibernian	W 2-1	Steven, Hateley	43,200
9	Oct	2 (a)	Raith Rovers	D 1-1	Hetherston (og)	8,161
10		6 (h)	Motherwell	L 1-2	I.Ferguson	39,816
11		9 (a)	Dundee U	W 3-1	Huistra 2, Hateley	11,262
12		16 (a)	St Johnstone	W 2-0	Huistra, Hateley	41,960
13		30 (h)	Celtic	L 1-2	McCoist	47,522
14	Nov	3 (a)	Hearts	D 2-2	Hateley 2	18,370
15		6 (a)	Kilmarnock	W 2-0	I.Ferguson, Huistra	19,162
16		10 (h)	Dundee	W 3-1	McCoist 2 (1 pen), I.Ferguson	38,477
17		13 (a)	Raith Rovers	D 2-2	Hateley 2	42,611
18		20 (a)	Hibernian	W 1-0	Gough	16,506
19		27 (a)	Partick Thistle	D 1-1	Huistra	17,292
20	Dec	1 (h)	Aberdeen	W 2-0	Hateley 2	45,182
21		4 (a)	Motherwell	W 2-0	Durie 2	14,069
22		11 (h)	Dundee U	L 0-3		43,058
23		18 (a)	St Johnstone	W 4-0	Hateley 2, Steven, Durie	10,056
24		27 (h)	Hearts	D 2-2	Hateley 2	45,116
25	Jan	1 (a)	Celtic	W 4-2	Mikhailichenko 2, Hateley, Kuznetsov	48,506
26		8 (h)	Kilmarnock	W 3-0	Hateley 2, Huistra	44,919
27		15 (a)	Dundee	D 1-1	Durie	11,014
28		22 (a)	Aberdeen	D 0-0		20,267
29	Feb	5 (h)	Partick Thistle	W 5-1	Durie 2, Mikhailichenko, McCall, Steven	42,606
30		12 (h)	Hibernian	W 2-0	Durie, Steven	43,265
31		26 (a)	Raith Rovers	W 2-1	I.Ferguson, Durie	8,988
32	Mar	5 (h)	Motherwell	W 2-1	Durie, Hateley (pen)	43,669
33		19 (h)	St Johnstone	W 4-0	McCall, Hateley, McPherson, Durie	43,228
34		26 (a)	Hearts	L 1-2	McCoist, Hateley	18,108
35		29 (a)	Partick Thistle	W 2-1	Gough, McCoist	14,706
36	Apr	2 (h)	Aberdeen	D 1-1	McCall	45,888
37		5 (a)	Dundee U	D 0-0		11,352
38		16 (h)	Raith Rovers	W 4-0	D.Robertson, McCoist, D.Ferguson, Mikhailichenko	42,545
39		23 (h)	Dundee	W 2-1	Durie 2	44,776
40		26 (a)	Motherwell	L 1-2	McCoist	14,050
41		30 (h)	Celtic	D 1-1	Mikhailichenko	47,018
42	May	3 (a)	Hibernian	L 0-1		14,517
43		7 (a)	Kilmarnock	L 0-1		18,012
44		14 (h)	Dundee	D 0-0		41,620

FINAL LEAGUE POSITION: 1st

Appearances: Maxwell 31, McCall 34, Wishart 5, Gough 37, Pressley 17, Brown 24, Murray 20, Ferguson I 35, Hagen 4, Hateley 40, Mikhailichenko 24, Durrant 14, Huistra 10, Steven 32, Vinnicombe 2, McPherson 27, Ferguson D 7, Stevens 28, Robertson D 32, Kuznetsov 4, Morrow 2, Miller 16, McCoist 5, Scott 23, Durie 8, Goram 1

Sub appearances: Maxwell 1, Brown 6, Murray 2, Hagen 2, Hateley 2, Mikhailichenko 10, Durrant 9, Huistra 11, McPherson 2, Ferguson D 1, Stevens 3, Kuznetsov 1, Miller 5, McCoist 1, Scott 1

Goals: McCall 3, Gough 3, Pressley 1, Ferguson I 5, Hagen 1, Hateley 22, Mikhailichenko 5, Huistra 6, Steven 4, Ferguson D 1, Stevens 1, Robertson D 1, Kuznetsov 1, Scott 7, Durie 12

1 own-goal

Scottish FA Cup

Rd	Date		Opponent	Result	Scorers	Att.
3	Jan	29 (h)	Dumbarton	W 4-1	Durie, Hateley (pen), Steven, D.Robertson	36,809
4	Feb	19 (h)	Alloa Athletic	W 6-0	McCoist 3 (1 pen), I.Ferguson, McPherson, Newbigging (og)	37,804
QF	Mar	12 (n)	Hearts	W 2-0	Brown, Hateley	41,666
SF	Apr	10 (n*)	Kilmarnock	D 0-0		35,144
R		13 (n*)	Kilmarnock	W 2-1	Hateley 2	29,860
F	May	21 (n*)	Dundee U	L 0-1		37,450

*Played at Hampden Park, Glasgow.

Appearances: 4, 6, 5, 1, 4, 3, 5, 6, 3, 1, 3, 5, 3, 6, 4, 5, 2

Sub appearances: 1, 2, 1, 3, 1, 2

Goals: 1, 1, 4, 1, 1, 1, 3, 1

1 own-goal

Scottish League Cup

Rd	Date		Opponent	Result	Scorers	Att.
2	Aug	11 (h)	Dumbarton	W 1-0	I.Ferguson	36,309
3		25 (a)	Dunfermline A	W 2-0	Steven, I.Ferguson	12,993
QF	Sep	1 (h)	Aberdeen	W 2-1	Hateley (pen), I.Ferguson	45,604
SF		22 (h)	Celtic	W 1-0	Hateley	47,420
F	Oct	24 (n*)	Hibernian	W 2-1	Durrant, McCoist	47,632

*Played at Celtic Park, Glasgow.

Appearances: 5, 2, 2, 5, 3, 2, 5, 1, 5, 1, 5, 3, 5, 1, 2, 1, 3, 4

Sub appearances: 2, 1, 1, 1

Goals: 3, 2, 1, 1

European Champions' Cup

Rd	Date		Opponent	Result	Scorers	Att.
1	Sep	15 (h)	Levski Sofia	W 3-2	Hateley 2, McPherson	37,013
		29 (a)	Levski Sofia	L 1-2	Durrant	50,000

Appearances: 2, 2, 1, 1, 1, 2, 1, 2, 2, 2, 2, 1, 2, 1

Sub appearances: 1

Goals: 2, 1, 1

Further match details for this season are continued on page 284

1994-95

Manager: W.Smith

Scottish League

Player columns (left→right): Goram, Murray, Robertson D, Gough, Boli, McPherson, Durrant, McCall, McCoist, Hateley, Laudrup, Ferguson D, Brown, Moore, Ferguson I, Pressley, Durie, Mikhailichenko, Miller, Huistra, Hagen, Wishart, McLaren, Scott, McGinty, Maxwell, Steven, Bollan, Cleland, Thomson, Robertson L, Caldwell

#	Date	V	Opponent	Result	Scorers	Att
1	Aug 13	(h)	Motherwell	W 2-1	Hateley, D.Ferguson	43,750
2	20	(a)	Partick Thistle	W 2-0	Hateley, Byrne (og)	15,030
3	27	(h)	Celtic	L 0-2		45,466
4	Sep 11	(h)	Hearts	W 3-0	Hateley 2, Durie	41,041
5	17	(a)	Falkirk	W 2-0	Boli, Laudrup	12,500
6	24	(a)	Aberdeen	D 2-2	Hateley, Moore	21,000
7	Oct 1	(h)	Dundee U	W 2-0	Hateley, Laudrup	43,030
8	8	(a)	Hibernian	L 1-2	Boli	12,118
9	15	(h)	Kilmarnock	W 2-0	Miller, D.Robertson	44,099
10	22	(a)	Motherwell	L 1-2	Philliben (og)	11,160
11	30(a*)		Celtic	W 3-1	Hateley 2, Laudrup	32,171
12	Nov 5	(h)	Partick Thistle	W 3-0	Miller, Hateley, Laudrup	43,696
13	9	(a)	Hearts	D 1-1	Hateley	12,347
14	19	(h)	Falkirk	D 1-1	Hateley	44,018
15	25	(h)	Aberdeen	W 1-0	McCoist	45,072
16	Dec 4	(a)	Dundee U	W 3-0	Laudrup, Huistra, Durrant	10,692
17	10	(a)	Kilmarnock	W 2-1	McLaren, Laudrup	17,283
18	26	(h)	Hibernian	W 2-0	Hateley, Gough	44,892
19	31	(h)	Motherwell	W 3-1	McCall, Laudrup, Durie	11,500
20	Jan 4	(h)	Celtic	D 1-1	I.Ferguson	45,794
21	7	(a)	Partick Thistle	D 1-1	D.Robertson	19,351
22	14	(a)	Falkirk	W 3-2	Huistra 2 (1 pen), McCall	13,495
23	21	(h)	Hearts	W 1-0	Miller	44,231
24	Feb 4	(h)	Dundee U	D 1-1	D.Robertson	44,197
25	12	(a)	Aberdeen	L 0-2		20,000
26	25	(h)	Kilmarnock	W 3-0	Durie, Laudrup, Durrant	44,859
27	Mar 4	(a)	Hibernian	D 1-1	McCall	12,059
28	11	(a)	Falkirk	D 2-2	Brown, Laudrup	43,359
29	18	(a)	Hearts	L 1-2	Laudrup	9,806
30	Apr 1	(a)	Dundee U	W 2-1	Durie, McLaren	11,500
31	8	(h)	Aberdeen	W 3-2	Durrant, Murray, Hateley	44,460
32	16	(h)	Hibernian	W 3-1	Durie, Durrant, Mikhailichenko	44,193
33	20	(a)	Kilmarnock	W 1-0	Mikhailichenko	16,086
34	29	(h)	Motherwell	L 0-2		43,576
35	May 7(a*)		Celtic	L 0-3		31,025
36	13	(h)	Partick Thistle	D 1-1	Moore	45,280

League appearances/goals summary

	Gor	Mur	RobD	Gou	Bol	McP	Dur	McC	McCo	Hat	Lau	FerD	Bro	Moo	FerI	Pre	Dur	Mik	Mil	Hui	Hag	Wis	McL	Sco	McG	Max	Ste	Bol	Cle	Tho	RobL	Cal
Appearances	18	14	23	25	28	9	16	30	4	23	33	1	10	19	13	2	16	4	21	15		3	24	3	1	10	10	5	10	5		1
Sub appearances	1	6					10		5				3	3	2	3		4	5		2	1		1		1	1	1				1
Goals		1	3	1	2		4	3	1	13	10	1	1	2	1		5	2	3	3			2									

FINAL LEAGUE POSITION: 1st
*Played at Hampden Park, Glasgow.

McKnight played number-12 in Match 36. 2 own-goals

Scottish FA Cup

#	Date	V	Opponent	Result	Scorers	Att
3	Feb 6(a*)		Hamilton A	W 3-1	Steven, Boli, Laudrup	18,379
4	20	(a)	Hearts	L 2-4	Laudrup, Durie	12,375

*Played at Firhill Park, Glasgow.

Scottish League Cup

#	Date	V	Opponent	Result	Scorers	Att
2	Aug 17	(a)	Arbroath	W 6-1	D.Ferguson 3, Hateley 2, McCall	4,665
3	31	(h)	Falkirk	L 1-2	Laudrup	40,697

Stevens played number-2 in Match 1.

European Champions' Cup

#	Date	V	Opponent	Result	Scorers	Att
1	Aug 10	(a)	AEK Athens	L 0-2		30,000
	24	(h)	AEK Athens	L 0-1		44,789

The Ibrox International Challenge Trophy

#	Date	V	Opponent	Result	Scorers	Att
SF	Aug 5	(h)	Sampdoria	L 2-4	Steven, Hateley	27,282
3/4	6	(h)	Manchester U	W 1-0	May (og)	30,186

Stevens played number-2 in Match 3/4. Fotheringham played number-14 in Match 3/4. 1 own-goal.

Other matches

#	Date	V	Opponent	Result	Scorers	Att
1	Jul 27	(a)	Aalborg	D 1-1	Hateley	7,300
2	29	(a)	1.FC Kaiserslautern	L 0-1		17,000
3	Aug 1	(a)	Ikast FS	D 1-1	Boli	4,265
4	Nov 1	(h)	Huntly *	W 5-2	McCoist 3, Huistra, McGinty	3,500
5	May 1	(h)	Rangers Int †	W 3-2	Mikhailichenko, Hateley, McCoist	27,705

*Floodlight Inauguration. †Scott Nisbet Testimonial Match.

Stevens played number-12 in Matches 1 & 2, and number-2 in Match 3. Dodds played number-14 in Match 4.

1995-96

Manager: W.Smith

Scottish League

Player columns: Goram, Wright, Robertson D, Gough, McLaren, Petric, Steven, Miller, McCoist, McCall, Durie, Durrant, Salenko, Gascoigne, Laudrup, Moore, Murray, Mikhailichenko, Cleland, Ferguson I, Brown, Scott, Bollan, Thomson, McGinty, McInnes, Van Vossen, Andersen, Snelders, Shields, Hateley, Reid

#		Date	Venue/Opponent	Result	Scorers	Att.
1	Aug	26 (h)	Kilmarnock	W 1-0	McCall	44,686
2	Sep	9 (h)	Raith Rovers	W 4-0	McCoist 2, Miller, D.Robertson	43,535
3		16 (a)	Falkirk	W 2-0	Salenko, D.Robertson	11,445
4		23 (h)	Hibernian	L 0-1		44,364
5		30 (a)	Celtic	W 2-0	Cleland, Gascoigne	34,500
6	Oct	3 (h)	Motherwell	W 2-1	Gascoigne, McCoist	37,348
7		7 (a)	Aberdeen	W 1-0	Moore	22,500
8		14 (a)	Partick Thistle	W 4-0	Durie 3, Gough	16,346
9		21 (h)	Hearts	W 4-1	Salenko 2, Gascoigne, Durie	45,155
10		28 (a)	Raith Rovers	D 2-2	Gough, Petric	9,200
11	Nov	4 (h)	Falkirk	W 2-0	McCoist 2	42,059
12		8 (a)	Kilmarnock	W 2-0	McLaren, Salenko	14,823
13		11 (h)	Aberdeen	D 1-1	Salenko	45,427
14		19 (h)	Celtic	D 3-3	Laudrup, McCoist, McKinlay (og)	46,640
15		25 (a)	Hibernian	W 4-1	McCoist, Miller, Durie, Dods (og)	13,558
16	Dec	2 (a)	Hearts	W 2-0	McCoist (pen), Gascoigne	15,105
17		9 (h)	Partick Thistle	W 1-0	Durie	43,173
18		19 (a)	Motherwell	D 0-0		10,179
19		26 (h)	Kilmarnock	W 3-0	Salenko, Durie (pen), Gascoigne	45,173
20		30 (h)	Hibernian	W 7-0	Durie 4, Miller, Gascoigne, Salenko	44,692
21	Jan	3 (a)	Celtic	D 0-0		37,000
22		6 (a)	Falkirk	W 4-0	McCoist 2 (1 pen), Durie, D.Robertson	10,581
23		13 (h)	Raith Rovers	W 4-0	Durie 2, McCoist, I.Ferguson	42,498
24		20 (h)	Hearts	L 0-3		45,096
25	Feb	3 (a)	Partick Thistle	W 2-1	Gascoigne 2	16,523
26		10 (h)	Motherwell	W 3-2	I.Ferguson, McLaren, McCoist (pen)	45,566
27		25 (a)	Aberdeen	W 1-0	Gascoigne	21,000
28	Mar	3 (a)	Hibernian	W 2-0	Laudrup (pen), Mitchell (og)	11,954
29		17 (h)	Celtic	D 1-1	McLaren	47,312
30		23 (h)	Falkirk	W 3-2	Andersen 2, Gascoigne	46,014
31		30 (a)	Raith Rovers	W 4-2	McCoist 3 (1 pen), Durie (pen)	9,300
32	Apr	10 (a)	Hearts	L 0-2		15,350
33		13 (h)	Partick Thistle	W 5-0	Andersen 3, McCall, Gough	46,438
34		20 (a)	Motherwell	W 3-1	McCall, Andersen, Gascoigne	13,128
35		28 (h)	Aberdeen	W 3-1	Gascoigne 3 (1 pen)	47,247
36	May	4 (a)	Kilmarnock	W 3-0	Durie 2, McCoist	17,056

FINAL LEAGUE POSITION: 1st

	Goram	Wright	Robertson D	Gough	McLaren	Petric	Steven	Miller	McCoist	McCall	Durie	Durrant	Salenko	Gascoigne	Laudrup	Moore	Murray	Mikhailichenko	Cleland	Ferguson I	Brown	Scott	Bollan	Thomson	McGinty	McInnes	Van Vossen	Andersen	Snelders	Shields	Hateley	Reid
Appearances	30	6	25	29	36	32	5	17	18	19	21	6	14	27	22	9	2	6	21	16	8	3	4	1	2	5	3	6	2	1		
Sub appearances							1	1	6	7	2	6	9	2	1		2	3	5	4	2	6					1	4				
Goals			3	3	3	1		3	16	3	17		7	14	2	1			1	2								6				

3 own-goals

Scottish FA Cup

#		Date	Venue/Opponent	Result	Scorers	Att.
3	Jan	27 (a*)	Keith	W 10-1	I.Ferguson 3, Cleland 3, Durie (pen), D.Robertson, Miller, Mikhailichenko	14,000
4	Feb	15 (a)	Clyde	W 4-1	Miller 2, Van Vossen, Gascoigne	5,722
QF	Mar	9 (a†)	Caledonian Th	W 3-0	Gascoigne 2, Thomson (og)	12,000
SF	Apr	7 (n‡)	Celtic	W 2-1	McCoist, Laudrup	36,333
F	May	18 (n‡)	Hearts	W 5-1	Durie 3, Laudrup 2	37,730

* Played at Pittodrie Stadium, Aberdeen.   † Played at Tannadice Park, Dundee.
‡ Played at Hampden Park, Glasgow.

	Appearances	Sub appearances	Goals
Goram	5		
Robertson D	5		1
Gough	2		
McLaren	5		
Petric	4	1	
Steven			
Miller	3		3
McCoist	2		1
McCall	4		
Durie	3	3	4
Salenko	4		
Gascoigne	5		3
Laudrup	2	1	3
Cleland	3	1	1
Ferguson I	3	1	3
Brown	3		3
Van Vossen	2		1

1 own-goal

Scottish League Cup

#		Date	Venue/Opponent	Result	Scorers	Att.
2	Aug	19 (h)	Morton	W 3-0	McCoist, Hateley, Gascoigne	42,941
3		30 (h)	Stirling Albion	W 3-2	Hateley, McCall, McCoist	46,686
QF	Sep	19 (a)	Celtic	W 1-0	McCoist	32,789
SF	Oct	24 (n*)	Aberdeen	L 1-2	Salenko	26,131

*Played at Hampden Park, Glasgow.

	Appearances	Sub appearances	Goals
Goram	4		
Wright	4		
Robertson D	3		
Gough	3		
McLaren	3		
Petric	3		
Steven	3		
Miller	4		3
McCoist	1	1	1
Durrant	1	2	
Salenko	2		1
Gascoigne	3		1
Laudrup	1		
Moore	2	1	
Cleland	1	2	
Ferguson I	1		
Hateley	2		2

European Champions' Cup

#		Date	Venue/Opponent	Result	Scorers	Att.
1	Aug	9 (h)	Anorthosis Fam	W 1-0	Durie	43,519
		23 (a)	Anorthosis Fam	D 0-0		12,000

Champions' League Group C

#		Date	Venue/Opponent	Result	Scorers	Att.
1	Sep	13 (a)	Steaua Bucharest	L 0-1		26,000
2		27 (h)	Borussia Dortm'd	D 2-2	Gough, I.Ferguson	33,209
3	Oct	18 (a)	Juventus	L 1-4	Gough	49,825
4	Nov	1 (h)	Juventus	L 0-4		42,523
5		22 (h)	Steaua Bucharest	D 1-1	Gascoigne	30,800
6	Dec	6 (a)	Borussia Dortm'd	D 2-2	Laudrup, Durie	35,800

	Appearances	Sub appearances	Goals
Goram	8		
Wright	6		
Robertson D	5		
Gough	8		2
McLaren	5		
Petric	6		
Steven	5	2	
Miller	4	2	
McCoist	7	2	
McCall	4	2	
Durie	2	4	2
Salenko	2		
Gascoigne	7		1
Laudrup	5		1
Moore	1	4	1
Hateley	2		
Reid	1		

The Ibrox International Challenge Trophy

#		Date	Venue/Opponent	Result	Scorers	Att.
SF	Jul	29 (h)	Steaua Bucharest	W 4-0	I.Ferguson, Gascoigne, Hateley, McCoist	18,225
F		30 (h)	Sampdoria	W 2-0	Durie, McCoist	19,493

	Appearances	Sub appearances	Goals
Goram	2		
Wright	1		
Robertson D	1		
Gough	2		
McLaren	2		
Petric	1		
Steven	1		
Durie	1	2	2
Salenko	1	1	1
Gascoigne	1	1	1
Moore	2		
Mikhailichenko	2	1	
Cleland	1	1	
Hateley	1		1
Reid	1		

Further match details for this season are continued on page 284

1900-01 continued
Other matches

No	Date	Opponent	Result	Scorers	Att	Dickie	Smith N	Drummond	Gibson	Neil	Robertson	Campbell	Cameron	Hamilton RC	McPherson	Smith A	Stark	Tutty	Crawford	Speedie	Graham	Sharp A	Brown	Hamilton JR	Munsie	McIntyre	McKinlay	Leslie	Taylor	Howden	Finlay	Johnstone	Knox	Donald	McKenzie	Kirkland
1	Aug 15	(h) Hibernian	W 2-1	McPherson, Cameron	3,000	1		3	4	5	6	7	9	10	8	11			2																	
2	16	(h) Partick Thistle	D 2-2	Cameron, R.C.Hamilton	2,000	1	2	3	4		6		9	10		11	5	8			7															
3	20	(h) St Mirren	D 0-0			1	2			5	6	7		9	10	11	4	8	3																	
4	22	(a) Clyde	W 2-1	R.C.Hamilton, Tutty		1		3	6	5	10	7		8		11		9	2								4									
5	29	(h) Celtic*	W 3-1	Tutty, Cameron, Robertson (pen)	4,000	1		3		5	6	7	9	10		11	4	8	2																	
6	Sep 3	(h) Sunderland	D 1-1	Robertson (pen)	3,000	1		3	4		6	7		10		11	5	9	2									8								
7	11	(a†) East Stirling	W 2-1	McPherson, Taylor	4,000	1	2		4		6			9	10	11	5				7						3		8							
8	Dec 8	(h) Hibernian‡	W 2-0	Stark, RC.Hamilton		1	2	3	4			7	8	9	6	11	5			10																
9	22	(h) Sunderland	L 0-3		4,000	1		3		5	6		8	9		11	4		2	10	7															
10	25	(a) Newcastle U	L 1-4	Speedie	8,000	1	2			5	6	7	9		8	11	4		3	10																
11	Feb 9	(h) Airdrieonians	W 5-3	Campbell 2, R.C.Hamilton, Speedie, Robertson	1,500	1	2	3	4	5	6	7		9		11				10		8														
12	23	(a) Dundee	W 4-3	Cameron, Speedie, Robertson, Longair (og)		1		3	6	5			9		11		4		2	10	7	8														
13	Apr 5	(a) Blackburn R	W 3-2	R.C.Hamilton 2, Neil	12,000	1	2	3	4	5	6	7			9	11				10		8														
14	6	(a) Bolton W	L 0-2		3,490																															
15	9	(a#) Linfield	W 8-1	McPherson 2, Speedie 2, A.Smith 2, Campbell, R.C.Hamilton	10,000	1	2	3	4	5	6	7		9	8	11				10																
16	10	(a§) Linfield	W 4-2	R.C.Hamilton, Speedie, Campbell, Sharp	1,500		2	3	4		6	7		9	1	11	5			10		8														
17	29	(h) Newcastle U	W 3-1	Speedie 2, Campbell (pen)	3,000		2		4		6	11					5		3	10	7	8								1	9					
18	May 4	(a) Caledonian	D 2-2	Untraced																																
19	6	(a) Aberdeen	D 3-3	R.C.Hamilton 2, Speedie		1		3		2	4	11		9			5			10		8										6	7			
20	7	(a) Arbroath	L 3-5	Untraced																																
21	8	(a) St Johnstone	L 1-2	Robertson																																
22	11	(a) Kilmarnock	W 2-1	Sharp, R.C.Hamilton																																
23	14	(a) Partick Thistle	W 2-0	R.C.Hamilton, Stark				3	6	5	11	7		9			8		2	10										1				4		
24	15	(a) Stevenston Th≠	D 1-1	Untraced			2	3		5	6	7		9		11	4			8															1	10
					Appearances																															
					Goals																															

*David Mitchell Benefit Match. † Played at Merchiston Park, Bainsford.
‡ League fixture abandoned after 55 minutes. # Played at Cliftonville Grounds, Belfast.
§ Played at Balmoral Grounds, Belfast. ≠ Stevenston Sick Nursing Association Benefit Match.
No further details available for matches 14, 18, 20, 21, 22 and 24.

6 goals untraced. 1 own-goal.

1901-02 continued
Other matches

No	Date	Opponent	Result	Scorers	Att	Dickie	Smith N	Drummond	Gibson	Neil	Robertson	Campbell J	McDougal L	Hamilton RC	Speedie	Smith A	Crawford	Stark	Wilkie	Goudie	Morton	McPherson J	Graham	McPherson N	Young	Hamilton JR	Lennie	Walker J	Mackie	Sharp	Miller	Campbell	Buchan	Wood	May	Grant	Richmond
1	Aug 15	(h) Hibernian	W 4-2	R.C.Hamilton 2, McDougall, Speedie	4,000	1		3	4		6	7	8	9	10	11	2	5																			
2	19	(a) Falkirk	W 2-0	R.C.Hamilton 2	3,000	1		3	6	5			11	9			2	4				10	7							8							
3	26	(a) Celtic*	D 1-1	Graham	5,000	1	2			5		11		9			3	4	10				7							8							
4	Nov 23	(h) Dundee†	W 2-1	McPherson, Graham	2,000	1			4	5				9	10	11	2	6			3	8	7														
5	30	(a) Kilmarnock	W 3-2	R.C.Hamilton 2, McDougall		1				5			7	9	6	11	2	4			3	8				10											
6	Dec 21	(a) Sheffield U	L 0-1		2,000	1						7		9	10	11																			8		
7	25	(a) Notts County	W 3-2	Graham 2, Robertson	3,000																																
8	Jan 2	(h) Notts County	L 2-3	A.Smith, Stark	6,000	1		3		5	11	7			8	10	2	6							4										9		
9	Feb 8	(h) Kilmarnock‡	W 3-0	R.C.Hamilton 2, Gibson	5,000	1	2	3	4	5	6	7		9	10	11			8																		
10	Mar 15	(h) Dundee	W 3-1	McDougall, Wilkie, J.R.Hamilton		1				5		7	11		10		2	4	9		6				3	8											
11	Apr 1	(a) Glentoran	W 3-0	R.C.Hamilton 2, A.Smith	4,000		2	3	4		6		8	9	10	11		5					7	1													
12	2	(a) Glentoran U	L 0-2		3,000				4			11	7	9	10		3				5			1	2								6	8			
13	16	(a) Beith	W 1-0	Wilkie		1			4	2	6	7	11		10			5	8						3												
14	22	(a) Rutherglen G§	W 4-0	Robertson 2, Wilkie, Drummond				3	4	5	8		11					6	9							10										1	2
15	Apr 24	(a) West Calder	W 4-2	Untraced																																	
16	26	(a) Dumfries Select	W 5-3	Robertson 2, Untraced 3	4,000	1	2	3	4	5	9	7			10	11		6	8																		
17	29	(h#) Newcastle U	L 0-5		5,000		2		4	5		7		9	10	11	3		8																		
18	May 5	(a≠) Victoria U	W 7-0	Untraced	3,000																																
19	15	(a) St Mirren¥	L 3-4	McDougall, McNab, Wilkie		1	4	3		2		7	11		10				8						5												
					Appearances																																
					Goals																																

NB. No further details available for matches 6, 7, 15, 18.
* Dan McArthur Benefit Match. † League fixture abandoned after 83 minutes due to fog.
‡ Scottish Cup-tie declared a friendly due to an icebound pitch. § Ibrox Disaster Fund Benefit Match.
# Played at first Cathkin Park, Glasgow. ≠ Played at Central Park, Aberdeen. ¥ Alex Wylie Benefit Match.

Munro played number-6 in Matches 3 & 19; Howden played number-9 in Match 13; Cunningham played number-7 in Match 14; Paterson played number-1 in Match 17; Knowe played number-6 in Match 17; McNab played number-9 in Match 19 and scored 1 goal. 14 goals untraced.

1902-03 continued
Other matches

No	Date	Opponent	Result	Scorers	Att	Dickie	Crawford	Drummond	Gibson	Neil	Robertson J	Graham	Walker J	Hamilton RC	Mackie	Smith A	Lennie	Smith N	Stark	Walker W	Speedie F	Fraser	McDonald	Wallace	Henderson	Brodie	McMurray	Paton	Rankin	Craigie	Thomson	Chalmers	Robertson G	Scullion	Howden	Dunlop	Lawrence
1	Aug 12	(a) Motherwell &Dis‡	D 2-2	Untraced				3	4	6		11	10	9			7	2	5		8			1													
2	18	(h) Hibernian	L 1-4	Graham	11,000	1		3	4	5	6	7	8	9		11	10																				
3	25	(a) Third Lanark RV*	W 6-2	Stark 2, Robertson 2, Lennie, J.Walker	2,000	1		3			9	7	10				11		5	8											2	4	6				
4	28	(h) Celtic†	D 1-1	Hamilton	4,000	1			4	5				9		11	10	2		8		3	7										6				
5	Sep 1	(a) Newcastle U	L 1-3	Untraced	3,000																																
6	Oct 25	(a) Morton	L 0-3		1,500		3		4		9					11	7		6	8	10	2		1										5			
7	Dec 25	(a) Preston NE	L 1-2	Untraced	5,000	1		3	4		6		10	9		11			5		8	2	7														
8	26	(a) Everton	W 2-1	Hamilton, A.Smith	9,000																																
9	Jan 2	(h) Hearts‡	D 2-2	Hamilton 2			3					7	8	9			11		5		2			1	4		10						6				
10	5	(h) Newcastle U	W 3-1	W.Walker 2, Brodie	9,000		3		4				10			11			5	9	6	2				7	8								1		
11	Feb 21	(a) Middlesbrough	D 1-1	Speedie	2,000	1			4		6		10	9	7	11		2	5		8	3															
12	Mar 14	(a) Partick Thistle	D 3-3	W.Walker, Speedie, Stark	2,000	1	3			5							11	2	6	9	8		7		4		10										
13	30	(a) Port Glasgow A	W 4-2	J.Walker 3, Thomson		1	2	3	6		11		10						5	9	8										7					4	
14	Apr 22	(h) Hibernian#	W 3-1	Mackie, Hamilton, Dunlop (pen)	4,000						6	11		9	8		10	2							4											5	1
15	29	(h) Newcastle U	D 2-2	A.Smith, Hamilton							6			9	8	11	7	2	5		10	3															1
16	May 4	(a) Clydebank J	W 4-1	Untraced																																	
17	5	(a) Hibernian+	D 2-2	Craigie (pen), Lennie	700																																
18	8	(a) Larkhall R Albert	W 3-2	Hamilton, McDonald, Speedie							6			9			11	2			8	3	7	1			10			5							
19	12	(a) St Johnstone	W 3-1	Untraced																																	
20	13	(a) Glasgow Perths	D 1-1	Untraced																																	
21	19	(a) Partick Thistle§	L 0-1						7		11				9				6		10	3			4											5	1
22	23	(a) Lanarkshire S≠	L 3-4	Speedie 2, J.Robertson																																	
					Appearances																																
					Goals																																

NB. No further details available for matches 5, 8, 16, 17, 19, 20, 22.
*Joe Simpson Benefit Match. †Jock Drummond Benefit Match. ‡Ibrox Disaster Fund Benefit Match.
#John McPherson Benefit Match. §Partick Nurses Benefit Match. ≠Motherwell Masonic Temple Fund Benefit Match.
+Leith Catholic School Building Fund Benefit Match.

Turner played number-3 in Match 14; Dalrymple played number-7 in Match 14; Eadie played number-4 in Match 15; Campbell played number-4 in Match 18 & number-2 in Match 21; H.Speedie played number-8 in Match 21. 12 goals untraced.

1903-04 continued
Other Matches

#	Date		Opponent	Res	Scorers	Att	Dickie M	Smith N	Fraser	Gibson N	Stark J	Robertson JT	Walker J	Mackie	Hamilton RC	Speedie FB	Smith A	Henderson GH	Drummond J	McDonald	Hartley	Campbell D	Watson JG	Neil RG	Chalk C	Paton T	Donaghy	Findlay J	Lloyd F	Gibson W	Gilchrist	Speedie W	Clark	Bolton	Kerr	Allan	Baxter	Black
1	Aug 17	(a)	Hearts*	W 4-2	Paton 3, Mackie	4,000	1	2	3		5	6	8	10	11	4						7				9												
2	19	(h)	Hibernian	L 1-2	Hartley	1,000	1		6				11	8	9	4					7		2			10							3		5			
3	24	(h)	Celtic†	D 2-2	Speedie, Hamilton		1	2	3		5	6	8	9	7	10	4					11																
4	25	(a)	Dunblane‡	W 5-2	Untraced		1					6			9				3																			
5	26	(a)	Dundee§	W 5-4	Mackie 2, Walker 2, Stark			2	3	4	5	6	8	9	10	11						7																
6	31	(a)	Clyde	L 1-2	Untraced		1		3			6	11	8	9							7	2												5			
7	Sep 1	(a)	Manchester C	D 1-1	Untraced		1	2	6		5		11	8	9	10	4		3			7																
8	Oct 3	(h)	Hearts	D 3-3	Mackie, Speedie, Walker		1	2	6				11	8		10	4		3			7			5	9												
9	5	(a)	Alloa Athletic	W 7-1	Untraced																																	
10	Dec 25	(a)	Bury	L 1-2	A.Smith	7,000	1		3		5		7	8	9	4	11																					
11	Jan 4	(h)	Bury			21,000			3			6	10	9		4						5	7	8												1	2	11
12	5	(h)	Third Lanark#	W 7-2	Mackie 3, Robertson, Untraced 3	20,000	1				7			9		12						6		5		11		8		2									
13	Feb 27	(a)	Hamilton A	W 3-2	Paton 2, Chalk	5,000																																	
14	Apr 9	(a)	Glentoran U	W 3-0	Untraced																																	
15	20	(n)	Queen's Park+	D 2-2	Untraced							6			10		9		4				3	1			11	8				7						
16	25	(a)	Yoker A	W 3-0	Untraced																																	
17	27	(h)	Newcastle U	W 2-0	Mackie, Paton						6	5		7		11	4					1				9	8			3	2		10					
18	May 3	(h)	Partick Thistle¥	W 5-1	Mackie 2, Speedie 2, Gilchrist						5	6	7	8	9							2	1				11			10							
19	11	(a)	Falkirk	W 6-3	Stark, Speedie, Untraced 4						5	8			9		3					6					11			7	2			10	1			
20		(a)	First Vienna	W 7-2	Untraced																																	
21		(n¶)	Boldklubben 93 K	W 9-0	Untraced																																	
22		(n¶)	Boldklubben 93 K	W 5-3	Untraced																																	
23		(a)	Vienna S-C	W 8-0	Untraced																																	
24		(a)	Prague Select	W 6-1	Untraced																																	
25		(a)	F.K.Prague	W 5-0	Untraced																																	

Appearances / Goals

No further details available for Matches 4, 6, 7, 9, 13-16 & 20-25.
*George Hogg benefit match. †Alex Smith benefit match. ‡Dunblane Town Band benefit match.
§Perth Disaster fund. #Jacky Robertson benefit match. +Played at Barr Head, Arthurlie benefit match.
¥Govan Distress Relief Fund benefit match. ¶Played in Vienna.

Kelso played number-3 in Match 12; Gourlay played number-4 in Matches 12, 18 & 19; Robey played number-10 in Match 12 and was substituted by A.Smith; Dunlop played number-5 in Match 15; McPherson played number-1 in Match 5; Chalmers played number-4 in Match 6; McDougal played number-10 in Match 6; Govan played number-3 in Match 18. 69 goals untraced.

1904-05 continued
Other matches

#	Date		Opponent	Res	Scorers	Att	Allan	Fraser	Gilchrist	Henderson	May	Robertson	Kyle	Mackie	Hamilton	Speedie	Smith A	Smith N	Stark	Easton	McColl	Donaghy	Walker, John (1)	Turnbull	Watson	Sinclair	McEwan	Campbell	Craig	Low	Chalmers	Steel	Chapman	Gibson	Galbraith	Lawrie	Chalk
1	Aug 15	(a)	Airdrieonians	L 1-2	Mackie		1		3	4			8		10				5	2			11	7	9	6											
2	17	(h)	Hibernian	W 2-0	May, A.Smith	3,000	1	2	3	4	5	6	10	9		8	11			7																	
3	18	(a)	Beith*	L 1-3	Donaghy			3											5	2		11	9		6								4	7	8	10	
4	24	(h)	Celtic†	W 1-0	A.Smith	3,000	1	3			4	6	9	10	7		8	11	5	2																	
5	Sep 8	(a)	Cumnock Dist‡	W 4-1	McColl 3, Untraced			3				5	6	10			11	2			9				4												
6	Sep 12	(a)	Port Glasgow A¥																																	
7	Dec 24	(a)	Preston NE	D 3-3	Speedie 2, Hamilton	2,000									9	8																					
8	26	(a)	Bradford C	D 1-1	A.Smith	9,000											11																				
9	Jan 2	(h)	Celtic§	D 0-0		60,000					4	5	6	10	7	9	8	11		2																	
10	4	(h)	Queen's Park#	D 1-1	McColl	10,000		2			4	6	8								9	11	10					5	1		3						
11	May 9	(a)	St Mirren+	L 0-3				7											4								1	2		3	11	9	8		

Appearances | 3 | 5 | 2 | 6 | 5 | 5 | 4 | 4 | 2 | 5 | 5 | 1 | 4 | 4 | 2 | 3 | 2 | 3 | 3 | 3 | 2 | 2 | 1 | 1 | 1 | 1 | 2 | 1 | 1 | 1 |
Goals | | | | | 1 | | | 1 | 1 | 2 | 3 | | | | 4 | 1 | 9 | | | | | | | | | | | | | 1 |

No further details available for matches 5, 6, 7, 8 and 11.
*Opening of Glebe Park, Beith. †Neil Gibson benefit match. ‡Cumnock Consumptive Sanatorium
benefit match. §League fixture abandoned after 65 minutes due to spectator encroachment.
#Nicol Smith benefit match. +Tom Jackson benefit match. ¥Goudie McNeil benefit match.

Dowall played number-1 in Match 3; Fitchie played number-7 in Match 10; Wylie played number-5 in Match 11; Drummond played number-10 in Match 11. 1 goal untraced.

1921-22 continued
Other matches

#	Date		Opponent	Res	Scorers	Att	Robb	Manderson	McCandless	Meiklejohn	Dixon	Muirhead	Archibald	Cunningham	Henderson	Cairns	Morton AL	Bowie	McDermid	Nicholson	Lawson	Hansen	Jameson	Smith, James	Laird	Smith JR	McKenna	Roberts	Fowler	Gould	Reid	Kirkwood	Morton J	Johnston	Gallagher	Wallis
1	Aug 29	(a)	Renfrew †	W 3-0	A.L.Morton 3												11																			
2	Sep 1	(a)	Helensburgh	W 5-0	Untraced 5			1	2	3	7					11	8	10	4								5	6	9							
3	5	(a)	Hamilton A ‡	L 1-2	Jackson	1,500	1					7	8		10			4	11							9										
4	14	(a)	Newcastle U	L 1-2	Cunningham	12,000	1					7	8	10				4	11							9										
5	Jan 4	(h)	Clyde §	D 2-2	McDermid, Hansen	5,000	8									10	5	11	9		3	4					1	2	6	7						
6	Apr 25	(h)	Newcastle U +	D 1-1	Archibald	20,000	1	2	3		5		7			9	10	11			4			6	8										
7	Jun 1	(a)	Copenhagen Sel	W 1-0	J.R.Smith	15,000	1	2	3	4	5	8	7			10					6	11			9										
8	4	(a)	Copenhagen Sel	W 3-0	Hansen 2, Muirhead	6,000	1	2		4	5	8	7			10					6	9	3												11
9	5	(a*)	Denmark	D 2-2	Cairns, Nicholson	20,000	1	2		4	5	8	7		9	10				6			3		11										

Appearances | 7 | 5 | 3 | 4 | 4 | 4 | 3 | 5 | 1 | 2 | 5 | 3 | 1 | 2 | 6 | 3 | 2 | 2 | 1 | 2 | 2 | 1 | 2 | 1 | 1 | 1 | 1 | 1 | 1 | 1 |
Goals | | | | | | 1 | 1 | 1 | | 1 | 3 | | 1 | 1 | | 2 | | | | 3 | | | | | | | | | | |

†J.Gilchrist Benefit Match. ‡Jock Hanlon Benefit Match.
§Tommy Singleton Benefit Match. +Andy Cunningham Benefit Match. *Played at Copenhagen.

No further details available for Matches 1-4. 5 goals untraced.

1953-54 continued
Other matches

#	Date		Opponent	Result	Scorers	Att.	Niven	Young	Little	McColl	Woodburn	Cox	Waddell	Grierson	Paton	Prentice	Hubbard	Caldow	Simpson W	Liddell	Stanners	Findlay	McMillan PH	Thornton	Brown	McCulloch	Rae	Gardiner	Rodgers	Neillands	Shaw	McKenzie	Gordon	Pryde
1	Aug 24	(a)	Queen of South	†L 1-3	Thornton	8,000								7					9	11	5	8		10	1		6			2	3	4	
2	Dec 8	(h)	Arsenal	‡L 1-2	McCulloch	80,000		2	3	4		6	7	8					9		5			10	1	11								
3	Feb 24	(a)	British Army	L 1-2	Paton	30,000			3	4	5		7	10	8		11	2						1			6	9						
4	May 16	(*)	Chelsea	W 1-0	Young (pen)	11,000	1			4	5	3	7	8			10	11	9								6							
5	19	(a)	Hamilton§	W 6-0	McCulloch, Hubbard, Paton, W.Simpson, Young, Thornton	10,000	1	2		4		3			8	10	11		9					5		9	7	6						
6	22	(a)	Ontario All St	W 4-1	Paton, Waddell, Prentice, W.Simpson	12,000	1	2		4	5	3	7		8	10	11		9								6							
7	24	(a)	B Columbia¶	W 9-0	W.Simpson 3, McCulloch 2, Hubbard 2 (1 pen), McColl, Paton	6,300	1	2		4	5	3			8	10	11		9								7	6						
8	26	(a)	Victoria	W 7-0	W.Simpson 2, Young, Paton, Prentice, Hubbard, Thornton	3,700	1	2		4	5	3	7		8	10	11		9								6							
9	29	(a)	Vancouver AllS	W 3-0	W.Simpson 2, Hubbard	8,000	1	2		4	5	3			8	10	11		9								7	6						
10	Jun 2	(a)	Manitoba AllS	W 5-0	Paton 2, Hubbard 2, Young	5,500	1	2		4	5	3	7		10		11		9								8	6						
11	5	(o)	Chelsea	L 1-4	W.Simpson	17,000	1	2		4	5	3	7		8	10	11		9								6							
12	6	(®)	Chelsea	D 0-0			1	2		4			7		8	10		3	9		5					11	6							
					Appearances		9	10	2	11	8	9	9	3	9	8	9	2	10	1	4	1		3	3	6	11	1		1	1	1		
					Goals		4			1			1		7	2	7		10					3		4								

†Charlie Johnson Benefit Match. ‡British Championship decider – official inauguration of Ibrox floodlights. *Played in Montreal, Quebec. §Hamilton & District All Stars. ¶British Columbia Mainland All Stars. oPlayed in Toronto, Ontario. ®Played in New York.

Grierson was substituted by Paton in Match number 4; Cox subbed by Shaw, W.Simpson by Thornton, Hubbard by McCulloch in Match number 6; Cox subbed by Little, W.Simpson by Thornton, Rae by Caldow in Match number 8; Young subbed by Caldow, Woodburn by Stanners, Cox by Shaw, W.Simpson by Thornton in Match number 9; Woodburn subbed by Stanners, Paton by Thornton in Match number 10; Hubbard subbed by McCulloch in Match number 11; Waddell subbed by Thornton in Match number 12.

1957-58 continued
Glasgow Merchants' Charity Cup

	Date		Opponent	Result	Scorers	Att.	Ritchie	Little	Caldow	Shearer	McColl	Baird	Scott	Simpson	Kichenbrand	Murray	Hubbard	Valentine	Austin	Niven	Davis	Moles	Millar	Telfer	Brand	Wilson	Queen	Duncan	Smith	Morrison	Robertson	Melrose	Hogg
SF	May 8	(h)	Celtic	D 1-1*	Murray	24,412	1	3		2		10				9				4		8	5		11		7	6					
F	12	(n†)	Clyde	L 0-4		18,000	1	3		2	4	10	7			9	11				6			5								8	
					Appearances		2	2		2	1	2	1			2	1			2	1	1	2	1	1		1	1				1	
					Goals											1																	

*Rangers won semi-final on the toss of a coin.
†Played at Hampden Park, Glasgow.

Other match

	Date		Opponent	Result	Scorers	Att.	Ritchie	Little	Caldow	Shearer	McColl	Baird	Scott	Simpson	Kichenbrand	Murray	Hubbard	Valentine	Austin	Niven	Davis	Moles	Millar	Telfer	Brand	Wilson	Queen	Duncan	Smith	Morrison	Robertson	Melrose	Hogg
1	Feb 17	(h)	Scotland*	D 1-1	Murray	55,217	1	3		2	4	6	7	8		9	11							5	10								
					Appearances		1	1		1	1	1	1	1		1	1							1	1								
					Goals											1																	

*World Cup Trial

1966-67 continued
Other Matches

#	Date		Opponent	Result	Scorers	Att.	Ritchie	Johansen	Provan	Millar	McKinnon	Smith D	Wilson	Smith A	Forrest	McLean	Johnston	Greig	Henderson	Setterington	Martin	Watson R	Willoughby	Jardine	Jackson	Paul	Reid	Hynd	Mathieson
1	Aug 6	(h)	Arsenal	W 2-0	McLean 2 (1 pen)	40,000	1	2	3	6	5		11			9	10	4	7		8								
2	Feb 15	(a)	Stoke C	L 1-3	D.Smith	13,719		2	3		5	10	11	8	9					1			4	6	7				
3	18	(a)	Leicester C	L 0-1		24,408		2	3		5	10	11	9	12					1		8	4	6	7				
4	May 10	(n*)	Sparta Prague	L 0-1		21,940		2	3		5	10	12	8			11	6	7		1		4					9	
5	May 17	(a)	Morton	W 2-1	R.Watson, Hynd	9,000		2	3		5	10	7	8			11	6			1	4						9	
6	24	(a)	Motherwell †	D 1-1	Hynd	11,384		2	3		5	10		8			11	6	7		1		4					9	
					Appearances		1	6	6	1	6	5	4	5	2	4	4	3		5	2	1	4	2	2	3			
					Sub appearances										1		1												
					Goals							1				2		1				1						2	

*Played Toronto, Ontario.
†Charlie Aitken Testimonial Match.

1968-69 continued
Toronto Cup

#	Date		Opponent	Result	Scorers	Att.	Martin	Jackson	Mathieson	Greig	McKinnon	Hynd	Henderson	Willoughby	Jardine	Smith D	Persson	Penman	Johnston	Johansen	Ferguson	Stein	McDonald A	Provan	Watson	Conn	Neef	Miller	McPhee	Smith A	Sorensen
1	Jun 1	(n*)	Tottenham H	L 3-4	Stein 2, Persson	10,506		3	4	5		7	6	11		10	2				9			8		1					
2	7	(n†)	Fiorentina	L 0-2		25,000		3	4	5		7	6	11	8	10	2				9					1					
					Appearances			2	2	2		2	2	2	1	2	2				2			1		2					
					Sub appearances																										
					Goals												1					2									

* Played at Varsity Stadium. † Played at CNE Stadium.

Other matches

#	Date		Opponent	Result	Scorers	Att.	Martin	Jackson	Mathieson	Greig	McKinnon	Hynd	Henderson	Willoughby	Jardine	Smith D	Persson	Penman	Johnston	Johansen	Ferguson	Stein	McDonald A	Provan	Watson	Conn	Neef	Miller	McPhee	Smith A	Sorensen
1	Jul 31	(a)	Tottenham H	L 1-3	Penman	37,998	12	2	3	4	5		7	8	6	11	9	10												1	
2	Aug 3	(h)	Arsenal	D 2-2	Greig (pen), Penman	60,000	1	2		4	5		7	6		11	9	10	3						8						
3	Jun 4	(n*)	Fiorentina	W 3-2	D.Smith, Penman, Stein	12,500		2	3	4	5		7	10	6	8	11	9						1			1				
					Appearances		1	3	2	3	3		3	2	3	2	3	3	1				1		1		1	1			
					Sub appearances		1																								
					Goals					1						1		3				1									

* Played at Randalls Island, New York.

1970-71 continued
Other matches

#	Date		Opponent	Result	Scorers	Att.	McCloy	Jardine	Miller	Greig	McKinnon	Jackson	Fyfe	Conn	Stein	McDonald A	Johnston	Penman	Henderson	Johnstone	Smith	McCallum	Parlane	Semple	Neef	Mathieson	Watson K (1)	McDonald I	Alexander	Denny	Watson RM
1	Jul 24	(a)	Hamburg	L 1-3	Mathieson	15,000		2		5		14	4	9	10	11	8		6	**7**						1	3			12	
2	28	(a)	Kaiserslauten	D 1-1	Penman (pen)	20,000		2		5			4	9	10	11	8		6	**7**						3	12			1	
3	Aug 3	(h)	Tottenham H	L 0-2		26,000		2	4	5			4	9	10	11			6	**7**						3				1	
4	Nov 16	(h)	Dinamo Moscow	W 1-0	Johnstone	55,500	1	2	3	5	6	12	4	**10**	8	11			7	9											
5	Dec 15	(a)	Hertha Berlin	L 0-3		14,000	1	2	3	4	5	6	14	8	10	12			**7**	9	11	15									
6	16	(a)	Hanover	W 2-1	Conn, Miller	13,000	1	2	3	4	5	6	14	**11**	9	8			7	12	10					1	3				
					Appearances		3	6	3	3	6	3	6	6	5	4	2		6	2	5				1	3				2	
					Sub appearances							4				1				1		1					1				
					Goals			1	1					1						1						1					

1971-72 continued
Gothenburg Alliance Jubilee Tournament

				McCloy	Jardine	Mathieson	Greig	McKinnon	McDonald A	McLean	Penman	Stein	Denny	Johnston	Conn	Jackson	Henderson	Smith	Fyfe	Johnstone	McDonald I	Miller	Parlane	Neef
SF	Jul 20 (a) G.A.I.s	L 3-4 Johnstone, Johnston, Conn	4,000	1	2	12	4	5	11	7			10	8	6	14			9			3		
F	21 (a) Organte	W 2-1 Greig, McLean	4,000		2	3	4			8	7		9	6	10			5	11		12	14	1		
		Appearances		1	2	1	2	1	2	2			1	1	2	1	2	1		1		1	1		
		Sub appearances				1														1		1	1		
		Goals					1			1			1	1						1					

Other matches

				McCloy	Jardine	Mathieson	Greig	McKinnon	McDonald A	McLean	Penman	Stein	Denny	Johnston	Conn	Jackson	Henderson	Smith	Fyfe	Johnstone	McDonald I	Miller	Parlane	Neef
1	Jul 26 (a) Halsingborg	W 4-0 Conn 2, A.McDonald, Greig	4,000	1	2		8	5	11	7			10	9	4	6					3	12			
2	Aug 6 (h) Everton	W 2-1 Johnstone 2	58,000	1	2	3	4	5	11	7			10	8	6	12			9						
3	9 (h) Tottenham H	W 1-0 Johnston	63,000	1	2	3	4	5		7		9	10	8	6	11			12						
4	Nov 24 (a) Chelsea*	W 1-0 Jardine	17,000	1	2	3	4		11			9	10	8	5	7	6								
5	Dec 7 (a) Hapoel/Maccabbi SD	0-0	15,000	1	2	3	4		10	8			9	11		7	6		5						
6	May 10 (a) Inverness S†	W 5-2 McLean 2 (1 pen), Mathieson, Johnstone, Giles (og)	7,000	1	2	3	12		10	7	8	9	11			6		5		4					
7	16 (a) St Mirren‡	W 5-2 Conn 3, Penman (pen), A.McDonald	8,000		2		12		11		7	9	3	14	8		6	10	5			4	1		
		Appearances		6	7	5	5	3	6	5	2	5	2	6	5	4	3	4	1	4		1	2	1	
		Sub appearances					2							1			1			1			1		
		Goals			1	1	1		2	2	1			1	5				3						

*Ron Harris testimonial match.
†Ally Chisholm, Ernie Latham and Chic Allan testimonial match played at Grant Street Park.
‡Paisley Charity Cup.

1 own-goal

1973-74 continued
Other matches

				McCloy	Jardine	Mathieson	Greig	Johnstone	McDonald A	McLean	Forsyth	O'Hara	Parlane	Smith	Conn	Denny	Scott	Young	Houston	Kennedy	Fyfe	Jackson	Hamilton	Morris	Hunter	McDougall	Mason	Donaldson	Miller
1	Aug 6 (a) Kilmarnock	W 2-0 Scott, McLean	5,000	1			4			7			9	6		2	8				5					11	10	3	
2	20 (h) Arsenal	L 1-2 Parlane	71,000	1	2	3	4	5	6	7	8	14	9		10		12	11											
3	Mar 4 (a) Hamburg	L 0-3	15,000	1	2	3	4	6	10	7		8	9					11			5								
4	9 (a) Manchester U	W 3-2 Greig, Johnstone, Parlane (pen)	22,215	1	2	3	4	6	10	7		8	9					11			5								
5	May 1 (a) Everton*	L 1-2 Jardine (pen)	10,730	1	2		3	5	10				9			8	7			11	6			4					
		Appearances		5	4	3	5	4	4	4	1	2	5	1	1	2	4			1	4			1	1	1	1	1	
		Sub appearances										1						1											
		Goals			1		1	1		1			2				1												

*Tommy Wright testimonial match

1974-75 continued
IX Trofeo Juan Gamper

				Kennedy	Jardine	Miller	Johnstone	Jackson	Forsyth	McLean	Young	Parlane	Fyfe	Scott	McDougall	McDonald	Greig	McKean	Denny	O'Hara	Hamilton	Stein	Mathieson	Sharp	Morris	Hunter	Steele	Henderson	McCloy	Dawson
SF	Aug 20 (a*) Athletic Bilbao	W 1-0 Jardine	100,000	1	8	3	6	5	4	7	9		10	11			2														
F	21 (a) FC Barcelona	L 1-4 Fyfe	100,000	1	2	3	6	5	4	7	9	8	10	11																	
		Appearances		2	2	2	2	2	2	2	2	1	2	2			1														
		Sub appearances																													
		Goals			1								1																		

*Played at the Nou Camp Stadium, Barcelona.

Other matches

				Kennedy	Jardine	Miller	Johnstone	Jackson	Forsyth	McLean	Young	Parlane	Fyfe	Scott	McDougall	McDonald	Greig	McKean	Denny	O'Hara	Hamilton	Stein	Mathieson	Sharp	Morris	Hunter	Steele	Henderson	McCloy	Dawson
1	Jul 16 (a) Malmö	L 1-2 Scott	4,900	1	2		6	5		7	11	9		8	12	10			4			3		14						
2	18 (a) Gothenberg A	L 0-2	3,231	1	2			5			7	9	14	11	6	10		4	12	8		3								
3	22 (a) Karlstad	D 0-0	3,000	1				5		7	10	9	11		2			4	6	8		3								
4	23 (a) Amal Alliance	W 9-0 Fyfe 2, Jardine 2 (1 pen), Hamilton, Steele, McLean, Scott, Parlane	3,000		4			5		7		9	11	8			6	10	12		3		15	1	14					
5	Dec 9 (a) Elgin City	W 8-1 Henderson 4, Parlane 2, Johnstone, Hamilton	6,000	1	2		10	5		7		8	11	15	4		3	12	6		14					9				
6	May 17 (a) Vikings Stav	W 5-0 McDonald 3, Henderson, Greig	7,000		3			5	7	11		14	15	12	10	2	8			6	4					9	1			
7	29 (a*) British Columbia	W 4-0 Fyfe 2, McDonald, McKean	9,532		2	5		14	7	9			11		6	4	10				8					12	1	3		
8	Jun 2 (a) Auckland	W 3-1 Johnstone 2, McDonald	16,000		2	8		5	7	11		14			10	6	12				4					9	1	3		
9	4 (a†) Canterbury ln XI	D 2-2 Greig, Stein	17,000		3	6		5	7	11		8			10	2	4				9						1	12		
10	8 (a‡) Australia	W 2-1 Parl;ane 2	32,000		2	6	5		7	10	9	11				3	8				4						1			
11	11 (a#) Australia	L 0-1	11,000		3	6	5		7	10	9	11				2	8				4					12	1			
12	15 (a§) Victoria	W 5-1 McKean 2, Parlane, Johnstone, Stein	35,000	12	2	10	5		7	6	9	14			4	8		11								15	1	3		
13	18 (a+) South Australia	W 2-1 Miller, Parlane	33,000		2	8	5		7	11	9				6	4		10									1	3		
14	22 (a¥) Western Australia	L 1-2 Johnstone	20,000	1		2	10	5		7	6	9	11			4	8											3		
		Appearances		5	4	9	10	10	3	13	12	10	8	3	4	6	10	8	4	3	8	4		1		3	8	5		
		Sub appearances		1				1				4	2	2			2		1	2			2		1	3		1		
		Goals			2	1	5			1		7	4	2		5	2	3			2	2				1	5			

*Played at Vancouver. †Played at Christchurch. ‡Played at Sydney. #Played at Brisbane.
§Played at Melbourne. +Played at Adelaide. ¥Played at Perth.

1975-76 continued
Other matches

				McCloy	Jardine	Greig	Forsyth	Jackson	McDonald	McLean	McKean	Stein	Johnstone	Young	O'Hara	Miller	Parlane	Denny	Fyfe	Dawson	McDougall	Scott	Kennedy	Boyd	Henderson	Hamilton	Armour	Munro	Watson K (2)
1	Aug 19a) St Mirren	W 2-0 McDonald, Fyfe	4,000	1	2	6		5	10	7	4	12	8			3	9		11											
2	4 (h) Hertha Berlin	L 2-3 Parlane, McDonald	41,000	1	2	6		5	10	7		4	8			3	9		11											
3	May 18 (a) Vancouver W	D 2-2 Hamilton, Johnstone	13,323	1		3	4	5	6	10	7		11			2	12								9	8		14		
4	22 (a) Seattle Sounders	W 1-0 McDonald	11,356	1		3	4	5	6	10	7		11			2	9									8				
5	23 (a) Portland Timbers	W 2-1 McLean, O'Hara	11,473	1		3	4		6	11	7	9	5		14	2	10								15	8		12		
6	26 (a) Minnesota Kicks	D 2-2 Stein, Henderson	11,000	1		3	4		6	7	15	10	5				12	14			2				9	8		11		
7	30 (a) Toronto M-C	W 2-1 Henderson, Miller (pen)	17,500	1		5	4		6	8	7	12	11			3			2						9	14		15	10	
		Appearances		7	2	7	5	4	7	7	5	3	7			6	4		2	2					3	4		1	1	
		Sub appearances									1	2			1		2	1							1	1		3		
		Goals							3	1		1	1		1	1	1		1						2	1				

1976-77 continued

Other matches

No	Date		Opponent	Result	Scorers	Att	McCloy	Miller	Greig	Forsyth	Denny	McDonald	McLean	Jardine	Parlane	Munro	Johnstone	Henderson	McKean	Hamilton	Jackson	Kennedy	Watson K (2)	Dawson	McDougall	Robertson	Steele	Stein	O'Hara	Morris	Armour	Brand
1	Jul 27	(a)	Werder Bremen	L 1-3	Johnstone	25,000	1	2	3	**4**		6	11	12	15		10	**9**	7	**8**	5			14								
2	30	(a)	St Pauli	L 1-2	Johnstone	3,000	1	2	3	4		6	7	8	9	11	10				5											
3	Oct 9	(a)	Aston Villa*	L 0-2		25,000		3	4		2	6			9	11		10	7	8	5	1										
4	Dec 20	(a)	Inverness Clach	W 8-0	O'Hara 3, Johnstone 2, McKean 2, McDougall	4,000		3		**4**		12		2		11	10	**9**	7	16		1	6		15	14			8	5		
5	21	(a)	Morton	W 3-2	Hamilton, Henderson, Watson	4,000	1		3	5		**10**	7	2		11	15	9		**4**			12		8				14			6
6	May 14	(a)	Trollhattans†	W 7-2	Hamilton (pen), McLean, Robertson, Parlane, McDonald, Greig, Morris	5,100			2	4		10	7		9	3	11		14	**8**	5	1	**6**			15				12		
						Appearances	3	4	5	5	1	5	4	3	3	5	4	4	3	4	4	3	2		1				1	1		1
						Sub appearances						1		1	1		1		1	1			1	1	1	2			1	1		
						Goals			1			1	1		1		4	1	2	2			1		1	1			3	1		

*Match abandoned 51 minutes – crowd trouble.
†Jet Cup – 75th anniversary of Volvo.

1977-78 continued

Other matches

No	Date		Opponent	Result	Scorers	Att	McCloy	Jardine	Miller	Forsyth T	Jackson	McDonald A	McKay	Russell	Parlane	Robertson	Cooper	McKean	McLean	Smith	Johnstone	Greig	Watson K (2)	Kennedy	Dawson	Hamilton	Morris	Henderson	Strickland
1	Jul 30	(a)	Ross County	W 4-0	Parlane, McDonald, McLean, Hamilton	4,500	1	2		4		6			**9**		11	8	7		5	3				10		12	
2	Aug 1	(a)	Nairn County	W 3-2	Greig, McDonald, Russell	4,000		2	14	6		10		4	12		11	**8**	**7**		5	3		1		15		9	
3	Apr 16	(h)	Scotland*	W 5-0	Greig 2, Russell 2, Johnstone	65,000	1	2		4	5	**6**		8			11		**7**	10	9	3	12						14
						Appearances	2	3		3	1	3		2	1		3	2	3	1	3	3		1		1		1	
						Sub appearances			1						1								1			1		1	1
						Goals						2		3	1				1		1	3				1			

*John Greig testimonial match.

1978-79 continued

Glasgow Cup

No	Date		Opponent	Result	Scorers	Att	McCloy	Jardine	Forsyth A	Forsyth T	Jackson	McDonald A	McLean	Russell	Johnstone	Smith	Watson K (2)	Urquhart	Parlane	Miller	Cooper	Dawson	Robertson	McDonald J	Armour	McKay	Morris	Strickland	Denny	Kennedy	McLaren	Richardson	Dalziel
SF	Mar 24	(h)	Partick Thistle	D 3-3*	Urquhart, J.McDonald, Miller (pen)	9,250	1		2	**4**	5			8	6	10		9		12	7	3		**11**				14					
F	May 16	(h)	Celtic	W 3-1	J.McDonald, A.Forsyth (pen), Strickland	3,000			3								6							11	10	7	9	8	**4**	1	2	5	12
						Appearances	1		2	1	1			1	1	1	1	1			1	1		2	1	1	1	1	1	1	1	1	
						Sub appearances														1								1					1
						Goals			1									1		1				2				1					

*Rangers won 4-3 on penalties.

Other matches

No	Date		Opponent	Result	Scorers	Att	McCloy	Jardine	Forsyth A	Forsyth T	Jackson	McDonald A	McLean	Russell	Johnstone	Smith	Watson K (2)	Urquhart	Parlane	Miller	Cooper	Dawson	Robertson	McDonald J	Armour	McKay	Morris	Strickland	Denny	Kennedy	McLaren	Richardson	Dalziel
1	Jul 29	(a)	Caledonian	W 6-3	Parlane 2, Smith 2, Johnstone, Russell	4,300	1	2		4		6	7	8	5	10			9	3	**11**			12									
2	Aug 1	(a)	Kilmarnock*	D 2-2	Johnstone, J.McDonald	7,000	1	2		4		6	7	8	5	10			9	3	**11**			12									
3	Jan 17	(a)	Clydebank	L 0-4		4,000	1	2	3	4	**5**	6	7	8	9	12	**10**		15	14	11												
4	mar 3	(h)	Ayr United	W 4-1	Jardine 2, Russell, Smith	4,500	1	4			5		14	8		10	**6**	9	15	**2**	16	3		12		7	11						
						Appearance	4	4	1	3	2	3	3	4	3	3	2	1	2	3	3	1				1	1						
						Sub appearances							1			1			2	1	1			3									
						Goals		2						2	2	3			2					1									

*Ian Fallis benefit match

1979-80 continued

Tennent Caledonian Cup

No	Date		Opponent	Result	Scorers	Att	McCloy	Miller	Dawson	Jardine	Jackson	Watson K (2)	McLean	Russell	Johnstone	McDonald A	Cooper	McDonald J	Smith	Stevens	Parlane	Forsyth A	Urquhart	Dalziel	McKay	Forsyth T	Young	Redford	Robertson	Richardson	Davies	Boyd G	McLaren	Watson G	Matthew	Stirton
SF	Aug 3	(h)	West Ham U	W 3-2	Smith 2, K.Watson	19,000	1		3	2	5	6	7	8	9	14	**11**		10		12									**4**						
F	5	(h)	Kilmarnock	D 2-2*	Smith, Dawson	20,000	1	2	3	**4**	5	6	7	8	**9**		11		10		14									12						
						Appearances	2	1	2	2	2	2	2	2	2		2		2											1						
						Sub appearances										1					2									1						
						Goals			1			1							3																	

*Kilmarnock won 5-4 on penalties

Glasgow Cup

No	Date		Opponent	Result	Scorers	Att	McCloy	Miller	Dawson	Jardine	Jackson	Watson K (2)	McLean	Russell	Johnstone	McDonald A	Cooper	McDonald J	Smith	Stevens	Parlane	Forsyth A	Urquhart	Dalziel	McKay	Forsyth T	Young	Redford	Robertson	Richardson	Davies	Boyd G	McLaren	Watson G	Matthew	Stirton
SF	Aug 15	(a)	Partick Thistle	W 2-0	Cooper, Smith	7,000	1	**2**	3	4	5	6	**7**	8	9	12	11		10						14											
						Appearances	1	1	1	1	1	1	1	1	1		1		1																	
						Sub appearances										1									1											
						Goals											1		1																	

Competition not concluded.

Red Leaf Cup

No	Date		Opponent	Result	Scorers	Att	McCloy	Miller	Dawson	Jardine	Jackson	Watson K (2)	McLean	Russell	Johnstone	McDonald A	Cooper	McDonald J	Smith	Stevens	Parlane	Forsyth A	Urquhart	Dalziel	McKay	Forsyth T	Young	Redford	Robertson	Richardson	Davies	Boyd G	McLaren	Watson G	Matthew	Stirton
1	Jun 13	(n*)	Nancy	D 3-3	J.McDonald 2, McLean (pen)	11,878	1		3		5		7	8	9		11	10		2		12				**4**		6								
2	15	(n†)	Ascoli	W 1-0	McLean (pen)	15,000	1		**3**		5		7	8	9		**11**	10		12		2		14		4		6								
3	18	(n‡)	Botafoga	D 1-1	Redford	22,000	1				5			8	4		11	10				3		9	7			6		2						
F	22	(n§)	Ascoli	L 0-2		10,000	1				5			8	**9**			10		2		3		11	**7**	4		6		12	14					
						Appearances	4		2		4		2	4	4		3	4		2		3		2	2	3		4		1						
						Sub appearances														1		1		1						1	1					
						Goals							2					2										1								

*Played at Calgary, Alberta. †Played at Toronto, Ontario. ‡Played at Montreal, Quebec.
§Played at Hamilton, Ontario.

Other matches

No	Date		Opponent	Result	Scorers	Att	McCloy	Miller	Dawson	Jardine	Jackson	Watson K (2)	McLean	Russell	Johnstone	McDonald A	Cooper	McDonald J	Smith	Stevens	Parlane	Forsyth A	Urquhart	Dalziel	McKay	Forsyth T	Young	Redford	Robertson	Richardson	Davies	Boyd G	McLaren	Watson G	Matthew	Stirton
1	Feb 13	(a)	Dumbarton	D 1-1	G.Boyd	3,000	1	4				**6**			**10**				**11**	5		3	**17**	**16**	**7**				**9**	**2**		8	12	14	**15**	**18**
2	25	(a*)	Al-Nasr	W 2-1	Johnstone, Smith	10,000	1	3		**2**	5	12	11	8	9	**15**	7		4	6					14			10				**16**				
3	27	(a†)	Al-Arabi	W 3-1	A.McDonald, Redford, Cooper	12,000	1	3		2	5	14		**8**	9	10	**7**		12	6					**15**	4		11								
						Appearances	3	3		2	2	1	1	2	3	1	2		2	3		1			1	1		2	1	1		1				
						Sub appearances						2				1			1				1	1	2							1	1	1	1	1
						Goals									1	1	1		1									1				1				

*Played at Dubai, United Arab Emirates. †Played at Al-Safat, Kuwait.

1981-82 continued
Other matches

#	Date		Venue/Opponent	Result	Scorers	Att.	McCloy	Jardine	Miller	Stevens	Forsyth T	Bett	Cooper	Russell	McAdam	Johnstone	McLean	Redford	McDonald J	Dawson	Johnston	McClelland	Jackson	Stewart	McKay	Black	Dalziel	Lyall	Robertson	McIntyre	McPherson	Clark R	Bruce	Forsyth A	Ferguson E	Watson G
1	Jul	20 (a)	IFK Trelleborgs	W 4-1	McDonald 2, Johnstone, Johnston	2,000	2			5	6	7	8	14	9	12	10	11	3	15	4		1													
2		22 (a)	Oland	W 5-0	McDonald 2, McAdam, Cooper, Bett	1,400	1	2		4	6	12	15	9	14	7	10	8	16	11	3	5														
3		24 (a)	Karlshamn	W10-0	Johnstone 2, McDonald 2, Russell 2, Johnston, Redford, Cooper, McAdam	1,400	2			4	6	7	8	14	9	12	10	11	3	15		5	1													
4		26 (a)	Hvidovre IF	D 1-1	McDonald	5,000	2			4		7	8	12	9	6	10	11	3			5	1													
5	Aug	1 (h)	Ipswich T	L 1-2	Dawson (pen)	30,000	2			4	6	7	8	14	9	12	10	11	3	15		5	1													
6		3 (h)	Manchester C	W 2-0	Johnstone, Johnston	22,500	2	3		4		14	8	10	9	7	6		12	11		5	1	15												
7	Nov	15 (h)	Everton *	D 1-1	Johnstone	25,000	1	2	3	4		6		8	15	9	17		11	14		5	12	7		10				16						
8	Dec	22 (h)	Liverpool †	L 0-2		40,000	2				6	7	8	4		12	10	11	3			5	1	14		9										
9	Jan	23 (a)	Kilmarnock	L 0-3		2,400	12		4		2	7	8	6	9		11		3			5	1			10					14					
10	May	9 (h)	Southampton ‡	W 1-0	Dalziel	20,000	2	15			6	7			9	12	10	11	3			4	5	1			8	14								
11		16 (a)	Southampton §	L 2-4	McDonald, Russell	7,000		2			6	7	8				17	10	11	3		4	5	1	14	16	9	15					12			
			Appearances				2	9	3	2	6	9	8	9	4	8	3	10	9	8	2	4	10	9	1		5								
			Sub appearances				1	1			2	1	5	1	7			3	3				1	3	1		2				1	1	1		
			Goals							1	2	3	2	5		1	8	1	3			1													

* Colin Jackson Testimonial Match – Rangers won 3-1 on penalties
† Official inauguration of Ibrox Stadium Redevelopment
‡ Sandy Jardine Testimonial Match. § George Horsfall Testimonial Match.

1982-83 continued
Other matches

#	Date		Venue/Opponent	Result	Scorers	Att.	Stewart	McKinnon	Dawson	McClelland	Paterson	Bett	Cooper	Prytz	McAdam	Redford	McDonald	Johnstone	Russell	McKay	Black	McPherson	Stevens	Robertson	Dalziel	Kennedy	Smith	McCloy	Davies	Lyall	Clark A	Bruce	Miller	Forsyth T	Ferguson D
1	Aug	8 (h)	Tottenham H	L 0-1		24,800	1	2	3	4	5	9	7	10		6	11		8				12			14				15					
2		11 (h)	China	W 3-1	Redford, McDonald, Paterson	9,500	1	2	3	4	5	6		7	16	11	15			14			10	9					8			12			
3	Mar	27 (h)	Swansea C *	W 6-3	Dalziel 2, Prytz 2, McDonald, Forsyth	10,000	8	2	3	5	6	7		10		14	11			16		15		9	1				12				4	17	
			Appearances				2	3	3	3	3	3	2	3		2	2		1			1	2		1	1				1			1		
			Sub appearances												1	1	1		1	1	2		1			1		2			1		
			Goals						1					2		1	2						2											1	

*Tom Forsyth Testimonial Match.

1983-84 continued
Glasgow Cup

	Date		Venue/Opponent	Result	Scorers	Att.	McCloy	Dawson	McClelland	McPherson	Paterson	Redford	Prytz	McCoist	Clark	Russell	Cooper	McDonald	Davies
SF	Aug	10 (a)	Clyde	W 1-0	Russell	4,700	1	2	3	4	5	6	7	8	9	10	12	11	
F		13 (n*)	Celtic	W 1-0	Clark	32,707	1	2	3	4	5	6	7	8	9	10	12	11	
			Appearances				2	2	2	2	2	2	2	2	2	2		2	
			Sub appearances														2		
			Goals											1	1				

*Played at Hampden Park, Glasgow.

Toronto Sun Sesquicentennial Series

#	Date		Venue/Opponent	Result	Scorers	Att.	McCloy	Dawson	McClelland	McPherson	Paterson	Redford	Prytz	McCoist	Clark	Russell	Cooper	McDonald	Davies	Stewart	Nicholl	Burns	Fraser S	McKay	Ferguson I (†)
1	Jun	15 (a*)	Toronto Blizzard	L 0-2		7,482		4	8	5	6		7			11	12	3		1	2	10	14		9
2		17 (n†)	VfB Stuttgart	D 1-1	E.Ferguson	9,000	3	4	8	5	6		7	12	10	11			14	1	2	15	9		
			Appearances				1	2	2	2	2		2		1	2		1		2	2	1	1		1
			Sub appearances											1			1		1			1	1		
			Goals																				1		

*Played at Hamilton, Ontario. †Played at Toronto, Ontario.

Metropool '83 (Antwerp, Belgium)

	Date		Venue/Opponent	Result	Scorers	Att.	McCloy	Dawson	McClelland	McPherson	Paterson	Redford	Prytz	McCoist	Clark	Russell	Cooper	McDonald	Davies
SF	Aug	5 (a)	K Beerschot VAV	L 1-2	Clark	8,000	1	2	4	6	5	3	7	8	9	10	11	12	
3/4		6 (a)	Berchem Sport	W 4-0	Clark 3, Prytz	7,000	1	2	3	4	5	6	7	8	9	10		11	
			Appearances				2	2	2	2	2	2	2	2	2	2	1	1	
			Sub appearances															1	
			Goals										1		4				

Other matches

#	Date		Venue/Opponent	Result	Scorers	Att.	McCloy	Dawson	McClelland	McPherson	Paterson	Redford	Prytz	McCoist	Clark	Russell	Cooper	McDonald	Davies	McKinnon	Mitchell	Stewart	Nicholl	Lyall	Stevens	Ferguson D	Kennedy	McAdam	Williamson	Walker	Burns	Fraser S	McKay	Munro	Ferguson E	Leeman	Bruce	Ferguson I (†)
1	Jul	21 (a)	Arlovs	W11-0	McCoist 3, McDonald 3, Redford, Russell, Clark, Prytz, McPherson	1,600	1	2	4	6	5	14	7	8	9	10	11	15	16	17						3	12											
2		23 (a)	Solvesborgs	W12-0	Clark 5, McCoist 4, Paterson, Redford, McDonald	1,000	1	2	4	6	5	3	7	8	9	10	17	11	16	12						15	14											
3		25 (a)	Norrstrands	W 5-0	McDonald 2, Stevens, Clark, McCoist	1,800	1			5			7	8	12	10	11	9	6	2						3	4											
4		26 (a)	Myresjö IF	W 4-2	Clark 2, McCoist, Cooper	2,928	1	2	3	4	5	6	7	8	9	10	11	14	16	15						12												
5	Aug	1 (h)	West Brom A	W 4-2	Prytz 2 (1 pen), Russell, Luke (og)	21,500	1	2	3	6	5	12	7	8	9	10	11	14								4												
6	Dec	13 (a)	Ross C	W 6-0	Williamson 3, McPherson, Clark, Russell	4,500	1	3		10	5		14		9	6	11		2							4		7		8	12						
7	Jan	11 (h)	Feyenoord *	D 3-3	Williamson, Redford, Prytz (pen)	16,900	3	4	10		6	7	14	9		11	15				12				5	8	1		2	16							
8	Mar	20 (a)	Linfield	W 4-0	McCoist, Clark, D.Ferguson, Walsh (og)	9,300	1	3	4	6	5		8	9		11	10		14		2		7		15							12					
9	Apr	10 (a)	Ajax Amsterdam	W 4-0	Russell 2, McPherson, McCoist	9,500	1		3	4	5	6	8	10	15	7	11				2					16	9	12	14		17						
10	May	15 (a)	Hearts	W 3-2	Clark 2, E.Ferguson	17,853		3	4	15	5		8	9	7	11	10		2				16		1	14			6	17		12					
11	Jun	7 (a†)	Australia 'B'	W 4-2	Paterson, Burns, McCoist, Cooper	6,500	1	3	4	10	5	6	8	12	7	11	14						2										9
12		9 (a‡)	New Zealand	W 3-0	McDonald, McPherson, I.Ferguson	6,000	1	3	4		5	6	8		9	15	11	10						12				14	17	16
13		13 (a§)	Minnesota S	L 2-5	Paterson, McCoist			3	4	5			7	9		11	10	12					1	2		6			8
			Appearances				10	10	11	12	11	6	7	11	10	9	12	6	1	4			2	2	3	1		3	3	3	1		2				2
			Sub appearances						1		2	1	1	3	1	5	3	4	1		1	2	2		3		2	2	1	1	2	2	1	1
			Goals						4	3	3	4	13	13	5	2	7						1	1			4						1

*KLM Challenge Cup. †Played at Newcastle. ‡Played at Auckland.
§Played at Minneapolis.

2 own-goals

1984-85 continued
Other matches

						Walker	Burns	Dawson	McKinnon	McClelland	Redford	McDonald	Fraser C	Ferguson I (1)	McCoist	Cooper	Fraser S	Ferguson E	Paterson	Russell	Clark	McPherson	Mitchell	McCloy	Prytz	McMinn	Fleck	Munro	Ferguson D	Johnstone	Williamson	McFarlane	Bruce	Durrant	Davies
1	Jul	28 (a) Einsiedeln	W 9-1 I.Ferguson 5, E.Ferguson 2, Redford 2	750	1	2	3		4	10			8		11		9	5	7		6														
2		29 (a) Solothurn	W 4-2 Clark 2, C.Fraser, E.Ferguson	1,050	1	2	12	3	14		10	7	15		16		11	5		9	4			6				8							
3		31 (a) FC Grenchen	W 5-1 I.Ferguson 2, C.Fraser, McPherson, Prytz	900	1	2	3		4		10	6	8		11		12		14	9	5		16	15				7							
4	Aug	3 (a) FC Sion	L 0-3	3,300	12		2		3	8		6	9	10	11			5	7		4		1												
5		5 (a) 1.FC Kaiserslautern W 2-1 I.Ferguson, Redford	10,000	1	12	3	2	5	8	15	6	9	10	11				7		4						14									
6		8 (h) Leicester C	D 2-2 I.Ferguson (pen), McCoist	17,250	1		3	2	4	5	14	8	9	10	11				7		6						12									
7	Oct	31 (h) New Zealand *	W 5-0 Fleck 2, McCoist, Mitchell, Prytz	5,560		2	14	3	10	16	4		8	11			5	7		6	9	1	13		17	15				12					
8	Nov	20 (h) Australia	W 2-1 Cooper 2	4,106	2	3	12		6	16	8	10		11			5	15		4	9	1	14	7											
9	Feb	13 (h) Dinamo Moscow	W 1-0 Paterson	11,392			12	2			14	10		11			5	8		4		1	6	7	16	3		9	15						
10		26 (a) Forfar A †	D 2-2 McCoist 2	1,429		3	4			8	10	6			9					1		7	12	11		5		2			14				
11	Mar	8 (a‡) Iraq	D 1-1 E.Ferguson	22,000	2		14			6	10	8		9				4		12	11	7			5		3	1							
12		10 (a‡) Iraq	L 1-4 Prytz	15,000		2				10	12	14	16				8		4		11	15	7		6	5	9	3	1						
13		12 (a§) Kuwait	W 2-1 McCoist, McDonald	14,000	2		5			16	6	10	8		9			4		1	11	7	14				15	3	12						
14	May	16 (a) Chelsea #	L 2-3 Durrant (pen), McCoist	7,329	1	2	3	4		12			15	10			5	8			7		11		9	14			6				
			Appearances		6	7	9	8	6	6	3	10	10	8	8		5	7	8	2	12	6	5	6	1	3	3	5	1	4	2	1			
			Sub appearances		1	1	2	3	1	1	5	2	3	1	1		1		2				2	3	1	4	1	2		3		2		1	
			Goals					3	1	2	9	6	2		4	1			2	1	1		3		2						1			

*Billy McKay Testimonial Match. †Stewart Kennedy Testimonial Match.
‡Played at Baghdad. §Played at Amman, Jordan. #Bradford City Disaster Fund.

1986-87 continued
Other matches

					Woods C	Dawson	Munro	Souness	McPherson D	Butcher	Russell	West	McCoist	Durrant	McMinn	Ferguson D	Fleck	Nicholl	Fraser	Cooper	Burns	Walker	McFarlane	Bell	Paterson	Roberts	Woods N	Phillips	Kirkwood	Williamson	Cohen	McCloy	Miller	Knell	Yule
1	Jul	20 (a) Union Solingen W 2-0 McCoist 2	2,900	1	2	3	4	6			10	9	8		7				11	12			5												
2		22 (a) Battenberg	D 1-1 West	2,500	1	2	3		6		7	8	14	10	11	12		4		15			5					9								
3		23 (a) Wurzburg H	W 1-0 D.McPherson	1,200		6	3		5		7	12	9	8	11		4	14	2	1									10	15						
4		25 (a*) 1.FC Cologne	L 0-2	5,400	1	2	3	4	5		7	8	9	10	12			11												6						
5		30 (a) Falkirk	W 3-1 Williamson 2, Fraser	7,800		2	3		4	7			11		9		6					8						10	5	1						
6	Aug	2 (a) Tottenham H †	D 1-1 Fraser	16,365		2	3	4	5			8	9	10	16	15	14		7	11	12	1							6							
7		5 (h) Bayern Munich	L 0-2	36,300	1	2	3	4	5	6	14	8	9	10	16	15		7	11	12																
8	Oct	13 (a) Cowdenbeath ‡	D 1-1 D.McPherson	2,942		6	3		5			9							2	1		7	8	12						4	10	11				
9		19 (a) Morton §	W 5-2 Fleck, Cooper, McSwegan, Burns, Nisbet	5,000	1		3		5	6			9	10		4	8	2		11	16	15	14	12	7	18							17	20	22	
10	Feb	20 (h) Bordeaux	W 3-2 Fleck, N.Woods, Souness	29,400	1		3	4	5	6			9		10	8	7				12				2	11										
11	May	11 (a#) Israeli Olm XI	L 2-3 N.Woods, McCoist	20,000	1	12	3	17	14	6		16	9	10		8	2	15							4	7	5	11								
			Appearances	7	8	11	5	10	4	4	5	9	8	3	4	3	5	2	3	1	3	2	2	2	1	1	3	3	1	1	1	1				
			Sub appearances		1		1	1		1	2	1		3	3	1		1	1	5	1	2	1		2					1		1	1	1	1	
			Goals				1	2			1	3			2		2	1	1		1					2			2						

*Played at Koblenz, Germany. †Paul Miller Testimonial Match. ‡Ray Allan Testimonial Match
§Jimmy Simpson Testimonial Match. #Played at Tel Aviv, Israel.

A.McPherson played number-14 in Match 8 & number-21 in Match 9; Beattie played number-15 in Match 8 & number-23 in Match 9; McSwegan played number-19 and scored in Match 9; J.Clark played number-24 in Match 9.

Glasgow Cup

					Dawson	West	Walker	Nisbet	McFarlane	Phillips	Kirkwood	Knell	Yule	McPherson A	Hamilton	Thomson	Milligan	McSwegan	Spencer	McEwan	Frith
SF	Apr	28 (a*) Clyde	D 1-1 Spencer	4,000	5			4		8	11	3	2	1	6	7	9	10	12	14	
F	May	7 (a) Celtic	W 1-0 Baillie (og)	15,109	5	10	1	8	4	3	7	14			6		9	11	12		
			Appearances	2	1	1	2	1	2	1	2	1	2	1	1	2	2	2			
			Sub appearances								1							2	1	
			Goals																1	

1 own-goal

1987-88 continued
Other matches

					Woods C	Nicholl	Munro	Ferguson D	McGregor	Cohen	Kirkwood	Falco	McCoist	Phillips	Cooper D	Fleck	McFarlane	Nisbet	West	Roberts	Butcher	Souness	McCall	Francis	Gough	Wilkins	Walker	McSwegan	Woods N	Spencer	Milligan	Dawson	McPherson A	Jess	Murray S (1)
1	Jul	15 (a) Solothurn	W 4-1 McCoist, Roberts, N.Woods, Durrant	800	1	2		7	5			9	3	11	10			4		6									8							
2		16 (a) SR Delemont	W 6-0 Fleck 3, McCoist 2, McGregor	1,400		14	3	7	2		9		12	5	16	10	8		11		4	6	15				1									
3		18 (a) FC Zürich	L 0-5	1,200	1	12	14	7	2		5		9	3	11	10	8				4	6														
4		21 (a) FC Wettingen	W 3-2 McCoist 2 (1 pen), Souness	1,000	1	14			12	2	5	7	9	3	11	10	16		15		4	6	8													
5		22 (a*) Lausanne-Sports	D 1-1 Fleck	1,500	1	14	3		12	2	5	7	9		11	10	15				4	6	8													
6		25 (a) Bayer 05 Uerdingen	W 2-0 Souness, McGregor	4,340	1	2	3		5	6	4		9	12	11	10			7			8														
7		28 (a) Deveronvale	W 8-0 Falco 3, West 3, Fleck, Spencer	1,300		6		5			9		3			8	2	11	10				1					14		4	7	12	
8		29 (a) Inverness T	D 3-3 Dawson (pen), Falco, West	2,400		6		5			9		3			8	2	11	10				1	14				12		4	7		
9	Aug	4 (a) Falkirk	L 1-2 Fleck (pen)	3,400									11			8	5	10	4					1	9			6	2	3	7		12
10	Nov	19 (a) AS Monaco	D 0-0	6,000	1		18	8	2	14	12	16	9	3	11	10	15		5	4			17	7	6								
11	Dec	8 (n) Everton †	D 2-2 Fleck, McCoist	8,000	1		12	11				9	3		10	8		2		14		7	6	5									
			Appearances	7	2	5	5	7	3	5	4	7	9	6	8	6	2	6	3	9	4	4		2	2	1	4	1	1	1	3	3			
			Sub appearances		4	3		2	1	1	1		1	1		3		1				2	1				2			1	2			1	1
			Goals					2			4	6			1	7		4	1		2							1	1		1			

*Played at Charbonnierres, Switzerland.
†Dubai Champions' Cup. Rangers won 8-7 on penalties.

Glasgow International Football Tournament

					Woods C	Nicholl	Munro	Ferguson D	McGregor	Cohen	Kirkwood	Falco	McCoist	Phillips	Cooper D	Fleck	McFarlane	Nisbet	West	Roberts	Butcher	Souness	McCall	Francis	Gough	Wilkins	Walker	McSwegan	Woods N	Spencer	Milligan	Dawson	McPherson A	Jess	Murray S (1)
SF	Aug	1 (h) Real Sociedad W 1-0 Fleck	14,617	1		3		2	7	9			11	10	8				12	4	6	5													
F		2 (h) Porte Allegre D 1-1* McCoist	19,041	1	2	3		5	6	7	10	9	14	11		12				4	8														
			Appearances	2	1	2		1	2	2	2	1		2	1			1	2	1	2														
			Sub appearances										1			1		1																
			Goals									1			1																				

*Rangers lost 5-4 on penalties.

Glasgow Cup

				Dawson	West	Walker	Nisbet	McFarlane	Phillips	Kirkwood	Knell	Yule	McPherson A	Hamilton	Thomson	Milligan	McSwegan	Spencer	McEwan	Frith
SF	Apr	13 (a) Partick T	W 2-1 Cooper, Spencer	4,500	4	3			8		5	7		2			6		1	9	10
		Competition not concluded	Appearances	1	1			1		1	1		1			1		1	1	1
			Sub appearances																	1
			Goals															1	1

A.Edwards played number-11

1988-89 continued
Other matches

					Result	Scorers	Att.
1	Jul	30	(a)	Raith R	W 2-1	McCoist, Gough	9,247
2	Aug	2	(a)	Kilmarnock *	W 3-1	McCoist 2, Wilkins	9,761
3		3	(a)	Clydebank †	W 1-0	Walters	8,000
4		6	(a)	Ayr U	W 4-1	McCoist 2, Walters, Furphy (og)	12,059
5		9	(h)	Bordeaux ‡	W 3-1	Butcher, Drinkell, McCoist	43,027
6	Sep	12	(a)	East Stirling §	W 6-1	Walters 3, Kirkwood 2, Brown	1,554
7	Oct	17	(a)	East Fife #	W 2-0	Drinkell 2	1,800
8	Dec	27	(a)	Kilmarnock	W 3-1	McSwegan, Walters, Spencer	10,032
9	Jan	9	(a)	Gretna Ω	L 1-2	McSwegan	2,000
10	Mar	1	(a)	St Johnstone +	D 2-2	McCoist, McSwegan	6,000
11		6	(a)	Gala Fairydean±	W 3-2	McSwegan 2, Morrow	5,000
12	Apr	24	(a)	Boness U ●	D 1-1	McSwegan	4,500

*Alan Robertson Testimonial Match. †Jim Gallacher Testimonial Match. ‡Davie Cooper Testimonial Match. §Charlie Kelly Testimonial Match, played at Brockville Park, Falkirk. #Jim McLaren Testimonial Match. ΩLockerbie Disaster Fund Benefit Match. +Dougie Barron Testimonial Match, Rangers' final game at Muirton Park, Perth. ±Floodlight inauguration. ●Lex Shields Testimonial Match.

Rouse played number-17 in Match 7, number-6 in Match 8 and number-8 in Match 11; Playle played number-3 in Match 8; McEwan played number-14 in Match 8; Scott played number-15 in Match 8 and number-12 in Match 12; Morrow played number-12 and scored in Match 11; Howard played number-6 in Match 12. 1 own-goal

1991-92 continued
Other matches

					Result	Scorers	Att.
1	Jul	27	(a)	Queen's Park	W 8-2	Hateley 3, Ferguson 2, Durrant (pen), D.Robertson, Spencer	5,200
2		29	(a)	Morton	W 1-0	Dodds	3,364
3		31	(a)	Dundee U *	L 1-3	McCoist	13,000
4	Aug	6	(a)	St Mirren †	W 3-2	Johnston, Spencer, Durrant (pen)	7,204
5	Oct	22	(a)	Forfar A ‡	W 5-2	McSwegan 4, Ferguson	1,000

*Maurice Malpas Testimonial Match. †Campbell Money Testimonial Match. ‡Rab Morris Testimonial Match.

Forum Cup (Kilmarnock International Tournament)

					Result	Scorers	Att.
SF	Aug	3	(n)	Coventry C	D 1-1*	Spencer	6,495
F		4	(a)	Kilmarnock	W 3-1	Hateley, McCoist, Steven	7,158

*Rangers won 4-3 on penalties.

1992-93 continued
Other matches

					Result	Scorers	Att.
1	Jul	20	(a)	Queen of South	W 7-1	Hateley 3 (1 pen), Durrant, McCoist, D.Robertson, Huistra	1,500
2		22	(a)	Queen's Park	W 3-1	Hateley, Rideout, McCoist	700
3		23	(a)	Dunfermline A	W 3-2	Rideout 2 (2 pens), McSwegan	2,444
4		25	(a)	Hamilton A	D 2-2	Gough, Brown	3,613
5		28	(h)	Marseille	L 1-2	Hateley (pen)	40,218
6		29	(a)	Caledonian	W 5-0	Ferguson 2, McSwegan, Rideout, Spencer	6,000
7	Sep	8	(a)	Exeter C	D 1-1	Gordon	2,200

*Billy Urquhart Testimonial Match.

McGregor played number-12 in Match 3; Vinnicombe played number-3 in Matches 6 & 7; Morrow played number-11 in Match 7; Scott played number-12 in Match 7.

1993-94 continued
Other matches

					Result	Scorers	Att.
1	Jul	24	(a)	Berwick R	D 1-1	Hagen	5,200
2		28	(a)	Sunderland *	W 3-1	Hateley 2, Hagen	21,862
3		31	(a)	Morton	L 0-2		2,600
4	Aug	3	(h)	Newcastle U †	L 1-2	Hateley	42,623
5	Feb	2	(a)	Clydebank	W 2-0	McPherson, Boyack	5,000
6	Mar	8	(a)	Morton ‡	W 1-0	McCoist	3,098
7		22	(a)	Barrow §	W 3-0	Patterson 2, Watson	4,000

*Gary Bennett Testimonial Match. †Ally McCoist Testimonial Match. ‡Martin Doak Testimonial match. §Glenn Skivington Testimonial Match.

S.Murray (2) played number-11 in Match 5; Boyack played number-12 in Matches 5 & 6, scoring once; Nicolson played number-14 in Match 5; Patterson played number-11 in Match 7, scoring twice. J.Robertson played number-12 in Match 7; Chisholm played number-14 in Match 7; Galloway played number-15 in Match 7; G.Robertson played number-16 in Match 7.

1995-96 continued
Other matches

					Result	Scorers	Att.
1	Jul	21	(a*)	Brondby	W 2-1	Hateley (pen), Gascoigne	9,500
2		24	(a)	Esbjerg	D 3-3	Mikhailichenko 2, Steven	6,950
3		26	(a)	Hvidovre	W 2-1	Hateley, Gascoigne	7,228
4	Aug	2	(a)	Clyde	W 4-0	Hateley 3, Gascoigne	5,000
5		4	(a)	Dundee U	W 2-1	Durie, Petric	7,035
6		14	(a)	St Mirren †	L 0-1		5,600
7	Oct	10	(a)	Dunbarton ‡	W 3-2	Durrant, Bollan, Boyack	1,500
8	May	10	(a)	Clydebank §	W 3-2	McCoist 2, Gascoigne	7,500

* Played at Grenaa. † Pheonix Honda Trophy. ‡ Dick Jackson Testimonial Match. § Ken Eadie Testimonial Match.

Dodds played number-14 in Matches 2 & 7; Boli played number-5 in Match 5; I.Nicolson played number-12 in Matches 5 & 6; Boyack played number-14 in Matches 5 & 6 and number-10 in Match 7, scoring once; L.Robertson played number-15 in Match 5 and number-14 in Match 8; Dair played number-10 in Match 6 and number-9 in Match 7; Wilson played number-5 in Match 7; Morrow played number-12 in Match 7; McShane played number-15 in Match 8; B.Ferguson played number-16 in Match 8. McCoist (65 mins) and McCall (67 mins) walk-off (no substitutes) in Match 8.

Rangers in the Scottish League

Analysis of Rangers' Results Against Other League Clubs

(Compiled to end of season 1995-96)

Club	P	W	D	L	Goals F	A	Points F	A	Club	P	W	D	L	Goals F	A	Points F	A
Celtic	240	93	73	74	352	317	259	221	Dumbarton	40	29	5	6	100	50	63	17
Hearts	224	126	45	53	419	267	297	151	East Fife	28	20	3	5	75	21	43	13
Hibernian	222	127	55	40	423	208	309	135	Stirling Albion	22	18	3	1	68	15	39	5
Aberdeen	206	90	60	56	306	237	240	172	Cowdenbeath	22	18	2	2	76	24	38	6
St Mirren	204	134	42	28	489	187	310	98	Arbroath	18	12	5	1	49	13	29	7
Motherwell	194	133	30	31	410	192	296	92	Albion Rovers	18	15	2	1	59	18	32	4
Dundee	194	106	42	46	399	225	254	134	Port Glasgow A	16	13	2	1	62	11	28	4
Partick Thistle	176	121	32	23	412	167	274	78	St Bernard's	14	11	1	2	45	21	23	5
Kilmarnock	150	102	26	22	379	136	230	70	Clydebank (Old)	14	10	3	1	39	11	23	5
Falkirk	138	101	22	15	349	121	224	52	Clydebank (New)	12	10	1	1	32	6	21	3
Airdrie	128	81	23	24	321	151	185	71	Leith A	12	10	1	1	37	18	21	3
Clyde	126	92	22	12	357	120	206	46	Abercorn	8	7	1	0	33	9	15	1
Morton	122	86	22	14	284	99	194	50	Renton	6	5	1	0	20	9	11	1
Dundee U	118	66	30	22	193	105	162	74	East Stirling	4	4	0	0	15	3	8	0
Third Lanark	116	82	18	16	298	131	182	50	Vale of Leven	4	4	0	0	20	2	8	0
Queen's Park	84	62	13	9	223	78	137	31	Cambuslang	4	4	0	0	16	4	8	0
Hamilton Ac	80	59	12	9	216	72	130	30	Alloa	2	2	0	0	4	0	4	0
St Johnstone	78	62	7	9	216	71	131	25	Bo'ness	2	1	1	0	4	2	3	1
Raith Rovers	76	55	9	12	205	80	119	33	Cowlairs	2	1	1	0	3	1	3	1
Ayr U	76	50	15	11	201	79	115	37	Totals	3,302	2,099	643	560	7,487	3,369	4,841	1,763
Dunfermline A	62	46	8	8	171	53	100	24	Play-offs	2	0	1	1	3	4	1	3
Queen of South	40	31	5	4	107	35	67	13	Totals	3,304	2,099	644	561	7,490	3,373	4,842	1,766

Rangers in 1907-08. Back row (left to right): J.Wilson (trainer), G.Wallace, G.Livingstone, A.Barrie, J.Macdonald, J.T.Butler, R.C.Hamilton, J.J.Dunlop, A.Newbiggin, J.Spiers, G.Law, J.Gordon. Front row: A.Craig, Jo.Bell, J.Galt, J.Dickie, R.G.Campbell, J.Currie, A.Kyle, G.R.Watson, A.Smith, On ground: J.May, W.Henry.

Analysis of Rangers' Premier League Results

(Compiled from Seasons 1975-76 to 1995-96)

Club	P	W	D	L	Goals F	Goals A	Points F	Points A
Celtic	84	27	27	30	110	112	81	87
Aberdeen	84	27	23	34	78	103	77	91
Hibernian	80	41	25	14	117	55	107	53
Dundee U	80	40	25	15	108	70	105	55
Hearts	68	38	15	15	124	73	91	45
Motherwell	68	51	3	14	129	58	105	31
St Mirren	60	36	12	12	103	48	84	36
Dundee	52	28	13	11	98	55	69	35
Partick Thistle	40	22	10	8	77	40	54	26
Kilmanock	28	19	4	5	54	12	42	14
Morton	28	18	8	2	65	16	44	12
St Johnstone	24	21	3	0	70	14	45	3
Falkirk	24	21	3	0	67	15	45	3
Dunfermline A	16	14	2	0	41	6	30	2
Airdrie	16	9	7	0	31	8	25	7
Ayr United	12	8	3	1	28	10	19	5
Clydebank (New)	12	10	1	1	32	6	21	3
Raith Rovers	8	5	3	0	23	8	13	3
Hamilton A	8	8	0	0	17	2	16	0
Dumbarton	4	3	1	0	9	4	7	1
Totals	796	446	188	162	1,381	715	1,080	512

	P	W	D	L	Goals F	Goals A	Points F	Points A
Premier Division	796	446	188	162	1,381	715	1,080	512
First Division 1922-23 to 1974-75	1,596	1,045	306	245	3,847	1,659	2,396	796
Total	2,392	1,491	494	407	5,228	2,374	3,476	1,308
1890-91 to 1921-22	910	608	149	153	2,259	995	1,865	455
Play-offs	2	0	1	1	3	4	1	3
Totals	3,304	2,099	644	561	7,490	3,373	4,842	1,766

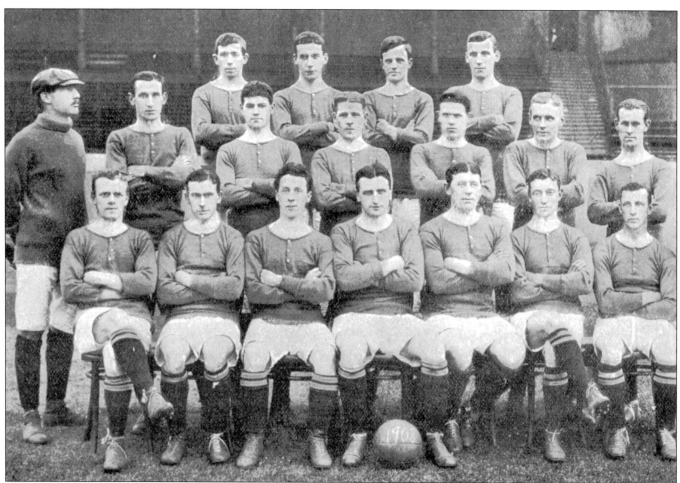

Rangers in 1908-09. Back row (left to right): Robert Noble, James Jackson, Alex Bennett, James E. Gordon. Middle row: Henry G. Rennie, James Galt, David Taylor, John Macdonald, John McArthur, George Law, Thomas Murray. Front row: Alex Craig, William MacPherson, Thomas Gilchrist, R.G. Campbell, James Sharp, George Livingstone, Alex Smith.

John Greig is hoisted high after the game against Motherwell in April 1978 as the jubilant Rangers team were confirmed the champions of the Scottish Premier Division.

Analysis of Rangers' League Results

Season	P	W	D	L	F	A	Pts	Season	P	W	D	L	F	A	Pts
1890-91	18	13	3	2	58	25	29	1948-49	30	20	6	4	63	32	46
1891-92	22	11	2	9	59	46	24	1949-50	30	22	6	2	58	26	50
1892-93	18	12	4	2	41	27	28	1950-51	30	17	4	9	64	37	38
1893-94	18	8	4	6	44	30	20	1951-52	30	16	9	5	61	31	41
1894-95	18	10	2	6	41	26	22	1952-53	30	18	7	5	80	39	43
1895-96	18	11	4	3	57	39	26	1953-54	30	13	8	9	56	35	34
1896-97	18	11	3	4	64	30	25	1954-55	30	19	3	8	67	33	41
1897-98	18	13	3	2	71	15	29	1955-56	34	22	8	4	85	27	52
1898-99	18	18	0	0	79	18	36	1956-57	34	26	3	5	96	48	55
1899-1900	18	15	2	1	69	27	32	1957-58	34	22	5	7	89	49	49
1900-01	20	17	1	2	60	25	35	1958-59	34	21	8	5	92	51	50
1901-02	18	13	2	3	43	29	28	1959-60	34	17	8	9	72	38	42
1902-03	22	12	5	5	56	30	29	1960-61	34	23	5	6	88	46	51
1903-04	26	16	6	4	80	33	38	1961-62	34	22	7	5	84	31	51
1904-05	26	19	3	4	83	28	41	1962-63	34	25	7	2	94	28	57
1905-06	30	15	7	8	58	48	37	1963-64	34	25	5	4	85	31	55
1906-07	34	19	7	8	69	33	45	1964-65	34	18	8	8	78	35	44
1907-08	34	21	8	5	74	40	50	1965-66	34	25	5	4	91	29	55
1908-09	34	19	7	8	91	38	45	1966-67	34	24	7	3	92	31	55
1909-10	34	20	6	8	70	35	46	1967-68	34	28	5	1	93	34	61
1910-11	34	23	6	5	90	34	52	1968-69	34	21	7	6	81	32	49
1911-12	34	24	3	7	86	34	51	1969-70	34	19	7	8	67	40	45
1912-13	34	24	5	5	76	41	53	1970-71	34	16	9	9	58	34	41
1913-14	38	27	5	6	79	31	59	1971-72	34	21	2	11	71	38	44
1914-15	38	23	4	11	74	47	50	1972-73	34	26	4	4	74	30	56
1915-16	38	25	6	7	87	39	56	1973-74	34	21	6	7	67	34	48
1916-17	38	24	5	9	68	32	53	1974-75	34	25	6	3	86	33	56
1917-18	34	25	6	3	66	24	56	1975-76	36	23	8	5	60	24	54
1918-19	34	26	5	3	86	16	57	1976-77	36	18	10	8	62	37	46
1919-20	42	31	9	2	106	25	71	1977-78	36	24	7	5	76	39	55
1920-21	42	35	6	1	91	24	76	1978-79	36	18	9	9	52	35	45
1921-22	42	28	10	4	83	26	66	1979-80	36	15	7	14	50	46	37
1922-23	38	23	9	6	67	29	55	1980-81	36	16	12	8	60	32	44
1923-24	38	25	9	4	72	22	59	1981-82	36	16	11	9	57	45	43
1924-25	38	25	10	3	76	26	60	1982-83	36	13	12	11	52	41	38
1925-26	38	19	6	13	79	55	44	1983-84	36	15	12	9	53	41	42
1926-27	38	23	10	5	85	41	56	1984-85	36	13	12	11	47	38	38
1927-28	38	26	8	4	109	36	60	1985-86	36	13	9	14	53	45	35
1928-29	38	30	7	1	107	32	67	1986-87	44	31	7	6	85	23	69
1929-30	38	28	4	6	94	32	60	1987-88	44	26	8	10	85	34	60
1930-31	38	27	6	5	96	29	60	1988-89	36	26	4	6	62	26	56
1931-32	38	28	5	5	118	42	61	1989-90	36	20	11	5	48	19	51
1932-33	38	26	10	2	113	43	62	1990-91	36	24	7	5	62	23	55
1933-34	38	30	6	2	118	41	66	1991-92	44	33	6	5	101	31	72
1934-35	38	25	5	8	96	46	55	1992-93	44	33	7	4	97	35	73
1935-36	38	27	7	4	110	43	61	1993-94	44	22	14	8	74	41	58
1936-37	38	26	9	3	88	32	61	1994-95	36	20	9	7	60	35	69
1937-38	38	18	13	7	75	49	49	1995-96	36	27	6	3	85	25	87
1938-39	38	25	9	4	112	55	59								
1946-47	30	21	4	5	76	26	46								
1947-48	30	21	4	5	64	28	46	Total	3,302	2,099	643	560	7,487	3,369	4,888

Top Appearances and Goalscorers

Rangers' League Appearance Records

	Player	Era	Total Apps	
1	Dougie Gray	1925-26 to 1945-46	667	(includes 177 wartime)
2	Sandy Archibald	1916-17 to 1933-34	514	
3	John Greig	1961-62 to 1977-78	498	(includes 4 as substitute)
4	David Meiklejohn	1919-20 to 1935-36	490	
5	Sandy Jardine	1966-67 to 1981-82	451	(includes 20 as substitute)
6	Tommy Cairns	1913-14 to 1926-27	407	
7	George Young	1941-42 to 1956-57	403	(includes 110 wartime)
8	Alex Smith	1893-94 to 1914-15	402	
9	Alan Morton	1920-21 to 1932-33	382	
10	Ally McCoist	1983-84 to 1995-96	378	(includes 38 as substitute)

Rangers' Top 10 League Goalscorers

	Player	Era	Total Goals Scored	
1	Jimmy Smith	1928-29 to 1945-46	300	(includes 74 wartime)
2	Ally McCoist	1983-84 to 1995-96	236	
3	Bob McPhail	1926-27 to 1939-40	233	(includes 3 wartime)
4	Willie Reid	1908-09 to 1915-16	177	
5	Jimmy Fleming	1925-26 to 1934-35	177	
6	Willie Thornton	1936-37 to 1953-54	164	(includes 20 wartime)
7	Andy Cunningham	1914-15 to 1928-29	163	
8	R.C.Hamilton	1897-98 to 1905-06	155	
9	Alex Venters	1933-34 to 1945-46	155	(includes 62 wartime)
10	Tommy Cairns	1913-14 to 1926-27	139	

Rangers' 'Old Firm' Goalscorers

	Player	Era	Total Goals Scored
1	R.C.Hamilton	1897-98 to 1905-06	35 (includes 6 non-competitive)
2	Ally McCoist	1983-84 to 1995-96	26
3	Jimmy Duncanson	1939-40 to 1950-51	22
4	John McPherson	1890-91 to 1901-02	20 (includes 3 non-competitive)
5	Alex Venters	1933-34 to 1945-46	18

Rangers' 'Milestone' League Goalscorers

	Player			Date
No.1	Jimmy Adams (og)	(h)	v Hearts	16 August 1890
No.1,000	Alex Smith	(a)	v Clyde	8 December 1906
No.2,000	Jimmy Gordon	(a)	v Kilmarnock	15 September 1919
No.3,000	Bob McGowan	(h)	v Cowdenbeath	20 December 1930
No.4,000	Jimmy Duncanson	(a)	v Dundee	25 December 1947
No.5,000	Alex Scott	(h)	v Ayr United	29 April 1961
No.6,000	Derek Parlane	(a)	v Hearts	19 January 1974
No.7,000	Ally McCoist	(h)	v Motherwell	9 December 1989

NB: The 'Milestone' records do not include the Scottish Regional League Western Division or Southern Leagues of World War Two.

Alex Venters